To Catherine, Dace and Ray
and
in memory of Gladys Shoard, Harold Shoard and James Clevett,
with thanks and love

'Nothing in life is to be feared. It is only to be understood.'

Marie Curie

Contents

Acknowledgements

Much of the pleasure in writing this book has arisen from countless chance encounters I have enjoyed with complete strangers in the street, on buses and trains, in day centres and care homes, cafés, parks and car parks; I am grateful to all of those involved for relaying their experiences and opinions to me about anything from the travel scooter they happened to be using to the joys of voluntary work or the pros and cons of using hidden cameras in care facilities. I have also derived a great deal of pleasure from the relationships I have had with people whom it has been my privilege to seek to help. At the same time, the various dimensions of later life are fascinating subjects to explore in their own right. I am grateful to the friends and acquaintances with whom I have discussed these matters, usually in the light of their own first-hand experience, and to the academics and professionals who have allowed me to benefit from their expertise.

For stimulating conversations on aspects of later life I should particularly like to thank Adela Austin, Dr Susan Chesters, Professor Luke Clements, David Cox, Jenny Desoutter, Ulriche Dono, Robynne Fletcher, Laurence Harper, Marion Hicks, Graham Hunt, Christa Monkhouse, Christine Read, Dr Justin Robbins, Glenda Watt and Philip Weaver.

Experts who have been kind enough to check through sections of the book and to whom I am grateful include Gary Bell, Liz Butterfield, Alison Carter, Allan Chapman, Amanda Cheesly, Dr David Cohen, Dr Jim Copper, Kevin Doughty, Dr Fionnuala Edgar, Rose Gallagher, Dr Reinhard Guss, Dr Rosie Heath, Dr Matthew Jones Chesters, John Johnson, James Kelly, Nick Kempe, George McFaul, Lorna Reid, Nick Rumney, Richard Rushworth, Alison Smith, Gina Starnes, Dr Jill Stavert and Matthew Wilkes. Any errors which remain are, of course, my responsibility.

Dr Susan Chesters, David Cox, Dr Justin Robbins, Val Selkirk and The Reverend Graham Trice have all commented on extensive sections of the manuscript and I am extremely grateful to them for taking so much trouble on my behalf.

My thanks go to the publishers of *Woman's World* and *Plus* (Atalink and the Christian Council on Ageing respectively) for allowing me to reproduce extracts of articles I had written for them on Intermediate Care, romance in later life and pets and older people. I should also like to thank the following authors and publishers for permission to quote from their work: Jan Morris (from *Trieste and the Meaning of Nowhere,* published by Faber), Elizabeth Garrett (from her poem 'Love in Midlife', published by Enitharmon Press) and Dr John Cockburn (from *Lonely Hearts: Love among the Small Ads,* published by Guild Publishing).

I am fortunate that Amaranth Books has provided an inspiring, patient and cheerful production team to complement my own helpers, and I am grateful to them all – Hazel Allison for help with typing, Elizabeth Henry for editing, Andrew Jamison for design and typesetting, Philip May for computer support and Dr Ray Canham for computer and other technical assistance.

I am grateful for the financial help I have received towards this project from Dr Robert Edmondson. I am also grateful for accommodation generously provided in various parts of the UK while I was researching the book by Dr Robert Aitken, Dr Ray Canham, George Pasteur and William Bennett, and Catherine Shoard.

I should like to thank Ann Widdecombe for her kind endorsement of this book and Christine and David Read for allowing me to photograph them for the front cover.

My special thanks go to my daughter, Catherine Shoard. Her playful and inventive spirit has enlivened many of my visits to hospitals and care homes. She provided a lively sounding board as I was researching and writing. Her grandmother, without whose difficulties this book would not have been written, would have been immensely proud of her.

Introduction

> The past is a foreign country, but so is old age, and as you enter it you feel you are treading unknown territory, leaving your own land behind. You've never been here before.
>
> Jan Morris, *Trieste and the Meaning of Nowhere* (2008)

Jan Morris describes a feeling familiar to all of us who are getting on: suddenly discovering we are living in an alien environment. We did not actively plan to go there. Rather, we knew we had arrived by clocking the reactions of those around us – the bus driver who assumes we have a free pass; the stranger who lifts our case onto the train unbidden. To journey into old age is compulsory, should we live long enough. And, once there, we can never leave. To enter it is to become an immediate, permanent resident. There is no tourist visa.

Not all is doom and gloom in this new world. Growing old today is far more congenial than it was even a few years ago. Cataract operations prevent people going blind, replacement joints enable them to walk, and stents stop people having strokes. Ingenious devices created by an army of unsung inventors enable us to side-step many difficulties. Today's nifty mobility scooters are a far cry from the donkey-drawn cart in which Jane Austen drove herself around the lanes of north Hampshire in the last years of her life. Bespoke digital hearing aids have replaced the ear trumpet and less sensitive analogue aid. Despite some trimming, pensioner perks provide a godsend to many – the Attendance Allowance available regardless of financial means helps offset the costs of disability and illness; and Guarantee Pension Credit provides a minimum income for everyone over state pension age whether or not they have ever worked.

Old age today is not only vastly different from what it was only twenty years ago, it is also fast changing. The loneliness that continues to bedevil many older people is at last being taken seriously and viewed as a real threat to physical as well as mental health. Evolving social mores mean older lesbian, gay, transgender and bisexual people can increasingly live their lives openly. Rather than embracing conventionality and getting married, many older men and women now embark on living-apart-to-gether relationships in which they stay over in each other's homes but keep separate households, thus preserving their domestic independence.

In her poem 'When I am an old woman I shall wear purple /With a red hat … ' Jenny Joseph encapsulated the exhilarating feeling of abandon many feel when they step into later life. In contrast to the extreme anxiety many young people feel about what their peers think about them and say about them on social media, many older people feel that at last they can do what they like, say what they like and wear what they like.

Joseph was only 29 when she penned that poem and certainly compared to our younger years, in later life we can be more much carefree. In theory at least, a grandparent can swan in and swan out – not shoulder the 24/7 burden of looking after a baby. Because they have fewer responsibilities, older people may feel that they can take more risks with their safety and do dangerous things – perhaps for the sheer joy of doing them, perhaps for fund-raising or political protest.

For many men and women, later life is a time in which at last they can separate the idea of activity to make a living from activity for self-fulfilment – work is often no longer something you have got to do to pay the rent but something that can have value in its own right. So we see older people embarking on new careers, setting up businesses of their own and volunteering.

Nonetheless, there is a very real downside to growing old in Britain today, and this book is designed to help you tackle this reality. If you are unlucky, you will develop a degenerative condition which will mean that you will struggle to look after yourself. This will affect your finances, but even more so your day-to-day life and perhaps even where and with whom you live. This might not be so bad were it not for our society's failure to address the dismal quality of life many people have to endure as they are helped – or neglected – by workers in care facilities or in their own homes, hired by commercial companies for which making a profit is of paramount importance.

Another unwelcome feature of ageing today is pressure to avoid looking old, or at least to look younger than you really are – pressure fuelled by the multi-billion-dollar beauty industry, the media and advertising. Some people respond positively to this cajoling, but others are intimidated, worried about the costs involved, and left with a nagging sense that they will never look as they feel they ought to.

The belief that we can hold off old age with pricey highlights or brain-taxing crosswords can mean that, should we develop a degenerative illness such as dementia, we can be led to feel that we have let ourselves go and failed. We can find ourselves attracting from others not loving, supportive empathy but rejection and stigma because, apparently, we have only ourselves to blame.

Amid the myriad challenges and choices about money, care, healthcare, housing, transport, appearance, friendship and romance which later life presents, we might in the past have turned to our own parents for answers. Thus, for instance, if we embark on a relationship when we are in our twenties, they may advise us on our prospective partner. But in our seventies, the questions to pose will be different. If we were disabled by a major stroke, would our new other half care for us? Or would we find ourselves on our own? As we grow older, the differences between individuals grow. You may find a new partner attractive but entering a relationship in later life may mean you would have to put up with political views entrenched over decades which you find distasteful. After decades living in what you see as an agreeable, scruffy muddle, how would you get on with someone who expects the house to be immaculate and tidy and everything put away out of sight? What complications might your grown-up children and grandchildren bring to your new relationship?

We look in vain for advice from our own parents and grandparents because we are now living not only in a very different social and cultural world from theirs, but also because we can expect to live out a previously unimaginable span. The media, too, can prove much less useful than anticipated. It may debate public policy on later life. It may provide revelations about people subjected to horrible abuse in care homes and celebrate the exceptional individuals who shin up Kilimanjaro to celebrate their 85th birthday. But it is singularly silent on how to find a good agency to provide practical help in the home for the hundreds of thousands of us who have no choice but to seek one out.

The ease of access to information on the internet can seem bountiful. But it gives us a false sense of control. Bite-sized, pre-packaged facts appear to be at our fingertips. Yet in fact negotiating the twists and turns of later life is much more about what you do not know you need to know than about what you suspect you might. It is also a world of endless interconnections – which is why this book seeks to be a comprehensive guide, rather than a series of separate volumes.

How can you judge a care home if you do not appreciate that when you are in your eighties your eyes will need at least three times as much light as when you were in your twenties? How will an out-of-town retirement village look if you have to surrender your driving licence? It is important to be able to understand the motivations of the many providers of facilities you may need. What is an exit fee in the world of retirement housing and is it necessary? How exactly is the equity-release provider expecting to make their money and what effect will mortgaging your house to it have on your freedom to move to another property later on?

A combination of ignorance, fear, denial, bravado and unrealistic expectations can leave us floundering.

This book is intended primarily for people approaching and experiencing later life, as well as those trying to improve the lives of older relatives and friends. But I hope professionals will dip into it too and acquaint themselves with areas outside their own specialisms. I have come across doctors and nurses recommending a move to sheltered housing yet blind to its drawbacks; accountants and solicitors blithely ignorant of the world of benefits and social services; church ministers unaware of the state benefits that could prove a real godsend to their flock.

My aim is to provide the kind of information I sought in vain when my own mother, fast becoming blind and developing dementia, was finding life more and more difficult. Now, twenty years on, I am beginning to find out what later life will mean for me. I hope I shall be better prepared than she was, and I hope this book will help you to be.

HOW THIS BOOK WORKS

You can never get a cup of tea large enough or a book long enough to suit me.

C S Lewis

How to Handle Later Life covers a wide range of subjects and does not have to be read from beginning to end (although you are welcome to do this). I have written it in the hope of enabling readers to live as happily and as healthily as possible by identifying and addressing the difficulties they may encounter.

If you have a particular subject in mind – how to get help in the home perhaps, how to choose a retirement flat, or an attorney, how to find romance in later life or what treatment to expect if you have had a stroke – I hope you will easily find the relevant section. You will not need to have read everything that appears before it. Throughout the book cross-references are provided to other sections likely to be relevant, and I hope these will enable readers to hop, skip and jump their way around what may seem at first a dauntingly hefty tome.

That said, **Part One: Growing Older**, is intended to form a basic framework for understanding the physical and psychological needs of older people and I hope all readers will take the time to look at it. Chapter 1: The Ageing Body, sets out some of the basic ways in which our body changes as we go into our sixties and beyond. Why and how does our hearing change as we get older? Does sexual desire automatically decrease in later life? Are strokes brought on by stress? Myths abound in this area, yet are easily exploded.

The body needs a certain amount of physical activity for it to remain healthy, just as it has needs for fluid, food and an equable temperature. In chapters 2 and 3, I explore these needs and consider to what extent they change when we are getting on. In chapter 4, I go on to examine their psychological counterparts, not least because meeting our emotional and spiritual needs can prove more challenging as we get older.

After this introductory section, the book proceeds subject by subject. One question many people ask as they approach later life is: should I move house? Some assume they must downsize; others that they should relocate to an idyllic country cottage. Adverts for retirement housing and retirement villages portray politely greying citizens playing bridge contentedly in plush surroundings. Other people may believe that a move to sheltered housing provided by their council or a housing association would deliver the security and care they feel they need. In fact, a move to retirement, sheltered or extra-care housing can prove successful, disastrous or a mixed blessing. In **Part Two: Housing**, I outline some of the many factors to be taken into account when deciding whether to relocate. But whether you move or remain in your existing home, I hope the suggestions made in the final chapter of that part, Staying put, will be of interest. It ranges over keeping your accommodation warm, safe and in good repair and making adaptations, major or minor, to cope with disability.

A small proportion of us move into a care home. Such a move involves not just a change in our physical space but also entry into a new social world as we go and live amongst other people (probably strangers) and rely on the home's staff to care for us and keep us safe. In view of the magnitude of the changes involved, I have devoted a companion volume to be published in 2019 to care homes. That said, you will find that care homes are discussed at many points in this book.

Staying in touch with other people is a basic human need, yet one which can become more difficult to meet in later life. Some older people look for new friends or lovers, others for a community of kindred spirits. People who can no longer get out and about look for someone who could visit them at home. **Part Three: Connections** addresses how we can find these sorts of contact. It also examines the problems that can arise in communicating with people as a result of sight or hearing loss, a major stroke, Parkinson's disease or dementia.

A surprisingly high number of older people decline to turn to the internet to pursue new interests, voice their views or find work (paid or voluntary) or plan a holiday. I outline the main ways in which electronic communication can enrich our life and help us stay connected. In the final chapter of Part Three, I look at factors to take into account if you are looking for an animal companion in later life.

Health matters form the focus of the following two parts. In **Part Four: The World of Healthcare**, I set out the rights to healthcare we all enjoy and how to ensure they are upheld, whatever our age. I go on to discuss how to make the most of GPs and other health professionals, from dentists to optometrists, whose input can do much to improve our quality of life. In **Part Five: Healthcare Provision**, I set out the sort of treatment we should expect from the NHS for such common conditions of later life as strokes, anxiety, depression, continence difficulties and dementia. I also discuss falls.

Part Six: Practical Help turns the spotlight on assistance with everyday activities. One of the welcome developments of the 21st century has been the invention of a host of ingenious gadgets to circumvent difficulties arising from disability and illness. These range from amplifiers for telephones to electric scooters which can cover bumpy terrain. I begin by discussing the range of equipment which might make life easier and go on to examine a range of products called 'telecare' – devices involving sensors which can do anything from sounding the alarm because we have left the bath running or had a fall to alerting someone that somebody with dementia has wandered outside a pre-set area.

The ministrations of paid care assistants can be a boon when we are getting on. In this part, I look at how to find such help and to make sure helpers act in the way we wish. However, care assistants turn up only at pre-arranged times. Many people come to need care on demand, often at unexpected times during the night, but prefer not to move into a care home. Live-in care – what can be involved and how to set it up – is discussed in the final chapter of Part Six.

The social services departments of local authorities can provide advice on what sort of help someone needs; they may also partly or wholly fund it. For people who need a lot of practical help because illness or disability is hampering their ability to look after themselves, advice, support and perhaps also financial input from the state can be invaluable.

However, many of us reach our sixties without ever having encountered social services. I therefore begin **Part Seven: Help from the Council** with an explanation of what social care is and the way the social care system works, including social services' involvement in countering the abuse of vulnerable older people. In the following chapter, I explain how to get help from your social care authority and how to ensure you are not short-changed at a time when councils' purse-strings are particularly tight.

I continue by examining the position of carers – friends and family members who provide unpaid care. I explain the range of support available to them, both from local councils and from the voluntary sector. Finally, I explain how to ensure your council does not charge you too much for care and support.

Retirement or semi-retirement can offer more time and freedom to explore the outdoors, but obstacles can stand in our path. In **Part Eight: Out and About**, I look at ways in which you can make your local area an easier place in which to move around, from getting path surfaces improved to pedestrian crossing times changed. Some of us have to give up driving yet have not used public transport seriously for many years. I offer suggestions for travelling by train, coach and bus, taxi, plane and ferry, and also explain your access rights in using these facilities if you have a disability. In other words, a taxi driver should not sail straight past you if they spot you in a wheelchair and should give you any help you need to get in and out of their cab.

Part Nine: Representatives and Advisors turns to a part of life many of us ignore, until it is too late. You could fall under a bus tomorrow, become too ill to think clearly or develop dementia, and you may not be able to do much to prevent such calamities. But you can stop your money being used in ways of which you would disapprove if you cannot supervise matters yourself, and you can protect yourself from being given medical treatment against your will or shuffled into a care home by those with no knowledge of your wishes.

I explain how to grant power of attorney and how to select your attorneys, and suggest ways in which you might consider circumscribing their powers. If you have no attorney, your relatives may find they have to apply to a special court to represent your wishes and I explain how they can do this. How can you ensure your attorneys or other representatives, or the health and social care officials who can come to wield a lot of power should you lose the mental ability to take important decisions yourself, behave in ways that best serve your interests? I tackle this crucially important area too. The final chapter in Part Nine examines more limited powers of representation, albeit ones that are widely used. It also puts forward suggestions for finding solicitors, advocates and advisors.

Part Ten: Money may hold surprises. It shows that even in a time of cutbacks in the welfare field, you may qualify for a range of means-tested and non-means-tested state benefits. Indeed, you may be one of the tens of thousands of older citizens who are unwittingly saving the state millions of pounds because they neglect to apply for benefits, perhaps because they are ignorant of their existence, perhaps because they assume they would be ruled out on grounds of wealth.

I go on to examine private financial matters. It can be tempting to offload large sums of money to your heirs before death; is this a good idea? At what age should you take your state pension? Many people are taking advantage of the ban on enforced retirement and are working well past the age of 65; I discuss their rights in the workplace.

Rights in hospital are addressed in the first chapter of **Part Eleven: Hospitals**. Many of us arrive in hospital with little idea of what to expect, let alone our rights. How can we ensure we go to the most suitable hospital where we will receive the best medical and nursing care? Should the hospital be laying on free transport to take us to appointments? What role can visitors most usefully play? In the following chapter, I turn to our rights as patients when facing discharge from hospital. This can be a fraught area, as cash-strapped hospitals are often keen to discharge patients as soon as possible, even before they are fully recovered.

Part Twelve: The End of Life sets out what sort of care you might hope to receive towards the end of your life and how to obtain it. In Britain, we cannot ask a doctor to help us end our life. I discuss how you can ensure you exert as much control as possible over your final weeks and hours, particularly if you are unable to express your views clearly at the time. I also touch on non-medical choices you may wish to make.

Finally, at the end of the book, in the Useful Contacts section, you should find the postal address, telephone number, textphone number if available and website address of all the organisations mentioned in this book.

Despite well-publicised differences in fields such as health and social care north and south of the border, the law and procedures in these and other fields are remarkably similar throughout the UK. In this book, I describe the situation in England, while pointing out differences in Scotland, Wales and Northern Ireland where these are significant. Where material relates only to a particular country, the name of the country is in a sub-heading or shown in bold in the text. If this is not your country, you can skip this bit.

I describe the situation as at 1st July, 2017. Amaranth Books will be publishing updates from time to time on its website.

Inevitably there are a huge number of interconnections in this book. I hope that the cross-references provided in the text, supplemented by the Glossary and the Index, will enable you to make best use of it all. Good luck!

PART ONE
GROWING OLDER

❝ *More than one in ten people over 65 have such a restricted diet that they are considered to be malnourished.* **❞**

PART ONE
GROWING OLDER

Ageing is a part of human experience about which we are almost as reluctant to think as we are about its inevitable conclusion. Yet ageing is not merely something that lies in store for all of us: it is a process which holds us in thrall from the very moment of our conception. We like to think of ourselves as static beings, treating our first grey hair as an affront to our sense of ourselves. In truth, however, we spend every second of our life locked into a process of physical and mental change which we may influence but cannot stop. Many of the frailties we observe in older people reflect much earlier developments. We may think of people in their nineties as enfeebled; in fact, we lose nerve cells in our brain from the moment we are born, while our muscle strength declines by 1.5 per cent each year from the age of 30.

Some people sail happily through old age, apparently untouched by physical or mental affliction. Others lose many faculties. What precisely does ageing of the body mean once we turn 55 or 60? Are our lives terminated by a death gene or could we live forever, replacing cells and organs as they wear out? How do the psychological drives and urges of youth translate into later life? Why are older people more at risk in cold winters and hot summers than younger people? How does sexual desire change with the advancing years?

To discover how we can help ourselves, we need to understand just what happens to our bodies and our minds as we grow older. In this introductory part, I examine:

▶ the main physical changes which occur to the body from about the age of 60, distinguishing between those which are inevitable, such as the loss of hair colour, and those which are more common in old age but will not necessarily occur, such as the development of significant hearing or sight loss

▶ the physical needs of older people for:

- food
- water
- an equable temperature
- physical activity

▶ psychological needs: these needs, whether for affection or a sense of self-worth, are crucial to our happiness and indeed our mental health, yet we may find meeting them more difficult than we did in our youth.

You will have to read other parts of this book to discover some of the ways in which these needs can be met. Thus, for example, I explore psychological well-being in such chapters as 9: Relationships, 10: Group activities, 13: Animal magic, 17: Anxiety and depression, 20: Dementia, 23: Human help, 27: Support for carers, 30: On wheels and water, 38: Staying in hospital and 40: End-of-life care. I hope the many cross-references and the Index will also help you navigate your way around.

Chapter 1

The ageing body

Although ageing has always been part of all our lives, scientists are still only beginning to understand it. Competing theories abound. In his 2001 Reith Lectures, Professor Tom Kirkwood of Newcastle University's Institute for Ageing argued that over time 'free radicals' (which are by-products of the body's use of oxygen) cause wear and tear to the DNA in our cells, and that this damage finally proves too much for our cells' repair systems.[1] So according to this theory, ageing is a bottom-up process of accumulated change and no 'death gene' exists that instructs our bodies to die after a set number of years.

However, some scientists argue the reverse – that a programme of ageing laid down in our genes does take place, just as the early development of embryos and infants follows a predetermined timeline. Still others maintain, for instance, that degeneration of the pathways along which cells communicate in complex organisms is the key to ageing.[2]

All we can say for sure is that individuals with the longest lifespans, such as the French woman Jeanne Calment, who died in 1997 at the age of 122 years (the oldest verified age on record), have demonstrated that the human body is capable of surviving the onslaughts of ageing for much longer than the traditional three score and ten.

Living to a great age is by no means a phenomenon of the 21st century. William Wordsworth, for instance, lived to see his 80th birthday (dying in 1850), while his sister, Dorothy, died at 84 and his wife, Mary, at 88. But long lifespans such as these were not common in past times: childhood diseases, childbirth, accidents and fighting in war killed many before they reached middle or old age. What has happened in Britain since the 19th century is that the average age on death of the entire population has increased steadily as a result of growing prosperity and improvements in nutrition, sanitation, town planning and medicine.

However, the bounty of the extra years of life which we can now enjoy comes with a downside – physical changes to our body. These changes fall into two types.

Some changes are an inevitable, universal feature of the ageing process and are not necessarily bad for our health; they include the greying of the hair and the cessation of the ability of women to bear children.

Other changes, such as the development of cataracts, hearing problems, osteoarthritis and the occurrence of strokes, are not universal. They are medical afflictions which are more common in later life, but they are not an automatic part of the ageing process. Ageing predisposes us to develop them, but it does not cause them, and many people will escape them completely. Unfortunately, many of these age-related conditions are incurable (although not necessarily terminal), and all that can be done is to seek to manage some of the symptoms.

Several factors combine to mean that no two people age in precisely the same way. Wrinkles and greying hair may make older people appear more similar to each other than children seem to other children, but in fact the differences between us increase markedly as we age. For some women, the menopause comes at 35, but for others at 45 or 55, or even later. Some people develop several chronic medical ailments in later life; others just one or none. Indeed, the appearance – or not – of conditions such as dementia and age-related macular degeneration is one of the main reasons why the experience of old age differs so widely between individuals.

Also, those who develop illness and disability react in different ways. For these ailments act on minds and bodies which vary massively – partly because of genetic endowment, partly because of life already lived. Because of this variability, doctors find it useful to consider a person's 'physiological' or 'biological age', which is reflected in their physical condition and the state of their main bodily functions, separately from their chronological age. As a result, they might conclude that a 90-year-old was sufficiently fit to survive a major operation while somebody much younger but in poorer health was not.

In this chapter, I look at the organ systems of the body in turn, teasing out those changes that are a universal part of the ageing process and those that often occur but do not affect everybody.[3]

Sense organs

Fortunately, the sense of touch does not seem to be much compromised by age. However, eyes, ears and our abilities to detect odours and tastes see several significant changes.

Eyes

Most of us know we are likely to become more long-sighted as we grow older because the lens in the eye becomes harder with age and thus less responsive to the attempts of the eye muscles to change its shape in order to focus. This change affects everyone over the age of 45 to some extent. Fortunately, it can be corrected with spectacles.

If sufficient light is to enter the pupil for normal vision, the muscles of the iris must contract. But as we grow older, these muscles become more sluggish. This change, coupled with an increase in the thickness of the lens suspended across the interior of the eye, means that less light manages to reach the retina at the back of the eye, where it is transformed into nerve impulses, allowing us to see. As a result, a 60-year-old needs three times as much light as a young person to see as well, while an 80-year-old needs four times as much.[4]

In view of this, it is hardly surprising that older people often find moving around out of doors after dark a strain. They need ample street lighting if they are to do this comfortably. Driving at night can also be stressful not just because older people need more light, but also because they are more sensitive to glare than younger people.[5] This increased sensitivity to glare means that an older person who is walking down a corridor towards light pouring through a window can become disorientated.

As we grow older, we experience a reduction in the ability to discriminate between colours, which appear less bright and show a lower range of contrast. There is a particular reduction in the ability to distinguish between shades of blue and green in the violet part of the spectrum.[6] This is why designers of products which need to be seen clearly by an older age-group should concentrate on colours like red and orange. Signs are most easily read if they involve yellow contrasted with black.

In addition to these changes affecting everyone, there are certain conditions whose frequency increases in old age. Fortunately, cataracts, which are very common, can be removed and vision restored. The development of laser technology to excise cataracts was one of the great medical advances of the 20th century and the benefits have been immense.

While low light poses problems for older people, it causes even greater problems for people suffering from age-related macular degeneration, or AMD. This is not an inevitable result of ageing, but it is the most common long-term visual impairment in later life, with nearly a third of people over 75 affected. For reasons which are unclear, the cells at the macula, a pinhead-sized area at the centre of the retina where most of the cells responsible for colour and acute vision are concentrated, progressively degenerate. This affects the centre of the field of vision, so objects seen straight ahead become smudged, blurred or blotted out. AMD can be very disabling, but does not cause complete blindness as people with the condition retain their ability to see around the periphery. Treatments to halt the development of the condition are available for the 'wet' form of AMD, but none has so far been found to treat the far more common 'dry' type. *(For information on gadgets to aid low vision, see page 461; on the Macular Society, page 328; on local council low vision teams, page 559; and on communicating with blind or partially-sighted people, pages 252–4.)*

Ears

From babyhood onwards, the tiny sensitive hairs in the inner ear, which convert sound into electrical signals, gradually die off. By the time we reach 40, this will have affected our hearing. As we grow older, other structural changes may make matters worse.[7] For some unlucky people, atrophy of the hearing apparatus is made much worse by its earlier subjection to the noise of guns in war, machines in heavy industry or very loud music. Significant hearing impairment is common in old age, affecting between half and two-thirds of people aged 70 and over in recent studies.[8]

However, older people tend to complain less about inability to hear than difficulty in understanding speech. This is because certain consonants critical to understanding speech, such as 's', 'sh', 'f', 'p' and 't', require high-frequency sound which is particularly impaired in age-related hearing loss. Thus, older people who are affected may feel that others are mumbling. Deciphering speech is more difficult when there is high ambient noise – at a party or when a TV weather presenter speaks against a background of wind noise. *(For information on gadgets which can help hearing, see pages 474–6; for tips on communicating with people who are hard of hearing, see pages 254–5.)*

Taste, smell and touch

All those tiny bumps on our tongues are papillae which detect taste through tens of thousands of taste receptors. In later life, the rate of cell replacement in our taste sensors slows down and as a result the number of receptors declines. A decline in the sense of taste may become apparent in people in their eighties and beyond.[9] Now, some people retain an acute sense of taste because they had higher than usual numbers of receptors to start with or their loss has been smaller. But in some people loss will be exacerbated by a condition such as dry mouth or the side-effects of medication.

Our sense of smell follows a similar path. One study pointed to a decline of more than 60 per cent among people over the age of 80 in the ability to detect odours.[10] This may mean becoming less able to detect, say, smoke, whether the pleasure of wood smoke or smoke that heralds danger. As the aroma of food is inextricably linked to its appeal, an increase in the threshold at which smell is detected can contribute to loss of appetite. As a result, older people may not get enough to eat and become malnourished *(as discussed on pages 43–7).*

Fortunately our sense of touch survives largely unimpaired till the end of our lives, so we can continue to benefit from the pleasures it affords. If you lose your sight, touch can take over as a vital means of communication and discovery. Touch can enable a blind grandfather to 'see' his grandchild. Stroking the hand or head of someone who is seriously unwell, perhaps dying, can do more than words to soothe and to convey love and empathy. Touch can also sidestep the need for words with a loved one, perhaps with advanced dementia, who can no longer comprehend them.

Sex

The reproductive systems of both men and women show very significant and dramatic changes as the body ages. The first such change, puberty, applies to both sexes; the second, the menopause, only to women. The menopause marks the cessation of egg release by the ovaries and of the monthly cycle. Women who hit the news headlines because they have given birth in their sixties do not do so naturally: they need donor eggs.

As the ovaries stop releasing eggs, they cut down the production of female hormones, resulting in various degenerative changes. The vagina becomes narrower, shorter and less elastic, while the glands which produce its lubricating secretions diminish. As glandular tissue in the breasts which produces milk is replaced with fat, breasts lose their firmness. But although women lose their fertility, they do not lose their capacity for sexual enjoyment.

For men, changes in later life are more gradual and, as with so many age-related changes, there is considerable variation between individuals in the timing and the scope of change. Men see no abrupt end to their ability to produce children as women do, and most men remain fertile throughout their lives. However, the reproductive organs of men do undergo some atrophy with age, which can have an effect on the efficiency of the system. Older men can take longer to achieve an erection and it may be less firm than that of a younger man. The force of ejaculation is often diminished and the amount of seminal fluid may be less. Furthermore, it usually takes much longer for an older man to be able to repeat ejaculation than for a younger man. None of this rules out sexual activity, and in practice the sexual pleasure of older women may increase, if only because the timing of the performance of older partners may be more to their taste than that of younger men.

The digestive system

Some parts of the digestive system change little with age, or if they do, the changes pose few problems. The stomach shows no important change; indeed, it is an organ which has such a large reserve in its capacity to function that even if four-fifths of it is removed, the remaining fifth can still keep the body functioning.

However, age-related changes in the stomach, liver and kidneys can combine to reduce the ability of the older body to process drugs. As a result, older and particularly very old people are more sensitive to medicinal drugs. The dosage required to generate the same result gets smaller as they age, and they are more susceptible to the side-effects of medication. The bodies of older people are also more sensitive to alcohol and recreational drugs.

What happens is this: the liver and the kidneys – the two major organs responsible for processing what we take in – become far less effective as we age. The volume of the liver and the rate at which blood flows through it decline by about 30 per cent in people over 65 years, so reducing its ability to process our intake. The kidneys also see an inevitable reduction in volume and rate of blood flow with age, while the stomach empties its contents more slowly. *(For the implications of these changes for the prescribing of drugs, see pages 294 and 309.)*

Teeth

Ageing can predispose us to dental problems. As teeth become older, they often lose some of their enamel covering, which makes them more susceptible to attack from sugars, and this causes decay. Also, as we grow older, we tend to lose bone tissue in the jaws, causing the teeth to loosen. Another common problem is gum disease, the main cause of which is build-up of plaque.

Although dental problems are not life-threatening, they can have a huge impact on quality of life. Sore teeth and gums can cause much pain and misery. When teeth are missing, the variety of food we can eat is reduced, along with the pleasure of chewing and biting, while unsightly teeth and ill-fitting dentures can affect our social life, making us too embarrassed to smile or kiss.

All this means that as we get older, we need to pay more attention to cleaning our teeth and gums, to arresting any developing problems through frequent visits to the dentist and hygienist, and to ensuring that we do not consume too much sugar. *(For more on sugar, see page 37 and on dental matters, page 305–7.)*

Hair and skin

Perhaps the most harmless changes involved in the ageing process are those that are most visible – those affecting the hair and the skin.

The greying and thinning of the hair are universal and inevitable features of ageing. Most people will find that by the time they are 50 about half of their hair is grey.

The thinning of hair and balding in men make them more susceptible to damage from the sun's rays, which can lead to skin cancer. That is why it is important for men (and women too) to protect their ears, necks, scalps and faces with wide-brimmed sunhats.

One inevitable feature of ageing is that structural changes to the elastic fibres in the skin reduce the skin's ability to smooth out. Gravity acts with these changes to cause wrinkles. The extent of wrinkling is a product of genes and also a lifetime's exposure to sunlight. At the same time, changes to the structure of the skin reduce its ability to protect itself from elements in the environment such as sunshine, so as we grow older we are more likely to develop skin blemishes, such as liver spots.

Other changes can affect older skin, particularly in people over 80. Small bruises can arise from very little trauma, particularly on the backs of the hands and the forearms, as the skin becomes increasingly thin and fragile – a condition known (charmingly) as senile purpura. A decrease in sweat and oil secretions from the skin also leads to dryness. This may be one reason why a condition known as pruritus, in which the skin is more vulnerable to itching in the absence of any obvious rash, is quite common amongst elderly people.[11]

Perhaps the most serious relatively common skin condition is a pressure sore. Pressure sores (also known as pressure ulcers and bed sores) can develop in people of any age but are much more common in very old people who are immobile and malnourished and when an area of skin is under great pressure, perhaps from body weight but also perhaps from the friction that can arise if someone slides down their chair or bed or is handled roughly. These factors can cause an area of skin with the fat beneath to die and an ulcer to form. This happens most commonly on the skin of the buttocks, heels, shoulders, toes and at the base of the spine.

Pressure sores are nasty things. The worst, classed as grade 4 ulcers, can kill tissue down to underlying muscle or bone. They can be extremely painful and take a long time to heal. If an ulcer becomes infected by bacteria which favour wounds, such as MRSA *(see page 917),* healing can take even longer. *(For more information on pressure ulcers, see pages 398–9, 813 and 913–4.)* Tissue viability nurses play a key role in safeguarding the integrity and health of the skin, not least in the prevention and treatment of pressure sores.

The skin infection shingles is relatively common in older people with a weak immune system. Do take advantage of the vaccine, which the NHS provides free for people aged 70 and over.

Skin and body temperature regulation

Changes to the skin affect the ability of older and particularly very old people to regulate their body temperature. The layer of fat under the skin acts as an insulator protecting body temperature and many people see a loss in thickness of this fat in later life.[12] Without as much insulation, the body chills more quickly if the ambient temperature is lowered and is heated more rapidly by hot temperatures outside the body. As a result, older people are more susceptible to overheating and hypothermia – both potentially lethal conditions.

A separate change to the skin also impairs the ability to cope with excessive heat. As we age, our sweat glands gradually atrophy, so reducing the efficiency of sweating – an essential mechanism in keeping the body's temperature at a safe level in a hot environment. As a result, older people, being unable to sweat as much as younger people, may overheat. *(I return to the special need of older people for well-heated rooms in winter and cool rooms in summer on page 49–52.)*

Incidentally, the reduction in thickness of the layer of fat under the skin can also make the skin less able to cope with pressure when we are sitting down. Hard benches can therefore be much more uncomfortable for older than younger people.

Muscles

One of the inescapable elements of the ageing process is a decline in muscle strength and power, starting from around the age of 30. Irreversible changes within muscles occur involving the loss of muscle fibres. We can seek to mitigate these changes through exercise, but we can never regain completely the muscle capacity that we enjoyed in our younger years.

These changes to our muscles don't really affect our day-to-day life until we approach old age. Then we can see their effects if we consider the minimum power necessary to carry out a particular function. So, at the age of 85, nearly half of women and a third of men are unable to rise unaided from a chair.[13] This means that the bench-like seating provided in shopping malls is often of little value to them unless they have some means of pulling themselves to their feet.

As we age, the nerve cells in our muscles which command them to act, decline in number. As a result, it will take us longer to respond to a stimulus such as the firing of a gun or the sounding of a fire alarm. This change, combined with reduced muscle power, means that people over the age of 80 find it more difficult to cross a road before the lights change than when they were younger. As a result, they may try to rush, trip and fall over.

Joints

In later life, the flexibility of our joints, such as those in the knees and elbows, declines, as a result of the deterioration of cartilage – the material covering the ends of those bones which meet in a joint and which prevents their wearing each other away. Cartilage also acts as a shock absorber, soaking up the impact imposed on our joints by movement.

In more than half of older people, this deterioration is sufficiently serious to take the form of osteoarthritis. This is a chronic, degenerative joint disease in which cartilage softens and disintegrates exposing bone ends and allowing them to rub together. In addition to knees and elbows, the joints most commonly affected are in the hips, neck, base of the spine, hands and feet. Osteoarthritis is slightly more common in women than men. Further stress and weight on damaged joints can worsen the condition.

Pain is a key feature of osteoarthritis. At first this may be relieved by joint rest, but as the disease progresses it becomes more common and more severe after activity. People with the condition also often experience stiffness after a joint has been at rest, as well as difficulty in moving joints as freely or as far as normal. So they may have trouble in climbing stairs, walking and bending.

Bones

We tend to think of our bones as the most inert part of the body. In fact, they are constantly replenishing themselves as bone cells die and are replaced with new ones. In women the menopause brings a drop in the female hormone oestrogen, and this causes the rate of renewal of bone cells to rise, which in turn weakens the bones.

As the amount of muscle fibre declines with advancing years, contracting muscles impose less pull on the bones; this in turn affects the strength of the bones. Lighter bones are much more likely to break in an accident. Osteoporosis is a disease which is an extreme version of this process and is characterised by low bone mass and deterioration of the support structure of the bones. It makes bones more fragile and likely to fracture, and thus makes injury more likely after a fall, even a minor one *(see page 386)*. It is thought to contribute to at least one bone break for a third of women at some time in their life. The risk amongst men is less, but still substantial. Many people do not realise that they have osteoporosis until they break a bone and a subsequent X-ray reveals that their superstructure of bone tissue is abnormally fragile.

Osteomalacia is also common among elderly people and in this case the bones soften. This condition causes pain in the joints and bones, weakness in muscles, and compression of the vertebrae, so height is lost. Slight cracks which can turn into complete bone breaks can appear. People who fail to make or consume enough vitamin D are at greater risk of developing osteoporosis and osteomalacia.

Kidneys and bladder

Many older people need to visit the lavatory more frequently than younger people. This is the result of changes in the kidneys and bladder. Structural changes in the kidneys reduce their ability to concentrate urine. As a result, more urine has to be passed to rid the body of waste products, so that many people find that their sleep is disturbed by a need to visit the bathroom.

Some older people also experience a delay in the sensation indicating the need to urinate until the bladder is almost full. This may mean that they don't know they need to pass water until it is almost too late to get to the lavatory. In men, enlargement of the prostate gland may make passing water more difficult, with the result that the person needs to urinate more frequently than normally.

These changes to our urinary system can make going out much more of a problem, especially as local authorities appear to have decided that many of the public lavatories the Victorians built are somehow no longer necessary and can be closed.

The changes do not, however, amount to urinary incontinence, in which somebody is unable to prevent loss of urine. This condition can have a number of different causes. It is not an inevitable part of the ageing process, but it is common: slightly less than a third of people over the age of 65 suffer from some degree of incontinence, often as a result of the tearing of the pelvic floor muscles during prolonged childbirth. *(Its causes, treatment and management are examined on pages 407–26.)* Faecal incontinence is much rarer than its urinary equivalent *(see pages 415–6)*.

Constipation is one of the bugbears of old age, and is one of the most frequent reasons for a visit to the GP. Much can be done to lessen or avoid the problem, such as the introduction of more fibre in the diet and an increase in physical activity.

Lungs

Inevitable changes occur to the lungs, their associated muscles and the tubes which lead into them (the bronchi) as we age, but they do not have a serious effect on health. However, damage to the lungs and bronchi built up perhaps over a lifetime as a result of cigarette smoking or the inhalation of coal or asbestos dust is the main cause of several serious respiratory conditions (emphysema, chronic bronchitis, lung cancer and asbestosis). These are therefore more common in later life.

Blood vessels and blood pressure

Hardening of the arteries is a universal feature of the ageing process and so will affect us all. Cross-linkages form between molecules in the walls of our arteries and calcium is deposited between them, making the arteries stiffer as we grow older. This process is progressive, irreversible and eventually harmful.

As arteries harden, fatty deposits are often, but not always, laid down on the insides of the blood vessels, causing them to fur up. This second process is not an inevitable result of ageing, but seems to occur when certain risk factors interact with the stiffening of the arteries to produce deposits. Risk factors include one's genes, high blood pressure, smoking, type 2 diabetes and a diet high in saturated fats and trans-fats *(see page 38)*.[14]

Both the hardening and furring of arteries are a major cause of rising blood pressure. This is a measure of the force with which blood presses on the walls of the arteries as it is pumped around the body. The stiffer and the more furred up the arteries become, the higher the blood pressure rises. This puts a strain on blood vessels, not least those which lead to the brain.

If arteries are narrowed greatly by the accumulation of deposits, then a piece of deposit may break off. In places where blood vessels are narrow, this is more likely to lead to a blockage. If this clot interrupts the supply of blood to the brain causing damage to brain cells, a stroke takes place.

Another type of stroke – a haemorrhagic or bleed stroke – arises when the extra strain on a blood vessel in the brain causes that vessel to burst and blood spills out, flooding surrounding tissues.

Strokes are a major killer of older people and leave many others severely disabled in all manner of different ways, depending on the area of the brain affected. *(Their causes and treatment are discussed in Chapter 16.)*

High blood pressure is not an inevitable result of the ageing process, and does not occur at all amongst people in parts of the developing world. In most people, high blood pressure causes no outward symptoms, so is completely invisible. But it is a dangerous condition, since it is implicated in many serious or life-threatening afflictions, not least heart attacks, strokes, heart failure and kidney damage. A woman is five times more likely to die from diseases affecting the heart or blood vessels – cardiovascular disease – than breast cancer.

The heart

As we grow older, our heart often has to work harder to maintain normal blood flow to all the organs of the body, mainly because of high blood pressure but also other factors, such as disease affecting heart valves. If a blood clot stops the flow of blood to the heart, the sudden blockage deprives the heart muscle of blood and oxygen, and someone is said to be having a heart attack. Heart muscle cells become damaged or die, and cannot conduct electrical impulses in the way that they should. If only a small area of heart muscle is affected, a full recovery is possible. But damage to a large area may cause sudden death or an incomplete recovery, because the heart has lost part of its pumping power. As the heart is an internal organ without pain receptors, the pain of an attack is not felt in the heart. Instead, it is usually referred to the chest or sometimes the shoulder, arm, neck or jaw, although small heart attacks can be painless.

The weakening of heart muscle through a heart attack may lead to the often long-term condition of heart failure – impairment in the heart's ability to pump sufficient blood around the body. Heart failure has several possible other causes, including lung disease, disease affecting the heart valves and disease in the main artery to the heart. High blood pressure too can cause heart failure by putting additional work on the heart muscle, which is thereby altered.

Heart failure makes walking more difficult because the person affected experiences shortness of breath. Other symptoms include coughing and swollen ankles. The condition usually gradually worsens and can be very disabling.

It is important to get blood pressure checked regularly and, if necessary, to take steps to bring it down to a safer level and also to address any other symptoms which might indicate cardiovascular disease. Treatment includes the use of drugs; and those affected can do much to help themselves by giving up smoking, taking appropriate exercise *(page 61)* and eating a healthy diet *(pages 37–41)*.

The brain

The health of the brain is closely linked to that of the cardiovascular system. As just noted, our arteries deteriorate as we get older, as a result of their inevitable stiffening; in many cases fat is deposited on their inner walls. The result is to slow down blood flow. This can be particularly significant for the brain, since it needs a lot of blood to function and has no mechanism (unlike our muscles) for storing the energy that blood contains. What this means is that the most important step we can take to ensure a healthy brain in later life is to keep our cardiovascular system healthy, so that blood can circulate freely to the brain at all times.

We shall see in a moment that the main significant impairment of the brain in later life – dementia – is often associated with an unhealthy cardiovascular system. Fortunately, most people in their eighties and beyond do not develop dementia. Nonetheless, certain changes to the brain are universal, whatever the health of the cardiovascular system.

As we age, there is a net loss of brain cells or neurones and of the connections between them. These connections, or synapses, are vital for passing information. Change starts young: from the age of 20, our brain experiences a steady reduction in the density of synapses. Were this to continue in people with no signs of dementia, it would reach the reduced density that is seen in Alzheimer's disease at the age of 130.[15]

The good news is that the brain is one of the organs of the body which possesses a large amount of spare capacity. This means it can cope even with a considerable loss of brain cells and synapses. Imaging studies have shown the brains of healthy people in their eighties to be almost as active as those of people in their twenties.[16]

The reduction in synaptic density is not evenly spread across the brain. It and other changes mean that the brain does not age as a single unit: different regions, responsible for different functions, show different types and rates of atrophy. These regions of the brain are interconnected, and the efficiency of these connections may also change with age and, again, not in a uniform manner. On top of this, there is much variation between individuals.

However, our brain cells can continue to make new connections in later life. Since learning requires the formation of new synapses, this explains why older people are perfectly capable of learning new skills and remembering new facts. To make matters even more complex – and fascinating – the brain has a remarkable capacity to reorganise itself and recruit different areas to compensate for any changes. That is why it is sometimes able to recover from the death of certain parts as a result of a stroke or injury in an accident.

One aspect of brain functioning which appears to be relatively exempt from the ageing process is the experiencing, regulation and processing of emotion.[17] As we see in a moment, even when someone suffers from the most common types of dementia, this area appears relatively untouched, at least until the dementia is far advanced.

However, the picture for 'cognitive functioning', which involves reasoning, remembering, planning and conveying thoughts in words, is more mixed. A team of researchers in Seattle carried out tests on cognitive functioning at regular intervals on a large number of individuals, in many cases the same people, over a 35-year period in an attempt to plot any changes over time. Once the participants were over the age of 65, the researchers observed reductions in the abilities to perceive speed, to reason through deduction and to orientate oneself in space. However, the ability to manipulate numbers, and even more so words, showed only a slight decline, being at an approximately equal level to that of people in their thirties.[18]

Scientists have also studied memory and observed changes which seem to be associated with the passage of time. While young people seem to be able to hold from five to nine items in their short-term memory at any one time, this number is slightly lower for older people.[19] This would account for the slight decline in the ability to learn new information or to store new material in the short-term memory which is often experienced in later life. This does not mean that older people cannot absorb new information – it simply takes longer and may require more effort.

However, other brain systems involved in memory react differently to ageing. Skills such as playing chess or a musical instrument rely on another type of memory, called implicit memory, and are maintained well with age, so long as there is continued practice. Autobiographical memory – the ability to recall our own life experience – also seems to be unaffected by the ageing process.[20]

Eminent psychologist Professor Patrick Rabbitt and the author of *The Aging Mind: An Owner's Manual* believes that changes in brain functioning associated with ageing are not that great. He believes that the key change that occurs as the brain ages is a significant decline in the speed with which it processes information.[21] This seems to be borne out by PD James' response in 2011 to the question whether age had affected her facility for creative writing. The crime writer, who was then in her nineties, replied that it had not, except insofar as she thought she was now slightly slower at calling to mind words and fashioning sentences.[22] In some people, this reduction in speed can be exacerbated by impairment in sense organs, so that the information feeding into the brain from the ears and eyes is degraded. The brain must then make more effort to recognise speech and the written word.

We can compensate for many of the changes in our brain in later life. If we cannot hold quite as many different items in our short-term memory, we can compensate by writing aide-memoire lists. A researcher measured typing speed in a group of older typists. Although they were slower at performing reaction-time tasks, they maintained their typing speed by compensating for this deficiency through reading and planning ahead.[23]

The wisdom of the old

Scientists distinguish between two kinds of intelligence. 'Fluid intelligence' is concerned with rapid on the spot problem-solving ability which does not rely on large amounts of previous learning. Studies have found that fluid intelligence, being related to brain-processing speed, declines with age. That is why older people don't make ideal fighter pilots.

'Crystallized intelligence', in contrast, relies on previous learning and is analogous with wisdom. It involves the taking of complex decisions relying not so much on speed of thought as on the possession and appropriate use of large quantities of relevant information, some perhaps arising from personal experience, and of the skills to solve complex problems.

Crystallized intelligence remains stable or even continues to increase with age. So, older people are often better suited to acting as judges, head teachers or managers than younger adults. In other words, there is real scientific backing for the idea of the wisdom of the old.[24]

Creativity in later life

If impressive intellectual ability can persist into old age undimmed, so too can creative ability. This is something else which does not demand lightning-quick responses. Richard Strauss, Haydn, Turner, Rembrandt, Verdi and Picasso all created important new work towards the end of their lives. Often the work of these and other artists took on new dimensions in later life. In his late fifties, Thomas Hardy set about writing poetry, produced eleven volumes over the next 30 years and was still penning new poems on the day before he died at the age of 88. Five of Ralph Vaughan Williams' nine symphonies were composed between his 60th birthday and his death, aged 86. His eighth and ninth, in particular, are very different from his earlier work, with much more colourful orchestration.

So, contrary to popular myth, which dictates that older people in general see their mental faculties decline, studies have shown that any decline in cognitive ability and memory in people not afflicted by brain disease is small, and that those affected can often adapt to or compensate for it. Perhaps as many as 10 per cent of older people show no deterioration whatsoever in their mental abilities as they grow older, except perhaps in extreme old age, according to studies conducted in Britain and the United States.[25]

Dementia

Where significant permanent decline in cognitive ability occurs in older people, it is almost always the result of the abnormal syndrome known as dementia. Dementia is a term for the progressive, irreversible loss of mental ability in many areas, including memory, language and the ability to reason, to plan and to cope with the activities of daily life. So, in the early stages, somebody may have difficulty in managing their finances; in the later stages, in washing and feeding themselves.

The most significant risk factor for the development of dementia is age. About one in ten people aged 80–84 have some degree of dementia, but the figure approaches one-fifth for those in their late eighties and 40 per cent for people over 95 years of age.[26] Of course, this means that four-fifths of people in their late eighties, for instance, do not have the condition.

The most common cause of dementia is Alzheimer's disease. This is characterised by changes in the configuration of nerve cells in the brain: for some reason, still unknown, types of protein (amyloid and tau) are deposited in brain cells giving rise to changes in the appearance of these cells.

The second main cause, known as vascular dementia, results from strokes, often tiny, imperceptible ones, which kill off brain tissue and result from an unhealthy cardiovascular system. There is considerable overlap, so that about half of people with Alzheimer's disease are thought to have some vascular dementia too.

Other less common types of dementia occur among older people such as Lewy body dementia, in which deposits of certain proteins are laid down in brain cells for unknown reasons.

Some people in their sixties and even younger develop dementia, but the condition is much rarer for these age groups. Nonetheless, 'early-onset dementia' affects 40,000 people under the age of 65 in the UK. Often those involved have Alzheimer's disease or vascular dementia but, as we see in Chapter 20: Dementia, other causes are more common in this younger age group that may give rise to changes in behaviour and personality rather than, as with Alzheimer's, memory.

Dementia manifests differently in different individuals. Differences arise partly from the type of dementia present and the brain cells affected, as well as the rate of progression of the condition. But differences also spring from the different personalities, experiences and skills of individuals. Thus some people manage to function fairly well, while others cannot. Some people with dementia seem not unduly troubled, while others are often upset, although as we see in chapter 20, the attitudes of those around the person with dementia can much affect the emotional impact of the condition. Many people finally succumb to some other disease and die with dementia, but not as a result of it. If the dementia reaches an advanced stage it affects many different parts of the brain, with the result that its impact is more similar between individuals.

One factor which may play a part in explaining differences in the impact of dementia on different individuals is 'cognitive reserve'. This is the brain's reserve against damage or the threshold beyond which damage to nerve cells has a noticeable impact on brain function. Genetics may play a part in the amount of cognitive reserve, but so too, perhaps, may the use to which the brain has been put in the past. Recent research has indicated that while education and use of the brain during adulthood cannot prevent dementia, they can sometimes compensate for its effects by lessening the severity of symptoms in the early stages. In this way, cognitive reserve can delay the time before brain degeneration has a significant impact on a person's ability to lead a normal life.[27]

Dementia is particularly challenging in its later stages because it is often accompanied by a significant loss of the ability to communicate, as people with the condition forget the vocabulary of normal speech. As a result, those who have lost the ability to communicate intelligibly cannot explain what dementia means to them on a daily basis or explain how they feel in other ways, from whom they would like to see to whether they have toothache. *(For tips on how best to relate to and communicate with people with dementia, see pages 257–64. For more on medical care for people with dementia, see Chapter 20. Further references to dementia occur at many points in this book; you can find them in the index.)*

No cure or means of prevention for dementia seems to be on the horizon, so for the foreseeable future attention must be focused on supporting the hundreds of thousands of people who have to live with the condition. One problem is that descriptions of dementia tend to focus on what is lost, not on what remains. People with dementia retain many things, including in many cases the ability to feel the full range of emotions until late on. This means that although their ability to reason and remember may be much diminished, they continue to be able to experience various different kinds of pleasure and pain, so can be injured just as easily as anybody else by hurtful behaviour and thrilled by, perhaps, a beautiful sunset.

The whole body

So far we have looked at the ways in which ageing affects particular organ systems. But in tandem with these changes, it also alters the whole body system, particularly in people in their eighties and over.

The body's reserves

One change involves the ability to cope with emergencies. If you are out shopping and the supermarket suddenly catches fire, your body needs to step up your heart rate and your respiratory rate and move speedily from the building. The ability to do this is known as the body's 'functional reserve'. It gets smaller as we grow older. The body organ systems of younger people contain reserves far greater than will be needed, whereas elderly people are living at the limit of their functional reserve. When all is well, the old manage as well as the young, but when they need extra acceleration or stamina, they may be unable to muster it.

For example, while younger people can function perfectly adequately while one lung recovers from pneumonia, in older people both lungs will already be working at their full capacity. Therefore, an attack of pneumonia can push the lung system over the edge. Similarly, the kidneys of older people do not have as much reserve capacity as those of younger people to cope with disease or trauma: they are under strain already. As a result, elderly people can become dehydrated more easily. Therefore when older people become sick, perhaps from some relatively minor affliction, they need expert care, otherwise they can go downhill very quickly.

Internal stability

The human body needs to maintain a stable internal environment so that the cells of the body can function properly. It needs to be able to regulate through constant adjustment the amount of water within cells, their temperature and the concentrations of various chemicals in the face of changes imposed from outside, such as a drop in temperature or an increase in the body's temperature as the result of an infection.

The ability to perform this intricate and complex task (known as homeostasis) depends on many organs of the body, including the kidneys and the part of the nervous system of which we are unconscious which is responsible for controlling heartbeat. As we grow older, our capacity to maintain homeostasis lessens. That is one reason why older people are more susceptible to overheating and hypothermia, for example. Also, if illness or stress to the system means that a part of the body responsible for maintaining homeostasis is not operating as it should, older people may go downhill more quickly than younger people.

Disability versus frailty

When a physical or mental condition has an impact on somebody's ability to function, this is called a 'disability'. For example, osteoarthritis in the knee joint may give rise to difficulties in walking and climbing stairs sufficiently serious for that person to be considered to possess a locomotion disability.

In contrast, frailty is not easily defined. It is, however, something you recognises when you see it. Somebody may have a disability, but in a body in which other organ systems, including the most of important of all, the lungs and heart, are in good order. So a child might have a locomotion disability because of a broken leg, yet be physically robust. But if impairments have built up in many systems of the body (rather than simply discrete diseases or injuries), so that the person has difficulty in carrying out ordinary day-to-day tasks and is very vulnerable to disease or trauma, they are said to be 'frail'.[28]

Not all of us will become frail just as not all will develop one or more disabilities. However, the chances of doing both increase with age.

Puzzling symptoms

Two further aspects of the physiology of the older body are worth noting. First, the knock-on effects of illness in older people mean that it is often not at all clear what is wrong with them. Sometimes the symptom with which a medical condition is diagnosed appears less strongly in an older person. A heart attack, for example, may involve less pain than in the case of a younger person. Or an older person may 'present', as doctors say, with symptoms apparently unconnected to the condition which has prompted them. If you get pneumonia when you are young, you will have symptoms such as a fever, chest pain and shortness of breath. But an older person suffering from pneumonia may have little in the way of respiratory symptoms. Instead they may start falling over and/or become temporarily confused, or temporarily incontinent, or unable to stand up.

Delirium is the term given to a confused state which is temporary – as opposed to the permanent confusion suffered by people with a brain injury or an illness such as dementia. It often develops in very old people and those who have dementia should they develop an infection, such as pneumonia. Some people with delirium are slow and sleepy, others restless and agitated but most are unable to speak clearly or follow a complicated conversation.[29] It is important that if the person involved needs to take an important decision at the time they are delirious, perhaps about whether they should move from hospital into a care home, that the decision should be deferred until the delirium subsides, if it is possible to do so, *as explained in Chapter 33: How representatives should behave.*

Medical care – the challenge

Many of these features of ageing may sound like bad news for older people – and of course they are, to some degree. But they do have one advantage: they make the field of geriatric or care-of-the-older-patient medicine extremely interesting. For one thing, the non-specific presentation of symptoms in elderly people means that diagnosing their ailments can resemble a detective puzzle, with some symptoms offering false clues to the nature of a malady. For another, several pre-existing conditions may well have to be taken into account in diagnosis and treatment. Someone turning up at a doctor's surgery with a chest infection may already be suffering from diabetes, hearing loss and depression. The drugs they are prescribed for one condition may have an effect on other conditions, or indeed on the body's reaction to other drugs. Whereas geriatric medicine used to be a Cinderella amongst medical disciplines, today it is attracting more and more high-flyers, fascinated by the extra dimension ageing itself adds to the challenge of treating disease.

The ageing body

* Ageing starts young.

* An 80-year-old needs four times as much light as a 20-year-old.

* Bones are not inert: they replenish themselves and change their density.

* Five times more women die of cardiovascular disease than breast cancer.

* Nearly 40 per cent of the over-75s have significant hearing loss.

* Changes to the kidney and liver make older people more sensitive to the effects of alcohol and drugs (recreational and medicinal)

* The ability to think quickly declines but not the ability to experience emotion.

* One in five people over 85 suffers some degree of dementia.

* The most important step to ensure a healthy brain is to keep one's cardiovascular system healthy.

* It may take detective-like skills to diagnose underlying conditions.

Chapter 2

Food, drink and temperature

We all know that our body needs fluid and food to sustain us and a temperature that is neither too hot nor too cold. Just how do these basic needs alter in later life? In this chapter I examine the nature of our needs for food, fluid and an equable temperature. I also look at some of the difficulties we may encounter in later life in meeting these needs.

Food

When we are growing older, we may assume that our nutritional needs pale into insignificance compared with those of children, pregnant women or sportspeople. As we don't appear to be growing, surely we don't need to build up new cells and body tissue? And as we have lived so long, we may jump to the conclusion that our nutritional requirements are being met perfectly adequately.

Another dangerous myth is that older people require a smaller quantity of food than younger people. Perhaps such thinking is prompted in part by one of the changes to the older body we noted in Chapter 1 – the replacement of muscle by fat. The resulting flabbiness in chins and arms may create the impression that we are eating too much, not too little. In the face of pressure everywhere to cut back on smoking, drinking and eating, older people may conclude they should be dieting even more energetically than the young.

Yet the truth is that good nutrition is extraordinarily important in later life and that malnutrition is common amongst older people – and not just those who are too poor to eat well. More than one in ten people over 65 have such a restricted diet, omitting many essential nutrients, that they are considered to be malnourished.[1] As Professor Susan Holmes of Canterbury Christ Church University points out, 'Appropriate nutrition has the potential to lead to additional years of productive life and improved functioning'.[2]

Older people don't need quite as many calories as younger people, and not just because they tend to engage in less physical activity: older bodies consume less energy than younger ones while resting, because of the reduction in the amount of muscle fibre which is an inevitable accompaniment to ageing. As a result, although we need carbohydrates – the sugars and starches that generate energy – when we are older, we don't need quite as many of them as younger people do, unless we are extremely energetic. Yet the requirement for virtually every other nutrient does not decline significantly with age. When you are 60 or 80 or older, an adequate intake of vitamins, fibre, protein and the other components of a healthy, well-balanced diet is just as essential as when you were 20. In some cases, the need for particular nutrients increases. It is worth understanding the main reasons for this.

Why older people need more nutrients

As we grow older, our body's ability to fight disease declines *(as explained on page 28)*. A healthy diet is vital **to enable the immune system to function efficiently.**

We also cut ourselves more easily than younger people as our skin becomes more fragile *(see page 17)*. Some older people also suffer from pressure sores or leg ulcers. The **healing of wounds** requires the formation of new tissue. Protein plays an essential part in this process in addition to adequate energy, fluid and micronutrients (vitamins, minerals and trace elements). In the absence of adequate quantities of protein, wounds heal more slowly, or not at all. In view of this, *The Oxford Textbook of Geriatric Medicine* recommends an older person should consume more protein than a younger person of the same bodyweight.[3]

A third reason why older people should pay attention to their diet is that ageing is associated with a gradual and progressive **loss of muscle mass,** together with a reduction in muscle strength and physical endurance *(see page 18–19)*. Good nutrition combined with exercise is the best means of maintaining muscle strength; consumption of adequate amounts of food which provide energy and protein are key.

But just how much protein should older people eat to maintain muscle mass? Nutritionists from many parts of the world came together at a workshop in Dubrovnik in 2013 to address this question. They concluded that healthy people over the age of 65 should consume at least 1.0 to 1.2 grammes of protein per kg of their body weight each day. This is higher than the amount (0.8 grammes/kg body weight) usually recommended for healthy adults of all ages.

In other words, if you are over 65 and weigh ten stone (64 kilogrammes), you should be eating 77 grammes or 2.7 ounces of protein each day, according to these fourteen experts – the equivalent of one, small, cooked chicken breast. For older people who are at risk of malnutrition because they have acute or chronic illness, the Dubrovnik nutritionists recommended a higher figure – between 1.2 and 1.5 grammes protein per kilogram of body weight each day, and an even higher amount still for older people with severe illness or injury. They also recommended that older people engage in physical activity every day, or aerobic exercise and resistance training to maintain muscle mass and strength.[4]

The Dubrovnik team's recommendations have not yet been adopted as standard advice in the UK, although they may be. What is clear however is that older people need a higher ratio of food providing protein to food providing energy (such as carbohydrates) than younger people. This means that should their overall consumption of food go down, their intake of protein should remain fairly constant.

A fourth area in which older people need more nutrients than younger people arises from the risk of **vitamin D deficiency.** Our bones contain thousands of cells which need to be constantly replenished if they are to remain strong, and the mineral calcium is essential to this process. Calcium is found in milk, milk products, tinned sardines (with the bones left in), tofu and fortified soya milk. Because today's older generation was brought up to believe that milk was especially nutritious, underconsumption of calcium is probably rare amongst them. But calcium is unable to build healthy bones without vitamin D, which helps transport it across the wall of the intestine.

Oily fish, such as mackerel and herring, contain vitamin D. But diet alone does not provide vitamin D in sufficient quantities. Luckily our bodies can manufacture it, in the fat just under the skin, but to do so, it needs sunlight.

As we grow older, our skin's ability to make vitamin D using the sun's rays diminishes. What is more, the lifestyle of some people means they are exposed to very little sunlight – most obviously those who are housebound or who live in institutions in which they are rarely able to go outdoors, since the key ingredients of sunlight cannot pass through glass. People who keep their skin covered or who, perhaps hailing from the Indian subcontinent, have dark skin should also bear in mind that they may be more at risk, since dark skins make less vitamin D than light skins. All these factors make us vulnerable to vitamin D deficiency and to the bone diseases associated with it, osteoporosis and osteomalacia, when we are getting on. We should therefore try to get out in the sun, particularly between April and September, when the sun is stronger, and try to expose our hands, face and arms or legs for at least a short time in order to build up sufficient vitamin D to last the whole year round. However, don't put yourself at risk of skin cancer, so apply sunscreen if you are going to be exposing ourselves to a lot of sunlight!

A useful safeguard is to take a vitamin D supplement. The National Institute for Health and Care Excellence (NICE) has recommended that groups considered at risk of vitamin D deficiency should take a daily vitamin D supplement in autumn and winter. In the adult population the groups are everyone over the age of 65, people who are housebound, those who don't get much exposure to the sun, people with darker skin and pregnant women.[5] The Scientific Advisory Committee on Nutrition (which advises the government on diet, nutrition and health) used further research to recommend in 2016 that everybody over the age of one year should consume a tiny amount of vitamin D every day.[6]

So particularly if you are at risk of deficiency, consider taking a supplement, at least during autumn and winter. You may wish to take a supplement in spring and summer too.

Supplements

With the exception perhaps of vitamin D, most people should be able to get all the nutrients they need from a healthy diet. Exceptional circumstances may call for supplements, for instance after an operation or if somebody is suffering from a disease which interferes with their ability to absorb nutrients, such as coeliac disease or Crohn's disease.

But nutritional supplements are intended to augment normal food intake, not substitute for it. If you are assessed as needing a supplement, you should be having normal meals (and any help necessary to consume them) as well, unless special considerations apply.

Certain vitamins, minerals and trace elements can be poisonous in large quantities and some supplements can be toxic to people with certain medical conditions. For example, large amounts of vitamin A can harm the liver and if somebody has a frail or diseased liver or is taking a lot of medication, excess quantities can cause serious damage. So before you take any supplement, consult your doctor. However, a one-a-day multivitamin/mineral capsule bought over the counter is unlikely to cause any harm to most people.

A healthy diet

In addition to larger amounts of protein and certain vitamins than younger people, older people also require the balanced diet required by people of all ages. This consists of:

- oily fish
- milk
- five portions of fruit and vegetables each day
- eggs and nuts
- foods rich in starch and wholegrain fibre such as bread, potatoes, cereals, rice and pasta
- plenty of fibre
- not too much salt, sugar, animal fat or processed fat

Let us look at these elements one by one.

Carbohydrates

We need carbohydrates to provide energy. The British Dietetic Association, which represents registered dietitians in the UK, recommends that a third of our food should consist of carbohydrates.[7] It is certainly true that if we take in more carbohydrate than we burn up as energy, the excess will be laid down as fat. But eating too little can lead to low blood sugar levels, which can leave us feeling weak or light-headed.

Look for carbohydrate-rich foods which do not also contain fat or too much sugar – bread, pasta, plain cereals and potatoes, rather than cakes, biscuits and puddings. Rice (use wholegrain) also contains fibre and vitamins.

Try to obtain your sugar from fresh fruit rather than cake – at least, most of the time! Prompted by concerns about the rising prevalence of type 2 diabetes as well as tooth decay, the World Health Organisation (WHO) followed by the Scientific Advisory Committee on Nutrition in Britain have changed their recommendations on the amount of sugar adults should consume each day. In 2015 they said we should obtain only 5 per cent of the calories we take in each day from sugar. For an adult of normal weight that amounts to about six teaspoonfuls.[8]

This seems a tiny amount. However, the experts could find no evidence of adverse effects from consuming sugar found naturally in fruit, vegetables and milk, so that is not included in the 5 per cent total. What the WHO and others are concerned about is an excessive amount of sugar that enters our diet for one of the following reasons:

- manufacturers and cooks have added it in anything from cakes and biscuits to fizzy drinks
- it is present in honey, syrups, fruit juices or fruit juice concentrates
- we have added it as consumers, for instance, to tea, coffee or fresh fruit

Fats

In spite of the bad image of fat as a cause of obesity, eating some fat is essential. Ageing does not alter this. However, some of the fats we consume are hazardous to health. So how do we separate the good from the bad?

Omega-3 oils

The most important oils to consume for good health are called omega-3 oils. They are a source of vitamin D, which is essential for building healthy bones. They have other key functions, too, in particular providing protection against heart disease. The best source of omega-3 oils is oily fish, such as herring, fresh tuna, mackerel, sardines, salmon and trout; they can also be obtained, in smaller quantities, in walnut, flaxseed, soya and rapeseed oils, broccoli, kale and spinach.

There is serious under-consumption of these oils. People over 65 in England were eating only 64 per cent of the recommended 140 grammes (5 ounces) of oily fish per week in 2012.[9]

Saturated fats

The fats found in meat, butter and cream – saturated fats – also provide a useful source of energy and of cholesterol, which performs several useful functions in the body. However, consumption of large amounts of saturated fat can increase cholesterol levels in the blood. This increases the risk of having a heart attack or stroke.

Most of us eat far too much saturated fat. Indeed, it has been estimated that halving our average intake of saturated fat might prevent around 30,000 deaths from cardiovascular disease every year.[10]

Trans-fats

Industrially produced 'trans-fats' are vegetable oils which have been processed to make them hard and less susceptible to spoilage by exposure to air or sunlight than, say, butter. They are found in many processed foods, from ice cream, salad dressings and soups to margarines, sweets and chocolate products. On the label they are likely to be described as 'partially hydrogenated vegetable oils'. Avoid them! They are considered so harmful to health that the National Institute for Health and Care Excellence, or NICE *(whose role is outlined on page 289),* has urged that they should be banned from food, as has already happened in Austria and Denmark.

Protein

Protein, which is found in meat, fish, eggs, milk, cheese, nuts, seeds, lentils and beans is important for many reasons for older people, as it is for younger people. As noted above, it is important in the healing of wounds and to prevent the wasting of muscle tissue. People who do not eat sufficient protein and energy can develop a condition called 'protein-energy malnutrition', which is associated not only with impaired wound-healing and impaired functioning of muscles, but lighter bones, impaired working of the brain and immune system and delayed recovery from surgery.

Fibre

We all need to consume fibre if our food is to pass through the intestine as it should and stools are to form properly. Lack of adequate fibre not only makes us constipated: it also increases the risk of cancer of the colon.

Fibre-rich foods include:

- wholemeal bread, cereals and rice
- dried fruit and nuts
- fruit and vegetables (eat the edible skins, such as those of potatoes)
- pulses such as lentils, baked beans and kidney beans

White bread has had the fibre stripped out of it, but some people prefer its taste to that of wholemeal. It is better to eat white-bread sandwiches than nothing, but if you really don't like wholemeal, why not try high-fibre white bread?

A well-balanced diet, especially including fibre, was one of the main recommendations of a group of health professionals who drew up guidelines for the management of constipation in 2006.[11] However, people who are constipated often take laxatives. While these can be useful in certain circumstances, they have drawbacks: some may reduce the absorption of some medicines, since they help them pass more quickly through the body than normal. If a laxative causes a sudden need to open the bowels and someone cannot reach the lavatory quickly, they may be deterred from going out or receiving visitors.

Vitamins, minerals and trace elements

Carbohydrates, protein and fat should make up most of our food intake in terms of volume, but there are other essential foodstuffs which differ from proteins, fats and carbohydrates in that they are usually required in very small amounts indeed.

Vitamins, minerals and trace elements, of which there are large numbers, play a huge variety of roles necessary for the healthy functioning of the body. Vitamin B12, for example, is involved in the normal working of every cell of the body. It can be found in fish, meat (especially liver), eggs, milk and milk products. Magnesium is needed for more than 300 biochemical reactions in the body. It helps to maintain normal nerve and muscle function, supports a healthy immune system, keeps the heart beat steady, helps bones remain strong and helps regulate blood glucose levels. Good sources of magnesium include peas, beans and seeds, almond and cashew nuts, bananas, avocados and dried apricots, soy flour, tofu and whole grains (such as brown rice and millet), and dark green, leafy vegetables. Although magnesium is essential, we need only about 420 milligrams (0.015 ounces) a day.

Vitamins A, C and E prevent disease by acting as 'antioxidants' – that is, they mop up the oxygen free radicals which cause the cumulative damage to cells that is thought to be a major cause of ageing and, ultimately, death *(see page 11)*. They can be found in tomatoes, peppers, carrots, spinach, curly kale, kiwi fruit, oranges and dried apricots, as well as eggs, nuts, seeds and dairy products.

Vitamin K is essential in blood clotting and also helps form a protein involved in hardening bones and thus preventing osteoporosis. It is found in spring greens, spinach and Brussels sprouts. The trace element selenium, which is present in high concentrations in Brazil nuts but also occurs in wheat, fish, shellfish, liver and kidney, may stimulate immunity and prevent cancer.[12]

Many of the benefits of trace elements are only beginning to be understood.

Fruit and vegetables

Key to obtaining sufficient vitamins, minerals and trace elements are fruit and vegetables. The government recommends that we should all consume at least five portions of fruit and vegetables every day – advice that is based on sound scientific studies. It has been estimated that if everybody ate five portions a day, this would reduce deaths from cancer, strokes and heart disease by 20 per cent.[13] Indeed, increasing fruit and vegetable intake is considered the most effective means of preventing cancer, after giving up smoking.[14] However, over two-thirds of adults under 64 and 60 per cent of people over 65 in England were failing to eat the recommended five portions each day in 2012, according to Public Health England.[15]

Montacute, a village in Somerset, has the highest life expectancy of men over retirement age of anywhere in Britain, according to an analysis of three million pension records in 2009.[16] When the residents were interviewed about why this might be, they pointed to the vegetable patches which most of them tended and which delivered them fresh produce almost daily.

Fruit, vegetables and eye disease

Age-related macular degeneration takes away the ability to see objects in the centre of the field of vision, or macula, and is the leading cause of severe vision impairment leading to near-blindness in people over 65, *as explained on page 13*. The cells in the macula, which is a tiny area near the centre of the retina at the back of the eye, deteriorate.

A study in the United States involving large numbers of people diagnosed with early AMD showed that those who took a particular supplement reduced their risk of developing advanced AMD by over a quarter.[17] The supplement contained the anti-oxidants vitamins C and E, zinc (as zinc oxide), copper (as cupric oxide), and two other substances, lutein and zeaxanthin. These latter form the pigment of the macula and act as a sort of sun-block, protecting it against potentially damaging blue light. Our bodies are unable to manufacture lutein, so it has to be obtained from food.

If you have a diagnosis of AMD, it is worth asking about this supplement. The NHS does not fund it at present, as it does not seem to help everyone. However, Action for Blind People advises patients to ask whether their particular health authority does pay for patients in its area to take it.[18] The National Institute for Health and Care Excellence (NICE) confirms that this supplement can reduce progression of AMD from an intermediate to advanced stage by up to 25 per cent.[19] Research has not found a conclusive link between consumption of this supplement or the individual nutrients it contains and a reduction in the risk of developing AMD in people who show no sign of the disease. However, consumption of vitamins C and E in the foodstuffs listed above and of lutein and zeaxanthin in kale, spinach, spring greens, cabbage and broccoli are unlikely to do you harm and could well be beneficial.

Barriers to healthy eating

I hope I have demonstrated that there are many important reasons why we should pay close attention to our diet when we are getting on in years. However, several factors militate against eating healthily. They include:

Shopping effectively

'Economy-size' packaging puts people who live alone and wish to buy in small quantities at a financial disadvantage. The price of a tin of baked beans large enough for one helping is much more, bean for bean, than that of a tin large enough for four helpings. As a result, people living on their own may not bother to prepare nourishing food very often, perhaps subsisting on bread and jam.

We can find getting to the shops and in particular returning home with our purchases a strain if we have to shop on foot. Around 60 per cent of people over 70 do not have a car, and the sheer weight of fresh fruit and vegetables may cause people to cut down the amount they buy, unless they can find somebody to help. Forty per cent of older people in Wales questioned in an Age Concern Wales survey reported that distance from food shops posed a problem. As one respondent commented, 'Imagine carrying home the required five portions of fruit and vegetables for one or two people, for seven days a week'.[20]

However, a revolution in shopping which offers enormous benefits to older people is the revival of the home delivery of groceries. Some companies have been set up simply to provide home deliveries. In addition, many supermarkets now offer home deliveries, as well, of course, as maintaining their stores. A new user creates their own account, logs in and places items in a virtual 'basket'. They then go to the online checkout, pay and specify a delivery time. There is a small delivery charge, but free delivery is offered if somebody is spending over a certain amount or has collected enough loyalty points, or if they request delivery at particular times (often unsocial hours).

For many, however, the barrier to home delivery is that the service has been developed with online customers in mind. Few supermarkets were offering a telephone delivery service at the time of writing, but more may do so in the future. Under the Sainsbury's Shop Online scheme, for example, a new user creates their own account, orders items, pays and specifies a time of delivery, all over the phone, rather than online; the delivery charge varies depending on the time of day they choose. This can be an especially useful service for people without a computer who tend to shop for the same sorts of items; the account 'remembers' their previous order and can automatically add items if required.

If a phone delivery service is unavailable, perhaps a friend or relative could order for you through the internet. Some Age UK groups offer this useful service too. Or perhaps a 'computer buddy' at your public library *(see page 247)* could show you how to place an online order.

'Click and collect' schemes, whereby somebody places an order with their local supermarket but collects their waiting shopping at the local store, saving them a trip round the aisles, are generally free. These can be invaluable if you find negotiating your way around the store challenging. However, supermarkets will usually provide an assistant to help someone who is blind or cannot move or stretch easily, if asked to do so. The Equality Act 2010 requires them to ensure that they do not discriminate against people with a disability in their provision of goods and services *(see page 688–91)*.

Past habits

Perceived wisdom about what constitutes a healthy diet has undergone a revolution in a comparatively short space of time. Yet many of us developed our tastes and cooking skills following such maxims as 'drink a pint of milk a day', 'go to work on an egg' and 'eat plenty of red meat'. As late as the 1970s, health guides were advocating sausage and bacon or fried kippers as a regular item at breakfast, along with two teaspoonfuls of sugar in every cup of coffee; recommended daily diets featured only two portions of fruit or vegetables per day.[21]

Compare standard cooking practice of 40 years ago with that of today. Then, we were told to boil vegetables; today we know that boiling leaches out vitamins and that vegetables should be lightly steamed, microwaved or eaten raw, if possible. However, some people will need vegetables boiled until they are soft, as that is the only way they can consume them because of difficulties in chewing or swallowing.

Changes to the senses of taste and smell

We are tempted to eat because we relish the flavour of food. That flavour arises from its taste and its aroma. Indeed, once food is in our mouth, the aroma of the food acts on our olfactory sensors to enhance the attraction of devouring it.

We noted in Chapter 1 that the senses of taste and smell see a decline in later life, mainly in people the age of 80. Not only may this reduce the pleasure people take in their food: it can potentially contribute to their becoming malnourished. Substances that enhance the flavour of food, such as a little curry powder, soy sauce, tomato or yeast extract or chemical flavour enhancers can encourage people to eat.

Illness

When we fall ill, we may be even more reluctant to eat – everything tastes like pulped cardboard. If illness takes away our appetite, so too can the drugs we take to cure it. A vicious circle may develop.

Teeth and digestion

The pleasure of eating can also diminish and the risk of malnutrition increase if eating is difficult. Missing teeth or ill-fitting dentures can make biting and chewing hard work. Gum or tooth disease can make eating painful. Studies have shown a close link between the state of teeth and the level of nutrients in the blood.[22]

Disability

Physical disabilities, too, can make consuming food challenging as we grow older. Impaired dexterity, perhaps resulting from arthritic finger joints, often causes difficulties in manipulating cutlery and opening cans and packets. Poor eyesight brings its own problems. Fortunately, plenty of gadgets have been invented to make preparing and eating food easier for those with impairments such as these *(as outlined on page 462)*. If you are in hospital, expect to receive any help you may need to eat and drink *(as explained on pages 912–3)*.

Dementia

People with dementia are especially likely to fail to eat enough and as a result risk becoming malnourished, as well as losing out on the pleasures of eating and drinking, both physical and social. If they cannot see or manipulate cutlery easily, they may not realise they need to ask for help to eat their food. They may be distracted at mealtimes so eat less than they might. They may not realise that what is placed in front of them is food, or what they should do with it.

Older people with dementia commonly lose weight. Between 20 and 45 per cent of people with dementia living in ordinary housing (not in a care home or hospital) lose a significant amount of weight over only one year, according to research examined by a group of experts brought together by Alzheimer's Disease International (ADI).[23]

Some of this loss may arise from the disease itself – the parts of the brain which regulate appetite and metabolism may become damaged. But much of the loss results from failure to eat enough food. Thus the ADI team reported on studies showing that up to half of people living with dementia in care homes were under-eating.[24]

If your relative has dementia, try to make sure they are eating and drinking as much as they can, so long as they are not eating far too much. If they are fast losing weight while living in a care home, talk with staff about their weight loss to see what can be done to address it. Is the home giving your relative what they want to eat and drink and any help they need to consume it? Is it reminding them to eat, if necessary? The ADI team urged that care homes and hospitals should put in place plans to monitor what people with dementia are eating and drinking and make sure they receive the food and drink that is best for them. Thus they should pay attention to the nutritional content of the food they serve, its variety and its suitability for people with eating difficulties. They should train their staff accordingly and also pay attention to the design of their dining room and the dining environment to make meal times as enjoyable as possible.[25] The ADI team's recommendations have no legal force, but you could reasonably expect any hospital or care facility in which your loved one is living to view them as best practice to which they should aspire.

Overweight or underweight?

The media bombards us with the unrelenting message that we should cut down on food intake. But weight loss can be dangerous when we are getting on. How can we establish and maintain a healthy weight?

What is important here is not your weight but your weight in relation to your height and body shape – or your 'body mass index' (BMI). If you have a large frame, you would expect to weigh more than if you are petite. Your GP or practice nurse should be able to calculate your BMI for you and tell you whether it is OK, but you can do so yourself using tables on the internet in which you enter your weight and height. A BMI below 18.5 is usually considered underweight, normal weight: 18.5 to 25, overweight: 25 to 30, and obese: over 30.

Obesity is clearly undesirable. It is known to increase the risk of high blood pressure, diabetes, strokes, dementia and both rheumatoid and osteoarthritis. What is more, older people who are overweight have a significantly higher risk of developing mobility problems and difficulties in carrying out everyday tasks.[26] The benefits of losing weight can be substantial. People who are overweight and manage to lose 5 kg (11 lb) can reduce their risk of developing knee osteoarthritis by 50 per cent over the following ten years.[27]

However, in later life, losing weight, particularly a lot of weight quickly, can be dangerous. The body of an elderly person is more susceptible to shocks to the system, of whatever cause *(see pages 28–9)*. If you are considering trying to shed a lot of weight, first go and talk to your GP.

There is compelling evidence that the BMIs considered acceptable or desirable set out above do not represent the ideal for older people. Researchers examined 32 studies which had examined the link between BMI and the risk of mortality from all causes in nearly 200,000 people over the age of 65. They found that mortality risk began to increase when it exceeded 33 (which is quite heavy), but it also increased when it was slightly below 23 – at 21, and even more so at 20. Indeed the risk was quite high: people with a BMI of 21.0–21.9 had a 12 per cent greater risk of mortality, while for those in the range 20.0–20.9 the increased risk was 19 per cent.[28]

If you are concerned about your weight, whether you think your BMI may be low or too high, go and talk to your GP about monitoring your weight and how it could be increased or reduced. Your GP could refer you to a dietitian, who can work with you to draw up a plan for gradual weight loss or gain, advising you on the foods you could usefully concentrate on. If you are going to lose weight, targeted exercise such as resistance training *(see page 64)* should ensure you preserve the mass and strength of your muscles while losing fatty tissue, perhaps around your waist and abdomen.

If you have lost a significant amount of weight unintentionally, do consult your GP. *The Oxford Textbook of Geriatric Medicine* advises that: 'Significant recent weight loss of greater than 5 per cent of original weight should never be ascribed to normal ageing.'[29] Unintentional weight loss could result from depression, infection, a side-effect of drugs, disease – or simply not eating enough.

Malnutrition

If your weight is less than that expected for somebody of your build, you may well be suffering from malnutrition. But you may also lack essential nutrients even if you weight is normal. As Susan Holmes observes, 'Many older adults may be suffering sub-clinical malnutrition but exhibit no overt signs of deficiency'.[30]

The National Institute for Health and Care Excellence (NICE) recommends that older people should be screened for malnutrition in the following circumstances:

- on entry to a care home
- on admission to a hospital ward
- at their first appointment as a hospital outpatient

- if they register at a GP surgery
- if there is concern about their health[31]

If nutrition screening shows that someone is at risk of malnutrition, they should first receive advice from their GP, practice nurse or another healthcare professional conducting the screening. If this step proves ineffective in preventing or treating the condition, they should be referred to a dietitian, who should carry out a full nutrition assessment. Apart from weight loss, other symptoms of malnutrition include weakness in the muscles, feeling tired all the time, a low mood, and an increase in illnesses and infections. The dietitian would work with the person and/or their carers to try to work out what might help – from changes in what they eat and how much, to how and where they obtain their meals. However, the problems created by malnutrition cannot always be overcome.

Salt

Too much salt is dangerous. It causes the body to retain fluid and the larger volume of blood which results causes blood pressure to rise. High blood pressure is associated with greater risk of serious illness such as heart disease, strokes, kidney disease and damage to the retina of the eye.

The recommended daily intake of salt is as little as 5–6 grams (around 0.2 ounces), which is roughly equivalent to one level teaspoonful. Yet average consumption is 9 grams per day (0.3 ounces). Cutting current salt intake down to the recommended level would lower blood pressure and thus help prevent some of the tens of thousands of strokes and heart attacks which take place each year in the UK.

This does not necessarily mean that we should all stop adding salt to the food on our plates. Salt added during cooking or at the table accounts for only about a quarter of our total intake. Nonetheless, reductions could usefully be made, perhaps by adding flavour with herbs, spices, lime, lemon, garlic, ginger, chilli or black pepper instead.

Most of our salt intake actually comes in processed foods. Biscuits, cornflakes, pizza, mayonnaise, sausages and bacon may not necessarily taste salty, but they often have high amounts of hidden salt. The British Dietetic Association advises that over 1.25 grams of salt per 100 grams of food (0.04 ounces per 3.5) is a lot, and suggests under 0.75 grams of salt (0.03 ounces) for food such as sauces and soups.[32] So scrutinise food labels carefully.

Several of the voluntary organisations concerned with health matters offer helpful suggestions for ways in which healthy diets can be as tasty as possible. For example, the British Heart Foundation publishes tips on nutrition with low-salt or no-salt recipes in its free monthly magazine, *Heart Matters.* Its website offers a facility for watching chefs prepare healthy versions of favourite dishes, such as lemon chicken stir-fry and spiced-apple bread pudding. As people of Afro-Caribbean background are more likely to develop high blood pressure and type 2 diabetes, the BHF has also produced recipe cards based on popular Caribbean dishes, but with reduced amounts of saturated fat, sugar and salt.

Don't worry about not having enough salt. Although our body needs it, the Food Standards Agency points out that, 'It's actually very difficult to eat too little salt.'[33]

Fluid

When we are older, we need to drink just as much fluid as younger people.[34] If water intake is insufficient, there is less water available to move into the bloodstream and our cells cannot function properly, with the result that blood pressure falls. Unless something is done, the drop in blood pressure causes severe damage to many organs, including the kidney, liver and brain; death follows.

Some dehydration can lead to temporary confusion when we are older. As many as one in six elderly patients admitted to hospital as medical emergencies was suffering from acute confusion related to dehydration in one study.[35]

How much fluid you need varies according to bodyweight. The more cells you have in your body, the more liquid you need. *The Oxford Textbook of Geriatric Medicine* recommends 30 millilitres of water every day for every kilogram of body weight. Generally speaking, older people need at least 1.5 litres (3 pints), or 8 to 10 cups of non-alcoholic fluid each day.[36] This is in addition to the water in food. If the weather is hot or you are exercising, or sweating as a result of stress, a fever or cold, you will need to drink more.

It is important that you should not rely entirely on strong tea and coffee for your fluid intake. These contain caffeine, so act in some degree as diuretics – in other words, they make you excrete more fluid than they provide. Herbal teas do not contain caffeine, so try to vary cups of ordinary tea and coffee with these, as well as squashes, juices and milk, if you do not always want water (though keep an eye on your sugar consumption, *as explained on page 37).*

It is easy to find yourself not drinking enough. The sensation of thirst often becomes blunted with advancing years, particularly into one's eighties and nineties. This means that by the time someone feels really thirsty, they may already have become quite dehydrated. So they should drink even if they do not feel thirsty.

If you are suffering from urinary incontinence *(discussed in Chapter 19)* you may be tempted to cut down on your fluid intake. Beware! It is important to maintain an overall fluid intake each day of 8–10 cups. Contrary to what might be expected, people who become dehydrated can become more prone to incontinence. This is because the less you drink, the more irritated the bladder becomes by concentration of the urine, and the more frequently you need to pass water.

There are other reasons why older people often drink too little. Some people have mobility problems which may deter them from going and getting a drink. Others cannot communicate easily their need for fluid, because their speech is impaired or they have dementia.

If your older relative develops even a minor illness, particularly in very hot weather, make sure they are drinking enough. If necessary, they should be prompted to drink hourly, as well as with their meals. If your relative is in hospital or a care facility and might have problems in drinking, perhaps because of dementia or sight impairment, make sure they are encouraged to drink frequently with a light, easy-to-manipulate container which they can easily reach. The Royal College of Nursing, which has drawn up tips for encouraging patients to drink, points out that water is best served fresh and chilled, not left in open jugs, and suggests nurses (or carers) say, 'Here is some nice cool refreshing water for you!' rather than, 'Do you want something to drink?'[37]

Approximately two-thirds of older people suffering from dehydration have an infection at the same time, such as pneumonia, a urinary tract infection or gastroenteritis.[38] Failure to take in sufficient fluid increases their risk of dying from the infection.

The right temperature

When we are getting on, and particularly when we are moving into our eighties and nineties, keeping warm in winter and cool in summer really can be a matter of life or death. Just as with food and drink, older people's requirements for an equable temperature differ from those of younger adults. It is important to understand these differences.

Every winter about 40,000 more deaths occur in Britain than in the rest of the year, and most of these involve older people. Only a small proportion (about 800 per year) are the direct result of hypothermia; most of the remainder involve the impact of cold surroundings on people suffering from respiratory or cardiovascular disease.

Our body maintains a constant core temperature through a sophisticated regulatory mechanism. In hot weather, the evaporation of sweat takes heat from the body and cools us, while heat is also released through the dilation of blood vessels close to the skin. In cold weather, the blood vessels near the skin constrict, so that body heat is conserved. In addition, we shiver and heat is generated by the muscular activity involved. As part of the ageing process, the efficiency of this mechanism declines, along with the reduction in homeostasis which is a key feature of ageing *(see page 29)*.

Also, our ability to tell how cold it is and thus alert our body to take action becomes blurred. So, elderly people are not quite as good at maintaining the constant body temperature needed for optimum health and may not realise that the ambient temperature is as low as it really is.

Another factor is also in play. As we grow older, the proportion of the cells in our body which are actively functioning, and therefore generating body heat, gets smaller. One way to generate internal body heat is to use muscles in work or exercise; another is to process food. So, elderly people who are immobile or not taking in enough calories are going to be particularly at risk in low temperatures.

The World Health Organization recommends a minimum indoor temperature of 18°C (65°F), but for rooms occupied by young children, handicapped people and sedentary older people, it recommends 20 or 21°C (70°F), day and night.

Keeping warm

In very cold weather, try to stay indoors, especially when it is windy. Wind whips away heat from the body: a strong wind on exposed skin has the same effect as a temperature drop of several degrees. Insulate your body as effectively as possible. Layers of clothing plus thermal underwear are better than one heavy layer. The clothing should be loose, to provide insulating layers of air, and lightweight, since heavy material slows down movement. Wool is a better insulator than synthetic materials such as polyester.

As half the body's heat loss occurs through the scalp, hats are extremely important. Scrooge's nightcap was extremely sensible. Try to stop heat loss through body extremities by inserting insulating insoles into boots or shoes and wearing thin pairs of gloves under woollen mittens. Cover exposed skin on legs, neck, face and ears as much as possible, ideally with two layers at least of scarves, stockings and so on.

In bed, several blankets will provide more insulation than one or two thick ones, and duvets are very effective. Although electric under-blankets have to be switched off before you get into bed, you can buy over-blankets which can be kept on during sleep.

Keep active, both to generate body heat from muscular activity and to keep the blood circulating properly. It is best to alternate physical activity with periods of rest, so spread housework over a longer period rather than doing it all at once and then resting for a long period. Even if you have difficulty moving, try to walk around the room or do exercises while sitting down. If you have to wait around outside, try to keep moving. One of the most dangerous things you can do is to sit immobile in a cold bus shelter for 20 minutes.

During cold weather you should have plenty of hot drinks and at least one hot meal every day. If you cannot move around easily at home, try to get somebody to make up a thermos for you. Keep your home as warm as possible and use a thermometer to check the temperature. If you cannot afford to heat the whole of your home to the required level, live and sleep in one well-heated room during spells of very cold weather. If you can get out, try to spend time in well-heated public buildings such as leisure centres and libraries. Take all the steps you can to insulate your home and to install effective heating systems. You may be eligible for help to install central heating on top of the Winter Fuel Payment which could go towards your fuel bills *(see pages 190–7)*.

Keeping cool

Elderly people are the chief victims of heatwaves, and rising global temperatures are likely to mean longer, hotter summers, including spells of extremely high temperatures. As we saw above, it is especially important to drink more than the usual 8–10 cups of liquid during hot weather, even if you don't feel thirsty, to replenish fluid lost through sweating. Hot weather often depresses appetite, but it is important to eat normally; salads and fruit are particularly helpful, as they contain water.

If a heatwave is forecast, plan ahead to keep out of the heat. Try to remain in the coolest rooms of your home and keep the heat out by drawing curtains and blinds and closing windows if the room is cooler than the temperature outdoors. Open windows at night to create a draught. Splash yourself several times a day with cold water, particularly over the face and the back of the neck, and take cool showers as well, if you can. Perhaps you can plan to spend long periods in air-conditioned public buildings, but if you do, avoid travelling to them during the hottest part of the day, between 11am and 3pm. Confine any strenuous outdoor activity such as gardening to the coolest parts of the day, and generally alternate periods in the heat with cooling periods. Out of doors, remain in the shade, wear a hat and loose clothing, preferably cotton, and take plenty of cold fluid with you to drink. At night some people dab their sheets with cold water, which absorbs heat in order to evaporate and keeps them cool.

A combination of dehydration and overheating can lead to heatstroke. What happens is that the body loses its ability to regulate its temperature, which allows its core temperature to rise dangerously. Apart from a temperature above 40° C (104 F), symptoms include a throbbing headache, dizziness, fainting, muscle cramps, confusion, feeling and being sick, intense thirst, a rapid heartbeat, seizures and darker urine than normal. These symptoms can develop within minutes or over several hours or days.

Heatstroke is a dangerous medical emergency. Call 999 at once. Try to move the person affected to a cooler place and cool them down by loosening their clothes, sprinkling them with cold water, wrapping them in a damp sheet and opening the windows or using a fan. If they are conscious, give them water or fruit juice to drink.

Food, drink and temperature

✻ Many people over 65 are malnourished, even if they are well-off.

✻ Drink 8–10 cups of non-alcoholic, non-caffeinated fluid every day.

✻ Consuming at least five portions of fruit and vegetables every day is just as important for the health of older people as the young.

✻ Being slightly overweight can benefit health in people over 65.

✻ Protein is important for the older body, especially for wound healing and muscle maintenance.

✻ Vitamin D is essential for healthy bones and a supplement may be necessary.

✻ People with dementia are at high risk of weight loss.

✻ A food supplement may reduce progression of age-related macular degeneration.

✻ In cold weather, wear layers of clothing and a hat, keep active and have lots of hot drinks.

✻ In hot weather, keep yourself out of the heat, wear loose clothing and drink a lot.

Chapter 3

Physical activity

When the vast majority of us were engaged in hard physical labour for most of our lives, the question of a need for physical activity would have seemed absurd – we were simply thankful for a rest. But just as our body needs to rest, so it also needs to move. And this is a need which, unlike our needs for food and drink, is not widely appreciated or understood. As a result, we could find we are doing too little in the way of physical activity when in fact we would be only too happy to do more. Or we might discover that our health is unlikely to benefit from an exercise régime which we find both punishing and tedious.

Physical activity and exercise – the difference

First, what is the difference between physical activity and exercise? Well, physical activity is any activity that uses muscles and bones in some form of exertion, whether it be walking or hoovering, gardening or cycling, swimming or playing tennis. In contrast, exercise involves structured, targeted physical activity, aimed at improving physical fitness in a particular way – for example, strengthening arm muscles with weights (which could be tins of baked beans!) or improving the heart and circulation system by running. So exercise is a form of physical activity, but not the only form.

Some older people are 'geriactives', climbing mountains or running marathons. Of course, people engage in activity such as this for reasons other than simply remaining physically fit – to enjoy the challenge or the scenery, for instance. The good news is that you can be fit and healthy in later life without going to lengths such as these.

Research has shown that:

- physical activity does not have to be vigorous or involve a huge amount of time to bring significant benefits to health

- improvement comes quickly – it does not involve months of dogged, repeated work to see any change. So people who have been sedentary have to exercise for only three or four weeks with an appropriate programme to see some improvement.

- the greatest health benefits come to those who have in the past done very little physical activity, but start to engage in a moderate amount

- the atrophy in our muscles that comes with ageing *(see page 18)* can be reversed by suitable exercise

What you can do depends on your taste, your level of mobility and general health, and the opportunities available. It could be canoeing or hill-walking. Equally, it could be dancing, playing ball games in a swimming pool or exercising while sitting down.

In this chapter I look at:

▶ the main reasons why we should engage in physical activity

▶ the amount of activity necessary for good health

▶ self-delusion about physical activity

▶ the different health benefits that come from some of the main types of activity

▶ why physical activity can be dangerous

▶ choosing between exercising in a group or on your own

Why physical activity matters

Physical activity reduces the risk of developing many of the common ailments of later life, or of preventing them getting worse. But physical activity is important for other reasons too. Stamina enables us to walk, swim or cycle long distances – as well as to survive illness. Flexibility enables us to retain a good range of movement in our joints and muscles, to play squash or do gymnastics – but also to walk correctly and not fall over. Strength in our muscles enables us to climb hills and play badminton – but also rise easily from a chair, reach up to shelves, and so remain independent of other people to help with daily activities.

Disease prevention

Physical activity does not provide a guarantee that an individual will not develop a serious chronic illness such as cardiovascular disease or diabetes. Other factors are involved in disease development, not least genetic inheritance. However, studies on large groups of people reveal a clear association between a certain minimum level of physical activity and good health. Here are the main ways in which physical activity can help prevent disease.

Strokes and heart attacks

People who engage in moderate exercise can see their risk of developing cardiovascular disease *(see page 21)* reduce significantly. It has been estimated that if everyone who led a sedentary life engaged in at least moderate physical activity, the incidence of strokes and heart attacks would fall by more than one third.[1]

A study of nearly 8,000 men living in 24 towns in Britain in the 1980s and 1990s examined the sort of physical activity that could prove beneficial. Researchers tracked the men first when aged between 40 and 59 and then in follow-up interviews at regular intervals, and calculated a score for physical activity for each of them.

The highest mortality from all causes was found in the men who were inactive. The lowest risk of death from all causes was found amongst the men who engaged in regular, moderate physical activity, such as walking or cycling for more than an hour a day and a range of weekend recreational activities. These findings applied both to the quarter of participants who had some cardiovascular disease at the start of the study and those who did not.

The findings of this and several other studies therefore dispel the idea that to be fit one has to spend hours on a treadmill at the gym or engage in very vigorous exercise for long periods. If we are looking to engage in physical activity to prevent serious disease, all that is needed is a moderate amount of activity. However, it has to be regular and sustained: occasional activity is insufficient. The researchers said:

> We have shown that sporting (vigorous) activity is not essential for reduction of cardiovascular risk, that regular physical activity for men over 60 brings a significant decrease in mortality, and that even light activities such as regular walking and weekend recreation can bring this benefit. … Light physical activities such as walking, gardening, DIY and light swimming or cycling undertaken regularly are highly desirable for middle-aged or older people, even for those with cardiovascular disease. [They] bring substantial benefits for cardiovascular mortality and longevity.[2]

What is also encouraging is that the men in this study who had led sedentary lifestyles but then became active showed the same level of reduction in mortality as those who simply continued to be physically active.

Again, this was true of both those who had pre-existing cardiovascular disease and those who did not.

Fewer studies have involved women, but one involving 72,000 nurses aged 40 to 65 certainly yielded similar results. Vigorous exercise for one-and-a-half hours each week or brisk walking for three or more hours per week reduced the risk of these nurses developing coronary heart disease by 30–40 per cent.[3]

Vascular dementia

Exercise which is good for the cardiovascular system is also good for the brain, since the health of the cardiovascular system and the brain are strongly related. If blood flow to the brain is impaired, the brain cannot function as well as possible. Vascular dementia, the second main cause of dementia after Alzheimer's disease, may develop if clots interrupt blood flow to blood vessels serving the brain.

Two thousand older people in the United States with normal mental functions were followed over six years. Their health was tracked, as well as the amount of physical activity in which they engaged. For every 1,000 of those who did not exercise, 40 developed dementia (all types). For every 1,000 of those who engaged in regular physical activity (such as walking, swimming and aerobic exercise), the number was 13.[4]

Diabetes

Research has shown that being physically inactive is a strong risk factor for the development of type 2 diabetes. A study of nearly 500 men and women showed that the risk of developing type 2 diabetes halved in those who switched from a sedentary lifestyle to one with moderate or vigorous exercise.[5]

If you don't want to get type 2 diabetes, don't put on too much weight! Obesity is associated with increased risk of developing type 2 diabetes. Physical activity helps keep body weight at a healthy level and holds off obesity.

A close link between diabetes and high blood pressure is another reason to avoid developing diabetes if you can. People with diabetes are at higher risk than others of having a stroke or developing diseases of the heart and circulation, such as the hardening and narrowing of the arteries which take blood to the legs. Indeed, diabetes doubles the risk of developing cardiovascular disease.[6]

Researchers examined the effect of exercise on the prevention of diabetes and on the further development of coronary heart disease in more than 300,000 people in 2013. They also compared the effect of exercise on these two conditions with that of drugs.

Exercise had such a beneficial impact on the prevention of diabetes and the further development of coronary heart disease that it was of the same order as the effect on these illnesses of drugs – the researchers could find no statistically detectable differences between exercise and taking medication for these conditions.[7]

Reduced efficiency of body functions

If we are immobile, the efficiency of many bodily functions decreases. So people who sit or lie for long periods increase their risk of a thrombosis or blood clot, which can be fatal.

In the case of the digestive system, material takes longer to pass through the colon if we are immobile, so we are more likely to become constipated. Not only is this condition uncomfortable and unpleasant, it can hinder mobility still further. This is because the pills taken to get the bowels moving may act so quickly that it is difficult to reach the lavatory in time (particularly if you have to manoeuvre yourself in a wheelchair). Constipation itself increases the risk of faecal incontinence *(see page 49)*. So an affected person may restrict outings, fearing potentially embarrassing problems.

Lack of physical activity has also been linked to an increased risk of developing cancer of the colon. This may be because movement of the body has the effect of reducing the time taken by food to travel through the digestive system.[8]

Of course, disease prevention is by no means the only reason for engaging in physical activity.

Power

One inevitable result of the ageing process is loss of muscle strength and power *(see page 18),* but regular physical activity can maintain and build up power in our muscles. This is important not just for people who wish to engage in demanding sports in later life. Physical activities which strengthen our muscles enable us to maintain what is known as our 'functional ability' – the ability to perform the activities necessary for everyday life, from walking up stairs and lifting heavy shopping to unscrewing a jam-jar.

Some people have no choice but to remain seated or in bed for long periods. They should do what they can to exercise their muscles and also consume enough protein *(as explained on page 35)*. Muscles which are completely unused waste away at an alarmingly fast rate: muscle mass shrinks to half size after two months of complete inactivity.[9] This means that as time goes on it becomes harder to become mobile again.

But some people who can stand and move a little, albeit with difficulty, are rendered immobile because others wait on them too much. They should insist on remaining as mobile as possible. Don't let your care-giver kill you with kindness!

Targeted exercise such as strengthening arm muscles by pulling against resistance bands can strengthen the muscles in the upper body. These are inexpensive wide elastic belts. Why not aim to exercise with one whenever the adverts appear on television? You could also increase your upper body strength with dumbbells or heavy household items.

Good upper body strength can improve our performance in sports such as canoeing and tennis, but equally it can enable us to do the ordinary activities of everyday life with greater ease. Good upper body strength can also prove important if we need to haul ourselves up after a fall. Without that strength, we might lie on the floor for a long time *(as explained in Chapter 18: Falls)*.

Stamina

Physical activity can increase our stamina, building up endurance and helping to keep our body going when it is becoming stressed. This may be as a result of extreme physical exertion, such as in running a marathon. Or it could be stress to the body arising from illness or injury. A healthy physical condition speeds general recovery. So, if you are in hospital, try to take exercise while there to maintain your muscle strength. Even if you cannot stand, you may be able to exercise your upper body and leg muscles while sitting down *(see below)*.

Flexibility

As we grow older, the tissues that connect our bones to our muscles lose some of their elasticity. As a result, our bodies become less supple. Physical activity can help maintain and develop flexibility. This enables us to move parts of our body more easily and allows us to continue to engage in many different activities. For instance, flexibility allows the joints to move through their full range, thus enabling us to walk without falling over.

How much activity?

Broadly speaking, for a range of health benefits, **aerobic physical activity** totalling two-and-a-half hours per week is considered desirable. This recommendation has been widely accepted, not least by the Chief

Medical Officers of England, Wales, Scotland and Northern Ireland, who prepared a major report on physical activity in 2011.[10]

'Aerobic' means any activity performed at moderate level of intensity over a relatively long period of time, so brisk walking or running at a moderate pace for a long time is aerobic exercise, but sprinting or lifting weights is not. It needs to involve enough exertion to make you feel warm and slightly breathless – not so breathless that you cannot talk, but sufficiently breathless that you cannot sing.

Aerobic exercise strengthens muscles throughout the body, while the breathing involved improves circulation, reduces blood pressure and strengthens heart muscle.

The recommended two-and-a-half hours of aerobic exercise each week could be divided into five 30-minute blocks. But aerobic exercise does not have to involve 30-minute sessions: it could be split into ten-minute blocks. If you are in your nineties and frail, hoovering a room could suffice.

However, some older people will want and be able to engage in far more energetic activity than this, such as sustained running. Seventy-five minutes per week of vigorous-intensity activity provides comparable health benefits to 150 minutes of moderate-intensity activity, according to the Chief Medical Officers.[11]

In addition to aerobic exercise, try to do **exercises which improve muscle strength and power**. The Chief Medical Officers recommend muscle-strengthening activities on two or more days per week. This might include the use of free weights, weight-training machines, resistance bands or exercise using one's own body weight. For frail, older people, the officers suggest the use of resistance bands, weights on the ankles and sit-stand activities. However, they say there is insufficient scientific evidence for them to recommend the precise amount of such effort.[12]

In addition, the Chief Medical Officers recommend that older people should perform **activities that maintain or improve their flexibility** on two or more days each week. They say these activities could include stretching on the spot or working through the full range of body movement during exercise or some other physical activity.[13]

There may also be specific exercises that could **help prevent or control any particular medical condition** you may have. For instance, the Chief Medical Officers recommend balance-training exercise such as tai chi for people at risk of falls.[14]

A core problem

Physical inactivity is now the default situation. Although human beings evolved as physically active animals, today many people lead very sedentary lives, sitting around in their homes or travelling by car. In 2011 the typical Briton was spending roughly 25 hours each week watching television.[15] During much of the 20th century, many people did not consider that they needed deliberately to engage in physical activity: they were only too pleased to put their feet up after long days of physical toil.

We have not yet realised that we should all now actively plan to ensure our daily lives contain sufficient physical activity. The figures are alarming. More than 400 residents of Dundee, aged between 65 and 84, were questioned in 2004 about the amount of physical activity in which they engaged and whether they thought it was sufficient to remain healthy. Nearly 80 per cent believed they were doing enough. Alas, this was probably true of only about 10 per cent of them.[16]

Other studies have thrown up similar findings and in view of the enormous impact physical activity can have on our health, it's worth asking just why older people are so reluctant to embark on physical activity.

The Dundee researchers felt that one of the main reasons why their participants engaged in so little physical activity was a lack of interest in it. Again, for today's older generation, this is understandable. Outdoor sport and gymnastics at school were often a boring, joyless trial, shivering on a hockey field or in an unheated, outdoor swimming pool.

Integrating physical activity into daily life

There are two ways in which we can increase the amount of physical activity in which we engage:

✓ by deliberately involving ourselves in activities such as swimming or playing badminton

✓ by changing our lifestyle so that we engage in more physical activity without actually trying. This means opting to walk rather than hop in the car or on the bus, to run around on the beach with our grandchildren rather than always sitting down to play games with them, and in general minimising the amount of time we spend seated.

Physical activity – the possibilities

Nowadays, many types of physical activity can offer far more fun than was the case a few years ago.

Swimming – non-weight-bearing exercise

Swimming can provide good aerobic exercise (so long as not too much gliding is involved), as well as improving stamina, strength and flexibility. It can help ease osteoarthritis by forcing joint fluid into and out of the cartilage of affected joints, thus lubricating and nourishing them. It can also help strengthen the muscles around the joints and keep them (and associated muscles and tendons) working, but without imposing weight and stress on damaged joints, as do running and walking. In view of this, the National Institute for Health and Care Excellence has recommended that:

> Exercise should be a core treatment for people with osteoarthritis, irrespective of age, comorbidity, pain severity or disability. Exercise should include local muscle strengthening, and general aerobic fitness.[17]

So, even if you have never learned to swim or ventured further than a paddle in the sea and the last thing you fancy is a trip to a public swimming bath, think again! Swimming pools and swimming as exercise for older people have undergone a revolution. Some parts of the typical pool are reserved for serious swimmers, but other zones with warm water, slides and wave machines tempt everybody, including people who cannot swim.

Some people may wish to do no more than move around in warm water, holding on to the side and using floats and engaging in, say, arm exercises. For these people, the water should be chest-high – sufficient to buoy up the body and take the weight off knee joints, but not deep enough to feel threatening. Other people may wish to learn to swim; while people who already enjoy swimming might like to join a group who play ball games or do aerobic exercises in the water. Many local council leisure centres offer free admission to pools and free swimming classes for older people.

Or perhaps you would prefer to see the exercise involved in swimming as incidental to other pleasures, such as enjoying the outdoors, listening to bird song and feeling water and weed against your body. If so, build swimming in the sea or an inland lake or river into your everyday life, insofar as you can. 'Wild swimming', or taking a dip in any enticing lake, pond, stream, river or sea you come across where it is safe to swim has become fashionable again, with guides published on the best swimming locations. Take sensible precautions – for instance, reservoirs can be dangerous as they contain underwater equipment; wear a wet suit if the cold might affect you.

Resistance training

Resistance training is different from aerobic exercise. It involves imposing force against something which is resistant to being pushed, squeezed,
stretched or bent.

Resistance training thus strengthens our muscles. What is more, the
physical demand imposed by muscles as they pull on bones in turn improves the strength of our bones, thus countering osteoporosis *(see page
20)*. Resistance training can increase the density of the minerals in bone
tissue, thus strengthening it.

Swimming is a form of resistance training: muscle effort is opposed by
the viscosity of the water. But there are other ways of engaging in resistance training without getting wet, such as rowing. This could involve
participation in a rowing club, but it could simply mean having fun on a
boating lake with your friends.

In the home, a resistance band is useful – a thick strip of elastic which
can be held behind the back with one hand holding each end. You extend
and relax an arm or a leg and in the process work against the elastic and
thus strengthen muscles and bones. Why not keep one of these in the
kitchen and use it whenever you are waiting for the kettle to boil?

Another simple form of resistance training involves pushing yourself
away from a wall:

- Stand facing the wall, an arm's length away, with your feet
  shoulder-width apart.

- Place your hands on the wall at shoulder height, fingers pointing up. Keeping your body in a straight line, let your arms bend
  so your shoulders move towards the wall.

- Then straighten your arms to bring yourself to an upright position. This part of the exercise, involving pushing up from the
  wall, should strengthen arm muscles and bones.

- Try to do ten such movements with a short rest between each
  one, keeping your stomach muscles tight throughout.

- If you want to impose more work on your arms, stand a little
  further from the wall.[18]

Cycling

In common with swimming, cycling is a form of non-load-bearing exercise. So, although the muscles are relaxing and contracting, the pressure
imposed by the weight of one's body on the joints is reduced. The Brit-

ish Medical Association explains in its book *Cycling: Towards Health and Safety* that cycling:

> …is potentially one of the most appropriate ways for individuals to maintain their fitness through the rhythmic contraction and relaxation of the large limb muscles. In contrast to running and jogging, which can place high stress on hips, knees, ankles and the Achilles tendons, there is very little risk of cycling leading to overstrain of muscles, ligaments, or other injuries from "overuse", particularly as the body is supported on a saddle, with pressure and effort distributed between two hands, two feet, and one backside.[19]

Of course, the reason why most of us engage in physical activity is that we enjoy it, not least the sensation of arms and legs swinging in the open air or moving through water. Doing this in surroundings we find absorbing can heighten our enjoyment still further. The poet Lascelles Abercrombie captured the exhilaration of cycling in his delightful poem 'For Bicycling':

> Poised on wheels as wondrously
> As on wings, I pass
> Through the green and golden land,
> Daffodils and grass.
>
> White the road beneath me slips
> A river with green shores;
> And glowing through my golden mind
> England's beauty pours.[20]

If you feel nervous about taking to a bike again, why not look to see whether your local council offers guided cycle rides?

Walking, playing badminton and other load-bearing exercise

Cycling and swimming provide good aerobic exercise, but they also help counter osteoporosis, as the tendons attached to muscles impose force on the bones as the muscles contract.

Walking and playing tennis also help strengthen bones in this way. But because they are types of 'load-bearing exercise', they help keep bones strong by imposing force on the whole skeleton as a result of gravity.

For people who prefer to walk with others, many local authorities as well as voluntary groups, from U3As to Ramblers' branches, offer group walks. These can of course offer a wide range of benefits, not least exploring hitherto unknown places and mixing with like-minded souls. Often walks requiring different levels of fitness are offered.

Walking with sticks, including Nordic walking, is becoming increasingly popular. These sticks contain little springs which help locomotion, enabling greater distances to be covered more easily. At the same time, the distribution of more of the effort of walking to the upper body reduces stress on knee joints.

Bones can be strengthened still further by exercises which involve high-impact force, such as jogging and skipping. However, these can be hazardous if they put too much strain on damaged joints. For more information about targeted exercises for people with osteoporosis, have a look at publications by the National Osteoporosis Society *(see Useful Contacts)*.

Dance

Dancing is for many the most enjoyable form of group physical activity. There are countless types from which to choose, from ballroom, Scottish, country, tap, Morris or line dancing to zumba, salsa, disco, jiving and Bollywood. Many dances have been devised for people who have to remain seated; a seated form of Hawaiian dancing can be fun, for instance.

Janetta Murrie, who runs dance and Pilates sessions in the UK and Argentina, sees social dancing as more than fun and exercise. She told me in 2016,

> Dance gives you the opportunity to express yourself freely to music and without words: it's as if you're expressing a deeper sense of yourself. The physical movement is just one part of a beautiful, multi-coloured jigsaw. Dance, for me, brings together the artistic, the emotional and the physical.

The physical contact with other people which dances from the tango and the waltz to the Gay Gordons involve brings an additional benefit. Professor of Geriatric Medicine Archie Young and Susi Dinan, a former dancer and now an expert on exercise for older people, explain that dancing, 'Permits the emotional benefits of socially acceptable touching, unconnected with dependence and the need for personal care'. They remind us of the cruel reality that, 'Touching is a rarity for many elderly people who are long bereaved.'[21]

Pilates

Pilates involves flowing movements carried out on mats on the floor or with large equipment with pulleys, springs, handles and straps which aim to increase the strength and flexibility of the whole body as well as improve balance, posture and breathing technique. Yoga is similar to Pilates, but does not involve a flow of movement or any equipment. Both emphasise the connection between physical and mental health, although yoga places more emphasis on relaxation and uses meditation.

Tai chi

Tai chi is a slow and graceful Chinese form of exercise which includes meditation and is often undertaken in groups. Moving weight from leg to leg is common to many tai chi exercises, as is extending and lifting the arms, legs and hands. This helps keep joints mobile but also strengthens the muscles that support them. Tai chi can be especially helpful in strengthening the muscles of the lower body and improving posture and balance, so reducing the risk of falls. As it is slow and gentle, it is suitable for people with illness and also joint and muscle impairments.

Chair-based exercises

Many different exercises can be performed while sitting down. These can be invaluable for people who cannot stand at all, but also for those who can stand but only for a limited period. Chair-based exercises need not only involve the upper body – strengthening arm muscles, for example. They could also involve marching with one's feet and swinging one's arms while seated. Thus chair cheer-leading features in exercise sessions promoted by Our Organisation Makes People Happy! (Oomph!), a national group that seeks to provide fun, yet effective exercise for older people.

It is easy to imagine that chair-based exercises are somehow casual, demand little effort and are not a serious form of exercise. Not so. Chair-based exercise aims to increase strength and functional ability and, if possible, reach a point at which participants can do the exercises without the need for chair support.

Chair-based exercise should be progressive, demanding a little more from the body on each occasion. As expert on exercise and older people Dr Afroditi Stathi of Bath University explained to me in an interview in 2012:

> There has been a misconception that if you do chair-based exercises, you always will. But no, the aim is to load the body so as to increase your strength, to increase your aerobic capacity in order to be able to do exercises standing up. There must be progress. There may be some very old, very frail people where improvement is not sufficient for them to be able to move on from chair-based exercises. But even for these people, their improvement will translate into better daily life. They will be able to do simple things that they

couldn't do before – such as reach things from a top shelf or stand up from a chair without the need for aids.[22]

Exercises to treat or manage specific ailments

Apart from preventing disease, exercise can play an invaluable role in treating some medical conditions. I have already referred to this when discussing the prevention of osteoarthritis and osteoporosis. But other ailments can be helped too.

Parkinson's disease

Parkinson's disease is a movement disorder, and particular exercises have been developed to help sufferers maintain walking ability and other movements necessary for everyday living, as well as to tackle slowness, stiffness and balance difficulties. If you have the condition, you should ask a Parkinson's disease nurse or other specialist such as a physiotherapist to point you to these targeted exercises. The value of physiotherapy in helping people with Parkinson's is recognised by the National Institute for Health and Care Excellence in its guidance on how the illness should be treated.[23] Parkinson's UK provides information about using Wii games to help people exercise at home. In a Wii game, you play with the same force as would be required when playing the game in question (such as tennis) in a normal situation.

Continence problems

One of the main causes of continence problems in later life is the weakening of the muscles of the pelvic floor; in women, reasons for this include natural childbirth and the reduction in oestrogen production after the menopause. But, just like any other muscles in the body, those of the pelvic floor get stronger if they are exercised. So pelvic-floor muscle exercises are a frontline treatment for continence difficulties and they can help prevent problems developing in the first place *(as explained in Chapter 19: Continence)*.

Dementia

Physical activity such as dance is often used as a form of therapy for people with dementia. In one form, Circle Dance, participants sit or stand in a circle and do a simple dance, drawing on traditional dances from many countries. The sense of togetherness this engenders can be especially useful for people who find conversation difficult. Accurate movements are unnecessary: the emphasis is on moving together with music. Circle Dance also provides the opportunity to touch and hold other people. The Alzheimer's Society publishes a free factsheet called *Exercise and*

Physical Activity, which describes types of exercise and physical activity which can help people at different stages of the disease.

Physical activity: warnings

In the field of exercise and older people, the idea that there is no gain without pain is wrong: if a type of movement hurts, it should be stopped. However, pain should not cause us to give up. Instead, we should adapt the exercise. If exercise performed standing up is putting too much weight on our joints and causing pain, we may be able to perform it sitting down.

Another example of a situation in which exercise might need to be modified: our body has ebbs and flows, so that if blood pressure rises, we might feel hot and bothered doing an exercise we coped with easily before. In that situation, it is best to stop and modify the routine, so that we do only what feels comfortable.

Here are one or two other warnings (in a group setting, the instructor would explain them in more detail):

✓ If you are going to engage in fairly vigorous movement, don't suddenly start at full throttle – do some form of gentle movements as warm-up first. Otherwise, you might injure your muscles. Similarly, do some gentler movements as a cool down, so as to bring your body temperature and heart rate down to pre-exercise levels gradually.

✓ If you feel sick, dizzy, especially stiff or tired, or you develop cold sweats, stop the activity at once and speak to a doctor.

✓ Don't turn your head sharply or tip it back suddenly to look at the ceiling: these movements can cause dizziness.

✓ Don't engage in vigorous physical activity if you feel unwell, tired or have just eaten.

✓ You are likely to feel tired and stiff after the first session or two of new physical activity, but if you continue to feel tired and stiff after several sessions, consult your doctor.

✓ Some physical activity brings its own risks. For instance, swimming can be hazardous not only because of the danger of drowning but also because you might have a heart attack in the water. If you are at such a risk, make sure the beach or pool has lifeguards on duty.

✓ Check that any swimming bath or gym you plan to use has a defibrillator. Vigorous exercise can unmask underlying heart problems.

✓ Before you embark on any new type of physical activity, talk to your GP. Some types of activity might be ill-advised, bearing in mind your state of health and any particular physical condition you have, such as asthma or previous injuries. Certain movements should not be undertaken by people who have had a triple bypass operation, fractured spine, heart attack, disc problems or a total knee replacement, for example.

✓ Not only starting but continuing to engage in some activities, such as vigorous exercise, can also cause damage, so talk to your GP if, say, you have osteoarthritis but are planning to continue with jumping or high-impact jogging.

Choices

When we are getting on, we may push weights in the gym or pound a treadmill for the same reasons as young people – perhaps to train for a sports event or to enhance body image. But as I hope I have persuaded you, there are many other, more diverting activities which can benefit health.

A good way of finding out what is available is to ask somebody in the relevant department of your local council (probably leisure services). They ought to be able to tell you over the phone about other activities the council arranges or knows of which might suit you. Depending on your physical condition, these activities might include sport – such as badminton, bowls, table tennis, stoolball and hockey (including sit-down hockey using small bean bags and upturned walking sticks) – as well as dance, exercise classes in the gym and outdoor walks or cycle rides.

You could also telephone your NHS health authority *(see page 277)*. These organisations often fund exercise programmes which are free or cheaper than the private exercise classes that take place in gyms or community venues such as church halls.

If you are from an ethnic minority, you may wish to seek out classes aimed at your group. Some authorities have developed classes designed to prevent cardiovascular disease which are targeted at African-Caribbean people, for instance, as they experience particularly high levels of diabetes and heart disease.

In a group or alone?

Of course, we can all start new physical activities on our own, but they may be more fun in a group situation. Group activity is also likely to be more effective in the long run. It is harder to cop out in a group situation and the mere presence of other people increases motivation.

Another advantage of exercising with a group rather than alone is the advice offered by the instructor in response to the way in which you exercise. For example, people often instinctively hold their breath when they exercise, but this puts up blood pressure so it is important to breathe in a relaxed way. Some people, especially those with osteoarthritis, hold their shoulders tensed up; an instructor would see this and encourage them to bring their shoulders down and relax. Participants can also learn a lot from other participants and spot each other's need to release clenched hands, and so on.

A trained exercise instructor should also ensure that you do not engage in any movements which are too violent for your body. If you go out and buy a yoga or an aerobics DVD and start exercising alone at home, you could hurt a tendon or cause other kinds of damage.

If you are really going to benefit from exercise in terms of strengthening muscles and bones, it needs to be progressive, so that you are demanding a little bit more from your body each time, whether walking a bit further or a bit faster, or increasing the resistance against which your body must work with weights or rubber bands. A trained instructor can provide invaluable help in devising ways of measuring this. In a group, an instructor trained in exercise for older people will be observing how members of the class are coping, asking how they are feeling and cross-checking continuously. Sometimes exercises will be modified if they are imposing too much strain on a particular part of the body. Crucially, monitoring enables the activities to form part of a steady progression which will bring greater fitness and body strength.

The job of an exercise instructor is a very responsible one. They must:

✓ make sure that participants do not come to harm

✓ take account of any medical conditions which participants may have – say, arthritis, breathing difficulties, heart problems, Parkinson's, MS and a hernia

✓ take account of the wishes of different participants to stand most of the time, to stand throughout or to sit, and adapt the exercises accordingly

✓ observe participants closely to see what effect the exercise is having on them

✓ make the session as much fun as possible, for instance with lively background music

Exercise instruction for older people does not attract a lot of cowboy operators trying to make a fast buck, but it is important nonetheless to make sure your instructor is suitably qualified and understands any medical condition from which you suffer as well as the characteristic features of the ageing body outlined in Chapter 1. There is a register of exercise professionals (REP), and you can check that a person is so registered. However, exercise is a vast field and somebody on the REP list may be an Olympic gymnast but have no knowledge of the older body, so make further inquiries.

One way of finding a good instructor is to look for one with training which has included attention to the special needs of older people. A swimming instructor might, for instance, have obtained the qualification for already qualified fitness instructors offered by the YMCA in 'exercise to music for older persons'. Generally, if an exercise class for older people is based in a local authority sports centre, a health service centre or a GP surgery, it will probably be led by instructors with appropriate qualifications.

Two organisations which offer exercise classes at many locations up and down the country are the Fitness League and Extend. At around 300 venues across the UK, the Fitness League offers classes which are part dance and part exercise. A non-profit-making organisation, its classes are inexpensive. Although they are for people of all ages, people in their fifties and sixties tend to be most numerous. The League emerged from the Women's League of Health and Beauty, and women predominate. Some Fitness League exercise will be similar to yoga. However, League exercise takes place to music and includes dance, while yoga is silent and dance-free.

Extend is an organisation which grew out of the Fitness League; it also offers classes at many venues scattered across the UK. It focuses on people who are less physically active. Trainers have specialised knowledge of the physical ailments of old age, the sort of movements which can help ease symptoms and also those which should be avoided by people with particular medical conditions. In many areas, Extend also offers classes for more active older people.

Both Fitness League and Extend classes are likely to involve some dancing. In Fitness League this could be, perhaps, the Charleston, jiving and salsa; in Extend there might be, say, barn dancing, possibly adapted if instructors consider that some of its movements might be ill-advised for particular participants.

Both Fitness League and Extend incorporate targeted exercises designed to improve balance, posture, strength, the flexibility of joints and muscle tone into their sessions. Some of these exercises may help to prevent falls (through improving balance, coordination and muscle strength). Pelvic floor exercises *(see page 412)* also have a place. Despite the serious purpose of the sessions, the emphasis is on having fun.

Extend instructors emphasise the 'personalisation' of exercise. In an ordinary all-age exercise class participants do the exercise if they can, but if they cannot, no alternative is offered. In contrast, Extend instructors insist on acquainting themselves with participants' medical history to ensure that they are not asked to do anything which might harm them and to devise exercises which would be particularly helpful for particular individuals.

However, getting out to a gym or church hall is not always easy, particularly if you live in a remote area. If you are planning to exercise at home, get hold of a good DVD or manual (Dr Muir Gray's book *Sod 70! The Guide to Living Well* contains a wealth of useful exercises with accompanying diagrams).[24] But discuss what you propose to do beforehand with your GP. To make exercising more fun, invite your friends to join you, perhaps with a Wii game. Or background music, so that you could move on to jiving and singing, as if you were in a musical …

Physical activity

* Most people don't engage in enough physical activity and don't realise they don't.

* Physical activity reduces the risk of heart attacks, strokes and vascular dementia.

* Most health benefits come to people who have done little physical activity in the past, but start to do a moderate amount.

* Make physical activity central to your everyday life.

* It is best to find an activity you will enjoy and perform it regularly.

* Try to do five half-hour sessions of moderate activity each week.

* Hoovering a room can be enough when you are in your nineties.

* Swimming is especially good for people with osteoarthritis.

* Exercise should be progressive: do a little more each time.

* Don't let others wait on you: do things for yourself.

Chapter 4

Psychological well-being

S ome older people are in prime physical condition and have plenty of money, yet they feel low most of the time. Others with major disability and little ready cash lead happy lives. While some people are thrown into permanent emotional turmoil by the death of their partner, others live happily after the deaths of spouses, brothers and sisters, even their own children.[1] Why? How do our psychological needs interact with our physical needs? Do those needs alter as we grow older? Do we have to find new ways of meeting them?

The pyramid of human needs devised by the American psychologist Abraham Maslow provides a useful and well-known framework for considering the range of needs we all share.[2] At the base of his pyramid Maslow placed our most fundamental needs – for water, air, food, sleep and an equable temperature. We all know that if any of these needs go unfulfilled, we die. But the four tiers that make up the remainder of Maslow's pyramid are almost wholly psychological needs. They include needs for affection, acceptance and self-worth.

In this chapter I use Maslow's pyramid as a framework for understanding our psychological needs when we are older. Of course, many people have no difficulty in meeting all their psychological needs. But not everyone. I consider whether those needs alter with advancing years and whether later life brings particular problems in meeting them.

Incidentally, Maslow's analysis need not be the last word on the matter – you may consider (as I do) that getting outdoors should also be identified as a real human need *(see page 671)*.

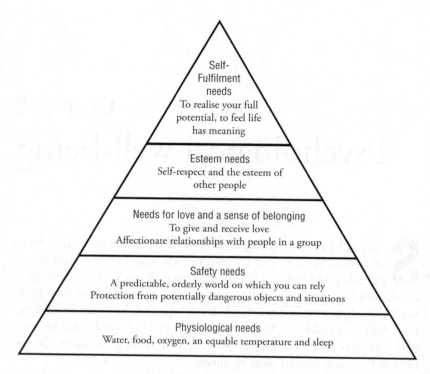

Abraham Maslow's hierarchy of human needs (based on Maslow, 1965 and 1970)

A need for safety

Maslow placed safety needs on the second tier of his pyramid. This category acts as a bridge between the basic physiological needs of the bottom tier and the psychological needs that make up the bulk of the pyramid. For Maslow believed that human happiness depended not only on physical safety (protection from hazardous situations and illness), but also on satisfying a deep-seated need to feel secure.

Today, one of the greatest fears for many of us when we are getting on is that we might be assaulted by a stranger in the street or even in our own home. For some, living in areas which see high levels of crime, this is understandable. But others are so fearful of violent crime that they never go out after dark lest they be attacked – even if they live in remote villages which rarely see any crime whatsoever. The media make much of the unfortunate victims of such events, yet statistically speaking, somebody aged between 16 and 24 is ten times more likely to become the victim of personal crime than someone aged 75 or over.[3]

Road traffic poses a greater danger than many realise. Older people make up a relatively small proportion of the total numbers of pedestrians involved in road accidents, but when they are involved, they are more likely to fare badly. So while 19 per cent of the pedestrians aged 20–24 involved in accidents in 2013 were killed or seriously injured, the figure rose to 26 per cent for people aged 60–64 and 38 per cent for 80–84-year-olds.[4]

Losing a safe space

Some of the most unsettling changes life can throw at us occur in later life. One is retirement from work. This is welcome to some, but for others it snatches away not just a source of income but also a familiar environment, a structure to one's days, a part of one's identity and the company of colleagues.

Another change which can be deeply troubling is a move away from what is perceived as the safe environment of our own home to a care home. Our home is our refuge from the outside world, the surroundings to which we long to return and the place from which we draw comfort and strength. It may actually be unsafe – perhaps from faulty electric wiring or clutter over which we may trip – but it *feels* safe, because we have inhabited it in the past without mishap, and its furnishings, ornaments and framed photographs embody times and people representing security. The older we are, the more time we have had to customise this refuge, and the more entrenched we may feel in it.

Tidy or untidy, spacious or cramped, with an extensive garden or a window box, our home is part of who we are. Small wonder, then, that when we find ourselves suddenly taken away from this environment to dwell amongst complete strangers, we can feel disorientated and alienated. Whether or not a particular care home provides good or bad care, a move into a home is a massive step, with as much potential for distress as divorce or getting the sack. Yet it is rarely acknowledged as one of life's major events.

Coping with bereavement

The loss of a partner of many years can also chip away at our feelings of safety and security. He or she may have given us a sense of physical safety by coping with practical matters, perhaps handling house repairs, doing the shopping and driving us around. They may have enveloped us in emotional and sexual security, as our confidante, best friend, lover and the only giver of hugs and kisses. The loss of that person demands that we reconfigure all those aspects of our life. So we might ask: what does this death mean to practical aspects of my everyday life? What is my identity without that person? What shall I tell other people? How can other people help me grieve? Will they think I'm mad if I tell them I talk to my dead partner every night?

Canon Dr Alan Billings, an Anglican priest and the then Director of the Centre for Ethics and Religion at Lancaster University, put the difficulties of adjustment like this on BBC Radio 4's 'Thought for the Day':

> The death of a loved one … also throws our life into the sharpest relief, exposing our fragilities to ourselves. The loss of one on whom we leaned, behind whom we sheltered, behind whom we hid, exposes us now to our lack of security. We miss them; we miss also the sense of safety and permanence they gave to our life. We have to find a way into the future wounded by that knowledge.[5]

Reaction to the death of a partner, relative or friend will depend on many factors, not least the relationship in life between the deceased and the one left alive. Some people are relieved when their partner dies, perhaps because they were trapped in an unhappy marriage. In other cases, death may have occurred at the height of a satisfying emotional relationship. Some people who lose a partner in later life die very quickly afterwards. Others may take a long time to adjust to the loss, since, as Billings notes, it can undermine the whole basis of life.

Grieving is natural when a partner dies, but for some people it becomes a long-lasting shadow blighting their life. Psychologists differ in how they distinguish 'normal' from 'pathological' grieving, as well as in how they think people should cope with either. During most of the 20th century, the fashionable view was that the bereaved should let go and move on to new relationships. However, studies published during the 1990s showed the importance to many people, particularly older people, of maintaining an ongoing bond with the dead partner, while forging new social ties. According to this view, if people find coping with bereavement difficult, they can be helped to look for ways in which they can create an enduring relationship with the dead person which is less painful. Thus they would not deny that their partner had died, nor avoid making necessary changes in the light of that death, but they would use their bond with deceased to help them make those changes – considering what the person who had died would have done in the circumstances and even talking things over with them.[6] *(I also discuss bereavement on pages 212 and 382).*

A need for affection and acceptance

Maslow called the next tier as we ascend his pyramid 'love and belongingness'. He felt that once basic physiological and safety needs were met, the next most important human need was to give and receive affection and to feel that one belonged and was accepted somewhere.

It is worth disentangling 'love' from 'belongingness'. Plainly, they can be closely related, as when somebody draws a sense of belonging from their family and at the same time gives and receives love and care within it. But a strong sense of belonging can be found in a diverse range of social groups, from choirs to knitting circles and political parties (within which 'love' may rarely feature).

Social activities amongst groups of people bring not only pleasure and interest: research has shown that they are surprisingly beneficial to physical health.

Researchers in the United States talked at length to nearly 3,000 people aged 65 and over in 1982, and subsequently re-interviewed them annually for 13 years. During the study, they collected information about which of their interviewees had died and the cause of death.

The researchers divided the activities in which these people took part into three types:

- 'fitness activities', such as walking, active sports, swimming and exercise
- 'social activities', such as church attendance, playing cards and bingo, visits to the cinema and participation in social groups, and
- 'productive activities', such as voluntary work, preparing meals, paid employment and gardening

Contrary to what many would expect, social and productive activities were found to be as beneficial as fitness activities in prolonging life. Indeed, the researchers found: 'Social and productive activities that involve little or no enhancement of fitness lower the risk of all causes of mortality as much as fitness activities do.'[7]

A more modest study in Britain was carried out by Dr Kate Bennett of Liverpool University, who examined the physical health and level of social participation of more than 1,000 older people in 2002. When she compared people of similar age, sex and physical health, she found that those with significantly lower levels of social activity were more likely to experience deteriorating physical health and to die sooner than the others.[8]

Barriers to social contact

Unfortunately, a web of factors combine to get in the way of fulfilling our need for social contact. Some of them affect young and old. Indeed, nearly half of adults of all ages who were questioned for a survey in 2010 believed that society as a whole was getting lonelier.[9] But older people are affected by some of these factors to a far greater extent than the young.

The single life

Many of today's older generation must meet their needs for affection and acceptance while living on their own. Indeed, as many as one in three people over the age of 75 lives alone.[10] There are several reasons. Divorce and separation have been increasing in recent decades, particularly among older people *(see page 208)*. Many people do not wish to team up with another live-in partner, or have never done so. Women in particular run into problems if they wish to find new love, since they tend to outlive men (although the lifespan gap is narrowing). To skew the odds further, older widowers and single men often prefer younger women as partners.

Some of those living alone will be struggling with sadness at having lost a loved one which prevents their engaging in many social activities. Being jollied along to a barn dance or some other group activity may make them feel more, not less unhappy. Yet when one member of a couple passes away, the survivor may live for 30 years or more without them. Many will not have the option of moving in with grown-up children: one in five people over 50 have no children, according to the campaigning group Ageing Without Children.

Fortunately, some changes in society can benefit older people who might otherwise feel unloved; in particular, increasing acceptance of openly gay relationships and the emergence of the phenomenon of 'LAT couples', that is, people who are 'living-apart-together'. In other words, couples go out together and stay over in each other's homes, but do not share those homes. *I turn to this lifestyle and to the steps that can be taken to find new love and new friends in Chapters 9 and 10.*

Disability

Common disabilities such as hearing and vision impairment create their own barriers to making new social contacts and retaining existing ones *(as explored on pages 252–56)*. So can difficulty in walking. This can rule out anything from group expeditions to strolling around your neighbourhood and chatting to passers-by.

If you cannot walk as far as a bus stop, you may miss out not only on particular visits which might have enriched your social life but also on informal contact with other people and the sense of being part of wider society while you are travelling around. In 2014, Professor Judith Green and others based in universities in and near London attempted to understand the way in which Londoners aged over 60 were using their concessionary bus pass to travel around. Through interviews with nearly 50 users, they discovered that buses provided not just a means of obtaining access to goods and services, but also an important space for social interaction. Chatting with other passengers served to mitigate loneliness. At the same time bus travel helped these older citizens to participate in the life of their city, rather than feeling relegated to the fringes. As the researchers reported, 'The key point here is that, for the older people we interviewed, to be on public buses is to be in *the* world and part of that world, however chaotic, and accounting for one's place in it.'[11]

Illness, especially if it confines someone to their home for a long time, is another common reason for social isolation and often also feelings of loneliness. So too is acting as a carer – a role which can bring a special kind of isolation, *as explored in 'the lonely carer' on page 225.*

Changes to communities

Whether you live alone or with other people, the sort of atmosphere you encounter when you step outside your front door can make a lot of difference to whether you feel part of a social world. In some places, you can go out to buy a newspaper and greet three, four, five, perhaps six people; even if you don't know them well, you know them by sight and exchange greetings.

But in other places, everybody else is out at work during the day. Perhaps a couple moved there when the man drove, but he has had to give up driving or has died, and his partner, who has never learned to drive, stays on, cut off from the world amongst neighbours who make all their journeys by car. Also, local amenities, from post offices and small shops to pubs and public libraries, in which people who might live alone and not travel very far can engage with the world at large have been closing.

One third of people over 65 questioned in 2009 said they felt lonely always, often or sometimes.[12] It is hard to prove a connection, but factors such as these must surely play a part in exacerbating social isolation and loneliness.

Older people from ethnic minorities

Problems of isolation and loneliness can be particularly acute for people from ethnic minority groups. They may have to grapple with lack of integration into British society, as well as difficulties in getting out and about. Although they may have lived in Britain for many years, they may remain unfamiliar with the organisation of British society and perhaps be hampered by lack of fluency in English and difficulty in reading English. These things can combine to create a formidable wall of isolation and sometimes also loneliness.

Lewisham in south-east London is an area with very high African-Caribbean and Asian populations. Researchers conducted in-depth interviews with 20 social care workers (social workers and managers of day centres) there in 2005, who told them that many of their elderly clients were accepting 'perpetual sadness as a norm' in their lives. Low mood and depression were alarmingly common.

The main reason given was social isolation. The black and Asian communities were being hit by social change of a kind that had affected white communities decades before. Children and grandchildren had become westernised and were focusing their attention on their careers, material wealth and their own nuclear families. If they moved away, elderly parents and grandparents became yet more isolated. As the manager of one African-Caribbean day centre put it: 'The strong family connection isn't there any more. A lot of older people are just left isolated, and they are not coping well.'[13]

Sexual orientation

There are one million gay, lesbian, bisexual and transgender (LGBT) people over the age of 55 in the UK, according to the campaigning and advisory group Stonewall. Many of them live alone. Various reasons may account for this. They may have lived for most of their adult life before same-sex relationships were accepted and may never have sought a long-term partner. Fewer LGBT than straight people have children. Some are ostracised by their blood families (although they often establish 'chosen families' for company and support, such as an older gay man treating a lesbian woman as he would his sister). Dr Jane Traies of the University of Sussex in Brighton has carried out a fascinating and important study of the lives of older lesbians, based on detailed questionnaires with 370 of them; the results were published in 2016. Half of the women in Dr Traies' study lived alone and one in four of these told her that loneliness was a problem for them.[14]

The social isolation of some older LGBT people may be compounded by the fact that they have come out to only a small number of people, fearing the stigma that might be prompted by revealing their true identity to the wider world. As a result, they may feel cut off, even alienated from most of the people around them.

Because LGBT people often live alone and lack family support, they are more likely than others to have to fall back on the care and support provided by day centres, extra-care housing, care homes and help in the home. But they can feel uncomfortable in a care environment. Care facilities can be 'heteronormative', in other words, they assume everyone is heterosexual, with much conversation revolving around life involving husbands, wives and grandchildren. An LGBT person living in a care home and attempting to keep their sexual identity secret lest they be rejected by other residents and even perhaps staff can feel very isolated and very lonely.

Dementia

Dementia, as we saw in Chapter 1, is relatively common as people move into their mid-eighties and beyond. One of the main effects of this condition can be increasing isolation from society as a whole.

One reason is the communication difficulties that can arise as someone with the condition forgets their vocabulary and eventually is unable to communicate through speech at all *(as explored in Chapter 12: Communication)*. Another reason is general rejection by other people. When somebody shows signs that they may be developing dementia, such as difficulty in expressing themselves clearly or remembering things that happened recently, some people react with feelings of warmth and empathy. However, others reject the person and see only the dementia. They seem to believe that somebody with dementia is less of a human being than everybody else and may even feel that the person's life can be written off as not worth living.

The stigma surrounding dementia is not helped by media focus on the things that people with the condition cannot do, rather than the wide range of ways in which they continue to be able to think and feel, just like everybody else *(see page 429–30)*.

Toby Williamson, Head of Development and Later Life at the Mental Health Foundation, wrote a report in 2010 based on interviews with people with dementia in which he showed just how much the needs and attitudes of people with dementia resemble those of people without the condition. He called his report *My Name is not Dementia,* in an attempt to encourage people to see the person who happens to have dementia, not simply the dementia itself.

When asked which aspects of their life they believed were important in giving them a good quality of life, Williamson's interviewees explained: 'It is very important to have a laugh ... something that can make you laugh, and being made to laugh is very important.' Another said: 'Meeting nice people, not necessarily nice people, but people that are interesting to me ... as long as they come over to me in a way that I can relate to and understand.'[15]

Sexual needs

Maslow placed sexual needs within love and affection needs but he also considered they could occur in the bottom level of his pyramid, as a physiological need, since sexual behaviour may arise from a sexual need alone or from a loving relationship.

Just as we can find meeting our needs for affection more difficult as we grow older, so too our needs for romance and sexual contact. But while society at least acknowledges a need for its older citizens to be in contact with other people for company and to pursue mutual interests, rarely does this extend as far as ensuring they can pursue their romantic instincts. Older people living in care facilities, for example, may spend much of their time thinking about romance and sex, yet romantic contact between them is rarely facilitated and often frowned upon not only by staff but also by their adult children.

In the famous horror film *The Shining,* based on the novel by Stephen King, one classic scary moment involves the leading character, played by Jack Nicholson, kissing a naked young woman when, horrors of horrors, she morphs into an elderly woman. How widespread is the idea that sex involving older women is repulsive? How often are the older man's sexual urges dismissed as 'dirty'? Is society's attitude to older people and sex more ageist than any other aspect of its attitudes towards them?

A need for self-esteem

Maslow's next tier ascending his pyramid was the need for self-esteem. Whatever our circumstances, we are more likely to feel positive about life if we have a sense of our own value. We are likely to get this from sensing that other people hold us in esteem and treat us with respect and we in turn believe in our own self-worth.

Self-esteem changes with age. Researchers in the United States conducted thousands of telephone interviews with people aged from 9 to 90 and discovered that there tended to be two crises of feelings of self-worth, one in adolescence and the other in later life. Feelings of self-esteem typically rose gradually through one's forties, fifties and sixties, then took a nose-dive after the age of 70.[16]

A later-life identity crisis

Expert on the psychology of later life Professor Peter Coleman of Southampton University believes that the crisis of old age is fundamentally a
crisis of meaning rather than self-esteem.[17] It is easy to see why. Retirement from paid work robs older people of much of the status society
accords citizens and they are simultaneously denied the status and value
derived from being parents and often also consumers.

Many older people lead lives they find deeply fulfilling. But however
meaningful we find our lives, the attitudes of family and friends can be
crucial in bolstering – or undermining – our feelings of self-worth.
When an older relative telephones with news of coffee and conversation
over a game of Scrabble, someone who has been at work all day may be
tempted to view those activities as trivial. Indeed, we are programmed to
do so: in the great scheme of things, a boardroom tussle or an exam crisis
is bound to be considered more meaningful.

How we look

Perhaps the key feature distinguishing older people is their appearance.
People who look old encounter ageist attitudes all the time. If your hair is
grey and you are introduced to a stranger at a party, you may encounter a
patronising attitude which assumes that you do nothing significant with
your time. If your hand hovers over the button to open the train door
yet it remains shut, the assumption of the younger person behind may
be not that the driver has not yet released the door-opening system but
that you are too dim-witted to know that you must press the button. In
other words, the appearance of age can proclaim to many that the person
involved is of little moment and probably slow, if not stupid.

As if this were not frustrating enough, older people also have to deal
with a world which dictates that the ageing body does not look 'right':
the norm to which we all should aspire is a youthful appearance. So,
fresh, plump skin is favoured and lines, wrinkles and grey hair are rejected – even despised. Whether this preference is an immutable feature
of human nature is open to question, but certainly the associations of
the ageing body with degeneration, mortality and perhaps also weakness
seem sufficient to make people reject it. A multi-billion pound industry,
of which makeover features in magazines and on TV are just one small
part, proclaims that it is wrong to look old, or at least to look as old as
one actually is.

Another key message of our time is that one should see one's body as
a sort of project, engaging in various self-care régimes to improve it and
thus become more attractive to potential employers, friends and lovers.[18]

The means deployed may involve no more than giving the face a more youthful appearance with make-up, dyeing one's hair or masking signs of ageing teeth through dental work. However, in 2010, 34,400 women and nearly 4,000 men in Britain went under the knife, many of them in their fifties and over. Some of the most popular procedures were face and neck lifts and blepharoplasty (the tightening of loose skin and removal of fat around the eyes).[19]

Botox is the most popular non-surgical treatment. It involves injection of botulinum (a poison) under the skin, usually of the face; this temporarily paralyses muscles, so reducing or smoothing out those lines caused by muscle contraction. Other non-surgical treatments include the injection of other types of filler and resurfacing the skin by means of laser beams. No reliable figures are available for Britain, but in the United States non-surgical treatments make up more than 80 per cent of all cosmetic procedures performed.[20]

Some will find such procedures a great help. Nonetheless, even when wrinkles on the face and hands have been ironed out, hands may give the game away, with their thickening joints and skin with a lifetime's accumulation of liver spots. Dyeing grey hair chestnut can bring glamour and the illusion of relative youth. Or, by drawing attention to the puzzling difference between apparent ageless beauty and the years betrayed by the tone and texture of the skin and white hair roots can make someone look older than ever. If hair colouring deceives at 70, will it do so at 90?

It is a cruel irony that while society applauds the efforts of younger people to improve their looks, attempts by older people to do the same can attract ridicule. Do grandchildren really respect a grandfather who paints his hair or a grandmother who opts for a facelift?

Changing circumstances

If the undermining of self-esteem through changes to our appearance were not enough, our circumstances may also conspire to erode our feelings of self-worth. If illness or disability takes away the ability to pursue a favourite hobby or feature of our working life, such as driving or playing sport, we can also lose part of our identity, and the part of our self-regard associated with it. Downsizing to a granny annex, retirement flat or care home often means getting rid of artefacts which remind us, as well as visitors, of this past. The deaths of close family and friends rob us of figures who reaffirm our self-image through the memory of past deeds and a common experience.

The myth of independence

Some people have a deep-seated fear of becoming dependent on other people, which they believe would strike at the heart of their self-esteem. As I write this, I have just received a letter from a woman in her mid-nineties. Although she suffers from much physical pain and discomfort and walking is very difficult, she can see well, hear with an aid and has a comfortable room in a nursing home, where she receives frequent visits from her family and friends. But she is racked by a feeling that her life is now utterly worthless. She spent decades caring for others, or more recently making things for needy children overseas. Now that arthritic fingers and general frailty prevent her from providing practical help to other people, she is convinced that her life has no value. When others offer to help her, all she can think of is the trouble this will cause them.

Another variation of dismay at dependency is fear of dependence on others to help with the necessary activities of daily life, such as washing, moving around or using the toilet. I have come across people who plan to sign an advance directive to refuse treatment *(explained on page 1017)*, instructing doctors to withhold the treatment necessary to keep them alive should they become dependent on other people for help with basic activities – and not because they are paralysed, in great pain or otherwise in extremis. Jane Miller, the 79-year-old author of *Crazy Age: Thoughts on Being Old*, told Jenni Murray during a *Woman's Hour* interview:

> I find the whole subject of being dependent on other people ter-rifying and the worse thing. ... If I'm stuck in any way and have to sit there looking at other people doing things for me, I think I'll go mad. ... It is a sort of torturing subject, I think, for those of us who are still all right.[21]

But Elizabeth Harbottle, a founder member of Christians on Ageing and the author of *Learning through Losses*, believes we should cut through what she sees as the illusion of independence and recognise that we are all dependent on one another. She told me:

> There is no such thing as independence. Instead, there are interde-pendencies, which shift through our lives. Driving a car does not mean that you are actually independent of help: you can drive the car, but you probably cannot manufacture it, or service it, and you need a filling station to be able to make it move. If you are in hos-pital and need people to look after you, you are not a lesser person. Frailty simply gives you a different sort of interdependence.[22]

We can help sustain the self-esteem of older, frailer people by showing that we value them for who they are – not what they do, or used to do. At the same time, younger, more 'independent' people can allow more apparently dependent people to help them, so that relationships are based far more on reciprocity, which in turn should enhance self-esteem. For instance, a friend in her mid-eighties whom I have helped to obtain Attendance Allowance is happy to do me a good turn by driving me wherever I wish to go. Another, in his mid-nineties, is only too happy to show younger people how to carry out DIY tasks, without actually wielding the drill or hammer himself. There is a huge amount of untapped reciprocal help out there which can benefit both parties. As we shall see when we look at help in the home, best practice now stipulates that paid care assistants should support people in doing things for themselves, rather than taking over and doing everything for them, as used to be the norm. Helping people to help themselves is now considered more likely to foster a sense of well-being in the person being helped, as well as help them retain and regain their own practical skills.

How to retain choice and control

Throughout our lives, expressing choice is an important means of expressing our identity. It's something easily taken for granted, whether we are choosing the clothes to wear, the food to eat and whether and, if so, where to go on holiday. But infirmity and with it perhaps a change of accommodation and reliance on help from other people can restrict choice and consequently undermine our belief in our own self-worth.

Restriction of choice can be particularly stark in some care homes, where residents may be able to exercise little control over the food which is served, the time of getting up or the number and destination of excursions. Management often allocate residents individual 'key workers', who are supposed to give them special care and be their best friend, but without allowing residents a choice in who that key worker will be. Yet research has shown that increasing residents' control over their own lives in care homes improves mental alertness, increases involvement in activities and speeds adjustment to surroundings.[23]

Care home residents could be offered more choice and more responsibility in many aspects of the life of the home. They could help to decide on the menu, the destination of trips and the type of activities offered. They could update the daily menu board, replenish flowers and run a library.[24] Prospective employees could be asked to meet residents, so that residents' comments could be fed back into the decision-making process: who is better placed to assess whether a candidate for the job of home manager would empathise with residents than the residents themselves?

Self-fulfilment

Maslow's final need, which he believed could only be addressed if the four lower needs had been met, was for self-fulfilment. This need, which Maslow called 'self-actualisation' involves feeling driven by a sense of personal mission, of belief in something beyond ourselves. Self-actualisation is not static but involves a personal journey of discovery, so that we feel our life has a meaning and that we have found a place for ourselves in the context of things. As this is an individual quest, it is perhaps a Western idea, so people from cultures which put more emphasis on groups than individuals may not feel quite the same way.

Maslow gave examples of people who seemed to have met their need for self-actualisation. One was a woman, uneducated and poor, who was a marvellous cook, mother, wife and homemaker. 'With little money, her home was somehow always beautiful. She was the perfect hostess. Her meals were banquets.'[25]

Self-actualisation could involve campaigning for a better world within lobby groups, including political parties. Here are two examples:

> Anneli Jones is an ardent activist in the peace movement, taking part in CND demonstrations in Trafalgar Square. 'Although I am 84, I feel like a spring chicken', she told her local newspaper.[26] Back home in east Kent, she fires off letters to her MP and submissions to parliamentary inquiries.
>
> Len Clark, aged 99, regularly drives to Godalming station in Surrey on his moped (proudly bearing L-plates), takes the train to London, then the Underground to attend committee meetings of the Council for National Parks. Len has devoted much of his free time over the years to the protection of the countryside and (as a former chair of the Youth Hostels Association), the provision of low-cost accommodation so that people of modest means, young and old can enjoy it. Len also regularly attends meetings of the Guildford Samaritans in which he has long played an active role. He posts a regular blog about the various campaigns in which he continues to be involved.[27]

Work can also be a means of self-fulfilment. Later life is a time when many people set up their own business and work for themselves. Of course, this may be because they struggle to land a job. Or it may be they are choosy and keen to spend time in an activity they find really fulfilling. Whatever the reason, there is a steep increase in the proportion of men who work for themselves after the age of 55. Nearly 30 per cent of men aged 60–64 who were in employment in 2009 were self-employed, with the figure rising to nearly 45 per cent for those aged 70 and over.[28] The Chief Medical Officer for England, Professor Sally Davies, has urged baby-boomers (people around 50–70 years of age) to remain in paid employment or engage in voluntary work to enhance their mental well-being as well as their physical health.[29]

Fulfilling spiritual needs can also help us find a wider meaning to our lives – as well as meet needs for affection and acceptance if pursued within a group such as a church, synagogue or mosque community.

Of all the needs of older people, it is the need for self-actualisation in people in advanced old age which society most often ignores. Do voluntary societies, political parties and faith groups do as much as they can to ensure that people who cannot walk easily or see or hear well continue to play as active a part as possible? Do family and friends do as much as they can to enable their loved ones to continue to perform roles in which they find a sense of personal fulfilment? Or do they let these activities fall by the wayside because the person can no longer get out to meetings or operate a computer keyboard?

Approaching death

The challenge presented by our own mortality does not necessarily diminish with the years. Perhaps you have enjoyed a long and happy retirement with your partner but are both now edging towards your nineties. How do you say goodbye to a world which continues to delight you and in which you savour every minute?

Facing death with a sense of self-actualisation, that our life has had significance in the wider scheme of things, however we define that, may perhaps help us cope with our passing. Swedish sociologist Lars Tornstam believes that we need to change our perspective from a materialist, rational outlook to a more cosmic and transcendent one if we are to achieve a sense of satisfaction with our life before we die. This would involve understanding not only ourselves but also our place within the wider scheme of things. That way we can see ourselves as part of a much bigger universe which will go on after our own death.[30]

So, rather than limiting our thinking to the material possessions we plan to hand on after our death to our loved ones, perhaps we should be much more explicit about the values, philanthropic causes, oral histories, skills, traditions, and objects of significance which do not feature in our wills but which we nonetheless consider an important part of our legacy.

Think about how you would like to be remembered. Are there particular stories, games, values or approaches to life you would like to be associated with? Write them down in a letter to be opened after your death. You could also use this opportunity to express feelings you might otherwise have been embarrassed to admit to in life. If you want your grown-up child to know they delighted you from the moment of their birth, say so.

Psychologist Joan Erikson sought to work out what Tornstam's thinking should mean for everyday life. She believed that older people should continue to involve themselves in life, but also remove themselves from it by focusing on what they will bequeath to the world. She advocated striving to develop a position in which they feel able to go with the flow, to accept their age as it really is, and to give death its own dignity by perceiving it as a necessary part of their own self-fulfilment.[31]

Intergenerational activities provide a unique opportunity to validate the experience and worth of older people and help them hand on skills and values – as well as enjoy themselves. Helping children with their reading at a local school is a common means of doing this. So increasingly are events at which children or teenagers and older people meet to talk and learn and engage in activities together. In imparting skills such as gardening or photography, older people can pass on something really useful, while they in turn can learn skills from the young, such as Skyping or using Twitter. When they involve reminiscence, older people can impress upon the young the hardships of life before a welfare state, for instance, and so feel that their life and experiences have continuing value. And as both young and old challenge the stereotypes of both groups, they can feel that they are also helping to restore what many see as a broken society.

Psychological well-being

✱ Human beings need to feel safe, loved and accepted and to have a sense of self-worth.

✱ Older people often find it harder to meet their needs for affection and a sense of self-worth and self-fulfilment.

✱ Some of life's most unsettling events – retirement from employment, a move to a care home and the death of one's partner – take place in later life.

✱ Disability, bereavement, poverty and a move to a care home can increase psychological difficulties.

✱ Physical manifestations of ageing can make people feel inadequate.

✱ People with dementia need to feel that they are loved and belong somewhere.

✱ Nobody, young or old, is truly independent.

✱ Social and productive activities such as voluntary work improve physical health.

✱ Friends, family and voluntary groups can ensure that older people play an active part in society.

✱ Intergenerational projects can help make older people feel valued.

PART TWO
HOUSING

> *Retirement housing may offer nothing that could not be provided in your current home without sacrificing much of your living space.*

PART TWO
HOUSING

Upping sticks often appears a good idea as we grow older. Finally, we sigh, we can swap a poky home in this rainy land for a villa with a swimming pool in Spain. New surroundings may enable new interests or even a new career. Or perhaps it simply seems sensible to downsize: the children have left home; now it's time to save on costs and release some capital.

In this part I explore some of the main options in the housing field, from where we might live and with whom to the type and design of housing that might suit us in later life, as well as the many pitfalls and false promises of these options.

Should I move abroad? To a different part of Britain? Alone or sharing? What type of property? The first chapter addresses such choices.

In later life, many people are drawn towards retirement housing or the equivalent when owned by a local council or housing association – sheltered housing. But they are often hazy about what it actually offers. This is to be expected: there is no legal definition, and retirement housing (I use the term to cover also sheltered housing) is not regulated and inspected by independent national agencies, as are care homes.

Also, what retirement (or sheltered) housing tends to offer has changed over the last decade or so, in particular with the widespread loss of resident managers. If people need paid practical help while living in retirement housing, they usually hire it in from outside. A growing number of schemes have a care agency on site; in this case the housing is called 'extra-care housing', but this too lacks a legal definition so there is no guarantee that any scheme will contain particular facilities. Retirement, including extra-care housing, is the subject of Chapter 6.

Retirement villages, meanwhile, usually offer care on site and more besides – a whole community in which you can shop, buy meals and engage in activities with other residents. In Chapter 7, I look at the advantages and drawbacks of moving into a retirement village, as well as some of the questions to ask before you do so.

Staying put raises issues of its own. Can you afford to remain where you are, given the costs of heating and maintenance? Could you adapt your surroundings to cater for any disability you may develop? In Chapter 8, I examine what can be done to better fit one's own home to the changing requirements of later life.

Care homes will be the subject of a companion volume (which will build upon an earlier analysis in my book *A Survival Guide to Later Life*). This is because a move to a care home brings with it far-reaching changes to your total living environment, from the provision of food and personal care to housing tenure; these all need to be weighed up thoroughly, together with the considerable financial ramifications.

Chapter 5
Shall I move?

Two questions tend to preoccupy us as we move into later life: 'Is my pension adequate?' and 'Should I move house?'

The housing question stems from the realities of later life but also from our dreams. Some people feel that if they have retired from paid employment, they should be seeking out the living space that will enable them to fulfil a lifestyle they could not enjoy while chained to an office. It seems natural to choose a property they spotted on holiday or imagined while daydreaming at work. Magazine features and TV programmes foster such fantasies: daytime TV is full of young and old in search of a place in the country, preferably a characterful property far from the madding crowd in which they will entertain and engage in ambitious schemes to renovate derelict outbuildings.

For other people – and sometimes the same people, after thudding back to reality – a house move in later life would enable them to downsize, shed the responsibilities of running a home bought to accommodate a family and also move closer to the shops, lest moving around should become difficult. A neighbour recently asked if he could take the empty cardboard boxes on my drive for his planned house move. His wife now finds walking a struggle and they have assumed that the best solution will be to swap their semi with garden and garage for a small terraced house in a town centre.

But are these sensible moves? Should we be seeking out dream home with seven bean rows and a hive for the honey bee as we edge towards later life? Might my neighbour be better advised to stay put, investigate grocery delivery schemes and suggest his wife buys a mobility scooter?

Other people, feeling they would like to see more of their children and grandchildren, may sell up and move into a granny flat, perhaps in another part of the country, in the expectation that their children will look after them if they become unable to care for themselves. All these options, and others, have advantages. But they also hold pitfalls for the unwary.

Whatever the reasons for a move in later life, there are factors to bear in mind over and above the considerations that affect us whatever our age.

Size

Downsizing brings obvious advantages. Smaller accommodation means lower running costs – not just council tax bills, but also those for maintenance and heating. Less maintenance means less bother, as well as less cost. However, space can be an advantage when we are getting on. Retirement or part retirement from paid work frees up time for hobbies. These often need space. So will the friends who might come and stay or the grandchildren we may look after.

Should we grow frail, space for guests can be even more important. When, in her mid-eighties, my mother's eyesight began to fail and arthritis made walking painful, I found my family and I were going to see her for long weekends far more frequently, to provide reassurance and company and to help her make small adjustments to her lifestyle. The fact that she had a house made a big difference. It wasn't just a matter of spare bedrooms: the run of a whole house and garden made staying a lot easier and pleasanter than it would have been had she been living in, say, a one-bedroomed flat in a retirement housing scheme, where we would have had to book the guest room in advance or, if it were not available, sleep on a sofa-bed in her living room.

Day visitors are more likely to visit if we have space for things which will interest them, such as a piano or games. These provide a potential focus for interaction, as well as reflecting our own interests.

Room simply to entertain is also important. Researcher John Percival conducted in-depth interviews with 60 older people on their feelings about their domestic space. Some of his interviewees who had moved to retirement accommodation with small kitchens and dining areas were dismayed not only at the loss of physical space for daily living but also of the role of playing host to their family.[1]

You may feel like abandoning your garden once you can no longer keep it in pristine condition, but you may live to regret giving in to this impulse. Your grandchildren may value a wild area in which to play or some grass on which to kick a ball. As Percival put it, 'Of course not all older people want the responsibility of the garden... But for those who value their own plot of land, a future without a garden can be rather bleak.'[2] *(I discuss ways of coping with challenging gardens on pages 199–201.)*

Perhaps you are perfectly healthy, in your seventies, and contemplating downsizing. Yet there may come a time when you need quite a lot of additional space for the extra support you come to need and by giving up space you may unwittingly be surrendering the possibility of continuing to live independently. For instance, if walking becomes painful and you wish to buy an electric scooter, you will need somewhere to store it and to charge its battery. A garden shed or a garage with a power supply is ideal. Indoors, wheelchairs and other mobility aids need space to manoeuvre, as well as to be stored out of the way.

You may come to need human help, too. You may want a friend to stay for a while when you come out of hospital. And if you need a live-in helper for any length of time, whether hired or a relative, you won't be able to have one if your accommodation is too small. One of Percival's interviewees had had to turn the dining room of her retirement flat into a bedsit for her live-in care-giver. I have just spoken to a distraught daughter trying to set up 24-hour care arrangements for her parents. Neither wishes to go into a care home, but that now seems to be the only option. The downsized accommodation to which they moved in their eighties contains only two bedrooms, and each, with very different care needs and lifestyle, requires a separate bedroom. So there is no space for the live-in assistant who would offer an ideal solution.

Even if you just want somebody to come in and help bathe you or do the laundry or some paperwork, you may find it is more difficult to attract staff if they see that working for you would involve navigating cramped surroundings. So, while there is no doubt a case for an older couple to move from, say, a five-bedroomed house to a three-bedroomed one, there is also a case for resisting the temptation to move to something smaller still.

Location

Perhaps you have had a lifelong dream of living within earshot of cathedral bells and padding along to evensong as the mood takes you. Or surely it is now time to take yourself off to that loch-side croft of which you dreamed so long at your desk? Or to a city centre, so that you can be a stone's throw from the shops, theatre and galleries?

To the seaside or the country

It is tempting to move to a seaside resort or village where you have enjoyed holidays in the past. But those who do sometimes come to regret their decision. In an area where you have not spent your life, you will lack the rich tapestry of human links enjoyed by the local older people. Though you may have longed to escape from the heavy traffic of London or Glasgow, you may come to miss the array of facilities available at the end of an underground or bus journey. Strolls by the sea or over the moors, particularly in winter, may prove insufficient compensation for lost human contact. At the seaside in particular, such facilities as do exist are often seasonal.

A move to the country will mean less choice of shops, restaurants and education centres and also of facilities you may not have imagined you would need. Sports and leisure centres provide not only the opportunity of using facilities such as swimming pools (and, *as we saw in Chapter 3,* swimming offers ideal exercise not least for people with osteoarthritis), but may also offer activities, such as formal exercise classes. You may come to need specialist health care, but physiotherapists and masseuses will cost you a lot more if they have to travel a long way to your charmingly remote home. Your teeth may require expensive treatment which would be much cheaper if carried out by a dentist working for the NHS *(see page 306),* but such dentists can be hard to find in some areas. A Citizens Advice survey in 2008 found particular shortages in south-west and north-west England.[3]

A dispersed rural population also reduces economies of scale for local authorities, so day centres, luncheon clubs and sheltered housing schemes, among other facilities, may be thin on the ground. Before you move, you may think you would never step inside a day centre, but should you become frail or disabled, the prospect of hot, home-cooked food and company can become very appealing.

The type and extent of services on offer vary greatly between rural areas. Researchers who looked at the provision of services including food shops, post offices, bus stops and free cash machines in sample stretches of countryside found that those in and around Stroud in Gloucestershire, for example, were twice as abundant as those in North Cornwall.[4]

In some rural and coastal areas favoured for retirement, councils are almost overwhelmed by the demands of their frail, older residents. The cause may be not only the underfunding by central government of social care services but also a shortage of young people who are willing to work as care assistants. On the other hand, an urban area may play host to a substantial young population and its council may have the wherewithal to sustain higher levels of public service. Even if the council is lukewarm, there may be supplementary facilities, whether private or located in the area of a neighbouring council with greater commitment to support for older people.

Regardless of whether you get help privately or through a local council, other problems may present themselves. Bad weather could cause floods or snowdrifts which cut you off and stop a care worker reaching you. If power lines are brought down, you may lose electricity.

Country-dwellers often have to be more self-reliant than those who live in urban areas, simply because fewer people may be available to fix things that go wrong or to help around the house and garden.

Transport

When researchers interviewed more than 70 older rural residents in England in 2006 about the realities of country living, the inadequacy of transport services emerged as the dominant theme.[5] Many people hesitate to confront the fact that one day they may no longer be able to drive. Sometimes a husband dies, leaving his wife, who has never learned, stranded. So check that your new home is accessible by public transport. Public transport in the British countryside is not always as bad as is supposed, particularly if you are flexible about when you travel. Pockets of the countryside may have very good bus services into a local market town *(a fact I highlight in the context of recreation on page 721)*, while nearby areas may have nothing – so study timetables and route maps. The relevant local authority should be able to advise you on the scope of conventional bus and train services and also of any other transport facilities such as community buses and dial-a-ride schemes.

What also concerned people in the survey of older country-dwellers was the cost of transport, whether by private car or other means. This made living in the countryside more expensive than elsewhere.[6] Local bus travel may now be free for older people, but this situation may not continue. What is more, there will always be journeys that cannot be made by bus; and there may come a time when you find getting on and off buses more of a struggle. Likewise, waiting at a stop that has no seat. So check the availability and cost of taxi journeys and whether any wheelchair-accessible taxis operate in the area *(see pages 719–20)*.

Once you have moved, start using public transport even if you continue to use a car. You don't want to have to navigate stops, destinations and timetables once failing eyesight has forced you from behind the wheel. There are also benefits in avoiding the stress of driving, being able to chat to your fellow passengers and enjoying the view over the hedgerows.

To the city

Some people yearn for the town, for the prospect of easy access to concerts, sports centres, parks and a wide range of shops.

Two friends of mine who had recently retired moved to a modern terraced house close to the centre of York. They enjoyed exploring their new surroundings and attending events in the city itself. Unfortunately, David died suddenly and unexpectedly. But Lynda feels she can cope better with his loss because there is so much going on within a short walk. Unlike a small settlement, York offers rich seams of opportunities for life outside the home.

If town life appeals, think outside the box. Retirement housing can tempt, but flats and houses available in the normal way, leasehold or rented, might suit just as well. You could obtain much of what is available in retirement housing, such as an emergency call system, in ordinary housing *(as outlined on page 486),* while enjoying more space than retirement housing usually affords. However, regular apartment blocks have two clear drawbacks for older people:

Other tenants: In an ordinary rented housing scheme, the tenants will cover a wide range of ages. They may be helpful or they may be noisy or even threatening. Even in a prestigious block of flats, other leaseholders may decide to sub-let, at least while the market is buoyant. Such tenants may be even less predictable.

Absence of a manager or warden: Retirement housing schemes usually have a manager present for at least part of the day, among whose tasks it will be to control entry to the property. The manager should also provide help in the event of an emergency. A manager who can offer help is unlikely to be present in a non-retirement scheme, while your fellow tenants or leaseholders may be unhappy with your giving keys or entrance-pass-numbers to any care assistants you may need to hire.

Or, how about a flat over a shop in the High Street, for instance? A retired friend of mine lives in a flat over a little supermarket in the heart of a small town in Herefordshire. His flat is extremely congenial – spacious, full of character, with a delightful, large garden. He has about ten times the amount of floorspace that one would normally find in a retirement housing flat, as well as a garden to tend or sit in as he wishes, as opposed to one shared by many other people and designed by a management company. The flat is rented, so Philip does not have to worry about the cost of maintaining or decorating it. True, he has to descend a flight of steps to reach the high street, but once there he is in the midst of shops, pubs, a library, other facilities and a vibrant community.

Similarly, a terraced house in a supportive community in or near a town or neighbourhood centre has many advantages as we grow older. Not only are facilities close at hand, but the close proximity of neighbours will enhance the security of the property and perhaps provide help in time of need.

Or how about a semi close to a neighbourhood centre, perhaps with a café, pub or day centre, among roads which are easy to cross and offer stress-free driving, and with a park close by and even a school in which you could offer to help with reading? Good public transport links to an urban centre, the countryside and seaside might enhance life even further.

Focus your mind on what really matters to you in your immediate environment. Would a dearth of green space in the urban location you have in mind bother you more than you are prepared to recognise? Would the leisure activities available in a particular small town, picturesque as it may be, really suit you? If you find pleasure and fulfilment in, say, embroidery or singing, and the town offers these in abundance, fine. If you like to learn and debate with others, then a place with a thriving U3A or adult education facilities should suit. But if you wish to be involved in political activity, a small town may not prove fulfilling in the long term.

Overseas

Lured by sunshine, cheaper housing, lower living costs and attractive landscapes and beaches, many of Britain's newly retired emigrate to France and other parts of southern Europe. Those in places which attract large concentrations of older ex-patriates, such as parts of the Costa del Sol, are more visible than the countless other older people who have moved abroad, often to live near relatives.

Moving overseas at any age is a massive step. Anyone seriously thinking of it in later life should carry out in-depth research beforehand. There are many matters to consider, not least what might happen should you become frail or disabled or fall out with those to whom you wished to be closer. So check up not only on the quality and any cost of medical care but also on that of practical help in the home. In some countries, older people rely far more heavily than in Britain on their own families for support, and domiciliary care workers are often few and far between. Although you would receive your State Retirement Pension abroad, you would not receive benefits such as Attendance Allowance to go towards help in the home, as you would in the UK. Check on the care homes:

you might thrive in a care home in, say, Spain, or you might find a régime of only a small tapas lunch, no afternoon tea, a late main meal and care workers speaking only their native tongue difficult to handle. As a result, you might be faced with the choice of moving back to the UK or trying for a place at one of the small number of Spain's expensive English-speaking care homes. There can also be difficulties in obtaining help from the state, including the NHS, should you return to this country after living abroad, as Independent Age explain in a useful free guide, *Moving to and Returning from Abroad: Benefits and Services.*

Social anthropologist Caroline Oliver carried out an illuminating study of expatriates living in Spanish coastal resorts in 2008. While her interviewees enjoyed many aspects of their lives, problems could arise as time took its toll. She writes:

> The march of the clock means that year on year, people who have retired to Spain face questions of how to maintain their chosen lifestyle whilst simultaneously negotiating challenges wrought by ageing: How much longer can they live in their *tipico* 'Spanish' house at the top of a steep, cobbled street? … Whilst the freedom from family responsibilities may be liberating, who will look after them if they fall?[7]

Dr Oliver draws attention to the constant influx of newcomers and the onus on older migrants to keep themselves looking young. Coupled with pressure to engage in much socialising, voluntary activity and the consumption of alcohol and rich food, this caused some of them to damage their health. Yet older migrants were not always willing to care for each other. She observes: 'Dealing with grief may be particularly hard … in a context … where people have a relatively small shared past with other migrants.'[8]

Plainly, many people lead happy, healthy lives in retirement overseas. But do consider the many ramifications before you take the plunge.

Immediate environment

Difficulty in walking is one of the commonest disabilities of later life. Whether you are contemplating a move to a city, village, the seaside or a Highland glen, try to think about how you would cope should you or your partner come to find walking difficult, perhaps even impossible, and also how you would cope if you were unable to drive. Include the following questions on your checklist:

✓ What would it be like to walk to the shops, GP surgery, pharmacy, bank, post office, library, places of worship, cafés, pubs, betting shop or whatever you would use from the property? Are any of them likely to close?

✓ Does this locality have clean, safe paths, pavements and alley-ways? Would they be wide enough for a wheelchair or mobility scooter? Are there plenty of dropped kerbs?

✓ Would walking over the pavements pose problems? Are they well maintained or cracked, uneven and strewn with litter and leaves on which you might slip?

✓ Are there comfortable benches in case you need to sit down for a rest? Are public lavatories within easy reach?

✓ Is the environment well lit and would you feel comfortable going out alone in the evening?

✓ Could you or somebody else park easily outside the property?

✓ How close is the property to bus stops and the railway station? When and where do the services go? Might they be reduced in the future?

Design

Whether you are thinking of moving to an ordinary house or flat or to housing marketed as dedicated to older people, it is important to check key design features. *(Further features are considered in the chapter on retirement housing which follows.)*

Some new-build housing has been designed to provide accommodation that can be used by everybody, from families with young children to older people with disabilities, under a scheme called Lifetime Homes. Houses and flats built to conform to this scheme should have basic features such as ramps that enable them to be used by parents with children's buggies and people with mobility problems who may be using a walker or a wheelchair.[9] A higher standard which provides more space for wheelchair users is set out in the Building Research Establishment's *Wheelchair Housing Design Guide*.[10]

Steps

If you are thinking of buying a flat, don't buy one above the ground floor unless there is a lift: many medical conditions common in later life make climbing steps difficult.

Similarly, avoid buying a house that has steps up to the front door, particularly steep ones. It is possible to install a ramp over these if there is plenty of space for the slope (which should be no steeper than 1 in 12, so a ramp to replace three steps needs to be 7.8 yards, or 7.2 metres, long) and even possible to install an outdoor stairlift. But of course you cannot guarantee that this will be an easy adaptation, or a cheap one, although your council may meet the cost through a Disabled Facilities Grant if you fulfil certain conditions *(see pages 186–9)*.

Stairs inside can also prove a problem, although many people do get stairlifts installed, with or without financial help from their local council *(see pages 87–90)*. The staircase must usually have minimum dimensions to accommodate a stairlift *(see page 184)*, so do check these before house purchase. Also check that any house you propose to buy could take a stairlift. Stannah Stairlifts offers a helpline to which you can send a photo of the staircase in a house in which you are interested so its consultant can advise you. Some people find they have no choice but to move to the ground floor of their house to avoid using the stairs.

Even single steps can prove a problem. That half-timbered olde-worlde country cottage in a remote location whose step down into every room you hardly noticed when you bought it becomes the most unsuitable place to live once you have fallen victim to, say, Parkinson's disease, or have a painful hip or knee.

Doors

Though door-widening is possible, it is obviously a good idea to check a wheelchair or other mobility aid could easily fit through before you move in. If possible, avoid even a small lip step between French windows and patio.

Bathroom, toilet and kitchen doors should open outwards to ensure that if somebody falls against the door, help can get to them. Many falls involving older people take place in the bathroom, often at night. If you collapse in the bathroom, lavatory or kitchen and the door opens out of the room, somebody can get in and rescue you. But if the door opens inwards and you collapse against it, they can't.

Windows

When we are getting on, we tend to spend more time at home than younger people. If unwell, we may be confined to the house for long periods. This can involve not just a physical difficulty, such as a broken bone, but a mental illness, such as anxiety, depression or agoraphobia. So the amount of natural light in our homes and the views from the windows can be extremely important.

It is easy to forget this when we look round, say, an apartment, assuming that the absence of a window in the kitchen does not matter as the lounge has windows. Perhaps the person showing you round points out the convenience of being able to eat in the kitchen, without having to carry food far. But would you really wish to dine in a room with no natural light? And if confined to the house more than usual, you may yearn for different views of the world outside.

Check that all the windows can be opened and closed easily. In a kitchen, the window behind the sink can be difficult to reach. Some medical conditions make older people feel dizzy if they bend their head back and reach up.

Plugs, sockets, lights

Electricity sockets at waist-height are ideal. If you property you are contemplating buying has sockets at skirting-board level, perhaps you could get at least some of them moved up. A dining room lit by many tiny lights in the ceiling is likely to cause much more trouble than one light with a long lead over the dining table which can be reached from a sitting position and so changed easily.

Choose the light bulbs you will use in different locations carefully once you have moved in. Many people find it harder to see as they get older (as explained on page 13) and a brighter energy-saving bulb costs less than £2 per year more to run than one with a lower lumen (a measure of brightness not the same as wattage). Rica (page 128) publishes an excellent, free guide called *Choosing Energy-saving Light Bulbs for your Home.*

Bathroom

If the bath does not have grab-rails, make sure there is sufficient space for them to be put in. If you are buying housing specially designed for older people, you should expect a bath with some kind of ledge at the non-tap end so that you can sit on it and then swing your legs over before lowering yourself down using handles already installed. Ideally, it should not be a full-length bath (6 feet or 1.7 metres), but a short one (5 feet or 1.5 metres). You cannot have quite such a nice wallow in this, but you will not accidentally slip down and drown or be unable to get out. So, when viewing, take your tape measure. There are also various specially designed baths with lifting devices as an option.

A walk-in shower can be useful feature: it should have no step but be flush with the floor and then drain downwards and have a stool to sit on. But regard housing for older people that offers only showers with suspicion. Some providers argue that older people get stuck in the bath, but in fact there are plenty of pieces of equipment on the market (or which may be provided free by the NHS or social services) to enable the less agile to get in and out easily *(see Chapter 21)*. Perhaps any omission to offer baths is in fact related to cost, as showers use less water than baths?

As far as the lavatory is concerned, you should look for sufficient space in case you need to have grab-rails or some other support installed and/or people to help you. If the toilet is squashed up into a corner, look elsewhere. Older people tend to spend more time in the bathroom and lavatory than the young, and it should offer as warm and pleasant an environment as possible.

Heating

As we grow older, we become more sensitive to temperature extremes *(as explained on pages 49–52)*. Is there a part of the property that would remain cool during a heatwave? Could the heating system maintain the temperature at 21°C (70°F) throughout the house or flat when the outside temperature is minus 1°C (30°F)? How much will heating the property cost? Is the insulation is adequate or could it be improved? *(I discuss grants for improving insulation on pages 194–196.)* In a compact, well-heated home, condensation can be a problem, so it is also worth ensuring that there is adequate ventilation.

Coping with severe disability

Suppose you or your partner has developed a chronic disease and you are proposing a move, perhaps to be closer to one of your children. It is very important to take full account of your disability when choosing a new home. The existence (or otherwise) of good primary care and social care services as well as friends and relatives to whom you can turn for advice and support may turn out to be a lot more important than the scenery.

Fred and Lindsay (names changed) were living in eastern England when Fred was diagnosed with Parkinson's disease in his mid-fifties. At first, he and Lindsay managed fairly well. The unpredictability of his arm and leg movements forced him to give up driving, but Lindsay took the wheel. Quite soon, however, she suffered a stroke – not a major stroke, but one that affected her eyesight, with the result that she too had to surrender her driving licence. The couple had three grown-up children, who took it in turns to drive long distances to spend the weekend with their parents, taking them shopping and on leisure trips and helping with chores.

As Fred's condition worsened, he and Lindsay decided to move to be nearer one of their children. Which one? One of their daughters was in a position to offer the most time and flexibility, as her own children had grown up. However, they had always disliked the town (Portsmouth) in which she lived, preferring the rural surroundings of their other daughter, although she had a young family to look after. They decided against moving to the small country town in which she lived, as it was hilly, which would have made walking difficult for Lindsay, who was overweight; this town also had few shops, and she liked to go shopping. She and Fred therefore opted for a sizeable town with no hills and a variety of shops, 15 miles (24 kilometres) away from this second daughter. The chalet bungalow they found seemed ideal: Fred could sleep on the ground floor, at the same level as the bathroom and living room, and the doorways proved wide enough to accommodate the wheelchair he now needed.

However, this property presented problems. Although the wheelchair could indeed be manoeuvred through the door entrances, there wasn't enough room for a helper to push him round many parts of the property. A chicane in the kitchen presented a particularly difficult obstacle.

A bigger problem was the couple's lack of friends in the town, since they were newcomers and their various ailments precluded making new contacts. Although their daughter was living what had seemed a short drive away, this wasn't close enough for her to deal with the many emergencies that began to arise. Parkinson's sufferers are prone to falling *(see page 390)* and Fred was no exception. What's more, although he received a regular dose of dopamine, he would sometimes 'freeze', so that he couldn't move at all. This might be, say, on the way to the bathroom. He would need to be given an extra dose of medication, which would take 20 minutes to kick in. In the meantime, he would need to be supported lest he should fall. If Lindsay popped out for only an hour, she might return to find her husband stuck somewhere or on the floor. She needed immediate help, but her daughter, though prepared to dash over at short notice, could not be present within minutes – and might in any case be occupied looking after her young children.

The couple did not know anybody else well enough to call on for help in situations like this. As they had not lived in the town for long, let alone worked or brought up their own children there, they had no social clubs or faith groups from which to seek support.

Nor had they had the opportunity to make friends. When their daughter came over to look after her father so her mother could go out, Lindsay had nobody to meet and nowhere much to go.

As the years passed, Fred's condition deteriorated. Quite apart from the freezing episodes, he now moved so slowly that it might take him two hours to get to the bathroom and back. Feeding was messy, as he could not control his movements; later he became incontinent. He would need Lindsay's help in the night too, so her sleep was often broken. Confined to the bungalow and with depression a side-effect of his medication, he became spiteful and difficult to live with. Lindsay, all of whose time was occupied with caring for Fred, came to hate him. A move to a care home, even for respite, was out of the question: her husband refused to enter a care home, fearing that he would never return home.

At first the couple had not contacted social services, as they assumed – incorrectly – that social services' remit covered only people of modest means, while they enjoyed both a state and an occupational pension. However, once they were put in touch with social services, they both started attending a day centre with transport provided, while a care assistant came to help with housework. More support might have been delivered, but the social worker did not inquire into problems which both Lindsay and Fred were too proud to spell out.

Finally, after a fall which made his condition worse, followed by good care in an acute hospital but an unhappy stay in a community hospital, Fred died. Only a few months later, Lindsay died, following another stroke. Both were in their late seventies.

Had the couple moved to live near their other daughter, they might have received higher level of support from social services, as Portsmouth City Council has enjoyed a good reputation for older people's services. Since it is a large town, it also has a wider variety of public and other facilities to hand. Had they moved while they were both still active, they might have built up a network of people who could have lent a hand or known who else might be able to help out.

Fred and Lindsay's life also might have been improved had they moved as close as possible to the daughter who could have supported them more easily and perhaps provided access to her social contacts. Or, had they remained in the town in which they had

> lived all their working lives and where they knew their GP, the local council, local councillors and voluntary organisations, they might have fared even better.

In other words, if you have a chronic illness or disability and are contemplating a move, don't allow the factors that would influence your choice in middle age such as attractiveness of the local environment to play too dominant a role. Also, you need to choose carefully between moving to an unknown area to be close to one of your children and staying in an area in which you have friends and with whose health and social support systems you are familiar.

With whom?

When we are getting on we may consider going to live with one of our children. There are, however, many other possibilities. Perhaps you would prefer to live among people of your own age who you believe would see things your way? Or are you prepared to cope with the stresses but also potentially greater rewards of sharing your life with younger people? If you want the society of your own peers, how exclusive do you want that society to be?

Relatives

If you decide to live with a relative, there are a number of options:

- living with a relative with whom you share living accommodation
- living with a relative but in separate living accommodation, such as a granny annexe or a separate floor of the house
- living with various relatives in rotation

In all these cases, you may run up against the fear of younger family members that if you go and live with them, they will have to care for you should such a time come. I have come across middle-aged people who would love a parent to come and live with them, but believe it would mean they would have to give up their job and care for the parent should they become frail or disabled. Other people would value their parents' company, but are themselves suffering from a chronic condition, such as ME, and so rule out the possibility because they know they could not physically cope.

In fact, sharing accommodation with somebody does not oblige you to look after them, no matter whether they are your father, mother, brother, sister or even spouse. In law we are no more our mother's keeper than our brother's. We have a legal obligation to care only for our children. A husband, wife or civil partner has a legal obligation to maintain their partner financially, but not to care for them should they be unable to care for themselves. The legal responsibility to care for somebody unable through illness or disability to look after themselves falls to the state, through local authority social services departments. Anyone is free to choose to become the carer of somebody living in the same house, however, and today such 'carers' have legal entitlements *(see Chapter 27)*.

Let us consider the situation of people choosing to live under the same roof as an older person, but not necessarily with the aim of caring for them.

Family relationships

When we move in with a relative we bring with us the baggage accumulated through a long relationship. How will it work out living under the same roof?

Moving in together can enhance our relationship with loved ones, but it can also cement unhealthy aspects. Also, once an older parent is living with their son or daughter, or perhaps a sister in her seventies or eighties moves in with her brother and his partner, all ties in the household are likely to change, as the dynamics of one relationship will impinge on those of another. It is important to recognise this and to plan for it, otherwise problems may develop which may cause much misery. For instance, would certain members of the household tend to gang up in a disagreement, isolating others?

There is also the important question of the resentment that can be generated by differential support. Let us suppose that a woman moves in with her middle-aged daughter. Another daughter lives 200 miles (320 kilometres) away and visits as often as she can. But annoyance builds up. Relatives ask why the faraway daughter could not have moved in with her mother, as she is single while her sister has children. She points to her brother, who lives near his mother but rarely visits, yet nobody apart from her is suggesting he should do more. In time, this daughter's visits to her mother, taking place in her limited time off work, become overshadowed by these family tensions. While her mother is alive, they simmer. At her funeral, they erupt.

Resentment may also work the other way. A son or daughter taking a parent into their home can generate jealousy among siblings. Suppressed competition for the parent's love in childhood can resurface. It may take the form of suspicion that the parent is being stripped by the sibling of assets that would otherwise have been shared equally in the will. If housing equity is pooled through a move into a bigger home, siblings may resent the acquisition of parental equity.

You may imagine that such monstrous thoughts could never surface in your family. Wait and see ...

Security of tenure

Your legal right to live in a property is an important consideration should you move in with friends or relatives. Here is a scenario which came to my attention. A woman goes and lives with her daughter and son-in-law in a granny annexe, because the daughter says she finds the drive to visit her mother burdensome. The relationship between mother and daughter had never been really warm; after the move, the daughter rarely takes her mother out and the old lady finds herself isolated in the wing of a house in a village in which she has no friends. Time passes and she develops continence and mobility problems. Care workers are difficult to find, particularly at night, and relations between the woman and her daughter and son-in-law become strained. The son-in-law and his wife hold legal title to the property and ask the old lady to move into a care home. She does not want to, but is placed under increasing pressure. Things come to a head when a medical crisis puts the mother in hospital and her daughter informs hospital staff that she will not accept her back. So, on top of her health problems, this lady, now in her nineties, has to cope with becoming homeless for the first time in her life, as well as the emotional impact of her daughter's betrayal.

Another scenario: an unmarried son gives up his job to devote himself to caring for his mother, who has Parkinson's disease, moving back into the large family home to do so. His brother and sister, both married, carry on with their own lives. Ten years on, the old lady dies. She has left her estate to be divided equally between her three children, believing this to be fair. The house is sold and the proceeds divided equally. The money comes in handy for the married children, who use it to support their children, but the unmarried son finds himself turned out of his home. No longer able after years of full-time devotion to his mother to re-enter his previous profession, he is forced to take a job in a field in which he has little interest. His share of his mother's estate is too small to buy him a house in the same locality and his new job pays too little for him to get a sufficiently large mortgage. He has to leave the area in which he has lived all his life to find new accommodation in another town.

Before you move in with younger or older relatives, or indeed with anybody else, it is crucially important to think through all the problems that could arise and leave you, or those with whom you will live, homeless. Don't think it can't happen to you. It probably can.

It is worth talking things over with a legal advisor and if necessary drawing up an agreement setting out the situation on rights to occupy the property as well as the financial arrangements in order to avoid future dispute. Essentially there are quite different ways of sharing the ownership of a home, with vastly different implications. Even by default, you will be choosing one. You need to know which and why. *(See pages 812–6 for tips on finding a solicitor.)*

One approach which has potentially wide application is the use of 'life interest'. The scenario involving the son who lost his home when the mother for whom he had cared died could have been prevented if the mother had left her property in equal shares in her will but added that the son should have a life interest in the property. That would have meant he could have lived in it until his own death or until he had obtained other accommodation.

Similarly, if you are becoming, or taking in, a tenant or lodger, you need to know not only the basis on which the arrangement will run, but also the exit routes for all parties.

Living arrangements

If you go and live with one of your children, you may assume that you will get on much as you did when they were younger. But there are almost certainly bound to be major issues to be sorted out. These include:

✓ **Food:** Who will do the shopping, cook the meals and decide what is to be to eaten? How often will everyone eat together? What about washing up?

✓ **Room temperature and open windows:** This is not just a matter of taste. Elderly people need a higher ambient temperature than younger people. Are you going to ensure that the temperature can be varied from room to room so that disputes can be minimized? Are you sure there will be no resentment when the heating bills come in?

✓ **Household tasks:** A daughter-in-law may feel put upon waiting on in-laws whom she considers could do more for themselves. Or older parents can easily find themselves doing more than their fair share of household tasks. They may feel they are bringing fewer resources to the party and so negotiate from assumed weakness rather than strength. So pre-existing relationships can make formal arrangements for the allocation of household tasks more rather than less necessary than they would in the case of strangers of the same age embarking on a flat-share, in which equal responsibilities would be automatically assumed to be the rule.

✓ **Self-esteem:** The division of domestic labour is likely to overlap with the creation of boundaries to protect each party's right to pursue their own interests. If you are doing much of the menial work while your son-in-law occupies himself with a prestigious job, your self-esteem may well be eroded. You need to feel appreciated for yourself, not just for what you do. How are members of the household going to feed and enhance one another's self-esteem?

✓ **Financial matters:** Familial factors make dividing up the bills harder, not easier. Older people may feel under pressure to contribute more than necessary to household expenses – or even to give money away. To people in their teens and twenties, grandparents can seem to be awash with money that they do not need, and they may push them to help out with school fees, medical bills or trips to the cinema. This is fine if the grandparents really want this role and won't need the money themselves at some point, perhaps for an electric scooter, medical treatment, a holiday or fees to pay for their care.

✓ **Benefits:** Benefits are a complex field and it is worth asking for a benefits check from a Citizens Advice Bureau or other organisation *(see page 869)* if you are proposing to share your household. For instance, if somebody is going to be your 'carer', they might be entitled to carer's benefits *(see Chapter 35 and 36)*. A self-contained granny flat housing a dependent relative of the owner of the main property is exempt from council tax.

But there is also scope for losing benefits. If you share your home with another adult, such as your grown-up son or daughter or a 'homesharer' *(see below)*, you may lose Council Tax Reduction or your single person discount for council tax, as these people are known as 'non-dependants' in your household and are assumed to contribute to housing costs *(see page 847)*. Also, if you receive an additional amount paid to people receiving the Guarantee element of Pension Credit called Severe Disability Premium, you risk losing this if another adult who is not your partner lives in the same house *(more information in Chapter 35).*

Many cases of fraud involve people receiving benefits and then neglecting to notify the Department for Work and Pensions when a grown-up child moves back home. Certain exceptions are allowed: for instance, if the person living with you is a student or is themselves receiving Guarantee Credit, you may still be entitled to Council Tax Reduction. Also, a 25 per cent reduction in council tax is available if somebody who is not a partner provides at least 35 hours a week of care for somebody who is receiving the high rate of Attendance Allowance *(this is explained in the section on council tax in Chapter 35).*

Rotating relatives

In a case of which I became aware, a lady in her eighties who was unable to look after herself lived in turn with two daughters and one son and their families, spending one month with each in different parts of the country. This worked well, and does in other cases too. The peripatetic parent can develop a circle of friends in each place and tensions which can fester when a couple knows that their frail relative will live with them indefinitely can be defused by the knowledge that they will soon move on.

However, this arrangement means more families have to find space in their homes for facilities such as ground-floor lavatories and extra bathrooms, and somebody in all the relevant homes may need to have time to provide care and company. Sometimes elderly people start to become disorientated moving from place to place, even though they may have spent a lot of time in each house in the past. It may be much more difficult to set up support arrangements such as paid help in the home if these should become necessary, whether or not this is steered by the local authority's social services department. So this modus operandi may prove to be only temporary – as indeed transpired in the case mentioned above.

An alternative possibility involves younger relatives moving in to provide care in rotation. This has the advantage that the older person remains in their own home environment with the social and support networks they have built up, from friends to their GP. Obviously, this arrangement can work only where relatives are free to come and go. In one situation of which I became aware, such a rota worked well. Two daughters and the son of a lady who needed a lot of help each lived with her for a fortnight in rotation. The siblings had all recently retired, none had a partner and they had deliberately ensured that their home commitments in terms of voluntary work, for instance, were sufficiently flexible to accommodate their absence for two-week stretches. Their mother benefitted not only from living with her children but also from experiencing their different food and cooking preferences, while they were returning to the pleasant city (Cambridge) where they had grown up. They acted as their mother's carers themselves, but paid for somebody from an agency to come in and give her a bath. When I spoke to one of the daughters in 2009, they had not obtained a carer's assessment from their mother's social services department *(see page 621),* but there seemed no reason why they should not do so.

Contemporaries

Some people prefer to live among people of their own age, with whom they are likely to share experiences, a cultural heritage and an understanding of the realities of ageing. It is possible to live in an environment peopled exclusively by older people, such as retirement housing, a retirement complex or a care home, or to live close to other older people in the wider community.

Buying a property close to people of your own age and interests whom you already know often works well. One such situation I have come across involves a number of elderly ladies who over the past few years have come to buy flats in the same block in a pleasant residential street in south-west London close to a suburban shopping centre. They already knew each other well, as they had lived in the area and attended the same church, but over the years they had separately come to the conclusion that they wished to move into a smaller dwelling close to shops and services, often after the death of their husband. Such a group can easily socialise informally and look out for each other. You have the advantage of independence, your own front door and greater security of tenure than you would enjoy in a care home or in much retirement housing. There is also the possibility of companionship and mutual help, and not just during the day – lots of elderly people do not sleep well and value the possibility of somebody to talk to during the long hours of the night.

If people in this situation decide they want to hire help in the home, they can often hire the same person or people. One professional care worker may thus be able to get a full-time wage by working for a small group. The presence of people of other ages nearby also means there is none of the feeling of ghettoisation that you can find in housing units accommodating only older people. If you move into, say, retirement housing, you may meet people of similar experiences and cultural heritage, but you run the risk (particularly in an enclosed retirement complex with its own facilities, such as shops) of engaging less and less with the outside world. However, a disadvantage of an informal move to be with older friends is that, at some point, there will be only one left.

Strangers

New means of sharing life to some extent with complete strangers are fast developing and attracting growing interest.

Communes

In theory, communes offer older people a great deal. A new approach in Britain called 'cohousing' is a type of commune. A small number of households – perhaps up to 20 – come together in a housing scheme, usually new build. Each household (whether a single person or large family) retains its own personal living space, but larger spaces and activities are shared to some degree or another. This may mean the community comes together to share one meal a week, for instance. Members are consciously committed to living as a community, so older people who would like company and a little mutual support – perhaps helping with children as well as receiving help themselves – should fit in well. Only a few schemes have been developed to date; information is available from the UK Cohousing Network.

Sharing your home

You could of course rent out part of your house to a lodger. But the lodger will not necessarily provide company – they may only exchange an occasional greeting at the front door, come and go at unpredictable hours and not even provide the reassurance of another person in the house at night.

Homeshare is a scheme that seeks to enable older people to benefit from companionship, a presence in the house in the small hours and some practical help in return for accommodation at a much reduced rate. Under arrangements run by an organisation called Share and Care Homeshare, an older householder (or it could be a younger disabled person) makes a modest monthly payment to the charity, while the sharer, a younger person, makes a slightly larger payment. No money changes hands between the two parties. In return for their own bedroom and shared use of the home's facilities, the sharer provides ten hours per week of practical support and undertakes to be present in the home overnight. Practical support could be shopping, light cleaning, dog-walking, driving or cooking – it depends on what the two parties agree. However, the requirement that the 'sharer' must be home at a reasonable hour and telephone if they are going to be late means that people who regularly come in from clubbing at three in the morning are ruled out. The sharer can be away from the home on only one weekend a month (although they may be away on other occasions by prior arrangement). They cannot bring partners to stay overnight.

Such conditions might be difficult to insist upon in a one-off situation agreed informally. Yet the existence of the organisation and the fact that both parties have signed an agreement makes it easier for requirements to stick. Sharers undergo reference and security checks and interviews. There is a short trial period. A facilitator from the organisation monitors the arrangement and if householder and sharer are unhappy with the arrangement, a new sharer may be sought; there is of course provision for notice. In 2016 Homeshare operated in parts of London, Bristol, Cumbria, Somerset and East Sussex.[11] Contracts are drawn up stipulating the number of hours to be worked, the proportion of household bills that the homesharer pays and which areas of the property are shared. They also stipulate that neither party can be a beneficiary in the other's will.

Of course there is nothing to stop you entering into such arrangements independently, and if you do so you could copy features of the scheme, although you would not have the benefit of a coordinator with whom to discuss problems and, if necessary, find a replacement homesharer. Do run your proposed agreement past a solicitor before you go ahead. You could fall foul of the law, for instance if the arrangement morphs into what is in effect the hiring of staff for homecare work and you fail to abide by the rules (see page 529–30).

Homesharing schemes also operate in some other countries, most notably Spain, about which information is available from Homeshare International.

Do not confuse Homeshare with Shared Lives. Under the latter, a family welcomes into their home a disabled or older person who lives as part of the family. Social care authorities organise the scheme, which has so far mainly involved people with learning disabilities.

The hiring of live-in care-givers is the subject of Chapter 24.

Shall I move?

* Moving house raises new issues in later life.
* Downsizing has significant drawbacks as well as advantages.
* Space is essential if you want visitors and may need live-in care.
* Check out public transport services before a move, especially to the country.
* Think about what matters most to you on your doorstep, such as green space and shops.
* Flats over shops in town centres can be ideal.
* You will lose your 25 per cent council tax discount if you are single and a relative moves in with you.
* Sort out responsibility for household tasks before you move in with your family.
* Buying an ordinary flat in the same complex as friends of a similar age can work well.
* Consider sharing with a young person who will provide help in the home in exchange for a low rent.

Chapter 6

Retirement and sheltered housing

S ome older people feel that they would rather live amongst people of their own age, with whom they are likely to share experiences and a cultural heritage. Their contemporaries will, they feel, be better able than the young to understand what going through later life means and thus offer support. They may also wish to offload the responsibility of managing a house and garden and hanker for the presence of somebody whom they could summon should they need help and who would provide support and care. For them, retirement housing – accommodation with other older people, mainly in apartments in a building that offers some additional facilities – seems the obvious solution.

It is important to distinguish these desires from the reality of retirement housing – or sheltered housing, which is the term used for the same facility when provided by housing associations and local authorities. People contemplating a move to such housing should think long and hard before they embark on this step.

So should those considering a move to extra-care housing. This is the term given to a small (about 10 per cent) but growing proportion of retirement housing that is more likely than other retirement housing to provide some practical help for individual residents.

Of course it may be that you are already living in retirement, sheltered or extra-care housing. If so, I hope this chapter will also be of use to you, not least the sections about the charges you have to pay to the organisation that runs your facility and the power of leaseholders to force a change to the management of their scheme.

In this chapter I therefore discuss:

▶ definitions of retirement housing

▶ providers of retirement housing

▶ what to take into account if you are choosing retirement housing

▶ charges

▶ how the management can be changed

▶ how to raise a concern or make a complaint

▶ security of tenure and moving on

▶ finding schemes

▶ supported housing

Definitions

There is no definition in law of retirement, sheltered or extra-care housing, and schemes in each category vary widely in what they offer. Apart from a minimum age for occupiers, such as 55, schemes tend to have the following features:

● self-contained accommodation: each resident has their own flat, or in some schemes a bungalow. Sometimes there are two bedrooms, but more often one, or the unit is a bedsit. Each resident's accommodation will include a kitchen and bathroom, and there may also be a balcony. If on the ground floor, it may give onto a small private garden and/or communal grounds. Couples may occupy larger units.

● a laundry room available to everybody

● a guest room where visitors can stay

● an emergency alarm system in each flat. This often takes the form of a long cord hanging from the ceiling which, when pulled, rings a bell in the scheme manager's office. The manager then goes to the flat in question to find out what is wrong, using a master key if necessary. If there is no scheme manager on site, pulling the cord alerts a control centre elsewhere, from which help is summoned, for instance by telephoning a relative, who is then expected to deal with the problem.

● an entrance lobby and various communal areas which all residents can use at any time, such as one or more lounges, possibly a dining area, corridors, stairs and probably lifts

- grounds, available to all residents
- car parking (although there is likely to be fewer than one space per resident)
- a property designed with the needs of older and frailer people in mind, perhaps through the provision of raised power sockets. However, retirement housing has not always been designed specifically for disabled people, so prospective residents need to check that the accommodation would be suitable should they develop disabilities, with doors wide enough to allow for wheelchairs and electric scooters, for instance.
- a 'scheme manager' or 'warden', who manages the property and keeps an eye on residents. What the manager actually does and when they are available vary massively between schemes. While some managers live on site and may be contacted during the night as well as the day, much more common is the situation in which the manager is available on site only during office hours or a peripatetic manager visits a couple of times a week.
- controlled access to the whole scheme provided by a keypad, swipe card, a manager stationed at the entrance or, for visitors arriving in the absence of the manager or other member of staff, a call centre
- storage space for electric scooters and other mobility aids; the location and size of this vary widely between schemes
- easy access on foot or by public transport to shops, places of worship, post offices, banks and other facilities
- the maintenance and management of the external fabric of the building, internal communal areas and the grounds by a management organisation. Individual residents must contribute a service charge to cover management and maintenance and for communal facilities such as the services of the scheme manager.

Bear in mind there is great variation between schemes. Many of them lack at least one of these features. You can find retirement housing with no communal lounges or controlled entry system, so that each resident has their own front door just as with ordinary housing and if residents get together it is in each other's flats or in the grounds. Some schemes have all these features and additional ones, such as a dining-room. If a scheme stands within a retirement village, it will probably have more features still, *as outlined in the description of a retirement village on pages 158–60.*

People contemplating a move into retirement including extra-care housing often think they will be receiving a package of care and support to meet their particular needs. Perhaps they have in mind something approaching a care home. Think again. Retirement housing is simply a type of housing, and any facilities which might come under the broad definition of 'care' may be provided, but equally may not. In other words, the key word in the name of these schemes is 'housing' – not 'care'.

This type of provision therefore differs fundamentally from a care home. The latter has a definition in law. It is a residential setting in which a number of older people live, usually in single rooms, with full board, including all meals; they also receive practical help with the ordinary activities of everyday life, whenever they need that help, day or night.

What care homes must provide and to what standard is set down and enforced through inspections from national agencies – the Care Quality Commission (in England), the Care Inspectorate (in Scotland), the Care and Social Services Inspectorate Wales and the Regulation and Quality Improvement Authority (in Northern Ireland). Anything from cleaning the premises to doing residents' laundry is the responsibility of the care home provider. So too is the provision of practical help to residents – whether to help them wash and dress, take a walk in the grounds, move into the lounge for a film show, eat their meals, take their medicines or use the toilet, day or night. A resident who cannot see or hear well may need different sorts of assistance; a resident with dementia may need help with other activities of everyday life, as well as supervision to make sure they do not come to harm.

Retirement and extra-care housing schemes are quite different. They are essentially a form of housing with other facilities that may – or may not – have been added. The most common is an alarm in each apartment and in the communal areas to be used to summon help in an emergency.

In some schemes, particularly extra-care ones, an agency which provides help in the home is based on the premises. Individual residents can enter into a contract with that agency to be provided with specified types of help at particular times. But this help is not on demand – it has to be pre-arranged – and it is up to the resident to arrange and pay for it, or for their social services department to do so on their behalf.

Any homecare service that offers personal care (help with washing, using the toilet and so on) provided within a retirement housing scheme is inspected by one of the national organisations listed above that inspect care homes, but the housing facility as a whole is not. Nonetheless, the providers of retirement, sheltered and extra-care housing will have their own checks and some will have signed up to various, often self-enforced, codes of good practice. In addition, there are rules and inspections in fields such as food hygiene and health and safety, as there are in other kinds of establishment. External controls also impinge through any funding provided, such as grants to housing associations from central government. But neither alone nor in combination are these checks equivalent to those made for care homes by statutory inspection agencies which look at the suitability of the premises for its older and often frail residents and the quality of care and support they receive in the round.

Extra-care housing

Extra-care housing also varies widely and lacks a legal definition. Some but by no means all extra-care housing schemes provide at least one cooked meal a day, together with an environment more obviously designed for disability than much retirement housing. However, residents are still expected to keep their own rooms clean and tidy and make their own breakfast and, if they need help with practical tasks, to obtain that separately. As I have said, in extra-care housing there is usually a care agency in the building which individual residents can pay to deliver help at particular times. Thus, someone might arrange for half an hour's help in the morning to get washed and dressed and take their medication and another half an hour in the evening to prepare for bed. There may be care staff in the building at night, providing pre-arranged help to any residents who have commissioned them to do this and providing help to others in an emergency.

Extra-care housing is sometimes known as 'assisted living housing' or 'close care housing'. The considerations to bear in mind are the same as those outlined below for retirement and sheltered housing, although some, such as the provision of care, may be more important to you than others.

Reference to retirement housing in the remainder of this chapter should be assumed to embrace both sheltered and extra-care housing too. In all these forms of housing, organised leisure activities may – or may not – be laid on.

Retirement housing providers

Private retirement housing took off in the 1970s and 1980s, after the founder of Britain's largest private retirement housing developer, John McCarthy of McCarthy and Stone, discovered that local authorities were readier to grant planning permission for retirement housing than for ordinary housing in town centres, since they believed that retired people would own fewer cars and generate less traffic. Developers were therefore able to place more housing units on one site, as they could allocate less space for garages and parking.

Today, around 150,000 older people live in retirement housing provided by the private sector in England and Wales. Some of this is rented, but most is sold on leases. When leased, a development company owns the freehold and sells individual leases, and it or a management company makes various annual charges on lessees. These include a ground rent and service charges, which cover overheads for the whole scheme, such as its maintenance and insurance and the employment of a manager.

In **Scotland,** in contrast, residents buy the freehold of private retirement housing, not a lease. Schemes are usually run by a management company, just as they are south of the border.

In the 1950s, local authorities starting building small flats for older people whose children had left home; in many cases, one member of a couple had died. These schemes, which came to be known as sheltered housing, were provided with a communal lounge and a manager who would keep an eye on residents; later, more were built to free up large council houses which older people were under-occupying. During the 1970s and 1980s, housing associations started to add schemes which provided, for example, guest rooms and a wider level of service from the manager. They now provide retirement housing to rent and to buy, including leasehold-shared-equity schemes, whereby somebody buys a proportion of the equity of the property.

Housing associations have often taken on sheltered housing formerly owned and organised by local authorities, which have been shedding much of their social housing in recent years. These associations may be small local organisations or large national ones. In Northern Ireland just one, Fold, provides much of this housing for older people, with private companies also providing a large amount.

Although private, local authority and housing association retirement housing schemes have been inspired by different motives, the various types have much in common. You will not necessarily find retirement housing in a private scheme superior to that in a housing association one, or vice versa.

Almshouses

Almshouse schemes have a different ownership structure: they are run by charities and usually governed by locally-based trustees. Some provide accommodation for people who have retired from particular occupations, others for older people in general, usually giving preference to people of modest means who have lived in the locality. The buildings involved are often in town centres and old and picturesque, though the interior will probably have been modernised. My anecdotal experience is that almshouses are more likely to have live-in managers or managers working longer hours on site, perhaps because decisions are taken by locally-accountable trustees.

However, housing tenure in almshouses is less secure than in other forms of retirement housing, with residents having the legal status only of a lodger. Check the security of tenure situation in any scheme in which you are interested. The Almshouse Residents Action Group monitors case law in this area *(see Useful Contacts)*.

Key factors

Here are some key factors to bear in mind if you are considering a move to retirement housing.

Food

One of the main ways in which retirement housing schemes differ is in the provision of meals on site. In some schemes a midday meal is cooked every day (including at weekends) in the scheme's own kitchen. In addition, the manager may provide refreshments at some other time, such as tea and biscuits in the lounge every afternoon.

In contrast, other schemes provide no main meals or regular refreshments, so residents make their own meals, go outside the scheme for them or receive meals-on-wheels. Any food served within the scheme is limited to particular events, such as an occasional fish-and-chip supper or a monthly coffee morning.

Clearly the presence or absence of food served on site has a big impact not only on the extent to which residents have to do their own shopping and cooking, but also on the opportunities available for social interaction with other residents.

If you are contemplating a move to retirement housing which offers meals, check on several occasions:

✓ whether the food is to your taste

✓ whether the food is nutritious. Older people need a healthy diet just like younger people, with five portions of fruit and vegetables each day, as well as oily fish, eggs, milk and nuts *(more details in Chapter 2)*.

✓ the size of helpings and the scope for seconds

✓ the social dynamics of the dining room: would you fit in?

✓ the cost of the meals

✓ whether the food would meet your cultural and dietary needs. Check carefully if you have strict requirements, such as for vegan food, kosher food or to cope with diabetes.

Think about what you might be eating day by day. How varied are the vegetarian options? Would the cook only ever and grudgingly make you an omelette? Or would they take pride in serving you an interesting range of vegetarian dishes?

The alarm

It is a basic feature of retirement housing that an alarm should be available for each resident so that assistance can be summoned quickly in the event of, say, a stroke or a fall, or simply getting wedged in the bath.

You might imagine that the alarm system in a retirement housing scheme would be superior to the pendant (or community) alarms *(described on pages 486–7)* that can be used in ordinary houses and flats and involve pressing a button worn on the person, but this is not necessarily the case. Indeed, alarms in some retirement housing units fall short of pendant systems in that they are less accessible. A long cord hangs from one corner of each room in a resident's flat. But if the resident should fall in another corner, they would not necessarily be able to reach the cord. One social worker told me that she had known many instances in which residents of sheltered housing had had a fall and then lain unattended for hours, as they could not reach the alarm cord. Others had sustained burns when forced to drag themselves across the carpet to reach the cord.

Housing schemes with cord alarm systems may offer you a pendant as well for an additional charge. If not, you could obtain one yourself. Rica, a charity which publishes information about equipment for older and disabled people, has a useful guide on choosing an alarm.

There are likely to be cords also in communal parts of the scheme, such as the corridors, the laundry and the lounge, but since reliance on pull-cords requires that you be close to them, you could not summon help from these areas either, unless you were able to reach the cord.

So, before you go in, establish:

✓ whether any alarm system provided in the scheme has advantages over a pendant alarm system

✓ if it has not, whether you could opt out of the scheme's system or whether you would have to pay for it anyway, through overhead charges

- ✓ the role the scheme manager plays in responding to calls for help through the alarm system
- ✓ whether there is anyone else on the premises day and night who would respond to an emergency call, whether made through a pull cord or alarm worn on the person

The involvement or otherwise of the manager in helping residents in an emergency will depend largely on how often they are on the premises and their overall brief. Before we turn to managers, it is worth pointing out that one of the major advantages of having a care agency on the premises, as often happens in extra-care housing and some other retirement housing, is that those care staff will often provide help in an emergency to any resident, whether or not they are receiving pre-arranged care from that agency. It is important to check carefully the arrangements for any scheme in which you are interested because, as I have stressed, there are no nationwide standards that apply to all schemes. The presence of care staff prepared to, say, summon an ambulance in the middle of the night and at short notice can be a godsend. This is particularly the case now that *(as we see in the next section),* many retirement housing schemes lack a resident manager so any call for emergency help when a manager is off the premises has to be diverted to a call centre outside.

The scheme manager or warden

Perhaps the best-known way in which retirement housing differs from most ordinary apartment blocks is the presence of a manager. But when you visit retirement housing, you will find widely differing arrangements. All scheme managers will manage the bricks and mortar, but there is wide diversity in their availability to help residents and to lay on activities.

Until relatively recently, the general rule was that retirement housing schemes had managers, then called wardens, who were available day and night to respond should a resident need help in an emergency and to provide general help to residents (although not personal care or housework). But more and more schemes have cut back the number of hours any on-site manager is available. Should a scheme offer on-site help at evenings and weekends, this will be because it has more than one warden, or because other managers fill in for the resident warden during part of office hours.

Another change has been the replacement of managers responsible for one scheme and available on-site at least during weekdays with managers responsible for a number of schemes. These peripatetic figures simply visit schemes, spending several hours per week in each.

This arrangement has several drawbacks. Peripatetic managers are likely to have less time to chat to residents or to provide them with information and general support simply because their time is divided between a greater numbers of residents. They are unlikely to run regular events and activities for residents.

A peripatetic manager should respond to the emergencies that arise when they happen to be at the scheme in question. Otherwise these are likely to be dealt with by a call centre, just like emergencies that occur when full-time wardens are off-duty at evenings and weekends. That call centre usually then phones a resident's named contacts, such as close relatives, or the emergency services (*as described on page 486*).

The call-centre system may work efficiently, but residents will miss out on the quick response provided by an on-site manager. Also, call centres tend not to provide reassurance and advice for the ordinary day-by-day concerns that do not constitute emergencies.

Manager arrangements also affect the ease with which visitors can gain access to residents. If a visitor calls at a scheme staffed by a manager present Monday–Friday during office hours, that manager should be available to vet any caller in order to decide whether it is safe to allow them past the front door. It can be a lot more difficult for prospective visitors to gain entry to a scheme which is run by a peripatetic manager, since there is no official on hand.

Even delivering a birthday card to someone in a sheltered housing scheme can prove difficult. In 2010, I was delivering leaflets about facilities offered by a local church in the small town in which I then lived. At one retirement complex, serviced by a peripatetic manager, I waited several minutes after ringing the buzzer before a voice asked me my business. The responder, who was based at the call centre of a group of schemes, told me she had no authorisation to allow me entry and that I should return in the afternoon two days later, when the peripatetic manager would be on site. When I duly did this, the voice behind the buzzer told me that the peripatetic manager had already left and that I would have to return on another occasion: the manager's hours could not be accurately predicted as she had to respond to problems as and when they arose at several schemes.

I had hoped to deliver the leaflets through each resident's letterbox and plainly could not do that. But nor could I post a handful through a communal letterbox: there was none outside the building. (Apparently the official postman is allowed entry.) Plainly this kind of approach is going to deter some visitors, and residents may miss out on useful missives, friendly notes or invitations.

The absence of a warden or manager takes on greater significance at times of danger. If and when the manager is absent, is the door entry system sufficient to prevent the entry of miscreants? Equally, what happens when someone needs to gain entry quickly?

Sheltered Housing UK (or SHUK) is a voluntary group which campaigns to improve the position of the residents of local authority and housing association sheltered housing, although its concerns could also apply to commercially-run schemes. When it polled 300 residents in 2010, it found that:

- nearly 80 per cent of respondents said wardens' hours had changed recently
- only 4 per cent of these people had been consulted on the changes
- more than 90 per cent of the respondents were unhappy with floating wardens
- more than 90 per cent said they would not have moved into their home had they thought there was any threat to the resident warden service.[1]

Checking on residents

When they are on site, a manager should respond if a resident triggers their alarm. But managers should also be taking steps to ensure that all residents are all right at other times.

In good schemes, managers take about two hours each morning to do a round of flats, checking on the well-being of residents. If there is no answer to their knock on a resident's door, they ask the next-door occupants if they have heard any noise. If they still get no answer, they ask somebody else to accompany them while they enter the flat using their own keys (as a security safeguard, managers should not be permitted to unlock a flat door on their own). A good manager will also stay with the resident and if necessary help them telephone the doctor to make an appointment. Ideally, the manager will make two daily visits, as otherwise somebody could fall just after the early-morning call and lie on the floor all day and night.

In schemes where the policy is morning visits, residents may be offered a waiver form to sign agreeing to forgo these calls. It is important that residents do not feel under any pressure to sign; if they do not want such visits, why are they living in retirement housing at all?

In some schemes, rather than visiting or phoning, managers contact residents each morning on the intercom and ask them if they are all right. However, this is not foolproof. A resident might say, 'I'm fine', while lying on the floor or ill in bed, eager to put on a brave face or to avoid troubling the manager. They may also be unaware of problems that are obvious to somebody else, particularly if they have sight or hearing loss. A face-to-face conversation is therefore preferable.

Some schemes expect residents to phone each morning to confirm that they are all right or to press a special button on a phone. At others, managers check by other means, such as noticing whether residents have pulled newspapers through their letterboxes. The housing provider may present this method as the more desirable because it is unobtrusive, but it is not reliable. Residents who have pulled their newspaper through their letterbox may still be unwell. Or somebody else may have taken it, either intentionally or absent-mindedly.

When looking for ways of cutting costs, a housing provider may make a full-time manager part time; or replace them with a peripatetic manager off site; or replace a requirement that the manager visit each flat every day with a call to each flat every day on the intercom; or make checking on residents a chargeable service. Before you enter a scheme, find out whether any such move is planned and whether residents would have any means of preventing it.

The replacement of onsite managers, whether resident or sleep-over, with peripatetic ones who visit residents in an emergency has caused much concern in several schemes. In Portsmouth, residents in high-dependency sheltered housing schemes engaged in an energetic campaign to overturn the decision of the housing provider, Portsmouth Council, to replace overnight managers with peripatetic ones, arguing that losing an onsite manager would take away their peace of mind. Their campaign culminated in a victory in court in London in 2009 in which they managed to get the decision quashed.[2] A similar case by residents in the London borough of Barnet was heard and won at the same hearing. But these are not easy steps to take and may not be successful.

Procedures and attitudes

There are other basic questions to ask managers:

✓ What is the procedure when they are out of the office as far as emergency calls are concerned? (Usually they will be able to divert calls to a call centre.)

✓ What is the maximum period for which they are permitted to do this?

✓ What happens when they go on holiday?

✓ What precisely are their duties?

Work out how the manager's duties are defined, as there is tremendous scope for individual variation. Every manager will have their own job description and code of conduct. Does it emphasise housing matters – making sure the buildings are kept in good repair and all bills are paid – rather than the support of residents or the provision of a sense of community? Does the manager's contract allow them to offer such help as extracting laundry from the machine for people who find this difficult or buying milk and bread for residents returning from a holiday or a stay in hospital?

It is important to know just what your manager can and cannot do. Have they had first-aid training and followed this up with refresher courses? Even if they possess first-aid skills, would they use them? Precisely what would they do if a resident had collapsed on the floor? If you ask them to give you an idea of the sort of problems with which they are summoned to deal, you could get a sense not only of what they would do in any particular situation but also of whether the scheme itself tends to create particular problems. If people are frequently getting stuck in the bath, there may be a flaw in the bathroom design.

Try to gain some insight into the way in which the manager balances loyalty to residents against loyalty to the company that owns or manages the scheme and pays their wages. As we shall see when we consider security of tenure *(on page 150)*, the manager occupies an influential position in deciding whether a resident should be encouraged to leave should their behaviour be seen to pose some difficulty, usually because they are developing dementia.

Suppose the manager is often away from their desk when the front door isn't secured, thus allowing criminals to slip into the building. Or they take a long time to respond to residents' enquiries. Or their friends are threatening or noisy. What mechanism is available to residents to complain about or even get rid of them? Are residents' complaints likely to have any effect? Is there a residents' council and what powers does it have?

Care

I explained at the beginning of this chapter that some retirement, especially extra-care, schemes offer the provision of practical help to individual residents in their own apartments through the presence on site of a homecare (or domiciliary care) agency. Any resident can commission help from that agency, depending on what they would like, what the agency can provide and the cost. The latter might be subsidised by the local social services department if the resident meets its eligibility criteria of need for help *(as explained on page 588)*. Assistance that an agency might, or might not, offer includes help with housework, paperwork or personal care (bathing, washing, using the toilet, dressing and so on, *as described in the Glossary)*. The management of an on-site care agency has to be separate from that of the housing scheme as a whole – if the two were managed by the same organisation, the facility would be classed as a care home and regulated as such.

If this care element is an important factor for you in moving into retirement housing, check out the agency carefully. Talk to them about the kind of help they provide and their charges, and look at the reports of inspections carried out by the Care Quality Commission (CQC) and its counterparts. *(In Chapter 23 I examine commissioning help in the home in general, whether to hire individuals or go through an agency, and the sort of matter to consider when talking to an agency.)* Do bear in mind that the CQC's reports on the agency will have involved only those residents who obtain care from it. Residents who do not will not have been questioned.

If an on-site agency does not offer the help you would like, or you do not wish to use its services for some other reason, check that the scheme would be happy with your hiring in help from outside. You should be free to hire help from an outside agency or from helpers on an individual basis *(as described in Chapter 23)* and the housing scheme should not insist that you use the agency on its premises – but it might try to.

As stressed at the start of this chapter, the care provided in retirement, including extra-care housing is not care on demand, as it is in a care home. It has to be pre-arranged and paid for separately. Think about what would happen should you need more care in the future. Could this agency provide it and could you afford the fees, or would your social care authority pay? Might you need the sort of care on demand that only a care home could provide? If your needs change so that you need more practical help than you can obtain or afford in the housing scheme, you will face the prospect of moving elsewhere, presumably to a care home. This additional move will bring its own disruption and costs.

If your needs and your behaviour are unpredictable, most obviously if you are developing dementia, extra-care housing might suit for a while but not work in the long term. You may have difficulty in settling in because you cannot learn your way around your new surroundings and communication difficulties may make forming friendships difficult.

People sometimes prefer extra-care housing to a care home, but if you come to need a care home you will have to start looking for accommodation once more and sell any lease on your apartment. As we will see *(in the section below on moving on)*, that can bring high costs.

Design

In the previous chapter, I outlined some aspects of any type of housing's physical fabric that it is worth bearing in mind if you are choosing new accommodation. Do have a look at that section *(pages 105–8)*. Consider the whole of the retirement housing scheme, not least the flat you would occupy, with these points in mind, since, as we noted above, the suitability of retirement (including extra-care) housing for people who develop disabilities is not guaranteed through any mandatory national specifications.

Individual flats

Think about the accessibility of the unit in which you might live. Would the kitchen and bathroom be suitable for you if you come to use a wheelchair? The kitchen may look top of the range, but would there be enough space for turning and would the worktops be at the correct height? If not, you might have to have doors widened and kitchen surfaces lowered at your own expense, only to have the work reversed when you or your heirs come to sell.

Another aspect of the internal design of individual flats concerns privacy. This can be undermined unless the flats are designed carefully, particularly if they are bedsits. Ideally, somebody standing at the door of the flat should not be able to see the bed. You want a hierarchy of spaces, with an entrance threshold area which has a different feel about it from the public part of the room where you would entertain visitors and the private part, where the bed is located. Even in a bedsit it is possible to maintain this hierarchy, perhaps through a combination of shape of the room (for instance, placing the bed in an alcove or one arm of an L-shaped room) and the way the furniture is arranged. A number of different sitting areas in the public space is also ideal, even if each one is small – perhaps on a balcony or by a window or two, as well as by the fire, at a dining table and around a coffee table.

Think too about your privacy in relation to your neighbours. You may come to build up mutually beneficial relationships with them, perhaps running errands when one or the other is unwell. They may become close friends. Or you might find them noisy, a nuisance or even frightening. Those who seemed polite over morning coffee in the lounge might not be delightful company in the middle of the night. They might behave noisily; they might bang on your door; they might pester you for help.

This is one important reason why you should try to stay overnight in the flat you are considering buying or renting on a trial visit. If the scheme says you must stay in the guest flat, take a stroll along the corridor near the flat in which you are interested at various times during the evening to check on any noise or disruptive behaviour. Ask other residents in the general vicinity what it is like to live there.

Amount of space

How would you live day by day in your apartment, bungalow or studio flat? Would you have sufficient space? Moving into retirement housing almost always means having to give up possessions because there is no room for them. Some are more important than others in terms of everyday life. Shelves of books may never be read, and anyway you could borrow them from the library, but if music is an important part of your life, a piano may be a different matter. There is unlikely to be space for one in your flat, and in any case playing it might disturb the neighbours. But is there a piano somewhere in the building which you could play? Ideally, are there other residents with whom you could share your interest?

Consider also:

✓ Is space provided for the storage of large items such as suitcases, ironing boards, mobility aids and wheelchairs (for frequent or occasional use)?

✓ Is there any additional storage space for items used only occasionally, such as toys and fold-up beds?

✓ Where could a battery-powered scooter be stored and where recharged?

Communal areas

As retirement flats are rarely spacious, you may often wish to go and spend time somewhere else, in the indoor communal spaces or the grounds. If you are considering moving into a scheme, sit in the various communal spaces and ask yourself whether you would enjoy spending time there. Do you like what would be your new surroundings?

Indoors

Think about ease of movement throughout the complex. It is important that you should be able to move easily through the various spaces, so that all the parts of the building are accessible. For instance, how easy is it to get down to the laundry or to take rubbish to the bins? Is there a lift? Does it often break down? When it is being mended or serviced, what arrangements are made for residents who find stairs difficult?

Doors can sometimes present problems, particularly heavy front doors and fire doors. A frail person finding it difficult to get out of the main front door might have to wait around in the lounge until somebody comes along to open it for them. Expect to see electronically operated doors so residents can let themselves in and out with fobs or keypad codes. Internal doors throughout the complex should close automatically to reduce the risk of a fire spreading. If doors are propped open by wedges, the building will not be protected from fire and the means of escape will fill with smoke.

It is of course important that the surfaces on which you walk are safe. Clearly, they should be non-slip and free of any rugs or obstructions on which people might trip. Also, check that floors do not have shiny, reflective surfaces, since older people can easily be dazzled by glare and become disorientated, which may lead to a fall. This can also mean they are temporarily blinded if looking at a bright light, for example when moving down a dark corridor with a light or window at one end.

Both in individual flats and communal areas, it is a good idea if important features are picked out in contrasting colours and tones because of the ways in which vision, in particular colour vision, changes as we grow older *(we come to see the red, orange and yellow part of the spectrum much better than the blue and green part, as explained on page 13)*. So look out for contrast in features such as handrails, stairs and changes in level or gradient. Within flats, contrast can be very helpful for doors, cupboards and the edges of the working surfaces in the kitchen.

Consider acoustic quality in the communal areas. Are the lounge and other places where people might converse fairly quiet? Many older people have some hearing loss in the high registers, so find it harder to distinguish certain consonants and as a result cannot understand speech as easily as they used to, particularly if there is a lot of background noise *(see page 14)*. Features which help sound absorbency can make a big difference, as can systems which deliberately enhance hearing, such as loop systems *(see page 476)*. You would expect a loop system to be present in the lounge and other communal rooms.

Outdoors

Sit in various spots in the grounds and consider whether they would interest and attract you all year round. Some people are happy amongst the low-growing, low-maintenance, evergreen bushes that dominate many communal grounds; others prefer more varied plants which reflect the changing seasons, or roses or herbs which are sweet-smelling. You don't want to find that in a matter of weeks you are regularly filling a flask and going to sit in a public park because you don't like the grounds you are paying for.

What could you do in the grounds? Would you feel happy picnicking out there with your family? Could your grandchildren play there? Could you do any work in the grounds if you wished? If you are a keen gardener, look for a scheme which encourages residents to carry on gardening, perhaps with some raised beds. If you would like to use a garden shed, ask – schemes do sometimes provide one. However, the housing provider may not permit residents to tend the grounds.

Many people who move into retirement housing have or later develop mobility problems. Loose gravel presents huge problems if you find walking hard work or have to push a mobility aid. Are the paths well maintained? Uneven surfaces, protruding roots and debris can cause falls.

Many people living in retirement housing have poor eyesight. The Royal National Institute of Blind People (RNIB) says in its guidance on gardens for visually impaired people that:

- a firm handrail should be provided on slopes and both sides of footbridges

- a change in the texture of paths should provide warning of any steps

- in addition to the handrail, there should be a handrail for people with sight problems – a so-called tapping rail about 7–8 inches above ground level for someone using a long cane

- garden furniture should not be placed where a visually impaired person might trip over it, but should nonetheless be in an area they could easily reach. It should be detectable by someone using a long cane.[3]

The RNIB also points out that gardens and grounds are more appealing for blind and partially sighted people if they contain:

- plants to smell (such as orange blossom, lavender, chamomile, lemon balm, mint, thyme and roses)

- things to hear (water playing or the breeze rustling through different types of leaf)
- things to touch (such as water, pebbles, boulders, and plants with a variety of texture)

Provision for guests

Is there at least one guest room? Is this accommodation sufficient to meet demand? Would it be likely to be available at short notice if a resident were ill? If it were not available, could guests stay in residents' rooms? Could grandchildren sleep on the sofa?

Using a car or mobility aid

Retirement housing schemes do not tend to provide as many car parking spaces per head as mainstream housing. Find out the amount of parking provided and any breakdown between residents, visitors and disabled parking. Are additional parking costs levied?

Locomotion problems are one of the most common disabilities amongst older people. If you rely on a car and/or cannot walk far from a parked vehicle, find out how parking spaces are allocated and where yours might be situated.

Perhaps you rely on a mobility aid, such as a walker, wheelchair or electric scooter. Some schemes welcome these aids, and residents can drive or wheel themselves right into their apartments, parking the device outside their own front door, or inside it if they wish. However, other schemes ban scooters indoors. Instead, a scooter park is provided outside, perhaps close to the wheelie bins. This is clearly far less convenient and may prove impossible to negotiate easily: residents with mobility problems will somehow have to get themselves from this parking place along a path, into the building and possibly down corridors and up a lift to get to their apartment.

Where could you leave an electric scooter or other mobility aid conveniently and safely and charge it up if necessary? You might not need a scooter or wheelchair now, but there might come a time when you do, either permanently or temporarily after an injury.

Communal living

One of the main advantages of retirement housing can be interaction with other residents. Residents may help each other in countless ways – collecting shopping, giving lifts and mending clothing or equipment. They may drop in on each other for refreshments or games. They may offer sympathy to those who have recently been bereaved. On the other hand, none of this may take place. Residents may be unfriendly or cliques may exclude newcomers who fail to meet certain criteria. It is important to know before you move in whether you would fit into the social structure, complex as it is likely to be.

Even if you plan to keep yourself to yourself, you will nonetheless be living in a community and you need to know beforehand whether you would find the company congenial. *(I discuss communal living in more detail in the next chapter, on retirement villages.)*

Men tend to be heavily outnumbered by women in retirement housing schemes, because women live longer and because supply and demand ensures that elderly widowers are more likely to remarry than elderly widows. Couples sometimes move into retirement housing, but seem more inclined than single or widowed people to remain in their own homes. As a man on your own, you may fit in well. You could invite similarly placed residents round to watch sport on television, and if necessary campaign or fundraise for the provision of more communal facilities likely to appeal to men, such as darts and billiards. On the other hand, you may feel isolated and out of place.

So, too, if you are gay or lesbian. You may feel you need to hide your sexual identity. A spokesperson for Stonewall Housing told an Age UK inquiry into retirement housing in 2013, 'There are a lot of people going back into the closet when they move into sheltered accommodation, because they don't feel able to tell people about who they choose to have as life partners. People take pictures off the wall, move books around, so that they don't have to out themselves.'[4] *(I return to the position of LGBT people living in retirement housing on page 152.)*

Any retirement housing scheme has its own complicated social structure of friendships and rivalries, involving countless interactions and subgroups, and you might find this too close-knit or even intrusive. Like it or not, gossip will probably feature. When people become less mobile they may compensate by taking more interest in the comings and goings of others. So stay in the guest flat for a few days to find out what it is like to live in the scheme 24 hours a day.

Find out about the rules covering aspects of communal living such as playing music in the lounge. To what extent are you and other residents able to alter such arrangements? Is there a residents' association and, if so, what powers does it have?

Establish precisely where you are allowed to smoke. You are likely to find that smoking is banned in indoor communal areas but may be allowed in individual apartments, so long as the bedding and furniture are made of fire-retardant materials. If so, might this change in the future?

In any scheme there is bound to be some noise, particularly if you live near the lift, the lounge or the laundry. If you live near or overlook the main entrance, there may be quite a lot of coming and going, potentially involving ambulances if the scheme is a large one. Could you cope with this?

Organised activities

Residents may organise activities themselves, perhaps around any games and other facilities provided onsite, such as a snooker table, darts board, table tennis, a music centre and board games. Would these appeal to you? The size of any scheme and the extent of shared interests amongst residents will affect the range of activities. One woman in a retirement flat in Reigate, Surrey, who was becoming less able to participate in activities in the town outside, told me that she had tried to organise a book club in her scheme. However, as there were fewer than 40 flats, she could not find enough takers.

Quite apart from the natural life of the community and activities organised by residents, there may be social activities organised by the scheme itself, either by the manager or even an activities coordinator. The range offered in retirement housing schemes varies enormously and is bound to affect life in the facility a great deal. Some schemes lay on a varied programme of activities and excursions, but others no more than a weekly or monthly coffee morning. The activities and social interaction in five extra-care schemes were examined as part of an investigation into the quality of life in these schemes carried out by Healthwatch Lambeth. *(I explain the role of local Healthwatch groups on page 330.)* In some of these schemes the local council provided activities, in others the housing provider did so, in this case a housing association.

In one scheme the researchers reported, 'No impression of strong friendships but regular opportunities for socialising and activities throughout the week', but in another, 'Isolated residents – situation exacerbated by remote location and limited activities programme with low participation levels; no trips.'[5] The other schemes featured somewhere between these two extremes. This is a small survey but it is nonetheless being aware that while extra-care facilities usually offer some care and support, they may well fail to provide activities. In contrast, although care homes are not required by law to do so, there does tend to be an expectation that some activities will be laid on.

Pets

The majority of retirement housing schemes do not allow pets. Some say that if you already have a pet dog you can bring it, but it must always be on a lead on site, never present in the public rooms and not exercised in the communal grounds, and when it dies you must not replace it. Cats, too, if allowed at all, are usually confined to individual flats. There are of course reasons for this – pets can be a trip hazard and cause allergies – but these rules can seem harsh for those with a strong attachment to their pets.

The Cinnamon Trust provides lists of retirement housing providers which allow residents to bring their pets *(see page 271)*. If you are keen to persuade a scheme to allow you to bring your pet, you could offer the suggestions in Chapter 13: Animal magic of ways in which you would manage your pet within the scheme.

Safety and security

Insurance companies often offer retirement housing residents lower premiums for household contents insurance, as they consider retirement housing less vulnerable to burglary than other types. It is, however, important not to be lulled into a false sense of security. Crime does occur in retirement housing and burglars do sometimes get in, particularly to ground-floor flats. So check that the security arrangements are adequate. Some schemes have no means of stopping anybody wandering into them, particularly at night when no manager or residents are likely to be around to question suspicious-looking characters. On the other hand, other schemes have swipe-card entry systems (though it is important to make sure that they are foolproof and that somebody could not get through simply by swiping another card, such as a credit card). Some schemes run to CCTV. Consider whether you would need to add security measures of your own, such as a chain on the front door or a burglar alarm. Would this be OK with the management?

The manager will have access to each flat or house through their own key. Find out what safeguards exist to prevent the abuse of this system. Is there a requirement that the manager can enter an unoccupied flat only if accompanied by somebody else, such as another tenant or lessee? Who has access to the safe in which all the flat keys are kept? There should be provision for the emergency services to get access when the manager is absent. Are you satisfied that this is foolproof?

What is the procedure in the event of a fire? How often is a fire practice held? How often is the fire alarm tested? If you are hard of hearing, how would you be alerted? (Flashing lights or vibrators under the mattress are devices used.) How does the fire service gain access to the premises if no manager is on site to let them in and nobody answers the call bell?

Some schemes ask people to remain in their rooms in the event of a fire lest they get lost or stranded in the communal areas, particularly as lifts would not be used. Would you feel happy with this? When I asked one manager for the first question she would ask if she were a prospective retirement housing resident, she replied: 'How often is the fire alarm tested? What happens in case of a fire? How can one manager get everybody out?'

Charges

There are many charges to think about when you move into retirement housing.

If you are a tenant, check to see whether you would be eligible for help with the rent from your local authority (or the Northern Ireland Housing Executive) through Housing Benefit *(explained on pages 861–3)*. Talk to your local council or the housing provider; many housing associations have their own benefits officer who helps tenants obtain a wide range of state and local-authority benefits.

Whether you are a tenant or lessee of retirement housing, you are likely to have to cover your own council tax, water and phone bills, household contents insurance and a television licence if you are under 75. Perhaps you are eligible for help with your council tax or at least for a concession reducing the amount for which you will be charged *(see pages 846–50)*.

As well as your own water and fuel costs, you may also have to pay something for the water and fuel for the communal areas of the scheme. There can be a long list of items for which you may be charged by the management company or housing association that runs the scheme. Schemes vary greatly in what they charge for and by how much. They have to ensure there is sufficient money in the kitty to cover any major repairs that may be necessary to the scheme as a whole. And they have to ensure that the insurance of the premises as a whole, the cleaning of the windows and general exterior and communal areas, the maintenance of the grounds, the administration of the scheme and the services and expenses of the scheme manager are all paid for. As a prospective tenant or lessee, you need to know whether what the company or association would charge you for is reasonable and by how much it might rise. You don't want to find you have to leave your retirement housing because you can no longer find the cash to pay the overheads.

If you are seriously interested in a property, the management company or housing association should send you a pack in which all charges are clearly spelled out. Clarify with the manager any about which you are unclear; they should be prepared to show you how the figures are arrived at.

Alongside the nature and size of the charges, it is important to look for guarantees that the money collected will be used for the purposes specified. So another important aspect of your checks should be to establish what obligation the company or association is under to do this.

You have probably realised by now that contracts involving retirement housing are complex and sometimes not very transparent. Go through the contract carefully, if possible with a solicitor who specialises in leasehold housing law. *See page 812–6 for tips on finding a solicitor.*

Here are some of the main items which you would expect to be included in the charges.

Ground rent

This is part of the whole system of leasehold housing law. The owner of the freehold can charge lessees a rent. It is up to the landlord to determine what this should be, although lessees can challenge it and other charges through an appeal to a leasehold valuation tribunal.

Check also for any timetable and formula for increasing the ground rent – the organisations which own the ground are increasingly building in review dates, typically at 25-years intervals, after which the rent is increased in proportion to the rise in the capital cost of the housing.

Repair costs

Any scheme should have a fund, which might be called a sinking or a reserve fund, into which residents have paid to cover any major repairs which may be required. Before you buy a lease or sign a tenancy, check that:

✓ the management company is covered by a watertight legal requirement to keep the property in good repair

✓ it has set aside sufficient funds for repairs

It is worth checking that the building and grounds do not require major repairs before you sign your contract, or that, if they do, sufficient money has already been set aside and that the company really is going to spend it. Ask to see recent structural surveys of the premises and study them carefully. One woman told me that she was unaware that the roof of the retirement housing scheme in which she and her husband had bought a flat was leaking. When they had looked round, the weather had always been dry; as they were not proposing to buy a flat on the top floor, they were oblivious to the rain damage caused to flats there. Her husband had since died and she was now trying to sell the flat, but could not do so until she could persuade the scheme's management company to take money out of its contingency fund, which had been set aside to pay for major repairs and into which residents had been paying.

Maintenance costs

The maintenance of the outside of the property and the communal areas will be the responsibility of the scheme owner or manager – a private company, local authority or housing association. It will be up to you to redecorate and generally maintain your own flat, but tasks such as periodic repainting of the external fabric, cleaning windows, cleaning and generally maintaining lounges, lobbies, other communal areas and the grounds should not be your problem.

Offloading these tasks is of course one of the main reasons why people move into retirement housing and why relatives often encourage them to do so. However, do be careful. For lessees, these maintenance costs will be paid for out of the annual service charge; for those paying rent, they will come out of the rent.

If you are a home-owner and are paying for repairs or window-cleaning or gardening direct, it is easy to determine exactly how and how often you wish these tasks carried out. In retirement housing, you may – or may not – be satisfied with the way in which the management company handles them. Some scheme management companies will be only too pleased to keep the property in tip-top condition. But if the management company fails to get the property repainted, litter cleared or the windows cleaned, the value of your lease will go down. And you probably will not be too happy living in property in which the paint is peeling and the grounds are strewn with rubbish and leaves.

On the other hand, you may be more concerned about over-expenditure on management and maintenance than under-expenditure. Organisations and companies keen to keep rents or leases at a high level may be inclined to overspend in this area. So find out what control or influence, if any, you would have as a lessee or a tenant.

A legal requirement on the part of the management company to maintain the overall shell of the property and the communal areas may be sound, but none of us likes to spend time and money going to court. What could you do if the company were to drag its heels over maintenance? What if the scheme's manager and their line manager took no interest?

Talk to other residents in the scheme about charges, maintenance, repairs and so on, and to the chair of the residents' association, if the scheme has one. Are there concerns in this area? What has happened about them? What might result?

As well as your fuel costs, you will have to contribute towards the heating costs of the communal areas of the scheme – this will be included in your annual service charge or your rent. Ask to see recent bills for your flat and for the scheme as a whole.

When was the complex constructed? What has been done to ensure heat is used efficiently, through insulation and the like?

Management costs

As well as general repairs, property maintenance and cleaning, you may find that the scheme in which you are interested (or in which you are living) levies all sorts of other charges. These might include:

- insurance for the whole complex
- the manager's salary
- the expenses the manager incurs
- the cost of the manager's accommodation
- the provision and maintenance of the alarm system in individual flats and also of any other security systems such as CCTV and/or door entry systems
- administration – the many and various charges under this heading can range from getting the accounts audited to preparing specifications for cleaners

Examine the size of these payments and ask questions before you commit yourself to paying them by signing the contract.

Exit fees

Some housing providers make yet another charge – an exit or event fee. This is a compulsory charge imposed when a leaseholder sells their lease or a family does so after a resident's death. It requires the owner of the lease to pay a proportion of the price or value of the lease when they sell or transfer it to somebody else.

It may be tempting to brush aside the exit fee if you are keen on a particular retirement flat, assuming that will be a matter for your heirs. Stop and reflect! An exit fee might perhaps work in your favour if it enables the housing provider to keep down its ongoing service charges, so that you defer part of your fees. But you could find you wish to move – perhaps on the death of your partner or because you need the 24-hour care of a care home. If that exit fee is high, it could restrict your choices.

Some exit fees are very high. A Law Commission inquiry in 2015 found fees of up to 30 per cent of the sale price, although 1 per cent was more usual.[6] I came across fees of 10 per cent being charged in 2013 in a scheme in which retirement apartments were valued at up to £600,000, so presumably their owners would pay £60,000. Even if you sold a flat for £250,000, you would be letting yourself in for a hefty charge.

Exit fees are sometimes justified by the housing provider offering free estate agency services when a lease is sold. However, estate agents do not of course charge 10 per cent for their services. And you might not wish to use the scheme's agents.

If an exit fee is included in a leasehold contract you are proposing to sign, challenge it. On what grounds is it being imposed? Why should it be necessary on top of the ground rent and service charge? And how can that particular percentage be justified? Could you pay a lower fee perhaps in return for foregoing any offer of free estate agency services?

Changing the management

Since 2002, lessees in England and Wales have had the legal right to replace the management company running their scheme if they are unhappy with it. The Commonhold and Leasehold Reform Act gives them the right to dismiss their management company and take over the management of their estate themselves or appoint managers of their choice if they have formed a 'right to manage' limited company, membership of which includes at least half of the lessees in the building scheme. They do not have to demonstrate fault on the part of the freeholder.[7]

The Act also usefully empowers lessees collectively to buy the freehold of their scheme, so long as half of them participate. And it introduces a new type of ownership called commonhold, which aims to provide a new system, as an alternative to the old freehold and leasehold system, for the ownership and management of schemes involving privately owned flats. Under the commonhold system, the 'commonhold association' owns all the common parts of a building; the association is a company whose members are the owners of the flats within it. Similar legislation has been enacted in Scotland,[8] but not in Northern Ireland.

More than 100 private retirement housing schemes have taken on management themselves, replacing the previous management company. A less extreme route is simply to switch to a different manager. Check whether the leases of your scheme allow for such a change through a simple vote in favour from leaseholders. The Campaign against Retirement Leasehold Exploitation (CARLEX) publishes advice about these options.[9]

Some have argued that the right to manage powers enjoyed by leaseholders should be given to tenants. This could perhaps mean that if a majority were dissatisfied with the way in which their scheme was being managed, they could vote to transfer it to another association of their choice or take management upon themselves.[10] This remains only a recommendation; tenants concerned at present about poor management should complain to their scheme manager or the regional or head office of the housing association. If a local authority scheme, they should lodge an official complaint to that council.

Concerns and complaints

What would you do if you had a serious concern about the housing scheme into which you had moved? If your grievance were a genuine one, would it be likely to be resolved in your favour?

Ask around amongst other residents about the concerns that have been raised in the scheme. And find out to what extent the management company or housing association has taken them seriously.

All schemes should have a procedure for lodging complaints. Ask to see it. Look for a procedure which clearly states who is responsible for receiving and investigating complaints and a guarantee that a response will be made within, say, four weeks. Good schemes will also have written procedures for handling residents' suggestions and ideas for improvement and an opportunity for these to be put forward within a formal governance process.

Look to see whether some recourse to mediation is mentioned. This can be useful: it should involve an independent and impartial third party facilitating discussion between the opposing parties so that they can voluntarily come to an agreed solution.

The sources of redress, should you be unable to resolve your concern within the scheme itself or through a regional manager, differ according to whether the scheme is sheltered housing run by a local authority or housing association, or retirement housing run by a private company.

In **England,** residents in local authority sheltered housing can complain to the Local Government Ombudsman, while those in housing association properties can approach the Housing Ombudsman.[11] Both have set procedures for pursuing complaints; they do not usually look at a complaint until it has gone through the complaints procedure of the housing provider in question.

The types of matters in which the Housing Ombudsman may get involved include the management of support services, poor maintenance, unauthorised or unexplained rent increases and anti-social behaviour; the Ombudsman does not tend to address complaints involving the level of rents and service charges.

If you are a leaseholder in a private scheme, you could still approach the Housing Ombudsman. He or she deals with complaints about the level or administration of service charges for leaseholders.

The **Scottish** Public Services Ombudsman, the Public Services Ombudsman for **Wales** and the Office for the Ombudsman of **Northern Ireland** handle complaints about schemes owned by local authorities or housing associations.

Two separate systems offer other possible routes for complainants. In England, a part of the legal system, the leasehold valuation tribunal service, provides independent tribunals sitting in five different regions which have the power to settle disputes about service and administration charges in private retirement housing. Tenants too can appeal about their rent, including the service charges that form part of it, to regional rent assessment committees of the Leasehold Valuation Tribunal. The tenancy involved must be a secure tenancy with a housing association or one with a private provider which dates before 1989.

Another approach could offer help if the manager of your scheme is a member of the Association of Retirement Housing Managers (ARHM). The Association represents most of the managers of private retirement and also housing association sheltered housing in England and Wales. Members agree to abide by such clauses in its code of practice as, 'The responsibilities of managers for repairs and maintenance should be clearly stated within the lease and managers should fully meet these obligations.'[12] You might be able to argue that this code has been breached. If so, the Association should approach the person involved to find out their side of the argument. They may be admonished and the matter put right. You can get hold of the code and the complaints procedure from the ARHM. However, approaching the ARHM is not part of any legal system.

If you will be moving into extra-care housing, ask about the way in which concerns and complaints are raised with the care provider as well as the housing provider and ask existing residents whether they are happy with this aspect of life in the scheme. Housing association managers to whom the Healthwatch Lambeth team spoke in the course of their investigations into five extra-care schemes in the borough told them that residents and their families faced difficulties in knowing where and how to raise concerns because of the split in responsibility between the land-lord and the provider of care.[13] *(See pages 523–5 for information about complaining about homecare services provided by an agency.)*

Security of tenure and moving on

Clearly, you want to ensure that your right to occupy your property is as secure as possible. Housing for rent provided for older people by local councils and housing associations is exempt from the right to buy. If you want to dispute whether this exemption applies to you, you must do so within 56 days of the landlord's decision.[14]

If you are renting, try to ensure you get an assured tenancy, which gives you much more protection than a licence or an occupancy agreement (the common form of tenure in almshouses and care homes respectively).

Despite the security of tenure that the law permits, the providers of retirement housing can insert clauses in tenancy or leasehold agreements which curtail the tenure of the tenant or lessee. The lease or tenancy, for private sector or public provision, might say that you occupy the accommodation as a person capable of independent living. Or there may be a statement in the literature about the scheme which points out that if a resident's independence deteriorates to the point where the sort of care that would be provided in a care home is needed but is not available in the scheme, the resident will be expected to move elsewhere.

Suppose you became severely incapacitated and could move around only in a wheelchair. You might wish to move elsewhere, but there again you might prefer to stay. A housing provider would probably need to se-cure a court order to evict you if you did not wish to go. But if it wished to see you depart, it could apply a lot of pressure on you or your family, arguing that you were not now capable of living independently and so no longer met the requirements of the scheme.

Contracts also often stipulate that lessees or tenants must not be noisy or a nuisance to other residents. This too might sound reasonable. After all, you would not wish to live amongst very noisy people. But what is involved is not a fine or other penalty if a resident behaves unsociably, but a limitation on their security of tenure.

Many private schemes have a preferred image of well-groomed people engaging in polite conversation around the bridge table. Not everyone will fit this. Some residents will get drunk, some will engage in apparently bizarre behaviour as a result of dementia, others will erupt into outbursts, perhaps prompted by the anguish of losing their sight or hearing. The impact of such behaviour on the life of the housing scheme will vary greatly. If a resident who is developing dementia starts walking up and down the corridors hammering on residents' doors in the middle of the night, that will clearly disrupt the life of the scheme. On the other hand, a resident who very occasionally walks along the corridors saying she is looking for a long-lost brother will probably not.

In deciding whether a resident should leave the scheme because their behaviour is unacceptable or they are no longer capable of independent living, the views of the scheme manager can be very influential. A sympathetic scheme manager will do what they can to help a resident who wanders a little, but an unsympathetic one may use wandering as evidence that the resident should move to a care home. Should the resident go into hospital, the manager might resist their return.

Scheme managers do have to protect the property and the community as a whole against anything which may pose a threat to it. The extent to which individual residents are seen to pose a threat and as a result encouraged to move out of their flats varies greatly, but this side of things makes the manager a policeman as well as a supporter. It is therefore worth trying to find out the proportion of people who have left any scheme in which you are interested, the reasons for their departure and the attitude the manager took in recent cases.

Also bear in mind that if somebody is developing dementia, a move into retirement housing will be probably be unhelpful in any case, unless they are living with a partner or carer. They will probably have difficulty in adjusting to their new environment as this requires learning many new things; as a result, they may well wander around in or outside the building and get lost.

In any event, look carefully at the wording of the lease or tenancy. Once you have taken it on, if you should become seriously disabled or develop dementia, you may decide to leave, but you obviously do not want to be forced out or feel uncomfortable about your position. Housing tenure law means that a housing provider will usually need to go to court to evict somebody who does not wish to go. However, many tenants and lessees may not be aware of the extent of their legal right to remain and may comply with a request to move on even when they could put up a fight and probably win.

Finding retirement housing

The most comprehensive source of information on retirement, sheltered and extra-care housing is the database held by the voluntary organisation the Elderly Accommodation Counsel, a voluntary organisation which seeks to help older people make informed choices about their housing and care needs, and publishes details of retirement, sheltered and extra-care housing, both to rent and buy, throughout the UK. It does this (together with other organisations) in a directory called FirstStop. You can type in the town in which you are looking for housing and will be given names and addresses and also in many cases details such as the size of the scheme, distance from bus stops, whether pets are accepted, and whether any support services (such as shopping and light domestic cleaning), care services (personal care, dementia care) and meals are provided.

FirstStop also provides general advice on housing and care matters, through printed publications, its website and a helpline, on which you can talk to an advisor about matters relating to housing, care and related finance.

Problems faced by LGBT people

Gay, lesbian, bisexual and transgender people can face special problems in finding and being accepted in retirement housing. Many heterosexual older people living today remember a time when same-sex relationships were frowned upon, indeed perhaps when they were illegal. Even now they may not view same-sex relationships with equanimity and may not welcome a new, openly-LGBT resident. For their part, a prospective resident may never have come out to more than a small group of selected friends, fearing disapproval from those around them. Once living in a retirement housing scheme, they may feel obliged to fake an interest in the conversations around them about heterosexual families and as a result feel even more out of place and alone.

Understandably enough then, when Dr Jane Traies of Sussex University asked nearly 400 older lesbian women for their preferences, three-quarters said they would prefer to live in a lesbian-only care home (she did not pose a similar question about retirement housing, but the answer would presumably be similar).[15] However, Britain has no exclusively gay or lesbian care homes. This situation may gradually change – in 2017, Manchester city council announced plans to build an extra-care housing scheme aimed at lesbian, gay, bisexual and transgender people, and other similar schemes may follow elsewhere. In the meantime, finding out whether any particular housing scheme is LGBT-friendly before you move in is not always easy.

Managers of retirement housing schemes and the staff who work in them or for associated care agencies are forbidden from discriminating against LGBT people: sexual orientation is one of the 'protected characteristics' cited in the Equality Act 2010 *(as explained on page 296)*. Some managers will do all they can to ensure the rights of LGBT people are upheld, but the residents in any retirement housing scheme are not covered by the Act, so they are free to welcome new residents whose sexual orientation differs from their own – or reject them. Tina Wathern, who provides advice and housing support to LGBT people at Stonewall Housing, told me in 2016 that she and her colleagues estimate that 90% of older people LGBT people go back into the closet when they move into retirement housing.

Should you tell the manager of a scheme in which you are interested that you are, say, gay? How can you be sure they would keep the information confidential? Stonewall Housing offers phone advice for older LGBT people throughout the UK about housing matters and can advise you on handling dilemmas such as these. It may be able to point you to a local organisation who could advise on whether they are aware that any particular housing schemes in your area are LGBT-friendly. It runs drop-in sessions in London at which people can turn up discuss housing issues and also offers advocacy support for older LGBT people, but only in London. There are regional groups in Birmingham, Brighton and Manchester.

One of Dr Traies' interviewees reported that in Florida groups of lesbian women had chosen particular housing schemes and then moved in, one by one, creating their own sub-world within the scheme within which they could socialise.[16] If you have a group of similarly placed chosen friends, that approach might work for you. *(See also page 117.)*

Supported housing

Some local authorities, housing associations and charities provide types of housing for people with particular needs. The support offered is tailored to those needs. So, for example, Action for Blind People provides specially adapted apartments with staff on hand 24 hours a day who can help with anything from shopping, personal care and preparing meals to managing finances, claiming benefits and enjoying leisure activities.

Other groups whom supported housing targets include people with learning disabilities, people with physical disabilities, people with mental health problems, homeless people, victims of domestic violence and people with drug- and alcohol-related problems.

Although older people do live in supported housing, it is different from the retirement housing discussed in this chapter. There may be controls that do not apply to retirement housing. Thus in Scotland, there are national standards for supported housing which require the providers of the support to respect basic principles for residents, such as their rights to privacy, dignity and equality.

Conclusion

A move into retirement, sheltered or extra-care housing needs careful thought. All housing by definition provides shelter, so just what does 'sheltered' mean in the particular scheme or schemes you are investigating? What does 'retirement' or 'extra-care' housing offer that could not be provided in your existing accommodation or in housing that does not suffer from the drawbacks of retirement housing, such as restricted space?

Take stock of the reasons why you feel that retirement housing would provide an amenable social environment. Some people move into retirement housing when they feel particularly isolated, for example after the death of their partner. It is important to be clear what a retirement housing scheme is likely to provide in such circumstances. Clearly, if you go into retirement housing some of the practical tasks your partner performed will be taken off your hands, such as, say, mowing the lawn. But you will still have to organise your own utility bills, redecorate your flat and do the shopping and cooking, and you may or may not find a substitute for the emotional support your partner offered.

Before any move into retirement housing, try staying in the guest flat for at least a week. Afterwards, you may find you cannot wait to move in permanently. Or points may occur to you which suggest that on balance you should stay put. I have met people who are very happy in retirement housing, having formed close friendships with other residents within a vibrant and stimulating community, and who would not wish to go back to the house in which they used to live alone. But I have also met residents in retirement housing who worry about what may befall them should they become mentally or physically frail. I have met others who find themselves in poky, lacklustre retirement flats with no green space to call their own. They say they left a house and garden with which they felt they could no longer cope, but one suspects they would give almost anything to go back. As with any change of accommodation, it will probably take at least two years to settle in. You need to be absolutely sure that this type of housing – and this sort of life – is going to be right for you before you take what is probably an irreversible step.

Retirement and sheltered housing

* Retirement housing schemes vary widely.

* A national care body will inspect any domiciliary care agency on the premises, but not the housing scheme as a whole.

* The functions exercised by managers or wardens also vary widely.

* An alarm worn as a pendant or on the wrist is better than a pull-cord fixed to the ceiling.

* Extra-care housing is likely to have staff on hand at night.

* When considering retirement housing, check the fire safety arrangements.

* Look out for unreasonable charges and high exit fees on leasehold properties.

* Look round at several different times of day and on different days of the week.

* Check that you would fit in with other residents.

* Stay in the guest flat and check for noise at night.

Chapter 7
Retirement villages

Agrowing number of retirement villages have been springing up in the UK over the last few years. Many have arisen as purpose-built facilities and, as land is the biggest cost involved, they have mostly been built on relatively large, cheap sites outside the Home Counties, often on the edge of settlements. Other retirement villages have been created through the conversion and extension of an existing building, typically a country mansion not far from a town.

There is no nationally agreed definition of a retirement village. They vary a great deal – in size, range of communal facilities and cost.

At the heart of a retirement village is retirement housing organised as described in the previous chapter. In other words, there is a collection of small housing units (usually apartments), occupied by older people and run by a scheme manager, accessed through a controlled entry system, and containing some communal facilities such as a lounge. Each flat will have a facility for summoning help in an emergency.

Perhaps the biggest difference between retirement housing and a retirement village is that a village is more likely to provide care through a team of paid helpers based on the premises, so residents who need some practical help can buy this from that team if they wish (or get it organised for them through social services). Care and support may be provided at various levels of need.

Another major difference is that many retirement villages contain a care home alongside the apartments as an integral part of the complex. This means that if somebody in one of the flats should need 24-hour support, they can relocate to that care home (if space is available and they can afford the fees), without having to move away from the village.

Here is an example of a retirement village:

Belong Warrington is one of several retirement villages provided by a not-for-profit provider in north-west England. Standing on the site of a former brewery not far from the town centre, it contains: apartments for older people in which care can be provided as in an extra-care housing scheme; communal facilities; and a care home providing round-the-clock care. The apartments and other parts of the complex look out over the grounds – a mix of lawns, paved areas, raised beds and seating.

Step inside the three-storey, brick-and-stone building that faces the road near a bus stop and, once past reception, you enter 'The Bistro' – a café/restaurant that is open to passers-by as well as people living in the village. There, residents from the apartments can enjoy refreshments with their relatives while their grandchildren can play close by. The food and drink are of high quality and the furniture and furnishings give the feel of a high-street facility.

Close to The Bistro there are other communal facilities that are also open to people living outside the village, including a hair and beauty salon, computer room and an exercise studio, which has a fitness instructor who devises personalised exercise programmes in consultation with physiotherapists and GPs.

Nearby stands The Venue – a function room with a jukebox and bar that hosts film shows, dances and other events; it also open to non-residents. The Venue's activities coordinator organises quizzes, craft sessions, computer workshops, film afternoons and 'knit and natter', which people living outside can also attend for a fee. The weekly chair-based exercise sessions at The Venue are based on a model devised by the social enterprise Our Organisation Makes People Happy! and they feature chair aerobics and chair cheerleading with coloured pom-poms.

The retirement/extra-care housing part of the complex consists of 18 flats. Each has a lobby with a cupboard and the control unit for the alarm system that enables the occupant to summon help in an emergency, day or night. The lobby gives onto a bathroom and also the main room, with a kitchen attached. Several of the apartments have two bedrooms. Each has a balcony. The total floor area of the larger apartments is equivalent to that of a small terraced house.

Residents have their own front door (with number and spyhole); in addition a keypad controls entry to the two apartment blocks. Within each apartment, residents wear a pendant alarm *(see page 486)* which connects to a control unit in their lobby. Or they can summon emergency help by speaking to somebody on site at any time through their control unit. Pets are allowed, so long as they do not disturb neighbours and can be looked after by their owner.

A care agency based in the village, called Belong at Home, provides a homecare service – care workers pay visits to residents in their apartments to help with practical tasks such washing and dressing, preparing food and going to bed. So, for instance, somebody who is developing dementia can obtain practical help through a support worker coming to their flat perhaps three times a day to help them. The Belong homecare service also supports people to attend appointments, join in social activities or pursue their hobbies. Belong at Home services are purchased separately from residents' housing costs; they can also be bought by people living outside the village.

If residents in the flats need nursing care, such as help with insulin injections, they obtain it from visiting district nurses employed by the local health trust. The village contains a guest room for visitors who wish to stay overnight.

Apartments can be rented or purchased on a lease, the latter either 100 per cent or on a shared ownership basis. In addition to the rent or purchase costs, flat residents pay a fee to cover services such as building maintenance and insurance, cleaning and maintenance of the communal areas. This fee also covers an emergency response service available day and night – offering a valuable facility not provided at many ordinary retirement or sheltered housing schemes that do not have a live-in scheme manager.

A 'buy-back scheme' provides that, if a lessee should leave, the housing provider guarantees to repurchase the lease at the price that the resident paid for it. There is no fee to move within the village or to leave it. In other words, no exit fee is levied *(unlike some private providers, which impose a percentage charge on the sale price, some as high as 10 per cent, on lessees who surrender their leases – see page 146).* If a resident needs to move into the care home, Belong would either buy back their flat or terminate their tenancy and then enter a different contract with them, requiring them to pay a fee for their residence in the care home.

The care home part of the village provides 24-hour care and support to 72 people living in six 'households', which each has its own family-like identity. Rather than residents' rooms giving off a long corridor, bedrooms in each household are clustered around a large central communal space, furnished with chairs, tables and sofas. Here, residents sit and chat, watch television or play games. Family and friends may visit at any time and stay for as long as they wish. A computer on a side table is used by staff and also by residents, for instance to Skype relatives overseas.

Each household's staff prepares meals for that household as well as snacks (including at night for people who cannot sleep). The kitchen area gives off the main space and has a shoulder-high divider so anyone can easily see into or enter it, as with an open-plan kitchen/diner. Tracy Paine, the operations director of Belong, explained to me in 2015 that staff are aware of any risk to individual residents of being in the kitchen but that even if they have dementia, 'In most people's long-term memory there is the knowledge of what a kitchen is, what it's used for, the fact that an oven or a kettle is hot and that what comes out of the taps is wet.' Should staff be called away and someone might be at risk, the kitchen can be sealed off with a small gate.

Household staff provide informal activities for residents, such as impromptu trips to local attractions and fish-and-chip and pamper evenings. There is an emphasis on meaningful occupation, so residents might be invited to help make the tea or peel carrots. And of course residents can take part in activities in the main communal rooms of the village. Each household has its own balcony, laundry room, and a bathroom with a deep bath that complements the walk-in showers of each en-suite bedroom.[1]

Belong Warrington has won awards. I hope it will provide a useful model against which you can measure any villages you investigate.

Regulation

Retirement villages are not defined in legislation. They are not regulated and inspected as such by a government-appointed national agency. This means no independent organisation is examining any retirement village in which you may be interested and establishing whether it meets the requirements of older people, whether in its physical fabric, the services it provides or the provision and training of staff. That is not to say of course that the companies and not-for-profit organisations that run retirement villages will not be doing their own checks, whatever they may be. And there are certain national laws with which retirement village providers must abide, on employment law and fire safety, for example.

This situation contrasts with the position on care homes. A care home is defined as a facility in which accommodation is provided to residents as well as personal and/or nursing care. Anybody who runs a care home has to be vetted by a national agency (in England the Care Quality Commission, in Scotland the Care Inspectorate, in Wales the Care and Social Services Inspectorate Wales and in Northern Ireland the Regulation and Quality Improvement Authority). Sets of regulations approved by national governments lay down rules and procedures about how homes operate, so as to ensure that their residents are well cared for. Teams of inspectors from the Care Quality Commission and its sister bodies periodically inspect all care homes to check that they are complying with these national regulations and standards of care; they can force improvements on homes which are performing badly and even force them to close.

However, many retirement villages contain care homes and these will be subject to regulation and inspection like any other care home. You could look up recent inspection reports (published by the national agencies on their websites) or ask the home to show them to you.

Another discrete element of a retirement village which will be subject to similar, independent inspection is any domiciliary care agency based in the village that provides help with personal care. Such agencies are also regulated and inspected by the CQC and its sister bodies, *as described on page 508.* (The accommodation and other facilities of a retirement village must be limited lest the whole facility should come within the definition of a care home and be regulated as such.)

If you are interested in a particular retirement village, ask to see the most recent inspection reports of any care agency on site, or obtain them through the relevant national agency. Bear in mind that only agencies that provide personal care are inspected, so the recruitment of staff for housework or other support that does not involve personal care, such as help with housework will not be covered by these regulations. *(For further information on the controls over domiciliary agencies, see pages 506–8.)*

Choosing a retirement village

There is much to consider before making a commitment to move into a retirement village. If you are thinking seriously about doing so, you may find the previous chapter on retirement housing useful, as the vast majority of the considerations outlined there also apply. As well as information about retirement housing schemes, the Elderly Accommodation Counsel provides information about retirement villages throughout the UK *(see page 151)*. If you are interested, go and look at a number of villages. Many have open days, or you could ask the manager if you could make a date to be shown round.

Here are one or two other matters on which you might like to focus when you tour a retirement village:

Security

Entry into a village tends to be controlled by a key pad or through visitors signing in at reception. In addition, villages often take CCTV to a high level. Lovatt's Fields, a large purpose-built facility on the edge of Milton Keynes, had many security cameras dotted throughout the complex and even a facility for residents to view what was being seen on all the cameras on their own TV screens when I visited in 2007. Plainly, this is likely to reduce the risk of burglary, as well as of threatening gangs roaming in the area.

All this can be reassuring. There have been few studies of residents' views of living in a retirement village; one of the most comprehensive involved researchers interviewing people living at a retirement village called Berryhill in Stoke-on-Trent, which was built on restored mining land. Many residents there told researchers that before they came to live in the village, they did not go out at night. Some had previously lived on quite dangerous housing estates and been frightened by the young people they either encountered or feared they would encounter on the streets: 'Inside at four o'clock and the doors and windows locked up tight, that was how it was.'[2] If the environment in which you live seems as threatening as this, the physical and psychological safety offered by a retirement village may be extremely welcome.

Some villages offer cash machines in the lobby and if you fear robbers looking over your shoulder at a cash machine in town, it can be reassuring to be able to take out money in a place from which many possible miscreants have been excluded.

However, you should nonetheless check on the effectiveness of the security system in any schemes in which you are interested. What kind of crime does take place there and why?

You might find any CCTV monitors viewable by residents not only reassuring in terms of safety, but also useful in other ways. You can see which residents are out and about on the 'streets' and in the communal spaces of the village and thus decide whether you wish to go and join them. If you are unwell, you can see what is going on even if you cannot participate. However, some people would find the presence of security cameras and the ability of their neighbours to see where they were going and what they were doing an undesirable invasion of privacy.

Activities

In a good care home, one would expect to find activities staff providing a range and choice of activities such as crafts, sing-songs, discussions, trips out and entertainment, usually free of charge. There is a general understanding that care homes should provide activities, although the law does not require this, and some homes do little more than pay lip-service to activity provision. In contrast in retirement villages, as in retirement housing schemes, one rarely comes across a full programme of activities which matches that of a good care home; very little may be offered.

So, find out what activities are offered on site and try to attend any that sound appealing. Would you enjoy them? Would they occupy as much of your time as you would wish? Could you afford any charges? Meet any activities organisers to see whether you would warm to them. What happens at weekends and when the activities organiser is on holiday? Many of the activities may be organised by residents themselves. Would you enjoy these?

Try to build a picture of what your life would actually be like in the village day by day. Work out whether you could easily get to facilities outside the village. Retirement villages tend to be located on the edge of towns, so, unlike much retirement housing, they are unlikely to be close to theatres, churches, public libraries and adult education centres. Is the village well served by public transport? Weekends in retirement villages which are far from any urban area and have no entertainment whatsoever provided on site can be lacklustre and tedious.

Pets

Could you bring your pet? And, if you do bring your pet with you when you move into an apartment, could you also take it into the care home, should you move in there at a later date? Belong Warrington is relaxed about pets and staff help care for them if care home residents can no longer do so, but many schemes forbid pets altogether. Nevertheless, there may be room for negotiation *(see pages 270–1)*.

Communal facilities

Retirement villages vary greatly in the type of facilities they provide, their size and any charges for them. Check whether the existing facilities would suit you and think about whether you would miss any not present. So, for instance, a library may sound appealing, but would the books be of the sort you would enjoy? Would you like to sit and read or write there, or would it be too noisy?

If you become unable to move around as freely as you can now and you live in a retirement village which is quite cut off, you will have fewer places to shop, since most of what you need will have to be found in the village store, or brought in from outside, perhaps through internet shopping. Do the goods and prices in the village shop match your taste and purse?

But of course a key feature of the attraction of communal facilities in a retirement village is that they stand within an environment which is easy to reach and which residents perceive as safe. Thus a shop can be useful not only because it provides things to buy, but also because you can reach it without going outside in the cold and rain and without going through streets in which you fear you might be mugged.

Berryhill contains a restaurant, shop, library, hairdresser's, greenhouse and woodwork and computer rooms as well as housing. Residents reported that they valued the opportunity to move around the complex safely, both during the day and in the evening. If all you have to do to attend an event is to go out of your front door and down a lift, you may well go to many more events and meetings, especially in the evening, than you did when you lived in ordinary housing.

Readiness to engage in social activities is also related to the presence of similarly placed people. A woman at Lovatt's Fields told me, 'Here I can go down to the bar on my own. Before, I would never have gone out in the evening.' She regularly attended events in the communal areas, including film shows and dances, at which she liked to chat to other people. As I was talking to her, she met a new resident in the foyer and persuaded her to go along to one with her. As a result, this resident too would be doing something active that evening, rather than perhaps remaining in her flat and watching TV. However, residents in another village might be less inclined to make friendly overtures to newcomers, leaving them feeling lonely, despite the presence of many other people.

It is easy to be bowled over by an impressive list of communal facilities in a retirement village. Investigate them all carefully. Are they sufficiently large to cater for the number of residents they seek to serve? Four benches in a woodwork room or four or five places in a computer room between 300 residents are not many; some may try to hog them. Can the facility be used at any time? How does any booking system operate?

Check whether the facilities can be used by people with disabilities. The resident in a wheelchair who showed me round one retirement village lamented that none of the tables in the greenhouse or woodwork room were sufficiently low for people in wheelchairs to reach. She pointed out that most of the raised flower beds were inaccessible even for the able-bodied: they would have to crawl over them on their hands and knees to reach the central area. Nor was her own flat suitable: she had had to spend thousands of pounds getting work surfaces in her kitchen lowered so she could reach them from her wheelchair.

The alarm system

An alarm system similar to that described for ordinary retirement or sheltered housing *(on pages 128–9)* should be in place. This should mean that any resident who needs urgent help, perhaps because they have had a fall and cannot get up, can summon assistance. This facility should be available to every resident, whether or not they are receiving any care and support services.

Check that the facility for responding to the alarm is available on site 24/7 and find out what sort of response you might receive to a call, day or night, bearing in mind the scheme's rules and the number of people available to help out *(see also page 130)*. Also, is reception manned day and night? Bear in mind that an on-site ability to respond to an emergency does not mean that care is available on demand, day or night.

Ask about the response to emergencies, as you would with retirement housing *(as outlined in the previous chapter)*. How is the building evacuated in the event of a fire?

Neutral space

A major difference between life in a retirement housing scheme and a retirement village is the provision of 'neutral' space for meeting other people, such as a bar and coffee bar. Of course, many retirement housing schemes serve coffee, but they tend to do so only at set times and in the lounge. In a retirement village, you may well find one or more drop-in coffee or bar facilities.

These neutral spaces can be welcome. They offer a place in which you can meet other residents or perhaps make a date to have a drink with a new acquaintance. While some people enjoy entertaining others in their own space, for some a bar and a coffee bar provide a very welcome alternative. After all, entertaining in your own flat can be hard work. You may wish to see your home as your own personal hideaway. Also, if you are in a neutral space it is easier to get away when you wish.

Mutual help

Retirement villages (and retirement housing schemes too) can involve a huge amount of mutual help, although, like so many other aspects of life in a community, that depends on the attitudes of the individuals involved. The point is that you are living very close to other people who may need the sort of help you are also looking for.

Help can take many different forms. It can mean agreeing with the resident living across the corridor that you will knock on their door or phone them if you notice that they have failed to draw back their curtains in the morning. It may mean picking up shopping for each other. It may mean looking after somebody's cat while they are hospital. A tradition can grow up in retirement villages of attending the funerals of residents who have died – 'rent-a-mob', as it was jokingly described to me. The village may provide a free-phone service whereby all calls made within the complex are without charge.

Retirement villages can be especially supportive environments for carers. The coffee shop, gym, library and so on are places in which a carer can get away from the confines of their own flat, perhaps while a paid care assistant is helping their disabled partner to get to bed. If any problems arise, they can be reached swiftly. Similarly a daughter might be having coffee downstairs or playing snooker, but if her mother or a care assistant should summon her, she can return speedily. A carer might ask another resident to sit with her sister while she pops into the shop; if a woman starts wandering, another resident could go and fetch her partner from the gym.

All this depends on the village being a friendly place. Some residents, however, will not find their village welcoming. There may be a variety of reasons why they do not mix well with other residents. Retirement villages can have their own cliques, just like ordinary retirement housing. Residents may find difficulty in finding their way around the many spaces and corridors, and this can intensify rather than diminish feelings of isolation, particularly for newly-arrived residents with mobility problems. As one Berryhill resident commented, 'It is just like living in a great big building on your own: the only thing you hear is the lifts,' while a doctor said, 'Going into somewhere large like that can actually be a bit overwhelming for one person on their own, unless they've got really good social skills.'[3] For reasons such as this, it is well worth staying in the guest flat of any village in which you are interested for several days before you commit yourself.

Getting out and about

Because of their size and their need for cheap land, retirement villages are often on the edge of settlements or in the countryside. Would you miss the ability to potter into a town as the mood takes you? The sales blurb may point out that the entertainment, healthcare and, retail facilities of a country town are close by. Stop and think! If at some stage you do not drive and have mobility difficulties, how are you going to get to it?

If you have a car, pay special attention to parking provision. Retirement villages tend to offer parking spaces rather than garages for residents. Are there enough, and what happens if the rules on allocated spaces are broken?

In 2013 a team of researchers examined provision of services and the general 'age-friendliness' of Denham Garden Village, a purpose-built retirement village in Buckinghamshire with more than 300 apartments, bungalows and houses for people aged 55 and over, together with a meeting hall, gym, swimming pool, GP surgery and café-bar. Here, leaseholders were given allocated parking spaces, but residents who rented their properties were not. Instead, they had to compete for parking with non-residents who visited the village to use the gym, café-bar and swimming pool. Some leaseholders complained that tenants had taken their allotted parking spaces. Some residents at Denham reported a dearth of disabled spaces.[4]

So focus your questioning first on the number of spaces (for residents, residents' visitors and other non-residents), but also the enforcement of the rules. What are the penalties and how energetically are they imposed? This could affect you even if you do not have a car. An insufficient number of parking spaces may result in parking on pavements and over dropped kerbs; this can make life very difficult for people with mobility scooters and wheelchairs.

Check bus services carefully, whether you drive or not. When and where do services run? Are the pavements outside the retirement village leading to bus stops well maintained? Is there a bus shelter with a seat? Even if you can drive, times may well arise when you are unable to, for one reason or another.

Some villages have their own minibus. There may also be local dial-a-ride services. Find out when and where you could travel around on both types of service. Would all this provide you with enough mobility? Investigate taxis too. Are there enough taxi firms? Are they reliable? Are any taxis in the area capable of taking a wheelchair while the occupant remains seated? Would the pavements alongside any road into the nearest town or village be wide enough for a mobility scooter or wheelchair?

Care and support

Retirement villages usually offer various support packages into which residents can buy, if they wish. These vary greatly. They may include help with housework, laundry, shopping, home maintenance and personal care, with the latter offered at various levels (from help with dressing or taking medication once a day to frequent visits involving help with bathing, washing, eating and using the toilet).

A key aim of providing care on site is that the village can be a home for life – in other words, you never have to move out. In some villages, people who need the sort of care that would be provided in a care home move to a care home in the complex; in other villages they remain in their own flats and care is provided there.

The presence of a care home on site has many advantages. If one member of a couple needs support in a care home, their other half could remain living in the flat (or relocate to a smaller one) and visit easily. If a resident should need short-term Intermediate Care *(see page 949)* in a care home, they may be able to get it in the home on site. If they should come to need care home support permanently, the overall environment will be familiar – although the staff in the home will probably be different from those they encountered in the complex outside.

But all this convenience might not work out in practice. The care home might not have space for you when you need it. You might not like that particular care home. It might be too expensive.

Even if you don't think you will need the care home or domiciliary care services provided on site, do examine them carefully. Although you may not need this kind of support when you move in, you may come to require it in the future. *(I outline what to look for in a care agency on pages 508–22 and in a care home in the forthcoming companion volume on care homes.)* Talk to the managers of both the agency and the care home and study the reports of inspections carried out on them by the Care Quality Commission (in England), the Care Inspectorate (in Scotland), the Care and Social Services Inspectorate Wales and the Regulation and Quality Improvement Authority (in Northern Ireland).

Have a look at Chapter 23 for an explanation of what obtaining practical help in the home can involve. Essentially, you can either buy help independently or obtain it through social services. In either case, help can be provided through a domiciliary care agency or individuals operating independently. Any agency based in the village would be the obvious source of helpers.

Unless your contract with the village specifically forbids it, you should be able to hire your own help from outside, if you wish to do so. However, one woman to whom I spoke who had done this through a direct payment from social services *(see page 637)* had had quite a fight on her hands with her housing provider, who had initially insisted that she must use staff based in the village.

It is also worth considering the extent to which the village offers or provides care and support separate from any provided to individuals. In any retirement village, between a fifth and a quarter of residents are likely to develop dementia once they are over the age of 85. This means they are likely to become confused as they move around the building. What are they to do all day? What provision has the village made for the reality of dementia? Are activity sessions provided and, if so, who runs them? A care home would be expected to have made specific provision through adequate numbers of trained staff and an environment designed to be comprehensible for people with dementia, for instance with explanatory pictures on doors. Inspectors from national agencies would check that this total environment was adequate. No similar check takes place for a retirement village.

Talk to as many members of staff as you can and try to ascertain whether they understand some of the problems that can arise in later life. Have they all received some training related to ageing or to working with older people? If a resident cannot attend an activity because they need someone to take them to it, would the village offer to help? If not, would the resident be able to obtain paid assistance, and how much would this cost?

Find out whether there is a local GP practice that you would like to use and that would accept you. Perhaps a GP calls at the village regularly? If not (and for other consultations), work out how you would get to the surgery. Could you walk, drive or take a mobility scooter? What would the trip be like in bad weather? Should you need the support of a paid assistant, would this be possible and how much would it cost?

Selling your lease

Retirement housing providers differ widely on the terms they stipulate when a lease is sold. The scheme might allow you to sell your lease on the open market. Or it might insist that you sell it to them when you leave. Or it might impose an exit fee, sometimes called a transition or an event fee *(as described on page 146–7)*.

You might imagine that you would not wish to move on once in the village and that the only sale would be on your death. But all sorts of eventualities might arise. You might choose to move to a different apartment. A relative might invite you to go and live with them. You and your partner might decide to separate. You might need to move into a care home, whether the one on site or one elsewhere.

If the village is one which levies exit fees, do talk through the situation should you wish to move within the complex. Is there any reduction on the fee imposed for moves within the village as opposed to a move away from it? If not, the levying of say, 10 per cent of the price for which you sell your apartment and the need to pay perhaps high weekly care home fees could prove prohibitively expensive.

Or perhaps the scheme insists that you sell your lease to it when you leave and at the price at which you purchased it. Would that be acceptable to you?

Security of tenure

Obtain a draft lease and study it carefully, not least on the question of the circumstances when you might be under pressure to leave. Retirement village providers no less than those of retirement housing are not keen on having residents wandering around who may harm their image of catering for the active over-55s. Should you come to need a lot of care and/or develop dementia you might feel under pressure from the housing provider and perhaps also from other residents to move elsewhere *(as discussed on page 150 in the context of retirement housing)*. As noted under 'Care' above, any care home on site might suit you – or not.

Guest accommodation

How much guest accommodation is available and how much does it cost? Just one guest room is woefully inadequate in a scheme in which many residents are bound to face illness, whether short or long-term.

Storage space

When you move to a retirement village you will probably be downsizing. Storage space could prove an issue, particularly if you have to find space for health or mobility equipment. In that case, you might find you have no choice but to devote part of your bathroom or any spare bedroom to storing your belongings. How much storage space does the village provide for its residents? Would this be enough for you?

Food

One of the advantages of living in a retirement village is that you can get a hot meal within the complex. Any care home within the complex will provide meals to its residents and these will be included in the fees. People living in flats in the village will prepare their own meals but can also eat in the village's restaurant, paying for their meals there as they take them.

Particularly if the village is in an isolated position with no other cafés, restaurants or take-aways in the vicinity, the type, quality, price and nutritional value of food served in the restaurant will be very important. So sample several different meals in the restaurant including over a weekend. Try to meet the chef and his or her team and use Chapter 2 to work out their level of understanding of the nutritional needs of older people. Questions worth addressing include:

✓ How much choice does the menu offer?

✓ How filling are the meals?

✓ Which dishes would you find appetising and which would you rule out for one reason or another?

✓ Would the meals help you achieve a healthy diet *(see page 37)*?

✓ Could the chef cope with any special dietary requirements you have?

✓ How often would you be able to afford to eat in the restaurant?

✓ Do its opening hours coincide with when you would wish to have a meal?

✓ Is the restaurant large enough for all the residents, say, at Christmas?

✓ Does the chef consult the residents about the menu and does he or she welcome feedback?

Consider also whether the cooking facilities in the individual housing units would suit you. At the Richmond Painswick village in Gloucestershire, which I visited in 2013, the apartments did not have an ordinary oven in their fitted kitchens. Residents could have a microwave, toaster and hob, but if they wished to have an oven, they had to have the kitchen altered at their own expense and return it to its original state, again at their own expense, when they left.

You may be pleased to put the task of cleaning an oven behind you. However, you may not always wish to use the restaurant all the time, however good the food. If the scheme is one that imposes an additional charge if you are unwell and wish to have your meal delivered to your room, you may not be able to afford to eat in that way over an extended period. Or perhaps you would simply like to bake a cake or cook a roast in an ordinary oven, once in a while.

Volunteering

Some schemes rely heavily on residents doing work in the various facilities in the village for free. For instance, the coffee shop and the library may be staffed entirely by volunteers, who may also offer activities for residents with dementia and essential back-up in the shop and restaurant. Find out what proportion of residents volunteer and the average number of hours per week that they contribute. Volunteering to help occasionally in the various facilities may appeal to you, and indeed provides a means of meeting other people, but check that you would not be expected to contribute a large amount of time for free unless you wished to do so. Running a coffee shop or organising outings for residents can be sheer hard graft. Look at the age profile of the village too: if volunteering is crucial to running activities and keeping facilities open and most residents are over 80, the village may well struggle to sustain them.

The ambience

Perhaps the most striking feature that hits the visitor to a retirement village is the preponderance of older people. Step inside a retirement or sheltered housing scheme and you will see older people to be sure, but the world they inhabit includes the world outside the housing, in which they shop, go to the bank and library, enjoy walks, see friends and so on – a world peopled by individuals of many different ages and backgrounds. Retirement villages tend to be larger than housing schemes and with larger communal areas. Virtually everybody you encounter in the village – in the foyer, shop, hairdresser's, corridors, restaurant, grounds, gym and so on – is old. Some are walking, others zipping around on mobility scooters or powered wheelchairs, but they are all of a certain age. Naturally, these residents venture out into the outside world sometimes. But they tend to have less need to do so.

Some people flourish in a world in which everybody is of a similar age to themselves, but others yearn for an age profile which more closely mirrors that of the world outside. It is important to know in which camp you fall before you take the plunge.

Retirement Villages

* Look at the recent inspection reports on any care home and also any care agency that provides personal care within the village.

* Do your own checks on support throughout the complex should you have a disability.

* How close to your apartment or house could you park your car?

* Where could you store any mobility equipment?

* Are the cooking facilities in your property adequate?

* How easy would it be to reach shops and other facilities outside the village?

* Where would your family stay if you were ill?

* Does the village offer activities that you would find fulfilling?

* Is the food provided to your taste and pocket?

* Does the scheme insist on an exit fee and, if so, how much is it and what would you receive in return?

Chapter 8

Staying put

Many of us feel rooted to our present homes. The impulse to stay put for as long as possible in the place where we have built memories and which we have fashioned to our taste is understandable. Yet as the years pass, maintaining our pride and joy can seem an overwhelming task. That once immaculate lawn could become ever harder to mow, its grass ever taller. There is the constant need to keep our house or flat clean, warm, safe, and secure from burglars.

Many properties have crumbling, uneven floors inside and out, awkward steps and rooms which are difficult to heat. Small wonder that managing property, not to mention improving it, can start to feel intimidating. But take heart: a surprising amount of help is available.

In this chapter I consider the following aspects of staying put:

▶ repairs

▶ adaptations

▶ security

▶ heating

▶ safety

▶ gardens

Repairs

Property repairs may pose problems for people who would have taken them in their stride when they were younger. One is disruption to their living space while modifications are made. Another is finding reputable workmen. Then there is the cost.

Disruption may be the easiest to address. It may be possible to go away while repairs are being carried out and for a relative come to stay in the property to oversee the work (together with consequential tasks, such as redecorating). One woman of whom I heard had made no improvements to her house for decades, not because she could not afford to do so but because she found the disruption and dust intolerable. With walking becoming increasingly difficult, she found it was as much as she could do to look after herself and her dog. However, she had to go into hospital, and while she was there, her legal representative organised all the house repairs that had become necessary and the installation of a washing-machine, tumble-drier and new carpets. When the woman returned from hospital, she was delighted with the improvements.

The older we get, the more vulnerable we can feel when negotiating with workmen with whom we have not previously dealt, lest we be persuaded to commission work that is unnecessary or exorbitantly priced. Or we may feel obliged to commission sub-standard builders whom we do not want to offend because we rely on them for other help and they live close by.

Friends or relatives can provide much help in tracking down honest traders, commissioning and evaluating estimates and then chivvying workers, monitoring progress and clearing up afterwards. But other help is at hand in many areas.

Care and Repair agencies

Dotted over the UK are over 200 Care and Repair agencies (also called Home Improvement Agencies or Staying Put schemes). These local, non-profit-making organisations aim to help people over the age of 50 to repair and improve their homes.

Care & Repair Cardiff and the Vale is a charitable organisation that seeks to help older people in Cardiff and the Vale of Glamorgan to repair, adapt or maintain their homes. It has a manager, nine case workers, three technical officers, four handypersons and five administrators, working from an office in Cardiff.[1]

Should someone ring the agency, perhaps wondering what they can do about a leaking roof or a broken boiler, one of the caseworkers will go and visit them and assess what work needs to be done, who would do the work and how it would be paid for. The inquirer could be of modest means or wealthy; the only restriction on this provision of free advice if repairs and home maintenance are involved is that the person must own their home or rent it from a private landlord, as it is assumed that tenants of council and housing association property will ask their landlord to deal with repairs. On average, 25 people each week are visited by Care & Repair Cardiff and the Vale's caseworkers.

The agency's own team of handypersons carry out about 50 practical tasks in people's homes each week. This work tends to be free, as there are grants available to cover the costs. Works carried out include fitting hand rails, stair rails and grab rails, installing smoke and carbon monoxide detectors, putting in new steps and repairing and widening old ones, and installing key safes and security door chains.

For large repair works, Care & Repair Cardiff and the Vale would suggest that estimates are obtained from contractors on its own list. These are tradespeople whom it has carefully vetted – for instance, they must comply with codes of conduct, have adequate insurance, offer fair prices and provide a complaints procedure. The agency monitors the way contractors on its panel treat their customers. If any behave badly, their name is removed from the list.

Care & Repair Cardiff and the Vale always recommends three quotes, particularly for works above £500. Its technical officers will put a contract in place between the older person and the contractor which outlines the work that is to be done, the timescale and the costs, if the client would like them to do so. No payment is made until the end of the job and both the client and the technical officer are satisfied that the work has been done to a satisfactory standard.

Care & Repair Cardiff and the Vale may help its clients find money to pay for the work. In the past, local authorities used to offer grants to householders to help pay for repairs, but in many areas these have more or less dried up. There are different types of funding sources in different areas.

In Cardiff, for example, the council is able to help older people in certain circumstances with an interest-free loan. Although the householder does not have to pay money upfront, a legal charge is placed on their property to require repayment of the loan when the property is sold, often after the death of the occupant. Five or ten thousand pounds is a lot of money to pay when a property is sold, but if it has prevented the roof from leaking it will have made the dwelling habitable and safeguarded its value. The work would not involve, say, the landscaping of a garden: it would be work necessary to enable someone to maintain their safety and independence in their home. This approach is very much local-authority-specific, so while the case-worker service would be similar in other Care & Repair agencies, any means of helping to pay for work will vary authority by authority. It is quite different from equity release, which involves the charging of interest.

Care & Repair Cardiff and the Vale can also look for other sources of funding, such as benevolent associations and charities specific to the individual – often they relate to the person's previous employment or any disability or religious affiliation. It also raises money to provide for a hardship fund that can help fund very urgent jobs. So if Mrs Jones contacts the agency and says her boiler has broken down, it can send a contractor out immediately; it tries to limit this kind of urgent spending to about £100 per job. If Mrs Jones' boiler needed to be replaced, the agency's two caseworkers who specialise in heating matters would step in and look to approach Nest (a source of funding in Wales to help people in fuel poverty *described on page 194 below*). In the interim, the agency provides heaters. These will not heat her whole house, but will heat a room while the repairs are going on.

A key feature of visits by Care & Repair Cardiff and the Vale is that caseworkers offer those they visit other advice about their homes, all for free. The caseworker would ask: what other problems do you have with your home that you want us to help you with? Or matters that require attention would emerge from checks that caseworkers carry out. Thus a home safety check would look at ways of preventing falls through modifying surroundings in the sort of ways outlined later in this chapter, while a healthy homes check would look at ways of rectifying dampness and other problems that might impair the occupant's health, as well as improving a property's security. As a result of this holistic approach, someone who had initially approached the agency concerned about draughty windows might also end up having a carbon monoxide detector installed, as well as grab rails to reduce the chance of their having a fall.

The agency's caseworkers who specialise in heating could also visit someone who might have inquired about something entirely separate. A (free) heating examination would look at:

1. **The energy efficiency of the property:** Is there adequate cavity wall or other insulation? Are the boilers the most efficient possible? Are windows and doors draught proof? Should other features that make the property cold be addressed, such as dampness?

2. **The use of energy:** The caseworker would offer tips for using energy as efficiently as possible.

3. **Energy purchase:** The caseworker would calculate the best tariff for the person to be on and switch them to it if necessary.

4. **The person's income:** The caseworkers also offer free checks to make sure that people are claiming the benefits to which they are entitled. Richard Thomas, Care & Repair Cardiff and the Vale's Chief Officer, told me in an interview in 2015: 'People are often not aware that there's a benefit to which they may be entitled that's not linked to their income but to their well-being and that makes a difference of £55 per week – Attendance Allowance. That sum can pay for taxis to the shops or help around the house.'

The checks on energy, home safety and income are also available to people who live in local authority and housing association property. It is the advice and work involving repairs and maintenance that is restricted to owners and private tenants.

Care & Repair Cardiff and the Vale carries out work to make people's homes safer free of charge to older people who rent their homes from social landlords, as well as private tenants and owner-occupiers. Rails are the most common form of adaptation – grab rails, hand rails, rails up the stairs or up the front steps, rails in the toilet, rails to help someone get out of the bath, including floor to ceiling poles – anywhere where there is a potential risk of a slip, trip or fall. The work is free because the Welsh government, two local councils in whose area Care & Repair Cardiff and the Vale operates and the local health board which finance this work consider it preventative – should someone have a fall and break their hip, the cost to the health and social care system might run to £30,000, whereas a grab rail costs just £30 to fit. There is a maximum spend of £350 per property. Many of these adaptations are put in quickly for people who are coming out of hospital and are facilitated by social workers and occupational therapists in the local hospitals. This scheme operates throughout Wales and is called the Rapid Response Adaptations Programme *(see also page 183)*.

If someone has a disability and one of Care & Repair Cardiff and the Vale's caseworkers considers that they need larger adaptations to enable them to live safely in their home, they would be referred to a team that assesses whether they would be eligible for a Disabled Facilities Grant *(described on pages 186–8 below)*. Care & Repair Cardiff and the Vale can arrange for work to be carried out that is partly or wholly paid for by Disabled Facilities Grants.

You can find any Care & Repair agency operating in your area by contacting the national coordinating bodies for these organisations – Care and Repair England, Care and Repair Scotland and Care and Repair Cymru; the Fold Housing Association performs a similar function in Northern Ireland.

Finding workmen

Should you be unable to obtain information about reputable builders from a Care and Repair agency, you could approach a local Age UK organisation, many of which have compiled a 'home services directory'. These are likely to give the name and address of traders, a description of the work offered and the hourly rate, any call-out charge and whether emergency work is taken on.

If you take names from lists such as these, find out what the compilation of the list has involved, for example whether police checks *(see page 507)* have been included. In the best such lists, each trader who appears has been evaluated, their references have been examined and a security check has been carried out on them. In addition, they have signed an undertaking that they will trade fairly and agree to adopt certain working practices, such as quoting prices inclusive of VAT and treating customers' property with care.

Sources of information such as this can be more useful than a tradesman's boasted membership of a trade organisation, which is likely to represent the interests of its members rather than those of customers. If you use a trade association to find a workman or woman, check what membership of these organisations means and whether the person you propose to hire really is a current member. Does the association offer any mediation facility in the event of a dispute?

Some local authorities, local Age UKs and other organisations provide a different sort of handyperson service which carries out such tasks as lifting carpets, moving heavy furniture and taking down and putting up curtains and curtain tracks. There is usually a small charge.

Paying for repairs

As noted above, Care and Repair agencies can offer advice on financing home improvement work. One possible source of finance is your local authority.

Local authorities have a discretionary power to give owner-occupiers, private tenants and, in Scotland, crofters financial help towards home repairs and improvement. In England, each council sets out its approach in its housing renewal assistance policy. This explains what kind of help is available, whether it is means-tested, the terms of any repayment, and any conditions attached. The law requires authorities to set out in writing the terms and conditions under which help is being given and to ensure that recipients have received appropriate advice and information about the extent and nature of any obligations (including financial) they will be taking on. Before making a loan or requiring repayment of a loan or grant, the authority must take account of a recipient's ability to pay.[2] Councils are not permitted to say that they never use their power to give these grants or loans.[3]

However, while these grants have helped many people in the past, in 2017 funding cutbacks meant that they were harder to obtain. Many local authorities were giving grants only in exceptional circumstances, where there was an imminent and significant risk to the grant applicant's safety or health as a result of the condition of their dwelling. It is nonetheless worth approaching your local authority, as your council may be one that bucks the trend; at least it may provide advice on obtaining repairs; or you may actually qualify for a grant. If you do not, you will have to consider dipping into your savings, borrowing the necessary money, downsizing to release cash, or entering into an equity release agreement. *(I consider equity release on pages 884–7.)*

If a local Care and Repair agency *(see above)* exists in your area, so much the better – it may be able to uncover new sources of funding or at least help oversee repairs that you pay for.

The situation is similar in Northern Ireland, where a state agency, the Northern Ireland Housing Executive, administers grants to owner-occupiers and private tenants to carry out repairs, improvements, security enhancement measures and adaptations to the home. The maximum amount available is £5,000 over three years, and grants are restricted to people with disabilities who are receiving Attendance Allowance, the Personal Independence Payment or Disability Living Allowance and those receiving Income Support or the Guarantee element of Pension Credit.

Adaptations to cope with disability

If you have difficulty in moving around, perhaps because of osteoarthritis, a few well-chosen adaptations to your home could make your life a lot easier and safer. If you have a significant amount of disability, adaptations to your home might make the difference between being able to continue to live there and having to move to a care home.

There are many straightforward ways in which your home can be adapted to help you cope with illness or disability. Care and Repair England has published useful guides that examine how common housing faults can affect our health and the range of ways in which we can change our day-to-day living conditions to better cope with illness and disability. In *Making your Home a Better Place to Live with Macular Disease*, Care and Repair England puts forward suggestions for changing lighting, increasing colour contrast, removing trip hazards and installing telecare equipment. It publishes similar guides on living with arthritis, dementia, heart disease, respiratory diseases and the after-effects of a stroke.

Many of the grants that local authorities give to help people adapt their homes to cope with disability are mandatory – in other words (unlike grants for home repairs), they must award them, so long as the person is assessed as needing the adaptation. First, though, what kind of adaptations might you make?

Minor adaptations

Adaptations could involve the addition of a ramp, a few strategically sited grab bars or a washbasin in a downstairs room which would enable it to be used as a bedroom, for example. Small changes such as these can be extraordinarily valuable. Expert on older people's housing Frances Heywood asked a sample of older people for their views about minor adaptations which had been made to their homes. They reported:

> …increased feelings of safety, ability to take a bath or shower, being more able to run the home and to go out and needing less help from others. Over three-quarters of those consulted said there had been a positively good effect on their health, and there were virtually no problems.[4]

Minor adaptations are usually inexpensive. What is more, you may be able to get one or more provided and fitted for free. The Department of Health has said that any home adaptation up to a ceiling of £1,000 (covering the cost of buying and fitting) should be provided free of charge to people living in England who are assessed by their local authority as needing it.[5] This provision should not be means-tested: if you are assessed as needing the adaptation, you ought to get it for free.

In **Wales,** the Rapid Response Adaptations Programme provides free, non-means-tested house adaptations as well as minor repairs for older and disabled people up to a ceiling of £350, *as explained in the case example box about the work of Care & Repair Cardiff and the Vale.* The scheme is often used to put in place small adaptations for people coming out of hospital, such as handrails and stair rails, or to carry out inexpensive tasks, perhaps getting a bed moved downstairs. If you are in hospital and think you might benefit, ask for appropriate adaptations to be included in your hospital discharge plan *(see pages 942–3).*

The **Scottish** Executive has decreed that local authorities should not charge for minor adaptations supplied to frail older people leaving hospital, so long as these are fitted immediately prior to discharge or within four weeks afterwards.[6]

The **Northern Ireland** Housing Executive provides some minor adaptations to the home to cope with disability for homeowners and private tenants free of charge. It also offers grants towards the cost of adaptations that are not paid for by health and social services trusts. Any minor adaptations for disability made to property owned by the Executive or housing associations are free.

Major adaptations

Major changes to the home to cope with disability include anything from the installation of a new bathroom to the addition of a ramp (indoors or out), the widening of doorways to cope with a wheelchair and the installation of a through-floor lift.

As one of the most common major installations is a lift up a flight of stairs, let us consider how to go about finding one and paying for it.

Stairlifts

Stairlifts can make the difference between using two floors of your property and living on one level only or moving house. But they can set you back several thousand pounds. Some people obtain a stairlift through the social services department of their local authority with the help of a Disabled Facilities Grant *(described in the next section).* In this case, the authority should carry out the necessary assessments to work out which would be the most suitable lift and should arrange for it to be installed and maintained.

However, many people end up buying their own stairlift rather than waiting while their application is processed. Or their need for a lift may not be sufficiently great to meet their council's eligibility criteria for one free of charge or at a subsidised price.

The most common type of stairlift involves somebody going up and down on a seat facing across the stairs. However, if the stairs are narrow and/or the person needs a lot of leg-room, they may need a 'flow chair' facing the direction of travel. Some stairlifts have an extra-wide base onto which a wheelchair can be driven or wheeled; these require a wide stair-way. There are also lifts with a platform on which somebody stands or perches. Flights of stairs usually have to be at least 27 inches wide, or 29 if curved, to accommodate any kind of stairlift (69 and 74 cms respec-tively).[7]

This is a major purchase. Before you contact a firm which sells stair-lifts, try to visit a Disabled Living Centre *(see page 458)*. There you can obtain advice and also try out a lift. Perhaps your son says you should have a stairlift, but when you sit or stand on a moving lift, you find the experience unsettling; were you to buy one, you would therefore be un-likely to use it. This may be particularly the case on a flow lift: you might feel giddy looking straight down the staircase.

Having decided that you need a stairlift and would use one, find an occupational therapist (OT) perhaps through the College of Occupa-tional Therapists *(see page 314)* and ask them for advice on your need for a stairlift in the context of your home environment. The visit should not take longer than an hour, so the cost should not be great.

Then invite prospective suppliers to visit. Or you could try to get the OT and a stairlift supplier in your house at the same time.

Obtain quotes from several suppliers. Apart from the price of the lift, make sure your discussions include the following points:

Your needs

✓ What type and size of seat would you need, bearing in mind your size and weight?

✓ In view of your height and the ceiling height(s), would there be sufficient room for your head?

- ✓ Would there be sufficient room for your legs, particularly if they are long and/or you have difficulty in bending them? Might you need a flow chair?
- ✓ Would you be able to manipulate the joystick, paddle or button controls easily, bearing in mind any eyesight or dexterity problems you may have?
- ✓ Would the controls be placed on the left or right arm?

The constraints of your property

- ✓ Could the staircase in your property stand the weight of the lift?
- ✓ Is the staircase the correct width?
- ✓ Is there space at the top where the lift could finish safely?
- ✓ Could any curved areas, short flights or platforms associated with the stairway be accommodated successfully and, if so, at what additional cost?

Ongoing use

- ✓ What happens if problems arise once the warranty period has expired? Would you be expected to take out a maintenance contract? What would be the cost? How long would it last?
- ✓ How frequently does the equipment have to be serviced to meet health and safety legislation? How will that be paid for? Is that servicing part of the initial contract?
- ✓ How quickly could a maintenance expert get to you? When are they on call? Who could you contact for advice about using the lift?
- ✓ If for any reason you have to dispose of the stairlift, would you get some of your money back? How much? (Some suppliers will buy a stairlift back then sell it on as a reconditioned lift.)

The matters listed above are also relevant if you are proposing to buy a second-hand reconditioned lift. So, for example, you should discuss whether the size of the seat is right for you and, if not, whether it could be altered. You would still expect a warranty, but it would not last as long as one for a new lift.

Any lift will depreciate in value, so consider hiring rather than buying a lift if you will need it only for a relatively short time. If you hire, you would have to pay a deposit and then monthly payments, with a minimum period for taking the product.

The Centre for Accessible Environments, a charity, provides detailed technical information about the design of stairlifts and other equipment and house adaptations to cope with disability. The Disabled Living Foundation *(see page 459)* also provides information, such as a free leaflet for the general public entitled 'Equipment for going up and down stairs'.

Ruth decided reluctantly to move to the ground floor of the house in which she had lived for more than 60 years. In her early nineties, she had had a couple of dizzy spells and was worried about using the stairs when she was alone in the house, particularly in the evening. She ruled out a stairlift, as she had been told by a stairlift company a few years before that a lift could not be fitted around a twist at the top of her stairs.

She and her sons thereupon set about getting estimates for the conversion and extension of the ground floor of her house to accommodate a bathroom, and they moved her bed, wardrobe and other bedroom furniture down into what had been her sitting room. Then I pointed out that stairlift technology was advancing all the time and that it would be worth making sure the previous advice remained true.

A different stairlift company which Ruth contacted assured her they could fit a lift up her staircase. Within a fortnight, they had installed the new lift and her sons had redecorated her upstairs bedroom and organised the delivery of a new bed. Now she enjoys the freedom of moving wherever she wishes in her house, travelling up and downstairs whenever she chooses. Her comfortable new bed and the new wallpaper in her bedroom are a daily remainder that the stairlift has given her back a key part of her life she had feared had gone forever.[8]

Grants for major adaptations to the home

If you have quite a substantial disability and live in England, Wales or Northern Ireland, you ought to be able to get a Disabled Facilities Grant. These grants can deliver quite a lot of money: the limit is £30,000 in England, £36,000 in Wales and £25,000 in Northern Ireland. They are mandatory grants – in other words, your local authority (or, in Northern Ireland, the Housing Executive) must give the grant if you meet the criteria.

Disabled Facilities Grants are typically given to:

- improve access in and out of a property
- improve access to the bathroom, lavatory, bedroom and principal living room
- facilitate food preparation
- improve lighting or heating

Often the work involved will be the installation of ramps, the widening of doorways or the provision of a track and hoist. These grants can also be given to facilitate access to a garden.

The definition of 'disabled' in this context involves a person whose sight, hearing or speech is substantially impaired, or somebody with any kind of mental disorder or impairment, or somebody who is substantially physically disabled as a result of illness, injury or impairment perhaps present since birth.[9]

Form of tenure is irrelevant, so grants are available to owner-occupiers and all types of tenant – private, council and housing association. The property involved could be a caravan or a houseboat. Recipients of grants have to sign a certificate stating that they will live in the property for at least five years after the works are completed, or a shorter period for health or other special reasons.

Although Disabled Facilities Grants have to be awarded to people who meet the criteria for them on grounds of disability, the actual amount they receive depends on their own income and savings and those of their partner. This means that people who are eligible for the Guarantee element of Pension Credit receive a far larger amount than those with a higher income and savings exceeding £6,000.

Disabled Facilities Grants can take quite a long time to process, so it is important to lodge an application promptly if you think you might be eligible. The need for assessment by the local authority's occupational therapist often causes delays, so you could ask the council whether it would accept an assessment from a therapist you commission yourself (see page 314).

In assessing applications, a local authority is not allowed to take its own resources into account. It has to pay the grant within 12 months of the date of application, so long as the work has been carried out.

Local authorities have to provide gadgets and human help to older people with disabilities or frailty only if they meet the council's own eligibility criteria (as explained in chapters 21 and 26). Councils do not have this flexibility when it comes to people meeting the definition of 'disabled' deployed in the context of Disabled Facilities Grants. Under the definition used in the Chronically Sick and Disabled Persons Act 1970 referred to above, local authorities *must* provide services to meet the needs of disabled people, including adaptations to the home, disability aids and equipment and human help.

If you cannot get your grant, or get it quickly, consider lodging a complaint *(see pages 578–80)*. This is an area in which you need to be prepared to assert your legal rights. Talk to your local Citizens Advice or any local organisation for disabled people in your area or ring the helpline of the charity Disability Rights UK about the steps you could most usefully take. If you think publicity would help, contact the local media: a press picture of you stranded at home because you cannot get up and down the front steps could give useful leverage to your campaign. Why not also contact your local councillor or MP?

In addition, local councils can give discretionary help for adaptations for disabled people either on top of the Disabled Facilities Grant or as an alternative to it; there is no ceiling on the amount. Such help can also be used as a means of enabling a disabled person to move to a more suitable property if that is more cost-effective than adapting their current home, even though the new property may itself need some adaptation.

If you have been living for a long time in accommodation that keeps you indoors and severely restricts your freedoms, it is easy to become disheartened and lack the motivation and confidence to fight the system. If you are in this position, think about getting someone to speak up for you who will challenge the authorities on your behalf. This could be a friend or relative or someone from a voluntary organisation that provides advocates who tackle health and social care authorities on behalf of people who are not getting the most that they should from the system or helps them to take action themselves *(see page 775)*.

Scotland

There are no Disabled Facilities Grants as such in Scotland, and the situation on local councils' grants for home repairs is different from that elsewhere in the UK too.

Local authorities in Scotland have to pay a minimum 80 per cent grant, whatever an applicant's income, for an adaptation to make a property suitable for the accommodation of a disabled person who is living in private housing (rented or owned), if the council assesses them as needing it. The adaptation must involve a permanent change to the home, such as the replacement of a bath with a walk-in shower, the construction of a ramp for easier access to the property or the fitting of lower work surfaces to make the kitchen easier to use. The council must pay the full cost if the applicant receives the Guarantee element of Pension Credit, Income Support, Income-based Jobseeker's Allowance or Income-related Employment and Support Allowance. Scottish local authorities can also give other improvement grants at their discretion to make property more suitable for disabled people.[10]

Security

Most aspects of home security will of course be the same as for younger people – window and door locks, participation in Neighbourhood Watch schemes and so on. You may find that a Care and Repair agency *(see above)* or the police will offer impartial advice on the various types of security devices available and put you in touch with a reputable tradesperson to install them.

One particular crime which targets older people is distraction burglary. A stranger knocks on the door, talks their way in and steals money or other valuables. Sometimes such villains claim to come from a public utility such as a water company, or even from the police. While the resident is out of the room, they rifle through drawers for wallets, purses and bank books.

Simple steps can be taken to improve protection. These include:

✓ Look through a spy-hole or window to see who is calling.

✓ Put the door chain on before you open the door. (But don't leave it on permanently, in case of fire or other emergency.)

✓ Open the door fully only when you are satisfied that the caller is who they say they are. A caller from a utility company ought to be able to quote your account number. If in doubt, ask them to return later when you have a neighbour or friend with you. A genuine caller will understand your concerns and give you time to check.

✓ Never allow somebody to step inside without identification. If in doubt, ask for their name and look for the name of their company, for instance on their van. Then go indoors, look up the number of the company in the phone book or on the internet and ask whether it has somebody on its books of that name. Never leave the door open while you phone: shut and lock it while you do so. Better still, arrange for the caller to come back later.

✓ When you make an appointment for someone to call, write down the name of the company and the name of the person who is going to turn up. If a different person appears, phone the company to check they have asked this person to come out to you.

✓ Keep an eye on the caller while they are in the house. Even genuine callers may be tempted to steal, so don't leave money or any other valuables lying around and don't leave the caller alone in a room, for instance while you go to find your purse. Ask them to step outside while you do so.

✓ If a stranger knocks on your door asking to use the phone, even to call the police, ask for details and then, with the door locked, make the call yourself.

✓ If you are suspicious of any caller, phone the police.

Heating

In Chapter 2, I explained that cold can pose a serious health risk to older people and that an ambient temperature which falls below 21°C (or 70°F), day and night, could threaten health. In that chapter I offer suggestions for ways of keeping warm in winter.

There are many steps we can take to improve heating in our homes and also keep a lid on fuel bills. These include:

✓ **Choosing heaters carefully and using them safely and efficiently:** For instance, if buying an electric fire, look at the different types on the market in terms of efficiency – electric bar fires don't heat a room as efficiently as fan heaters. Make sure that rooms which contain gas fires and appliances are ventilated, and never go to sleep with a gas fire left on. Gas fires need to be checked and serviced regularly. Energy companies have to give older people free safety checks on any gas appliance, including water heaters and boilers, under the Priority Service Register *(see below)*.

If you have an open fire, think about putting in an enclosed stove, as this can minimise the heat loss out of the chimney. If you don't use your fire, get the fireplace sealed (leaving a small hole for ventilation), to prevent heat loss up the chimney. The Solid Fuel Association offers advice on buying smokeless-fuel fires and their safe management.

✓ **Maximising the heat in your home** by, for instance, leaving plenty of space around radiators, since more fuel will be used up to heat the room if you place furniture in front of a radiator. Keep your thermostat away from draughts or cold spots, so that heat is not wasted.

A lot of heat can be lost from the back of radiators, but if you hang aluminium foil behind them with the shiny side towards a wall, you can prevent some heat from escaping. This is especially useful on external walls. A small shelf above the radiator helps the warm air to circulate. Add lining to your curtains, even cheap fleece, and keep doors closed.

✓ **Insulating your home** with loft insulation, cavity wall insulation and double-glazing. The main energy companies provide insulation for free for some people, *as explained below.*

✓ **Maintaining your heating equipment, such as boilers, regularly:** You could be paying more for your fuel because your boiler or other parts of the system are not operating efficiently. If you can afford it, replace all or part of your system if it is inefficient. You may be eligible for a free replacement boiler *(see below).*

✓ **Choosing the cheapest method of paying fuel bills:** Direct debit paid monthly is usually cheaper by at least 15 per cent than a quarterly cheque or pre-payment meter. An energy company's internet tariff is usually cheaper than its standard tariff; your bill is emailed rather than posted.

✓ **Choosing the cheapest supplier in your area** and shopping around for special deals and discounts. There are sites on the internet which compare prices and deals offered by various companies.

✓ **Taking advantage of free services for older people from fuel suppliers:** Under a scheme called the Priority Service Register, suppliers must provide anybody over state pension age with free services as a condition of their licence to provide power. These services include:

> ✓ gas appliance and installation safety checks
> ✓ the provision of bills in such formats as large print, Braille or by cassette
> ✓ help to overcome difficulty in using appliances

191

✓ the relocation of a meter which is in a position which makes it difficult to read

✓ a personal password system for gas and electricity staff to use whenever they call, to confirm they are genuine

To join the Priority Service Register, contact your gas or electricity supplier or phone the Energywatch helpline or log on to its website.

Some suppliers offer in addition an electronic cold alarm which makes a noise if the temperature drops below 12° C (54° F). This is very useful in warning people, perhaps while they are asleep, that the room temperature has fallen to a dangerously low level.

✓ **Remembering that gas and electricity companies are not allowed to cut off older people** between 1 October and 31 March for failing to pay their bills, unless they can clearly afford to pay or there are younger people living in the household who could be expected to pay.

✓ **Making sure you are receiving the Winter Fuel Payment,** which offers a sizeable annual sum to everybody of state pension age, rich or poor *(as explained on pages 834–5).*

✓ **Checking that you are receiving the Warm Home Discount from your energy supplier,** if you are entitled to it. The Warm Home Discount is well worth having – it is an annual credit of £140 made by energy supply companies to people who are receiving the means-tested benefit called the Guarantee element of Pension Credit *(see page 854).*

The Department for Work and Pensions passes to the energy supply firms details of people receiving Guarantee Credit, and the companies should then automatically apply the discount to these individuals' bills. If you receive Guarantee Credit and you do not receive the Discount (payments are usually made in winter), approach your energy supplier direct.

The scheme also provides for suppliers to give the Discount to other people who are on low incomes and have a disability or long-term illness; the energy suppliers have their own eligibility criteria. If you think you might fall into that category, approach your supplier.

Only the large energy suppliers (those with more than a quarter of a million customers) are covered by the Warm Home Discount. Smaller suppliers are not obliged to give the Discount, but some do, so check. Bear this in mind if you are proposing to change to a smaller supplier. If you run into difficulties, ask Citizens Advice for help.

✓ **Checking you are receiving a Cold Weather Payment,** if you are entitled to it. This is a payment of £25 per week from the Department for Work and Pensions made during very cold weather to people who are receiving the Guarantee element of Pension Credit or Income Support. The average temperature must be equal to or below zero degrees Celsius for seven consecutive days. If you do not receive the payment and you think you should, contact the Pension Service of the DWP *(see Useful Contacts)*. As with all state benefits, there is provision for appeal against refusal *(as explained on page 869–71)*.

✓ **Seeking advice:** Care and Repair agencies offer advice on energy efficiency in the home *(as explained on page 179)*. Citizens Advice has a consumer service that ranges over a wide range of consumer matters and offers information and advice about the best way of paying gas and electricity bills and cutting costs. The Energy Saving Trust offers advice on energy efficiency and how to generate your own energy. Home Energy Scotland has advice centres and a national helpline *(see below)*. The writer and broadcaster Martin Lewis provides tips on how to save money on heating (as well as in other areas) on his website moneysavingexpert.com.

Help to improve heating

The government has been keen to help people who face 'fuel poverty', that is, people whose heating costs form a high proportion of their income. In the past help was given mainly through government grants but, in many parts of the UK, it now comes predominantly through the main energy companies which are required to contribute as part of the 'Energy Company Obligation' (ECO) placed on them by Parliament.

The ECO applies to all electricity and gas suppliers which have more than a quarter of a million domestic customers and supply more than a specified amount of electricity or gas. They must meet targets for the reduction of home heating costs and carbon emissions. This usually means help to consumers, particularly those worst off, to make their homes more energy efficient. Each of the large energy suppliers has to provide figures and other information on how they have met their obligations to the Office for Gas and Electricity Markets (Ofgem), which can enforce the ECO.

In England, energy companies provide grants to domestic consumers through a part of ECO called Affordable Warmth. These grants help fund the replacement of inefficient central heating boilers with new energy-efficient ones and pay for the insulation of lofts, cavity walls and solid walls where this is needed. Eligibility is restricted to people who own or privately rent their property and are receiving a means-tested benefit, such as the Guarantee or Savings element of Pension Credit or Working Tax Credit (so long as their household income does not exceed about £16,000). If an applicant is receiving one of the means-tested benefits for people lower than pension age they must also be eligible for a premium to that benefit on grounds of disability.

The main energy companies have to offer other assistance on top of Affordable Warmth, as part of the ECO. What is on offer varies, but can be quite a lot. For example, British Gas offers free loft and cavity wall insulation, regardless of income. You may not have to be one of the customers of a particular company to qualify and it is worth shopping around and comparing current offers.

If you are unsure whether you would be eligible for ECO help, contact an energy supply company or the Energy Saving Trust, which gives advice in this area. Another option is to contact any Care and Repair agency, as described above for Wales. If you run into difficulties in getting help, contact your local Citizens Advice or Ombudsman Services, which seeks to resolve disputes between consumers and suppliers in the energy industry. Failing these, contact Ofgem.

Wales

In Wales the scheme for help with heating is called Nest. This funds or part-funds the replacement of boilers, the installation of insulation and air-source heat pumps and draught-proofing. The property must be owner-occupied or privately rented and the applicant must be receiving one of the following benefits to qualify: Pension Credit, Council Tax Reduction (but not the single-person discount), Housing Benefit, Income-based Job Seeker's Allowance, Income-related Employment Support Allowance and Working Tax Credit (if earnings are less than about £16,000). As elsewhere, housing association property in a shared equity scheme is eligible. The Welsh government chips in some money for Nest, but the bulk comes from the energy companies.

To apply for a grant, you could contact Nest *(see Useful Contacts)*. However, the grant application can take some time to complete as Nest will wish to establish the degree to which your home is energy inefficient and thus whether or not to offer you help. It is worth first approaching any Care and Repair agency in your area. Its officials may well help you make the application to Nest. But if you are not eligible, it may offer you other advice and support. Thus if you would be ruled out of Nest on grounds of income, it may help you work out what action is needed to improve your home's energy efficiency and help you find a contractor to carry out the work *(see pages 176–80 for information about Care and Repair or Staying Put agencies)*.

Scotland

The Scottish government provides a wide range of help to home-owners and private sector tenants to improve the insulation and heating of their homes through a scheme called Warmer Homes Scotland. Grants are given to older and disabled people who receive certain benefits, as well as interest-free loans for those without a qualifying benefit. Unlike the situation in England or Wales, in Scotland the non-means-tested Attendance Allowance is a qualifying benefit.

The items for which a grant or loan might be given to someone whose home is considered relatively energy inefficient include wall insulation, loft insulation, draught-proofing, central heating and measures to provide renewable energy. To obtain a grant, you must fall into a category linked to receipt of a benefit.

The qualifying benefits are: Universal Credit (or any of the benefits which it will replace including Working Tax Credit and Housing Benefit), Council Tax Reduction, Disability Living Allowance or the Personal Independence Payment, War Disablement Pension, Industrial Injuries Disabled Benefit and Attendance Allowance.

You may qualify for a grant if you are:

- aged over 75 and receiving one of the benefits listed above
- aged 60 or over, receive one of the benefits above and have no working heating system
- have a disability and receive either DLA or PIP
- are a carer and receive Carer's Allowance
- have been injured or became disabled while serving in the Armed Forces and receive Armed Forces Independence Payment or War Disablement Pension

- have an injury or disability arising from an accident or disease caused by work and receive Industrial Injuries Disablement Benefit

The final criterion on which the awarding of a grant depends is the energy efficiency of the property. If you phone Home Energy Scotland, one of its advisors will go through a home energy check with you, asking about your insulation, heating, type of windows and so on to work out whether the energy efficiency of your home is sufficiently low to qualify.

The energy companies in Scotland also have schemes of their own as part of ECO, but they do not embrace such a wide range of measures as Warmer Homes Scotland. You could contact the companies yourself and ask them what they offer (you do not need to be an existing customer). Or ask Home Energy Scotland to signpost you.

All local authorities in Scotland must have an energy discount scheme (under climate change legislation) which allows householders to claim a one-off discount on their council tax bill when they have made improvements to the energy efficiency of their property. So, if you have made any such improvements, ask your council about this.

Northern Ireland

The Northern Ireland Housing Executive oversees help from government and from energy suppliers to domestic consumers to implement energy-saving measures. There is a range of measures, in addition to Affordable Warmth. Many of these offer help to people who would be ruled out of Affordable Warmth because their income is too high. For instance, a householder aged 70 or over with an income of up to £35,000 may be eligible to receive a fully-funded gas heating system and up to £800 towards cavity wall and/or loft insulation. Some schemes are directed at people living in social housing. To find out whether you would be eligible, contact your local council, the Northern Ireland Housing Executive or a home improvement agency. Or have a look at the Northern Ireland Sustainable Energy Programme, which sets out all the schemes and is available on the website of the Northern Ireland Housing Executive.

Throughout Britain social landlords are required by law to ensure that the property they let meets energy efficiency standards – for instance, that it is insulated and the boiler reaches a set minimum level of efficiency. Many local authorities and housing associations offer their tenants advice about reducing their heating costs and also claiming state benefits.

Heating and park homes

More than 100,000 older people in England and Wales live in park homes or static mobile homes. Residents of park homes should be eligible for much of the help outlined above, such as the Warm Home Discount scheme. But many park homes are very expensive to heat. They often lack adequate insulation, particularly those built before 2005, when a British Standard for Park Homes was brought in; the addition of insulation over the outside walls can be expensive. At the same time, residents may have little choice in their sources of fuel: the remoteness of some parks means they may not be connected to the main gas grid, while residents may not be free to shop around if they are bound by a fuel supply agreement with the owner of the site.

Insulation therefore remains a major problem for many. In 2015, Age UK was urging government to help older park home owners by giving them special grants for insulation.[11]

Safety

Falls can cause serious problems in later life *(as we see in Chapter 18)*. There are countless straightforward ways in which we can reduce the risk of a fall at home.

Obstacles

Go round your home and look out for anything over which you might trip or on which you might slide. Trip hazards could include items of furniture such as cupboard doors which are left permanently open or do not close properly, cables and wires running over the floor, flooring or carpets in need of repair, rugs with curled-up corners, low side-tables and general clutter. So:

✓ Check that stair-carpets are secure

✓ Move low items of furniture out of the way to clear broad paths along which you can move freely

✓ Remove any unnecessary rugs, especially those at the top or bottom of stairs

✓ Tape any cords or wires to the floor or tuck them away

✓ Work out where equipment to increase safety should be installed, such as grab rails. They cost little to buy and fix to the wall; social services will often pay for or subsidise installation. Care and Repair agencies often install these *(as explained on page 177).* Grab rails provide much firmer and safer support than tables, radiators or the bathroom basin.

Lighting

Older people need three or four times as much light as 20-year-olds to see as easily *(see page 13).* So make sure lights are especially bright in parts of the house where you are at greatest risk of tripping, such as the landing and staircase. Switch on the lights at night whenever you visit the bathroom (and take a portable alarm).

If your eyesight is poor, mark out the edges of stairs and steps with white or yellow strips. If you are making major changes, such as refitting the kitchen, consider buying kitchen units and working surfaces with highlighted edges, *(as explained in the section on kitchen design for people with vision impairment on page 462).*

Levels

Both bending and stretching can lead to falls. Try to reduce the need to do either by thinking creatively. For example, could you:

✓ hook a basket behind the letterbox, so you don't have to pick up your post from the floor?

✓ get an electrician to move power points, or at least those in most use, to waist level?

✓ reorganise furniture so that you don't have to reach across it to draw the curtains? Might a curtain pull-cord be safer?

✓ put in long-lead fittings to make changing light bulbs easier?

✓ place items you use frequently on the lower shelves of wall cupboards or on work surfaces?

Behaviour

In addition to addressing physical obstacles and hazards, we can adapt our behaviour to reduce the risk of a fall. Here are a few tips if you have difficulty in moving or are unsteady on your feet:

✓ Reduce the need to keep going up and down stairs by performing all your tasks upstairs before coming down in the morning, and have duplicates of items you often need on each floor. Carry small items you often use in a bag slung across your front.

✓ Go up and down stairs sideways, so you can hold on to the banister with both hands for extra support.

✓ Use high furniture, as it is easier to get in and out of. Armchairs should have a firm seat. When getting out of a chair, don't pull on anything in front of you – it may tip over (this includes a Zimmer frame). Instead, slide to the front of the chair and use the arm-rests to push yourself up. Lean forwards and use your leg muscles to straighten your knees.

✓ Consider buying an electric bath seat *(see page 464)*. Not only can these help if you have difficulty in getting in and out of the bath, but they also reduce the risk of falling by removing the need to lower or pull yourself up: you sit on the seat and let that lower or raise you.

✓ Avoid the temptation to stand on stools or chairs. A fall from even a small height can fracture a bone. If you must stand on something, non-slip steps with safety features should be used. Avoid looking up for long periods if giddiness is a problem.

✓ Place a cushion in a plastic bag on the seat before getting into a car; this should enable you to slide in more easily, particularly if you go in bottom first (while minding your head) and then swing your legs in. Remove the bag when the car drives off, lest you should slip down. Or buy a swivel cushion from a disability shop. Special swivel seats can be installed in cars *(see page 698)*.

✓ Buy a high bed or a deep mattress to reduce the height by which you need to lower and raise yourself. Make sure there are no long bedspreads, electric wires or other bedside clutter on which you might trip.

✓ Don't get up too quickly from your bed, whether in the morning or during the night to go to the lavatory, as your blood pressure may not adjust quickly enough from the lying position and this may make you feel dizzy. Rise slowly and carefully, and if you do feel dizzy, take a few deep breaths and wait until the dizziness disappears. Tense your muscles to get them working. As you get up, make sure the bed is behind you, so if you lose your balance, you will fall onto it. If you wear spectacles, always put them on, even if you are walking only a short distance from your bed.

Gardens

An unruly jungle where faultless lawns and weedless flower beds once spread can cause dismay by providing an ever-present reminder of decline in physical abilities. Some people reluctantly give up their house because they can no longer manage the garden. What can be done?

You could think about hiring help. If you have trouble finding a gardener, contact a local organisation such as Age UK or Care and Repair, which may keep a list of reputable gardeners or even have its own volunteer gardeners. Some Scottish local authorities offer basic garden maintenance services (mainly grass cutting and hedge trimming) for older residents.

Find out whether a garden-share scheme exists in your area. In several places including Edinburgh, Wandsworth, Sheffield, Stratford-upon-Avon, Totnes and Brighton, voluntary organisations have set up Garden Partner schemes. These seek to match people who are too frail or too busy to manage their plots with others who wish to grow their own food, but lack the land to do so. Schemes usually screen potential gardeners with security checks and character references (although it is worth checking that they have done so). The garden owner can remain as much in control as they wish, but clearly the more requirements they stipulate, the smaller the chance of a match. No rent is involved. Ask your local Age UK, Care and Repair agency or any Transition town local group whether a garden share scheme exists in your area.

If you enter into a garden share agreement independently, check that your house insurance would cover you if the gardener were to have an accident, and try to obtain security checks or at least character references on the gardener and anybody else they wish to bring onto your land, if you do not know them well.

A wide range of gadgets have been developed to make gardening easier for people who have difficulty in kneeling and bending *(see pages 464–5)*. Tools that make bending unnecessary include trowels with long handles and a device which will sow rows of seeds through a drill. The Carry on Gardening website and Arthritis Research UK in its free booklet *Gardening and Arthritis* offer advice and ideas. The Disabled Living Foundation also provides much information online, in particular through its question-and-answer facility AskSARA. Responses to questions you type in relate not only to useful gadgets, such as the just-mentioned long-handled tools for weeding the garden, but also tips on how to make gardening safer – for instance, how to prevent garden paths becoming slippery. Ask your GP or physiotherapist for advice about posture while gardening: they might recommend kneeling on thick cushions and bending forwards with your head down, rather than squatting and craning your neck.

Finally, there are plenty of ways in which a garden can be refashioned so that it requires less work, or at least less work at ground level. These include:

- replacing annuals with perennials which will not need planting each year, such as daffodils, tulips, valerian and cranesbills

- introducing plants which require little maintenance and crowd out weeds, such as heather

- introducing plants for which any management can be done without bending, such as roses. Perhaps you could fence off one area with a trellis and give it over to roses, while paving another area in which you place tubs and hanging baskets (not too high).

- installing tubs and raised beds to enable a gardener to sit while working, perhaps from a wheelchair

- replacing grass lawns with lawns which do not need mowing and also perhaps have a fragrant smell, such as thyme or chamomile

Why not adjust your own thinking about what a garden should look like? A switch from frequently-trimmed lawns from which any non-grass species have been banished to ones in which different grasses are encouraged to seed and wild flowers to invade would fit in with the fashion for wildlife gardening and be likely to attract more birds and butterflies. You and your visitors might come to find the results more attractive and more interesting.

Staying put

* Care and Repair agencies provide much useful advice.

* National governments offer many home adaptations free of charge.

* Disabled facilities grants are available to fund expensive home adaptations.

* A stairlift enables you to use more than one floor of your home if you cannot do stairs.

* Try out a stairlift in a display centre before you buy or rent.

* Distraction burglars can be very cunning.

* Apply for grants to improve heating efficiency.

* If you receive Guarantee Credit, make sure you get a discount on your fuel bills.

* There are many ways of reducing back-breaking work in the garden.

* Citizens Advice gives a wealth of guidance on consumer rights.

PART THREE
CONNECTIONS

“ *How could I not be happy with that lovely, wee, cheery face? I depend on you. You make me happy.* ”

Remark to a befriending scheme volunteer

PART THREE
CONNECTIONS

Man, unlike the solitary wolf or the companionable ant, is both a loner and a herd animal. While we are fit and well and enjoy a reasonable income, we may feel able to choose whether we shut ourselves away or party every night. However, if growing older curtails our mobility, kindred spirits die and perhaps our health and wealth suffer, choice about how we interact with our fellow human beings can seem to diminish. Indeed, we may feel faced with two options, both ghastly: a hermit-like existence perhaps stretching to 20 or 30 years, or reluctant participation in group activities jollied along by an excruciating organiser. How can we find the sort of contact we actually want?

In this section I examine some of the myriad sorts of relationships with other people in which we may engage in later life and also some of the difficulties that we may face in sustaining and initiating relationships with family, friends and lovers.

When we are getting on, we can find ourselves single for one of several different reasons. Our partner may die. We may find that our partner wishes to end the relationship. Or we may go down that route ourselves. Some divorced, separated or bereaved people will not wish to embark on a new quest for love and will swell the numbers of those who have long been single. Some will avoid a new relationship; others will actively look for closeness. Some will find it unsought. How do you master the dating game when you are in your sixties – or nineties? How does later life change the process of establishing a new relationship?

Our relationships with members of our own families and friends face new challenges too. How do we negotiate family relationships when we are older? How should we respond to our children's requests to care for our grandchildren? Freed of the demands of work and family (at least, to some extent), how can we engineer the kind of friendships, family contact, connections with groups of like-minded spirits and romantic relationships we really desire?

The reality is that today many older people live solitary lives. While many delight in living alone and venturing forth to seek out contact with others only when they wish, other people feel lonely some or most of the time. Surveys show that those most likely to experience loneliness include people with a disability or long-term illness who live alone and also un-paid family carers. How can these people find new friends? How can they find people who will visit them in their own homes?

For many people who get out and about, group activities from Men in Sheds to volunteering to amateur dramatics yield new friends. They also offer the singular experience of being part of a group of kindred spirits.

But how do you venture forth into a new social world or communicate effectively with your loved ones if you have one of the many difficulties in communicating with other people that can arise in later life? I examine how some of the barriers that can arise from vision loss, hearing loss, Parkinson's disease and dementia can be tackled.

Computers, tablets and the internet are sometimes perceived as a bar-rier cutting off older people from the modern world. In fact, as I try to show, they provide a unique means of enriching our contact with the wider world. They also offer valuable means of reducing obstacles to communication for people with hearing and sight problems.

A pet can help us socialise and keep fit, as well as providing company. I also examine the pros and cons of pet-keeping in later life.

So, Part Three explores the following areas:

▶ romance

▶ family

▶ friendship

▶ overcoming loneliness

▶ clubs and societies

▶ day centres

▶ faith groups

▶ the internet

▶ listening and talking to people with disabilities

▶ animal companions

Chapter 9
Relationships

Our most important relationships tend to be with family members, close friends and romantic partners. How do these ties change when we reach later life? How can they be strengthened? In this chapter I examine:

▶ finding new love

▶ romance

▶ family relationships

▶ loneliness

▶ finding new friends

▶ befriending schemes

▶ getting people to come to you

▶ telephone contact

Romance

Graham Greene wrote of 'the indifference of old age' in his autobiographical work *A Sort of Life*.[1] But the poet Elizabeth Garrett reminds us to be alert to the possibility of new romantic excitement in her poem 'Love in Midlife':

> Trust in your sudden thought –
> Like finding the buried pulse
> Still quick at your quiet wrist.[2]

Differences towards attitudes to romance in later life also arise from our circumstances. People who have been bereaved may find their experience of closeness and intimacy with one person makes contemplating a committed relationship with somebody else very difficult. But other people whose partner has died will actively look for new love. So too will some of the large numbers of older people who get divorced. While the total number of divorced people in England and Wales has been falling steadily since the mid-1990s, the number of people aged 60 and over who are getting divorced has been rising.[3] Then there are the many single people who would like to find love in later life, whether they have had many partners or none at all.

If you are looking for love, should you go on a world cruise to find it or might a new Mr or Ms Right be living round the corner? If so, how do you engineer a meeting? And if you find someone who will form a significant part of your life, how do you handle the reaction of other people, such as your children? In this chapter, I first discuss finding love and then consider some of the issues that settling down with a new partner in later life can bring.

Finding romance

One thing that will have changed since your teenage fumblings is that systematic searching for love has lost its stigma. Introduction agencies, personal ads and internet dating are now routine in a world where traditional social networks have broken down and time is scarce. Increasingly, both old and young are happy to announce that they met their partner in this way.

Online dating

There are many opportunities to look for love through the internet. You could find a dating website, fill in your details, add a photograph and wait for a response, while approaching others on the site to whom you think you may be drawn.

Choose the site you use carefully. Some, such as Tinder, offer easy registration and almost instant access to many possible contacts. Apart from casual sex, this can encourage short-term liaisons and shopping around – with so many possible matches people may endlessly seek someone better. If you are looking for a serious partner and possible matrimony, look for a service that takes a lot of trouble to match people. With eHarmony, for instance, you need to answer up to 40 pages of questions before you are offered any matches. On the other hand, if you have specific requirements, a niche site might suit you better, for country dwellers, people of Indian origin, professional people or Christians, for example.

If you are planning to use an all-age internet site, think about the age-range of your competitors. Older women may well be passed over in favour of younger women. If they do go ahead on an all-age site, they may find it worth having their photograph taken by a professional photographer. But it may be better to use one of the several online dating services that have been created specifically for older people.

Internet dating can work well and it is an inexpensive way to find people you may wish to meet. However, as with any facility through which you try to make many romantic contacts, it is important to bear in mind that many – even most – of them may be completely unsuitable. Yet you will have the time and trouble of contacting people, sometimes meeting them and sometimes coping with the emotional anguish when you discover that they do not wish to see you again.

Then there is scamming to consider. While teenagers are targeted by criminals on online sites for sex, scammers seek out older people mainly for their money. So beware online romance scams both on dating sites and, increasingly, through unsolicited email. A criminal (typically part of an international criminal group) sets up a phoney identity using stolen photographs and pretends to develop a romantic relationship with somebody they have selected online. They flatter their victim and get help from others such as members of their organised crime circle to convince the victim that the person with whom they are in contact is real – faking a profile to seduce their victim. After escalating the emotional content of the relationship, the main perpetrator pretends to be in urgent need of money and asks for help.

More than a quarter of a million people in Britain may have been conned by romance fraudsters, according to Professor Monica Whitty and Dr Tom Buchanan of Leicester University. The financial losses of the victims have ranged between £50 to £800,000. Victims receive a double-hit from this crime – the loss of the money, but also the loss of a relationship with someone whom they have never met but nonetheless may have fallen deeply in love. Many of the victims Whitty and Buchanan interviewed found it difficult to let go of the relationship, even though they knew they had been scammed; this made them vulnerable to a second wave of scamming.[4]

The classified columns

Personal classifieds (once known as 'lonely hearts columns') are a more familiar world to many older people. You select a newspaper or magazine which reflects your social background, outlook, interests and sexual orientation and place an ad. Often this does not cost much, even in prestigious publications. It may be free, and you pay only to collect responses. If you are especially keen to find somebody who likes, say, sailing or bird-watching, you could advertise in sailing or bird-watching magazines. You can of course add whatever additional information you choose, such as the area in which you live and your sexual preference.

However, as with online dating – and most publications now also exist online – you have to rely on your own ability to screen out people who are time-wasters and potentially dangerous, or simply not Mr or Ms Right. Many of the people who place or respond to personal ads and online dating may not be scammers, but are nonetheless not truthful. Yet, meeting them out of their usual environment, you rely on them alone for information about themselves. Some may be looking to marry for money, not love. Others may be looking for a carer, as they have an illness which they do not disclose. Some may be married and simply desire an affair – although they may pretend otherwise.

If you wish to understate the sexuality of the first encounter, go for a day-time meeting.

Whenever you meet, consider your safety. Both women and men should always arrange to meet a date arising from an advert or an online contact in a public place and tell a friend beforehand where they are going to be. Women in particular can feel pushed into situations such as allowing a man to pick them up from home on the first date, but it is important that they should not reveal their home address or telephone number (even a mobile one) during the first few meetings. Use the facility on many lines of withholding your number by dialling 141 first.

If you and your date are ready to exchange phone numbers, perhaps after two or three meetings, and he or she is reluctant to do so, become suspicious: why should taking calls at home cause difficulty?

On the other hand, if you are corresponding with someone online and they do not wish to meet you within the first month, you should also become suspicious. They may have created a fake identity to set you up for a scam. Or they may not really be available.

Introduction agencies

Introduction agencies take a pro-active role in bringing people together. Some compile a database of men and women looking for romance (whether with the opposite or the same sex) and try to match them up, either using computers alone or complemented by human sifting. Then they send their clients lists of possible matches and leave them to take things further.

If you go down this road, try to find an agency specialising in older people, otherwise you may find the number of people of your age and tastes and in your area on the agency's books very small. It is crucially important to know how many people are available to be matched with you before you sign up. Some introduction agencies offer new clients a special deal: lifetime membership. Reject this: it offers no financial incentive for the agency to find you any matches and certainly not quickly.

The Association of British Introduction Agencies can provide a list of its member agencies and advise you on which might be best for you. Member agencies have agreed to comply with the Association's code of practice and it is worth getting hold of this to see what good agencies should do and whether or not an agency you are considering is a member of the ABIA. However, this code of practice is not legally enforceable.

Another type of introduction agency, the search agency, relies on head-hunting. It interviews new clients at length, then proactively searches for matches for them on an individual basis by placing adverts on their behalf in suitable newspapers and magazines – golf, caravanning, antiques-collecting or whatever. The people who reply will not of course be known to the agency, so it vets them, interviewing them face to face, sometimes for hours, to find out about their background, life history and interests, checking documents such as passport and divorce certificates and telephoning them unannounced at home. If all seems well, the agency draws up a profile and recommends a meeting to its client. The whole process can take months and the cost run into thousands of pounds; it is well worth comparing the prices of different agencies if you are going down this route. Also, check how thoroughly they carry out the vetting.

As introduction agencies have to pay a higher charge to place personal adverts in magazines than individuals seeking matches themselves, you can save yourself a lot of money by penning your own personal classified ad. But you need to be confident that you can sift out inappropriate responses.

Meeting informally

Those wary of organised approaches can of course still look for love through events and activities in their local community. In that way they are able to meet people in context and find out about them in ways other than relying, at least initially, on what they choose to reveal about themselves. Drama groups, dances, tennis, bowls and computer classes all present possibilities.

If you are considering this approach and you have a special interest, such as steam trains, so much the better. What's more, if you don't find instant romance in an interest group or community activity, you may well make new friends. Friendships and romantic relationships both seem to thrive on joint projects and shared experiences.

Clubs which bring together people not only with shared interests but also similar levels of wealth and attitudes to life, such as local Rotary or Probus groups, political parties, sports clubs and business people's organisations, can also be means of finding a new partner. If you are a professional person or in the world of business, enjoy attending meetings and events and are of a philanthropic bent but avoid religious and political groups, your local Rotary may be an ideal venue for meeting somebody with whom you would be compatible on many different levels. *(I also discuss clubs and societies in the following chapter, on page 227–30.)*

In society as a whole, more than 60 per cent of all relationships start at work. For many older people, this could be voluntary work. Involvement in voluntary work can open up a wide range of opportunities to mix with others while also contributing to a cause you hold dear. Such social interaction could lead to friendship and/or romance. *(I discuss volunteering on pages 238–9.)*

Potential complications

Nobody should take on looking for love lightly, particularly if they have not dated or had a partner for a long time. It is easy to forget how much time and emotional energy romance can take up and that falling in love can be a state of being which utterly consumes us, defies control and often goes awry.

Denise Knowles, the magazine and radio agony aunt and a counsellor with Relate, told me: 'We sometimes tend to think that as people get older they're less vulnerable and less likely to feel hurt. Actually, I find the opposite is true.'[5]

Recovering from bereavement

In later life, people may face particular difficulties if they are considering embarking on a new relationship. Those recently bereaved may be desperately searching for love after coping with the long illness and death of a partner. Yet they need to accept that no other person is likely to fill that void. Also, their lives may for years have revolved around hospital or care home visits, and in the process of caring and supporting, they may have lost any sense of their own identity outside their role as carer.

Jane Pendlebury, a counsellor based in the West Midlands, believes that to be ready to embark on a serious new relationship after a bereavement we need to recognise what we could give as well as what we might receive. She told me:

> You need to be happy with yourself. If there is a void in your life,
> it won't be man- or anybody-shaped. It's self-shaped, and no other

person can fill it. You need to know yourself and be happy with yourself before you can give. And to know what you are giving.

Discussing your feelings about your bereavement with a professional may help *(see pages 382–3)*, especially if, for one reason, or another you face complex issues and feel unable to talk to family and friends about them. For example, perhaps the person whose death you are grieving was your long-term lover but the relationship was secret, as he or she was married. Or perhaps the relationship was same-sex and you have never come out. In each case, you may have felt marginalised at the funeral, if your position was acknowledged at all. Now, perhaps you feel unable to talk about your sadness as you believe the relationship should continue to remain secret. Or perhaps you fear rejection by other people should you try to share with them your feelings of sadness and recollections of happy times with your deceased partner. Psychologists call this 'disenfranchised grief', in other words, 'The grief that persons experience when they incur a loss that is not or cannot be openly acknowledged, publicly mourned or social supported'.[6]

Sex

Sex can be a real obstacle to relationships in later life for many reasons. You may not have slept with anyone new for decades and fear you would not know the form these encounters now take; you may be concerned about the appearance of your body, perhaps after surgery; while any loss of sexual function can undermine self-confidence. Therapy and counselling on these matters can be extremely beneficial. Relate may be able to help from one of its local centres. The British Association of Counsellors and Psychotherapists provides lists of therapists qualified to help in this field.

A visit to your GP may also help *(as explained on page 463)*. Viagra is well known as a drug which can help men overcome loss of sexual ability, but women can be helped by medical prescriptions too. For example, many women experience loss of lubrication in the vagina after the menopause, as a consequence of the reduction in the female hormone oestrogen in their bodies. Many probably assume that nothing can be done to help – we so often assume that many of the physical aspects of ageing are not only inevitable but also untreatable. In fact, however, low doses of oestrogen, delivered locally through creams or by small tablets, can be very effective in relieving dryness and soreness.[7]

Next steps

Two questions arise for those contemplating embarking on a love affair in later life: would such an attachment be preferable to close friendship? And should it lead to cohabitation?

Romance can of course be enormously rewarding, not least for the company and physical intimacy it offers. However, people often have deeply held and sometimes conflicting ideas about why one should look for love. When Professor Kate Davidson of the University of Surrey conducted in-depth interviews with older widows and widowers about entering new partnerships, she discovered that, broadly speaking, while the widows were looking for a man to go out with, the widowers were searching for somebody to come home to.[8]

Participants in a romantic relationship may also have widely differing views about the form such a relationship should take and may conclude that it has failed if it does not follow their expected pattern. Contrast this with friendship: when you embark on a new friendship, you are starting from scratch. You have greater freedom to create its shape or simply allow it to develop. If you fall out, the ramifications can be upsetting, but they are unlikely to involve having to find a new home or dispose of assets as with a couple who have been cohabiting.

However, there is no need to let stereotypical ideas of the form relationships should take dictate our lifestyle. In later life, we should feel freer to customise all our alliances. This can be important, because as we grow older, the differences between us increase. A lifetime's attitudes to how we behave in our own homes can make entering into cohabitation quite difficult, no matter how deep our affection may be. If you always take your shoes off when you step inside your house, and expect others to do so, or if you leave the kitchen spotless after every meal, how do you live with somebody to whom such behaviour is foreign?

These differences can of course be negotiated, but it is not always easy, particularly for people who are used to taking charge of all aspects of their life and unused to renouncing some control.

Living apart together

One way in which older couples try to circumvent problems such as these is through entering into 'LAT' relationships: living apart together. They meet often, go away together, stay over in each other's homes, but maintain separate households and their financial independence. This has obvious appeal to people who have felt weighed down with domestic commitments in a previous relationship. Sometimes the initial impetus for entering into what becomes an LAT relationship is loneliness. As one

80-year-old interviewee put it, 'I know many elderly people who start an LAT relationship simply for the sake of companionship. ... Weekends are awful for people who live alone.'[9]

Living apart together enables people to carry on pursuing interests in their own way and avoid conflicts about the time and manner in which they get up, have their meals and so on. LAT relationships also neatly side-step potential difficulties with grown-up children – perhaps disapproval of the relationship and concern over inheritance, since each member of the couple can retain equity in his or her own property. While some lesbian, gay and bisexual people opt for living apart together to retain their freedom and independence, others may do so to hide the nature of the relationship; it has been estimated that LAT arrangements are three times more common amongst LGBT people.[10]

LAT relationships can involve very deep bonds, as a recent study of more than 100 older people in LAT relationships in Sweden revealed. Without ties involving possessions or household activities, the relationships focused on the giving and receiving of emotional support.[11]

However, LAT relationships require participants to be mobile, wealthy and with accommodation large enough to maintain a household which can accommodate someone else when required to. People living in retirement or sheltered housing could find their accommodation too small.

The apparent attractions of the set-up may blind people to its downsides. For example, health or social care officials may take little notice of a LAT partner when dealing with someone who has had a major stroke (unless they have been appointed as an attorney or been given consultee status – *see page 782*). People might find LAT partners less ready than cohabitees to stand by them if they become ill. A relationship with an LAT partner might prove less useful than a network of trusted friends.

Impact on the family

Should you find love in later life, you may have to bear in mind its impact on your adult children. Some people like to see a new man or woman in their parent's life, not just because they are pleased to see their parent happier but also because the new partner may relieve them of the burden of support. Others, however, put as many spanners in the works as they can – because they dislike the idea of their parent being intimate with someone other than their own parent, or perhaps because they fear that they will lose their inheritance or because they are simply jealous.

On marriage, the husband or wife inherits the spouse's assets automatically if they die intestate. However, it is perfectly possible to draw up a will in favour of your children. Often people embarking on marriage in later life bequeath their house or flat to their grown-up children on condition that their spouse can continue to live in it until death. A wills lawyer can provide advice tailored to individual needs.

More intractable and agonising problems may arise when two older people fall in love but one has a partner who is living in a care home and has dementia. Their relationship status may hang in a sort of limbo for years. The husband or wife may no longer even be recognised by their spouse. To whom do they turn for emotional support? If they feel attracted to somebody else, they may feel guilty.

In such circumstances, Denise Knowles recommends accepting the relationship between husband and wife as it has become and at the same time recognising each partner's physical and emotional needs.[12]

Bruce Covill has been able to do this successfully. He left work to care for his wife, Jan, when she developed dementia. When her condition deteriorated after a fall and she moved into a care home, he was devastated. He planned his own suicide, but did not go through with it because of the duty of care he felt towards his wife. By chance he met Nina, the widow of an old friend, and she asked him whether he would like to take a holiday with her, as a companion. Their relationship developed into a romantic one and this has given Bruce much happiness, but it has also given him the emotional strength to provide better support to Jan. Nina's grandchildren's desire to engage with Jan through play have opened up new ways of visiting her.[13]

Family

Family circumstances are one of the key factors that differentiate the lives we lead when we are getting on. Some people in their sixties have no parents still living and no children. Others have elderly parents as well as children and grandchildren. Indeed, the increased acceptability of divorce and remarriage mean that some older couples, perhaps in their second or third long-term relationships, may have many step-grandchildren as well as six or more people whom they think of in some sense as 'Mum' or 'Dad'.

Plainly, the relationships we develop with members of our families can enrich our lives. But family circumstances can get in the way of developing an enriching social life. When we retire, it is easy to find ourselves taking on many family responsibilities simply because the main excuse hitherto – going out to work – has disappeared. As a result, we may stop paid work or go part-time only to find ourselves continuing to work just as hard, albeit for no pay, as the carer of elderly relatives or grandchildren, or both – and with the freedom that we had imagined retirement delivering somehow snatched away and remaining a distant dream.

Alison Johnson ran a seminar entitled 'Retirement: Promised Land or Barren Wilderness?' three months before she retired from paid work as a writer and consultant in 2009.[14] Mrs Johnson gave examples from her own experience of grandparents whose lives revolved around the care of grandchildren. Some were committed to collecting them from school every day, giving them a meal and looking after them until late evening; others to weekly long-distance commutes to stay over for several days as their grandchildren's carer. She asked: 'Is it selfish to refuse: "I've done childcare already"?'

In other words, although grandchildren can be a powerful force for good in their grandparents' lives, engaging them in a wide range of activities and the interests, tastes and expectations of a new generation, they can also burden their grandparents with chores and responsibilities which can leave them exhausted. Taking on the care of grandchildren can be one of the choices in retirement which we do not make consciously, but by going with the flow. We can live to regret not recognising and addressing these decisions at the time.

There are no easy answers, particularly for people faced with demands for childcare, perhaps to support families in the wake of divorce or those who are struggling with alcohol and drug issues. But we owe it to ourselves to think how we wish to spend our remaining years, work out priorities and, if necessary, learn to say no.

If you are considering looking after grandchildren, try to be realistic about how much care you are prepared to provide, bearing in mind that looking after young children can be exhausting. The discussion forum of the website Gransnet publishes views and tips on such care. As one of its contributors observed in 2015, 'When I first started looking after my grandson, I had forgotten about the unrelentingness of it all. Love them to bits but as the cliché goes, parents are young for a reason!'

Try to establish before you start:

✓ the days and hours (and make sure everyone sticks to them)

✓ whether you will be expected to provide more care during school or nursery holidays

✓ if you provide food or nappies, whether and, if so, when you will be reimbursed

✓ what the parents expect you to do with their offspring

✓ whether there any aspects of child-rearing on which you may disagree

✓ whether you will be reimbursed for expenses incurred in taking the children out, such as public transport or petrol costs, entrance charges, the cost of ice-creams and so on

✓ whether you will be paid for looking after the children: perhaps a proportion of the fee a child-minder would command?

✓ whether there are any other expenses for which you would like to be reimbursed, such as heating and laundry costs

A choice which faces couples entering retirement is whether they should create for themselves a joint life, in which all social engagement is in the company of each other, or whether they should develop different social networks, as well as those in which they appear as a couple. This is another choice that may not be made deliberately and which happens by default. But if you do everything together, the one who survives is likely to feel that much more at sea. Perhaps consider developing parallel, or slightly different, lifestyles as well as doing some things together?

Friendship

When we retire we may face similar choices with existing friends as with our own families. While retirement from paid work brings an opportunity to spend a lot of time with friends, it also removes perhaps the main reason for not seeing them. Do you spend every afternoon with your friends? Do you wear yourself out visiting a succession of friends in different parts of the country?

That is – if you have them. Many people find themselves without many friends as they grow older, particularly when they retire. During our working life our friends and acquaintances are often people we know at work. This means that when we leave paid employment, retirement can bring a gaping void. Almost overnight, we can find ourselves socially isolated, especially if we live alone. It is therefore a good idea to begin to develop a social network outside work before you retire.

Finding new friends

Many older people lose touch with existing friends, work-related or not, and wish to find new ones in later life. How to go about doing this? One way is through group activity – in other words, pursuing interests we enjoy in a group setting. These can of course be interesting and fulfilling in themselves. New friendships – or romance, as noted above *(see page 212)* – can be a bonus.

Older people who are fit and mobile can of course find kindred spirits in the myriad of ways open to anybody, young or old, such as shared interest clubs and societies, paid work and volunteering. Learning something new is a good way of making new friends – and a new skill does not have to be advanced computing. Some classes in particular lend themselves to striking up new friendships – dancing, singing, painting, many crafts or learning cookery or a foreign language. *(I explore group activities at greater length in the next chapter.)*

If disability hampers participation in an activity, there may be an organisation to help. For instance, Conquest Art is a voluntary body which trains volunteers to run classes to help people (young and old) with physical disabilities to express themselves through art. Each participant chooses whichever art medium and style they would like. Key features of Conquest Art's ethos are encouragement and friendship.[15]

Combating loneliness

Sometimes new friends can be hard to find when you are older. Bereavement may have taken its toll and connections may have been severed through divorce, separation or migration to another part of the country. Factors such as these can lead to isolation and loneliness, which is common in people over 65 *(as we saw on page 81)*, but is particularly prevalent in people over the age of 80.[16] People with sight or hearing problems or in poor health are also more likely than others to feel lonely.[17] So what can you do if you feel lonely?

You could advertise for friends. Friendship columns are springing up in newspapers and the internet also offers possibilities. The psychologist Dr John Cockburn, who interviewed 200 people who had used personal lonely-heart advertisements for his book *Lonely Hearts: Love among the Small Ads,* reported:

> One older widow I spoke to explained how she expanded her friendship group by placing ads for friends in the personal columns of her local newspaper. Now she is seldom lonely and this whole group of elderly people meets together regularly throughout the week, bringing companionship to each together. Many older people could do the same and transform the loneliness of the later years. Romance might even blossom – who knows?[18]

Getting people to come to you

Keeping in touch with others is perhaps most difficult for people who cannot get out and about easily and may even be housebound, whether living in their own home or that of a relative or in a care home. Yet for many older people, face-to-face contact with others is valued more than anything else. When 200 people aged 90 and over were interviewed about their various leisure pursuits, the most popular was talking and chatting – more so than watching TV, reading, doing crafts or listening to music or the radio. Exchanging news, views and advice provided not only interest and pleasure but also a sense of self-worth. As one of the interviewees reflected, 'I feel I am here for some good.'[19]

Visitors may also exchange views and impressions and expand our own horizons as they offer a fresh angle on things and propose new interests. Furthermore, the anticipation of a visit, the preparation and the tidying up afterwards keep us more active and help give shape to our lives. But how do you bring the world to your door and even form rewarding friendships if you cannot get outside to mix with other people?

Befriending schemes

Countless informal befriending schemes have existed for a long time, run by faith groups and voluntary healthcare groups, for instance *(pages 236–7 and 326–7)*. Here is an example of a more formal and an extremely valuable initiative. Bear in mind its features if you are looking for a scheme; details of local schemes should be available at your public library.

The Broomhouse Elderly Befriending Scheme, based in a small community centre in a suburb of tightly-packed housing in western Edinburgh, is the kind of operation that can offer a real lifeline. Twenty volunteer befrienders pay weekly visits to twenty older people, lasting between one and two hours, and at the same time and day each week to ensure continuity. The scheme has been in place since 1997, and when I visited it in 2015 discussions were under way to extend it. What follows is a description of the service at the time of my visit; since then the scheme has changed slightly in various ways. It now covers a larger area of Edinburgh and is called Vintage Vibes.

Weekly contact may involve chatting, usually over a cup of tea, playing a game or watching a quiz together on television. Some befrienders take their companions out to the shops, the park or the country, after the scheme's manager has conducted a risk assessment. The service is free to clients; volunteers' expenses are covered.

Volunteers hail from all walks of life and are of all ages. The majority are working, so visits often take place in the evenings. Clients are in their 80s and 90s. Many live alone and would rarely see people were it not for their visitor. One befriender explained: "I recently asked my client what she gets out of the experience. Her response was: 'I love it. How could I not be happy with that lovely, wee, cheery face? I depend on you. You make me happy'. ... She tells me how happy she is we met. ... I don't like the word client, as to me she is a dear friend."

The Broomhouse scheme is meticulous about recruitment, not just to screen out volunteers with evil intent but also to ensure that befrienders possess suitable qualities. First, an applicant visits Phyllis McFarlane, the Project Manager, for a chat, then they fill in an application form and two references are taken up, as well as a check with Disclosure Scotland *(see page 507)*. If all seems fine, the volunteer is given two, two-hour sessions of training, after which Mrs McFarlane decides who to match with whom. She accompanies the volunteer on their first visit and, after introductions, leaves client and visitor for ten or fifteen minutes, returning to see how they get along. If all is well, the two embark on a trial period of one month of visits. Each is free to step away after that, but if not, visiting continues.

The training visitors receive before they first meet a client covers the role of the befriender and includes such tips as trying to engage in as much eye-to-eye contact as possible; sitting by the good ear of someone who is deaf; planning the visit so if refreshments are offered this is done early on; and ten minutes at least before departure, the visitor should start paving the way for their farewell. Just over half the clients have some degree of dementia and training includes an explanation of the nature of dementia and suggestions for communicating with someone with the condition. Training on lone-working is important too: visits often take place in the evening, in bad weather and on an estate in which houses and flats look similar and in which the atmosphere can be threatening. Mrs McFarlane points out from the start that the relationship may end in loss – through death or through the deterioration of someone with dementia who is no longer able to benefit.

Once a befriending situation is established, other types of training are offered to volunteers. These include first-aid (with an annual refresher), and moving and handling. Although visitors are not expected to help clients with practical tasks, they may occasionally need to be able to help them sit down and should know what action to take should their client have a fall.

After a month has passed, Mrs McFarlane reviews a new befriending situation and thereafter every three months, seeking the views of client and volunteer. Telephone contact with the organiser is always available if either the client or visitor needs help or advice within the befriending situation. Should a client die unexpectedly, Mrs McFarlane contacts the visitor and asks them to drop by and see her rather than go on their planned visit. Then she sits down and talks to them about what has happened. She always attends the funeral with the visitor, if they would like.

Visiting plainly benefits clients who live alone, cannot get out and would otherwise be isolated. Some, especially those with dementia, might not settle easily into a day centre and a befriending service may be the only help they are willing to accept. Befriending also helps any family carers: 'It's the carer's time to go and do something. It's amazing what you can do in an hour. We've had carers who just want to go into their bedroom and read for a whole hour, which they can't do, especially if they are caring for somebody with dementia, because you're constantly on the go', Mrs McFarlane explained.

Older people befriended through a scheme in Buckinghamshire similar to that at Broomhouse said they were pleased with the results. They said they, 'Particularly valued the individualised and stimulating conversations which they believed to be rare in group activities for older people. The service was also supportive at specific times, as following the death of a spouse or close friend, or during recovering from an illness.' Relationships often developed beyond the service remit, involving outings, shopping and the provision of care.[20]

I found the Broomhouse befriending scheme through Befriending Networks, a voluntary organisation based in Edinburgh, which has drawn up a list of befriending schemes throughout the UK, with details of any particular types of people the schemes seek to help, such as carers and people from ethnic minority groups. It has drawn up a code of practice for befriending schemes and evaluates them by reference to this code. The Broomhouse scheme came out with flying colours but not all will, so it is worth checking that key features of the Broomhouse scheme operate in any scheme you may use, such as security checks on volunteers and training for them. Keen to encourage the development of more befriending schemes which reach out to people with dementia, Befriending Networks has published a pack putting forward advice for people who wish to befriend people with dementia.[21]

Contact outings

People who find it hard to get out of their homes can easily miss out on the pleasure of going out with others on outings. A voluntary organisation called Contact the Elderly has been combining the offer of friendship with a monthly outing since its formation in 1965.

A typical Contact group consists of volunteer drivers, helpers and hostesses. It takes out eight to ten people in four or five cars on an outing one Sunday afternoon each month. The outing may consist simply of going to the home of one of the Contact hosts and enjoying tea and company. Or there may also be a trip to the country or seaside.

The criterion for being befriended by a Contact group is that you have to be 75 years old or over, living on your own and without much social support. Because the same passengers and drivers are involved at each outing, people get to know each other.

There are nearly 400 local Contact groups across Britain. You can refer yourself, or perhaps your GP or day centre manager could pass on your name.

Library services

The arrival of somebody on your doorstep to change your library books and DVDs can bring a welcome connection with the outside world if you cannot get out and about. Many public libraries proactively help housebound people by organising volunteers to borrow books and audio items on their behalf. Volunteers are given a special ticket so that they don't have to use their own library card. Many councils offer special help to people with significant sight impairment, permitting them to take out audio material and DVDs for free. Most DVDs come with subtitles for people who are hard of hearing.

Paid company

Hiring help in the home, whether somebody to help with housework, cooking or gardening or even personal care such as bathing, can bring regular, informal yet invaluable contact with other people. Care assistants are often portrayed as uncaring people who rush around providing minimum assistance and rarely exchanging a word with those they are helping. In fact, they can become real friends, and their visits are often anticipated with pleasure. Even hiring a gardener often involves chatting over coffee as part of the arrangement.

In the past wealthy older people might be accompanied by a companion, who would provide company and perhaps friendship as well as help. While this remains possible for the well-heeled, for others paying somebody simply to visit can bring much benefit.

For example, when my mother had dementia and was living in an NHS long-stay facility, my brother and I hired somebody to visit her for two hours every day during the week, when we found it harder to visit. Initially we found visitors through a care agency; later, we hired a visitor direct ourselves so that we could select her and so that my mother could develop a long-term bond with her. In the early days, the visitor would take my mother for walks in Ramsgate in her wheelchair or they would chat together *(see also page 260)*. Later, when my mother's dementia had worsened and she was also nearly blind, the visitor would sit beside my mother, hold her hand, chat to her and respond imaginatively to her often unintelligible speech. A tangible warmth grew up between them.

The lonely carer

In 2016 NHS Highland surveyed its older citizens to find out how many often felt lonely and why. They found some risk factors to be those explored in chapter 4, such as living alone and the presence of a disability or long-term illness. But the team also discovered that acting as a carer (in this case providing ten or more hours of unpaid care a week) was also often associated with feelings of loneliness.[22]

It is easy to see why. Carers are often confined to the house with limited freedom to get out and socialise. They are likely to be spending a great deal of time with the person for whom they are caring. But that contact may not give them joy: perhaps the person involved is a partner whose company they once cherished but who has now been changed by a physical or a mental illness *(as for instance in the case example on pages 108–11)*.

Some possible solutions will not be available in a remote rural area like the Highlands. But for carers in general, the presence of other people nearby, such as neighbours, family members, perhaps residents in a retirement housing scheme may help. Computers and the internet offer the opportunity of joining chat-rooms and discussions and playing games with other people all over the world from your own living room, at any hour *(see pages 241–3)*. The phone can be also be a lifeline, particularly if a friendly voice can be called up at times when the carer feels most desperately in need of contact, as with The Silver Line.

Telephone contact

The Silver Line is a national phone befriending scheme for older people founded by the television personality Esther Rantzen; its chief executive, Sophie Andrews, used to serve as national chair of the Samaritans. Anyone over the age of 55 – including, of course, carers – can phone the line, which is based in Blackpool and manned by paid staff and volunteers, for a one-off conversation at any time of the day or night. Or they may have preplanned, regular contact over the phone with a particular volunteer, called their Silver Line Friend. Although the provision of friendly contact is the main aim, callers can also obtain information about services local to them, such as lunch clubs. Five per cent of the calls taken involve reports of abuse and neglect.

These services complement national and local phone befriending schemes, such as Independent Age's national service, as well as local schemes often operating in remote areas where travelling takes a long time. For instance, Age UK Norfolk runs a befriending scheme which focuses on weekly phone calls. Sometimes regular visiting operates in tandem with telephone contact. Thus the Salvation Army's community centre in inner-city Portsmouth provides both phone and visiting befriending services to 200 isolated older people (of any or no religious belief). Many local faith groups operate informal phone befriending schemes, to complement face-to-face contact.

Phone befriending clearly has the potential to reach many more socially isolated people than one-to-one visiting. What's more, if like The Silver Line it runs at weekends, during the evening and even at night, it offers immediate help at the time a need arises. On the other hand, one-to-one visiting enables a completely different sort of relationship to develop. This can be especially important for people with dementia who may find phone contact with a stranger difficult to engage with, particularly if their powers of verbal expression diminish.

But no doubt the most widespread telephone befriending involves families keeping in touch with older relatives through regular phone calls. It is hard to under-estimate the importance of keeping in touch in this way, particularly with people who have lost their partner. When a partner dies, the ability to put things into perspective can be lost. It can be a great comfort to look forward to the sound of a ringing phone, heralding the moment when the worries of the day can be chewed over with somebody else.

Relationships

* Systematic searching for romance has lost its stigma.

* Online dating sites are cheap and often effective, but require care.

* Meet in a public place at first and tell a friend where you are going.

* A new partner is unlikely to heal the pain of bereavement – counselling and therapy may be more useful.

* Friendships and relationships thrive on shared interests: join a club or take up a hobby.

* Take charge of your time: don't get pressured into unwelcome tasks.

* A retired couple can lead parallel lives to avoid swamping one another.

* To find new friends, advertise, look online, join a befriending scheme or get in touch with Contact groups.

* Don't forget the library – it can help housebound people.

* Paid assistants or a hired gardener can provide valuable companionship.

Chapter 10

Group activities

We saw in the previous chapter that clubs and societies can offer a valuable means of finding new friends. However, for many people, the group experience, whether pursuing an interest or perhaps engaging in voluntary work, is invaluable in itself. Groups have a life of their own, quite separate and distinct from the life involved in a relationship between two or a small number of people. A group provides company in which people can pursue their interests or simply socialise. They may not feel they could claim members of the group as friends, but they nonetheless mix with them in a companionable way and connect to the group as a whole.

Groups can also offer their own unique sense of support in times of trouble. A regular attender for more than 20 years at an annual jazz festival told me that although he had no contact with attenders between festivals, while at them he enjoyed a sense of friendly camaraderie with about 100 others. This proved invaluable one summer when he was trying to cope with the recent death of his son.

One of the pluses of moving into later life today is the wealth of clubs and societies that offer a diverse range of opportunities for engaging in activities with like-minded souls, young or old, from singing to restoring steam engines, amateur dramatics to playing badminton. Furthermore, social change means that an older woman is likely to have fewer inhibitions about going out solo to join, say, a metal-detecting club or a dancing group than she would have had 30 years ago. A visit to your local public library or browse of the internet is likely to throw up all manner of clubs and societies offering regular activities. If you move to a new area, joining one of the long-established societies can be a quick way of finding new friends, but also a social life within a group. Within the National Federation of Women's Institutes, for instance, are many local institutes (nearly 140 in Worcestershire alone), so if one does not suit, you could try another not far away.

Alongside societies for all age groups, such as the women's institutes, is a growing number specifically for older people. The Ulysses Club, for example, formed in Australia in 1983, provides rides and stop-overs for motorcyclists over the age of 55. Branches have sprung up in many countries, including the UK. Members can join in local meetings but also enjoy hospitality on foreign trips from members overseas.

In addition, a galaxy of organisations offers opportunities for older people simply to get together with other people of a similar age. Some of these offer mainly talks and social activities, others volunteering and campaigning, and some both. In many areas, you will find a range of active retirement clubs, pensioners' groups and clubs for retired people from particular trades and professions.

All these types of group tend to have been formed by older people themselves. If you cannot find one that suits you, why not consider forming a group, whether you devise it completely de novo or use an existing template? For example, a growing number of people, mainly men, are setting up local clubs called men's sheds in which they get together to engage in activities such as carpentry, furniture renovation, repairing bicycles, upholstery and gardening. Participants share skills and enjoy working and chatting together. A UK Men's Sheds Association was formed in 2013 to swap ideas and support people who might be considering setting up their own shed.

Two other types of group which also depend on the energy and ideas of their members but which are sometimes misunderstood are the University of the Third Age (U3A) and older people's forums. A type of provision which may be ruled out by people unaware of just what it offers is the day centre and, to a lesser extent, older people's drop-in centres. In this chapter I explain what the following groups can offer:

▶ the University of the Third Age

▶ older people's forums

▶ day centres

▶ drop-in centres

▶ faith groups

▶ organisations that welcome volunteers

University of the Third Age

Some people imagine that the University of the Third Age (U3A) attracts only serious-minded people with daunting qualifications getting together to follow university courses or engage in esoteric debate. Not so. Much stimulating intellectual activity does take place in the 1,000 U3A local groups scattered over the UK, but essentially the U3A allows older people to enjoy interests with others of a similar bent, making use of any special expertise members are prepared to offer. No entry qualifications are necessary and learning is pursued not for paper qualifications but sheer enjoyment.

Each local group usually meets monthly to listen to a speaker, enjoy refreshments and find out what is on offer for the coming month. Alongside this, interaction occurs within interest groups. Some of these involve subjects for study with members getting together to learn. New groups are always encouraged: all that it takes is three or four people who share expertise and enthusiasm.

CASE STUDY

The South Durham U3A has 180 members living in the Darlington and Cockerton areas of County Durham. Its interest groups explore local history, art appreciation, photography, current affairs, reading, music for pleasure, gardening, canasta, bridge for beginners, poetry appreciation, creative writing, boules, play reading, theatre and mah jong. In addition, there is a lunch group, dinner group and occasional coach outings. South Durham U3A has two walking groups: hill walking and intermediate (covering four to five miles), while 'Discoverers' meets to explore a particular site that is, as far as possible, accessible for people who use mobility aids. Six other U3As exist nearby, including a thriving Darlington U3A; sometimes they all meet for joint events, such as quizzes.

Each local U3A group in the country is autonomous and runs its own affairs, so there is considerable variation in terms of activities and interest groups. Some U3As have large numbers of interest groups – Bromley has 44, Malvern 98 and York U3A (with 1600 members) 134 interest groups. The Third Age Trust, the majority of whose members are elected by local U3As, supports and represents them at national level.

In addition to activities organised by local groups, national U3A study events and field visits are held, as well as regional events, which may include discussions about matters of general interest, such as education policy. All these can offer opportunities for finding out about new areas of interest but also for keeping in touch with one's professional life, for although U3A members are no longer in full-time employment, many relish the chance of chatting to people who have shared a similar working background.

Perhaps you often stay with friends or relatives in another part of the country and would like to meet like-minded people of your own age there? The U3A membership subscription is low, so why not join a group in that area too? Or you could probably visit once or twice using your membership card from another area.

Older people's forums

Older people's forums offer social contact through meetings and outings, but much of their activity involves campaigning for improvements for older people in the locality in which they have sprung up. It is difficult to paint a picture of an entirely typical older people's forum: the key characteristics are localness, independence and democracy. They are rather adventurous organisations, developing in whichever direction their membership takes them.

North Tyneside Older People's Forum is a case in point. When I interviewed its vice-chair, Dr Joyce Lesson, in 2011, the Forum had 400 individual members and many local affiliated organisations in Tynemouth, Shiremoor and Whitley Bay in Northumberland. It was organising some social events, such as coach outings, visits and talks, but the focus was on campaigning.

The Forum had responded to a consultation by the local authority on personal budgets in social care, but had itself lobbied to be consulted on other areas of council activity; indeed, it pressed for the creation and later updating of the North Tyneside Older People's Strategy. It had campaigned for the introduction of more seating on the streets, better bus shelters and the installation of outdoor exercise equipment for older people in parks. The Forum's efforts to improve the local environment were not based solely on its desire to create a safe and congenial place for older people to move around: members who actively campaigned in this area were also firmly committed to the need for green policies, so they had also sought to change council policy on sustainable development and climate change.

The North Tyneside Forum sets its own campaigning agenda. So when members were concerned about the proposed withdrawal of the cheque facility by banks in 2009, it wrote letters and lobbied local MPs without needing to feel it was acting within the campaigning framework of a larger organisation.

Broadly similar local groups may go by other names, such as the Newcastle Elders Council, Wirral Older People's Parliament, the Fife Elderly Forum and the Medway Pensioners Forum. Some areas have several older people's forums. Belfast has six local forums; representatives of each meet together monthly on the Greater Belfast Seniors Forum, which exchanges information about events and facilities, and represents the views of older people at city level. It was involved in the drawing up of the plan for Belfast as an age-friendly city *(page 683)* and has helped implement the plan through developing intergenerational projects and surveying the accessibility of streets, parks and buildings for older and disabled people. The Scottish Seniors Alliance is the umbrella body for forums north of the border. Older people's forums are different from local Age UK groups. The latter tend to provide services, *as we see on page 803,* and while they may campaign for change tend to do so within a framework agreed by the national organisation.

Many older people's forums are affiliated to the National Pensioners Convention (NPC), which campaigns at national level, mainly about pensions and other benefits, housing and social care. Its annual Pensioners' Parliament brings together older people's forums, NPC local groups, other organisations, and individuals. If you are keen to debate issues of special interest to older people, why not join in? Or perhaps take part in the debating opportunities provided by the Northern Ireland Pensioners Parliament or the Scottish Older People's Assembly?

Day centres and local hubs

Day centres offer the opportunity for older people to meet together regularly for conversation and refreshments. They can also provide a vital means of alleviating loneliness and isolation. As one user of the Claremont Project, a centre for older people in Islington, north London, remarked, 'Loneliness ends when I walk through the doors at Claremont.'[1]

Yet many older people shun day centres. Those who manage to overcome any initial aversion will discover they can offer a place not only to engage with other people but also to learn new skills and engage in a range of activities, as well as enjoy a midday meal.

Day centres for older people are usually open to anybody over the age of 60, wealthy or of modest means, able-bodied or less so. They vary a great deal in their ambience and activities, although most tend to be geared to people in their seventies and older rather than late fifties and sixties.

Day centres are not part of any national system and there are no hard and fast rules. Some are run by local authorities, others (now probably the majority) by a wide range of voluntary organisations. They should respond to what attenders would like to see – a pool table, links with the local U3A, outings to the races, or whatever.

In England in particular, charges at day centres have risen considerably since about 2010. However, you may be able to get your local council to partly or wholly fund your attendance at a centre, if you can show them that this is necessary to meet your needs for practical and emotional care and support *(more details in Chapter 26)*. You could argue that attendance would be an effective means of reducing the likelihood of your need for care and support such as practical help in your home developing or increasing in the future; local councils are supposed to pay special attention to preventative measures in this area *(see page 604)*.

Farncombe Day Centre in the little town of Farncombe near Godalming in Surrey shows what a typical centre offers. It celebrated its 25th anniversary in 2013 and is run by an independent charity, Age Concern Farncombe. Every weekday morning about 40 people arrive at the centre, which is housed in a light, airy, refurbished former Victorian school. Many are picked up from their homes and travel in the centre's own minibus, with a volunteer helper as well as the driver. After sitting and chatting over hot drinks and snacks, followed by playing games, they eat lunch – a two-course meal, cooked each day on the premises, with baked potatoes, salads, omelettes and sandwiches as alternatives. After lunch, some people make their way to a lounge, where there are magazines, large-print books, games and a computer, on which staff will provide any help needed to use the internet or email. In another lounge, people sit and chat. Or they may walk in the very pleasant gardens, with flowers, plenty of seats and wide paths which easily accommodate walking aids. Many then enjoy such activities as listening to musical entertainers, playing bingo, whist or other games, taking part in quizzes, crafts and exercises, and greeting a Pets as Therapy or PAT dog *(see page 283)*.

A bathing assistant helps some attenders on a rota basis, using a bathroom in a sheltered housing scheme next door. Nurses, opticians, chiropodists, hearing specialists, a beauty therapist, hair-dresser and a mobile clothes shop make visits. The centre tries to make full use of its minibus, so offers trips to local places of attractions as well as the seaside and local supermarkets, while on some summer Sunday afternoons the bus ferries people to concerts at the bandstand in the town's main park.

Staff at the centre can help with filling in forms and making appointments to see health professionals, but there are too few staff to help attenders move around or use the lavatory, so they must be able to look after themselves.

My impression was that people appreciated first and foremost the company and fun the centre provided and the hot, nourishing meals. The convenience of getting a bath or seeing a chiropodist or hairdresser in a place to which you were going anyway also went down very well.[2]

Older men in particular may shun day centres without perhaps realising how much they might enhance their lives. Professor Kate Davidson of the University of Surrey at Guildford carried out a study of the social and emotional well-being of older men which found that older men who live alone tend to be much more socially isolated than their female counterparts.[3] Should an older man lose his partner, he may find coping more difficult than would a woman in the same situation, since older men do not tend to gain emotional support from their male friends, unlike women, whose friendships with members of the same sex tend to involve much more emotional closeness. Professor Davidson's interviewees felt day centres attracted a stigma and perceived them as providing a service to 'much older' people (even though many of them were in their eighties). Yet a hot meal every weekday can be a godsend.

Some centres are geared to specific disabilities or conditions. At some of these, the building is designed to make it user-friendly for, say, blind or severely disabled people, and activities are geared towards these groups, although attenders will probably need to be able to move around the premises under their own steam and use facilities such as the lavatory unaided. In contrast, at day-care centres, staff and/or volunteers can usually provide one-to-one help, including with personal care.

Some care homes provide day care for people living outside *(as described at Warrington Belong on page 159, for example)*. Some day-care facilities specialise in people with particular conditions, such as dementia.

These can be a godsend, not only for the person with the condition but also by providing time off for any carer.

Some day centres, day-care centres and lunch clubs specialise in provision for particular cultural groups. For instance, Jewish Care provides a wide range of facilities for the Jewish community in London and the South East, from disability services, homecare and talking books to respite care and meetings for Holocaust survivors.

Here is a day centre provided with the needs of Sikh people in particular in mind, although older people from all cultural backgrounds are welcome.

The Guru Nanak Day Centre in Gravesend, Kent, welcomes 80 elderly men and women, who attend on two, three or five days each week. They selected the colours for the entrance hall – rich golds, ochres and earthy browns, rather than British institutional cream or magnolia. The walls display paintings in rich pinks and turquoise made by attenders and reflecting the lives they have left in the Punjab.

The men occupy the first floor of the centre, where they often watch television and play cards and snooker. The women meet together on the ground floor. They told me they would not laugh and talk freely were the men present.

The Centre's own minibus brings in people from within a two-mile radius. In the mornings the women take part in seated exercises, music or craft activities; after lunch they may listen to people reading, perhaps do some knitting or watch Indian programmes on television and enjoy tea and refreshments. Much of the activity is spontaneously generated by the women themselves – if a relative has got married or a child has been born, the mother or grandmother involved will throw a little party, with singing and dancing. On Wednesdays all this gives way to prayers, hymns and readings from holy books. Once a week, staff take attenders to the nearby gurdwara, pushing those in wheelchairs. There are occasional trips to the seaside or shops.

Language continues to cut off many people from ethnic minority backgrounds. Many of the women at this centre spoke hardly any English, although they had lived in Britain for decades. But it was not only the ability to converse and the familiar colours and furnishings that attracted them to this centre: 'We think alike too', one told me.

Unlike most day centres, where personal care is not provided, staff at this centre will help people as necessary. They are bilingual, and helping to organise appointments and referrals is an invaluable facility provided by the manager, Ravinder Atwal. The seminars she organises are even more valuable than they would be to a white audience since many attenders do not watch British television or read British newspapers, so have little idea of what the state could provide. Seminar topics range from pensions (with a check by pension officials that people are receiving the amounts to which they are entitled) to continence and dementia. It can come as welcome news that equipment is available to help with disability and that it is possible to get help in the home with personal care and other practical tasks.[4]

The best way of finding out what day or day-care centres are available and what might be suitable for you is through directories of local organisations produced by local councils or available in public libraries or held by local Age UK organisations. Some centres take people who apply to them direct; others, or often the same ones, take people referred by social services. If you find a centre which looks promising, show an interest early, as there may be a waiting list.

Drop-in centres

Drop-in centres for older people are more informal than day centres. You simply turn up and partake of whichever activities take your fancy. Local Age UKs run some centres, as does the Royal Voluntary Service (RVS). The latter's centre in Chatham, Kent, for instance, is open six days a week for those who would like to drop in, chat to other people and enjoy drinks or a hot lunch. It offers art classes, computer courses, and reading, creative writing and knit-and-natter groups. For a small fee, you can obtain beauty treatments and one-to-one instruction on how to Skype or use a mobile phone or a digital camera. Citizens Advice provides advice sessions within the centre.

Faith groups

Faith groups run a vast array of social activities, often without any overt religious dimension. In other words, these are available to anybody, regardless of their beliefs. You may find drop-in coffee-and-cake mornings, help with learning computer skills, meetings with a talk and refreshments (these may start with a hymn and a prayer), lunch clubs, barn dances and many other activities. Faith groups may also offer one-to-one help to individuals in various ways, again without the recipient necessarily subscribing to the beliefs of the group in question.

Those who participate more fully in the life of a faith group should find a second family and another 'home'. Apart from our blood families, faith groups provide one of the few other structures which bring together people of all ages and backgrounds. For some older people, meeting children and perhaps becoming involved in their activities can bring great joy, particularly if they have no grandchildren of their own living nearby. Others may value the opportunity to talk to others across the generations and engage in voluntary activity with people from different backgrounds and of different ages – faith groups offer people the opportunity to go on contributing, working and giving. The range of possibilities is wide and could include helping at fundraising and other social events, attending committees and discussion groups, taking part in dramatic productions, singing in choirs, organising outings, welcoming people to services, helping with children's activities and participating in study groups.

Care and kindness – outreach to all

The provision of friendship and help in time of need to anybody are key aims in most faith groups.

One field which can be of particular value when we are getting on is support during a stay in hospital. Older people make up more than 60 per cent of the hospital population. Visiting patients in hospital is part of the staple of many faith groups' pastoral activities. Visitors can provide not only company, interest and support but also help with the day-to-day challenges of a hospital stay, from obtaining hearing-aid batteries to bringing in favourite food, battling with the card system to secure access to a television or to connect to the internet and wheeling the patient down to the coffee bar *(as discussed in Chapter 38)*.

Faith groups may manage to provide lifts not only for patients but also for their visitors, particularly if they are frail themselves. This is worth bearing in mind at a time when hospitals are being concentrated onto fewer and fewer sites and hospital visiting frequently involves long and complicated journeys.

Care and kindness to others are usually provided in Christian churches by teams of lay members of the congregation, who may be allocated individuals to whom they offer friendship and help, but not spiritual support, which is usually the role of the minister. Most frequently, the provision of care and kindness involves friendship, visits and the guarantee that if people need help, there is somebody to whom they can turn. Naturally, some faith groups will be more energetic and/or better organised in this area of support than others. There are no national standards to which they are expected to conform, as in the case of state support.

Some faith groups also offer help to people with particular needs. Some specialise to a considerable extent, for instance offering a range of meetings for people with learning difficulties. A growing number are waking up to the special needs of people with dementia. Some churches in the Leeds area, for example, have set up 'friendship clubs' one morning a week for the carers of people with dementia. Copying the format of the mother-and-toddler group, volunteers provide coffee and cake; they can look after the people with dementia while their carers chat or interact together.[5]

CASE STUDY

St Stephen's church in Chatham, Kent realised it wished to do more for people with dementia when someone with the condition attended services in 2004 and church members were unsure how best to help him. They invited local professionals and other churches and voluntary groups to a day conference; from this came a ten-week course about the nature of dementia, how best to relate to people with the condition and how to support them spiritually. St Stephen's then set up a support group and invited a group of younger adults with dementia to tend the church garden. They organised another conference, which attracted 150 participants.

The next step was to increase space in the church premises for community activities especially for people with dementia, and £64,000 was raised over one weekend to do this. As soon as building was finished, the church began to invite various groups – people with the illness and their carers and professionals such as Admiral nurses – to use the premises. It organised more courses, not least for carers. When I last visited in 2016, the church was playing host to meetings of people with dementia and their carers as well as a self-help anxiety and depression group, meetings of the local branch of the Parkinson's Society, and osteoporosis and fibromyalgia groups. In addition, the church was running two afternoon friendship clubs for older people involving talks, trips and socialising, one on a local housing estate, the other in the church premises. Individual church members were regularly visiting people living in care homes in Chatham, often making use of their expertise in relating to people with dementia. They were also visiting housebound people in their own homes.

None of this is of course exclusive to Christian churches. Sikh gurdwaras, for instance, attract young and old as volunteers, and the strong ethos of hospitality in Sikh culture means that gurdwaras offer hot food free of charge to anybody who steps through the door. If you are not a Sikh but respect Sikh practices, you are likely to be welcomed. Muslim, Hindu and Jewish mosques, temples and synagogues act as a focus for people of all ages in their local communities and often offer special support to older people. Some mosques run social clubs for older members and organise visits and outings, perhaps socialising with similar groups elsewhere. Larger synagogues run day clubs and organise outings for older members.

If you are looking for a faith group that will send out a visitor to you or an older relative, ask about its policy on safeguarding – that is, ensuring its volunteers have been cleared to make sure they have never engaged in some misdemeanour that could make them a danger to vulnerable people. A good faith group will get all their volunteers DBS checked as they consider this good practice, even if it is not strictly necessary. But it would be if, say, someone visiting a vulnerable older person later started doing their shopping or driving them to hospital appointments (*as explained on page 507*).

Volunteering

Participating in the activities of a group as a volunteer can offer more satisfaction, interest and sense of doing something worthwhile than anything we achieved during our working lives. It offers more opportunity than paid work to participate on your own terms. You choose how much time you are prepared to give and what you are willing to do. You can make new friends and experience team work.

Ray volunteers on several days each week at Woodchester Mansion, an architecturally interesting, historic country house outside Stroud in Gloucestershire. Retired from a career in computer security, Ray provides IT support that ranges from updating the Mansion's website, keeping the computers working properly to programming new tills in the shop. He also takes visitors on conducted tours and crepuscular expeditions to watch the Mansion's bats. He drives the Mansion's minibus, helps in the tea-room and represents the trust at meetings.

Netta visits elderly people in retirement housing in Rochester, Kent every day. She arrives at 7.30 a.m. (weekends included) and remains until noon, chatting and helping residents to continue to live independently. Unlike a paid homecare worker, she spends as much time as she needs to with each person. In the afternoons, she sorts donated goods and takes some to a charity shop while loading others to be taken in lorries to help needy people in Kosovo. She also finds time to help at her local church, serving refreshments, visiting sick people and giving lifts in her car.

Alan volunteers on two days a week at a charity bookshop in Canterbury, Kent. The work involves opening the shop for business, greeting and helping customers, keeping a record of takings and answering questions about the charity. On another day each week, Alan helps people with physical and mental disabilities to grow vegetables in a community garden in nearby Faversham.

These three people, in their late sixties and early seventies, told me they find their voluntary work extremely satisfying. Alan, for example, enjoys the exercise in working in the garden but also the satisfaction of helping people learn new skills, make friends and take pleasure in being outdoors. He told me, 'I've learned so much from seeing and hearing how fellow members of the garden cope with and often overcome their disabilities. This is the most rewarding aspect of volunteering, for me.'[6]

Age and infirmity present no barrier to many voluntary activities. Alan, living in extra-care housing in Strood, Kent and unable to walk after a medical accident, travels in his wheelchair twice weekly to a local school to help with reading and to teach chess. Ingrid, who lived in sheltered housing in Portsmouth, led a campaign to stop her council from withdrawing night-staff from its high-dependency sheltered housing (see page 132). Later, when housebound, a volunteer from a befriending service would visit Ingrid to chat and bring in her shopping. At the same time, Ingrid was acting as a volunteer phone befriender, offering friendship to other people almost until the day she died in 2015.

The Royal Voluntary Service (RVS) commissioned a survey by academics in 2012 which showed that volunteering in later life improves both the feeling of well-being and the physical health of volunteers. In another study those aged over 60 reported even greater increases in their perceived health and sense of life-satisfaction than their younger counterparts.[7]

Group activities

* Groups can be stimulating.
* Groups can improve your social life.
* Campaigning groups can provide new friends and a sense of usefulness.
* Day centres and lunch clubs can provide company, activities, outings and meals.
* Bereaved men can find day centres beneficial.
* Approach a day centre early: most have waiting lists.
* Some day centres provide special support for ethnic minorities.
* Faith groups provide contact with people of different ages.
* Faith groups usually welcome everyone.
* Volunteering can be rewarding in unexpected ways.

Chapter 11

Computers and the internet

Computers and the internet are often seen as among the primary inventions of modern life which cut off older people, particularly from the young. They should be the opposite, breaking down barriers for online, age, appearance and many disabilities melt away. In this chapter I explain how.

Many older people are highly computer literate – 72 per cent of people aged between 55 and 64 reported using a computer daily or almost every day in 2015.[1] But that still leaves many people for whom computers and the internet are a closed book. I explain the advantages of learning how to use these facilities and where to find help to do so.

More and more of the facilities we use day by day are shifting online. It is still possible to use a bank account or fill in an application for a state benefit without using a computer, but this is becoming harder. Life could become much more difficult for people unfamiliar with computers after 2020 – the year by which the government has said that 'digitalisation by default' should be in place, with central and local government engaging with the public without the use of paper.

Things you can do on the internet
Here, first, are a few of the ways in which the internet can open up new opportunities and interests.

Communication
In the past, grandparents could see grandchildren in Australia only if they journeyed across half the world to see them, or posted photographs, films or videos. Phone calls were expensive. Now, grandparents can talk to grandchildren in real time in front of a camera within their computer for

free. They can not only hold a conversation but also bring in other people (and pets), show items, demonstrate skills, perform dances, whatever.

If you are lonely in the evening and fancy chatting to somebody but cannot think of anybody to call, you can 'talk' to other people in one of many so-called 'chatrooms', typing your thoughts and sending and receiving responses on the screen in front of you. You don't have to give any personal information about yourself; you can go under a nickname, such as Irene23. A chatroom might bring together people exchanging thoughts about a TV programme or hobby or offering mutual support. For instance, Gransnet is a popular website which hosts discussion forums, including one about caring for grandchildren *(see page 217)*. All you need are basic skills in typing and using a computer.

Using Facebook you can create a circle of acquaintances, friends, family and anyone else you like and hear regularly what they are up to while telling them what you are doing. This can be invaluable for giving and receiving support through difficult periods. Twitter enables you to send messages of your own to the outside world and to receive regular messages from people you select, including celebrities.

(I discuss using the internet to find new friends and new romantic relationships on pages 208–9 and 219.)

Having fun

You can also play games using the internet, either with people you know or complete strangers, whom you find through websites or by yourself. A carer who cannot get out of the house in Broadstairs can play chess with a like-minded person in Los Angeles.

You can buy a games console which enables you to play competitive games on your television screen. Other electronic games enable players to fight dragons and hunt criminals. You can play the equivalent of bowls in your living room by swinging your arms as if you were indeed playing the game, with your actions translated into the movement of a ball on the screen. Such games are used in some care homes.

Emailing

Emailing is a fantastic facility. You write a letter which arrives at a destination instantly. You can send it at any time of day and it can be read and replied to at the recipient's convenience. You can send photographs, videos or music recordings with your message. Less deliberate than a written letter, and less intrusive and more formal than the telephone, emailing provides an ideal means of exchanging information and getting to know somebody, perhaps if you are deciding whether you wish to actually meet them.

Although you can exchange written messages with people you know or don't know through 'instant messaging', email gives you time to compose a communication more thoughtfully. You can type slowly, with one finger, and nobody who receives the email is going to know. Nor will anybody know that your handwriting is wobbly. Thus, electronic communication can be a great leveller. What is more, you can communicate with the young through a means familiar to them, so breaking down generational barriers.

Emailing is ideal if you are hard of hearing and find spoken conversation difficult. Say you wish to finalise arrangements to meet a friend. You can give and receive details about times and places without having to worry about whether you have taken down information correctly over the phone.

Instead of writing you can speak if necessary, using a voice recognition dictation programme whether to pen an email or a document that you can print out. You simply speak clearly and slowly and your words are converted into text.

Catching up on old programmes

Many television and radio programmes are available online, sometimes for a week, sometimes for much longer after the time at which they were broadcast, so you can watch or listen to them at your convenience. Programmes from long ago can also be called up. By downloading TV shows, films and radio programmes onto your computer, you can keep them forever.

Experiencing places and live events

For people who cannot easily get and about, to be able to tour a building or landscape through a video or to experience a live event as it is happening can help to alleviate isolation. A variety of buildings are presented on the internet in the form of 'virtual tours', from Buckingham Palace to Dover Castle's secret wartime tunnels. You can participate in a public event on the other side of the world as it is actually happening. Plainly, you will not be able to interact with others in quite the way that you would if you were not viewing what was happening on a screen, but it is misleading to talk about experiencing events online as 'virtual' – they are very real.

Influencing the public realm

If you wished to voice your views about public policy in the last century, you would pen a letter to the editor of a newspaper. Often your letter, competing for spaces with many others, bit the dust. Today, the internet offers countless ways of offering your opinions. Newspapers enable you to respond to articles online, and you can read and comment on the comments that other readers submit. The internet is ideal for running a campaign – you can send round petitions for people to sign, alert them to events, organise meetings, send out information and so on.

Finding information

The internet makes a vast amount of information instantly available. Not just encyclopedias and reference books, but a wealth of other resources is available, often for free. The internet has the edge on traditional printed material in that:

- Information can be constantly and more or less instantly up-dated. Not only can you read about news as it is breaking, you can take advantage of updated versions of countless sources of information without having to wait for, say, new editions of books and encyclopedias to be printed.

- Size is no barrier – an internet website can contain thousands and thousands of pages, but you don't have to carry a weighty tome or make a trip to the library to consult it. Not only a wide range of reference books but also such compilations as records of births, marriages and deaths, for instance, are available on-line too.

- Material closely related to a particular subject is readily available. You want to go to the theatre? The internet offers an easy way of finding out what is showing, reading reviews from many sources and obtaining the phone number of the theatre you choose to visit as well as its location details, whether it offers a bar, cloakroom and so on. Usually you can buy your tickets over the internet too.

- Cross-referencing is effortless. On any webpage, whether a theatre review or an article about growing tomatoes, some words and phrases are highlighted in a different colour: they are called hyperlinks. This means if you click on that word, you are instantly transported to another document relevant to it. So instead of having to leaf through others books or newspapers if you wish to look up something on the same subject, you need only click your mouse or press your touchpad.

- Since there are no costs for printing or distribution online, much information is available there which would never be printed otherwise. Recently, I was keen to discover which birds I would be likely to see if I visited sites in the Greater Manchester area. Through looking up this subject via a search engine, I was instantly presented with a website of which I had never heard: Manchester Birding. On this, bird-watchers had written detailed descriptions of large numbers of sites favoured by birds in Greater Manchester, and added photographs of the sites involved. I printed off about 30 pages and took them with me on my expedition.

- The information available on the internet has revolutionised many areas. Perhaps you wish to move to a part of Britain with which you are unfamiliar. No longer do you need to visit or phone all the estate agents in the area to ask them to send you details of properties they are marketing, since the vast majority subscribe to one or two websites which display all the property for sale or to rent in any particular area – you simply type in the town or district in which you are looking and the size of accommodation you require or its price range. Not only can you see photographs, a description and a floor plan, you can press 'street view', which enables you to pass along the street in question and even around corners. Your church is important to you and you are concerned lest you would not find one to your taste? The majority of churches have websites and many of them offer the facility of listening to past sermons, thus saving much time and expense.

- Information provided by consumers is one category of information rarely found in printed form that abounds on the internet and can be extremely useful. You can read about the experiences of people who have drunk in particular pubs, eaten in restaurants, stayed in hotels or patronised guest-houses.

- Because more and more people are using the internet rather than printed material, official bodies are producing information that is available only online. For instance, in 2011 a website was launched (police.uk) which enables anybody to find out which crimes have been carried out in particular streets recently and which police officers are responsible for those areas.

Seeing how things work

The internet contains plenty of pictures and videos which can be useful in showing what items are like and how they work. Check out the site called YouTube. This is especially useful if the item being demonstrated is unfamiliar, say, a hip protector *(see page 393)*. Little online clips can include instructions, for instance on how to bathe somebody with dementia. Do bear in mind, however, that some of this material, useful as it can be, is in effect advertising.

Reading more easily

Looking at books and pamphlets can be difficult if your eyesight is impaired, but on the internet you can adjust a page from a website or a document you have downloaded or been sent to make reading easier for you, by, for example, increasing the font size. (E-book readers also allow for changing print size.) You may also be able to change the colour of the document (black against yellow is usually most helpful for people with sight impairment).

Another useful facility is the rough translation of documents into other languages. This is yet another way in which the internet can overcome problems that would act as barriers in ordinary life.

Shopping

Shopping online saves much time and energy. On the internet you can easily browse through catalogues and also call up reports evaluating products. A large number of retailers, including supermarkets, offer online shopping, so you can place an order through the internet and your goods will be delivered to your door, although there is usually a charge for this *(see page 42)*.

If shopping for a new outfit alone with your computer seems a bit bleak, why not invite round a few friends, ask them to bring their laptops or tablets and share opinions about what might suit each other over a cup of coffee?

Booking doctors' appointments

A growing number of general practitioners are providing their patients with the option to book appointments and order repeat prescriptions online. This can be a lot easier than using the phone or sending the surgery a repeat prescription form. The procedure is simple.

Help to use a computer

Many opportunities exist for learning how to use a computer and the internet. Local authority adult education classes offer a range of courses as do many local Age UKs. For example, Age UK Leeds offers free and low-cost courses which range from an introduction to computers and sending emails to coping with viruses and using a Smartphone in its Silver Surfers digital inclusion programme. There may be other possibilities in your area, perhaps at a local community centre.

Perhaps you do not want to learn how to use a computer and the internet and would simply like someone to help you go online when you need to. Most computers available for free, public use are to be found in public libraries, so ask library staff what help may be available. For instance, Age UK Faversham in Kent provides a 'computer buddy' whom anyone can request at the local library. Older people's community hubs and day centres often have computers for attenders, with help provided if required. Some retirement housing facilities and care homes offer their residents computer access and help.

Accessibility for people with disabilities

Most computers have facilities to:

- magnify parts of the screen
- change the contrast between background and words
- have text on the screen read out loud
- have the computer recognise your speech and type out what you have said

In addition, various ingenious devices have been invented to overcome specific problems. For example, there are alternatives to a mouse for people with stiff wrists or painful fingers, keyboards designed for single-handed use and, for visually impaired people, screen magnifiers and keyboards with large keys and high colour contrast.

AbilityNet is a leading authority on the accessibility of digital facilities for people with disabilities and its website provides guidance on ways in which you can maximise facilities on a computer to cope with any disability, for instance by making text larger. AbilityNet's helpline answers questions about ways in which computers can be specially adapted for the needs of disabled people. Expert information is also available from the Royal National Institute of the Blind (RNIB), Rica *(see page 459)* and Disabled Living Centres *(page 459)*.

Tablets

If you are unsure about buying a computer, be it a laptop or desktop, a perhaps easier first step into the world of the internet is to buy a tablet. Tablets are simpler to use than computers and also smaller and more portable, though with a much larger screen than on a mobile phone. A tablet is usually cheaper than a laptop.

You may have seen a very young child sitting on a train using a tablet. Tablets work intuitively – you simply touch a point on the screen or swipe it to bring up a new image or new information. So you can easily look through images of photographs you have stored on the device or browse the internet. As with a computer, the tablet is ideal for people with vision impairment – you can alter the size of the font as well as the screen brightness, and you can hold the device as close to your eyes as necessary.

Tablets cannot usually connect to the internet through the cellular network like a mobile phone. You usually need a wifi signal, though these are available in coffee shops, libraries or other public places. Even if you are not connected, you can read and view material you have downloaded already.

You can download onto a tablet hundreds of your favourite TV programmes, films, radio shows and music albums. With a set of headphones, you can then enjoy them wherever you are, without disturbing others or needing a big TV set and video player. This can be a godsend in hospital, say, or on a long journey.

The drawbacks of a tablet compared to a computer may – or may not – matter to you. You will still need a broadband connection to access the internet at home. A computer will probably have more storage space. It is also likely to have more ports through which you can connect other devices such as a microphone and printer.

You can write documents and emails on a tablet – a virtual keyboard pops up on a screen whenever you want to write something and larger, detachable keyboards can be added. However, if you plan to do a lot of typing and altering documents or handling spreadsheets, a computer, with its keyboard and mouse, will probably be easier to use.

Computers and the internet

* The internet is not an obstacle: it can break down barriers.

* It provides information that is constantly updated, infinitely expandable and generally free.

* You can adjust the size of the typeface on screen and often the background colours and the language as well.

* Email and messaging hide some of the deficiencies that ageing brings.

* Take advantage of free computer classes.

* Explore chatrooms featuring your interests.

* Use Skype to make free video phone calls.

* Explore your local area from the comfort of your home.

* Join in a debate on public issues.

* Tablets can be easier devices to start with than laptops or desktops.

Chapter 12

Communication

Several of the most common long-term conditions of later life bring in their wake difficulties in communication. Failing eyesight can become a formidable barrier, removing the surroundings of our everyday world which forms the stuff of so much conversation. Failing hearing brings with it the problem of deciphering what others are saying and endeavouring not to be cut out of conversations. Both can result in people becoming marginalised and their opinions not being sought.

Parkinson's disease, a major stroke and dementia can each create different and potentially serious barriers to communication. People with Parkinson's disease may be unable to speak when and how they would like, or to show the facial expressions they would wish. After a major stroke someone may struggle to find particular words or understand other people, or the muscles that make speech possible may have been damaged.

Dementia can have an impact on communication in a different way again. In the middle to later stages, people often forget some of their vocabulary and so struggle to bring to mind the words with which to convey their thoughts and wishes; later they may lose the whole idea of what is encapsulated in the words that others are using.

In this chapter, I put forward suggestions for reaching out to people struggling to communicate freely, focusing on those whose ability to talk and listen has been affected by vision problems, hearing problems, Parkinson's disease and dementia. *(I examine communication problems arising from a major stroke in Chapter 16: Strokes.)*

Whatever the cause of the difficulty – and there are many other medical reasons why people find talking and listening difficult – perhaps the most important rule of thumb for other people is to put oneself in the place of the person with the difficulty and try to relate to them. The difficulties visually-impaired people face in engaging with social activities can contribute to their becoming socially isolated and lonely. So if a blind person is sitting and waiting alone in a bank or by the supermarket check-out, see if they need any help or would welcome a chat. Or perhaps you see someone sitting alone in a shopping mall or park and looking confused and unhappy. They may have dementia, be waiting for their carer, but worried about where they are and why. Do reach out: you may be able to reassure them. I shall never forget occasions when my mother, partially-sighted and in the early stages of dementia, was cold-shouldered by strangers in a pub or while waiting on a park bench.

Sight impairment

One in five people over the age of 75 have some form of vision impairment that cannot be corrected with spectacles; the figure rises to one in two for people over 90.[1] Many of these people are partially sighted or blind. Unless others take the trouble to explain, they will be unable to understand conversation about what is happening around them. As a result, they can feel cut off from life and from other people.

Conditions such as cataracts, glaucoma and age-related macular degeneration affect sight differently (see page 13). If you know from which eye condition somebody is suffering, you could adjust your behaviour accordingly. For instance, people with age-related macular degeneration (AMD) often have residual sight at the periphery of their field of vision, even if the centre presents itself as an opaque blob.

Adjustment to sight loss which develops in later life brings its own challenges. Those affected have not learned to cope with the help of trained teachers, as do children and young people. People around them may not be as ready as, say, the parent of a young child to adjust their own behaviour and may not compensate for someone's inability to see and respond to things of interest in the world around them by explaining what is out there.

Vision problems can also exacerbate the difficulties posed by other conditions, such as dementia or the aftermath of a major stroke. But for the majority of people who lose their sight in their later years, vision problems can simply make coping with everyday life highly challenging, even with the help of the sort of equipment described in Chapter 21. How do you remember what you have to do if you can no longer see to write and read lists? How do you choose what to wear when you cannot see the contents of your wardrobe? Simply selecting and then donning your clothes can feel like an epic task.

Here are a few tips for communicating with somebody who is blind or nearly so:

- ✓ don't touch them if you might startle them
- ✓ gain their attention by speaking or moving into their range of vision and face them at eye level
- ✓ check that any spectacles are being worn and are clean
- ✓ make sure lighting is evenly distributed and prevent glare and bright reflection
- ✓ be ready to use expansive gestures
- ✓ reinforce your message with visual, auditory and tactile cues
- ✓ use large-print written material with clear contrast and definition *(see page 13)*

If the person is blind, say 'hello' and introduce yourself. Address them by name, if you know it. If you do not, show you are speaking to them by a light touch on the arm. Say that you about to leave before you move away.

If you are guiding somebody who is blind, let them take hold of your arm with their fingers in the crook of your elbow. This way, they will be half a step behind you and should be able to tell more easily when you are turning by the movement of your body.

Announce ahead if there are any obstructions. For instance, if you are approaching a kerb, say so, and whether it is 'kerb up' or 'kerb down'. If you pause at the kerb before stepping down or up, the blind person will feel the change in your body movement through the arm they are holding.

When you are approaching a set of stairs, ensure the blind person is on the handrail side and guide their hand to the rail. Let them ascend one step behind you. They will start to move when they feel your arm move as you place your weight on the first step. When you have reached the last step, tell them, then stop and allow them to find it with their foot. They will know you are both on the level when they feel their arm resume its normal position. When going downstairs, allow the person who is blind plenty of time to feel the edge of each step with their foot, while they hold securely on to the handrail. Again, descend one step ahead, then stop at the bottom and announce that there are no more steps.

If you are going through a door, let somebody who is blind pass on the hinge side. Open the door with the arm with which you have been guiding them, so that they can tell whether the door is moving inwards or outwards.

If the person has a guide dog, walk on the opposite side from the dog.

The RNIB issues useful free factsheets on guiding blind and partially sighted people, which offer advice on such situations as getting through turnstiles, dealing with rows of seats and getting into a taxi.

Hearing impairment

Nearly 40 per cent of people over the age of 75 have significant hearing loss and, *as we saw on page 16,* this frequently results in difficulty in comprehending speech. In many cases, hearing loss can be rectified with a hearing aid – but not always. Even if an aid can help, it is unlikely to result in perfect hearing. At the same time, many people go for years before they seek help. All these groups of people may face a variety of challenges in communicating with other people.

If you cannot hear well, maintaining attention and concentration in a conversation takes much effort. You are trying to follow what is being said, probably relying to some extent on lip-reading. You are having to deal with interruptions, background noise, different accents and softly -spoken people, and you may be mishearing sounds. This on top of tackling all the usual demands of social engagement.

It is easy to fail to appreciate how awkward and embarrassing it can be for a person who is hard of hearing to engage in a conversation. They may have to violate social rules by asking people to repeat themselves or to move and talk to them in a place where background noise (wind, traffic, the radio, piped music) is absent. They may feel a fool if they have been unable to follow a joke; they may feel sad if no longer able to keep up with family banter or to whisper sweet nothings. Some people around them will view a hearing aid, no matter how discrete, as a reminder of their own mortality and choose to avoid seeing one.

Researchers have identified three sorts of communication breakdown between couples in which one member is hearing-impaired. First comes misunderstanding, because the hard of hearing person may not hear properly, answer or give appropriate responses. Second, frequency of interaction declines, as it is stressful and tiring. Third, the content of discussion becomes restricted. People try to make themselves understood only about important, necessary things, and so the interest and companionship arising from engaging in everyday conversation can be lost.[2]

Try to pay heed not only to the physical difficulties someone who is hard of hearing is facing, but also the psychological impact of their hearing loss. Unlike children or younger adults who lose their hearing, people who become deaf in later life have developed personalities and ways of life in which their ability to hear is assumed. Along with the challenge of finding ways of improving their hearing, they may have to deal with feelings of sadness, anger and frustration at their loss, as well as hurt in social situations in which they would once have been at ease.

So as unobtrusively as possible, be ready to enhance the experience of someone whose hearing is impaired by:

- ✓ avoiding or reducing background noise
- ✓ speaking clearly and slightly more slowly than usual
- ✓ ensuring your face is well lit
- ✓ sitting or standing face to face about a yard (a metre) away
- ✓ moving your lips but without distorting your face
- ✓ writing things down if necessary and
- ✓ paraphrasing if you are not being understood

One of the most hurtful reactions when asked to repeat is, 'Never mind: it's not important.'

Dual sensory impairment

For many people the challenge of coping with hearing loss is exacerbated by vision impairment. So someone may have glaucoma and also be hard of hearing. Their sight loss will mean they have difficulty seeing their hearing aids – where they have left them, putting them in and making a note that they must obtain replacement batteries.

As many as 24,000 people in the UK are deaf-blind, which means they have little or no useful sight and little or no useful hearing. The majority are over 60. Many are very old – perhaps having lost most of their eyesight through age-related macular degeneration while already being very hard of hearing. Younger people may learn specialist communication techniques such as Braille and sign language, while some deaf-blind amateur radio operators communicate on two-way radios using Morse code. But it is often very difficult to adapt to the loss of both hearing and sight in later life. Communicating with and supporting someone who has become deaf-blind in old age requires a great deal of imagination, patience and determination.

The voluntary group Sense campaigns for people who are deaf-blind and provides advice, information and support, including specially adapted housing, to help deaf-blind people of all ages, from those who were born with the condition to those who develop it, perhaps gradually, in later life.

If someone has great difficulty in communicating, those around them must not assume they are mentally incapable of making decisions. Mental incapacity *(see Glossary)* results from an impairment of the brain, not the sense organs. Only if someone is mentally incapable of making a decision because of a brain impairment or of expressing their views even through moving an eyelid are others entitled to step in and take decisions on their behalf *as explained on pages 727, 775 and 777.*

Parkinson's disease

Parkinson's disease can affect communication in a variety of different ways. Much as they would like to, someone with Parkinson's may find it impossible to respond to a question until long after it was posed. If they can respond at the time, they may speak very quietly. Their speech may be slurred, lack variation in tone and expression and be hoarse and tremulous. They may have difficulty in starting to speak, but then get faster, with the result that they stammer.

Inability to respond promptly is the result of the 'on-off' nature of Parkinson's – marked fluctuations in ability, which is a result of the condition or of the wearing off of the effects of drugs used to treat it before the next dose is due. As a result, someone's voice may be louder and easier to understand when they are 'on' but much quieter and less intelligible when 'off'.

Parkinson's sufferers often have to contend with muscle rigidity and slowness of movement. This means they may find smiling or frowning difficult, especially spontaneously, so that their face often seems frozen in one expression. In one study, the response of health professionals to people with Parkinson's was compared to their response to people with heart disease. Worryingly, the professionals assumed that those with Parkinson's were more anxious, hostile, suspicious, unhappy, bored and tense and less intelligent.[3]

Parkinson's disease does not in itself cause a reduction in cognitive ability or memory, although some people with Parkinson's also develop dementia. So people with Parkinson's do of course understand the world around them and whether people around them are ignoring or patronising them, just like anybody else.

There may be yet more difficulties. People with Parkinson's may have restricted ability to gesture with their hands, head and neck, through nodding for example. Conversely, they may be unable to control shaking or turning of their head. So a person with Parkinson's may seem to be responding to somebody in a way which seems inappropriate and can easily be misconstrued.

In a social situation, people with Parkinson's sometimes find difficulty in following a wide-ranging conversation and interjecting as appropriate. They can also have difficulty comprehending subtle nuances such as irony, sarcasm and shorthand speech – 'Tea?' Just as with people with hearing impairment, those around people with Parkinson's may stop communicating about anything but the bare essentials of life – visiting the lavatory, going to bed and so on.

Patience is key to supporting people with Parkinson's. They need time to talk and extra time to respond. So don't insist that they pronounce each word perfectly and don't interrupt when they are trying to say something. Give them time to speak and resist the temptation to jump in and answer for them or complete their sentences.

As with other conditions which make communication difficult, it is frustrating and demeaning if somebody pretends to understand when they have not. If you don't understand, ask for a repetition of what has been said, but more loudly or in another way. Listen carefully. Give the conversation your full attention, maintain eye-to-eye contact and above all don't shout and don't walk away while being spoken to. Inspire confidence by holding a hand if that seems appropriate. When you speak, talk normally, but use short sentences and stress key words, making sure that you can be seen and heard.

Do bear in mind that some of the behaviour I have suggested is inappropriate in some non-western cultures, such as holding somebody's hand or eye-to-eye contact (where lack of such contact is a mark of respect).

Dementia

Generally speaking, dementia involves a progressive loss in the ability of the brain to think logically, plan, remember, carry out practical tasks and, in the later stages, speak intelligibly *(as explained on page 26)*. These features of the illness can make communication more and more difficult. Yet the parts of the brain responsible for the emotions tend to remain relatively untouched so that people with dementia experience anger, frustration, boredom, pleasure, excitement and other feelings, just like anybody else and, naturally, will wish to express them. They may feel frustrated and angry that they cannot express themselves easily.

Things go wrong much more often for people developing dementia than for others. They may lose things and be unable to work out how to find what they have lost. Should they themselves become lost, they may be unable to find their way home. All this can make them feel stressed and more and more cut off from a world which is becoming an increasingly difficult and scary place. As noted in Chapter 20: Dementia, the provision of love and understanding by those around can be more important than anything else in improving quality of life.

The experience of dementia varies greatly between individuals. Some people have a diagnosis of dementia yet their powers of expression and ability to construct complex sentences, at least at first, seem hardly affected, although they may frequently repeat themselves. Often, however, the ability to converse is affected. How do you talk to someone who has forgotten much of their vocabulary and whose utterances are often unintelligible? You turn up to visit your father but he is no longer eager to find out how your week has been. He may not initiate any conversation at all. He may struggle to recall his connection with you. So the onus is on you to work out new ways of reaching him. In working out how to communicate and how to demonstrate your continuing affection and support, you may find the following suggestions useful.

Be positive and avoid correcting

A key feature of dementia is difficulty in laying down new memories. If you try to correct someone, whether over a minor or major point, they may well be unable to remember that correction, let alone adjust their thinking in the future in the light of it. However, the experience of being corrected, particularly if this happens frequently, will undermine their self-confidence.

Don't probe or ask direct questions

Direct questions can also highlight memory problems and undermine self-confidence, particularly if the person with dementia senses that a ready answer is required. So tread carefully if you are introduced to somebody and you don't know whether they could easily respond to the sort of inquiries we customarily make.

Once, at a time when her dementia was not far advanced, I arranged for my mother to receive visits from a volunteer visitor. Soon after the introductions, this cheerful man asked my mother where she lived and how many children she had. Retaining her ability to sense the tone of social encounters and that she ought to know the answers but was unable to deliver them, she became confused and upset.

John Killick is a writer and poet who has worked alongside people with dementia over many years, trying to understand what they are trying to convey and transposing some of their thoughts into poetry. He teamed up with psychologist Kate Allan to write a ground-breaking book called *Communication and the Care of People with Dementia*. More recently Killick has distilled his guidance on how to communicate with people with dementia into a short but also invaluable book called *Dementia Positive*.[4]

Allan and Killick advise that if there is an item of information some-one with dementia is trying to convey to you unsuccessfully, you should be patient and give gentle prompts. Say something like, 'I'm not sure of the exact details of what you are saying, but I am picking up that you are very excited/troubled/angry about something.'[5] Don't complete sentences for the person: that may erode their sense of self-worth too.

Tone and body language

In *Dementia Positive*, John Killick recommends that when you speak to someone with dementia, do so in a voice which is soft, kind, unhurried and relaxed, using short, simple sentences. Stay on the same level as the person, so you are face to face. Make sure the person can see and hear you as well as possible. Check they are wearing their glasses or hearing aids, if they need them. Pay attention to your body language and make sure the expression on your face and your tone of voice are encouraging. If it seems right, you could convey more reassurance perhaps by holding the person's hand.[6]

Listen, then respond

Again, in *Dementia Positive*, John Killick explains that you should not feel you need to talk all the time. 'Make it clear that you have chosen to be there with the person, and that this time is for them', he says. Do not to be afraid of silence. Your companion may be thinking or perhaps having difficulty with language or too tired to engage with you.

Try to work out the reason for silence. Killick and Allan: 'In a situation where silence is occurring because thinking is occupying the energy and capacity available to the person with dementia, it is *vital* that you allow the process to take its time, and do not interrupt in any way.'[7]

Let the person living with dementia direct the course of and set the frame for the conversation, as far as possible. Respond to what they are saying, after getting the ball rolling. If they seem to ramble, let them – such talk may well be connected by links which are meaningful to them.

At the same time, be sensitive to the pace of the encounter, taking your cue on pace from them. Make sure you don't inadvertently start speaking quickly. If your speech speeds up as it would in normal conversation, someone with dementia may lose your drift.

Initiating encounters

How do you begin an interaction, whether it involves spoken conversation or communication through body language? Below are some examples from my own experience at different stages of my mother's dementia.

My advice is to experiment and see what works for you. Try to enter the mental world of the person with dementia as it is in that moment. This can be difficult for casual visitors, who may simply see the person they knew in the past and assume that their focus remains the same as it was before their illness. They may breeze in with news of recent holidays, traffic conditions or the birth of grandchildren, rather than to trying to meet the person with dementia on their own terms by engaging with the mental universe that they now inhabit.

Turning the pages and chatting about the content of the local newspaper had been a familiar part of the repertoire of encounters between me and my mother before her illness and it seemed a good idea to continue the rhythm of doing this. At one period which lasted for perhaps two months, she could be absorbed in news of minor disasters. I would paraphrase aloud a story from the newspaper of a man who had been cycling along a path close to the edge of (soft) cliffs my mother knew well. He had accidentally tumbled over the edge. But he survived unharmed, as he had landed on a dumped mattress. My mother seemed genuinely interested in this story. I think she could picture the scene and comprehend the tale. But as she would promptly forget it, I could retell it over and over again.

During my mother's stay in an NHS facility my brother and I hired a visitor who would go in and engage with her one-to-one for two hours every weekday, with family visiting at weekends. The visitor would chat to my mother and sometimes pretend that the two of them were making an apple pie or marmalade together. In doing this, my mother could offer a few words of agreement and advice and so feel positive about herself, without being challenged to recall particular occasions in the past when she had actually carried out these complex tasks.

Perhaps a year or two later on, I turned up to visit my mother to find her silent and apparently very withdrawn. At that stage she had lost much of her vocabulary and I recall wondering whether we would ever have a conversation again. After a while, I asked her what she was thinking. To my amazement, she proceeded to relate, with such limited words as she could rustle up, a cops-and-robbers story which was clearly absorbing her completely. The events being played out in her imagination seemed just as real and important to her as would the news of world events being conveyed by a television newscaster. And I believe that she felt validated by being able to share her story and by the genuine interest I tried to convey in my voice (by this time my mother was nearly blind).

Communicate during another activity (real or imagined)

John Killick reported that many successful and significant conversations he had had with people with dementia took place when they were engaging in another activity at the same time, such as walking, watching events or other people, handling an object or looking at pictures.

The broadcaster Sally Magnusson has chronicled her experience of interacting with her mother, Mamie, when she developed dementia in a book entitled *Where Memories Go*. Magnusson recalls, 'Flashes of her lovely personality remained and could be nurtured. "This is the best day of my life," she would enthuse regularly, after a trip to the seaside or just a walk to pick blackberries in the sunshine.'[8]

Because the experience of dementia varies so widely, impinging on different individuals with pre-existing likes, dislikes and experiences, I recommend experimenting on a trial-and-error basis to find activities and ways of being that enable you to create a connection. I have listed some possibilities below. But be ready to switch rapidly to another pursuit if one you try does not work out. Ideas include:

- going for walks
- going for a drive or an outing on a bus or train
- gardening
- looking at photographs (without turning this into a memory test)
- meeting babies
- patting dogs
- feeling things such as modelling clay, soil, play-dough or cake-making ingredients
- watching films that involve slapstick comedy

I mention the last because some intriguing research found that many of the relatives of 48 people with dementia questioned by researchers in 2015 reported a change in their loved ones' sense of humour towards the fatuous and the farcical. They even laughed at natural disasters and mistakes such as badly parked cars.[9] Why not try films and programmes featuring Mr Bean or Laurel and Hardy? Not only may your loved one enjoy the slapstick: watching films may consolidate the bond between you and perhaps remind you of earlier, similar, shared joys.

Activities such as these can at least distract someone with dementia and at best bring laughter, happiness, absorption and a sense of self-worth.

Mirroring

Shared activities can also be enjoyed through what Kate Allan and John Killick call 'mirroring'. This, 'Involves being engaged in one-to-one inter-action, focusing closely on the person's movements, and reflecting back what they do, and in the style they are doing it, essentially following the leads that they give. So if the person looks at something and points, you would do the same.'[10]

For example, I have shared happy times with an elderly man I used to visit in a care home. We would sit side by side and turn the pages in an il-lustrated book about the Wild West or football. We communicated little through speech, as dementia had taken away most of his vocabulary and he certainly could not have read aloud any of the words. Instead, each of us would point to the cowboys' hats or their horses or a dramatic goal-kick and make an approving or surprised noise and receive some kind of response from the other. Once we had finished the book, we would start again, as my companion had forgotten he had seen it all before.

Be prepared to compromise yourself

Communicating with somebody with dementia can, however, throw up real ethical dilemmas. For example, if your mother thinks you are her husband or her father or mother, should you disabuse her? If she thinks she is back in her childhood home with her own parents and siblings, should you tell her that this is wrong?

With my mother, my instinct was always to try as much as possible to reassure her – no matter how ridiculous I might appear to onlookers. Sometimes she thought that I was her mother, and when she did so I sought to maintain her illusion, indeed was flattered that she thought I was a sympathetic soul (by then she had long forgotten my actual rela-tionship to her).

This approach is advocated by Oliver James in his book *Contented Dementia*. He aims to help the person with dementia to find a safe ver-sion of reality where they can remain relatively content. So one would go along wholeheartedly with the person's delusion that they were living at some stage of their own past, agreeing with everything they said and not asking direct questions. James also suggests that one finds a default state of an activity with which the person with dementia would have been very familiar and to which they may now be seeking to revert, and supports them in doing this. This might involve activities such as sorting and shuffling papers, packing and unpacking a suitcase or mixing the ingredients of a cake, for instance.[11]

On the other hand, therapist Naomi Feil recommends 'validation therapy' – finding ways of responding to the emotion behind the mistaken belief of the person with dementia.[12] In my mother's case this would have involved my showing that I really understood why she missed her own mother, thus validating her anxiety and helping her find the comfort she sought – but without faking a reality which was not there.

John Killick counsels going along with the person with dementia's belief, but not too wholeheartedly: 'I am sure that ... correcting the person is counter-productive. You may only upset them and make them feel inadequate. And it is disrespectful. Whilst not actively agreeing to what is said, surely we should maintain an encouraging stance? Everyone needs to talk, and to be listened to, however unlikely the narrative.'[13]

What is clear is that it would have been disastrous if I had announced that my grandmother was dead and so missing her was pointless, as this would have upset my mother terribly. What is more, if she had later forgotten this news, as she presumably would have, I should have had to repeat it, giving rise to distress once again.

Use any aids you can find

The market is responding with the invention of many ingenious devices to help people with dementia remain connected with those around them. For instance, Sam Dondi-Smith, an occupational therapist working in east Kent, has produced a device for a tablet or iPad that enables people to summon at the touch of the screen their favourite music, photos of their family or favourite places. He visits the person with dementia and their family, and together they decide what array of pictures, music or audio material would give the person with dementia most pleasure and enable them to interact with their own life story.[14]

Sally Magnusson found that playing familiar songs could help her mother connect with her old self and through that with her loved ones. After her mother's death in 2012, Magnusson set up a charity Playlist for Life, which encourages families to create a sequence of music that would have been well known to the person in their early life and place them on an iPod.

'Talking mats' are an older invention, based on the fact that many people who can no longer communicate verbally can often understand pictures. You might have one group of pictures which depict types of food and drink which someone might wish to ask for; another items they may need, such as money or scissors; a third group might be health-related – such as 'I have a headache' or 'I need some medicine.' Another group might help people express how they feel, showing pictures of happy, sad, fearful or anxious faces. Disabled Living Centres *(see page 459)* stock devices to facilitate communication. Your local branch of the Alzheimer's Society or Alzheimer Scotland should be able to point you to any additional devices available in your locality.

Cherish the person

So far in this chapter I have concentrated on communicating with people with quite advanced dementia, but it is also important to be sensitive to the feelings of people whose dementia is at an early stage. For these people too you might like to bear in mind the techniques outlined above. Above all it is important to try to relate to the person rather than the illness and to avoid bruising throwaway remarks.

Once a high-flying civil servant in New Zealand, Christine Bryden has lived for more than 20 years with dementia. During this time she has explained in talks and books what this means. She urges people to see the person, not the dementia – a message also promoted by other experts, such as Toby Williamson *(see page 83)*. 'We are still fully human, worth relating to, but our personhood is so often denied us', Bryden explained in 2015. She went on:

> Without connectedness with others, we lose an important sense of identity – of meaning in life…. And yet people with dementia are often excluded from human relationships. Others say of us, 'She won't remember I visited', 'He doesn't make much sense,' 'She never asks about how I am.' These are all devastating statements, as they are all self-centred, assuming that if another person has nothing to give, then they are no longer worthy of human relationship.[15]

Bryden emphasises that the deep-seated psychological needs explored in chapter 4 – for affection and acceptance, self-esteem, and a belief that our life has meaning in the wider scheme of things – are also felt by people with dementia. And, as we have noted several times in this book, people with dementia often retain their emotions for far longer than their cognitive powers.

Communication

* A major stroke, Parkinson's disease, dementia, hearing and sight impairment can all affect the ability to communicate in later life.

* Impairments associated with ageing can cause embarrassment. Hearing impairment in particular may attract a stigma.

* There are tried and tested ways of talking and listening to people with reduced capacity to communicate.

* Adjust your behaviour according to the different types of impairment.

* Think of ways you can help practically – for instance, working out how a blind person can make lists of things they need to remember

* It is often much harder to adapt to vision or hearing impairment when you are older.

* People with dementia still feel emotions when understanding has declined.

* It can be hurtful to those with dementia to correct what they say.

* Try to imagine what it would be like to have dementia.

* Try to engage in an activity with someone who has dementia, even if it is imaginary.

Chapter 13

Animal magic

One day a friend asked June Thompson if she would take a grey-and-white border collie named Shadow for walks, as arthritis prevented Shadow's owner from walking her himself. Ms Thompson expected the arrangement to last for a fortnight; in fact, it was to last for four-and-a-half years, until Shadow's owner died. Asked to adopt Shadow, she didn't hesitate: 'I knew what a quiet, loving dog she was.'

June Thompson believed that Shadow brought her two important benefits: company and exercise, in the little Surrey town of Dorking where she lives. The two are inextricably linked. She told me:

> I am out of the house walking Shadow for two or three hours every day. I used to go for walks because I couldn't stand being in the house all the time. Now it's much more fun, because I speak to so many people who would have passed me by before. Today, coming through the market, a little girl wanted to stroke her.[1]

Certainly most of us would testify that being greeted by a pet when we return home, stroking it by the fireside, watching it play, taking it for a walk and getting into conversation with other pet owners are all things that keep us in touch with other people and thereby enrich our lives. Exercising a pet can also mean we ourselves engage in more physical activity, which should benefit our health. Research shows that pets act as 'social catalysts', leading to greater social contact between people.[2] Perhaps more than anything else, they provide companionship.

What are the considerations to bear in mind in taking on a pet in later life?

Choosing a pet

Anybody taking on a pet has to consider the cost of feeding it, microchipping it, insuring it and paying vets' bills, but some of the responsibilities and challenges of pet-keeping become more burdensome as we grow older, not least exercising a dog and hoovering carpets strewn with moulted hair. Also, the likely lifespan of the creature becomes a more significant consideration. It can be heartbreaking to think that your beloved pet will be put to sleep because you have to go into hospital or a care home which does not accept pets and no one can be found to look after it. So, if possible, involve your family or friends when you select a pet, on the understanding that if you are unable to care for it, they will take it on.

Older people often do not want a very young animal which they will need to house-train and which may well outlive them. A reputable rescue centre is one place to acquire an older animal, such as those run by Cats Protection, the Dogs Trust, the Blue Cross, Battersea Dogs and Cats Home and the Royal Society for the Prevention of Cruelty to Animals (RSPCA). Such centres will know the sort of environment to which the animal is accustomed and try to match temperament and lifestyles; they ought to be able to narrow down your choice and offer you three or four possibilities. If the pet turns out to be unsuitable, a reputable centre will take it back and you can try again.

Cats' relative independence makes them a very attractive proposition for elderly people. They do not need to be exercised, and older cats are often more than happy to curl up on a lap and so provide comfort.

Small caged animals such as birds, gerbils and hamsters do not of course have to be taken out for a walk and are relatively easily transported to somebody else if you are going on holiday. If your eyesight is poor, you still know where the animal is, although grooming may be difficult, as can retrieving a bird let out of its cage.

Fish can be extremely restful and interesting to watch, and although tortoises cannot now be bought new, they are easy to look after and they respond to their owners.

Nonetheless, many people prefer a dog. Small dogs can be easier for older people to manage, but they can be very bouncy and easily tripped over. Also, they tend to live longer than larger dogs: terriers, for example, can live to 18 or even 20. Though large dogs may have a more manageable lifespan, however, it is not a good idea to have a dog that could pull you over or that you could not lift in and out of the bath or to take to the vet or whose tins of dog food you might struggle to carry.

Are there particular breeds which suit older people? Frail people should avoid dogs bred for working, such as German shepherds, springer spaniels and border collies, as these need a great deal of physical and mental exercise. Setters can be extremely affectionate, but they are often difficult to train, highly-strung and need a huge amount of exercise. However, every dog and every situation should be judged on its own merits.

Cavalier King Charles spaniels can make good pets for older people, although they may be prone to particular medical problems. Dachshunds, corgis and terriers can also make good pets, although terriers are bred for ratting, so they are quite active, and may be yappy. Shetland sheepdogs make good companions, but need a lot of grooming and quite a lot of exercise. Some of the very tiny exotic breeds also need a lot of grooming, but are of course very light to pick up. Whippets are very gentle, sweet-natured and quiet, and of course have short coats; greyhounds need surprisingly little exercise (although they can be heavy to lift). Although Labrador retrievers are large and highly demanding until about the age of six, an older Labrador can be gentle and extremely companionable. Mongrels, if they combine the good traits of the breeds from which they are derived, can also make very good pets.

Support for pet-keeping

Two daunting problems can arise if you have a pet and are getting on in years. What will happen to your pet if you have to move somewhere which does not accept animals, whether suddenly into hospital, or long term into a care facility? And if you are of modest means, how will you pay the vets' bills?

Although there is no NHS for pets, we are extremely fortunate in having nationwide organisations which help people of modest means should their pets become injured or ill. The Blue Cross and the People's Dispensary for Sick Animals (PDSA) provide medical treatment for pets free at their own hospitals and they also reimburse the fees charged by private veterinary practices.

To qualify for help from such organisations you need to demonstrate that your income is low. The most straightforward way of doing this is to show that you receive a means-tested benefit, such as Council Tax Reduction, Housing Benefit or the Guarantee element of Pension Credit. However, if you are of modest means and do not receive such a benefit, it is still worth approaching these organisations. Ring up the national office of each and talk through whether it has a clinic near you or, if not, what other help it could provide.

The third organisation you could try is the Royal Society for the Prevention of Cruelty to Animals. The RSPCA provides similar help to the Blue Cross and the PDSA at RSPCA hospitals and private veterinary practices, except that it does not cover the whole cost of treatment and the amount of financial help varies between the local branches which provide it.

There are also differences between these three organisations in the costs they are prepared to cover in addition to those for medical treatment. The Blue Cross, which is particularly keen to keep down the numbers of stray animals, will pay for neutering; some RSPCA branches will help with the costs of neutering or microchipping; the PDSA will subsidise but not pay the whole cost of neutering, flea treatments, microchipping, deworming and vaccination.

The Cinnamon Trust is a little-known charity which offers different support from the mainstream pets' organisations: it seeks to help elderly people look after their pets should they become ill or incapacitated. Volunteers scattered across the country provide practical help when some aspect of pet care poses a problem, from the management of a cat's litter trays or the cleaning out of a budgie's cage to walking a dog or fostering a pet whose owner has to go into hospital. Help is free, non-means-tested and short-term or long-term.

The Trust also offers two other invaluable services: it publishes a directory of care homes which accept pets and it offers a scheme whereby elderly (or younger, terminally ill) owners can ensure that the Trust takes over responsibility for their pet should it outlive them. In this eventuality, it finds a foster home for the pet, while itself caring for very infirm pets at 'home-from-home' sanctuaries with sofas and attractive gardens.

Pets in care homes and retirement housing

Whether a retirement housing scheme, retirement village or care home accepts residents' pets can be of enormous importance. It can be devastating to move into new surroundings bereft of the company of your pet because the scheme operates a 'no pets' policy, as many do. The challenge of settling in is then compounded by grieving over loss.

If a housing scheme or care home looks otherwise attractive but pets are barred, it is worth challenging the rule, particularly if live-in staff keep pets themselves. Counter possible practical objections. Think ahead of answers to such questions as:

✓ How much freedom should the pet have? In which parts of the scheme or home, including the grounds, should it be allowed to roam freely and from which should it be banned or taken in only on a lead?

✓ Who is going to buy and pay for pet food?

- ✓ How are vets to be summoned?
- ✓ How often will walks take place? When? Who will take charge? What will happen in bad weather?
- ✓ Who will be responsible for breakages?
- ✓ What will happen if you are ill or have to go into hospital?
- ✓ What will happen to the pet if you die?
- ✓ What will happen if the pet fails to settle in?[3]

Pets for people with dementia

Pets can be especially rewarding for people with dementia, since they are affectionate and do not discriminate against people as human beings often do. They can bolster self-esteem, both through interaction and by providing the opportunity to give care. Frena Gray-Davidson, the author of *The Alzheimer's Sourcebook for Caregivers*, recommends that carers who are looking after somebody with dementia should seriously consider obtaining a pet, such as an adult cat.[4]

Enjoyment without ownership

If you are in hospital or a care home, you may wish to see if Pets as Therapy (PAT) is operating in your area and ask whether a pet could visit if visiting does not already take place there. The PAT scheme has 4,500 dogs and 90 cats which, with their volunteer owners, visit people in hospitals, hospices, schools and care homes. Only dogs which pass tests covering health, temperament and behaviour can enter the scheme.

If you enjoy taking a dog for a walk but do not welcome the responsibilities and cost of owning one, why not contact a local animal rescue centre to see whether it would like you to help exercise its dogs? As I write this I have just heard of somebody who, recently retired after years of sitting at a desk, is aiming to improve his fitness and enjoy the open air by taking rescue greyhounds on two-hour walks several times a week.

Animal magic

* Pets are not just good company: they encourage us to take exercise and to chat to with other people, thus benefitting our health. However, pet keeping can be more onerous for older people.

* Involve family and friends when you select a pet, on the understanding that they will take it on if that proves necessary.

* Select the type of pet carefully. Cats are ideal. Some types of dog are more suitable than others.

* Rescue centres can be a good place to find a suitable pet.

* The Blue Cross, RSPCA and PDSA provide concessionary veterinary treatment for the pets of people on low incomes.

* If you go into hospital, look for a pet fostering scheme.

* In hospital or a care home, press for a PAT dog or cat visiting scheme.

* Many care facilities and retirement housing schemes say they forbid pets; make sure they really mean this, as they sometimes relent.

* If you move, cannot take your pet and have nobody to hand it to, contact a pet rehoming service.

* The Cinnamon Trust runs a scheme to find a new home for pets which outlive their owners.

THE WORLD OF HEALTHCARE

> **❝** *NICE pronouncements often attract criticism if NICE has declined to recommend a particular drug for use in the NHS. You may therefore be inclined to dismiss NICE guidance in general. Please do not. It can be extraordinarily useful when working out what treatment you should expect to obtain.* **❞**

PART FOUR
THE WORLD OF HEALTHCARE

As we grow older, healthcare tends to separate into two areas. First, there is care if we suddenly fall ill or have an accident. Our main concern then is the same as when we were younger – to receive the best treatment as swiftly as possible.

But as the years advance, long-term issues loom much larger. Ongoing medical conditions such as asthma, which we may have developed when younger, continue to need attention, along with the unexpected ailments which may come along, from gallstones to pneumonia. But in later life new long-term illnesses and disabilities may also develop, from heart disease and loss of sight to type 2 diabetes and cancer.

Much of our information about the health service still comes from what we see on television, such as dramas set in hospital A&E departments. These tend to focus on emergency treatment to save the lives of (mostly) young people who have met with dramatic accidents or sudden illness. They dwell less on the work of an army of other health professionals, such as physiotherapists, audiologists and occupational therapists, who can greatly enhance the quality of life for older people with medical conditions.

Those moving into later life may be completely unaware of the help available in these non-emergency areas, let alone their rights to receive it. Therefore, the first chapter of this part considers the legal rights and government pledges that underpin the whole of the NHS system throughout the UK. These apply both to the world of primary care (that is, outside hospitals) and to hospitals. They include anything from free healthcare to the right to see one's medical records or to refuse a particular treatment. These rights also include an expectation that certain types of treatment will be offered.

In the second chapter of this part, I describe the expertise of the main professionals who can do much to improve our health and quality of life when we are getting on. These professionals are subject to controls to ensure they have the necessary experience and expertise and that they behave professionally.

These healthcare professionals and other staff work through the organisations which hire them, such as hospital trusts, pharmacies and dental surgeries, and I outline the controls which apply to these organisations to ensure that patients receive good, safe treatment.

Voluntary organisations from the Patients' Association to the British Heart Foundation do much to improve the experience of patients, both through the information and support they provide and the lobbying in which many of them engage. I outline the ways in which voluntary healthcare organisations might be able to help you.

Finally, at the end of chapter 15, I outline the various options open to anybody concerned about the way in which they have been treated by a healthcare professional or provider organisation, from suing for negligence to lodging a formal complaint.

This part therefore examines:

▶ the organisation of the NHS

▶ the right to free care

▶ the right to see medical records

▶ the right to consent to or refuse a treatment or test

▶ patient choice

▶ the right to tests and treatment

▶ the right not to be discriminated against

▶ the scope of work of various healthcare professionals

▶ how healthcare professionals are regulated

▶ controls over the organisations that provide healthcare

▶ sources of information about healthcare

▶ how voluntary organisations can help

▶ what to do if you have a concern about treatment

▶ organisations which can help with concerns

Chapter 14

The NHS: Rights and pledges

We are often told that our health service is the envy of the world and that it costs the country a very large amount of money. At the same time, there is an almost constant stream of stories of patients denied expensive treatments or substandard care on hospital wards. Just what are our rights as patients?

In this chapter I explain these rights one by one, from a right to see our health records to a right to refuse treatment. First, though, a quick word about the organisations that provide NHS care and also their relationship to those that provide closely-linked social care *(defined below)*.

NHS organisation

Although the organisation of the NHS is complex, don't worry too much about understanding who does what. In this book, I use the terms 'health authorities' and 'health bodies' to cover whichever organisation is involved.

In **England,** local clinical commissioning groups (CCGs) commission a wide range of services for patients, from district nursing to ambulance and hospital provision. A national body, NHS England, commissions the services of GPs, dentists, opticians and pharmacists, although CCGs are increasingly involving themselves in this area too.

In **Wales,** NHS health services are both commissioned and delivered by local health boards.

Health boards have performed this dual function in **Scotland** too, but a law passed in 2014 provides for health boards and the local authorities that administer social care to run services more closely together.[1] They have the option of fully integrating some or all of their functions and appointing an integrated joint board to take responsibility. Alternatively, the health board or the local authority can take the lead in any particular geographical area, performing the functions of both using delegated powers.

In **Northern Ireland,** health and social care services have long been administered hand in hand. Services are delivered on the ground by six health and social care trusts. A separate body, the Health and Social Care Board, which covers the entire province, commissions services from the trusts on behalf of citizens.

How government influences healthcare provision

Our Westminster Parliament and the legislatures in each country of the UK influence healthcare provision in various important ways, not least in deciding the amount of money available to commissioning bodies to buy services from providers such as GP practices.

For potential patients, trying to establish just what care they should receive, the instructions government issues to NHS providers are invaluable. In England, the Department of Health issues 'guidance'. This guidance has more force than the word might suggest: the courts expect health authorities to comply with 'policy guidance'; in other words, it has the power of law. In this book I often quote policy guidance because it can be helpful to patients to know what health providers are expected to deliver in case they are failing to do so.

Sometimes 'practice guidance' is relevant. This is different: it sets out the ways in which the Department of Health considers that a health organisation should go about particular tasks. Health bodies have a legal duty to take practice guidance into account, but do not have to follow it in such an absolute way as policy guidance: if challenged in court, a health body would simply have to explain why it had chosen not to do so. Thus while policy guidance tells an authority what it must do, practice guidance tells it how it should go about doing it.

Elsewhere in the UK, arms of the Scottish government, Welsh government and Northern Ireland Executive perform a similar role in shaping policy and practice on the ground.[2] Contrary to public perception – fuelled by media attention to the differences – official guidance and regulations issued in Edinburgh, Cardiff and Belfast are often very similar to those drawn up by the Department of Health for England.

Health rights

Whichever body provides or commissions their healthcare services, citizens on the ground enjoy a number of rights in the field of NHS healthcare provision. These include:

- the right to receive healthcare services and healthcare equipment free of charge, subject to limited exceptions
- the right to refuse a physical examination and/or treatment
- the right to see their medical records
- the right not to be discriminated against on grounds of race, gender, disability, religious belief or sexual orientation. (Age discrimination has also been introduced, but with limitations, as we see in a moment.)

These healthcare rights apply wherever somebody is living – at home, in a residential or nursing care home, in hospital, prison or a hospice.

In addition to legal rights, the government has made some important pledges on what patients can expect to receive from the NHS. Both the legal rights and the pledges have been brought together in *The NHS Constitution* and the *Handbook to the NHS Constitution*, which accompanies it. Both can be obtained by post or on the internet from the Department of Health.[3] Although these documents are important, they are not well known. They should be.

Clinical commissioning groups in England, the NHS Commissioning Board and the Secretary of State for Health are all required by law to have regard to the principles, values, rights and pledges set out in the NHS Constitution when they are carrying out any of their functions in relation to the health service.[4]

Although written for England, the principles that underlie the Constitution have been accepted by the health administrations in Scotland, Wales and Northern Ireland.

In addition, the Scottish Parliament has passed its own Patient Rights (Scotland) Act 2011 and the Scottish government has compiled a Charter of Patient Rights and Responsibilities. The Charter provides a useful guide and extends patients' rights beyond those provided in the NHS Constitution in the area of guaranteed treatment times *(see below)*.

Here are some of the rights and pledges on healthcare provision – many of them set down in the NHS Constitution and the Scottish law and Charter – that can be particularly useful in later life.

Free healthcare

Free provision for all is perhaps the best-known central tenet of the NHS. It means that any NHS service should be free at the point of delivery, unless it has been specially exempted. The NHS Constitution states: 'You have the right to receive NHS services free of charge, apart from certain limited exceptions sanctioned by Parliament.'[5] 'Services' cover not only care and expertise, but also equipment. So your hearing aid or surgeon's scalpel, as well as the work of your surgeon, GP and many more medical professionals, should be free.

What are the 'limited exceptions'? Four years after the establishment of the NHS in 1948, the government of the day realised that the provision of universal free dental care would be far too expensive in a population whose teeth were in poor condition, and it introduced charging for dental treatment. Today, there is special provision for people of modest means who need dental treatment *(set out on page 306)*.

Hearing aids are free *(see page 475)*, but spectacles and contact lenses are not. Free healthcare does not include blanket provision of free transport to obtain it, and older people often need to make frequent visits to hospital. However, transport to hospital is free in certain circumstances *(as explained on pages 933–4)*.

Drugs obtained on a prescription are another of the exceptions that have been made to the general rule. However, prescriptions have been made free for certain groups, including people over 60 throughout the UK. (In Wales, Northern Ireland and Scotland prescription charges have been abolished for everybody.)

Social care

Social care forms the largest single exception to the principle of free care at the point of need. If you have an illness or long-term health condition such as osteoarthritis, you may need not only tests and treatment from healthcare services, but also help with the practical difficulties resulting from your condition, such as in getting dressed or preparing a meal. If you have dementia, you may need someone to keep an eye on you so you do not come to harm. Help provided to cope with such practical matters is called 'social care'.

The need for healthcare and social care thus springs from a common source – illness, disability or general frailty. But while healthcare provision is automatically free, social care is not (although, as we see in Part Seven, various types of social care are, in fact, free).

Another difference is that while healthcare services are administered by the NHS or organisations working for it, social care is the responsibility of local authorities. However, health and social care authorities are expected to work closely together and sometimes services are run jointly.

Patient records

Another important right gives access to an individual's healthcare records, under the Data Protection Act 1998. So all your records – recently computerised ones as well as paper ones, including consultants' letters and the results of tests – should be available to you. The law applies to all information relating to your physical or mental health which is recorded by a healthcare professional, such as a GP, hospital doctor, dentist or physiotherapist, whether working for the NHS or in private practice.

You may find perusal of your medical records useful for the following reasons:

● it provides a means of better understanding your own current medical conditions

● it provides a means of calling to mind past conditions which may recur

● it provides data which may be useful if you are engaged in a dispute over healthcare provision

● it enables you to check that your records are correct

● it enables you to know whether your records contain any instructions with which you might disagree. For example, if doctors have inserted a 'Do not attempt resuscitation' instruction yet you would like attempts made to keep you alive should your heart stop beating, then you could try to get the instruction altered *(see pages 1014–5).*

You do not need to explain why you wish to see your medical records or say which parts of the records you are interested in. Simply telephone your GP practice and ask to be sent an application form to view your records. You will be asked to provide proof of identity (or of your status as a patient's representative). The GP practice manager or another official will be present when you examine your records and you can ask them to photocopy items, for which a small charge may be made.[6] The law says that records have to be provided within 40 days, although government guidance says healthcare organisations should respond within 21 days.[7]

If you are offered online access to your GP records, you may receive only a summary covering the medication you are taking, your allergies and any adverse reactions to drugs. The Patients Association publishes a useful, free guide called *How to Obtain Access to your Medical Records.*

Waiting times

The NHS Constitution pledges that patients should not have to wait for longer than a set period in certain situations. These include the following:

- When a patient arrives in Accident and Emergency (A&E), they should not have to wait for more than four hours until they are admitted to a ward, discharged from the hospital or transferred (the Constitution does not say where to).

- If a patient has an operation cancelled for non-clinical reasons on or after the day they are admitted to hospital, including the day of surgery, they must be offered another binding date within 28 days. Or their treatment must be funded at the time and hospital of their choice.

- A patient must be seen by a cancer specialist within a maximum of two weeks from a GP urgent referral where cancer is suspected.[8]

- A patient who is referred for investigation of breast symptoms must not wait longer than two weeks to see a specialist, even if cancer is not initially suspected.

- A patient must not wait longer than 31 days from diagnosis to their first treatment for all types of cancer.

- Any consultant-led treatment for a non-urgent condition must start within a maximum of 18 weeks from referral.

In the last two cases, the Constitution lays down that if the NHS body that commissions and funds the treatment is unable to deliver it itself, it must take all reasonable steps to offer a suitable alternative provider.[9]

Patients in Scotland also enjoy a right to another maximum waiting time. The Charter of Patient Rights and Responsibilities says that any planned treatment which a doctor has agreed with a patient must start within 12 weeks and gives as examples of treatments covered by this guarantee: hip or knee replacements, hernia surgery and cataract surgery. The Charter further provides that if a health board cannot provide treatment within that time, it must explain the reasons for this, give the patient information about how to make a complaint and take steps to ensure they start their treatment at the next available opportunity, taking account of other patients' clinical needs. Some treatment is exempt from this treatment-time guarantee, including organ transplantation and assisted reproduction.[10]

Treatment in Europe

If your treatment on the NHS will become available only after an unacceptable delay, you could require your NHS body to pay for it in another European Economic Area (EEA) country or Switzerland. Under a European Union regulation, if your NHS consultant considers that you should be offered a particular treatment on the NHS and the NHS cannot provide it without 'undue delay', and that treatment is available from a state provider in an EEA country or Switzerland, you can apply to be treated there, with your health costs met by the NHS.[11] Ask for form S2. The NHS Constitution and Scotland's Charter of Patient Rights and Responsibilities confirm this right.[12]

A court case in 2006 established that health authorities are not permitted to refuse to fund treatment elsewhere on the grounds that they do not have the cash to pay for it.[13] However, bear in mind that if nationals in the member state where you wish to obtain treatment themselves have to pay a proportion of that treatment, say, 20 per cent, you will be expected to do so too. Do also be aware that if the operation goes wrong, you will probably have to pursue any complaint in the country in which the treatment took place.

Consent

As patients, we do not have the right to insist that a particular treatment or test be offered to us by the NHS. However, we do have the right to refuse any medical treatment or examination we are offered, unless we are unconscious or have been detained under mental health law. In normal circumstances, any medical professional who gives us a physical examination or treatment without our consent is acting unlawfully. When we go to see our GP, our implied consent to the tests and treatment they offer us is assumed, and when we have an operation, a hospital will ask for our written consent. But it is important to be aware that we can withhold consent at any time.

The rules on consent are set out in the Department of Health's publication *Reference Guide to Consent for Examination or Treatment*, issued in 2009. This begins by establishing that:

> It is a general and ethical principle that valid consent must be obtained before starting treatment or physical investigation, or providing personal care, for a person. This principle reflects the right of patients to determine what happens to their own bodies, and is a fundamental part of good practice.

Fundamental to obtaining consent is acquainting patients with facts so they can make an informed decision. So expect your doctor to ensure that you understand:

✓ the nature, benefits and risks of any investigation or treatment they are offering

✓ the nature, benefits and risks of any alternative investigation or treatment

✓ the consequences of not receiving any treatment

If you have difficulty in communicating, perhaps because of sight or hearing problems or limited grasp of English, expect your doctor to take all necessary steps to ensure that you can comprehend what they are saying, including writing things down if necessary.[14] If a health professional fails to obtain proper consent and you subsequently suffer harm as a result of treatment or a physical examination, failure to explain adequately may be a factor in a claim of negligence against the doctor or nurse involved.

Patients can also refuse to participate in teaching if they wish. Any consultant who breezes up to a patient's bed with an entourage of students and asserts: 'Mr Smith, you don't mind, do you?' should know that is bad practice. Any patient should be consulted properly beforehand and given the opportunity to refuse if they so wish. There are strict rules on seeking patients' consent for participation in research.

Some people are so certain that they do not wish to receive certain forms of treatment that they have drawn up an 'advance directive to refuse treatment' (similar to a 'living will'). This directive is a statement of wishes to refuse specified forms of treatment in the event of being unable to give consent at the time treatment is necessary *(I discuss it on pages 1017–20)*. Plainly, if you make an advance directive, you should also ensure it will be easy to find in an emergency.

Consent for people with impaired mental powers

You may be tempted to skip this section – don't! Any of us at any moment could become incapable of giving consent for a medical examination or treatment because we are unconscious or delirious, we have had a major stroke or other brain injury, or we have developed dementia. In this situation, when the considered consent of the patient cannot be obtained, any healthcare professional must take whatever action they or a medical team considers would be in the best interests of the patient.[15]

When working out what these best interests might be, doctors and nurses must take into account the person's past and present wishes and feelings, the beliefs and values that would be likely to influence their decision if they had mental capacity *(defined in the Glossary),* and any other factors that would be likely to influence their decision. They must also seek the views of certain other people before they can go ahead, if is practicable and appropriate to consult them. A key person here is any attorney with powers to take proxy decisions in the health field whom the person had previously appointed, *as explained on pages 782–5.*

Any patient in England and Wales who lacks the mental capacity to make a decision about whether to accept significant medical treatment such as major surgery or to convey their decision must be given a special 'advocate' to represent their interests. In Scotland, any adult with a mental disorder is entitled to be given an advocate.

In 2016 a new law on mental capacity for Northern Ireland was passed. However, it is unlikely to be brought into effect for several years *(see page 750).* In the meantime, you could expect its provisions (which are similar in many respects to the mental capacity legislation for England and Wales) to guide best practice. *I discuss the rules governing consent for people who lack mental capacity in more detail in Chapter 33.*

Patient choice

A patient cannot fully exercise their right to give or withhold consent without understanding the implications of refusing or accepting a test or treatment that a doctor is offering. So patient choice is inextricably bound up with patient consent.

The NHS Constitution places patient choice centre stage, declaring: 'You have the right to be involved in planning and making decisions about your health and care with your care provider or providers, including your end-of-life care, and to be given information and support to enable you to do this.'[16]

This right to choice so firmly proclaimed by the government poses a fundamental challenge to the paternalistic doctor-knows-best attitude. However, genuine shared decision-making and choice pervading every aspect of patient care is only going to materialise if patients seize the opportunity to ensure that it does. You may need to prompt, even over apparently minor matters. If, say, your doctor says they are sending you for a consultation at a foot clinic, make sure they consult you about which hospital or clinic will be involved. The facility the doctor has in mind might be in a location you would find inconvenient, and you may regret not having discussed alternatives when you face a half-an-hour wait for the bus to take you there.

Another example: if you object to the method by which medication is delivered to you – perhaps large tablets rather than liquid – ask your doctor about the alternatives and expect to be fully involved in the decision that will be made when the prescription is written. The possibilities for involving patients in choice, whether over decisions made by doctors, nurses, pharmacists or other professionals, are endless. Here are three areas in which you may care to exercise choice.

Choice of GP

While we have no choice of, say, social worker, we can choose our own doctor. As GPs are the first port of call when we have an ailment and are also the gateway to much healthcare provision, wise choice of GP practice is very important. The NHS Constitution states, 'You have the right to choose your GP practice, and to be accepted by that practice unless there are reasonable grounds to refuse, in which case you will be informed of those reasons.'[17]

Particularly in inner cities and rural areas, the most favoured GP practices are likely to have full lists and to operate tight geographical boundaries. However, if you live within a practice's area, it must accept you, unless its list is full. Practices are allowed to turn down prospective patients within their area only if they close their lists to any new patients. This rule is designed to prevent practices cherry-picking patients and rejecting those with multiple health needs likely to involve the practice in much time and trouble.

If you are choosing a GP practice, go and talk to the practice manager and ask around; in England, the website MyNHS allows some comparisons to be made.

If you prefer to see one doctor in the practice rather than others, say so. The NHS Constitution states that, 'You have the right to express a preference for using a particular doctor within your GP practice, and for the practice to try to comply.'[18]

Named GP for people aged 75 or over

Since 2014, the contract in England between the government and GPs has said that patients who are aged 75 or over should be assigned a named GP in their practice who will take lead responsibility for ensuring they receive whatever services they need from the practice. This GP will not always provide services – a patient could still be seen by someone else, such as a member of the practice with a particular specialism. (A named care coordinator, who might be the named GP or another professional, could also be brought in.)[19]

The GP contract says that patients should be simply informed of their allocation to a particular GP. If you have built up a good relationship with another GP, you may not wish to change to a GP to whom the practice has assigned you. If so, object, quoting the pledge in the Constitution above. The NHS tells GP practices, 'Where the patient expresses a preference as to which GP they have been assigned, the practice must make reasonable effort to accommodate this request.'[20]

Out-of-area patients
Patients in England can, in theory at least, register with two GP practices. The government has introduced the option for practices to register patients from outside their geographical boundaries, without any obligation to provide those patients with home visits.[21] Although this facility is of most obvious benefit to people who commute long distances to work and whose chances of seeing a GP during practice opening hours are minimal, the option is not confined to working people. So if, for instance, you often stay in another part of the country, you could also consider applying to take advantage of this opportunity.

Choice of specialist healthcare provider
As choice is a fundamental tenet of the NHS Constitution, patients throughout the UK should expect choice in the specialist to which a GP or hospital doctor refers them.

In England, a system called Choose and Book has been set up to enable patients to exercise choice in this situation. It allows patients to choose a hospital for referral anywhere in England. This could be in their own locality or far away; it could be an NHS hospital or a private hospital which offers the NHS service required. The website chooseandbook.nhs.uk provides information to enable people to make comparisons between hospitals.

Choose and Book does not cover treatment requiring speed, such as for chest pains and suspected cancer. Also, the system allows patients to choose a hospital, but not the particular staff in that hospital. So it can be useful in allowing somebody to choose to go to a hospital with low rates of hospital-acquired infection or expertise in a particular area, but it does not provide a guarantee that they will be seen by the consultant of their choice, although there is no reason why they should not make a request to be seen by a particular person. Choose and Book includes both physical and mental health services. (*I examine Choose and Book in more detail in the chapter on staying in hospital, on pages 905–6.*)

Personal health budgets

An increasingly popular way in which care for people with long-term chronic conditions is being funded in England is through personal health budgets. The principle of free healthcare is retained, but the health authority gives the patient or their representative a sum of money to buy the healthcare services it would otherwise have organised for them, thereby giving them greater choice over the way in which the money allocated for their care is spent.

Personal health budgets are not given for routine aspects of NHS provision, such as emergency treatment at A&E or a consultation with one's GP, but for the treatment of ongoing illnesses, palliative care and NHS Continuing Healthcare *(explained below)* – situations in which choice can be exercised across a range of types of treatment, such as fitness classes, physiotherapy, psychological therapy and attendance at a day hospice. A health professional discusses with the patient or their representative the services that could be commissioned and their cost. A support plan is then drawn up, setting out how the money will be spent; this must be agreed by both parties before the budget is handed over.

One field in which personal health budgets are firmly established is NHS Continuing Healthcare. This is a form of NHS funding allocated to a small number of people (about 60,000 people in England, for example) who need a great deal of care on account of a serious medical condition or conditions, or because they are terminally ill. It provides free social care regardless of means, as well as healthcare, and the amount of money given per patient can run into tens of thousands of pounds every year. The care involved can be provided in an NHS facility, a nursing home or the home of the patient or a friend or relative.

It can be especially helpful to exercise choice in the form in which NHS Continuing Healthcare is received, *(as we see on pages 963–8)*. NHS England has said that people awarded NHS Continuing Healthcare have a right to have a personal health budget (though this is not a legal right), and that, 'People with long-term conditions who could benefit should have the option of a personal health budget'.[22]

If you think you would like a personal health budget, raise the matter with your GP or hospital consultant. It may not have occurred to them to offer you one. Mental healthcare is included. The website Peoplehub. org.uk publishes video stories of people who have experience of using personal health budgets to cope with depression, motor neurone disease, Parkinson's disease and dementia, and to manage an NHS Continuing Healthcare budget.

Whatever the area of healthcare for which you are offered or ask for a budget, make sure that it does not leave you short-changed. Cash-strapped health bodies may be tempted to provide less than is necessary to buy the services and equipment recipients need, in the hope that they will top up the budget out of their own resources. If clinical commissioning groups do this, they will be flying in the face of the central tenet of the NHS that healthcare is free to those who need it. So make sure your personal health budget is large enough to cover the costs of the healthcare you should be receiving. Health bodies should not be trying to introduce charging for services by the back door by declining to give people enough money. Also, don't allow a personal health budget to be foisted on you, perhaps to relieve NHS officials of the task of organising your care. As the NHS has said, 'Personal health budgets ... will always be optional for patients.'[23] *(See also page 966.)*

The right to treatment

You cannot demand that a doctor gives you a particular treatment: it is offered to you if a doctor considers that it might help you and would not be futile. However, a well-established feature of the NHS, restated in the NHS Constitution, is that patients have the right to the drugs and other forms of treatment that the National Institute for Health and Care Excellence has recommended for use in the NHS, so long as their doctor says they are clinically appropriate for them.[24]

NICE

The National Institute for Health and Care Excellence, or NICE, is an organisation based in London which commissions teams of experts from many disciplines to draw up detailed guidance on the way in which particular medical conditions should be treated. The treatment it recommends includes anything from medication to physiotherapy and surgery to nursing care.[25] NICE pronouncements often attract criticism if NICE has declined to recommend a particular drug for use in the NHS. You may therefore be inclined to dismiss NICE guidance in general. Please do not. It can be extraordinarily useful when working out what treatment you can expect to obtain.

Once NICE clinical guidance is published, health professionals (and the organisations that employ them) are expected to take it fully into account when deciding what tests and treatments to offer people. NICE guidance should be followed by both medical professionals and the organisations that employ them in whatever location NHS healthcare is provided. This could be a general, specialist or community hospital, a patient's home or a residential or nursing care home.

However, NICE clinical guidance does not replace the actual knowledge and skills of individual health professionals who treat patients; it is still up to them to make treatment decisions in consultation with the patient and/or their representative *(or one of the other categories of consultee listed on page 782)*. In other words, a patient's right to treatment recommended by NICE is not absolute: it comes with the proviso 'if the doctor considers it is clinically appropriate'. So, while doctors are expected to take NICE guidance into account when coming to decisions about individual patients, they are not forced to prescribe any particular drug or treatment. However, if a doctor denies a patient a drug or other treatment recommended by NICE and is taken to task, their health organisation would have to demonstrate why the doctor did not consider it was appropriate for that particular patient's condition.

NICE guidance published to date covers conditions such as diabetes, glaucoma, heart failure, high blood pressure, Parkinson's disease, prostate cancer and the wet form of age-related macular degeneration. *(I refer in detail to NICE guidance on dementia, depression, falls, urinary continence and strokes in Part Five.)* Since 2013, NICE has been also drawing up guidelines in the field of social care.

NICE guidance is available on the internet. It is worth noting that although NICE publishes guidance for the general public, the clinical guidelines issued for professionals (released in full and summary forms) are often more useful if you are checking to see that you are receiving the best treatment you can reasonably expect.

NICE clinical guidance operates to varying degrees over the UK. It applies in England and Wales. In Northern Ireland, the Department of Health, Social Services and Public Safety assesses guidance published by NICE and decides whether it should be implemented; much NICE guidance has been so endorsed. In Scotland, a similar body to NICE, Healthcare Improvement Scotland, examines NICE guidance and often recommends its adoption or that of a group of healthcare experts called the Scottish Intercollegiate Guidelines Network (SIGN). SIGN's recommendations are often very similar to NICE's. The Patient Rights (Scotland) Act 2011 says that the healthcare citizens receive must be based on current clinical guidelines.[26]

Tests and treatments required under the GP contract

The GP contract, agreed between doctors' representatives and the NHS every year, forms the basis on which GP practices operate. It sets out what

GPs have to do in return for their payments from the state. The contract was agreed in 2004 and it is modified slightly each year. It is divided into a core contract, which sets out the essential services that practices must provide in return for a basic payment, and other services which GP practices can choose to offer their patients. Since 2013, there have been separate contracts for England, Scotland, Wales and Northern Ireland, but they tend to be similar to the one described here for England.

Annual health checks for patients over 75
One element of the core contract is a requirement that all patients aged 75 and over should be given a general health check every year by their GP practice. This check is a general consultation, 'In the course of which [the practice] shall make such inquiries and undertake such examinations as appear to be appropriate in all the circumstances'. It should take place in the patient's home if their medical condition makes it inappropriate for them to visit the surgery. This annual health check is in addition to normal consultations and to the appointment of a named doctor for patients aged 75 and over described above.[27]

One advantage of a general health check – a sort of MOT – is that medical conditions previously unknown to the doctor or the patient can be picked up, for instance late-onset type 2 diabetes. A study of 40 GP practices in Nottinghamshire found that as many as a quarter of annual checks for older people carried out revealed a problem previously unknown to the patient's doctor.[28]

The catch is patients have to request the health check – GPs are not instructed to offer it automatically. This is a shame, because many people will be completely unaware of the facility, yet their GPs are receiving payments from government on the assumption that it is being provided. If you think this general health check would be of benefit to you, ask for it. It is unlikely it would not be.

You may need to press. A survey published by the British Geriatrics Society (an association of medical professionals interested in the care of older people) uncovered the shocking statistic that as many as 68 per cent of residents in care homes were not receiving a regular planned medical review by their GP in 2010. Yet the vast majority of people who live in care homes are well over 75 years old.[29]

Medical condition payments
On top of the core payment for essential services, practices can opt to try to meet targets in another part of the contract, called the Quality and Outcomes Framework (QOF). This singles out certain (not all) medical

conditions and, for each of these, sets out a system of steps GPs should take to address the condition; compliance with each of these attracts a separate payment for the GP practice.

For each of the selected categories of ailment, the practice must assemble a register of all patients in the practice who are suffering from it. For several conditions, this register forms the basis of a complex tier of further standards and rewards. Thus for diabetes, different tiers of reward are given if a practice has given particular tests to patients with the condition, as well as rewards for particular treatments. A complex panoply of rewards is also offered for tests and treatments for asthma, chronic obstructive pulmonary disease (such as emphysema), coronary heart disease, epilepsy, and stroke and transient ischaemic attacks.

However, by no means all of the common chronic conditions of later life have been selected for the QOF incentive system. GPs are expected to give the best possible treatment to their patients with other conditions too, but obviously there is a danger that the basic tests and treatments required under QOF do not spring to mind so readily for other conditions or that GPs do not always devote as much time and energy to those for which QOF offers no or only a very basic reward.

This danger was borne out by a study of the quality of care for 13 different conditions in England in 2008. Eight-and-a-half thousand people over 50 were interviewed about the care they had received. While 75 per cent of them reported that they had received good care for conditions which were covered by the QOF, the figure was only 58 per cent for non-QOF conditions. Some conditions performed particularly badly: for example only 29 per cent of patients who were interviewed who had osteoarthritis (still not within QOF) seemed to be receiving good care.[30]

In Part Five I discuss what you might reasonably expect from a GP if you suspect you may be suffering from a few of the most common conditions of later life. The majority of the conditions I discuss are either not covered or covered only in a very basic way by the Quality and Outcomes Framework.

Services from pharmacies

Like GP practices, pharmacies also have their own contract which lays down the essential services they must provide in return for payment from the NHS. These services include ones we might expect, such as the dispensing of medicines, but others which can also be invaluable.

Pharmacies must provide **support for self-care services.** These are aimed not only at people who are trying to care for themselves, perhaps with a long-term condition, but also for unpaid carers. Both groups must be provided with, 'Appropriate advice to help them self manage a self-limiting or long-term condition such as diabetes or osteoporosis, including advice on the selection and use of any appropriate medicines'.[31] Pharmacists must also ensure that carers and people managing a long-term condition are given information by pharmacies about the treatment options they have, including non-pharmacological ones.

As another essential service to the public, pharmacies must provide **advice on healthy living.** If you have a question about diet or exercise, you could ask your pharmacist.

All pharmacies are also required by their contract with the NHS to signpost people who need help that cannot be provided by the pharmacy to other providers of health and social services and support organisations.

Pharmacies must also offer a **minor ailments service,** in other words, they must offer advice and if necessary medication on such ailments as:

- skin conditions, including mild acne, mild eczema and athlete's foot
- coughs, colds, nasal congestion and a sore throat
- minor cuts and bruises
- constipation and haemorrhoids (or piles)
- hay fever and allergies
- headaches, earache and back pain
- indigestion, diarrhoea and thrush
- warts, verrucas, mouth ulcers and cold sores

There are also so-called Advanced Services that pharmacies can choose whether to provide.[32] Advanced Services attract additional funding from the NHS. These include the **New Medicine Service.**

When we are given a new medicine, many of us stop taking it within a short time because of side-effects or difficulties in taking it. The New Medicine Service is designed to help patients understand a newly prescribed medicine for a long-term condition, so that they take it as the doctor intended. The consultation should take place in a private area and be followed by a subsequent meeting or phone conversation in about a fortnight and then a final consultation between three and four weeks after starting the medicine. If a significant problem persists, the pharmacist may refer the patient to their GP.

Another service which pharmacies may sign up to provide is **Medicines Use Reviews.** When a pharmacist conducts such a review, they sit down with a patient in a private consultation area, assess the patient's use of their existing medicines and attempt to identify any problems they may be experiencing. The Review can be conducted regularly, say, every year, or when a significant problem with someone's medication comes to light or when a drug is being dispensed. The pharmacist can refer any issues on to the patient's GP.

Medicines Use Reviews and the New Medicine Service are potentially valuable and it is certainly worth asking for a consultation if you think it might help you. Not all pharmacies offer these services: if your pharmacy does not, ask which pharmacies in your area do.

We have already noted *(see page 16)* that drugs have a different effect on the body as we grow older. Changes to the liver and kidneys which are an inevitable part of the ageing process mean that we become more sensitive to drugs, because our body cannot process them as effectively as it could when we were younger. This has implications for dosage. Also, older people are more likely to develop side-effects to drugs. These can of course be harmless, but can also be dangerous. Some drugs can increase the risk of falls, for instance *(see page 390)*.

Expect the following questions to arise during a Medicine Use Review or in a subsequent consultation with your GP:

✓ Are my drugs continuing to help whatever condition they were selected to address? One study of medication reviews for care home residents revealed that in nearly 50 per cent of cases the recommendation was that a drug should be stopped; in an astonishing two-thirds of these cases, there was no stated reason for the medicine having been prescribed in the first place.[33]

✓ Are the drugs being delivered in the correct form? If they are being given as tablets, might a liquid form or patch suit me better?

✓ Should anything be done to help me take my drugs? For instance, should the pharmacist offer a dosette (a device with little compartments indicating time and day of the week)?

✓ Are any of the drugs, both those newly prescribed and those that have been taken for some time, giving rise to undesirable side-effects? Can anything be done about these side-effects? Or should a different drug be selected?

✓ Are there any drugs that might be of benefit that are not at present being prescribed?

Pharmacists may also sign up to provide an **Appliance Use Review Service,** which can be conducted in a private consultation area or in the patient's home by the pharmacist or a specialist nurse. It would help people having difficulty with using a stoma, for instance.

In future, pharmacies are likely to become more and more involved in health promotion and prevention by encouraging people to look after their own health and to self-manage ongoing medical conditions, such as diabetes, high blood pressure and asthma. As more and more people wear telehealth monitors *(see pages 494–5),* pharmacies are likely to play a key role in helping people to interpret the results. They are also likely to become more involved in NHS health checks for the likes of skin cancer, respiratory disorders, diabetes, high blood pressure and an irregular pulse rate.

Respect for human rights

The NHS has a legal obligation to respect every patient's human rights. Parliament has decreed that it is unlawful for a public authority to act in a way that violates one of the human rights set down in the European Convention on Human Rights.[34] These rights include:

- Article 2: the right to life
- Article 3: the right not to be subjected to inhuman or degrading treatment
- Article 5: the right not to be deprived of one's liberty, except in clearly defined circumstances
- Article 6: the right to a fair hearing or trial
- Article 8: the right to respect for one's private and family life, home and correspondence
- Article 14: the right not to be discriminated against in the enjoyment of any other Convention right

The legal duty to respect these rights applies not only to public bodies (such as the NHS and the social services departments of local authorities) but also to organisations performing a public function. These might be a private hospital carrying out work for the NHS, or a GP practice, or a private care home looking after people through a contract with the NHS, or a housing association fulfilling housing functions on behalf of a local council. If any of these bodies fails to provide someone with a fair hearing in a dispute or subjects them to degrading treatment or fails to respect their private life, for example, it can be taken to court.

The more harm the breach of somebody's human rights has caused, the stronger the case – including for compensation. In mounting a defence for a breach of a human right, it is not permissible for a public body (or one carrying out a public function) to excuse its behaviour by saying it did not have sufficient money to act in the way it should have done or that its actions arose out of ignorance rather than deliberate intent. In other words, a hospital ward could not say that it lacked the cash to employ sufficient numbers of staff to ensure that patients were not left in urine-soaked sheets, nor that staff were ignorant of the way in which the human rights of patients should be upheld. What matters is that somebody has suffered harm because their fundamental human rights have been breached. However, the courts are reluctant to direct public authorities to take action where the allocation of resources is involved. So it is not always possible to force an authority to provide a particular service or treatment, unless someone is being mistreated or suffering harm.

The outlawing of discrimination

Since the European Convention on Human Rights was drawn up and the British Parliament required public bodies to comply with it in 1998, further thinking has refined just what the protection of an individual's human rights should mean. Public debate and campaigning in Britain have focused on safeguarding the position of people who might be discriminated against, such as those with a disability. The Equality Act 2010 addresses the protection of human rights in a different way from the European Convention; both approaches have proved very useful.

The Equality Act, which applies in England, Wales and Scotland, forbids any provider of goods and services whether private or public from discriminating against someone or treating them differently from other people in a similar situation because they possess a so-called 'protected characteristic'. These characteristics are:

- the presence of a disability
- their age
- their race
- their religion or belief
- their sex
- their sexual orientation
- their gender reassignment
- their being married or in a civil partnership

- their being pregnant or being a parent[35]

This means that a hotel, bank or betting shop as well as a hospital could be penalised by a court if it does not make its goods and services equally available to say, people of a particular race or religion or age, unless the service provider in question could persuade a court that its action (or inaction) is justified.

In a case of which I became aware a deaf man had to wait three weeks in a hospital in Scotland for his health board to provide the sign language interpreter he needed. The delay was unfortunate, but an interpreter might never have been forthcoming had he not enjoyed the legal right not to be discriminated against when services were provided. For the Equality Act (together with the rules on gaining patient consent) mean that any doctor providing a patient with the information they need to make an informed consent to treatment must take steps to ensure they are not discriminated against because of any disability. The doctor must do what they can to ensure the information is available in a form in which the patient can absorb it and that they can express their views. If the patient cannot speak English, the doctor would need to provide an interpreter. It is the forbidding of discrimination against people on grounds of race and disability that has prompted the provision of information about services in different languages and in large-print, audio and Braille formats. *(See also the so-called public sector equality duty on page 692.)*

Age discrimination

As we have just seen, age is one of the protected characteristics under equality law in Britain. So it is against the law to treat someone less well when goods or services are being provided to them because they are of a certain age (whether they are young or old), whether the provider is a golf club or a GP practice. However, protection again age discrimination is not absolute – certain limitations have been introduced.

The government has told doctors, nurses and other professionals, as well as the commissioners and providers of health and social care services, that they, 'Can continue to treat people differently because of their age. However, they will need to show, if challenged, that there is good reason (or objective justification) for that different treatment.'[36]

What does this mean in practice? Take the age cut-off points in the mass screening for particular diseases. These are often difficult to defend on medical grounds, so they might be overturned by court decisions in the future.

Women are sent routine invitations for breast screening every three years only up to the age of 73. Yet 40 per cent of breast cancer cases occur in women over 70, and women over 80 are the group most at risk.[37] Women over 73 should therefore ask for breast screening themselves.

There are many other ways in which you might encounter age discrimination in healthcare provision. Your doctor suspects you may have Parkinson's disease but declines to refer you to a specialist when they would have referred a younger person; they could be guilty of age discrimination. If your local health body refuses to provide you with a physiotherapist within a certain period, yet provides such a service to a younger person with the same medical condition as yours, that too could constitute age discrimination. Or if you suffer a major stroke and the nursing home in which you are living fails to summon emergency help, it could be guilty of age discrimination, since a stroke in someone of any age should be treated as a medical emergency *(see pages 349–52)*.

If you are concerned that you have been discriminated against on grounds of age, the question you need to be able to answer in the affirmative is: has the health professional or health body treated me less favourably than it would have treated somebody else in a similar situation but of a different age?

How can you tell? Well, to start with, you could have a look at the NICE guidance that sets out the tests and treatment that health bodies and professionals should provide for many different medical conditions *(see pages 289–90)*.

The follow-up question must then be: is there any good reason why I should have been treated differently? A doctor might argue that they declined to offer a patient a particular treatment because they thought it would be futile. For instance, they might decide against trying to restart somebody's heart if it had stopped beating because they thought the procedure would not work because the person was too weak. However, a doctor must not base their clinical decision on the patient's chronological age. None of us ages in precisely the same way, as we discovered in Chapter 1. The more refined approach, which a doctor should adopt, is to look at somebody's 'biological age' *(as explained on page 12)*. In other words, a doctor must not refuse to attempt resuscitation simply because their patient is very old.

If a health professional or organisation denies you a test or treatment, referral to a specialist or provision of a type of NHS funding, that decision has affected you badly and you think it was based on your age and could not be objectively justified, ask the person responsible to reverse or amend the decision. If you fail and need speedy action, consider the steps to resolve urgent healthcare problems outlined in Chapter 15. If immediate action is not called for, consider lodging an official complaint *(see pages 336–41)* and/or taking a claim of age discrimination to your local county court (in England or Wales) or sheriff court in Scotland. If you win your case in court, the judge or sheriff could make a ruling that the discrimination should be put right, so you would be given the test or treatment which had been withheld on grounds of your age. The judge or sheriff could also award you compensation, including for any hurt feelings. Mention that you might lodge a complaint or go to court, thus showing awareness of your legal rights, could work in your favour, even if you would not in fact seriously consider going that far.

Before you take steps to pursue the matter in court, talk to your local Citizens Advice or a helpline advisor of the Equality Advisory Support Service *(see page 691),* as you would have to pay a court fee to make a claim (though you may be eligible for legal aid), and if you lose your case you may have to pay the legal costs of the other party. The Equality and Human Rights Commission publishes guidance on how the law should be complied with and what might be deemed to be unacceptable discrimination, *as explained on page 689.*

If you plan to take a claim of age discrimination to court, make sure you leave yourself sufficient time. The Equality Act lays down a time limit for making a claim of six months from the date of the alleged act of discrimination to which a claim relates. If you first try to pursue the matter another way, perhaps as an NHS complaint, you might run out of time. Fortunately, the legislation allows for discretion on the part of the court, saying that a case may be heard after such period as the county court or sheriff 'thinks just and equitable'.[38] But note: *may.*

No legislation barring age discrimination in Northern Ireland had been drafted at the time of writing.

I also explore the use of the Equality Act in the field of disability discrimination on pages 687–92 and in age discrimination in the workplace on pages 882–3.

National Service Frameworks for Older People

Quite apart from the Equality Act, there are older anti-age-discrimination directions which can prove useful.

The Welsh Assembly published a *National Service Framework for Older People in Wales* in 2006. This sets out standards which the Assembly expects healthcare providers to attain. Unequivocal in its disapproval of discrimination on the grounds of age in the provision of health services, the first standard, called 'Rooting out Age Discrimination', states:

'Health and social care services are provided regardless of age on the basis of clinical and social need. Age is not used in eligibility criteria or policies to restrict access to and receipt of available services.'[39]

If you feel you are being denied a drug or other treatment or examination on grounds of age in Wales, then you could challenge your doctor or health board, if necessary quoting Standard One.

Standard Two, called 'Person-centred Care', could also be useful. It states: 'Health and social care services treat people as individuals and enable them to make choices about their own care.'[40] In other words, an older person should not be treated in a way which does not treat them as an individual. If, for instance, you have been admitted to hospital after suffering a stroke and a doctor proposes to send you for acute care to a geriatric ward rather than the stroke ward where you think you would receive better treatment, discuss the matter with them and mention this standard if necessary. *(See also pages 358–9.)*

Not only does the Framework set general standards which the Assembly considers the health service (and social services) should reach in areas of key importance to older people, it also contains detailed recommendations for best practice in particular areas, including the use of medicines, falls and bone fractures, mental health (including depression and dementia), and the care of older people in hospital. The Framework is available by post from the Welsh Assembly Government and on its website.

Although this National Service Framework does not, strictly speaking, apply to England, Scotland or Northern Ireland, it would be difficult for a health organisation in these places to argue that the injunctions and standards set out for Wales should not also apply to them. In fact, a similar and potentially useful framework for England was promoted by the Department of Health in 2001. It remains available, although it is rarely referred to by government.[41]

Rights in care homes

All the rights described in this chapter apply equally in care homes whether residential, nursing or specialist, such as homes for people with dementia. So your right to see your GP or obtain free disability equipment or clothing such as a wheelchair or continence pads is unaffected by your residence in a care home. Similarly, if you or your relative needs a referral to an audiologist for a hearing aid or to a clinical psychologist to help with problems associated with dementia, ask your or their GP for one – just as you would if you or they were living at home. The fact that a nurse is required to be present at all times in a nursing home *(see Glossary)* should not affect your health rights.

The NHS: Rights and pledges

* The NHS Constitution sets out important health rights, but it is not well known.

* Entitlement to free healthcare includes equipment such as hearing aids and continence pads.

* Make sure a personal health budget will cover the costs of your healthcare.

* Choose your GP carefully, after a preliminary consultation.

* Appoint attorneys or named consultees to give or withhold medical consent if you should become incapable of doing so.

* Watch out for treatments and tests that you might want to refuse.

* Exercise your right to choice in treatment, GP and hospital.

* Expect NICE guidance to be followed for your ailments.

* Ask for your annual health check if you are 75 or over.

* Get your own copy of your patient records.

Chapter 15

Practitioners, organisations and concerns

I n this chapter I turn to the main professionals involved in healthcare provision for older people, from dentists and nurses to chiropodists and physiotherapists. I explain what these professionals do and how to find one, as well as the system that seeks to exclude people without the relevant qualifications or lacking a professional manner from practising.

As users of the NHS and also of private healthcare provision, we are also protected through the inspection and regulation of the organisations that deliver healthcare services, from nursing agencies and hospital foundation trusts to care homes. I outline the way in which this separate regulation works too.

Voluntary organisations, from Macmillan Cancer Support to the Stroke Association to Action on Hearing Loss, also play a crucial role in supporting people affected by particular illness or disabilities. The scope of this sector is outlined as well.

Finally, I address what you can do if you are unhappy with your treatment.

This chapter therefore covers:

▶ the work of individual healthcare professionals

▶ protection from unqualified or disreputable people

▶ the way in which healthcare services are regulated

▶ sources of information about healthcare

▶ the work of voluntary organisations involved in healthcare

▶ what to do if you have a concern about healthcare treatment

▶ organisations which can help with raising concerns and lodging complaints

Doctors, nurses, pharmacists and other professionals

Many different types of healthcare professional can make a huge difference to our quality of life when we are older. Some are familiar; others not. Before I explain what they do and how to find one, here is a brief explanation of the way in which these professionals are regulated.

A system of compulsory registration covers many of the professionals whose area of expertise is outlined in this chapter, including:

doctors	physiotherapists
dentists and other dental professionals	pharmacists
speech and language therapists	nurses
optometrists and other eye care professionals	chiropodists
occupational therapists	clinical psychologists

This is how compulsory registration works. The title 'dentist', 'chiropodist' and so on is said to be 'protected': only people who have been accepted onto a special register can lawfully call themselves, say, a dentist, and if they behave unprofessionally, their name can be struck off the register, leaving them unable to work in that field. Or their registration might be suspended for a limited period, perhaps for failing to communicate clearly with patients or provide the best treatment.

Anybody who wishes to check that somebody claiming to be one of these professionals is bona fide can contact the organisation holding the particular register. If they wish to complain about somebody who is practising, they do so to the same body.

Doctors, nurses, pharmacists, dentists and eye care professionals have their own bodies to supervise their registers. For the other professionals covered by compulsory registration, this task is carried out by the Health and Care Professions Council.

Before an organisation such as the Health and Care Professions Council or the General Medical Council (for doctors) places someone's name on its register, it looks at their competence in the relevant field, most obviously if they have gained certain qualifications and experience. It considers whether that individual might pose a danger because they might abuse their position of trust by harming a patient, whether physically, sexually, financially or emotionally. The organisation does this by consulting lists of people who have been convicted of a criminal offence and/or abused a vulnerable older person or a child in the past or are considered to pose a significant risk of harming vulnerable older people or children in the future. *I explain how this system works when discussing the hiring of care staff in Chapter 23 (on pages 507 and 528).* There is a considerable number of people whose names are on these lists.

Let us now examine the work of the healthcare professionals who can offer valuable help in later life.

Doctors

The majority of doctors practise in thousands of GP practices scattered over the country. A minimum of five years at university and a year in a hospital is followed by three years' training to become a GP. Once GPs have qualified, they are expected to keep abreast of developments by attending updating courses. They are remunerated through money paid to their practices by the NHS, from which they allocate themselves a salary, which may run to £100,000 per year. Other doctors work in NHS hospitals and other facilities and independent practices, clinics and hospitals.

Before anybody can lawfully practise as a doctor in any setting in the UK, their name must be entered on a register held by the General Medical Council (GMC), and they must also possess a licence to practise.

Applicants for the GMC's register must possess certain qualifications, follow a code of professional behaviour, and be reassessed for their fitness to practise every five years. The GMC has powers to take a doctor to task if they behave unprofessionally and can have their name struck off the register, temporarily or permanently. If they then continue to practise as a doctor, they can be prosecuted and sent to prison. In other words, registration is compulsory and titles such as 'doctor' are legally protected, so other people cannot adopt them without breaking the law.

At least as well known as the GMC but quite different from it is the British Medical Association. The BMA is a professional association of doctors which lobbies on their behalf, represents their interests and provides services for them.

The role of doctors is discussed at many places in this book, not least in relation to particular medical conditions, such as strokes, in Part Five. The role of doctors in hospitals and hospices is discussed in Parts Eleven and Twelve.

Dentists

Many teeth problems can emerge or worsen when we are getting on, not least tooth decay, gum disease and gum shrinkage *(as outlined on pages 16–17)*. As we come to outlive the life expectancy of our teeth, major work may become necessary. At the same time, the maintenance of good oral health can be difficult if dexterity problems prevent us from cleaning our teeth and gums properly.

Dentists have to study for four or five years as undergraduates, followed by further training for general dental or specialist work. The General Dental Council maintains a list of people who can lawfully practise as dentists in the UK, whether in the NHS or in private practice. It also compiles lists of specialists, such as those with expertise in diseases of the gums and special care dentistry (dental care for people with physical and mental illnesses and impairments, including dementia).

Dental hygienists focus on the prevention of problems, for instance through removing plaque, polishing teeth and sealing fissures. They too must register with the General Dental Council, once they have successfully completed a two-year course at dental school.

However, in stark contrast to medical care, neither check-ups nor dental care are provided free through the NHS. You can obtain free treatment by an NHS dentist only if it is carried out by an NHS hospital dentist or, if outside hospital, if you receive Income Support, Guarantee Pension Credit, Universal Credit or income-based Employment and Support Allowance or Jobseeker's Allowance. If you have been accepted by the NHS Low Income Scheme, your charge may be reduced *(see Chapter 36 for these qualifying benefits and the Low Income Scheme).*

Some people obtain treatment from a dentist who has a contract to carry out work for the NHS, even though they are not eligible for free care. They do, however, benefit from lower charges than those of dentists acting privately, who can charge whatever they consider the market will sustain. If you receive treatment from an NHS dentist, your costs are capped: you pay a set amount falling into one of three cost bands. The lowest band covers check-ups and the most expensive covers complex treatment, such as work on crowns and bridges. As dental work can be very expensive, you could save a lot of money if you use an NHS dentist.

Lists of dentists prepared to carry out treatment under the NHS are held by primary care organisations – clinical commissioning groups, health boards and, in Northern Ireland, a national agency – the Central Services Agency.

However, there is a serious shortage of dentists prepared to carry out work for the NHS, so many people who would like dental treatment through the NHS end up going private. Because of the high charges levied by some private practitioners, many people probably forego dental treatment altogether.

Getting to the dentist

A separate problem which many people face is difficulty in moving around and so getting out to a high-street dental practice. They must therefore try, somehow or other, to find a dentist prepared to visit them at home.

Few private dentists offer this facility and those that do are likely to charge a call-out fee on top of the charge for treatment. However, every primary care commissioning organisation should have a roving team of NHS dentists who visit patients in their own homes or in care homes, if they cannot get to surgery. On the ground, these teams vary according to the resources the health body is prepared to devote to them. But they can be invaluable. If you are looking round a care home or an extra-care housing scheme, it is worth asking whether the community dental service calls regularly.

Nurses

When we are getting on, the nurses we most frequently encounter outside hospital are practice nurses and district nurses.

Based in GP practices, practice nurses carry out tasks such as syringing ears, removing stitches and changing wound dressings, and they often run clinics for conditions such as blood pressure or asthma. Although you are most likely to see the practice nurse in his or her office, they do visit patients in their own homes.

District or community nurses, on the other hand, always treat patients where they are living – in their own homes or in residential care homes, visiting them to give injections and change dressings, catheters and feeding tubes. (In nursing homes the home's nursing staff should carry out most of the tasks that a district nurse would otherwise perform.) District nurses sometimes share premises with GP practices but operate separately from them, reporting direct to the organisation that employs or commissions them, such as a health board in Scotland or a clinical commissioning group in England. Often district nurses visit patients recently discharged from hospital.

Alongside these general nurses is a range of specialist nurses with whom you may come into contact. These include:

- tissue viability nurses (specialising in wounds and the prevention and treatment of pressure sores)
- continence nurses (very important, as continence difficulties affect many older people and much more can be done to alleviate distress than is often realised)
- care-of-older-people specialist nurses
- community psychiatric nurses or CPNs (providing support for patients with mental health problems living in their own homes or non-NHS institutions such as care homes)

- palliative care nurses (specialising in the care of people with illnesses that may result in death and of people who are coming to the end of their lives). They include Macmillan nurses, Marie Curie nurses and hospice-at-home nurses *(see Chapter 40)*.

- nurses specialising in particular medical conditions, such as diabetes, Parkinson's disease or heart failure. Dementia specialist nurses seek to help people with dementia and to give practical, clinical and emotional support to their families. In Scotland dementia specialist nurses are based in health boards; in England, they are called Admiral nurses and are provided by the charity Dementia UK

(The various types of nurse encountered mainly in NHS hospitals, including nurse associates and apprentice nurses, are described in Chapter 38.)

In addition, many nurses work outside the NHS, in private hospitals, nursing homes and for nurses agencies. These organisations are inspected and regulated the Care Quality Commission and its equivalents in other parts of the UK *(see pages 320–3 below)*.

The Nursing and Midwifery Council is responsible for registering and disciplining nurses, so check registration details about anyone you propose to hire privately with the NMC. Also find out about their area of expertise – working as a nurse in the operating theatre is very different from caring for someone who has heart failure or Parkinson's disease.

Pharmacists

Pharmacists are the third most numerous healthcare professional in the UK. They train for five years – one year less than a doctor and one year more than a nurse. This training equips them to do far more than dispense prescriptions, and their expertise is increasingly being used more widely, not least to reduce the workload of GPs of whom there is a shortage in many parts of the country.

The General Pharmaceutical Council holds the lists of pharmacists and also pharmacy technicians who are registered to practise, and can take to task anyone who does not behave professionally.

The vast majority of pharmacists work in pharmacies on the high street, but many people do not benefit from their expertise as much as they could. Here are some of the advantages of consulting one:

A pharmacist will have knowledge about **minor ailments** which may not require a visit to a GP and may be treatable with medication which does not need a prescription, such as a sore throat or an allergic reaction.

This is a walk-in service offered by most high street pharmacies and can be more convenient to use than a GP appointment.

A pharmacist will have special **knowledge and experience of drugs**. They may know more than a GP about the advantages and drawbacks of particular types of drug, which ones work best in particular circumstances, the side-effects and – crucially – the way in which different prescribed drugs as well as over-the-counter medicines interact.

Pharmacists are taught to ensure that patients use drugs in the best possible way. This means that a consultation with a pharmacist should cover not only what drug or drugs would benefit you, but the form in which they should be given and the way you are using them. They should seek to involve you in making decisions about the selection and use of your drugs. This is called **medicines optimisation**.[1] *As explained on page 294,* not all pharmacies offer these consultations, but many do.

Take asthma, for instance. By the time we are in our 60s, it is easy to be complacent about the symptoms of asthma and put up with them. Do you understand what your asthma medication does? Are you using the correct inhaler? Do you know how to use it? Do you know how you can avoid or manage any side effects of the medication in the inhaler? Do you know how to reduce your chances of needing to use it?

A consultation with a pharmacist can therefore be useful. Apart from their special expertise they bring, pharmacists tend to have more time to see patients than the standard ten minutes offered by GPs.

If you are **starting a new medicine**, it is worth talking to a pharmacist about it, so that you understand how it works and can sort out any difficulties in taking it. Ten days after starting a medicine, almost a third of people are not taking it properly, according to research. Of these, more than half are unaware that they are failing to do so.[2] If you fail to take your medication as prescribed, you will miss out on the treatment you need.

If you are concerned about a medicines prescription, perhaps given you by a hospital, talk to your pharmacist. They can double-check that any new drugs will not cause problems by interacting with your existing medicines. They may suggest a different dose. Or perhaps a doctor has suggested anti-psychotic medication to control the behaviour of a loved one with dementia. Sometimes this medication can be helpful but if it would be unsuitable for your relative yet you are under pressure to sanction it, your pharmacist could prove a useful ally; the General Pharmaceutical Council has produced a resource pack to support pharmacists who wish to oppose such prescribing.[3] *(See also page 450.)*

One reason people fail to take medication is **swallowing difficulties**, which are common in people in their eighties and above. Indeed, half of the residents in any care home may have swallowing difficulties.[4] As a result, they may be unable to swallow tablets whole. The same medication in liquid form is often more expensive, while some drugs are not available in liquid form. It can be tempting to crush tablets or dissolve them in water or even melt them, but this can be dangerous. Some drugs are designed to release their dose slowly over a long period; if crushed, the active ingredients are released immediately and this could result in an initial overdose, with potentially dangerous side effects. Also, the drug will not treat the condition as intended and, after the initial burst of drug, a period without any medication will follow.

Some tablets are coated to disguise the taste and so make them easier to swallow or to protect the lining of the stomach so that they are released only after the drug has passed through the stomach. Crushed tablets could taste horrible and/or damage the lining of the stomach.

Always seek the advice of a pharmacist if you face problems in the form in which you are able to take the medication. If there is no alternative to crushing, a pharmacist would explain how to crush the tablets and how to take the medicine. *(I discuss the delivery of drugs for people receiving end-of-life care on page 984–8.)*

As well as giving advice on medication, some pharmacists conduct special reviews for patients of the medicines they are taking; *I discuss these Medicine User Reviews and other services which pharmacies must or may provide, including help for carers and help with the management of long-term conditions on pages 292–5.*

Hospitals have their own pharmacists; some are based in GP practices. Pharmacists on the high street and in GP practices play an important role in providing medication to care homes and may visit the home; they may also visit individual patients in their own home.

Eye care professionals

Optimising eyesight is important not just in order to be able to see and enjoy the world around us. The world is a more dangerous place if we cannot see well. Driving is clearly more hazardous, but so too is moving around our homes or streets, particularly negotiating stairs. In a study of 200 elderly patients admitted to hospital after a fall, more than half had impaired vision; in nearly 80 per cent of cases the cause could have been corrected.[5]

Eye tests

Eye tests are valuable for three main reasons. First, they can detect eye problems which are amenable to correction with spectacles or contact lenses, such as long-sight. Second, the professionals qualified to perform tests, optometrists, can detect serious eye conditions such as glaucoma and cataracts, which, if left untreated, could result in serious loss of vision. Third, optometrists can detect other health problems not primarily centred on the eye, including diabetes, tumours and high blood pressure, although these conditions will not definitely be picked up by an eye test.

Everybody over the age of 60 is entitled to a free NHS eye test every two years. Some people are entitled to a free test annually. They are:

- people over 70
- people with diabetes or glaucoma
- people who are partially sighted or blind
- people over 40 who have a close family member with glaucoma

It is well worth taking advantage of this facility; in any case, you should consult a doctor or an optometrist immediately if you are worried about your sight.

People with mobility problems and those living in care homes are entitled to a 'domiciliary eye test'. This means that an optometrist will visit them at home and the NHS will pay for the test and the optometrist's visiting costs. Local primary care organisations have lists of opticians who offer this service, as do GP practices and opticians' practices, some of which make a business decision not to offer domiciliary eye tests but should know of someone in the area who offers the service.

Bear in mind that the optometrists who perform eye tests, prescribe spectacles and carry out examinations for eye disease in people's homes are unlikely to carry all of the most sophisticated testing equipment found at a high-street practice, although they should carry perfectly adequate portable equipment, such as that specified in a code of practice issued by the College of Optometrists.

Help with managing poor eyesight

Dispensing opticians fit and dispense devices to aid vision, principally spectacles. Many people are unaware of an important service offered by both optometrists and dispensing opticians: advice on how to cope with low vision through appliances other than spectacles, such as magnifying lenses, magnifying spectacles, telescopes and screen readers (electronic devices that use your computer or TV screen to make material easier to decipher). There is now a wide range of such devices, and advice on which ones are most suitable can be very useful. *(Some of this equipment is described on page 460–1.)*

Both optometrists and dispensing opticians acquire competence in helping people with low vision as part of their basic training, but many do not use it much or keep up with new developments. About one in 50 dispensing opticians, however, have obtained a special qualification in this area. It is called a diploma in low vision and is awarded by the Association of British Dispensing Opticians. The Royal National Institute of Blind People (RNIB) has a database of practices that offer a low vision assessment or a low vision aid service.

Both optometrists and dispensing opticians are regulated by the General Optical Council, which sets standards for training and conduct and maintains a register of people qualified and fit to work in the field.

Registration, regulation and complaints

We have already seen that doctors, dental professionals, pharmacists, nurses and eye care professionals are covered by a system of compulsory registration carried out by the General Medical Council, General Dental Council, Nursing and Midwifery Council, General Pharmaceutical Council and the General Optical Council. Another body, the Health and Care Professions Council, performs the same role for many other healthcare professions, such as dieticians, physiotherapists, occupational therapists and chiropodists. As with the GMC and so on, the HCPC is UK-wide.

The Health and Care Professions Council holds the registration lists and provides a single port of call for people wishing to check the registration of the professionals in question. It also operates a mechanism for reprimanding or striking off people who do not behave in a professional manner.

Before the advent of the HCPC, many of the professions involved operated a system of control over who could practise through their own professional bodies, such as the Royal College of Speech and Language Therapists. Many of these older bodies still exist, acting as trade groups protecting the interests of the profession but also offering information to the general public. They can be a useful source of information about the type of work undertaken by the profession in question and also about how to find a professional, should you wish to hire privately. Cutbacks in NHS funding may mean that the NHS will not offer you a referral to, say, a physiotherapist or will give you only a few sessions when more would be far better, or that there will be a long delay before you see the professional. Or perhaps only the first appointment will be with a fully qualified practitioner and the remaining with a less-qualified assistant.

Complaints about the conduct of individual professionals covered by compulsory registration can be made to the Health and Care Professions Council, the General Medical Council, General Dental Council, Nursing and Midwifery Council, General Pharmaceutical Council or the General Optical Council. Each of these has the power to reprimand professionals or strike them off its list.

If you are concerned about a healthcare professional such as an NHS dentist, you could also consider contacting the health body that has commissioned them. Failing resolution, contact the relevant Ombudsman (*see page 340–1 below*).

In 2007, the General Dental Council set up a useful but little-known facility – a dental complaints service to help people who wish to complain about any dental professional, whether NHS or private. The complaint might involve, for instance, treatment, cost, unnecessary pain or giving (or not giving) consent to treatment. If a complaint is justified, the service encourages a dentist or other dental professional to say sorry for what happened, refund the fees and/or pay for treatment to put matters right.

Here are the main professionals encountered in later life who are overseen by the Health and Care Professions Council:

Physiotherapists

Qualified physiotherapists probably know as much about the skeletal and muscular systems of the human body as do doctors. They can help people suffering from arthritis and osteoporosis, weakness in the muscles, walking difficulties, trouble in retaining balance, and breathing problems. Treatment can be administered to relieve pain, and particular exercises and movements encouraged.

The Chartered Society of Physiotherapy is the professional, educational and trade union body for physiotherapists. It maintains a list of registered practitioners in addition to that held by the Health and Care Professions Council.

Occupational therapists

Occupational therapy developed after the Second World War to help injured servicemen and women adapt to injury and disability. Therapists take a three- or four-year university course leading to a degree in occupational therapy.

The majority of occupational therapists (OTs) work in the public sector, mostly in the NHS. They help people who have to cope with illness and disability to manage their day-to-day living. Someone who has lost the use of an arm after a stroke might be taught new ways of performing household chores such as meal preparation and shopping, and personal care tasks such as dressing and bathing. Occupational therapists are also trained in psychology and can help people cope with both the physical and mental challenges that ageing, illness and disability can present.

Occupational therapists are experts in the gadgets and home adaptations that can help people with dexterity and mobility problems. Social services departments employ OTs to advise on such matters in the homes of older people and to assess whether somebody meets the criteria to receive adaptations and gadgets for free. Their advice on how to reduce the risk of a fall in the home can be invaluable *(see Chapter 18)*. As noted above, registration of OTs is controlled by the Health and Care Professions Council. Their professional body is the College of Occupational Therapists.

Dieticians

State-registered dieticians are usually based in large NHS hospitals. Many older patients in hospital are malnourished, and dieticians are called in to work out their nutritional needs and how these can be met. They can recommend particular diets both for people who can take food in the normal way and also for those who can be fed only by other means, such as a tube which passes direct into the stomach. But they can also come up with recommendations for older people in their own homes, community hospitals and care homes.

Dieticians take a four-year full-time course or a two-year post-graduate diploma, after a degree in, say, physiology or biochemistry. Their professional association is the British Dietetic Association *(some of whose recommendations are mentioned in Chapter 2)*.

Speech and language therapists

This profession originally developed to help people disabled in the First World War. Speech and language therapists have usually taken a three-year or four-year university course. Their work with older people includes helping those whose mechanisms for swallowing and speaking have become impaired, for example after a major stroke or as a result of Parkinson's disease.

If you are looking for a private practitioner, contact the therapists' professional body, the Royal College of Speech and Language Therapists, or the Association of Speech and Language Therapists in Independent Practice.

Chiropodists

In later life some foot problems arise as a side-effect of a medical condition. For instance, people with diabetes often develop a condition in which the nerves in the feet are damaged by high blood sugar levels and the foot or toes become numb and sometimes painful; the person involved may therefore cut their foot without realising they have done so.[6] In other cases, corns, bunions, callouses, in-growing toenails, fungal infections and so on arise as a result of a problem which develops in the foot itself.

Chiropodists or podiatrists (as they are sometimes called; there is no clinical distinction between the two terms) examine feet and treat or refer patients on for further treatment of any medical condition of the foot, including surgery. They also provide foot care through cutting nails, cutting back corns and so on.

Chiropody should be available on the NHS free of charge, usually through a GP referral. However, primary care organisations impose their own eligibility criteria, which means that whether somebody receives free treatment depends on the severity of their condition and how quickly it needs to be treated. You may find that there is a waiting time of three months unless you are considered to need urgent treatment, perhaps because you are in extreme pain and there are signs of infection. You may find that you are eligible for some free treatment, but between visits you need to pay for treatment to remain comfortable.

If you are looking for a chiropodist privately, be careful. Chiropodists can be invaluable – or cause harm. Somebody who has not been properly trained can give wrong advice and treatment, and as a result make your condition worse. Or they could fail to spot potentially serious problems. The terms 'chiropodist' and 'podiatrist' are protected in law, so a person who has not registered with the Health and Care Professions Council cannot lawfully use them. A 'foot health practitioner' or 'foot health professional' is unlikely to be a qualified chiropodist – they may be giving themselves one of these titles because any qualifications they may have fall short of those required for registration as a chiropodist. Find out where and for how long they have trained and what exams they have passed.

You may be able to reduce the frequency of the help you will need from a chiropodist by cutting your own toenails, perhaps with nail clippers, or long-handled, angled toenail scissors if you have difficulty in bending to reach your toes. You could also keep your nails and hard skin in check by filing them. Ask a chiropodist to show you how to do all these things first and to recommend appropriate files and clippers.

Many chiropodists specialise, in fields such as the analysis of the mechanics of gait; rheumatism, arthritis and other disorders of the muscles, joints and ligaments; diabetes; and artificial devices to support weakened or abnormal joints or limbs. They can be invaluable in working out why someone is having falls and what can be done to prevent further falls *(see page 389)*.

In some places volunteers who have been trained by chiropodists in basic foot care offer a nail-cutting service. This is likely to be cheaper than a private visit to the chiropodist.

Mental health specialists

How do psychiatrists, psychologists, counsellors and psychotherapists differ one from another? Well, psychiatry is a branch of medicine: after training first as doctors, **psychiatrists** pursue a minimum of three years' post-graduate study in psychiatry. They can prescribe drugs, but psychologists, counsellors and psychotherapists cannot, although they may make recommendations to a GP or a psychiatrist. Psychiatrists are registered with the General Medical Council. Psychiatrists who specialise in care for older people are sometimes called psycho-geriatricians.

While GPs often think of referring older people to a psychiatrist, they might not consider a **clinical psychologist.** Yet these professionals can be very useful. They treat conditions such as anxiety, phobias, dementia, depression, psychosis and schizophrenia with various kinds of talking therapy. The approaches taken to the treatment of anxiety and depression *(as described in Chapter 17: Anxiety and depression)* give a good idea of the way clinical psychologists approach their work. They may be asked by care homes for help with the care of people with dementia. Or a relative could ask a GP for a referral for their loved one.

Nobody can lawfully call themselves a clinical psychologist without being registered with the Health and Care Professions Council. The clinical psychologists' professional body is the British Psychological Society, which holds a register; some clinical psychologists practise privately, but of course they must be on the HCPC register.

Counsellors and psychotherapists

Counsellors and psychotherapists tend to deal with less serious mental health problems than psychiatrists and clinical psychologists. Both offer help through talking either to one person or a small group, such as a family.

The terms 'counsellor' and 'psychotherapist' are not easy to distinguish in terms of their approach or their role. There is much crossover, with some people calling themselves psychotherapeutic counsellors. To complicate matters further, there are different approaches to therapy within the disciplines of psychotherapy and counselling – for instance, some practitioners focus on getting to the root cause of problems, while others try to alter the behaviour that is causing the problems without concentrating too much on the causes.

The terms 'counsellor' and 'psychotherapist' are not protected titles. Anybody can call themselves either, even if they have no qualifications or experience, without breaking the law. Fortunately, two reputable professional bodies have themselves compiled registers to which people can turn to find out whether somebody has adequate training to practise as a psychotherapist or a counsellor and has agreed to abide by standards of professional behaviour. Do check that any practitioner you plan to hire or to whom you are referred by your GP has opted to register with one of these bodies. All sorts of problems can arise during counselling or psychotherapy and it is vital that the counsellor or therapist should have the training and experience to handle them and treat what you tell them in confidence.

To become an accredited member of the UK Council for Psychotherapy, somebody must have a first degree or equivalent (which could be in an unrelated subject) followed by four years' part-time training and supervised practice. If you are in any doubt about a practitioner's status, seek confirmation from the Council, but look for an accredited psychotherapist.

For a counsellor, look for an accredited (not just an ordinary) member of the British Association of Counselling and Psychotherapy (BACP). They will have had at least three years' training and a minimum of 450 hours of practice, will have agreed to adhere to a code of ethics and a code of practice and to subject themselves to the BACP's complaints procedures. Senior accredited members have practised for at least five years.

The lists drawn up by the UK Council for Psychotherapy and the BACP have been approved by the Professional Standards Authority (PSA). This organisation oversees the work of the Health and Care Professions Council, General Medical Council and other bodies which operate systems of compulsory registration. Just as it checks on the way in which compulsory registration works, so it has the power to approve procedures for voluntary registration.

Both the UK Council for Psychotherapy and the BACP are happy to give guidance on the sort of professional who could best help and to point inquirers to reputable professionals operating in their localities. Some counsellors and/or psychotherapists specialise in bereavement for instance, others in relations within families, workplace difficulties, addiction and relationship problems. The BACP publishes useful factsheets about the various approaches of counsellors and psychotherapists.

Practitioners outside the HCPC system

Reflexologists, chiropractors and medical herbalists are among the many other professionals in the world of healthcare whose help can be invaluable. But how do you know whether the aromatherapist or the injector of Botox you may use has any more knowledge of what they are doing than might be obtained through consulting a website or subscribing to a correspondence course?

Look first to see whether the title of, say, reflexologist is protected through registration. If so, which organisation acts in a way similar to the HCPC in protecting the public against unqualified people claiming this title?

If the field does not involve compulsory registration, is there a professional organisation which operates its own voluntary register, as does the BACP? If so, ask whether the register has been approved by the Professional Standards Authority. If it has not, ask the holder of the register how practitioners get their names onto it. For instance, do they have to obtain regular checks through the Disclosure and Barring Service *(see page 528)*, possess a certain level of training, and agree to work to certain standards of professional behaviour?

Pressure has been building up for the introduction of compulsory registration for certain other practitioners. For instance, a review by the NHS's medical director in 2013 urged the introduction of controls over beauty therapists who inject dermal fillers to smooth out wrinkles, unless they have been properly trained and hold a formal qualification.[7] However, at the time of writing, the government had not announced compulsory registration for this sector; the Scottish government was considering tighter controls.[8]

Pressure for greater safeguards for the public has also come from the Royal College of Surgeons. Someone who carries out cosmetic surgery must be a registered doctor, but they are not required by law to have a specialist cosmetic surgery accreditation based on training, qualifications or experience in the field. To help patients judge whether the surgeon who might operate on them is up to the task, the Royal College of Surgeons launched its own certification system in 2016. The system is not compulsory, but a surgeon can apply to have their name placed on this register. So if you are looking for a cosmetic surgeon, check to see whether the Royal College of Surgeons has accepted their name on its list of accredited cosmetic surgeons. The Royal College has also published information on its website about matters prospective patients should consider carefully, not least the potential complications and drawbacks of any procedure. It urges them to reflect for a fortnight between a consultation and agreeing to surgery.

Healthcare assistants

An increasingly familiar professional in the health service is the healthcare assistant. Different assistants perform widely differing tasks. In hospital, you may encounter them on the ward, monitoring patients through blood tests, bathing them, helping them with personal care and talking to them and their relatives. In a GP practice, a healthcare assistant may be relieving the practice nurse of work by taking blood samples, checking blood pressure, sterilising equipment or interviewing new patients. The role of healthcare assistant is not tightly defined. Essentially, assistants do whatever a GP practice manager or a hospital ward manager asks them to do.

Some healthcare assistants do an excellent, professional job; others not so good. The background of heathcare assistants varies widely. Some may be students of an unrelated subject working in their college holidays who know virtually nothing of the working of the human body; others people who trained as, say, midwives in their own country but are unable to work as nurses here.

The term 'healthcare assistant' is not a protected title so there is no bar on anyone calling themselves a healthcare assistant whether or not they have passed any examinations or signed up to a code of conduct. However, they should have received some training. This is because the organisations that provide health (and personal care) must ensure their staff have the qualifications, competence and experience to provide care safely.[9] This means staff should have had some induction training in health and care, which might have involved obtaining the 'care certificate' *(see page 514)*, and instruction in the tasks the assistant is asked to perform.

If you are concerned that the healthcare assistant who turns up to, say, help manage your urinary catheter is not up to the task, ask to speak to the professional who is supervising them and ultimately responsible for them. Remember that your consent is required for any medical test or treatment. The Royal College of Nursing has set out the principles that it considers nurses should follow when delegating work to healthcare assistants, including crucially whether the assistant can carry out the task involved competently and whether delegation is in the best interests of the patient.[10] The care certificate framework also sets out the principles on which delegation should be based which also make clear that supervisors are accountable for the decision to delegate care and that those to whom work is delegated must be appropriately supervised and supported.[11]

The providers of healthcare service

Up till now in this chapter we have looked at individual practitioners – their qualifications, field of expertise and the way in which the state tries to protect the public against ill-intentioned or unqualified people. But the state separately regulates organisations that provide healthcare services, from GP practices to hospices, cosmetic surgery clinics, nursing agencies and care homes. Institutions and businesses are required to present themselves to a national agency before they can provide particular services and are then subjected by that agency to periodic inspection.

The Care Quality Commission

In England, the Care Quality Commission (CQC) is responsible for protecting and promoting the health, safety and welfare of people who use health and social care services through inspecting health and social care providers. These providers include GP practices, hospital trusts, care homes, and nursing and domiciliary care agencies.

The law singles out certain activities as 'regulated activities'. Any person or organisation that wishes to offer one or more of these must first obtain a registration certificate from the CQC. Regulated activities include:

- the treatment of disease, disorder or injury under the supervision of a healthcare professional or a social worker (or a multidisciplinary team)
- surgery
- diagnostic and screening procedures
- ambulance services
- nursing care
- personal care
- the provision of accommodation for people who need personal or nursing care[12]

(If any of these activities are carried out in the course of a family or personal relationship and for no commercial reward, they do not fall within the definition of a regulated activity.)

The provider of a regulated activity, such as a hospital trust, care home or dental surgery must obtain a certificate of registration, and the manager of such a facility also has to obtain one. The certificate relates to a particular facility, so, for example, someone known as 'the responsible person' would be registered to provide certain regulated activities at a particular clinic or care home. An applicant for registration must satisfy the commission on a number of counts, including that they:

● are of good character

● are physically and mentally fit to carry on the regulated activity

● possess the necessary qualifications, skills and experience to do so

● can supply the CQC with specified information about themselves, for instance, a full employment history and an explanation of any gaps in employment[13]

The CQC can impose conditions on the registration, for instance, that a GP practice can (or cannot) carry out minor surgery, or a care home can accommodate only a certain number of residents. A provider can apply for a modification of the conditions – for example, a residential care home that wishes to be allowed also to provide nursing care to residents.

Any person or organisation carrying out a regulated activity without possessing a certificate of registration or in contravention of conditions set down in such a certificate is acting unlawfully and can be fined, potentially a large sum of money. Thus, for example, in 2012 the CQC successfully prosecuted a cosmetic surgery treatment company for carrying out liposuction procedures at independent clinics in Wakefield and London without having obtained the necessary registration. The CQC's inspectors carried out an unannounced inspection of the Wakefield clinic after receiving a tip-off from a member of the public. Magistrates ordered the company to pay a £40,000 fine.[14]

The CQC has a range of tools to force providers who are registered to act within the terms of their registration. Thus it can order them to make improvements within a certain period; as a last resort, it can remove their certificate of registration. This means they will have to cease to offer the activities for which registration is required.

Regulations on how providers are to behave

Once a responsible person has been given a certificate of registration to carry out regulated activities at a named facility, the CQC ensures that they carry them out to a certain standard through meeting regulations approved by Parliament. Failure to comply with these regulations constitutes a criminal offence.

The regulations are intended to be a catch-all safety net protecting those who are using the service and are cast in very wide terms. They seek to protect users against risks such as:

- unsafe or unsuitable premises
- unsafe equipment
- care or treatment that is inappropriate or unsafe
- unsafe use and management of medicines
- catching infections
- inadequate nutrition and dehydration
- abuse (including physical or psychological ill-treatment, theft and neglect; *see page 565*)

The regulations also seek to make sure that the provider makes suitable arrangements to ensure, amongst other things, that:

- users of the service are enabled to participate in making decisions about their care or treatment
- users are notified of any safety incident that has occurred and given support in relation to it, as part of a requirement that registered people must act in an open and transparent way with clients in relation to their care and treatment
- the service has a system for responding to comments and complaints, and
- everybody employed to carry out the regulated activity is of good character, has the necessary qualifications, skills and experience, and is physically and mentally fit for the work.[15]

The Care Quality Commission has published what it calls 'fundamental standards'; that is, the ways in which it expects the regulations to be met. The regulations and standards can be obtained from the CQC.[16] They are extremely useful in giving patients a clear idea of what to expect in such facilities as hospitals (NHS and independent), hospices, nursing agencies, clinics, pharmacies, GP and dental practices, as well as from services which come within the area of social care, such as care homes and domiciliary care agencies. CQC inspectors regularly go and inspect services they have registered and when they do so they base their examination around five questions. These are:

- Is the service safe?
- Is it effective?
- Is it caring?
- Is it responsive to people's needs?
- Is it well-led?

The CQC then publishes a report of its evaluation and gives the service in question one of the following ratings: inadequate, requires improvement, good or outstanding.

NHS Improvement

A separate body, NHS Improvement, seeks to help healthcare providers in England to improve the quality of their services so as to meet the standards set by the CQC. To this end it publishes guidance on its website and visits individual providers to offer tailored advice and support. But NHS Improvement has a separate function too – to keep an eye on the financial viability and management of the organisations which provide NHS services and help those with large deficits to get into the black, since the collapse of providers such as hospital foundation trusts or care home chains can have far-reaching consequences. NHS Improvement also involves itself in competition law, so if, say, two hospital foundation trusts propose to merge, it will examine the implications.

Healthcare Improvement Scotland (HIS)

In Scotland, the situation is different in two ways. First, a single body both regulates and inspects healthcare services and also helps providers to improve the quality of their services. But HIS restricts itself to healthcare: a separate organisation, the Care Inspectorate Scotland, has responsibility for regulating and inspecting social care facilities, including care homes, although both bodies often carry out joint inspections.

When Healthcare Improvement Scotland inspects registered healthcare services, it does so using clinical standards prepared by the Scottish Intercollegiate Guidelines Network (a body similar to NICE), as well as other national standards and best practice statements published by the Scottish government, HIS or one of its predecessor bodies. Like the CQC, it is very concerned to ensure that services are safe and so carries out inspections to check on the safety and cleanliness of hospitals, for example. But it also focuses on particular areas both in its inspections and in seeking improvements, such as, in recent years, chronic pain care;

the treatment of older people with delirium; and the care given to older people in acute hospitals. Have a look at the report of the inspection it carried out in 2012 on the care of older people in Dumfries and Galloway Royal Infirmary or its joint inspection with the Care Inspectorate in 2015 on services for older people in Glasgow (both on HIS's website) to get an idea of the range and depth of its inquiries and the criteria it uses; the results of inspections such as these are also invaluable if you are thinking of relocating to a different area.

Healthcare Inspectorate Wales

This is responsible for inspecting all NHS and independent healthcare providers, from a large acute hospital to a mental health establishment, a hospice to a private clinic in Wales. As with the other national healthcare regulators, you can see reports of its inspections and the standards, regulations, policies and guidance used in evaluating services on its website. Healthcare Inspectorate Wales has the additional responsibility of monitoring the way in which the mental health legislation is working on the ground. So, for instance, it keeps an eye on the way in which local health boards and local authorities use their powers in relation to people with dementia, amongst others. *As noted below, community health councils also evaluate NHS services.*

A separate body, the Care and Social Services Inspectorate Wales, registers and inspects care agencies and care homes *(see pages 531 and 963).*

The Regulation and Quality Improvement Authority (for Northern Ireland)

We noted in the previous chapter that health and social care are administered jointly in Northern Ireland. In line with this approach, a single body, the Regulation and Quality Improvement Authority (RQIA), regulates and inspects both health and social care services. These include not only the health and social care provided by public organisations but also those provided by independent organisations, both commercial and not-for-profit, from care homes to private hospitals.

Like its counterparts in other parts of the UK, the RQIA undertakes special reviews where there appears to be a systemic failure in a particular service and publishes its findings, as it has done on the control of infections in hospitals in Northern Ireland, for example.

The voluntary sector

Alongside and in many ways complementing the efforts of the health service is an array of charitable organisations. The vast majority of these focus on a different illness or disability, from blindness to strokes, diabetes to Parkinson's disease. These organisations keep themselves acquainted with the latest breakthroughs in their field and sometimes commission research themselves into causes and treatments. This informs the areas in which they may promote research, the campaigning work in which many of them engage and the advice they offer individuals. This advice is rather different from that usually proffered by the NHS. If you go and see your GP about your cancer, they can give or refer you for medical treatments and tests, but they are unlikely to be able to tell you to which state benefits you are entitled while taking time off work nor non-medical ways of living with the condition, such as how to find a volunteer who will visit you and help keep your spirits up.

I have sketched out below some of the many ways in which voluntary groups can help. Bear in mind that unlike state operations, the work of voluntary organisations is not subject to independent inspection to ensure it meets set standards of service. This means the type and quality of help groups even within the same organisation provide on the ground varies. At the same time, you may well find that more than one group could help you: there are separate voluntary organisations for different types of cancer as well as for cancer in general, just as there are different charities to help people with different kinds of vision impairment, in addition to the Royal National Institute of Blind People, for example.

The provision of information and advice

The information available to laypeople on the causes, treatments and ways of living with various conditions has vastly improved over the past few decades. Contrast for instance what little was available 20 years ago for migraine sufferers with the free handouts provided today by the Migraine Trust, covering anything from prevention to drugs and their side-effects and the forms which migraine can take in later life.

Some of the larger national groups provide a huge amount of information. Thus the RNIB and Action on Hearing Loss publish many information sheets and catalogues about the wide range of equipment available to help people with vision and hearing problems. The National Kidney Federation publishes a website running to more than 5,000 pages, and distributes its own magazine, *Kidney Life*, free of charge four times a year to more than 19,000 people. Many groups are expert in the complex field of state benefits too – for instance, Macmillan Cancer Support provides invaluable information and guidance about the benefits to which people with cancer may be entitled.

The large national voluntary organisations in healthcare operate helplines; that of the National Kidney Federation, for instance, takes about 200 calls a week. Trained staff discuss with callers the particular problems they are facing. Some voluntary sector organisations employ advice workers on the ground, who are aware of the services available in their localities and may visit people in their homes, offering suggestions not only about local support but also about how to cope day by day.

Some groups provide people called advocates who will pursue individual cases, helping people to secure the services they need and, if that is what the person wishes, representing them at meetings *(I explore the world of advocacy in Chapter 33).*

Contact with other people with your condition

Carole Whitbread has the lung condition emphysema and she reflected in 2013 on the support she had received from a local support group, Breathe Easy Medway:

> It's a lifeline for some people. When you're diagnosed, you think you're the only person in the world that has it. When your whole life has been active and all of a sudden you're not capable of doing things … you go down that deep, dark, hole.[17]

The sense that you are the only person in the world coping with a serious illness is a common reaction to a diagnosis. Talking to other people who have had the same experience not only helps you feel you are not alone – indeed, that you are treading a well-trodden path – it enables you to receive and share tips and information about possible ways of living with the condition in your locality.

Support for carers

The same goes for carers. Many voluntary healthcare organisations run carers' groups, some for carers on their own, some which the people for whom they are caring also attend. At these, carers can share tips and offer mutual support – and, let's hope, enjoy themselves too.

Say you have cared full time, night and day, for your mother for five years. She dies or moves into a care home. What then? Coping with the transition to life after caring can be daunting. Some groups provide one-to-one support for people in this situation, others events to bring former carers together socially. *(See also page 630.)*

Befriending

Some groups seek to break any isolation a person is feeling by teaming them up with a befriender, who may chat to them or take them out *(see Chapter 9)*. Befrienders may also provide practical help. A friend of mine, Cecily, who was nearly blind and lived in a care home received weekly visits from a volunteer associated with the Surrey Association for Visual Impairment. He would take Cecily for a walk, help her with paperwork, set up equipment (such as her DAISY CD player for listening to talking books) and provide the listening ear of someone who really understood the everyday challenges she was facing.

Day and day-care centres

Some groups provide day centres or day-care centres, such as local branches of the Alzheimer's Society. These can provide a welcome break for carers not just for a few hours but for whole days. The person for whom they care returns home refreshed from a change of company, activities and food. *(See also pages 231–5.)*

Internet contact

Several voluntary groups provide a means for sufferers of particular conditions and carers to swap experiences and provide mutual support through an online chat room. This is invaluable for people who cannot get out of the house easily. *(In Chapter 11, I outline some of the other ways in which the internet can break down social isolation.)*

The web facility at healthtalk.org.uk features short video clips by people facing a range of illnesses from multiple sclerosis to asthma, reassuring others living with the condition that they are not alone. It also publishes perspectives from carers, and it addresses choices about care and all-round support at the end of life *(see page 1023)*.

Taking part in fund-raising and campaigns

Voluntary groups often also offer opportunities for taking part in fund-raising and campaigns. These can help you feel you may be making life easier for people who develop the condition in question in the future. Relatives who find visiting difficult or impossible might be happy to go on a sponsored walk or organise a fund-raising quiz.

Age-related macular degeneration (AMD) is very common and can cause many problems as people progressively lose the ability to see in the centre of their field of vision *(as noted on page 13)*. The Macular Disease Society is a good example of the range of support even quite a modestly-sized voluntary organisation can offer. The Society's national office publishes information and advice on anything from the causes of macular disease to the ways in which changes to diet may reduce the severity of symptoms or the various types of treatment available for the rarer, 'wet' type of AMD. It keeps track of research in the field, such as clinical trials involving stem cell therapy. But many of its factsheets concentrate on the impact of macular disease on everyday life and how people with the condition can cope – one sheet explains how mobile phones, tablets and computers can be used to help, for example.

Advisors on the Society's national helpline provide free, confidential help on any aspect of living with macular disease, although not medical advice. Friends and family members are also welcome to call. The Society also has a team of professional counsellors, all members of the BACP *(see page 317)*, who provide emotional support over the phone. They help people talk through their feelings about sight loss and find ways of dealing with them.

The Society considers that talking things through with someone living in your locality who also has macular disease can be very beneficial. Dotted across the UK is a network of local groups involving people with the condition. Groups meet regularly; invite guest speakers; run social events; arrange outings and holidays; fund raise; help raise awareness of macular disease; get involved in campaigns; and work with local eye-care professionals.

Skype groups facilitated by the Society give people the opportunity to talk to others affected by macular disease from their own home. 'Treatment buddies' are those who have had treatment through injection into the eye for wet AMD and reassure others over the phone who are apprehensive about it. The Society also trains volunteers who teach people to use the vision they retain more effectively. 'Steady eye strategy' involves learning a new way to read text, while 'eccentric viewing' helps people to make most use of their peripheral vision.

Working in tandem with groups targeting medical conditions is the Patients Association, which provides information and guidance in print and on its website about the rights of patients, such as how to access one's medical records. The Association's helpline advises people about difficulties with healthcare providers, whether NHS or independent. It is perhaps best known for its impressive lobbying work to improve patient care.

Healthwatch

If you are interested in trying to improve healthcare services in your locality, look for your local Healthwatch branch, if you live in England. Branches are actually provided for by legislation but operate much like voluntary bodies but with potentially greater clout. Their purpose is to gather experiences and views about local health and social care services which receive some public funding and use them to seek improvements. They may sit on local health bodies such as clinical commissioning groups in order to feed in the views of consumers. Local Healthwatch organisations are obliged by law to enable local people to monitor the standard of provision of health and care services and they must make reports and recommendations about how local services could and ought to be improved. Their remit also includes providing information and advice about local health and care services.

In order to carry out their inquiries, local Healthwatch organisations have the power 'to enter and view': this means they can tell, say, a local care home or dental practice that they wish to come and see what is going on and talk to users of the service, their relatives and carers, as well as staff. The provider of that facility is legally obliged to allow someone who has been authorised by the local Healthwatch to observe activities on the premises, so long as this does not affect the provision of care or the privacy or dignity of people using services. This means that a Healthwatch observer would not be permitted to enter residents' bedrooms in a care home, but they should be granted access to communal areas such as the lounges, dining room and grounds.

The reports that local Healthwatch draw up can be influential. They may send them to the local commissioning health body, national Healthwatch, the Care Quality Commission, the Department of Health and the Secretary of State for Health, if they wish. The people and organisations to whom local Healthwatch send recommendations for service improvements are under a legal duty to have regard to these recommendations when they are commissioning, providing, managing or scrutinising health or social care services.[18] Local Healthwatches vary considerably on the ground; the activities of Healthwatch Lambeth show what a good Healthwatch can achieve.

Catherine Pearson, the energetic chief executive of Healthwatch Lambeth, and her small team of staff and larger band of volunteers seek to discover the views of people living in Lambeth – an inner London borough bounded to the north by the Thames near Waterloo station and running due south through Brixton to Streatham. They try to improve services by drawing together residents' views and channelling suggestions to the providers of services.

Were it not for the actions of Healthwatch Lambeth, those voices of users would go unheard. For example, in 2015 it carried out enter-and-view visits in five extra-care facilities in Lambeth, talking at length to residents, their families and staff. Extra-care facilities provide accommodation and some level of care and support, but they are not inspected as such by the Care Quality Commission (as are care homes, *as explained on pages 124–5*). Healthwatch Lambeth's team not only published reports of their findings and circulated them widely: they also made a film in which residents explained their views about living in the facilities.

Healthwatch Lambeth's enter-and-view system was developed by a retired CQC inspector living in the borough. A team of staff and volunteers have received special training in how to carry out these visits. They have undertaken visits and published reports about a variety of other facilities, including A&E departments, older people's hospital wards, dementia services, pharmacies and homecare services.

Lambeth may lie in inner London, but it is not Mayfair, and nearly one third of children in the borough live in poverty; black people and those from other ethnic minorities make up a quarter of its residents. The organisation is constantly trying to think of ways of reaching all of Lambeth's citizens, particularly those who might otherwise be excluded. To this end it has appointed a trustee with experience of working with young people in the borough and another with an Afro-Caribbean advocacy organisation. People with learning disabilities helped in its survey of pharmacies.

Apart from publishing the findings of its surveys, Healthwatch Lambeth seeks to improve services through meetings with providers and officials in the local council and the NHS, as well as representation on local organisations, such as the governing body of Lambeth's clinical commissioning group. It also canvasses the

In tandem with the work of the local organisations, the national body, Healthwatch England, carries out nationwide investigations, based largely on reports by local Healthwatch groups. It might, for instance, draw up a report about problems with podiatry services across England (waiting times for NHS treatments vary considerably). Organisations such as local authorities and the NHS Commissioning Board are required by law to inform Healthwatch England in writing of their response to such reports. Healthwatch England is actually a committee of the Care Quality Commission and has a legal duty to report annually to the Commission on standards of health and social care service provision and whether and, if so, how they could or should be improved.[19]

State-funded organisations for patients

Some state-funded organisations give patients advice on their illnesses; others with handling the health service and resolving concerns about treatment they have (or have not) received.

NHS 111

Perhaps your painkillers do not seem to be working in the middle of the night. Or you develop a pain and are unsure whether to call a doctor or go to Accident and Emergency.

NHS 111 is a 24-hour, 365-day phone helpline through which trained operators field calls and provide information and guidance. Calls are free from UK landlines and mobile phones. Operators do not have access to patients' medical records and are not medically trained. Essentially, they proceed through pre-set pathways and checklists. But they can consult qualified personnel. An NHS 111 operator should be able to give you a sense of whether you should go to A&E immediately or your condition can wait. They can give advice and signpost to particular healthcare professionals and organisations. They can call an ambulance there and then, if necessary. They may be able to book you an appointment to see your GP or another professional. But if you think you need urgent medical care, phone 999 (or go to A&E). If you are keen to talk to a doctor immediately outside GP practice hours, contact the out-of-hours GP service; NHS 111 may in any case refer you to this.

NHS 111 also provides general information in paper form and on its website about illnesses and treatments, including guidance on different medicines, their side effects and ways in which food and alcohol interact with them. It also holds information about health services provided locally, such as NHS dentists.

NHS 111 was first established in England and Scotland and is being introduced in Wales, where it will eventually replace a previous number *(all these numbers are in Useful Contacts)*. At the time of writing, NHS 111 had not been established in Northern Ireland.

NHS Inform

In Scotland, NHS Inform provides information through a website and over the phone about a wide range of ailments and how they should be treated. It also gives information about local health services as well as the support that is available from voluntary organisations. So, if you are trying to find a stroke club or an NHS dentist, NHS Inform is the body to contact.

The Patient Advice Liaison Service (PALS)

Patient Advice Liaison Services (PALS) are support hubs for patients in England, paid for by health bodies but operated independently of them. Some PALS offices are based outside hospitals and help patients find primary care services and support them if they run into difficulties, perhaps in their dealings with their GP practice. Other PALS offices are based in large, acute hospitals, often near the main entrance. Advisors there should be able to help patients with queries about that hospital and with, say, obtaining hospital transport, finding an interpreter or working out what will happen to their state benefits during a stay in hospital. Indeed, if you have any query which you cannot immediately solve, contact PALS. It may be able to direct you to a person or organisation which could witness a will or a power of attorney or visit your relative in hospital or accompany them to outpatient appointments, for example.

Perhaps PALS' most valuable function is to mediate between patients and NHS professionals. You may wish to follow up a concern with your hospital consultant but find the prospect daunting and confusing. You may be concerned about the treatment you have received and, rather than lodge a formal complaint, would like an apology and the assurance that steps will be taken to ensure the mistake is not repeated with another patient. Go to PALS, who have direct access to consultants and other professionals and can help sort things out. If this does not work, PALS can give you information about how to lodge a complaint and direct you to advocacy services which can help you do so.

In some places, PALS are overwhelmed. Your local Healthwatch may be able to help instead, at least with the provision of information about local services.

The Patient Advice and Support Service (PASS)

In Scotland, patient support is organised differently. It is paid for by the Scottish government and run independently of government or the NHS by Citizens Advice Scotland. Advisors in local offices give information and guidance about patients' rights and support those who wish to raise concerns or make complaints. Advisors in the same office (or the same person) can help with other matters which can be important when we are unwell, such as employment, housing, travel and benefits.

Complementing this system is a network of patient advisors, one in each of the 27 health board areas. They help patients who have complex problems or who need ongoing or specialist support. They also help patients make a complaint, write letters, make phone calls and attend meetings on their behalf.

Community health councils

The seven community health councils of Wales are coterminous with local health boards, but independent of them. They provide information and advice about local health services. But they also investigate the quality of NHS services from the patient's point of view and urge improvements where required. This includes carrying out an annual check on all major hospitals in Wales. Community health councils have powers to inspect premises owned or controlled by NHS bodies of all types as well as services provided in private facilities but commissioned by the NHS, for instance in a hospice or an independent hospital.

Community health councils also help people with a healthcare grievance to decide what to do and then support them in lodging an official complaint, if they wish.

The Board of Community Health Councils in Wales coordinates the activities of the health councils, so if you think a community health council might be able to help you, contact one in your local area or ask the Board to direct you to your nearest council.

The Patient and Client Council

In Northern Ireland the Patient and Client Council proactively seeks out the views of the public on health and social care provision and tries to ensure that trusts address them when providing services, focussing on themes which the public say are important, such as the treatment of pain.

Much of its work involves helping people who wish to complain and then seeking to improve services in the light of these complaints.

Trouble-shooting

If something is wrong with the healthcare provision you or somebody else, perhaps for whom you act as attorney, have received, what could you do?

Serious concerns which require a prompt response

If you have a serious concern about any aspect of healthcare which demands immediate action, first talk to the manager of the facility involved in the hope of persuading them to put in place the changes you need. There will be a hierarchy of professionals to whom you could put your case: on a hospital ward for example, the ward manager, unit manager, matron and, at the top, the chief executive of the hospital trust *(as explained on pages 908–10)*.

If you fail to secure the change you wish, look for help outside. A sympathetic MP or councillor can often cut through the red tape to get decisions changed and action speeded up. Consider alerting the local press, radio and television. A few TV cameras – or the threat of them – can work wonders. For example, in 2005, a 64-year-old man who was suffering from Parkinson's disease needed rehabilitation care after two operations. The hospital where he had been treated insisted that he must relocate to a nursing home, as there was a shortage of hospital beds. However, his wife, a retired nurse, knew that the therapy crucial to his rehabilitation would be available only in the hospital. She contacted the local newspaper and within two days of an article appearing on the front page the hospital had found a rehabilitation bed.[20]

Abuse

One form of harm that often demands immediate attention comes under the broad heading of abuse. 'Abuse' in a healthcare setting has an official definition and could involve any of the following actions or inactions:

- physical assault – hitting, slapping and so on
- the prescription or administration of medicine that is not licensed for the purpose used – such as anti-psychotic medication given simply to keep somebody quiet
- sexual assault
- neglect – this might be failure to give somebody the food and drink they need or failure to care for them properly, perhaps by

leaving them in wet sheets or failing to tape protective padding to prevent the development of pressure sores

- psychological abuse – this could involve threats of harm or abandonment, humiliation, coercion and verbal abuse
- theft

If you are subject to any of these types of behaviour or you see somebody else who is, or you fear that you or somebody else will be harmed in one of these ways, raise the matter immediately with the manager of the unit involved, such as a hospital or care home. Facilities such as these must have procedures in place for dealing with cases of suspected abuse, and a hospital will have a member of staff responsible for 'adult safeguarding', as the protection of vulnerable people from abuse is known. You could also contact the police or the social services department of your local authority, which both have responsibilities for responding to abuse 24 hours a day, seven days a week. *(I discuss elder abuse on pages 564–71.)*

Less immediate problems

If your problem is not one that demands an immediate change but is nonetheless likely to be long-standing unless something is done, first try to resolve it amicably with the person with whose action (or inaction) you are dissatisfied. For example, if your GP is refusing to refer you to a specialist, go and talk the matter through with them. You could put your request in writing to demonstrate that you are serious. Or you could try to find somebody else who might be more responsive, such as another member of the practice.

If you have to write to restate a request to a doctor, you could mention that if they refuse to take action, you will consider lodging a formal complaint about the practice. GP practices – indeed, all providers of NHS services – have to pass on details of formal complaints to the bodies that commission their services, so are likely to try to pre-empt them.

Professional misconduct

Perhaps you consider that a particular professional such as a GP, dentist, pharmacist or nurse, whether in the NHS or the private healthcare system, has behaved unprofessionally. Bodies exist to protect the public against unprofessional behaviour on the part of practitioners in all the main health professions (the General Medical Council, the Health and Care Professions Council and so on) and you can talk to them about your concerns before lodging a complaint. These organisations examine cases of professional misconduct, such as negligence, and can prevent professionals from practising, *as explained on pages 305–18.*

Poor practice

Perhaps you have been the subject of a botched operation or some other medical malpractice has harmed you. If so, you could sue the doctor, the health trust or a private hospital. The Law Society has a list of lawyers who specialise in clinical negligence and *I discuss the use of solicitors in the field of negligence on pages 811–2.*

Lodging a complaint

Often, however, what people want more than financial compensation is an inquiry into the cause of what went wrong, an apology and an assurance that the same will not befall another patient. Mediation perhaps with the help of a patients' organisation such as PALS may not be enough to satisfy them. In this case, lodging an official complaint can be the best means of redress.

All the organisations that provide services for the NHS – GP practices, pharmacies, hospital trusts, mental health trusts and so on – must have a complaints procedure in place. The NHS Constitution states:

> You have the right to have any complaint you make about NHS services acknowledged within three working days and to have it properly investigated. ... You have the right to be kept informed of progress and to know the outcome of any investigation into your complaint. ... You have the right to compensation where you have been harmed by negligent treatment.[21]

In a moment, I will outline the procedure involved in lodging an official complaint. It is worth stating at the outset, however, that going down this road is unlikely to sort out a problem quickly. Indeed, essentially the problem is buried while the complaint goes through various procedures.

Also, you should bear in mind that, particularly in England, the investigation of complaints is not a quasi-judicial process involving independent investigators examining and if necessary cross-examining witnesses. While the procedures for NHS complaints in Scotland, Wales and Northern Ireland do allow for the possibility of independent people becoming involved, in England, NHS complaints are essentially investigated by the part or parts of the NHS system about which the complaint is being made. Only after that has been done can a complainant turn to a body outside the healthcare system – an ombudsman.

Advice on lodging complaints

Before you embark on lodging a complaint or suing a professional, it is worth discussing the matter with an advisor. Perhaps the most easily accessible source of advice is Citizens Advice. You can sit down at a local bureau and talk through how you might best approach your concern or complaint about health or social care. In **Scotland,** Citizens Advice provides the Patients Advice and Support Service, which specifically offers information, advice and support for anybody who wishes to raise concerns delivered by NHS Scotland *(see also page 333).*

Elsewhere in the UK there are organisations which specialise in advising and if necessary supporting people in the field of NHS complaints. Some of them also provide general advice about NHS services.

In **Wales,** community health councils *(see page 333)* help people raise concerns and lodge complaints. In **Northern Ireland** this function is performed by the Patient and Client Council *(see pages 333–4).*

In **England,** the Independent Complaints Advisory Service (ICAS) seeks to help patients and others aggrieved by action (or lack of it) taken by people and organisations funded by the NHS. Staff working for the organisations which have contracts to provide services for ICAS will help you lodge a formal complaint, but they will also help you work out whether to lodge a complaint or whether to take some other action, such as pursuing a claim for compensation citing clinical negligence or reporting the inappropriate behaviour of a professional to the GMC, for example. You can obtain contact details of the organisation that carries out ICAS's work in your area from your local PALS or through the internet or phone book.

If you decide to lodge a complaint against a healthcare organisation, an advocate working under contract for ICAS should, if you wish, help you make that complaint, writing and sending a letter for you to the appropriate person or organisation, such as the chief executive of a hospital trust. The advocate would draft a letter setting out your complaint and explaining how you have been affected by what went wrong. The letter would be sent back to you for approval and then, once it is OK, dispatched. ICAS itself does not have powers of investigation: advocates simply help you work out what action to take and help you take it. But an advocate might also support you at a meeting to help make your complaint more effective.

ICAS takes an interest in the provision of hospital care and primary care for the NHS through various types of institution, including GP practices, pharmacies and NHS trust hospitals, but also private hospitals and private nursing homes. (In a nursing home, the NHS-funded care would include any nursing care paid for by the NHS as 'free nursing care' *(see page 962)* as well as Intermediate Care *(see pages 947–83)* and NHS Continuing Healthcare *(see pages 953–98).)*

NHS complaints

If you are going to complain about an NHS service, you will find that complaints procedures involve a number of fairly straightforward stages. Below I offer some tips for handling complaints, using the procedures in operation in England. I hope that readers in Wales, Scotland and Northern Ireland will also find these tips useful. They will need, however, to apply the slightly different procedures in operation outside England, for instance involving different time periods permitted at different stages.

1. Find out to whom you should complain. Every organisation that delivers an NHS service from a GP practice to a large hospital has to have in place procedures for the use of members of the public who wish to complain about their actions (or lack of them). Such procedures will explain to whom you should lodge any complaint, the time within which you can expect a response and who you should approach if you remain dissatisfied.

2. Lodge the complaint. This can be done by letter, email or the spoken word. If you make your complaint orally, make sure that the body to which you are complaining makes a written record of your complaint and provides you with a copy. However you make the complaint, ensure that it is clear what you are doing. Say, for instance, that you are making a formal complaint about the care given to you while a patient on a particular ward in a particular hospital on a particular date or during a particular period. Give a brief account of the matter about which you are complaining, such as the treatment you received or the care you did not receive. The organisation concerned may have a form which you fill in. If you are unsure to whom you should write, address your complaint to the chief executive of the hospital trust, health board or manager of the GP practice, for example.

   The person who lodges a complaint does not have to be the patient or their representative, such as an attorney. The English rules say that anybody may complain if they are, 'A person who is affected, or likely to be affected, by the action, omission or decision of the responsible body which is the subject of the complaint'.[22] The organisation receiving the complaint has the discretion to decide whether or not somebody falls into that category, so be prepared to argue why the effect is significant in your case if you are not the patient (or their representative) but their partner or a close relative or friend.

3. Include in your letter any steps you took to try to sort things out and the responses of staff, with times, dates and names if possible. Enclose photocopies of any relevant documents. Ask the chief executive or practice manager or someone performing a similar role to investigate the matter.

You can also say what you would like to come out of your complaint. This could be, perhaps, a change in practice, an urgent investigation into a particular area perhaps of hospital practice, reimbursement for a loss you have sustained, such as the loss of your personal belongings while on a ward, or an apology and explanation. If somebody is signing the letter on your behalf, they should explain their relationship to you.

The organisation to which you are addressing your complaint should send you an acknowledgement promptly, but if you want to be sure that it has received your complaint, send it by recorded delivery. If complaining by email, use the request receipt facility. If you complain in person or over the telephone, bear in mind that it may be difficult to confirm what was said at a later date.

If you do not receive a prompt acknowledgement, get in touch again. Perhaps there is some confusion: perhaps the organisation does not realise that this is an official complaint. Restate the position if necessary.

In whatever form a complaint is made, the organisation that receives it must acknowledge it no later than three working days after the day on which it was received. The acknowledgement can be made in writing or orally. At the same time as it does so, the body must offer to discuss the complaint with the complainant. (This offer to discuss is one of the main ways in which the procedures in England differ from those in Wales, Scotland and Northern Ireland, where it is not a formal part of the procedure at this stage.)

The discussion should take in three main areas – the length of time that investigation of the complaint is likely to take; the way in which the complaint is to be handled; and the outcome you want. During that period, the responsible body must keep the complainant informed, as far as reasonably practical, about the progress of the investigation. So, at that initial discussion, try to secure a timescale as short as is consistent with a proper investigation.

Discuss how you will be informed about progress. Make sure you know the name of the person who will be conducting the investigation and how you can contact them. If the matter in question presents a continuing risk to your health, you should expect the organisation involved to investigate it as quickly as possible and should press them to do so. If you consider they are not taking matters as seriously as they should, contact the Ombudsman *(see below)*.

Under the English system, if you make a complaint orally and it is resolved to your satisfaction no later than the next working day after you make it, then it does not have to go through the procedures I describe here.

Be on your guard against being dissuaded from lodging or pursuing a complaint, wherever you live. Health (and social care) providers are very keen to minimise the number of formal complaints that come to them and will clearly wish to deflect complaints if they can. This is because they have to release information about the number of formal complaints lodged against them, the number that turn out to have been well-founded and the number referred on to an ombudsman. All this is potentially very embarrassing and affects a provider's standing with commissioning bodies like clinical commissioning groups.

If the original complaint was made orally, the body to which you are complaining must make its own written record of the complaint and provide you with a copy of this before it investigates. Of course, you may disagree with its interpretation of your complaint – which is why it is usually best if you can set your complaint down in writing yourself at the outset.

There is usually a time limit for making a complaint – one year after the date that the matter occurred or from the date that you first became aware of it; there is discretion to waive that limit if the complainant has a good reason for delay (perhaps extreme trauma or grief), or if it is still possible to investigate the complaint effectively and fairly despite the delay.

The report that the organisation sends to the complainant must set out how the complaint was considered and the conclusions reached, including any matters where remedial action is needed, together with a statement saying whether the responsible body is satisfied that any action needed as a consequence of the complaint has been taken or is proposed to be taken.

People who remain aggrieved after having gone through this complaints procedure should approach the Parliamentary and Health Service Ombudsman. The Ombudsman considers complaints that government departments, a range of other public bodies in the UK and the NHS in England have not acted properly or fairly or have provided a poor service.

In Scotland, Wales and Northern Ireland, complaints about the NHS are investigated by the Scottish Public Services Ombudsman, the Public Services Ombudsman for Wales and the Northern Ireland Ombudsman.

The Ombudsman usually considers cases only after they have gone through the NHS complaints procedure. They can make recommendations such as an apology, financial compensation and the drawing up of action plans to prevent similar mistakes occurring in the future.

Practitioners, organisations and concerns

* Some healthcare practitioners are strictly controlled, but others are not.
* Unqualified, inexperienced healthcare and beauty practitioners can cause much harm.
* Before using a private healthcare practitioner, check that they are on a reputable register.
* If a healthcare assistant in hospital or a GP practice seems incompetent, refuse treatment.
* Voluntary healthcare organisations offer a wide range of information and advice.
* Voluntary organisations advise carers on how to protect their own physical and mental health.
* If healthcare treatment goes wrong, complain.
* There are organisations that advise on lodging complaints.
* Approach the Ombudsman if you remain dissatisfied.
* Swifter action may be obtained through the media, your MP or a councillor.

PART FIVE
HEALTHCARE PROVISION

" *Much is at stake in testing for dementia. Diagnosis can provide a gateway to help of various kinds. But incorrect diagnosis can be unhelpful, since it may lead to changes in somebody's control over their own life that do not occur with a diagnosis of a physical illness such as cancer or diabetes.* "

PART FIVE
HEALTHCARE PROVISION

We have just examined the rights we enjoy of access to healthcare under the NHS and have looked at the professionals who deliver healthcare, both in the NHS and the independent sector. But what does this actually mean should we, say, have a stroke or suspect we have dementia? What sort of tests and treatment could we reasonably expect to receive through the NHS and so be in a position to demand if they were not offered?

Some of the most common medical conditions of later life are the subjects of the chapters in this part – strokes, depression, anxiety, continence problems and dementia. Not all of these have been selected as medical conditions for which doctors are rewarded with special financial incentives for testing and treatment under the GP contract *(as described on page 291)*. Where they are included, the rewards provided under this system are rudimentary. Several of these conditions attract a stigma, making people reluctant to seek help. I try to explain the nature of these conditions and the sort of help to seek if it is not offered.

Having a fall can be one of the most feared events of later life and the worry of a fall can lead people to circumscribe their activities. I also explain what the consequences of falls can be, how to deal with falls and what can be done to prevent them in the first place.

When we are young we take it for granted that we will recover quickly from an infection, accident or operation, even quite a major one. When we are getting on, speedy recovery is not automatic. As explained in Chapter 1, the older body takes longer to recover and its systems have less capacity to cope with change. So, in this part I also examine rehabilitation – what it actually means and how it can be facilitated – in the context of strokes and of an operation to repair a hip fracture.

Chapter 16
Strokes

Strokes are one of the most common causes of death, with nearly 40,000 people dying every year in the UK as the direct result.[1] They are also one of the largest causes of disability among adults: 600,000 people have to live with moderate to severe disability as a result of a stroke.[2] So how can we maximise our chances of surviving a stroke and avoiding long-term disability?

Many people do not seem to realise that quick admission to hospital is very important if they are having a stroke and that, even if they experience one in which the symptoms disappear quickly, they should nonetheless seek medical advice urgently. In this chapter, I first consider why strokes should be treated as a medical emergency and then the acute care that should be offered during the first few hours and days.

Subsequent action to help regain faculties that have been affected by a stroke is also crucially important. Indeed, as we shall see later in this chapter, strokes provide a good example of the need for rehabilitation to be a key part of the treatment that people should receive for a number of conditions in later life. Rehabilitation, whether after a stroke, an operation, an infection or an accident, involves examining the damage that has been done to an organ or a part of the body, how this is affecting bodily functions (for instance, difficulty in moving around or passing water) and the ways in which both of these things influence somebody's prospects of stepping back into the life they led before.

But how far should rehabilitation go? How hard should somebody try to recover lost faculties? What rehabilitation does is try to restore someone to the optimum physical, mental and social capacity that is consistent with their needs and desires and those of their family. For instance, if two people have had a leg amputated, but beforehand one was playing

18 holes of golf a day but the other was barely able to walk, the goals of their rehabilitation will be different.

In this chapter, I examine:

- ► how to tell when someone is having a stroke
- ► the causes of strokes
- ► the prevention of strokes
- ► why even fleeting symptoms need emergency action
- ► medical treatment for a stroke
- ► nursing care in hospital
- ► stroke units in hospitals
- ► rehabilitation
- ► making decisions for the future
- ► support from the voluntary world

Causes

Strokes arise from damage to the brain. The most common cause is a clot in an artery which blocks off blood supply to part of the brain. The second most common cause is the bursting of a blood vessel in the brain, causing blood to spill out. It is important to know whether the cause of a stroke is a clot or a bleed, as somebody who has had a stroke resulting from a blockage could benefit from drugs that disperse clots (thrombolytic drugs) or reduce the tendency of the blood to clot. However, these drugs would worsen the condition of someone suffering from a brain haemorrhage.

Many people believe that strokes are prompted by stressful events such as a burglary or bereavement, but this is rarely the case. Most occur as a random event in a susceptible person. High blood pressure is the main indication of susceptibility and this has usually been present for many years.

There is another less well known cause. A condition involving an irregular heartbeat called atrial fibrillation is thought to be responsible for one fifth of strokes. The heart rhythm disturbance causes a blood clot to be thrown from the heart and lodge in the brain. These strokes usually result in a larger area of brain death than other strokes and a higher risk of death and disability. If you have irregular palpitations or an irregular pulse, tell your doctor so that they can monitor your heart rhythm and if necessary give you drugs to reduce the risk of a stroke. This is a relatively neglected but important area where strokes could be prevented.

Symptoms

One difficulty is knowing that you are actually having a stroke. There are no hard and fast rules, but it is important to get emergency treatment at hospital if you think you may be having a stroke or have just had one. Watch out for the sudden onset of unusual weakness or numbness in a limb, dizziness, difficulty in reading and writing, slurred speech and difficulty in finding the right words and in understanding what somebody is saying. Your consciousness may be a little impaired, so you may feel slightly spaced out. But many other symptoms may occur, depending on which part of the brain has been affected and the extent of the damaged area. Sometimes strokes make people drowsy or unconscious. Sometimes they occur during sleep, without the sufferer realising anything has happened; only on waking is the victim aware that something has changed, for instance, that they cannot see properly.

The 'FAST' test emphasises the need for speedy action. It encourages people to apply the following checks if they suspect that they or somebody else is having a stroke:

✓ *Face:* Has their face fallen on one side? Can they smile?

✓ *Arms:* Can they raise both arms and keep them there?

✓ *Speech:* Is their speech slurred?

✓ *Time:* It is time to call 999 if you see any one of these signs.

This is a useful and memorable test. However, do bear in mind that the symptoms of strokes vary considerably and also that people who suffer a major stroke often have a depressed level of consciousness, so if you ask them to raise their arms or smile, they may be unable to understand what you are saying. That said, the very fact that their consciousness is depressed should alert you to the need for urgent action. For instance, I was having dinner with a friend, John, and we were chatting happily when he abruptly stopped speaking, gazed blankly at one spot and was unresponsive to anything I said or did. His only action was to feel one arm with the opposite hand. I dialled 999 immediately and the paramedics who arrived within minutes confirmed that he was having a stroke.

Sudden eyesight problems can indicate a stroke or something very similar. If the stroke is not treated, the sight impairment could become permanent, with such repercussions as a bar on driving.

An early warning sign of stroke is called *amaurosis fugax*. It is a temporary total or partial loss of vision in one eye, quite unlike a migraine. If a stroke is to occur, it is likely to occur within three weeks of this event. So anybody suffering a sudden change in their vision, especially those with a history of blood pressure or circulatory problems, should go straight to A&E and bypass their GP.

Amaurosis fugax is a type of 'transient ischaemic attack', or TIA. In a TIA, symptoms such as loss of vision in one eye or weakness in a limb last for a shorter time. But TIAs, minor strokes and major strokes represent a continuum, so any stroke-like symptoms should be taken very seriously and the sufferer seek urgent medical advice. The factors that led to a TIA or a minor stroke may lead to a major stroke.

However, the kind of stroke I want to consider in this chapter is a major stroke, the type people usually mean when they say somebody has had a stroke.

Acute care

Wherever you are living, your first instinct should be to treat a stroke as a medical emergency. Failure to do so can mean that the patient dies or suffers long-term disability, and this can be avoided or lessened if immediate action is taken.

After suffering his stroke, John was rushed to A&E, where he was given further tests and a brain scan. Then, after his attorney had been consulted (since he had lost the ability to understand what anybody was saying, let alone mentally capable of weighing up the pros and cons of having treatment), thrombolytic drugs were administered. Of course, I cannot tell whether the stroke might have killed him if he had not received such prompt attention, but I do know that the paralysis that had taken hold down one side of his body from the onset of the stroke (the reason why he was trying to clutch his arm in the restaurant) disappeared within 24 hours; the doctors put this down to the action of the drugs.

Although strokes most frequently occur as random events, they are sometimes associated with a fall in blood pressure after major stress to the body, such as an operation or a heart attack. As a result, some people who suffer a stroke are already in hospital. But that does not mean they will necessarily receive the best possible treatment for the stroke.

If you or your relative are in hospital when a stroke occurs, try to get admitted to a stroke unit *(see page 358 below)*. If the stroke occurs outside hospital, try to get to hospital as quickly as possible, making sure that the emergency services recognise the stroke as an emergency, and when you have arrived, try to get admitted into a specialist stroke unit.

Clot or haemorrhage?

Once an apparent stroke victim has been admitted to hospital, medical staff should work out the cause of the stroke (usually a clot or a haemorrhage), assess the extent of damage to the brain and establish that a different condition (such as a brain tumour or a migraine) is not to blame. Another possible condition, particularly in elderly people, is a subdural haematoma: a relatively minor head injury causes slow oozing of blood over surface of the brain, which in time causes symptoms similar to a stroke. But unlike a stroke, the onset of symptoms is gradual; urgent surgery is often required.

Two main techniques are used to diagnose a stroke. A CT (computerised tomography) scan uses X-rays to take pictures of the brain from different angles, which are added together by a computer to construct an image of the brain. An MRI (magnetic resonance imaging) scan can give more detailed information, but takes longer than a CT scan. The fiendishly clever technology involved magnetises hydrogen atoms in water molecules and fires radio waves at them which can trace blood flow; an MRI scan can differentiate between different types of soft tissue.

Brain imaging should be carried out promptly. If as a result doctors rule out a haemorrhagic stroke, they should attempt to disperse the clot with thrombolytic drugs which dissolve it, thereby improving blood flow to the part of the brain being deprived of oxygen. The National Institute for Health and Care Excellence (NICE) says this procedure should be done within four-and-a-half hours of the onset of stroke symptoms. Then, within 24 hours of the stroke and over the following fortnight, the patient should be given aspirin, which makes blood platelets less sticky, so preventing further clotting while also accelerating the dispersal of clots. Thereafter, patients should receive long-term treatment to prevent further strokes, according to NICE.[3] *As noted on page 289,* doctors should abide by NICE guidance unless there is a particular reason not to. Similar guidance is in force north of the border.[4]

Aspirin is not used initially, as thrombolytic drugs are much more powerful. They cause a clot to disperse, so the blocked artery re-opens and brain damage is reduced. They can be extremely useful not only in preventing death but also in reducing the chances of major long-term disability. However, they need to be administered within hours of the stroke by staff specially trained in handling them and carefully monitoring their effects.

Thrombolytic drugs also come with risks. Some stroke patients have minor bleeds in the brain as well as the clot that is causing the main problem. Plainly, clot-busting drugs may prevent those bleeds clotting, with the result that the patient may suffer a brain haemorrhage. Some patients may also have an ulcer from which bleeding would be dangerous. Therefore not all patients, even those whose strokes have been caused by a clot, are treated with these drugs, because the risks of the treatment may outweigh the benefits.

Not all hospitals offer clot-busting drugs. Of those that do, not all can offer them at evenings and weekends, as they would need to have radiographers on hand round the clock to operate the brain scanner and radiologists to interpret the results. It is therefore worth doing some homework in case you should have a stroke in order to find out which hospitals in your area have such facilities working round the clock.

From 2016 a quite different treatment was being rolled out, after its approval by NICE and endorsement by Healthcare Improvement Scotland.[5] Thrombectomy involves the mechanical removal of a blood clot. A catheter tube is inserted into a leg artery in the groin region and threaded along blood vessels to the brain where, with the help of X-rays, doctors remove it with a tiny device attached to the catheter which grabs and traps the clot and in which it travels down arteries and out of the body. Thrombectomy is more effective at opening blocked blood vessels than thrombolytic drugs, which may be used at the same time. NICE insists that only highly trained and experienced staff should perform thrombectomy and at the time of writing it was available at only a small number of hospitals. It is worth keeping track of whether any can provide it in your locality.

A range of other medical treatments may be helpful. Treatment could be offered to address atrial fibrillation. Some patients need surgery to facilitate the flow of blood through a narrowing of the main artery leading to the brain, the carotid artery.

Nursing after a stroke

Getting a brain scan and emergency treatment is by no means the only reason for going to hospital after or during a stroke. Another important reason is the reduction of possible complications which can have serious effects in themselves. They relate to:

Fluid intake

Stroke victims must receive sufficient fluid lest they become dehydrated.

If someone cannot take fluid by mouth, they should be given a nasogastric (passing through the nose) tube, an intravenous drip or an infusion of fluid under the skin, called a subcutaneous infusion, which has advantages over a drip (see page 985).

NICE recommends that everyone who has had an acute stroke should have their hydration assessed on admission to hospital and reviewed regularly. Good nutrition is important too: NICE also says that all hospital inpatients should be screened for malnutrition and the risk of malnutrition on admission.[6]

Pressure ulcers
These can develop quickly in somebody who is not moving, can take a long time to heal and can hinder the rehabilitation process. However, straightforward action can be taken to prevent them *(see pages 913–4)*.

Swallowing difficulty
It may be tempting to offer a stroke victim a cup of tea. But this could be dangerous. Strokes frequently reduce the ability to swallow, though usually only temporarily. If swallowing mechanisms have been impaired, liquids such as tea or water may go down the wrong way and end up in the lungs, where they can cause pneumonia.

So, while it is crucially important that somebody who has had a stroke has sufficient fluid to combat the risk of dehydration and is taking in the correct nutrients, it is also important to establish just how they should consume their food and fluid, since mistakes can be fatal. Anyone who has suffered a stroke should have their ability to swallow assessed very soon afterwards. Nurses can do this, but the specialists in this area are speech and language therapists *(see page 314)*, who will run tests to find out whether somebody's throat muscles are working properly.

In view of this, NICE recommends that all patients who have had an acute stroke should have their swallowing screened on admission to hospital before they are given any food, fluid or medicines. If the screening shows up problems, a specialist assessment of swallowing usually by a speech and language therapist should follow, preferably within 24 hours of admission and certainly within 72 hours.[7] If swallowing has been impaired, a speech and language therapist or a nurse will decree that the patient's diet or method of taking food, drink and medication should be modified. Often this means that the patient must be given only liquids which have been specially thickened – a process which will ensure that nothing passes into the respiratory rather than the digestive system. However, if someone is unable to take food or fluid orally, they would usually be given a tube which passes through the nose into the stomach, bypassing the throat. Failing this, they might need a 'PEG feeder', which requires the insertion of a tube straight into the stomach through the side of the body; a minor surgical procedure is necessary.

Urinary catheters

When somebody who has had a stroke is in hospital, relatives should also be alert to decisions being taken about the insertion of a urinary catheter. Catheters have significant drawbacks, including a heightened risk of developing a urinary tract infection, although they can be useful in certain circumstances *(see page 419)*. The Royal College of Physicians recommends that any incontinence should be managed by high levels of nursing care during the acute phase of a stroke and that, 'People with stroke should not have an indwelling (urethral) catheter inserted unless indicated to relieve urinary retention or when fluid balance is critical.'[8] The patient or their representative should be asked for their consent before a catheter is inserted. If one is put in place, they should expect the need for the catheter to be reviewed regularly and for their consent to be sought for it to remain. *(See also pages 419–23.)*

If your relative or friend has had a stroke and has sight or hearing impairment or dementia, you may wish to remain with them for as long as possible. When my mother, who was already suffering from dementia and nearly blind, suffered a stroke, family members took it in turns to be at her bedside through her waking hours for the first few days. We were keen to make absolutely sure that she did not consume unthickened liquids, took her medication, had sufficient food and fluid, did not topple out of bed, did not fall over should she get up, did not pull out her intravenous drip or her urinary catheter and, later, that her continence pads were changed frequently. This as well as the provision of company and reassurance.

Deep vein thrombosis

Lying immobile in bed increases the risk of deep vein thrombosis, or DVT. Steps can be taken to reduce that risk, including improving circulation in the limbs with the use of inflatable sleeves, gloves or boots, encouraging a patient to sit out of bed and walk and, if they are unable to do so themselves, to regularly reposition them while in bed.

Prevention of strokes

Strokes can not only be treated, they can also be prevented. It is very important that your hospital consultant (or your GP if you do not go to hospital) should be involved in the prevention of further strokes, since people who have suffered a stroke are at significant risk of having another. The time of greatest risk is soon after the first stroke. *(As noted above, this is also the case for minor strokes and TIAs.)*

The Royal College of Physicians, which has drawn up its own guidance accredited by NICE emphasises 'secondary prevention', saying that, 'People with stroke or TIA should receive a comprehensive and personalised strategy for vascular prevention including medication and lifestyle factors, which should be implemented as soon as possible and should continue long-term.'[9] Treatment might involve drugs to lower blood pressure or cholesterol levels or to make the blood less sticky and so less likely to clot. Or drugs might be given to control the heart rate and thus prevent atrial fibrillation.[10] A stroke patient may be advised to lower the amount of salt in their food *(see page 47)*, eat a healthy diet *(page 37)*, reduce alcohol consumption, give up smoking, and exercise more frequently and more vigorously *(pages 57 and 61)*. Some people buy an inexpensive device to monitor their blood pressure themselves *(page 494)*.

Take advantage of any screening that is offered. For example, abdominal ultrasound for aortic aneurysm screening can detect a dangerous swelling or aneurysm of the aorta (the main blood vessel running from the heart through the abdomen to the rest of the body). A burst aneurysm is often fatal. Men over 65 are invited for screening as aneurysms are more common in men over that age than in women or younger men.

Rehabilitation

Of people who experience a stroke, about a third die, a third recover more or less, and a third are left with significant disability. The extent to which people are permanently disabled after a stroke depends partly on the location and degree of the damage to brain tissue and partly on the extent to which the brain can continue to operate the parts of the body controlled by the damaged cells through side-stepping them and forming new nerve pathways. These new pathways enable parts of the brain that are not permanently damaged or can recover, together with those that have survived intact, to take on the functions of the damaged parts. This process takes place either spontaneously or through will-power and practice.

The most common types of disability that occur after a major stroke are paralysis, muscle weakness, difficulties in swallowing, difficulties in speaking and disruption of balance. The rate of recovery varies considerably between individuals, but also between different impairments in the same person. Thus, swallowing and balance difficulties tend to resolve quickly, but language problems and arm paralysis more slowly.

It is hard to overstate the difficulty that everyday tasks can pose if the relevant part of the brain has been impaired. Eating can involve slopping food all over the place; going to the lavatory can take a long time; crossing a room can seem next to impossible. Forcing oneself to do things that have suddenly become impossible can become very important. A major part of rehabilitation after a stroke involves seeking to regain lost functions, usually through repetitive training. Rehabilitation also involves learning to cope with disabilities that will only slowly (or may never) be overcome.

Of course, practice in doing everyday tasks can be daunting. People who have suffered a major stroke can feel shocked and overwhelmed by what they fear they have lost. However determinedly they may try to, say, feed themselves again, they do not know whether that faculty will ever return. Some people find it particularly difficult to summon up the motivation to relearn old skills, especially if they are suffering from a challenging pre-existing condition. And after a stroke, when a person is often feeling very tired as well as concerned about the future, depression can easily set in and worsen an already difficult situation. You may be a very intelligent, optimistic, driven person, but if you have lost a large number of brain cells as a result of a stroke, there is nothing you can do about it, in the same way that you cannot will yourself to get better from cancer.

Many people do of course regain lost abilities spontaneously or with specialist help. Others impose their own retraining régime and some go to extraordinary lengths to maximise their chances of regaining faculties. After author and headmaster Martin Stephen suffered a major stroke, he was unable to write, stand up, hold a cup or speak without a heavy slur. Dr Stephen determinedly forced himself to write out the alphabet for two hours a day, recite poetry, play a computer flight simulator game (which required hand-to-eye coordination), type, walk up and down stripes on his lawn without crossing the lines and bounce a tennis ball. After two-and-a-half months he felt he was returning to something like normality and within six months he felt he was cured.[11]

Dr David Cohen, the director of the stroke unit at Northwick Park Hospital in Harrow, Middlesex, told me that the chances of successful rehabilitation after a stroke are improved by:

✓ a considered and realistic rehabilitation programme implemented by specialist staff supporting the patient

✓ understanding of the rehabilitation programme by family, friends and non-specialist staff who are providing care

✓ encouragement by everybody

✓ therapy that begins early

Recovery is fastest in the first few weeks after a stroke, when the brain seems to be more responsive to the changes necessary for faculties to be regained. A further 5–10 per cent of recovery takes place between six months and one year.[12] However, some people improve even after a year.

Although Dr Stephen's régime, devised apparently largely independently of professionals, worked wonders, do keep in close touch with professionals if you can. That way you will benefit from their expertise in working out exactly what exercises and other interventions would best suit your particular situation, and can take advantage of any new research findings in this area. The mechanisms of rehabilitation and recovery are only beginning to be understood and experts disagree on such questions as at what point treatment should start, the intensity required to produce an effect and the nature of the exercises and other interventions (including drugs) that may be helpful. For instance, it has become apparent that repetitively carrying out the same movement – say, straightening your fingers or flexing your elbow joint – may not be the best way of regaining particular faculties. Rather, changing the movement to take in a wider range of variations more akin to real-life situations may be better.[13]

Therapists

Several types of therapist can play an invaluable role in aiding recovery. Physiotherapists help stroke victims regain the ability to move around by getting muscles and joints back up to speed; they also help people regain their balance when, as often happens, this has been affected, and advise on aids such as sticks or walking frames if it seems unlikely that sufficient muscle strength will return for unaided walking. *(I discuss the role of physiotherapists on page 313.)*

Occupational therapists focus on helping people recover their ability to perform their normal activities. Washing, dressing, cooking and other activities around the home figure here, but also the leisure and other activities that give life meaning. Having the goal of, say, cooking a meal or driving a car can be powerful motivation to persevere with rehabilitation exercises.

Inability to voice thoughts and feelings often follows a stroke. Indeed, communication problems are common. They vary widely. Some people can put across their wishes or views but only in very short sentences or single words, so they can get out only a tiny fraction of what they would like to put across. Others may be able to speak more easily but are unable to find the right words, or utter one word when they mean another. Some people can speak easily and use long sentences, but what they say does not make sense. Still others struggle to understand what others are saying to them or to read the written word. Communication difficulties such as these are not only frustrating but can be terribly isolating. They can make life difficult for family, friends and carers too.

Speech and language therapists can work wonders. Thus, for instance, my friend John *(see page 349)* received speech and language therapy in the hospital stroke unit to which he was moved from A&E. There the restoration, over about three weeks, of much of his ability to communicate seemed little short of a miracle.

As the chances of therapy providing greatest benefit are in the days and weeks immediately after the stroke, it is important to press for an assessment of the need for any type of therapy as soon as possible. Be alert to the possibility that cutbacks in services may mean delays and less therapy than is needed. A survey in Scotland in 2008 found that many people who had survived a stroke were not receiving the speech and language therapy from the NHS they needed to cope with communication problems. One third of people reported that they did not receive any such therapy after leaving hospital and in some parts of the country the figure was two thirds. What is more, over half of those who did receive speech and language therapy outside hospital said that they did not get enough and wanted more.[14] If you have enough money, you may wish to consider hiring a speech and language therapist, physiotherapist or occupational therapist privately if the NHS does not provide one promptly *(see pages 313 and 314)*.

Stroke units

In its *National Service Framework for Older People*, the Department of Health urged acute general hospitals to set up specialist stroke units and many hospitals now have one; by 2012, about 180 hospitals in England contained a stroke unit.

Stroke units can be good places to be in the immediate aftermath of a stroke, since the staff there will be used to diagnosing the cause of stroke or stroke-like symptoms and averting possible complications. But perhaps the units' greatest strength lies in the benefits they can offer during rehabilitation. If you are in hospital, a specialist stroke ward is usually a much better place to be for rehabilitation than a general medical or a geriatric ward. Studies have shown that patients in stroke units receive more therapy than those elsewhere in hospitals as well as closer monitoring of their condition and the provision of treatments to minimise complications. Some stroke units provide both acute care and rehabilitation; others acute care only or rehabilitation only.[15]

358

The National Institute for Health and Care Excellence (NICE) drew up a set of recommendations for the rehabilitation of people who had had a stroke in 2013. The first recommendation was: 'People with disability after stroke should receive rehabilitation in a dedicated in-patient stroke unit and subsequently from a specialist stroke team within the community.'[16] Do get hold of this guidance, as many of its recommendations are helpful and, as explained *(on page 289)*, health professionals and health bodies are expected to follow NICE's recommendations. The guidance is available free on NICE's website *(see Useful Contacts)*.

Nurses working on specialist stroke wards should have a deeper understanding of rehabilitation, and specifically rehabilitation after a stroke, than general nurses. This means they will be well equipped to help patients continue with therapy after, say, they have seen the physiotherapist in the gym. Also, since nurses on stroke wards are used to dealing with conditions that frequently arise with strokes, such as fatigue and temporary speech or continence difficulties, they are better placed than a nurse on an ordinary ward to anticipate such problems.

Finally, nurses on stroke wards are more likely to understand and support emotionally people who have lost a significant part of their abilities or are taking a long time to recover faculties. For instance, a nurse on a stroke unit ought to be on the lookout for symptoms of depression, so that this condition receives prompt treatment. Many people suffer from depression after a major stroke; indeed, it occurs in one third of cases. However, it can be treated, for instance, with antidepressant drugs.[17] *(See also Chapter 17: Anxiety and depression.)*

Family and friends

Just as the staff nursing a stroke victim can help recovery or adjustment by providing support and encouragement, so can friends and family. Their ability to do this will be much enhanced if they understand the rehabilitation programme, and in particular its goals and targets. Families need to know precisely how much, if any, help they should give to a loved one encountering serious difficulties in, say, feeding themselves. So, make sure you are involved in devising the rehabilitation programme for your relative, partner or friend. Doctors should involve the patient's family, if only to obtain information about the environment to which the patient will return.

Keeping spirits up may be challenging, quite apart from encouraging patients to practise skills they find difficult. Go round a stroke unit and you will find it probably shares the major drawback of all hospital environments: there is little with which patients can amuse or occupy themselves, and of course they have none of the tasks that demand attention and effort at home. Friends and relatives can help by bringing in things which will prompt their loved one to try to take action, whether to operate a laptop or dress themselves. Day clothes as opposed to pyjamas or hospital gowns foster a sense of normal life. Sitting in your night clothes by your bed in a place where you expect things to be done for you can induce the feeling that you should be taking things easy rather than doing what you can to regain any skills and faculties affected by the stroke.

Making decisions for the future

Be alert to any assessments that are taking place in hospital, particularly where these will influence when you or your relative are discharged, where to, and with what support. A social care needs assessment (by which a social worker, often with the help of an occupational therapist, works out what practical help somebody might need at home or indeed whether they should relocate to a care home) should form a key part of the assessment, so you need to know when this is taking place and prepare for it *(see Chapter 26)*.

Beware of anybody, even a nurse, saying early on after the stroke, 'He should get his house onto the market because he will need to go into a care home now.' An off-the-cuff assessment is masquerading as a systematic assessment, and may be taking place far too early. A care home may indeed turn out to be the only realistic option, but in the early weeks it is usually best to wait and see.

Dr David Cohen believes that, for many people, recovery from a stroke is variable, so an assessment of prognosis and thus any permanent change to a person's living arrangements should not take place until six weeks after the stroke has occurred; this is likely to be long after they have left hospital, as the average length of hospital stay for a stroke was about 17 days in 2012. There are some people of whom quite an accurate prognosis can be made before six weeks is up, particularly those who are going to do very well and those who are going to do very badly. It is the middle group of patients, who are making a moderate recovery and showing some progress, who require time before assessments are conducted and crucial decisions are taken.

So, relatives need to be careful about taking over decision-making for somebody who has had a major stroke, since mental abilities may return. Relatives often do not realise that while somebody with dementia will usually see a progressive deterioration in their mental powers, somebody who has had a stroke may see a steady or a sudden improvement in theirs. You don't want to put your father in a care home only to find that his mental powers return and he is dismayed at your precipitate action. In such a situation, you would find that you had flouted one of the key principles of the mental capacity legislation – that those who take decisions for those whose mental capacity is impaired must allow the person involved to take as many decisions as possible for themselves and that if there is any question of fluctuating capacity, they should wait until such a time as the person being represented can exercise choice themselves *(see page 773).*

If you plan to act as the person's carer, ask for a carer's assessment *(see pages 621–3).* The Royal College of Physicians has rightly pointed out that: 'Stroke is a family illness'. Relatives and partners need information to be able to support their loved one through the initial period after a stroke but they will also themselves need support to cope with any long-term effects of the stroke, whether practical, emotional, social or financial.

Rehabilitation at home

Some people who have had a stroke will do better if their rehabilitation takes place at home rather than in hospital. This is not only because of the risks that a lengthy hospital stay can bring *(outlined on pages 902–3).* In studies, patients who were undergoing rehabilitation at home took the initiative and expressed their goals for recovery more often than those whose rehabilitation was taking place in hospital.[18] Also, it is easier for both patients and health professionals to identify the problems that patients are likely to encounter in their home environment and so adjust the rehabilitation programme accordingly, building up the necessary physical ability but also the confidence to enable them to, say, catch a bus or drive their car.

Rehabilitation at home is not likely to be so successful, however, without the speech and language therapists, physiotherapists and others who might be needed. Whether you are in hospital, your own home or a care home, it is crucially important to obtain the ministrations of the healthcare specialists who can help with rehabilitation. If you live in a remote rural area, for example, you may be better off remaining in hospital, where the therapists you need are closer to hand.

Care homes

If you are planning to move to a care home, it is important to check that a high proportion of the staff have had training in stroke awareness and are aware of the need to apply the FAST test and treat a stroke as a medical emergency.

If you move to a care home from hospital after a stroke, whether permanently or for a temporary period, it is important to continue to pursue any rehabilitation activities and exercises that might help you. A survey of more than 11,000 care home residents found that those who engaged in rehabilitation were more likely to return from the care home to their own home and less likely to die than those who did not.[19]

Some rehabilitation exercises may be specific to particular residents, but general rehabilitation activities can also produce encouraging results. In one study, a number of people affected by strokes and living in 12 care homes were given a small amount of occupational therapy, involving practice with tasks such as dressing and moving around as well as targeted exercise. The researchers found that the residents who received additional occupational therapy were significantly less likely than a control group to deteriorate in their ability to perform these activities.[20]

If you are not receiving good rehabilitation services in your care home, complain to the home, but also raise the matter with your GP or the hospital from which you moved to the home. The Royal College of Physicians says, 'People with stroke, including those living in care homes, should continue to have access to specialist services after leaving hospital, and should be provided with information about how to contact them.'[21] Similarly, NICE points out that, 'Hospital trusts and other health bodies should, 'Ensure that people with stroke who are transferred from hospital to care homes receive assessment and treatment from stroke rehabilitation and social care services to the same standards as they would receive in their own homes'.[22] These are potentially very useful sticks with which to beat your local NHS organisation, such as mental health trust or clinical commissioning group.

GPs and strokes

There is much that a GP can do, including providing treatment to prevent further strokes, making a referral for specialist therapy and treating conditions that may arise as a result of the stroke, such as depression. A GP could refer a patient to specialists working in primary care and also ask a hospital to provide rehabilitation.

You could also ask your GP about primary prevention of stroke – whether you should be taking steps to reduce the risk of any stroke, however minor, ever occurring. This could involve stopping smoking, losing weight if you are obese and checking your cholesterol and blood pressure levels, for example.

Help from the voluntary world

If you or a loved one has had a stroke, it is well worth contacting the Stroke Association.

The Stroke Association is one of Britain's most impressive voluntary organisations. It offers support to people to maximise their recovery and rehabilitation and do what they can to prevent further strokes.

The Stroke Association offers support at national, regional and local level (including visits to people in their own homes). Callers to the national helpline can obtain immediate information about strokes and their impact, and can be directed to whatever services are available in their local area. They may be sent helpful factsheets on such subjects as driving after a stroke, high blood pressure and stroke, swallowing problems after a stroke, and emotional changes after a stroke; these are also available online.

The charity also campaigns, funds research, provides training, runs conferences and administers a welfare grants scheme, providing small one-off grants to help people affected by strokes with anything from paying for driving lessons to buying a washing machine. TalkStroke, a chatline hosted by the Association's website, also provides a means for people affected by a stroke to connect with each other and swap tips and anecdotes.

This help at national level is complemented by action on the ground by paid advisors and support coordinators together with teams of volunteers, operating from 200 local centres. These helpers do not offer medical advice, but a wide range of other support. For instance, they may visit people in their homes and offer emotional support. If a stroke has left somebody feeling isolated from society, they try to help them work out how to feel comfortable again in social situations. This may mean accompanying them on a visit; it may mean putting them in touch with a stroke support club in their area. These clubs, which are run by volunteers, involve people coming together and sharing their experiences, helping each other to regain confidence, perhaps by relearning skills and trying out new things. 'We aim to walk alongside the person who has had a stroke and provide whatever support they need at whatever stage they have reached', Elaine Roberts, the Association's

Director of Life after Stroke Services of the north of England, explained to me in 2012.

Local coordinators also offer advice on simple gadgets *(see Chapter 21)* to help people whose ability to move around or carry out everyday activities has been affected by their stroke. This could be equipment to help somebody peel potatoes with one hand, for instance *(see page 462)*.

Money can be a headache if you find yourself suddenly incapacitated by a stroke. The Association's local offices provide advice on benefits from sick pay to Attendance Allowance, and may be able to help fill in an application form or point a person to an organisation offering this service, such as a local Citizens Advice or a disability advice centre.

In some places, Stroke Association staff actually form part of the multi-disciplinary stroke team of their local hospital, working alongside social workers, therapists, doctors and so on to plan the care of the person who has had the stroke and help the family cope with what has happened and what might come next. Although part of the stroke team, Association staff remain part of a quite separate organisation and as a result feel free to champion the interests of the person and their family.

Even where Association staff are not formally part of a stroke team, they have close contact with it and can help people find their way through the health and social care systems. So should a family carer need extra support, they would try to establish just what might be the best form of assistance, perhaps the provision of additional equipment or human help, or perhaps a regular break. Respite care, as this is known, which usually involves the person being cared for going into a care home for a short period, can make the difference between a carer who is providing a great deal of support being able to continue to do so and their loved one having to move permanently into a care home. Association staff may also lend their backing in other arenas, for instance giving evidence at a tribunal in support of an appeal against the refusal of a state benefit *(see pages 869–72)*.

Stroke Association staff and volunteers also support people in their efforts to prevent a further stroke occurring. Elaine Roberts again:

People are terrified of having another stroke. We explain the things you can do to reduce the risk. We encourage you to follow your doctor's advice. This might be to take medication such as statins or warfarin. It might be to alter your lifestyle – changing your diet, reducing salt intake, stopping smoking, reducing the consumption of alcohol and taking gentle exercise. We try to improve people's chances of success by helping them to make simple changes and encouraging their wider family to support them in doing so.

Straightforward steps can help. If, for instance, an Association co-ordinator should visit somebody and notice that they are not taking prescribed medication to prevent further strokes, perhaps because they are unclear when they should take it or their tablets have got muddled up, they might ask the pharmacist to sort the tablets for them, so that they are provided in a dosette, with separate compartments containing the correct tablets and dose for a particular day or time of day. If the problem of failing to take medication is a serious one, they would contact the local stroke team.

The Stroke Association also offers help with communication problems from about 160 other centres, also staffed by paid employees and volunteers. As noted above, professional help from a speech and language therapist should be the first point of help in this area. However, people often benefit from more one-to-one help than the state is prepared to fund, and trained volunteers may help with practising the use of numbers and handling money or practising writing skills by writing letters and talking about stories in the news. Activities such as these (as well as normal social contact) can be useful means of enabling somebody whose speech has been affected to regain some of their skills or find new ways of communicating. Also, staff and volunteers work with the whole family to find out the best means of communicating – for instance, family members providing a prompt of the first letter of a word which cannot be found or encouraging the person who has had a stroke to write or draw what they are trying to convey.

The Stroke Association offers services throughout the UK (apart from Scotland), including the Channel Islands and Isle of Man. In Scotland and Northern Ireland, two other organisations also provide much help – Chest, Heart and Stroke Scotland and Northern Ireland Chest, Heart and Stroke.

In addition, a variety of other voluntary organisations provide support to people and their families affected by stroke on the ground. Conquest Art, for instance, which has branches mainly in southern England, seeks to help people with physical disabilities to regain their ability to draw and write and at the same time derive enjoyment from creating works of art *(as explained on page 219)*.

Strokes

* Strokes can be both prevented and treated.

* Find out which of your local hospitals has a good stroke unit.

* A stroke is an emergency: prompt treatment is essential.

* Drugs to disperse blood clots can be invaluable, but must be taken soon after the stroke.

* Don't drink anything after a stroke until your ability to swallow has been assessed.

* Question plans to insert a urinary catheter after a stroke.

* Therapy can work wonders but should start early.

* Make sure your family understand how to help you recover.

* High blood pressure damages organs irreparably and increases the risk of heart attacks and strokes.

* Moderate exercise reduces the risk of strokes.

Chapter 17

Anxiety and depression

O ur emotions and the chemistry of our brains are inextricably inter-twined. Being in love causes the levels of the chemicals dopamine and oxytocin to rise – without, of course, our being aware this is happening.

So too with anxiety and depression. Worrying about something or feeling low both involve complex chemical changes in the brain. It is of course perfectly normal sometimes to have a low mood or to worry about things. But sometimes anxiety or depression – and sometimes both together – are severe enough to affect our lives day by day.

Researchers do not know the precise cause of depression. They believe it may be caused by a combination of circumstances in the environment together with psychological, biological and genetic factors. Fortunately, both conditions can be treated, however they have been caused. Drugs are available, as are talking therapies; indeed, there is plenty of research evidence for the success of both.

However, many people suffering from anxiety or depression do not seek help. Older people go to see their GP almost twice as often as other age groups, but only a third of older people who have depression raise their symptoms with their GP.[1]

Dr Fionnuala Edgar works as a clinical psychologist for the NHS in Dumfries and Galloway. Concerned at the low uptake of talking thera-pies among older people, she and her colleague Mary Hughes did some research in 2013 to try to work out why when launching a campaign to increase awareness of the benefits of therapy. In an account of that research and in an interview with me in 2016, Dr Edgar highlighted the following factors:

- older people often consider that having a low mood is an inevitable part of the ageing process. In fact, feeling tired of life may mean you have depression, which could be treated.

- they may feel that their depression or anxiety is an inevitable accompaniment of any physical health condition they have

- they may be unaware that their anxiety or depression is responsive to treatment

- a stigma around mental health – people may be reluctant to seek help because they fear what others may say

- they have feeling of worthlessness, perhaps the result of or exacerbated by depression. So someone might say, 'I shouldn't complain – there are other people worse off than me.' Dr Edgar would respond: 'Why are *you* not anybody else? This is having an effect on your ability to enjoy life and if we can help you have a better quality of life, then why not?'[2]

In this chapter I examine:

▶ the definitions of anxiety and depression

▶ problems to which anxiety and depression can give rise

▶ some of the common causes amongst older people

▶ how both conditions are diagnosed

▶ types of talking therapy

▶ drug treatment

▶ how to get the best treatment

▶ how therapy can help people facing bereavement, carer stress and sleep problems

Anxiety: definition, symptoms and causes

At what stage is anxiety different from just being understandably concerned about things in everyday life? Where does normal end and abnormal begin? The answer is when that worry starts to become present much of the time and the person has difficulty in controlling it.

Apart from near constant concern, generalised anxiety disorder (GAD) may have other symptoms. Somebody may become easily upset. Their sleep may be disrupted. They may have difficulty in concentrating, tension in their muscles and a feeling of being constantly jittery and on edge. They may have panic attacks.

Essentially, someone with GAD over-estimates a threat and under-estimates their ability to cope with it. As a result, their life starts to centre around their anxiety and the fear of what might happens leads them to avoid doing things. This can result in a vicious circle. Some people have what is known as social anxiety, so that they are constantly nervous of prompting negative reactions from other people. That may prevent them from going out. That isolation in turn perpetuates their anxiety, because they never learn that their social interactions in the outside world can be all right. Remaining at home may lead to loneliness, which may in turn lead to depression.

Similarly, some older people fail to step outside their front door because they have an intense and abiding fear of falling over. As with social anxiety, what they perceive to be safe behaviour sustains the belief that is fuelling their anxiety – and also denies them the benefits of going out and mixing with other people. Some people who fear going out develop agoraphobia, which involves anxiety in situations in which the person might find escape difficult or embarrassing, such as open spaces, crowds or public transport.

Being over-anxious about your health is another common form of anxiety. Having an illness or disability can cause people to worry a great deal. In some illnesses, the development of anxiety is a part of the physical illness. But in other cases it arises because someone is worried about their health, and it can become so severe that it makes dealing with the illness or disability more difficult to handle.

Some people worry about their health even though they have no physical illness. They are constantly checking for symptoms, seeking yet more information on the internet and frequently consulting their doctor. There again, some people may develop GAD not because they themselves are ill, but because they find themselves caring for someone else who is seriously ill. Carers are often even more reluctant to seek help for anxiety or depression than other people. Yet they could benefit much from learning how to manage carer stress. This not only helps them feel happier: it also helps ensure that the caring situation is more sustainable and does not break down because of the carer's mental condition.

One reason to seek help with anxiety is that it can lead to the development of depression. Someone who never goes out because of social anxiety may become intensely lonely, which in turn may lead to depression. About 40 per cent of older people who have depression also suffer anxiety disorders and in most cases of comorbidity (the two conditions existing side by side), the anxiety preceded depression.[3] So address anxiety as early as possible.

Depression: definition and symptoms

In 'Depression in later life: a personal account', Bronwen Loder recalled: 'About a year after retirement, I had become apathetic, withdrawn, and unable to concentrate and was sleeping badly. ... I had a particular problem with procrastination: was unable to open letters, pay bills or, at times, communicate with anybody. I felt I had lost my purpose in life.'[4]

Dr Loder had some of the common symptoms of depression. These include low mood but also fatigue, insomnia, loss of appetite, apathy and loss of interest or pleasure in the ordinary activities of life, experienced for at least a fortnight.[5] You do not need to have all these symptoms to have depression. As the National Institute for Health and Care Excellence (NICE) has pointed out, 'Depression is a broad and heterogeneous diagnosis. Central to it is depressed mood and/or loss of pleasure in most activities'.[6]

If someone has symptoms of depression, changes in the brain have probably taken place that include higher than normal levels of hormones associated with stress and a change in the levels of a chemical called serotonin. The ability of the person involved to function day-to-day may be impaired, so that they cannot look after themselves properly or lead a normal life.

The symptoms of bipolar disorder, formerly known as manic depression, are quite different. Genetic factors seem to play a larger part in triggering bipolar than other types of depression. It is far less common amongst older people than clinical depression and I do not consider it here.

What is the difference between depression and a feeling of being fed up? As with anxiety, depression is deemed to be present when a low mood starts to affect someone's day-to-day functioning. If they are depressed, they are probably not sleeping or eating properly. They may be thinking about suicide, as they feel life is no longer worth living. They may be withdrawn socially – from friends, from family, and from the activities they previously enjoyed.

Depression can make coping with other medical conditions more difficult. It can reduce the incentive to avoid other illnesses – by getting a flu or shingles jab, for example. You may not get enough to eat nor obtain enough exercise. Depression can have a massive impact on our social and emotional lives: lack of interest and pleasure in life can make us less entertaining company, so that the friends and even the partner who might have given support drop away.

Some people who have symptoms of depression take their own life. Nearly 500 men and more than 200 women aged 60 and over in the West

Midlands committed suicide between 1995 and 2004, for instance.[7] Various studies indicate that between about two-thirds and three-quarters of older people who killed themselves had showed symptoms of depression beforehand.[8] The attempts of older people to kill themselves are more likely to be successful than those of younger people: cries for help – attempts to influence other people without strong intent to actually die – are less common amongst older people.[9] As depression is treatable, much death and subsequent heartache could potentially be preventable.

Causes of depression

While anxiety is linked to fear, depression often stems from loss. Later life is a time when we tend to see many losses. It is also a time when we have time to contemplate those losses, and perhaps other losses that occurred earlier in our lives but at a time when we were too busy with family or work to process them. So what are the losses that can lead to depression in later life?

They are not difficult to find. There is the loss of one's job – and with that loss of income, self-esteem and a structure to one's life *(as discussed on page 84)*. There is the loss of loved ones – someone might move away from their friends and family to live in another part of the country. Or people to whom they have been close, perhaps for decades, may die.

Illness and disability can give rise to losses. Thus loss of your eyesight is devastating in itself but so too can be the ramifications, such as having to surrender your driving licence, no longer enjoying particular places on holiday or having to leave one's home to relocate to a care facility or live with relatives. That disability is often associated with depression is hardly surprising. The after-effects of a major stroke, chronic heart or lung disease for instance, bring daunting psychological challenges. Thus my father had to cope during the last ten years of his life with progressively losing his ability to move around. Once he had scampered up cliff-sides with me and my brother; 15 years on, emphysema meant that he struggled to catch his breath when climbing stairs and could walk only a few yards before resting. In those days (the mid-1970s), mobility scooters and many of the other inventions for helping people who find walking difficult were pretty well unknown. My father bore his increasing confinement to his small terraced house imaginatively and cheerfully, but many people, myself included, would have bowed under the mental strain.

But while some people are unhappy as a result of changes in their lives such as these, they do not go on to develop depression. What is crucial is how people respond to situations – their attitudes and their behaviour.

That response may be shaped by their character, their resilience and the support or lack of it from others around them.

Resilience developed earlier in life can buffer the impact of loss. But sometimes emotional problems experienced much earlier, even in childhood weaken our ability to cope in later life. One study revealed higher rates of anxiety disorders, current sleep disturbance and emotional distress amongst survivors of the Holocaust than other people of a similar age.[10] Another has shown an association between the forcible displacement of people during World War Two and higher levels of anxiety together with lower levels of resilience and life satisfaction 60 years later on.[11]

A key feature of later life that can affect whether or not we develop anxiety or depression or indeed both is time and commitments. Retirement affords people a lot more leisure to think about their past experiences, both negative and positive. Some people will have experienced abuse in childhood or domestic violence during adulthood. Some will have experienced the loss of a loved one, such as a child, at a time when one was supposed to get over such loss quickly and perhaps never talk about it. Many things can happen to us in life which we do not process emotionally at the time, whether because we are told that is wrong or because the pace of work and family life preclude it. But when we come to retirement, that changes. And in our reflections, we will pick up on regrets or things that have not gone so well.

Dumfries and Galloway attracts many older people in retirement, perhaps taking advantage of low property prices and the benefits Scottish older people enjoy compare with their counterparts south of the border. Indeed, it has a higher proportion of older people in its population than any other region in Scotland. Dr Edgar explained to me:

> Often someone retires into the local community and then develops physical health problems. They have retired with high expectations of what retirement will look like, so they have lots of ambitions and plans for their retirement, but then suddenly these hopes are thwarted because of a physical health problem, such as a stroke. Because they've retired away from their support systems, with friends and family scattered elsewhere, they may not have local support. This combination of the stress of a serious health concern, coupled with a lack of support and an altered future can contribute to the development of low mood and anxiety. There may be other factors predisposing them to develop depression such as negative experiences in the earlier part of their lives which reduce their ability to cope with such difficulties in later life.

Diagnosis of anxiety and depression

Diagnosis of generalised anxiety disorder involves a GP or other health care professional using an assessment tool to try to work out whether the symptoms and the severity someone is feeling conform to those seen in GAD. There is no simple blood test. As we have noted, anxiety often arises in association with a physical illness. Now sometimes, this anxiety is indeed a characteristic symptom of that illness, but in other cases it develops separately. The doctor has to try to establish which is the case.

The diagnosis of clinical depression is not straightforward either: again, there is no simple blood test or brain scan. The first step is to rule out other medical causes for the low mood and any other symptoms being experienced. These can arise as a side-effect of medication (including certain cancer drugs, steroids, tranquillizers and beta-blockers). In addition, digestive disorders, diseases of the blood, thyroid problems, vitamin deficiencies and a brain tumour can all give rise to similar symptoms to depression.

Having ruled out other possible causes for symptoms, a GP will then seek to establish their nature, intensity and duration and the severity of their effect. There is doubt here too: it is unclear how low one's mood has to be before it becomes clinical depression, as opposed to a natural response to a depressing set of circumstances.

Expect to come away from seeing your GP with answers to the following questions:

✓ Have I got depression?
✓ If not, what is the cause of my symptoms?
✓ Should they be treated and if so, how?
✓ How bad is my depression?
✓ Is it possible to establish why I have developed depression?
✓ What treatment will I receive?

Take somebody with you to see the doctor, if possible. Your low mood may mean you fail to explain all that the doctor needs to know. You will probably not be in a fit state to press for a referral if your GP seems keen to write off your low feelings or simply give you tablets without considering any other approach. Also, another person can be invaluable in helping you monitor the effects of treatment and the side-effects of any medicines. Indeed, the attitude of those around somebody with depression is important: in a talk on depression among older people living in care homes, Professor Anthony Mann of King's College London recommended that such people should be positive and talk of recovery, as people suffering from depression struggle to see a future without their depression.[12]

Even if your symptoms are not too bad at present, your GP should take them seriously. About 25 per cent of people with mild depression go on to develop severe depression within two years.[13] That said, many people (about 30 per cent) recover from their anxiety or depression without treatment.

Your GP should follow guidance published by NICE on anxiety or depression. The guidance NICE has issued is concise and readable and can be obtained free of charge from its website. Look for NICE Clinical Guideline 113 entitled *Generalised Anxiety Disorder and Panic Disorder in Adults: Management* (published in 2011) or Clinical Guideline 90: *Depression in Adults: the Treatment and Management of Depression in Adults,* (published in 2009). As depression is between two and three times more common in people with a chronic physical health problem and NICE considers that, 'Treating depression in people with a chronic physical health problem has the potential to increase their quality of life and life expectancy', it has also issued *Clinical Guideline on Depression in Adults with a Chronic Physical Health Problem: Recognition and Management* (published in 2009), to be read alongside its general guidance on the treatment of depression in adults.[14] The equivalent body to NICE in Scotland, the Scottish Intercollegiate Guidelines Network, has published broadly similar guidance.[15]

The voluntary organisations Depression Alliance and MIND offer a wealth of information and advice. They also have helplines, so you could ring up and talk to someone about whether you might perhaps have one of these conditions.

Help for which your GP can provide a gateway could take various forms:

Drug treatment

There has been much research into medication for both anxiety and depression in recent years and a psychiatrist would choose between a range of drugs which have antidepressant or anxiolytic (relieving anxiety) effects or both. This is a complex field in which the doctor is looking for a drug which is effective yet does not cause the person to become dependent on it or give rise to undesirable side-effects, such as making them sleepy. A psychiatrist would prescribe the drugs in the first instance and a community psychiatric nurse would visit the patient at home and monitor their effectiveness and any side effects. NICE recommends selective serotonin reuptake inhibitor drugs (known as SSSRIs) for depression and generalised anxiety disorder, although other drugs are also available.[16]

Talking therapy

For non-medics, talking therapy is easier to understand. It would be carried out by a psychotherapist, counsellor or clinical psychologist *(these terms are defined on pages 316–7)*, although, as we see in a moment, self-help manuals are available which can help some people. The types of therapy most frequently used to treat anxiety and depression are as follows:

Cognitive behaviour therapy (CBT)

This is the most widely used approach and is based on the idea that people are not mentally disturbed by things in themselves, but by the attitudes they take towards them. The therapist would meet the person for a number of sessions and try to alter the way they think about their situation, rather than focusing on the roots of the problem. Together, the patient and therapist try to identify unhelpful thoughts, beliefs and types of behaviour to which the depressed person finds themself automatically reverting, and the situations that often prompt them. They then develop strategies for avoiding or altering those situations, or intercepting or modifying the thoughts.

Cognitive behaviour therapy for GAD would look for the situations or events and the automatic anxious thoughts which tend to trigger the anxiety. The therapist would go on to examine with the patient how this process can be interrupted or changed. Anxiety is often associated with a need for control and an inability to tolerate uncertainty. As a result, people try to control situations as much as they possibly can, in order to alleviate their anxiety. As we see in a moment, talking therapy can help them relinquish some of that control and accommodate uncertainty in their lives. The therapist might also teach the patient techniques to help them relax, such as deep breathing, progressive relaxation of the muscles and imagining pleasant situations. They might also consider sleep management *(see below)*. CBT has also been shown in research studies to have a high success rate for people with panic attacks and phobias. Treatment for agoraphobia involves desensitising the person to the thing that prompts their fear but with someone else alongside them, in a graded way, accompanied by relaxation and with CBT helping the person to develop skills to cope with their problem.

Interpersonal therapy

This is also a time-limited treatment (perhaps 12 to 16 sessions) in which someone is helped to assess the quality of their relationships with other people. Might recent changes in these relationships have led to their depression? Interpersonal therapy does not view interpersonal difficulties as the only cause of someone's depression but does try to explore their relationships with other people and develop methods of improving them.

Interpersonal therapy can be used to help someone depressed after a death. Discussion may reveal that grief at the loss of a partner is compounded by previous bereavements, and therapy could help the person process and adapt to these various losses. It may also be used to deal with disputes, transition in role (perhaps involving retirement), and difficulties in establishing and maintaining supportive relationships, for example.

Mindfulness

If someone is depressed and often ruminating about the past or worrying about the future it can be useful to focus on the here and now. Mindfulness seeks to enable someone to be aware of and open to their internal mental state and the external world at the present moment and in a non-judgmental way, without defining things as good or bad. It involves various techniques that help people to do this and is often used in conjunction with CBT.

Other therapies

Other therapies used might for instance help you to identify the activities in your life that give you most pleasure and help you plan to include them to a greater extent and increase the pleasure you take in them.

A therapist might help you identify activities which bring a sense of accomplishment. If you find yourself engaged in tasks which seem to have no end and thus offer no sense of achievement along the way, it is easy to fall into a low mood.

A good therapist will give whatever form of therapy would best suit the person and their situation – the various therapies can be adapted. So, if therapy should reveal that childhood abuse is affecting the situation now, they might try to tackle the problem through trauma-based CBT. Or the therapist may consider they would get better results from interpersonal therapy and look at relationships throughout the person's life and how these have been affected by early abuse. Often the process of disclosure of abuse itself can be cathartic, so that the therapist simply helps the person process the memory and resolve some of the feelings of shame and guilt that they have felt, perhaps over decades.

Make sure your therapist takes account of any difficulties you have, such as with hearing, vision or understanding. They should be ready to adapt their approach so as to proceed at a pace with which you are comfortable and if necessary give you material in large-print form.

The therapist will include other people close to you if that might be helpful and you agree. For instance, NICE recommends behavioural couples therapy for people with a physical health problem and moderate depression where their relationship with their partner may affect that depression.[17]

Self help

If your anxiety or depression is quite mild you could try to help yourself by using a manual which takes you through your problems using (mainly) cognitive behaviour therapy. There is an excellent series of books called the Overcoming series such as – *Overcoming Depression, Overcoming Anxiety* and *Overcoming Low Self-Esteem*.[18] They contain many sound suggestions for all of us, whether or not we have depression or anxiety. These books were originally published by Robinson, now by Little Brown.

Taking yourself through one of these manuals or perhaps a similar online package offers advantages – treatment at your convenience without taking time off work or other activities, being able to work at one's own pace and of course privacy and freedom from the stigma some people feel if they attend clinics. However, you do need sufficient self-motivation to take yourself through a self-help manual.

Another possibility is to attend group sessions provided by a voluntary organisation. For instance, many carers' centres *(page 631)* provide sessions for carers to help them manage stress.

Help through the NHS

If you go to your GP and your anxiety or depression is mild, you may well be referred to 'guided self-help', in other words, you go through a manual or workbook, but you have someone to support you in doing so. You may get help one-to-one or in a workshop or group. Your therapist might set you homework and/or phone you mid way between sessions to see how you are faring.

Cash has been put into the NHS in recent years to pay for guided self-help for psychological conditions that are at a mild stage; thousands of people have been trained to provide CBT-based talking therapy in a little-known government initiative called Improving Access to Psychological Therapies (IAPT).

You should not have to wait long for a referral. Waiting time targets set down in the NHS Constitution state that 75 per cent of people should receive treatment within six weeks and 95 per cent within 18 weeks if they have been referred to the IAPT programme. Scotland uses a similar approach but does not call it IAPT. There, supported self-help often uses an online resource called Moodjuice.

In many centres you can self-refer for IAPT. Or a friend or family member could refer you, with your consent.

However, many people will need more help than this, because their anxiety or depression is more serious or the causes complex. Sometimes a stepped approach is tried with guided self help going on to one-to-one therapy if the former does not provide enough help.

In the past, GPs often gave patients medication without considering talking therapy. There are pros and cons with each approach; much depends on the cause of the condition and its severity. Talking therapy can provide a toolkit for managing depression in the short-term, as well as a strategy should the condition return. That said, drugs can also be effective, particularly if the depression is severe. Sometimes a combination of drugs and therapy works best.

Doctors may have given antidepressants to patients with symptoms of depression as a matter of routine in times past, but they should not be doing so now. NICE enjoins doctors as follows: 'Do not use antidepressants routinely to treat persistent subthreshold depressive symptoms or mild depression.' Instead, doctors should consider them only for people with a past history of moderate or severe depression; those with symptoms which do not seem to reach the threshold for classification as depression yet have been present for a long period (typically at least two years); and in cases of subthreshold depression symptoms or mild depression which persist after other treatments have been tried.[19]

For people with moderate or severe depression, doctors should offer patients, 'A combination of antidepressant medication *and* a high-intensity psychological intervention (cognitive behaviour therapy or interpersonal therapy)'. (my emphasis)[20]

The National Service Framework for Older People *(see page 300)* takes mental health seriously, devoting a chapter to the condition. For depression it recommends treatments not involving drugs as the 'first line management wherever possible, such as cognitive behaviour therapy and individual counselling and support'.[21]

Overcoming anxiety and depression is not always easy. Not everyone will respond to the treatment first offered to them. Be ready to ask to try different medication or at a different dose. If you don't develop a rapport with the therapist allocated to you, ask for another.

Mental health is covered by the Choose and Book system, which provides choice for patients in England who are referred for specialist treatment *(page 905)*. Wherever you live in the UK, expect to be offered a choice in the way you are treated: patient choice is a fundamental principle of the NHS Constitution *(see page 285)*.

If you or your loved one has dementia and also has depression the latter should be addressed as recommended by NICE *(explained on page 289)*.

Practical support

Enlist your therapist or GP's help to address any problems which are adding to your anxiety or depression. For instance, if you are struggling with anxiety or depression related to being a carer, ask your therapist or GP to help you secure practical help to enable you to cope. They could write to social services and ask that you be given a carer's assessment of the practical support you need *(as explained on page 621)*. In any case, if you are a carer do make contact with your nearest carers' centre *(page 630)*. These centres can provide a gateway to much help and some provide group sessions in relaxation and managing stress, as well as one-to-one counselling.

Uses of therapy

Finally, let us look briefly at the ways in which talking therapy can be used for some common causes or symptoms of depression and anxiety in later life.

Sleep problems

Many people particularly with anxiety but also with depression do not sleep well. A therapist would look at basic sleep hygiene – how someone is preparing their body for sleep. They would consider the temperature of the room and any other physical factors that might prevent or disrupt sleep such as noise or the consumption of a large amount of food or alcohol before going to bed. Another is the need to go to the toilet. If someone needs to go frequently, the therapist would suggest they consult their GP about possible causes – perhaps an overactive prostate gland.

Relaxing before going to bed is important. So a therapist would suggest winding down activities and teach relaxation exercises.

However, sleeplessness often results from worry – someone wakes during the night and a constant, pervasive concern prevents their getting back to sleep. That worry might be about a family situation, perhaps, or money matters or illness.

The therapist would try to help the person work through it – accepting that there are aspects of the situation they cannot alter, thinking what practical steps they could take to do something about it and helping them tolerate uncertainty.

Another common cause of insomnia is rehearsing in the mind something you have done that day or anticipating all the things you have to do. Professor Colin Espie is the author of the excellent self-help guide *Overcoming Insomnia and Sleep Problems*; therapists often use Professor Espie's suggestions. So they might encourage you to devote a short time in the early evening to putting the day to rest – writing down on paper what has happened and what you felt good about and what has troubled you. You would also write down a list of things you need to do and set down anything you are unsure about, considering in advance things you are looking forward to and things you worry about. All this should leave you feeling more in control. Another simple tip is to keep a piece of paper beside your bed so you can write things down in the middle of the night to be dealt with the following morning.

Blocking distracting thoughts can also be helpful. Professor Espie recommends thinking the word 'the' to oneself slowly and calmly every two seconds. He believes that helps block out other thoughts, disconnects us from the outside world and helps us fall asleep.

Bereavement

If you have lost a loved one such as your partner and are finding it difficult to get through your grief, you could approach Cruse Bereavement Care. Trained bereavement support volunteers give one-to-one help and group support throughout England, Wales and Northern Ireland; Cruse Bereavement Care Scotland provides a similar service. Trained volunteers also give help via a phone helpline and responding to email messages. The emotions you are feeling may be perfectly normal but it can be difficult to know whether they are, as coping with bereavement is not much discussed in our society.

If you are continuing to feel low six months after the death of a loved one, do go and see your GP and ask for a referral to a counsellor, psychotherapist or clinical psychologist. He or she should help you cope better with your bereavement. Some people feel that they should be over a bereavement, say, a year after it has taken place. But response to bereavement is very individual and much of the therapy may involve helping you to normalise your reactions. It is OK to have good days and bad days and to move forward on that basis.

Therapy often involves not trying to work your way through the stages of grief that were used in the past[22] but helping you cope with inevitable fluctuations between being able to function and then suddenly being thrown into a raw state of grief by a trigger such as an anniversary. Rather than expecting you to progress in discrete stages, the process should be dynamic and changing; this is the dual process theory of bereavement.[23] The aim would be to ensure that the swings you experience between matters related to loss and those related to restoration gradually result in the latter becoming more prominent over time. But the therapist would try to help you cope with prompts such as seeing a photograph or visiting a grave, rather than avoiding them.

Dr Edgar told me:

> Sometimes it is about finding out about the relationship someone had with the person who has died and their beliefs and thoughts on moving forward. Often there can be guilt about carving out a new life for themselves without the person who has passed away; for some people, it can be about giving them permission to move on. The therapist helps them realise that moving on isn't going to affect their memory or the memories that they have with that person, but it is about supporting them to find a new normal. It's not like life getting back to normal, because life is never going to be the same as it was, but it's about carving out what they want the rest of their life to look like. Often it can be reflecting on if the reverse had happened: if they had died, would they want their spouse or partner to live like this, with this kind of homage to the previous relationship? Or would they want them to move forward? So we are trying to explore what are the barriers to them actually living life the way they would like to live, what were their expectations of life and how can those expectations be met in a different way, without their loved one.

Anxiety and depression

* Depression is not an inevitable part of growing older.
* Difficulties with bereavement, the psychological challenges of illness and disability, family situations, carer stress, sleep problems and many others can be helped by talking therapy.
* Anxiety is often related to fear and depression to loss.
* There are sophisticated self-help manuals which can help some people.
* Recent research has shown that talking therapy and drugs are often effective.
* Don't be ashamed of having depression or anxiety
* Two thirds of older people with depression have never discussed it with their GP.
* Suicide attempts by older people are much more likely to succeed.
* Involve friends and family in your treatment and find a support group if possible.
* Enlist the help of your doctor to get changes in your living conditions, say, in a care home, if they are making you anxious or depressed.

Chapter 18

Falls

O f all the hazards posed by moving around when we are getting on,
a fall is probably the most feared. It is also the fear that the young
find most difficult to comprehend. Children, footballers, tennis
players fall over all the time. Why should falling be such a hazard in later
life?

In this chapter I examine:

▶ why older people are more likely to fall and hurt themselves

▶ problems which falls may cause

▶ medical conditions which increase the risk of falling

▶ trip hazards in the home and outdoors

▶ alarms to summon help in the event of a fall

▶ how to get up after a fall

▶ hospital care for a fractured hip

▶ help from your GP

▶ falls prevention exercises

▶ fear of falling

Falls and the older body

Staying upright and balanced is only achieved through a miracle of physiology. We constantly assess whether we are upright or off-balance through
the information fed into our brain from our eyes, balance mechanisms in
our inner ears and touch receptors in our muscles, skin and joints. As we
grow older, some of these mechanisms become less sensitive. Meanwhile,
those that enable us to correct our body position and stop or break a fall,
such as swaying, staggering and putting out an arm, are less instantane-

ous. They may come into play, but often not quickly enough. This means that factors which may cause falling at any age, not least uneven paving or a drink too many, are more likely to result in a fall when we are older.

In addition, there are a number of medical conditions that tend to occur in later life and can increase the risk of a fall, from poor eyesight to a painful knee or a stroke. Older people tend to take a wider range of drugs than younger people and the side-effects may include unsteadiness. Internal factors such as these can combine with hazards such as a pet underfoot or unfamiliar surroundings to cause a fall. So, when we are older, a fall often results from a combination of external and internal circumstances.

The good news is that many of the risk factors for falls are actually reversible to some extent or other. We can remove trip hazards around our home and urge our council to repair broken paving or improve street lighting. If a fall is caused, or partly caused, by a medical condition, we can get treatment for it and/or advice on ways of lessening the risk of falling. We can also obtain equipment that can alert other people if we have had a fall, even if we are unconscious.

Bizarre as it may sound, a fall can be a useful – if disconcerting – symptom of a medical condition from which we hitherto did not know we were suffering. 'Falls are a key syndrome in medical gerontology. They may be the first indicator that all is not well medically, and they should prompt a diagnostic appraisal aimed at early detection and intervention', in the words of Professor Cameron Swift, former president of the British Geriatrics Society.[1]

It is therefore important to seek medical advice after a fall which has not obviously been caused by a physical obstruction, even if you have not sustained an injury.

Why falls pose problems

There are about one million falls every year in the UK, the vast majority involving older people. They would not be such serious events were it not for the fact that they can have a range of effects on older people. One in ten falls (again, most involving older people) results in significant injury such as a bone fracture, head injury, cuts or serious damage to the soft tissues of the body.

One of the main reasons for the damage a fall can cause to the older body is the widespread occurrence of osteoporosis and osteomalacia – diseases which weaken bones and thus makes them more likely to break. A fractured wrist, shoulder, arm or leg can cause pain, temporary disability and much inconvenience. But perhaps the injury older people most dread from a fall is a hip fracture. It is common, with 65,000 occurring in England, Wales and Northern Ireland each year.[2]

A hip fracture is the name given to a break in a narrow piece of bone which connects the shaft of the thigh bone or femur to its head. This vulnerable piece of bone is called the neck of the femur and it is situated in the hip area. A fracture here usually means pain, an operation and a lengthy period of recovery. For very frail people, a broken hip can be fatal in itself or herald the beginning of a final period of decline.

Falls can have a wide range of less severe but sometimes far-reaching effects. A fall may confine somebody to hospital or their home while they are recovering, so depriving them of all the benefits of getting out and about. It can also erode self-confidence. So someone may stop going out to meet their friends or doing voluntary work to avoid places where they think they might fall.[3]

A fall and its injuries can also result in moving into a care home. Indeed, a fall is thought to be a contributory reason for as many as 40 per cent of admissions to nursing homes.[4]

Internal causes

As we have seen, in older people falls are far more likely to be caused by an underlying medical condition than they are in younger people. Here are some of the conditions that may lead to a fall or make a fall more likely:

Stroke

A stroke may cause someone to fall. The majority of strokes occur because a clot forms in one of the small arteries in the brain, temporarily cutting off the blood supply to that part of it. As a result, the sufferer may become unconscious and collapse. *(See Chapter 16 for more information about strokes.)*

Low blood pressure

A stroke usually results from abnormally high blood pressure, but low blood pressure in the arteries can also cause a fall. In this case, the amount of blood flowing to the brain and other vital organs is restricted and someone can feel dizzy and unsteady. Reasons why someone might have abnormally low blood pressure include the side-effects of some drugs and a heart attack, which prevents the heart from pumping blood around the body, while some people experience a lowering of blood pressure as they grow older.

A condition known as postural hypotension is quite common: one fifth of older people are affected. What happens is this. When somebody is lying down, their blood pressure is low, but when they get up suddenly, their blood pressure has to rise quickly. In some people, it takes a little while for this increase to kick in. So if they get out of bed too quickly, early in the morning or the middle of the night, they may feel faint and fall.

A doctor can check for postural hypotension by measuring blood pressure when somebody is lying down, immediately they are standing and every 30 seconds for more than two minutes after they have risen. Treatment can include medication and changing medication for other conditions which may be exacerbating the problem. If you are affected, avoid rising quickly: sit on the edge of the bed for a few minutes and then stand up slowly. Rather than standing quickly after sitting in an armchair, wiggle your legs before moving.

Syncope

Sometimes an elderly person feels faint or loses consciousness momentarily and falls as a result of a decrease in the amount of blood arriving at the brain because the heart has suddenly stopped pumping. The heart then recovers spontaneously. This condition is known as syncope. Diagnosis and treatment can prevent this happening again.

Drop attacks

In a drop attack, somebody drops to the ground without warning. One moment they are on their feet, the next on the ground, with no idea why. They do not lose consciousness or suffer stroke-like symptoms. They may feel helpless, almost paralysed, when lying on the floor, but recover immediately when they are helped back onto their feet. A drop attack is usually caused by a temporary drop in blood supply to the brain; syncope is one possible reason.

Continence difficulties

Men and women with continence difficulties (a common condition in later life) may need to use the lavatory more frequently and/or have to rush to reach it in time. In doing so, they may fall over, not least at night. *(I discuss continence matters in Chapter 19.)*

Diabetes

Non-insulin-dependent, or type 2, diabetes is about ten times more common amongst older than younger people. Insulin, produced by the pancreas, is essential to transport glucose in the bloodstream to the muscles, where it is converted to energy, which can be used immediately or stored until it is needed. However, in people with diabetes, the body develops resistance to the effects of insulin or does not produce enough to meet the body's needs. As a result, the level of sugar in the blood increases. Diseases which damage the pancreas can lead to diabetes, but the main risk factor is obesity, as this causes insulin resistance. Some types of people inherit a greater risk of developing diabetes than others – south Asian men, for instance.

Many people think diabetes poses only a minor inconvenience. In fact, abnormally high blood sugar levels can affect almost every organ system in the body, from the brain to the kidneys and a woman's reproductive system. As a result, diabetes can lead to kidney failure, blindness and gangrene, amongst other serious conditions. People with diabetes are up to five times more likely to develop cardiovascular disease and so to be at increased risk of strokes and heart attacks.

There are several reasons why diabetes can lead to a fall. In order to dilute the abnormally large amount of sugar in the urine, the kidneys excrete additional water. As a result, someone with diabetes may need to urinate frequently, and this can increase the risk of falls.

If somebody with diabetes has taken insulin in the morning but then not eaten enough, they can develop a condition called hypoglycaemia, which will make them feel faint; this too may lead to a fall.

People whose diabetes has not been controlled may develop gangrene in their feet and/or vision defects, both of which can increase the risk of falling.

Some people with diabetes lose the ability to feel sensations in their toes because high blood sugar levels have damaged their nerves. This 'peripheral neuropathy' can cause them to fall because they don't realise that their foot has hit an obstruction.

Many people are unaware that they have diabetes. The charity Diabetes UK estimates that there are 2.5 million people in the UK with diabetes but a further half a million who do not know they have it. If you think you might have diabetes, seek medical advice quickly.[5]

Foot problems

Apart from loss of nerve sensation in the toes, several other foot problems may lead to falls. Corns, calluses and long toenails can cause somebody to stand in an abnormal way, move with difficulty and as a result lose their balance. People with painful or swollen feet may wear slippers which are too large for them, or pull the laces out of their shoes. As a result, they may shuffle or drag their feet, or trip over their own footwear.

Parkinson's disease

One person in 50 over the age of 80 has Parkinson's disease, a disorder of movement affecting the muscles. It arises because a chemical called dopamine, which is connected with movement, is not secreted in adequate amounts by the brain.

Parkinson's disease affects individuals differently, but typically leads to falls for various reasons. Somebody with the condition may be unstable, with their centre of gravity in the wrong position; their gait may be shuffling; they may have difficulty in starting to move and then in stopping; they may start to make a movement and adjust their weight to anticipate it but then freeze, so the movement is aborted, but, unable to return to their previous position quickly enough, they may lose their balance and fall.

People with Parkinson's must be given their dopamine-replacement drugs at the correct time to ensure their symptoms are controlled as well as possible. The duration of action of these drugs is quite short, so if a dose is delayed, movement difficulties and with them the risk of falling return.

Medication

Drugs can have a range of effects on the older body which can increase the risk of falls. Sedatives of course induce sleepiness and can impair balance. Diuretics or water tablets are frequently taken to encourage the kidneys to remove water and salts from the blood as treatment for high blood pressure, heart failure or swelling of the ankles and feet. But in lowering blood pressure, these drugs increase the risk of falling. Also, people taking them need to pass water more often and more urgently, and they may fall while hurrying to the lavatory. The risk of falling may be greater if someone is taking many different drugs.

Gait abnormalities

If somebody is not walking correctly, perhaps because of a temporary injury or a long-term problem, their risk of a fall is increased. For instance, degeneration of joints caused by osteoarthritis increases the risk of falling, while a painful hip or knee can cause somebody to walk in a one-sided manner. Knees may simply give way. The risk is greater if muscles are weakened – another reason to perform muscle-strengthening exercises if you suffer from osteoarthritis. *(See page 63.)*

Vision problems

The older eye, even without additional impairments, needs four times as much ambient light as the younger eye *(as explained on page 13)*, so low levels of lighting can be hazardous. Also, as we get older, we become more sensitive to glare, so may not see objects on a highly polished floor that is reflecting light. Our eyes also take longer to adjust to changes in light levels, so we may be confused and trip as we move from a dark room to a brightly lit one. As if that were not enough, vision impairments such as cataracts and age-related macular degeneration may mean that our ability to measure depth or recognise objects such as kerb-sides is reduced.

Fortunately, many eye problems can be corrected or reduced through a change of glasses, the removal of a cataract, more lighting or the reduction of glare.

Depression

Depression is common in older people and it can lead to falls for various reasons. Depressed people may not eat as much as they should and thus become weakened. They may not sleep well and, while drowsy, fall. The side-effects of some anti-depressant drugs include tiredness and confusion. Depression can also reduce the motivation to prevent falls by tidying away clutter at home or avoiding hazards out of doors. *(I discuss depression in Chapter 17.)*

Dementia

As long as people with dementia are mobile, they run a high risk of falling. Indeed, they are twice as likely to have a fall as other people.[6] People living with dementia may simply forget that obstructions exist (as my mother did when she fell headlong down a step, *as mentioned on page 429*). They may misinterpret their environment and mistake objects for other things. Several types of dementia can affect spatial awareness, coordination and balance, while the movement difficulties which people with Lewy body dementia often experience and which are similar to those in Parkinson's disease increase the risk of falls.

External causes

Of course, falls often result wholly or partly from objects in our home or other surroundings that cause us to trip. These trip hazards include:

✓ low-level obstructions, such as side-tables, foot-rests, stools, and kitchen cupboard doors which do not shut properly

✓ objects which can only be reached by bending down, such as electric sockets at skirting-board level, or stretching up, such as overhead kitchen cupboards or a light bulb which needs changing

✓ clutter on the floor (say, magazines around the base of an arm-chair), electric and telephone wires

✓ too much furniture

✓ fitted carpets with holes, warped flooring and rugs, particularly if they have curled-up corners

✓ pets which run freely and items deposited by pets

✓ wearing the wrong glasses or glasses which are dirty

✓ using mobility aids incorrectly or using the wrong aid – for instance, carrying as opposed to using a Zimmer, using a stick when a walker-on-wheels is called for or being unable to coordinate two sticks

✓ footwear which is not properly fastened or poorly fitting; baggy clothes over which you might trip

✓ lack of equipment such as grab-rails

✓ inadequate lighting and glare

✓ kerbs, uneven paving, potholed paths and alleys, wet or slippery pavements and clutter on pavements, such as advertisement stands

Action

Fortunately, there are many straightforward steps you can take to improve your safety:

✓ Make sure your footwear is comfortable, gives a good grip and fits well.

✓ See a chiropodist regularly.

✓ Ensure your glasses provide the best possible vision and that there are no blind spots, for instance with bifocals.

✓ Obtain equipment which reduces the risk of falling, such as long-handled devices for retrieving things off the floor. Perhaps place one in each room?

✓ Obtain a walking aid, such as a stick or walker, if it would help, after seeking advice from an occupational therapist or physiotherapist, ideally at a Disabled Living Centre *(see page 458)*. Make sure you use any mobility aid correctly.

✓ Obtain an alarm to enable you to summon help in an emergency without having to telephone *(as outlined below)*.

✓ Ensure that movement around your home and garden is as safe as possible *(as suggested in Chapter 8)*.

✓ If you think you might need help, ask for it. As I write this, I just have heard of an elderly man who was living contentedly in a residential home. Proudly independent, he would seek help from the staff when using the lavatory only if he felt unsteady. One day, he did not summon help quickly enough, took a tumble and broke his hip. His happy life in the home, shared with an elderly woman whom he had met only a couple of years before, was over: the fall prompted a two-month stay in hospital and then relocation to a nursing home. Three months later, he died.

✓ Apply pressure to get pavements and paths repaired and the fabric of your locality maintained well, if necessary by taking to task your local council or other organisations, from football clubs to churches *(see pages 674–7)*. If you live in Wales, you could point to the Welsh Assembly's *National Service Framework for Older People in Wales*, which urges local authorities to prepare community strategies to prevent falls; these should include, 'Ensuring that pavements are kept clean and in good repair, and that there is adequate street lighting'.[7]

✓ If you (or your relative) are frail, consider obtaining a hip protector. This is a protective device designed to absorb the physical energy of a fall, so that it is not transmitted to the body. At its simplest it consists of two foam shock-absorbers, held in place in pockets in special pants, each on the outer side of the hip. Hip protectors can prevent hip injury and also increase the wearer's confidence to move around independently.

However, this is a field in which one has to be careful. The early protectors consist of a hard shell, which can be uncomfortable. In the event of a fall, they can damage the body if they do not fit well or are dislodged or not positioned correctly in the first place. Some of the newer protectors, though softer and more comfortable, can be bulky and incompatible with continence pads, as they absorb fluid. But biomedical engineering is a fast developing field, with new materials and new means of fitting protectors being brought out regularly (as has happened with cycle helmets, for example). If you or your relative are in a care home and at high risk of falling, it is worth finding out whether a type has been developed that might help.[8]

In 2013, however, the research evidence did not suggest that hip protectors provided a great deal of benefit – when the National Institute for Health and Care Excellence's team examined this evidence in the process of drawing up guidance for health bodies, they went no further than to say there is, 'Some evidence that hip protectors are effective in the prevention of hip fractures in older people living in extended care setting who are at high risk'.[9]

Garments with similar pockets for knee protectors – pieces of foam which absorb the energy of an impact – can be useful if you often fall forward; they can also offer extra comfort when kneeling.

✓ Take special care in times and places which are particular risky. Here are some examples:

Between a quarter and a half of falls amongst older people occur **away from home.** These are more likely to occur amongst healthy older people and the risk of injury is higher than for falls in and around the home.[10] So, take special care if you are in a hotel or hospital or staying with a friend – the spiral staircase that looked charming by daylight may be hazardous if you are hurrying down it in the middle of the night, perhaps after a few drinks or still befuddled from a sleeping tablet. Also bear in mind that you may be away from the help you would rely on if you had a fall at home, such as a falls detector *(see the next section).*

The first few weeks after a permanent **change of home** can also be hazardous, before you are familiar with your new surroundings. The World Health Organisation estimates that the incidence of falls can double when older people move to a new environment, but returns to baseline after three months.[11]

Wherever you are living, **night-time** can bring hazards. You rise quickly from bed to go to the bathroom. But standing quickly after lying down for some time can cause a significant drop in blood pressure and make you light-headed *(as explained on page 388).* Or perhaps as you move out of your bedroom you are only half awake, still affected by a sleeping pill. You reassure yourself that you are so familiar with your surroundings that there is no need to switch on the light or put on your glasses or slippers or take your walking stick. Beware! Any of these omissions could increase your risk of tripping or slipping. Your bare feet might slide on your stair carpet, for instance, and before you are aware that anything is happening, you have painfully wrenched your shoulder in grabbing a rail to prevent a fall headlong down the stairs.

Raising the alarm

If you cannot get up after a fall or think you may have injured yourself, there are important reasons for summoning help speedily. The cause of the fall, such as a stroke, may demand urgent medical attention. Any injury may need attention. It is possible to die simply from lying on the floor, if help does not arrive swiftly enough. This is because changes in our temperature regulation mechanisms as we grow older mean we are more vulnerable to hypothermia. Therefore if we don't have the physical strength to get up off a cold floor and aren't discovered within a couple of hours, we may die, even though the injuries involved are not that serious. Conversely, over-heating can cause or contribute to death.

Cilla Black, the singer and television personality, died as a result of a fall in August, 2015, aged 72. The arthritis from which she had been suffering had caused falls in the past. On the day of her death, she seems to have fallen over when she got up after a siesta on the balcony of her holiday home in Spain. She fell backwards, hitting her head against a wall. This rendered her unconscious. The fall also caused a brain haemorrhage, which can cause loss of consciousness but does not normally lead to death. However, the fact that she lay undiscovered for several hours and on an afternoon of high temperatures exacerbated the situation. The coroner considered that Cilla Black's life could have been saved had she been discovered sooner.

An alarm system to call for assistance quickly can literally save our life. A fixed alarm, such as a wall button or a hanging cord, does not offer as much protection as a pendant alarm worn round the neck. A falls detector worn on the belt, which alerts a control centre automatically if moved in a certain way, without the wearer needing to press a button to raise the alarm, may be even better; both these types of device are explained in *Chapter 22: Telecare.*

I was recently chatting with a woman on a bus and asked why she was wearing a neck brace. Five weeks before, as she was crossing the landing getting ready for bed, her cat had slinked between her legs, causing her to trip, fall down the stairs and hit a wall. She heard a vertebra in her neck break. Had she been wearing an alarm, she would only have needed to have pressed a button on her wrist or round her neck to summon assistance. A falls detector would have summoned help all by itself. But, without either device, and no mobile phone, as it had fallen out of her pocket during the fall, she had – in excruciating pain – to reach up and open a door, drag herself over the floor, causing burns to both forearms, and pull a landline phone down from a table to dial for an ambulance.

Getting up after a fall

If you think you may have broken a bone in a fall, do not move that part of your body – and do not allow anybody except a paramedic to do so.

If you think no bones have been broken and you can get up, be careful about how you get to your feet or onto a chair. When we fall, our instinct is to sit up quickly and get off the floor as soon as possible. But raising the head abruptly and sitting up quickly can mean hurting your back and/or becoming dizzy, because your blood pressure may not yet have realigned from the lying-down position. It is better to use a technique called backward chaining.

What you do is to roll onto your side, bend your legs, stay there for a little while, then ease yourself halfway up, leaning on an elbow and a hand. Stop again to let your blood pressure readjust. Then move onto your hands and knees and – slowly throughout – edge yourself to a firm surface which you can use to support yourself, such as the seat of an armchair. Facing the chair, get yourself into a standing position, then turn and sit down.

If you are unable to get up from the floor or summon help and know that a rescuer will not turn up for a while, perhaps several hours, it is easy to assume that the best plan is to lie still and even try to sleep. However, if you lie still for several hours you increase your risk of deep vein thrombosis and pressure ulcers as well as hypothermia. What you should do is to make lots of noise in the hope of attracting help. Also, keep moving, even though you are on the floor. This will help to keep your blood circulating, avoid stiffness in the joints and reduce the likelihood of pressure sores developing. If a part of your body hurts, you should not move that part, but move other parts instead. If you have fractured your hip, you can still move your arms, for example.

Do what you can to keep warm, for instance by pulling a blanket or rug over yourself. If you are lying in a wet spot, try to edge yourself out of it, as the evaporating liquid will chill your body. Try to get comfortable by placing a cushion or rolled-up clothing under your head.

Hospital care for hip fractures

Paramedics are trained to assess how somebody who has fallen should be moved. They will also assess the likely cause of the fall. They will then decide whether the patient should go to hospital.

If a fall has caused a hip fracture, the injured person should get to hospital as quickly as possible in order to relieve pain, stem the bleeding and get the healing process started. One indication of a broken neck of the femur is the fact that when the two legs are side by side, the one that has suffered the break will be slightly shorter than the other and the foot will be pointing outwards (although this phenomenon does not always occur and a hip fracture can be difficult to diagnose). If the neck of the femur has been broken, the rough edges will cut against internal tissue, causing bleeding and giving rise to often severe (sometimes referred) pain.

It is extremely important that somebody with a fractured hip has someone they know with them in A&E to provide constant help and reassurance. Two helpers are ideal, so that one can remain with the injured person while the other is free to go and get whatever or whoever is needed.

The list of challenges with which an older person with a fractured hip must cope is daunting: the pain from their injuries, the shock of the fall, the trauma of the journey to hospital and the fear of what lies ahead. Sometimes an older person who has broken their hip develops temporary confusion.

In the mid-1990s there was considerable concern about the way in which hospitals were dealing with older patients with fractured hips. Long waits in A&E were common, as were long waits for operations, which might be postponed and might be conducted by unsupervised junior surgeons. A report in 1995 by the Audit Commission entitled *United They Stand* urged a number of improvements. When, five years later, the commission carried out a further study, they found that some progress had been made.[12]

To improve care further, in 2007 a team of specialists from the British Geriatrics Society and British Orthopaedic Association drew up recommendations for hospital care for hip fracture patients in what they call the

Blue Book.[13] Later they set up the National Hip Fracture Database. This gathers patients' records from a large number of hospitals and shows the way in which patients are treated, including for instance the length of time patients wait for their operation.[14]

Despite the improvements in patient care that have been made since the mid-1990s, it is worth knowing what you should expect, just in case you need to press for the care you or a relative need. Some of the main steps you would expect to be taken when somebody has fractured a hip include:

1. Sophisticated **pain relief** as soon as the patient has been examined and before any X-ray has been performed. If possible, it should be given through a drip, so that it can act speedily. The Scottish Intercollegiate Guidelines Network (SIGN – Scotland's equivalent of NICE) has brought together health professionals, patients and researchers to draw up recommendations for best practice on the prevention and management of hip fracture in older people; those on the care of patients with hip fracture are broadly similar to those in the *Blue Book*. Thus, for instance, SIGN recommends that pain relief should begin as soon as possible, in the ambulance if necessary.[15]

   If you are accompanying somebody with dementia, be ready to press for pain relief if it is not offered. The Department of Health's National Dementia Strategy, which seeks to improve care for people with dementia, deplores the fact that people with dementia admitted to hospital for hip fracture received less than half the pain relief of non-sufferers in one study.[16]

2. Hip fracture patients are at risk of developing pressure sores, which can be extremely painful and greatly impede recovery from other conditions *(page 913)*. Indeed, the Blue Book says, 'One third of hip fracture patients will develop pressure sores, most of which could be prevented by good anticipatory care.'[17]

   Action to **prevent the development of pressure ulcers** should therefore be taken, beginning in the ambulance and continuing through the patient's stay in A&E and later on the ward. Any parts of the body that are particularly vulnerable, such as the heel and the hip, should be given special protective cushioning. *(I also discuss the prevention of pressure ulcers in hospital on pages 913–4.)*

   SIGN recommends that, 'Patients judged to be at very high risk of pressure sores should ideally be nursed on a large-cell, alternating-pressure air mattress or similar pressure-decreasing surface' and that the heel and hip areas of all patients in emergency departments with a suspected hip fracture should be protected using soft surfaces.[18] In the *Blue Book*, the British Orthopaedic Association and British Geriatric Society recommend that all patients with hip fracture are assessed for the development of pressure sores when admitted to hospital and at least twice a day while they are immobile. Any early or superficial damage to the skin should immediately trigger care to prevent ulcers, or reverse any which might develop. 'Risk factors such as pressure, shearing forces, friction, incontinence, pain and malnutrition should be addressed, and if problems arise the patients should be referred to an expert on tissue viability.'[19]

3. An **operation should take place** as soon as the medical condition of the patient permits and certainly within 48 hours, according to the *Blue Book* team. They also urge that patients who have fractured their hip are cared for from the time of their admission to hospital on an orthopaedic ward that has routine access to specialists in the care of elderly people with bone fractures.[20]

    Involvement of specialist surgeons is important not only because different types of break may occur but also because fixing together broken bones which have been weakened by osteoporosis can make surgery more challenging. After the operation, elderly people with multiple conditions need skilled care from geriatricians, with surgeons keeping in close touch in case of surgical complications for instance.

4. If there is a delay in operating, **intravenous fluids should be given.** Patients should not be denied food and water for an unnecessarily long time before surgery. A report by the Audit Commission commented: 'Research has shown that a four-hour period is usually sufficient. But in some hospitals food is withheld by routine; patients scheduled for surgery in the morning are starved from midnight, those scheduled for the afternoon list from 6 a.m. ... To minimise the risk of dehydration, water and food should be denied for no more than four to six hours, calculated individually for each patient by counting back from the time of operation. If food and drink are withheld for more than eight hours, intravenous fluids should be given.'[21]

5. **Mobilisation** after the operation should be encouraged. If someone lies still in bed for a long time, the risk of their developing deep vein thrombosis, pneumonia and pressure sores rises. The *Blue Book* recommends that patients should be out of bed and weight-bearing on the day after their operation if possible.[22]

   However, moving and walking after the operation can be very painful. Drugs to relieve pain need not only to be effective, but effective at the right time – for instance, before somebody is turned or gets up to wash. Pain or the fear of pain can pose a real hurdle to the movement necessary for recovery.

6. Expect the post-operation ward to be well-lit, with handrails, non-slip floor surfaces and well-signposted doors, exits, toilets and bathrooms, to **reduce the risk of falling** again. Beds, chairs and toilets should be at the appropriate height for individual patients, who should enjoy easy access to their glasses, hearing aids, walking aids and personal belongings.

7. We noted in Chapter 2 the importance of **good nutrition** in helping the older body to heal. But some patients will feel too weak to feed themselves or, if they have dementia, may not understand the need to do so. Expect your or your relative's intake of nutrients to be monitored and assessed; if specialist advice is called for, you should be referred to a dietician. In addition, expect any help needed with eating and drinking to be given. As the *Blue Book* points out, 'It is crucial that all staff dealing with patients recovering from hip fracture understand the importance of adequate dietary intake, and that specific attention is given to helping people eat at meal times.'[23]

   (Other nursing matters to which it is worth paying attention in hospital are discussed on pages 910–52.)

8. **Rehabilitation** seeks to ensure that patient's physical, mental and social abilities can be restored so that they can live the sort of life that they wish to live *(as explained in the context of strokes on pages 355–8)*. Rehabilitation strategies should not be one-size-fits-all: they need to be precisely tailored to the needs and circumstances of the individual. Patients should expect to be fully consulted about their own rehabilitation strategy and relatives and/or carers involved too.

   The *National Service Framework for Older People (see page 300)* states that rehabilitation plans after a hip fracture should aim to:

- teach awareness of hazards and how to avoid them

- teach the patient how to cope in the event of another fall. If possible, they should be trained in how to get up from the floor *(see page 396)*. Methods of summoning help, including use of pendant alarms, and strategies for preventing hypothermia and pressure sores should be discussed.

- encourage the patient to improve the safety of their environment by removing or modifying any hazards

- increase the patient's stability when they are standing, walking, transferring from one place to another, such as getting out of bed, and other movements. This should be done through strengthening the muscles around the hip, knee and ankle; increasing the flexibility of the trunk and lower limbs; offering balance training; and providing appropriate mobility and safety equipment

- help patients to regain their independence and the confidence to carry out the tasks required for everyday living, if necessary by relearning and practising them

- help patients to stop themselves falling and to cope successfully with everyday tasks

- establish a network of community support if necessary. This might include befriending services provided by the voluntary sector to relieve isolation and support the patient's rehabilitation.[24]

Help from GPs

If you have fallen but there is no obvious external cause, go and talk about your fall with your GP, even if it has happened only once and there appear to be no ill-effects. Even if you save yourself from falling, or suddenly find you have to hold on to things in order to keep your balance while walking, go and find out what is wrong. Some older people give up activities which they have greatly enjoyed because they have been frightened by a couple of 'funny turns'. As we have seen, a fall can serve as a useful symptom of an underlying condition and remedies are often available. A trip to the GP could save you from staying at home unnecessarily. Your GP might review the medication you are taking to see whether that is the cause, or refer you to a vision specialist if your eyesight might be a contributory factor, for example.

An older man who already suffers from angina suddenly starts having falls in which he loses consciousness for brief periods. He goes to his doctor, who wires him up to a box which looks a bit like a personal stereo and takes recordings from his heart over a 24-hour period. The information is fed into a computer, which translates it into data about the rhythm of his heartbeat. This reveals episodes when his heart beats with an abnormal rhythm, pumping less efficiently, so that blood flow to the brain drops and consciousness is lost – the condition known as syncope *(outlined on page 388)*. Treatment involves putting in a pacemaker or giving the man a drug that smooths out the rhythm and thus stops the falls.

Falls prevention

How can you prevent yourself having a fall? Be especially careful when moving around in an unfamiliar environment, for instance a hospital ward or in a hotel or friend's property. If in doubt, ask for help.

If you have had a fall (whether it injured you or not) or feel unsteady on your feet, ask your GP for a falls assessment. This should tease out the factors that may cause you to fall and point to the steps that could be taken to reduce the risk of falling and the risk of injury should you fall.

The National Institute for Health and Care Excellence has said: 'Older people who present for medical attention because of a fall, or report recurrent falls in the past year, or demonstrate abnormalities of gait and/ or balance should be offered a multifactorial falls risk assessment. This assessment should be performed by a healthcare professional with appropriate skills and experience, normally in the setting of a specialist falls service.'[25] NICE guidance should be followed by healthcare professionals *(as explained on page 289)*.

The risk factors NICE cites are:

- any vision impairment
- any continence problems
- the patient's gait, balance and mobility
- footwear that is unsuitable or missing
- any cognitive impairment
- any health problems that may increase the risk of falling

- the medication being taken
- whether the person is suffering from syncope *(see page 388 above)*
- the patient's falls history, including the causes of past falls and their consequences, such as a fear of falling

Even if you have not had a fall, you should expect an assessment of your risk of falling to form part of your annual health check if you are 75 years of age or older. If a patient over 75 requests a health check they should be given one under the terms of the GP contract *(see page 291)*.

Osteoporosis

If you have a fall and fracture a bone, your doctor should pursue the possible presence of osteoporosis. Not all bone fractures amongst older people indicate osteoporosis, but often they do. A bone scan, which can measure the density of minerals in your bones, is the most reliable diagnostic tool.

Treatment is usually through medication – calcium and vitamin D supplements and, in more serious cases, drugs which slow down the turnover of bone cells.

There are some very useful (and easily comprehensible) guidelines on how osteoporosis should be treated from the National Institute for Health and Care Excellence (NICE) and the Scottish Intercollegiate Guidelines Network (SIGN).[26]

Weight-bearing exercise helps counter osteoporosis *(see page 65)*. Check with your GP before engaging in any new exercise, both to find out whether it is appropriate for you and, if so, to what level of fitness you should aspire. Taking in sufficient amounts of calcium and vitamin D also counters brittle bone disease *(page 35)*. Rich natural sources of calcium include milk, yogurt, hard cheeses, sardines in oil, tofu and calcium-fortified soya milk.

Exercises for falls

Quite apart from exercises to prevent osteoporosis, there are exercises that improve balance and coordination and thus help prevent falls. These are often offered as an element of exercise programmes for older people, for instance those offered by Extend *(see page 72)*.

Specific routines have been devised for people with heightened risk of falling. For frail people who have had a fall or perhaps have a recognised walking or balance problem, exercises are likely to involve using the back of a chair as support during the first few weeks in order to improve balance and coordination. Participants progress to moving around and also stretching, doing pulse-raising exercises and moving from one exercise to another, often to music. They practise adapting to circumstances – for instance, through starting or stopping or changing pace or direction suddenly, as well as learning to cope with crowded areas. These exercises can be made more difficult by having to count, talk or carry something while walking. One other important element of falls exercises is instruction on the safe way of getting up off the floor after a fall, through the technique called backward chaining *(described above, page 396)*.

Falls prevention classes are also likely to involve education on nutrition, osteoporosis, the causes and prevention of falls, appropriate footwear, how to maintain an active and healthy lifestyle and any help available locally to do these things. Participants are encouraged to practise exercises and to make changes to their home to reduce trip hazards.

If you are at risk of falling, ask your GP for a referral to a falls prevention class if this is not offered. The National Institute for Health and Care Excellence has pointed out:

> Those most likely to benefit are older people living in the community with a history of recurrent falls and/or balance and gait deficit. A muscle-strengthening and balance programme should be offered. This should be individually prescribed and monitored by an appropriately trained professional.[27]

Fear of falling

Some people are so worried that they might have a fall that they rarely step outside their homes; some even develop agoraphobia. Agoraphobia as well as generalised anxiety disorder are treatable conditions, whether by medication or talking therapy or both *(as explained in Chapter 17)*. If you are in this situation, do seek help.

Falls

* Falls are more frequent and more damaging when we are older.

* One in ten falls amongst older people results in serious injury.

* A fall contributes to 40 per cent of nursing home admissions.

* Falls may indicate an underlying medical condition.

* Falls can be prevented and their ill-effects treated.

* Pendant and wrist alarms are more practical than wall alarms.

* If you are waiting for help after a fall, do not go to sleep: make a noise and move your body.

* If in A&E after a fall, ensure prompt action is taken to prevent the development of pressure sores.

* Dementia sufferers with hip fractures tend to receive less pain relief in hospital than non-sufferers.

* Exercise can help prevent falls.

Chapter 19
Continence

To find that you have lost control over your bladder can be one of the most devastating experiences. Yet although this seems an intensely individual concern, it is an experience which is widely shared. Continence difficulties are certainly not a universal feature of growing older. But more than one in five of men and women over the age of 65 experience bladder problems.[1]

Many people who develop continence difficulties circumscribe their lives thereafter. They stay in hotels or with friends only if sure they can cope with their problem successfully and in secret. They avoid long journeys by car, as they feel too embarrassed to ask the driver to make frequent or unplanned stops. Even short walks can come to seem impossible, not only because of the management of the problem itself but also because of fear of 'an accident' – viewed as a great embarrassment in our society. And the difficulties of moving around out of doors are not helped by the widespread closure of public lavatories.

Home life can see major changes. Sleep may be frequently disturbed. Couples who have slept together for decades may take to separate beds. Dealing with a large amount of laundry can come to dominate life.

Continence difficulties can be very hard to wrestle with psychologically. They can cut away at our sense of attractiveness and sexual appeal. The problems in everyday life to which they give rise can seem overwhelming and depressing. Yet the stigma and embarrassment associated with bladder and bowel difficulties deter people from discussing their problems with anyone at all. Women may take up to ten years before they turn to their GP for help.[2] Men may turn to improvised containment devices such as plastic bags, wads of paper tissues, and cut and modified plastic bottles.[3] Yet an impressive body of expertise now exists not just on managing the problems but also on curing them.

The Royal College of Physicians estimates that 70 per cent of people suffering from incontinence will respond well to treatment.[4] Lecturers in nursing Hazel Heath and Irene Schofield report:

> With a comprehensive assessment leading to a correct diagnosis and the appropriate treatment, incontinence can often be cured and, if not cured, at least better managed. Simple nursing interventions can achieve cure rates of up to nearly 70 per cent.[5]

In this chapter I examine:

▶ the causes of urinary incontinence

▶ treatments to cure urinary incontinence

▶ ways of managing incontinence

▶ faecal incontinence and how it can be treated

▶ special underwear and equipment, including catheters

▶ entitlement to free pads

▶ urinary catheters

▶ how care homes should approach continence matters

Causes

Several changes which occur to our body as we grow older lead to some lessening of control over urination. In both men and women, the maximum amount of urine that the bladder can hold declines with age, as does the ability to postpone passing water after feeling a need to do so. In women, the reduction in oestrogen levels in the body that occurs after the menopause causes the muscles in the urinary system to weaken, so they are not as effective at controlling the outflow of urine. In men, the prostate gland often enlarges and this may affect the flow of urine. Changes such as these, which occur in most people, may mean they need to visit the toilet more frequently when they are older. Or perhaps they suddenly feel a need to use the toilet when they arrive home in cold weather or when they are anxious in a way which did not occur when they were younger. These changes can make life slightly less easy to manage than in the past, but they do not involve the uncontrolled leakage of fluid. When incontinence occurs, it commonly does so because one or more of the organs of the urinary system has become more significantly impaired.

Three parts of our anatomy can play a key role in the development of continence problems:

The pelvic floor muscles

Stretching like a sheet from the base of the backbone to the pubic bone in front are the muscles of the pelvic floor. Three exit passages from the body pass through these muscles: for women these are the urethra (for urine), the vagina (for reproduction) and the back passage. If the pelvic floor muscles are in poor condition, they are unable to perform effectively in keeping urine in the bladder. Weakening of the muscles may occur as a result of prolonged births or surgery, as in a hysterectomy. While muscle weakening associated with a reduction in oestrogen after the menopause does not itself cause continence problems, it can make matters worse. However, just like other muscles, those of the pelvic floor strengthen if exercised and, as we shall see in a moment, special exercises have been devised to tone them.

In men, the pelvic floor muscles, which are penetrated by only two passages – the back passage and the urethra – also respond to exercise. Weakening can occur after an operation on the prostate gland.

'Stress incontinence' arises largely from weakness in the pelvic floor muscles. The person involved cannot stop themselves expelling urine when an activity such as sneezing, coughing, exercise, lifting a heavy object or even sometimes standing up from sitting or lying suddenly increases pressure within the abdomen. The extent of the problem varies according to the strength of the pelvic floor muscles and also of special sphincter muscles which control the output of urine through the urethra in men and women.

The bladder

The bladder is a sophisticated organ of the body, shaped like a balloon, which fills up with urine, stores it and then expels it on urination. Nerve endings in the bladder wall respond to a sense of whether the bladder is full or not; a full bladder ought to send a message to the brain that water needs to be passed.

Various things can go wrong with the bladder. Some people do not completely empty their bladder as they should. This may be because the nerves supplying the bladder wall have become damaged, perhaps as a result of diabetes, over-consumption of alcohol, a neurological condition or problems in the backbone which impinge upon the bladder. In this case, the bladder becomes so full that it overflows.

Conversely, in some people, the nerves in the bladder wall tell the bladder muscles to contract and thus expel urine even when the time is not right, so with little warning the bladder empties itself completely. This may be because nerves in the brain have been damaged, perhaps through a stroke or a form of dementia, or because the bladder itself is being irritated, say, by a cystitis infection, a bladder stone or bladder cancer. In fact, in many cases the cause of overactive bladder muscles is unknown.

'Urge incontinence' is the name given to the type of continence problem caused by overactive bladder muscles which cannot be properly controlled by the brain. As a result, quite large amounts of urine may be lost, day or night. Or the person involved may be able to control their bladder to some extent.

The prostate gland

Enlargement of the prostate gland is a common cause of continence problems in men. Although the prostate gland functions in the reproductive rather than the urinary system, it can easily affect urination, as the bladder sits on top of the prostate and the tube which drains it (the urethra) actually passes through the prostate. This means that if prostate tissue grows inwards towards the urethra, perhaps as a result of prostate cancer or benign enlargement of the prostate (common in men over the age of 50), urination can become very difficult. To expel urine, the bladder muscles need to work harder to push it past the obstruction, but frequently they have weakened as they have aged. As a result of all this, the bladder can become distended, fail to empty properly and overflow.

Help

If you have continence problems, go and see your GP. He or she is the gateway to expert analysis and treatment of your difficulties, as well as management of any that cannot be eliminated. As a first step, your GP should assess precisely what the difficulties are in your particular case. You might be suffering from stress or urge incontinence, or a combination of the two, and your GP should work out the likely reasons. They should also examine the severity of your symptoms and the impact they are having on your life, as well as offer treatment and/or help to manage the problem.

Another reason why you should contact your GP about any change in your toilet habits is that they can be a symptom of conditions that are potentially very serious if untreated, in particular kidney, bowel or ovarian cancer.

Some people are embarrassed about discussing continence matters with their GP, although of course they should not be. However, they may prefer to contact a continence nurse direct. The continence service is provided by community health teams and is a walk-in part of NHS provision, so an appointment can be made without a referral from a GP, although this facility has seen cutbacks in recent years. Contact details of continence nurses can be obtained from primary care organisations and from the Bladder and Bowel Foundation, a voluntary organisation which holds a list of the centres from which continence nurse specialists operate across the UK.

Whether you refer yourself to the continence service or are referred by your GP, the main professional with whom you are likely to come into contact is a continence nurse specialist. This nurse should be able to:

- analyse your difficulties and offer you first-line treatment, such as pelvic floor muscle exercises

- discuss ways of managing your problem while you are trying to get it cured, for instance continence pads or, for men, penile sheaths (*see below*)

- offer advice on handling the problem, for instance, the need to wash well every day, to dry yourself with a soft towel or small hairdryer, and perhaps to use a barrier cream to help prevent soreness

- tell you where you can obtain products to manage the problem, such as pads and bedsheets, and advise on the relative merits of different pads and items of underwear

- explain your entitlements under the NHS to receive the pads, underwear and equipment you need for free

Other specialists working in the continence field include continence physiotherapists (who should have a similar range of knowledge and skills to a specialist continence nurse) and doctors from the urology department of hospitals, since some treatments require (often minor) surgery. For instance, a small probe can be inserted which carries an electrical current that stimulates the muscles controlling the exit through which urine passes out of the body. This can help people for whom, for one reason or another, pelvic floor muscle exercise cannot deliver sufficient control. The success rate for this treatment is impressive: up to two-thirds of patients obtain substantial improvement in their symptoms or become continent after sacral nerve stimulation.[6]

Another possible specialist is a hospital gynaecologist, since repair operations such as for a prolapsed womb may resolve the problem.

Let us now look at the most common treatments in more detail.

Pelvic floor muscle exercises

These exercises are essentially simple. You slowly squeeze in and lift up as if you were trying to prevent yourself passing urine or faeces and hold the muscle contraction up to a slow count of ten (or as many as you can manage), then rest for a few seconds – say, a count of four. Then you contract again, repeating the exercise up to a maximum of ten times. Breathe evenly and naturally throughout – don't hold your breath. Avoid tightening your abdominal or buttock muscles – all the muscular action should involve the muscles controlling the urinary system.

As these exercises are invisible, you can do them while waiting in a queue or whenever you wash your hands, for example. The organisation Extend (see page 72) incorporates pelvic floor exercises into its general exercise classes for older people.

Another exercise is simply to draw up and tighten the pelvic floor muscles as quickly as you can, then let go straight away. Wait about a second, and then repeat until you tire or can no longer feel the muscles working. If you suffer from stress incontinence, be ready to draw up and tighten the pelvic floor muscles as quickly as you can whenever urine might leak, such as when you cough, sneeze or lift a heavy weight.

The National Institute for Health and Care Excellence (NICE) recommends, 'A trial of supervised pelvic floor muscle training of at least 3 months' duration should be offered as first-line treatment to women with stress or mixed urinary incontinence.'[7] As already noted (on page 289), any treatment recommended by NICE or an equivalent body should be given unless there are clear reasons why it would not be appropriate for a particular person. Exercise expert Dr Joan Bassey of the University of Nottingham Medical School has written, 'Specifically designed exercises for the pelvic floor have been shown in a single-blind randomised controlled trial to be significantly more effective than other forms of treatment or no treatment at all.'[8]

It is helpful to do these exercises even if you are not experiencing problems. If you are, you should be taught how to do them one-to-one by a continence nurse or specialist continence physiotherapist. They can check that you are doing them correctly and give you extra help if you experience problems.

Hormone replacement therapy

Sometimes a targeted type of hormone replacement therapy is helpful for women. Localised hormone replacement therapy in the form of creams or a pessary can be placed in the lower end of a woman's urethra and help restore muscular power in that area and in the pelvic floor muscles.

Drugs

Medication is the most common treatment for an overactive bladder and many different drugs are available. Another type of medication seeks to reduce the amount of urine produced for a temporary period, such as at night, by temporarily reducing its formation. These drugs can be particularly helpful for people who pass large amounts of water at night but perhaps can control outflow during the day. The Scottish Intercollegiate Guidelines Network (SIGN) publishes guidance on the treatment of medical conditions which is often very similar to that prepared by NICE. SIGN's guidance on urinary incontinence (available free on its website) contains a useful evaluation of the various drugs available.[9]

Bladder retraining

By the time we are 70 or 80, passing water eight times a day and twice at night is normal (four times during the day is normal for a much younger person). But sometimes people need to pass water much more frequently because their bladder is telling them they need to go before it is actually full. In this case it may be possible to retrain the bladder to hold its content as it should until it is full, so increasing the time between urination.

Another kind of bladder retraining which may be necessary seeks to help people who find that they are wet after three or four hours. In this case the key is to find the time at which the bladder has voided its contents and then to encourage the person with difficulties to use the lavatory just beforehand – say, every two-and-a-half hours.

NICE recommends: 'Bladder training lasting for a minimum of 6 weeks should be offered as first-line treatment to women with urge or mixed urinary incontinence.'[10]

It is possible unintentionally to make matters worse by getting into the habit of passing water before one really needs to. Worried lest they will be unable to find a toilet when they need one during a journey, somebody might pass water before they set off, to be on the safe side. But if they make a habit of doing this, their bladder will readjust, so that it always wants to pass water when only part full. A continence nurse would recommend methods of gradually building up the capacity of the bladder to its full extent.

Altering food and fluid intake

Part and parcel of any assessment by a GP or continence nurse of continence problems should be an examination of what goes into the body – food, liquid and drugs.

Healthy functioning of all the cells of our body requires intake of between eight and ten cups of non-alcoholic fluid every day *(see page 48)*. But we also need to drink sufficient quantities of fluid to flush bacteria out of the urinary system. If we do not, we lay ourselves open to developing infections of the urinary tract. These are unpleasant and can make us extremely unwell.

If we don't drink enough fluid, we will develop constipation. This will make us feel uncomfortable and disinclined to move around, which in turn may worsen the constipation. This can lead on to faecal incontinence as a result of the impaction of the faeces *(see below)*.

If your problem is an over-active bladder, the cause may be not how much but what you are drinking. The caffeine in tea and coffee stimulates the bladder and also has a diuretic effect – it increases the body's excretion of water and thus the production of urine. So, if you finish the day with a large cup of tea, you may be exacerbating problems overnight. Try drinking herbal tea earlier in the evening instead.

Alcohol also aggravates the bladder and acts as a diuretic, so can cause particular problems during the night if large quantities are drunk in the evening. It is easy to find yourself trapped in a catch-22 situation: you drink alcohol, which causes continence problems, which make you depressed, so you drink more alcohol …

A continence nurse would also help you consider whether what you are eating is exacerbating any bowel or bladder problems. Are you consuming sufficient fibre? *(See page 39.)* Would the addition of prunes or apricots at breakfast help any constipation problems, or perhaps Fybogel, which is essentially fibre and can be obtained at the pharmacy? As a last resort, a laxative or an enema may be needed.

Changing medication

Different kinds of medication can cause or exacerbate continence difficulties. As a result, the type of drug used may need to be changed or the drug taken in a different way. Diuretics, for instance, which are often given to treat heart failure or high blood pressure, increase urine production, so someone taking them will need to use the toilet more often and perhaps urgently. In view of this, the timing of taking a diuretic may need to be adjusted so that it takes effect when there is easy access to a toilet. Continence expert Professor Adrian Wagg considers that, 'The importance of a medication review and alteration in the management of urinary incontinence in the elderly should not be underestimated'. However, he points out that, 'Data from the National Audit of Continence

Care for Older People suggest that, at best, this is only done for 33 per cent of older people in primary care'.[11]

Surgery and care after prostate surgery

The cause of continence difficulties is sometimes an overactive bladder together with outflow obstruction as a result of an enlarged prostate gland. In these cases, surgery is often the most effective treatment.

Sometimes men experience some degree of incontinence after surgery for prostate cancer. Various treatments can help, including the implantation of an artificial urethral sphincter muscle to improve control of the discharge of urine.

If the problem cannot be cured, a penile sheath might be the solution. These are soft, one-piece, self-adhesive sheaths which fit over the penis and collect urine, which drains down a tube into a storage bag. The bag is often worn on the inner calf, taped to the leg under trousers.

Penile sheaths come in various sizes and it is important to get the correct size and to learn how to fit it and use it correctly; the tubing to the leg bag also needs to be the correct length. As the drainage bag must remain securely in place to prevent the sheath becoming detached, a night drainage bag should be used in bed.

If you have continence difficulties after prostate surgery, ask for a referral to a continence nurse. In an analysis in 2006, specialist continence advisers David Williams and Sandra Moran deplored the frequent failure to refer men for specialist continence advice after prostate surgery. As a result, their problems would often have been managed with a urethral catheter left in place long term, which brings the risk of a urinary tract infection, as *explained below*.[12] A continence advisor might well have suggested a penile sheath instead.

Faecal continence problems

Faecal continence problems are less common than those involving urine, but they are nonetheless not rare: prevalence in people over 80 ranges from 12 to 22 per cent, according to studies; men and women are affected equally.[13] People with faecal incontinence often have urinary incontinence as well. But, as with urinary continence, the main causes are eminently treatable.

Constipation is the most common cause of faecal incontinence in frail older people. The stools become hardened and cannot be ejected; additional waste matter overflows and leaks out without the person involved being able to prevent this.

Common causes of constipation are immobility, certain drugs, lots of different types of medication being given together, lack of fibre in the diet and lack of fluid. A doctor, nurse or continence nurse specialist should address these causes – for instance, ensuring that somebody has plenty of fluid and any help necessary to drink it, sufficient fibre in their diet, help to move around if needed or a change in the drugs they are taking.

Diarrhoea is another common cause of faecal incontinence. In this case the presence of lots of loose stools overwhelms the sphincter muscle which controls outflow and which may have become weakened by age. In this case, leakage takes the form of loose stools.

What are the causes of loose stools? They may form as a side-effect of certain drugs, but probably the most common cause is excessive use of laxatives. Again, addressing the cause or causes of the constipation for which the laxatives were prescribed is the route to treating faecal incontinence.

A third common cause of faecal incontinence is difficulty in getting to the toilet in time. Poor mobility thus increases the risk of faecal incontinence. It is also a major cause of constipation *(as explained on page 59)*. So, poor or complete immobility can sit at the centre of a circle of self-perpetuating bowel problems.

There are other causes of faecal incontinence. People who have suffered a major stroke are sometimes affected temporarily. People with advanced dementia sometimes lose control of defecation. Weakening of the pelvic floor and other muscles as a result of childbirth can also play a part.

As with urinary continence problems, the key is to get a medical professional to carry out an assessment of the cause or causes of the problem and then seek to treat them. But again, the instinct of care providers, such as the managers of nursing homes, is often simply to manage the problem rather than seek a cure. The Royal College of Physicians carried out a wide-ranging evaluation of continence care in England, Wales and Northern Ireland in 2010 and came to the shocking conclusion that 'Vulnerable groups in particular (frail older people, younger people with learning disability) continue to suffer unnecessarily and often in silence with a "life sentence" of bladder and/or bowel incontinence.'[14] In other words, you may need to press to get a proper assessment and/or referral to a continence nurse or other specialist.

Review of problems

Continence is a complex subject and problems often change over time. So you may need to ask your GP or continence nurse to review your needs or carry out regular checks. For instance, you might come to need a different strength of pad or to try a different exercise or other treatment.

Underwear and equipment

The range of underwear and equipment available to manage continence difficulties comes as a welcome surprise to most people.

First, there are gadgets and pieces of equipment which cut down the time taken to reach a toilet equivalent, in particular commodes and urinals. Hand-held urinals come in many different designs according to sex, manual dexterity, the intended situation in which they will be used (whether in bed, seated or standing) and the capacity required. Disposable urinals can be especially useful while travelling.

Commodes can be hired from the British Red Cross and also from many local disability organisations; this is a useful facility if somebody is coming to stay.

Types of underwear have been devised to help people who need to be able to use the lavatory quickly yet are held up by difficulties in manipulating their underclothes, perhaps because of sight or dexterity problems. These include wide-legged knickers which fasten with Velcro at the front of the crotch. Or perhaps you could alter your existing clothes, for instance by fixing an extra tab on a zip to make it easier to find quickly, or replacing buttons or zips with Velcro openings.

Of all the undergarments developed to lessen the difficulties caused by bladder problems, perhaps the most useful is the continence pad. Women who develop continence problems are often tempted to buy a packet of sanitary pads. However, sanitary pads are designed to cope with a far smaller volume of liquid and offer much less absorbency than continence pads, which may seem more expensive but actually offer better value.

Continence pads are surprisingly sophisticated. They come in varying degrees of strength and size and incorporate an anti-bacterial device to counter odour. What is appropriate will vary with the amount of urine being passed and gender: continence pads for men are shorter than for women and designed to be differently located.

Special stretch pants are available which are designed to keep a pad in place. Some people prefer pants fitted with a pouch, waterproof on one side, into which the pad fits. Disposable pants can be useful when travelling.

As noted above, penile sheaths can be a useful tool for managing urinary continence in men.

Continence pads, so long as they are of the correct strength, ought to be able to take up all the urine expelled, but people who lose very large amounts at night may feel reassured if they sleep on a quilted absorbent undersheet or bed-pad. These soak up fluid and spread it, thus keeping the body comparatively dry; they are far more comfortable than plastic undersheets.

Chair pads can give people extra confidence as well as comfort if they are sitting for long periods, whether at home or if staying away or perhaps during a car journey.

Enuresis alarms are electronic devices placed in a bed or on underwear which provide an alert should they detect moisture. A wireless signal emits a warning in a care-giver's room, perhaps next door, or the person themselves receives the alarm. These devices are often used to help children with bed-wetting problems; they are intended to help them learn when to use the toilet. Plainly, many elderly people will not be able to jump out of bed and go to the bathroom should their alarm be triggered. If they can, it may be too late. But these devices can be very useful if someone is trying to retrain their bladder to conform to a particular time régime or ascertain the reason for night-time continence difficulties.

Obtaining underwear and equipment

If a nurse or doctor on behalf of the NHS assesses you as needing pads and/or other types of continence underwear and equipment, you should receive them free of charge, in line with the basic tenet of the NHS that healthcare is free at the point of delivery *(see pages 293–4)*. The nurse or doctor will set down how many pads of a particular absorbency you need. If you use large numbers, the cost alone is a good reason for consulting your GP. You could save yourself a lot of money.

Primary care organisations often have their own guidelines on the numbers of pads they will issue, but the Department of Health has made clear that these should guide the choice of pad only and should not be seen as hard-and-fast rules. Everybody should receive the number and type of pads they are assessed as needing, for free: allocation should be solely on grounds of clinical need. The Department of Health has told the health organisations that finance continence services that:

> Pads should be provided in quantities appropriate to the individual's continence needs. Arbitrary ceilings are inappropriate. Guidelines should be developed for the Primary Health Care Team to aid product choice, but these should not be seen as rules. ... It is unacceptable to have waiting lists for pads as a means of rationing the service.[15]

If you are unhappy with the amount or type of pad or other equipment or service which you have been allocated, you could appeal to your health organisation – clinical commissioning group in England, health board in Scotland, local health board in Wales or health and social care trust in Northern Ireland. You could also raise the matter with a local patients' group, such as a local Healthwatch in England *(see page 329)*.

Some people will wish to obtain pads and underwear or equipment privately for one reason or another, or their problem may not be sufficiently serious to be given these items by the NHS. Many continence products are zero-rated for VAT, so if you buy privately in a shop or through a catalogue or the internet, check that VAT has not been added *(see page 479)*.

View as wide a range of products as possible, since there is much variation in price and suitability for individuals. Disabled Living Centres *(see page 458)* display continence underwear and equipment and can tell you how to obtain it. The Bladder and Bowel Foundation provides a range of helpful information. Its catalogue sets out a wide range of equipment and underwear and it also provides helpful comparisons between products, such as disposable as opposed to reusable items. Its helpline is staffed by continence nurses. You could also ask your own continence nurse to recommend catalogues.

Urinary catheters

A urinary catheter provides another means of managing (as opposed to treating) continence problems. A small-bore plastic tube is inserted directly into the bladder usually through the urethra. Urine drains through the tube into a plastic bag, which is emptied by turning on a tap. The catheter may be kept in for a matter of hours, days, months or longer.

The question of whether or not to accept a catheter often arises when someone goes into hospital for an acute condition, such as a stroke. There may be perfectly sound reasons for the insertion of a catheter. Perhaps the bladder or another part of the urinary system is blocked and a catheter would effectively bypass the blockage. It is important to distinguish reasons which might benefit the patient from those which benefit only nursing staff: a catheter can be seen as an easier way of managing urination than helping somebody to use a lavatory, commode or bedpan or changing their continence pad. In other words, patients already relying on continence pads when they come into hospital should not be given a catheter simply for the convenience of hospital staff.

Urinary catheters have several drawbacks. Insertion is not a pleasant procedure and can cause discomfort. However, this should be minimised if the smallest bore possible is used and insertion is carried out by an experienced, trained professional who uses a lubricating gel.

Another drawback is psychological: lying or sitting alongside a catheter bag can erode self-esteem and, if the bag is visible, also diminish one's dignity. The equipment provides a constant reminder of the problem.

In hospital, the fact that a catheter rules out sexual intercourse is not relevant but it will be if the catheter remains in place when the patient returns home or to a care home. It is also worth bearing in mind that catheters can cause painful erections, particularly during sleep.

The main physical health risk to which catheters give rise is infection. Indeed, urinary tract infections are the most common form of infection acquired from the provision of healthcare. The introduction of a catheter provides a surface on which bacteria can travel into the bladder, circumventing the body's normal defence mechanisms. Other bacteria may enter the urinary tract from the connecting point between the catheter and catheter bag or from the urine inside the bag. For anatomical reasons, women run a higher risk of infection.

Not everyone who develops a urinary tract infection has symptoms but many do, and infection can cause someone to feel very unwell. Treatment with antibiotics is often successful, but it can take some time. However, infection can prove fatal. The risk of infection increases with the length of time the catheter remains in place.[16]

Use of a catheter also has repercussions for the ability to use the toilet. After about six weeks, someone who has an ongoing catheter removed must relearn how to control their urine outflow. This is because the presence of a catheter causes the bladder, a muscular organ, to shrink, so when it is taken out, the bladder must be trained to regain its former size and potential. Retraining can take a long time and may be impossible. However, as we see below, catheters with a special valve are available to address this problem.

Dr David Cohen has had much experience of taking decisions about catheters as head of the stroke unit at Northwick Park Hospital in Harrow, Middlesex, since temporary and sometimes permanent urinary incontinence can occur after a stroke. He told me in an interview that the issue of whether to insert a catheter was one whose importance should not be under-estimated:

> In my view, a catheter should never be used except as a last resort to manage incontinence. There are very few reasons to try to put a catheter into somebody, and most of them involve a blockage to the flow of urine. If for some reason the urine is there but it is not flowing out, then I would put a catheter in. In almost all other

circumstances a catheter carries more hazards than the problems it solves. It should never be put in for convenience: I feel very strongly about that. There are all sorts of ways of managing incontinence, from toileting people regularly to making sure they can call a nurse easily or giving them pads. Pads these days are very strong and can soak up large quantities of urine. In the case of somebody who could not speak and therefore not attract a nurse's attention or was unconscious, I would manage their incontinence with pads rather than a catheter, because pads carry no hazard to the patient at all.

Dr Cohen explained that the other circumstances when he thought an indwelling catheter might be a legitimate last resort involve somebody completely immobile at home but desperate to remain there even though social services can run to only three visits a day, so that after passing urine between visits they would be wet. 'There may be reasons to use a catheter rather than pads here', said Dr Cohen, 'but that's a long way down the line from the first few hours after a stroke'.

In view of these drawbacks, the Royal College of Nursing has drawn up detailed guidance for nurses and healthcare assistants on the use of catheters. In this, the Royal College stresses that nurses must discuss fully the pros and cons of catheterisation in seeking consent to insert a catheter, pointing out that 'catheterisation is an invasive procedure with associated serious risks, therefore obtaining documented, valid consent is vital prior to the procedure'.[17] (This guidance does not have the force of law, but it does represent the best practice on which nurses know they should base their work.)

If you feel pressed to agree quickly to a catheter, stand your ground (unless the situation is an emergency) and expect the nurse involved to explain fully the case for and against catheterisation so that you are in a position to give informed consent (or not). As the Royal College says, in the process of gaining consent, the patient, 'Should be provided with supportive written information in a format they can understand' and understand the rationale, the alternatives and the consequences of not being catheterised. It also says, 'Never catheterise or continue catheter usage for nursing convenience'.[18]

Someone who does not understand why their catheter is in place may pull it out, while they may find its insertion puzzling and disturbing. The Royal College of Nursing says, 'Catheterisation of patients who are agitated and/or cognitively impaired is best avoided where possible.'[19]

If a healthcare professional wishes to insert a catheter in someone who lacks the mental capacity to grant consent, they must by law consult certain people if it is practicable and appropriate to do so *(listed on pages 782 and 789);* these include any attorney and unpaid carer and anyone the patient had previously named as someone to be consulted. The healthcare professional can take the final decision about whether to go ahead with any treatment that is being proposed, but they must take that decision in the best interests of the patient. In working out what those best interests are, they must take into account the views of these consultees.

If you are dissatisfied with what the medical staff intend, ask to speak to one or more of the following people:

✓ your relative's consultant doctor

✓ their named nurse

✓ the ward manager

✓ the hospital's continence nurse specialist and

✓ the hospital's director of nursing

If you remain unhappy with a decision about a catheter, insist on the agreement of a date at which the decision will be reviewed. The Royal College of Nursing again: 'When an indwelling catheter is inserted the nurse should consider and plan for early removal as the infection risk increases on a daily basis.'[20]

Types of catheter

If it is decided that a catheter is necessary, make sure that the right type is chosen. Two types of catheter use do not share all of the drawbacks of one that is left in place for several weeks or longer. 'Intermittent catheterisation' involves the person involved inserting a urinary catheter themselves and using it whenever they need to drain their bladder, perhaps three or four times a day. This type is often used for people who have had a spinal injury which has stopped the sphincter muscle at the exit from the bladder relaxing and contracting in the normal way. Plainly, however, the patient has to be sufficiently flexible to perform what can be quite a tricky procedure. Or a nurse could perform intermittent catheterisation.

A 'supra-pubic catheter' involves a tube inserted through the wall of the abdomen direct into the bladder, after a minor operation. Like an ongoing catheter, a supra-pubic must be emptied frequently, and the whole tube must be changed regularly, every few weeks. This type and intermittent catheterisation have the advantage that sexual activity is not logistically compromised.

For frail, older people, the indwelling urinary catheter remains the most common type in use. It should be a type which incorporates a valve, so that rather than draining the bladder continuously, the valve allows it gradually to fill up with urine, which is then dispelled when the valve is turned on. This should help to retain the natural functioning of the bladder. Ask whether your catheter has been coated with a substance that reduces the risk of infection, such as a silver alloy (which is expensive). Sometimes catheters are impregnated with antibiotics.

Management

The plastic bag in which urine is held should be emptied regularly. If it gets too full, your bladder could become infected by urine ascending back up the tube. Also, if you are standing up and walking around and your bag is too full, it will pull on the catheter tube and that will hurt.

You can of course drain off fluid from your catheter bag yourself. In hospital, healthcare assistants often help with catheter management, including emptying the bag. An assistant who drains fluid from a catheter bag should do so sensitively, to avoid embarrassment.

If you are unhappy with the prospect of a particular healthcare assistant managing your catheter, says so. The Royal College of Nursing says that assistants can undertake various tasks in catheter management (not catheter insertion or removal), so long as the risks of doing so have been assessed by a registered nurse; the assistant can perform the particular task competently; the employing health body authorises healthcare assistants in general to do it; a registered nurse sanctions the delegation of that task to a particular assistant; and the patient consents.[21]

Every few months, the whole tube should be taken out and a new one inserted; if not, it can become blocked with mineral deposits. Changing a catheter would be done by a hospital nurse or a district nurse if you are outside hospital. The changing of a urinary catheter by an untrained person without the use of a lubricating gel can cause excruciating pain.

If you have continence problems and have not had a catheter inserted, make sure that you or nursing staff are changing your continence pads sufficiently frequently, that the pads themselves are of the correct absorbency, that you are washing sufficiently often, and that you are being given a barrier cream to prevent soreness.

Help with personal care

Helping people cope with continence difficulties is frequently included in the personal care for which they may receive help from care assistants. Care assistants may be hired independently *(see Chapter 23)* or obtained through the social services department of a local authority *(Chapter 26)*.

If help with personal care is obtained through social services, some people in England, Wales and Northern Ireland will be asked to contribute towards the cost, while for others it will be free *(as explained in Chapter 28)*. However, people living in Scotland should automatically receive this help free, as tasks involved in continence management are specifically mentioned in the definition of 'free personal care' which all older people assessed as needing it should receive, regardless of their income. The rules say that free personal care should include not only any help necessary to change pads, but also changing and laundering the underwear and bedding of somebody who is incontinent, making their bed and caring for their skin to make sure that it is not harmed.[22] (The insertion and changing of a catheter should be carried out for free in any part of the UK by an NHS district nurse; if somebody is living in a nursing home, this would be carried out by a registered nurse in the home at no cost to the resident under the free nursing care provisions *described on page 962.*)

Care homes

Continence is a very important matter to talk about if you are going to live in a care home or you are arranging entry for a relative, yet it is often little discussed. It is important that the home understands continence matters and their importance and will ensure you receive treatment which addresses your particular difficulties, rather than be slotted into a one-size-fits-all régime of continence management.

Sometimes care homes treat continence difficulties as inevitable, and indeed they are a difficulty which many care home residents have to face day by day. Yet, as we have seen, continence problems can often be cured, or at least the severity of the symptoms lessened. It is important that care homes ensure their residents obtain the free advice and treatment to which they are entitled from GPs, continence nurse specialists and other NHS healthcare professionals, just like people living outside care homes. Recognising the importance of good advice to care home residents, the Department of Health has told health bodies responsible for primary care: 'Residents of care homes, including those providing nursing care, should have access to professional advice about the promotion of continence.'[23]

If you live in a care home and have continence problems, these should be assessed and a plan drawn up to treat and/or manage them; the contents of this plan should be incorporated into your care plan.

All care home residents are of course entitled to receive continence equipment, underwear and pads for free through the NHS, just like everybody else. Sometimes the local continence service of the NHS sends care homes the numbers of pads needed for their residents, or they may send homes the money to purchase pads instead. The important point for the user is that pads should be free of charge, just as they are for people living in their own homes. So if you are living in a care home (residential or nursing) and are charged for continence pads or continence equipment, you should object. If the home says that you should pay for some of your pads because you need more than the number supplied, ask for a reassessment of your continence needs: perhaps you now need more, or a more absorbent type of pad.

I discuss finding a toilet when you are outdoors and the 'Can't Wait Card' scheme on page 678.

Continence

* Continence problems can often be cured.

* GPs and continence nurse specialists can provide invaluable help.

* There is a range of ways of treating and managing incontinence.

* Continence pads are surprisingly sophisticated.

* Penile sheaths can work well.

* Catheter use can cause urinary tract infection.

* Continence pads, underwear and equipment are free on the NHS.

* If you buy continence underwear, pads or equipment, check that VAT has not been added.

* Amongst frail, elderly people, constipation is the most common cause of faecal incontinence.

* Expect a plan to assess, treat and manage any continence problems if you move into a care home.

Chapter 20

Dementia

O f all the common illnesses of later life, dementia has experienced the most rapid change in public attitudes during the current century. Twenty years ago, when my mother developed the condition, most people had only a vague notion of the word's meaning. Myths abounded – not least, that someone with dementia would take on an entirely new personality or that the impact was much worse for family and friends than for the person with the condition.

Since then, dementia has come out of the closet, the taboo about discussing it beginning to disappear, just as did that for cancer during the 1980s. The Alzheimer's Society and Alzheimer Scotland have worked tirelessly to educate professionals but also crucially the general public about the nature of the condition. Celebrities have written about their experience of the condition within their own families. Films as well as television and radio soap operas frequently feature the dilemmas dementia poses. Groups of citizens in many localities are considering how people with dementia can better be supported through creating 'dementia-friendly communities'. Public libraries promote reading material for people with dementia and guides for their carers. Organisations from carers groups to local council adult education centres offer courses on how best to support someone with dementia.

People with the condition have themselves become more assertive and keen to raise awareness of what living with the condition actually means. Activists have formed local groups which lobby to improve services in their particular locality and to educate, often delivering training to professionals. Their approach is based on the mantra 'nothing about us without us'. Impelled to feel part of something bigger, they have formed a network of groups called the Dementia Engagement and Empowerment Programme.

But although public awareness and understanding of the condition has grown, many aspects of the experience of having dementia or of supporting a loved one with the condition have not progressed very far. A cure for dementia seems a long way off. Techniques of diagnosis have advanced little. The decisions that my mother and her family faced are similar to those faced today. Many people – even those who have experience of dementia in their own family – have little idea of how to relate to someone with the condition. Equally tragically, some people still say that were they ever to receive a dementia diagnosis, they would wish to end their lives.

In this chapter, I discuss:

▶ the symptoms of dementia

▶ the advantages and drawbacks of obtaining a diagnosis

▶ how to obtain a diagnosis

▶ medical and non-drug treatments for dementia

▶ how other people should relate to people with dementia

▶ advance and contingency planning

▶ social care entitlements and rights to advocacy

▶ help with other medical conditions

▶ the use of anti-psychotic drugs and tranquillizers

What is dementia?

When someone develops dementia, structural and chemical changes occur in their brain which give rise to a progressive decline in their intellectual functions.

As explained in Chapter 1 *(on page 26)*, dementia occurs most often in people over the age of 85. In that age-group it is common, affecting one in five people. Whatever the age at which the condition develops, the main cause is Alzheimer's disease and the reasons why someone develops Alzheimer's as well as the majority of other types of dementia, such as Lewy body dementia, remain unknown. However, the cause of the second most common cause, vascular dementia, is understood – an unhealthy cardiovascular system. This causes tiny strokes to take place which are often imperceptible at the time but which lead to the death of brain tissue. Dementia can also arise after a major stroke; one-fifth of people who have a major stroke develop dementia in the following six months.

The symptoms of most cases of dementia typically involve progressive difficulties in remembering, understanding, reasoning and planning, as well as the ability to orientate oneself in space. There is much variation in the rate at which dementia develops. In time, people with dementia usually lose the ability to perform the ordinary tasks of everyday life, including, in the advanced stages, the ability to communicate intelligibly through speech. Yet their emotions remain far less affected than their cognitive powers.

The early symptoms of dementia can vary considerably.[1] Neither the person themselves nor those around them may realise that dementia is the cause. I had noticed my mother's deliberate handwriting style had become a little uncertain. Then, one day, she said she never wished to play Scrabble again – a game she had long enjoyed and in which she had excelled. My family and I should have asked her the reasons, but we did not like to probe; she seemed slightly withdrawn at the time. Soon afterwards, she tumbled down a step in a house to which I had moved a few months before, we should have wondered why she had failed to remember its existence. Instead, we, and indeed the A&E department to which we took her, investigated only whether she had broken any bones, not the root cause of the accident.

My mother's decision about Scrabble may well have been related to recognition on her part of a growing difficulty in mastering the reasoning involved in playing. She may have fallen because she had not been able to process a fresh memory about the layout of my new house. Failure to lay down new memories may become apparent because somebody repeatedly fails to keep appointments or remembers where they have arranged to meet friends. Later on, as the disease progresses, they may be unable to recall how to find their way home or what they have just been doing. Thus nine months after her fall in the kitchen, my mother would ask me many times in the middle of the day whether she had had her lunch.

Difficulty in planning to which dementia can give rise does not only involve planning a journey or a complex task. In fact, what we think of as quite simple tasks, like dressing, involve a long succession of different actions that need to take place in the correct order, and dementia can interfere with this. So someone may put on their clothes in the wrong order or put on two pairs of trousers.

It is important to realise that people with dementia retain many aspects of brain ability, even if they lose aspects which Western society prizes in particular, such as the ability to remember and to reason. Thus when researchers Beatrice Godwin and Fiona Poland talked to very old people with dementia living in nursing homes whose intellectual abilities were considered to be zero or at a very low level, they found that the emotions of these people remained more or less intact. So did their sense of right and wrong. Professors Godwin and Poland reported: 'Asked questions relating to conscience and the superego, even people with a cognitive score equivalent to zero ... expressed awareness of the moral implications of their actions, still wishing to act as agents for good.'[2]

The various types of dementia cause differences too. For example, in Lewy body dementia (which accounts for about 10 per cent of all cases), memory is not much affected in the early stages: rather, symptoms can involve confusion and alertness, delusions, visual hallucinations, changes in thinking and reasoning, and a hunched posture, rigid muscles and balance problems similar to those seen in Parkinson's disease.

While deterioration of mental faculties tends to be gradual in Alzheimer's, with vascular dementia it often occurs in steps, so someone may be functioning well but then suddenly deteriorate and find they have lost the ability to do something. About 30 per cent of people with dementia have both Alzheimer's and vascular dementia.

Alzheimer's disease and vascular dementia are common amongst people who develop the condition before the age of 65. However in this group with 'early onset dementia' there are other types that are less common in older people, such as a form of dementia which develops in the fronto-temporal part of the brain. In this, memory and visual-spatial skills are usually little affected: instead early symptoms can include apathy, loss of social inhibitions, changes in behaviour and personality and difficulties with language.

Symptoms tend to become more similar as dementia advances and people can come to need a lot of practical and emotional support. Dementia is often the underlying cause of someone's death but not the immediate cause, which may be perhaps pneumonia or a stroke. In these cases and in others where the dementia is milder, people die with the condition, but not from it. They all need sensitive care when they are dying, just as they do earlier on. *(I discuss palliative care and dementia on pages 1004–5.)*

The Alzheimer's Society has trained 'dementia champions' to give informal talks about dementia and one of their key messages is 'You can live well with dementia, with support.'

One sees evidence of this frequently. This Saturday morning in February, as I strolled along a riverside promenade in Kent, I got chatting to a man, perhaps in his 70s, who was using exercise equipment the council had provided. He showed me how he enjoyed sitting on one piece of equipment and pushing his legs up

CASE STUDY

and down while looking at the river, the clouds and buildings on the far bank. We discussed sea fishing in this stretch of the river. After a while, he explained that he has a memory problem so cannot recall many recent events. However, the sight of an ancient church close by reminded him of a recent visit with his carer, who takes him out twice a week. They had parked there and he told me he had enjoyed exploring the church and experiencing its special atmosphere.

How dementia is diagnosed

As we will see in a moment, there are drawbacks as well as advantages in having a formal diagnosis. But let us first look at the process of seeking to establish whether someone has dementia.

There is no easy diagnosis for dementia, no pinprick blood test, although much research is being devoted to finding one, particularly for Alzheimer's disease. What happens is that doctors carry out tests on the symptoms of the condition; in particular, they look at somebody's mental ability and try to work out whether it has declined significantly. If it has, the assessor may infer that the person involved has dementia. However, dementia can be diagnosed with complete accuracy only through analysis of the brain after death.

Diagnosis of all forms of dementia is complicated by several factors. Some changes to the brain are considered normal in older people, such as difficulty in remembering names *(see page 24)*. If there is a slight further decline in faculties which is greater than expected for somebody's age and level of education but does not interfere notably with the activities of their daily life, they may be said to have 'mild cognitive impairment' (MCI). If the decline is greater still, they may be diagnosed with dementia. For instance, someone with MCI would be likely to have some difficulty in finding words and forget why they had gone into a room more often than someone without it. When someone has dementia, forgetting such things occurs a little more frequently. But the distinctions are not absolute and there is a spectrum within which at some points normal behaviour becomes abnormal.

Just because someone has MCI does not mean they will necessarily go on to develop dementia. Over three years, one third of patients with MCI spontaneously improve (perhaps because their symptoms were caused by depression or anxiety), one third remain the same, and one third go on to develop dementia.[3]

A person is said to have dementia when the decline in their brain power is more marked and widespread and symptoms such as the inability to remember recent events are sufficiently severe to interfere with their everyday activities. But in the early stages of the illness this decline does not prevent the person involved from living independently.

As the disease progresses further, people often lose more and more of their vocabulary as well as their abilities to perform ordinary tasks.

The key role of the GP

GPs can put patients on the road to diagnosis and also provide a gateway to various kinds of treatment and other help. A good GP will also ensure that other medical conditions not directly related to dementia are detected and treated. GPs can play a vital role in:

- referring somebody for formal diagnosis and then, particularly if Alzheimer's disease is present, for drug treatment
- referring somebody for psychological therapy
- referring somebody to social services for practical support
- signposting to voluntary groups which provide support
- referring somebody for one or more types of talking therapy
- the provision of medical treatment for vascular dementia
- the provision of medical help for other conditions
- the provision of palliative care, if necessary through referral to specialists

As GPs provide the gateway to help, the first stage in obtaining it is for the person who may have dementia to go and talk to their GP. A GP who has seen a patient regularly over many years should know what level of cognitive ability is normal for that person and thus whether there has been a significant progressive decline.

If you are going to talk to your GP, it is worth getting hold of a booklet published by Alzheimer Scotland entitled *Getting help from your doctor: a guide for people worried about their memory, people with dementia and carers* or a factsheet from the Alzheimer's Society entitled *How the GP can support a person with dementia*.[4] You could also ring the helpline of one of these voluntary organisations to talk through your situation. The reassurance that many people have trodden this path before and have received support can be particularly helpful at this early stage, when it is easy to feel that you are facing a daunting challenge alone.

The first task of the GP (or a hospital-based doctor) is to screen out other medical conditions from which you might be suffering, as your symptoms could be caused by an entirely different condition, such as an under-active thyroid gland, the side-effects of certain drugs, infections such as pneumonia or a urinary tract infection (which can cause temporary delirium) or a brain tumour (benign or not).

Your doctor should also consider whether you might be suffering from depression. The two conditions share certain symptoms, with the result that dementia may be mistaken for depression or may be masked by depression. *(I discuss the diagnosis of depression on page 375.)*

It is of little help if your GP merely speculates: 'I think you may have a dementing illness.' A more practical step is to refer you for assessment by a team of mental health professionals, often based in a 'memory clinic'. This facility should contain a consultant psychiatrist (who can prescribe Alzheimer's drugs) and other professionals such as clinical psychologists *(see page 316),* social workers and dementia nurses *(page 310).*

It helps to have someone who knows you well at the memory clinic, so the assessors there can establish whether any loss of memory you are reporting is part of a significant, gradual decline, perhaps over the past year. If someone has lost their cognitive powers rapidly or has recently started behaving in a confused manner, perhaps wandering at night, delirium is more likely than dementia, while someone who is excessively preoccupied with memory loss may actually be suffering from depression, not dementia.[5]

The Mini Mental State Examination, or MMSE, is often used. This involves tests such as asking somebody to spell words like 'lunch' backwards and to name common objects placed in front of them. The maximum score is 30; people with moderate dementia may score somewhere between 10 and 20. Sometimes factual questions are asked, such as 'Who is the Prime Minister?' and 'What year is it?'

When tests such as the MMSE are conducted, it is important that adjustments are made to take into account circumstances which may result in a score lower than the true cognitive ability of the person involved. Communication difficulties with the assessor may be an issue. For instance, people with Parkinson's disease often take a long time to respond to questions, even though they are well aware of the answer they would like to give. Other people may be very hard of hearing or have difficulty in speaking, perhaps as a result of a stroke. There is also the question of fluency in English. Some of the people being assessed may not be fluent in spoken English; sometimes the accent of the assessor means that their speech is not easily intelligible.

The assessor should take all the steps necessary to overcome any such problems. If hearing might be an issue, cards can be offered with questions written down on them, or the assessor can refer the person involved for a specific hearing test before continuing with a dementia assessment. They should also make sure that the tests do not rely on knowledge of which the person being tested may well be ignorant, and make adjustments if necessary. Objects that are common in some cultures – a Qur'an-holder, say – are unfamiliar in others. Asking somebody who had just arrived in Britain from Ghana to name the country's last two prime ministers would probably fox them, as would the same question posed to a British person who had recently moved to west Africa.[6]

Some GPs and other assessors in primary care use a different tool from the MMSE called the General Practitioner Assessment of Cognition. This is shorter than the MMSE, less likely to be influenced by cultural and linguistic background and places more focus on the ability of the person being assessed to function day to day.

If a memory clinic considers that dementia is a possibility, the patient should be sent for a brain scan. An MRI scan cannot give a definitive answer but can help in arriving at a diagnosis, as it can show a loss of brain volume and thus atrophy in areas of the brain associated with functions such as memory. The more powerful PET scan can reveal the clumping of amyloid proteins – a sign of Alzheimer's disease – while another technique, SPECT, can help diagnose fronto-temporal dementia.[7]

It is important to know what type of dementia is involved, as this affects medical treatment. For instance, particular drugs have been developed to treat Alzheimer's disease and Lewy body dementia, while anti-psychotic drugs which may be used for behaviour problems are especially dangerous for people with Lewy body dementia.

In the past, GPs often failed to refer people whom they thought might have dementia for formal diagnosis, as they did not think any help or treatment was available. In 2011, only about 40 per cent of people who had dementia had been formally diagnosed, according to a survey by the Alzheimer's Society and Alzheimer Scotland. The situation on the ground varied widely: nearly 70 per cent of people in Belfast had had a diagnosis, for example, compared with only 25 per cent in Dorset.[8] In fact, as we shall see, various types of treatment and support are now available.

If your GP fails to refer you to a consultant psychiatrist or a memory clinic, you could point out, as diplomatically as possible, that the National Institute for Health and Care Excellence (NICE) has told doctors in its special guidance on dementia that 'Memory assessment services (which may be provided by a memory assessment clinic or by community mental health teams) should be the single point of referral for all people with a possible diagnosis of dementia.'[9] As already explained *(on page 289)*, it is a fundamental principle of the NHS Constitution that patients in England and Wales should be offered all the treatment recommended by NICE. The NICE guidance on dementia has also been endorsed as applicable in Northern Ireland.

The Scottish Government has published *Standards of Care for Dementia in Scotland*. These lay down that everybody has the right to a dementia diagnosis and that NHS boards 'will ensure that GPs and hospitals can refer people with suspected dementia to services that specialise in the diagnosis of dementia and that these will have initial contact with the person within four weeks'.[10]

Wherever you live in the UK, if you fail to secure a referral, write formally to your GP practice and if necessary also your health authority, pressing your request. *(See page 335 for other steps you could take if your GP drags their feet in referring you on.)*

Possible implications of a dementia diagnosis

Much is at stake in testing for dementia. As we shall see in a moment, diagnosis can provide a gateway to help of various kinds. But incorrect diagnosis can be unhelpful, since it may lead to changes in somebody's control over their own life that do not occur with a diagnosis of a physical illness such as cancer or diabetes.

For instance, anybody who develops a condition which could affect their ability to drive has to inform the driving licensing authority *(as explained on page 697)*. Dementia is one such condition, and diagnosis could result in the DVLA restricting a person's licence in some way, such as requiring that they apply for renewal after a certain period or even removing it completely. These requirements exist of course to safeguard the person with dementia and others on the road. But an incorrect diagnosis could lead to unnecessary restrictions.

An incorrect diagnosis could also affect the choice of where somebody lives. Should they need to go into a care home, a dementia diagnosis will mean that a home which is not registered to care for people with dementia is unlikely to admit them. Yet if they have a slight cognitive impairment which does not develop into dementia, an ordinary non-specialist care home may suit them better.

Perhaps the most important reason why an incorrect diagnosis can be unhelpful is that a dementia diagnosis is the first stage in establishing that somebody lacks 'mental capacity', or the mental ability to take certain decisions at certain times *(see page 775)*. If it is thought that someone's mental capacity is limited to the point where they cannot take an important decision – such as whether they should move into a care home – somebody else will be entitled to take it for them. This could be their legal representative, such as an attorney. Failing suitable representatives, it will be the social services department of their local authority, *as explained on page 782*.[11]

If you have dementia, it will be important to get the help of other people in running your affairs and taking decisions that you are no longer able to take. But if you do not actually have dementia, you do not of course want other people to assume control over key elements of your life (although as we see in Chapter 33 there are legal safeguards intended to prevent this happening).

The fact is that if you think you might be developing dementia, you will know that something is wrong, and it can be helpful to know for sure and obtain all the help that is available, whereas if you have a different condition which is causing dementia-like symptoms, such as depression or delirium, it will be important to get that treated. But if you are being pressed to subject yourself to an assessment for dementia and of your mental capacity by someone you do not completely trust, perhaps who could gain financially should you lose control of your affairs, tread carefully. If you consent to testing, ask somebody reputable outside the situation and who knows you well to accompany you. They can ensure that the types of assessment that are proposed are clear, that your consent to assessment is secured properly and that any reasons why your score in an MMSE or similar test does not truly represent your mental ability are taken into account. They can also make sure that help is given to overcome any difficulty that might be confused with mental impairment in the assessment process *(as explained on pages 774–9)*.

If you cannot find somebody to accompany you, ask a health or social care official to provide you with an independent advocate *(see page 804)* or tell you where you can find one. There is no rule to which you could refer to absolutely insist on this, but you could point to the encouragement or (in Scotland) the requirement to provide an advocate to people who have dementia *(outlined on pages 785–6)*. If advocates should be provided for people with dementia, why not for people who are facing this crucial assessment? If you get nowhere, you could refuse to take the test.

If there is doubt about whether you have Alzheimer's disease, ask for a PET scan. As noted above, an MRI scan is insufficiently powerful to detect the abnormal deposition of amyloid proteins, although a PET scan is not absolutely conclusive.

In fact, much help can be obtained without a formal diagnosis, so if you are having trouble managing the practical aspects of your life, social services ought to help you whether or not dementia has been formally diagnosed. The NICE guideline on dementia says: 'People who are suspected of having dementia because of evidence of functional and cognitive deterioration, but who do not have sufficient memory impairment to be diagnosed with the condition, should not be denied access to support services.'[12] But plainly some forms of follow-on help, most obviously potentially invaluable medication for Alzheimer's or Lewy body dementia and targeted programmes of talking therapy and cognitive stimulation, cannot be given without a doctor being as convinced as they can be that somebody is suffering from the condition.

Let us now look in more detail at the help for which a dementia diagnosis can be useful (but is not always essential).

Drugs to treat Alzheimer's disease

There is no known medication which can prevent or cure Alzheimer's disease. However, certain drugs have been developed which can help people with the condition.

The first category can delay the development of certain symptoms mainly in the early and middle stages of the disease; they have been recommended for use by NICE.[13] These drugs prevent the breakdown of an enzyme called acetylcholine that is essential for the transmission of messages between nerve cells and is found at lower than normal levels in the brains of people with Alzheimer's disease. By increasing the amount of acetylcholine available in the brain, these drugs can temporarily inhibit the symptoms of Alzheimer's, in particular cognitive decline, and also improve behaviour; people can be 'more themselves' for a useful period of time.

Although the acetylcholine-targeted drugs can be very useful, their success in an individual case is by no means guaranteed. Some patients find they are better able to concentrate, remember and carry out the activities of daily living, as well as feeling more motivated and less anxious. But in about one third of patients, the drugs seem to have little or no effect. Where they work, the effects tend to be only modest, lasting for between six to twelve months. This variation in effect is not surprising: Alzheimer's has several variants and is a complex disease. If side-effects of the drugs such as nausea or diarrhoea prove troublesome, a different brand may be tried or the patient may have to come off the medication. This type of medication has no effect on the underlying progress of the condition. Studies to see whether it can prevent the development of Alzheimer's in people with mild cognitive impairment have been inconclusive.[14] But this is a fast-moving field and other drugs which may arrest the progression of the disease (although without reversing earlier change to the brain), such as the anti-depressant trazodone could join the armoury.

The second main group of drugs developed to date can have a beneficial effect on people with Alzheimer's in the moderate to severe stages of the disease. Memantine, also recommended by NICE, can help stabilise the condition of somebody with severe dementia and maintain such skills as walking and feeding oneself. It may also improve any agitation, aggressive behaviour and speech problems. The chemical basis for the action of memantine is different from that of the drugs just described for the early stages of Alzheimer's. It protects brain cells by blocking the effects of a chemical called glutamate which is released in excessive amounts when brain cells are damaged by Alzheimer's disease.[15]

Medical treatment for vascular dementia

The second most common kind of dementia is vascular dementia, which results from problems involving the supply of blood to the brain, usually because the person's cardiovascular system is unhealthy (see page 26). Damage to the brain may arise from the occurrence of many tiny strokes which each create a small patch of dead brain tissue, a major stroke which kills off a large piece of brain tissue on one side of the brain or disease of the small blood vessels deep in the brain.

Steps can be taken to improve the health of your cardiovascular system and thus try to arrest any dementia it has precipitated. Expect your GP to do whatever is necessary to treat risk factors – in particular high blood pressure, high cholesterol level and diabetes. Smoking, obesity and excessive alcohol consumption can make matters worse; if you need help to bring drinking, smoking or over-consumption of the wrong foods under control, ask your doctor to give it to you, for instance, through referral to a dietician.

Non-drug treatments for dementia

Various types of therapy have been devised to help people with dementia. They will not prevent the further development of the condition, but they can help people adapt to it, keep themselves orientated in their present situation and gain comfort and support from other people.

Therapy in a group

Meeting other people who have dementia, and perhaps any carers they have, can be invaluable. It enables those with dementia to see they are not alone and to receive encouragement from others who understand their situation.

Types of non-drug therapy offered to people with dementia include dance, art therapy, singing, music therapy and pet therapy (a grand term for allowing somebody to pat and stroke a dog, cat or other pet). At the very least – and importantly – these activities can provide distraction and interest and a sense of connecting with other people. They may help in other ways. For instance, art therapy can enable somebody whose word-remembering skills have declined to express themselves and to be creative. This can improve their sense of self-worth and identity – feelings considered especially important for people with dementia *(as discussed on pages 257–64)*.

Cognitive stimulation therapy is different. Typically, it involves a group of people with mild to moderate dementia meeting together with two facilitators for twice-weekly sessions over about seven weeks. The group builds its own identity through starting each session with its special song and a game of softball. Each 45-minute session focuses on a different subject. Much use is made of the stimulation of all the senses, so exploration of 'childhood' might include tasting sweets and playing with old-fashioned toys, while discussion of recent events in the news and in participants' own lives aims to keep people orientated in the present-day world. Leaders, who do not require expensive training, try to be supportive and do all they can to boost the confidence of participants.[16]

Cognitive stimulation therapy embraces reminiscence therapy and orientation therapy, which can be given separately. Any therapy of this nature should be conducted with great sensitivity. Therapists should be supportive and seek to boost the confidence of people with dementia, not put them under pressure to remember particular facts or come up with particular answers. Quizzes can be particularly cruel.

The National Institute for Health and Care Excellence considers that cognitive stimulation is sufficiently beneficial to recommend that 'People with mild/moderate dementia of all types should be given the opportunity to participate in a structured group cognitive stimulation programme.'[17] Your GP should provide you with services recommended by NICE unless there is a reason why they would be unsuitable for you *(as explained on page 289)*.

One-to-one therapy

Professionals such as clinical psychologists and psychotherapists, who specialise in talking therapy, can be invaluable in helping people cope. Ask your GP or psychiatrist for a referral, or hire a professional yourself, if you can afford to do so *(see pages 316 and 317)*. Here are one or two approaches used in dementia care.

Occupational therapy involves a therapist working with a person with dementia and their carer at home (or care-givers in a care home) to analyse the day-to-day difficulties the person is encountering, help them overcome them and give the care-giver some coping strategies. Here is an example of what might be achieved:

Richard, who has dementia, and Anne, his wife and carer, were struggling to cope with daily life. Richard had stopped gardening and preparing the vegetables – two tasks he had hitherto enjoyed – and seemed to Anne to be passive and to take little pleasure in any activities. The therapist helped Anne to see that she needed to adjust her norms and goals to enable Richard to continue to garden and wash vegetables, even though the end-results might seem substandard. She also needed to show appreciation for what Richard could do. After the therapist's help, Anne commented: 'I need to learn to set smaller goals, to use a slower pace, and to concentrate on Richard's happiness and pleasure in activities, instead of just how the garden looks'.

The occupational therapist also provided advice on a range of ingenious gadgets to help Richard with gardening and with dressing himself.

As a result of the therapist's input, Richard started gardening and preparing vegetables again and also rejoined a choir.[18]

Therapy can help carers to learn to go with the flow of the illness and let go of past expectations. If someone with dementia cannot remember, say, how to make a cup of tea, or if they always get lost when left in the town centre while you pop off on an errand, the key is to act with understanding and empathy and accept that this is how things are going to be now. In other words, try to set aside your old expectations and prioritise providing love and support to the person with dementia. Certainly do not get angry and blame them.

Professor Linda Clare of Bangor University has pointed out that people in the early stages of dementia can be helped a great deal simply through ordinary memory prompts and devices to reduce the need to remember, such as:

✓ labelling cupboards as a reminder of where things are

- ✓ labelling the doors to rooms (with a word and simple diagrammatic clue)
- ✓ always keeping special items like keys or spectacles in a particular place
- ✓ putting important information on a message board[19]

Plainly, although one-to-one consultations with professionals are ideal, these types of therapy are often not rocket science and could be used at least in part by non-professionals.

Doll therapy, which involves giving somebody a doll or soft toy and encouraging them to care for it and talk to it, can help people in the middle to late stages of dementia. The doll or toy can bring comfort and security, and it can also help somebody cope with their feelings by transferring them onto the doll. In addition, it can help them feel needed and useful as they care for the toy.[20] One woman whom I used to visit in a care home kept a soft toy rabbit in a bag under the handle of her walking frame. Whenever anybody spoke to her she would proudly show them her creature. She would dress the rabbit, talk to it, cover it in kisses and try to knit garments for it. Doll therapy is not for everybody, of course: some people would find no comfort in a soft toy; they (or their relatives) might feel insulted by the idea.

Love as an answer

So long as their physical needs are met, the quality of life of somebody with dementia will depend more than anything else on the extent to which those around them, whether they be family carers, friends, neighbours, care assistants or staff in a hospital or care home, can bring them empathy and love.

Professor Tom Kitwood wrote a ground-breaking and widely-acclaimed book, *Dementia Reconsidered: The Person Comes First*, in which he set out a framework for the way in which other people should support and relate to people with dementia. Kitwood argued that the central need of people with dementia is love and that we can all help people with dementia by fostering the following aspects of their lives:

- **Attachment to other people:** Human beings like to feel part of a group, and if people with dementia feel socially isolated, they are likely to feel unhappy.

- **Identity:** Even if someone can no longer remember where they fit into the world around them – their name, where they used to live, whether they have a partner and children, for instance

– they nonetheless still need to feel they have a special identity and belong somewhere.

- **Comfort:** Somebody with dementia may be grappling with a sense of loss, perhaps arising from failing abilities or transfer to a care home. The provision of warmth and strength can be especially helpful.

- **Occupation:** The need to be occupied in doing something is instinctive. What is more, occupying yourself can provide absorption and also enhance self-esteem.[21]

(I explore Kitwood's approach in the context of communicating with people with dementia on pages 257–64.)

A team at Bradford University has used Kitwood's framework to work out how people with dementia should be cared for. Rather than a one-size-fits-all approach, it places the person with dementia centre stage. The team has set out its thinking in a useful guide, explaining that 'enhanced person-centred care' for people with dementia should encompass:

- **valuing** people with dementia and those who care for them and promoting their rights as citizens

- treating people as **individuals** – appreciating that everyone has a unique history and personality

- looking at the world from the **perspective** of the person with dementia and seeking to empathise with them

- recognising that people with dementia need to live in **social** environments which both compensate for their impairment and foster opportunities for their personal growth.

As a memory jogger, the team use the acronym VIPS – Very Important Persons.[22]

Advance planning

One of the advantages of knowing that somebody (probably) has dementia is that it enables the family to get started with planning for the care needs that lie ahead. In common with the person with dementia, families are often in denial – they know something is wrong but prefer to ignore it. As a result a common scenario is that the person involved has some kind of accident as a result of their dementia, such as a fall or even a road accident, and the family is then catapulted into having to make major decisions about their care in a crisis situation.

Early diagnosis made in a non-crisis situation, in which the person with dementia is simply becoming worse while living at home, enables action to be taken under less pressured conditions. If dementia is diagnosed, a son or daughter might ask: Can my father remain safely and happily at home with help? If so, for how long? Could he come and live with me or another relative or friend? What does he want to do? Should he go into a care home? These are major questions which demand time to ponder their considerable financial, legal, caring, medical and other implications.

The person with dementia will probably wish to be fully involved in this decision-making. If they have not yet granted power of attorney, they should do so *(see Chapter 31)*, and they may also wish to consider an advance directive to refuse treatment *(see page 1017)*. A dementia diagnosis does not in itself rule out the granting of power of attorney or the making of an advance directive: what is necessary is that the person involved should have the mental capacity to understand what they are doing and to make real choices *(see page 772)*.

Of course, plenty of people consider care, legal representation and other matters because it is clear that they are becoming mentally frail yet they do not have a formal dementia diagnosis. Some people will know their loved one has dementia and not wish to subject them to tests that they might find traumatic. Some will fear the impact that knowing the diagnosis will have on their loved one. That said, I have come across day centres in which the words 'dementia' and 'Alzheimer's' are never mentioned in front of those with the condition. There is a great deal of use of euphemism in the world of dementia. Some people take a test for dementia but opt for the result to be relayed to somebody whom they nominate rather than to receive it themselves.

Clinical guidance drawn up by NICE emphasises the importance of people with dementia having care plans. These should be drawn up jointly by health and social care staff, take into account the changing needs of the person with dementia and any unpaid carers, and be endorsed by the person with dementia and their carers. Importantly, they should be regularly reviewed.[23]

The care plan should lay out not only medical matters but also the guiding principles for the care of the person involved, for example whether they should be able to go out on their own, perhaps while being monitored with telecare equipment. This is an example of the way in which the medical condition of dementia prompts consideration of a range of ethical and practical matters in a way which does not quite follow with physical illnesses.

Other entitlements and support

People with dementia are entitled to expect adjustments in the way that services are provided – not only health services but also those provided in anything from hotels to shops – so that they are not unduly disadvantaged by their condition. This is because dementia is defined as a disability within the meaning of the Equality Act 2010 *(I give more details on page 688).*

The social services departments of local authorities often provide help to people with dementia. They have a duty to carry out assessments of individuals' care needs *(see page 588),* which may result in the provision of various services. Social services may also put people in touch with the support available from voluntary organisations, such as the Alzheimer's Society (covering England, Wales and Northern Ireland) and Alzheimer Scotland. These societies provide advisors, day centres, carers' support groups and the provision of various kinds of therapy, amongst other things. However, such services are not provided uniformly throughout the UK.

You can refer yourself to social services by ringing them up and asking for a care needs assessment *(as outlined on page 588).* Or your GP can approach social services direct and ask if somebody can contact you. As noted above, a formal dementia diagnosis is not essential in securing social services support. Many people receive all kinds of practical help through their social services department because it is clear that they probably have dementia and that it is causing various problems in their everyday lives.

Advocacy

In Scotland, people with dementia, and indeed any mental disorder, are entitled to be given an 'advocate' to support them and if necessary represent their views *(as explained on page 787).*

This legal requirement does not apply south of the border. However the National Institute for Health and Care Excellence says in its guidance on dementia that 'Health and social care professionals should inform people with dementia and their carers about advocacy services and voluntary support, and should encourage their use. If required, such services should be available for both people with dementia and their carers independently of each other.'[24]

Also in England and Wales, if somebody whose mental capacity is limited as a result of dementia is facing an important decision such as whether to move to a care home or receive major health treatment and they have nobody suitable to represent them, they are entitled to the services of an 'independent mental capacity advocate' *(this facility is ex-*

plained on pages 784–5). In Northern Ireland, legislation passed in 2016 incorporates a similar approach, but it is not expected to come into force for several years *(see pages 892–3).*

The Scottish government's National Dementia Strategy 2013–2016 sets out ways in which people who have been diagnosed with dementia can be better supported. It states that by 2016 everybody diagnosed with dementia should have a named and trained individual (called a link worker) who will provide support for at least a year after diagnosis in helping the person understand the illness and manage its symptoms; think about decisions they needed to make for the future; help them plan their future care; and help them keep in touch with their existing social networks. This is a potentially valuable entitlement.[25]

Medical help with other conditions

People with dementia do of course still fall prey to other illnesses, from the common cold to cancer. Make sure you or your loved one receive the assessment and treatment you or they need for any other illness.

However, people with dementia do not always get all the medical help they should *(see page 1005).* Certainly professionals have told me of cases in which, for example, an optometrist had declined to refer somebody for specialist treatment for eye disease because they had dementia, with the implicit assumption that they mattered less than other people. Somebody might even say, for example, 'She doesn't need palliative care because she's got dementia'.

If you need to, deploy the following recommendation from NICE: 'People with dementia should not be excluded from any services because of their diagnosis, age or coexisting learning disabilities.'[26] Health bodies in England, Wales and Northern Ireland are expected to follow NICE guidance *(as explained on pages 289–90).*

However, the identification of new medical conditions, assessing their severity and evaluating the impact of treatment can be difficult if someone develops the communication difficulties discussed in Chapter 12. If they cannot find the words to explain that they have a headache or feel sick for instance, these conditions run the risk of going untreated.

GPs play a key role here. They should be aware that they must give someone with dementia plenty of time to explain their symptoms. If someone has advanced dementia and has forgotten most of their vocabulary, the GP should seek to detect symptoms by other means – consulting the person's medical records, talking to family or friends, interpreting body language – for instance, somebody who is in pain may rock from side to side.[27]

If a GP has known someone for some time before they developed dementia, the GP is more likely to be able to diagnose a new condition and treat them effectively. This is a compelling reason for somebody who develops dementia to retain a GP who has talked to them and treated their various ailments over the years, rather than switch to a practice whose members have not met them before. Such a switch may happen when someone moves into a care home that encourages its residents to switch to a GP practice with which it has a special relationship, possibly financial. In this situation, it is important to consider carefully the pros and cons but bear in mind that we all have a right to choose our GP and residence in a care home does not affect this right *(see pages 286–7)*.

Depression and anxiety, *discussed in Chapter 17,* can exist alongside dementia and make the latter much more difficult to cope with. Ask your GP for help, perhaps through a referral to a psychiatrist or a clinical psychologist. Challenge any doctor who announces that depression is a normal and untreatable aspect of dementia: it should be addressed seriously on its own terms. NICE has said that cognitive behaviour therapy may help people with dementia who have depression and/or anxiety, while people with dementia who also have a major depressive disorder should be offered anti-depressant drugs.[28]

There is growing awareness of the need to pay special attention to the care of people with dementia if they go into hospital, *as explained on pages 919–22.*

People who have advanced dementia need special care if they have a terminal illness or they are dying. The person may be unable to comprehend that any pain will in time subside or put it in the context of a life enjoyed without pain. They may be unable to be distracted by another activity. Talk to the GP well in advance about how good palliative care can be delivered to a loved one with dementia *(as outlined on page 1004).*

We can help ourselves by avoiding places or situations in which we might develop infections. In the case of Alzheimer's disease there is an additional reason for doing so. Infections seem to increase the rate of cognitive decline in people who already have Alzheimer's disease. In a study involving 300 Alzheimer's patients, Professor Clive Holmes of Southampton University found that those who had had an infection experienced a threefold increase in their rate of cognitive decline over a six-month follow-up period.[29] Take up vaccinations against flu, shingles and pneumonia. If you develop an infection, make sure it is treated swiftly. Do not forget mouth care in this context: someone with dementia may not remember to brush their teeth properly, and poor mouth hygiene can lead to infection of the gums *(see page 16–7).*

The effects of dementia on behaviour

Many people with dementia become restless, agitated or even aggressive at some stage in the development of their illness. They may wander around or repeatedly call out. Some experience delusions or hallucinations. Some lose some of their sexual inhibitions. Behaviour such as this may cause no problems for other people and demand only that the person with dementia be given empathetic care. For instance, my mother often experienced hallucinations in which she could 'see' young children hiding under chairs. This did not seem to trouble her; indeed, she seemed to find the presence of the children reassuring (she had worked as a playground supervisor). But what would have been unhelpful would have been for somebody to have ridiculed her claim. In that case, I am sure she would have become very upset, as those children were as real to her as I was, sitting at her side.

My mother could not walk by this time, but had she been able to go in search of the children, perhaps calling loudly for them, wandering around and looking under seats on which other people were sitting, or if somebody had tried to stop her in her quest and she had remonstrated with them or even slapped them, this would have been classed as 'challenging behaviour'. This is the term used to describe behaviour engaged in by people with dementia that is deemed to be troublesome by those around them.

The first response to any such behaviour should be an attempt to understand it and act accordingly. One consultant clinical psychologist told me of a care home resident who insisted on going outside and searching under bushes at a certain time every day. If thwarted, he would do all he could to ensure he could continue. It transpired that he had lived on a farm and was accustomed to searching for hens' eggs around the farmyard at that hour. Once the home's staff knew this, they left eggs hidden in the grounds for him to discover on his round each day. His 'challenging behaviour' ceased.

Frustration at being unable to express yourself and so tell others that you are cold, lonely, frightened, need the toilet, wish to do something, see somebody or go somewhere can be another reason why you might become agitated and perhaps engage in behaviour which other people find challenging, such as lying down on the floor in the middle of a corridor.

Or you may be in pain. A study in 2011 involved more than 350 people with moderate or severe dementia living in nursing homes in Norway. Half of the participants were given painkillers at every meal. After eight weeks, the researchers found a 17 per cent reduction in agitation in those who had been given painkillers.[30] This is hardly surprising: many older people take analgesics daily and there is no reason why people with dementia should need them less than other people. However, if they cannot express themselves clearly and those caring for them are not alert to any pain they may be feeling, they may well miss out on drugs which could alleviate it. As we noted earlier *(on page 264),* some care homes use 'talking mats' – cards on which somebody with dementia can point to pictures to indicate that they are in pain, wish to use the toilet or need to see a dentist, amongst other statements and requests.

Anti-psychotic medication

Another response to challenging behaviour has been to give drugs to people with dementia. The drugs involved were originally developed to calm younger people with schizophrenia, but were found also to calm people with dementia, often making them drowsy.

Until about 2010, these drugs were in widespread use for people with dementia. Sube Banerjee, a psychiatrist and professor of mental health and ageing who carried out pioneering work in this field, estimated that they were being given to up to a half of people with dementia in the UK in 2009.[31] Yet, as he pointed out, these drugs can bring serious threats to physical health, arising largely from the drowsiness which the drugs induce. Patients who are drowsy are less likely to drink as much as they should, thus increasing the risk of dehydration *(see page 48).* They are also less likely to move themselves and clear their chest as much as usual, which means that infections such as pneumonia are more likely to take hold. People with dementia are more likely to have a fall than others, and drowsiness increases the risk still further. Professor Banerjee calculated in 2009 that anti-psychotics for people with dementia could be causing 1,800 additional deaths every year in the UK, as well as an additional 16,000 strokes.[32]

Anti-psychotic drugs can help in some circumstances – if a patient is severely distressed or at immediate risk of harming themselves or other people, according to the National Institute of Health and Care Excellence. But it says they should be prescribed only after an assessment has been carried out of the factors that cause, aggravate or improve their socalled 'challenging behaviour'.[33] NICE says that this assessment should be comprehensive and include:

- the person's physical health
- possible undetected pain or discomfort, depression and the side effects of medication

- the person's background, including their religious beliefs and spiritual and cultural identity
- psychosocial factors
- the physical environment

It should also include an analysis of the person's behaviour and ability to function, conducted by professionals with specific skills, in conjunction with carers and care workers. Then, an individually-tailored care plan should be drawn up to help carers and staff address the behaviour that is considered challenging. This plan should be recorded in the person's notes and reviewed regularly.[34]

In other words, anti-psychotic drugs should not automatically be given to people with dementia who are behaving in unusual ways. Instead people caring for the person should set out to understand what lies behind the behaviour. By observing it carefully, they should try to identify patterns. It may be occurring in a particular place at a particular time. It could indicate frustration at anything from a noisy environment to lack of privacy, meaningful occupation or access to the open air in someone who can no longer express themselves verbally.

If the behaviour cannot be prevented or modified by caring for the person in a different way, more specialist staff should be brought in to help work out what should be done, such as an occupational therapist, community psychiatric nurse or clinical psychologist. Only if further attempts to modify care based on their suggestions have failed should anti-psychotics be considered.

Concern about the effect of anti-psychotic drugs seems to have been having an effect. Between 2006 and 2011, the number of these drugs prescribed by GPs in England halved. However, it seems unlikely that the considerable number of people continuing to receive these drugs reflects a real need for them since rates of prescribing vary widely between areas: from 2 per cent of patients in London to 13 per cent in north-west England in 2011, for example.[35]

If your relative is already taking an anti-psychotic drug or a doctor proposes to prescribe one, check that the following matters have been considered:

✓ For how long has the drug been/will the drug be prescribed and when will its use be reviewed? (Even if the drug causes an improvement in behaviour, it should be reviewed regularly: the need for it may change as the dementia progresses.)

✓ Is the drug being started on a low dose and are the effects on the behaviour that it aims to affect being closely monitored?

✓ If your relative is currently taking a high dose, could that be reduced gradually?

✓ If they are currently taking a low dose, could they be taken off the drug immediately?

✓ Are any possible side-effects being closely monitored and are all necessary steps being taken to reduce the likelihood of side-effects in the first place? (For instance, steps should be taken to ensure that a patient is given any help they need to drink.)

The Alzheimer's Society publishes free factsheets about anti-psychotic drugs and about tranquillisers and sleeping tablets, which might also be suggested as a means of controlling behaviour.[36] It also publishes a free guide for health professionals about the care of people with moderate to advanced dementia with an emphasis on non-drug treatment; this contains useful questions which family and friends could pose about how their loved one is being looked after.[37]

Pharmacists are also a key professional with whom to talk; *as noted on page 310,* their professional body has issued a resource pack to support pharmacists who wish to oppose the prescribing of anti-psychotic drugs to people with dementia.

Dementia

* Dementia is common amongst older people, but the majority will not develop it.

* Alzheimer's disease is the main cause of dementia; its cause is unknown.

* The second main cause of dementia, vascular dementia, arises from an unhealthy cardiovascular system.

* Drugs can delay the onset of some symptoms of Alzheimer's and help in other ways, but they cannot cure it.

* It is important to plan arrangements early, including the appointment of attorneys.

* Diagnosis of dementia can bring help, but there are drawbacks as well as advantages.

* Try to avoid colds and other infections if you have Alzheimer's, as they can worsen the condition.

* Pain relief often reduces agitation in people with advanced dementia.

* Anti-psychotic drugs should be used to control the behaviour of people with dementia only as a last resort.

* The main need of people with dementia is for the love and support of those around them.

PRACTICAL HELP

" *One aspect of our lives which has changed dramatically over the last 50 years is the range of gadgets which enable those of us with some disability to remain independent and make the most of life. A host of inventors, largely unsung, have come up with ingenious practical solutions to everyday problems.* **"**

PART SIX
PRACTICAL HELP

Most people prefer to remain in their own homes when they are older, but this can prove a challenge if they develop conditions which give rise to difficulties in everyday living. If osteoarthritis prevents you from climbing stairs, if a stroke has left you in a wheelchair or if frailty means you lack the energy to do your housework, what can you do to get round the difficulties presented by living in your own home?

The solutions lie in two distinct areas, each of which can be pursued on its own or in combination with the other.

You could obtain equipment to help, from long-handled pincers to pick things off the floor if you cannot bend to flashing lights to show that somebody is calling if you cannot hear the doorbell. A new range of equipment known as 'telecare' is helping keep people safe in their homes by alerting a control room should they have a fall or leave the gas on.

As well as obtaining equipment, you could hire people to help you. This could range from assistance for a few hours a week to live-in care. You could hire helpers direct or enter into a contract with a care agency to provide them. I explore both avenues and consider the pros and cons of each.

This part is not intended only for people who live alone. Having a partner, relative or friend living with you does not mean that you may not benefit from help brought in from outside. Your house-mate may not be capable of providing the help you need, or they may not wish to do so, perhaps fearing that helping with personal care would damage your relationship.

Whether you are rich or poor, using social services or acting independently, the most straightforward source of additional revenue to help cover the costs of practical help in the home is Attendance Allowance.

Many relatively wealthy people do not apply for Attendance Allowance because they assume that it is given only to people of modest financial means. They are wrong – the applicant's income and savings are irrelevant. The sole grounds on which Attendance Allowance is paid is disability. To qualify, you need to be experiencing a certain basic level of difficulty in performing ordinary daily living tasks or you must have a need to be supervised to some extent, perhaps because you have dementia. I discuss this benefit and how to get it in the chapter on state benefits *(see pages 835–40)*. Recipients are free to spend their Attendance Allowance as they like. Other possible sources of funding for help in the home are discussed in this part.

Part Six therefore covers:

▶ equipment to make life easier and where to find it
▶ telecare equipment
▶ obtaining help in the home through a care agency
▶ hiring care staff direct
▶ live-in care
▶ paying for care

Chapter 21

Equipment

One aspect of our lives which has changed dramatically over the last 50 years is the range of gadgets which enable people with some disability to remain independent and make the most of life. A host of inventors, largely unsung, have come up with ingenious practical solutions to everyday problems such as washing your feet if you cannot bend to pouring from a kettle if your hand shakes. Such aids can be tremendously empowering.

However, these are areas in which you can spend a lot of money and, without sound impartial advice, not very effectively. Whether what you are looking for is a large-digit keyboard or an electric scooter, it is important that you investigate a range of possibilities before anything is bought.

Using disability equipment is a sensitive area for many people: gadgets from hearing aids to walkers can seem to some to proclaim inadequacy. In view of this, I offer reflections on ways in which family and friends can adjust their behaviour to provide support.

This chapter examines the following areas:

▶ viewing and trying out equipment

▶ gadgets for use in the home

▶ gadgets to help mobility

▶ gadgets to help hearing

▶ buying equipment privately

▶ obtaining equipment through the health service or social services

▶ inclusive design

▶ adjusting to life with disability equipment

Certain related matters are discussed elsewhere in this book:

- structures which are permanently fixed to a property, such as stairlifts and ramps, in Chapter 8: Staying put

- equipment to help with continence problems in Chapter 19: Continence

- state benefits awarded on grounds of disability and unrelated to income in Chapter 35: Universal state benefits.

Viewing equipment and trying it out

It is easy to assume that the best way of selecting disability equipment is to go to a local shop or order catalogues from providers found on the internet. Not so – for many reasons. The suppliers might not offer the full range of what is available. The items might be more expensive than you would find elsewhere. You might not obtain impartial advice on what would suit you or the difficulties that might arise with it. For example, might the power on a stairlift fail, leaving you stranded halfway up the stairs?

For many types of equipment, not least mobility aids, it is also vital to see and handle before you buy: various aspects might not be right for you, and you might have difficulty operating the equipment or getting it repaired. Some types of equipment, not least the telecare devices explored in the next chapter, are unfamiliar to most of us, so there is a special need for explanation and demonstration by impartial advisors.

Dotted across the UK are about 40 Disabled Living Centres. There, a large range of equipment from different manufacturers is on display (not for sale). Trained staff provide impartial advice, with the help of a 16,000-item database. Many centres have their own resident occupational therapist to give more specialist advice. (You may need to telephone ahead to make an appointment to see the OT.) Although it is best to see and handle equipment and discuss its usefulness face to face, you can phone for advice if you cannot visit.

All the items at Disabled Living Centres are priced, so you can easily make comparisons, and centres give information about local suppliers. (Those in remote locations act as vendors too.) It is extremely important to buy from a reputable supplier who will also provide or arrange ongoing maintenance, for instance for electric scooters or wheelchairs. Many centres also hold information about obtaining second-hand equipment. Information about all the centres is provided by the Disabled Living Foundation (*see below and Useful Contacts*).

Once you know what sort of equipment would best suit you, also look at commercial catalogues and compare quality, suitability and price. Catalogues can be especially useful in fields in which technology is developing very fast, such as telecare.

Some voluntary organisations, such as the Stroke Association, the Royal National Institute of Blind People (RNIB) and Action on Hearing Loss (formerly the Royal National Institute for Deaf People or RNID), have online shops and also provide information about equipment.

The Disabled Living Foundation, based in London, collates information about the location and hours of opening of all the Disabled Living Centres in the UK. Its website displays a huge number of pieces of equipment, and the Foundation also publishes factsheets and provides a helpline as well as an online advice tool from which you can obtain the answers to a wide variety of questions, such as what types of equipment can minimise bending in the garden and how to prevent garden paths from becoming slippery.

Rica (standing for Research Institute for Consumer Affairs) is an independent consumer research organisation publishing reports which evaluate equipment for its suitability for people with disability and for older people in general. So not only are textphones, electric scooters and adaptations to cars, for example, examined, but also digital televisions and set-top boxes and domestic appliances such as toasters and electric kettles. Many of Rica's publications are available at Disabled Living Centres.

Some readers will be offered equipment through the health service or through the social services department of their local authority *(see pages 480–1)*. They should nonetheless have a look at the full range of what is available. They may prefer equipment of a different colour, style or capability. Viewing the full range, as one can in a Disabled Living Centre, provides the basic knowledge needed to ask for something different or for a voucher covering the cost of the equipment the state would provide. People can then go and make their own choice, perhaps adding to the voucher any cash they can afford. Viewing the full range also offers the opportunity for them to see items for which they would definitely not be deemed eligible by the state but which they might care to buy from their own resources.

The home

First let us get a flavour of the range of equipment that is available to help us in our homes.

The living room

Most people will be familiar with armchairs with a side lever which raises a support for legs in the front and another lever which lowers the back, enabling us to recline or even lie flat. Perhaps less familiar are armchairs whose seat can be made to tilt forwards at the push of a button to help rise, or to lower to help with sitting down.

If you think such a chair would help you, look for one which is comfortable, provides firm support for your back, which you can handle confidently and which, if it is lifting you up, will do so without making you topple over.

From the comfort of a chair you can now, thanks to remote control equipment, open and close curtains, windows and doors, control lighting and even operate domestic appliances such as hoovers.

Reading stands are helpful if your hands tremble or are easily tired. If reading small characters is difficult, plenty of magnifiers can be found. Some contain an in-built light; some will hang around your neck; some are mounted on a stand; some are adjustable. Don a pair of prism glasses if you want to read while you are lying flat – the glasses will change the angle, so you can rest an open book on your stomach and still read it.

Arthritis may stop you holding a pen easily. Fortunately, a range of ingenious and sophisticated pen grips is available.

Changing a light bulb is exactly the kind of simple task that can become impossible if you cannot climb onto a stool or ladder or fear that you will fall off. So why not obtain a light which hangs on a long cord from the ceiling so it can be easily reached when the bulb needs changing?

There are large wall clocks which also show the date, and talking clocks for people with impaired eyesight.

Telephones with large numbers are widely available. Those which store your most frequently used numbers save a lot of dialling. If you have difficulty remembering which button dials whom and the labels are too tiny to read, look for a phone which has space for a photograph alongside each of the memory buttons. There are also phones which have a voice-activated dialling facility.

Phones, TVs, keyboards and books

Mobile phones and cordless phones can of course be a great help, but for older people miniaturisation is not necessarily a boon. Fortunately, however, inventors have been developing mobile phones (and many other gadgets) for people who find it hard to read small digits. Thus there are now mobile phones with large numbers, mobiles equipped with magnifiers, and talking mobiles which require no reading, as everything is spoken.

Computer keyboards adapted for various degrees of sight impairment are available. There are keyboards on which the letters and numbers are imprinted in bolder print than usual and others furnished with 'monster keys', or keys in different colours. E-books can be easier to read than print books because you can adjust the size of the font and the colour contrast.

Remote controls for television also come in large-digit forms. If you have sight problems, you might also benefit from 'audio description', a free service where, as you watch, a narrator fills you in on the movements, expressions and body language depicted on screen.

Not only books, playing cards and Scrabble, but also the weekly TV and radio schedules now come in large-print format. A sophisticated, though expensive, device, called a video magnifier, can enlarge by up to 80 times on a screen newspaper print, crosswords, photographs, pages from books and so on.

Audiotapes of books have long been of great value to people who cannot read the printed page. A more sophisticated version is the DAISY talking book (the acronym stands for Digital Accessible Information System). The DAISY CD player's 'jump' function allows you to begin either at the start of a chapter of a book or halfway through it. The function buttons are large and are picked out in a colour that contrasts with the background. A compact, portable DAISY player has also come onstream. Another array of gadgets convert printed material into speech: devices will scan a newspaper, for example, and then read the content aloud.

Disabled Living Centres display gadgets for helping visually impaired people. But phones, scanners, keyboards, video magnifiers and audio devices are probably best viewed at the headquarters of the Royal National Institute of Blind People in London, situated only a short distance from King's Cross and St Pancras stations. Helpful staff are on hand to explain what is available and how the items work. The RNIB has other resource centres around the country, but they tend to show a smaller range. The RNIB publishes a comprehensive catalogue of equipment. Look out for Sight Village exhibitions too. Local authorities' sensory teams *(page 559)* also hold equipment. *See also Chapter 11: Computers and the internet.*

The kitchen

Various types of kitchen furniture and gadgets have been devised for different kinds of disability. Or you may be able to adapt your existing kitchen surroundings.

Many older people suffer from tremor, particularly if they have Parkinson's disease. There is a variety of equipment to help cope with tremor. A cup is available which is almost impossible to knock over, however much your hand shakes. It sits on a wide base with rubber underneath to stop it sliding, narrows at the waist and has handles either side of the upper part. Non-slip placemats prevent a plate from sliding on a table. These can also be invaluable for people who have had a stroke and are trying to recover their skills with crockery and cutlery. Useful too is cutlery with a large grip, and a fork with a cutting edge which enables somebody to feed themselves using one hand.

Clamps, too, can be invaluable if you can use only one hand: they can enable you to do anything from prepare food to file your nails. A useful work station for the kitchen consists of a slab of hard plastic with spikes coming out of it on which you can place a potato which you can then peel with one hand, or a piece of meat which you can carve.

For weak hands and wrists, there are scissors which need no force to be applied as they rely on a spring mechanism. Various simple jar and bottle-openers are available. However, for people who do not have the strength or dexterity to use these openers, the answer could be a robotic jar-opener, powered by a battery. You place it on the jar and press a button; the opener grips both jar and lid before rotating the lid to loosen it.

Perhaps you find a kettle of hot water heavy or difficult to control? If so, have a look at a kettle-tipper. The kettle rests on a stand with a spring, which allows it to tilt over only one way and to bounce back. You keep the kettle on its stand so that it faces into the sink. When you pour, you don't need to lift the kettle but simply hold its handle; it is kept in place with special guides.

If your eyesight is poor, try picking out the edge of work surfaces and the edges of cupboards, the sink and other features in a contrasting colour to improve their visibility. Work surfaces are available with a raised outer edge to prevent liquids falling on the floor – a slip hazard. People who cannot see well need a lot of light; you can obtain cupboards which light up when opened, like a fridge. Inside the cupboard, a 'penfriend' is a device for labelling tins and bottles, as well as CDs and tapes, by recording an audio label through the pen.

If you cannot see the divisions on your kitchen scales, you could place pieces of hard red rubber on them to emphasise the fine lines, or you could buy talking scales. You can even buy a talking thermometer, a talking measuring jug and a talking microwave. If you cannot see easily when a cup is full, you can buy a simple and cheap device – a 'liquid level indicator' – that will hang over the edge and make a noise when it is covered.

Various safety devices are available. An inexpensive 'magic plug' can be placed in the sink (or bath) before filling it. If the weight of the water exceeds a particular threshold, indicating that the sink or bath is too full, the pressure of the water forces the plug up and out.

Many safety devices, such as a gas safety system which can detect natural gas or carbon monoxide emit an alarm if gas is at a dangerous level. They cut off the gas supply through a special valve. Another device, a flood detector placed by the sink or bath, provides an audible alarm and alerts a call centre if it detects too much water. These types of 'telecare equipment' are discussed in the next chapter.

The bedroom

There are many different gadgets available to aid dressing and undressing, such as devices to help put on socks or stockings without bending far. Some Disabled Living Centres contain a clothing department, in addition to providing free factsheets and advice booklets on clothing. There are five different factsheets on footwear alone, for example, as swollen feet call for different considerations from corns and bunions. Centres also provide catalogues, for example for Cosyfeet, a company offering shoes and other footwear for swollen, painful or wide feet.

If you find difficulty in getting yourself up from lying down in bed, look for a bed with a lever similar to those on some armchairs and hospital beds. Another clever gadget is a rope-ladder bed hoist. It is tethered by strings to the bed posts and you pull yourself up by putting hand over hand up the small ladder. You can also obtain a foot-rest to stop yourself slipping down the bed when you are sitting up as well as an adjustable back-rest and a device for raising part of the mattress.

If you have difficulty getting in and out of bed, it is often a good idea to raise the bed itself so you have less distance to move; this can be done with steel brackets on which the bed sits and which are fixed to vertical tubes on castors. If you are hard of hearing, you can be woken by an alarm clock with a flashing light or a vibrating pad under your pillow.

Problems with erectile function are a notorious bugbear of old age *(see page 15)*. Gadgets can play a useful part here too. But for the full range of options from drugs to psychological therapy or other treatment in what is a rapidly developing field, talk to your GP.

The bathroom

A broad board is the most basic device to help you get in and out of the bath. You place it across the bath, sit on it and then swing your legs over and into the bath. However, with a board you cannot sit under the water and enjoy a proper soak: instead, you have to ladle water over yourself, or get a helper to do so.

A bath lift is more sophisticated and helpful. Battery operated, it consists of a little plastic chair which you place in the bath (or leave there). You turn it towards you, sit on it, swivel round, then press a button and find yourself lowered down. You sit on the seat while you wash, then press another button to be lifted back to bathtop height. The whole apparatus can be installed in an existing bath, with the control unit screwed to the wall just above it.

Body dryers help people who find drying themselves difficult. Warm air is blown out of a tall unit and dries someone from top to toe without the need for towels.

For somebody who has trouble getting on and off the lavatory seat, a raised toilet seat can be clamped onto the existing one, raising the height by 6 inches (15 cm). A more sophisticated aid is a lavatory seat which tilts backwards and down to help a person sit on it and forwards to help them get off; this is operated with a press button. To help somebody lower and raise themselves, grab-rails can be installed either side, or support bars which are pushed up against the wall when not in use.

A more sophisticated toilet can incorporate a heated seat, a bidet system of warm-water washes and warm-air drier, and a seat that can push up to aid standing after use.

If you will be taking tablets in the bathroom, you may have seen a pill dispenser with separate compartments indicating the times each day when the pills they contain must be taken. These are helpful for people with limited dexterity and those who find it difficult to remember whether they have taken their medication. Another device is available which announces at a pre-set time that somebody should take a tablet and sends a signal to a telecare call centre *(page 486)* if they fail to do so.

The garden

A range of light gardening tools, from trowels to spades, made from materials such as aluminium and plastic, has been devised for people who can no longer manage heavy versions. Another range offers tools which are especially heavy, to counteract tremor. One handy device is a padded stool on which you can kneel, with a firm handle on either side to push on when you want to stand up. Turned over, the 'garden kneeler' becomes a seat for resting or doing waist-high tasks. All ideal birthday presents!

Thrive and Gardening for the Disabled provide advice in this area, in addition to that provided by the Disabled Living Foundation.

Walking aids

Walking problems are some of the most common disabilities of later life, affecting as many as 25 per cent of women and 14 per cent of men over 65. The most common cause is osteoarthritis.[1]

Some people prefer a four-wheeled shopping trolley to a walking aid, which they feel proclaims their infirmity. Beware! An ordinary shopping trolley is not designed to provide support to the user, does not usually have a brake and is not adjustable in terms of height, so if it isn't right for you, it could give you backache. Also, if you are unsteady and intend to rely on a shopping trolley for support, you could be putting yourself in danger. Should you start to fall and catch the handle, the trolley will go flying.

You can obtain a shopping trolley with a brake, and a hard top and sides on which you can sit. But again, its purpose is to carry shopping, not to support somebody who cannot walk easily.

There is, however, a wide range of equipment designed specifically to help with walking. The reason(s) why you might find a walking aid helpful include:

- to distribute your weight and thereby lessen pain from particular joints, muscles or ligaments
- to provide stability and balance
- to help you move around more quickly
- to improve your posture and help you stand upright
- to increase your confidence in your own walking ability, perhaps after being frightened by a fall

It is important to obtain specialist advice on which piece of equipment would best suit your particular needs. There is also the environment to consider: indoors or out, in confined spaces, up and down steps, and so on. More than one type of aid may be called for. Does the aid need to be lightweight and collapsible because you want to take it with you in the boot of a car, or does it need above all to provide a stable support for movement indoors? You also need to consider hands and forearms. It is possible to find an aid with arm-rests, which allows weight to be borne through the forearms rather than the hands, and with contoured hand grips which spread pressure more evenly through the palms. Other physical considerations may be relevant; for example, arthritic fingers may make the manipulation of fiddly equipment difficult.

The best approach is to get your GP to refer you to a physiotherapist or occupational therapist or to see an OT at a Disabled Living Centre. They can work out exactly which of the many different models available would best suit you. They will ensure that the one selected fits you in terms of height, weight and type of hand grip, and will show you the correct way to use it and how to maintain it. Even an ordinary walking stick needs regular checking to see that the rubber ferrule on its base – which should be slip-resistant – is not worn, cracked or loose, and that the stick itself has not cracked.

Measure significant dimensions before you choose your aid: your doorways may be too narrow for some types of equipment.

Once you acquire a mobility aid, it is important that you use it safely *(see page 470)*.

The main types of walking aid are:

Zimmer frames

These are waist-height frames with four feet in contact with the ground, about 12 inches (30 cm) deep, slightly wider than the user and widening by four inches from front to back. Zimmers provide safe support for walking indoors and are usually provided by the NHS. Their width and four feet make them especially helpful for people who are unsteady.

The main disadvantage of a Zimmer is you cannot get into small spaces, nor walk in the normal flowing manner, as you have to keep stopping and starting in order to pick up the frame, and then move it forwards and step into it.

To improve manoeuvrability around the home, narrower frame Zimmers have been developed. However, they are less stable than the wide version and unsuitable for anyone who puts much of their weight on one side of their body. In some models of Zimmer, the front two legs have wheels attached, and there may be castor wheels or glides on the back legs. But the front wheels do not swivel and so do not manage corners easily.

The Zimmer should be at a height which is comfortable for you and allow you to maintain a slight bend in your arms. In most models, the height is adjustable – you choose a model in one of three or four height ranges and can then adjust it by one inch increments. Some models can be folded. The type of hand grip can be varied too.

Rollators

These are substantial two- or four-wheeled walking aids with largish wheels which are used outdoors. There is often a shopping basket or string bag on them, and perhaps even a little seat on which you can sit and rest. You can choose the type of brake and hand grip.

Rollators can be enormously useful but they tend to be heavy, so if you have steps up to your front door you need to think about where you would leave one or who could carry it into your house. It is important to feel confident that you can control the equipment easily so that it does not run away with you.

Triangular outdoor frames

Triangular frames with large wheels suitable for outdoor use are versatile and popular. They have the advantage over the four-wheeled type in that they can be folded and thus stored more compactly and manoeuvred through narrow spaces. Again, you can choose between different types of braking system, hand grip, basket and bag. If you opt for a frame with a shopping basket attached (perhaps with a hard lid for sitting on), you will not be able to fold it. Instead, you could hang a folded shooting seat from the handlebar; indeed, you could add a walking stick there too, if necessary.

Like rollators, triangular frames tend to be quite heavy (in order to provide stable support). The control to keep the brake on and the bar to secure the frame in the open position may be difficult to manipulate if you have arthritic fingers.

Tripods and quadrupods

These are walking sticks which divide at the base into three or four legs; they are more stable than a single pole and are particularly helpful for people with poor balance. Also, unlike a stick, they do not fall over when you let go of them, perhaps to open a door.

Tripods and quadrupods will enable you to get into spaces which would be too small for a Zimmer frame. However, you have to be careful that you don't trip over one of the legs.

Sticks

Sticks are much easier to use than tripods and quadrupods if you are walking any distance. It is important that you get one which is the correct height, but the height of metal sticks can be adjusted, and they tend to be stronger than wooden sticks.

It is important to be aware that if you are using a stick to reduce the weight on one side of your body, perhaps because you have a painful knee, then the stick should be used in the opposite hand; the leg with the painful knee and the stick should move forwards together.

Walking sticks have a different structure from canes for blind and partially sighted people. Such canes are never used for support: you hold them across the lower part of your body to protect it and to check the existence and height of obstructions such as steps. Attend a training course before acquiring one. Blind or visually impaired people who need the support of an ordinary walking stick can obtain a white one. A piece of red tape around the stick indicates that the person using it is also deaf.

Electric scooters

Battery-powered scooters provide transport rather than an aid to walking. Social services departments and health organisations do not fund the acquisition of scooters – unlike most of the other types of walking equipment described here, including wheelchairs. So you should select one with care, as you will be paying for it yourself and you could waste a lot of money if you later find you cannot use it.

The vast majority of electric scooters seen out and about in the UK come in two main types, differentiated mainly by size and whether or not they can be dismantled. The smaller ones can be taken apart, move more slowly than the larger scooters (maximum speed of 4 as opposed to 8 miles per hour) and are often called boot-scooters, as they will fit into the boot of most cars.

Only the larger scooters (officially called class 3 vehicles, as opposed to the smaller class 2) are allowed to go along roads and, because of this, they must be fitted with lights, indicators, a horn, rear-view mirrors and rear reflectors. Although exempt from road tax, scooters that go on the road must be registered with the DVLA. They are not allowed on motorways, bus lanes or cycle lanes. If driven on footpaths, the speed must not exceed 4 mph (6 kph).

The type you choose (and there are many different varieties within these two broad groups) depends mainly on where you most wish to use the vehicle. Clearly, the large scooter is more appropriate if you need to drive along the road and the boot-scooter if you think you are more likely to take it with you in a car. Thus, on holiday, you could leave a boot-scooter in a car boot, lift out the battery only and take it to your hotel room for overnight recharging.

All scooters need to be recharged regularly. The distance they will run before recharging varies with such factors as the weight they must carry and the number of hills to be negotiated, but they are unlikely to go for more than 25 miles (40 kilometres). Recharging takes eight hours; users often remind themselves to recharge when the evening news comes on television. If the battery is run down too much, it can never be recharged.

If you are considering purchasing a scooter, think about where you will store it: you need to find a secure waterproof space near to the power point you will use for recharging. (If you do not have sufficient space, consider getting a folding self-drive electric wheelchair instead, *as explained below.*) Consider whether the dimensions and turning circle will allow you to drive the scooter into your home, your favourite supermarket, or wherever. Both types of scooter can theoretically be driven indoors, but some will work better in some situations than others. Three-wheel scooters tend to be more agile, with smaller turning circles, but they are more unstable than four-wheelers. Stability is especially important not only if you are proposing to cover rough, rural terrain, but also if you will need to negotiate kerbs which have not been lowered. *(See page 675 for advice on getting kerbs lowered.)*

A combination of scooter and train can be a very successful means of getting around. Staff on stations and on trains ought to give you help with ramps to get you on and off the train *(see page 706)*. But as scooters come in different sizes and weights, check with the train-operating company beforehand that your scooter could fit in the train and would not be too heavy for the ramp. National Rail Enquiries lists contact information for these companies on its website. Or you could phone National Rail Enquiries or ask at a station. You can take a boot-scooter on a plane.

If possible, visit a Disabled Living Centre *(see page 458 above)* to try out different scooters and obtain information about local suppliers. (You may qualify for advice and help with obtaining a scooter through Motability, *as explained on page 701.*) Don't go first to the manufacturer or a salesperson: they may try to sell you the model they are trying to get rid of or on which they will get the most commission, and it may not be the best type for your needs.

Before you buy a scooter, make absolutely sure you understand:

✓ how to maintain the vehicle

✓ what you should do if it breaks down

✓ how you are going to get it repaired and the likely cost of repairs

✓ whether a replacement will be loaned if it has to be taken away

If you are planning to buy second hand, look at the range of new scooters first, so you know which kind would suit you best. And have the scooter checked thoroughly before you spend your money: it may not have been serviced for years and break down soon after you have bought it.

Tuition on how to drive is crucially important. One user explained to me that although she considered herself au fait with vehicles generally (she had driven for 60 years and cycled until she was 80), she had experienced difficulty in understanding how to operate her scooter when she first bought it. Instruction had been given in the shop, but she wished she had been shown how to operate it in the environment in which she was going to use it. So, insist not only on adequate tuition but also on trying out the vehicle, ideally in your home environment. Not all manufacturers offer this last facility, but some do, and it can be extremely useful in revealing unexpected problems.

Although scooters can be tremendously liberating, they can also be dangerous. They offer little protection if you collide with a car or lorry, whether you are driving your scooter along a road or crossing one. In 2014, there were 209 road crashes involving mobility scooters in England and Wales in which nine people were killed.[2] Some deaths and injuries also arise from the unsafe driving of scooters in pedestrian areas and even within buildings.

Some local police forces offer training in driving electric scooters and, as we see in a moment, Shopmobility centres *(see below)* may offer training. Plainly, when you go out on a scooter, you should obey the Highway Code. If on a footpath or pavement, drive slowly and give way to pedestrians. Use lowered kerbs wherever possible and reduce your speed when going up and down kerbs and round corners. The organisation Help My Mobility advises people to practise using their scooter in a safe area before taking it out on the pavement. It also suggests trying out a new scooter in fine weather before going out in the rain and increasing the length of trips gradually, both to build up confidence and to test the battery range of the vehicle.

At the time of writing, it was not a legal requirement to obtain insurance for driving a mobility scooter, but this may change. If you have an accident and cause damage – say, knocking a ladder standing on a pavement and causing a window-cleaner to fall off and hurt himself – you could be sued. You should therefore obtain third party insurance and public liability cover. A company called Mark Bates Limited, based in Grantham, specialises in this type of insurance.

Motability allows people either to buy through hire purchase or to hire a powered wheelchair or scooter. However, the qualifying conditions to enter the scheme are very tight *(as explained on page 701)*.

The world of scooters is developing rapidly so if you are contemplating buying one, it is worth doing research on new types of scooter that may be developed. For instance, the TravelScoot is lighter than the traditional electric scooter. It has three rather than four wheels, with a platform on which to rest your feet and place luggage. The Tramper, in contrast, is a much heavier vehicle that can cover rough terrain, ideal for people who wish to explore the countryside. Trampers are sometimes offered for hire or loan at local authority country parks and the like, as well as being available to buy. An organisation called Countryside Mobility offers trampers (and sometimes also wheelchair-accessible boats) for hire at outdoor attractions in south-west England.

Wheelchairs

Wheelchairs come in two forms: one has to be pushed and the other can be propelled by the user. While some (pushed or self-propelled) rely on human power, others have a battery-powered motor.

Unlike scooters, wheelchairs are often provided for free, through referral from a GP or other health professional, on long-term loan from the NHS. You have to be assessed as needing a chair, and health authorities vary in the eligibility criteria they use to decide what type of wheelchair to provide and how soon to provide it. You may not need to be unable to walk to qualify – my mother, for example, was given a new, sophisticated chair at a time when she was still able to walk but found walking more than a few hundred yards painful. The chair enabled her to cover much greater distances when family and friends went for walks with her along the promenade at Broadstairs.

The NHS Wheelchair Service, to which doctors refer patients who need wheelchairs, has centres throughout the UK at which people who have permanent difficulties with walking are assessed and provided with chairs. They are usually evaluated individually by a physiotherapist for their own chair, and their precise requirements in terms of size of wheel, height and type of cushions are taken into consideration. All this is very important and many factors need to be borne in mind *(many of them are similar to those outlined above for scooters).*

Even the cushions of the wheelchair have to be considered: they are important not only for comfort but also in reducing the risk of pressure sores in vulnerable individuals. They come in many varieties, including gel cushions for people at high risk of developing sores, and one-way-slide cushions, so that the sitter does not slide out.

Although an NHS wheelchair should be of high quality, it will not necessarily be top of the range. If you want to buy a more expensive chair than your health authority will provide, it should give you a wheelchair voucher representing the value of the chair it is prepared to provide, so you can top it up. It is even possible to buy a wheelchair which climbs and descends flights of steps or enables the user to stand upright to reach high items, perhaps on supermarket shelves. And of course if you are not offered a chair by the NHS or prefer to go private, you will want to see the full range of what is available.

Somebody proposing to push a wheelchair should get advice on matters such as the height and weight of the chair, as pushing can damage the back. Indeed, it is a good idea if both the pusher and the person to be pushed are assessed for the most appropriate chair. One factor to take into account is the weight of the chair, particularly if the pusher is likely to be lifting it, perhaps in and out of a car boot. Chairs with a motor are especially heavy. Some cars have been adapted to allow a wheelchair to be pushed up a ramp through the back door and affixed to the floor, so that its occupant can sit in it throughout a journey. Information on such vehicles, on ways in which cars can be adapted for disability in general and on related equipment such as that used to lift heavy items into car boots is available from Rica *(see page 698)*.

People going into a care home should take their NHS wheelchair with them, as it may well be a much better vehicle than any provided by the home. In any case it should have been designed specifically for them.

It is important to sort out who is going to take responsibility for ongoing maintenance in a care home: you don't want your wheelchair sitting unused for weeks on end with flat tyres or a missing foot-rest. Make sure you are shown how to keep your chair, or any mobility aid, in working order, and if you will be pushing a wheelchair, be certain the supplier shows you how to minimise the strain on your back and how to ease the chair up and down kerbs smoothly.

Wheelchairs can also be borrowed from the Red Cross (as can other items, such as commodes). You might borrow one when a relative is coming to stay, for example, or when you are on holiday with somebody who cannot walk far. As explained above, manual and electric wheelchairs can be borrowed or hired from Shopmobility centres for the day or half-day.

In recent years, a type of self-propelled electric wheelchair has come onto the market that can be folded. This makes it easier to store and may be the solution for people who would like to have an electric scooter but lack anywhere sufficiently large to store it safely overnight. An electric wheelchair has a joystick, so you can drive it just as you can a scooter.

Shopmobility

Shopmobility is the name of a group of independent organisations which provide mobility aids for hire or loan, typically electric scooters and wheelchairs, both manual and powered. The organisations are based in town centres, often in malls. At any typical centre, you telephone beforehand and say that you would like to borrow a piece of mobility equipment on a particular occasion. When you ring, you will usually be asked your weight (as this affects the type of vehicle offered) and told what you need to bring with you – usually some form of identification, such as a household utility bill. The service is intended for people who have temporary or permanent mobility problems, so you should not need to be registered as disabled (say, for a Blue Badge parking permit). Nor is the service likely to be confined to local residents. Some centres loan out equipment for free, others make a small charge. If provision is free, you will be encouraged to make a donation when you return the equipment.

The centre will hire or loan its equipment only if it is satisfied that it is appropriate for you (in terms of size and type) and that you can manoeuvre it safely. The first time you borrow you are likely to have to make an appointment for an assessment and, if necessary, tuition. If all is well, you will be given a number.

As the centres have to meet their own safety and insurance requirements, the equipment is likely to be of high quality. Push-wheelchairs will probably have brakes which occupants can apply as well as those on the handlebars. The equipment is likely to be frequently serviced. The scooters may well have shopping baskets and facilities for carrying walking sticks or crutches.

Once you go out, you will be given a phone number to ring in case of breakdown or, say, a puncture. If this happens, staff from the centre will usually go out to you with replacement equipment which can be swapped for the damaged vehicle.

You borrow or hire vehicles for a day or half a day. There is nothing to stop you hiring frequently. The vehicles are not intended for use on roads, but you can use them on pavements (for instance to get to a hospital appointment) and in shopping centres or parks. There will usually be provision for disabled parking places close to the centre; these may or may not be free of charge.

Helping hearing

Hearing aids are programmed precisely to the audio impairment of a particular individual. Many other devices to help hearing are not. This means that they are much cheaper to buy and more straightforward to use and maintain. Some can be used with a hearing aid, some without. Let us look at these first.

Often we wish to focus on particular sounds. Inexpensive headphone systems can connect to a TV or radio; there are models for people who wear hearing aids and people who do not. If you want to amplify sound and focus on a particular sound while also reducing background noise, say in a group discussion or a lecture hall, you could look for a 'conversor'. The person whose voice you wish to hear speaks into a small discreet microphone which transmits sound to a device connected to your hearing aid and worn round your neck. If you do not use a hearing aid, the sound can be sent to a special receiver to which you can listen.

There is an impressive range of devices to facilitate telephone conversation for people who are hard of hearing. A simple portable amplifier suitable for use with or without a hearing aid could be taken to work or on holiday. Other devices amplify the sound received down the phone (landline or mobile) and transmit it to a hearing aid.

How can people who are hard of hearing know that the phone is ringing or a fire alarm is sounding? If a phone with a loud ring is insufficient, you could look for a flashing-light device that indicates that the phone is ringing. Fire alarms for people who are hard of hearing include a device placed under the pillow which vibrates in the event of a fire.

Disabled Living Centres do not usually display hearing equipment such as phone amplifiers, conversors and hearing aids, though some do. Sometimes the regional information officers of Action on Hearing Loss stage demonstrations, so you could telephone to find out whether one is planned in your area. If you cannot manage to view equipment, look at the range of possibilities in a catalogue. You can select a product from Action on Hearing Loss's catalogue and try it at home. If it does not suit, there is a money-back guarantee. Action on Hearing Loss also sells devices to help people cope with tinnitus, publishes factsheets and provides a helpline.

The Next Generation Text (NGT) is an impressive service which helps people with hearing loss to communicate by telephone with people who can hear. The hearing-impaired person speaks down the phone but the reply from the hearing person comes back on screen; an intermediary transcribes the voice message. Or the hearing impaired person can type a message which is read out to the hearing person.

NGT replaces Type Talk, a similar service in which the hearing-impaired person needed to have a textphone, which is a device for communicating down the phone by text. But NGT can also be accessed by a smartphone, tablet, laptop or computer with an internet connection.

Hearing aids

If your hearing loss is significant, you should seriously consider a hearing aid. The problem will almost certainly not go away, and will probably worsen. As it does so, you will not only miss out on information which could be important but are likely to become more and more isolated and even withdrawn. *(The causes of hearing loss are examined on page 14 and some of the psychological effects to which it can give rise on pages 254–5.)* However, in contrast to spectacles, obtaining, operating and maintaining a hearing aid in later life can be daunting.

To begin with, how do you know whether you have hearing loss? You could ask your GP, who will do a simple screening test to work out whether there might be a problem that should be examined further through a more sophisticated test. Or you could telephone Action on Hearing Loss' telephone hearing check service. It will carry out a test over the phone and let you know the result.

Hearing aids are available privately or on the NHS. The advantages of going private have largely disappeared: waiting times for NHS aids are relatively short in most areas and high-quality aids are provided. These can be programmed to amplify (or play down) sound at particular frequencies. If your ear has lost the ability to detect a particular frequency, nothing can be done: a hearing aid cannot create sound. But if your ear is simply weak at picking up particular frequencies, for example the frequencies at which we utter consonants (the key to understanding speech: *see page 14),* a digital aid can amplify them.

Both the aids and the batteries needed to power them are free on the NHS. To obtain a hearing aid, you need to be referred by your GP to an audiologist in a hospital. They can diagnose hearing loss, recommend the most useful type of aid and show you how to use one. In addition, they train people, such as staff in care homes, on how best to help people with hearing loss.

The first time you put in a hearing aid the world can seem very strange and the aid distracting, with lots of noises louder than hitherto. If you find it tiring to get used to your aid, try to build up use, wearing the aid a little longer each day. If you persevere with it over a fortnight or so and continue to find it troubling, go back to your audiologist, who may need to adjust it. When we obtain spectacles, we rarely need to go back to the optometrist to ask for a change to the lens. But programming a hearing aid is a sophisticated process and not infrequently the new user needs to return and ask the audiologist to reprogram it.

All this means that it is important that you should be able to pay a return visit to your audiologist relatively easily. If you decide to go private, discuss with the dispenser the ease and cost of return visits.

Some people have a hearing aid yet find that communication remains very difficult. Perhaps their hearing aid has not been checked or adjusted.

Hearing is likely to change, whether a hearing aid is worn or not, so it should be reassessed every three years. However, some unscrupulous private dispensers make money by telling their clients that they need a new hearing aid when in fact the old aid could be reprogrammed successfully.

Hearing aids are easily lost, so if you have one, insure it and label it. If you live in a care home, this is especially important, but it is also true in other circumstances: your aid might be mislaid and inadvertently mixed with that of another patient during a hospital stay, for example.

Hearing aids need to be cleaned and maintained, so make sure that your NHS audiology department or your private dispenser will carry out any work you cannot manage yourself. If you are moving into a care home, ask whether any members of staff know how to maintain hearing aids and whether hearing specialists such as audiologists from the local hospital make visits to the home. Some audiologists make home visits, but by no means all.

A hearing loop consists of a microphone to pick up speech, for instance from a post-office counter assistant, an amplifier which processes the signal and then sends it through a wire placed around the perimeter of a particular space, such as a service counter or a meeting room. This radiates a magnetic signal into any hearing aid or aids which are switched on to the T or telecoil setting to receive it. Hearing loops not only magnify sounds but they also cut out background noise.

Buying equipment privately

Equipment of the kinds I have described can be bought privately or obtained through the health and social care systems. However, equipment is provided by the state only if the prospective user has a sufficiently serious need for it and thus meets the eligibility criteria all health and social care state organisations use to allocate resources from their limited budgets.

Some people pay for disability equipment (and home adaptations, such as ramps and lifts between floors, to cope with disability) themselves for various reasons. Perhaps the equipment involved is of a type which neither the NHS nor social services normally provides or subsidises – such as electric scooters or boats specially designed or adapted for disabled people. In other cases, a local authority has deemed that somebody's need for equipment is not sufficiently high to meet the threshold for provision in its care needs assessment *(explained in Chapter 26)*. In other cases, a local authority or the health service says it will provide equipment but there is a long delay before it arrives.

Buying at home

Despite the advantages of viewing and trying out equipment in Disabled Living Centres, some people buy disability equipment from salespeople who call on them in their own homes. Doorstep selling certainly has the advantage of convenience for the purchaser, and people who are housebound are often tempted to buy from a door-to-door salesperson. But there are many possible pitfalls.

Door-to-door salespersons can play on the vulnerability of older people who are perhaps unable to get out to the shops or to log on to the internet to compare prices. On their own in their living room with the salesperson, they will lack the advice of an impartial professional occupational therapist on the range the market offers and the suitability of particular items for them. The mobility aid the salesperson seeks to convince them will be invaluable might actually cause back problems or fail to give the stability they need. It might be equipment the salesperson is trying to get rid of or on which they will earn the highest commission.

Complaining about goods which do not work as advertised or in the way that was described and getting a refund or a replacement at a later date can be both difficult and time-consuming. If the mobility scooter for which you have paid hundreds of pounds will not go up kerbs in the way the salesperson told you it would, you may have to spend a lot of time getting a refund or a different model.

If you do nonetheless buy disability equipment from home, plainly you need to be absolutely clear about whether the product is good value, whether you really will use it, whether you can afford it and whether it best suits your needs. On the last point, a reputable seller of disability equipment will carry out an assessment of your needs. But this is unlikely to be as objective and wide-ranging as one you would obtain at a Disabled Living Centre (see page 458).

Here are a few questions you may wish to put to a doorstep salesperson:

✓ Could I have details of at least two previous customers with whom I can discuss the service and the reliability of the goods and your company?

✓ Does the company charge extra for delivery and installation?

✓ Does the price include VAT? (Much disability equipment is exempt for people who need it, as outlined below.)

✓ How can I get the product repaired? Do I have to use an approved supplier of replacement parts?

✓ Are there any possible future trade-ins after the product has outlived its use?

✓ What happens if it breaks down?

✓ How can I contact you again?

✓ Does the contract of sale include a cancellation notice?

A cooling-off period is vital and is provided for by law.[3] Traders selling goods or services worth £35 or more to people in their own homes, their workplaces or in the home of another individual are legally required to give the consumer a written notice of their right to cancel the contract; this notice must be given at the time the contract of sale is made. The cancellation notice must provide for a seven-day cooling-off period, starting from the day the consumer signs the contract. If no cancellation notice is given, then the contract of sale can be seen as not enforceable.

The effect of the cancellation notice provision is that if goods or services cost more than £35, a consumer has seven days to change their mind (for any reason) and cancel the order (this must be in writing), without having to pay anything. This is in addition to the usual rights consumers possess when an item is bought from a shop.

Beware of a salesperson offering you a discount for, say, an electric scooter so long as you sign to allow the contract to come into effect immediately. If you agree, you lose the cooling-off period and cancellation notice facility.

If you cancel, do so by recorded delivery letter.

Citizens Advice provides advice on consumers' rights in the purchase of goods and services at its own centres and also through its Adviceguide service of free leaflets, online information and a consumer helpline (see Useful Contacts). The trading standards departments of local authorities enforce consumers' rights on the ground.

VAT relief

Much disability equipment should be free of charge, as explained below. Thus continence clothing, pads and equipment such as hand-held urinals can be obtained free on the NHS, so long as you are assessed as needing them. Social care authorities also provide many types of disability equipment free to people they assess as needing them. However, delays in assessment may mean you end up buying your own. Or you may have only a relatively minor difficulty so would not qualify for state help. The good news for people buying privately is that there is a long list of types of disability equipment for which the purchaser should not be charged any VAT. In some cases, such as a yacht designed or adapted for someone in a wheelchair, this relief can be worth a lot of money.

The VAT rules (promulgated by H M Revenue and Customs) state that equipment designed exclusively for disabled people should be zero-rated for VAT purposes. This includes wheelchairs, textphones, long-handled pick-up sticks and vibrating pillows to alert deaf people of danger. The exemption does not apply to equipment which may be used by disabled people but is not specifically designed for them, such as reclining armchairs or air-conditioner units. But if you go into a shop or buy equipment over the internet or by mail order that a manufacturer has designed for disabled people, you should not have to pay any VAT on it.

Although this exemption applies to continence equipment and clothing, you will have to sign to confirm that the products are for your own personal use if you buy more than 200 disposable continence pads, ten pairs of leak-proof underwear, five collecting devices or 50 washable pads.

The VAT rules also say that a wide range of products and home adaptations can be zero-rated so long as they are sold to an eligible customer. Anybody who has a physical or mental impairment which has a long-term and substantial adverse effect on their ability to carry out everyday activities, or have a condition which the medical profession treats as a chronic illness, such as diabetes, or are terminally ill, qualifies for this relief. The item has to be bought or the adaptation to existing equipment or building made for the personal use of such a person (in other words, it does not apply to a business such as a nursing home).

To obtain the relief, you should ask the supplier for a form which you complete, declaring that you are chronically sick or have a disabling condition and giving a description of that illness or condition. The types of disability equipment covered include wheelchairs, chair lifts, stairlifts, adjustable beds, hoists, commodes, support devices around lavatories, low-vision aids, boats, alarms which enable somebody to call for help in case of illness or injury, lifts between different floors of a private residence, ramps and the widening of doorways. Services to adapt or install equipment or some other device are also exempt, as are repair and maintenance.[4]

Obtaining equipment through the state

A basic principle of the NHS is that health services and health equipment are free to those who need them (*see page 280*). Hoists, adjustable beds, pressure-relieving mattresses and feeding tubes, for instance, are all items of medical or nursing equipment which you should expect to obtain free on the NHS through your GP or hospital doctor and often with the advice of a physiotherapist. (Large equipment is likely to be loaned rather than given.)

The NHS also provides free mobility equipment such as wheelchairs, rollators, crutches, Zimmers and walking sticks. What it will not provide for free is electrically powered scooters or motor cars.

Hearing aids and batteries are free on the NHS *(as explained on page 475)*. However, spectacles are not: only if you are receiving the following means-tested benefits are you eligible for a voucher towards the cost of your glasses or contact lenses – the Guarantee element of Pension Credit, Income Support, Income-based Jobseeker's Allowance or Income-related Employment and Support Allowance.

Unlike equipment provided by the NHS, that provided through the social care system is not automatically free. However, the government has told social care authorities that the equipment they provide should be free in certain circumstances to everybody, whatever their financial means. Thus social services departments in England must provide equipment free of charge, whatever its cost, to everybody whom they assess as needing it to cope with frailty or disability.[5] Furthermore, the Department of Health has told councils that people assessed as needing adaptations to their homes to cope with disability or frailty should also receive these free, so long as they do not cost more than £1,000.[6]

How do councils decide whether somebody needs equipment and so should receive it for free? They do so as part of a care needs assessment, which takes a holistic view of someone's needs for care and support arising out of illness or disability. *(I describe this process in Chapter 26: Social care assessments.)* Councils must all work within eligibility criteria which provide a safety net to ensure that anyone who has reached a certain threshold of difficulty will receive help, and some councils offer help to people below their threshold. However, you may face delays in getting equipment through social services. There may be a delay in being given the assessment and/or a delay before the equipment actually arrives.

Assessment by local councils for gadgets, except the most rudimentary, usually involves an appraisal of the level of need and of the type of equipment which can best meet that need by one of the local authority's own occupational therapists (OTs). These people are highly trained but spread pretty thinly in most areas, with the result that it is by no means unusual to wait several months for their assessment.

In these circumstances, what can you do? Well, you could commission and pay for your own assessment. A local council would hesitate to disagree with such recommendations unless it could produce its own professional OT to question them, which it would of course be hard pressed to do. Check with your local council what their response would be before you go ahead. You can find the names of fully qualified and registered OTs who work privately from the College of Occupational Therapists *(see Useful Contacts).*

Sometimes a council says it will provide equipment, but a long wait will be involved. If this is the case, you should consider seeking the help of your local councillor and/or MP to hurry things along, lodging an official complaint with the health or social care authority in question and even building a campaign through the media if necessary.

Charging

If councils in England charge someone for equipment, they must do so within tightly defined government rules *(described on pages 654–64).* Although equipment that someone is assessed as needing must be free, councils have the discretion to charge to service equipment; that charging too must be in line with these rules.

Inevitably, users and social services departments sometimes disagree about whether their need is sufficiently great to qualify for equipment. They may also disagree on the proportion of any costs a council proposes to charge them. *(I discuss how to challenge social services' decisions on charging on pages 664 and 573–9.)*

Outside England, the situation is broadly similar. However, in Scotland, there are certain key differences. 'Free personal care', which older people enjoy north of the border, includes equipment as well as services and those assessed as needing personal care receive it free, whatever their income. However, by no means all helpful gadgets are included: the legislation defining 'free personal care' mentions only 'devices to help memory' and 'safety devices' and does not explain precisely what these might be.[7] *(Free personal care is examined in more detail on page 587.)*

If equipment does not fall within these categories, a local authority in Scotland may charge for it; again, any charging must conform to national rules.[8] There is a useful blanket exemption: Scottish local authorities are expected to provide equipment free to frail older people leaving hospital. The Scottish Executive has told local councils that they should not charge frail older people for equipment and minor house adaptations arranged through social services if these are supplied and fitted within four weeks after or immediately before hospital discharge.[9]

Types of equipment that involve adaptations to the home such as stairlifts and ramps are covered by a different form of funding – Disabled Facilities Grants *(see pages 186–8).*

Inclusive design

Of course most of us use items in our everyday lives which are not specifically designed for people with particular disabilities. Inclusive – sometimes called accessible – design differs from the equipment we have considered up till now (in other words, items especially for people with disabilities) and involves making equipment easy to use for as wide a range of people as possible. Some manufacturers – by no means all! – have been focusing the design of their products increasingly on older consumers, who are often not as agile or dexterous or readily able to read small print as younger people.

Fortunately, the British Standards Institute has drawn up a standard on inclusive design.[10] Products which comply with this standard have been designed to be useable by most people, with clearly written instructions, considered use of colour (such as black against yellow, which is most easily visible by people with vision impairment) and fail-safe design (so if the product is used or assembled incorrectly, it will fail without posing a hazard to the user). Look for items bearing this standard.

The British Standards Institute does not enforce its standards, but they are often used by trading standards officials. Also, it is an offence to claim conformity to a standard when in fact this is untrue, so firms can be taken to court by individual consumers as well as organisations if they are suspected of doing this.

Bespoke devices

If you cannot find the equipment you need, you may be able to find a supplier who provides bespoke equipment. Such suppliers do exist up and down the country, sometimes involving volunteers using skills developed in the world of engineering earlier in their lives. Ask at your local Disabled Living Centre or the social work or occupational therapy department of your local authority.

Adjusting to life with disability equipment

Perhaps you have gone to great lengths to obtain gadgets for an older relative or friend, only to find them rejected. It is easy to forget that actually using these things often requires considerable psychological adjustment. You may imagine that your father would be delighted to be taken out in a wheelchair; he may find the prospect very upsetting. He may feel frightened, frustrated and helpless, and think everybody will be staring at him. It may help to wheel him in an area in which he is not known until he gets used to the chair. Even pushing a walker can seem to be taking a person out of mainstream society and into a victim class which they do not wish to inhabit.

To make matters worse, many conditions, and therefore the equipment that can help people deal with them, attract a stigma. Unlike sight loss, hearing loss for instance is stigmatised, perhaps because it is more closely associated with old age. Sometimes it is confused with mental frailty. So, unlike glasses, hearing equipment that helps may be rejected by those who need it.

This is by no means true of everybody. Many people are fiercely assertive and point to the social model of disability, which says that disability is caused by the way society is organised, rather than by a person's impairment or difference. In other words, the onus is on society to remove barriers that restrict the life choices for disabled people, whether physical or psychological.

But others, probably at present the majority of older people with disabilities, do not fall into this camp. This second group need sensitive support to encourage them to use disability equipment. Partners, friends and relatives should try to lighten up in their approach, so that these gadgets are not viewed with dismal seriousness, as is so often the case. Equipment whose design is infused with an element of dash and glamour may prove more acceptable than more obviously practical models. Also, any opportunities to customise the equipment so that users can stamp their own individuality on it may enhance its acceptability.

It is also important to be sensitive to the placing of equipment in the home. Wheelchairs, alarm systems, commodes and so on can seem to invade a person's home, eroding their sense of privacy and autonomy over individual space and providing an ever-present reminder of dependence and infirmity.

Equipment

* The range of equipment for people with disabilities is unexpectedly vast.

* Disabled Living Centres are the best places to view it and to get impartial advice.

* Expect to receive much equipment free through the NHS or social services, if you are assessed as needing it.

* If the NHS or social services drag their heels over providing equipment, make an official complaint and contact your councillor and/or MP.

* If you buy complex or expensive disability equipment privately, get professional advice from an occupational therapist on what would best suit you.

* Make sure you are not charged VAT on any equipment or clothing for disability, including continence pads.

* Attendance Allowance is a state benefit for rich and poor and helps cover the costs that disability can bring.

* Family and friends should be sensitive to the psychological barriers around the use of disability equipment.

Chapter 22

Telecare

S ince the turn of the century a new type of technology has been developing in many exciting directions. Known as 'telecare', it uses sensors to alert others if a person is facing some kind of danger. It can thus be an invaluable means of enabling all of us, but especially frail and disabled people, to live safely. It can also provide reassurance to relatives living some distance away that a loved one is less likely to come to harm.

A woman of whom I heard lived in a remote location in the Lake District. Her greatest joy was to play her grand piano and enjoy the views over the fells. However, she was prone to leaving the gas on or the front door open by mistake. Safety devices were installed in her home which alerted a control room should she do so, which in turn would alert two nearby contacts prepared to help in an emergency. As result, she was able to live for another two years in her own home; without these safety measures, she would probably have moved earlier to a care home.

There is no very clear definition of 'telecare', but, unlike the equipment explored in the previous chapter, the term tends to be used for devices, systems or services that use information or telecommunication technology to support somebody.

Telecare includes equipment with which we are familiar, such as an ordinary landline telephone or a computer and variations of both. Skyping, for example, involves talking to somebody in real time through a microphone built into a computer; you can see as well as hear the person with whom you are conversing, so this could be used by, say, a son to check more effectively than through a phone call that his mother was OK.

Here are a few devices with which you may be less familiar.

Pendant or community alarms

One of the first types of telecare device to become widely known was the pendant alarm, sometimes called a community alarm. This is worn round the neck or on the wrist. If the wearer needs urgent assistance, perhaps because they have fallen over and cannot get up or are unable to get themselves out of the bath, they press a large red button on the device. This sends a wireless signal to a 'home unit', a box in their home which is linked to their landline telephone system and which looks like a standard phone or modem unit. Through this, an alarm automatically goes through to a call centre; an operator then speaks to the user through the home unit, to find out why they pressed the button. The home unit acts as a loud, hands-off, two-way phone, reaching the user anywhere in their house or garden, so long as the distances are not too great.

Sometimes people press the button by mistake. In that case, they simply explain this to the operator when they call them. But if the operator contacts someone who has pressed their alarm but receives no response through the home unit or if they consider that the person who pressed the button needs help, they ring prearranged numbers. These are those of relatives, friends or professionals such as care assistants living nearby who have agreed to help out in this situation and have been given door keys or lock codes to gain entry. Some call centres offer their own 'rapid response service', in which case control-room staff make an immediate visit; one such service is described in the case-study box below. Or the operator may summon the emergency services themselves.

If you have a pendant alarm, it is important to have it with you all the time when you are on your own property, in the garden as well as in the house, including the bathroom. Many people have falls going to the bathroom during the night and cannot summon help because they have left their alarm by the side of the bed. Whenever you get out of bed you should put your alarm round your neck and take it off only when you get into bed or into the bath. When you do so, place it close by.

It is the pendant alarm's portability and ease of use that give it the edge over possible alternatives. A pendant alarm really can save your life. An acquaintance of mine moved into a glorious flat in the centre of a quiet, leafy country town, having looked forward for years to escaping from noisy, busy south London. In her new flat, she said that she would think about obtaining an alarm should she start having falls. But, one night, only a few months after moving in, she did fall, not near her phone but in her bathroom. When she was discovered there the following day, it was too late. Had she been able to summon help from the bathroom, she would probably have survived to enjoy many years in her much-loved new surroundings.

A variation of the pendant alarm provides two additional buttons which can be pre-programmed to call particular people direct, in addition to the button which alerts a call centre. The user can have a two-way conversation in each case.

You can obtain a community alarm independently or through social services. Your social services department should be able to give you details of providers in your area, whether councils, private companies or voluntary organisations.

If you are obtaining an alarm independently, it is worth shopping around, as prices vary greatly. You should be able to rent the equipment or buy it. There should be the option of an ongoing maintenance service contract too. If the equipment is linked to operators in a call centre, you will have also to pay an ongoing charge for their services. This in itself will vary according to what the centre does. The charity Rica (Research Institute for Consumer Affairs, formerly Ricability) publishes information to help people choose equipment such as community alarms.

Retirement housing schemes often have alarms involving the pulling of a cord in an emergency. However, these suffer from the drawback that you may not be near the cord when you wish to summon help and have to crawl over the floor to try to reach it (see page 128). A pendant alarm is therefore a safer option.

Response services

As noted above, some response services do no more than contact pre-agreed phone numbers or the emergency services, but others have their own team of people ready to go out and help. What might the latter type of response service provide?

CASE STUDY

Riverside Careline operates in Carlisle and parts of north Cumbria. If one of its clients lives outside a 12-mile radius of the organisation's base in Carlisle, the call centre will contact only nominated friends, relatives, volunteers, professionals, or the emergency services if a client is in trouble. But within a 12-mile radius of the control room, Riverside Careline will respond with its own 'rapid response service', if required. In other words, staff answer the phone but are ready to respond with a home visit if necessary. They have received training in, amongst other things, first aid and manual handling. This means that when they arrive they won't simply confine their help to summoning other people but will, if necessary, offer first aid or help someone to their feet after a fall. They are prepared to perform practical tasks too. If there has been a small fire, there may be clearing up to be done. If a flood detector *(see below)* has found water on the kitchen floor because a tap has been left on, a follow-up visit can include mopping up.

Riverside Careline will also do what they can to help a client feel safe and confident after an incident. For instance, if a smoke alarm sounds, a speech path is immediately opened up with the client so that the control-room operator can ask whether they are all right. If there is no answer, the call centre will contact the fire service. If the client replies that there was a fire but it is now under control, the call centre will alert the person's named contacts and suggest that they go and check that everything is OK. Or Careline staff will make a visit themselves.

Clients can also contact Riverside Careline if they need reassurance. An operator may talk them through getting into bed, for instance. Somebody with dementia may worry about the arrival of their meals-on-wheels or be unable to remember whether a meal has been delivered that day and make frequent calls to Riverside Careline. It will respond to such enquiries with empathy and understanding – and certainly not treat them as a nuisance.[1]

Response services vary in price, partly according to the level of help you can expect from them. It is worth shopping around. You can find lists of all the services that have been accredited by the Telecare Services Association. This is an organisation whose members provide telecare. It accredits those which meet certain standards. Riverside Careline is one of the few services that has been awarded premium membership of the association because it has achieved high standards.

Any call centre that is going to provide a response over and above alerting named contacts should keep such information about each client as:

● their name and address

● how they prefer to be addressed

● the names and visiting times of any care assistants

- the name and contact details of their GP and close family members
- the contact details of people who have agreed to respond in an emergency
- the types of sensor installed
- how any rapid response team is to gain access to the property and
- any relevant medical information.

The centre will also hold a calls and alarms history, so that if somebody regularly has a fall at a certain time in the morning, they might suggest that a care worker should call earlier.

Whichever response system you choose, check that:

✓ the organisation has sufficient operators to cover at night

✓ the operators are well trained and so able to offer advice in the event of an emergency

✓ if the call centre does not offer its own rapid response service, the operator stays on the line to reassure the caller until help arrives

✓ the equipment will be mended or replaced immediately if it goes wrong or is damaged

✓ the equipment is maintained frequently

Community alarms are enormously valuable. It is important not to wait until you have had a fall before you get one. You may never need to use it, but it could save your life.

Falls detectors

A falls detector resembles a community alarm in that it sends a signal to a call centre via a home unit. However, in this case the wearer does not need to activate it – the device is worn on an elastic belt and any sudden movement at an acute angle triggers its detector, which transmits an alarm signal to the home unit. At the call centre, the operator opens up a two-way speech facility so that they can speak to the user and assess whether help is needed and who should provide it. Sidestepping the need for the person who has fallen to raise the alarm can be important, as they might be concussed or too shocked to press a button. However, a falls alarm also has a button which its wearer can use to summon help.

If you are obtaining a falls detector, find out what happens if you drop the alarm or if you fall gradually, perhaps sliding to the floor. Would dropping the detector cause false alarms that you would find difficult to handle? Make sure the setting is adjusted to suit your size and shape and likely pattern of falls.

Home sensors

Most of us are familiar with smoke alarms, but a home unit can be set up so that several other sensor devices feed into it. Sensors that detect and respond to abnormally high levels of smoke, natural gas, carbon monoxide or water on the floor would send an alert to a call centre without the need for the user to raise the alarm. So would sensors registering a very low temperature – resulting perhaps from someone failing to turn on their heating or leaving a door open – or a very high temperature, perhaps the result of a cooker being left on.

The response could not only alert the person in the property involved but other people too. Devices that detect carbon monoxide or natural gas will normally activate gas shut-off valves as well as sound the alarm.

If in addition to signals passed through the home unit, the response would also involve the emission of a loud warning sound, consider:

✓ What would it sound like? Would you be able to hear it? If you are hard of hearing, could you have a non-audio alarm – a flashing light perhaps?

✓ Sound alarms can scare us when they go off. Would the sound worry you? If so, ask whether a different sound or one set at a lower volume could be provided. Failing that, ask for a different means of alerting you.

✓ How sensitive is the alarm? Environment sensors can be very sensitive. A low level of smoke at the cooker or a small amount of fluid on the kitchen floor may be sufficient to set off an alert. Make sure you know what to expect and that you can confidently turn off the alarm sound when it is triggered.

✓ If the system is for somebody with dementia, would they be disorientated or distressed by the sound of the alarm?

Remote-control operators

Telecare environment controls are not confined to responding to danger – they can also involve the remote control of equipment around the home. You can turn your heating up or down, open or close your curtains, doors or windows as well as switch your television or DVD player on or off remotely from a single unit.

Reminder devices

It is easy to forget to take tablets on time or to get muddled if you have to take several different types. As noted in the previous chapter, you can obtain small plastic, compartmented containers labelled with times and dates that you or your pharmacist fills with tablets beforehand. If you are likely to forget to take these, however, you might find it useful to have a device which sounds at pre-set times to prompt you to take your tablets. Some medication reminders are incorporated into a wristwatch.

Another category of reminder device is aimed at people, mainly in the early stages of dementia, who might leave the house, wander off and get lost. If they are going down their hall, a movement detector triggers a pre-recorded message reminding them to take their keys. Other reminders could involve telling them to do things at particular times of day, such as to get dressed or have their breakfast.

Night-time detectors

A useful device detects through sensors under the mattress that some-body has got out of bed. Once triggered, it causes lights to be switched on, illuminating the route to the bathroom. Another signal turns them off when the person returns to bed. The pre-programming takes into account the fact that one user may take five minutes to visit the bathroom during the night while another, with mobility difficulties, may take 15.

Many of these devices can be invaluable to carers living on-site. A son, for instance, might worry that his mother is getting out of bed, wander-ing around and falling over while he is asleep. A detector in her bedroom could alert him to her movements, perhaps through a 'pillow buzzer', a vibrating device placed under a pillow, so he could know when she is getting out of bed and then listen for the sound of her returning to bed.

This equipment can be programmed so that an alarm goes through to a call centre if the person involved fails to return to bed within a specified time. If that happens, the operator will ring and ask whether they are all right. Are they unwell? Have they fallen over? Or have they simply gone to the bathroom and then downstairs to watch television?

Sensor pads can also be placed on chairs. They tend not to be placed under mats, say by the side of beds, lest they pose a trip hazard.

Front-door devices

Devices are also available that can open the front door remotely, protect against unwanted intruders, or send an alert if somebody is out of their house for longer than a pre-set period.

Perhaps you want to be able to let callers into your house or flat without going to the front door. An intercom system that can unlock the door remotely can be invaluable. A variation is ideal for people in wheelchairs: it opens the door, then closes and locks it after a pre-set interval. You can even obtain a door entry device which can be used outside the home, perhaps by a family member.

If protection is required, various 'bogus entry systems' are available in addition to the ordinary button on a community alarm or the intruder button that comes with a burglar alarm. One involves somebody pressing a button when they open their front door so the call centre of the community alarm can hear and record what is going on and, if necessary, send somebody round. A miscreant would hear a voice coming from the home unit saying, 'Mrs Jones, we've heard this and we're on our way', and would, one hopes, take flight.

If a person is prone to wandering off, perhaps because of dementia, sensors on the front and back doors can alert a call centre to the fact that they have been out for longer than a certain time. Again, the signal would go through to a call centre and the information be relayed to, say, a family carer through their mobile phone.

If somebody else were living in the house, these sensors would be disabled or modified accordingly.

Door sensors could also record the length of time other people had been in the dwelling, such as, say, visiting care workers, who would have a particular PIN number to type in when entering and leaving so as not to set off the alarm in the call centre.

Person locators and tracking devices

A person locator is a means of summoning help outdoors. You wear this small device or keep it in your pocket and if you press a button on it, pre-arranged contacts are alerted. You do not have to say where you are because the device pinpoints your location through a satellite tracking system or GPS. So if, say, you have a fall in the street, you could press the button and immediately alert your daughter. She would then call you on the locator and, armed with your location, tell you she is coming to help. If you do not respond, she could come anyway.

A person locator can also be used to summon help inside a building, but in this case the satellite signals needed to locate the wearer will not enable the person called to track where they are.

Support for people with dementia

Many of the types of equipment already described could be helpful for people with dementia. A device that automatically cuts off the supply of water should a bath tap be left running could be very useful, as could a sensor that detects that someone has got out of bed at night and remained out for an uncharacteristically long time.

It is very important, however, that alarms do not worry or disorientate a person with dementia. If they are preparing to leave the house and a disembodied yet perhaps familiar voice tells them to remember their keys, or even not to go out at all, they might wonder what is happening. Where is the person? In this case, a better response would be a call from the control room.

Sometimes people with dementia forget to have meals or look after themselves in other ways. One means of addressing this is to use monitoring equipment to check what they are doing. An infra-red sensor similar to a burglar alarm sensor could be placed in the corner of the ceiling of a downstairs room to register whether somebody was moving around there – or not, which might indicate that they were unwell or wandering outside. It could be programmed to alert the call centre to contact the user if they had not appeared by a certain time in the morning.

Devices that can locate somebody out of doors can be invaluable for people with dementia who wander away and get lost, or, when they are out, forget about a rendezvous.

Both person locators and GPS systems on mobile phones can locate somebody out of doors. An app on an iPhone, for example, registers that you want the phone to track a certain person and orders it to locate their phone. The spot that appears on your screen enables you to find them.

Both person locators and GPS apps on mobile phones can have a 'geofence' incorporated into them. If somebody strays outside this fence, the device they are wearing or holding can generate an automatic call to a carer or monitoring centre. The zone can vary from around 250 yards (229 metres) to several miles and be adjusted in the light of circumstances.

Privacy and ethical issues

Safety has to be balanced, however, against the intrusion some of these devices bring with them. Some people would find them unpalatable.

It is important to be aware that there are serious ethical issues in introducing surveillance into somebody's life through devices that allow other people to track them and even observe what they are doing if they have not been able to give consent to the monitoring themselves. If, perhaps as an attorney, you are planning to install monitoring equipment for someone who has dementia or another brain disorder that is sufficiently serious to mean they lack the mental capacity to decide whether they should accept this equipment, you should authorise its installation only once you have involved the person in question as fully as possible in the decision, decided that the equipment proposed would be in their best interests and established that it would be the least restrictive means of ensuring their safety. *(The way in which decisions should be taken is explained in Chapter 33.)* If social services sanctions the monitoring equipment, it must first go through a special process of authorisation designed to safeguard the interests of the person who lacks mental capacity called the deprivation of liberty safeguards *(I discuss the use of secret monitoring equipment on pages 547–8.)*

Viewing equipment

You can see telecare equipment at Disabled Living Centres *(see page 458)*. There are also some demonstration 'smart homes' with equipment in place; your social services department ought to be able to tell you about any display facility in your area.

Voluntary organisations and centres of excellence such as the Royal National Institute of Blind People and the Dementia Services Development Centre (DSDC) at Stirling University hold information about new equipment. The DSDC publishes free guides on its website about telecare equipment for people with sensory impairment, learning disabilities, mental health problems and physical disabilities as well as dementia, and also on how telecare equipment can help to prevent falls.

Obtaining equipment

Buying telecare equipment is unlike buying an electric kettle. Most of us are completely unfamiliar with this type of gadgetry, so it is important to try out a wide range of equipment and to be able to address questions to people who are both knowledgeable and without a pecuniary interest in a sale. The equipment has to suit your needs and your situation. Some devices will help you, others will not. You need to feel confident that anything you obtain can be easily integrated into your everyday life. Also, it is crucially important that the equipment is installed correctly, maintained and repaired, and adjusted or replaced if the nature of the risks you face changes.

The social services departments of local authorities usually have experts in telecare to hand. They also fund or part-fund this equipment *(as outlined on page 481),* but you may not be eligible for funding. Whether you are or not, do contact your local social services department and request a telecare assessment. Ask for a social worker and an assessor working for an accredited company to carry out a detailed assessment of the risks and the way they might be managed within your home. (A telecare assessment might also be carried out after a more wide-ranging social assessment, as described in Chapter 26.)

A telecare assessment needs first to establish whether telecare really could help reduce the risks you face. After all, telecare does not offer a fail-safe solution and if, say, you are developing dementia, you might be safer and generally better looked after in a care home. If telecare could help, the professionals need to work out precisely how the risks could be managed, which equipment should be installed and how it should be programmed. Then they need to obtain information to advise the control room on how best to respond. They should make follow-up visits to ensure you can handle the equipment and also to review whether it is helping you, whether its programming should be tweaked, and whether changing circumstances call for a different response.

If telecare is recommended, do:

✓ investigate the range of equipment available and shop around – equipment and response systems vary in price

✓ establish what kind of equipment would work for you, now or in the future

✓ work out what type of equipment would best suit any carer you may have, now and in the future

✓ make sure the equipment is correctly installed, so that the sensors are appropriate for your situation and are programmed correctly

✓ ensure that the equipment will be regularly tested and maintained and can be mended swiftly, for instance if a child should inadvertently damage it

✓ ensure that there is provision for back-up if, say, mobile phone signals, internet or landline access should fail

✓ make sure you and at least one member of your family receive all the training you need in how to work the equipment. You and at least one other person should be sufficiently confident with the technology to tell if it is malfunctioning.

Look for a supplier with Telecare Services Association accreditation. If you go to the TSA's website *(see Useful Contacts)* you can find lists of suppliers with accreditation in different parts of the country. For instance, Fold is the leading and an accredited provider of telecare and telehealth devices in Ireland. If your service does not come up to scratch, contact the TSA and it should seek to resolve the matter with any supplier it has accredited. Contact your social services department if you encounter problems with equipment it has authorised.

Telehealth

Telecommunications technology is also increasingly being used in the world of healthcare. Monitors can track weight, blood pressure, heart rate and blood sugar, for instance, and the results be sent to a doctor using a secure website. The doctor logs on, examines the results and responds if there is cause for concern, perhaps by phone or Skype.

Telehealth can be invaluable in helping people manage long-term medical conditions such as diabetes or heart failure. It may enable them to return home from hospital earlier than they otherwise would have. Equally importantly, telehealth monitors can prevent emergency admission to hospital. They can also be useful for people who are receiving palliative or end-of-life care in their own home.

None of these devices should be an excuse for failing to give someone face-to-face attention. Telehealth is not a substitute for human help: the two approaches should complement each other.

Talk to your GP if you think telehealth might help you. Pharmacists are already involved in the prevention of disease and in helping people to manage long-term conditions such as high blood pressure, and it seems likely that they will do this through telehealth equipment to a greater extent in the future.

Some telehealth devices are already available over the counter. You can obtain a health monitoring device and a prompt to take medication as apps to download onto a mobile phone.

All iPhones come pre-fitted with a health app, which allows you to track the number of steps you have taken each day and to upgrade for more in-depth fitness tracking. It is worth keeping abreast of developments in this fast-moving sphere. It is easy to foresee a time when health and fitness software becomes more sophisticated, especially when smartphones are superseded by devices worn on the body, such as the Apple watch.

Telecare

* Obtaining telecare equipment involves considering what would work for you. Ideally, get advice from an occupational therapist who visits you at home.

* A community alarm or a falls detector could save your life.

* Take any help alarm with you when you go to the bathroom during the night.

* A person locator can enable you to summon help out of doors and for others to work out where you are.

* Think about how you will be alerted if you have flood and other detectors in your home – you don't want the sound to worry you.

* Flashing light devices can alert you if you are hard of hearing.

* Disabled Living Centres display the range of telecare equipment available.

* Social services departments have expertise in telecare and may contribute towards its cost.

* Monitoring equipment can be intrusive: tread carefully lest you infringe privacy unnecessarily, particularly the privacy of someone with dementia.

* Telecare equipment should complement, not replace, human contact.

Chapter 23

Human help

As you get older, help from equipment, no matter how sophisticated, is often not quite enough. If you need human assistance in the home and cannot or do not wish to obtain it from friends, family, volunteers or neighbours, paid help may be the answer.

If you decide to look for domestic support, the sooner you get the wheels turning, the better. This is because accepting the help of strangers often requires considerable psychological adjustment. If you have long been used to doing everything yourself, the idea of strangers in the house can seem unsettling, especially when you feel frail and anxious about what the future holds. Using paid help early on gets you accustomed to this state of affairs before the tasks involved become too intimate.

There are other reasons for finding paid help. Without it, you can easily find life dominated by the challenge of the day-to-day. Things which once made life enjoyable, such as getting out and seeing friends, may be squeezed out. There is also the danger of becoming over-reliant on one person, such as your partner, son or daughter. If they should suddenly fall ill, a crisis could occur. It is always easier to have adjusted to having paid help and to know to whom you could turn in an emergency before events force you into action.

Help can be hired for a couple of hours a week or 24 hours a day; it can be hired privately or arranged by a local authority social services department (social work department in Scotland; health and social care trust in Northern Ireland).

This chapter is written for people who will operate independently of social services. It is nonetheless also relevant to people who will have some contact with social services but otherwise organise their own care through a direct payment. In this case, social services pay all or part of the cost of the care but the recipient chooses how that care will be delivered *(as explained in Chapter 28)*.

The first question that usually confronts anybody contemplating hiring staff to help them in their home is whether to do so on a one-to-one basis or enter into a contract with an agency that provides helpers.

In this chapter I examine:

▶ obtaining staff through a homecare agency as opposed to hiring helpers direct

▶ how to choose and work with a homecare agency

▶ how to hire staff direct

▶ what to expect staff to do

▶ paying for homecare

This chapter is confined to hiring staff who come into your home for particular periods during the day or night. Live-in care is explored in the following chapter.

Homecare agency or individual personal assistant? Pros and cons

Homecare agencies (often called domiciliary care agencies) are organisations which have people on their books (often called care assistants) whom they send into the homes of clients to carry out a range of tasks. Typically these tasks could be help with housework, ironing, gardening, paperwork, driving, shopping, paying bills and personal care. The latter means help with washing, bathing, dressing, mouth care, eating, drinking, using the toilet, managing continence, and the care of skin, hair and nails. If someone is physically capable of engaging in these activities but unable to understand that they should, personal care involves prompting and supervising them.[1]

The agency (sometimes called a domiciliary care agency) will organise its care assistants, sending either the same ones most of the time to a particular client, or many different workers. The agency will pay them and take on the other legal responsibilities of being an employer, such as dealing with tax, National Insurance and holiday pay.

The vast majority of homecare agencies are private, commercial companies run to make a profit. Some voluntary groups such as the Red Cross and local Age UK organisations offer the same service, also for a fee, but they are far fewer on the ground. A few local authorities have their own teams of homecare workers, but if you want to use these you will have to be assessed by the council: their homecare services cannot be bought privately.

A homecare agency will take a cut of the money it charges you. The proportion varies, but it might mean that up to a half of the hourly fee you are paying goes to fund the agency's administration overheads and profits, leaving the remainder for the care assistant. If you need help over several years you will obviously end up paying the care agency a great deal, so you need to be sure you are getting more for your money than you would if you hired a worker or workers yourself.

The alternative to using a homecare agency is to select and hire your own individual helper yourself – to commission them direct to do whatever tasks you wish, whenever you want them done. People who work as care or personal assistants in this way have often previously worked for care agencies but have quit in order to have more control over their working conditions and their clients and to earn more money. They may work as a personal assistant for several clients within a small locality.

Both approaches have advantages and drawbacks. These include:

Bang for your buck

If you hire staff direct, you will get more help for your money. Without the agency's cut to fund its own costs and profits, you will have more money with which to pay staff direct. You could use the extra cash to attract higher-quality staff and to pay for more hours of help.

Choice of helper

If you recruit your own staff, you are in a position to select somebody you consider will be competent and reliable, understand your needs and treat you with respect.

If you go through an agency, it will decide which helpers to send you. This could mean that you get the same workers frequently, but it could mean that many different people come through your door every week.

Timing of visits

A personal assistant will know that you may dismiss them if they fail to turn up on time consistently and with no good reason. At the outset, you will have discussed at what time or times they will arrive and for how long they will work.

If you go through an agency, it will slot you in at a time when it has workers available. Most people who want an early visit would like a helper at 8am and those who want a lunch-time visit would like somebody to appear about 1pm. But the agency might say it cannot give you an early morning visit before 10am and that your lunchtime visit is slotted in after 2pm. To satisfy more clients in this way, agencies have to hire more staff, but they may not wish to do this, so it can be more difficult to secure the time slot you want with an agency than with an assistant you hire yourself.

Choice of tasks

If you go through an agency, a manager from the agency will come and talk to you beforehand about the tasks with which you would like help. When you agree a list, these will be written down in your 'service user's plan'. You may well find that an agency is rigid about what it will and will not do. Thus an agency providing personal care may say its workers never do housework. If you hire staff direct, you can of course ask them to do whatever you like – housework, help with personal care, cooking, driving, help with paperwork and so on.

Flexibility

An agency is likely to expect the same tasks to be performed on each occasion. This is inevitable: if different helpers are coming, they need a clear list of tasks to work through and will not have time to respond to a variety of requests.

With your own personal assistant, on the other hand, you could aim to follow the same pattern at every visit, or to vary week by week within agreed limits. You could ask your assistant to do whatever calls for attention, from sewing on buttons or helping to clear out a cupboard to taking you to appointments or helping you to have a bath.

Hiring help direct yourself also allows you to bring flexibility into pay rates. For example, you could offer a lower hourly rate for less skilled tasks such as walking your dog but a higher rate for, say, helping with paperwork or driving and accompanying you somewhere.

You are also likely to find it easier to vary the time your personal assistant works for you than you would with an agency. This might be important if a relative often stays and can do some of the tasks that your assistant would otherwise perform. Of course, you will need your personal assistant's agreement to such variation, and you might find that they need to be sure of a guaranteed number of hours of work from you each week and only within certain time limits. Agencies, however, tend to have strict policies in place on the cancellation of visits – in other words, you still have to pay for the visits unless you cancel well in advance. You should agree a minimum cancellation period with a personal assistant too, but they might be more flexible than an agency.

Availability of staff

One major advantage of using a homecare agency is that it should be able to provide staff whenever they are needed. If you rely on your own personal assistant and they are sick or on holiday, you may find yourself in difficulties, particularly if that sickness is unexpected. In contrast, a contract with a homecare agency will require the agency to provide staff at the times agreed, regardless of illness or holidays.

Some people who hire staff themselves get round this by loosely teaming up with others so that personal assistants can fill in when others are unavailable. Or the personal assistants themselves may know of others working in a similar capacity in the locality who would be prepared to cover. Or you could hire help from an agency to fill in if and when needed.

Administration

Perhaps the greatest drawback and most daunting aspect of hiring staff yourself is the responsibility you take on as an employer, involving income tax and National Insurance payments, among other things. Tax and National Insurance will not be your responsibility if your assistant is self-employed, of course, but you will need to check that they really can claim that status *(see page 530)*.

Familiarity and consistency

If you go through an agency, you may (or may not) be able to influence the selection of the helpers it sends you *(see page 511)*. Each agency assistant arriving for the first time (and perhaps on other occasions) will have to familiarise themselves with the nature of the help you require and the layout of your property. Of course, if you hire a personal assistant, you will have to explain what you would like them to do, where everything is kept and your likes and dislikes, but this should be necessary on only one or two occasions. If you are hard of hearing or partially sighted, briefing many different care assistants who turn up on your doorstep can be quite a headache, not to say time-consuming and costly.

With one helper, you should enjoy a consistent service. As a result you can begin to forget about day-to-day tasks and devote more of your energy to less mundane matters.

Perhaps you do not need care yourself but are arranging it for somebody with dementia, as their attorney. If so, you will almost certainly find care provided by the same person or a small number of people better than care from many different helpers. For one thing, the person with dementia may have difficulty in explaining what needs to be done and how, and where everything is kept. A regular helper should also be able to develop an understanding of your loved one – their daily pattern of behaviour, any mood swings and what they are trying to say if they have difficulty in articulating their views and preferences. What is more, the helper should be able to build up experience of dealing with the other professionals involved.

The protection of human rights

Any domiciliary care agency that provides personal care wholly or partly funded by a local authority or arranged by a local authority must respect its clients' human rights as set down in the European Convention on Human Rights *(see page 295)*. If an agency worker subjects someone to, say, discriminatory behaviour or degrading treatment or infringes their right to a private life thereby causing them harm, they can be sued and made to pay compensation. This provision in law, which applies throughout the UK and was enacted in 2014,[2] should mean that care agencies take steps to ensure that the human rights of their clients are understood by care assistants and upheld. It does not apply to assistants hired on an individual basis and with no financial involvement by social services. However, you can nonetheless expect any personal assistant to behave in a way that respects your religious beliefs, private affairs, liberty and so on and does not subject you to degrading treatment.

Training, competence and conscientiousness

Part and parcel of the regulations that govern home care agencies which provide help with personal care is that they must ensure their helpers have been adequately trained and are competent to carry out their tasks.

Nonetheless some agency workers may not have been trained adequately and of course a personal assistant may or may not have been trained at all. The difference is that you rather than the agency would ask for documentary proof before hiring them.

However, while training is very important, many people would argue that competence and motivation are more so. For many people, the difference between a good and a sub-standard care assistant comes down to motivation and character. Some care assistants are competent, conscientious and feel motivated to deliver a good service; others fail to make use of the training they have been given and do the minimum amount of work they can get away with. If, for example, one of the set tasks is to do the washing up and the client involved is partially sighted, a conscientious assistant will wash the dishes well, rinse them, dry them and ensure that all the crockery and cutlery are put away, lest the client knocks some and injures themselves. They will draw up a chair by the sink so that the client can chat to them while they work swiftly, cheerfully and efficiently.

In contrast, an unmotivated worker will fail to wash up all the dirty dishes and leave the crockery and glasses out to drain, despite the danger to the client. They will not bother to engage in conversation with their client. But they may have received training. Some excellent care workers have no paper qualifications because they started work many years ago and have never been required to obtain a qualification.

Motivation and diligence are especially important where people with dementia are concerned, as they may not be able to remember what an assistant has done or should be doing. An irresponsible assistant would opt not to change bed sheets which they discover to be damp and someone with dementia might not be able to comprehend the situation or report poor care.

Relationships

For older people who live isolated lives, care assistants provide potentially invaluable human contact. If you choose your own staff, you are free to choose somebody (or more than one person) with whom you think you will get on well. You may want to keep the relationship on a work footing. But you may wish to develop a close rapport with your personal assistant which may lead to other forms of help being offered. Your assistant's partner might bring you fresh vegetables from their garden, for example, or provide occasional help with tasks around the home.

These things are of course possible with agency workers. I have met many agency workers who are deeply committed to their clients and prepared to walk miles through deep snow to help them. But the potential of developing a rewarding relationship with one or two people you hire yourself is probably greater.

However, for vulnerable older people who are highly dependent on others, reliance on one person and little contact with others can be dangerous if the person on whom they depend is likely to abuse their trust and cause harm, perhaps through stealing. A variety of helpers and the background presence of an agency may lessen the chances of harmful practices. Of course if you hire direct, you can reduce the chances of abuse by selecting your helper carefully and obtaining security checks on them.

Coping with difficulties

Where a good agency may have the edge over one personal assistant is in having experience of difficult situations. It is not always easy for older people to cope with failing faculties or increased dependence on others and they can react against this by digging in their heels in what can be a rapidly dwindling number of situations in which they can flex their muscle. As a result (or for some other reason), some people will object to bathing or showering, for instance, or taking their medication. Also, some clients will have alcohol-related mood swings. As agencies have more clients than an individual, they may well have built up more experience in dealing with difficulties such as this and be able to offer valuable advice.

Regulation of individual assistants and agencies

We saw in Chapter 15 that many types of healthcare professional, such as nurses and dental hygienists, are subject to a compulsory registration scheme which seeks to exclude people who are unqualified or might harm their patients. Care assistants are different: they do not have to pass examinations and a character check and register with a national agency in order to work lawfully in the field, except in Scotland.

By 1 January 2020, care assistants working for domiciliary agencies in Scotland will have to apply to register with an independent body, the Scottish Social Services Council (SSSC), within six months of starting care work. The register will record the person's name, home address, place of employment, any qualification and also any details of restrictions on their registration – for instance, if they have been temporarily suspended from the register, the reasons for suspension and the length of the suspension.[3] The register will be open to the public and so can be consulted equally by homecare agencies as well as individuals proposing to hire staff. Names are likely to start appearing on the register in late 2017.

Registration will thus provide a means for anyone to check the registration of a homecare worker. What is more, they can contact the SSSC if they are concerned about the way in which a care worker is behaving. As a result, the Council might suspend a care worker's registration.

When considering an application to join its register, the SSSC will check that the applicant does not appear on a special list of individuals thought to pose a risk of harming their clients should they seek work in care and certain other fields. Fortunately, although no formal registration is planned for domiciliary care workers outside Scotland, individuals as well as organisations everywhere in the UK can obtain information from these very same lists about people they are considering hiring (or engaging for voluntary work).

This is how the system works. Anyone on these lists who seeks work (paid or unpaid) in what are called 'regulated activities' is committing an offence. For 'vulnerable adults' *(see below)*, the regulated activities are:

- healthcare
- personal care (such as help with washing, dressing and using the toilet)
- social work
- help with household affairs (with cash, bills or shopping)
- help with the conduct of someone's affairs (this would include people holding power of attorney and those appointed as deputies)
- transporting someone for health, personal or social care reasons as a result of their age, illness or disability[4]

The lists in question are held by national agencies – the Disclosure and Barring Service or DBS (for England and Wales), Disclosure Scotland and Access Northern Ireland. They hold information about the past criminal records of individuals and also whether their names are on lists of people who have been barred from working with people because they have been found to have abused someone in the past or are otherwise considered to pose a risk to vulnerable people. *As noted on page 565,* 'abuse' involves the abuse of trust by harming a vulnerable person, whether it is physical, sexual or psychological (such as humiliating or taunting someone) or neglecting to provide necessary care. The term 'vulnerable adult' in this context is wide-ranging: it applies to any adult who is receiving one of the following services: healthcare, personal care, help to manage their affairs, help with household matters by reason of age, illness or disability, or is being driven around.[5]

Information for the DBS and its equivalents comes partly from police sources (from the Criminal Records Bureau, which it part replaces) but also from other organisations that have compiled information about people known to have abused vulnerable adults in the past. These latter lists have been compiled over many years and the number of people on them is surprisingly high. For instance, 180 people on average were added to the list for England each month during 2005. About one third of the referrals during that year involved neglect; slightly fewer involved physical abuse such as slapping; a quarter involved financial abuse which might be fraud or simply putting pressure on someone to hand over cash.[6] It is important to be aware that records of many cautions and convictions are removed from the lists after a specified period.[7] A similar system exists in Scotland and Northern Ireland.

Medium-sized and large organisations apply to the DBS and its equivalents themselves – for instance, the General Medical Council in deciding whether to place people on their register of doctors. Small organisations and individuals cannot themselves apply direct for a DBS check on a prospective employee or volunteer but have to go through an 'umbrella body' approved by the DBS. *I also discuss this system on page 528.*

Some domiciliary care agencies are subject to separate regulation. No homecare agency providing personal care can operate lawfully without first obtaining a registration certificate from a national body – the Care Quality Commission (in England), the Care Inspectorate (in Scotland), the Care and Social Services Inspectorate Wales and, in Northern Ireland, the Regulation and Quality Improvement Authority. Once, say, the CQC has given an agency a certificate of registration, CQC inspectors make visits to check it is complying with regulations sanctioned by Parliament in its day-to-day operations. If an agency breaches one of these regulations, the national organisation can order it to put matters right. It can even withdraw an agency's registration, which means that it would have to close.[8] *(This system is described more fully on pages 320–3).*

Agencies which provide help not classed as personal care, such as housework are not covered by this system. Nor are people hiring staff whether for housework or help with personal care on an individual basis. However, I recommend that you do a DBS check on any staff you plan to hire yourself.

These various factors mean there are pros and cons of going down both the agency and the independent routes. So let us examine each in a little more detail. If you decide to use an agency, how you do you choose a good one and use it to best advantage? If you hire direct, how do you find and retain a good personal assistant?

Choosing a homecare agency

Home care agencies vary considerably in the quality of help they give. How do you find an agency which will deliver a dependable service of consistently high quality?

Obtaining information

You can obtain a list of care agencies operating locally in the *Yellow Pages* or the internet equivalent, yell.com. The United Kingdom Homecare Association (the professional organisation for homecare agencies) provides, through its website or by telephone, a list of agencies which support its code of practice.

Your local authority social services department should also be able to provide you with a list and also answer questions. Every social care authority in England has a legal duty to set up and maintain a service for providing people in its area with information and advice relating to care and support.[9] This requirement relates to all adults in the local authority's area, not just people whom social care is supporting or whose needs it has assessed.

But perhaps the most straightforward and useful source of information about agencies providing personal care is one of the four national organisations listed on the previous page which are responsible for deciding whether to give agencies that offer help with personal care a registration certificate.

If you look at the website of the Care Quality Commission or one of its sister bodies, you will find basic information about every homecare agency it has registered to provide personal care; simply type in your postcode to find agencies in your area.

The CQC and so on carry out inspections of registered agencies and publish their reports on their websites. These reports provide a useful initial means of evaluating an agency and thus screening out agencies before you go to the trouble of approaching them. If you do not have access to the internet, ask the homecare agency in question to send you its most recent inspection report.

However, do not rely too heavily on inspection reports or on any grading system (perhaps 'outstanding' to 'requires improvement') based on them. The national agencies tend not to inspect care agencies frequently, and much can change between inspections. Thus, the manager may change and care staff come and go; this is in a sector known for high staff turnover. Also, agencies that provide help other than with personal care such as cleaning, shopping and sitting are exempt from this inspection system.

The majority of domiciliary agencies provide help only with personal care and/or housework. However, some agencies offer a wider range of care services, such as a sitting service, occasional checks to see that someone is all right through to live-in care, care for complex medical conditions and end-of-life care. If you think you may need a variety of different kinds of assistance over the years, it might be worth investigating this second type of agency. *(Live-in care is considered in detail in the following chapter.)*

Care versus profit

When choosing an agency, the key factor to bear in mind is that there is an unavoidable conflict between the demands of good care and the imperative to make a profit. Care costs money – in particular to:

- provide high-quality training
- pay staff a wage which reflects the importance of their work
- hire a sufficient number of staff, so that assistants are not rushed off their feet
- pay staff for the time they spend travelling between clients, so they are not under pressure to leave early and rush to their next call
- ensure that assistants have enough time to talk to their clients

Different agencies make the judgement on how to balance profit and quality of care in very different ways. So, work out, from whatever evidence you can assemble, how any agency in which you are interested has chosen to resolve this conflict. Your initial enquiries will not be able to range over every aspect of care which might matter to you, but you can look for clues to an agency's underlying priorities and ethos.

Talking to the manager

If you think an agency looks promising, telephone for a preliminary chat, explaining the sort of help you need and asking for information about the agency's hourly rates. If you want to take matters further, ask the agency to send you a pack which includes information about:

- the nature of the services the agency provides
- its fees
- the terms and conditions under which it would offer you a service (in other words, a draft contract)
- its complaints procedure
- the qualifications of its staff, not least its care assistants
- the most recent inspection report from the Care Quality Commission or its equivalent

The manager should be only too pleased to send you these items.

In Scotland, Wales and Northern Ireland, the standards that the national regulation body has developed to show how homecare agencies should abide by official regulations are more detailed than those for England. They set out what a 'service user's guide' should contain – basically, the items I have listed above.[10] Standards at this level of detail no longer apply in England. But there is no reason why you should not expect the more detailed standards that apply in Scotland, Wales and Northern Ireland to be regarded as best practice in England.

Study the introductory material that is provided before you go and meet the manager. You could also consult past inspection reports in addition to the most recent one to see whether recurring problems have been noted. Why not also look at inspection reports on agencies which you do not plan to visit but which have received a top rating even in another part of the country, so that you can see what can be achieved?

Have a look at the care standards by which the national regulatory body in your part of Britain measures the performance of agencies, so that you have a good idea of what should be standard practice.[11] Another useful briefing document is the guideline published by the National Institute for Health and Care Excellence (NICE) on homecare.[12] NICE wrote this for people using services as well as the organisations that commission and provide homecare, so that users could see how it should be planned and delivered.

Here are a few areas on which you might focus when you go and interview the manager of an agency in which you are interested:

Which helpers will be sent?

The provision of care is big business and in such a competitive field a client ought to be in a position to press for choice in the helpers who will be sent. Could the agency comply with any preference you may have to be helped by assistants with particular expertise? Could it guarantee to send not more than say, six different people – or fewer if you have special difficulties such as poor hearing or eyesight.

You need to be sure you could trust the agency to comply with any important requirements on the selection of staff. When my mother had dementia and was being cared for in an NHS long-stay unit, my brother and I used an agency for several months to send visitors for two hours every day to complement visiting by the family at weekends. I insisted that I should meet any worker the agency proposed to send, so that I could feel sure that they understood the nature of dementia and would be likely to take the trouble to empathise with my mother. This system worked well at first. However, after a few weeks the agency started sending other visitors, saying that those whom I had met were unavailable. For instance, they reassured me that one whom I had not met was a trained nurse, but when I met her, I discovered that her background was in the operating theatre, not in general nursing let alone providing help to older people with dementia. Living a three-hour journey away, I found the situation on the ground difficult to monitor, let alone control. My brother and I finally terminated our contract with the agency and hired visitors direct; this worked much better.

Timing of visits

One area in which wires can get crossed is the time a care worker arrives and the length of time they remain. Resentment can soon build up if they are consistently late in the morning or arrive too early in the evening, particularly if they are supposed to help somebody rise or go to bed or to take medication on time.

Clearly the first thing to do is to agree times of arrival and departure. It is important to establish from the start of your interview at what time the agency would send you helpers. It would be annoying to discover at the end of a long discussion that the early morning visit you need would not take place before ten. Clearly, if an agency really wants your custom and all the slots are already taken, it will simply have to hire more staff, but it may not be willing to do this. So clarify this early on.

Make sure each visit will be long enough, particularly if you are arranging help for someone who is frail and/or whose eyesight, hearing, mobility or cognitive abilities are poor. They may become upset and confused if rushed.

Travelling time

An agency's assistants will often be travelling considerable distances, as they will be visiting many different clients, especially if the agency covers a large geographical area. Establish with the agency who pays for the time the assistants spend travelling between calls – you or it. If you pay for an hour's help and the agency includes in this hour the quarter of an hour the assistant spends reaching your house or flat, plainly you will receive only three-quarters of an hour's care, yet you will be paying for an hour's service.

You may care to find out what reward the agency gives care assistants for driving to clients' properties, as this can provide a useful indication of how much it values good care over maximising its profits. One agency might pay its assistants for the time they spend travelling between calls, as well as a mileage rate (to acknowledge the cost of petrol and wear and tear on their vehicles). Another agency might pay only a mileage rate, and set that very low. Those assistants are thus receiving no payment while behind the wheel, putting them under pressure to drive as quickly as possible to their next call and even to leave one client earlier than they should; as a result, that client's fee covers their travelling time. Some agencies may pay travelling time to some workers but not others.

Recruitment of staff

People working for care agencies vary greatly in background, training, character, skill and motivation. Many are conscientious and kind, committed to ministering as well as they possibly can to their clients. They will go the extra mile and, if their clients are unwell, will ring up to see how they are and/or pick up shopping in their own time. Others are on an agency's books because they offer few attractions to a prospective employer and have not been able to get any other kind of work. They may have little motivation for the work and, in a situation outside the public gaze perhaps involving someone who is no longer able to think and speak clearly, imagination and motivation are crucially important. Some care workers will have an unblemished record but others will have committed offences and even perhaps abused elderly people in the past.

Quiz the manager on how they recruit staff. It is part and parcel of the requirements for agencies which provide personal care and which are enforced by the Care Quality Commission and its sister bodies that each agency should have the following information on staff: their identity, a recent photograph, two written references and a full employment history, together with a satisfactory written explanation of any gaps in employment. Care assistants who provide personal care also have to provide information about any qualifications and training they possess and a statement about their physical and mental health.

Security checks

Work in the closed world of someone's home offers many opportunities for criminal activity, not least theft. Someone helping you get dressed or hoovering your lounge might pilfer money from your wallet or slip a piece of jewellery into their pocket. There is also the possibility that a worker might abuse their position of trust in some other way. They might put pressure on someone who is physically or mentally frail to hand over money. They might even physically harm them. *(I explain the various forms that the abuse of vulnerable older people can take on page 565.)* The dangers are greatest when a client cannot see or hear well or has some kind of cognitive impairment, such as dementia.

Fortunately, as noted above systems are in place that allow people and organisations to check whether someone they might hire has a criminal record and also whether they might be the sort of person who would harm vulnerable elders. If a care agency is going to provide personal care, it has a legal duty to carry out these checks on every prospective employee.

When you talk to the manager, look for an awareness of the limitations of this system for people who have not lived long in Britain, since these checks will rely only on convictions and other records for the time somebody has worked within the UK. Does the manager obtain and verify references from previous employers overseas? Could an applicant create an email address and write a bogus reference for themself?

Training

A good care agency will have well-trained staff, with qualifications in care work. Care agencies are required by law to ensure that their staff have the qualifications, competence and experience to provide care safely.[13] But the regulations do not specify just what the qualifications should be. Look for a high proportion of staff with at least Level 2 in the Regulated Qualifications Framework's (RQF) Diploma in Health and Social Care or the Scottish Qualifications Authority's (SQA) Scottish Vocational Qualification in Social Services and Healthcare.

Not all staff will have a level 2 diploma. Indeed, 37 per cent of care staff in England (working for care agencies or independently) had no recognised qualification whatsoever in 2016.[14]

A separate requirement from each national administration is that domiciliary care agencies should ensure that staff who provide personal care have undergone induction training. This is important because the care sector sees a high turnover of staff, with newcomers joining from sectors outside care, such as retail and the hospitality industry.

In England, new care staff in agencies must be given induction training within three months of starting work, and it is likely to involve studying for the 'care certificate'. Devised by the government agencies Skills for Care, Skills for Health and Health Education England, the care certificate seeks to provide basic understanding and expertise in person-centred care, fluids and nutrition, communication, privacy and dignity, the nature and prevention of elder abuse, infection prevention and control, and awareness of mental health, dementia and learning disability.[15] Students have to demonstrate they can perform practical tasks as well as answer questions about facts.

However the care certificate differs from qualifications such as GCSEs in that employers are permitted to teach and assess students and there is no system of independent scrutiny, let alone standardised national assessment. *(I also discuss training within the context of paid, live-in carers on page 543.)*

Expect this initial training to be followed by a period in which new staff shadow people who are doing a similar job to that which they will be asked to do. The agency's manager or its training supervisor should then look at the skills the new member of staff possesses and the way in which they are carrying out their work and sign them off as having successfully completed their induction training only if satisfied that they can safely work unsupervised – in other words, alone in clients' homes.

Wherever you live in the UK, it is worth bearing in mind that managers have a financial incentive to get new staff working as swiftly as possible, so minimal training may be followed by minimal shadowing. Ask about the precise form and duration of induction training, how soon it starts, and the period within which it must be completed. How long does the process of shadowing a more senior member of staff take?

A good care agency will solicit feedback from its staff and clients about how staff are performing. It will carry out spot checks on staff, with the agreement of clients. It will provide means of motivating staff and reinforcing a professional approach to their work by providing training in new skills, as well as refresher training.

Staff who shop, clean, sit and walk the dog

The regulations that cover agencies which provide personal care do not apply to those which provide other types of help, such as with housework, gardening or looking after pets.

However, there is nothing to stop an agency securing enhanced security checks on staff they are going to use to provide non-personal care and being scrupulous in the securing of references. Nor should the lack of a legal requirement stop them providing training, for example on how they should handle clients' money if shopping is requested and how to communicate effectively with people with some of the communication difficulties examined in Chapter 12.

I explained above *(page 507)* that there is some other control over people who help with household affairs through doing shopping, paying bills and handling money or driving someone, or who help with the conduct of someone's affairs as their attorney or deputy. This control operates regardless of whether the person is working through an agency or independently.

Working out an agreed list of tasks

If you are going ahead with an agency, you will need to work out a list of tasks which you wish its care assistants to perform. It is important to be clear about this from the outset. Without clarity about what care assistants are expected to do, confusion, misunderstandings, resentment and bad feeling can easily arise.

If you are setting up arrangements for a parent who is living at home and has dementia you may perhaps be considering four visits each day. The first might involve helping her with taking medication, preparing her breakfast, washing up, tidying, making the bed and showering or bathing. Obviously, much will depend on why the person involved needs help and what they can do and would like to do for themselves. At the beginning of Chapter 26 I give the example of the help given to a man named Jack. This was written in the context of help arranged through social services but it could equally apply to help arranged independently.

All registered domiciliary care agencies have to carry out an assessment of the needs of the person they are going to support. (This requirement is regardless of any social services involvement.) Thus the regulations for England stipulate that a registered person (who will usually be the agency's manager) must:

- carry out an assessment of the needs and preferences for care and treatment of the 'service user' in collaboration with them

- design the person's care or treatment with a view to meeting their preferences and ensuring their needs are met

- enable the user to understand the care or treatment choices available to them.[16]

The guidance that accompanies these regulations explains that the assessments of a client's needs should include all their needs – including health, personal care, emotional, social, cultural, religious and spiritual ones. It also explains that people using the service must be given opportunities to manage as much of their care and treatment as they wish and are able to, and should be actively encouraged to do so.[17]

A similar situation exists elsewhere in the UK. In Wales, for example, the regulations explain the process of assessment and preparation of a service user's plan in a way that is perhaps easier to understand. They say that a manager in an agency who is trained and competent for the task must carry out an assessment of the needs of the service user and in doing so, and subsequently preparing a service user's plan, the manager must fully involve the user as well as any carers and representatives they may have. They must also communicate with the user in such a way as to ensure they are fully involved. The assessment of needs might include not only the help the person requires but also matters which bear on how support should be given, such as dietary requirements and food preferences, any dexterity or mobility problems, religious and cultural needs and sight, hearing and communication considerations.[18]

Wherever you live, expect your service user's plan to set out in detail the action that care assistants will take, so that any assistant could do all that is necessary by following it. For instance, if care assistants are to apply creams, expect the care plan to contain a body map to show where the cream should be applied. Make sure that everything that is necessary is included. Help with oral care is often overlooked, perhaps because helping someone clean their teeth seems highly intrusive and some people do not like to admit that they cannot clean their teeth properly. Yet good mouth care is extremely important, *as explained on pages 16–17.*

The plan should also set out all necessary background information, such as contact details for the GP and for any legal representative such as an attorney, deputy or guardian. It should be signed by the service user or their representative and given to the service user in a language and format that they can understand. The plan should be reviewed regularly and more frequently if changes in circumstances require this. The agency should provide the service user with a copy of their plan in a form in which they can best read it, perhaps large-print. It should be available in their home for them and visiting care assistants to consult, with separate space for visiting assistants to make notes reporting what they have done and any problems which arose.

Don't wait until you and the agency's manager sit down together to draw up your service user's plan. Consider beforehand the tasks you would like its helpers to perform *(as outlined in the case study below).* Otherwise, you could find yourself slotted into a system providing standard help which does not meet your particular needs.

I am writing this chapter on help in the home while staying for five days with a friend, John, with the intention of working out just what help he needs and getting his care package off to a good start. He has been in hospital and then a nursing home after suffering a major stroke. He is partially sighted, hard of hearing and has some cognitive impairment.

I arrived to bring him home from the care home to his spacious flat in a converted country mansion a few miles outside Edinburgh

CASE STUDY

and to work out how a local care agency his family had already engaged could best help him. Before my visit he had been assessed by social services as needing help with personal care, but nobody was clear just what that help might consist of. In fact, it has quickly become apparent that John does not need the sort of help that is often provided – with washing, showering or dressing. The help he needs arises mainly from his sight impairment and from the tiredness and confusion that come upon him in the early evening. For example, it would be helpful if somebody could place toothpaste on the brush ready for him to use and select his clothes the night before, lest he puts on garments which are dirty or inside out. He also needs somebody to spot items he has unknowingly knocked over and to find items he has lost.

Although John is able to brew coffee and serve himself with cereals, he cannot see sufficiently well to spread butter and marmalade on his toast. Any hot meal has to be prepared by somebody else. They then must cut up his food, tell him where it is on his plate and check that he has eaten everything.

I insisted that all these small yet significant tasks be spelled out in John's service user's plan, so that any new care worker would know precisely what to do. Although the agency's workers do not do housework, I persuaded them that they should sweep under John's dining chair if necessary, as he is apt inadvertently to let food fall, pointing out that this is a task closely associated with personal care as defined in Scotland.[19]

John loves to get out in the fresh air and his ground-floor flat giving onto attractive grounds is ideally suited for short walks. He can walk unaided even over uneven ground, but does sometimes suddenly feel weak and have difficulty in returning to his flat. I therefore ensured that the care plan stipulated that a care assistant should accompany him on a walk outside twice a day.

Having spent weeks away from home, John takes great delight in moving around his flat once more, sorting things, moving things and doing everyday tasks in the way he used to. It seems to me important that the care workers should help him with tasks which he considers important, even though they might not seem so to an outsider, such as taking food waste to the compost heap in the gardens – a task which is an important means for John to express the conservation ethos he holds dear.

I am staying long enough to monitor how the care assistants go about their tasks and to tweak the arrangements as necessary. John's family have been anxious lest problems should occur during the night. In fact he sleeps well, has few problems in using the bathroom during the night and is alert in the mornings. However, as the day wears on he becomes increasingly confused, with the result that he needs more intensive help and supervision in the early evening. It is important that the early evening care assistants encourage him to go to bed by 7.30pm.

If you (or a close relative or friend) are going to need quite a lot of help, it is worth getting somebody to stay for a few days, as I did with John, to help with drawing up a list of tasks for the agency workers and then to monitor how well the support system is working and whether it could usefully be altered. This can involve working out whether somebody needs equipment: when assessments are made by social services of the need for physical supports such as grab rails, the assessors inevitably spend only a limited time with somebody in their house or flat and so may miss out on some of the tasks they will perform which might be facilitated by, say, handrails in particular places.

Time-keeping

Discuss with the agency's manager how times of arrival and departure are to be recorded. It is important that this is done accurately and in a way which cannot be disputed. A reliable record of attendance by care assistants is invaluable should you wish to make a complaint.

The traditional method of recording attendance by care workers has been a paper time-sheet. This has space for each care worker to insert their time of arrival and departure and for the care recipient to sign to confirm the times. However, you may wish to think about a more sophisticated system, particularly if you are organising help for somebody who, perhaps because of poor eyesight, cannot check the time-sheet on every occasion.

Electronic devices have been developed. One uses the worker's mobile phone and a call-tracing system which indicates their location, another a smart card which is slotted into a mobile phone to show that the worker is in a particular house. An alternative: a daughter, say, could ask that each homecare worker text her from her parent's mobile when they arrive and leave. Some agencies enable a client to pay by blocks of 15 minutes of care actually received, rather than for a pre-set amount of hours every week. In this case, an electronic monitoring device showing times of arrival and departure is essential.

A traditional time-sheet for use in care work has space for other information to be inserted on each visit and it is worth providing such a facility, whether the sheet is used as the only time-record or not. It could set down, for example:

- the time and dose of any medication given. If a client refuses their medication or misses a dose for whatever reason, this should be set down.

- any financial transactions undertaken on the client's behalf

- any accident (however minor) to the client or care worker, and

- details of any changes in the client's circumstances, health, physical condition or care needs. The care assistant might perhaps note that the client was refusing food and might be sickening for something, so the next assistant could be alert to this possibility.

The contract

In any agreement with an agency, the service user plan and the contract are the key documents. The service user plan sets out the help you will be given; the contract the underlying arrangements between you and the agency. Make sure you are happy with the terms of the contract in the following areas. If you are not, push for suitable amendments. Areas to check include:

✓ the fees payable for the service and by whom they are to be paid. Is any VAT included?

✓ whether the agency is paying all necessary tax, National Insurance, staff travelling expenses and employer's liability insurance

✓ the areas of activity that homecare or support workers will, and will not, undertake

✓ the rights and responsibilities of you on the one hand and the agency on the other

✓ the liability if there is a breach of contract or any damage in your home. Ask to see all relevant supporting documentation, such as the agency's employer liability insurance.

✓ the circumstances for one-off cancellations

✓ the circumstances in which you or the agency can terminate the contract

The following matters should also be set down in writing, ideally in the contract:

- the supplies and/or equipment to be made available by you and by the agency
- the arrangements for the supervision of staff by the agency
- the arrangements to cover holidays and sickness
- the contact numbers for the agency's office, including for out-of-hours and emergency help
- the arrangements for updating your needs assessment and service-user care plan
- key holding and other arrangements for entering or leaving your home

On the last point, consider giving other people, such as neighbours, a spare set of keys lest the care assistant cannot get into your home for some reason.

How care assistants should behave

Quite apart from their qualifications and background and the list of tasks they should be carrying out, just how should you expect care workers to behave? What is considered professional behaviour in this field?

First and foremost, a care assistant should be carrying out the tasks set out in the service user's plan to the best of their ability. However, if your plan says you need help to wash and dress, the assistant should be helping you as and when you need help, not taking over and washing and dressing you as they would a doll. In doing so, they should address you in the way you wish, respect your dignity and privacy as far as possible and make any necessary adjustment for any special needs you have, such as vision impairment or dexterity problems. They should show respect to your culture in the way they talk and behave.

The regulations and care standards in each country of the UK lay down the basic principles which should guide the behaviour of care workers. Thus they must treat the service user with dignity and respect, not discriminate against or harass them on any of the grounds set down in the Equality Act (disability, sexual orientation and so on, *see page 296),* and they must offer the service user 'support to maintain their autonomy and independence in line with their needs and stated preferences'.[20] Do have a look at the regulations and standards in your part of the UK.

Make sure these standards work for you. As I write this, an elderly lady has just told me of the distress she felt when a care assistant from an agency refused to give her the help she needed, insisting that she should do more to help herself. Yet this woman had a severe, unrelenting tremor which prevented her from performing many tasks she would have been delighted to accomplish unaided. So, ask if you need more help, and if a care assistant refuses to give it, contact the agency's manager for clarification and, if necessary, change your service user's plan.

Expect assistants to have time to chat. Care whether at home, in a care facility or in hospital is supposed to be 'person-centred'. The NHS in England singles out 'communication' as one of the six key elements of good nursing care *(see page 911)*. Scotland's Care Inspectorate reported approvingly that a client at a care facility in Dumfries had said: 'Staff are respectful, professional and can have a good banter and a laugh and a joke with us'.[21] If that is in case in Dumfries and is supposed to be the case for busy nurses on hospital wards, why not also with the helpers sent by the agency you are proposing to use?

If you are arranging care for somebody whose mental abilities are limited, perhaps as a result of dementia, you should expect care assistants to understand and abide by the principles of the mental capacity legislation *(outlined on pages 770–4)*. This is important, as in the privacy of, say, you mother's home, an untrained or unmotivated care worker might well fail to ensure that they involve your mother as much as possible in the decisions of her everyday life as they should.

For example, your mother should choose the clothes she would like to wear each day. If she cannot do this easily, the care assistant should help her make her choice. If she cannot contribute to the process of choosing, the care assistant should make sure that the clothes selected reflect your mother's tastes and preferences.

If things go wrong

Problems may well be unforeseen. Staff sent by an agency could arrive poorly briefed and/or late. They could fail to do what has been agreed. They might steal from you or even physically harm you.

Take plenty of precautions. Hide away valuable items. I have come across cases in which people have been convinced that an assistant has stolen from them, usually jewellery. The assistant has maintained that they have not but that their client often loses items. The police have failed to act, leaving the person who needs help annoyed and frustrated.

However, should you encounter criminal activity such as stealing or assault by an agency's workers (or helpers you hire direct), do contact the police. If care staff engage in any type of abuse (such as intimidation, physical harming or neglect), contact the adult protection team of your local authority *(see page 566)*. It does not matter that you have obtained your help independently, without the involvement of social services; social care authorities must have teams of professionals to investigate cases of possible abuse. They can take a range of steps to stop the abuse and prevent further abuse taking place, *as explained on pages 566–71*.

But what of the far more common problem of care assistants not doing what they should or when or how they should?

Lateness may be an issue. You should expect assistants to arrive within 15 minutes of the time they are supposed to. Running later than this should be an infrequent occurrence; if and when it happens, expect the agency to telephone you to alert you, explaining the reason for the delay.

If you encounter problems such as assistants often turning up late, or failing to carry out the tasks agreed or in a way you do not like, ring up the manager of the agency and try to resolve them informally. The manager might respond by sending you a different assistant, clarifying any misunderstanding in your service user's plan or changing schedules so assistants always arrive earlier, for instance. However, if problems persist, lodge a formal complaint to the agency; every agency is required by law to have a procedure for handling complaints.

Many people hate complaining, but it is worth grasping the nettle and sorting out any problems rather than soldiering on, hoping matters will improve without prompting. Of course you could terminate your contract with the agency involved, but there may be few other agencies providing homecare in your area and you might encounter similar (or worse) problems with another one. If your homecare arrangements fail to deliver and you rely heavily on help, you may feel there is no alternative but to go into a care home, however much you may dislike the idea.

The Care Inspectorate (in Scotland), the Care and Social Services Inspectorate Wales and the Regulation and Quality Improvement Authority (in Northern Ireland) take up individual complaints and seek to resolve them; contact one of these organisations for information on how to do this. In England, the Care Quality Commission does not pursue individual complaints. That role falls to the Local Government Ombudsman, who is responsible for handling complaints from individuals who pay for their own care. However, you could contact the CQC nonetheless: it may decide to pursue a particular area of an agency's activities on its next inspection. If your concerns are serious, it could make an extra inspection as a result of them and take enforcement action. This may help your particular situation, but will not be aimed primarily at resolving your concern.

The role of the Local Government Ombudsman in England

The Local Government Ombudsman in England has powers to get involved in complaints by people funding their own care, in addition to its main work responding to concerns about local government. Often these individual complaints involve care homes, but the Ombudsman can also investigate domiciliary care, so long as it relates to 'personal care'. The service is free.

You can complain to the Local Government Ombudsman by phone, email, letter or text. The Ombudsman will expect you to have already complained to the care agency in question without a satisfactory response. However, they have the discretion to take up a matter without a complainant first having approached a care provider.

An official in a regional office will see whether they can resolve the matter informally. If not, they will call for evidence from all parties in a quasi-judicial manner. They will then draw up a report and give both sides the opportunity to comment on it. The report may or may not be amended before the Ombudsman issues their decision.

The Ombudsman may make recommendations of various kinds: these could be that the complainant should receive an apology, compensation should be paid, charges should be refunded or changes be made to the services the agency provides (such as the facilities provided, the equipment or the training of staff). The Ombudsman must send a copy of their report to the complainant and the care provider. They may also send copies to the local authority in whose area the agency operates and to the Care Quality Commission.

A care agency that has been the subject of an Ombudsman investigation with recommendations must send to the Ombudsman a statement of the action that it has taken or proposes to take within one month of receiving a report from the Ombudsman. If no such statement of action is received within the time period or if the Ombudsman judges that the provider is not proposing to take any action or is not satisfied with the action taken or proposed, they can publish an 'adverse findings notice', for example in a local newspaper. This sets out what the Ombudsman has found and the action they have proposed. But although the Ombudsman can name and shame care providers in this way, they have no powers to enforce change. Also, not every case is taken up: the Ombudsman has to be convinced that a significant injustice is involved before they will go ahead. However, you may find you get some benefit merely from showing awareness of your right of recourse to the Ombudsman.

Hiring home care staff independently

Hiring staff direct rather than through an agency enables you to have much more control over who turns up on your doorstep, what they do and when *(as we saw on pages 501–2)*. So just how do you find staff and, if you need to actually employ people rather than hire self-employed staff, how do you go about paying them and coping with income tax?

More than a million people work in the care sector in the UK, some working independently for people in their own homes, some for care agencies, some in care homes, many in a combination of these. The problem for the consumer is that care work inevitably involves inviting a worker into a situation in which theft or even sexual abuse can occur. Also, care work has traditionally been an area in which people can work without paper qualifications. And in the absence of a professional background on a par with that of nurses or teachers, just what should you expect from a care assistant?

Finding staff

To find staff, whether employed or self-employed, you could ask around, advertise (for example, in a local Job Centre) or use an employment agency. Your local Age UK, carers trust organisation or independent living centre may hold lists of suitable people. An organisation called PA Pool provides a means of matching people who are seeking work as a personal assistant to people who are looking for one; it operates online only.

When you provide information for prospective helpers, you could consider including the following items:

✓ the qualities you are looking for in your helper

✓ any qualifications you expect them to possess

✓ the tasks with which you require help

✓ basic rules with which you would expect helpers to comply, such as:

> ✓ arriving at the correct time, ready for work
>
> ✓ giving notice if they are going to be more than ten minutes late
>
> ✓ discussing any problems that arise as soon as possible

✓ treating your working relationship, including details of the help they give you, as confidential

✓ respecting your possessions and equipment and only using your facilities with prior consent

✓ abiding by the Code of Practice of Social Care Workers

This Code has been drawn up by national organisations seeking to raise standards in social care work (amongst social workers as well as care assistants). It is available free of charge and in many different languages as well as in audio and large-print forms from the Health and Care Professions Council, the Care Council for Wales, the Scottish Social Services Council and the Northern Ireland Social Care Council.

The Code is pretty basic, but it does set out key components of professional behaviour and has the imprimatur of government bodies in each of the four countries of the UK. If a care assistant fails to conform to its precepts, you could reasonably expect them to change their ways.

The Code tells every social care worker that they must, amongst other things:

● promote the independence of service users while protecting them as far as possible from danger or harm

● not abuse the trust of service users and carers or the access they have to personal information about them or to their property, home or workplace

● respect the dignity and privacy of clients, and

● respect the different cultural behaviour and values that clients may have

There is no reason why you should not also use the minimum standards for domiciliary agencies that relate to how care workers should behave *(referred to on page 521)* when you work out how you would expect your staff to go about their work.

On the job application form, as well as obvious elements such as name, address and phone number, you could perhaps include space for the following:

✓ Do you have any experience of care work (or whatever other forms of help you are looking for)?

✓ Why do you wish to work as a personal assistant?

- ✓ Do you have any relevant qualifications, such as a current driving licence or a qualification in the provision of care?
- ✓ When would you be free to start work?
- ✓ Which times of the day and of the week would you be available to work? What about school holidays?
- ✓ How early could you start and how late finish each shift?
- ✓ Could you work extra hours at short notice or be free to make a later additional call occasionally (for example, if a prescription needs to be collected urgently)?
- ✓ Do you have any necessary business car insurance?
- ✓ Have you had an enhanced security check from the Disclosure and Barring Service (DBS) (for England and Wales), Disclosure Scotland or Access Northern Ireland, and if so, what is its date? Explain that you will expect to see documentary proof of this at a later stage. I explain this checking system below.
- ✓ Could you give the dates, job titles and duties of previous paid work?
- ✓ Could you give the name, address and phone number of your current or last employer?
- ✓ Could you give the names, postal addresses and phone numbers of two referees, one personal (but not a member of the family) and one professional (current or most recent employer)?

When you write and offer somebody a position, it is important to get the details correct: a contract of employment is formed as soon as somebody tells you that they accept the position. So do not make a firm offer for the position until you are satisfied with the references, the record from the Disclosure and Barring Service or its equivalent, and anything else you consider important. A trial period can be useful: it is difficult at an interview to get a sense of whether somebody is conscientious and would work well and you would get along with them.

Qualifications and training

I have already outlined the qualifications and training to be expected from a care assistant (*see page 514*). Examine any certificates an applicant shows you: in this field it is easy to amass certificates simply by attending a day's course rather than by passing an assessment; I have many of them. If your prospective assistant has a paper qualification, probe a little on just what they have had to do to secure it. Work out what skills they actually possess. Crucially, try to work out how they are likely to go about their work. This is why references are so important. As noted earlier in this chapter, there are plenty of excellent personal assistants with years of experience who do not possess a fistful of certificates.

Security checks

We noted above *(page 507)* that lists have been compiled of people who are considered to pose a risk to vulnerable older people (and also children) and that homecare agencies which provide personal care are required to use this system to obtain security checks on the people they plan to hire. If you hire somebody independently, the law does not force you to obtain a security check, but you would be well advised to do so.

As also noted above, the lists of people who might pose a risk are held by national agencies. If you apply to one of these, such as the Disclosure and Barring Service or DBS, for a 'standard or basic disclosure' you will obtain information about whether someone has been convicted of an offence if the rehabilitation period set for that conviction has not yet expired. However, a standard disclosure will not provide the 'soft' information that the police holds – that is, the intelligence that the police has on someone, such as that they have never been convicted of an offence but have been questioned on numerous occasions. Nor will it reveal whether the person is on a barred list – in other words, they have committed a type of abuse in the past or are considered to pose a significant risk of harming a vulnerable adult *as explained on page 507.*

So you would be advised to apply for an 'enhanced disclosure'. This will contain a comprehensive list of all that person's convictions together with any information held by the police that did not lead to a conviction but may indicate that the person is a danger to vulnerable adults.

The result of the application to the DBS is sent to the person who is the subject of the inquiry. So you will have to ask the person you are proposing to hire to see it.

You could make any job offer conditional on seeing an up-to-date record from the DBS or its equivalent. It is also worth asking the DBS or equivalent to notify you of any change in the status of a particular person in relation to the barred list, just in case they should commit an offence or otherwise misbehave with someone else without your knowledge.

Do not rely wholly on security checks. The DBS lists, though extremely useful, should not be seen as a 100 per cent guarantee that someone is well-intentioned. Many people who have stolen from or otherwise mistreated older people in their care have never been brought to book. Some may have misbehaved in foreign countries in which there is no record of the abuse or from which information is difficult to obtain in Britain. So pursue your own investigations through references as well, even if you are hiring somebody for only a short period or a few hours a week.

People who apply for work in certain fields including the provision of personal care and help with money matters are themselves breaking the law if their names are on the DBS list, *as explained on page 507*. Don't rely on your prospective care-giver to disqualify themselves from working for you because their name is on the DBS list and they fear being found out. Ask them to produce documentation from a very recent DBS check *(as outlined on pages 507–8)*.

Keeping a distance

When you are employing somebody in your own home or that of a relative it is easy for the boundaries between work and domestic life to become blurred. This can mean that people you are paying to help overstep what you see as the mark, perhaps making themselves drinks whenever they choose. And you may forget that you should be playing your part as an employer – giving them adequate holiday time and holiday pay, for example.

The legal obligations of employers

If you employ staff, there are many legal implications. For instance, you have to pay them at least the National Minimum Wage or the National Living Wage and provide the minimum rest periods set down in the European Union's Working Time Directive. You may have to enrol your worker into a qualifying workplace pension scheme and obtain employers' liability insurance.

Then there is tax and National Insurance to consider. Usually, a worker in your home is considered to be employed by you. This means you are responsible for deducting National Insurance Class I contributions and tax from their salary under PAYE.

If you are paying your assistant less than a set weekly amount, called the lower earnings limit (£112 in 2017), you do not need to worry about National Insurance. But if you are offering more than this amount, you will have to pay employer contributions, and deduct these from what you pay and send them to Her Majesty's Revenue and Customs (HMRC). Tax is different: whether you need to deduct it depends on your employee's total earnings from all their sources of employment. If your employee's only job is with you and you are paying less than the personal allowance (£221 in 2017), no income tax is payable. But if they are earning more than this amount from working for you or you and other people, they will have to pay tax on their total earnings. It will then be up to you to deduct tax pro rata from their earnings from you and send it to HMRC.

If your assistant is self-employed, you will not have to make any tax or National Insurance deductions. For this reason, some people who need a lot of help in the home choose to enter into contracts with several personal assistants, each self-employed. But it is important to be sure the assistant really can claim that status. Neither you nor they can choose whether they are considered self-employed: this is up to HMRC, applying certain rules. Telephone HMRC to confirm the status of your prospective assistant before you go ahead.

All this may sound daunting but plenty of people employ staff, including individuals and very small businesses, and much guidance is available.

Guidance

The ins and outs of hiring staff are described in many free sources. The voluntary organisation Disability Rights UK is one: it provides information on its website and in paper form about many aspects of hiring staff, from the form of a contract of employment to the difference between employed and self-employed staff. It also has a helpline *(see Useful Contacts)*.

Many free booklets describe how to recruit and hire staff and the relevant laws on employment and insurance law which have been written for people who receive direct payments (in other words, they organise their own care but their council pays for it). Look in particular at the Department of Health's *A Guide to Receiving Direct Payments from Your Local Council: A Route to Independent Living* and the Scottish Government's *A Guide to Receiving Direct Payments in Scotland,* wherever you live in the UK.

Some of the independent living centres and independent living councils *(see next section)* also provide free guidance on hiring staff. The Surrey Independent Living Council is a good example.

All this is in addition to the information provided by the government on the hire of staff for any purpose, not only care work. Go to the government's website gov.uk and then the 'Employing People' section; HMRC's New Employer Helpline also provides information on the responsibilities that come with being an employer and how to set up a PAYE scheme.

Support

It is worth trying to link into a system that supports people who are hiring care staff, as a way of reminding both you and the person or people you plan to hire of the reality that this is a work situation. This will also enable you to obtain advice and support with the various technicalities involved in hiring helpers, from paying a minimum wage to not employing people living in Britain illegally.

Up and down the country there are a number of independent living centres or independent living councils. They provide support for people who are receiving payments from their local authority to organise their own care. These payments are known as 'direct payments' and I discuss them much more fully in Part Seven. I am mentioning them here because these organisations are often happy to help 'self-funders' too. They do not always advertise the fact in their publicity material, but if you are interested, phone one of them and ask. They may help you with the whole of the process, from advertising for staff to paying them. Some run pay-as-you-earn (PAYE) schemes for their clients; others will put clients in touch with other organisations that will do so.

Keys and back-up

Who will help you if your assistant is unwell or on holiday? Make sure you put in place back-up arrangements. Sometimes several older people who are living close to each other and are friends hire the same person. They can therefore discuss and to some extent share the burdens of engaging staff and make similar arrangements for cover in the event of their helper being unwell or on holiday *(see pages 117–8)*.

Also, make sure you tell your assistant what they should do and whom they should contact in the event of an emergency.

Will you let them in each time or will they have keys? An alternative is a key-safe fixed to the wall near your door which enables people who know a code to open the safe, take the key and let themselves in. There is less chance of the wrong people getting that key copied than if you give someone a key to take away. Should you no longer wish someone to gain entry because they no longer work for you, you simply change the code. A drawback is the presence of the safe, which proclaims the presence of unusual door entry arrangements perhaps because the house occupant is frail. So consider putting the safe by a back door instead. Whichever route you go down – keys or key-safe – it is useful to have at least one neighbour who holds an extra set of keys or knows the key-safe code.

Paying for homecare

Some people are under the misapprehension that they would be ineligible for a subsidy from their social care department to help fund the costs of their homecare. Perhaps they believe that anyone who owns their own home is ruled out of help. This is wrong. The ownership of someone's home affects their entitlement to council help if the costs of care are taken in a care home, but not in their own home or that of somebody else. What matters most in this context is whether their savings are lower than about £23,000 and their needs for care meet a threshold. *(This is explained in Chapter 28.)*

Attendance Allowance is different. It is a benefit paid on grounds of disability or illness regardless of financial means and can provide the recipient with up to £82.30 per week which they can put towards the costs of homecare. *(I discuss Attendance Allowance on pages 835–40.)*

A Disabled Facilities Grant can run to tens of thousands of pounds and fund or part fund the adaptation of someone's home to cope with illness or disability. Check whether you would be eligible for a grant *(pages 186–8)*. You might find you would need less human help in the home if you obtained one.

You will find suggestions for raising money out of your own resources to pay for help in the home in the section on paying for live-in care in the next chapter.

Human help

* You could hire a helper to do anything from drive you around to doing the cleaning or helping with personal care.

* Take time to work out exactly what you would like your helper(s) to do and how.

* You may get more value for money if you hire helpers direct rather than going through a homecare agency.

* You could hire helpers direct and use a domiciliary care agency to fill in when your helpers are unavailable.

* Your local independent living centre may lend you a hand if you are employing staff direct.

* Get an enhanced security check with barring on anybody who works for you in your home.

* If somebody you plan to hire says they will be self-employed, make sure they are making the necessary arrangements.

* Expect helpers to help you help yourself, not do everything for you.

* There are bound to be some difficulties with individual helpers or agencies. Sort them out as they arise – don't leave them to fester.

Chapter 24

Live-in care

f you need practical help and have at least one spare bedroom in your home, live-in care may be the answer. It is an option with a long history – live-in paid staff who were expected to provide practical help, care and company whenever it was needed have been used at least by wealthier families for centuries. Many people rule out live-in care as they assume it would be prohibitively expensive. Yet the cost can vary widely (from over £1,000 per week to less than £100), depending on the amount of support the care-giver provides, the way in which the arrangement is organised and the extent to which the person (or people) paying the bill can take advantage of state entitlements.

What does live-in care look like on the ground? Here is one situation I have come across:

Christina lodged in a house in London with Alice (names changed), who was frail and in her nineties. She did not care for Alice, but organised her care. After posting adverts on university noticeboards, Christina hired several care assistants (who had trained as nurses in their own country) and organised them into three shifts each day. They helped Alice with personal care, ensuring this was not rushed – a meal might take two hours, as Alice had become very slow at eating. As Christina was present much of the time, she was able to ensure that the assistants carried out tasks in the way she and Alice wished. She insisted the assistants take Alice out each day in her wheelchair, perhaps to the shops, perhaps to Mass. But exercise was important too, so they were also expected to help Alice move around as much as possible. Thus each day they would accompany her on a walk. Even if it was only to the end of the street, the walk also meant that Alice dressed herself smartly with a hat and gloves, as was her custom.

Christina also insisted that the care assistants help Alice upstairs to bed every night. This would take half an hour, but again was considered important for exercise and a change of scene. Indeed, variety was deliberately built into Alice's life, with care assistants lining up a range of television programmes for her to watch.

Live-in care can also take place on a more modest scale or for a temporary period. As live-in paid care is customised, you negotiate with the live-in carer or their agency to establish the range of responsibilities. Here are one or two situations in which live-in care can prove useful.

You live on your own and develop an illness such as pneumonia that saps your strength but for which you are not sent to hospital. No friends or family offer to come and stay. A live-in carer who shops, cooks, cleans, looks after your pets, provides a reassuring presence in the house and accompanies you on outings could transform what might otherwise be a bleak few weeks.

Or perhaps you are about to be discharged from hospital after an illness or operation and are advised that you should move permanently into a care home, as you now struggle to look after yourself. But you do not wish to leave your own home. A live-in carer could be hired to help you move around, wash, dress, take medication, do the housework, cooking, shopping and look after your pets. In time, they might come to provide companionship and emotional support.

Another scenario: you and your partner are finding difficulty in continuing to look after yourselves but do not wish to leave your home and relocate to a care home. Neither needs a great deal of help and a live-in carer who could provide light-touch care and support could make life easier.

Or perhaps you have only a few weeks to live and your partner is happy to look after you but you both feel that an additional pair of hands day and night to complement help from visiting nurses would be a great relief.

Some older people with room to spare offer free or low-cost accommodation to, say, a student or young person in return for a set number of hours per week of practical help, although not usually help with personal care. They also enjoy the security of knowing somebody is in their house or flat at night. Such arrangements may be negotiated as part of a Homeshare scheme or independently between the two parties. Clearly they can be tailored to a wide range of individual requirements. *(I examine this option in the discussion of housing choices in Chapter 5).*

Live-in care versus a care home: pros and cons

If you go and live permanently in a care home, you no longer have to worry about house maintenance or household tasks. All your meals and other refreshments are provided, as well as any help you need with practical tasks and aspects of personal care such as bathing, dressing and using the toilet. Indeed, help can be summoned day or night. In addition, the home is likely to provide various types of entertainment and activity. In a care home, you will be able to enjoy communal spaces and the company of other people, but your own private space will be confined to your own bedroom (which may be en-suite and include a television and phone).

On the other hand, if you have a live-in care-giver, you can continue to enjoy all the amenities of your home – not just the house or flat and any garden, but also features associated with it that you may value such as your neighbours and the locality, as well as any pet (the majority of care homes do not accept pets). You continue to be responsible for running your home, although your care-giver may help with many aspects of it, such as doing the laundry, exercising your dog and entertaining your guests. Help will be on hand with any tasks such as moving around, bathing or helping you eat your food that you have pre-agreed the assistant will do, as well as general support from putting your favourite tracks on the CD player to taking you out or helping you with your correspondence. Your contract with the helper (or with an agency) should also have specified when and for how long they will have free time, and you (or the agency) may need to provide a replacement at that time.

The individual care provided in a care home can never involve as much as that provided by a live-in carer. In a care home, residents have to share the services of care assistants with other residents. Although care homes are supposed to offer personalised support, the sheer pressure of caring for many people means that the care given tends to be task-driven – getting residents washed and dressed, taking them to breakfast, serving them breakfast, taking them to the lounge afterwards, and so on. There does not tend to be much time to, say, sit down with a resident or group of residents and read the newspaper aloud. Many homes employ activity organisers but they tend to have pre-set programmes of activities and little time to respond to spontaneous requests from individual residents.

That said, the live-in care-giver will have plenty to do and will not have the time and energy to provide diversions all the time. But they should have more time for one-to-one support and interaction than would a care assistant in a care home. And they should be better able to respond to spontaneous wishes.

The one-to-one nature of the arrangement coupled with the fact that care is taking place in the person's home environment means that live-in care should be well-placed to reflect a client's tastes and interests. Dominique Kent, the Operations Director of The Good Care Group, a company that specialises in live-in care, told me in an interview in 2015 that the service her care-givers provide:

> is much more than what I call the task of caring. It's about saying to somebody, "What's really important to you about your life? How do we ensure that we enable you to carry on with this in the best possible way for you?" If we know somebody loved the opera and is no longer able to get out to the opera, we bring the opera to them – through music, through films, through books, through radio, whatever it might be.

Nonetheless, it is worth considering the alternative before going down the live-in care route. Care homes have had a bad press, but there are plenty of good ones. In a good care home you will receive not only 24-hour care and your meals, but also the company of people of your own age and a range of activities to enjoy, such as crafts and games. Life with a live-in helper in your own home or in a granny annexe can work well – or it can be lonely and unstimulating, particularly if you feel that your family are only allowing you to live in an annexe of their home on sufferance.

Costs

Before you consider live-in care in detail, work out whether you could raise the funds to pay for it. Live-in care is difficult for most people to fund because although the fee to be paid to the live-in assistant (or assistants) or to an agency is of the same order as to a care home, there are significant additional costs: your own and the care-giver's living expenses, as well as the maintenance of your home and possibly a car. Yet the funds you would release to pay care home bills – through the sale of your home – are not available.

Live-in care obtained through a specialist agency could set you back over £1,000 every week, or £50,000 a year – to be found out of post-tax income. Releasing money through equity release is one option, *and I examine how it works on pages 884–8.* However, equity release might not deliver enough money, and there are significant drawbacks such as a reduction in money to pass on to heirs. Also, an equity release contract would require you to keep the property involved in good repair. Getting substantial work such as rewiring carried out while an elderly relative, perhaps with dementia, and their live-in care-giver are occupying it may not be feasible.

If you are looking to buy an annuity and/or to release money through equity release, obtain advice from an independent financial advisor: the deals that are offered vary widely. If you have a serious, ongoing health condition consider buying an impaired annuity, which will give you more than a standard annuity. *(I examine impaired or enhanced annuities in Chapter 37, on page 879.)*

Some families pay for live-in care by sharing the costs between individual family members – perhaps children chipping in to fund live-in care for their parent. Taking it in turns to provide cover when the assistant has time off could bring down the costs further. If you share care costs, plainly you need to be sure each person is fully committed and will continue to be able to pay their share for as long as it is required. Each person may wish to be reimbursed after the death of their loved one, rather than relying on the terms of a will. If so, ask a solicitor to draw up a contract, perhaps paying a small amount of interest to family members on what is in effect a loan, so that it can be a debt against the person's estate after their death.

In this situation the older relative receiving live-in care might themselves be of modest means and eligible for financial subsidy from the state towards the costs of their care. That might bring the overall cost of live-in care down to a level that would bring it within the family's budget.

Social care authorities (usually local authorities) help pay for practical help in the home for people whom they assess as having care and support needs and whose financial means are deemed too low to expect them to pay all or part of the cost *(see pages 654–64 for a detailed explanation).* When councils carry out financial assessments of the ability of the person who is to receive care to fund that care, they are not allowed to take into account the financial resources of family members, including any partner who is living with the person involved. In other words, other people could top up whatever amount the social care authority will contribute.

Anyone receiving a subsidy towards their care costs from their social care authority should be able to choose the way in which that subsidy is delivered. One means is through a 'direct payment' – a sort of voucher that enables the person receiving the subsidy (or their representatives) to organise the care and support they need, *as explained on pages 642–52.*

Free healthcare

Healthcare provided through the NHS is free whatever one's financial means. Various types of NHS care might reduce the amount of live-in care that someone needs.

If you have high-level care needs arising from a medical condition you might be eligible for NHS Continuing Healthcare. This is a form of funding provided by the NHS regardless of the financial means of the recipient to cover the costs of the provision of healthcare and also the social care that is normally means-tested involving practical assistance, for instance with personal care. NHS Continuing Healthcare can be taken in your own home and, although it should cover all the health and social care you need, it might not cover all the help you would like to have. You could hire a live-in carer to provide additional assistance, perhaps with cooking, housework and for general support at night. *(I discuss NHS Continuing Healthcare on pages 953–68.)*

If you or your loved-one are likely to die from terminal illness in the near future you could be eligible for a fast-tracked form of NHS Continuing Healthcare *(see page 961)*. Again, a live-in carer could provide company and support when nurses and carers provided by the NHS were not on your premises.

I discuss other types of free NHS care in Chapter 14, so do have a look to check that you are not missing out on any of these. For instance, if you are terminally ill and not eligible for NHS Continuing Healthcare, you should still expect whatever healthcare you need to be provided free by the NHS. This could include care through a hospice, much if not all of which may be provided in your own home *(see pages 997–1000 for a discussion of hospice-provided care)*.

Other goodies

Several other valuable types of state provision that are not means-tested and thus available whether you are of modest means or a millionaire include:

- Attendance Allowance, Disability Living Allowance and the Personal Independence Payment – state benefits awarded on grounds of disability, not income *(see pages 835–44)*

- an assessment of someone's care and support needs from social services, thus giving them the benefit of expert advice *(page 560 and Chapter 26)*

- equipment from the NHS to cope with disability and illness *(pages 480–1)*

- equipment from social services to cope with disability and illness *(pages 480–1)*
- house or flat adaptations from social services to cope with disability and illness *(pages 182–90)*
- full exemption from council tax for someone with a severe, permanent mental impairment which affects their ability to live a normal life and is entitled to Attendance Allowance, Disability Living Allowance or the Personal Independence Payment; this covers many people with dementia *(see pages 847–8)*
- a care-giver's disregard for council tax *(see page 848)*

Choice of arrangement

If you think you could afford live-in care, should you set up the arrangements yourself, as Christina did for Alice, or hand over the work involved to an agency?

The factors to be weighed up in coming to a conclusion are similar to those explored in the previous chapter on organising domiciliary care that is not live-in. Essentially, if you commission an agency to provide your live-in care, you pay more because you have an agency fee to cover, but you are relieved of the responsibilities of hiring and managing staff, as well as the reassurance that helpers will be provided despite illness and holidays. On the other hand, hiring staff yourself would enable you to select your care-giver (although a good agency should allow you to meet them beforehand or at least send someone else if you find you do not warm to each other).

Some domiciliary care agencies described in the previous chapter offer live-in care as part of a wider portfolio. Two types of specialist live-in care agency have emerged. One is like an employment or introduction agency: it finds live-in care-givers for clients and should have undertaken checks on the expertise and integrity of the people it offers and may have provided training. But once it has matched live-in care with client, the ongoing management of the situation including the formal hiring of the helper(s) is left to the client. This type of agency is not regulated by the Care Quality Commission and its equivalents.

The other type of agency matches a client with one or more care-givers and also oversees the situation, paying them and providing overall oversight. It should guarantee that it will provide a care-giver for as long as you need one, providing cover if any regular live-in helper it sends you is ill or on leave. This type is regulated by the Care Quality Commission and equivalent bodies, as explained in the next section.

In 2015, thirteen agencies came together to form the Live-in Care Information Hub *(see Useful Contacts)* with the objective of raising the profile of live-in care. The hub provides information on its website and in written form about how live-in care can work. Whether you are considering approaching an agency or finding live-in care-givers yourself, it is worth reading the Hub's material to give yourself a sense of the way in which live-in care can work.

Finding an agency

To find agencies that might be able to help you, trawl the internet and ask around. Perhaps there is someone at your local independent living centre or Age UK who has used one? You could ask social services or health service personnel if they know of good agencies in your area. But do not rely on word-of-mouth recommendations – an agency is only as good as the staff it hires, while the manager too may have changed since your contact was one of the agency's clients; the domiciliary care industry sees high staff turnover.

All agencies that provide live-in care-givers who provide personal care must be vetted and then registered by the Care Quality Commission (in England), the Care Inspectorate (in Scotland), the Care Standards Inspectorate for Wales or the Regulation and Quality Improvement Authority (in Northern Ireland). After that, agencies are appraised by CQC or equivalent inspectors. The inspection reports that result are available online. Read them – the most recent and any past ones. Why not also read those of agencies that have attracted high ratings by national inspectors and/or won awards (such as The Good Care Group), so you get a sense of what you could reasonably expect? If you are looking for an agency that provides only a facility for finding a live-in care-giver and is not therefore registered with the CQC, ask for a list of those in your area from the UK Homecare Association.

If some agencies seem promising and you think you could afford the fees they would charge, talk to their managers over the phone and if you remain interested, try to arrange face-to-face interviews.

Here are some suggestions for points you could consider when you talk to an agency's manager. Do also refer to the checklist of considerations *(on pages 508–15)* for choosing a domiciliary care agency. They are even more important than if you were hiring staff for limited periods: over time you are likely to be paying the agency an even larger sum of money, while the opportunities for theft, substandard practice and even abuse and neglect are even greater than in the world of visiting domiciliary care assistants.

Recruitment

Probe the agency's manager on how checks on the honesty of staff, their work-permit status and their suitability to work with potentially vulnerable people are carried out. Expect:

✓ checking of work-permit status

✓ verification of identity and qualifications

✓ several written references

✓ interviews and aptitude tests

✓ enhanced security with barring disclosures *(page 528)* and for these to be renewed regularly, perhaps every three years

✓ attempts to pursue checks of police records overseas where necessary

Training

Expect a live-in care agency's personnel to have much more expertise than that provided through the induction training outlined in the previous chapter, *on page 514.* So expect any care-giver sent to you to have at least level 2 in the Regulated Qualification Framework's Diploma in Health and Social Care or of the Scottish Qualifications Authority's Scottish Vocational Qualification in Social Services and Healthcare, or better still, level 3. In addition, expect to see proof that assistants you will be sent have received specialist training in any area relevant to you – such as how to care for someone with dementia or after a major, disabling stroke and/or at the end of their life. In the isolated world in which they work, standards could easily slip. How does the agency ensure this does not happen? How does it remind them of the professional standards that should underpin their work and bring them up to date with any changes in good practice? Look for evidence of audits and spot checks by managers and also regular refresher training.

Ask about the guidance the agency provides to help live-in care-givers look after their own emotional needs. Working and living alone, far from friends and family, perhaps in a foreign country and perhaps for someone with contrasting background and views can be challenging. At the same time, the work can be physically tough and emotionally hard; and simply dealing with people all day long brings its own difficulties.

Time off

What provision does the agency make for its workers to have time off and does it provide replacement at those times if you need it?

If someone requires a lot of care, particularly at night, an agency would usually send in a care-giver for a week or fortnight and then send a replacement for a couple of weeks, alternating the two so neither helper suffers burn-out and their client enjoys continuity of care. Nonetheless, the assistant will need time off during the period in which they are at work. How much time does the agency allow? Would this work for you? Would a replacement be needed or perhaps a relative could step in at those times? If a replacement must be hired, will this be your or the agency's responsibility?

If a client does not need continuous supervision or care, an agency would send in a care-giver for several weeks, even longer perhaps. Plainly, days off as well as a certain number of hours each day must be factored into the arrangements. Again, what does the agency propose? Would these arrangements work for you and how would you cope when your helper is off-duty?

Continuity of care
If you get along well, would the same live-in care-givers be sent to you?

Preparation
The agency should send a manager to meet you in the environment in which you would like to be cared for. They will assess precisely what tasks the helper should perform and then come up with a proposal for the level of support you need and the cost. The manager will also want to check that he or she would have adequate living conditions and that the working environment is all right. Expect them to point out any hazards, such as rugs over which you might trip, and discuss with you what might be done about them. A formal specification of how the caring situation will work should be drawn up.

Expect to meet the care-giver(s) before they work for you or your relative. If this is impractical, expect detailed information about them and their qualifications and the offer of a conversation with them through Skype. If you do not meet the assistant and find that when you meet you fail to gel, expect the agency to do what it can to provide a replacement and promptly.

Expect a formal review of how things are going and whether the care-giver's tasks should be tweaked within the first month. Sometimes the situation will not change much, but if the person who is being looked after has a condition that can result in the development of new care needs, such as dementia, reviews will be more important.

Back-up

Problems can arise both for you and for your care-giver, even in the middle of the night. Perhaps they will not do what you expect of them. Perhaps you refuse to play ball, for whatever reason including, perhaps, the influence of alcohol. Expect the agency to provide a back-up phone service, day and night, so if either you or your care-giver needs help to sort out a problem that has arisen within the caring situation, they have easy access to someone capable of resolving it.

Should your assistant become unwell or particularly tired – perhaps because you have been unwell and they have been up at night caring for you – expect the agency to be able to send in a replacement.

Feedback

A good agency will regularly seek the views of both their clients and their staff, whether or not any problems have arisen. They will send out client satisfaction and carer satisfaction forms every six months and respond to any issues that arise. Expect the manager to phone regularly to check that all is well and to make visits without alerting the helper beforehand. Whether or not any problems have arisen, expect the manager to meet care-givers regularly to discuss how things are going.

Charges

Make sure the agency will not ask you for further payments that it has not specified. Do not expect to have to fork out for Disclosure and Barring Service fees, for example *(see pages 506–7)*.

Hiring a live-in carer yourself

The suggestions for recruiting, hiring and managing personal assistants as well as the responsibilities that come with hiring staff outlined in the previous chapter should be helpful if you are hiring a live-in helper independently. Thus, for instance, when you are looking for staff:

✓ check the immigration status of your care-giver. Insist on seeing original documents, not copies.

✓ obtain an enhanced disclosure with barring from the Disclosure and Barring Service or its equivalent

✓ check paper qualifications

✓ if in Scotland, check that the applicant is registered with the Scottish Social Services Council *(see page 506)*

- ✓ obtain references of both character and competence in all the fields in which you hope your live-in care-giver will provide help, from personal care to driving
- ✓ if possible, go and meet your prospective assistant's referees

You are able to exercise more choice over the personality of your assistant if you hire staff direct than you would if you go through an agency. Consider whether you would find their company congenial. Would your live-in helper be friendly and chatty? Would that suit you, or might they be too garrulous to your taste? Conversely, would they retire to their own room at every available opportunity and thus not provide the company you are seeking?

Look for somebody who really enjoys working as a live-in helper. One young woman to whom I talked, who was caring for an elderly woman much incapacitated after a stroke, told me she had looked after her grandmothers and liked elderly people. When I commented that the person she was looking after was beautifully dressed, she explained that each morning they would discuss what she would wear, what jewellery she would put on and how she would style her hair: 'We're girls together!'

If you are hiring live-in help yourself and you need 24/7 cover, you will of course need to find one or more other helpers to cover when your main helper is having time off. Indeed, if you need a lot of help, you will need a whole team of carers, perhaps some live-in and some to provide back-up who live off your premises. You will also need to have some arrangement to retain staff should you need to spend time in hospital.

It is important clearly to define the scope of live-in workers' tasks and to be realistic about what you expect them to do. Draw up a list to avoid resentment building up, perhaps because the assistant finds themself expected to perform tasks they consider unnecessary. You might find the sort of approach to listing tasks I took when I worked out a list for a friend in Scotland useful (see pages 517–9).

Practicalities

Whether going through an agency or hiring independently, you also need to consider matters which arise only when somebody is sharing property. For instance:

- ✓ How will household bills be handled?
- ✓ Will the care-giver have the run of the whole of your property?
- ✓ Can they receive visitors there?

Life for your live-in helper

Whether you are contemplating live-in help through an agency or independently, it is important to consider the life the care-giver would live in your house or flat. You are likely to be happier and better cared for if your helper feels relatively content with their life. So:

✓ make your surroundings as congenial as possible for them, with a pleasant room, a comfortable bed, large-screen television and so on in their room.

✓ respect the assistant's need for equipment to prevent their damaging themselves when lifting you or your equipment. Don't expect them to lift you in and out of a car, for instance. Obtain gadgets such as car swivel seats and lifts for loading and unloading wheelchairs from car boots *(see page 472)*.

✓ consider which tasks you could offload from the care-giver. Perhaps a family member could do a big shop every few weeks or you could organise home deliveries? Perhaps you could hire somebody else to do the cleaning and the gardening?

✓ find friends for the care-givers if you can. Life for live-in assistants can be isolated and dull. Perhaps you or your friends know people of their age with whom they could socialise? Perhaps your friends and acquaintances, for instance from your local faith group, could offer diversionary activities and/or support?

Many of the other services outlined in this book could also help to keep you in contact with the world and at the same time provide respite for your live-in helper, not least befriending *(pages 220–3)* and day centres *(page 231)*. If you can no longer get out to meetings you used to enjoy, perhaps your assistant could help you host them in your home?

A secret camera?

As with any situation in which someone is working closely with someone else, it is worth setting in place a system for regular review of how things are going. Various points might have occurred to one or other party that could develop into ongoing concerns if not addressed early on. And regular discussion should also bring to light ways in which the situation could be tweaked so that you are both happier with it.

Perhaps you are planning to hire live-in care for someone who will live alone with their helper and might not speak up were their care substandard or even were the care-giver to take advantage of their vulnerability and perhaps put pressure on them to hand over money or even bully or physically abuse them. The potential for the abuse of people who are blind, deaf, deaf-blind or who have another kind of serious physical disability and/or a mental condition such as dementia in this private world is enormous. So too is the potential for slipshod service.

Try to ensure that someone from outside can visit frequently if you are unable to do so, including at times when visits would not be expected, to check that all is well. You could also consider installing some kind of recording device to find out what is going on. This could be anything from motion sensors or a sound recorder to a video camera with the sound switched off or on.

If you record and do not tell the live-in carer they might be annoyed and perhaps justifiably so. Far better to tell them at the outset. If they perform their job well, they should have nothing to fear. Indeed, you might end up praising their efforts and raising their wages. Dominique Kent of The Good Care Group told me in 2015 that if a carer is doing their job properly, a camera should not concern them: 'My stance is if you're confident about the service you provide, it shouldn't matter.' However, she pointed out that it is important to respect the dignity of the person who is being cared for. If the camera is recording continuously in their bedroom, they will be filmed behaving in ways which most people prefer to keep private, including the provision of help with personal care.

The consent of the person who will be filmed in this way should first be obtained. If they lack the capacity to give that consent, their legal representative should be approached (who may of course be you). In making any decision on behalf of someone who lacks the capacity to make it themselves, anyone representing them must conform to the principles of the mental capacity legislation *that are explained on pages 770–4.* They must go ahead only if the decision is in the best interests of the person involved.

Make sure the installation of secret recording equipment does not flout any contract of service with an agency or indeed with an individual live-in care-giver. If other people might be captured on film too, such as visitors or cleaners, they might consider their human rights had been infringed. They too might consider taking legal action against you, although general guidance issued by the Care Quality Commission in 2015 about the use of cameras noted that it was not aware of any instance in which recording equipment used by family members had been legally challenged.[1] Nonetheless, it is worth getting your own legal advice before you go ahead.

You should also consider what will happen to the film footage. Who will view it and will they be in a position to know whether the ministrations of the assistant represent good practice or not? What will happen to the footage after viewing? Who will destroy it and when?

Let us hope that the worst that you pick up through any camera or other recording equipment is sub-optimal care. You might find that the care-giver does not respond as promptly as you think they should to calls for assistance at night. Or perhaps they give your relative their meals in front of the television when you know they would prefer them at the dining table or in the garden.

However, many of the most terrible scandals involving care homes and domiciliary care in recent years have come to light and been acted on only because of the evidence provided by cameras. If you fear that you or your loved one has been or may be abused or neglected, contact the police or social services, *as described on pages 565–6*. The wilful neglect or ill-treatment of another person who lacks mental capacity by somebody who is caring for or in a position of trust or power over them is a criminal offence *(see page 568)*.

Support from social services

We see in Chapter 27 that unpaid carers (often family members) have a right to an assessment by their social care authority of their own needs for support when they are caring for someone. Paid carer-givers, live-in or not, do not enjoy that right. However, social care authorities have the discretion to help them. A live-in care-giver could find they are being expected to perform tasks for which they consider themselves ill-equipped and in that sort of situation, social services could be asked to help sort out the problem; *I describe a case in which this took place at the end of Chapter 27, on pages 629–30.*

Social services can also be approached for advice, perhaps by the person seeking live-in care or their family. Social care authorities have a responsibility to provide advice to anyone who might need care and support, whatever their financial circumstances. They must carry out an assessment of the care and support needs of individuals if asked to do so, again regardless of financial means *(see Chapter 26)*. This assessment is well worth having and can inform the sort of care you may be seeking. If you cannot obtain an assessment swiftly from your local council, you could consider approaching an independent social worker *(page 582)*.

Live-in care

* Live-in care varies greatly in cost.
* Some families club together to pay for live-in care.
* NHS Continuing Healthcare funding can cover much of the cost.
* Someone paying for care, however wealthy, is likely to be entitled to several valuable free services from the state.
* Choose any live-in care agency carefully.
* Hiring live-in care-givers yourself brings more responsibilities but should give greater choice.
* Look for a care-giver who enjoys their work and the company of older people.
* Think about the life your live-in helper will lead and how you can improve their quality of life.
* Live-in care focuses on the individual, but care homes offer more company.
* Consider how you will monitor care, particularly for a relative with dementia.

HELP FROM THE COUNCIL

> " *Stigma and ignorance can put people off approaching social services, yet social services departments, which may employ hundreds of people, many with years of experience and a passion for helping people facing difficulties, can be invaluable.* "

PART SEVEN
HELP FROM THE COUNCIL

U nlike state healthcare provision, which we looked at in Part Four, social care aims to mitigate the practical and emotional difficulties that life can throw at us. When we are older, it can help us cope with the challenges to daily life that illness, both physical and mental, can give rise.

However, many people who might benefit fail to do so because they assume that social care is restricted to people of modest income. This is not true – the system should offer something to everybody who is experiencing problems in their everyday life, and legislation for England and for Wales passed in 2014 stressed this wide-ranging role.

Another reason why people fail to use social care is that, unlike the health service, it suffers from a confused and negative image. I therefore begin this part with an introduction to the world of social care. This includes a brief explanation of the involvement of social care in such fields as elder abuse and help for people with eyesight problems.

In the following chapters of this part, I explore the ways in which we can make the best use of the social care system. Chapter 26 examines the hoops we must go through to get practical and/or emotional help and Chapter 28 the different ways in which help from social services can be delivered, with tips on which options could work best for you. Chapter 28 also examines at the ways in which social care authorities charge users for services.

Many older people look after their partner, relative or friend as a 'carer', often without realising that they are a carer and that carers can obtain help through the social care system. I explain how this is provided and the sort of support they can typically obtain – perhaps more diverse and more extensive than they might imagine – in Chapter 27.

Incidentally, the help given to carers to care for others through the social care system is usually called 'support' to distinguish it from that to people with needs for help for themselves, termed 'care and support'.

Media stories about cutbacks in local authority funding for social care might cause you to rule out even considering looking to your council to help you cope with daily tasks in your own home. Think again! Although *(as we shall see in Chapter 26)*, councils are expected to distribute help to individual older and disabled people using criteria set nationally country by country, in fact, particularly in England, they vary considerably in the amount they are prepared to spend on citizens who need help. (This variation reflects differences in councils' political priorities, the amount they can raise locally through business rates and council tax, and the level of their funding from central government.) This means that in some places you are likely to find attracting support easier than in others.

Another fact to bear in mind is that although the number of people receiving publicly-funded care services in England fell by a quarter between 2011 and 2016, 90 per cent of the people who did get publicly-funded social care were satisfied with the care and support they received.[1] And, as I try to show in this part, the help which social care can provide, including to those whose financial means rules them out of council subsidy, extends into many areas beyond the provision of practical help in the home.

Chapter 25

The world of social care

The state system for delivering care for older people has two arms. In Parts Four and Five we looked at the first of these, state healthcare provision. Social care complements healthcare by homing in on the practical and emotional difficulties that life can throw at us. For older people, these often arise as the result of illness or disability, such as osteo-arthritis, which can impair somebody's ability to walk and even to wash and dress themselves.

While it is a basic principle of state healthcare that provision is free at the point of delivery, the local authorities that usually provide social care can charge users for services. However, social care is sometimes free to everyone; where services are charged for, there has to be a safety net to prevent the poorest citizens being denied services because they cannot afford to pay for them. As a result, means-testing, while absent from state healthcare provision, is a characteristic of social care.

In this introductory chapter, I examine the social care system, in particular:

▶ its organisation

▶ how it can help older people and carers

▶ how it is involved in admission to a care home

▶ its role in the investigation and prevention of elder abuse

▶ the legal and financial constraints on social care authorities

▶ controls over social care authorities by central government

▶ the difference in charging for health and social care services

▶ tips on handling social services departments

▶ access to records held by social services

► raising concerns and lodging complaints
► consulting an independent social worker

Origins and legacy

Social care does an enormous amount to enhance the lives of Britain's older citizens. But unlike the health service, it suffers from a muddled and sometimes unflattering reputation which puts off many of those who could benefit from it.

One problem is that while some local council services such as education and waste collection are provided to everybody, social care is offered only to people who need assistance for particular reasons. While we all encounter teachers and refuse collectors from an early age, many people never encounter an official from their social work department or, if they do, it is only at a particular time in their lives – for instance, if they have a disability or have had a child with a learning disability. This restriction of social care to people who need certain types of help means most of us are unfamiliar with social workers on the ground.

We look in vain to the media to remedy our ignorance. Social workers are not usually depicted on television and film informatively, still less with the glamour accorded to doctors and nurses.

The origins of social care do not help its present-day image. While the roots of the health service are in the post-war dream of a better Britain in which every citizen has an equal right to top-class healthcare, social services' origins lie in the earlier idea of local communities having responsibility for people in the parish who could not look after themselves, such as unmarried mothers or the frail infirm. If parishes would or could not look after such people, they put them up in the workhouse, where they were expected to be grateful for the parish's largesse and ashamed of the needs that had laid them low. Today, social care arranged by local authorities still carries something of this ancient stigma.

Stigma and ignorance can therefore put people off approaching social services, yet social services departments, which may employ hundreds of people, many with years of experience and a passion for helping people facing difficulties, can be invaluable.

Organisation

Social care is the responsibility of local authorities. In England these are county councils, unitary councils and metropolitan borough councils. In Wales, social services departments are based in local unitary authorities.

This is also the case in Scotland, where the social services departments in the country's unitary councils are called social work departments.

In England, Wales and Scotland, moves are afoot to bring the running of health and social care closer together. In Northern Ireland, social care has been administered for some time alongside healthcare by six regional health and social care trusts.

In all these cases, if you wish to enquire about social care provision, simply telephone the council or trust involved and ask for the social services (or social work) department. Should you contact the wrong local authority, such as your district rather than your county council in England, you should be referred on to the correct tier of local government.

Social work departments

The social work departments of local authorities are often huge. Some of the people there will be addressing the plight of children who need help, while others will be working with disabled people, people with learning disabilities or asylum seekers, for instance.

Social workers are the key professionals in any social work department. In order to practise, they must have a social work degree and have spent a year in employment involving the development of particular skills. Once this has been completed, they can apply to have their name entered on a national register and then they must agree to abide by a code of practice and make themselves accountable for their actions to the agency that holds the register. Social workers can be taken to task for unprofessional conduct and reprimanded or even struck off the register for a limited period or indefinitely, in the same way that doctors and dentists can be removed from their professional registers if found guilty of professional misconduct *(as described in Chapter 15)*. The national agencies that hold the registers for social workers are the Health and Care Professions Council (in England), the Scottish Social Services Council, the Care Council for Wales, and the Northern Ireland Social Care Council.

Social workers are also expected to abide by the code of ethics of their professional body, the British Association of Social Workers. This sets the core values on which social workers' conduct should be based, including the promotion of the right of the individuals they seek to help to make their own choices and decisions.[1]

The section of a social work department responsible for helping older people will also contain assistant social workers. Many of these are care managers, and they should have a different, non-degree qualification. They carry out assessments of the needs of individual older people and assemble care and support for them. Care managers are supervised by social workers and, if the assessment is complex, the case will be passed to a social worker.

Another tier of people you might come across is the contact assessor or customer advisor, particularly if you telephone social services and say you think you may need help. These advisors will answer straightforward enquiries and pass your name on to a care manager if they consider this necessary and/or you ask them to do so.

Occupational therapists are also likely to feature in the adult social care section of a social services department. OTs offer advice on the ways in which people can cope with illness or disability in their daily lives, including through the provision of walking aids and other disability equipment and the modification of a person's home through ramps and the like.

One section of the department will focus on dealing with cases of abuse of older people and this will probably contain the highest concentration of social workers. It will have close links with the health service and the police through its adult safeguarding board *(see below)*.

The support of people with mental health problems is the role of social workers who have undergone additional training to become 'approved mental health professionals', or 'mental health officers' in Scotland.

Other departments of a social work department with whom the adult social care section works closely include the hearing and vision team and the team that supports carers. Some social workers are employed in hospitals, where they play a key role in the discharge of patients *(see Chapter 39.)*

If you are unclear whether a particular person from social services is a registered social worker, you could contact one of the national agencies that register social workers to find out whether their name is on the official list. If you consider that a social worker is behaving unprofessionally, contact the Health and Care Professions Council, the Scottish Social Services Council, the Care Council for Wales or the Northern Ireland Social Care Council.

Activities

Here are the main ways in which social care authorities are involved in the lives of older people:

Information and advice

Councils have long provided a wide range of information about social care matters. In England, for example, the Care Act 2014 confirms this by laying a duty on social care authorities to establish and maintain a service for the provision of information and advice about care and support for adults and support for carers.[2] Councils cannot wriggle out of this requirement by saying it does not apply to so-called 'self-funders' – people whose financial means rule them out of a subsidy from the council – or people whose needs for help do not meet a particular threshold of severity. For the government says, 'Importantly, this duty to establish and maintain an information and advice service relates to the whole population of the local authority area, not just those with care and support needs or in some other way already known to the system.'[3] Councils in England are also legally obliged to provide information and advice to help people plan and pay for any care costs they may incur *(the duty about financial advice is discussed on page 665).*

Hearing and sight impairment

Many social care departments have 'sensory impairment teams' who visit people of all ages with hearing or vision difficulties, or both, and offer practical help. This can include the provision of equipment to help people who are hard of hearing to make phone calls or visually impaired people to use their kitchens safely, as well as support to counter problems such as anxiety and isolation that can arise from sight or hearing problems. Social services have duties to help people with hearing and sight impairment separate from their obligations to help older people in general who are facing difficulties. Do not worry too much if your name is not on a special register of people with sight or hearing impairment: the government has said provision of services should not be limited to people whose names are on these registers.[4]

Family issues

Social workers are trained to help people cope with their emotional responses to situations and also with family problems. They can provide invaluable help, often by breaking the deadlock that can arise within families and that may seem intractable. In one case of which I became aware, an elderly mother was becoming frail, but while her two daughters were growing increasingly worried about her and wanted her to obtain help in the home, their brother (who held power of attorney over the old lady's considerable estate) resisted this idea strongly. His sisters contacted social services for advice and the old lady was allocated a social worker who used her training in dealing with family relationships to explain the nature of his mother's difficulties to the son. As a result, his resistance to his mother hiring help melted away – much to her benefit.

Practical help and support

This is provided to help people when they are facing difficulties such as disability and general frailty, and typically involves the provision of assistants who help with personal care tasks like washing and dressing and/or practical chores like shopping and cleaning. As we shall see in the remainder of this part, sometimes social services organise the provision of care services to individuals, but they are being encouraged instead to offer them a pot of cash and leave them to make their own arrangements, albeit with some organisational support. Social care authorities also provide or subsidise lunch clubs and day centres.

If it is established that somebody needs practical support, such as help to get up or go to bed, social care authorities must ensure it is provided, even if they have to foot the entire bill.

Social care authorities have a legal duty to arrange care and support for somebody who needs services yet lacks the mental capacity to arrange them themselves and has nobody suitable to do so on their behalf. In these ways, social care acts as a safety net for people unable to look after themselves and/or unable to pay the costs involved.

Someone whose financial means rule them out of any subsidy can still ask social services to organise the provision of a package of care and support for them under what is known as 'the right to request' *(see page 666).*

Equipment and adaptations to the home

Social services are also the gateway to a wide range of equipment as well as to adaptations to the home to make life easier and safer for people with illness or disability. These range from pendant alarms to stairlifts and include 'telecare' – alarms and detectors which can help people, including those with dementia, to live safely.

Despite cutbacks in public spending, provision is often free. Thus all social services departments in England must provide for free equipment as well as house adaptations up to the value of £1,000 to anybody they assess as needing them. *(This area of social services activity is discussed in Chapter 21: Equipment, Chapter 22: Telecare and Chapter 8: Staying put.)*

Help for carers

Carers are people who provide care at home without remuneration for loved ones who need help. Innumerable possibilities exist. Parents (of any age) may be caring for a child with a physical disability, mental health problem or learning disability. Couples in their eighties may be acting as each other's carer – perhaps one has mobility problems while the other suffers from depression. Carers in their sixties may be looking after a frail parent or an older relative or friend who needs support. Social services have special responsibilities to help carers, *which are discussed in Chapter 27*. Most social care authorities have a senior manager with responsibility for supporting carers and developing a strategy to help them.

Signposting

Not everyone who approaches social services will qualify for equipment, home adaptations or services, because their degree of need for them will not be considered sufficiently high. However, they will still be able to benefit from free advice and support. Social care officials are able to sign-post people to a wide range of facilities and organisations in their local areas, from carers' support groups to befriending schemes to benefits advice centres. Social services should also help people find advocacy organisations – that is, bodies which can offer individuals one-to-one help in negotiating the care system and and/or representing them *(see Chapter 34)*.

Solving problems

Social workers can tap into their knowledge of the ways in which problems can be overcome and of how to help people square up to difficulties psychologically. Perhaps an older man who has walked to the newsagent's every day has a stroke and can do so no longer; his social worker puts him in touch with a befriending group one of whose volunteers takes him there twice a week. Perhaps an older woman hoards piles of old magazines in her flat; her social worker persuades her that they should be removed and, having secured her agreement, organises their disposal.

People with mental illness

Social workers seek to help people with mental health problems. As mentioned earlier, mental health social workers receive special training. Some of them work with health professionals in teams which seek to help people living long-term with mental health problems. Others work in teams which deal with crisis situations, sometimes 'sectioning' patients, who can be compulsorily placed in hospital if they have a serious condition such as schizophrenia, bipolar disorder or dementia and refuse to accept treatment for it, even though detention and treatment are necessary for their health and safety or for the protection of other people, and appropriate medical treatment is available. Patients can appeal against detention and can also ask for the order placing them in hospital to be reviewed. This legislation is complex and is not considered in detail in this book. You can find out more about it from the voluntary organisations Mind, Mind Cymru, the Scottish Association for Mental Health, and the Northern Ireland Association for Mental Health.

Care homes

When people live in a care home they receive practical help with everyday tasks made difficult by illness or infirmity at any time, day or night. They also receive their accommodation and food in the home, and laundry and cleaning are undertaken by the home's staff. In addition, homes often provide activities and outings.

There are 20,000 care homes in the UK. The vast majority are owned by commercial companies, a smaller number by not-for-profit organisations such as charities. Local authorities, which used to own many homes, now own few, especially in England. However, social services are still involved in the world of care homes in the following ways:

1. The provision of advice

Social services offer advice to people contemplating a move to a care home. Anybody, whatever their financial means, has a right to an assessment by social services of their need to go into a care home; this can be invaluable, as some people move into a care home when they do not need to, or go into a nursing home when a (cheaper) residential home would be adequate. These assessments have always been free. They are called care assessments and I explain how they work in Chapter 26.

2. Action for people who lack mental capacity and need care

Social services cannot force somebody to go and live in a care home against their will: they are overstepping the mark if they do more than advise. However, this is not the case if a social care assessment shows that somebody needs the round-the-clock care that can only be provided in a care home, they lack the mental capacity to take the decision and there is nobody suitable to act in their best interests, such as their attorney *(mental capacity and attorney are defined in the Glossary)*. In this kind of case, social services can move the person involved into a home, even against their will. Such a situation often arises when people are in hospital, are developing dementia and are considered by social services unlikely to be able to care for themselves should they return home.

However, there are safeguards which protect the human rights of the person who might be treated in this way. Before a social care authority in England or Wales can place somebody of limited mental capacity in a care home, it must appoint an 'independent mental capacity advocate' who will form their own view on whether the proposed move would be in the best interests of the person involved. Social services must take the advocate's conclusions into account when reaching their final decision on how they should act.

In addition, if social services in England or Wales proposes to restrict the liberty of somebody with limited mental capacity, for instance by placing them in a care home in which they will not have the freedom to come and go at will or indeed restricting their freedom of movement in their own home, they must go through a procedure called the 'deprivation of liberty safeguards'. In Scotland, an application to a sheriff court must usually be made for the authority to take on special guardianship powers to enable them to take these steps. *(I discuss this complex field in Chapter 33.)*

3. Paying residents' care home fees

Care provided in a care home is usually considered to be 'social care' and thus the recipient of it must pay. However, safety nets are in place to ensure that care home residents do not have to use all of their savings to pay care home bills, as fees can run to more than £30,000 each year for residential care and £50,000 for care in a nursing home. In each country of the UK, a savings threshold is set below which social care authorities must pick up the tab – the resident continues to contribute their income, but their savings must not be depleted below a certain level.

In **Wales,** savings are safe from care home bills as soon as they have been depleted to £30,000, or if they have never reached that level.

The other countries operate two thresholds. In **England,** once somebody's savings are down to £23,250, social services must begin to contribute. A sliding scale determines the size of the resident's and the local authority's respective contributions until the resident's savings have been depleted further, to £14,250. If this lower threshold is reached, the resident's savings are completely off-limits and social services must pay all that is necessary. The same two thresholds obtain in **Northern Ireland.** In **Scotland,** there are also two thresholds, at £26,250 and £16,250.

Many people have never had savings above the threshold and move into a care home with social services organising the contract with the home and paying whatever is necessary by way of fees, after the resident has contributed their state pension and any other weekly income. Others start as 'self-funders' in care homes, but later come to rely on social services to pick up the tab if their savings are depleted by paying care home fees.

The threshold safety nets described above operate throughout the UK, but in **Scotland** social care authorities also make two non-means-tested contributions towards their residents' care home fees.

The provision of 'personal care' is free to people in Scotland aged 65 and over assessed as needing it, *(as explained on pages 659–60)*. The amount a council contributes varies according to how much help somebody needs, but if it is provided in a care home, it makes a flat-rate contribution towards a resident's fees.

In addition, councils in Scotland make a flat-rate payment to cover the costs of nursing care for people in care homes which provide nursing (nursing homes). In England and Wales, in contrast, these payments (known as the Registered Nursing Care Contribution or free nursing care) are made by health bodies, and in Northern Ireland by health and social care trusts *(as explained on page 962)*.

4. Loans to pay care home fees

Care home residents whose relative wealth means they must pay their own fees can ask their local authority for a loan to cover the cost. This ensures that they do not need to sell their homes when they move into a home. Under a 'deferred payment agreement', social services pay the care home bills until such time as the resident dies or decides to repay; they then refund social services the loan. Social care authorities have been empowered to provide loans under these agreements for several years and they have been free of interest. Since 2014, however, councils in England have been empowered to charge interest (subject to a set limit) on the loan and to require reimbursement of their costs in negotiating and setting up the agreement.[5]

Hospital patients

Although most social care staff are based in council offices, some are located in large hospitals. There may be a social worker in A&E; there may be one in the palliative care team. Social workers perform a pivotal role in discharging people from hospital and putting in place practical support while they are recuperating after leaving hospital *(this is explored in Chapter 39: Leaving hospital)*.

People at risk of abuse

Should we become frail and unable to protect ourselves, we can be just as vulnerable to harm from those claiming to look after us as young children. Indeed, elder abuse has much in common with violence against children. Both often occur in a domestic setting, in a relationship in which one person has far more power than the other, and may involve violence which cannot be justified. So, blows, slaps and beatings may be inflicted on, say, a frail, elderly parent living in their son or daughter's home or a frail person living in a care home, just as on a child. But, also as with children, the abuse of older people can include neglecting to give someone the food, drink and care they cannot obtain for themselves. Most people are well aware that social care authorities involve themselves in cases of the abuse of children. It is important to know that they also play a key role in protecting older people against abuse.

For harm to an older person to be classed as abuse in the world of social care, the abuser has to be somebody acting in a position of trust. So, a stranger who mugs an elderly man in the street is not an abuser in the sense it is used here, but a care assistant who slaps, ridicules or steals from him is. Of course, most people are perfectly capable of standing up for themselves. Social care authorities' responsibilities relate only to people considered 'vulnerable'. In England and Wales, this is defined as people who:

- are experiencing or at risk of abuse including neglect
- have needs for care and support, and
- as a result of those needs are unable to protect themselves against abuse or neglect or the risk of abuse or neglect[6]

A similar provision exists in Northern Ireland.[7]

The definition of adults at risk of harm in **Scotland** is slightly different. They are people who:

- are unable to look after their own well-being, property, rights or other interests
- are at risk of harm, and
- are more vulnerable to being harmed than others because they are affected by disability, mental disorder, illness or physical or mental infirmity[8]

Throughout the UK, the types of harm and neglect (in other words abuse) with which social services concern themselves include:

- physical abuse, such as hitting or slapping
- the misuse of medication so that it inflicts unnecessary harm
- sexual assault or sexual acts to which the adult at risk has not consented or was pressured into consenting

- humiliation, intimidation, swearing, harassment, bullying and other forms of psychological abuse

- neglect, such as withholding adequate food, drink, heating and medication or ignoring medical or physical care needs

- theft, fraud, exploitation and pressure in connection with property or money

A study in 2007 estimated that one in 25 older people living in mainstream housing (not care homes or hospitals) were affected by abuse of one kind or another during that year – 39,000 people in Wales alone.[9]

Social care authorities have special responsibilities and powers in the field of abuse. They have a legal duty to investigate cases of abuse that has happened or it is feared will occur to vulnerable people, *as defined on the previous page*. So in England and Wales, the abuse must involve people who need care and support (whether or not their needs are being met); and they must be unable to protect themselves against this threat as a result of their needs for care and support.[10]

Social care departments usually have a section devoted to 'adult protection' or 'adult safeguarding', staffed by their most experienced social workers. They should work closely with the police and health services in their area. Indeed, local authorities with social care responsibilities must set up safeguarding boards seeking to ensure that the activities of the police and NHS bodies in their areas in tackling abuse are as well coordinated and effective as possible.[11] In Scotland the equivalent bodies are called adult protection committees and in Northern Ireland adult safeguarding partnerships.

Anybody can ring social services at any time to say that they or somebody else has been, is being or may be about to be abused. Social care authorities provide a 24-hour phone line for such calls, so they should be available to talk not only at any time during office hours, but also during the night and at weekends. If the matter is very urgent, an official may make an immediate visit to the place where the alleged abuse has taken place or where it is feared it will occur, if necessary with a police officer. Anybody concerned about abuse, such as physical or sexual assault or neglect could also contact the police direct.

When alerted to a case of possible abuse, (unless the matter demands immediate intervention), social services officials acting alone or in conjunction with the police and health services consider:

✓ Is there a significant risk of harm to this person?

✓ How vulnerable are they?

- ✓ What is the nature of the abuse being alleged?
- ✓ Over what length of time has it been taking place? Is it one-off?
- ✓ Is there a risk to other people?
- ✓ Could the abuse get worse? Could there be an escalation?

If the person who is being abused or is at risk of abuse would have sub-stantial difficulty in being involved in the inquiry into the abuse and so-cial services in England consider there is nobody suitable who is available to represent and support them, (including if this is because the person considers a willing candidate unacceptable), social services must appoint an independent advocate to help the person engage with the inquiry and express their views.[12] This advocate will come from an agency which pro-vides advocacy services; people who provide care or treatment for the person in a professional capacity or for remuneration are ruled out of acting as their advocate. *(Advocates are discussed in Chapter 34.)*

If the abuse were considered potentially serious, social services would convene a 'best interests meeting', drawing in all officials who might have some knowledge of or bearing on the situation, including the person's GP. Possible courses of action would then be discussed with the person who had been abused or was at risk of abuse, unless they lacked the mental capacity to be involved. In this case, their legal representative (attorney, deputy or guardian), or their partner or relative would be involved – un-less these people were the suspected perpetrator of the abuse.

The response to the abuse could be the taking of one or more of a wide range of different steps, taking no action, or monitoring the situation to see whether action might become necessary in the future.

Punishment

There are legal remedies for many types of abuse. Theft, types of physical assault and various sexual offences are all acts for which people can be prosecuted in the criminal courts and be sent to prison. Another exam-ple: making abusive comments and insulting gestures linked to some-one's age or disability does not only constitute psychological abuse: it is a form of discrimination under the Equality Act 2010, for which there are remedies exist in the civil courts *(as explained on pages 691–2)*.[13]

There are also tools which enable abusers to be pursued through an injunction requiring them to desist from molesting someone or barring them from that person's home. Thus in **Scotland,** social care authorities can make a 'banning order', barring access by a third party from a speci-fied place or places (which would normally be the place where the person at risk was living); this order, which can be temporary or permanent, needs the consent of the local sheriff.[14] Orders such as these are not usually granted without the agreement of the victim.

In **England** and **Wales,** the Court of Protection can be asked to make a 'contact order', which prevents an abuser from entering the home of someone they have abused, although it cannot be used if the abuser has the right to occupy the property. However, a 'domestic violence protection order', made through the police, can bar someone from having contact with their victim for up to 28 days and from access to the victim's home.

Helpfully and separately, anybody who has been found guilty of committing elder abuse has their name placed on a special register. This covers not only types of abuse for which someone could or might have been prosecuted, but also other types which do not constitute an offence at law. These registers provide a means for ensuring that people do not work with vulnerable older people (or with children) if they have been found to have abused a child or an older person, even if this has not involved a criminal activity. *(I explain how this system works on page 528.)*

People with dementia are particularly vulnerable to abuse. They may not be able to defend themselves, either by fighting back verbally or physically against those who are hitting or humiliating them, or by obtaining or insisting upon being given the food and water that those who are neglecting them are failing to provide. What is more, they may be unable to explain who has been harming them and how.

In view of this extreme vulnerability and the terrible suffering that can be inflicted through abuse, a new criminal offence was introduced in England and Wales in 2005. Somebody who is caring for or in a position of trust or power over a person who lacks mental capacity and who is ill-treating or wilfully neglecting them is committing a criminal offence; a person found guilty can be fined or sent to prison for several years.[15] The perpetrator might be a family member, an attorney or deputy or someone being paid to care, perhaps in a hospital, care home or the person's own home. Separate laws in Scotland and Northern Ireland contain a similar provision.[16]

Another way of punishing an abuser, and also possibly taking them out of the environment in which the abuse has occurred, is through reporting the matter to a professional body in a position to take disciplinary action, such as the General Medical Council or the Nursing and Midwifery Council. These bodies have the power to strike individuals off the lists of professionals who are able to practise *(as explained in Chapter 15)* and often do so. For example, the conduct of a nurse in a nursing home who gave residents powerful sedatives and put call bells out of reach so that she could have an 'easy night' was brought to the attention of the Nursing and Midwifery Council in 2010. It struck her off its register.[17]

Training and Support

By no means all abuse results from malevolence on the part of the abuser. In a care home or hospital, staff might neglect residents' or patients' needs not through lack of concern for the welfare of those for whom they are caring, but because the provider of the facility has failed to provide them with adequate training or equipment or to hire sufficient numbers of staff. For example, if a care assistant is ignorant of the technique of turning somebody with the aid of a slip-sheet or has not been provided with one, then the chances of rough, painful man-handling and therefore abuse increase. The same problem could arise within a domiciliary care agency which fails to ensure that the assistants it sends to provide care to people in their homes have received adequate training or have sufficient time for their assigned tasks.

In these situations, social services will take up the matter with the care home, hospital or domiciliary agency. They might well also bring in the national organisation that regulates and inspects these facilities – in England the Care Quality Commission, in Scotland the Care Inspectorate, in Wales the Care Standards Inspectorate for Wales and in Northern Ireland the Regulation and Quality Improvement Authority. These regulatory agencies have the power to insist on improvements and ultimately to force a provider to close down if remedial action is not taken.

Financial abuse

The main way in which the abuse of older people differs from that of young children is harm involving material goods. Often sitting on greater wealth than those around them, older people who cannot stand up for themselves may be pressurised into making gifts and bequests or cheated out of their money by unscrupulous attorneys, friends, relatives and neighbours as well as accountants, care assistants, gardeners and other hired helpers. The law provides many means of dealing with anyone who gains unauthorised access to someone else's finances and takes money belonging to them. They can be charged with such criminal offences as theft, forgery, blackmail or dishonestly and intentionally taking advantage of their position to extract money.

If the alleged financial abuse involves the attorneys or other representatives of people whose mental capacity is limited, the Office of the Public Guardian can be asked to become involved. The Guardian, together with the Court of Protection, can investigate cases of improper use of such powers and remove or revoke them if necessary *(as explained in Chapter 31).*

But the abuse involved might be quite different from an attorney defrauding the person they are representing. For instance, whenever a boy visits his great-grandmother, who is nearly blind, he filches money from her purse. She knows what he is doing and he probably knows that she knows, but is aware that she wishes to remain on good terms with his parents and that exposing the theft and in particular bringing in the strong arm of the law would sour relations. So he knows she will probably allow the situation to continue.

One of the great benefits of the involvement of social services in elder abuse is that somebody in a difficult situation such as this can talk it through with an experienced professional and discuss a range of solutions which may not have occurred to them. In this case, for example, social services might be able to arrange for somebody, such as a care assistant, always to visit at the same time as the boy. Or he might be made aware that another person knows about the situation and might take action if the stealing does not stop. This person could be a social worker or a police officer. (Visits by the police to discuss with the woman what she would like to happen would be made in an unmarked car to avoid embarrassment with neighbours.)

Abuse and the provision of support services

The provision of support services is another way in which social services respond to cases of elder abuse. For instance, a devoted husband looking after his seriously ill wife without any help and at the end of his tether might, one night, lash out with his fists. Alerted to the situation, perhaps by a neighbour who has heard shouts and screams, social services could step in, make sure that the woman is not in imminent danger of more harm and then sit down with the husband and the wife (if she is able), as well as any other individuals or professionals who might usefully be involved, to work out whether the caring situation is really sustainable and, if it is, how the man might be supported in his role as his wife's carer. The result of the discussion with the professionals could be that the woman attends a day centre for several days each week, thus giving both her and her husband a break from their domestic situation. Social services might help secure complete time off for the man through his wife staying in a care home for a short period of 'respite care'. A range of free support may be available for him in his role as her carer *(as outlined in Chapter 27).*[18]

So although abuse is horrible, it can provide the trigger for the provision of support services by the state, or at least advice by professionals. Indeed, the possibility of abuse or the fact that it has taken place is one of the key eligibility criteria used by councils when determining whether somebody (in the above example the woman) is eligible for practical support in their own right *(as explained in Chapter 26)*. In other words, the abuse in the case above could increase her chances of securing help in the home herself, such as with washing and dressing, thus freeing up her husband to provide more in the way of emotional support and leaving him less tired and stressed.

What social services cannot do

Social care authorities thus possess powers in a range of areas, but it is worth being aware of the limits on what they can do.

Legal constraints

Local councils can only take action which the law has specifically empowered them to take. Parliament has divided these actions into those that are 'mandatory' and those that are 'discretionary'. Mandatory powers are those that local authorities have a legal duty to use. For instance, they must provide education for children. If the words 'shall' and 'must' feature in the law involved, the power is mandatory. If a council fails to use a mandatory power, a court can force it to do so.

Other actions by local councils result from the use of discretionary or permissive powers. For instance, councils have a discretionary power over whether to charge individuals for the provision of social care services. The vast majority do, but they do not have to. In the case of discretionary powers, the relevant Act of Parliament will contain the words 'can' and 'may'.

Plainly, it can be tempting for councils to rule out any use of discretionary powers which would involve them spending money. This is wrong: a local council cannot rule out the use of a discretionary power on all occasions. Binding itself in exercising its discretion is called 'fettering discretion', and it is unlawful. A council could be taken to court for doing this. It may establish internal guidelines, but it must be prepared to make exceptions on the basis of individual cases. *(See page 612.)*

So, if your local authority says it never uses a certain power or never subsidises a person by more than a certain amount, you could point out that it is fettering its discretion. If it fails to change its behaviour, you could lodge an official complaint and if necessary bring the matter to the attention of the relevant Ombudsman. You could even take your council to court (or threaten to do so). These forms of redress are described at the end of this chapter.

Respect for human rights

Local authorities have to respect certain principles of behaviour deemed to be 'human rights', such as the right to respect for one's private and family life and the right not to be subjected to inhuman or degrading treatment. These obligations apply to all public bodies in the UK and to organisations acting on their behalf *(I explain them in the context of the National Health Service on pages 295–6).*

Financial constraints

Much of the cash that local councils spend on social care comes from central government, whether channelled through the Department of Health, the Scottish Government, the Welsh Government or the Northern Ireland Executive. This money, along with locally generated income such as that from council tax (or in Northern Ireland domestic rates), pays for the work of local authorities.

Governments can influence the behaviour of local authorities by the amount of funding they give them and whether or not particular pots of money are ring-fenced. If money is not ring-fenced, it is available to be spent in a range of areas and the choice is in the hands of the local authority. Social care tends not to be ring-fenced, so it has to compete with all other claims on a council's resources.

For many years, national governments have underfunded social care. It is seen as the poor relation of its natural twin, healthcare. So, while national governments feel they must flag up their protection of NHS spending, in the past they have often omitted to mention that social care also needs large amounts of public cash.

Control by central government

National governments also influence how local authorities behave through issuing official instructions and guidance to councils which set out how they should be using the various powers they have been given. In England, the Department of Health issues regulations, directions, orders and 'policy guidance', all of which have the force of law. Policy guidance is often the most useful and revealing means for people outside the system to know how official bodies are expected to behave, and I often quote it in this book.

The Department of Health also publishes 'practice guidance', which sets out how it considers a social care organisation should go about particular tasks. Practice guidance (sometimes called best practice guidance) is weaker in status than policy guidance and does not have to be followed slavishly. Nonetheless, if challenged in court, a local authority would have to explain why it had not been followed.

Inspection

Central government monitors, to a greater or lesser extent, the actions and decisions of social care authorities. Published reports of inspections of individual social services departments by national agencies can be useful if, for example, somebody is considering moving to a different part of the country and wonders what sort of support they might expect from the local council there. If you are moving to or within **Scotland** or **Wales,** have a look at the reports of inspections of local authority social care departments which the Care Inspectorate in Scotland and the Care and Social Services Inspectorate for Wales carry out regularly.

In **Northern Ireland** the Regulation and Quality Improvement Agency publishes across-the-board studies of service provision, such as those for people with severe hearing and/or vision impairment, throughout all five health and social care trusts, rather than annual or periodic assessments of each health and social care trust in the province.

Unfortunately, in **England,** the Care Quality Commission no longer carries out annual or periodic inspections of local authority adult social care departments; it stopped doing so in 2010. Instead, the Commission expects councils to produce annual reports on the quality of adult social care in their areas for local scrutiny.

Charging service users

A key difference between social care and healthcare provision is that while the latter is free to users, local authorities are free to charge users for certain social care services.

On the ground, the system works like this. A 70-year-old man has a major stroke, apparently out of the blue. It leaves him paralysed down one side of his body. While he is in hospital, perhaps for rehabilitation over a period of weeks, the NHS pays for his care (and for his meals and general accommodation). Once he is discharged from hospital, any further medical and nursing care he needs is free. But any practical help he needs (perhaps to wash and dress, prepare meals, make his bed, do his shopping and so on) in his own home, or the 24-hour care provided in a care home, is classed as social care, even though the need for it arises from a medical problem. So the unfortunate man has to pay for it or, if he is too poor to do so, his local authority with social care responsibilities must step in and meet the shortfall.

This may sound at odds with the idea of a cradle-to-grave welfare state. The idea, however, is that older people suffer from frailty and disability affecting their ability to carry out everyday tasks from which they can never be cured and which should not therefore be considered 'medical'. In practice, of course, many people find this distinction at best unclear and at worst preposterous and grossly unfair.

In fact, charging for social care is more complex than this. First, the government has decreed that social services must provide certain services and facilities for free. We noted above that equipment which a social services department in England has assessed somebody as needing on grounds of disability or illness must be provided free, and other free dispensations are discussed elsewhere in this book, such as those that apply when people come out of hospital *(see Chapter 39)*.

A second basic principle is that the poorest people do not have to pay. As a result, there are clear rules about leaving people with sufficient money of their own so that they are not impoverished by paying for care. So, were the man who has had a stroke living in his own home with help brought in from outside, his council would have to pay the costs if he were of modest means. Were he to move into a care home, his social care authority would have to pick up the tab if his savings (including the value of any house or flat he owned) were lower than the thresholds listed above *(see page 563)* and his income were low. In addition, the state would have to provide him with a small weekly sum for personal spending.[19]

Handling social services

Some social services departments are very easy to work with, but others drag their feet over performing even the tasks that the law demands. Many come somewhere in between. In Chapters 21 and 22, I discuss the ways in which social services could help you obtain equipment, in Chapter 26 practical help in your home, and in Chapter 27 support if you are a carer. In all these areas a few ground rules come in handy when handling social services departments. (You might also find them useful when dealing with officials in other areas, such as health or housing.)

Before you deal with any social services department it is a good idea to take a cool look at yourself and try to modify your behaviour if necessary. Are you naturally an assertive, confrontational person who readily takes people to task, or are you a conciliatory soul, always seeing the other person's argument and hating to make a fuss? Those in the first group risk antagonising those with whom they must deal, so making negotiation less easy; those in the second group risk being denied the services they could get if they were a little more assertive. My experience is that many of the older people who most need social services help are deferential to authority and reticent about pushing their own case. The suggestions below have been devised to provide that group in particular with a little more confidence and so reduce the likelihood that they will be short-changed.

✓ If any member of a social services department should visit you for the first time, expect them to give their full name and job title, explain why they are contacting you and how they received any referral (perhaps from your GP or the manager of a hospital ward), and provide their full name and contact details in written form. This behaviour is regarded as good practice in the world of social care.

✓ Keep your own record of all dealings with social services. File all the letters they send you, keep copies of all the letters you send them and of any completed forms, and retain your own notes of all meetings with them. That way, you will have a comprehensive record to hand if you wish to raise concerns or even lodge a complaint.

✓ Note all phone conversations with social services, logging the name of the person to whom you speak and the date and details of what is said. That means you know whom to ask for if you telephone again. If you cannot reach that person, you could ask for their line manager. Everybody in social services is supervised by a line manager, so there is a tight chain of command from the first point-of-call to the director of the department and, above them, elected representatives. Within the department, the buck stops at the director of social services: that person is responsible for and therefore in theory could be sacked on account of the mistakes of the lowliest customer advisor.

✓ Do not countenance delays simply because an official from social services with whom you have been dealing is away, perhaps on holiday, even if only for a day. Ask instead to speak to their line manager.

✓ Line managers are also useful if you are unhappy with what somebody from social services tells you. Ask: 'Would you mind if I just checked that with your line manager?'

✓ Make sure that you know that anybody to whom you send an email or a letter receives it, unless the matter involved is not serious. Always use the request receipt facility for emails and send letters by recorded delivery. This is particularly important if you want to make sure that correspondence is acted upon promptly. If you have not written by recorded delivery or emailed using the facility to request a receipt, you may have to write in again (and again).

✓ If you think you need help swiftly, say so. There is always a means of fast-tracking services and equipment and fast-tracking the money to provide them.

✓ After a phone conversation with somebody in social services, it is a good idea to write to confirm anything useful that emerged, for instance that the official agreed to do certain things. If the authority does not subsequently write back and deny that these commitments were made, any subsequent investigation would deem that they were.

✓ If social services write to confirm a situation, perhaps the result of a discussion about your care, scrutinise the letter carefully to ensure that it does not contain mistakes or omissions. If it does, write back and say so; try to get any document involved, such as a care plan, amended accordingly.

✓ Social services should never start charging for anything without having agreed with you a written set of terms and conditions beforehand. If it does, phone or write in immediately. Be ready to show your awareness of the option of lodging a complaint, even if you never plan to make use of it.

✓ Don't be pushed into any course of action you do not want to take. Apart from in exceptional circumstances (*outlined on page 782*), social services can only advise, not coerce.

✓ If you think an independent person might help you in your dealings with social services and no friend or family member would fit the bill, you may be able to obtain the services of an 'advocate'. (*Advocates are considered on pages 804–10.*)

✓ If you have difficulty in obtaining information from the council, such as background papers to its policies, you could contact its monitoring officer. Usually the monitoring officer is the chief legal officer in the council and their brief is to ensure all the council's actions are lawful and fair.

Records

Social services maintain a file on each person with whom they have dealings. These people have a legal right to see them in their entirety. The Data Protection Act 1998 makes accessible any record of personal information held by a health or a social care authority for the purposes of their health and social services functions. The information covered is not simply factual material, but also 'any expressions of opinion, and the intentions of the authority in relation to the individual'.[20] In other words, you ought to be handed the entire file, unsifted unless there are special circumstances, most commonly that it contains material about another person.

If you wish to see your social services record, telephone your local authority to ask to whom you should write to view it, as this can save time; and you could post your letter by recorded delivery, lest the authority should claim it never received it. The Data Protection Act 1998 says that the information should be disclosed 'promptly' and in any event within 40 days. There is no need to say why you want to see your records. Attorneys, deputies and guardians also have the right to see the records of the person from whom they hold proxy powers; they have to provide proof of their status.

Trouble-shooting

If you are dissatisfied with the way you have been treated by social services, what can you do? Perhaps the homecare assistants whom social services have organised to help you fail to perform the tasks they should. Perhaps the council refuses to fund the services you consider you need.

In the first instance, you should chase up the relevant officials, if necessary in writing. If you get nowhere, lodge a formal complaint to social services. This step costs nothing and requires no recourse to a solicitor. It can result in a change, if necessary retrospective, in the way in which your case has been handled. Social services are more likely to take a problem seriously if it has the status of an official complaint than if it is simply raised orally as a concern.

You could also raise the matter with your local councillor or MP. They should in turn contact the council about your case and this intervention may help secure the action you wish. Particularly if your problem requires quick action, do think about side-stepping the complaints process and approaching your councillor and/or your MP and asking them to pursue your case. You could also try to interest the media, although bear in mind that once the media are involved, it is hard to control the course of events.

First, though, it is worth talking to local voluntary organisations whose members or officials have had experience of handling social services on the ground, such as a local carers' or Age UK organisation or Citizens Advice. They may have or be able to put you in touch with advocates *(see page 804)* who can help you lodge a complaint, if that is what you decide to do. In Northern Ireland, the Patient and Client Council supports people who are making complaints involving health or social care.

Lodging a complaint to social services

Lodging a complaint performs a special function in the world of social care. Not only is it a means of signalling someone is concerned about something: it is usually the only means of appealing against a particular decision which the council has made about an individual.

This may sound odd. After all, in other spheres of public life there are usually specific avenues for aggrieved people to appeal against decisions. For instance, if a developer is refused planning permission by a local council or an applicant refused a state benefit by the Department for Work and Pensions, they appeal against that specific decision. Not so in social care. There the complaint performs that function.[21]

This presents a potential problem for the would-be complainant. Most of us do not like to be seen to be awkward, and, because of that, are deterred from making a complaint. We should not be. Dr Jackie Gulland of the University of Edinburgh has made a special study of social care complaints in Scotland. She told me, 'There is no formal appeal procedure in social care: people can only complain. That can seem like moaning and whingeing. It is not: people should use complaints procedures to keep local authorities up to the mark.'[22] Furthermore, social services departments often receive quite a lot of complaints, so they are unlikely to label an individual as a troublemaker if they resort to a complaint.

Scope of complaints

It is important to be aware that the subject of any complaint is restricted to the way in which a council has discharged (or failed to discharge) one of its functions. However, this covers many actions (or inactions).

For example, Liverpool City Council had undertaken to provide an elderly disabled man with help to enable him to continue to live in his own home. However, the care agency that the council commissioned to provide this help did not deliver the support properly. The case was referred to the Local Government Ombudsman, who said: 'This situation has the potential to put some of the most vulnerable members of the community at serious risk. It is simply unacceptable.' The Ombudsman recommended that the council take action to address the problem with the care agency, monitor the care it delivered to the man in future, and also pay him £700 as compensation for the inconvenience and distress that the council's failings had caused. The council agreed to take these steps.[23]

Complaints procedures cannot be used to criticise or challenge a political decision a council has made. So there is no point in using this procedure to complain about a council's decision to withdraw hot meals at all sheltered housing in its area or to restrict help to certain categories of people – unless you can show that it did not use the correct procedures to come to the decision or did not discharge its functions correctly.

The possible need to lodge a complaint was one of the reasons I gave above for keeping a record of all dealings with a social care authority. For instance, if a council fails to provide a ramp within a reasonable time to enable somebody who is disabled to reach their front door, it would be useful for them to have kept a note of the date when the ramp was promised, by whom it was promised and any attempt they have subsequently made to chase up the equipment.

Complaints procedures

Every local authority has to have procedures in place for handling complaints about the way in which it has behaved. So, if you wish to lodge a formal complaint, ask your social services department for details of its complaints procedures. These might be set out in a leaflet with a detachable form on which you set out your complaint. If not, you should write a letter to the Director of Social Services (Social Work in Scotland) asking them to treat the letter as a formal complaint concerning the discharge of their authority in respect of you or somebody whom you name.

In your letter, you should set out the complaint clearly, explaining:

● what you are complaining about
● the names of the social care staff with whom you have dealt (if you know them)
● the dates of important events, such as when care assistants organised by the council turned up late and by how much.

Explain briefly why this matters so much – for instance, the difficulties caused by the failure to deliver your ramp on time or the late arrival of the homecare workers. Enclose copies of any relevant papers. Say that you require the complaint to be investigated as quickly as possible by the authority's complaints manager and give any phone numbers and email addresses on which they can contact you.

In England, you should make your complaint within 12 months of the date of the action (or lack of it) about which you are complaining, or 12 months from the date when you first became aware of it. Slightly different time limits and procedures operate in the different countries of the UK, so the first thing to do is to find out what those are in your local authority. In England the procedures for social care complaints are the same as those for complaints about NHS-funded healthcare. *(I explain them and offer tips on lodging complaints on pages 338–40.)*

Professor Luke Clements is a leading authority on social care law, based on many years of experience as a solicitor in this field in England and Wales. He offers sample letters which can adjusted and used to lodge complaints on his website.[24]

If your complaint is upheld, your council should take steps to rectify the problem in question, although it is not usually under an absolute obligation to do so. Or it might reject your case. What then?

The Ombudsmen

Those who get no joy through the official complaints system of their local councils can seek to involve – again for free – a separate and independent organisation, the Ombudsman. Contact the Local Government Ombudsman (in England), the Scottish Public Services Ombudsman, the Public Services Ombudsman for Wales or the Northern Ireland Ombudsman.

Local authorities tend to be embarrassed by the fact that they are under scrutiny from the Ombudsman, so you could mention that you are prepared to refer the matter to the Ombudsman early on in the local authority complaints process, if that seems appropriate. The Local Government Ombudsman will usually examine a concern only if the complainant has already gone through the local authority's complaints procedure, but that is not hard and fast, and you could always approach the Ombudsman at an earlier stage if you wish. The Ombudsman tends to be a quick and effective means of resolving concerns. They have the power to look at local authority files and to compel people to give information. The Public Services Ombudsman in Wales sometimes does a 'quick fix', seeking to resolve a problem without an investigation.

However, the Ombudsman's writ extends only to administration. They cannot help you overturn a council decision to which you object, unless the process by which the decision was taken did not conform to procedures the council itself or central government has laid down. The

Ombudsman cannot challenge, let alone alter, a council's policy decision or substitute their own judgement for the council's. But when the Ombudsman upholds a complaint, they can make recommendations to put things right, including the payment of compensation.

Judicial review and mediation

Judicial review involves taking a council to court in order to get a decision overturned. The High Court of England and Wales, the High Court of Northern Ireland or, in Scotland, the Court of Session review the lawfulness of the decisions made by a public body (whether it be a local authority, an NHS body or a government department).

While the remedies outlined above are free of charge, judicial review can be financially very risky, as high costs can be involved, perhaps around £30,000.[25] However, help from the state in the form of community legal service funding (which has replaced legal aid) is available to people of modest means and whose case is considered to have merit. If you receive the Guarantee element of Pension Credit *(see page 854–9),* you will automatically pass the means test for this funding.

The Public Law Project (a charity which offers advice to lawyers and members of the public about how judicial review works and how to obtain state funding to bring cases) and the government's Community Legal Service can point you in the right direction to obtain advice on your particular case. A complainant must start judicial review action within three months of the date of the decision or action in question and have exhausted or at least considered alternatives to bringing proceedings, not least complaints procedures.

Mediation is being increasingly discussed as an alternative to pursuing a judicial review case in court. This costs money, but not as much as pursuing the case in court. What happens is that the person who has been affected by the decision sends a letter to the public body that made the decision setting out details of the decision, why they consider it to be unlawful, what they want the public body to do about the matter and a deadline within which the body must respond. The letter from the complainant must state that judicial review proceedings will be issued if they do not receive a satisfactory response within the time limit. Once the public body has responded, negotiation between the two parties and a settlement may be possible.

Judicial review (or the threat of such action) can be effective in convincing a public body to reconsider its decision or in forcing it to take action or secure a compromise. That decision may then act as a precedent for other cases. However, judicial review does not allow consideration of whether a public body has made the right decision; rather, it questions whether it has taken a decision or an action which was unlawful and for which there is no adequate alternative remedy for the person who is aggrieved. The action (or inaction) might have involved a local council failing to respect the complainant's human rights or fettering its discretion *(page 571)* when ruling out the provision of a service, for instance.

Various outcomes are possible if the case goes to court, and more than one may result. The court may quash the original decision and order the public body to take the decision again, this time lawfully. It may order the public body to take an action which it has a statutory duty to perform. It may prohibit it from doing something unlawful in the future. Courts rarely order authorities to pay damages in judicial review cases.

Independent social workers

As local authorities have shed qualified social workers on their staff as a consequence of the austerity cuts, a growing number have begun to offer their services privately. The social workers' professional organisation, the British Association of Social Workers (BASW), holds a list of independent social workers available for hire.

You might perhaps consult an independent social worker for advice on getting the most out of the social care system provided by your local authority or on seeking redress if something has gone wrong in your dealings with it. If you wish to obtain help in the home or live-in care or are looking for a care home, the advice of a qualified social worker could be invaluable. You are entitled to such advice (for free) from your local authority, but if for some reason you do not wish to use your council's services, you could contact an independent professional instead. Or you could use both. The BASW's directory holds information about each independent social worker's location and areas of expertise.

The world of social care

* Social services can help wealthy as well as poorer older people.
* Social care can help carers, people with sight or hearing impairment and people with mental illness as well as those challenged by illness, disability or frailty.
* Social services cannot place you in a care home against your will, unless they can prove that you lack mental capacity.
* The state provides a cushion so nobody need use all their savings on care home bills.
* Loans from councils can help people who do not wish to sell their own home to pay care home fees.
* Elder abuse is a betrayal of trust by somebody who should be providing help.
* Social services have expertise and legal duties in the field of elder abuse.
* Abuse can increase the chances of obtaining council-funded support.
* Keep your own record of all your dealings with social services.
* Don't be put off appealing against a council decision because you have to lodge a complaint.

Chapter 26

Social care assessments

I n Chapters 23 and 24, we examined the ways in which staff could be hired to help with tasks in the home. But many people cannot afford this – or, at least, cannot afford to hire as much help as they need in order to continue to live independently. Other people may need a lot of care and support, but feel anxious about hiring care assistants without advice. Both groups can obtain help from the social services department of their local authority.[1]

If you need a lot of practical help, particularly with personal care, approaching the council is vital: it is the only gateway to services which would be extremely expensive if you had to bear the cost entirely yourself. For the many people who cope with a number of disabling conditions, the cost of hiring help independently would become overwhelming without outside financial assistance. You could receive a significant subsidy from your council, resulting in hundreds of pounds each week – thousands of pounds over a number of years – to help cover the cost of enabling you to remain in your own home.

Local councils are allowed to charge people for social care services, unlike healthcare. However, there are major exceptions to this rule and a safety net to ensure that people with only modest savings or income do not have to pay.

In this chapter I look at the process by which councils work out whether individuals need help in their homes and how they go about drawing up plans to provide for those needs. I look at the wider benefits of these needs assessments and suggest ways in which you can prepare for one. There are ways in which the system can short-change you and I explain what you can do to avert this danger.

Many older people look after a partner, relative or friend as their carer, often without realising that they are a carer and can therefore obtain help through the social care system. *I explain how this is provided and the sort of support carers can typically obtain, which may be more diverse and extensive than you imagine, in the following chapter.*

In **Scotland,** everybody, rich or poor, who wishes to access the free personal care that the state provides must obtain an assessment of their care needs from their social work department.

Wherever you live in the UK, obtaining an assessment of your care needs and a package of care and support financed partly or wholly by your local council involves four stages. These are:

- working out what help you need
- preparing a 'care plan' setting out the help you should receive
- establishing an amount which social services will pay towards the costs of your care
- organising the delivery of your care

How provision of council-organised services can work

What do care and support services facilitated by local authorities look like on the ground? Here is an example (the name has been changed):

Jack had complex hip problems which made walking and bending very difficult. He lived in a sheltered housing scheme in which a hot meal was provided daily. Social services carried out an assessment of his care needs. As a result, he was provided with a walking frame on wheels and two visits each day by care workers from a local homecare agency: in the morning they would help him wash and dress, and in the evening get ready for bed.

One year on, Jack's mobility problems had worsened. Social services reassessed his needs and came up with a new care package. They provided an electric wheelchair in which he could move himself around, and the morning helper was given additional tasks. As well as helping Jack wash and dress, she also made his bed and prepared and served breakfast (since the small size of his kitchen made manoeuvring his wheelchair in it while also carrying plates and cups almost impossible). And before helping Jack get ready for bed, the evening assistant also prepared and served a light meal and filled a thermos for drinks during the night.

A new visit was introduced at lunchtime, when a care assistant would wheel Jack to the dining room of his sheltered housing facility. While he was having lunch, she would return to his flat to clean, wash up, take his washing to the launderette room and put out the rubbish.

The result of this care package was that Jack was able to continue to enjoy living amongst his friends in his much-loved housing scheme, which was close to shops and social facilities. Without this care and support, he would have spent hours struggling with everyday tasks, leaving little time or energy to socialise or go out.

As Jack was of modest means, his council bore much of the cost of his care services.

The services that come within the ambit of care and support, many of which Jack obtained, include:

- personal care: help to wash, dress, bathe, use the toilet, deal with continence matters, eat, drink, care for nails, skin, mouth and teeth or prompt someone to carry out these tasks themselves and supervise them while doing so, if they are unable to decide to undertake them themselves[2]
- the preparation and serving of food[3]
- help to take medication
- other practical help, such as housework, bringing in shopping and being accompanied while shopping
- the delivery of meals to the home
- services to enhance social contact, such as attending day centres, eating out, going to clubs and befriending

These services are sometimes known as community care services. A needs assessment can also result in the provision of equipment to help cope with illness, frailty and disability. *(This is discussed in Chapters 21 and 22.)*

Needs assessments

Before anybody can receive services such as Jack's through their council, they must have been the subject of an assessment of their need for help. This is not a test of their own abilities or of those of any care-givers who may be helping them. Rather, it is an assessment of the type and amount of help they need. Social care authorities throughout the UK have a legal duty to assess the need for services of people living in their area who may need help. Thus the Care Act 2014, which applies in England, says:

> Where it appears to a local authority that an adult may have needs for care and support, the authority must assess
>
> a.   whether the adult does have needs for care and support, and
>
> b.   if the adult does, what those needs are.[4]

A council cannot refuse to give somebody a needs assessment on the grounds they will probably be ineligible for help. Nor can it do so because it considers they are wealthy enough to organise services for themselves or that a relative could do so for them. Nor can it refuse if a relative or friend is providing or intending to provide the care and support they need. If someone might be in need of care and support and would like to have an assessment, they must be given one. An assessment of their financial situation should come after the needs assessment and must not affect the local authority's decision to carry out the needs assessment. Similar provisions apply in Scotland, Wales and Northern Ireland.[5]

You can request a needs assessment yourself or you can ask somebody to do so on your behalf. Sometimes health professionals such as GPs or district nurses pass a name to the local authority's social services department, which should then approach the person in question and ask whether they would like an assessment. Needs assessments are often carried out when somebody is to be discharged from hospital, to establish whether they need help with the practical tasks of everyday life when they return home *(as explained in Chapter 39)*.

Types of need

No council can meet the needs of everybody who might ask for help: all councils have to ration the money they spend on individuals in one way or another. What they do is to rate the importance of meeting a need according to certain eligibility criteria.

As a result of this evaluation, certain needs emerge as so serious that they are termed 'eligible needs'. Once a need is so rated, the local authority must ensure it is met if the person so wishes; this applies even if the council has to foot the entire bill. Other needs identified during an assessment are called 'presenting needs'. They are not serious enough to cross the threshold to become eligible needs, but it can be helpful if they are set down in the assessment nonetheless. They can form a useful benchmark: needs change and a presenting need may go on to become an eligible need at a later date; indeed, people's needs can increase quite rapidly.

At the same time, the way in which eligible needs are met can be informed by presenting needs. For example, if a presenting need is to keep someone in touch with their ethnic group and an eligible need is to ensure they are given a meal because they can no longer prepare one, the result might be that their council pays for them to visit a day centre which meets the needs of that particular cultural group, even if to do so would cost more than their attending another centre or the provision of meals-on-wheels in their own home.

If someone has one or more eligible needs, the council has to draw up a care and support plan. After that, it carries out a financial assessment to establish what proportion of the cost, if any, the recipient should pay for services provided to meet those needs. These financial assessments have to conform to national rules *(as described in Chapter 28)*, so that the recipients of care and support services are not impoverished by paying for them. If the person who is going to receive the services cannot afford to pay, social services must pay, unless the person involved does not want them to. (There are national exceptions to this rule. Thus in Scotland, everybody, rich or poor, gets the personal care they are assessed as needing paid for by the state.)

The onus is thus on the local authority to ensure that eligible needs are always met. Once in place, services to meet eligible needs cannot lawfully be taken away. The only way this can be done is if an assessment at a later date concludes that the person no longer needs them.

Eligibility criteria

How are councils to work out whether a need is sufficiently serious to rate as an eligible need and one which they must therefore ensure is met, if the person involved so wishes?

Each of the four national administrations has published a national framework for ranking needs to determine whether they should be eligible, which they expect their social care authorities to use. It is worth understanding these frameworks.

In England, councils must work out whether a need is an eligible need in the following way. First, it must be caused by a physical or mental impairment or illness. Second, as a result, the person involved must be unable to do two or more things *(see below)*. Third, the upshot of all this must have or be likely to have a significant impact on their well-being. All three conditions must be met.

The things two (or more) of which someone must be unable to do include:

- obtaining their food and drink, preparing and consuming it
- maintaining their personal hygiene, including washing themselves and laundering their clothes
- managing their toilet needs
- being clothed appropriately
- being able to use their home safely
- maintaining a habitable home environment
- developing and maintaining their family or other personal relationships
- accessing and engaging in work, training, education or volunteering
- making use of necessary facilities or services in their local community, including public transport and recreational facilities
- carrying out any caring responsibilities for a child[6]

How does a local authority judge whether someone can do any of these things or, as the government calls it, 'achieve a particular outcome'? Does someone have to be experiencing some difficulty in, say, dressing themselves – or be completely unable to put on their clothes? According to the Department of Health, someone is unable to achieve an outcome, if doing so without help:

- causes them significant pain, distress or anxiety, or
- endangers or is likely to endanger their health or safety or that of other people, or takes significantly longer than would normally be expected.

The Department of Health gives as an example of what this means: 'An adult with a physical disability is able to dress themselves in the morning, but it takes them a long time to do this, leaves them exhausted and prevents them from achieving other outcomes.'[7]

Finally, social care authorities must consider the likely effect of failure to achieve two or more outcomes on the person's well-being. Parliament has laid down that well-being can relate to any of the following aspects of someone's life:

- their personal dignity (including treating the person with respect)

- their physical and mental health
- their emotional well-being
- their protection from abuse and neglect
- control by the individual over their daily life, including over any care and/or support which is provided to them, and the way in which it is provided
- their participation in work, education, training or recreation
- their social and economic well-being
- their domestic, family and personal relationships
- the suitability of their living accommodation and
- the individual's contribution to wider society[8]

This final focus on well-being brings an additional individual dimension to the assessment. It may not matter too much to someone that they cannot, say, use recreational facilities in their local area, but it may matter massively that they are unable to keep in contact with their family. Or vice versa. The authority should consider whether the cumulative effect of being unable to achieve the outcomes is likely to have a significant impact on the person's well-being.[9]

Don't worry too much about ploughing through the complexities of the eligibility criteria. The important thing is to know that your council should be using them and that in doing so they should consider your emotional as well as your physical needs and your overall well-being.

My anecdotal evidence from speaking to social workers is that many councils in England use their own screening tools to further rank needs, using categories such as 'low', 'moderate', 'substantial' or 'critical'. A council will decide that it will rate needs as eligible only if they reach its chosen threshold, often 'substantial' or 'critical'. However, different councils vary in how much they spend on adult social care *(as noted on page 554)*, while the national rules permit them to meet needs not deemed eligible, if they wish. Also, research has shown that social services officials sometimes reinterpret the criteria to bring needs up into the eligible category and thereby secure services to meet them.[10]

Once eligible needs have been established, a council can apply a formula to determine whether the person involved should contribute to the cost of meeting them *(as described in Chapter 28)*. Some people will end up paying quite a lot of the cost; others will pay little or nothing. However, the contribution the council will have to make should not be a factor in its determining whether or not a need is met: once the council has accepted a need as eligible, it must ensure that it is taken care of, if the person involved so wishes.

Care and support plans

After establishing somebody's needs and then whether they can be considered eligible, the person carrying out the needs assessment should draw up a 'care and support plan'. Wherever you live in the UK, you can reasonably expect this plan to contain the following elements:

- a summary of your presenting and eligible needs. This should indicate their intensity, predictability, complexity and the risks they present to your well-being if they are not met. The plan should distinguish between presenting and eligible needs and also indicate any non-eligible needs that the council is nonetheless prepared to meet. Try to ensure it also explains why you have a particular need. For instance, does your need for help with dressing stem from difficulties with bending, or dexterity, or stamina, or perhaps dementia, which might impair your ability to work out how to dress yourself? Ensure the plan states the outcomes you consider important for your well-being – perhaps walking to the park every day

- the part you will play in caring for yourself

- details of what any carers (family or friends providing unpaid help) are prepared to do

- details of any help carers need to enable them to care

- details of any support to be provided to meet carers' needs

- contingency plans to cope with emergencies, for instance if a family carer is ill

- advice and information about other steps that can be taken to meet or reduce your needs and to delay or reduce needs which might develop in future

- the amount it would cost to meet your eligible needs; this is known as your 'personal budget'

- which needs are to be met through this payment and how often and how much will be paid

- any contributions which you will have to make towards your personal budget

- whether the council is to give you a 'direct payment' so you can organise your care and support yourself

- a date when your care and support plan will be reviewed and details of how it will be monitored
- the name of the person responsible for implementing, monitoring and reviewing the plan[11]

The information about what any unpaid carers are prepared to do (the third item above) is important. In establishing needs, councils must disregard any help to meet them that is being provided by a carer. So, if your husband helps you, say, to dress yourself, that help should be noted, and also the help he provides. The logic involved is that should your husband's help later not be available, you would continue to need it and, if an eligible need, the local council would then have to ensure that it was met. But in drawing up your care and support plan, the council is permitted to take account of your husband's contribution, after checking with him that he is prepared to provide it. As the guidance to councils in England states: 'The local authority must identify, during the assessment process, those needs which are being met by a carer at that time, and determine whether those needs would be eligible. But any eligible needs met by a carer are not required to be met by the local authority, for so long as the carer continues to do so.'[12]

The **Welsh** Assembly government takes a broadly similar approach to needs assessment and care and support planning. All social care authorities are required to use a national eligibility framework to determine eligibility of needs, and this has been expanded in a set of regulations and a code of practice.[13] Like the framework for England, eligibility involves testing the severity of a need by reference to outcomes.

The first condition in the framework operating in Wales says a need must arise from circumstances such as physical or mental ill-health and second, the need must pass an outcome test involving reference to well-being and outcomes. The third condition in Wales effectively says that if an unpaid carer is providing the help someone needs or they are obtaining it from a service in their community, then the need cannot be an eligible need.

However, this does not mean that someone in Wales who has a carer should be denied a needs assessment – the Code of Practice accompanying the Welsh care law of 2014 points out that, 'The Act entitles anyone to have an assessment where there appears to be a need for care and support – even if that care and support is being met by a carer.'[14] The reason behind this is that a need which a carer is meeting can become an eligible need if the carer ceases to meet it. In that case, the local authority must undertake a reassessment of the person's care and support needs.[15] Importantly, the Code stresses that the local council must satisfy itself that the carer really is willing and able to provide care.[16]

In **Northern Ireland,** the system is simpler. The Department of Health, Social Services and Public Safety tells health and social care trusts to place any need within one of four categories of severity – low, moderate, substantial or critical – and that if a need meets the substantial threshold or higher (critical), it becomes an eligible need which trusts must ensure is met. A need falls within the substantial band if as a result of that need:

- the person is unable to carry out the majority of personal care and domestic tasks; and/or
- they have or will have only partial choice and control over their immediate environment; and/or
- they have been or will be abused or neglected; and/or
- they cannot or will not be able to sustain their involvement in many aspects of work, education or learning; and/or
- they cannot or will not be able to undertake the majority of their family and other social roles and responsibilities; and/or
- there is the possibility that they will be admitted inappropriately to hospital or a care home[17]

Finally, trusts should look at the extent to which the need poses a risk to the person's health, safety and independence.

In **Scotland,** social care authorities also use a national eligibility framework involving placing someone's needs into one of four bands (low, moderate, substantial or critical). Councils are expected to meet any needs considered as at least substantial, in other words where failure to meet the need would pose a substantial risk to the person's independence or health and well-being. The Scottish government has said it expects councils to provide everyone with needs assessed as substantial or critical to be provided with services within six weeks.[18]

The single assessment process

Healthcare and social care organisations are being encouraged to work more closely together. As a result, assessments are often carried out which take in both health and social care needs; these are called 'single assessments' (in Wales 'unified assessments' and in Scotland and Northern Ireland 'single shared assessments').

Single assessment is an approach to the assessment of older people and disabled people which is supposed to subsume a social care assessment within a wider picture of somebody's health, housing situation and mobility. Someone's right to have a social care needs assessment and their rights within that assessment process are not affected if the social care assessment forms part of this wider assessment.

Single assessment can produce better results than one which looks only at social care needs, since it places the person involved in a wider context. Also, it encourages professionals in different disciplines – housing, health, social care and so on – to work together to a greater extent. As they share the information in the assessment, this can save time. For example, if somebody has had a fall, single assessment should remove any need to repeat to different professionals identical information about the incident and the problems to which it has given rise.

Professionals outside social services can carry out a single assessment. If an urgent referral is received for a social care assessment, perhaps from a GP, and a district nurse is the first person to call, they would do the assessment. However, social services must have overall control of the process of social care needs assessment within a single assessment.

Needs assessment and care planning: your rights

Your right to have your needs for social care services assessed by your local authority is supported by guidance issued by government on the way assessments should be carried out. Particularly at times of great pressure on councils' resources, it can be extremely useful to know what you should expect. If it is not provided, you can then indicate to the social services department that you know what it should be doing and are prepared to take action to ensure that it does so. As in so many areas of life, it is often the squeaky wheel that gets the oil.

In discussing rights, I often refer to guidance issued by the Department of Health for England about how the Care Act 2014 should be implemented. This is statutory, policy guidance and councils must act in accordance with it.[19] Social care authorities in Scotland, Wales and Northern Ireland are also expected to follow the (broadly similar) guidance on assessments and care and support planning issued by their own administrations.

What can you reasonably expect when your council carries out your needs assessment and draws up your care and support plan?

A wide range of needs

Plainly, your need for help with personal care (such as washing, dealing with continence problems and taking medication) will be an important feature of your assessment. However, planning for social care needs has long acknowledged that assessments should be wider than simply personal care matters, important as these are.

The courts have held on a number of occasions that community care assessments have to investigate a wide range of possible needs. For instance, a court which considered the adequacy of an assessment carried out by the London Borough of Haringey in 1998 found that the council had restricted itself to personal care needs and omitted to consider social and recreational needs. This restriction was deemed unlawful and the assessment had to be redone to investigate all potential needs.[20]

Focus on the inclusion of a wide range of needs, not just those necessary for physical survival, has been recognised in the Care Act 2014, which lays a legal duty on social care authorities in England to promote the 'well-being' of the individuals whom they help *(defined on page 591)*. Similarly, the Social Services and Well-being **(Wales)** Act lays down that the promotion of the well-being of people who need care and support should underpin the assessments of their need for help.[21]

The **Scottish** Parliament has coined the term 'self-directed support' for help for people with care and support needs. 'Self-directed support is intended to support, promote and protect the human rights and independent living of care and support users in Scotland', says the Scottish government – in other words, not simply to provide for their physical care needs.[22] In the same vein, a set of rights drawn up in 2012 by the Scottish government for people with dementia asserts: 'I have the right to be as independent as possible and to be included in my community.'[23]

In **Northern Ireland,** too, assessments should be wide-ranging. The statutory guidance says that they should range over not only someone's ability to carry out the practical tasks of everyday life but also their social networks and lifestyle and the adequacy of their housing.[24]

A one-time head of the inspection agency for social care provision in England has helpfully summed up the purpose of a care needs assessment that might apply anywhere in the UK. It is, she said, 'Supposed to be all about you: your needs, the life you lead and what you want to keep in touch with'.[25]

Residence

Suppose you are seriously considering having your mother come to live with you, but are unsure whether your local authority would provide sufficient support. So long as your mother has firm plans to move, the social services department in your area should carry out an assessment.

If you move when you have a care package in place, the duty of the local authority in whose area you plan to move is triggered once that authority has been notified of your intention and is satisfied that intention is genuine.[26] This should ensure that there is no interruption in the care and support you receive. However, it is unlikely to be identical, as the two authorities may differ in their readiness to class a need as eligible and their approach to charging for care and support services.

Your views

In the past social workers often simply slotted older people facing difficulties into the services that happened to exist: they did not begin by focusing on the person and then considering which out of many possibilities might best suit them. For instance, in the late 1990s a social worker arranged for my mother (then living at home and struggling with practical and psychological problems arising from the onset of dementia and the loss of her eyesight) to attend a nearby day centre. No doubt the social worker meant well, and indeed she accompanied my mother to the centre on what she had assumed would be her first visit of many. A day centre in a converted school building may sound appealing. But my mother had never been to a day centre. To walk into a room of people, most of them strangers, when you are baffled by changes taking place to your brain and struggling with worsening eyesight is a massive challenge. Will you feel awkward? To whom will you talk? Where is the lavatory? There was the added factor that my mother had been to primary school in the building. She found the visit stressful and never returned.

Today, you should expect your views about any service which you might be offered to be treated very seriously. The law and government guidance emphasise the need for assessment to place the person who may need services centre stage.

So the Care Act 2014 tells social care authorities in England (and similar instructions have been made for Scotland, Wales and Northern Ireland) that when carrying out a needs assessment and subsequently drawing up a care and support plan they must pay attention to:

- the views, wishes and feelings of the person involved
- the importance of that person participating as fully as possible in the decisions involved
- the need to ensure that decisions are made with regard to all that person's circumstances and are not based on their age or

appearance or any other condition or aspect of their behaviour which might lead others to make unjustified assumptions about their well-being[27]

In explaining how councils should implement the Act, the Department of Health has told them: 'Putting the person at the heart of the assessment process is crucial to understanding the person's needs, outcomes and well-being, and delivering better care and support.'[28] It goes on, 'The purpose of an assessment is to identify the person's needs and how these impact on their well-being, and the outcomes that the person wishes to achieve in their day-to-day life.'[29]

The key role of the person who needs help in working out what sort of support they should be offered has been given an extra boost through the coining of the currently fashionable term 'personalisation'. This concept also seeks to counter the old approach of social services, which was felt by many to be rather paternalistic, restricting rather than encouraging any consultation with the individual who was to be helped. Personalisation:

> means starting with the person as an individual with strengths, preferences and aspirations. It means putting them at the centre of the process of identifying their needs and making choices about how and when they are supported to live their lives.[30]

Involvement is central to the concept of self-directed support in **Scotland.** The Self-directed Support Act 2013 says the person concerned must have as much involvement in the assessment of their care needs and the provision of support services as they wish. This involvement is one of the key principles underlying care planning set down in the Act.[31]

Help to convey your views

Not only should you expect your views and experiences to be fed scrupulously into the care planning process, you should expect any help you may need in putting your views across to be forthcoming. Perhaps you are worried because you are hard of hearing, your vision is poor or your English not fluent? If so, you ought to have somebody with you during the assessment to help put forward your views. Indeed, your council would be contravening equality legislation *(see pages 295–9 and 687–92)* if it were to fail to provide a translation facility or help for people with a disability such as blindness or deafness to play as full a part as they wish in their assessment.

Some people have a brain impairment, such as dementia or arising from a stroke which prevents their being able to take particular decisions. The law requires councils to provide these people with an advocate to support them *(see pages 784–5)*. Many others do not have any brain impairment but would still have great difficulty in getting on top of the various matters involved in their care assessment.

Social care authorities in England have a legal duty to provide people undergoing needs assessment with an independent advocate if they would have substantial difficulty in engaging with the process of assessment.

The tests by which a local council would ascertain whether someone would have substantial difficulty in being involved are as follows:

- Can the person understand the relevant information?
- Can they retain that information long enough to weigh up their options and make decisions?
- Can they use or weigh the information as part of the process of being involved?
- Can they communicate their views, wishes and feelings?[32]

If the answer is 'no' to any of these questions, an advocate should be provided.

The substantial difficulty might arise because someone has some mild cognitive impairment or they are very unwell or feel confused or very upset for some reason *(as discussed in the section on advocates, on pages 806–7)*.

If the council considers someone would have substantial difficulty, it must first consider whether there is a family member or friend who could support the person in their assessment. If there is nobody willing and available or if the person being assessed does not want that family member or friend to be involved, the authority must appoint someone quite outside the situation to support and represent the person and to enable their involvement in the assessment – an independent advocate.

Difficulty in being involved might not be apparent at the start of an assessment. If it becomes apparent only while the assessment is underway, an advocate must be instructed as soon as it does become known.[33] *(I discuss advocates on pages 804–10. In **Scotland**, anyone with a mental illness or impairment must be provided with an advocate, whether or not they are undergoing a social care assessment.)*

Carers' views

Perhaps you have a friend, neighbour or family member who provides you with some practical support, but not for remuneration. If so, you may wish this carer to be present during your assessment so that their views can be fed in and the support that social services are willing to sign up to complements whatever they are prepared to give. If the person being cared for so wishes, the council must involve any carer they have in their needs assessment; if they have more than one carer, they too should be involved. The council should also involve 'any other person requested'.[34]

If you would like your carer and/or anybody else to be present during your needs assessment, make this clear beforehand to social services.

Carers are entitled to assessments in their own right to examine whether they should receive support in their caring role and these 'carer's assessments' can take place at the same time as an assessment of the needs for the person being cared for *(as we see in the following chapter)*.

Consultation with others

Quite apart from any carer you may have, there may be somebody who you think could usefully contribute to your needs assessment and discussion about your support arrangements. This could take place during your assessment or as a separate consultation. If so, expect social services to approach them, too, if you request this.

The Care Act 2014 makes specific provision for this consultation. It says that the authority must consult any other person if the person who is the subject of the needs assessment asks them to do so. It does not say who that other person might be.[35] You could put forward somebody who knows well the sort of problems you face, such as a neighbour. They should be separate from your carer and also from anybody who is helping you to convey your views more effectively.

Perhaps you would simply like a relative or friend to sit alongside you at the assessment to give you moral support or fill in some details. If so, tell social services that you would like to bring this person with you to the assessment. Social services should have no problem with this.

Location of the assessment

An assessment can be carried out over the telephone, but this is hardly ideal, as it is important that the assessor is able to understand the person's problems. So if you think a social services official is carrying out a needs assessment over the phone or is proposing to do so and you are unhappy with that, say so and ask for a home visit. Councils know they should be prepared to carry out the assessment in the person's own home as a matter of good practice. It is much harder to understand the nature of the problems somebody is facing if they are not seen in their everyday environment. *(I also discuss phone compared with home assessments below.)*

Expertise

You should expect social services to bring in any expertise which is needed to inform the assessment and care planning process.

Expertise, or at least access to it, should be available throughout the assessment process. This starts either when an official starts to talk to someone about how they are coping and what they might need or when someone phones social services and asks if help might be forthcoming. We see in a moment that the people who carry out these phone 'contact assessments' are unlikely to be registered social workers, but they should be suitably trained for the task. As the Department of Health has pointed out:

> Local authorities must ensure that assessors are appropriately trained and competent whenever they carry out an assessment. ... The training must be appropriate to the assessment, both the format of assessment and the condition(s) and circumstances of the person being assessed. They must also have the skills and knowledge to carry out an assessment of needs that relate to a specific condition or circumstances requiring expert insight, for example when assessing an individual who has autism, learning disabilities, mental health needs or dementia.[36]

Other professionals may be brought in. Frequently a care manager asks an occupational therapist to visit somebody in their home environment to work out whether particular gadgets and/or house adaptations such as ramps or grab rails might help; the results of this will be fed into the needs assessment. Ask before the assessment who will conduct it and whether any other professionals will be present or their advice sought; if the answers seem unsatisfactory, make suggestions of your own.

If you are unhappy with what is being proposed for your care and support plan, you can ask for the views of a particular professional to be canvassed or for such a person to be present at the assessment.

In one assessment of which I became aware, social services recommended that an elderly man who could walk, albeit with great difficulty, should hitherto remain in his wheelchair, where care workers would wait on him, lest he should have a fall. The man involved reluctantly agreed but, understandably enough, came to find his enforced immobility difficult to cope with psychologically. The expertise of a mental health professional such as a psychologist or community psychiatric nurse would have been invaluable. In additional, a nurse or GP could have made the important point that enforced immobility would further weaken his muscles and exacerbate his constipation. If a situation such as this should confront you, point to the likely impact of what is proposed on your overall well-being, since well-being is supposed to be central to care planning today.

Expertise brought in from outside may increase your chances of securing help. For instance, if you suffer from depression, you could ask your GP to explain to social services that in view of this it is important that you should be enabled to keep in regular and close touch with other people, perhaps through attending a drop-in facility or a day centre. Social services often find it difficult to ignore such missives.

Speed

If you desperately need support services, delay could make a bad situation much worse. Get back to social services if they drag their feet in providing you with a promised assessment. Assessments should be carried out within a reasonable time.

Government guidance for England does not lay down just what 'a reasonable time' should mean. If the situation is serious, for example, if a carer who provides a lot of care has been taken into hospital, the general assumption in the world of social care is that an assessment should take place on the day that social services hears about the problem, whether through a GP, hospital or carer's emergency card *(see page 632)*. Indeed, in the case of a carer being taken ill, many social workers would be phoning or visiting within an hour. All social services departments have the capacity to carry out an assessment on the day they hear about a problem, and there is always an out-of-hours service, so an urgent case should not have to wait overnight for a social services' response. If the situation is not urgent but nonetheless serious, expect a phone call within a day and a visit from a social worker within three or four days. If social services receive a phone call from a GP or from the person themselves, staff will usually assume that there is a need that demands their prompt attention. But be prepared to explain your problem when they contact you: do not understate your needs.

Many local authorities publish a timescale within which they aim to respond to assessment enquiries. If you experience a delay, phone the council (or look on its website) and see what timescale it has set itself. This could provide you with valuable ammunition.

If you have to wait longer than three or four days for an assessment for a serious but not critical situation, phone social services and ask why there is a delay. Consider lodging a formal complaint *(as outlined on page 579)*. This will be passed to a senior member of staff, who will have to investigate it. However, local authorities dislike receiving complaints, as they have to reveal the number and nature of complaints lodged against them, so you might elicit immediate action simply by threatening to complain. You could also threaten to take your case to the Local Government Ombudsman (or equivalent in other parts of the UK); delays in the provision of services are often examined by the ombudsman service on the grounds of maladministration and councils also dislike their actions being scrutinised by the Ombudsman.

If you have been or fear you will be mistreated or neglected in ways which could be described as elder abuse *(page 565)*, draw this to social services' attention: it could prompt officials to fast-track your assessment. Councils can do this in cases where needs are particularly urgent.

The services arising from an assessment should also be provided within a reasonable time, and quickly if the need is immediate. Indeed, councils have the power to provide services temporarily without carrying out a prior needs assessment if they believe that the person involved requires care services as a matter of urgency.

Support for independent living

Although many care homes offer excellent care, many people wish to live independently in their own homes or those of relatives or friends. The care assessment and plan preparation should help make this possible, if that is what they wish.

The Department of Health, Social Services and Public Safety of the Northern Ireland Executive makes a specially useful statement about independent living in its guidance to health and social care trusts, saying:

> The central objectives of community care services remain:
>
> - helping people to remain in their own homes or in as near a domestic environment as possible, for as long as they wish and it is safe and appropriate to do so
>
> - providing practical support to carers to support them in their caring role; and
>
> - ensuring that residential care, nursing home and hospital care are reserved for those whose needs cannot be met in any other way.[37]

Expect any social care official anywhere in the UK to abide by those basic objectives. They are reflected in guidance elsewhere. For example, 'Supporting people to live as independently as possible, for as long as possible, is a guiding principle of the Care Act', according to the Department of Health.[38] The main law in Wales on community care, the Social Services and Well-being (Wales) Act 2014, stresses the importance of promoting independence wherever possible, while the Scottish government enjoins councils to give people the freedom, choice, dignity and control which it believes underpin independent living.[39]

Preventing the escalation of care needs

Councils should not only be dealing with crisis situations in which serious problems such as abuse will occur or people will spend hours to get themselves washed and dressed if help is not provided, but should be looking proactively for ways in which people in their areas can be helped to prevent any needs for practical help arising or growing.

The Care Act 2014 (at Section 2) lays on councils a duty to provide or arrange for the provision of services and other facilities or take other steps that will help to prevent or delay needs for care and support. Facilities might include exercise classes to help prevent falls, telecare *(see Chapter 22)*, stress management classes for carers, and older people's hubs that promote social contact. Prevention measures must be aimed at people who have no current health or care and support needs, as well as those with eligible needs, and carers.[40]

The duty to provide or arrange for the provision of preventative services could provide ammunition for local pensioners' forums and the like who are lobbying their councils to fund, say, befriending schemes or day centres. It could be useful for individuals too, who are asking their council to provide them with house adaptations *(Chapter 8)*, Reablement *(see below)* and various types of equipment *(see Chapter 21)*.

On an individual basis, councils have been told that in cases where none of the needs of someone they have assessed meet the eligibility criteria, they should give them information and advice about the steps that can be taken to meet or reduce their needs and what can be done to prevent or delay the development of needs for care and support in the future. Expect to be given more than a few phone numbers and left to make your own enquiries: the Department of Health has told councils that this should be information and advice to prevent or reduce needs relevant to that person.[41] A general reference to prevention services or a website would therefore fall short of the mark.

Awareness of the assessment

Last, but by no means least, is a provision which could help the many people whom social services probably think they have assessed but who were unaware that the assessment was happening and were therefore unable to participate in it fully. In a case in 1998 involving Bristol City Council, the judge took the view that somebody who was unaware of being assessed had not been assessed.[42] So, if social services tell you that they have carried out an assessment on you or your loved one and that comes as news to you or them, demand a new assessment, referring to this case.

Access to your care and support plan

We all have a right to see our own social care records *(see page 577)*, but it is clearly much better to see documents at the time they are being drawn up. Your care and support plan should be as freely accessible to you as it is to social services and you should expect social services to send you a copy of it promptly. The Care Act 2014 says that the local authority must give a copy of a care and support plan to the person for whom it has been prepared and must supply a copy to any carer and any other person if the person who has been assessed asks it to do so.[43]

If what is set down in your care plan and needs assessment does not reflect what was agreed during the drawing up of these documents, get back to social services and say so. If they fail to provide details that you think would be helpful, such as those I have itemised above, say so.

If you have difficulty reading your plan, ask for a copy of it in large print or a language other than English or whatever you need. Your council is forbidden by law (the Equality Act 2010) from discriminating against anyone by reason of disability or race (amongst other 'protected characteristics') when providing goods and services *(see pages 767–72)*.

Keep your plan with you if you go into hospital. Your care needs may be reviewed while you are there and it can be useful for you to have to hand what has already been agreed.

Appeals

You may wish to appeal against what is contained in your plan. Perhaps you consider that your council should have established that certain of your needs were eligible for support.

Examine your council's reasons. If it decides that your needs do not meet its eligibility criteria, it must explain its reasons to you in writing.[44]

Unfortunately, there is no simple appeals system in the field of social care service provision. Instead, anybody who wishes to challenge the way in which their council has handled their assessment and care planning has to use their local authority's complaints system. Nonetheless, the use of the complaints system is recognised in this context. In other words, making a complaint is the equivalent of appealing *(as discussed on page 578)*.

Grounds for a complaint might be, for instance:

- your council has failed to give you a needs assessment when you have asked for one
- it has given or proposes to give you an inadequate assessment
- it has failed to assess you within a reasonable period or
- it has failed to recognise your needs as eligible when you think they meet its eligibility criteria

As councils dislike receiving complaints, simply threatening to lodge one may be sufficient to have the desired effect. If you do file a complaint, the process is straightforward *(see page 579)*. The grounds of the complaint have to be that the rules and procedures were not applied properly in a particular case; complaints cannot be used to object to a political decision the council has made.

Preparing for a needs assessment

If your council is one of those which is pleased to arrange and pay for sophisticated and generous support in the home, you may find your assessment and care plan proceed without a hitch. If, however, your council has other priorities or (as so many do) has very limited resources, expect to fight. Such councils may underestimate or ignore your needs, try to palm you off with an assessment which denies your rights in the care assessment process, put forward inadequate proposals to support you or deny you important information.

So, before your assessment, it is worth doing a little homework. Think about what help you need. You could keep a diary over a week and jot down the things that cause you special difficulty. Write down how long it takes you to carry out everyday tasks and the nature of the difficulties you face. This should help you when you describe your difficulties.

It is important to be as specific as possible and, while not exaggerating your difficulties, certainly not leave any of them out. Also, explain the ways in which those difficulties have, or could have, an impact on other areas of your life, such as your social life and your relationships with your family. These two aspects are singled out in the eligibility criteria *(page 591)* and there may be others to which you could refer.

According to research, older people tend to under-report the amount of help they need.[45] The reasons are quite revealing: they have low expectations of their quality of life; they do not know what help might be available; and they are too proud to acknowledge the extent of their difficulties.

Think about the sort of support you would really like to have. If you can get an idea beforehand about the type of solutions to your problems your council favours, perhaps by talking to local voluntary organisations with experience of care provision in the area, so much the better: that will give you time to consider whether you think they are right for you. Try to relate this to your idea of how you wish to live your life; the Care Act says that in England councils should be looking at the outcomes people wish to achieve from the help they are offered.[46]

If your needs are considerable, try to find out the maximum amount by which social services might subsidise your care at home, so that you have some concept of the boundaries of discussion. Some councils publish this figure, but many are reluctant to do so; you may therefore have to probe, asking your council and/or local groups, such as a local older people's forum, Age UK or carers' organisation. Often councils subsidise support in the home up to the amount they would pay for somebody to live in a low-dependency care home – in other words, to the tune of several hundred pounds a week. That said, councils are not allowed to refuse to fund support above that figure. To do so would involve 'fettering their discretion' *(see page 571)*, so they can use that care-home figure only as a guideline.

If you have serious, complex social care needs arising from a medical condition, you may be eligible for a form of NHS funding called Continuing Healthcare. *(I explain how eligibility is determined and the way in which this funding can be delivered, including in someone's own home, on pages 953–62.)*

Benefits of a needs assessment

If you wish to continue to live independently in your own home, the main benefit of a needs assessment should be to enable you to do so. But if you suspect your needs are unlikely to reach the eligibility level your council insists upon or that your council's policy on charging for domiciliary care services will mean you will have to foot much of the bill for any services offered, you may consider an assessment not worth your time and trouble. Yet a needs or community care assessment can be invaluable in many ways other than in opening the way to the provision of services to meet eligible needs and/or a council subsidy.

Gadgets and house adaptations

An assessment can provide a gateway to gadgets and adaptations to your house or flat to help you cope with disability and frailty. This is because the needs assessment ought also to examine your need for equipment and adaptations to the home to cope with illness or disability. As we saw, councils have to provide equipment and house adaptations up to the value of £1,000 for free for people assessed as needing them in England, for instance. Even if you are not deemed eligible to receive equipment or adaptations through your council, the advice of its professionals about the type of equipment and adaptations that would work best for you could be invaluable.

General expert advice and referral to other services

A care manager or a social worker conducting a needs assessment in your home environment should be able to give an informed perspective on your situation and the problems you face. They should be able to bring expert knowledge of what is available, particularly locally. For instance, they might put you in touch with the fire service for help with fire safety; or a Care and Repair agency for advice on house or flat renovation *(see page 176)*; or a local voluntary organisation such as a local Age UK that offers the particular help you need.

A good social worker will pick up on problems you might be having not just from what you say but also from, for example, the state of your clothing or whether you are underweight. Their imagination and experience ought to be able to help you. *(I list examples of the range of advice which can materialise from a social care assessment on pages 558–61.)*

The social worker might also give you a referral to another service, for instance to a falls clinic or the council's benefits advisor, who might help you fill in an application form for a state benefit such as Attendance Allowance. Or they might notify the relevant professionals if, in the course of a needs assessment, they spot medical or housing needs which are not being met. This might, for example, result in somebody in an upper-floor council flat being offered ground-floor accommodation or somebody in private rented accommodation being offered sheltered housing. Again, although you might obtain such a referral without a social care assessment, the chances are probably higher if a social worker sees you in your own home and discusses your problems with you face to face.

Obstacles during the assessment process

Social care needs assessments can offer a wide range of benefits. However, cash-strapped local councils often try to keep down their costs by offering older people less than they should, both in terms of the type of assessment they conduct and the commitment to spending on their part set out in the care plan. This is how they do this.

1. Contact assessments

If you ring up social services and say you think you may need help, the person at the end of the line will ask you a few questions. This may lead to their passing your name on so that you later receive a full social care assessment. But it might mean that your help ends with this chat. The person comes to the conclusion that your needs are unlikely to pass the eligibility threshold and gives you the phone numbers of organisations in your local area which may be able to help you, such as commercial homecare agencies. The contact assessor, who has in effect carried out an assessment of your needs for care and support, tells you to ring back if your circumstances change.

Sometimes the 'contact assessment' system works well. Perhaps the person phoning has a specific enquiry, such as how to obtain a bus pass or the contact details of a local agency which offers gardening. But if they are experiencing real difficulties in their everyday life, this more superficial assessment could result in their being screened out of the system right at the beginning, without even benefitting from an in-depth assessment of their needs, let alone the provision of services.

Who are the people doing these initial contact assessments? Well, they are unlikely to be social workers. They may not even be social work assistants or other social work personnel. As in many areas of public service, social work professionals have been replaced with less well-trained personnel in order to cut staff costs. More than 40 per cent of contact assessments were being carried out by non-social-work staff, according to a survey in 2011.[47] Another study revealed that people were often screened out too early during contact assessments, or not given adequate directions to other types of help, or their needs were insufficiently explored.[48]

Councils must provide their contact assessors with adequate training, just as they are required to provide training for all assessors *(see page 601)*. Expect too that a contact assessor will be ready to seek advice from a registered social worker if they cannot answer your questions.

If asked to justify offering only a superficial assessment, a council can point out that the government has indicated that assessments need not always be in-depth and cover every possible matter, but can be proportionate to an individual's needs. Fair enough: somebody whose life has not become circumscribed through, say, continence problems does not need help in that area. But talking to someone about the needs they do have and the range of ways in which these might be addressed is an entirely different matter from assessing somebody over the phone.

If your council does not offer you a full needs assessment, you can still ask for one, and your request ought to be successful – after all, you have a right to one if you might have needs for care and support *(page 588).*

As mentioned earlier, when you first telephone social services, do not minimise your problems. Be prepared to explain difficulties at that stage. The official at the end of the phone line is likely to have a form in front of them and will ask you whether you can dress yourself and carry out similar tasks. If you simply answer 'yes' to every question, the official will tick all the boxes and conclude that you are coping pretty well. It is easy to say 'yes', but if it takes you a great deal of time and effort to get dressed, say so. Be prepared to explain your difficulties.

One social worker with whom I explored the problem of getting a full assessment thought that a request might be more readily complied with if an older person asked somebody else to make it on their behalf. So perhaps you could ask your GP, a neighbour or the manager of a lunch club you attend to approach social services. Their voice might well add weight to the request, as it suggests a third party considers you need help.

Another tack: you could tell the official trying to conduct a contact assessment that you feel you cannot convey your situation well over the phone, perhaps because you cannot speak or hear well, and ask if a social worker could come and see you instead. Councils are required by law to make reasonable adjustments to ensure that people are not discriminated against in the provision of services by any disability they may have. If a council is prepared only to provide an assessment on the telephone, this could be argued to impose a barrier for somebody with, say, a hearing or a cognitive impairment and so would be unlawful.[49] *(See pages 687–92.)*

Contact assessors must consider whether the person to whom they are talking is having substantial difficulty in being involved in the conversation about their needs and, if they are, the council should consider whether to provide them with an independent advocate, just as people who are doing a fuller assessment.[50]

One way of increasing your chances of receiving a full needs assessment in your home quickly is by pointing out that you are being abused or neglected or might be abused or neglected unless action is taken. Perhaps somebody with whom you live or who comes into your home is stealing from you, intimidating you, hitting you or simply failing to take the necessary care of you. If this is the case, say so when you call social services. Social services departments tend to regard adult protection, like child protection, as a field in which the involvement of fully qualified social workers is essential. They are forbidden from delegating their responsibilities in this area to outside organisations.

2. Self-assessment

'Self-assessment' sounds empowering, suggesting that the person being assessed plays the central role in determining what services they will receive. Beware! If you agree to self-assess, you may secure less than you would through a needs assessment carried out by a social worker or an assistant social worker or care manager.

This is how it works. You are given a form which you are asked to fill in yourself, with little or no discussion with a social work official. The form asks, for instance, how much personal care you need and also how much help you receive from family and friends. So, if you need constant care and get none from family and friends, you might get the maximum score.

However, plainly what you lose out on if you self-assess is the expertise of a social worker or other official from social services who can talk to you about your situation and who knows how the system works.

One danger of operating without this expertise is that you underestimate your need for help. We noted above that older people often do this. Also, you may find it hard to put your needs into categories. Or you may find it difficult to fill in the form to best advantage for other reasons.

If you understate your need for help, your council will underestimate the amount of money necessary to meet your care and support needs *(a matter to which I return on page 650)*. Unless you can afford to top up out of your own resources, potentially for years, you will not receive the amount of help you need. You could then find life a greater and greater struggle and you might find you have to move into a care home when, with adequate support at home, you could have stayed put.

Ninety-nine per cent of social workers questioned for a survey in 2011 thought that potential service users could not complete the paperwork relating to assessments without support.[51] This is hardly surprising: social work is a sophisticated discipline *(as explained in the previous chapter)*. Yet the whole point of self-assessment is that potential recipients of care fill in their forms on their own.

In fact, the Department of Health has warned councils against avoiding their responsibilities through self-assessment. It has told them that any self-assessment should be viewed as 'supported self-assessment', with the council giving the person any support they need:

> Whilst it is the person filling in the assessment form, the duty to assess the person's needs, and in doing so ensure that they are accurate and complete, remains with the local authority. ... If the person does not wish to self-assess, then the local authority must undertake an assessment following one of the other processes outlined above.[52]

However, the department does not spell out how much help a council might provide, and plainly it could be minimal. The processes referred to are those I have outlined.

If you are being pressed to self-assess, you could simply say, 'I would prefer somebody trained to assess me'. Failing this, you could ask for a trained social services official, ideally a social worker, to help as you fill in the form, citing the Department's words. Stand your ground and if necessary point to your right to a supported needs assessment. In an important court case in 2009, a judge said that a council could not, 'Avoid its obligation to assess needs etc by failing to make an appropriate assessment themselves, in favour of simply requiring the service user himself to provide evidence of his needs'.[53]

3. Ruling out services

Particularly at a time when local authorities are desperately trying to make their resources go as far as possible, it can be tempting for them to rule out any use of some of their discretionary powers and thus save themselves money. For instance, faced with a case in which an older person needs a lot of community care services, including perhaps a visit by a care assistant in the late evening, a council might say it never funds such visits after 8pm (when they would be more expensive). This is wrong: a local council cannot rule out the use of a discretionary power on all occasions. Similarly, it cannot say that it will never fund home help involving housework such as cleaning. Binding itself as to the way in which it will choose between possible options is called 'fettering discretion' and it is unlawful. A council may establish internal guidelines, but it must be prepared to make exceptions on the basis of every individual case.

So, if your local authority says it never uses a certain power or imposes blanket across-the-board ceilings on the amount of financial support it gives to individuals, you should point out that it is fettering its discretion. If it fails to change its behaviour, lodge an official complaint, and if necessary approach the Local Government Ombudsman or the equivalents in Scotland, Wales and Northern Ireland *(see page 580)*.

4. Reablement

Reablement involves the provision of free social care in the home, without any financial means-test, for a limited period – usually up to six weeks. The focus is on helping people with poor physical or mental health to live with their illness by learning or re-learning the skills necessary for daily life. Reablement was originally envisaged for people who had had a temporary setback, such as an infection or operation, and needed help to regain their competence at home skills. Since then, it has also come to be used by social services departments to provide short-term help for people living at home who are experiencing problems. Rather than having a full social care needs assessment when they contact social services, they are given Reablement for a short period. An assessment might follow at a later date if they continue to experience difficulties.

Reablement has much in common with a scheme called Intermediate Care *(which is discussed on pages 947–52)*, but while the latter is funded by the NHS, Reablement comes out of local authorities social services' budgets.

Regulations in England forbid local authorities from making any charge for Reablement services for the first six weeks of the period they specify for which Reablement should be given or, if the specified period is less than six weeks, during that period.[54] Similar provisions pertain in Scotland, Wales and Northern Ireland.

Councils can consider whether a period of Reablement should be given to someone in order to maximise what they can do for themselves before the council undertakes a further assessment of needs. So someone contacting social services might be given a community care needs assessment. Or they might be given an assessment to see whether they should be given Reablement services. These would be provided for a set period, after which the person would be reassessed. They might have Reablement for, say, a fortnight, at which point their ability to look after themselves might plateau out. They would then be given a more holistic assessment of their needs through a community care assessment.

Reablement is potentially useful as a means of helping somebody get back on their feet and gain the confidence to look after themselves after a temporary setback or to relearn skills lost during a period of illness or disability. Furthermore, for people whose means would rule them out of any council subsidy towards ongoing community care services, it may provide the only free care services they can obtain, albeit for a limited period.

If you think Reablement services could help you yet they are not being offered, press your case. You could perhaps ask your GP to write a letter of support.

But dangers lurk in Reablement. One of the main objectives of Reablement for councils is to cut their overall spending on social care. This can mean that people who need ongoing help can fall through the net.

Isobel (name changed) received Reablement after a period in hospital. She was not aware that any formal assessment of her needs was taking place before she left hospital, perhaps because she was hard of hearing, but she was delighted to receive the ministrations of care workers each morning after she returned home to the rented flat in which she lived alone. When this help came to an end, she was dismayed – not only because she valued the practical assistance she had been given but also because she had come to look forward to the regular social contact involved. She asked her care assistants to tell their supervisor that she would like help to continue, but did not know who to contact to try to secure this herself. No further social care help or assessment ever materialised.

Quite separately from the condition for which she had been hospitalised, Isobel was suffering from diabetes and heart failure; her flat was accessible only via many flights of steps and was in an isolated rural location. Swelling in her legs made walking more and more difficult, while her heart condition also meant that she became breathless after only minor exertion. As a result, she became progressively less able to do household tasks and increasingly isolated in her flat.

Isobel's heart condition deteriorated; one morning her legs had swollen to such an extent that the pain in them was intolerable. She phoned the ambulance and was admitted at once to hospital. She might have been spared that emergency transfer and would certainly have spent a less distressing last few weeks in her home had she received ongoing support initiated by a wide-ranging social services assessment, not only for help with personal care and household tasks but also to address her social and emotional needs.

As this case study shows, there is a danger that people might receive Reablement for a short period but then find they are left with no help at all, even though they desperately need it. Therefore it is important to be aware of the fundamental differences between Reablement and the ongoing provision of community care services.

Assessment for Reablement focuses on rehabilitation, but it does not consider someone's wider social, cultural and emotional needs, let alone whether they are being met adequately. In other words, Reablement can help somebody regain their mobility after a fall, but not help them cope with the long-term problems that may arise from it.

What is more, receipt of Reablement services can reduce your chances of obtaining long-term care and support. For if you receive Reablement, you are likely to forego, at least for the time being, both a proper needs assessment and the possibility of ongoing care services subsidised by your council. It is therefore important not to be sidelined into Reablement when ongoing service provision would offer a better long-term option.

So, make sure you do not go unprepared into an assessment. If you think you are being assessed by an official (social care or health), establish precisely what type of assessment it is. If you are being assessed for Reablement services and you think ongoing support would be better for you, insist on a full needs assessment.

If you are offered Reablement services, make sure that:

✓ your council does not charge you for them: they should be entirely free of charge for up to six weeks unless the council has specified a shorter period[55]

✓ you are given a full needs or community care assessment at the end of the Reablement period if you might need further support

✓ the help you are offered really will be designed to help you to regain your skills and faculties

If you are going to receive Reablement services, discuss with your care manager what form the help will take in order to ensure it is fashioned towards your particular needs. As Reablement should focus on helping you to maximise your potential to look after yourself, clear goals should be set at the beginning in terms of, say, enabling you to walk to the shops, and every effort should be focused on meeting them. Care assistants should help you to help yourself and be able to adapt the timing, duration and content of their visits as your needs and abilities alter. At some stage you may need practical help; at others, the focus may need to be on encouragement and reassurance.

Reassessment

A local authority has a legal duty to keep its care and support plans under review and must conduct a specific review if it receives 'a reasonable request' by or on behalf of the adult covered by a plan.[56]

Reviews are important. Several of the most debilitating illnesses common in later life are long-term and degenerative. Your social care needs if you have Parkinson's disease, for example, are likely to change. If you have dementia, your needs for practical and emotional help may well increase. As a result, new needs could become identified as eligible. This could also happen because the delivery of your care and support changes. Perhaps the son who is caring for you decides he must take a full-time job. In these cases a formal reassessment leading to a revision of your plan should give you the enhanced care and support you have come to need.

However, some reviews will not necessarily lead to a formal reassessment, but simply involve an examination of how a care and support plan is working; the result might be that the arrangements for implementing it are tweaked so that it works better. The Department of Health says that the first pre-planned review should be a light-touch look at the planning arrangements (not of the person's needs for care and support) between six and eight weeks in.[57] That first date will probably be set down in your care and support plan.

However, don't assume you can only raise the mechanics of the plan's operation six or eight weeks after it was approved. If you think your plan is not working in the way that was intended at any time, go back to social services and ask them to have a look at it. But if your needs or circumstances change substantially, consider requesting a formal reassessment.

Your rights of involvement and eligibility for help in a formal care needs assessment are the same as for a first assessment. So your needs should again be examined on the basis of the eligibility criteria outlined above. And the local authority must involve you, any carer you have and any other person whom you wish to be involved. If you have no family or friends to help you to engage, the council must bring in an independent advocate.[58]

Of course, a reassessment brings risks. Your council might conclude that your needs no longer meet the threshold for eligibility and as a result withdraw services. Still, a council cannot lawfully remove services for which you have been deemed eligible without showing that you no longer need them. You will have the opportunity to demonstrate why your needs should be eligible, and you might care to involve other people to help you make your case, *as described above for a first care needs assessment.*

Social care assessments

* The council may subsidise help in your home.
* Social services can help even wealthy people by organising their care.
* Your local council must assess your needs for social care services if asked.
* Needs assessments should cover more than practical help with physical tasks.
* Your views should be a key factor in your assessment and the preparation of your care plan.
* Take a friend, relative or advocate with you to your assessment.
* Contact assessments and self-assessments are not suitable for everybody.
* Free disability equipment and six weeks of Reablement support are available to all.
* Appeal against the result of your assessment if you are unhappy with it.
* If you have a complex medical condition, you may be able to obtain free social care alongside free healthcare.

Chapter 27

Support for carers

Acting as the unpaid carer of a friend, partner or relative is common when we are getting older. Many people care for their partners; indeed, one may be caring for the other and vice versa – perhaps a husband caring for his wife, who is developing dementia, who in turn is caring for him, as he has emphysema. Many people care for older relatives, while others (and sometimes the same person) care for their adult children, who perhaps have a learning disability or are incapacitated after an accident. Audrey Butler, whom I met at a carers' event in Lincolnshire in 2005, told me she had been a carer from the age of four, first for her mother, who was deaf and blind and had had a limb amputated, later for her husband, who had diabetes, and for many years for both. Some people care for much shorter periods – like the painter J M W Turner, who looked after his father, or Philip Larkin, who cared for his long-time close friend Monica Jones when she was incapacitated for nearly three years; Larkin died while still caring for her.

In the past, the ministrations of carers were often taken for granted. But since the late 1990s, the social care system has taken the needs of carers much more seriously. Supporting them in their caring role not only helps them and those they are looking after, but also saves the state money. Legal responsibility for caring for people who are unable to look after themselves now rests with the state, and were it not for carers, the state would have to pick up the tab. By supporting carers to help them care and to tackle any adverse effect the caring is having on their well-being, the state helps ensure that caring situations are sustainable in the long term.

Several types of service are provided to carers. The one with which people are probably most familiar is 'respite care', or care so the carer can take a break. This could involve someone coming and sitting with the cared-for person so the carer can go out. Or respite can involve the cared-for person going to a day centre, or on an outing, or for a stay of perhaps a week or two in a care home.

In fact, the range of help given to carers is much wider than this, mainly because social care authorities can give carers a direct payment *(explained in the next chapter)* to enable them to buy whatever help they would like. Some might buy help with housework, others a mobile phone or driving lessons, for instance. In addition, social services can arrange for the person being cared for to receive practical help, such as help with personal care, if the carer does not wish or is unable for various reasons to undertake some care for the person they are looking after.

Much support for carers is channelled through carers' centres that are dotted over the UK, from west Glasgow to Brighton and Hove, and Cambridge to Mourne. These receive some funding from social care authorities, some from the health service and some from other sources. Social care authorities have delegated to some carers' centres the power to carry out carers' assessments and prepare support plans for carers. But the centres can also provide help over and above this to carers who do not meet their council's eligibility threshold for support and those who are eligible for some help but could benefit from additional support. This additional assistance may range from counselling and training to advice on benefits. *(I outline the range of support these centres provide on pages 630–5.)*

Definitions

In the context of social care, a carer is understood to be someone who provides or is going to provide unpaid care for someone (such as a relative, partner or friend) who is ill, frail or disabled. Thus the term does not apply to a paid care worker or someone providing formal voluntary work. The carer does not have to be living with the person for whom they are caring. They may be caring for a short or a long time.

The care that carers provide takes many different forms. For instance, as a child Audrey Butler used to accompany her mother on the bus, guiding her and buying the fares. Someone caring for someone with a mental health problem might have to spend much of their time prompting them to care for themselves and providing moral and practical support to help them to go out and mix in the community. Someone caring for someone with advanced Parkinson's disease might spend a long time helping them to eat and move around and ensuring they take their medication on time.

To get help through social care, a carer does not have to be providing a huge amount of support. The legislation in England and Wales defines a carer as 'an adult who provides or intends to provide care for another adult who needs care'.[1] In **Wales** a carer is simply 'a person who provides or intends to provide care for an adult or disabled child'.[2] In **Scotland** and **Northern Ireland,** a carer is defined more tightly – as someone 'who provides or intends to provide a *substantial* amount of care on a regular basis' (my emphasis).[3] However, on the ground, there is probably not much difference. The Scottish government has told carers, 'No definition of "substantial" is given, but most people who want to see if they can get support with their caring role are likely to be able to get an assessment.'[4]

Carers' assessments

The gateway to help from a social care authority is a carer's assessment. This is not a test of the competence or the commitment of a carer: it is an assessment of any needs they may have for support to help them in their caring role. Social care authorities throughout the UK have a legal duty to carry out a carer's assessment if they consider that a carer may have needs for support, whether currently or in the future.[5] You may have to ask for a carer's assessment: it will not always automatically be offered to you. But if a social care authority considers that you may need social care support, it cannot refuse to give you an assessment of your support needs.

Whether or not the person you are caring for is eligible for care as a result of an assessment described in the previous chapter is irrelevant to your right to a carer's assessment. This is because the latter focuses on the carer and the impact the caring is having. You do not need to have already become a carer to get an assessment. This is important, because the degree of help you might get from your local authority may well help you decide whether to become a carer or not. If you live away from, say, your father and are seriously considering whether to go and live with him to act as his carer, you have a right to an assessment of your needs as a prospective carer by the social services department in your father's area.

Normally an assessment for a carer would take place at the same time as a needs assessment of the person for whom they are caring or planning to care. This combined assessment of the needs of both carer and cared-for person can ensure that the person who needs care receives it and the carer receives any support they need, including at times when the carer is unable or unwilling to provide help, perhaps because they go to work. A co-ordinated package of support can therefore be assembled. However, if the cared-for person is not having an assessment – maybe because they have already had one or do not wish to – then the carer can have a free-standing assessment. Both the carer and the cared-for person can insist that their assessment takes place in private, separate from that of the other, if they so wish.

Carers can ask for an assessment at any time. Some people will have been acting as a carer for years without an assessment. The provision of support services is only one possible benefit of an assessment – for instance, the conversation with an outsider with expertise can help them clarify in their own mind what they are doing and get their caring role recognised, perhaps within their own family.

As with people who may need care, carers often have assessments when somebody is going to be discharged from hospital and may need more practical help than they did before they went in *(see page 946–7)*. At this time, the willingness or otherwise of a carer to take on practical support can take centre-stage.

Social care authorities can offer older people a wide range of services, but some people are disinclined to approach them, perhaps believing (erroneously) that social services help only people of modest means. If you fall into this camp, find your local carers' centre *(see page 632)* and go and talk to the advisors there. If they think you would benefit from an assessment, they will tell you how to obtain one and may have delegated powers to carry one out themselves.

The ways in which social care authorities should behave during a carer's assessment are virtually the same as for an assessment of someone who might need care. Thus the detailed guidance on how social services should carry out a needs assessment and draw up a care and support plan for someone who might need care *(outlined in Chapter 26)* also applies to assessments and the preparation of support plans for carers. As a result, carers should be able:

✓ to have a friend or advocate present at the assessment, as well as an interpreter or other person if there may be language, communication or comprehension difficulties

✓ to have an assessment that focuses on the outcomes they would like and takes account of their personal views and wishes

✓ to have an assessment that takes a holistic approach to their needs

✓ to have an assessment within days if their need for support is urgent

✓ to have an assessment that is in sufficient depth and is carried out by someone who has been adequately trained to conduct it

✓ to receive a copy of their assessment and support plan

✓ to receive any support they require if they self-assess their needs

✓ to request a review of their assessment at any time should their circumstances or those of the cared-for person change

✓ to retain any service for which they have been assessed as eligible: no service should be taken away from them without a reassessment of their needs that concludes they no longer require it.[6]

It is worth preparing for a carer's assessment, and the tips offered *(on pages 608–9)* for people who are to be assessed for their needs for care may be useful. Think ahead about whether you would like to ask someone to be present at the assessment to support you (as well as the person for whom you are caring or proposing to care). Also think about the forms of respite care that would be most helpful, and how caring could tie in with other parts of your life, such as earning a living. If you are already a carer, keep a diary of the problems you have faced, such as lack of sleep, frustration and fatigue. Try to list all the difficulties you are facing or anticipate that you will face as a carer, and the things you think you need or anticipate that you will need. The voluntary organisation Carers UK publishes useful free guides to carer's assessments applicable to each country of the UK, setting out the precise rules councils use. Guidance issued by the Northern Ireland Executive to social care bodies in Northern Ireland lists questions about caring situations that can serve as a useful prompt for people anywhere in the UK preparing for a carer's assessment.[7]

Eligibility for support

Just as councils use eligibility criteria to ration support for individuals who need help, so too for carers. Here, first, is the situation in England.

The eligibility criteria for carers are quite different from those for people who themselves need help: they bring into the equation such considerations as whether the carer's health is at risk as a result of caring and whether caring significantly affects or is likely to affect their working life, as well as their caring obligations to other people, not least their children. These considerations can mean that a carer is eligible for various kinds of help from social services although the person for whom they are caring does not meet the separate and rather different eligibility criteria for people who are being cared for, which turn on their degree of need for care. But as with the rule for eligibility for people who need care, if a council decides that a carer's need is an eligible need, then that council must ensure it is met, if that is what the carer wishes.

The first eligibility criterion is that the carer must be providing 'necessary care': in other words, the need must arise as a consequence of the carer providing necessary care to an adult – not help that the person is perfectly capable of providing for themselves.[8]

The next question that is asked is whether the carer's physical or mental health is or would be at risk of significantly deteriorating as a result of the caring they are carrying out or are going to be carrying out.

Many carers have health problems that arise from their caring situation. They may hurt themselves trying to move their loved one, for example, or they may not get enough sleep or develop depression or anxiety. If any health issue is relevant in your case, ask your GP to write and explain it to social services to increase your chances of obtaining support. But also ensure that the issue itself is addressed. For instance, if you are putting your health at risk by lifting your loved one, ask for training on safe moving and handling techniques. After all, this is provided as part of the initial induction training given to paid care workers.

If the health of the carer is not or is not likely to deteriorate significantly as a result of their caring, the assessor considers whether the caring situation will pose a serious risk to the carer's life outside caring, recognising that carers have a right to a full life, including time to enjoy themselves, to work, to obtain education and training, and to enjoy family and personal relationships. This stage of the process also considers whether the carer's ability to care for other people will be seriously affected, so the assessor should ask whether, as a consequence of caring, the carer will be unable to do any of the following:

- to care for any child for whom the carer is responsible; this includes grandchildren,[9]
- to provide care to other persons for whom the carer provides care
- to develop and maintain family or other family or other significant personal relationships
- to engage in work, training, education or volunteering
- to access necessary facilities or services in the local community
- to participate in recreational activities and have leisure time
- to maintain a safe home environment (whether or not this is also the home of the adult needing care)
- to do essential shopping and prepare meals for their family[10]

How do councils work out whether any of these things (called outcomes) are being undermined by caring for someone? Well, they are expected to use a similar approach as that outlined above *(page 591)* in relation to outcomes for people who may need care. In other words, 'being unable' to achieve an outcome includes circumstances where the carer:

- is unable to achieve the outcome without help

- is able to achieve the outcome without help, but doing so causes or is likely to cause significant pain, distress or anxiety

- is able to achieve the outcome without help, but doing so causes or is likely to endanger the health or safety of the carer or any adults or children for whom the carer provides care[11]

If the answer is 'yes' to any of these questions, the assessor considers whether the impact of caring on the carer's health or the difficulty of achieving outcomes is having or is likely to have a significant impact on the well-being of the carer. A significant impact on the carer's well-being is the third and final condition for determining whether a carer's need meets the eligibility criteria that the government has set. So, just as well-being is central to the assessments of people who may need care, it is the same for carers, and the same definition of well-being applies in each case *(see page 593)*.

The Department of Health has given case examples of how the weighing up of all these factors might work on the ground. In one case, a woman was caring for her neighbour, working part time and collecting her grandchild from school. The Department postulated that a local authority would conclude that she was certainly busy, and a local carers' organisation could advise her on ways in which she could manage her commitments more easily (for instance, through doing her neighbour's shopping online rather than carrying it home), but that as she found her caring roles fulfilling, her well-being was not significantly affected and so she did not have any eligible needs for support. In another case, a divorced father worked full time and had two children who lived with him every other week; he also cared for his mother, who had dementia, by visiting daily and doing her cooking, shopping and laundry. The Department envisaged that a local authority would give this carer a direct payment to pay for a care worker to visit his mother for three days every other week to check that she was all right and to make her a meal. It would also direct him to a carers' organisation that could tell him about his rights at work both as a parent and a carer.[12]

You may find that even if the needs of the person for whom you are caring fail to meet the eligibility criteria, yours as their carer do, with the result that more support from your council will be forthcoming than if the person for whom you are caring had been assessed on their own.

The system for establishing that a carer's need is an eligible one in **Wales** uses a similar approach involving tests of well-being and outcomes to that in England. This means that in Wales, too, the carer may be eligible for help while the person for whom they are caring is not.

Apart from eligibility criteria involving well-being and outcomes, the Welsh rules go on to say that a carer's need cannot be eligible for local council help if that need can be met through the support of other people willing to provide it, or with the help of services in the community to which the carer has access. Finally, the criteria stipulate that the carer must be unlikely to achieve their outcomes unless their council provides or arranges care and support to meet their needs.[13]

In **Scotland** and **Northern Ireland,** social care authorities establish whether a carer's need for support is sufficiently serious to make it an eligible need by using a four-level framework which classes the severity of a carer's need according to the severity of the risk posed if that need goes unmet – whether that is low, moderate, substantial or critical. In Scotland, for example, a need is considered critical if, 'There is a very high risk that the carer will not be able to begin caring for someone, or continue to care for someone, without having major problems in their own life, health or relationships, and they need to get support immediately'.[14] It is considered substantial if, 'There is a risk that the carer will not be able to begin or continue caring for someone without experiencing some major problems in some parts of their life, and they need to get support very soon'.[15] Although the Scottish government has not laid down that carers with low or moderate needs must not be offered help, it has said that, 'Each council is different, but usually it is only people with critical or substantial needs who are given a full package of support, as they would be at risk if the council did not provide a service to them.'[16] It has also pointed out that people with low or moderate needs should be given information, advice and details of other support that is available, but may not receive any services from their council direct.

Willing and able

A key consideration that must take place during the assessment process involves the recognition that carers are not forced to care, at least by the state. Local councils must ask whether the carer is able and willing to provide some or all of the care that the person being looked after needs.

This question reflects the legal reality that the ultimate responsibility for caring for frail, ill and disabled people lies with the state, not with relatives or even spouses. The work that unpaid carers assume saves the state a huge amount of money and it is in the state's interests to ensure that caring situations work well and do not unduly exploit a carer.

National governments have told social care authorities that they should not make any assumptions about the level or quality of support available from carers. It is up to carers to say how much they are prepared to do.[17] In any consideration of the role of a carer, whether during a carer's assessment, the assessment of someone who may need care or a combined assessment, social services are not allowed to press a carer to provide more support than they wish. Always a social care authority must ask: is the carer 'willing and able' to care?

This question provides an opportunity for a carer to explain the amount and type of care they are prepared to carry out. Although social services must not press a carer to provide care, councils have a compelling incentive to see carers do as much as possible, as this saves them money. Social care authorities are obliged to meet eligible needs for care, but they are not obliged to do so if a carer is willing and able to meet them.

So, before an assessment, think carefully about just what care you are prepared to provide. Think of the times and/or tasks you would like to avoid (or have to, perhaps because of work commitments), and in order to increase your chances of obtaining support, try to link them to the outcomes listed above.

Someone who is living in the same house as the person who needs care might say they are happy to provide care during the evenings, weekends and at night, as well as meals, but not during the day, when they go to work. Another carer might say they will provide care for their mother except on Friday mornings and Tuesdays, when they go to college, or a knitting group, or have a weekly hairdressing appointment, or whatever it may be. All these things would count as 'education' or 'accessing local facilities' or 'recreational activities', for instance.

The 'willing and able' provision provides an opportunity for a carer to say they are unwilling to perform certain care tasks, even though they may have the time to do so. A daughter could say she was unwilling to help her father with aspects of his personal care, as she felt to do so would undermine their relationship.

A carer can also request a reassessment of their needs at any time. Perhaps someone is looking after an older relative and their own child has a baby in another part of the country. They could ask for a break to visit them – say, a week – in order to 'maintain other family relationships'. This would probably be made possible by a week's stay in a care home for the person for whom they were caring. However, it might not. One social worker who dealt with such a case told me in 2015:

We put in a plan that was about respite at home for the mother, as her daughter was very concerned about her going into a care home. We arranged for people to come in five times a day to provide the care that the daughter had been providing. She was still anxious, but we got through it, and the new granny returned home refreshed. This experience changed her attitude: it made her see it was OK to ask for help. There's a guilt thing – an "I should be shouldering this myself" feeling. But carers should absolutely not.

Carers' services

As we have just seen, provision for a carer to have a week away can be facilitated through the cared-for person going to live in a care home for the week. Or, if they do not need care on hand all day and night, it might be provided by visiting domiciliary care workers. While some services to support carers are provided direct to them, whether by their social care authority or as a direct payment, several are actually delivered as a service to the person for whom they are caring. In these cases, the person being cared for is assessed for their need for care and that care is then provided to them. They may be charged for it, unless they are of modest means (*as discussed in Chapter 28*). Social care authorities can charge carers for support services, although in the past they have rarely done so.

Likewise, although a need for other types of respite care may arise out of a carer's assessment, they are not in fact a service delivered to the carer. The carer is assessed as in need of a break from the caring role, which is set down in their carer's assessment; the person being cared for is then assessed for the additional support that will enable the carer to take a break, and this is documented in their care needs assessment. For instance, if the carer is assessed as needing a break every Tuesday for three hours, the cared-for person might then be assessed as needing a sitting service for three hours every Tuesday. That sitting service would be provided as a service for them, not a service under the carers' legislation.

As we will see in a moment, some services for carers are provided by carers' centres, which are charitable organisations. Others are provided by other public authorities. For example, the Care Act empowers social services in England to ask another part of the local authority, such as that responsible for the provision of housing, to cooperate with it in supporting a carer (or indeed someone with needs for care). If it does this, the local authority approached must comply with the request.[18] This provision could be useful where caring could be helped through a switch from one council house or flat to another, for example.

The support plan

Once the needs of a carer have been teased out and evaluated, a social care official should lay down how their eligible needs will be met as well as set out their non-eligible needs (the so-called presenting needs discussed *on page 589*) in a 'support plan'. The plan should also clearly set out the extent of the care that the carer is prepared to provide. This will enable the local authority to respond to any change in circumstances more effectively – for instance, if the carer is unwell or decides they no longer wish to provide care.[19]

Talking through caring

Even if you do not get many services as a result of a carer's assessment, there can be real advantages in having an assessment or simply a conversation with an advisor in your local authority or carers' centre. These include information about the various facilities that a carers' centre and other voluntary organisations may provide to carers in your area, but also:

- recognition of your role as a carer
- peace of mind from knowing how to make contact in the future
- a chance to talk through the issues and consider your own needs
- information about the condition of the person for whom you are caring and its likely progression
- information on other support in your area, for instance through carers' groups attached to organisations such as the Alzheimer's Society

Services for paid, live-in carers

Local councils also have the discretion to carry out carers' assessments on people who are being paid to care or are caring in a voluntary capacity. They do not have to, but they can look at the care-giver's needs for support for the part of the care they are providing that falls outside their contractual or voluntary arrangements.[20] One social worker, for example, told me a GP had referred to her local authority a live-in care assistant who was struggling with aspects of the personal care she was expected to carry out for a client who had had a colostomy. The social worker, who also had expertise in nursing, carried out an assessment of the man's needs and concluded that his well-being was being affected by the lack of assistance in this aspect of his personal care. As a result of this assessment, and in agreement with the care-giver, the man and his family, social services provided (and funded) 15 minutes' help twice daily to support the paid assistant. The social worker reasoned that the help could be considered to fall outside the tasks the live-in care-giver could reasonably be expected to undertake and that live-in care blurred boundaries. As she said, 'You're not talking about someone who can toddle off at 5 o'clock and resume their life: it is a big commitment if it's done properly.' *(Live-in care is the subject of Chapter 24.)*

Help from carers' organisations

There are two main national voluntary organisations that seek to support carers – Carers UK and the Carers Trust. Each provides a wealth of information and guidance *(see Useful Contacts for their contact details)*.

The Carers Trust oversees a network of more than 140 carers' centres, dotted across the UK, where people can obtain one-to-one help. It was formed through the amalgamation, in 2012, of the national bodies Crossroads for Care and the Princess Royal Trust for Carers, and here and there local Crossroads organisations remain separate from their local carers' centre, albeit working closely with it. Crossroads provides care in the home to enable carers to take a break.

As noted above, people who might feel reluctant, for whatever reason, to approach their social care authority could go instead to their local carers' centre, which will have close links with social services. To find your centre, contact the Carers Trust by phone or through the internet. Most centres bear the name 'carers' centre', but some retain the name of a previous organisation that has become part of the centres network, such as the Derbyshire Carers Association.

Gloucestershire Carers is typical of the sort of help that carers' centres offer to carers in their areas. It was providing the following range of support in 2013:

A carer's helpline: Any carer in the area could phone the helpline for information and general guidance. It was available every weekday from 8am until 8pm.

Carers' assessments: The centre carried out carers' assessments on behalf of Gloucestershire County Council. These examined the needs of carers for help both to support them in their role as carer and to have a life of their own.

Carers who were considered to need a lot of support received a direct payment – in other words, a weekly payment they could spend on obtaining help, such as paying somebody to come in regularly to help them. To obtain a direct payment, a carer had to meet the eligibility criteria for carers set by Gloucestershire County Council. From April 2015 it has been the eligibility criteria set by national government described above.

Flat-rate yearly payment: Many carers who did not meet the eligibility criteria for a direct payment received a payment of between £300 and £500 per year. They could use it to buy whatever seemed best for them – perhaps a washing machine, driving lessons, gym membership, alternative therapies or somebody to help out with cleaning. The amount they were allocated turned not on the severity of the needs of the person for whom they were caring but on the impact on their own life (including their physical and mental health) of their care work.

The provision of free short breaks from caring was also a feature of carers' support in Gloucestershire, as it is in many other areas. In Gloucestershire, this involved free breaks of a few hours a week. Helpers from Crossroads would go to the carer's home and look after the cared-for person for the assessed time, usually a few hours. The figure was determined by whatever the carer was assessed as needing. The carer could then go out, or take advantage of the opportunity of enjoying space in their own home without the presence of their loved one if the latter had been taken out. There was a men's 'pub club': small groups of men were collected and taken to the pub for two hours.

Provision of training: Gloucestershire Carers worked in partnership with Gloucestershire County Council to deliver a programme of training called Positive Caring. This involved six training sessions covering such subjects as help available locally for carers, manual handling techniques and ways in which carers can look after themselves, for instance through relaxation techniques. Occasional courses were also provided for particular groups of carers, such as those caring for people with a learning disability or people with dementia. These provided not only information and advice but also the opportunity for carers to exchange ideas with each other. The training was free and available to any carer.

A counselling service: This was also free and available to any carer. When somebody embarks on caring, there may be issues arising from the relationship they have had with the person for whom they are caring that would benefit from being worked through. Unlike the situation when we become a parent, acting as a carer takes place alongside a past relationship with the person we are looking after. If that relationship has been a troubled one, difficulties may surface that compound the problems intrinsic to the caring situation. Counselling also gives carers space to think about themselves and to get things into perspective. It usually involves between six and ten sessions, but there may be more.

Of course, to take advantage of services such as those offered in Gloucestershire, a carer would probably need to find somebody else to look after the person for whom they were caring while they were out of the house. However, enabling them to access support services is one of the objectives that should be viewed as legitimate in their own assessment. Or a carers' organisation might organise care for the person separately, through somebody from a local Crossroads coming to the house and standing in for a while.

A carer's emergency card: One of carers' biggest worries is what will happen to their loved one if they are unable to care. So, emergency cards were issued free to the Gloucestershire carers to provide a means of putting in support if they were suddenly unable to care, perhaps because of an accident or illness. They could carry the card in their wallet and it contained a phone number with an instruction to ring it in case of emergency, together with that particular carer's reference number. Anyone who rang the number would get through to a call centre. The centre would then call a nominated person to tell them what had happened – perhaps a neighbour who had agreed that in the event of an emergency they would go in and, say, give medication to the person being cared for.

However, in some cases, more support would have been necessary. The call centre would have then made use of information it had obtained previously to put in place care for 48 hours, until the carer could return or while longer-term arrangements were being made. This information would have already been provided to the local branch of Crossroads for Carers and it would dispatch care assistants; Crossroads would have held information on where medication and food (including cat food!) was stored in the house or flat to enable this interim support to be as seamless as possible.

Caring arrangements that would have elicited this more comprehensive help would have been based on information gathered by Carers Gloucestershire at a carer's assessment. The organisation carried out assessments on behalf of Gloucestershire County

Council which examined the needs of carers for help both to support them in their role as carer and to have a life of their own.

Help with obtaining benefits: This was available both for the carers themselves and for the people for whom they were caring. Gloucestershire Carers staff told carers about the benefits to which they might be entitled and helped applicants fill in the forms. They also advised on appealing against benefits decisions. Some carers' organisations represent applicants at appeals, but in Gloucestershire another organisation did this. *(In Chapters 35 and 36 I highlight the benefits to which carers may be entitled, in particular if they are eligible for the Guarantee element of Pension Credit.)*

Meetings: Meetings took place in which carers heard a talk, perhaps about an aspect of healthcare services in the locality, and could chat to each other.

As in other aspects of life from employment to housing, local Citizens Advice offices can also provide invaluable help to carers. Phone the office beforehand and ask for an appointment, pointing out any restrictions in the times you are available because you are a carer.

Support for carers

* Carers have a right to an assessment of their needs for support in their caring role.

* Carers can obtain an assessment of their needs for support without needing to inform the person they are caring for, if that is their wish.

* Carers' assessments look at carers' lives in the round.

* The criteria used to work out whether a carer is eligible for support from their local social care authority do not turn on the degree of help the person they are caring for requires.

* Carers may be eligible for support even though the person they are looking after is not eligible for social care services.

* A carer should get support if their health is or is likely to deteriorate significantly as a result of caring.

* The support that is provided could be a voucher to pay for help with housework or to buy driving lessons.

* Carers' organisations may provide one-off payments, training, counselling and other help.

* Councils fund respite care to enable carers to take a break, whether for a day, part of a day or a week or more.

* Ensure you have emergency arrangements that can be called on should you suddenly become unable to care.

Chapter 28

Organising and paying for care and support

I n Chapter 26 I looked at how the social care system seeks to ensure that older people who need practical support because of age, illness or disability can obtain it from social services through first having their needs for help assessed. In this chapter I look at the way in which that care and support is delivered and funded. I also address the provision and funding of support for unpaid carers.

Social care, unlike healthcare or education, is not free but charged for, mainly according to financial means, although with exceptions such as Scotland's provision for free personal care. Here I outline what to look out for when your council informs you how it proposes to divide the costs of your care and support services between you and it, and what you can do if you disagree with its proposed charges.

Wealthy people might assume they should not try to involve social services when setting up their care arrangements. I explain the reasons (not just financial) why social services involvement can help them too.

This chapter therefore examines:

► how individuals can ensure their services are delivered in the way that best suits them

► how councils work out how much money to contribute towards the cost of somebody's care and support

► how they work out how much an individual should pay

► the benefits for relatively wealthy people of asking social services to be involved in the organisation of their care and support

► how carers can ensure their support is delivered in the way that best suits them

► the rules on charging for support given to carers

Organisation of the delivery of care and support services

In the 1990s and before, care delivery was handled by social services with little input from the recipients. A social services care manager would visit somebody who was struggling to cope in their home, decide what would help them, then go away and organise provision, usually through handing details to the council's team of homecare workers or to a domiciliary care agency with which the council had a block contract. The care assistants thus dispatched to the person's home would arrive at set times and perform a list of set tasks that the care manager had stipulated. The council would also work out whether the service user should contribute towards the cost and, if so, send them a bill. So homecare was a service that was done to people rather than one with which they could engage and which they could arrange to suit their lives and needs.

Many younger disabled adults – people in their thirties or forties, perhaps blind or using wheelchairs – who wished to live as independent and mainstream a life as possible resented this paternalistic approach. The last thing such people wanted was for bureaucrats to organise all their homecare support: they wanted as much control and choice as possible in this as in all other areas. Campaigning by their voluntary organisations bore fruit in legislation in the late 1990s which enabled local authorities to offer 'direct payments' to service users. This meant that rather than the council organising the provision of care, the individual could commission their own, from individual helpers or domiciliary care agencies as well as other organisations such as day centres, using a voucher from their council equivalent to the cost of providing the care they needed or the proportion of that amount which their council will contribute. Direct payments are now available for people who need care and support throughout the UK.

Choice has moved on further still. Nowadays, social care authorities are expected to offer service users choice in the way in which their services are delivered, whether themselves operating a direct payment; the local authority organising the provision of their services; or their organisation by a third party (known as a 'brokerage agency'). Choice in delivery is called 'personalisation' in England and in Scotland it is a key element of 'self-directed support' *(page 596)*. As in the past, service users are told how much they must pay for their services, but they should also be told how much their council is contributing in their 'personal budget', or 'individual budget' as it is known in Scotland.

There are two senses in which this budget is personal – first, plainly, it relates to one individual; but second, it brings with it personal choice. Part and parcel of a personal budget is that the individual in question has a choice about who organises the spending of the money involved in their care and support and how this is done.

Thus the Department of Health has pointed out to councils in England that, for the person eligible to receive services, a personal budget means:

- having clear information about the total amount of the budget, including the proportion the local authority will pay, and what amount (if any) the person will pay
- being able to choose from a range of options for how the money is managed …
- having a choice over who is involved in developing the care and support plan for how the personal budget will be spent
- having greater choice and control over the way the personal budget is used to purchase care and support, and from whom[1]

A similar approach in **Scotland** is set down in legislation called the Social Care (Self-directed Support) (Scotland) Act 2013. The same principle of choice and range of alternatives outlined above is enshrined in this law and explained in detail in guidance to councils from the Scottish government.[2] There is a website provided for people who wish to find out about self-directed support in Scotland which includes a user's guide and case studies. This site, called Self-directed Support in Scotland, provides a helpful sense of what choice in the method of delivery of care and support services might mean on the ground anywhere in the UK.

A similar approach involving personal budgets operates in **Northern Ireland. Wales** has direct payments, but personal budgets do not form part of its social care system. However, councils in Wales have a legal duty when organising social care services to ascertain and have regard to the individual's views, wishes and feelings insofar as this is reasonably practicable.[3]

In view of this, expect your council to explain that you have a choice in how your services are delivered and to be able to answer your questions, so that you can work out which alternative (or alternatives, because you can mix and match) would suit you best. Officials should certainly not imply that only one way is possible. As the Department of Health has explained: 'People should be encouraged to take ownership of their care planning, and be free to choose how their needs are met, whether through local authority or third-party provision, by direct payments, or a combination of the three approaches.[4]

If the social services official who talks to you about the way your services could be delivered cannot answer your questions about, say, what a direct payment might mean for you or the extent to which you could influence services organised by the council or a third party, ask to speak to somebody who can. A conference on self-directed support in Glasgow in 2013 heard reports of staff who were doing social care needs assessments but were unfamiliar with aspects of direct payments, such as the responsibilities of acting as an employer.[5] There should be a dialogue between the social services official who is presenting the options and the person who is to receive the services that enables the latter to understand the implications of each approach and make an informed choice.

Let us look at each of the three alternatives by which care and support can be delivered in more detail.

Organisation of care by the local authority

Although direct payments arose as a reaction against what was seen as excessive control by social services, in fact there are undeniable advantages in allowing social services to manage your personal budget for you. They will shoulder the tasks and the responsibilities of finding your help and managing it week by week, and this may be an appealing rather than irritating prospect, particularly if you are coming into the care system at a time of crisis.

Another advantage is that you may well obtain more care for your money than you would if you were entering into a contract with a care agency as an individual. Councils can use their dominant position as large-scale purchasers of care to beat down the prices care agencies charge, partly because the administration costs for the agency will be much smaller per person helped than if they were dealing with all those people on an individual basis.

You should also expect far more involvement in the way in which social services set up your arrangements and monitor how they are working than was the case in the past: councils are enjoined by national government to allow service users much involvement and control, whatever the actual means by which their services are delivered.

If you allow social services to manage your personal budget for you, it is nonetheless worth taking a little time to understand the system of care delivery it will use – occasionally a council's homecare team, but usually a commercial domiciliary care agency. In Chapter 23: Human help, I explain how I helped set up care and support arrangements for a friend in Scotland when he was awarded free personal care by his council; I could not have done this without prior knowledge of how care agencies operate. If you read Chapter 23, you should get a sense of what you can reasonably except from care agencies and from the care assistants they send out. Although that chapter is written for people setting up their care and support arrangements independently of social services, much of it should also be useful if you are going to obtain agency help via your local authority.

For instance, it is important to clarify precisely which tasks care workers will provide help with and which they will not. Make sure that you have a copy of the instructions your council is proposing to send or has sent to the agency or to its own team, so that if they are incorrect or defective, you can try to get them changed.

Misunderstandings and disagreements can arise from inadequate briefing. When social services arranged help through an agency for my mother, we frequently found assistants would claim they had been asked to do certain tasks while we understood that they had been asked to do others (usually more). Those who worked only at weekends were often different from those sent during the week and poorly briefed. Yet we could not get hold of the care manager at weekends to clarify matters and she resented my providing any instructions to the assistants direct.

In Chapter 23, I also explain that care agencies have to comply with certain regulations by law. These regulations, and the associated standards or guidance, can be obtained for free. It is well worth reading them so that you understand that agencies (and council-run domiciliary care teams, which are governed by the same rules) must, for instance, put in place an adequate system for recording attendance by care workers. A time-sheet, with space for each care worker to insert their time of arrival and departure and for the care recipient to sign to confirm those times, or an electronic device *(as described on page 519)*, is essential for ensuring that care workers spend as long in your property as they should.

The second reason for briefing yourself on the ways of care agencies is to empower yourself to exercise choice in the way in which the council commissions care on your behalf. Although you are unlikely to have as much choice as you would if you handled all the arrangements yourself, as in a direct payment, you may well wish to have some degree of choice, and a little background knowledge could inform your thinking in suggesting ways in which your services could be delivered.

In what ways would you like the system to work for you? Local authorities will vary in the extent to which they accommodate individuals' suggestions, but it is worth discussing your ideas with social services well before they send instructions to the care agency or to their own team of care assistants.

For instance, you could specify how you would like your religious practices to be respected, perhaps in terms of diet. You could ask for a particular care agency to provide your care, perhaps one that you are using to obtain services independently as they are not considered by social services as meeting your eligible needs – for instance, walking your dog or doing housework. You could seek to bank your paid care time to days when no relative is available to help out.

Councils vary in the extent to which they charge brokerage fees. If your council proposes to charge you a brokerage fee to manage your personal budget, check to see whether you would have to fork out to pay that yourself separately. It should be included in your personal budget allocation. Your council might charge you a fee to organise additional services to those necessary to meet your eligible needs, which you might be paying for separately. If you are not entitled to any financial subsidy from the council and ask it to organise your care package for you, it will almost certainly charge you a fee *(see page 665)*.

Once your homecare arrangements are up and running, be ready to iron out hiccups or solve serious problems. Perhaps your assistant is supposed to arrive at 9am but often does not turn up until 10.30am and is then in a rush to go to their next client. If care assistants frequently fail to turn up on time or to perform the tasks set out in the plan, or if the arrangements are unsatisfactory for some other reason, you should report problems to the manager of the agency and keep your social services care manager briefed; ask them to raise matters with the agency if necessary. If concerns remain, be prepared to go further and file (or threaten to file) a formal complaint to social services *(as described on page 578),* since social services is ultimately responsible for the provision of your care, even though it has been outsourced to a non-council body.

Make sure you have the contact details of both the care agency (or the council's homecare team, if no agency is involved), as well as your social services care manager. Get contact names and numbers for any problems which arise outside normal office hours or when your care manager is unavailable. *(See also the tips on handling social services on pages 575–6.)*

Care provided through care agencies often works well. However, even apparently small problems, such as the lateness of helpers, can have a cumulatively deleterious effect. I have come across several people who needed a lot of help but who were disinclined to report lateness, oversights by care workers or other ways in which the agency was not doing what it was paid to do. These people shrugged their shoulders, preferred not to make a fuss and hoped things would improve. Over time, their homecare arrangements proved unsustainable. In every case, these people ended up moving to care homes when they would have much preferred to have continued to live independently.

Brokerage agencies

Brokerage agencies manage personal budgets on behalf of the recipients, hiring staff for them or entering into contracts with care agencies and their providers and handling the week-by-week running of the arrangements. Some brokerage agencies are voluntary bodies which offer brokerage in addition to other services including the management of direct payments. Other brokerage agencies are private companies, which often offer brokerage as an adjunct to the main work of the agency, which is to provide domiciliary care services.

If you ask any brokerage agency to manage your personal budget, the money will go direct to it and it should set up the provision of your care services and carry out all of the administration involved in running them. In other words, it should handle every aspect of your personal budget. If it also provides care services, it may deliver your care services itself.

Plainly a brokerage agency can be useful if it is going to take upon itself the recruitment, management and responsibility of hiring helpers for you. But, just as in the case of your council organising your care, it is important to establish just how much control you will have over who will help you and how and when they will do it. To what extent will the agency consult you about the services it is commissioning on your behalf? Will you, for example, have the opportunity to meet the helpers who are to be sent to care for your mother, who has dementia, beforehand?

A brokerage agency will almost certainly keep a proportion of your personal budget to cover its own administration costs. So, if you propose to use such an agency, find out how much this will be and make sure that it is included in your personal budget and is thus paid for by your local authority if you are eligible for a subsidy on financial grounds.

If the brokerage agency is part and parcel of a domiciliary care agency, will it really commission services from an agency other than itself if that is what you wish? Conversely, might it sub-contract your care out to another agency without first consulting you? Be aware that the choice and control that a personal budget is supposed to embody may turn out to be an illusion. Also, consider how easy it would be to complain if the agency providing the services was the same as the one commissioning them.

A final element of a personal budget may be sent by social services to the brokerage agency to spend on 'other support'. How is the agency to decide how this should be spent? Will it consult you? As the manager of a large homecare agency in London explained to me in 2011:

> There will always be the incentive to spend this amount on the services that an agency provides. So all this can act as a smokescreen for greater independence for the client. The brokerage agency is acting as social services used to act: it's just that the agency will have an incentive to spend the money on things it provides.

He pointed out that an agency might, for instance, use the money provided by social services to obtain equipment for the client to which they are entitled free of charge *(see pages 481–2)*. So, if you do hand your personal budget over to a brokerage agency, you still need to spend time checking that it is obtaining value for money, acting in your best interests and looking at all possible options rather than passing work to itself or to organisations with which it has a special relationship.

Direct payments

Under the system called 'direct payments', the council gives you the money it would otherwise have spent on providing your care services and leaves you to make the arrangements to find somebody (or an organisation) to provide those services. You might decide to commission services from a domiciliary care agency, for instance, or you might decide to hire direct one or more individuals as personal assistants to provide the help you need at home.

The advantages of direct payments

The advantages direct payments offer as against care organised by the council or a third-party include:

- greater choice over who provides help – you select your own staff or your own homecare agency

- greater choice over how and when help is given – you tell your staff or agency how you wish tasks to be done and you work out timings with them

- more control – if any problems arise, you deal with the person responsible yourself

- greater flexibility – as you are in charge, you can change the timing of help and the tasks to be carried out

- familiarity with helpers – you are in a better position to ensure that the same assistants come regularly. As a result, your help should be more consistent than if a variety of assistants turn up, each with their own strengths and weaknesses.

A direct payment can also be used to pay for care services outside the home. For instance, if part of your personal budget is intended to meet your need for a hot meal and company, you could opt to take that element as a direct payment and choose to spend it on, say, attendance at a day centre or lunch club, buying meals in a pub, café or restaurant, or hiring someone to come and help you prepare a meal (or meals, placing others in the fridge for later). At a time of cutbacks in local government services, you are unlikely to be given sufficient cash to enable you to dine like a king, but you should have control over where you spend that money.

How direct payments work

Direct payments can involve large sums of money – perhaps £400 each week. It is a condition of receiving a direct payment that you must handle it separately from your other money. This might be via a dedicated bank account into which your council will make regular payments or a pre-paid card in which your council places the money at regular intervals. Then you either hire one or more helpers (often called personal assistants) yourself or you enter into a contract with a homecare agency to provide you with helpers or organise your care through a mix of these means.

> The combination of care and support you obtain with your direct payment and who provides it is in your hands, so long as it meets your eligible needs. The Scottish government's guidance to local authorities on how direct payments should work gives the example of Mr Scott, who lives in a rural area. He was using his payment to hire five personal assistants, all of them self-employed, to provide 30 hours a week of care and support in 2007, of which 17 involved free personal care.[6]

The rules on the way in which direct payments can be used and administered are similar throughout the UK.[7] Here are some of the main features.

You must use the money for the purpose for which the council has given it to you – to meet the assessed needs written down in your care and support plan. Although you have choice in how those assessed needs are met, you cannot use your direct payment for another purpose. If you do, the council is entitled to protest, and this may lead to the withdrawal of the direct payments facility and a demand for repayment of the misspent money. For example, if you are receiving direct payment money for help with personal care and you use it to pay somebody to do the decorating or to give you aromatherapy, you will be in trouble. Not only will you be misusing public funds, but you will also be missing out on help which you have been assessed as needing. Your council will expect you to put in place monitoring systems, such as time-sheets and receipts, to show that you are using your direct payment in the way intended.

There are no general restrictions on whom you hire, except that you are not allowed to use your direct payment to hire a relative or partner with whom you live to provide your care. However, if you can convince your council that this is necessary to meet your eligible needs, it may allow you to do so, perhaps because you live in a remote valley where the only person who could provide care for you also lives with you, for example.[8] But the use of a direct payment to hire a relative or friend who does not live with you is generally permitted.

Councils do not give people direct payments to fund their stay in a care home as a long-term resident (although it is possible the rules may change to allow this in the future). However, if you are living in a care home and wish to try out independent living to see whether you could live independently, your council may give you a direct payment to enable you to do so.[9]

More commonly, direct payments are used to purchase a short stay in a care home. This may occur because an unpaid family carer is assessed as needing a break and they, the person they are looking after and their social care authority consider this could best be provided through a short stay in a care home during the carer's absence. Under the direct payment rules, the stay cannot be longer than four consecutive weeks in any 12-month period. But if two stays are more than four weeks apart, they are not added together. This respite care could be funded through a one-off direct payment purely for that purpose or as an element of a direct payment that also provided other services, such as day care once a week. Although the respite care arises from a carer's need, in fact it is the person receiving care who receives the service and the associated direct payment.[10]

A growing number of people in England are using a personal health budget provided by their local NHS body to buy some elements of the healthcare services to which they are entitled *(as explained on page 288)*. This too requires the recipient to report on how they have been spending the money involved. If you are receiving a health budget from the NHS, you may wish to combine that pot of cash with your direct payment, to give you greater flexibility and bring the monitoring of spending in one place. Your council and local health body should be prepared to consider cooperating to do this, nominating one of the organisations to keep an eye on how you are spending the money.[11]

A direct payment is usually paid net of any contribution the person receiving the payment may be required to make if a financial assessment shows that they should make a contribution. While the direct payment someone receives from their council may include cash which they have already paid to social services for their care and support, more often it will not and the recipient will be expected to add the sum necessary to bring the payment up to the level at which they can purchase the services they are assessed as needing.

The recipient of a direct payment is also free to add separate cash out of their own pocket to buy more care or to get their eligible needs met in a different, more expensive way, if they wish and can afford to do so. However, it is important that the possibility of topping up is not seen by the council as a way of giving someone less money than it should to ensure that their needs are met.

Support to operate direct payments

The main drawback of direct payments is that the recipient of care takes on board the responsibilities and work involved in hiring staff. For instance, if you take on staff as an employer, you will take on legal responsibilities such as paying tax, and if you use people who say they are self-employed, you will have to make sure they really can claim that status. I explain these matters and also set out where information and advice can be obtained, such as through Her Majesty's Revenue and Customs' New Employer Helpline and from booklets issued by government, at the end of Chapter 23, *on page 530*. In that chapter I also discuss how to go about finding a personal assistant, from advertising for one to using an organisation that tries to team up people who need a personal assistant with those offering themselves for this work.

However, what many people want is face-to-face advice and the option of handing over at least part of the task to people with relevant expertise. Fortunately there is a network of usually voluntary organisations throughout the UK that support people using direct payments. Direct payments have been available since the late 1990s and the government has encouraged social services authorities to fund organisations to support people (including younger disabled people and people with a learning disability) who are receiving them.

The Kingston Centre for Independent Living, a voluntary organisation, supports people in the Royal Borough of Kingston-upon-Thames in south-west London who are receiving or are about to receive a direct payment from Kingston Council. It provides one-to-one advice (by phone, in its office in the heart of the borough or through home visits) on how to obtain a direct payment, how to find staff and how to manage them, including how to run a payroll. It applies for enhanced security checks for direct-payment holders, so they can be clear whether the people they may hire have been convicted or suspected of an offence that could jeopardise their homecare work. It also organises the securing of all direct-payment holders' employers liability insurance, and is reimbursed for this separately from Kingston Council so that this element does not feature in the direct payments of individuals.

When Kingston Council initially proposes a figure for someone's direct payment (the 'indicative amount' *referred to on page 652),* the Centre advises on whether this would be sufficient to cover all the costs involved in meeting that person's eligible needs. If it considers it is too low, it puts forward a case for more money on behalf of the prospective direct-payment holder.

Kingston Centre for Independent Living also supports people who are receiving a personal health budget from their local clinical commissioning group because they have been assessed as eligible for NHS Continuing Healthcare. *As explained on page 943,* this funding covers all the healthcare as well as social care costs of people with serious and unpredictable conditions and it can be taken in the person's own home, with nurses and care assistants visiting them there. Kingston Centre for Independent Living helps recipients (or their representatives) to establish whether the budget the NHS body proposes is sufficient, to organise their teams of helpers and to pay them where necessary.

The Kingston Centre for Independent Living has been seeking to help disabled and unwell people in the Royal Borough of Kingston-upon-Thames for over 45 years. In addition to its work in the fields of direct payments and personal health budgets it offers other services, such as the administration of holiday grants made by Kingston Council to help pay for disabled and/or unwell people of modest means to take a holiday. It also gives advice on welfare benefits.[12]

What support agencies such as the Kingston Centre for Independent Living do varies: some will operate a payroll for you, others will not, a few will help with personal health budgets. Most will help with recruiting staff and give information and support in such areas as insurance, health and safety at work, contracts of employment and so on *(pages 529–31)*. If such a system exists in your locality, you are likely to find the operation of direct payments much easier. As noted *(on page 531),* these agencies may also provide help to people who hire care staff outside the social services system. A complete list of these organisations is available from Disability Rights UK.[13] They are scattered over the whole of the UK. Some have the words 'independent living centre' in their name, others do not, such as the Darlington Association on Disability. This list contains other organisations many of which give advice on handling direct payments.

If there is no support system such as this in your area, your social services care manager ought to be able to provide some assistance, but they cannot take on the responsibility for running the system for you. You can, however, appoint somebody else, perhaps a son, daughter or partner, to act on your behalf as an agent, or you could set up a trust to administer it, which might include a solicitor.

Many people who have a direct payment get a friend or a member of their family to organise it for them. These can become 'nominated persons' by the person entitled to the direct payment and then the payments can be made direct to them. You may be able to persuade your council to add an element in your direct payment to cover an administration payment to this person. Councils in England have the discretion to include such an element to pay someone living with the person who is receiving services for their efforts. If you do not live with the person, you could nonetheless ask for a payment; the administration of a direct payment can involve a lot of work if the arrangements are complicated and involve several different paid assistants or agencies.

If a voluntary organisation that supports people using direct payments helps you and charges you for its services, ask for this amount to be included as part of your direct payment.

People whose mental abilities are limited and direct payments

Perhaps you would like to have a direct payment but do not have the mental capacity to come to a reliable decision on whether that would be the best means of organising your care. If you also would not be able to administer a direct payment but know of somebody prepared to organise it on your behalf, ask that person for their views. If they consider a direct payment a good idea, could the council give you a direct payment channelled through this person? It should consent if it considers a direct payment an appropriate way of meeting your needs and your 'authorised person' suitable to receive and manage the direct payment on your behalf.

Similarly in **Scotland** and **Wales,** a direct payment can be made to the legal representative of somebody who lacks the mental capacity to make choices about a direct payment. This representative would be an attorney, a deputy or a guardian *(see Chapters 31 and 32).*[14] The **Northern Ireland** Executive also seeks to ensure that people who cannot manage a payment themselves perhaps because they have a mental illness are not disbarred from benefitting from one.[15]

Mixing and matching

You may already be receiving council-organised care services and be wondering whether you could switch to direct payments. The answer is yes. You can come out of the social services system at any time – there is nothing to force you to remain there forever. Or you can mix and match, organising some of your services through direct payments but getting social services to organise the remainder. This is a good way of trying out direct payments if you are nervous about them. If they do not work for you, you can go back into the social services system.

If you are in the social services system and wish to switch to direct payments, a good time to do this is when social services reassesses your needs, either on its own initiative or as a result of a request from you.

Obtaining a direct payment

Surveys show that people who have direct payments value them.[16] However, on the ground take-up has been low. In Scotland, for example, councils have been able to make direct payments to older people since 1996. Yet by 2012, only 5,049 adults were receiving them – just 8 per cent of the total receiving homecare services. Of the recipients of direct payments in 2012, half were aged 50 and above. The first direct payment to be signed in Scotland involved Edinburgh City Council, and it has far exceeded any other council in its number of direct payments – at 16 per cent of the total. Several other Scottish councils had fewer than 100 people receiving direct payments in 2012.[17]

This situation is mirrored in other parts of the UK. What seems to have been at the heart of care managers' reluctance to offer direct payments, particularly to older people, has been patronising attitudes about their ability to manage direct payments, low awareness among social care staff of direct payments, and lack of information about them on the part of the people who might have asked for them had they known of their existence.[18]

This final factor remains significant because, although councils are expected to give people choice when setting up their care and support arrangements, they are not strictly speaking under a legal obligation to offer a direct payment per se. The law in England says a direct payment must be requested either by the person who wishes to have it or, in the case of someone without the mental capacity to choose a direct payment, an 'authorised person' acting on behalf of the person involved.[19]

If a council receives a request for a direct payment, it must allow the person to organise their services in this way unless it considers that they are not capable of managing the payment themselves or with the help the authority thinks they will be able to obtain or that a direct payment is not an appropriate way of meeting the need or needs in question.[20]

If you face a fight with your council, ask a local agency which supports people who handle direct payments for advice about the arguments you could advance. If your council continues to refuse to give you a direct payment and you consider its objection unreasonable, lodge an official complaint to your social services department and, if necessary, take the matter to the Local Government Ombudsman or its equivalents in Scotland, Wales and Northern Ireland *(as described on page 580)*. Councils must provide written reasons for a refusal to give someone a direct payment, make them aware of how they can appeal against the decision through their council's complaints system and also explain the steps they might take to get the council to change its mind.[21]

In theory, your council should be only too pleased to give you a direct payment. Certainly the Department of Health has said that direct payments, 'Remain the Government's preferred mechanism for personalised care and support'.[22]

Refusing a direct payment

Direct payments are probably most attractive to people who need many hours of support, wish to select their own helpers and vary the sort of help they receive day by day (although keeping to a pre-arranged total number of hours) and are happy to take on the responsibilities of organising their own arrangements (with or without help).

Do not take on a direct payment if you do not want one. One woman in her fifties, much disabled through multiple sclerosis, to whom I talked, was in a direct payments scheme because her council had never told her that an alternative existed. She needed a considerable amount of help, and organising that help was not easy. She operated through care agencies because she felt too frail to hire staff direct. Fortunately, a friend came round weekly to help sort out the finances, handle paperwork and make phone calls. Her council provided no administrative support whatsoever and the woman in question felt that the council was using the direct payment as a means of offloading the burden of managing her care.

The council's behaviour was completely wrong: in law nobody can be required to have a direct payment: they have to agree to receive one.[23] As the government has said, 'People must not be forced to take a direct payment against their will, but instead be informed of the choices available to them'.[24] Today, had this woman opted to continue with a direct payment, she could have asked for an additional sum to pay her friend to administer it.

The amount of your direct payment

A direct payment will usually be paid to you net – in other words, you will receive the contribution which the council makes and, if you have been financially assessed as able to contribute, you will be expected to chip in your contribution to get the services you are assessed as needing.

Plainly, it is crucial that the council's contribution really does cover the true cost of obtaining services. If it is too low, you will be unable to buy sufficient services to meet your eligible needs. Or you will end up topping up the council's contribution by more than you should, if you can afford to do so.

The main element in the direct payment may well be the cost of obtaining care through a care assistant. A good support organisation *(see page 647)* should be able to advise you on whether your payment or budget is sufficiently large. If you are unsure, do some research on how much a care assistant's services will actually cost before you go ahead with your direct payment. Ask local homecare agencies how much care they would be able to deliver for that amount of money. Or find out how much you would have to pay a personal assistant. If the result differs significantly from the care you think you need, challenge your council.

Underpayment can arise because social services calculates the cost of care on the basis of what they would pay an agency to obtain the support you need. Yet they will pay less than you, as they will be in a position to enter into block contracts with agencies to buy many hours of care for large numbers of people.

Underpayment can also arise because the council underestimates your need for care. That is why it is very important to explain fully your needs and their severity at your assessment and, if you think you might underestimate the help you need, to insist on the involvement of a trained professional and certainly not agree to self-assess your needs without any professional help *(see pages 611–2)*.

Your direct payment should include any costs you incur as a result of finding and appointing assistants as well as ongoing overheads. The latter include fulfilling the legal obligations involved in the hiring of staff *(as outlined on pages 529–30)*. All these costs should be itemised and provided for in your direct payment. As the Department of Health explains:

> The local authority should have regard to whether there will be costs such as recruitment costs, employers' National Insurance contributions, and any other costs by reason of the way in which the adult's needs will be met within the direct payment. If these costs will be incurred their amount must be included in the personal budget (and thus direct payment) if it is appropriate for the adult to meet the needs in a way which incurs the costs.[25]

If you employ someone or treat them as if they are an employee, you must obtain employers liability insurance *(see page 529)*. The Department has also said: 'The direct payment should include an amount to cover the cost of employers' liability insurance and any other insurance that is required in order that the person can meet their needs in the way specified in the care plan.'[26]

Perhaps there is a change in your circumstances – you go and live somewhere else or even die. If you or your legal representative have to meet financial liabilities such as a redundancy payment, the direct payment should include provision for these too. As the government states in relation to redundancy payments, 'The local authority must ensure that the direct payment is sufficient to meet these costs if it is appropriate for the adult to meet their needs by employing someone.'[27]

A major part of the administration of a direct payment is paying staff and sending tax to HMRC if you employ them. Some people pay an agency to run the financial side of their direct payment; this cost, too, should be covered. If a relative administers your direct payment for you, you could pay them for their trouble. For while the direct payments rules prohibit paying a relative who lives with you to provide care under most circumstances, the government guidance does allow the holders of direct payments to pay a relative living with them to administer their direct payment, so long as the local authority agrees.[28] The Department of Health gives the example of a couple, David and Gill. Gill provides unpaid care for her husband. In addition, David has a direct payment which funds the hiring of several personal assistants who come in to help cope with his fluctuating needs for care. He and Gill persuade the council to let her take over the running of the direct payment, summoning staff when needed and paying them. The local authority reimburses her for her trouble, while saving the one-off payment they had made in the past to an agency to administer the direct payment.[29]

The care manager who drew up your care and support plan will probably not work out precisely how much money their council will offer you as a direct payment. This will be done by another section of the council responsible for the allocation of resources who will come back with a figure called an indicative amount. Once that figure has been obtained, the care manager should finalise your care and support plan with you and confirm the actual amount of your direct payment.

The indicative amount can be challenged. Councils often try to pre-empt such challenges by insisting that they have used standard procedures to calculate someone's indicative amount and that figure is the maximum it can possibly pay and it has no discretion to depart from it. Yet in fact it is unlawful for a council to say it never varies the amount by which it subsidises an individual or the services it is prepared to give or commission. This is 'fettering its discretion' *(page 571)*. If you encounter problems, ask a local Citizens Advice or independent living centre for advice or call the helpline of Age UK or Independent Age.

Carers and personal budgets and direct payments

Unpaid carers also have a personal budget. In their case, it sets out the cost of enabling them to meet their eligible needs for support in their caring role and to reduce any adverse effect the caring is having on their well-being. It should also set out how the cost of their support is divided between them and the local authority. *(In Chapter 27 I gave examples of the sort of support a carer might receive.)*

Carers should expect choice in the way in which the support services they are assessed as needing are organised, just as people who are to receive care services are offered choice. The injunction from government to give choice over the method of delivery of services, whether by a local council, a brokerage agency or a direct payment or a combination of these set down in the English guidance applies to carers just as much as to people receiving care services.[30] Scottish legislation specifically states that when a local authority has decided to provide support to a carer, he or she should be given the same choice on how that support is delivered as is provided to a person needing support for themselves.[31] Whether or not a legal right to choose exists, social care authorities throughout the UK know that the provision of choice to carers about how their support should be delivered constitutes good practice.

Carers who receive a direct payment should expect to do so under the same terms as people who receive a direct payment to pay for care services for themselves, so they must be able to manage one with such help as is available and they must usually request one.[32] Not all social care authorities make clear that direct payments are available for carers, but they should.

A direct payment can work well when carers wish to use their personal budget to pay for help with housework, taxi fares, counselling, relaxation therapy, driving lessons or the purchase of a computer or a mobile phone, for example. The network of carers' centres *(see page 632)* as well as the Carers Trust and Carers UK should be able to advise you about operating a direct payment. Talk to them or Citizens Advice if you wish to challenge the size of the personal budget your council proposes.

As noted above, sometimes a carer will be eligible to receive support because they meet their council's eligibility criteria for support for carers, whereas the person for whom they are caring does not meet the (different) eligibility criteria for care and support for individuals. As a result, a carer might receive 'replacement care' or 'respite care' – in other words, care for their cared-for person so that they can take a break from caring. A local authority may decide not to charge for this care, but if it does, the cared-for person will be financially assessed to see whether they should contribute towards its cost, not the carer.

Complaints

If you have any concern or complaint about a direct payment or a personal budget, you should first try to resolve it with your local council, if necessary using their formal complaints procedure *(see page 581)*. This sounds bizarre, but in fact it is the recommended way of resolving disputes in the world of social care, *as explained on page 580*.

If you remain dissatisfied, take your complaint to an outside body – the Local Government Ombudsman (in England), the Scottish Public Services Ombudsman, the Public Services Ombudsman for Wales or the Northern Ireland Ombudsman.

Reassessment

Your needs for social care services may be reassessed at any time, and if they are, you want to know that this is happening so you can think beforehand about what you want to say, arrange to have somebody with you if you wish and ensure that all the rights you enjoy during an assessment *(as outlined in Chapter 26)* are upheld.

Why might you be reassessed? The obvious reason is that your needs have changed: perhaps you are particularly tired, as you are receiving chemotherapy, and so need additional practical support. Perhaps your arthritis has got significantly worse. Or perhaps there has been a change in the provision of care – your son, who acted as your unpaid carer, has moved away, for instance – which means you need help from somebody else.

Beware of a fourth reason why you may be reassessed: your local authority has decided that it does not want to spend as much money on you as it has up until now. It is not allowed simply to stop or scale down services it is already providing – it can do so only if, after reassessing you, it decides that your needs have diminished so that they can no longer be classed as eligible needs. If the council writes and tells you out of the blue that your services are going to be downgraded or the size of your personal budget reduced without any new assessment having been proposed or carried out, you should immediately lodge an official complaint or threaten to do so. *(See also page 576.)*

Charging for social care services

However your care services are delivered, a decision has to be made on what proportion of the costs you on the one hand and the council on the other should bear. It will send you a statement setting out what, if anything, it expects you to pay and how it has arrived at that figure; it should do this before you are billed for any services. In making its calculations, it will work out your 'assessable income', that is, the amount from which charges for care services might be made, after disregarding certain elements of your income and expenditure.

How much you have to pay for homecare services varies widely across the UK. In Scotland, councils are forbidden from charging anybody aged 65 and over for personal care, regardless of their income and savings. In Northern Ireland, health and social care trusts are not allowed to charge people aged over 75 for homecare, as well as any adult who is receiving Income Support (or the equivalent for older people, the Guarantee element of Pension Credit). The Welsh government forbids councils from charging any user more than £60 per week, regardless of their income or savings. In England, a means-tested system means that people with modest income and savings do not have to pay, or they share the cost with social services.

The governments of each country of the UK have issued guidance to all the social care authorities in their areas setting out the overall approach those social care authorities should take. Whichever country you are living in, it is worth getting hold of the national rules *(referred to below)*, so that you can check that your own council is complying with them when it calculates your charges. For instance, in Scotland you could check that your local council is not charging you for a service that in fact falls within the definition of personal care. As we shall see, that definition contains some elements which may surprise you.

So long as it conforms to national parameters, every social care authority has the freedom to draw up its own policy on charging. This is the second reason for the postcode lottery on what price people pay for homecare across the UK. Authorities actually have the option not to charge for homecare services at all. While the vast majority do charge, their approach depends partly on their own political priorities and partly on their financial resources, which can vary hugely.

If you need or might need a lot of care services and are considering moving house, find out about the charging policy of the council in whose area you might live. A survey by Which? in 2011 found that while Derbyshire County Council and Newham and Tower Hamlets borough councils in London were not charging for homecare services, Surrey County Council and Poole and Cheshire East unitary councils were charging around £20 per hour.[33] This means that somebody in Redhill could have been £100 per week worse off than somebody of the same financial means in Derby who was receiving the same number of hours of care.

Another study in Wales found that some local authorities were charging nearly three times the hourly rate for homecare services as other councils; the maximum weekly charge being imposed ranged from £16.50 to £200, with some councils not operating any maximum charge at all.[34]

The best social care authorities set out precisely how they calculate charges for services. Unfortunately, some councils volunteer only scant information. If yours is one of these, ask for clarification. You may wish to dispute the charges. It is important to get any disagreement about the level of charges sorted out as soon as possible, lest you find yourself getting into arrears. If you refuse to pay and it is later established that the council was entitled to what it demanded, you may find yourself running up debts which the council will be entitled to pursue.

England

In England, a safety net seeks to ensure that nobody uses up much of their income and all of their savings on paying for their care (just as a slightly different system safeguards the savings of people receiving care in care homes).

The safety net works like this. If somebody's savings are (or have fallen through paying care charges) below a threshold (£14,250 in 2017), their social care authority must pay all the costs of providing care to meet their eligible needs. People with savings above this level and up to an upper threshold (£23,250 in 2017) have some protection in that their savings between these two figures are converted to a notional income (of a weekly income of £1 for each £250) which is added to their income from other sources. Only if their savings exceed the upper threshold is any council subsidy ruled out.[35]

These savings have nothing to do with whether you own your own home and councils are forbidden from taking into account the value of your house or flat. Only if you are to receive care in a care home are they permitted to take this into account. Yet I have heard of cases in which councils have told people that if they own their own home they are ineligible for any financial help towards homecare. Nothing could be further from the truth.

National rules also seek to protect the weekly income of poorer citizens. Councils are forbidden from allowing care charges to eat up so much of someone's resources as to leave them with an income only 25 per cent above the level of Income Support (or the equivalent for people of about 63 and over – the Guarantee element of Pension Credit). People do not have to be actually receiving Income Support or Guarantee Credit for this protection to apply to them. If they are receiving a premium (such as disability or carer) on top of the basic amount of Income Support or Guarantee Credit, it is 25 per cent of that higher, total figure.[36]

It is important to stress that these concessions apply only to the care that somebody is considered to require as a result of their needs reaching the threshold of eligibility, which *(as noted in Chapter 26)* is set at a fairly high level. As a result, someone might find themselves paying a great deal of money for their care but receiving no state subsidy because their needs do not meet the severity of needs threshold.

If you are living in England, check the following points when your council sends you notification of the charges it proposes to make for your care at home:

✓ If the charges your council wishes to make would reduce your income below Income Support or Guarantee Credit plus 25 per cent, ask your council to waive them. If your income is at or below that level you should not expect to have to pay for social care services at all.

✓ Check that when the council assesses your wealth it is not taking into consideration the value of the property that you occupy as your main or only home. Councils are strictly forbidden from doing this.[37]

✓ Check that the council disregards any earnings. The government has said that councils must disregard earnings from current employment or self-employment when working out how much they should pay, to encourage people to remain in or take up employment.[38]

✓ Check that you are not being charged for any disability equipment you have been assessed as needing or for any house adaptations unless the latter exceed £1,000 in cost. These should be free if you are assessed as needing them to cope with disability.[39] *(See Chapters 8 and 21 for further information.)*

✓ Check that you are not being charged for any health service provision. You should not be paying for help from a continence nurse or dietician, for instance, since this would fly in the face of the NHS principle that healthcare is free at the point of need *(see pages 279–80).*

✓ Check that you are not being charged for any 'Reablement' services. This is a scheme whereby somebody is given social care services to help them maintain or regain to ability to live independently at home; it is often provided after a hospital stay *(as explained on page 950).* The Department of Health has told councils they must not make a charge for Reablement support services (which can involve housework as well as help with personal care) for the first six weeks of the period during which someone needs them or, if the specified period is less than six weeks, for that period.[40]

However, as many as one in five councils in England were charging for Reablement services in 2010, according to research by Community Care magazine.[41] Charging for Reablement services is unlawful and the people involved were paying when they should not have been. The only circumstances in which you might pay while receiving Reablement would be if you had been receiving social care services before you received Reablement and these services were continuing alongside your Reablement services. *(I also refer to Reablement on pages 612–5.)*

✓ Check that your council is disregarding any housing-related costs you are liable to meet for your main or only home. These include council tax, rent or ground rent, mortgage repayments, insurance and service charges.[42]

✓ Check that your council is disregarding any of the following disability benefits you receive: Attendance Allowance, Disability Living Allowance or Personal Independence Payment. It should also disregard any Armed Forces Independence Payment as well as any direct payment.[43]

✓ Councils have been told they must also disregard disability-related expenditure, which Parliament has defined as including, 'Any community alarm system, costs of any privately arranged care services required including respite care, and the costs of any specialist items needed to meet the adult's disability'.[44]

Think about whether there are any other costs that arise from disability that you could put forward, as the definition above is not exclusive. You may be spending more money than you otherwise would on laundry because you suffer from night-time incontinence; you may have above average heating costs because of illness or disability; you may be paying for a cleaner, a gardener or domestic help as a result of illness or disability. And/or you may have spent a lot of money buying equipment such as an electric scooter.

Keep the receipts for any of these services and for any pieces of equipment which you have bought out of your own pocket to cope with any disability or frailty, and ask the council to deduct these, as well as any other relevant ongoing costs, in calculating your assessable income. The financial benefit could be considerable.

Day-centre attendance and meals-on-wheels are often charged on a different basis from personal care and other practical help in the home. Some councils heavily subsidise day centres and charge all users relatively little, on a flat-rate basis. So you may find that you would receive a larger subsidy for these services than you would for practical support in your home.

It may be tempting deliberately to get rid of income and assets that would count as capital in order to reduce your liability for care charges. Don't! Councils look out for what they call 'deliberate deprivation of assets'. If your council considers you have done this, it will treat you as possessing the income of which you have deprived yourself.[45]

Carers

If a local authority provides care to the person whom a carer is looking after which eases the load on the carer, the council must not charge the carer. Any costs must be borne by the person being looked after and/or the council. This care could take the form of, say, help with personal care or attendance at a day centre or respite care in a care home to enable the carer to take a complete break for a little while.

But councils are free to charge carers for other services and equipment which help them in their caring role. In the past, they have tended not to do so, but austerity cutbacks could mean they do so in the future. If a local authority does charge a carer for the whole or part of the cost of, say, the provision of housework or driving lessons, it must abide by all the rules set out above for people receiving care, such as ensuring that charging does not reduce the carer's income more than 25 per cent above the level of Guarantee Pension Credit or Income Support.[46]

Although a council could charge a carer for the whole or part of the cost of, say the provision of housework or driving lessons, they are not permitted to charge carers for preventative services – in other words, support to a carer that is intended to prevent or delay the development by the carer of a need for support.[47]

Scotland

The rules within which councils operate north of the border are quite different from those in England. In Scotland, anybody, rich or poor, aged 65 or over does not have to pay for any personal care that their social care authority assesses them as needing.

In this context, 'personal care' is defined as help with:

- washing, cleaning teeth, trimming nails, bathing and showering
- getting dressed, getting up and going to bed
- taking medication, including eye drops, creams and dressings
- the use of surgical appliances, manual equipment and prosthesis
- going to the toilet or using a bedpan or other receptacle
- the use of a catheter or stoma
- bed-making, changing and laundering clothing and bedding, and caring for the skin, if the person is incontinent

- food preparation and the fulfilment of special dietary needs; and also
- the management of behaviour and psychological support
- the provision of safety devices and devices to help memory and
- dealing with problems arising from immobility[48]

Check that you have not been charged for any service which might fall within any of these categories: there may be some charges, perhaps over food preparation, that you could dispute. Food preparation in the context of free personal care is defined to include cooking, heating or re-heating pre-prepared fresh or frozen food; serving food; the preparation of food ingredients; and cutting up or puréeing food to help eat it.[49]

Local authorities in Scotland are free to charge for other social care services, but with other important exceptions.

As in England, Reablement is given to adults of any age most often after discharge from hospital to help them regain lost skills and to continue to live independently. It involves free help in the home with personal care and also other practical tasks usually for up to six weeks.

Two other provisions could help those not assessed as needing Reablement. First, anyone aged 65 or over on the day of discharge from hospital assessed as needing Intermediate Care (which is similar to Reablement) or additional homecare should receive it free for up to 42 days.[50] The final provision, probably the least used, which has the status only of guidance and dates back to 2001, says that anyone aged 65 and over on the day of discharge should receive free homecare for up to four weeks, if assessed as needing it. The homecare can include housework, meals-on-wheels, laundry and shopping, as well as help with personal care.[51]

After these periods, local authorities can revert to their normal charging policy of providing free personal care for people aged 65 and over but having the option of charging for other care and support services. Thus they can charge people below 65 for personal care services. And they can charge any adult of any age for services that do not involve personal care, such as housework, shopping, meals-on-wheels and attendance at day centres. Different councils approach this in different ways. However, in drawing up their policy on charging, they are expected to conform to guidance drawn up by the Convention of Scottish Local Authorities or COSLA, which is based on government laws and regulations. Thus, for instance, councils are not expected to charge anything for social care services if the recipient of those services does not have savings that exceed £10,000 if they are at least state pension age, or £6,000 if they are younger. If someone is assessed as being able to pay for their care and support services, they should not be impoverished by doing so – there is the same provision as in England that they should be always be left with an amount equivalent to the level of Income Support or the Guarantee element of Pension Credit plus 25 per cent of that figure (as in England this applies to anyone, not just people receiving those benefits). *See also page 656.*

As elsewhere in the UK, the value of someone's main property should not be taken into account in working out their assessable income for homecare purposes. In Scotland, while healthcare equipment must be provided free of charge to people who need it, councils have the discretion to charge for equipment provided through the social care system (unlike the situation in England, where it is free). However, 'devices to help memory' and 'safety devices' (which should include much telecare equipment) are free, as they come within the definition of personal care.[52]

We noted in the section above on charging in England that councils must disregard expenditure someone has incurred related to their illness or disability, but that the range of items listed as potentially eligible is short. The COSLA guidance encourages greater generosity on the part of local authorities. It recommends local councils should be proactive in asking people about additional disability-related costs so that they can take them into account when assessing someone's financial resources. It says that these additional costs may relate to but are not restricted to:

- additional heating needs
- the purchase, maintenance and repair of disability-related equipment
- specialist dietary needs
- specialist clothing
- help with cleaning and other domestic tasks[53]

COSLA also recommends to Scottish social care authorities that they should exercise discretion, so not impose charges harshly or inflexibly. Usefully, COSLA also recommends that authorities should waive charges for social care services for people under 65 years of age who have a progressive illness from which they are expected to die within six months. This is a recommendation only, so not all councils will include provision for it in their policies. But if you are under 65 and expecting to die within six months from a progressive disease, you could ask your council to waive your charges pointing to a provision in its own policies or at least to

COSLA's recommendation for flexibility in deciding what, if anything, individuals should be charged.

Carers

Although councils have the power to charge for support they arrange or provide to carers, the Scottish government has forbidden them from doing so, telling them they must waive charges involving support to carers. It also says that charges for replacement or respite care provided to a cared-for person as part of the support provided to a carer to give them a break from caring must also be waived.[54]

Wales

In Wales there is no universal guarantee of free personal care regardless of income, as in Scotland. However, there is an across-the-board cap on costs. Councils are forbidden to charge people more than £60 each week for domiciliary services; these are not restricted to help with personal care. This cap operates regardless of financial means. So if somebody receives services that cost more than £60 per week, their social care authority must cover the excess.[55]

The only exception is for services which replace ordinary living costs, such as laundry services or meals received at home or in day care. Councils often charge for these at a flat rate, without carrying out a means assessment.

However, they are not permitted to charge for transport to attend a day centre or day-care service where the transport is provided or arranged by the local authority and where attendance at the day service and transport to it are included in the person's assessment of need.

How do councils work out what, if anything, to charge people for domiciliary services up to the £60 per week limit? Well, in evaluating someone's assessable income (from which charges may be levied), they must disregard any earnings and also any savings credits the person receives. They must not include the income of any partner of the person receiving services. In establishing the person's outgoings, they may take into account expenditure that is incurred by any unpaid carer.

The rules laid down by the Welsh government say that if councils use savings limits to determine ability to pay, they must set the threshold at £23,250; if people have savings below this limit, the local authority must pay for all of their care.

Finally, the net income of the person receiving services must not fall below a total figure that consists of:

- their basic entitlement to Income Support, Employment and Support Allowance or the Guarantee element of Pension Credit
- a buffer of 35 per cent of that entitlement and
- at least 10 per cent of the amount they spend on coping with any disability

As elsewhere in the UK, check that you are not being charged for:

✓ healthcare equipment or services *(see pages 279–80)*

✓ Reablement or Intermediate Care services *(pages 947–51)* or

✓ equipment or home adaptations you are assessed as needing which should be free *(page 481–2 and 182–9)*

Carers

Carers in Wales may be charged for services and there is no £60 maximum in their case. However, they are also covered by the requirement that their income must not be reduced by having to pay charges for their support services to a level lower than that of Income Support plus the additional elements outlined in the previous paragraph.[56]

Carers may be charged only for services provided to them and not for any services provided to those for whom they are caring. So, if the latter goes to a day centre once a week so that their carer can take a break, the cared-for person is liable for any charge.

In working out the charges, if any, to be imposed on a carer, a local authority must take into account any costs they bear, such as for:

- the purchase of clothing or cleaning
- additional transport or other costs such as taxis that arise unavoidably because they cannot be away from home for long
- adaptations that have been made to the carer's home, for example, where the cared-for person moves into the carer's home
- the private purchase of care, for example to allow short breaks from caring or where this is needed to enable the carer to maintain employment or to fulfil their obligations as a parent[57]

Northern Ireland

In common with the situation in Wales and Scotland, the administration in Northern Ireland offers a type of universal free care. In this case, health and social care trusts are forbidden from charging people aged 75 and over for homecare services. Younger people who are receiving Income Support or Guarantee Pension Credit also receive services free.

The range of services which can be provided free is far wider than personal care and includes cleaning, shopping, laundry and preparing and cooking food as well as dressing and undressing, washing and bathing and other personal care tasks.[58]

What of the people who are liable to be charged for homecare services, such as people in their late sixties? Trusts are not allowed to take into account the value of the property in which the person involved or their spouse is living.[59] When assessing savings, health and social care trusts must disregard the first £3,000; above that, savings are converted to a notional weekly income. Earnings are taken into account, although there is a small disregard for the first few pounds. Each person is given an allowance, and their assessable income is worked out only once that allowance has been taken into account. Different amounts apply to single people, couples, people with disabilities and people receiving Pension Credit.

As elsewhere in the UK, check that you are not being charged for:

✓ any healthcare equipment or services *(see pages 279–80)*

✓ any Reablement or Intermediate Care Services *(pages 947–51)*

✓ any equipment or home adaptations you are assessed as needing which should be free *(pages 481–2 and 182–9)*

Carers

Health and social care trusts can levy charges on carers if they wish.[60] The Department of Health, Social Services and Public Safety has declined to issue rules on the way in which charges may be levied. However, my anecdotal impression in 2017 was that trusts tended not to charge carers for support they assessed them as needing.

Appeals and disputes

As you can imagine, charging for domiciliary services can be the subject of very bitter struggles between councils and clients. It is one of the main causes of complaints to local councils.

Try first of all to resolve any difficulty by talking and writing to social services. For instance, if the council has (deliberately or inadvertently) failed to take into account a cost which should have been included when working out your assessable income, write and point this out: it should result in an adjustment of their calculations. If you have already been paying, ask for a refund.

If you consider that the charge your council proposes to levy on you is wrong or you feel you cannot afford to pay, request a formal review of it. Some councils have panels that consider such appeals.

Alternatively, you could lodge an official complaint to your social care authority. The lodging of a complaint is viewed as a means of appealing against various decisions taken by councils in the field of social care *(as explained on page 578)*.

As far as charging is concerned, keep your situation under review yourself. Many councils use a savings threshold and anybody with savings above this threshold is expected to foot all or most of their entire bill, once other considerations have been taken into account. If such a threshold is in place with your council and your savings come down over time to less than the threshold, ask your council to review its assessment of your ability to pay. Your council is unlikely to know that your savings have dropped to below the threshold unless you tell it.

Wealthier people and the involvement of social services

Wealthier people often assume that there is no point in approaching social services should they need practical help in the home. In fact, there are a number of compelling advantages in doing so.

The first is that social services must provide everybody with **information and advice** about care and support services in their area, and this includes financial advice. They must provide sufficient information and advice for people to consider the financial implications of meeting their needs for care and support and how to make plans for paying the cost of care and support in the future,. This should include information about financial entitlements and provisions (such as deferred payment agreements) and also where they can obtain independent financial advice on funding care and support. These duties refer to everybody in a local authority's area, regardless of whether they have needs for care and support or whether any needs they do have meet the eligibility criteria.[61] So expect your council to provide you with at least some information and advice on paying for your care, regardless of whether you are wealthy.

Secondly, in every country of the UK there is an element of **free provision of care** that is not dependent on the recipient's means. For instance, in Scotland, the Scottish government will cover the cost of the personal care you are considered to need by your council from the moment you first receive that care, so long as you are aged 65 or over, regardless of your financial means. Another example is the free provision of social care through Reablement or Intermediate Care throughout the UK. Other examples are outlined in the sections on the different countries of the UK above *(pages 655–64)*.

If your financial resources rule you out of council subsidy, you can ask your council to arrange homecare support to meet your eligible needs under what is known as '**the right to request**'. The guidance in England states clearly that councils must accede to this request and should take steps to make people aware that they have the right to request the local authority to arrange care and support to meet their eligible needs. The local authority is permitted to charge a fee to cover their administration costs, but forbidden from applying an arrangement fee on top.[62]

There are non-financial reasons for getting social services to organise your care for you. First, you are saved the hassle of doing so yourself. Second, local councils can bulk-buy care from domiciliary care agencies and as a result obtain a lower rate per hour of care than an individual is likely to be able to negotiate. So if social services enter into a contract with an agency for you, you ought to be able to obtain more care for the same amount of money.

This will not apply if you wish to commission your help from personal assistants you hire direct yourself. But if you plan to obtain help through a care agency and you need a lot of care, the difference in cost could be significant. In addition, you will benefit from councils' knowledge and expectations on the way that a domiciliary care agency should behave.

You do not have to undergo a full financial assessment if you ask your council to arrange your care and support. Councils are empowered to do a 'light-touch financial assessment' instead: basically, to convince them-selves that you have sufficient money to reimburse them for the payments they will be making to the care provider and to cover any cancellation fee these providers might levy.

Organising and paying for care and support

* Check carefully any charges your council tries to levy for social care. There are strict national rules on what they can charge for and many items should be free regardless of means.

* Check that your council is not charging you for Reablement services, whatever your income.

* If in Wales, check your council is not charging you more than £60 per week for help in the home.

* Expect your council to give you the choice between organising your care, asking another organisation to do so or organising it yourself through a direct payment.

* A direct payment should give you more choice and more control.

* If you use a direct payment, it is you and not the council who will take on the responsibilities of hiring or commissioning staff.

* People with dementia can obtain a direct payment if they have someone to manage it for them.

* If you plan to use a brokerage agency, check whether you would lose control and what it would charge.

* If a social services department or a brokerage agency is organising your care, make sure you have a copy of the instructions it provides to the workers it has commissioned before they arrive on your doorstep.

OUT AND ABOUT

> **❝** *To see foreign parts gives I think more of the feelings of youth to those of an advanced age than anything they can engage in.* **❞**

Sir Walter Scott[1]

OUT AND ABOUT

L ater life, at least for those who retire from full-time work, offers
more time to explore environments familiar and new. Cruises and
tours provide opportunities for the relatively well-heeled to see the
world, and in doing so to pursue all manner of interests. Some people
hike and cycle and engage in energetic sports. Others prefer to explore
where the whim takes them, travelling slowly perhaps with their bus pass,
or covering longer distances by train, plane, coach or car.

There are plenty of guides available to help you explore your surroundings if you are able-bodied. Not so however if you are one of the ten per
cent of adults who cannot walk more than a quarter of a mile without a
rest or who cannot manage a flight of steps.

In this part, I look at ways in which we can make the most of opportunities to get out and about in later life but I also address the challenges
that people with disabilities can face in walking both in town and country and in using various forms of transport.

For many people, getting outdoors is a basic psychological imperative.
As many as 90 per cent of the 300 older people in Britain interviewed for
a study in 2007 said it was very important to them to get outside their
house or flat. Participants often talked about how bored or depressed they
became if 'stuck indoors' for a few days. As one put it, 'It's a psychological
thing about escaping from the flat. I get cabin fever and a load comes off
my mind when I go out.' Another: 'It's my great pleasure in life; I can't
bear to be indoors all day. I have a different feeling about myself when I
get home after being out.'[2]

However, more than half of those interviewed reported problems –
physical barriers to free movement, such as flights of steps, and the absence of necessary facilities, such as public lavatories.[3] In the first chapter

of this part, On foot, I examine how some of these difficulties for pedestrians can be overcome.

In the second chapter of this part, On wheels and water, I go on to examine some of the opportunities and difficulties in using cars, buses, coaches, taxis, trains, trams, ships and planes we may encounter in later life, whether in our home area or on holiday.

This part therefore covers:

▶ the challenges of moving around the urban environment on foot or with a mobility aid

▶ the challenges of moving around the rural environment on foot or with a mobility aid

▶ how equality law can secure better access

▶ driving in later life – the joys and difficulties

▶ controls on older drivers

▶ parking for people with disabilities

▶ public transport – opportunities, difficulties and information

▶ concessionary travel arrangements

▶ disability when travelling

▶ alternative holiday possibilities

Chapter 29

On foot

A national survey in 2005 asked people aged 65 and over which was the most common disability they faced. The one most often mentioned was difficulty in walking and climbing stairs.[1] In later life this usually arises from a medical condition such as osteoarthritis, osteoporosis, emphysema or heart disease.

Were our environment fashioned to cope with this reality, exploring towns and cities and popping along to the shops would be much more of a pleasure than it actually is for many. Broken pavements, poor street lighting, a dearth of seating or of public lavatories, and pedestrian crossings that do not allow enough time to cross the road are among the problems that make journeys on foot in our towns and cities less enjoyable for everybody. When we are getting on, they can pose real problems.

Problems in moving around outdoors are not confined to walking. Changes to the kidneys mean that we all need to visit the toilet more frequently as we grow older, and between four and six million Britons, many of them over 60, have continence problems. Many older people have conditions such as cataracts and age-related macular degeneration that seriously impair their eyesight. And if we should trip and fall, we are more likely to break a bone than when we were younger.

What can we do to make our environment, urban and rural, easier to negotiate on foot? In this chapter I look at some of the obstacles that can impair the enjoyment of moving around, particularly if we have a disability. I outline the steps businesses and local councils must take to improve accessibility and discuss the activities of organisations which may support calls for better provision. Finally, I look at the way in which equality laws have made Britain much more accessible than it was ten years ago, and how we can use them to secure improvements.

The urban environment

If you face problems in moving around your local area arising from defects in the infrastructure, try to tackle them head on. Talk to your local councillor in the first instance. Focus on routes you would like to follow. Walk – or get a friend to walk – along them, identify any problems and consider what improvements you could seek. Here are a few of the ways in which you might be able to secure improvements.

Seating

Seats do more than anything else to help people with walking problems move around their town, city, suburb or village. But as more and more people have come to use cars, much public seating along roadsides and on street corners has fallen into disrepair and not been replaced. Bus stops rarely provide comfortable seats – often only narrow perches. New public seating tends to be concentrated in urban parks or places popular with tourists, such as seaside promenades and historic streets. Regular walking routes are often ignored. Yet 10 per cent of adults cannot walk a quarter of a mile (400 metres) without a rest, and 5 per cent cannot cover 55 yards (50 metres).[2] For the second group in particular, strategically sited seats are essential.

No law forces local councils to provide seating anywhere. However, the Department for Transport publishes guidance which you could deploy to try to persuade your council to install more seating. It recommends that, 'In commonly used pedestrian areas, transport interchanges and stations, seats should be provided at intervals of no more than 50 metres' (55 yards).[3] If you cannot get your council to match this standard, it may still respond to some degree. Even a single extra seat might prove a vital help.

Where seating is inadequate in shopping malls, or where what is provided is uncomfortable or lacks a back or armrests, it is the property company or the scheme manager to whom you should turn. (Armrests are an important means of helping people to get to their feet: *see page 19.*) Keep a watch on any new shopping developments proposed in your area: is adequate seating (among other facilities) guaranteed? It is often easiest to obtain new facilities at the planning stage, when developers have to offer the public something in return for the profits they hope to make.

Think of the future too. Many families erect a seat in a public place in memory of a loved one. If you would like that to happen, tell your family and suggest a place for it. Donated seats tend to be concentrated in particular places – parks, viewpoints and famous places, such as along Edinburgh's Princes Street. But seating might often be more appreciated along the streets in everyday use.

Dropped kerbs

People using electric scooters, wheelchairs or walking frames on wheels all depend on dropped kerbs, while those with a walking stick often choose to cross the road where the step down or up is shallowest. Lowered kerbs are also useful for blind and partially sighted people if accompanied by tactile paving, which lets them know they are close to the edge of a pavement and a place where crossing the road should be safer.

Securing a new dropped kerb can be straightforward. In the early 2000s, I used to take my mother for walks along the promenade at Ramsgate in a wheelchair, as she could no longer walk. But to get the wheelchair up onto the promenade, I was forced to push her far along the road until we reached one of the few dropped kerbs. I wrote to the highways department of the local council, explained our problem, and it agreed to put in dropped kerbs where I had requested them.

If it had refused, I could have challenged it under disability discrimination legislation, now incorporated in equality legislation. As we see in a moment *(pages 688–92),* the Equality Act of 2010 is an extremely useful law which can be used to challenge the provider of any service if somebody finds difficulty in using it because of a disability.

'Disability' in this context is defined very widely: as a substantial, adverse and long-term physical or mental impairment which affects a person's ability to carry out normal day-to-day activities, *as explained on page 688.* The impairment could be an arthritic knee or hip, continence problems, lung disease causing breathlessness on exertion, and many other such things. The legislation decrees that people and organisations providing services must make 'reasonable adjustments' to ensure that people with disabilities are not discriminated against. Helpfully, the 'reasonable adjustments' stricture applies to the highway authorities responsible for the maintenance of the vast majority of roads, public footpaths and bridleways.

Clearly, dropped kerbs are not going to be installed everywhere: which places might be deemed reasonable? The Department for Transport says that dropped kerbs or raised pavements *(see below)* should be provided, 'At all zebra and controlled crossings and at other places, side roads, access points to parking areas etc used by pedestrians.' It goes on to say they should be provided on longer side roads and residential roads at 100 metre (110 yard) intervals where possible.[4] Use this recommendation to urge your council to step up to the plate.

Raised pavements

Even better than a dropped kerb is a 'raised pavement' – in fact, a road built up to pavement level so a pedestrian goes straight across while road traffic goes up. Forcing vehicles to go over the rise slows them down, so making the road safer for pedestrians. Because of this, raised pavements are often installed as part of traffic management schemes. So, if your neighbourhood is plagued by rat-running, you might be able to link your demand for easier pedestrian mobility with those of other people, such as the parents of young children who are concerned about safety. Living Streets is a group which campaigns for more user-friendly streets and may be able to give you help.

Pavement surfaces

In England and Wales, local highway authorities have a legal duty to make sure that publicly-maintainable roads, footpaths and bridleways are looked after and safe to use.[5] So report any defects such as badly maintained pavements, uneven slabs and holes which pose trip hazards to your council and ask it to take action to mend or replace the broken or missing structures.

Do not forget alleys. These are also covered, so long as they are public rights of way. We are fortunate that far-sighted Victorian town planners provided this alternative transport network, but much of it is now woefully neglected and beset by potholes and weeds, not to mention litter and dog dirt. So you might need to remonstrate with your council not only about repairing surfaces but also dealing with littering or fouling.

Highways authorities must also ensure they do not discriminate against people with disabilities when providing services, such as rights of way. In addition, as public bodies, they are under a legal duty proactively to promote equality of opportunity between disabled people and others – the so-called 'public sector equality duty' *(explained on page 692)*. So if you face an additional problem arising from disability, such as difficulty in walking as a result of osteoarthritis or painful feet, refer to this duty too if your authority drags its heels.

Sometimes paths which are not rights of way but nonetheless used by the public have been covered in gravel – the most difficult material to cross with a wheeled aid, after sand. Paths around country mansions which are open to the public (usually on payment of a fee) often sport gravel paths. In cases of private routes such as these, the organisation to approach is the owner of the land. You could simply point out the difficulties that are encountered and ask them to replace the gravel with a hard surface. Tarmac is more expensive than gravel, but resin-bonded gravel, in which a small amount of gravel is compacted onto the surface, is much cheaper. Failing that, if the difficulties you face on account of a disability are significant, you could take the owner to task using the equality legislation *(as outlined on pages 688–92 below).*

Road crossings

Many journeys on foot require the crossing of busy roads. If older pedestrians are involved in accidents, they are far more likely to be injured or killed than younger people. Children accounted for one third of total pedestrian casualties on Britain's roads in 2008 but only 9 per cent of the pedestrians who were killed. In contrast, people over 70 were involved in 9 per cent of pedestrian casualties and 35 per cent of pedestrian fatalities.[6]

More than half of accidents involving pedestrians arise when the person is crossing the road. Speeding is often involved. Have a look at the places where you cross the road and think about your safety. If you have to cross a major road and the illuminated crossing does not give you sufficient time, write to your highway authority and ask it to increase the length of time allowed. Or you may need to ask for an entirely new crossing, or seek improvement to basic crossings which lack the full panoply of lights and a pedestrian crossing.

If you think speeding is a danger at a particular place, ask your local highway authority to introduce traffic-calming measures. Ring your council before writing to find out which is the most appropriate department to which to address your request – it may be a road safety section or an accidents investigation unit. (You do not have to have been involved in an accident to write to such a unit and they do not restrict their attentions to accidents involving serious injury.) Failing that, address your letter to a general official, such as the highway officer or the transport officer. If you feel you need to step up the pressure, copy the letter to your local councillor or MP. Joining forces with groups such as the parents of children who walk to school can increase pressure for change.

Lighting

Dark streets not only increase the risk of tripping but may prompt concern about street crime. Unfortunately, there are no statutory requirements on numbers of streetlights. However, contracts are regularly placed for the replacement of street lighting, so it is worth lobbying your local council. If it says there is no space on the pavement for lamp-posts, ask whether they could be affixed to buildings instead. Ask for white lighting, as yellow sodium lighting does not permit the perception of colour.[7] If you fear night-time muggers, ask for CCTV cameras. The Department for Transport's *Manual for Streets,* published in 2007, which aims to show how good design can make streets more people-friendly, gives an idea of what might prove possible.

Lavatories

Our Victorian forebears acknowledged the importance of public lavatories and laid on such facilities (along with drinking fountains) as a matter of civic pride. But huge numbers of those provided by local councils have been closed, largely to save money. The first ten years of the 21st century alone saw the closure of an estimated 40 per cent of public toilets in the UK, according to calculations by the British Toilet Association.[8]

This loss hits older people particularly hard. They often need to use the lavatory more frequently than younger people or to get there more quickly *(as explained on pages 20–1).*

The dearth of public lavatories can therefore cause considerable anxiety when we are getting on and severely restrict where and when we go out. Many people's route around town is dictated by the presence – or absence – of lavatories. Age UK have put it like this: 'Lack of public toilets is a significant contributory factor in the isolation of older people, and the situation will worsen as toilet provision continues to decline.'[9]

Garages, pubs and restaurants often insist that their facilities are for customers only. Failing to get to the lavatory in time is a nightmare scenario for many. How does it feel to have to venture into an unfamiliar restaurant or garage to ask to use the lavatory when you are desperate?

In this situation, a 'Can't Wait Card' can be invaluable. This is the same size as a bank card and states that the holder has a medical condition and needs to use a toilet quickly. You produce it in a shop, restaurant or other facility when you need to go and there is no public toilet to hand. Cards are available from the Bladder and Bowel Foundation, Multiple Sclerosis Society and the IBS Network (for people with irritable bowel syndrome). You may also be able to obtain a card from one of these organisations with a translation of the 'Can't Wait' message which can be used in various countries overseas, such as Denmark and Pakistan.

Better for everyone, however, are public lavatories available to everyone that are easy to use: well lit, with handrails, supports and contrasting colours for fittings. Yet where new public toilets have been provided in recent years, they are often only urinals to prevent men resorting to the street.

The types of lavatory a council could provide come in many different sizes, from the one-off facility to a block with an attendant. Some councils are exemplary. East Lothian council in Scotland considers public lavatories are a vital resource not only for local people but also for tourists and it has opened several new ones in recent years. The toilet block in the centre of Haddington, for example, was not only spotlessly clean but decorated with vases of flowers, replenished by an attendant when I visited in 2005.[10] Some councils in areas favoured by tourists, such as South Devon, provide more toilets open for longer than those in other areas. A relatively new endeavour, the community toilet scheme, involves councils entering into arrangements with private bodies such as pubs, restaurants and shops to make their toilets available to the public.[11] The City of London Corporation, for instance, has entered into agreements with many business to provide these facilities.

Toilets made available under the community toilets scheme as well as others available to the public at train stations, shopping centres, libraries and in facilities provided by councils are shown on the Great British Toilet Map. This is a useful facility that enables you to pinpoint the location of toilets through an interactive map. You type in a postcode and the five nearest toilets available to the public appear on your screen. You can scroll around on the map and other toilets hove into view. Coverage is not universal but where it exists (for instance, for central London and some of the London boroughs) the information is invaluable.

So what could you do to persuade your council to create more toilets, keep others open or arrange for businesses to allow the public to use their facilities? You could try to rope in your local councillor to help you lobby your council to provide more. You could approach your MP too. A parliamentary cross-party committee on public lavatories has been set up, so MPs should be aware that the severe lack of public lavatories is an issue which should be addressed. The British Toilet Association is the main campaigning group and can provide advice, although it does not have local branches.

If a toilet is provided but is of no use to you, perhaps because you have difficulty in bending and there are no handrails or support bars, you could challenge the service provider under the equality legislation to make reasonable adjustments so you can use it *(as described on pages 688–92 below)*. Handrails cost very little.

Model lavatories for disabled people are not confined to those provided by enlightened councils. Disabled facilities at stations along the Settle–Carlisle railway line, such as that at Settle, which is managed by Northern Rail, are roomy, spotlessly clean and offer rails on either side of the hand basin as well as by the toilet itself. No step obstructs entry. Use examples such as these to shame providers into action. You can obtain examples from the British Toilet Association's 'Loo of the Year' awards shortlist.

Information

If you visit a town with which you are unfamiliar, it is useful to know in advance about any obstacles – fixed features such as steep steps, or temporary obstacles such as street works or lifts that are out of action – which could make life difficult if you cannot walk or climb stairs easily. Try telephoning the town centre manager employed by the local council. Many town centres, including those in suburbs, employ such people. They patrol their areas frequently and are more likely than anybody else to know of any difficulties, permanent or temporary.

The last ten years have seen the writing of guides that provide information for people with mobility problems about access to shops, public facilities and tourist attractions that would have seemed unimaginable in the last century. These have often been devised by younger people struck down by illness or injury who are determined to be able to use as many facilities as before, despite their disability.

CASE STUDY

Craig Grimes is one of the pioneers. While studying in Wolverhampton in 1997, he had an accident that broke his spinal cord in four places and forced him to rely on a wheelchair. I met him in Barcelona in 2005 where he was then living, and photographing good and bad features from the disabled access point of view. He was drawing up a map of the city showing obstacles and provision, partly to lobby local government but also to show people with problems where they could go. This information was fed into AccessibleBarcelona, a website which explains how to see the attractions of the city if you are disabled, showing steep hills and cobbled streets but also accessible toilets and bars. When I met him, Grimes was also testing hotels in Barcelona, taking his wheelchair into each one to check manoeuvrability in the rooms and lifts and providing further data for AccessibleBarcelona. He was also extending his coverage to other European cities, as well as organising the provision of adventure tourism for disabled people.

Grimes later returned to Britain and worked as a consultant for Open Britain – a one-stop shop that provides information about the accessibility for disabled people of tourism destinations and places to stay in Britain, from caravan and camping sites with accessible toilets and shower rooms to city-centre hotels. Open Britain, which exists as a book and a website, also contains handy tips for disabled people about travelling by various forms of transport. Grimes is currently running Experience Community, which organises expeditions and residential holidays for wheelchair users and people with lower-limb difficulties in the countryside of northern England.

Other web-based facilities have been devised. Sage Traveling (also set up by a young man, John Sage, who suffered a spinal cord injury while skiing) offers information about the accessibility of tourist attractions, hotels, ferries and so on in Europe. For the UK and Ireland, Gregory Burke, a young wheelchair user, set up Disabled Go, which provides detailed accessibility information about cafés, restaurants, museums, parks, hotels, pubs and universities – whether there are ramps, a hearing loop, automatic doors, a wheelchair-accessible toilet, information in large print and also, importantly, whether staff have received disability awareness training. You type in your postcode and details of accessible facilities in the category you choose appear on your screen. Accessible Countryside for Everyone (ACE) provides information about walks, countryside and green spaces, camp sites and other holiday accommodation, taxis, pubs and restaurants in the UK which are accessible to people using wheelchairs and mobility scooters.

Local guides are also springing up. In 2013, Euan MacDonald, who uses a powered wheelchair, and his sister Kiki set up Euan's Guide – a website which publishes reviews of the accessibility for disabled people of hotels and other facilities in Edinburgh. Euan's Guide has since widened its coverage to include reviews sent in by users across the UK (though with a concentration in major cities), and some countries overseas.

Joint action

Action to make the urban environment easier to negotiate may sound like a lot of work. It need not be. A letter or a conversation with your local councillor to prompt a small reallocation of spending may be all that is necessary. Any journey is a sum of its parts and you may find yourself having to negotiate with a number of organisations to get improvements. But take heart: the necessary action need not involve massive public works. A repaired pavement, a resurfaced public footpath, seating at a suburban street corner, additional lighting in an alleyway, a CCTV camera, a community toilet scheme – these are all things for which local councils have budgets, even in cash-strapped times.

681

Coping with disability when trying to move around on foot can feel isolating. It is easy to imagine that nobody else has faced the same physical problems or the feeling of being excluded from the world inhabited by everybody else. In fact, a growing number of groups are seeking to tackle the difficulties for everybody.

Local access groups

Throughout Britain, concerned citizens have set up access groups which seek to improve the environment for people with disabilities. The Tunbridge Wells Access Group in Kent, for example, meets quarterly in the centre of town to discuss access problems encountered by people with physical disabilities or sensory impairment. It draws attention to difficulties and negotiates on anything from the shortage of taxis that can cater for disabled passengers *(see page 758)* to accessibility to public buildings. In 2015, Patricia Stone, a resident who needs to use a mobility scooter, presented a report with photographs by a friend on the obstacles she faces – poor surfaces, potholes and a lack of lowered kerbs. The access group presented the report to Kent County Council and has roped in its local MP to press for action.

In the far west of Wales, the Pembrokeshire Access Group campaigns for improvements to infrastructure to benefit disabled people, both residents and holidaymakers. It has successfully campaigned for the provision of special beach wheelchairs with large tyres that can cross sand to be available on Pembrokeshire's most popular beaches. It has drawn up its own map of dropped kerbs with tactile paving in towns throughout the county, which is invaluable both for people with vision and mobility disabilities. *(See also the slightly different countryside access forums discussed on page 687 below.)*

Older people's forums

Some of the older people's forums that have been springing up in recent years are keen to improve facilities for moving around outdoors *(see page 230)*. If one exists in your area, you could see whether it is interested; perhaps like-minded members would join you in taking action on this front? Older people's forums pride themselves on being both local and independent – their agendas are set locally by their own members and they act independently of other organisations.

The older people's forum of North Tyneside, covering Tynemouth, Shiremoor and Whitley Bay, for example, was regularly lobbying its local highways authority and other bodies when I talked to its vice-chair, Dr Joyce Lesson, in 2011. It was seeking everything from greater spending on the maintenance of pavements and the prevention of pavement parking to the placing of benches in public places suitable for older people and the introduction and enforcement of speed limits in residential and shopping areas. The Forum had been involved in the installation of new seating on the street and improved signage at a local hospital for people arriving by bus.[12]

Citizens Advice
Local Citizens Advice bureaux spend much time helping people deal with instances of alleged age and disability discrimination. If you go and talk to one of their advisors they will tell you what you could most usefully do to remedy the situation *(page 691)*. They are likely to be familiar with the providers of services and infrastructure in your locality and discrimination issues which have arisen in the past. Not only will they help you resolve your particular case, they may also refer your case to their own local research and campaigns team and so channel your concern into a concerted campaign to improve facilities.

Age-friendly cities
Age-friendly cities is a World Health Organisation initiative which seeks to make the physical, social and economic facilities of urban areas more accessible to older people and the whole environment thus more inclusive. Cities can apply to join its global network and twelve in the UK have successfully done so.[13] The WHO stipulates that age-friendly cities must assess the age-friendliness of their city in a number of areas including transport and outdoor spaces and buildings. So if you live in an age-friendly city, expect it to take a keen interest in any deficiencies you spot. In Newcastle and Belfast, for example, older people's forums have been involved in surveys of the accessibility of the city centre, streets and parks.

The rural environment
What do you do if you move to the countryside because rambling is your passion but later disability makes getting around difficult? Whereas a town may offer parks and promenades with seating, the countryside can seem much more forbidding for people with mobility issues. They are restricted in where they can set foot to public rights of way (roads, public footpaths, bridleways and byways) and open spaces where public access is either of right or tolerated by landowners. In many parts of the country this means the possibilities for access are limited, even for able-bodied people. They are more so if such public paths and accessible open areas as

exist are impassable because their physical state means they are unusable by people with walking difficulties.

Information

One way of finding where you are likely to encounter fewest problems is to consult guides that offer information on access for people with disabilities. For instance, the Sussex branch of The Ramblers has published an online guide to walks accessible to people with disabilities. Many national park authorities and some local authorities provide such information and offer special guided walks for people in wheelchairs or with vision impairment. The organisation DisabledGo provides information about facilities for disabled people at rural tourist attractions in its online guide. The National Trust publishes information about the suitability – or not – of its properties for people with mobility and other disabilities, as do some other landowners, from county wildlife trusts to the owners of stately homes.

Action

Councils and others such as the National Trust providing open-air recreation facilities such as country parks sometimes provide one wide, surfaced path suitable for wheelchairs but little by way of plentiful seating and obstruction-free paths suitable for the larger numbers of people with less serious, albeit real mobility problems. Use the equality legislation to lobby for better provision. But far more of the countryside could be opened up through improvements to the public paths network, which runs to 140,000 miles in England and Wales.

One of the biggest problems is the stiles that interrupt public footpaths, particularly if they are high and rickety. Where farmers have ceased to keep cattle or sheep, stiles are no longer necessary for land management. Legally, gates and stiles are the responsibility of the landowner. You could ask your highway authority to try to persuade landowners to remove or alter stiles and gates which present problems.

Lincolnshire is a county with many redundant stiles. The county council has been removing them, on behalf of landowners, on routes favoured by walkers at the rate of about 100 a year. In about a third of cases, the landowner has been happy to leave a gap where the stile once stood; in other cases, they have asked for a gate instead. Where the council can, it puts in a self-closing gate, since this is accessible to wheelchairs. Where it cannot persuade the landowner to accept a self-closing gate, it has installed kissing gates, which landowners often prefer, although they are impassable for a wheelchair, unless very wide.[14]

Many other councils have replaced stiles with gates or persuaded landowners to remove stiles altogether. Thus Buckinghamshire County Council has removed over 2,000 stiles since the millennium and in the Chiltern Hills 'Miles without Stiles' booklets showing public paths along which all stiles have been removed have been published. However, often councils do not list the locations where work has been done, so you may need to contact your local authority and ask for details.

What may matter more than the existence of stiles is the state of the path. If it is always muddy and slippery, or trenched by deep ruts, people who are unsteady on their feet, depend on a wheeled aid or cannot see well may have to turn back. However, highway authorities own the surface of public rights of way and are required by law to keep the surface in good repair. So, if you encounter a path whose surface prevents you from using it because you have a walking or vision disability, ask your highway authority to take action, perhaps by filling in deep ruts or resurfacing sections of the path. Refer both to its duty to keep the path surface in good repair and to its obligations under the disability discrimination legislation *discussed on pages 675 and 687–92.*

Several voluntary organisations might lend you support and expertise. The Ramblers has a wealth of experience of encouraging and if necessary forcing councils to comply with their statutory duties on rights of way in the countryside and it has local branches which do this on the ground. Disabled Ramblers and the Fieldfare Trust campaign for better provision for those with mobility problems and may be able to offer additional advice. Perhaps you could rope in your local access forum *(see page 687).*

Opening the countryside to people with walking difficulties may seem a tough task, but, as with the urban environment, take heart: as the case from Lincolnshire shows, some local councils have been taking action.

Furthermore, since the year 2000 highway authorities in England and Wales have been required by law to suggest improvements to public paths in 'rights of way improvement plans', which have to be reviewed every ten years. One of the key objectives of these plans is to facilitate access to rural paths for people with disabilities: each plan must contain an assessment of, 'The accessibility of local rights of way to blind or partially sighted persons and others with mobility problems'.[15] Typically, plans include policies, 'To reduce the number of unnecessary barriers to using public paths' and 'to develop a network of key routes in conjunction with disability groups'.

Core path networks are also being developed in Scotland, and throughout Britain local access forums are seeking to develop access opportunities on the ground. So, if you have difficulties or spot ways in which access could be improved, contact your local highway authority and/or your local access forum.

Mobility aids such as walking frames and wheelchairs (push or powered) are treated, like pushchairs, as 'natural accompaniments' for pedestrians using public footpaths in England and Wales. This means pedestrians enjoy a legal right to take them.

However, the situation on electric scooters is less clear and those who rely on them should keep in touch with organisations such as Disabled Ramblers so that they find out if and when this is tested in case law. If you are driving an electric scooter at no more than 4 miles per hour (6 kilometres an hour), which is normal walking speed, you will probably be fine. But if you exceed this speed, in other words you are driving a type 3 vehicle over the 4 mph maximum attained by type 2 vehicles *(see page 468),* your scooter will probably not be seen as a natural accompaniment and so taking it on a public footpath would be classed as trespass.

The right to roam

Since the turn of the century, local authorities and national park authorities have been establishing the right for people to move freely over whole stretches of land under 'right to roam' legislation. In England and Wales the new right applies only to about 10 per cent of the countryside – designated common land and open moor, mountain, down and heath, usually indicated on Ordnance Survey maps. A narrow belt of land around the coast of England is gradually being added.

Unlike public rights of way, where people are entitled only to move along the route, the right to roam legislation gives a legal right to move freely over all the land in question. As with public footpaths, you would be within your rights to take an aid to mobility with you, but if you wished to drive a powerful electric scooter over the land in question, including one of the all-terrain scooters known as trampers, you would be outside the rights conferred by the right to roam legislation.[16] However, the owner of the land, which might be a local council, has the option of lifting this restriction, so do check online, on the signboards posted up on site or by contacting the countryside section of your local council. *(See page 471 for a note about hiring trampers.)*

In Scotland the situation is different. There, the right of access is not restricted only to particular types of land: it runs everywhere (with exceptions such as people's gardens and fields of growing crops), so long as it is used responsibly. If you need a mobility aid to exercise your right of access, including a vehicle with a motor, you can take it, since the code that sets out people's rights under the access provisions says, 'Access rights extend to being on or crossing land in a motorised vehicle or vessel which has been constructed or adapted for use by a person with a disability and which is being used by that person.'[17]

Users of mobility vehicles in Scotland should be aware that horse-riders and cyclists have a right to use paths running through land covered by the right of access, so they should keep a look out for them. Local authorities employ access officers, who are responsible for ensuring that any conflicts between users are minimised, so it is worth contacting the access officer to find out whether a path you wish to take is often used by a riding school, for instance.

No legal right to roam has been introduced in Northern Ireland.

Countryside access forums

These rural-focussed forums have a wider remit than the access groups *described on page 682.* They seek to improve public access to the country-side for the purposes of open-air recreation and enjoyment, whether that be along rights of way, over access land open under the right of access or over land whose owners voluntarily offer access (or can be persuaded to do so). The forums also seek to improve access for people with disabilities, although that is not their main role.

Unlike the access groups set up by concerned people in various places, countryside access forums are statutory bodies which local authorities must establish in their areas. They advise on the ways in which public access to land for the purposes of open-air recreation and enjoyment could be improved, and such other matters as government may prescribe. Each forum usually includes a member with special interest in access to the countryside for people with disabilities. As the forums are set up by councils and contain councillors, they are well placed to secure improvements on the ground. So if you live in Devon, for instance, you could approach the Devon Countryside Access Forum for information and suggestions. Contact information for countryside access forums is available from the government agencies Natural England and Natural Resources Wales. Forums perform a similar role north of the border where they are coordinated by Scottish Natural Heritage.

How equality legislation can help

We noted above that help is at hand to enable people with physical and mental impairments to get around outdoors, both in town and country, in the form of laws which outlaw discrimination on grounds of disability. These laws can be useful not only when pressing a local council to make the sort of improvements to pavements and footpaths discussed above, but also in making buildings and services provided by a wide range of other organisations, both public and private, easier to use. Disability discrimination legislation is a real breakthrough. It seeks to ensure that nobody with a disability should be at a disadvantage when receiving a service from a very wide range of providers. Furthermore, organisations exist to help individuals to use the opportunities the laws have provided.

The legislation applies to virtually all types of people and organisations which provide a service to the public. The service could be provided by a corner shop, hairdresser, estate agent, off-licence, private landlord, football club, betting shop, stately home open to the public, taxi, church, library, education facility, leisure centre, railway station, railway train, coach or bus vehicle or station, for example.

It operates through the Equality Act 2010, which brings together anti-disability discrimination and also that in other fields. The Act makes it unlawful to discriminate against someone in England, Scotland or Wales because of their age, disability, race, religion or belief, sex, sexual orientation or state of marriage or civil partnership. *(I discuss making use of the prohibition against age discrimination in healthcare provision and employment rights on pages 297 and 881 respectively.)* It is the disability aspect of the law which is particularly useful in the context of wheeled transport and moving around on foot.

A widespread misconception is that the law affects only people with very significant disabilities, such as blind people and people in wheelchairs. In fact, it can and does strengthen the position of people with many levels and types of disability. 'Disability' is defined in a broad way in the Act – as a physical or mental impairment which has a substantial and long-term adverse effect on somebody's ability to carry out normal day-to-day activities.[18] 'Long-term' is defined as having existed for at least 12 months or being likely to last for at least 12 months or for the rest of the life of the person affected. The threshold for 'substantial' is 'more than minor or trivial'.[19]

The legislation can therefore apply to someone whose arthritic knee has a substantial and long-term effect on their ability to move around, someone with a hearing problem (whether or not they use a hearing aid), someone with heart disease who becomes breathless on exertion, someone with continence difficulties who needs easy access to a lavatory, someone who cannot handle objects easily because osteoarthritis has impaired their manual dexterity, and somebody with a mental condition such as a learning disability, autism or dementia which affects their normal day-to-day activities, to take a few examples.

The Act makes it unlawful for the providers of services to the public to discriminate against disabled people and requires them to make 'reasonable adjustments' so their services are accessible to them. What is considered reasonable? It is not the intention of the legislation to put small operators out of business by requiring substantial costly rebuilding – requiring every bed and breakfast establishment to install a lift, for instance. Fortunately, the Equality and Human Rights Commission (EHRC), the independent agency that helps enforce the law on discrimination, publishes plenty of guidance on what it expects.

The Equality and Human Rights Commission explains how it expects service providers to adapt their premises and/or their behaviour to comply with the legislation in free, detailed guides such as *What Equality Law Means for your Business*. For instance, it says it would not expect a small bookshop which employs only one member of staff to install ramps and lifts. But it would expect handrails by any front step, help from staff for people who cannot reach the higher shelves, and strong lighting to make use of the premises easier for visually impaired people. If the bookshop were larger and part of a national chain, much more would be expected, such as the installation of a level or ramped entrance, more improvements to lighting and signage, provision of low shelves or trained staff to help locate books out of reach.[20]

Much of the EHRC's guidance was originally issued by the Disability Rights Commission (DRC), which joined forces with anti-race and anti-gender-discrimination organisations in 2007 to form the Equality and Human Rights Commission. (The EHRC has offices in Manchester, London, Glasgow and Cardiff.) Useful booklets published by the DRC as well as material the EHRC itself has prepared are available on the EHRC's website. Readers in Northern Ireland, where similar legislation outlaws discrimination on grounds of disability, should contact the separate, similar Equality Commission for Northern Ireland.[21]

Discrimination involves more than failure to make the physical fabric of buildings accessible. Unlawful discrimination is also considered to take place in the following situations:

- if a service provider refuses or deliberately neglects to provide a service to a disabled person because of their disability
- if a service provider offers a service at a lower standard to a disabled person because of their disability, or offers a service on different terms to a disabled person because of their disability

Service providers must also make sure that none of the staff or organisations operating on their behalf discriminate. So contractors and subcontractors are also covered.

In the past, discrimination was common. If somebody could not manage the steps up onto a station platform to take a train or wave a relative goodbye, tough. In the mid-1990s, my mother and I were waiting at a bus stop in Gilbert White's village of Selborne in Hampshire for one of the infrequent services to Alton railway station five miles away, to take the return train home to London. We had borrowed a wheelchair so I could push my mother around the village, as her arthritis meant that she found walking more than a short distance painful. But when the bus drew up, the driver refused to let us on, saying he did not accept wheelchairs, so we were stranded.

The legislation enacted since that incident makes such disability discrimination unlawful, except on limited grounds. The main justification allowed is health and safety, so the bus driver would have been acting lawfully if my mother had insisted that he should lift her and/or her wheelchair on board and he feared this would damage his back. A service provider can also consider the health and safety of the disabled person. If, for instance, my mother had insisted on remaining in her wheelchair on the bus in a place the driver considered dangerous for her, he would have been entitled to refuse her access. But the EHRC advises that disabled people are entitled to make the same choices and take the same risks as other people, so if she had said she was willing to take the risk of not being able to vacate the bus swiftly in the event of an emergency, she should have been allowed on board.

The legislation offers enormous opportunities. If a retirement housing scheme or a care home lounge, a church or a meeting hall you use lacks a hearing loop system, you can ask the proprietor to put one in, referring if necessary to the legislation. If you cannot get up a step into a shop or move around within it as you have a mobility disability, you can complain. If you cannot use a lavatory because you have bending difficulties and it lacks the bars and supports you need, you can challenge the service provider. (However, bending difficulties would not enable you to challenge the provider if they had not provided any lavatories for anybody.)

The Act can do much to make leisure facilities more accessible too. The owners of garden centres, zoos, stately homes, football clubs, swimming pools and so on can all be called to account if necessary – and wealthy organisations like the National Trust are expected to do more by way of provision than a small café or field centre.

Controls over alterations to historic buildings should not let a service provider off the hook. If, say, a flight of stairs at the front of a stately home open to the public prevents disabled people entering it and a ramp or outside platform lift would be unsuitable as the building is listed, the EHRC would expect some other means for disabled people to get into the building, such as through an entrance on ground level at the back of the building used by staff or for deliveries.

Some categories of service provider have gone the extra mile and issued guidance on ways in which they themselves consider their facilities could be made more accessible. Thus the librarians' professional body, the Chartered Institute of Library and Information Professionals, has advised its members to make sure that library use for older people is facilitated through, among other things, shelving which is neither too high nor too low; the provision of gadgets such as magnifiers, enlarging photocopiers and hearing loops; good lighting; plenty of space between aisles; and the provision of large print and audio material in a suitable location.[22] So, if facilities such as these are not provided, ask for them.

A small number of categories of service provider are exempt from the disability legislation, notably airlines. However, as we shall see when we consider airlines *(pages 709–12)*, where exemptions exist under the Act, there is usually a code of practice with which service providers are expected to comply.

Resolving a grievance

If you face problems using, say, a hairdresser's or your local cricket club on account of disability and you are not sure what to do, go and talk to your local Citizens Advice *(see page 682)*. Their advisors' familiarity with the law, local circumstances and perhaps similar concerns to yours that have been raised by other people will enable them to give you a sense of whether what you have experienced could be classed as discrimination. They will advise you on your options and help you to take whatever course of action you choose. They might write a letter to support your grievance.

You could also have a word with the Equality Advisory Support Service (EASS) – a national helpline covering England, Wales and Scotland, which answers queries about equality and discrimination matters. Its advisor will go through with you the steps you could usefully take. These include first trying to sort out the matter amicably with the service provider. If you get nowhere and the EASS considers you have good reason to complain, it might write a letter to the person or organisation about whose actions or inactions you are concerned. For instance, if you take someone out in a wheelchair and need a kerb to be lowered at a particular point or a deeply-rutted public path to be smoothed over and your highway authority offers you no convincing reason for its failure to act, the EASS might write to the authority and remind them of the law and ask them to take action and to get in touch with you.

The EASS helpfully publishes a template letter on its website for individuals to use when their problem is not solved by persuasion and negotiation. You insert your individual story, explaining that you were treated less favourably, at a particular time and in a particular place, for a reason related to your disability, than the way in which somebody without that disability would have been treated. You might also explain any inconvenience, distress or discomfort you experienced as a result. The EASS suggests you remind the service provider of the legislation and ask why you were treated in that way and what steps the provider intends to take to deal with the situation and by what date. Request a written reply within a reasonable time, such as 14 days, pointing out that after this you reserve the right to take the matter to court under the equality legislation.

In that case, you could make a civil claim for disability discrimination in the county court in England or Wales or the sheriff court in Scotland. *For information about the procedure and the costs, see page 299.*

If you win your case, the court can issue an injunction to prevent future or continuing acts of discrimination. Or it can order the service provider to pay you compensation for any actual financial loss you have suffered or injury to your feelings.

The EHRC takes up some cases it considers have significant implications for other disabled people. If you think yours has wider importance, alert the EHRC, perhaps through the EASS.

For concerns such as the failure of a highway authority to provide ramps in its buildings or make a public footpath available for disabled people, there is an additional weapon a complainant could deploy. The 'public sector equality duty' in the Equality Act 2010 means that any public body or a private body acting on behalf of a public body must actively take steps to promote equality of opportunity between people who might be discriminated against, whether on grounds of disability, age, sex, race, religion and so on *(see page 296)*. They must have due regard to the need to eliminate discrimination and to advance equality of opportunity.[23] This duty could also be used against a public body which failed to provide information in say, Braille or Polish.

On foot

* Difficulty in walking and climbing stairs is the most common disability in people over 65.

* Seating is important because many people need a rest when walking more than a quarter of a mile.

* Online guides provide information about the accessibility of buildings for people with disabilities.

* Point to the equality legislation to get toilets provided, kerbs dropped and gravel replaced with a hard surface.

* Older pedestrians involved in road accidents are more likely to be killed or injured.

* Rope in the parents of young children and groups such as Living Streets to push for traffic-calming.

* There is a legal right to use walking frames and wheelchairs (even if powered) on public footpaths and bridleways.

* Highway authorities are legally required to take into account the needs of the less able-bodied.

* If public path surfaces are rutted or otherwise impaired, tell your highway authority to make them useable by all.

* Landowners can sometimes be persuaded to replace stiles and gates which pose problems for some people.

Chapter 30

On wheels and water

When we reach 17, our first instinct may be to get a driving licence. When we are 70, we may be beginning to wonder how we would cope if we could no longer drive, especially if we have not set foot on a bus or train for 40 years. Need driving be more difficult when we are getting on? How do we tackle public transport after a lifetime behind the wheel? How can we handle any disabilities when we are using any type of wheeled transport?

In this chapter I take the main forms of wheeled transport in turn – car, train, underground, tram, plane, ferry, coach, bus and taxi – and look at how to find out what services are available and how any difficulties in using them can be overcome. For instance, on driving I look at ways in which older people can make driving easier (such as car-sharing and avoiding night-time driving), as well as the help available for drivers and passengers with disabilities (from Blue Badges to personal parking bays). I also explore ways of going on holiday in Britain for non-drivers.

(Specially designed mobility vehicles such as wheelchairs, electric scooters and trampers are examined in Chapter 21: Equipment.)

Motoring

When we are getting on, it can seem that only personal, private, motorised transport will preserve our independence. What are the factors we need to take into consideration?

Behaviour

Sometimes older people find that driving makes them more tired than when they were young. Also, as roads get more crowded, driving becomes increasingly stressful. A survey of 1,500 drivers by the Civil Service Motoring Association in 2008 found the stress of modern driving to be 'worryingly high'. And while most drivers questioned estimated that they had been the victim of road rage between two to five times, the figure for most of those over 55 was an astonishing 50 times.[1]

But this figure is perhaps not surprising in view of the impatience generated by what is seen as the slowness of elderly motorists. They can find themselves tailgated and then overtaken by a swearing and gesticulating driver.

Older drivers are not more dangerous than their younger counterparts, whatever the latter may think. Exuberance and aggression cause more trouble than frailty. 'Drivers over the age of 70 are significantly safer than drivers under 30 and are at no greater risk to other road users than middle-aged drivers', according to the Institute of Advanced Motorists, which has analysed government statistics on accidents. However, when older drivers are involved in road accidents, they are more likely than younger people to suffer fatal injuries.[2]

The fatigue older people often feel at the wheel can be compounded by afflictions of the body, even apparently insignificant ones. Our reaction times increase as we grow older *(as noted on page 25);* also the amount of light we need to see well increases *(as explained on page 13),* which is why night driving can be particularly challenging. Joint and muscle stiffness can also affect ease of driving.

We can help ourselves. If we find driving more taxing, we can try to avoid it at times and in places which make particular demands on us. So we may cut down on driving at night, for long distances, or on unfamiliar roads. The Automobile Association (AA) publishes tips on its website of ways of making driving easier in later life.

If driving continues to prove burdensome yet you still need motor transport, you could investigate car sharing. Or perhaps a relative could drive you sometimes. In one case of which I heard, an older couple were regularly driven by their children in their own car from their home in Birmingham to their holiday destination in North Wales. At the end of the holiday, the children returned to drive them back home. Their parents had the use of their car while on holiday but without the stress of a long drive there and back. Perhaps you could advertise for someone to drive you?

Sometimes women in long-term relationships do less and less driving, but it is important that they retain their skills. Not only does this mean that the burden of driving can be shared: it also ensures that a woman can continue using a car should her partner die or become unable to drive.

Or could you use public transport instead? Today we live in a world in which media messages bombard us relentlessly with the notion that car travel is the norm and that public transport is in a dreadful state and to be avoided at all costs. Yet when car drivers unfamiliar with buses and trains do take to them, they are often very pleasantly surprised and wonder why they never let the bus or the train take the strain many years before.

Controls

Contrary to popular belief, there is no bar on driving after any particular age, but there are age-related requirements. These are designed to prevent drivers taking to the road who have developed a condition which could make them unsafe to themselves and other road users, such as severe vision impairment, giddiness, a tendency to lose consciousness momentarily or dementia. At any age you have a legal duty to disclose any new disabilities, such as worsening eyesight, which could affect your driving ability. Since many medical conditions which can affect the ability to drive safely develop in later life, 56 days before your 70th birthday the Driving and Vehicle Licensing Agency (DVLA) sends you a form on which you have to declare that you are still sufficiently mentally and physically alert to carry on driving.

If a medical problem develops which affects or could affect your ability to drive, the DVLA may decide that you can nonetheless keep your licence but tell you to contact it again to report any change in your condition after a specified period. On the other hand, it might revoke your licence immediately. However, that does not mean that you can never get it back: somebody in their nineties who develops a cataract, for example, may have their licence returned after an operation to remove it. Nor does a particular diagnosis necessarily mean an automatic ban on driving, so somebody newly diagnosed with dementia may be told that they must apply for the renewal of their licence every year, and may indeed get it renewed for several consecutive years, so long as they can still drive safely.

Drivers also have a legal duty to inform their motor insurance provider if they develop a medical condition which affects or could affect their ability to drive.

GPs or consultants who consider that a medical condition is making a patient's driving hazardous have a duty to raise the matter with them. If a GP fails to persuade a patient to stop driving, or discovers that a patient is continuing to drive contrary to advice, they must disclose the relevant medical information immediately to the medical advisor at the DVLA. Before doing so, however, they should inform the patient. Things are then up to the DVLA.

Users of electric scooters are not required to hold a driving licence. However, several nasty accidents take place each year involving these vehicles, so do seek medical advice immediately if you develop a medical condition which might affect your ability to drive one safely. Some people obtain a scooter when they lose their driving licence, but scooters can kill both the driver and other people. *(I discuss the safe use of mobility scooters on page 470.)*

Disability

Many people do not suffer from a condition which could make them a hazard on the road but do have a disability which makes handling a car difficult. If you are in this situation, find out about the myriad ways in which cars can be adapted for disabled people. The possibilities are enormous: adaptations range from altering hinges so a door opens wider to positioning the seat back further, altering seat height, installing a swivel seat (which makes getting into and out of the car easier) and changing the controls.

A charity called Rica *(see page 487)* provides a wealth of pointers in this area. It also publishes valuable guidance on the various types of adaptation which can be made to a car to cope with disability (including to the controls); choosing a wheelchair-accessible car; and driving with various medical conditions, such as with arthritis or after a stroke. Rica's information is available by post as well as online. You could also obtain literature from Motability *(see below),* even if you are not eligible for the scheme it operates.

Parking

The internet has brought help to motorists trying to find somewhere to park, particularly in an unfamiliar location, with Sat Nav and Parkopedia. You type your postcode into Parkopedia and receive information about the location and price of parking spaces nearby. Click on a particular car park and you will be told about the hours of opening, maximum length of stay, whether there are any charges, disabled parking spaces, CCTV and any restrictions, such as for customers only.

For some people, the problem lies not in physical difficulties while driving or finding a parking spot but in walking from their vehicle to their front door, perhaps because of chronic lung or heart disease or an amputation. If you find yourself in this situation and have no form of off-street parking, you may be able to get a parking bay installed outside your house or flat to minimise the distance between your front door and your car or any vehicle which drops you off. Councils often do not publicise the fact that they will install personalised parking bays for disabled people if asked to do so, so if you have serious mobility problems, apply to the council for one. An occupational therapist will normally assess you and, if approval is given, drop kerbs will be put in and any street furniture which is in the way will be moved. Once the bay is installed, however, anyone who is disabled and has a Blue Badge *(see below)* can park in it, so you may find your 'spot' occupied by somebody else.

The Blue Badge scheme

The Blue Badge scheme involves giving a badge to people with severe mobility problems. It enables its holder to park not only in any disabled parking bay but also on single and double yellow lines, except where other restrictions operate (for instance, in cycle and bus lanes and in places where loading is not permitted). The purpose is to allow disabled people to park close to shops and other facilities. The Badge is given to the person, not the vehicle, so a badge-holder can use it whether they are travelling in their own vehicle or that of somebody else.

The Blue Badge map is an online facility provided by the government which provides information on the location of Blue Badge parking bays across the UK, as well as Shopmobility centres *(see page 473),* taxi ranks and accessible public lavatories.

Although the Badge does not apply in off-street car parks, some of these may provide spaces for people with disabilities, for whom charges may be waived. It does not apply on private roads or in certain locations, such as central London. (Blue Badge-holders are, however, exempt from the London congestion charge and special places for them to park have been allocated.) The scheme operates in most European countries, under partnership arrangements.

To qualify for a Blue Badge, one of the following conditions must apply. These are that the applicant must:

- have a permanent and substantial disability which means they are unable to walk or have very considerable difficulty in walking
- be registered blind
- have a severe disability in both arms which prevents their turning a steering wheel by hand
- receive the higher rate of the mobility component of Disability Living Allowance
- of the possible criteria for the mobility component of the Personal Independence Payment, meet the one that says the person

cannot stand, or can stand but is unable to walk more than 165 feet (50 metres) *(see page 841)*

- as above, but meet the PIP criterion that indicates someone cannot follow the route of a familiar journey without another person, an assistance dog or an orientation aid

- receive a War Pensioners' Mobility Supplement or

- have received a lump sum benefit within tariffs 1 to 8 of the Armed Forces and Reserve Forces (Compensation) Scheme and have been certified as having a permanent and substantial difficulty that causes them to be unable to walk or to have very considerable difficulty in walking

It is illegal for non-disabled drivers to park in disabled bays unless a passenger in the car has disabilities and a Blue Badge. If drivers do so, they can be fined as well as incurring an additional penalty for the original parking offence. If the enforcement officer decides that the vehicle is parked in such a manner that is potentially dangerous and/or an obstruction to other road users, it can be towed away. Nonetheless, many able-bodied people abuse the system by parking in disabled parking spaces. Traffic wardens, police officers and local authority parking attendants all have the right to inspect Blue Badges, so if you suspect misuse, try to alert one of these officials.

Make sure you do not lose your Blue Badge or leave it at home while you are motoring around. This is because if you fail to show it to an enforcement officer if and when required, you will be found to be in breach of the law and could be hit with a penalty of up to £1,000. Also, if you allow your Badge to be misused, it can be withdrawn.

To apply for a Badge, contact your local authority if you live in England, Wales or Scotland. If you live in Northern Ireland, contact the Roads Service of the Department for Regional Development.

As noted above, the situation in off-street car parks, for example those belonging to supermarkets and airports, is different. There, operators make their own decisions on charging for parking and themselves enforce the exclusion of motorists from parking bays they have set aside for disabled people. So if you observe an able-bodied motorist parking in a disabled space in a supermarket car park, you should contact the manager of the store or car park, who may ask the motorist to move from the reserved space but will not necessarily insist that they do so.

In Scotland, the Disabled Persons' Parking Places (Scotland) Act 2009 lays a duty on local authorities to use their existing powers to promote parking specifically for disabled people. It also requires them to negotiate arrangements with the owners of private car parks, including supermarkets, in order to enforce disabled persons' parking places in them.

Motability

More than 400,000 people in the UK are registered users of a valuable yet little-known scheme called Motability, which enables severely disabled people to obtain a car, adapted if necessary to take account of their disability, with ongoing support. Unfortunately, the qualifying conditions rule out many older people, but some do qualify. If you are severely disabled and have not yet reached 65, or you are severely disabled as a result of service in the armed forces (and are of any age), this scheme could be a godsend.

If you enter the scheme, you hand over your weekly disability state benefit to the charity Motability and in return it provides you with a car (or, if you prefer, an electric scooter or a powered wheelchair) and covers its on-road costs, apart from petrol. Every three years, you receive a new vehicle.

More than 300 types of car are available in this way. But if you prefer a more expensive brand, you can do so by topping up with an advance payment.

Motability also advises on a large range of alterations which can adapt a car to the disability of the driver. If minor adjustments are needed, for instance push-and-pull hand controls or left-hand acceleration for somebody who cannot use their right foot, Motability covers the cost. If expensive adaptations are required, such as a swivel seat or a boot large enough to store a wheelchair, the user must pay. However, Motability administers means-tested grants to cover such additional costs.

Up to two people can be named on the disabled person's lease of the vehicle as nominated drivers; these could of course include the disabled person themselves. A third driver can be added for an additional cost.

The qualifying state benefits are the higher rate of Disability Living Allowance, the enhanced rate of the mobility component of the Personal Independence Payment and the War Pensioners' Mobility Supplement. The qualifying conditions for each of these are quite restrictive and to receive one of them you are likely to have to find walking very difficult.[3] If you might qualify under DLA or PIP, you must apply before you turn 65. This is because DLA and PIP are not open to new entrants after that age (Attendance Allowance comes into play thereafter). However, if you obtain the DLA higher mobility supplement or the enhanced rate of the mobility component of the Personal Independence Payment before you are 65, you can keep it and thus your Motability vehicle.

Public transport

Car ownership drops dramatically among older people. While some carry on driving until they drop, others have to give up because they develop a medical condition which makes driving unsafe. A third group surrender their licence voluntarily because they are finding driving too difficult or stressful, for one reason or another.

Many of these people will have doggedly carried on driving for as long as possible. Yet those who give up driving after decades at the wheel, perhaps not having used buses and trains for years, may well find public transport less troublesome than they expected.

In many ways, the experience of using public transport has improved hugely in recent decades. Digital displays show when buses will arrive at many main bus stops in urban areas. Apps and mobile phone texts can tell you which bus to catch and how long before it arrives at a particular stop, whether you are waiting there or in your living-room. Modern bus stations too are often very different from those of the past, with large, covered shelters, shops, toilets and refreshments, lifts and ramps.

We can thank the equality laws, in particular the disability discrimination elements discussed in the previous chapter, for many of these improvements. At the same time, the rail pass for older (and for disabled) people and free off-peak bus travel for seniors throughout the UK have slashed the costs of public transport for older and for disabled people.

However, some problems remain. In some areas bus services are very poor in the evenings and on Sundays. Many people, after years behind the wheel, find public transport puzzling. So, where can you find information to help you plan a journey? And where can you obtain advice on using buses, trains, planes, taxis and ships if you have a disability?

Information

Public transport timetables are available from several sources. If you have access to the internet, you could simply type a request into a search engine (such as 'buses St Ives to Zennor'), and up-to-date service details should appear at the click of your mouse. Transport Direct is an online journey planner which provides information on door-to-door travel for both public transport and car journeys throughout Britain. In Northern Ireland, Translink, the province's integrated bus and rail transport company, provides a journey planner on its website.

A useful source of help for planning a journey by public transport any-where in Great Britain, and provided over the phone as well as online, is Traveline. Calls are answered by a person, not a recorded voice. Different types of public transport are covered, as are matters relating to disability, such as whether low-floor buses run on particular routes. *(Other sources of timetable information, such as National Rail Enquiries, where the information provided is confined to one transport mode, are considered below.)*

If you are planning a holiday or considering moving to a different part of the country, you may wish to browse through timetables of local services rather than simply ask for details of specified services as you do when you use Transport Direct, Translink or Traveline. Local tourist information offices are a good source of timetables, as are public libraries and the websites of the relevant local authorities.

Trains

Obviously public transport (apart from dial-a-ride and similar bus services which collect people from their own doorstep) cannot offer the flexibility and door-to-door advantages of personal motorised transport. However, public transport does have many pluses. Here are some of the advantages of train over car travel:

- routes away from roads, so the journey is more relaxing
- no need for any member of the party to drive, so offering the opportunity for all to read, chat, play games, interact with grandchildren and so on
- easy evening travel, without the additional stress that can arise from driving at night
- the ability to get up and move around at any time, helping blood circulation and preventing knees from becoming stiff
- warm, well-lit compartments and the possibility of a table for books and refreshments
- opportunities for chatting with fellow passengers
- the ability to take pets free of charge (except in very few circumstances), and space on the floor for the pet to relax
- the possibility of using the lavatory at any time; many trains have support bars in toilets
- the possibility of travelling in a wheelchair, with staff helping you on and off with ramps; on many trains there are special seats for people in wheelchairs with additional space and tables

at a comfortable height (though they may have to telephone ahead to book these on long-distance services)

- in many but not all trains, the freedom to buy refreshments on the journey

CASE STUDY

On August bank holiday 2015, I met a friend at St Pancras station for a trip we had planned to Margate. Carolyn had arrived by taxi from Euston, as she could not walk far. I asked an official on the concourse if he could make her journey easier by wheeling her to the train we were to catch. Within minutes, he returned with one of the wheelchairs provided on demand at the station for this purpose. When we arrived at the platform, the official unfolded one of the ramps kept on each platform and wheeled her on board.

This official asked where we were going and whether we would like someone with a wheelchair to meet us at Margate and wheel Carolyn to the taxi-rank there. Without any further prompting on our part, a Margate station official with one of that station's chairs appeared outside our carriage on arrival. When she left us, she told me to ask for help when we returned to Margate station later. This I duly did and Carolyn was wheeled by another cheerful, helpful official along platforms, up and down lifts and finally up a ramp he unfolded between the platform and our London-bound train.

That official phoned St Pancras, so when we drew up on the platform there at 8 pm, another official with a wheelchair was waiting for us outside our carriage. He wheeled Carolyn to the taxi rank. She was delighted and also surprised with the help she had received during the day. She had been under the impression that help such as this was rarely provided and, if it was, four days notice was necessary and some kind of documentary proof of disability would have to be shown. Not so.

Some people are under the misapprehension that train travel from the north to the south of Britain is difficult for people with bulky luggage or mobility problems as it always involves breaking the journey to cross London. This is no longer true. St Pancras railway station offers a very easy means of travelling north–south without the hassle of crossing London by taxi or tube, and it is furnished with plenty of lifts, lavatories, shops, seats and cafés. For instance, you can travel direct from Brighton (which itself connects with many lines along the South Coast) to St Pancras, go to another platform and travel on to Leicester. Or you could cross the road to neighbouring King's Cross station and catch a train to York, Newcastle-upon-Tyne, Edinburgh, Cambridge, Lincoln or stations in north London and Hertfordshire.

Many key towns outside London also now perform an important role as junctions which avoid the need to cross London at all. Reading, for instance, enjoys direct services to London; Bristol and Bath; South Wales; the West Country; Bournemouth and the New Forest; Oxford, Coventry and Birmingham; Guildford and Gatwick Airport; East Croydon and Brighton; Worcester, Ledbury and Hereford; Sheffield, York, Durham, Newcastle-on-Tyne, Edinburgh and Glasgow; while an airport bus connects Reading station with Heathrow airport. The station is easy to use, with plenty of seating, lifts, waiting rooms, refreshment rooms and station attendants.

Preston also serves as an extremely useful rail transport hub. Just over two hours from Euston, it offers direct rail links to the Lake District, Blackpool, Lancaster, Carlisle, Glasgow, Bolton, Blackburn (and thence to stations in the Ribble Valley), Leeds, Bradford, Manchester and the delightful little country stations of Arnside and Silverdale, just south of the Lake District. Preston is a delight to use, with its brightly painted canopies, plentiful seating, ramps and lifts.

There are also plenty of long-distance routes you could take which involve no change or a straightforward one at an uncomplicated station, such as the route from Aberdeen and Dundee to Plymouth and Penzance.

Information about fares and timetables throughout the UK is available from National Rail Enquiries, through its phone line and website.

Cutting the cost

Train travel is often assumed to be expensive. It can be – if you turn up on the day of travel with no concessionary cards and hope to travel on the next long-distance train. But you can cut costs.

There are several ways of doing so. One is to travel off-peak. Another is to buy your ticket ahead. An advanced ticket will cost you far less than any other – but you have to travel on the particular service specified. More information is set out in a helpful leaflet available at stations called *National Rail Guide to Buying Tickets.*

The other means of cutting the cost of rail travel is by buying a concessionary railcard. The Senior Railcard is available for people aged 60 and over. It costs £30 and entitles the holder to a reduction of up to one third on all journeys anywhere in Britain for 12 months. The exception is during the morning peak period, Monday to Friday, on journeys made wholly within the London and South East area. There is a substantial saving if you buy your Senior Railcard online for a three-year period.

A Disabled Person's Railcard might suit you better if you have a disability. It also costs a small amount to buy, but entitles not only the holder of the card but also a companion to travel at up to a one-third reduction. To purchase it, you have to provide proof of your disability, for instance a copy of the letter awarding you a disability benefit *(see pages 835–41)*.

Residents of Northern Ireland enjoy free rail (and bus) travel in the province from the age of 60 and throughout Ireland from the age of 65.

Disabled access

If you have a disability all railway staff should be prepared to give you any help you need. Railway stations come within the full scope of the equality legislation, so services provided must be accessible to people with disabilities. This means that somebody with vision, hearing, mobility or dexterity problems, for instance, should be given all necessary help both when purchasing tickets and locating their train. *(See pages 688–91.)*

The companies that run train services should also be prepared to provide help during journeys and in boarding and alighting, lest travellers with a disability are discriminated against. If you wish to take a wheelchair or large mobility aid on board, you ought to be able to get help through the provision of a ramp when you turn up, but you may wish to contact the station or the train operating company beforehand to tell them that you will need assistance. You may also wish to check that your vehicle could be transferred onto the train and fit inside it, as some large scooters are too heavy for ramps and some older trains cannot carry wide vehicles.

Requirements for the provision of help to use trains (and also coaches, buses, taxis and trams) are set out in a document entitled *Provision and Use of Transport Vehicles: Statutory Code of Practice,* available from the Equality and Human Rights Commission.

Supposing you draw into a station and unexpectedly find that you cannot alight because of the presence a large gap between train and platform. In that case, ask somebody to help you: either station or train staff ought to provide you with an arm to lean on or get out one of the portable ramps that are folded up on platforms. If, however, when you set off on your journey you know that you are going to alight at a station where there is a gap, ask the station or train staff to phone ahead to the station to tell them that you will need help. They should pass on details not only of the particular train on which you are travelling, but also the number of the coach in which you are sitting.

Large stations often have vehicles in which disabled people and their luggage can be transported from one platform to another, or to the taxis or a bus stop. Again, you can ask for this when you arrive at a station and help ought to be given. But as any station is only likely to have one such vehicle, you will have to wait if it is already in use or has been booked ahead of time. So give the train company notice, ideally 24 hours if you can, via its assisted travel helpline.

To help pre-empt potential problems, if your disability is not obvious you could travel armed with some proof of it, such as a letter from your GP or, say, a Blue Badge parking permit. What you do not need for this purpose is a Disabled Persons Railcard – although of course if you have bought one to take advantage of the fare reduction it offers, it may be worth producing it.

How do you find out whether a station which you have never used has lifts between platforms and space at the entrance for a car to pick you up? The National Rail Enquiry Service provides information on the accessibility of stations through its phone line and website. On the website, you type in the name of the station in which you are interested and receive details on many matters, including staffing levels, the presence or absence of lifts to platforms, the number of disabled parking places, whether the booking office has a hearing loop, whether the station is furnished with waiting rooms, refreshments and lavatories (and whether these are disabled-friendly), and whether the platforms are edged with tactile surfaces.

You can also obtain a useful free booklet called *Rail Travel Made Easy* as well as a *Map for People with Reduced Mobility* at main stations. The booklet lists the phone numbers of all the railway companies. These can provide further information, and you should contact them if you wish to ask for assistance in advance. Information attached to the Disabled Persons Railcard also contains contact details for the railway companies.

A word of warning: it can be much more difficult for people with disabilities to travel if train services are disrupted and they are told to use a replacement bus or coach. This may well involve waiting at a stop outside the station (with or without seating) and then clambering up steep steps into the vehicle. The replacement of scheduled train services with buses happens most often on Sundays and public holidays, to allow repair work to be carried out, and it is usually advertised well in advance. If you are planning to travel on a Sunday or public holiday, check at stations. The train times provided online by National Rail Enquiries are adjusted continuously to take account of changes arising from planned engineering work and also last-minute delays.

(For information about taking a mobility scooter on a train, see page 469.)

Underground and tram systems

Subway and tram systems introduced since the 1980s, such as the Tyne and Wear Metro, the Docklands Light Railway and trams in Sheffield, Croydon and Manchester, tend to be relatively accessible for disabled people. However, older underground systems, like those in Glasgow and London, present difficulties. The main problem is the dearth of lifts (except on very deep lines and in new or refurbished stations), and some people feel unsteady on escalators.

In London, one way round this is to travel on trains running at ground level, which usually have lifts where necessary. The London Overground, which traverses the capital from Richmond in the west to Stratford in the east, is extensive. Look at a map of the Overground and you will see you could travel from Acton, Harringay or Highbury and Islington to Hampstead Heath, for example, using stations that are all step-free. Another ordinary train line which crosses London and has many stations along the route runs from Bedford to Brighton; stops include Farringdon, St Pancras International and City Thameslink (near St Paul's Cathedral).

Transport for London gives out information about all forms of transport in the capital (although it does not have a phone facility for help in planning journeys). To work out how to get from A to B, go to the journey planner on its website. If you have a disability or difficulty, take the advanced option. This will show you the easiest route if, for instance, you cannot manage stairs or, alternatively, you prefer not to use escalators and need a stairs-only route.

London Underground Customer Services (LUCS) publishes a useful guide *Getting Round London – Your Guide to Access*. This describes the access situation for people with disabilities at all tube stations. Although the Underground can look forbidding and impersonal, station staff are usually happy to help unless they are very busy. If you are nervous about travelling, phone the LUCS (with lines open from 8am until 8pm), and ask it to notify the station supervisor beforehand that you would like help. You could also phone before you leave to check that you will not encounter unexpected problems, such as a lift out of operation on the day; LUCS is notified of any such difficulties.

The Strathclyde Partnership for Transport provides information on using the Glasgow Metro.

Flying

Large airports are among the easiest places in which to move around if you have difficulty in walking or climbing stairs. They have plenty of seats, lifts, lavatories and level surfaces. They have to comply with the equality legislation and so must make reasonable adjustments to ensure their facilities are accessible to people with disabilities; shops at the airport are of course also covered by the law. But although airports must comply with the Equality Act, airlines have been granted exemption. This means that they differ in the amount of adjustment they make and the help they provide.

Airports

In addition to the rights provided to disabled people by the equality legislation described in the previous chapter, the position of disabled passengers at airports in the European Union has been clarified and strengthened by the introduction of a number of important requirements on airlines covering disabled people and 'persons with reduced mobility', laid down in an EU regulation. Key points of this regulation include:

- airports must provide help to disabled passengers and those with reduced mobility from the point of arrival at the airport to their seats on the aircraft or, if they are returning, from their aircraft seats to their point of departure from the airport

- airports must designate points of arrival and departure at the airport, both inside and outside terminal buildings, at which disabled and reduced mobility passengers can announce their arrival at the airport and ask for help. They should not be charged for this help.

- 'All essential information provided to air passengers should be provided in alternative formats accessible to disabled persons and persons with reduced mobility, and should be in at least the same languages as the information made available to other passengers.'[4] So expect information to be fully accessible, including in Braille or large print form or in your own language.

Airlines

As noted earlier, however, airlines vary in the amount of help they are prepared to offer. While some have been helpful, others have refused seats on their planes to disabled people or have charged them for the provision of help when embarking or alighting.

The EU legislation referred to above says that airlines and tour operators may not refuse to accept a reservation from a passenger or refuse them permission to board an aircraft on the grounds of disability or reduced mobility. They can refuse a reservation only if the size of the aircraft doors makes it impossible to take the passenger on board, or on grounds of safety. However, an airline cannot simply invent safety requirements: they must be requirements established by international, EU or national law. Furthermore, airlines must make these safety rules available to the public, as well as any restrictions on the carriage of disabled people or on that of mobility equipment due to the size of the aircraft. (In order to meet safety requirements, airlines or tour operators may insist that passengers be accompanied by somebody who can provide the assistance they need.)

If mobility or other problems connected with a disability mean you need help to take a flight, give at least 48 hours notice of your requirements to the airline, its agent or the tour operator. If no notification has been given, the regulation says that all reasonable efforts to provide the help should be made as follows:

- if an airline refuses to permit a passenger to board on the grounds of disability or reduced mobility, the passenger should be offered reimbursement of their fare or conveyance on another service

- if a wheelchair or another kind of walking aid is lost or damaged during handling at the airport or during transport on board the aircraft, the owner should be compensated

- the staff of airlines and airport managing bodies must receive training on disability awareness, and those who provide help to disabled people must have knowledge of how to meet the needs of people of various disabilities and levels of mobility impairment

In the context of this EU regulation, 'disabled' includes people with impaired sight or hearing and those with impaired intellectual abilities (which would include people with learning disabilities and people with dementia). Those with reduced mobility include 'people who would not normally be classed as disabled, such as older people or those with a temporary mobility problem'.

Airports and airlines must comply with the requirements set out above. The Civil Aviation Authority has the power to enforce them, so if you have any difficulty on the ground you could say that you will take the matter up with the CAA. The CAA's Consumer Protection Group has published a useful summary of the law.[5] The Equality Advisory Support Service *(page 691)* and the Consumer Council for Northern Ireland can advise if you wish to lodge a complaint.

In the air

Although airlines are exempt from the equality legislation, the Department for Transport has published a useful code of practice on how people with disability should be helped when travelling by air.[6] Compliance with this code is not a legal requirement, as with the EU regulation. However, travel agents, tour operators, airlines (scheduled, 'no frills' and charter), UK airports, ground handling companies and retailers are all expected to comply with it. In addition, it can be useful because it refers to many situations not covered by the regulation.

When you are booking your airline tickets, according to this code, the person booking them should ask whether you or anybody in your party requires help at the airport or during the flight. If you book on-line, make sure that you explain any difficulties at least 48 hours before the flight. You do not have to be seriously disabled to expect help. The Code suggests the question, 'Would any member of your party have difficulty walking 500 metres?', explaining that this is intended to address any problems for people with walking difficulties proceeding between the check-in and the gate, but 'would also capture those people who do not consider themselves disabled but who would have difficulty in the airport environment'.[7]

The code says that airlines should provide help with activities, including those listed below, 'upon request' – in other words, you may need to ask for it. The activities are:

- proceeding to the gate
- boarding and disembarking
- stowing and retrieving baggage
- providing an on-board wheelchair
- moving to and from the aircraft lavatory
- transferring someone between a mobility aid and the passenger seat
- providing limited assistance with any meals and enquiring periodically during a flight about a passenger's needs
- individually briefing disabled passengers and their escorts or companions on emergency procedures and the layout of the cabin
- proceeding to the general public areas or, in some cases, to a representative of another operator
- giving help to passengers in transit[8]

If an airline drags its feet, it is worth pointing out that you are aware of the Code and are prepared to pen a letter of complaint to the chief executive of the airline concerned, perhaps with copies to the chief executive of the airport, the Department for Transport, your MP and the local press.

However much support you get from the airport, airline company or any other organisation involved in a flight, some difficulties will be unavoidable. It is often a long way from the departure lounge to the gates. You may have to go upstairs to get on board. Economy class is usually cramped and uncomfortable, and it costs a great deal to upgrade. If you want to move around as easily as possible, ask for an aisle seat, but this will mean you will be required to get up whenever your neighbour wants to do likewise. Extra leg-room may be available, but will probably be expensive. Lavatories at airports are often excellent, but those on board will be cramped.

Flying can be dangerous if you have a medical condition, so check with your doctor before you book. There are many restrictions on what you can carry on board, so check before trying to take large amounts of liquid medicine or medical equipment, including portable oxygen.

Ferries and cruises

Ports, in common with railway stations and airports, are covered by the equality legislation, so they should be disabled-friendly. However, it is well worth phoning to check beforehand about any facilities which would matter to you.

However, ships are not covered by the Equality Act 2010. Fortunately, the European Union has set out rules with which ferries and cruise liners which use ports in the UK or any other EU Member State and travel by sea or inland waterway must comply. They must:

- carry any disabled person who wishes to travel on them, so long as this is safe and the design of the vessel or terminal makes it possible for the passenger to board and disembark

- provide assistance to disabled passengers or those with reduced mobility. The passenger should notify the ferry or cruise operator at least 48 hours before they need help, but if they give less than 48 hours notice, the operator must still make all reasonable effort to help them

- allow any assistance dog to accompany the passenger on board

- refrain from charging for taking onto the vessel any mobility or medical equipment that is reasonably necessary for the passenger's needs during the voyage.[9]

In addition, ferry (but not cruise operators) have to allow free passage for anyone whom a disabled person needs to help them with personal care such as feeding, taking medication or using the toilet.

Cruise operators cannot allow mobility scooters and wheelchairs to be left in corridors as this would be unsafe, impeding the evacuation of all passengers in an emergency. There will be a limited number of cabins large enough to store mobility equipment, so book early.

The EU disability regulations do not apply to vessels certified to carry fewer than twelve passengers, those not propelled by mechanical forces, ferry journeys of less than 500 metres (0.3 miles) one way, and pleasure excursions not involving at least two nights' accommodation.

Whatever the vessel, contact the operator in advance about how any disability could be addressed. For instance, perhaps you could board the ship in your wheelchair via the car deck and a lift, if ramps are too steep. Give advance notice of any help you will need. Ask the port and/or the ship operator about:

✓ the availability of lifts and ramps in the terminal building(s) and on board

✓ the availability and location of wheelchair-accessible toilets in the terminal(s) and on board

✓ the availability of wheelchairs to help you move between the terminal and the ship

✓ accessibility at ports outside the EU

✓ arrangements for travelling overnight

✓ any relevant conditions of carriage

Coaches

The main advantage of coach travel is that fares are relatively low. What is more, people over 60 can buy a Senior Coachcard that enables them to travel at peak and off-peak times throughout the UK at two-thirds of the usual price.

Coaches are far more comfortable than they were a generation ago. Many have a lavatory on board; there may be refreshments for sale. Some are double-decker. In London, most coach services converge at Victoria Coach Station, so travellers do not have to transfer between separate terminals.

Most coaches do, however, have several steep steps up to the door. By 2020 they must be low-floor in order to comply with the requirements of the Equality Act 2010. Many coaches have already been made wheelchair accessible – the driver unfolds a ramp which extends over the steps to the pavement, so that someone in a wheelchair can ascend and place themselves at the front of the passenger area, from which two seats have previously been moved aside. Telephone the passenger assistance helpline of the bus company at least 36 hours before you travel to be sure of receiving this help.

If you have a choice between train and coach, however, train will still probably be preferable. Many coaches will have a ramp for getting on board, but once you are inside, moving around will be harder. The central gangway will probably be too narrow for a mobility aid such as a walker. Any toilet will probably be more cramped. You are unlikely to have refreshments delivered to your seat, as often on a train. You may find yourself thrown around more violently than would be likely on a train.

You should be able to take a lightweight mobility scooter on board a coach, so long as it can be dismantled for storage in the boot. But as the coach driver has the last word on whether mobility vehicles will be permitted, it is worth checking beforehand if you propose to take any mobility vehicle including a wheelchair. If you plan to sit in your chair during the journey, make sure it would fit in the space provided. If your vehicle is to be stored in the boot, check how it will be protected there. If you have any concerns about damage, you may decide that you would rather not take any risks and hire or borrow a chair or scooter at your destination instead. So inquire about these things when you book your ticket.

Rica *(see page 487)* publishes a free guide for older and disabled people on public transport. This sets out information about using coaches belonging to the main coach companies and includes phone numbers for inquiries.[10]

Two other differences between coaches and trains: whereas you can take a pet dog free of charge on the majority of train services, on coaches you can take only an assistance dog, and while a train station may have a fleet of taxis outside or a local taxi office next door, coach stations or coach stops often lack taxi ranks. Holiday coach organisers, on the other hand, often provide unrivalled local pick-up facilities. You may find that a coach tour to the Baltic has a pick-up point just down your road, or even that the organisers lay on taxis to and from a town-centre rendezvous.

Buses

Free bus travel is one of the universal state benefits for older people which would have seemed unimaginable to our grandparents. It must have enhanced the lives of countless people since it was introduced in England in 2008 (two years earlier in Scotland).

In 2017 it seemed doubtful that the bus pass would remain a completely universal benefit indefinitely, with one of the most likely changes being some restriction so that wealthier people would be ineligible. Whatever happens to the pass in future, however, it will probably remain available to older people of modest means, if not everybody. And it has already changed behaviour, with many older car-owners using buses now, although they may not have done so for years. *(For more on the arrangements for free bus travel see the next section.)*

Along with free bus travel there has been a general improvement in the experience of bus travel. One area of progress has been in the provision of information about the location of buses along their routes. A growing number of operators are providing real-time information about buses which take into account delays and cancellations. Information is provided as a digital display at bus stops and interchanges in many of our larger towns and cities. Apps are also available that enable you to locate the nearest bus stops in any area, the bus services that stop at them and how soon any bus will arrive at that stop. Some local authorities or transport providers provide a facility for texting the time of arrival to a mobile phone, so you can leave the house when you know the bus is on its way.

Another area of improvement has been in ease of use for people with walking aids, including wheelchairs and mobility scooters. All buses (single- and double-decker) had to be low-floor by 2017. Low-floor buses are much easier to board: the height of the floor of the old standard bus is 12–15 inches (300–400 mm) off the ground, but that of a low-floor bus is 7 inches (200 mm), and the driver can drop it to less than 4 inches (100 mm).

Further improvements made to many vehicles include priority seats for older and disabled people at the front and handrails in and outside the bus that are non-slip and tactile, a ramp that can be extended, and dedicated space inside the bus for somebody to travel in a wheelchair. The button you push to signal that you wish to alight at the next stop if you are in a wheelchair is low down and emits a distinctive sound, so the driver knows when someone using a chair is planning to get off. He or she can then lower the floor so it is flush with the pavement or extend a ramp at the second door to bridge the gap between bus and pavement. To help partially sighted people, the destination and numbers are picked out in yellow and black. On any kind of bus, low-floor or traditional, it is important to tell the driver when you get on if you have mobility or balance difficulties, so that they can give you time to sit down before moving off.

Unfortunately, the bus is not an option for many. Perhaps they live in a village without a regular bus service. Or the bus stop is too far to walk to and to carry shopping from. In this situation, a 'demand-responsive service', running as and when there is a demand and collecting customers from their front gate, can be invaluable - especially when it provides a regular meeting for people living in isolated properties in a rural area for a trip to town. (Don't expect the journey to be short though, as it will take a circuitous route to its destination or destinations!) Some demand-responsive services, often called dial-a-ride, have special provision for passengers with mobility problems, perhaps accommodating several wheelchairs in which passengers can remain during the journey, if they wish. Fares on these buses are often quite high; the free bus travel facility does not normally apply. Traveline Scotland sets out a list of demand-responsive services with phone numbers for inquiries on its website and you can phone it for information.

Free bus travel
The arrangements for free bus travel vary slightly country by country.

England
In England, everybody above a certain age *(explained below)* is entitled to free off-peak travel on all local buses anywhere in England. 'Off-peak' means all day at weekends and on bank holidays, and during the week between 9.30am and 11pm. To benefit, you must obtain a concessionary travel pass from your local authority, or passenger transport executive if you live in a metropolitan area apart from London (where borough councils are responsible). As elsewhere in the UK, free travel using the pass is confined to the particular country of the UK in which you obtained it, so if you travel from England into Wales on a pass obtained in England, you will have to pay a fare at the border to continue your journey. Travel on dial-a-ride buses and other community transport schemes not running to set timetables tends not to be included in the bus pass scheme.

Local authorities have the discretion to extend the facility, for instance by providing extra cash to enable older citizens to travel free before 9.30am. In many metropolitan areas there is provision for free travel on modes of transport other than buses, so holders of the bus pass in Greater Manchester, for instance, can also travel free on trams and trains within that metropolitan area. The Freedom Pass in London entitles older Londoners to travel free not only on off-peak buses but also on off-peak underground and national rail services within Greater London. However, older people living outside London benefit only from free off-peak travel on buses within the capital, just as eligibility for free local tram and train travel within Greater Manchester is limited to older people residing within that area.

If you have to travel before 9.30am on a service which is free only after that time, buy a ticket to the place the bus should reach then. At that stop, go back to the driver and check in through your bus pass. Some drivers helpfully call out at 9.30, 'Anyone using a pass?'.

In England, but not elsewhere in the UK, the age at which somebody becomes eligible for their bus pass was changed in 2012. No longer 60, it is linked to the pensionable age of women, which is rising so that it will be the same as that for men (65) in 2018 (*as explained on page 824*). Men do not have to wait until they are 65 to receive their bus pass – a man becomes entitled to his bus pass when he reaches the age at which a woman born on the same day becomes eligible for her state pension.

If you would be entitled to a bus pass but cannot use buses you could apply instead for a travel token, sometimes called a taxi token. These are issued by some local authorities to people who have a permanent disability such as blindness or serious walking difficulty that prevents them from using buses; your GP would probably need to verify your claim. Tokens are given to a driver in lieu of the fare: you need to check beforehand that the taxi or dial-a-ride service you propose to use will accept tokens.

If age rules you out of a free bus pass in England, perhaps you are eligible for one on grounds of disability? To qualify, one of the following conditions must apply: you must have a disability or have suffered an injury which has a substantial and long-term effect on your ability to walk; be blind or partially sighted; be profoundly or severely deaf; have a learning disability; be unable to speak; or have long-term loss of the use of both arms.

Wales, Scotland and Northern Ireland

In Wales, Scotland and Northern Ireland, the rules on the provision of the older person's bus pass are more generous than in England. Everybody aged 60 and over is eligible. There is no peak-hour restriction, so people aged 60 and over living in Wales, for instance, travel free on local buses at any time. In Scotland, long-distance bus and scheduled coach services are also covered. Some local councils fund concessions on ferry and train travel.

Northern Ireland was the first part of the UK to introduce free bus travel for older people. All residents over the age of 60 are entitled to a SmartPass, which gives them free travel at any time on any scheduled bus or rail service within Northern Ireland. Residents aged 65 and over can obtain a Senior SmartPass, which also entitles them to free travel bus and rail services within the Republic of Ireland. Both passes are issued by the public transport operator Translink.

Cutbacks in government spending could see a reduction in these concessionary fares. This would be a shame, as older people would benefit from their extension rather than their reduction. Thus Age UK Scotland has been campaigning to extend the bus-pass scheme to include all community transport services for older and disabled people. Another extension that could be advocated is to make the system UK-wide, so that people could use their bus pass in any country of the UK, thus enabling a resident of Orkney to enjoy free bus travel in London and vice versa.

Taxis and minicabs

Taxis and minicabs can come to take on huge importance if you find you can no longer drive or use public transport. You enter a new world in which your life is circumscribed or enhanced by the attitudes of taxi and minicab drivers and the business that employ them and also by the availability of vehicles adapted for conveying people with disabilities.

Taxis – quaintly called hackney carriages – are public hire vehicles which can ply for trade by driving around until flagged down by a member of the public or which wait for business in taxi ranks. Private hire vehicles or minicabs cannot find trade in those ways – they must only pick up passengers who have pre-booked their journey via a licensed operator.

The Equality Act 2010 applies to taxis and minicabs just like other services, but has only done so since 2016. This means you may have to exert extra pressure on drivers and businesses to comply with the law, as they may be unfamiliar with it.

Drivers and the firms that employ them are now forbidden from:

- discriminating against anyone because of their disability
- offering a lower standard of service to someone because of their disability
- offering a service to someone on different terms because of their disability

As a result, a taxi or minicab firm is behaving unlawfully if it refuses to accept a booking by a disabled person who says they will be accompanied by their assistance dog. Any taxi or minicab driver who refuses to take an assistance dog with a passenger or who charges extra for conveying the dog is breaking the law; they can be taken to the county court in England and Wales or the sheriff court in Scotland for flouting the equality legislation, *as described on pages 691–2*. (Drivers are permitted to apply for exemption that allows them to refuse to convey an assistance dog for medical reasons, such as asthma. Any driver who holds an exemption certificate must display it in their vehicle.)[11]

The equality legislation also means that all drivers of taxis and minicabs must make reasonable adjustments to ensure that the overall service they provide is accessible to disabled people. You should therefore expect the driver to give you any assistance you need to guide you to the vehicle and to get in and out of it.

All taxis and minicabs have to obtain a licence before they can lawfully operate and this provides an important safeguard should a driver behave badly and/or discriminate against you, perhaps on grounds of disability. Licensing is the responsibility of local authorities on the British mainland; in London is it the Public Carriage Office, which is part of Transport for London. This means that if a passenger has a complaint they can contact the licensing authority. So if, for instance, a driver refused to take you and you suspected it was because of your disability, you could take him or her to the county or sheriff court *(see page 692)*, but you could also (and perhaps more easily) tell the licensing authority, which might impose a penalty or even withdraw the driver's licence. If you think you might make a complaint, note down the driver's name and number and the time and date of the incident.

Some licensing authorities impose more particular requirements than others, and some firms make more provision for people with disabilities than others. For instance, some taxi and minicab firms train their drivers in disability awareness; some require drivers to undertake a test of spoken English. Some firms ensure that some of their vehicles have a passenger swivel seat, which can swivel round when the passenger has lowered themselves onto it, thus making entry and exit much easier.

Licensing authorities do not expect every taxi and minicab to be able to take a wheelchair with a passenger sitting in it during the journey. Instead, they licence a certain number of designated wheelchair-accessible taxis. Minicabs are usually family saloon cars and cannot accommodate someone sitting in a wheelchair during the journey – passengers need to be able to get out of their chair and sit in the cab while their wheelchair is stowed in the boot. Some minicabs do have special vehicles which can accommodate a passenger sitting in a wheelchair, but they tend to be uncommon. Black taxis are the most numerous hire vehicles which can accommodate a passenger sitting in their chair, through the use of a ramp which the driver unfolds. All taxis in London and many other cities have been licensed to take people in wheelchairs. Make sure you apply the brake inside and sit facing or looking away from the direction of travel – not sideways.

A consequence of being on the list of wheelchair-accessible taxis and minicabs is that the driver is obliged by law to undertake the following duties:

- to carry the passenger while in the wheelchair
- not to make any additional charge for doing so
- to carry the chair if the passenger chooses to sit in a passenger seat
- to take such steps as are necessary to ensure that the passenger is carried in safety and reasonable comfort; and
- to provide reasonable assistance to enable the passenger to use the taxi[12]

If you need a wheelchair-accessible taxi, contact your licensing authority to find which ones operate in your area or ask individual firms whether they are licensed to do this. These taxis tend to be most numerous in large towns and cities – Edinburgh had 1,300 in 2012 and Aberdeen nearly 500, for example. But less densely-populated areas had some – South Lanarkshire, for instance, had more than 30, in addition to more than 50 wheelchair-accessible minicabs.

All this means that if you are considering moving (including into a care home) and you rely on vehicles which can take you sitting in your wheelchair, check beforehand that firms exist which offer this service in that area. You may find that a dial-a-ride service would take you out in the day, but that you would find great difficulty in going where you wish in the evenings and weekends without black taxis or private hire vehicles adapted to take seated wheelchair passengers.

The laws governing taxis and minicabs in Northern Ireland are broadly similar to those on the British mainland.[13] The Driver and Vehicle Agency of the Northern Ireland government is responsible for issuing licences.

As noted in the previous section, some local authorities provide taxi or travel tokens which can be used to help pay taxi fares to people entitled to a bus pass but whose disability means they cannot use an ordinary bus.

The RNIB issues TAXI signs to help blind and partially-sighted people to hail a taxi. As noted above, a taxi must take you and must take your dog, unless there are proven medical reasons why the driver cannot. Some taxis have a hearing loop, but by no means all.

Holidays using trains and buses

The range of holiday possibilities for wealthy able-bodied people is of course enormous. Many older people, whether fit or with some disability, opt for an organised holiday; if you do that, check beforehand that you will not face unexpected problems, such as flights of steps without lifts. Other older people would relish the freedom to plan their own excursions and holidays but believe that without a car the possibilities would be extremely limited. Perhaps they imagine that public transport services in rural Britain barely exist. This is wrong. There are of course places where services are thin on the ground, but there are also countless areas where excellent networks of public transport services still exist, offering a wide range of holiday opportunities.

If you have had to give up driving, the days of stopping off at farmhouse B&Bs in the heart of the countryside are probably going to be over, unless you can afford taxis. But farmhouse B&Bs have their disadvantages, principally their isolation. Instead, you could base yourself in one of the many attractive market towns which continue to act like the hub of a transport wheel, with regular bus services plying along the spokes and a railway station providing an easy means of reaching the settlement from further afield. These bus services are largely designed for country dwellers to get into town, but you could use them in the opposite direction, to get into the heart of the countryside. Here are a few examples; some of these places offer the delights of the seaside too: Berwick-upon-Tweed, St Ives, Barnstaple, Exeter, Penzance, Wareham, Dorchester, Chichester, Eastbourne, Lewes, Arundel, Whitstable, Broadstairs, Sandwich, Canterbury, Dover, Norwich, Aylsham, Sheringham, Cromer, Lowestoft, Great Yarmouth, Lincoln, Derby, York, Harrogate, Beverley, Shrewsbury, Hereford, Leominster, Ledbury, Great Malvern, Ambleside, Keswick, Windermere, Settle, Kirkby Stephen, Barnard Castle, Durham, Ballymena, Derry, Inverness, Dumfries, Blair Atholl, Nairn, Elgin, Fort William, Perth, Swansea, Carmarthen, Cardigan, Aberystwyth, Bangor (both in North Wales and County Down).

Another area with plenty of attractions easily accessible by public transport is the Isle of Wight. Fast trains link the island with London, Reading and many other places and the main bus station stands next to the ferry terminus at Ryde. There are frequent bus services providing access all over the island, with B&Bs and hotels in glorious settings along the bus route.

Some local authorities publish booklets designed to help people on holiday or taking day trips by public transport – such as Norfolk County Council's *Days out in Norfolk by bus and train*. The website countrygoer.

co.uk focuses on the national parks of Great Britain, including Snowdonia, the North York Moors and Dartmoor. For these and a few other locations, it includes timetable information and suggests towns suitable for people holidaying without a car.

On wheels and water

* Keep up your driving skills – you would need them if your partner could no longer drive.

* Cars can be adapted for a disabled driver or passenger in many ways.

* A personalised parking bay and a Blue Badge can be a godsend.

* Even if you drive, get used to using public transport.

* Phone apps and text messages can tell you when a bus will come.

* Airports are covered by disability discrimination laws but airlines are not.

* Airlines should nonetheless provide assistance if asked.

* Taxis and minicabs must not charge you more because you are disabled.

* Many long-distance coaches can take people in wheelchairs.

* Train travel has many advantages for people with mobility problems.

REPRESENTATIVES AND ADVISORS

> **"** *More than half of us believe mistakenly that we have the automatic right to make end-of-life treatment decisions for our next-of-kin.* **"**

REPRESENTATIVES AND ADVISORS

When we are getting on we rely on two main types of representative. Those we appoint as executors to carry out the wishes set down in our wills have the responsibility of ensuring that the people and organisations we have singled out as beneficiaries really do receive the cash and goods we had in mind. Clearly, selecting executors you can trust is very important and much guidance on how to make a will and choose executors already exists.

During life, however, another type of representative has much more power to influence how we live – those who act as our proxy should we be unable to take decisions for ourselves. Whatever your age and state of health, it is well worth setting in place arrangements to ensure that a proxy or proxies can act for you if you lose the mental capacity to make decisions for yourself. You could step in front of a bus or suffer a major stroke at any time and at best be temporarily unable to handle your affairs, at worst permanently brain-damaged. You might develop a long-term, progressive brain impairment, such as dementia. You could simply be too ill for a temporary period to make decisions. Much rarer is the situation in which you are able to think clearly and make decisions but are completely unable to convey them, not only verbally (perhaps because your muscles have been paralysed after a stroke) but even through blinking. About two million people in Britain are thought to lack 'mental capacity', or the ability to make a particular decision at a particular time or to convey a decision, for one or more of these reasons.

To safeguard your position against such eventualities, you should appoint one or more proxy decision-makers who could step in on your behalf should the need ever arise. The power may never be used, because you may retain the ability to decide and to communicate until your death. But you and your family will enjoy the security of knowing the power is there should it be needed.

The 21st century has seen the enactment of significant legislation on mental capacity which strengthens the safeguards for people who are represented in this way. In England and Wales, the Mental Capacity Act of 2005 introduced the concept of the 'lasting power of attorney'. This comes into two forms.

The first is the power to appoint one or more 'property and affairs attorneys' to take decisions in the finance and property realms; they may be authorised to take decisions for the person who granted them their power – the donor – over a narrow or wide range of financial and property matters.

This proxy power in the field of finance and property has replaced the old power to grant 'enduring power of attorney'. But the new Act has also introduced an entirely new type of attorneyship – the 'personal welfare attorney', who can act in the fields of health and welfare. Personal welfare attorneys can be important not just in determining whether you would want to be kept alive artificially if you were terminally ill and in distress, but also in a host of medical, nursing and care decisions. For example, should you find yourself living in a care home but with limited mental powers, your attorney would have considerable status to influence a multitude of decisions taken by the professionals looking after you.

This framework of two types of attorney – one for finance and property and the other for health and welfare (with the possibility of granting both types in one document) – also obtains in **Scotland.** So do the other elements of the basic structure of representation, although, as we shall see, there are differences, mainly in nomenclature and in the public bodies that are responsible for overseeing the system. The description that follows refers to the situation in England and Wales; I highlight the most significant differences north of the border in separate sections.

A new law on mental capacity in **Northern Ireland,** including provision for lasting power of attorney, was passed in 2016. However, at the time of writing, no date had been set on which this law would come into effect and it may not do so for several years. In the meantime, the main power of representation in Northern Ireland remains as it used to be in England and Wales – the enduring power of attorney.

In the past, many people in England and Wales granted an enduring power of attorney. These earlier powers can still be used. However, any enduring power of attorney made after 1st October 2007 (when the Mental Capacity Act 2005 came into effect) is not valid. Since that date, only a lasting power of attorney can be made.

If someone has failed to nominate an attorney or attorneys (of whatever type), representation of their views and interests will nonetheless be needed if they lose the mental ability to make decisions themselves (or lose their ability to convey their decisions to other people). In this situation, a judge acting within the Court of Protection of England and Wales can appoint one or more people to represent the person involved, as their 'deputy'. Similarly, in Scotland, a sheriff in a local court can appoint a 'guardian'.

Do not be put off granting power of attorney because you fear high legal costs. Fees (relatively low) have to be paid to the national organisations that administer the system, but you do not need a lawyer to grant attorney or to use the system as a whole: the forms have been devised so that they can be readily used without the involvement of a solicitor. The exception is **Scotland,** where a solicitor (or a doctor) has to be involved in certifying that the person granting attorney has the mental capacity to do so, although they do not have to have drawn up the document or have been involved in any other way. However, you may decide it is worth seeking legal advice on your particular situation.

Attorneys, deputies and guardians often have enormous power over the lives of those they represent and many decisions to take. In what circumstances should they step in and take decisions on behalf of the person they are representing? And how should people (such as doctors, social workers, the managers of care homes and care assistants) working for remuneration for people whose mental capacity is impaired behave?

The legislation lays down basic principles which these representatives and others working for pay or in a professional capacity have a legal duty to observe. These include that all decisions taken on behalf of somebody whose mental capacity is limited must be in that person's best interests and must involve the least possible curbs on their freedoms.

A major feature of the new legislation is to recognise that mental capacity is not a black-and-white, all-or-nothing attribute. There is a very wide spectrum of mental capacity, which will depend to some extent on the degree of brain impairment. So somebody may be mentally capable of making simple decisions which have few ramifications, such as whether they choose to take part in a sing-song, but not more complicated ones, such as whether they should have an operation. Or their ability to make any decision may fluctuate according to their medical condition and any medication they are taking. In other words, the absence of mental capacity is not classed as a general symptom to which a condition like, say, dementia or a learning disability gives rise. Rather, it is defined (mainly) as the ability to take a particular decision at the time it needs to be taken.

The new legislation also recognises the reality that the world of proxy decision-making opens up much scope for fraud and the manipulation of vulnerable people. This part also therefore explains how the procedures seek to minimise the risk of the abuse of power by representatives, how disputes are addressed and what anybody who is concerned that they or somebody else may be exploited or misused by the system can do. Again, you do not have to use a solicitor to use these safeguards, but, if you do, legal aid may be available.

If somebody does not have the capacity to take decisions about their care, social care officials may do so on their behalf if there is nobody suitable and available to do so for them. For instance, perhaps somebody is coming out of hospital and it is unclear whether they should return home or move to a care home. If it is established that they do not have the mental capacity to take such a decision and there is nobody suitable such as an attorney to take it for them, officials from social services, or in Scotland social work, will step in and act for them. Those powers too offer much scope for abuse, and the checks on the powers of social care authorities to protect the human rights of the person involved are set out *in Chapter 33.*

The powers granted to individual attorneys, deputies and, in Scotland, guardians are usually wide-ranging and ongoing. But sometimes, representation of someone's views and interests will be needed for a one-off decision, or a range of decisions with a narrow focus.

A relative or a public official might wish to apply for authorisation to take money out of someone's estate to make specified purchases. Or somebody might wish to authorise somebody else to take decisions over their financial affairs for a limited period. Or somebody who fears they might be kept alive against their wishes, perhaps after a major stroke, might wish to instruct that medical treatment offered to keep them alive be withheld in certain circumstances if they lack the ability to communicate their views at the time.

A range of legal powers are provided for these and other eventualities. Chapter 34: Limited authorisation, advisors and advocates examines many of these. It goes on to consider sources of advice, the use of solicitors and also of a new type of representative in the world of health and social care called an 'advocate'.

In Part Nine, I therefore examine the following matters:

▶ lasting power of attorney in the field of finance and property
▶ the equivalent power in Scotland
▶ enduring power of attorney

- the situation in Northern Ireland
- lasting power of attorney in the field of health and welfare
- the equivalent power in Scotland
- the system of deputies and, in Scotland, guardians
- how people with proxy powers should behave
- the powers of public authorities to act on behalf of people with limited mental capacity
- the concept of mental capacity and how it is determined
- safeguards to prevent abuse of this system
- limited representation, advice, advocacy and the use of a solicitor

This may all seem quite complicated. However, people in England and Wales can skip sections which mention Scotland or Northern Ireland (often indicated by a sub-heading), if they wish; those interested in granting power of attorney will not need to read the chapter on deputies and guardians; while not all the types of limited authorisation discussed in Chapter 34 will be relevant to your situation.

Chapter 31

Powers of attorney

Y ou can give other people proxy power to make decisions on your behalf through granting power of attorney over your financial and property affairs or your health and welfare or both. In this chapter I discuss:

▶ the legal powers involved in the creation of a 'property and affairs lasting power of attorney' (PALPA) and the factors to bear in mind when selecting attorneys and considering what powers to give them

▶ the role of the Court of Protection

▶ the equivalent 'continuing power of attorney' in Scotland

▶ enduring power of attorney

▶ the situation in Northern Ireland

▶ the legal powers involved in the creation of a 'personal welfare lasting power of attorney' (PWLPA) and the factors to bear in mind when selecting attorneys and considering what powers to give them

▶ the equivalent power of welfare attorney in Scotland

Property and Affairs Lasting Power of Attorney (PALPA)

To create a lasting power of attorney that relates to property and finance you must first secure the agreement of one or more people whom you wish to become your attorney(s). Then you should obtain the necessary form (free from the Office of the Public Guardian). You need to line up somebody prepared to certify that you know what you are doing and that you are not being subjected to inappropriate pressure to grant power of attorney by your prospective attorneys. Then you fill in the form and ensure that you, your attorney(s) and your 'certificate provider' sign it.

The powers granted by a donor (known as a 'grantor' in Scotland) through a property and affairs lasting power of attorney range over many different types of activity. They can include:

- dealing with bank and building society accounts
- collecting money to which the donor is entitled, such as pensions and rent
- making purchases, such as clothes and holidays
- paying care bills
- buying and selling property
- managing investments
- sanctioning the expenses of the attorney(s)

Attorneys can also make gifts of the kind the donor would have made, for instance at birthdays, as long as the terms of the attorneyship do not prevent this.

Since, if unlimited, the power gives the attorney(s) pretty well unrestricted access to the donor's assets, those proposing to grant a property and affairs lasting power of attorney should think carefully about whom they ask to represent them in this way. As theirs could be an onerous responsibility, prospective attorneys should also consider carefully whether they are prepared to take on the role and *some of the considerations they should bear in mind are outlined on page 743.*

However, attorneys take on their powers only when they have successfully applied to an official body, the Office of the Public Guardian, to 'register' them; they cannot lawfully use their powers until this has happened. Some donors decide to include in the powers they grant a 'springing clause' which says that their attorneys can apply to register their powers only if and when they (the donor) has lost mental capacity. In other powers of attorney, probably the majority, there is no springing clause and the donor themselves applies for the powers to be registered soon after the power of attorney has been signed. Attorneys and donor then wield the powers simultaneously, deciding how they should divide up the tasks. If at a later stage the donor should lose capacity, the attorney takes on all the power the donor granted them in the original form and acts alone, without the need to apply at that stage for registration [1]

Should I restrict the attorney's powers?

If you are proposing to grant power of attorney, you should consider whether to impose limitations on the powers you are granting. For example, you could specifically exclude the power to sell your house or flat. However, although it is tempting to limit power, it is usually best not to do so but to exercise careful choice in the selection of the attorneys. If attorney powers are hedged around with all sorts of conditions and eventualities, the person who has to act on your behalf may find they have a lot more work to do or certain matters may remain unaddressed. If you have to go into a care facility, for example, but your attorney lacks the power to sell your property to help pay the bills, they will have to make an application to the Office of the Public Guardian to try to extend their powers. Or your bank account may continue to make payments for goods and services you no longer need simply because nobody is authorised to cancel these payments on your behalf.

As well as placing restrictions on the power of attorneys, you can also issue guidance on the way you would like them to behave. This guidance, unlike the restrictions, is not legally binding, but attorneys are expected to take it into account. Perhaps you have always made a donation to a particular charity and feel strongly that this should continue. Perhaps there are particular companies in which you wish your attorneys to invest for ethical reasons. If considerations such as these matter to you, set them down in the space on the form earmarked for guidance. Attorneys are supposed to consider the donor's past wishes, values and beliefs when they handle their affairs, but matters such as whether investments are ethical or not might not occur to them.

People with dementia

There is a mistaken belief that a person with a diagnosis of dementia, or indeed any other brain impairment, cannot grant power of attorney. This is wrong. What they must have is sufficient mental ability or, as it is called in the legislation, mental capacity. This means that they must be able to grasp the implications of granting attorney powers and weigh up the choices involved in an informed way at the time they grant the power. *(I explain the meaning of mental capacity in more detail on page 774.)*

However, it is important for people with a dementia diagnosis to grant attorney quickly if they have not already done so, lest their mental condition deteriorate to a stage at which they are not deemed to have sufficient capacity to take this step. They may also wish to make an advance statement to refuse treatment, formerly known as a living will *(and discussed on page 1017)*. They should also make a will if they have not already done so: a will can be contested successfully if it is shown that the person making it lacked the mental capacity to know what they were doing.

What to look for in an attorney

Clearly, choosing on whom to bestow the power to act on your behalf in financial and property matters is an extremely important decision. So, what features and qualities should you look for in your attorney(s)?

First and foremost, look for somebody who would be competent to manage your affairs and prepared to give some thought to investing your money or capable of obtaining sound advice and acting on it. Obviously you also want somebody you can trust, as, if the power is not limited, the attorney will be able to do virtually anything you could have done. It is also a good idea to choose somebody younger than yourself, in good health, who lives close to you and who will have sufficient time to apply themselves to the task.

You should also think about who should step into the breach should your attorney die or lose their mental capacity. The person to whom you grant attorney cannot nominate a substitute, so you need to make provision for a fallback alternative in the power of attorney you sign. Some people appoint their partner to be their main attorney and their children in the event that their partner is no longer able to manage their affairs.

How should I share powers between my attorneys?

If you appoint more than one attorney you have to decide whether you will allow them to act separately and independently – known as 'several' power of attorney – or whether they will need to obtain each other's agreement for every decision and so act together, in which case it is a 'joint' attorneyship. If the attorneys are appointed jointly, both or all their signatures will be required on every cheque, and they cannot reach decisions unless they are in agreement. If one of the attorneys is unable to act, perhaps being unwell or out of the country, the attorneyship can have no force.

Another possibility is to make the attorneyship 'joint and several'. For instance, if you consider Peter is going to be on hand to do most of the work but you want Paul to have some involvement, you could grant a 'joint and several' attorneyship, with specified areas of authority for Peter. Or you could provide for several powers, so that each attorney can do what they are good at without constant reference to the other(s). But you could require that both (or all) the attorneys sign for transactions above a certain sum.

You also need to consider whether any conflicts could arise between your own interests and the interests of the attorneys, particularly if the latter are the main beneficiaries of your will. Most obviously, they might scrimp on spending on your care as that would deplete the estate from which they eventually hope to benefit. On the other hand, you want people prepared to take some time and trouble to ensure that your money generates as much income as possible. If the attorney stands to inherit some of your cash at the end of the day, that may provide an additional incentive.

Attorneys can claim reasonable expenses. They must not derive personal benefit from their position, but they may be paid a fee – this is something to be negotiated with them and set down clearly in the form granting power of attorney. The job can involve much time and effort and a time-related payment could help sweeten the pill, particularly if the attorney is not a beneficiary of your will. Of course, a solicitor or an accountant will expect payment commensurate with their professional position if you appoint one as your attorney; this could impose a considerable drain on your estate over a long period. It may be better to appoint relatives or friends as your attorneys and allow them to commission work from professionals such as solicitors, estate agents and financial advisors, if they wish.

Safeguards

This system of representation offers huge potential for abuse, not least fraud. A number of measures are designed to reduce the risk of abuse or to deal with it when it occurs.

1. Setting up the attorneyship: scrutiny by outsiders

The creation of an attorneyship cannot involve the donor and their attorney(s) acting alone. In England and Wales, the donor must find at least one person who will agree to take on the role of 'certificate provider' – an independent person who is prepared to say that the person granting attorney understands the purpose of the attorneyship and the scope of the powers it confers, that no fraud or undue pressure is being exerted on them to create the attorneyship, and that there are no other reasons why the attorneyship should not be created. The certificate provider should discuss the attorneyship in private with the donor, and the attorneys should not be involved in this discussion. Certificate providers can thus play an important role in guaranteeing that attorneys are not imposing pressure on a donor to grant them attorney powers and, indeed, in acting as a witness should a dispute about the attorneyship arise subsequently.

An individual whom the donor selects as their certificate provider has to have known the donor for at least two years and to explain briefly why they consider that they have the necessary skills to perform the role, unless they are a registered social worker, a registered healthcare professional, a lawyer or an independent mental capacity advocate *(defined on page 784)*. The following people are forbidden from acting as the certificate provider:

- prospective attorneys
- care workers
- the spouses or partners of the donor

2. Registering the attorneyship before it can be used

Attorneys cannot lawfully use any of the powers granted in the power of attorney until a successful application to register it has been made to the Office of the Public Guardian. As noted above, registration may take place only once the donor has lost mental capacity; in this case, the attorneys apply to register the attorneyship. The alternative is to register the powers soon after the attorney form has been signed, even though the donor retains mental capacity. In this case, the donor can apply to register the power.

Say your father starts making uncharacteristic purchases. Perhaps all is well and he is simply exercising his right to spend his money as he wishes, even though you may consider the purchases unwise. But perhaps his brain functions are becoming impaired as a result of illness and he has lost the ability to understand the implications of what he is doing. In that case, if he has previously appointed you as his attorney, you should apply to use your powers as his attorney by applying to the Public Guardian to register the attorneyship. On the other hand, if the power of attorney had been registered soon after it was made, you as your father's attorney would be empowered to act at once.

The requirement for registration provides an important safeguard for the donor, since it provides an opportunity for the Public Guardian and their staff to step in if they consider that something might be amiss.

It is important that attorneys realise that they cannot lawfully act as such unless the power of attorney has been registered. So if, say, they sell the donor's house to pay for care home fees without registration having taken place, the sale is invalid.

There are heavy penalties for making a statement known to be false when applying for registration. For example, an attorney of evil intent who, when applying to register a power of attorney, claimed that the grandmother who granted him his power had lost mental capacity when in fact she remained of sound mind could face a hefty fine or imprisonment for up to two years.

3. Checks by friends and family who are not the prospective attorneys

Out of the thousands of applications to register powers of attorney that arrive in their office, how is the Public Guardian to identify the ones about which they should be concerned and which might need to be referred to a visitor (*see below*) or otherwise investigated further? One way is through being alerted by people outside the attorneyship who are concerned that all may not be well. Often these will be people named by the donor on the form granting power of attorney.

This is how the system works. When setting up power of attorney, the donor has the option of selecting up to five people. These could perhaps be family members not named as attorneys, such as nieces and nephews. They could be friends or work colleagues. An application to register a PALPA triggers a mechanism for alerting these people, thereby giving them the opportunity to lodge an objection to the registration of the attorneyship, if they wish.

In addition, the donor themselves must be notified of the registration application. However, if no useful purpose would be served by this last notification, the Court of Protection can agree to dispense with it.

4. Oversight by the Public Guardian and Court of Protection

If the Public Guardian has a concern about an application to register a power of attorney, they can enter into correspondence with the people involved and investigate what is going on. The result might simply be the provision of advice to the parties involved. But if necessary, the Guardian can refer the matter to a special court called the Court of Protection with which it works closely. This might be because they consider that some part of the attorneyship is unworkable, or its meaning is unclear, or they have concerns about the motives and integrity of an attorney.

In England and Wales, the Court of Protection has ultimate power to decide whether the registration of an attorneyship should be approved. The Court has its own 'visitors' who can be dispatched to investigate matters on the ground. Some are 'general visitors'; others 'special medical visitors', who must be registered doctors with expertise in the many ways in which brain functions can be disturbed or impaired.

Court of Protection judges hear cases involving disputes arising from the system of representation at regional courts in England and Wales.

They can make their own case law and are equivalent in status to judges in the High Court. They act as the final arbiter in all disputes over attorneyships. The Court is based at the Royal Courts of Justice in London.

If you have a concern about possible abuse of the attorney system or other parts of the representation apparatus, your first port of call should be the Office of the Public Guardian. If, for instance, the son of an acquaintance of yours is spending money from the estate of his mother, for whom he says he is an attorney, on himself rather than his mother, or is perhaps proceeding to sell his mother's house and move her into a care home and you are concerned that her rights are being overridden, you should contact the Public Guardian. Investigations might reveal that the son does not in fact hold registered power of attorney. In this case, the Court of Protection will investigate the matter further and perhaps appoint a deputy to handle the mother's affairs on an ongoing basis, if she lacks the mental capacity to appoint a new attorney. Or it might transpire that the son does hold registered power of attorney but needs advice on how to operate it, which the Public Guardian or a Court of Protection visitor could provide. Or perhaps he is deliberately acting in his own – and against his mother's – best interests. The Court of Protection might then amend or even cancel the attorneyship and appoint a deputy.

Anybody can contact the Public Guardian, which is an executive agency of the Ministry of Justice. A good care home manager, for example, will do so if they consider that attorneyship powers relating to residents in the home are being abused.

A National Mental Capacity Forum in England, set up in 2015, seeks to educate the public about the mental capacity legislation, especially the principles on which attorneys should base their behaviour.

When donor and attorneys hold powers concurrently

The type of attorneyship we have tended to concentrate on so far is the type that stipulates that the attorneys' powers can be registered only if and when the donor should lose mental capacity. In the second type of PALPA, the donor does not have to lose mental capacity before attorneys can act on their behalf in the property and affairs realm.

Attorneys using this second kind of PALPA (the type of attorneyship probably most often recommended by solicitors and other professional advisors) can act alongside the donor, sharing the responsibility of financial and property decision-making. This can be helpful if, say, the donor has difficulty reading documents or spreadsheets and would like the reassurance that somebody they trust is taking on at least some of the decision-making. Such an attorneyship can be tailor-made to suit individual circumstances, with a selected attorney or attorneys handling particular areas which the donor would like to delegate.

The arrangement could act as a useful safeguard for relatives slightly worried about what a parent, perhaps living some distance away, might do. There are plenty of unscrupulous salespeople looking for opportunities to exploit older people who, if isolated, can be very vulnerable to their advances.

One example: a man who does not wish to embarrass himself in front of his family finds himself in need of a large sum of money. An individual specialising in equity release schemes persuades him to mortgage or transfer 50 per cent of his property in return for that sum and recommends a solicitor to handle the transaction. Perhaps the firm and the solicitor are perfectly reputable; on the other hand, perhaps not. If an attorney's signature were also required for such transactions, that would provide an additional safeguard. The attorney might carry out checks on the company or the solicitor which the man had omitted to do. Relatives should in any case try to take a healthy, yet not intrusive, interest in their older loved ones' financial affairs.

Another advantage of creating an attorneyship and registering it as soon as it has been made, or soon afterwards, is that it avoids any delay should the donor lose mental capacity. Perhaps someone is becoming forgetful and neglects to pay credit card and other bills or to carry out essential maintenance to their property. Early registration can be helpful during difficulties that often occur if someone is losing their ability to run their own affairs but exerts exclusive control of them. What is more, if the attorneyship contains a springing clause, there is bound to be a delay before attorneys can take charge. Six weeks have to pass to allow for any objection to be raised to the registration. Finding a doctor to certify that somebody has lost mental capacity takes time, and it usually takes a while for a family to realise that something is amiss in the first place.

However, a delay during registration may not always pose a problem. For instance, if an attorney has to sell the donor's house or flat, registration of their powers would probably not be required until exchange of contracts. If you have a special need for speedy registration, you could ask the Office of the Public Guardian to fast-track your application.

An attorneyship in which attorneys take on full powers while the donor remains mentally intact could have attorneys holding concurrent powers for many years, perhaps decades. In this case, the donor should work out what this will mean in practice. Will they give their attorney keywords to access their bank accounts throughout this period, or only when they are going abroad or into hospital? How will attorneys keep PIN numbers and the like secure? What would happen in the event of the theft of their papers or identity? Should a dispute arise between donor and attorney, the donor enjoys the safeguard that they are free to revoke the power of attorney, so long as they have the mental capacity to do so.

Day-to-day practical matters

Whether or not a property and affairs attorney is operating alongside the donor of the power or instead of him or her, the attorney must keep the donor's money and property separate from their own and they must keep accounts of transactions carried out on behalf of the donor. They must not delegate their powers to someone else, although they can seek advice (say, from a financial advisor) to enable them to come to a decision. And they must keep the donor's affairs confidential, except in certain circumstances. Attorneys cannot give up their role without notifying the donor and the Public Guardian, whose guidance on how the role is relinquished must be followed.

Property and affairs attorneys must comply with any directions given to them by the Public Guardian or the Court of Protection, perhaps to provide information or to perform a wider range of tasks than granted in the original attorneyship. They must act in good faith, in other words with honesty and integrity, and not use their position for their own advantage. And they have a 'duty of care', which means that they must apply the same skill, care and diligence in acting as attorney as they would in making decisions about their own life. If they are professionals or are being paid, they should be able to demonstrate a higher level of care and skill; professionals should follow their profession's rules and standards.

It is important that donors keep the document granting attorney in a safe place and make sure that attorneys and certificate providers know where it is stored. Also, they should ensure that their attorneys have all the information they need to take over bank accounts, tax affairs, shares, property, insurance and so on. The attorneys will need to be able to locate passwords, PIN numbers and National Insurance and tax numbers, so it is important to make a list beforehand to make life easy for them.

I consider the principles that must guide the behaviour of attorneys acting on behalf of a donor whose mental capacity is limited in Chapter 33.

Deciding whether to become an attorney

Anybody contemplating acting as an attorney or applying to become a deputy *(see page 761)* should think carefully about the implications before going ahead. These forms of representation can involve a lot of work.

As an attorney, you will have to use a separate bank account for the attorneyship and keep all the money connected with it separate from your own. You will need to keep receipts, file them carefully and keep full accounts. For instance, if you propose to claim the cost of travel and accommodation for frequent visits to, say, your uncle in a care home 200 miles away, you will need to keep a careful record of your expenditure. The British Banking Association produces a useful leaflet entitled *Banking for People who Lack Capacity to Make Decisions*.

As we shall see in a moment, deputies have to submit annual accounts to the Public Guardian and consult him or her about certain decisions. Although attorneys have more freedom to act on their own initiative than deputies, they have to be prepared to respond should the Guardian raise questions about their actions. They need to cover themselves so that they can show they have not misappropriated money and that the steps they have taken were in the donor's best interests.

Unforeseen work may arise. If staff have to be hired, attorneys will be responsible not only for paying them but also for ensuring that the law is observed on anything from statutory sick pay to National Insurance contributions *(see pages 529–30)*. Legal action on behalf of the donor may need to be taken; legal action may be taken against the donor. A donor's property might require attention.

Performing the role of attorney (or deputy) is a serious business. Attorneys and deputies may be held personally liable if the donor's money is not handled in a responsible manner – if, say, state benefits are paid for which the donor no longer qualifies, perhaps because an able-bodied adult has moved in with them, so removing entitlement to the single person's allowance for council tax *(see page 847)*. Whatever informal arrangements may have been made between attorneys, for instance that one should focus on certain areas and the other on others, are irrelevant in this situation: both heads are on the block if a mistake has been made.

Attorneys have to behave in a way that conforms to the Mental Capacity Act, and in doing so they must have regard to the Code of Practice that accompanies it. Have a look at that Code *(outlined in Chapter 33)* before you agree to become an attorney.

Of course, people usually agree to become attorneys in the hope that their relative will remain mentally able, so they will never need to step up to the plate. They take on the role because nobody else is prepared to do so. But the potential extent of the responsibility remains the same.

Reviewing power of attorney

It may be tempting to grant power of attorney and then put the attorney-ship form away in a drawer and forget about it. Do not do this – review it every so often. Your circumstances and your views may change over time, as may the circumstances of those you have appointed as your attorneys. Remember that you can alter the attorneyship, or revoke it and grant another, but only so long as you retain the mental capacity to do so. The procedures are similar to granting power of attorney in the first place.

Or perhaps as an attorney you find that you lack sufficient powers. Perhaps your powers do not include the power to claim state benefits yet you discover that the donor is eligible for, say, Attendance Allowance or Pension Credit. In that case, you could apply for an extension to your power – perhaps through becoming the donor's appointee *(see page 799)*, while continuing as their attorney. Or perhaps the donor specifically ex-cluded the power to sell their property in the powers they granted and you now find that you do need to sell the property, perhaps to pay care home bills. In that case, contact the Public Guardian to discuss how you could apply for the additional powers you consider you need.

Do you need a solicitor to create an attorneyship?

Many solicitors offer to prepare attorneyships for clients. Often this is suggested when somebody approaches a solicitor to make or alter their will. As noted above, it is only in Scotland that the involvement of a solicitor is specifically required when attorneyships are created. If you live south of the border, should you involve a solicitor or not? And in Scotland, should you ask the solicitor to do any more than sign the cer-tification form?

Much will depend on what the solicitor offers. If they help you work out how to choose your attorneys, what powers to grant them and, in-deed, all the various matters discussed in this chapter, such help may be invaluable. A good solicitor can also be useful if there are sensitive dis-cussions to be had, perhaps explaining to one daughter that you would prefer her sister to become your attorney. If your attorneyship is complex in particular areas, such as financial matters or the division of powers be-tween attorneys, or if you simply feel worried about ensuring the forms are correctly filled in and signed, help from a solicitor could be very use-ful. But beware solicitors who are jumping on the attorney bandwagon and demanding high fees to set up an arrangement which you could easily set up yourself.

I have heard reports of solicitors who fail to discuss the terms of the attorneyship with their clients and do no more than ensure that minimal entries are made on the form, that it is signed and witnessed, followed by an immediate application for registration of the powers. In return for little work, they demand a high fee. They fail to discuss matters such as the pros and cons of delaying registration, provision for replacement attorneys, whether or not the powers of attorneys should be limited, and whether donors should set out their wishes on how their attorneys should behave. They fail to explain to prospective attorneys just what is involved in being an attorney or point them to the code of practice linked to the mental capacity legislation.

There is another point too. If you hire a plumber, you tell them what outcome you would like and then leave them to tackle the tasks necessary to achieve it, without any further input from you. Commissioning a solicitor to draw up a power of attorney is different. You and your attorneys, not the solicitor, will be using the powers granted on a daily basis and you need to ensure the arrangement will work. You need to know precisely which powers you will be giving to your attorneys and they need to be happy with how they think they are going to use those powers before the attorneyship is signed. It is they who will be called to account by the Public Guardian if they fail to act correctly. Asking a solicitor to set up the attorneyship can lead to the dangerous illusion that the solicitor will have some continuing involvement or oversight, which is by no means necessarily the case. They will be involved in the future only if asked to do particular things or if selected as an attorney or if they are the sort of solicitor who keeps a watchful eye on their clients.

That said, it is worth talking through what you propose before you finalise your power of attorney. If you do not take legal advice, have a word with acquaintances with experience of using powers of attorney. You could also contact your local Citizens Advice and/or the helpline of the Alzheimer's Society and Alzheimer Scotland. Plenty of information about setting up attorneyships and managing them is available from the Public Guardian's office; you can put questions by phone or email.

If you decide to involve solicitors whether in setting up the power of attorney or as one of your attorneys or both, you may find the section on choosing and working with a solicitor on pages 812–6 useful.

Financial powers of attorney in Scotland

In Scotland, the system of creating and registering powers of attorney covering property and financial matters is broadly similar to that in England and Wales. Under the Scottish legislation, a 'granter' can grant powers to one or more attorneys over their property and financial affairs through a 'continuing power of attorney'.[2]

As in England and Wales, this power of attorney must be registered before it can come into effect. The granter can opt to apply to register the powers at any time, for instance soon after they or their attorneys have signed the attorneyship form. Or they can choose to include a 'springing clause' stating an event that must take place before the powers can be registered, most obviously if and when they lose the mental capacity to take certain decisions. If you go down this route, consider what decisions you should specify and how many professionals you should stipulate must assess your capacity – perhaps two rather than just one, to help protect against possible abuse of the system.

Unlike the situation south of the border, if you want to grant a continuing power of attorney in Scotland, you must involve a solicitor or doctor when you sign the form. The solicitor or doctor has to certify that they interviewed you just before you signed the form and are satisfied, either because of their own knowledge of you or because they have consulted other people (named in the certificate) who have knowledge of you, that at the time the continuing power of attorney was granted, you understood its nature and extent. Their signature also certifies that they had no reason to believe that you were acting under undue influence or that any other factor invalidated the granting of the power.

The Office of the Public Guardian for Scotland (which is separate from the Public Guardian of England and Wales) plays a key role in financial attorneyships. Sheriffs in local sheriff courts hear and determine cases rather than a national court with regional sittings (the Court of Protection), as happens in England and Wales.

The procedure for registering continuing powers of attorney is as follows. If a power of attorney in Scotland specifies that it can be registered only after a reduction in the mental capacity of the granter, the attorney or attorneys must provide medical evidence of this to the Public Guardian. Before they register the attorneyship, the Guardian checks that the attorney(s) are willing to act. The Guardian sends a copy of the registered document to the granter and also notifies any other people previously specified by the granter – on the original form granting attorney powers, the granter can name up to two individuals or officials whom they would like to be sent a copy of the attorneyship once it has been registered. This can be a useful means for ensuring that, say, a distant relative or an old friend is aware of the situation.

The Public Guardian in Scotland has the power to investigate any concerns they may have or to which members of the public have alerted them about the financial and property affairs of an adult. The Guardian has teams of investigators who can go out and examine cases and interview the people involved. On an application for registration, the Guardian then decides whether or not to approve the registration. If the case is contested, for instance over whether or not the person involved has really lost mental capacity, the Public Guardian will take proceedings to a sheriff court for resolution.

In Scotland, the Guardian's functions in supervising and investigating powers of attorney are confined to property and financial matters. The supervision and investigation of attorneys in the field of health and welfare are the responsibility of local authorities; this is a major difference from the situation south of the border *(to which I return on page 757)*.

The Office of the Public Guardian, based in Falkirk, provides advice and information about the system, including sample powers of attorney documents that cover many possible variations of type, appointment and power. The Scottish government publishes detailed free guides.[3] Alzheimer Scotland also publishes much useful guidance.

Enduring powers of attorney (EPA)

Some people reading this book will be much more concerned about enduring powers of attorney granted before the mental capacity legislation came into force than about creating new powers of attorney.[4]

In Scotland, the situation is straightforward: the equivalent of enduring power of attorney – powers granted under a contract of mandate or agency with powers relating to property and financial affairs, or welfare, or both granted before the Adults with Incapacity (Scotland) Act came into force – are automatically converted into continuing powers of attorney.

In England or Wales, existing enduring powers of attorney which were made before 1st October, 2007 (when the Mental Capacity Act 2005 came into force) can still be used, but not any made after that date.

Although earlier enduring powers of attorney can be used in England and Wales, the 2005 Act lays down a new procedure for registering them which provides tighter safeguards for donors than existed in the past.

These procedures are as follows.[5] If an attorney has reason to believe that the donor of the EPA is or is becoming mentally incapable, they must, as soon as practicable, make an application to the Public Guardian to register the power. At the same time, they must notify at least three close relatives of the donor.[6] Separately, the attorney must notify the donor, although they do not need to if the OPG agrees that such a step would be impracticable, undesirable or serve no useful purpose. Those relatives who have been notified have five weeks to object. Objection is dealt with by correspondence, but if this does not enable the Public Guardian to come to a decision, the Court of Protection holds a hearing.

The donor or other relatives may object on one or more of the following grounds:

- that the power purported to have been created by the attorney-ship is not valid
- that the application is premature because the donor is still mentally capable
- that the attorney has committed fraud or put unnecessary pressure on the donor to grant the power of attorney
- that the attorney is unsuitable to hold that role

If the Court is convinced, it can direct the Public Guardian to refuse registration. Thereupon, the attorneyship is cancelled. Anybody who makes a false statement when applying to register an EPA can be fined, imprisoned or both.

Even after an EPA has been registered, the Court of Protection, working closely with the Public Guardian, has powers to investigate and, if appropriate, modify or cancel the EPA. For example, it can order EPA attorneys to produce accounts and the records they have used (bank statements, receipts and so on) to compile those accounts. It can require them to produce details of the expenses they have claimed; if it considers these were excessive, it can require them to pay them back. If there are questions or disputes about the meaning of the attorneyship, the Court can intervene and determine what should happen. And if it considers that serious irregularities are occurring or that the EPA was unsound to start with, it can direct the Public Guardian to revoke it.

What this means is that there are plenty of powers which the Court of Protection can use to monitor the use of existing powers of attorney and thus respond to any concerns that an EPA is being abused. This is why it is important that the wider community – not just people chosen as attorneys or professionals in the care world – should know of the existence of the Court of Protection and understand the scope of its powers.

Any donor of an enduring power of attorney which has not yet been registered should seriously consider revoking it and replacing it with a PALPA, since this is a more effective and transparent tool than an EPA, with greater safeguards against abuse. Or they could keep their EPA but also grant a personal welfare lasting power of attorney (PWLPA). In the past, people holding enduring power of attorney have often been consulted on health and welfare matters, and indeed made them on behalf of those they represent. But this has been a grey area; a PWLPA *(see page 751)* offers more reliable representation by people chosen specifically for the purpose by the donor.

The situation in Northern Ireland

In Northern Ireland, the enduring power of attorney is a far more important tool than on the British mainland, since it remains the main legal tool of long-term representation until the provisions of the Mental Capacity Act (Northern Ireland) 2016 come into force, which may not be for several years.

Nonetheless, the same considerations on granting power of attorney – choosing whom to appoint and deciding what powers to give them *(described above under lasting power of attorney)* – obtain for enduring power of attorney, so readers planning to grant an enduring power of attorney may care to refer to those sections *(pages 735–7)*. If more than one attorney is appointed, the power can be joint or several *(as described on page 736)*. Also, an alternative attorney can be appointed in case an existing attorney is unable to continue.

A donor can revoke a power of attorney at any time, but doing so after they have lost mental capacity requires the consent of the Office of Care and Protection. This office, based in Belfast, oversees the representation system in the province and is part of the Family Division of the High Court. It publishes information about the procedures involved.

Essentially, the procedures involved in setting up an enduring power of attorney and in registering the power bear a strong resemblance to those for lasting power of attorney in England and Wales.[7] Attorneys can start acting on behalf of the donor in financial matters as soon as the attorneyship is signed and witnessed: in other words, their power does not wait to be used until the donor loses mental capacity. But it can cover that eventuality too; indeed, a donor can stipulate that the powers cannot come into effect until the attorneyship is registered because they have lost mental capacity. If that should happen, the attorney(s) would apply to the Office of Care and Protection to register the attorneyship.

Specified people must be notified of the application to register. These are the donor (unless the Office agrees that to do so would cause too much distress) and a minimum of three relatives in the order of priority set down in legislation (starting with the donor's spouse or civil partner). If no objections to registration are raised, the office notifies the attorneys that registration has taken place. If objections are raised and cannot be resolved, the office makes a ruling.

Anybody concerned about the possible abuse of an enduring power of attorney should contact the Office of Care and Protection.

Lasting power of attorney in Northern Ireland

A new law, the Mental Capacity Act (Northern Ireland) 2016 provides similar powers for individuals to create lasting powers of attorney as those in contained in the Mental Capacity Act 2005, which apply in England and Wales. However, this Act is unlikely to be commenced for several years, during which regulations and official guidance will be drafted. When it does so, the new system of lasting power of attorney will operate alongside the existing system of enduring power, not replace it as is the case in England and Wales.

The new Act provides for a donor to grant a lasting power of attorney covering finance and property. The donor can declare that the powers of donor and attorney(s) can be used concurrently or that the attorney's powers can be used only if and when the donor loses mental capacity. Powers can be given jointly or severally to attorneys, and the donor (but not the attorney) can appoint one or more replacement attorneys. There is provision for a certificate provider when a power is set up and for registration of powers to take place in a similar way as in England and Wales. Donors will also be able to appoint attorneys covering health and welfare decisions, *as explained below.* However, these cannot be used until the donor has lost mental capacity.[8]

Once the Act comes into effect, the Department of Justice of the Northern Ireland Assembly Government will appoint a new official in Northern Ireland called the Public Guardian, with similar powers to the Public Guardian in England and Wales. Thus they will establish and maintain registers of lasting powers of attorney and receive reports they request from people who are acting (or claiming to act) under a lasting power of attorney. The Guardian will be able to investigate complaints or any fraudulent activity that might emerge.[9]

No special court equivalent to the Court of Protection is proposed for Northern Ireland. Instead, the legal body with authority in this field will continue to be the High Court. If capacity is unclear or there is a dispute, the High Court will determine the matter. It will also be able to revoke a lasting power of attorney, if the donor does not have the mental capacity to do so. The Public Guardian and Court Visitors will investigate the working of powers of attorney on the ground. The Public Guardian will direct Court Visitors to people about whose actions they are concerned and the Visitors will prepare reports of their findings.[10] Anyone who becomes concerned about the terms of or operation of a lasting power of attorney under the new system should contact the Public Guardian in the first instance.

Personal Welfare Lasting Power of Attorney (PWLPA)

Just as a property and affairs attorney can take any decision in the management of money and property which the donor of the attorneyship would have enjoyed, so a personal welfare attorney can take a wide range of decisions which the donor would have taken had they sufficient capacity to do so, but in the areas of health and welfare.

Welfare attorneyships (PWLPAs) differ from property and affairs attorneyships (PALPAs) in that while the donor of a PALPA has the option of decreeing that registration and thus activation of the attorneyship can take place while they retain mental capacity, a personal welfare attorneyship can be registered only in the event that the donor loses capacity.

It is often assumed that the only matter in the health field about which older people need to concern themselves is whether they would wish their life to be sustained artificially if they became so unwell that this was necessary. In fact, however, there are a huge number of other very important decisions in the fields of health and welfare over which a welfare attorney would be well placed to exercise influence.

Let us take two examples. Your loved one, whose mental capacity is much reduced, goes into hospital, perhaps after suffering a stroke. Nurses propose to insert a urinary catheter. This action has significant drawbacks – not least, catheters can cause infections and cause the bladder to shrink so that it becomes difficult to return to normal urination *(see pages 420–3)*. The patient's consent is required, unless the situation is a medical emergency. So you, as personal welfare attorney, should expect consent to be sought from you instead. To make sure that you are, you should explain to the medical staff at the outset that you expect this to happen and that you hold power of personal welfare attorney.

Second example: your father, who suffers from dementia, goes into hospital after a fall. When he is ready to be discharged, a social care official at the hospital tells you that he should move to a care home. As his legal representative, it is you, not social services, who decides where he should live – whether in his previous home, or with a friend or relative, or in a care home. If he is to move to a care home, you decide which one, making the decisions in your father's best interests. If social services will be responsible for paying the bills, you as his legal representative should be fully consulted at all stages and you should be able to exercise your father's ability to choose which home to go to *(as explained on pages 972–3)*. Once your father is living in a care home, whoever is paying the bills, you as his legal representative should be consulted on decisions that he is unable to take himself, not least whether he should share a bedroom with another resident.

None of these, or similar, attempts to assert the interests of loved ones by partners, friends or relatives including next-of-kin are ruled out at present. But the chances of real success in championing the interests of loved ones are likely to be higher for people who are personal welfare attorneys.

There are only a small number of areas where the writ of a welfare attorney does not run. These are casting a vote, giving consent to a marriage or civil partnership or to the divorce or dissolution of such relationships, consenting to sexual relations and consenting to medical treatment being given for a mental disorder to somebody who has been detained under the Mental Health Act of 1983.

On the ground, the main difference between a PALPA and a PWLPA is that welfare attorneys are likely to have to refer to the person they are seeking to represent more frequently than does a property and affairs attorney. This is because somebody who is unable to manage their money and property may be perfectly capable of taking many decisions about everyday life – what to wear or who to see – and the mental capacity legislation requires that attorneys enable donors to take as many decisions themselves as they can and to support them in doing so. If the person who is being represented lives in a care home, care staff would take decisions about their daily lives in accordance with the principles of the Mental Capacity Act *(see pages 770–4)*, but they must allow the person to take as many decisions themselves as possible and to support them in so doing. If someone is unable to take a particular decision, their attorney (and others) should be consulted. The attorney of anyone who moves into a care home should sit down with staff and discuss how this situation should be tackled, providing general guidance on their views and singling out any particular categories of decisions on which they would like to be consulted in future.

The procedure for appointing welfare attorneys is precisely the same as that set down for property and affairs lasting power of attorney; indeed, many people will wish to grant both types of attorneyship at the same time. The same safeguards are provided through the requirement that a certificate provider be involved in the attorneyship *(as described on page 737)*. Unlike the situation with PALPAs, personal welfare attorneys may not exercise their powers concurrently with the donor; they can do so only if and when mental capacity is lost. The statement of wishes section of a personal welfare attorney power provides an opportunity for donors to set down what they would like to happen, not least at the end of their lives, *as discussed in Chapter 41.*

The status of next-of-kin

Many people assume that the next-of-kin can make decisions on behalf of someone who lacks mental capacity. This is wrong. It is true that they may well be consulted by health or social care staff, and their wishes may be those that are put into effect, but this will not necessarily happen. As we see when we examine the categories of people health organisations must consult when deciding, say, whether to give medical treatment to someone who is unable to state their wishes at the time, next-of-kin is not one of those categories – although someone who is next-of-kin may well fall into one of the other categories.

Several pieces of research have shown that people are surprised to find that the next-of-kin cannot make decisions for another adult. For example, research cited by the voluntary organisation Compassion in Dying has shown that more than half of the public mistakenly believe they have the right to make end-of-life treatment decisions for their next-of-kin.[11]

Partners and relatives can find the ability to see their loved one's medical records useful when they are discussing matters with doctors and nurses. But while personal welfare attorneys have the automatic right to see the medical records of the people whom they representing, next-of-kin do not. As Amanda Odd, the then manager of the award-winning Amherst Court care home in Chatham, Kent, which looks after more than 100 older people with dementia, told me in 2013, 'Relatives seem to think that just because they're next-of-kin they've got this automatic right to see all health and medical records that we have on their loved one. That is not the case whatsoever. Unless they've got lasting power of attorney on health and well-being, they have no legal right to see the records.'[12]

Attorneys may be consulted even on matters which fall outside the scope of their legal powers simply because their status is an indication of the trust placed in them. So the Code of Practice that accompanies the Mental Capacity Act and explains how it should be implemented states:

> It is good practice for decision-makers to consult attorneys about any decision or action, whether or not it is covered by the lasting power of attorney. This is because an attorney is likely to have known the donor for some time and may have important information about their wishes and feelings.[13]

Nonetheless, hospitals may accord someone's next-of-kin special status in deciding what should happen to a patient who is unable to speak up for themselves. If your next-of-kin is not someone you would wish to be consulted, make sure you appoint a health and welfare attorney and/or nominate individuals to be consulted over health and social care decisions *(as explained on page 782–3)*.

Shaping a welfare attorneyship

The choices confronting the donor of a welfare attorney are the same as those facing the donor of a property and affairs attorney – in other words, they must select an individual or individuals whom they ask to act as attorney and decide whether these attorney(s) should be able to act independently of each other or only together. The donor should also consider whether they wish to restrict the powers through conditions and whether they should set down guidelines for their attorney(s).

As with PALPAs, any conditions or restrictions you place on the welfare attorneyship limit the power of the attorney. Attorneys cannot act outside them. If they do, the attorneyship becomes invalid. A condition might be, for example, that your attorney must always talk to a particular person before making certain decisions on your behalf – say, about where you live or whether you should receive life-sustaining medical treatment. It is important that these conditions are not too complicated; they could prove an additional headache for the attorneys. What is more, the Court of Protection reserves the right to cancel conditions or restrictions which it considers too complicated or impractical.

Again as with PALPAs, the guidelines you might set down for your personal welfare attorney(s) are different from conditions: they are not binding on attorneys, but are intended to guide them when they make decisions on your behalf. Guidance, sometimes known as 'a statement of wishes', can be as long or as brief as you wish (or non-existent). You might specify, for instance, that, should you have to move to a care home, you would prefer one which does (or does not) permit pets, or is located in a particular place, or has a particular cultural or religious dimension. However, if your attorneys cannot find a home which meets any of these requests but do find one in which they nonetheless consider it will be in your best interests to live, they are within their powers to move you to that one.

The statement of wishes can also guide attorneys when they have to weigh up risks. For example, I should wish to make it clear in my attorney document that, were I to lose capacity, I should like to spend as much time as possible out of doors, even though this might pose a risk to my health. I imagine that, should I develop dementia, the ability to derive pleasure from seeing a beautiful sunset or watching rain fall would probably persist, even though I might no longer be able to name such objects as clouds or the sun. People with dementia usually retain their essential personality and their capacity to feel emotions for far longer than their cognitive powers.

As with PALPAs, you may wish to restrict decision-making in a particular area to one of your attorneys but not the other, through granting 'several' powers *(as explained on page 736)*. Or you may wish to ensure that neither can act in all or only certain areas without the agreement of the other. If you do not specify that your attorneys can act independently in some areas, it will be assumed that they have been appointed together, so they must all agree on all decisions.

Decisions about whether to accept life-sustaining treatment such as the administration of antibiotics or the artificial delivery of food and fluid are considered so important that the donor of a welfare attorneyship has to give a special indication on the form that they intend granting this power to their welfare attorney(s). Only if the donor expressly does so by completing a particular part of the attorney form will the attorney(s) hold what is in effect the power of life or death. If donors do not give attorneys power in this area, those decisions will be taken by health professionals after consulting attorneys and any other people in the categories specified, if it is practicable and appropriate to do so *(as explained on page 782). I explain the relative status of a power of a welfare attorney and an advance directive to refuse treatment on page 1019.*

Choosing your welfare attorneys

Should you appoint the same or different people as your welfare attorney(s) and your property and affairs attorney(s)? In view of the considerable amount of work involved, it might seem a good idea to divide a lasting power of attorney in this way. Christine, for example, living hundreds of miles from her father, might suggest that she should look after the financial side of things and take on the property and affairs attorneyship, while Tom, living much closer, should concern himself with the actual care of their father and thus become his personal welfare attorney. But this approach, logical as it can seem, has dangers.

The reality is that in the field of eldercare, legal and financial matters are inextricably bound up with supervising care. If you are hiring somebody to visit your mother in a care home, you will want to know how you can get the most value for money from the arrangement while ensuring she receives the best care. The person on the ground who sees how good or poor the service actually is will have more impact in ensuring that it remains of high quality if they are also authorising payment. Someone dealing with the financial side far away may not have the incentive to generate as much money as possible from the estate so that better care can be delivered, because their involvement is too intermittent and their grasp of the needs on the ground too tenuous.

If you do propose to appoint different welfare and property and affairs attorneys, bear in mind the likely relationship between them and the extent to which they are likely to agree or seek to thwart the wishes of each other. This is important because the holders of PALPA will not have the legal authority that a welfare attorney has to make decisions in the care field, while the reverse is also true, although each must consult the other. So, if your welfare attorney decides that it would be in your best interests to move you to a particular care home but your PALPA, who would be responsible for organising your financial affairs to enable your estate to pay the care home bills, would be likely to disagree, you need to bear that in mind in your choice of individuals.

Sorting out difficulties

Perhaps you are concerned that powers of welfare attorney are being misused. If so, you should consult the Office of the Public Guardian, as you would if you were concerned about the abuse of a property and affairs attorneyship. The Guardian might need to refer the matter on to the Court of Protection to make a ruling about the capacity of the person involved or about the way in which the attorney powers should be used.

The Court of Protection can also make rulings about the welfare of people who have lost capacity which do not involve attorneyships or deputyships directly. For instance, perhaps your sister is looking after your father, whose cognitive powers are impaired, in her own home and refuses to allow you to visit him. You would like to see your father and also to be consulted about his care. In this case you could apply to the Court of Protection for an order allowing you contact with your father and giving you the right to be consulted. The Public Guardian provides information on how to do this.

Power of welfare attorney in Scotland

The Scottish equivalent of the power of personal welfare attorney in England and Wales is the power of welfare attorney. There are many similarities between the two legal instruments. Differences are confined mainly to the type of organisation responsible for administering the operation of the powers on the ground.

Powers of welfare attorney cannot be lawfully used until they have been registered, and the Public Guardian in Scotland is responsible for scrutinising registration applications. The document conferring power of attorney may contain a condition that the Guardian shall not register it until after they are satisfied that a particular event has occurred, most obviously a loss of mental capacity. If all is in order, the Guardian adds details of the power of attorney to a public register. However, while the Public Guardian supervises financial powers of attorney, other organisations supervise welfare powers.

Sheriffs sitting in local sheriff courts are responsible for dealing with any disputes about powers of welfare attorney, performing a similar role to judges in the Court of Protection of England and Wales. If someone wishes to appeal, perhaps that the event specified in a power of welfare attorney has not occurred, they do so to the sheriff. A sheriff has the power to order a welfare attorney to report back about the way in which they have exercised their powers during any period. The sheriff can also revoke any of the powers of the attorney or indeed the appointment of the attorney. Somebody aggrieved about a sheriff's decision can appeal to the Sheriff Principal or ultimately the Court of Sessions and then the Supreme Court.

Another option for a sheriff concerned about the operation of a particular power of welfare attorney is to order that it be supervised by a local authority. In this case a social worker with special training in the field of mental health matters and mental capacity, known as a mental health officer, would become involved. So local authorities play a role in way they do not south of the border.

If an attorney finds they do not have powers under their power of attorney that they consider they need, they could seek further power from the sheriff through an intervention order *(page 802)* or a guardianship order *(pages 764–6)*. The Scottish Government has set out clearly how welfare attorneys should go about exercising their powers in a document entitled *Code of Practice for Continuing and Welfare Attorneys*.

Local authorities have the responsibility of investigating complaints about the exercise of welfare powers and any suspicious circumstances of which they become aware. If such complaints are not investigated satisfactorily by a local authority, the Mental Welfare Commission for Scotland is empowered to make investigations itself. The Commission is an independent organisation funded by government which works to safeguard the rights and welfare of everyone with a mental disorder, including dementia. Anybody dissatisfied with the way in which a local authority has investigated a concern raised about the behaviour of a welfare attorney can approach the local authority or the Mental Welfare Commission for Scotland.

Local authorities also have to provide information and advice to people exercising welfare functions under the Scottish legislation when asked to do so. So, if you need advice on operating welfare powers of attorney, the social work department of your local authority should be your first port of call.

Local authorities' involvement in welfare functions under the mental capacity legislation is explained clearly in a free document which can be obtained from the Scottish government.[14] The Mental Welfare Commission for Scotland also provides a range of guides and a free phone helpline. Alzheimer Scotland provides guidance and a free 24-hour helpline.

Power of welfare attorney in Northern Ireland

Until the Mental Capacity Act (Northern Ireland) 2016 is commenced, no power of attorney in the field of health and welfare exists in Northern Ireland. Once the law is brought into effect, any adult will be able to grant a lasting power relating to care, treatment and personal welfare, so long as they have the mental capacity to do so. A personal welfare power will not be useable until the donor has lost mental capacity, and if it involves the granting of power to withhold life-saving treatment, that must be specified on the attorney form. The other provisions on welfare attorneyships are the same as those outlined for lasting power of attorney in the property and finance field *(see page 750)*, so the powers will be able to be used jointly or severally or both, and attorneys will be unable to appoint someone to replace them in their role – only the donor can appoint replacements. The involvement of the Public Guardian and the High Court in the new system in Northern Ireland will also work as described for property and finance powers. *I discuss the relative status of power of welfare attorney in Northern Ireland and an advance directive to refuse treatment on pages 1019–20.*

Powers of attorney

* Any of us could become incapable of handling important decisions over our lives because of brain injury or illness.

* Appoint one or more attorneys to act in your place if you should lose mental capacity.

* Choose your attorney carefully and don't automatically appoint your closest relative.

* Without an attorney, you could find court-appointed proxies or your local council taking control of your affairs.

* A personal welfare attorney can challenge care decisions.

* You don't need a solicitor to grant power of attorney, except in Scotland.

* Make fallback arrangements in case your attorney is unable to act for you.

* Attorneys are acting unlawfully unless their powers have been registered with the Public Guardian.

* Use the safeguards the system provides.

* Dementia does not prevent you from granting power of attorney.

Chapter 32

Deputies and guardians

Y ou hear that your aunt nearly burnt down her house because she left the gas on. Subsequent tests reveal that she has dementia. She will probably be unable to grant you power of attorney because she will be deemed incapable of understanding what she is doing. What steps can you take to safeguard her interests?

The Court of Protection cancels a power of attorney because attorneys have abused their power. What happens now?

An attorney has died or is too ill to act, and the donor, who has now lost mental capacity, failed to nominate a replacement attorney in the original attorneyship. Who can take over?

Deputies

In these situations anybody can apply to the Court of Protection to act as the 'deputy' for a person who has lost capacity. There can be one deputy or more than one; if more than one, they may act independently or together, as with power of attorney. A similar tool, called 'guardianship', is available in Scotland *(as explained below)*.

Deputyship differs fundamentally from attorneyship. As a deputy, you are authorised not to act on behalf of someone else, but on behalf of the Court of Protection. What happens is the Court assumes control of the individual's affairs but delegates specified tasks to one or more deputies, and the Office of the Public Guardian administers the system. So there is a layer of accountability and control involved additional to what obtains with attorneyships, designed to protect the person being represented in view of the fact that they have not selected their deputy and the deputy might have an ulterior motive. In other words, a deputy takes on the work and responsibilities that an attorney shoulders *(outlined in the previ-*

ous chapter), but at the same time has to account for their decisions and actions to the Public Guardian.[1]

A deputy usually has to report back to the Public Guardian annually and can be told to report more frequently: the Court of Protection possesses the discretion to require deputies to submit to the Public Guardian, 'Such reports at such times or at such intervals as the court may direct'.[2] Only if the assets of the person being represented are below about £20,000 and the Guardian has no concerns is a deputy relieved of the requirement to make an annual report (although the Guardian may still make inquiries about what the deputy has been doing).

For deputyships involving estates worth more than £20,000 an annual report must be submitted and the Guardian chooses one of three levels of supervision.[3] In addition, if the deputy proposes major spending, say, on property repairs, they may have to ask for the Guardian's permission to use the money of the person being represented to carry them out and submit estimates to the Guardian. The Guardian may seek the help of a visitor from the Court of Protection *(page 739)* to meet a deputy whom it considers needs advice or about whom it is concerned. In the latter case the visitor might perhaps talk to the deputy about the way in which they are making decisions or ask to see bank statements or health records.

An attorney – in contrast – is not obliged to send reports or seek authorisation from the Guardian unless the Guardian has so requested in that particular case. In view of this, many people who are deputies are relatives – perhaps nieces and nephews – of people who simply omitted to grant power of attorney and no longer have the mental capacity to do so. The deputies involved often have to do a lot of hard work, even more so than attorneys. They are bound to wish that the person they are representing had taken the relatively short time necessary to grant them power of attorney instead. They may well also regret the annual fee that the Public Guardian charges for supervision, which must be paid out of the estate of the person being represented.

Deputies are advised to keep their client's money separate from their own in a bank account opened in the name of the person being represented, as in an attorney situation. If a deputy sells somebody's property in order to pay care home bills, the money from the sale would be placed in that account. Deputies are advised to obtain advice from a financial advisor about where they place funds to provide a regular income for care home fees, and can pay for that advice with the assets of the person they are representing (although they cannot give any of their decision-making responsibilities to someone else). If they wish, deputies may use the Court of Protection's 'special account' to keep the money of the person they are representing. This is a safe place in which to place investments, as it is backed by the government. However, in 2017 it paid a low rate of interest, far less than National Savings (also, of course, government-backed).

Although much of the work of a deputy with financial powers is likely to involve paying bills, deputies are permitted to spend money on activities or items they consider would improve the quality of life of the person they are representing, so long as the terms of their deputyship allow this. If that person is living in a care home, money might perhaps be spent on paying for them to be taken out or to buy new clothes or items to enable them to pursue their hobbies. A deputy is allowed to make gifts as long as the powers the Court of Protection has given them allow this. Gifts might be made to charities that the person involved would have made or to people (including a deputy) on occasions such as birthdays when the person being represented has customarily made a gift, provided that the value of the gift is not unreasonable in the circumstances, not least the size of the person's estate.[4]

In most cases, a deputy is a family member who knows the person well. Sometimes however the Court of Protection decides to appoint a professional person, particularly if the person's financial affairs or care needs are complex. This could be the director of adult services of the local authority in whose area the person involved is living; it could be a solicitor who specialises in a particular area of law.

The Court of Protection can authorise that deputies be paid a fee for discharging their functions, to be taken from the estate of the person they are representing. If the Court appoints professional accountants or solicitors as deputies, their charges will eat into the older person's estate. In addition, the Guardian exacts fees for their own services. They impose a fixed fee to assess the level of supervision that will be required and then another fee to supervise the deputyship each year.

To apply to become a deputy, you should obtain a form from the Public Guardian. It is broken down according to the possible categories of activity in which you seek authorisation to act and asks for information about the person to be represented, such as the state benefits they receive and the extent of any business interests they have. You send the form to the Guardian, together with a fee. The Court of Protection will also need medical evidence to satisfy itself that the person involved is incapable of managing their own financial affairs because of a mental disorder, so you will need a doctor to fill in a form, for which they will probably charge a fee.

Sometimes attorneys find they do not have sufficient powers yet the person who granted the power is no longer able to give them extra powers under a power of attorney as they have lost the mental capacity to grant one. In that situation, the attorney could seek further powers by applying for a deputyship order.

Deputies have to comply with the principles of the Mental Capacity Act and have regard to the Code of Practice, just like attorneys (as described in the following chapter). Also, they must make sure that they only make the decisions that the Court of Protection has authorised them to make: their powers may be restricted because the Court considers it is unnecessary for them to cover certain areas or that the person being represented can still make certain decisions and rule that they should be allowed to do so.

If you are a deputy, it is worth notifying all the people and organisations such as banks and care homes that might make decisions about the person you are representing and about which you would expect to be consulted or notified, so long as these decisions fall within the scope of your deputyship.

Before the Mental Capacity Act came into force in 2007, 'receivers' performed a similar role to deputies. Those who were appointed before the Act came into operation are now treated as deputies and must behave in the way that a deputy created under the Act would. So, for instance, they must have regard to the Code of Practice that accompanies the Act and they must abide by the five principles of the mental capacity legislation (explained in the following chapter).

Deputies do not tend to be given powers in the field of health and welfare such as deciding where somebody should live. Major decisions in these areas can be made by the Court of Protection itself or by social care or health bodies. The Court is likely to appoint a deputy involving health and welfare only if a series of linked welfare decisions are likely to be required over time and it would not be beneficial or appropriate for each to be determined by the Court, or there are serious disagreements within the family which could have a detrimental impact on the person's care unless a deputy were appointed to make decisions.[5]

Guardians in Scotland

The equivalent to a deputy in Scotland is a 'guardian'. Anyone with an interest in the affairs and well-being of the person in question, such as a friend, relative, partner or lawyer, can apply for a guardianship order from a local sheriff court. The court will provide them with the relevant form to complete; it has to be submitted with supporting information – a report from a mental health officer of the local authority on the suitability of the applicant to be a guardian and two medical reports, no more than 30 days old, about the mental capacity of the person whom they are seeking to represent. The sheriff considers the applicant's suitability for the role, taking into account:

- their ability to manage financial or welfare matters
- any conflict of interest
- any adverse effect their appointment might have on the person to be represented
- their ease of access to them
- any undue concentration of power over that person which is likely to result

Sheriffs also consider whether the person in question actually needs to have a guardian. They might decide that an intervention order *(see page 802)* would be sufficient instead, for instance. Sheriffs are empowered to appoint an independent person (known as a 'safeguarder') who can elicit the views of the person in question and report them to the court to help the sheriff reach a decision. If the sheriff grants the guardianship order, the court will notify the person to be represented, the local authority where they live and the Public Guardian in Scotland, who will place details on a public register. If any welfare matters are covered, the Mental Welfare Commission for Scotland will also be notified *(see page 766)*.

Full details of the procedures for applying for guardianship powers and detailed guidance on how guardians should behave are set out in a code of practice for guardians published by the Scottish government.[6] Useful guidance is also published by Alzheimer Scotland and the Dementia Services Development Centre in Stirling.[7]

Anybody who held office as curator bonis when the Scottish legislation came into effect in 2001 automatically became a guardian of the adult involved with the power to manage their property and financial affairs.

As with deputies, guardians are frequently not relatives but officials in local authorities or professionals such as solicitors. Various fees must be paid, including a fee to the sheriff court to make an application; a fee to register the order with the Public Guardian; fees to the two doctors for their reports on the person's capacity in relation to the powers requested; and fees to solicitors if engaged. It is worth seeking legal advice before applying for an order, to make sure that the order will benefit the person concerned and is appropriate under the circumstances. Legal aid without a means-test is available for applications for guardianship orders that involve welfare powers. As with deputies in England and Wales, guardians can seek additional powers, in their case from the sheriff, although it is best to secure all the powers you think you will need when lodging the original application.

Local authorities must apply to the sheriff to take on guardianship powers themselves in cases where no other means are sufficient to safeguard the interests of the person involved.

Supervision of guardianships

In Scotland, the Public Guardian supervises guardianships involving property and money; they have the power to investigate any concerns. Anybody worried about the way in which guardianship powers are being used should approach the Public Guardian.

Local authorities are responsible for the supervision of guardianships involving welfare powers, just as they are for welfare attorneyships in Scotland. They must visit guardians and the person they represent within three months of the appointment and thereafter at intervals of six months. They have a duty to provide information and advice to all those exercising welfare functions under the mental capacity legislation. They are also responsible for investigating complaints about guardians, welfare attorneys and interveners *(see page 801)*.

As an additional safeguard, the Mental Welfare Commission for Scotland monitors the actions of local authorities in this field. It can carry out investigations if it believes that a person who is the subject of a guardianship order has not received adequate care or treatment or that they might have been ill-treated or neglected. This could mean challenging the way in which a local authority has carried out its powers as a guardian.

Deputies and controllers in Northern Ireland

The Mental Capacity Act (Northern Ireland) 2016 Act has enacted provisions involving deputies which, like the situation with power of attorney, mirror those obtaining in England and Wales. However, these provisions had not been brought into effect at the time of writing but were awaiting the drawing up of regulations and guidance to deputies and other legal representatives in the form of a code of practice.

The 2016 Act provides for the High Court to appoint a deputy for someone who lacks mental capacity in relation to a matter or matters about which a decision or decisions have to be made. Deputies will be able to be responsible for property and finance or health and welfare, although deputies (unlike attorneys) will be unable to refuse consent for life-saving treatment. The High Court will be empowered to revoke a deputy powers and Court Visitors will be able to make inquiries about how powers are being used, just as in England and Wales this is done by the Court of Protection's Court Visitors. The Public Guardian in Northern Ireland *(page 750)* will supervise deputies whom the Court has appointed. The Guardian will be responsible for receiving reports from deputies about the way in which they are discharging their responsibilities and reporting to the High Court on any matter relating to deputies.[8]

Until such time as the 2016 Act is brought into force, the situation in Northern Ireland is as follows. There is provision for the appointment of the equivalent of a deputy, called a 'controller'. Controllers cannot determine whether somebody should have medical treatment or where they should live – they are responsible only for financial affairs. The High Court, working through the Office of Care and Protection (OCP), appoints controllers, and the person being represented is known as 'the patient'. A relative, friend or professional such as a solicitor can apply to become somebody's controller if they produce medical evidence of the patient's lack of mental capacity.

The powers granted to controllers are usually quite specific, for instance to release money to pay bills, to carry on a business or to sell property, although the Court can vary them if it wishes at a later stage. If the patient should regain their mental powers, the OCP would discharge the controller.

If nobody wishes to act as somebody's controller or controllers disagree between themselves, the head of the OCP, known as 'the master', can order that an officer of the High Court is appointed. If the patient's assets are quite small, this can be done under a short procedure order.

The OCP publishes a detailed guide for controllers.[9] Fees to pay for the work of the OCP in handling controller matters are paid out of the patient's estate. Every health and social care trust has a legal duty to inform the OCP of any person within its area who is incapable as a result of a mental disorder of managing their property and affairs and who does not have anybody who is doing so or going to do so on their behalf. The trust could ask the OCP to take specific action such as to freeze their bank account or make an order allowing an official of the trust to take specific actions.

As elsewhere in the UK, it is a good idea to to choose your own attorneys and decide which powers you wish to give them if you can, rather than find yourself represented by a controller or an official of a health and social care trust.

Deputies and guardians

* In England and Wales, the Court of Protection can appoint a deputy to represent somebody who has not granted power of attorney.

* Deputies can be solicitors or ordinary individuals.

* Deputies are subject to more scrutiny and control than attorneys.

* Deputies are more expensive than attorneys.

* Well-meaning relatives and friends find their lives easier if they hold power of attorney.

* Deputies usually deal only with financial and property matters.

* In Scotland guardians are appointed by local sheriffs.

* The chief social work officer of a Scottish local authority may be appointed as somebody's guardian.

* Approach the local sheriff court or the Mental Welfare Commission for Scotland if you are concerned about the way a local authority is using its powers.

* In Northern Ireland, the Office of Care and Protection can appoint a proxy to act for somebody with limited mental capacity.

* Notify all the people and organisations whom you wish to learn of your status as deputy or guardian.

Chapter 33

How representatives should behave

How are deputies, guardians and people with registered power of attorney to act day by day as proxy decision-makers for people with limited mental capacity? Should they step in and take every decision for the person they represent, or just a few? What should they do if their view of the way a matter should be decided conflicts with the wishes of the person themselves?

And how should care assistants, doctors, nurses, social workers and others working in a professional capacity or for remuneration for people with limited mental capacity approach proxy decision-making? In this chapter I discuss the principles that the law stipulates should guide the behaviour of these people too.

Key to the system of representation is the concept of mental capacity. This usually means the mental ability to take a decision at the time it needs to be taken. In other words, it is task or decision specific. Somebody might be incapable of managing their financial affairs, yet be capable of deciding whether they would like to go swimming or who they wish to care for them. So just how can mental capacity be determined? And what can be done if the assessors have wrongly concluded that somebody lacks mental capacity?

Health and social care authorities have the right to take certain major decisions with potentially far-reaching consequences on behalf of people who lack mental capacity if those involved do not have anybody such as an attorney suitable and able to take the decisions for them. These decisions include whether somebody should receive important medical treatment and whether they should move from their own home into a care home, even if they do not wish to do so.

In this chapter I examine:

▶ the principles that should underlie the behaviour of legal representatives and people working for remuneration looking after those whose mental abilities are limited

▶ the concept of mental capacity, how it is determined and what to do if you wish to challenge an assertion that your or someone else's capacity is, or is not, impaired

▶ the powers of health and social care authorities to take major decisions on behalf of people with limited capacity and the safeguards to ensure they do not exceed their power or act unwisely

Guiding principles on behaviour

The Mental Capacity Act 2005 sets out how people who are representing those whose mental capacity is impaired must behave. This law applies in England and Wales; as we shall see in a moment, very similar instructions apply elsewhere in the UK. The law puts forward five principles and lays on representatives and others a legal duty to respect them.[1]

The Lord Chancellor has produced a Code of Practice which explains how these principles should be put into effect in England and Wales.[2] The people to whom it applies *(see below)* must 'have regard to' the Code when acting or making decisions on behalf of somebody who lacks the capacity to make a decision for themselves and must be prepared to explain how they have had regard to it.

The categories of people to whom the five principles and the Code applies are:

● attorneys acting under a lasting power of attorney

● deputies

● anybody acting in a professional capacity in the care or treatment of somebody who lacks capacity

● anybody who is being paid to carry out work involving the care or treatment of somebody who lacks capacity

● independent mental capacity advocates *(explained on pages 784–5)* [3]

In other words, attorneys, deputies, doctors, nurses, social workers, care home managers homecare agency managers, healthcare assistants, care assistants, physiotherapists, occupational therapists, independent mental capacity advocates and other people caring for people who lack mental capacity should all ensure that all their actions and decisions comply with the Act and have regard to the Code.

Unpaid family carers, other family members, friends, neighbours and professionals such as police officers and accountants are not legally obliged to do this. But the Act and Code nonetheless provide an invaluable framework to guide their actions and attitudes.

So, what are the guiding principles set down in the legislation?

Principle 1: A person must be assumed to have capacity unless it is established that they lack capacity

This important principle effectively states that everyone has the right to make their own decisions and must be assumed to have the mental capacity to do so until proven otherwise.

In other words, nobody must assume someone lacks capacity because they are old or have an unusual appearance or have a diagnosis of, say, Down's syndrome or dementia. Some people with dementia retain the ability to make complex decisions for years, perhaps for the remainder of their lives. The onus is on others to establish that the person in question lacks the mental ability to make a particular decision at a particular time.

In the past, relatives, social workers, doctors and others often took decisions on behalf of older people because they considered that they must know best. Often the wishes of the older person were disregarded and by no means all the decisions that resulted were actually in their best interests. For example, somebody who had had a stroke might be moved into a care home by their relatives or social services or both acting together, on the assumption that they were now incapable of deciding where they should live and others automatically knew what was best for them.

The legislation states quite clearly that everybody in such a situation – professionals, relatives and so on – must assume that the individual has the mental ability to make their own decisions and to communicate them, unless it can be demonstrated that they do not.[4] If the capacity to take decisions is likely to improve, then the decision on whether somebody has capacity should be delayed until that time.

Principle 2: A person is not to be treated as unable to make a decision unless all practicable steps to help them to do so have been taken without success

This principle means that we all have the right to be supported to make our own decisions. All reasonable assistance should be given to help somebody to make their own decisions and to communicate those decisions before it can be assumed that they have lost capacity.

The Code of Practice accompanying the Mental Capacity Act stresses that every effort must (not should: *must*) be made to enable the person involved to make the decision themselves, and explains that this might mean:

- writing things down for people who cannot hear
- obtaining the help of an interpreter
- providing material in large print in the individual's mother tongue
- communicating by sign language or through pictures[5]

Implications

Clearly, principles 1 and 2 should inform the way in which staff in care facilities should behave towards people who may or may not have lost capacity. They should allow somebody who is perhaps in the early stages of dementia to determine as many aspects of their life as possible, and support them in doing so. Staff should not automatically choose how the person involved should spend their time, or whom they should see, or what they should eat.

An implication of principles 1 and 2 is that the donors of powers of attorney may well continue to make all sorts of decisions even after the attorneyship has been registered. This is because, as the Public Guardian says: 'There is no one point at which you are treated as having lost capacity to manage your property and affairs. Your attorney(s) must help you to make as many of your own decisions as you can.'[6]

In practice, then, much day-to-day decision-making should remain with the donor: although they may lack the capacity to weigh up all the factors in, for example, deciding whether to accept medical treatment which could have damaging side-effects, they may still be perfectly capable of coming to a decision about the myriad of less complicated and less far-reaching choices which pepper our days. Attorneys (and deputies) should therefore only take decisions which, on the balance of probabilities, the donor cannot take. And they must support the donor to take as many decisions as they can.

Principle 3: A person is not to be treated as unable to make a decision merely because they make an unwise decision

All of us make unwise decisions all the time, or decisions that appear strange to other people. The legislation asserts that making an unwise decision is not to be taken as evidence of lack of mental capacity. If somebody decides, for example, that they wish to live frugally so as to channel most of their wealth to an animal rescue centre, that decision is theirs to make and does not point to a loss of their mental capacity to weigh up the pros and cons and take that decision.

Older people can find themselves under pressure from relatives and from health or social care personnel to take steps to reduce the risks of having accidents such as falls. An elderly woman who has broken her hip through a fall and spent a long time in hospital recovering may find the hospital's social care staff urging her to go and live in a care home where they claim she will be safer. She may or may not be safer there, but she is entitled to take her own decision, even if it will leave her at higher risk of another fall. Only if she lacks the mental capacity to weigh up the pros and cons and take the decision herself could somebody else force her to move into a care home, and this would entail particular procedures.

Principle 4: An act done, or decision made, under this legislation for or on behalf of a person who lacks capacity must be done, or made, in their best interests

In other words, the decision must be in the best interests of the person involved, not those of anybody else, such as their child or partner. *(I explore this important principle further on pages 781–92.)*

Principle 5: Before the act is performed, or the decision is made on behalf of someone who has lost capacity, regard must be had to whether the purpose for which it is needed can be as effectively achieved in a way that is less restrictive of the person's rights and freedom of action

This means that any decision taken on behalf of someone who lacks capacity must be the option that least restricts their rights and freedoms. So if the woman in hospital after a fall lacks the capacity to decide where she should live and her attorney(s) or social care authority decide that it is in her best interests that she should move to a care home, they must ensure that her rights and freedoms are restricted as little as possible. This might mean, for instance, that she should enter the home as a temporary resident in order to keep open the option that she might move back to her own home if her condition should improve.

Scotland

The main piece of Scottish legislation on representation for people whose capacity is impaired, the Adults with Incapacity (Scotland) Act 2000, also focuses on principles on which the behaviour of attorneys and others should be based. Some are similar to those for England and Wales. Thus, emphasis is placed on presuming capacity; any intervention on behalf of someone who lacks capacity must be the one which involves the least restriction on that person's freedoms; and certain categories of people must be consulted before a decision is taken *(listed on page 789)*. The Scottish principles go further than those in England and Wales in saying that, where practicable, attorneys, guardians and care home managers should encourage people who lack capacity to exercise their skills concerning their property, financial affairs and personal welfare and to develop new ones. And while action taken in England and Wales must be in the person's best interests, the criterion in Scotland is that it must benefit the person, and that benefit could not reasonably be achieved without the intervention.[7]

Scottish ministers are required by law to prepare codes of practice providing guidance for people and organisations exercising functions under the mental capacity legislation. The Scottish government has published detailed, separate, free codes for attorneys, guardians, local councils and people with intervention order powers.[8]

How mental capacity is assessed

Whether somebody does or does not possess mental capacity is clearly key to the operation of the system of attorneyship and deputyship. But just what is capacity?

The Mental Capacity Act of 2005 defines a person who lacks mental capacity as follows: 'A person lacks capacity in relation to a matter if at the material time he is unable to make a decision for himself in relation to the matter because of an impairment, or a disturbance in the functioning of, the mind or brain.'[9]

A determination that somebody has lost capacity is thus a two-stage process. First, it has to be established that some impairment or disturbance in the brain or mind is present; second, the question as to whether this impairment or disturbance prevents the person involved being able to make a decision must be addressed.

In other words, a medical diagnosis is insufficient under the provisions of the Act to establish that somebody has lost mental capacity. What matters is whether the balance of probabilities suggests that they are capable of making a particular decision at a particular time.

The most common reason why older people see a significant permanent reduction in their mental ability is the onset of dementia *(see pages 26–7 and 428–30 for a description of the nature of the condition)*. They may well have many years of life ahead of them and thus many different decisions to take. Deciding whether or not they are capable of making their most important decisions themselves is thus of key importance.

The first stage in establishing whether somebody with suspected dementia lacks the capacity to make a particular decision, for example whether they should go and live with their son or move into a care facility, is to establish whether they do actually have an impairment or disturbance of the brain, such as dementia.

Yet establishing whether somebody has dementia is not straightforward. There is no simple test, such as a blood test. Instead diagnosis relies largely on identifying symptoms of the condition through carrying out tests of mental ability and trying to work out whether the results point to a progressive reduction in the person's mental powers. Yet development of this condition does not affect somebody's mental ability in a clear-cut way. Dementia develops gradually, and different individuals are affected in different ways in terms of their ability to think logically, to reason and to remember.

If a brain impairment or disturbance such as dementia is diagnosed, the person establishing capacity then has to consider whether this means that decision-making ability has been lost. The Mental Capacity Act explains that somebody is to be considered unable to make a decision for themselves if they are unable:

- to understand the information relevant to the decision
- to retain that information
- to use or weigh that information as part of the process of making the decision, or
- to communicate their decision (whether by talking, using sign language or any other means).[10]

In other words, to be able to make a decision, somebody must be able to understand the likely consequences both of deciding one way or another and of failing to make the decision. Should they forget the information relevant to the decision later on, that should not prevent their being regarded as able to make the decision at the time that they make it.[11]

Establishing capacity is a complex task. It may well require the assessor to set aside plenty of time and brief themselves on legal and financial matters pertaining to their patient. In Chapter 4 of the Code of Practice associated with the Mental Capacity Act 2005, the Lord Chancellor sets out how assessors should approach their work.

Take the case of a solicitor or perhaps a doctor trying to establish whether somebody has the mental capacity to make a will. To possess the necessary capacity, the person involved must be able to understand the nature and effect of making a will, the overall extent of their estate (not necessarily down to the last penny) and the claims of those people whom they have included and those they have excluded but who might expect to benefit from their estate. Finally, to have the capacity to make a will, the person must not have a mental illness which influences their ability to make bequests they would otherwise have included – for instance, one which gives rise to delusions or paranoia about particular individuals, whom they may proceed to disinherit.[12]

It is not only attorneys and others acting for people who lack capacity who are required by law to abide by the principles of the mental capacity legislation: so too must people trying to establish whether someone has the mental capacity to take a decision.[13] So they should recognise that capacity can fluctuate over time, with the ability to make decisions varying according to time of day, feeling of well-being and level of support. Delirium can cause somebody to become temporarily confused; a major stroke or a brain injury can impair someone's mental powers, but these may be recovered. Assessments of dementia and of capacity should be delayed until the patient recovers their maximum mental ability. Or they should be timed to take into account temporary fluctuations of ability. My friend John *(whose homecare arrangements I described on pages 517–9)* was mentally acute in the mornings but by the evening, speaking incomprehensibly. Any assessment of capacity should therefore have taken place in the morning, when he was most lucid, and been adjusted to ensure that John's hearing and eyesight limitations did not affect the assessment of his cognitive ability to take a decision.

Often the question of capacity arises when somebody is extremely ill and coming towards the end of their life. Perhaps decisions are to be faced about whether medical treatment designed to cure them should be continued. Again the patient's condition may fluctuate and any test of capacity should be taken when their mental powers are at their most acute. But it may be clear that they have only a minimal grasp of what is going on around them. As we see below, if the person lacks capacity to declare whether they wish to receive the medical treatment that a doctor is offering, then the doctor can take the decision, after consulting particular individuals. However, if the patient has made an advance directive to refuse treatment, the treatment must not be given *(see page 1017)*.

Inability to convey thoughts and wishes

There is a chance that an accident, or perhaps a stroke, might take away somebody's means of conveying thoughts and wishes, even though the mental apparatus to devise such thoughts and wishes remains intact. In very rare cases this takes the form of 'locked-in syndrome', in which somebody retains the mental capacity to make decisions about their life but lacks the wherewithal to verbally communicate them because the muscles of their face have been paralysed.

If somebody can communicate in some way, even if only by blinking, yet their mental abilities remain intact, they are deemed to possess mental capacity. If they cannot communicate their views at all, they are deemed to be in the same situation as somebody whose mental capacity is impaired. Hence part 'd' of the definition of inability to make a decision *(quoted on page 775)*.

Mental incapacity in Scotland

North of the border, the definition of someone considered to lack capacity is slightly different from that in England and Wales: it also includes having the ability to act and also to remember that one has made a decision. The legislation states that someone is considered to lack capacity if they are incapable of:

- making decisions; or
- communicating decisions; or
- understanding decisions; or
- retaining the memory of decisions, or
- acting[14]

The reason for their being unable to do any of these things must be that they have a mental disorder or they are unable to communicate because of a physical disability. However, if this inability to communicate can be remedied, whether by some mechanical aid or human help, they are not considered to lack mental capacity.[15]

Differences in the definition of capacity probably do not result in significant differences in the proportion of people north and south of the border being assessed as lacking capacity. In most cases assessment of capacity in Scotland turns on whether someone can make a particular decision at a particular time, just as it does in England and Wales.

Challenging assessments of mental capacity

Assessments of mental capacity can be helpful as a means of authorising attorneys and other representatives to take action for people who lose the ability to make decisions for themselves. However, some people commissioning an assessment may not have the best interests of the subject in mind. A son aggrieved that his father has recently changed his will in favour of his new partner might seek a formal assessment of capacity to prove that his father could not have understood what he was doing. Or a daughter keen to take over her mother's affairs might have an assessment carried out to support her application to register a power of attorney and thus get her hands on her mother's estate.

Ignorance can undermine the system too. A representative taking decisions on behalf of somebody else might confuse temporary delirium with impaired mental capacity. Or they might assume that somebody who has a diagnosis of dementia necessarily lacks the ability to make decisions they are in fact perfectly capable of making. Or they might be unfamiliar with the circumstances in which an assessment of capacity is called for.

This ignorance may not be confined to lay people, A worrying survey, albeit some years ago, in 2010, by the Mental Health Foundation found that in 25 per cent of cases where professionals were making decisions on behalf of somebody with alleged lack of capacity, they assumed the person's lack of capacity to make that decision on the basis of their illness, disability, age, behaviour, appearance or because they thought they were making an unwise decision – not an assessment of their actual mental capacity. This although the first principle of the legislation is to presume that somebody has capacity unless proved otherwise.[16]

Appealing against an incorrect assessment of mental capacity

A key weakness of the present system in England and Wales is the lack of any formal appeal system for somebody who has been assessed as lacking mental capacity. Somebody so assessed by just one professional can be transferred against their wishes to a care home or other institution with little or no access to appeal. And once in the institution, they may have little prospect of ever being able to leave.

This is in striking contrast to the situation of people who are 'sectioned' – that is, admitted against their will for treatment for a mental condition, but under mental health legislation. In that case, three independent recommendations are required. The person involved has access to legal representation and at least two rights of appeal. This for admission for only 28 days.

So, what can you do if you consider that you (or somebody else) have been wrongly assessed as lacking mental capacity in deciding, for instance, whether you should move to a care home or be given a particular medical treatment?

Try to find out:

✓ when the assessment took place (the date and the time of day)

✓ who did it and their qualifications

✓ whether anybody else was present

✓ the method used

✓ what steps were taken to compensate for any factors which might have affected your (or the person's) true mental capacity

For instance, you might find out that the assessment of capacity was carried out by a doctor who had little understanding of the legislation. In an investigation in 2014, a House of Lords select committee noted that GPs were identified as having poor understanding of the Act and recommended that their training in this area should be improved.[17]

Armed with such information as you can discover, write to the chief executive of the social services authority or hospital trust involved and urge them to set in motion an urgent review of the assessment. Point out why you think it was flawed. Speed is advisable, because after assessment of capacity, social services often take charge and decide where somebody should live. So, the sooner you can interrupt the process, the better. When you approach the social care or health body, explain that you propose to take the matter to other organisations if necessary.

None of these steps will be easy, particularly if you are operating on your own from a hospital bed. If you are, ask PALS or in Wales, the local community health council for help *(see page 332–3)*.

If the organisation responsible for the assessment refuses to set it aside, try to persuade it to refer the case to the Court of Protection *(described on page 739)*, which can adjudicate on capacity in cases where it is disputed. Health trusts should refer disputes involving major decisions concerning medical treatment to the Court, as should social care authorities for disagreements involving decisions that affect the welfare of people who lack mental capacity.[18]

If the trust or authority fails make a reference, you could do so yourself if you are the person whose lack of capacity is alleged or you are a friend, relative, professional, paid carer or advocate (including an independent mental capacity advocate – *see below).*

Taking a case to the Court of Protection sounds daunting, but it need not be. You do not have to instruct a solicitor to act for you: the Court has been designed to be accessible to those without legal representation. If you do use a solicitor, legal aid may be available. An organisation called Community Legal Advice holds lists of solicitors who deal with Court of Protection work and legal aid cases. A handy guide to accessing the Court, written for friends and relatives of people who may lack capacity (as well as professional social care and health staff), is published by the Social Care Institute for Excellence.[19]

Other steps that might help are to lodge an official complaint about what has happened to the social care or health body responsible. You could also ask the relevant ombudsman service to investigate. If your complaint is against a social care organisation in England, go to the Local Government Ombudsman; for a health complaint in England, approach the Parliamentary and Health Service Ombudsman. The Public Services Ombudsman for Wales investigates complaints in both areas as does the Northern Ireland Ombudsman. *(I discuss complaints in the fields of social care and health on pages 575–83 and 334–41 respectively.)*

The Care Quality Commission has no direct powers to enforce the mental capacity legislation, but you could contact it nonetheless, as it registers and inspects health and social care facilities and services in England. In Wales, you could contact the Healthcare Inspectorate Wales, which registers and inspects healthcare services and also monitors the working of the mental health legislation. You may also wish to alert patients' organisations such as, in England, Healthwatch *(pages 329–31).*

Another line of attack is to challenge the assessment of the brain impairment that is the first stage in an assessment of mental incapacity. Again, try to find out some details of the circumstances of this diagnosis, whether it be of dementia, learning disability, brain impairment through a stroke, or whatever. As this is a medical assessment, you could ask for a second opinion of it. Try to establish:

✓ when the assessment took place (the date and the time of day, which might affect mental powers)

✓ who did the assessment and their qualifications

✓ whether anybody else was present apart from the person being assessed

✓ the method used

✓ what steps were taken to compensate for any factors which might have affected the person's understanding or ability to communicate, or masked their true mental powers

The factors in the last category could include difficulty in speaking, hearing or seeing, unfamiliarity with spoken English or with the culture that informed the questions posed to test mental powers. *(See page 433–4.)*

Challenging capacity assessments in Scotland

For people in Scotland, the system of appealing against decisions involving capacity can seem more accessible compared to that south of the border as it involves local courts, and plainly most people will be far more familiar with their local sheriff court than those in England and Wales will be with the Court of Protection. What is more, the legislation north of the border specifically states that anybody who wishes to appeal against a decision about incapacity – whether the person affected or anybody else claiming an interest in their property, financial affairs or welfare relating to the purpose for which the decision about incapacity was made – can do so to the sheriff.[20] So, if you believe that your attorney is trying to take on their powers on the false assertion that you or somebody else has lost mental capacity, get in touch with the local sheriff court. Anybody who wishes to challenge the decision of such a court can appeal to the Sheriff Principal or, failing satisfaction there, the Court of Session. Before you go ahead, you could seek advice from the Office of the Public Guardian or the Mental Welfare Commission for Scotland.

In Chapter 32 we noted that if a social care body wished to take on the powers of a 'guardian' (and thus, perhaps, place someone in a care home against their will), it had to apply for guardianship powers to a sheriff court. In other words, the matter is taken outside the closed world of social care (in which it remains in England and Wales) into the courts system. That application must be supported by two independent medical reports of incapacity, which are based on an examination and assessment of the person involved. Anybody wishing to challenge the request for guardianship powers and/or the assessment of incapacity should contact their sheriff court.

Special rules for health and social care officials

Health and social care authorities and the officials acting on their behalf must comply with the five principles discussed above when acting with or on behalf of somebody with limited mental capacity. So they must act in the best interests of the person concerned, for example. But there are certain additional rules and procedures which apply specifically to them. It is important to know what these are, as failure to comply with them can have disastrous consequences for people with real or alleged limitations in their mental powers.

Supposing somebody needs medical treatment such as a pain-killing drug (which will of course have side-effects and drawbacks) or an operation (which might save a life or, on the other hand, possibly kill or maim). A doctor would have to obtain the patient's consent before administering the treatment *(as we saw on page 283)*. But what if the patient lacks the mental capacity to weigh up the pros and cons and grant or withhold consent? In that case, the healthcare official can go ahead and provide the treatment, but only after going through procedures designed to safeguard the interests and human rights of the patient.

Or perhaps social care officials consider that somebody should move to a care home, but the person involved lacks the mental capacity to handle such a complex decision themselves. If they have nobody suitable to act for them, social services can step in and make the necessary decision, even if it is contrary to the person's wishes. But here too safeguards exist to protect the person additional to the requirement that social services must act in the person's best interests and have regard to the Code of Practice.

Here are the safeguards obtaining in England and Wales.

1. Requirement to consult

In working out what the best interests of somebody with limited mental capacity might be both health and social care officials in England and Wales have a duty under the mental capacity legislation to take into account the views of that person and also those of certain other categories of people, if it is practicable and appropriate to consult them. These categories are:

(i) any attorney or deputy

(ii) any unpaid carer

(iii) anyone 'interested in the welfare' of the person involved

(iv) and 'anyone named by the person as someone to be consulted on the matter in question or on matters of that kind'[21]

Although next-of-kin are usually consulted, the law in England and Wales does not require this; next-of-kin are often consulted by virtue of their status as unpaid carers or attorneys. I set out the similar list of people who must be consulted according to the legislation in **Scotland** below *(see page 789)*.

It might seem odd that an attorney or deputy has to be consulted, but that attorney or deputy might not be aware of the situation or might not be in a position to act, perhaps because they themselves are unwell, live far away or have died.

What does the proviso 'if it is practicable and appropriate to consult them' mean? Well, Parliament's intention certainly was not to let decision-makers off the hook easily. The government's explanatory notes on the legislation explain:

> No consultation may be possible in an emergency situation and it might not be appropriate for every day-to-day decision (such as whether to watch television). For significant, non-urgent decisions, including where there is a series of minor decisions that cumulatively become significant, consultation will be required, as being both practicable and appropriate.[22]

Plainly, anybody who wishes to be consulted and considers they fall into one or more of the categories above should approach health and/or social care to say that they expect to be consulted, just to be on the safe side. After all, the legislation says that people must be consulted only if it is practicable and appropriate to consult them, or in **Scotland** only 'insofar as that can be ascertained by any means of communication'. If you think a key decision on carrying out a test or an examination might be taken without seeking your views, explain to the relevant professional that you expect to be consulted.

For example, when my mother, who had dementia, was admitted to a hospital ward suffering from a stroke, nobody asked for my consent (as her attorney) before inserting a urinary catheter. There are pros and cons to this procedure and it distressed my mother. I regret not making it clear to the ward manager that I expected my consent to be sought *(see also pages 419–22)*.

If you have no attorney, deputy, close relative or carer, do think seriously about selecting somebody (or more than one person) who would fall into the fourth category above. You might perhaps ask a friend or current or former work colleague whom you trust and who knows you well whether they would agree to be a named person to be consulted.

But a named consultee can also be helpful when the views of consultees in the other categories are being sought. A son acting as attorney might, for example, be much influenced by social services, who tell him that there is no alternative to his mother moving to a particular care home. Perhaps that would be the best environment for her; perhaps another arrangement would be better. A close friend of his mother, acting in her capacity as a named consultee, could be invaluable in illuminating the choices involved, particularly if the son lives in a different area, has not visited his mother frequently and is not well acquainted with her current tastes and way of life.

The named consultee has to have been authorised by the person involved. This is not the case for somebody in the third category, who is 'interested in the welfare' of the person involved. Perhaps you are a neighbour or friend who visits an older person who has no attorneys or close family and you are keen that any decisions about their care should be as well-informed as possible. Why not put yourself forward as somebody interested in their welfare?

In my experience, health and social care officials often treat somebody who shows concern but is not a blood relative with suspicion. So, if you wish to be recognised as falling into categories three or four, draw up a formal letter or statement, signed and dated, which explains your role and that your status arises from the Mental Capacity Act 2005, Section 4 (7). If possible, find somebody with standing to give it their imprimatur. For example, I acted as the named consultee of a woman whom I had got to know over many months as her church visitor during the mid-2000s. Anxious about her future welfare, I asked our church minister to ask her whether she would like me to act in this way. When she replied that she would, he wrote an authorisation letter which I used when she was living in a care home and later moved into hospital.

2. Independent Mental Capacity Advocates

The requirement to consult as described above relates to decisions in which the best interests of the person involved have to be weighed up. But when certain decisions with potentially very far-reaching consequences are to be taken by health and/or social care officials, they are expected to seek out the views of an entirely different category of consultee. This is an 'independent mental capacity advocate', or IMCA. A health or social care body has a legal duty to 'make such arrangements as it considers reasonable' to enable an IMCA to represent and support somebody if they lack capacity and they have no family or friends who are available or considered appropriate to be consulted on their behalf. The types of decision which trigger the requirement for an IMCA are as follows:

- a move into a care home for more than eight weeks (this includes a move from one care home to a different one)

- a move into hospital for more than 28 days (this includes a move to a different hospital)

- significant medical treatment, such as major surgery, chemo-therapy, artificial ventilation and the withdrawal of artificial feeding or provision of fluid

- restriction of a person's freedom; this could involve placing somebody in a care home and restricting their ability to leave it, *as explained in the next section.*[23]

The independent mental capacity advocate must talk to the person involved, represent their views and consider whether the steps health or social care proposes are in their best interests. Health and social care must take the IMCA's views into account when reaching their decision, although they are not obliged to go along with their recommendations. When working out what course of action would be in the best interests of the person involved, IMCAs must have regard to the detailed Code of Practice on the Mental Capacity Act *(page 753)*. They are legally obliged to comply with the five principles underlying the Act *(as explained on pages 770–4)*.

Despite the legal requirement laid upon them, the extent to which health and social services authorities actually commission IMCAs varied widely, according to a House of Lords select committee's examination on the working of the mental capacity legislation in 2014.[24] If you have not been offered an IMCA and you think you qualify, ask for one. An IM-CA's familiarity with the health and social care systems ought to help you secure the outcomes you want; they might also be able to support you in applying to the Court of Protection or doing so themselves, for instance. But consider whether the person who is sent would be helpful *(perhaps by using the criteria for advocates of all types on pages 808–10)*. The Lords reported that not all IMCAs are as good as they might be in championing the interests of the people they are supposed to serve.[25]

Social care authorities are separately required to provide an independent advocate to support someone for whom they carry out various other assessments and who would have substantial difficulty in being involved. This right embraces people who lack mental capacity, but it is not restricted to them. *(See pages 806–8 for more information.)*

3. The deprivation of liberty safeguards (DOLS)
The third safeguard in England and Wales involves procedures which must be gone through if somebody with reduced mental capacity is being deprived of one or more of their basic freedoms.

Perhaps a doctor considers that somebody without the capacity to agree should be kept in hospital for treatment against their will. Perhaps someone is living in a care home and those responsible for their care wish to place an ongoing restriction on their ability to move freely in and out of the front door. 'Deprivation of liberty' is usually considered to involve more than simply locking a door to stop somebody coming to harm on one or a small number of occasions. Rather, it involves situations in which restraint is frequent, cumulative and ongoing, or if there are other factors present.

Some of the other ways in which the liberty of somebody might be constrained and in which the DOLS procedures would apply include preventing their:

- going out without close supervision

- getting out of bed through the use of guard rails

- moving freely in a particular room or suite of rooms

- remaining alert through the administration of anti-psychotic drugs or tranquillisers *(see page 448)*

The Deprivation of Liberty Safeguards have been devised to comply with human rights legislation by safeguarding individuals against unwarranted restrictions on their liberty. They lay down that nobody who lacks mental capacity can be deprived of their liberty in a hospital or care home unless that deprivation has been authorised.[26]

An important legal judgement in 2014 widened the range of locations where the safeguards must be used. The UK Supreme Court held that deprivation can occur in people's homes so long as the state (in other words, usually a social care authority) is responsible for imposing the arrangements. It also laid down rules in other areas. Also, before this judgment, it had sometimes been argued that if someone was failing to protest against their confinement, a deprivation of liberty procedure was not needed. Not so now. The Supreme Court stated that the conditions when a DOLS is called for are simply that the individual in question:

- lacks the mental capacity to agree to arrangements for their care or treatment

- is under continuous supervision and control and

- is not free to leave[27]

This means that if a family prevent their relative with dementia from leaving the house perhaps through withholding a door key or putting barriers in their path, they can do so lawfully. But if this restriction is made with social services' involvement, a formal DOLS consent must first be obtained.

If the place where the deprivation of liberty is proposed or is already taking place is a hospital or a care home, the 'managing authority' – the hospital or home where the person involved is living or is to live – must apply for authorisation to deprive somebody of their liberty from a 'supervisory body'. The latter is the relevant local authority social services department or NHS organisation. The managing authority must be able to demonstrate that the restriction that is proposed:

- is in the person's best interests
- is necessary to prevent harm to them and
- is a proportionate response to the risk of harm

Before authorising the deprivation, the supervisory body must carry out assessments of the mental health of the person, their mental capacity and what action would be in their best interests. Two assessors must be involved. An IMCA *(see pages 784–5)* must be appointed in the absence of anyone suitable to consult about what would be in the person's best interests. The maximum period for which an authorisation to deprive somebody of their liberty can be granted is 12 months. An authorisation can be reviewed, renewed or ended at any point.

The Lord Chancellor has drawn up a lengthy code which sets out how the safeguards should work. Just like the main code for the mental capacity legislation, this has the force of law. It says that assessors should ensure that:

- deprivation of liberty is avoided whenever possible
- it is permitted only where it is in the best interests of the person involved and it is the only way to keep them safe
- it lasts for as short a time as possible and
- it is made only so that a particular plan of treatment or course of action can be accomplished.[28]

If the restrictions on someone's liberty are taking place or are proposed in other locations, such as in their own home or that of a relative, social services must apply for authorisation to the Court of Protection *(page 739)*.

If you are concerned that these safeguards should have been used in your case or that of somebody else, tell the social care or health body involved in the first instance. You may wish to ask the Office of the Public Guardian for advice or even contact the Court of Protection.

Perhaps you are concerned about a situation in which the freedoms of a vulnerable person including someone who lacks mental capacity seem to be restricted in a domestic situation that has not involved social services and in which DOLS would not apply. Approach the social services department of the local authority in which the person involved is living and ask to speak to the adult safeguarding officer. The situation of which you are aware could be associated with elder abuse and social services has a duty to investigate cases of possible abuse *(as explained on page 566)*.

Safeguards in Scotland

North of the border, the apparatus that seeks to protect people with real or alleged limitations in their mental capacity against actions by social care authorities that are not actually in the person's best interests is different from that in England and Wales. Instead of the system of independent mental capacity advocates and deprivation of liberty safeguards (neither of which apply in Scotland), the outside world of sheriff courts provides a check on the actions of social work departments.

If a social work department in Scotland wishes to move somebody who lacks mental capacity to a care home against their will, a move that would amount to a deprivation of their liberty, and they do not have a welfare attorney or a guardian, the department must seek authorisation by applying to its local sheriff for special powers – a welfare guardianship order *(see pages 764–6)* or an intervention order with relevant decision-making powers *(page 802)*.[29]

The chief social work officer (who makes the application) must produce two medical certificates confirming incapacity. If the application involves welfare powers, as it would for placement in a care home, they must also submit to the sheriff a report from a mental health officer of the local authority.

A welfare guardianship granted by a sheriff to the chief social work officer of a council and implemented day by day by its mental health officer might grant powers to:

- decide where the person involved should live
- organise the provision of care, including care in the person's own home
- decide with whom they should or should not have contact
- make decisions on their social and cultural activities

- consent or withhold consent to medical treatment
- provide access for them to healthcare services

A sheriff could decide that the order should be time-limited, particularly if the person might regain some or all of their mental abilities. It might be renewed at a later date.

Anybody concerned about an application by a local authority for guardianship or intervention order powers should approach the sheriff *(as outlined on page 746)*. They could seek advice beforehand from the Mental Welfare Commission for Scotland and/or the voluntary organisation Alzheimer Scotland.

In Scotland the rules laying down which people must be consulted if a health or social care authority wishes to intervene in the life of somebody who lacks the mental capacity to consent are as follows:

- the person for whom the intervention such as medical treatment or a test is proposed, so far as they can be ascertained by any means of communication
- the nearest relative and the main carer
- any attorney or guardian (the Scottish equivalent of a deputy)
- anybody who appears to the person responsible for deciding whether the test or treatment should go ahead to have an interest in the welfare of the patient
- anybody whom a local sheriff has directed must be consulted[30]

Sheriffs play a key role and can instruct that a particular person must be consulted about a social care or health matter. The Scottish legislation does not make provision for the person lacking capacity to nominate consultees, as can occur south of the border *(see page 784)*.[31]

Advocates

In Scotland, there is no equivalent of the independent mental capacity advocates of England and Wales. However, people with dementia benefit from a right to independent advocacy which goes much wider than that south of the border – it extends to any adult with a mental disorder.[32] 'Mental disorder' is defined in this context as any mental illness, personality disorder or learning disability; it could therefore include depression, schizophrenia, dementia and agoraphobia.

The right to advocacy is free-standing: it is not restricted to particular circumstances or procedures, such as whether the person involved has representatives or next-of-kin. Local authorities, in collaboration with their local health boards, have a duty to ensure that they make available an independent advocate to people with a mental disorder living in their areas and that these people have the opportunity of making use of the advocates' services.[33] The purposes of these advocacy services are support and representation, to enable the person involved to have as much control of, or capacity to influence, their care and welfare as is appropriate in the circumstances. The advocate must be independent, which means not provided by the health board or the local authority for that particular area. Further information is available from the Scottish Independent Advocacy Alliance. *(See also pages 804–810.)*

The situation in Northern Ireland

At present, mental capacity issues and interventions by health and social care organisations are largely governed by the common law in Northern Ireland, in other words, case law developed by the courts. Essentially, that provides that people over the age of 16 should be presumed to have capacity, that anyone who wishes to show they lack capacity should have to demonstrate this through a test, and that those acting for someone who lacks capacity must act in that person's best interests.

The Mental Capacity Act (Northern Ireland) 2016, which is likely to come into effect at some point before 2020, will provide a comprehensive system for the representation of people who lack mental capacity in the future. The definition of 'mental capacity' in the 2016 Act is similar to that described for England and Wales. So too is the definition of 'best interests'. There are similar guiding principles to those established for England and Wales on the way in which attorneys, deputies and others should act so that they do so in the best interests of the person they are representing.

Other safeguards to protect people with real or alleged limitations in their mental capacity provided for in the Mental Capacity Act (Northern Ireland) 2016 also echo those for England and Wales. The six health and social care trusts, as well as others such as private providers who provide health and social care services in Northern Ireland will have to go through deprivation of liberty safeguard procedures if they propose to deprive someone who lacks capacity of their liberty while they are receiving care or treatment (which could be in a hospital, a care home or in the person's own home or that of someone else). Trusts will also have to appoint an independent mental capacity advocate (IMCA) to advise them if they propose significant compulsory action for someone who lacks capacity, just as health and social care authorities must in England and Wales. The circumstances when an IMCA must be appointed include when serious compulsory medical treatment is proposed or a restriction on where someone must live or a deprivation of their liberty.[34]

The new system in Northern Ireland gives prominence to the 'nominated person'. Rather than embarking on the more complex process of donating a personal welfare power of attorney, any adult with the mental capacity to do so will be able to appoint a 'nominated person', who thereby acquires consultee status if and when a health or social care official has to make a decision on their behalf, should they lose the capacity to make it themselves. The donor and the nominated person will enter into a written agreement, signed in front of a witness, who will certify that the donor understands the effect of the nomination and has not been subject to undue pressure. Health and social care trusts will have a duty to consult the nominated person if it is practicable and appropriate to do so and to take into account the views of the nominated person in deciding what would be in the best interests of the person involved.[35]

Under the provisions of the new Act, if someone who lacks capacity had not already appointed a nominated person, a default arrangement provides that someone else can take on that position. There is a list of people who will be asked to do so by default, with the person's main carer at the top of the list, followed by their spouse or civil partner, then someone who has been living with the person as if they were their spouse or civil partner for at least six months, followed by their child, and so on.[36] A new Review Tribunal, which will work closely with the High Court, will be able to appoint someone else to that role if there is no nominated person or the nominated person is unsuitable. If a nominated person objects to a proposed significant treatment, additional authorisation will be required before it can go ahead.

However, the Mental Capacity Act (Northern Ireland) 2016 will not come into force until the Northern Ireland Assembly commences its provisions once it is ready to be fully implemented, and this may not be for several years. In the meantime, you could reasonably expect that the basic underlying ethos of the Act will be used as best practice until it does become law. Thus you could expect that health and social care professionals taking decisions on behalf of someone who lacks the capacity to take them themselves will abide by the principles of the Act, taking all reasonable steps to help the person involved to take the decision themselves. When taking a decision on behalf of someone, expect officials to take into account the wishes and beliefs of the person when they had capacity and to consult individuals close to the person. In acting in the person's best interests, they should consider not only the person's health but also their general well-being, including their spiritual and religious welfare.[37]

At present, most matters involving capacity are handled by the High Court in Northern Ireland. It resolves disputes and can make a declaration on whether someone lacks capacity in relation to a particular matter. It will continue to do so when the new system provided by the Mental Capacity Act (Northern Ireland) 2016 is working, with health and social care professionals dealing with straightforward cases involving capacity.

How representatives should behave

* When acting on behalf of somebody who lacks mental capacity, attorneys, deputies and professionals are required to abide by certain principles.

* Attorneys and others must act in the best interests of the person they are representing.

* Attorneys and others must allow the person involved to take as many decisions as possible.

* A code of practice sets out in detail how attorneys and other representatives should behave.

* Establishing that someone has lost mental capacity has enormous implications.

* Somebody who is completely incapable of communicating their wishes is treated as lacking mental capacity.

* Beware professionals and others assuming lack of capacity on the basis of age, appearance, illness or disability.

* Health and social care organisations must consult before taking decisions on behalf of somebody who lacks mental capacity.

* You can name friends other than your attorney, deputy or unpaid carer to be consulted if health or social care are proposing to act on your behalf.

* You could put yourself forward as someone to be consulted.

Chapter 34

Limited authorisation, advisors and advocates

The powers of attorney examined in Chapter 31 are designed for circumstances in which a proxy takes many different decisions and actions on behalf of somebody else, particularly if they no longer have the mental ability to act for themselves. Similarly the powers of deputies and guardians examined in Chapter 32 tend to be quite wide. Alongside these potentially wide-ranging proxy powers is a menu of much more limited ones.

Perhaps you are going into hospital and wish to be able to authorise somebody to handle some of your financial affairs while you are out of action. Or perhaps you can no longer get out to the bank or post office and would like to enable somebody else to collect money on your behalf or pay bills for you. Perhaps you visit somebody in a care home or extra-care facility and would like to buy items you know they would value but you have no means of accessing their funds and they have lost the mental capacity to grant you authorisation to do so. A range of powers exists for these strictly limited authorisations.

The most useful tightly circumscribed tool in the field of health and welfare is the advance directive to refuse treatment (ADRT). If you fear being given medical treatment at a time when you are mentally incapable of refusing it, you can set down your wishes in such a directive and medical staff must abide by them.

As well as authorising others to take action or make decisions, you may be simply looking for advice. In this chapter I set out the range of third sector organisations, such as Age UK and the Carers Trust, that provide information and advice about many of the choices that confront us in later life.

However, phoning a helpline of a voluntary organisation may not deliver more than general information. If you would like advice from somebody about your particular case, and perhaps the option of getting them to act on your behalf, you may wish to contact an 'advocate'. This is the term given to a new group of people who act in this way in the field of health and social care; their services are usually free.

Alternatively, you may wish to use a solicitor. Apart from the areas such as buying and selling property, getting a divorce and making a will in which we all tend to use solicitors as a matter of course if we can afford to do so, there are particular fields we may encounter in later life in which the input of a solicitor can be especially helpful, such as medical negligence and approaching the Court of Protection *(see page 739)*. So, I also outline how to go about finding an advocate and a solicitor who will best suit your situation.

In this chapter I therefore consider:

▶ limited powers which a donor can grant over their financial affairs, such as ordinary power of attorney

▶ proxy powers involving finance for which a prospective proxy can seek authorisation

▶ limited authorisation in the health and welfare field

▶ the range of voluntary organisations that provide information and advice on matters of special interest to older people

▶ advisors who pursue individual cases as advocates

▶ what to look for in an advocate

▶ some of the areas in which solicitors can be especially useful and how to find one

First, let us turn to the representatives we can appoint to take circumscribed powers over our financial affairs.

Types of limited financial authorisation that can be granted by a donor

There are several tools to choose from if you wish to authorise somebody else to take your place in a limited range of financial transactions.

Bank and post office proxies

The most restricted of the various proxy powers that can be granted in the financial field enable someone who cannot get out to the bank, building society or post office to appoint somebody to deposit or take out money on their behalf.

Perhaps you wish somebody you trust to have access to some or all of the funds in your bank or building society account. There is no question of your lacking the mental capacity to handle your money: you simply wish somebody else to be able to spend or deposit money on your behalf. In this case, it is possible to grant them one of several levels of access to your resources.

The highest level of access is provided through a joint account: you allow somebody to have access to money you hold by setting up an account jointly with them. You and the other account holder have the same card and personal identification number (PIN) and both have unrestricted access to the funds in the account. You are both liable if the account goes into the red. Of course, you can safeguard your overall position by placing only a limited amount of your money in this joint account.

If someone with whom you hold a joint account at a bank loses mental capacity, you can no longer lawfully use that account. Use can only be resumed if the bank receives new instructions from a person or persons acting on behalf of that person, such as somebody holding a registered enduring, lasting or continuing power of attorney *(see Chapter 31)*. In Scotland, however, an 'either or survivor' account will suffice, provided only one signature is needed on cheques.

The British Bankers' Association publishes a free leaflet entitled *Guidance for People Wanting to Manage a Bank Account for Someone Else,* which applies in England and Wales. A separate version is available in Scotland called *Banking for People Who Lack Capacity to Make Decisions.*

Many (but not all) banks as well as building societies provide a 'third party mandate' facility. This enables a named individual to access someone's bank or building society account. Sometimes the account holder has to fill in a form every time they authorise another person to act on their behalf at the bank; in other cases, a single form suffices.

Another option, which carries fewer risks, is to instruct the bank or building society to transfer a fixed sum of money regularly to somebody else's account by standing order. This facility could be used to transfer money to pay somebody to do housework or buy shopping.

However, not all of these options are available for people who have a basic or an introductory bank account. These are accounts set up mainly to pay in pensions and other benefits, to deposit cheques and to pay direct debits, but the account holder is not given a cheque book.

Collecting your state pension and other benefits

Most people now receive payments such as their state retirement pension direct into their bank or building society account. The drawback is that this does not provide cash in hand, as did weekly collection from a post office. So those wishing to spend a portion of their weekly pension or other financial benefit on their shopping have to find a way of collecting cash if they do not wish to pay with a debit, credit or contactless card.

One way of having cash to hand is to collect your pension or benefit at the post office. If you do this, you will be given a plastic card and PIN number, and you will have to use this card to get your cash. You can apply to receive your pension in this way to the Department for Work and Pensions (DWP).

If you wish somebody to collect your pension regularly on your behalf, you can set up a facility for them to do so by applying to the post office. The person you mandate to collect your pension and/or other benefits will be given their own card and PIN number to enable them to collect your pension. Of course, this facility to collect a benefit yourself or to permit a proxy to do so on your behalf is available only when the post office is open: there is no 24-hour hole-in-the-wall access to this money.

Ordinary power of attorney

Perhaps you know you are going to be incapacitated for a temporary period during an illness or recovery from an operation. Although you may have the mental capacity to manage your affairs and be perfectly able to speak or write, you anticipate that you will be too unwell to do so. Or perhaps you are going to be abroad at a critical time, perhaps in the middle of buying and selling property. Clearly it would help if you could hand over your affairs temporarily to a trusted representative. You could hand them over to a solicitor, but they would of course charge a fee. Instead, you could grant 'ordinary power of attorney' to a trusted friend or relative.

With an ordinary power of attorney, you grant powers to a person, or more than one person, to enable them to act on your behalf. The power of attorney may end on a specified date or you can cancel it before that date if you cease to need it. It can be a general power to handle all your financial and legal affairs or it can be limited to a particular act, for example buying a house or selling shares. You can specifically exclude, say, the power to write out cheques above a certain amount or to collect the rent for any property you own.

An ordinary power of attorney becomes invalid if you lose mental capacity. Without capacity, you are no longer in a position to monitor what your attorney is doing and they could therefore use your money for their own ends.

Limited financial proxy powers that are granted by an official body

We saw in Chapter 32 that a court can appoint a deputy or, in Scotland, a guardian, to handle the financial affairs of somebody who has lost mental capacity and did not appoint attorneys while they retained capacity. These representatives can be empowered to handle all of a person's financial affairs. But simpler powers over a more limited range of matters also exist. These are not granted by the person who is to be supported in this way (as with power of attorney), but applied for by the prospective proxy from an official agency or, in some cases in Scotland, a sheriff court. In Scotland, there is a provision for limited power in the welfare realm too.

Appointeeship

Perhaps someone in England or Wales is incapable of managing their own finances because of mental incapacity and their financial affairs are fairly simple, involving the receipt of benefits such as pensions and the paying of certain bills. They have not granted power of attorney. In this situation there is an alternative to full-scale deputyship: an 'appointee' may be appointed by an official body to act for them.

A friend or relative could be appointed as could an organisation, such as a firm of solicitors or a local authority. The system is administered by the Department for Work and Pensions, which usually takes the view that a close relative who lives with the older person or visits frequently is the most suitable candidate. Sometimes people living in care homes lose mental capacity and have no relative who is prepared to take on appointeeship. In this case the manager of the care home may be authorised to act as their appointee. Only one person or organisation can be appointed, either for a temporary period or permanently.

If you are applying to become the appointee of somebody whose main income is their state pension, contact the Pension Service. Before granting the power, officials have to satisfy themselves that the person involved is unable to handle their affairs and that the prospective appointee is a suitable person to claim and spend the benefit(s) instead. So an official will arrange to visit the person for whom you propose to act to assess whether they need an appointee and to interview you to establish that you are suitable. The interviewer will help you fill out the appointee application form and, if your application is successful, the DWP will send you a form confirming your appointment. You will not be authorised to act if the person involved already possesses a deputy or an attorney.

As an appointee, you will:

- claim and receive state benefits for the person involved

- make payments for them, such as charges for their care

- ensure that, if they are living in a care home and their bills are funded partly by social services, they receive the personal spending money from the state to which they are entitled each week (their Personal Expenses Allowance)

- report any changes in their circumstances to the DWP

If the benefit that you are seeking authorisation to administer is Attendance Allowance or Disability Living Allowance, you should phone the disability benefits helpline of the DWP in the first instance. If it is the Personal Independence Payment, contact the PIP claims line; if a tax credit, you should complete the appointeeship section on the tax credits form. For all other benefits, contact Jobcentre Plus.

Officials from the DWP can investigate an allegation that an appointee is not acting appropriately or in the person's best interests and, if necessary, revoke the appointeeship. So if you are concerned about the possible abuse of appointeeship powers, you should contact the DWP.

Appointee arrangements can also be made for people with a serious physical disability, but they are not designed for people who simply no longer wish to manage their affairs or are unable to get out to the bank or post office.

The powers and procedures for appointees are similar in **Northern Ireland.** An appointee will not be appointed if a controller is already in place. Prospective appointees should apply to the Social Security Agency, which is based in local social security and jobs and benefits offices.

Appointees, withdrawers and interveners in Scotland

Appointees can also be authorised in Scotland. However, the reason for using an appointeeship north of the border will probably be to help somebody who cannot manage their financial affairs for reasons of serious physical disability rather than mental incapacity. This is because Scotland has two other more sophisticated powers designed only to help people who lack mental capacity.

In Scotland, a 'withdrawer' can be authorised to access the bank or building society account(s) of somebody who is mentally incapable of looking after their money. Funds can be withdrawn from one account for specified purposes, such as to pay utility bills or care bills, buy clothes or engage in leisure activities. This simple tool has the potential for much beneficial use, for instance, if somebody has not granted power of attorney but their bank account contains money which could be used for their benefit for everyday items such as favourite luxuries or extra services. A withdrawer cannot be appointed if somebody already has an attorney or a guardian.

The system is not administered by the Department for Work and Pensions, as for appointeeships in England and Wales, but by the Public Guardian *(see page 746)*. A prospective withdrawer should contact the Guardian to obtain an application form. This must be accompanied by a medical certificate from a medical practitioner such as the person's GP to say that they lack the mental capacity to manage their own money. When an application is received, the Guardian must send a copy of it to certain other people, including the person's nearest relative, primary carer and any other person who may have an interest in the application. The person themselves must also be notified, although this requirement is suspended if two medical practitioners confirm to the Guardian that notification would pose a serious risk to the person's health. It falls to the Guardian to confirm or refuse the application; they may pass the matter to a local sheriff for a decision.

Once the withdrawer has a certificate of authorisation from the Public Guardian they should set up a special account at the bank or building society in their own name on behalf of the adult involved. The account can be used in the normal way, for instance with direct debits. It cannot be used for the receipt or expenditure of funds other than those specified in the certificate of authority granted by the Public Guardian.

Withdrawers should keep records of spending and bank statements and may be asked to show them to the Public Guardian. If they find they need to cope with an unexpected expense, they can apply for a variation of their certificate to the Guardian.

Withdrawers must abide by the principles of the mental capacity legislation *(outlined on pages 770–4)*. Thus, any action or decision taken must benefit the adult being represented, should be the option that is least restrictive on their freedom, must take account of their wishes and should take account of the views of others, including the nearest relative. Finally, the withdrawer should, as far as possible, encourage the person to exercise whatever skills they have relating to property, financial affairs or personal welfare and to develop new such skills.[1]

More than one individual may be appointed, so that there are joint withdrawers. If only one withdrawer is appointed, a reserve may also be appointed, to act while the withdrawer is on holiday, for example. The consent of the Public Guardian is required for a joint or a reserve withdrawer, either at the outset or through later application. Further information about acting as a withdrawer is available in a free publication from the Scottish government.[2]

Intervention orders

Sometimes what is called for is the power for someone to take one-off or time-limited actions or decisions on behalf of a person who lacks the mental capacity to do so themselves. The 'intervention order' has been designed for this eventuality.

Only one person is allowed to be nominated as an 'intervener'. The sort of areas in which they might be appointed include:

- the sale or purchase of property
- opening, operating or closing a bank account
- winding up someone's business affairs
- selling jewellery or paintings to obtain necessary income

The process of applying for an intervention order is quite complicated, but the Scottish government has published a template and examples of completed applications.[3] It is similar to the procedure for applying for guardianship powers *(see page 765).*

People empowered under intervention orders are expected to keep full records of correspondence, expenses, payments and so on involved in using their powers. They must work within the principles set down in the mental capacity legislation.[4]

Limited authorisation in the health and welfare field

Limited proxy decision-making powers can also be granted over health and welfare matters.

In England and Wales, an advance directive to refuse treatment (ADRT) enables someone to refuse specified forms of treatment in advance, should they be unable to withhold their consent at the time. *(This power is discussed in Chapter 41: Final decision-making.)*

Welfare intervention orders

In **Scotland,** but not elsewhere in the UK, there is a facility for individuals to obtain powers to enable them to act as proxy for someone who lacks mental capacity in certain specified areas. The powers involve a variation of the intervention order described above.

If, for example, someone is unable to give their consent to an operation or to significant medical or dental treatment, a sheriff could authorise someone to be their intervener, saying yea or nay in respect of that decision alone. Or it might become apparent that someone could not make a particular decision that could significantly improve their life. Or perhaps someone is a guardian or an attorney but the scope of their powers does not extend to making the decision or taking the action in question. In cases such as these, they could apply to a sheriff for intervention powers.

Legal aid without a means-test is available for applications for intervention orders which include welfare powers or a mix of welfare and financial powers (as it is for applications for guardianship).

Local authorities supervise welfare intervention orders if told to do so by the sheriff. If nobody else is applying to be someone's financial guardian or their welfare guardian or for a financial intervention order, the authority can itself apply to the sheriff to take on those powers. More information about welfare intervention orders is available from the Scottish government.[5]

Advisors

In the course of this book we have come across a wide range of voluntary organisations that provide information and advice. Some of these specialise in particular fields and I often refer to them in this book when discussing their field of expertise, such as Action on Hearing Loss, the National Kidney Federation and the Relatives and Residents Association. *(Groups concerned with particular illnesses are discussed on pages 325–8.)*

Alongside these specialist groups are national organisations that provide free advice and information over a range of fields. The most wide-ranging of these, Citizens Advice, provides one-to-one advice in areas ranging from tax, benefits and immigration to consumer affairs, social care and housing tenure at more than 3,500 venues across the UK (as well as through helplines and webchat). Foremost among the national groups that offer advice in areas of special interest to older people are:

Age UK

The information and advice Age UK provides cover anything from welfare benefits to selecting a cruise and finding a computer course to aspects of social care. It publishes invaluable free guides and factsheets, adjusted for national variations, and also provides expertise through a phone advice line. Age UK and its partners Age Scotland, Age Cymru and Age NI also lobby for improvements in the lives of older people.

A network of local Age UKs vary in the services they offer; these may include the provision of information and advice by phone or in person, drop-in centres, face-to-face or phone befriending, and shopping, bathing and handyperson support. Age UK is linked to an international charity which helps older people in developing countries. Another arm of Age UK provides goods and services such as insurance. Age Scotland provides its own helpline.

Independent Age

This charity is smaller than Age UK but also provides valuable advice in a range of fields including staying in hospital, choosing a care home, obtaining help in the home and financial benefits. As well as free guides and factsheets, it provides a phone advice line; you can book for half-and-hour's discussion with an advisor. It also provides befriending through phone calls, visits and phone discussion groups.

Independent Age covers the whole of Ireland as well as Great Britain. It campaigns for improvements in the lives of older people, particularly involving state benefits and care homes.

Carers UK

Many older people provide unpaid care for partners, parents, other older relatives and friends and sometimes their own adult children. Carers UK seeks to ensure that people realise that they are a carer and that help is available. It provides useful free guides and factsheets, an advice line, and also a listening service for people to talk through their caring situation. Carers. In addition, campaigns for greater recognition of the value of carers and for improvements in state support for them.

Carers Trust

The Carers Trust also provides advice and information at national level, including a chatroom. However, its focus is the delivery of advice and support through nearly 150 carers' centres dotted across the UK. These may provide advice and information through their own helpline or face to face, as well as advocacy. *(I refer to the support that Carers Gloucestershire, for example, provides on pages 630–3.)*

The Carers Trust was formed in 2012 through the merger of the Princess Royal Trust for Carers and Crossroads Care. However, the two organisations sometimes continue to exist separately on the ground, albeit working closely together.

Advocates

If you ring a helpline, you should get information and advice on the subject of your enquiry, and this may include an explanation of the choices you face. But the assistance offered by most helplines does not usually involve the advisor carrying out their own investigations into your case, offering detailed advice specific to your circumstances and helping you take things further by representing you or sitting alongside you at meetings if, for example, you wish to challenge a decision by social services about your care. Help is at hand in the shape of a new type of supporter – a so-called advocate.

Advocates are based in organisations that provide advocacy services. Not to be confused with the Scottish and American term for a lawyer, advocates do not represent people in court but help them navigate their way through the care system and secure whatever entitlements they may have in both health and social care. Some will suggest steps they might take, others will act for them – writing letters on their behalf, speaking up in meetings and so on. Advocacy is usually free.

Some advocates help people obtain the best outcome from particular decisions or situations. For instance, somebody may be in hospital and wondering whether they should move from there into a care facility or rely on care and support provided in their own home. Other advocates work with their clients on a long-term basis, supporting them over a period of months or even longer. They may be helping someone with dementia over a period of months, or even years. However, advocates do not provide befriending or counselling.

There are three main reasons why advocacy can be useful:

- both health and social care are complicated fields: people frequently have little notion of their legal rights and still less how to secure them

- people often need to take issue with, say, the manager of a care facility or a local council at a time when they are feeling unwell or frail. Additional difficulties such as sight or hearing impairment or mental frailty may prevent their putting across their views as forcefully as they otherwise might or appreciating the possible consequences of particular courses of action.

- conflicts of interest may arise between older people and the close relatives and friends who might assume that they will represent them. It may be more helpful to have someone outside the family situation who is also more knowledgeable about health and social care.

How do you find an advocate? The Scottish Independent Advocacy Alliance maintains a register of advocacy services operating through that country. At the time of writing, no comprehensive register for the whole of England, Wales or Northern Ireland was in existence. However, voluntary organisations such as local Age UKs, Carers Trust centres and local branches of voluntary organisations associated with particular ailments as well as social care departments often have contact information about advocacy organisations operating in their areas. Some of these voluntary groups offer advocacy themselves. Or you could contact one of the organisations, such as VoiceAbility, which is paid to provide advocacy in several parts of the country and ask whether it provides a service in your area or is aware of an organisation that does.

When you have a legal right to an advocate

There are certain situations in which the state must provide you with an independent advocate. In Scotland, you are entitled to an advocate if you have a mental disorder *(as explained on page 787)*. Plainly, this entitlement could mean that you have an advocate to support you in various arenas over several years.

In England and Wales, entitlement is restricted to particular situations – there is no blanket entitlement as there is north of the border.

An independent mental capacity advocate or IMCA has to be provided by a local authority or health body if someone is facing certain decisions with far-reaching consequences, such as whether to have an operation, lacks the mental capacity to tackle the decision and has no family or friends who are available or considered appropriate to stand in for them. *(For details about IMCAs, see pages 786–7.)*

People in England are also entitled to receive help from a 'care advocate'. The Care Act 2014 laid a duty on local authorities to arrange for the provision of an independent advocate if they propose to carry out certain social care procedures and the person who is to be subject to one of them would be likely to experience 'substantial difficulty' in being involved, and the local council considers that there is nobody suitable to represent or support them. The legislation does not restrict the provision of advocates to people whose difficulties are the result of a brain impairment or mental illness and who lack mental capacity *(defined in the Glossary)*.

The procedures when an advocate might be necessary are:

- an assessment of somebody's needs for care
- the preparation of a care and support plan setting out the ways in which the local authority will help the person meet their care needs
- a revision of someone's care and support plan
- an assessment of someone's needs for support as a carer

- the preparation of a carer's support plan
- the revision of a carer's support plan
- an inquiry that examines whether somebody has been abused or is at risk of abuse[6]

(I discuss the assessments and plans to which this duty relates in Chapter 26: Social care assessments and Chapter 27: Support for carers.)

What does 'substantial difficulty' mean? Well, it means that the person is likely to experience substantial difficulty in one of the following areas:

- understanding the relevant information
- retaining the relevant information
- using or weighing it as part of the process of being involved
- communicating their views, wishes or feelings[7]

In deciding whether someone would experience substantial difficulty, councils are told to have regard to the person's health and any disability they have (which could be physical, mental or learning). They are also told to consider whether the person involved is experiencing or at risk of abuse including neglect, whether they had previously refused an assessment, and the degree of complexity of their circumstances.[8] But a diagnosis of a mental condition such as dementia or a learning disability is not required for provision of an advocate – only that there would be substantial difficulty. So someone who is easily confused or vulnerable to coercion or perhaps feels overwhelmed by a serious illness or, say, anxiety or grief and so feels unable to get their head round the matter apparently ought to qualify.

So if your local authority plans to give you a carer's assessment *(page 621)* or a needs assessment *(page 587)* or to work out whether you have been or might be at risk of abuse *(page 566)*, and you have real difficulty in mentally engaging with what is involved and there is nobody suitable to speak up for you or support you, ask your local authority to provide you with an advocate. Remember: advocacy is free.

Or perhaps severe hearing or speaking problems are hampering your ability to communicate your views, wishes or feelings and the provision of information in different formats such as large-print, Braille or audio is insufficient to enable you to engage with your care assessment or other procedure. In that case, too, an advocate should be provided if you have nobody to help you convey your views. Advocates are available wherever you are living. You can obtain one when you are living in your own home, or a care home, in prison, or while you are staying in hospital.

Broadly similar provisions apply in **Wales.** Local councils must arrange for the provision of an independent advocate when someone would face difficulty in participating fully in a care assessment. The difficulties are defined in the same way as in England using the four possibilities listed above (understanding, retaining information and so forth). The range of procedures when an advocate could be appointed in Wales is wide and includes not only a care needs assessment but also the preparation of a care and support plan, review of a plan, investigation of alleged elder abuse, assessment of someone's financial resources to decide whether they should be charged for social care provision, and the provision of preventative services and direct payments.[9] Local authorities in Wales must ensure that people who may need advocacy are aware of the service and are able to access it, in particular if they live in sheltered housing or a care home.[10]

There is no requirement in **Northern Ireland** that a council must appoint an advocate to help someone who would find considerable difficulty in engaging with a care needs or other assessment. The Mental Capacity Act (Northern Ireland) 2016 makes provision for the appointment of IMCAs *(as explained on page 790),* but this statute had not been brought into force at the time of writing.

However, as elsewhere in the UK, you could request an advocate from your health and social care trust, even if you are not strictly speaking entitled to one. Seek advice on the best way to approach your trust from one of the organisations in Northern Ireland which provide advocacy, such as Age NI, the Belfast office of the Alzheimer's Society, CAUSE (for carers), Disability Action, Inspire (formerly the Northern Ireland Association for Mental Health), and the Irish Advocacy Network.

Choosing an advocate

Whether you are looking for an advocate to commission independently or whether you are being offered one by social services, it is worth asking one or two questions. Many advocates offer excellent help, but advocacy is a relatively new profession and as yet there is no requirement for an advocate to have their name accepted on a register of professionals considered suitable to practise, as is the case for social workers, nurses or solicitors, for example. Points to check include:

✓ **Your relationship:** Is the advocate going to help you with a particular decision or provide support for a longer period? If the latter, what sort of help might they provide and for how long?

✓ **Prior knowledge:** What training has the advocate received? City and Guilds offer qualifications in independent advocacy that have been approved by the Qualifications and Credit Framework. Expect a City and Guilds certificate or diploma in independent advocacy to at least level 3 or its equivalent, accredited by the Framework.

✓ **Experience:** Advocates act in different situations and for different types of people. Thus some advocates will help in care needs assessments, while others support people facing medical decisions or mental health problems, or they support carers, for example. Has the advocate you are being offered had training and experience relevant to your situation?

✓ **Effectiveness and independence:** Try to get a sense of whether the advocate has been effective for other people in the past. Can they give you examples (without naming names) of instances in which they have challenged recommendations by health or social care organisations?

✓ **Your wishes or their views?** A distinction also exists between an advocate pursuing a client's wishes and one pursuing what they consider to be the client's best interests. It is important to find out which you are getting. Ideally, you want someone who will explain clearly the pros and cons of particular courses of action and give you unqualified support whatever you decide to do.

✓ **Your security:** Much advocacy is carried out by extremely reputable organisations which train their staff and carry out thorough checks on their suitability to work with people who may be vulnerable. However, advocacy is a new field and there is no national register of accredited advocates, so in theory someone of evil intent could set up as an advocate. You therefore need to establish beforehand that security checks have been made, for instance through character references and Disclosure and Barring Service checks *(see page 507)*.

✓ **Style of working:** Ask advocates for information about the way in which they work. Expect them to refer to a code of practice. The Scottish Independent Advocacy Alliance is at the forefront of working out how advocates should operate and has drawn up a code, which is available by post or through the internet. It has also drawn up additional guidelines for particular types of advocacy.

Expect any code of practice (and therefore your advocate) to say that they will spend a reasonable amount of time talking to you in private to understand where you they are coming from. Advocates should rely on views and information they have obtained themselves, rather than hearsay. If the advocate is going to help you in complex areas of your life, you should expect preparatory work to take several hours.

Clarify whether there is any information you might give which they would not treat as confidential. Although you would expect everything to be confidential, an exception would probably be made if you revealed that you were being abused and it emerged other people might also be at risk.

✓ **Availability:** Make sure the advocate will keep you abreast of developing situations. How easy would it be to reach them if you wished to discuss your situation further? Try to judge whether they might often be unavailable. This could pose problems if a replacement who did not know you well were sent by the advocacy organisation to represent your views at an important meeting.

If you are happy with your advocate, give them consent to speak for you and inform any close family or friends that you have done so. Also, be prepared to fill in the advocate on all relevant background. Sometimes clients do not reveal the existence of family rifts. This can make matters difficult for an advocate when a family member favours a different course from their client's preferred direction.

Solicitors

There are many situations in which the help of a solicitor can be invaluable, from pursuing a case of unfair dismissal to buying a house and signing a tenancy to making a will. But it is often difficult to know whether a solicitor is necessary and, if one seems to be, whom to instruct.

Take the case of granting lasting power of attorney. Many high street solicitors offer help with drawing up a power of attorney. In fact, however, the forms and procedures have been devised so that recourse to a solicitor is unnecessary (apart from the requirement in Scotland that a solicitor be involved at one point). What is more, total reliance on a solicitor in drafting a power of attorney can be dangerous, *(see page 745).*

On the other hand, a good solicitor who has a wide range of experience in this area, is prepared to consider what the terms of a particular power of attorney might be, help with any complicated aspects of it and later check that things are working smoothly, can be invaluable. If you are considering involving a solicitor in setting up a lasting power of attorney, have a word with a number of possible solicitors over the phone *(as described below).*

There is a strong case for using a solicitor in such areas as:

- equity release
- rights in the workplace
- entering into a lease or tenancy, for instance, with a retirement housing provider
- entering into a care home contract

It is worth taking a real interest in all these matters yourself, but also finding a solicitor with expertise in the area. They should be able to spot clauses that could be challenged, for instance involving exit fees in leasehold retirement housing *(see page 146),* and also have a sense of whether the financial amounts proposed are reasonable.

Other areas in which a solicitor's expertise can be useful include probate applications and divorce. Good solicitors with experience in probate will not only be able to go through the process of obtaining a grant of probate and administering someone's estate, but also spot inheritance tax calculations which can be challenged. Similarly, a firm of solicitors with expertise in wills should check not only that your wishes can be put into effect but also that the will is as tax-efficient as possible.

Medical negligence

An area of the law in which a growing number of people are involving themselves is seeking compensation in the case of an accident or medical negligence.

Say your operation has gone wrong or you have developed a pressure sore while lying on a hospital trolley. You could lodge a formal complaint to the health trust involved and it might offer you compensation. But you would probably extract more money if you used a solicitor.

As with such areas as personal accident, it is probably best to use a firm that specialises in this area: few high street solicitors are likely to have pursued many cases of medical negligence and the field in which negligence might occur is wide and complex. If the action, or failure to act, is what is known in the field of negligence as a 'never event', you will probably be successful in obtaining compensation, as never events involve situations which should never occur, such as a surgical instrument or a swab being left in someone's body, or a patient being injured through climbing out of a bed to which the hospital has added bedside rails or falling from an open window without a safety bar. Some other areas are not quite never events but they involve things that should not happen, such as a misdiagnosis of a condition that later turns out to be very serious, a failure to prescribe necessary medication or the development of a pressure sore. For medical negligence claims to succeed, the patient must have suffered harm, whether physical or psychological. So, for instance, the failure to prescribe medication must have had adverse consequences. A claim is made through the civil courts.

A firm specialising in medical negligence is likely to work on a conditional fee basis, or 'no win, no fee'. That means the client does not have to pay anything upfront and the solicitor is paid only if they win the case, although the charging may not be clear cut *(see below)*.

A formal complaint to the NHS can still be useful. Often people have complaints about their care that are justified, but medical negligence is not necessarily involved, for instance if a member of staff handles somebody very roughly or behaves unsympathetically or rudely towards them. But sometimes a solicitor will advise their client to make a formal complaint in order to extract information from the health body that can be used in pursuing a case of medical negligence.

The circumstances in which legal aid is always available for medical negligence are extremely limited, mainly involving injury at birth. It is available in some other areas, for example, if somebody wishes to approach the Court of Protection because they consider they have been incorrectly assessed as lacking mental capacity *(see page 779)*.

Finding a solicitor

Whether you are looking for a solicitor to take up a negligence case or perhaps one involving employment law or an approach to the Court of Protection *(page 739)*, how do you find one?

The Law Society represents the solicitors' profession in England and Wales; sister bodies are the Law Society of Scotland and the Law Society of Northern Ireland. Each publishes lists of solicitors or firms of solicitors who have the necessary certificate allowing them to practise. Other useful sources are *Chambers Directory* (issued each year by Chambers and Partners and covering the whole of the UK) and *The Legal 500*. In all these lists, solicitors are categorised not just according to geographical location but also speciality. They may also be ranked through accreditation schemes.

If you find solicitors who specialise in the area in which you are interested, look at the website of the firm involved. It will probably give you information about particular professionals within it.

There may be a consumers' organisation that could help you find a solicitor. For example, Action against Medical Accidents (AvMA) is a charity which provides advice and support through a phone helpline to people who have suffered injury from treatment by healthcare professionals. It has solicitors to whom it refers enquirers.

Armed with your list of solicitors or firms of solicitors, you should then ring up several, perhaps six, and talk to somebody who might help you. Do not expect to have to pay for this preliminary chat, but check beforehand that this is so. Ideally, you would ring up and your details be taken by a junior member of staff who would then pass them to one of the solicitors who might handle your case, who would then ring you. Factors to consider when you are selecting a solicitor include:

Expertise

Does the solicitor have an in-depth knowledge of the area in which you wish to instruct them?

Take the pressure sore example again. This is an almost always preventable type of harm to a patient, since it develops only when someone who is vulnerable to the development of a sore is in a situation in which one might develop and those caring for them fail to prevent it. A solicitor with experience in compensation claims involving pressure sores would be interested in whether the patient had been assessed for their likelihood of developing a sore using a well-respected tool and whether the correct steps had been taken to prevent a sore from developing, such as the use of a special air mattress and repositioning of the patient at frequent intervals.

Approachability

Would you find the solicitor the sort of person with whom you would feel comfortable in person or over the phone? If you are hard of hearing or English is not your first language, would they take adequate steps to ensure these difficulties were overcome?

Convenience

Do you need to use a solicitor close to where you live? Could the solicitor visit you at home if you have difficulty getting out and about? Does the solicitor offer out-of-hours appointments?

Success

Look for evidence that the solicitor has succeeded with similar cases. If you are enquiring for a medical negligence or an unfair dismissal case, for example, ask how much compensation was secured in similar cases and the proportion of that sum the solicitor retained as a fee.

Conciliatoriness

Look for evidence that the solicitor is keen to get the best outcome for their client even if their own earnings are less than they might be. If you are getting divorced, for instance, is the solicitor committed to ensuring you can resolve your difficulties with your partner in the best possible way rather than automatically engaging in a legal process? Do they suggest relationship counselling before concluding that a divorce is the only option?

Charges

Solicitors vary considerably in what and how they charge. If there is an hourly charge, it is important that you get an estimate at the outset of the likely total cost of pursuing your case. You could insist on a fixed spending limit and ask the solicitor to contact you and seek your agreement before continuing if the costs approach this limit.

You should also ask for regular updates of the cost of your case as it progresses. The work carried out should be itemised clearly, not left vague – for instance, work carried out between two dates three weeks apart.

Establish how charging by time works and how much time is likely to be involved if, say, the solicitor agrees to write a letter on your behalf. If you phone them, will you be charged? How are such charges rounded up? Many solicitors charge in six-minute blocks, so you will be charged the same amount whether you talk for one or six minutes.

No win, no fee arrangements are often offered for personal injury claims, fighting unfair dismissal or seeking compensation for medical negligence. The understanding, as mentioned earlier, is that you do not pay the solicitor a fee unless the case succeeds. If the claim is successful, the solicitor will charge you a success fee. It is important to be clear about such matters as:

- If you lose the case, will you have to pay the other side's costs? How much is this likely to be? What are the chances of this happening? Could they be covered by an insurance policy?

- If you win, what proportion of the compensation you are awarded would the solicitor take as their success fee?

- Would there be any additional charges? There may be disbursements to pay, such as a medical report in a negligence claim or search fees if you are buying property.

- Would you be eligible for legal aid? Your local Citizens Advice ought to be able to tell you about eligibility for legal aid and may suggest solicitors in your area who handle legal aid cases. The Community Legal Service also has lists of solicitors who do legal aid work. LawWorks is a charity which puts people ineligible for legal aid and who cannot afford to pay a solicitor in touch with lawyers who provide free legal advice.

Read up about charging before you instruct a solicitor to act for you. The Legal Ombudsman, which handles complaints about legal services in England and Wales, has published useful free information, including a leaflet entitled *Ten Questions to Ask your Lawyer about Costs;* a template for no win, no fee contracts; and a short report called *An Ombudsman's View of Good Costs Service.* Here are one or two points to check:

✓ Before going ahead, make sure the solicitor writes and confirms: i) that they are happy to take on your case; ii) that they themselves will actually be handling it

✓ If charging is time-based, get an estimate of the amount of time the case will take and the costs involved and agree any spending limit

✓ If you are proceeding on a no-win, no-fee basis, establish all the costs you might have to cover, the compensation the solicitor considers you might win and the proportion they would take as their success fee

✓ Make sure you have written confirmation of i) any advice the solicitor has given you and ii) any information they would like you to supply

Solicitors for the Elderly

Solicitors for the Elderly is an organisation of solicitors who specialise in fields such as mental capacity and power of attorney; paying for care (including appeals against decisions about local council care and NHS Continuing Care); and wills, estate planning, trusts and probate. Look for a 'full accredited member' (rather than an associate member). The former are listed on SFE's website by specialism and geographical area. To be accepted, the qualified solicitor, barrister or legal executive must have at least three years post-qualification experience, be spending at least half of their time on the law relating to older clients, have completed an SFE course and an online assessment, and agree to abide by the organisation's code of practice. Expect an SFE member to offer home, hospital and care home visits as an alternative to seeing them at their office, although consultations outside their office may incur an extra charge.

Complaints

If you have a complaint about a solicitor, you should first pursue it through that firm's complaints procedure. If you get no joy, approach the Legal Ombudsman (for complaints in England and Wales). Probably the majority of complaints concerning solicitors arise because people feel that the solicitors have given them poor service. Perhaps they have dragged their feet in writing letters, written letters that are unclear, lost documents or charged what seems to be an excessive amount. The Ombudsman deals with complaints about poor service from solicitors and can order the solicitor or the firm to apologise, refund fees or pay compensation.

The Solicitors Regulation Authority, which regulates solicitors in England and Wales, has set down the principles that should underlie the behaviour of solicitors – that they should behave independently, fairly and with integrity to best serve the interests of their clients and the public interest. It handles complaints about alleged failures to comply with these principles. It does not have the power to order that a client be compensated, but it can issue various reprimands and ultimately stop a person or firm from practising. If you approach the Legal Ombudsman when your complaint would fall within the remit of the Solicitors Regulation Authority, it will be passed to the other organisation.

In **Scotland,** the Scottish Legal Complaints Commission handles complaints about the service a solicitor has provided and the Law Society of Scotland deal with complaints about solicitors' professional behaviour.

In **Northern Ireland,** the Law Society of Northern Ireland handles complaints about solicitors, and the Lay Observer, an official appointed by the government and the Lord Chief Justice, can examine the way in which it has dealt with a complaint.

Limited authorisation, advisors and advocates

* Powers are available to enable you to grant others control over part of your financial affairs, perhaps while you are out of the country or in hospital.

* You could mandate someone else to collect your pension or to access your bank account.

* Official organisations can authorise other people to have tightly defined access to the financial resources of someone who lacks mental capacity.

* Third-sector organisations provide useful advisory factsheets and guides as well as phone helplines and internet chatrooms.

* In the world of eldercare, advocates are not lawyers but people who advise and represent others in the fields of health and social care.

* Anybody with a mental health disorder in Scotland has a legal right to a non-legal advocate.

* Anybody in England and Wales facing major decisions and lacking the mental ability to decide what is best has a right to an independent mental capacity advocate.

* Ask for an advocate if you are not offered one.

* Solicitors can be particularly useful in such fields as care home contracts, medical negligence and approaching the Court of Protection.

* Compare the expertise and prices of solicitors before you commission one.

MONEY

> **"** *'Gold,' said Shelley, 'is the old man's sword. He should be careful before he relinquishes it.' Paying for 24-hour care because a major stroke has clipped your wings might cost a sum undreamt of when you handed over your spare cash to pay for your grandchildren's gap years.* **"**

PART TEN
MONEY

As a group, older people vary far more than the young in terms of prosperity. They have had a lifetime in which to make (or lose) a fortune, inherit one (or fail to), invest it successfully (or disastrously) and to incur (or avoid) financial setbacks arising from divorce, accidents, illness and redundancy. Once people have reached the age of 55 or 60, many of the decisions relevant to their financial well-being in later life have already been made.

Nonetheless, many choices still present themselves: should I take my state pension when I reach retirement age or defer it? What should I do with privately accumulated pension entitlements when I gain access to them? To what extent should opportunities for paid work feature in any decision I make about moving to another area? Should I release capital from my property through equity release?

In this part, I touch on choices such as these. I also draw attention to choices you may not realise are open to you. Many older people do not claim state benefits from which they assume – mistakenly – their financial means would exclude them. Others struggle on with only their state pension to keep them going, unaware of the state financial safety net that would give them an additional £37 per week (2017 figure). Still other people assume – incorrectly – that their age or receipt of a pension rules them out of all the benefits available to people of what used to be considered normal working age.

Everybody's circumstances are of course different, so what matters for one person will be irrelevant for another. The range of basic knowledge about financial matters also varies massively, from those who plan for their retirement unaware that their state pension is taxable to those who study the stock market on a daily basis. What I therefore do in this part is to provide an overview and to concentrate on sources of cash, especially particular state benefits, of which, in my experience, people fail to take advantage.

In the first chapter of this part, I focus on benefits awarded on grounds of age, regardless of the recipient's financial means, such as the state retirement pension, free eye test and free television licence. Another set of non-means-tested benefits are linked not to age but disability: eligibility is based on the practical difficulties that can arise as a result of disability caused by illnesses such as osteoarthritis, Parkinson's disease or dementia.

In Chapter 36, I turn to means-tested benefits. Foremost among these is the Guarantee element of Pension Credit that brings the weekly income of anyone roughly at or above state pension age to a minimum level and also provides access to other benefits. I also discuss means-tested benefits for people below pension age, such as Universal Credit, and benefits for adults of all ages, including Housing Benefit.

This information is important because while the government will proactively contact us about receiving some benefits, such as our State Retirement Pension or the Winter Fuel Payment, this not the case for the vast majority of benefits. First we have to know of the existence of a particular benefit. Second, we have to obtain an application form and post it in or find it online and send it in electronically.

Council tax can pose a special headache when we are getting on, particularly if we find ourselves with only a limited and perhaps dwindling income living in a large property that attracts a high council tax bill. However, councils must allow a range of council tax discounts and concessions, regardless of financial means. In addition, they must help people who struggle to pay their council tax bills because their income is low. These are all discussed in the section on council tax at the end of Chapter 35.

Despite the austerity cutbacks, much free advice on benefits is available over the phone, internet and in person at advice centres. I explain where to get advice and where to submit applications. If you are turned down for a state benefit, it is often well worth appealing against the decision and/or trying again later. Many people do appeal, and many appeals are successful. You do not need a solicitor to represent you. These matters are discussed in the sections called 'Benefits administration and advice' and 'Tips on applying and appealing' at the end of Chapter 36.

In Chapter 37, I examine private financial matters, including private pensions, inheritance, the release of cash through equity release, and the pros and cons of working in later life. Paying for care is discussed in Chapters 24 and 25.

Chapter 35

Universal state benefits

Whether you are rich as Croesus, a pauper or somewhere in between, certain financial privileges are available without means tests – the so-called 'universal' state benefits. Some of these may seem irritatingly piffling, and some may seem patronising, but together they add up to a degree of financial advantage it would be rash to ignore.

In this chapter I discuss these non-means-tested benefits, in particular:

▶ the State Retirement Pension

▶ health-related goods and services

▶ free television licences

▶ the Winter Fuel Payment

▶ public transport concessionary fares

▶ the Christmas Bonus

▶ disability and illness-related benefits: Attendance Allowance, Disability Living Allowance and the Personal Independence Payment

▶ Carer's Allowance

▶ discounts, exemptions and concessions on council tax

Many people are well aware of universal benefits such as the state pension, bus pass, TV licence and Winter Fuel Payment, and for several of these the government makes the first move and informs those entitled to receive them. This is not the case for disability benefits such as Attendance Allowance or the Personal Independence Payment. These can provide an extremely useful source of cash, as well as a means of obtaining other benefits. Many people miss out on them because they are unaware of their existence or unaware that they are eligible, often assuming they are only for people of modest means or those who are on some register of disability. Still others miss out because while it is a simple matter to obtain the free TV licence and little qualification is required other than age, there is nothing inevitable or automatic about receiving a disability benefit. You need to be prepared to put in effort to complete your application. I therefore explore the disability benefits in more detail than the automatic entitlements.

The final section in this chapter, on council tax, outlines discounts, exemptions and concessions that are available without a means-test. For completeness, I also discuss the means-tested benefit available to help people on low incomes to pay their council tax bills.

The State Retirement Pension

About four months before you reach your age of entitlement for the State Retirement Pension, the government's Pension Service should get in touch with you and explain how to apply for your pension. So you do not need to worry about not knowing when you come of age (although if you do not hear within three months of your birthday, you should contact the Pension Service; *address in Useful Contacts*). However, the state pension is a complex area and it is important to check that you are receiving your full entitlement.

Changes in the pension age

For many years, the age at which you could claim your state pension remained the same – 65 for men and 60 for women. Now, however, the age at which we are entitled to receive our pension is in the process of being raised.

There are two elements to this change. First, the age at which women can receive their state pension is in the process of being brought into line with that of men; this change, which started in 2010 will be complete by November 2018.

A second change is a planned hike in the state pension age for both sexes, to take place after the pension age of women has reached the age 65 level. This will mean that the pension age for both sexes will rise to reach 66 in October 2020. The government has said it will increase further, to 67, between 2026 and 2028. Thereafter, it is likely to rise further still.

Some groups of people have lost out under this change, not least half a million women born in the early 1950s who expected to receive their pension at the age of 60 but now have to wait. Many will have based their financial planning on the expectation of being able to retire at 60. At the time of writing the government was considering whether transitional arrangements should be introduced to soften this blow – perhaps providing for these women to receive their pension earlier than the new rules provide. However, if a woman opts to do this, it looks likely that she would have to accept a smaller pension for the remainder of her life.

If you are not already receiving your state pension, the easiest way to work out when you will be entitled to do so is to contact the Future Pension Centre, which is part of the government's Pension Service. You can contact the Centre by post, phone or over the internet *(see Useful Contacts)*. It can also give you a forecast of how much you are likely to get.

Changes in the nature of the state pension

The nature of the state pension changed for people who are entitled to receive it on or after 6 April 2016, that is, men born on or after 6 April, 1951 and women born on or after 6 April, 1953. The post-April-2016 pension is known as the 'Flat-rate Pension' or 'Single-Tier State Pension'. The main aim is to simplify the previous system and to provide a greater incentive for people to work and build up pension contributions.

The new Single-Tier State Pension (at £159.55 per week in 2017) is higher than the Basic State Pension which people who retired before 6 April 2016 received and will continue to receive (at £122.30).

People who reached pension age before 6 April 2016 are not affected by the Single-Tier Pension and receive their pension under the previous rules (including if they have deferred taking it). For the foreseeable future, the two different pension systems will run in parallel. Both pensions are taxable.

The pre- and post-April 2016 pensions: similarities and differences

The main differences between the old and the new state pension are as follows:

Period of necessary contributions and credits

Men and women who claimed their State Retirement Pension before 6 April 2016 are entitled to a state pension if they have 30 years of National Insurance (NI) contributions or credits *(defined below)*.

Eligibility for the new Single-Tier State Pension is based on National Insurance contributions and credits for a longer period – 35 years.

Amount of pension received

The pre-6-April-2016 state pension is awarded solely on grounds of these contributions or credits, regardless of the amount earned. However, different people receive different amounts. Not everybody who retired before 6 April 2016 gets the full basic state pension. Some people have not built up sufficient years of contributions or credits and the amount they get is reduced proportionately. But some people get more. This situation arises from the Second State Pension.

Under the old system, many people who were employed (not self-employed) paid additional NI contributions that entitled them to an additional Second State Pension. (This additional pension is based on two earnings-related state schemes called SERPS and S2P and meant that there was a wide range of accumulated entitlement to the basic and the additional pensions.)

The Second State Pension has been completely replaced by the new Single-Tier State Pension. People who in the past built up an additional state pension entitlement continue to receive it if they retired before 6 April 2016. However, if they retire or retired after that date, they receive a higher amount than the basic Single-Tier Pension as an extra payment on top of their single-tier amount.

For people who have built up entitlements to a higher pension in the past, the Department for Work and Pensions works out what they would have received on the pre-April-2016 pension rules based on their National Insurance record. It compares this figure with what they would receive under the Single-Tier Pension and the higher of the two amounts becomes that person's single-tier amount. This means that the state pension someone receives under the new system is not lower than it would have been had they received it under the old system.

Some people contracted out of the Second State Pension in return for a broadly similar occupational pension and payment of a lower National Insurance rate. This has come to an end and under the new system all employees pay the same rate of National Insurance. The government has said that amounts built up in schemes to 2017 will continue to be paid.[1]

For these reasons then, the amount which different individuals receive under the pre-April 2016 pension varies considerably. But what of the Single-Tier Pension? It had been widely assumed that variation would be largely eliminated under this replacement, often called the flat-rate pension. In fact, however, there is quite a lot of variation in what people receive under this scheme too.

As just noted, people who built up entitlements under the pre-April-2016 arrangements will get more than the full amount of the

Single-Tier Pension. Indeed, the Institute for Fiscal Studies has estimated that 23 per cent of people reaching state pension age between 2016 and 2020 will receive more than the full single-tier amount.[2] But it has also calculated that 61 per cent of people reaching state pension age between 2016 and 2020 will receive less than the full amount (with 17 per cent receiving the full amount).

The reason some people receive less than the full amount of the Single-Tier Pension is that their National Insurance record fails to qualify them for it. Those who reach state pension age with fewer than 35 years of contributions or credits receive a pro-rata amount. So, if they have 30 qualifying years, they will get 30/35 of the full amount: each qualifying year is worth 1/35th of the full Single-Tier Pension. However, everyone needs a minimum qualification of between seven and ten years to receive anything at all. If they have less than this, they do not receive any Single-Tier Pension.

What of high-earners under the Single-Tier Pension? Well, the provision under the pre-April 2016 system for high earners to reap the benefit of their high earnings in the form of a higher state pension has been removed, since the new system aims to equalise the amount of state pension people receive, whatever their circumstances may have been during their working lives. The better-off pay more in contributions because National Insurance involves a percentage levy on earnings, but they do not receive more in pension than poorer people.

Employees have to enrol separately into a workplace pension scheme which should deliver them additional income when they retire.

Indexation

The triple-lock provides for an annual increase in the basic state pension determined by the growth in earnings, price inflation or 2.5 per cent, whichever is the higher. It applies to both the old and new pensions. Since the lock is often attacked for unfairly advantaging the old over the young, it is far from certain that it will last.

Relationship to means-tested back-up

Now and in the older system, the State Retirement Pension is complemented by a benefit that provides a safety net for those for whom the state pension fails to provide what is considered the minimum needed to live on.

If someone claimed their state pension before 6 April 2016 and their weekly income, whether from their pension and/or other sources, is lower than £159.35 per week and their savings stand at less than £16,000, they can receive a top-up to bring their income up to £159.35. This top-up is called the Guarantee element of Pension Credit *(and I go into it in more detail in the following chapter)*. It can thus add £37 to the weekly income of a single person who receives only the Basic State Pension, or more if they have less income than this. The Guarantee Credit maximum figure for a couple in 2017 was £243.25.

In contrast, as one of the aims of the Single-Tier Pension is to reduce reliance on means-tested benefits, the amount of that pension has been set higher than the level of eligibility for Guarantee Pension Credit.

However, it has been set at only slightly more than Pension Credit. At the same time, many people are not entitled to the full Single-Tier Pension because they lack the necessary record of contributions and/or credits. So these people too will look to Guarantee Pension Credit to top up their income.

Derivation of pension rights

A major difference between the pre- and post-April 2016 systems involves inheriting or deriving state pension rights. Under the pre-April-2016 system, a spouse or civil partner can benefit from the state pension entitlement of their other half. National Insurance contributions built up by a spouse or civil partner can entitle them to a pension as a single person or as a couple. Thus a married or civilly-partnered person receives 60 per cent of their spouse or civil partner's entitlement to the basic state pension, if this is greater than their own entitlement. Also, if the spouse or partner who built up state pension entitlements should die, the surviving member of the couple can inherit 100 per cent of the pension of the person who built up the entitlement. People can also inherit up to half of their spouse or civil partner's additional state pension entitlements on the death of their spouse or partner. In addition, a divorced person can claim a pension based on the contributions of their former spouse or civil partner for the period of the marriage or partnership. All these entitlements remain in place for people who claimed or deferred their pension before 6 April 2016.

Under the new Single-Tier State Pension, spouses and civil partners are unable to inherit or derive state pension rights from their other half: they have to rely on any state pension entitlement they have built up for themselves.

The government has said there will be transitional arrangements, although at the time of writing it had not explained what these will be. Transitional arrangements will be important, as plainly this is a massive change. Many married people, men as well as women, have planned their lives in what they thought was the certainty that should the spouse who was making National Insurance contributions die, they would inherit that person's state pension entitlement.

Pension deferral

One major decision you have to make when you reach the age at which you become entitled to receive the state pension is whether to put off receiving it. If you do, you get a higher weekly amount later on. This means that if you reach state retirement age and have all the income you need perhaps from investments and earnings, it usually makes sense to defer and thus build up the amount your state pension will deliver when you do decide to take it.

Deferral has been possible under the pre-2016 system and is possible under the flat-rate system too. However, unlike under the old system, there is no option to receive a lump sum as part of the deferral payment.

If you defer under the new system, you have to defer for at least nine weeks and your pension increases by 1 per cent for every nine weeks that you defer, or just under 6 per cent for every full year you put off claiming. However, you cannot defer if you receive certain benefits – Income Support, Pension Credit, Employment and Support Allowance (income-related), Jobseeker's Allowance (income-based), Universal Credit, Carer's Allowance, Incapacity Benefit, Severe Disablement Allowance, Widow's Pension, Widowed Mother's Allowance or Unemployability Supplement. Nor can you defer and thus build up extra pension if your partner receives any income-related benefits such as Income Support, Pension Credit or Universal Credit. If you are in prison, you are not allowed to defer receipt of your pension until you leave.

National Insurance (NI) credits

Under both the pre- and post-April 2016 systems, you can obtain a contribution to your state pension from working, whether as an employee or a self-employed person. But there is also a system for the crediting of unpaid activities. If you are unemployed, sick or have limited capability for work, you can obtain credits that are acceptable in lieu of earnings.

Many people are unaware that you can also obtain credits if you are a carer, whether of a child or a disabled person. This facility is particularly valuable for women, whose working lives are more volatile than men's because of the caring responsibilities so many of them have for children and/or their parents. The requirement under the new pension system for 35 years of contributions or credits means it is even more important that everyone should understand their rights in this area.

You can obtain a credit for the period during which you are awarded child benefit for a child under the age of 12 or you live with someone who is awarded child benefit for a child aged less than 12 and you share responsibility with that person for the child. Foster carers can claim these credits too. And there is a facility for the person entitled to child benefit to transfer it to someone else in their family if they look after a child aged under 12 for at least 20 hours a week; these are called Grandparent Credits.

If you are the unpaid carer of someone who is receiving a disability benefit you can also obtain an NI credit, known as Carer's Credit. You must be caring for 20 hours a week or more and the person you are looking after must be receiving one of the following disability benefits:

- Attendance Allowance *(see pages 835–7)*

- Constant Attendance Allowance *(pages 844)*

- Personal Independence Payment – the daily living component, at the standard or enhanced rate *(pages 840–2)*

- Disability Living Allowance care component at the middle or highest rate *(pages 840–2)*

- Armed Forces Independence Payment *(page 844)*

If the person(s) for whom you are caring does not get one of these benefits, you may still be able to get Carer's Credit. On the form you obtain from the Department of Work and Pensions (England, Wales and Scotland) or the Disability and Carers Service (Northern Ireland), you give details of the care needs of each person you look after and find a health or social care professional to sign it. The professional might be a district nurse, occupational therapist, social worker or community psychiatric nurse – someone who understands well the care needs of the person you are looking after.

You do not have to be receiving the state benefit Carer's Allowance (for which the qualifying criteria are stricter, *as explained on page 844*) to qualify for Carer's Credit. Nor do you have to be someone's sole carer: your 20 hours a week could involve your acting as the unpaid carer of several people.

You can backdate a claim for Carer's Credit, although the earliest you can ask for it to start from is the beginning of the previous tax year.

If you have a query about one of these credits, contact the National Insurance Helpline (tel: 0300 200 3500 or textphone 0300 200 3519). This helpline also answers questions about NI rates and thresholds, NI statement requests and gaps in contributions.

Choices

What choices are available as regards the state pension? Choices break down into three types, depending on your situation.

If you may postpone taking your state pension

If you have not yet taken your state pension, consider whether you would obtain a higher state pension if you paid more in NI contributions now.

The first step is to obtain a forecast from the Future Pension Centre *(see Useful Contacts)* of what your state pension will be. It is especially important to do this if you are over 50, as you have limited time in which to build up additional contributions to your NI record. Plainly you cannot engage in any financial planning if you do not have an indication of the amount of state pension you are likely to receive.

For people who did not reach state pension age until after the single-tier system started, the government has advised them to wait until it can provide an estimate of their Single-Tier Pension before they decide whether to make voluntary National Insurance contributions beforehand.

Armed with these figures, consider whether it would be worth paying more in NI contributions to increase the amount of state pension you will receive. The advantages and drawbacks compared with, say, deferring receipt of a pension are complex. Much will depend on your circumstances. Thus if you are self-employed and a low income means you are not required to pay NI contributions (Class 2), it may well still be worth your while paying them, in order to build up your entitlement to your state pension. On the other hand, would making these contributions require a lot of sacrifice and render you ineligible for Guarantee Pension Credit once you reach state pension age? If so, it would almost certainly not be worth your making them.

The decision on whether to defer is complicated, with many factors to take into account. The Pension Service publishes a useful, free 60-page guide entitled *Deferring your State Pension.*

The Pensions Advisory Service gives advice on the pros and cons of deferral and also other aspects of the state pension. It is an independent organisation, funded by government, whose staff and volunteers armed and volunteers with specialist knowledge answer questions from enquirers over the phone or by email, web-chat or post. All advice is free and impartial. The Pensions Advisory Service also covers private pensions *(as I explain in Chapter 37).*

You may also find other organisations helpful, such as savvywoman. co.uk and the Money Advice Service. If you think you need a financial advisor to give you detailed advice, *turn to page 890.*

If you are about to take your state pension

If you are about to take your state pension, three choices present themselves. You could:

- take the state pension in full and give up working

- take the state pension in full, but continue to work. (People who work after state pension age do not have to continue to pay National Insurance contributions.)

- continue to work and put off claiming your state pension, so you receive a higher weekly payment when you do claim and for the remainder of your life. You can postpone for as long as you like. There is also the option of deferring your pension even if you have already started drawing it, to obtain a higher sum later on.

If you are already receiving your state pension

If you are already receiving your state pension (or are about to receive it), check that you are receiving the maximum amount to which you are entitled. Here are two matters you may wish to check:

1. In calculating your pension, has the DWP taken into account credits to which you are entitled in addition to NI payments you have made?
As explained above, if you have been looking after a child below the age of 12, you are entitled to credits for the years in question. If you have been caring for a disabled person or persons for at least 20 hours a week, you are entitled to Carer's Credit.

2. Could you receive more money if you were to rely on NI credits built up by your spouse or civil partner (or former spouse or civil partner)?
Under the pre-April-2016 system, any spouse or civil partner can claim a retirement pension through their spouse or partner's NI contributions. However, this gives a couple substantially less than twice the rate of a basic state pension for two single people.

Some people who are married or in a civil partnership and have built up their own state pension entitlement might nonetheless be better off claiming the state pension under their spouse or partner's NI record, particularly if they opted for the scheme that closed in 1977 whereby married women could pay a much reduced NI contribution.

You cannot claim using your spouse or civil partner's NI record unless they have reached pension age. Claims using a spouse or civil partner's record will not affect the amount that the spouse or civil partner who built up the contributions receives. People whose relationships have not been formalised by marriage or civil partnership are not covered by this provision.

Another source of additional pension of which I have found many people unaware is the entitlement of divorced people to credits to their own state pension based on their former spouse's contributions. Supposing you were married for ten years and during that period either did not earn or you did but paid reduced contributions. If your spouse was working during that period, they would have built up National Insurance contributions and you will be entitled to a state pension based on those, even though you are now divorced, so long as you have not remarried. Your ex does not have to be told that you are claiming, but you will need their NI number to be able to do so. Divorced people can also apply for a share of any second state pension.

The state retirement pension is taxable and requires National Insurance contributions. However, there is a raft of non-means-tested, non-contributory, non-taxable benefits available to older people.

Healthcare

A wide range of goods and services is free to older people through the NHS. These include:

- prescriptions *(see page 280)*
- sight tests *(page 311)*
- hearing aids *(page 475)*
- continence pads and clothing *(pages 424–5, 479 and 481–2)*
- disability equipment, such as wheelchairs *(pages 466–8 and 470–2)*

(I explain means-tested help to pay for goods and services for which the NHS makes a charge, such as dental treatment, on page 306.)

Free television licences

For people aged 75 and over, television licences are free. It does not matter if the eligible person is living in a household containing younger people, as long as the licence is in their name.

The TV licensing service has no automatic means of knowing when licence holders reach 75 – if you do not apply for your free licence, you will not get it.

Two groups of people under the age of 75 qualify for a reduction in their licence fee. If the licence holder or somebody with whom they live is blind or severely sight-impaired, they qualify to receive a 50 per cent reduction in the fee. Secondly, people who live in care homes or sheltered housing and wish to watch television in their own separate accommodation can receive a concessionary licence (called an Accommodation for Residential Care Licence), which is a fraction of the cost of the usual licence. Ask the manager of the care home or sheltered scheme to help you apply for one. You must be retired, disabled or aged 60 or over, and live in accommodation which is eligible. Refunds are available for people who have paid their full licence fee but later in the year qualify for this concessionary licence.

Further information about concessionary and free television licences is available from TV Licensing.

The Winter Fuel Payment

The Winter Fuel Payment is perhaps the best-known of the raft of non-means tested, non-contributory, non-taxable benefits available to all older people. This particular benefit reflects the special needs of older people for a warm living environment *(explained on page 49)*. However, as it involves a relatively large sum and benefits millionaires as well as poorer people, it could fall victim to moves by the government to bring some universal benefits within the scope of means-testing in order to reduce public spending.

At the time of writing, anyone who has reached the qualifying age for women to receive Pension Credit *(see page 855)* is entitled to this annual one-off payment of £200. People over 80 receive £300.

If you share your home with people who are not eligible, you should still receive the full amount as long as you have reached the qualifying age. However, if other eligible people share your home, you will not receive the maximum. If you live with someone else who also qualifies, you each receive only £125. If you are over 80 and live in the same household as another person over 80, you each receive only £200.

If you live in a care home, you should receive a lower-rate payment – £125 or £200. However, care home residents who receive a government contribution to their fees in the form of Guarantee Pension Credit are not eligible for Winter Fuel Payments.

The Winter Fuel Payment should be paid automatically. Check that you are receiving the correct amount. If you are living in a self-contained flat in a multiple occupancy building, perhaps a retirement housing scheme or a tenement block, you should be receiving the higher amount.

However, the person deciding what you receive might assume that you are living in a communal setting, as you would be in a care home. If you think you are receiving less than you should, call the Winter Fuel Payment Helpline; people in Scotland can ring the Scottish Helpline for Older People. As with all benefits, there is provision for appeal against decisions *(see pages 869–72)*.

Public transport concessionary fares

Free bus travel is available for older people throughout the United Kingdom. There are slight variations in what is offered between countries *(these are explained on pages 716–8)*. In Chapter 30: On wheels and water, I also describe additional free public transport provision, such as on the underground for older residents of London. The Senior Railcard, offered by the rail industry rather than the government, is also considered in that chapter.

The Christmas Bonus

The Christmas Bonus is a small sum (£10) paid automatically to people receiving at least one of a wide range of benefits, including the State Retirement Pension, Widow's Pension, Attendance Allowance, Carer's Allowance and Pension Credit. It should be paid automatically, but if you do not receive it by the end of December, you should inform the Department for Work and Pensions or your local Jobcentre Plus office.

Bereavement Allowance

Formerly known as Widow's Pension, Bereavement Allowance is available to widows, widowers and surviving civil partners who were at least 45 years old when their spouse or civil partner died and who are themselves under state pension age. It is paid only for up to 52 weeks after the death, and entitlement depends on National Insurance contributions.

Attendance Allowance

Attendance Allowance provides anybody – pauper or millionaire – aged 65 or over with a weekly payment of up to £83.10 as long as they meet disability conditions. It can be invaluable for people with illnesses from osteoarthritis to Parkinson's disease which make movement painful or difficult, partially-sighted and hearing-impaired people, and those who need supervision perhaps because they have dementia, for example. What is important is not the diagnosis of an illness but the extent to which the person is disabled as a result, with Attendance Allowance providing help to cover the additional costs arising from the disability.

Unlike help provided through local authorities' social services departments, there is far less focus on help with personal care. Also, there is no postcode lottery, as the money is administered by the Department for Work and Pensions. Recipients are free to spend their money however they wish. So you might spend your Allowance on paying a cleaner, a gardener, a care assistant, or on taxi fares or extra heating or better food, and you could vary what you spend the money on week by week.

To get Attendance Allowance (AA), you must make a claim for it – you will not receive it automatically. But when you claim, you do not have to reveal anything about your financial circumstances. You can use the money however you wish and you do not have to report back on exactly how you have spent it. You do not have to pay tax on Attendance Allowance. It does not count as income if you are applying for means-tested benefits such as the Guarantee element of Pension Credit, so you will get it on top of that benefit if you are eligible. It is not included in the benefit cap. You can qualify for AA whether or not you work. You do not need to have bought a single National Insurance stamp in the whole of your working life to receive Attendance Allowance: it is a non-contributory benefit. You can receive it if you are living in your own home, but if you are living in a care home and paying your own bills, you can get it too. However, if you recover from your disability or illness, you must tell the Department for Work and Pensions (in fact, the DWP's Disability and Carers Service), in which case they might withdraw the benefit or pay it at a lower rate.

Eligibility

The conditions for receiving Attendance Allowance stipulate that you are so severely disabled, mentally or physically, that you require one of the following:

- help throughout the day in connection with your normal bodily functions

- prolonged or repeated attention from someone else in connection with your bodily functions during the night

- continual supervision during the day in order to avoid substantial danger to yourself or others

- somebody else to be awake for a prolonged period or at frequent intervals at night to watch over you so as to avoid substantial danger to yourself or other people

'Bodily functions' are anything you do in connection with your body, such as going to the lavatory, washing, dressing, walking, eating or communicating. 'Continual supervision' is different: it is about being kept safe by the presence of a third party who can make sure you do not harm yourself or other people.

Attendance Allowance is payable at two rates: a lower-rate of £55.65 and a higher rate of £83.10. To qualify for the higher rate, you must satisfy one of the daytime and one of the night-time conditions.

Do not assume that Attendance Allowance is provided in order for you to buy disability equipment (such as grab rails or a device to help lower you into the bath) or to make adaptations to your home (such as installing a stair lift or a ramp). The state provides separately for people to receive disability equipment and adaptations, often for free *(as explained in Chapters 21 and 8 respectively).*

You can obtain an application form for AA from the government's website (gov.uk) or at advice agencies such as Citizens Advice centres. If you ask for a form from the DWP, it will date-stamp it. You then have six weeks in which to fill it in and return it.

To receive Attendance Allowance, you have to be present in Britain at the time of your claim and to have been present in Britain for at least 104 out of the previous 156 weeks. (These conditions also apply to Personal Independence Payment, Disability Living Allowance and Carer's Allowance.)

You must also have needed the help you describe in the application for six months before your claim and to need it for another six months (in other words, there is a time-qualifying condition, to stop people with a short-term temporary disability applying or somebody waiting for an operation likely to remedy their problem, such as a knee replacement).

You also have to be ordinarily resident in the UK with an unlimited right to reside (so asylum seekers, for example, are ruled out).

Anybody who has a progressive illness and is not expected to live for more than six months as a result of that disease is entitled to be fast-tracked to the higher rate of Attendance Allowance under what are known as 'special rules'. *(This is explained in Chapter 40: End-of-life care, on page 1007.)*

You might consider that the amounts Attendance Allowance provides are paltry. It is true they are not large. But AA can indirectly provide other financial benefits. If you are getting a means-tested benefit, receipt of AA can provide a gateway to an additional amount on that benefit. It can gateway an unpaid carer to their own weekly payment, Carer's Allowance *(see page 844)*. Furthermore, it can unlock means-tested benefits to people who would otherwise be excluded on grounds of income. *(I explain how this works on pages 856–8.)*

Tips on applying

Attendance Allowance is therefore a potentially valuable benefit. The main problem is that it is quite difficult to get. I wish I had sought advice before filling in my mother's application form, as her first application failed. Here are a few tips:

✓ Be prepared to spend a lot of time filling in the form. To maximise your chances of success, you should give plenty of detail to back up your argument that you are no longer able to do certain things without help or supervision. One benefits advisor for a housing association told me that completing a single Attendance Allowance application form on behalf of one of her tenants took on average four hours – and she is a professional!

✓ Try to get somebody who knows you well and/or is used to filling in AA forms and has a high success rate to do so on your behalf, rather than completing the form yourself. For instance, if you are living in sheltered housing, your housing association may have a benefits advisor who will do so. The main reason is that many people find it hard to write the worst about themselves. They probably try to make light of their problems as much as possible, simply to cope with them psychologically. They may even be in denial of, say, continence problems.

✓ When you fill in the form, it is a good idea to work out whether you are trying to meet the 'frequent attention' or the 'continual supervision' condition, or both. What you have to do is to paint a picture of all the different ways in which you need help or supervision. You may well still be carrying out various bodily functions unaided, but you have to explain how and why you find them difficult. For instance, perhaps it takes you a long time to dress in the morning because you get breathless, or you cannot bend or see well. Your living arrangements are relevant, so if you have great difficulty in walking and have only one lavatory up a flight of stairs, say so. Some people adapt to disability by avoiding bathing or changing their clothes frequently, so it is important to think of all the bodily functions which you would like to perform, even if you do not currently do so.

✓ Try to describe your worst day. If you have osteoarthritis and you are filling in the form on a sunny day, you may feel a lot better. Try to remember what problems you face and how you feel when the weather is cold and your joints are stiff and movement painful, if not impossible.

✓ If you live in sheltered housing, say so on the form. Although there are plenty of people living in sheltered housing who are hale and hearty, the fact that you are there suggests some infirmity or disability. What is more, you may be paying for some 'care' through payments to the warden for the alarm system and for a cooked lunch on the premises (not all these facilities apply to all sheltered housing schemes). Both these considerations should help your case.

✓ If you are waiting for an operation which is likely to reduce your problems, such as a hip replacement, wait until six months after the operation before you file the application. The DWP takes the view that an operation is likely to improve somebody's situation, so are unlikely to give a new award until six months afterwards, by which time it should be clear whether the operation has remedied the problem.

✓ Keep a copy of everything you send in. Don't fill in the form online unless you can print off or save a copy. If the application is queried or it is turned down and you appeal, you will have nothing on which to base your response.

✓ There are significant advantages in sending in a paper form. You can enclose supporting information and evidence and use extra pages to explain why you think you qualify.

✓ You can always send in additional pieces of information at a later date as well. For instance, if during the application phase you find you have another relevant medical condition, write in, quoting your National Insurance number, and ask for this follow-up to be added to your application.

✓ Be alert to the possibility that the Department for Work and Pensions may phone you after you have submitted your application, or even when you are receiving Attendance Allowance, to ask how you are. Some people are lonely and welcome a chat with somebody on the phone apparently interested in their well-being; others may be hard of hearing or not pay attention. If you fall into any of these categories, be on your guard if somebody from the DWP rings you up. If you tell the official at the end of the phone that you are fine, you risk losing your Allowance or having your application fail.

There is space on the form for corroboration – a statement from somebody else. You need to find somebody to fill in this section who is prepared to draft it carefully and who knows you well; this might be a home help, carer, relative or friend, or the district nurse, if they visit often. People sometimes ask their GP, but this is not necessarily a good idea. GPs often simply offer a medical opinion of the ailments from which somebody is suffering, whereas what is needed on the form is a description of the help needed in daily life. To be in a position to give this, a GP would need to have a much better idea of a person's daily life than they often do. (The Department for Work and Pensions may send along another doctor to verify that an applicant really is suffering from a particular medical condition, but that is a different matter.)

What you could also do, however, is to ask your GP and/or other health professionals to write a letter as supporting evidence for your application, explaining your medical condition and the limitations it imposes. Make sure you include the contact details of any such professionals.

You may have equipment to help you and this may remove your need for attention or supervision. For instance, if you have a commode, you might not need somebody to help you get to the toilet at night. On the other hand, you may still need help. It is important to explain how far any equipment can help, and in particular whether you still need help from somebody else despite the equipment.

You could seek help to submit your application from Citizens Advice or a voluntary group, such as a local Age UK or carers' organisation, but also from the social services department of your local council. Some departments will visit at home for this purpose – a successful application can enable them to save money they might have spent subsiding help in the home, since they are entitled to take Attendance Allowance income into account when they assess people for homecare charges.

Personal Independence Payment (and Disability Living Allowance)

For people under the age of 65, the equivalent of Attendance Allowance is the Personal Independence Payment (PIP). Like AA, PIP is designed to provide cash to help people with problems of the mind as well as the body. Again like AA, you must make your own claim.

PIP replaces an earlier equivalent to Attendance Allowance called Disability Living Allowance (DLA). Applications for DLA are now closed. People who are currently receiving it will continue to do so until the DWP tells them they must apply for PIP instead, but they will not automatically be transferred to PIP.

PIP (and DLA) are similar to Attendance Allowance in that they do not require National Insurance contributions, they do not form part of the benefit cap, they are not taxable, and although they are given to help people cope with the additional costs of disability and illness, how recipients use the money is up to them. The residence conditions outlined for AA *(see above)* also apply to PIP.

However, PIP is more complex than Attendance Allowance in that a wider range of levels of payment is available. Whereas Attendance Allowance is payable at only a low or a high rate, PIP has two components and within each component there are several possible levels of payment. It is possible to receive different levels of payments from each or both components.

Like AA, PIP can enable a carer to obtain Carer's Allowance and higher payments under the means-tested benefits Income Support and Universal Credit. Recipients of PIP may be entitled to a concessionary travel card and a Blue Badge; in most cases these are available through local authorities *(see pages 717 and 699–701)*.

You cannot normally apply for PIP once you are 65 or over. However, if you are already receiving it when you reach that age, you may well decide that it is worth remaining on it, as you can obtain more money from PIP than AA if you qualify for its 'mobility' as well as its 'daily living' component.

Eligibility

To qualify for the standard daily living component of PIP, you have to demonstrate that your ability to undertake specified 'daily living activities' is limited by your physical or mental condition, that this has been the case for three months and that it is likely to continue for a further nine months.

If you are deemed 'severely limited' by your mental or physical condition, you are given the enhanced rate. This is also given to people who are terminally ill. As with Attendance Allowance, there is a mechanism for fast-tracking these people for receipt of PIP. They do not need to meet the one-year condition.

In 2017, the daily living component of PIP was paid at the standard weekly rate of £55.65 and the enhanced rate of £83.10. The standard weekly rate of the mobility component was £22 and the enhanced rate £58. So the maximum it was possible to receive each week through PIP was £141.10.

Your ability to perform daily living activities is assessed in relation to ten activities. They are: preparing food; eating and drinking; managing therapy or monitoring a health condition; washing and bathing; managing toilet needs or incontinence; dressing and undressing; communicating verbally; reading and understanding signs, symbols and words; engaging with other people face to face; and making budgeting decisions.

Assessment for the mobility component of PIP involves two activities: the extent to which you can stand and then move; and planning and following journeys. Points are scored in the second category if you need someone else, an orientation piece of equipment or an assistance dog to help you make journeys, or if the planning and following of a journey would cause 'overwhelming psychological distress'. So again, PIP can provide financial help to people with a mental illness such as dementia that causes difficulty in moving around, even though they might be physically fit.

Making a claim

You cannot obtain an application form for PIP at a Citizens Advice or other advice centre, as you can with AA. The Department for Work and Pensions requires applications to be made through the internet or over the phone. To start off a phone claim, call 0800 917 2222 or textphone 0800 917 7777. If you find phoning difficult, get somebody else to make the call for you, so long as you are sitting beside them. You or they will need to have the following information to hand:

- your date of birth
- your National Insurance number
- your bank or building society details
- your doctor or health worker's name
- details of any time you have spent abroad or in a care home or hospital
- your contact details

Phoning to ask for a form actually sets your claim in motion; thereafter you have only one month from the day the form was sent to you in which to complete it, so think before you make that initial call about whom you might ask to write letters to support your claim and contact them. Have a look at the suggestions above on Attendance Allowance for the sort of people you could usefully ask to write supporting letters.

If you cannot find someone to phone for you, ask the DWP for form PIP1 by writing to Personal Independence Payment New Claims, Post Handling Site B, Wolverhampton WV99 1AH. The DWP says this form can be used in exceptional circumstances.

If the DWP considers that you might be eligible for PIP, it will send you an individually bar-coded form to complete in which you will be asked to explain how your disability affects various daily living and mobility activities.

Take trouble over completing this: draft your entries first on rough paper and then ask someone who knows you well to read them through and let you know if you have missed out any points. For instance, when describing any difficulties you have with dressing, don't forget to include putting on your shoes and stockings. You may need different amounts or types of help on different days. If so, explain this and how often you need different types of help.

Bear in mind that the assessors will consider whether you can undertake any particular activity, such as bathing and washing, 'reliably'. This means they will consider whether you can, say, bathe yourself safely, in a way that is unlikely to cause harm to you or anyone else, to an acceptable standard, as often as is reasonably required, and within a reasonable length of time. This time should be no more than twice the maximum taken by someone without disabilities or health problems. So, when you complete the form, explain if an activity takes you longer than is normal or you can never perform it satisfactorily.

Many activities can be undertaken more successfully with the help of a piece of equipment. The assessors will expect you to use suitable equipment. You will score highest if the activity in question cannot be reliably carried out even with the help of equipment.

Have a look at the tips for applying for Attendance Allowance *(above)*, and send in any supporting evidence you can muster (after keeping copies for your own files). The DWP allows only one month for claimants to fill in this form. If you cannot meet that deadline, phone the DWP and ask for an extension.

An independent medical professional will examine your claim form and supporting evidence. In most cases, applicants are then interviewed. You can take someone along with you to this consultation and it is well worth doing so: they can help you explain the difficulties you face. If you fail to attend this consultation without good cause, the DWP may terminate your claim.

The disability or illness associated with your application for PIP must last at least a year – the rules say that you must have met the disability conditions if assessed at any time in the previous three months before their application and be likely still to meet them at any time during the following nine months. However, you can be awarded PIP if the assessor considers that you will satisfy this total period in the future.

These rules apply in England, Scotland and Wales. It is likely that a similar approach will be taken in Northern Ireland, but none had been announced at the time of writing. The Northern Ireland Assembly Government or a voluntary group, such as Carers Northern Ireland, will provide information as soon as plans have been finalised.

Constant Attendance Allowance

This benefit offers cash at four different weekly rates for people who receive Industrial Injuries Disablement Benefit or a War Disablement Pension and need daily care and attention because of a disability.

You can obtain an application through the government's website (gov.uk) or at a Jobcentre Plus office.

Armed Forces Independence Payment

This provides financial support to personnel and veterans of the armed services who are seriously injured as a result of service to cover the extra costs they may have as a result of their injury.

Applications are handled not by the DWP but Veterans UK, part of the Ministry of Defence *(see Useful Contacts)*.

Carer's Allowance

A specific state benefit is offered to carers called Carer's Allowance. The bad news is that the amount is small (£62.70 per week in 2017). However, entitlement to Carer's Allowance can provide a gateway to other sources of money. This is important for older people because many of them act as carers yet do not receive Carer's Allowance.

The qualifying conditions to receive Carer's Allowance are that you must be providing care for at least a total of 35 hours a week and the person for whom you are caring must be considered to be 'severely disabled' – defined in this context as someone receiving one of the following benefits:

● Attendance Allowance
● the daily living component (higher or lower rate) of the Personal Independence Payment

- the care component (highest or middle rate) of Disability Living Allowance
- Armed Forces Independence Payment or
- Constant Attendance Allowance in respect of a disability incurred through war or industrial accident

The 35 hours spent caring can include supervision as well as assistance, at night as well as during the day. They can include doing practical tasks such as cooking and keeping an eye on the person so they do not come to harm, as well as physically helping them. You do not have to live with the person you are looking after, and the caring hours can include clearing up after the visit of a disabled person and preparing for them to be with you, although it cannot include your travel time in getting to their house or flat.

You can earn up to £110 a week (after deductions of tax, National Insurance and half of your contribution towards an occupational or personal pension) and receive Carer's Allowance. If you are self-employed, you can also deduct expenses incurred in the course of your business. But if you earn more than £110, you cannot get any Carer's Allowance. So, someone who is perhaps working part time and not earning much while caring for an older relative at weekends and in the evenings could see a modest increase in their income from Carer's Allowance.

You can receive Carer's Allowance only in respect of one person for whom you are caring, even if you are caring for someone else as well.

Do not assume that if you receive Carer's Allowance you must be caring for 35 hours *every* week. You are entitled to certain holiday weeks under Carer's Allowance, so you can continue to receive it even if the person for whom you are caring goes into a care home for short periods of respite care. However, if they lose their Attendance Allowance, PIP or DLA, your Carer's Allowance stops too. This will happen if the cared-for person goes into hospital or enters a care home, say, for intensive care for longer than 28 days, or for two periods shorter than 28 days which are separated by less than 28 days and the local authority is contributing to that cost.

Carer's Allowance continues for up to eight weeks after the death of the person being cared for.

Older couples and Carer's Allowance
Many older people are caring for their partners and sometimes each provides care for the other. One might have severe osteoarthritis that limits their movement, for instance, and the other severe vision impairment.

The bad news is that if you are receiving the full state retirement pension, you are not eligible for Carer's Allowance, as this is considered an 'overlapping benefit'. However, should your state retirement pension be less than Carer's Allowance because of gaps in your National Insurance record, you will benefit by the difference between Carer's Allowance and that pension.

Bizarrely, although earnings over £110 per week or the pre-April-2016 Basic State Pension rule you out of receipt of Carer's Allowance, application for it and a response that you would otherwise have been entitled to it can increase the level of other benefits.

Take a husband and wife (or unmarried partners). Perhaps the woman has mobility problems and the man sight impairment, and each is caring for the other, struggling by on only a partial state retirement pension. If they had not previously applied for Attendance Allowance and were each eligible, this could increase their weekly income. But they could also each apply for Carer's Allowance, since it is possible for one person to receive Carer's Allowance as well as Attendance Allowance.

If this couple were entitled to the Guarantee element of Pension Credit, the increase in their weekly income would be greater still. This is because entitlement to Carer's Allowance (even if it is not actually paid because of an overlapping benefit) automatically entitles the receiver to the Carer's Additional Amount. This amount increases somebody's 'applicable' or 'appropriate amount' for Guarantee Pension Credit from the basic amount by £34.95 per week. That might not sound very much, but you may nonetheless feel it is worth having. Furthermore, if the other member of this couple were similarly eligible for the Carer's Additional Amount, their joint income could rise by nearly £70 each week. *(We see in Chapter 36 that an additional disability payment on top of your carer payments should bring your joint weekly income from Guarantee Pension Credit alone up to £430.45.)*

To receive the Carer's Additional Amount, you must be entitled to Carer's Allowance. But you do not actually have to be receiving it; most older people who could receive it choose to receive their state retirement pension instead.

Council Tax

It is well worth checking that you receive any reductions on your council tax bill to which you may be entitled, regardless of financial means. They are many and various. In addition, local authorities provide help to people of modest means to pay their council tax bills.

The council tax on a property is determined partly by the valuation band in which it has been placed by the local authority in whose area it lies. Like anybody else, an older person can always shift down a valuation band by moving to a smaller property, or move to a part of the country where council tax bills are lower.

Whether or not you relocate and whatever your means, you may find you are eligible for at least one of the following discounts and concessions:

Council tax exemptions and discounts

Some types of dwelling are completely exempt from council tax. Other exemptions and discounts arise from the circumstances of the people living in them.

Exempt dwellings

If your property is unoccupied because you live elsewhere as you need to be cared for in hospital, in a care home or with relatives, your property is exempt from council tax. There is also an exemption for carers: if property is unoccupied because the person who lives there has gone to care for someone else, that property is also exempt from payment of council tax.

A self-contained granny annexe is a separate property for council tax purposes but it is exempt if lived in by a 'dependant relative' of somebody living in the main part of a dwelling. A dependant relative in this context is someone who is aged 65 or over or who is substantially or permanently disabled or severely mentally impaired. The latter category can include people with a learning disability or with dementia or those who have had a stroke which has affected their mental ability.

Exemptions and discounts for people

The best known of the discounts arising from the circumstances of somebody living in a property is the 25 per cent reduction for people who live alone.

There are other less well-known discounts and sometimes complete disregards. People who are living in a care home or staying long-term in hospital are themselves exempt from payment of council tax. Now, they may already benefit from an exemption for their property, as described above. However, if the property is not empty but one other person remains living there while the person is in hospital or care, that other person will now be classed as living alone and so attract the 25 per cent discount.

There is also an exemption for severely mentally ill people. To attract this disregard, there are three qualifying categories: The person must have a severe impairment of intelligence and social functioning which appears to be permanent; or possess a certificate confirming this impairment from their GP or consultant; or be entitled to one of the disability benefits – Attendance Allowance, Disability Living Allowance or the Personal Independence Payment. If someone meets all three conditions they are disregarded; if they meet less than three, they may pay a reduced rate.

Another disregard involves carers. Unpaid carers are disregarded for council tax so long as they live with and provide at least 35 hours of care a week to somebody who is sufficiently disabled to be receiving Attendance Allowance, Disabled Living Allowance or the Personal Independence Payment. However, this disregard does not apply to the partner or spouse of the person for whom they are caring (nor the parent of a child under 18). But it does mean that a household consisting of a daughter, say, caring for a mother with dementia should not have to pay any council tax: each is disregarded in their own right. If one other person were living in the household, they would be classed as a single person occupying the property and so receive the single-person reduction.

In certain circumstances paid live-in carers are exempt. However, the circumstances are so restrictive that they rule out many: the live-in carer must be paid no more than £44 per week; be employed by the cared-for person to look after them for at least 24 hours a week; provide care on behalf of a local authority, government department or charity; and have been introduced to the situation by a charity.

Lowering of council-tax band for property adapted for disability

Another rule with which all councils must conform is the 'disabilities scheme'. According to this, local authorities must treat a property as if it is one council-tax band lower than its valuation if it has one or more of certain features which are essential or of major importance to the well-being of somebody who lives in it and is substantially and permanently disabled. The features are:

- extra space within the dwelling to allow for the use of a wheelchair
- an additional bathroom or kitchen needed by the person with the disability or

- any other room (except a lavatory) which is predominantly used by the disabled person. This extra room can be an existing room: it need not be specially built.

This provision is intended to help people who live in larger properties than they would need had they not been disabled, or in which the living area for normal use has been reduced.

Your council will not give you any of these exemptions and discounts unless you apply for them, as it will not know that your circumstances qualify you. In some cases, special forms are provided to apply for them.

Council Tax Reduction

In addition to these exemptions and discounts given regardless of the financial means of the person involved, local authorities also administer schemes that provide help to people to pay their council tax bills on grounds of income. In **Scotland** and **Wales,** there are national schemes within which councils must work.[3] In England, local authorities are each free to devise their own schemes (sometimes called council tax support schemes), but within certain limits, and the government has provided a default scheme for councils which have not devised their own.[4]

If you think you might qualify, ask your council to send you details of its scheme or look online.

Whether you live in England, Scotland or Wales, you should receive 100 per cent reduction on council tax if you receive the means-tested Guarantee element of Pension Credit – in other words, you pay nothing, so long as no non-dependant adult (such as your son or daughter) lives with you. If you have reached state pension age but do not get Guarantee Pension Credit (perhaps because you have never got round to applying for it), your income is low and your savings stand at less than £16,000, you may still be eligible for Council Tax Reduction.

Council Tax Reduction replaced Council Tax Benefit (a national scheme funded by central government but administered by local councils) in 2013. When this change took place, government cut the funding from national government to local authorities. However, older people were shielded from the impact of this reduction. This means that in England while people over pension age are eligible to receive 100 per cent reduction of their council tax liability if they qualify on low-income grounds, people under pension age can receive only a maximum reduction of 80 per cent, even if their income is tiny. In Scotland and Wales, 100 per cent reduction has been maintained for adults of all ages who qualify on income grounds.

Perhaps even after reading the information provided by your council, you remain unclear about the qualifying criteria for Council Tax Reduction. Bear in mind that local authorities are not permitted to keep secret the rules they are applying. Somebody might ask, for instance: do I have to be receiving a state benefit such as Universal Credit to receive this benefit from my council? Is there any link between my assessment for Council Tax Reduction and some other aspect of my council's activities, such as a social services assessment? If you think you may be unaware of all the instructions that the officials assessing applications are working to, do not hesitate to ask your council. It must make all this information available under the Freedom of Information Act 2000, Section 1.

Council Tax Reduction benefit is a qualifying benefit for Funeral Expenses Payments *(see page 863–4)*.

In **Northern Ireland,** residents pay rates, not council tax, and the equivalent of Council Tax Reduction is called Housing Benefit for Rates (HBR). The rules are similar to those for Council Tax Reduction in Great Britain. Thus if you receive Guarantee Pension Credit or Income Support, your HBR covers the whole of your rates bill, so you have nothing to pay. If you do not receive this benefit, you may still be able to claim it if you have capital of less than £16,000, or £50,000 if you are over the age of 60. Your income is also taken into account. There is also a Rate Relief provision for people on low incomes who are not entitled to HBR; if you make an application that is unsuccessful for HBR, you will automatically be assessed for Rate Relief. The amount of any award is increased if you are disabled or a carer.

The schemes are administered by the Land and Property Services Agency (for owner-occupier applicants) or the Northern Ireland Housing Executive (for tenants). There is information about them on the Northern Ireland Assembly government's website, at nidirect.gov.uk, and also in Citizens Advice publications.

universal state benefits

* Millions of older people fail to apply for valuable benefits for which they are eligible.

* The Pensions Advisory Service offers free, impartial information and guidance about the state pension and all types of private pension.

* If you have enough money for your current needs, it usually makes sense to defer receipt of your state retirement pension and receive a higher weekly sum later.

* Claim through the state pension entitlement of your spouse or civil partner if it will get you a better deal.

* Divorced people can have their state pension boosted by their former spouse's contributions.

* Disability benefits do not require the disclosure of financial details.

* Granny annexes are often exempt from council tax.

* Properties adapted for use by a disabled person should attract a lower rate of council tax.

* The single person council-tax discount may be available on top of a reduction because your house has been adapted for disability or there is a carer living there.

* All poorer people can apply for a council tax reduction and those receiving Guarantee Pension Credit are entitled to a 100 per cent reduction.

Chapter 36

Means-tested benefits

niversal state benefits for older people such as the Winter Fuel Payment remain under threat, and the rises in the state pension age will deliver large savings to the government. However, a focus on the poorest pensioners ensures that means-tested benefits remain more or less unchallenged. A minimum income remains provided for all who need it, even if they are neither ill, disabled or looking for work. This benefit, called the Guarantee element of Pension Credit, not only provides often vital cash, but entitles the beneficiary to other valuable assistance, such as 100 per cent relief from council tax.

I begin this chapter by examining Guarantee Pension Credit (GPC) and go on to outline other means-tested benefits available for younger adults and for adults of all ages.

Finally, I look at how to obtain information and advice about benefits in general and what to do if your application for a benefit is turned down.

Unlike universal benefits such as the State Retirement Pension, you must proactively apply for means-tested benefits – the government will not contact you about them automatically, even though it knows that you would qualify.

This chapter examines:

▶ Guarantee Pension Credit
▶ Universal Credit
▶ Savings Pension Credit
▶ Housing Benefit and Local Housing Allowance
▶ the benefit cap
▶ Funeral Expenses Payments
▶ the Cold Weather Payment

► the NHS Low Income Scheme

► one-off loans and grants

► general tips on applying for benefits

► the bodies that administer benefits

► where to go for free benefits advice

► appealing against a refusal of benefit

Guarantee Pension Credit

The Guarantee element of Pension Credit is the equivalent for older people of Income Support and it provides all those over a certain age with a minimum level of financial support if they cannot find this from their own resources. They may be receiving a full or partial state pension at the same time as GPC, or no pension at all. Unlike the state pension, Guarantee Credit does not require National Insurance contributions or credits. Age and relative poverty alone are enough to secure this guaranteed weekly income from the state.

The basic amount you receive as GPC (£159.35 or £243.25 for a couple in 2017) is known as the 'standard minimum guarantee'. The Department for Work and Pensions looks at your income and works out whether it falls short of that guaranteed level. If it does, you are given a top-up. In this way, GPC (and most other means-tested benefits) provides recipients with an amount that varies person to person – unlike most non-means-tested benefits, such as Attendance Allowance, which provide flat-rate amounts.

The minimum income guaranteed through Guarantee Pension Credit is £37 per week higher than that provided by the basic, pre-April-2016 state retirement pension *(as explained on page 827)*. Financial life for those who end up on GPC is in some ways easier than for those struggling to get by on their own resources, particularly if their only source of income is that state pension. If you have no more than the pre-April-2016 basic state pension to live on, GPC is well worth the form-filling it entails. It is impossible to buy a private pension as good as Guarantee Pension Credit on the open market, and if it were, it would cost a great deal. Yet 30 per cent of people eligible to receive Guarantee Pension Credit were neglecting to claim it in 2013/14.[1]

What of the situation for people who became or will become eligible for their state pension after April 2016, when the pension just described was replaced by the Single-Tier Pension? Well, that pension has been set at a level slightly higher than GPC rather than substantially below it.

However, *as we saw on page 826,* many people are not eligible to receive the full Single-Tier Pension. So they too may benefit from GPC.

The age of entitlement to GPC is complex. It is the qualifying age at which a woman becomes entitled to her state pension (which, *as we saw on page 824,* is different for men). This means that if your date of birth is before 6 April 1950, your qualifying age, whatever your gender, is 60, whereas if your date of birth is after 5 December 1953, the qualifying age is 65 or over. If your date of birth lies between 6 April 1950 and 5 December 1953, you can find your qualifying age by looking at a table available on the government's website (gov.uk) or on other websites *(listed on page 868)* or by telephoning the organisations that give information and advice on benefits *(listed on page 868–9).*

While some people who receive GPC simply receive a top-up to their state pension, many receive more than this. The reason might be that they do not qualify for a basic, pre-April-2016 state pension, so they need more than the £36.30 difference. However, some people receive more money than others through GPC because the state deems that they need a higher amount than the standard minimum guarantee on which to live, possibly because they have to cope with additional costs connected with their housing, or as a result of disability or acting as a carer. They thereby qualify for an amount higher than the minimum provided by GPC.

If someone qualifies for one or more of these additional payments, or premiums, as they are known, the DWP tops up their income to the level of GPC plus the premium, so they receive more than would someone receiving only the basic GPC. Also, people who would be ruled out of the basic GPC because their income is too high now find they qualify for GPC because the larger amount the DWP considers they need to live on is higher than their weekly income.

Applying for Pension Credit

If you apply for any means-tested benefit, you will obviously have to reveal details of your income. Income from many sources is taken into account when an assessment is made to see whether somebody is eligible for Guarantee Credit; these include pensions, earnings above a small threshold, payments from equity release schemes and income from annuities. All are assessed after any tax has been paid.

Savings are also taken into account: they are converted into notional income and assessed as such. First, savings (in bank accounts and shares, for instance) are added up. If they total less than £6,000 (or £10,000 for care home residents), they are ignored. But if they exceed these figures, every £500, or part of £500 over a threshold of £6,000 (or £10,000 if the person lives in a care home) is assumed to contribute an additional £1 a week to their income. This means that savings totalling £14,700, for example, would be assumed to give an income of £18 per week. This conversion of capital to income helpfully provides flexibility, so that people with relatively high savings but low income as well as those with low savings but a higher weekly income can both be eligible.

The list of types of income and savings that are disregarded or taken into account is long and complex. Income from disability benefits (Attendance Allowance, for example) is disregarded. The forms available for claiming GPC explain the various types of income and savings that must be declared, as well as how they are treated (usually after any tax has been paid).

Here are the three additional payments for which an applicant for GPC might qualify:

Help with housing costs

Guarantee Pension Credit contains a facility for obtaining additional help on top of the standard minimum guarantee if you face ongoing costs because you own or lease your property. Perhaps you have bought the lease to your flat and face annual maintenance or service charges, ground rent, mortgage payments or interest on a loan you have taken out for repairs and improvements. If so, you may be able to receive a higher amount to cover these costs.

One useful provision is that you can receive help with your housing costs even if you are away from home for up to 52 weeks. This includes absences because you are in hospital, are providing care for somebody or are living in a care home for short-term care or for a trial period to see whether you wish to move permanently to the facility.

If you need help with paying rent on your home (whether to a private landlord, local authority or housing association), you need to apply for a separate benefit to your local authority – Housing Benefit (see below). People who receive GPC are eligible for Housing Benefit at the maximum rate.

Extra help for disabled people

You can also qualify for an additional weekly payment through Guarantee Pension Credit if you are coping with illness or disability. In this case, you would receive a Severe Disability additional amount. In 2017 this was worth £62.45 for a single person and £124.90 if both partners qualified.

To qualify for the Severe Disability amount, you must already be receiving one of the (non-means-tested) disability benefits discussed in Chapter 35 – Attendance Allowance, Disability Living Allowance or the Personal Independence Payment.

As noted above, the existence of this additional disability amount can be invaluable not only for people on the lowest incomes, for it brings within eligibility for GPC people whose income was slightly higher than the basic amount for GPC. So a successful application on the part of such people for Attendance Allowance would not only increase their income by the amount of the Attendance Allowance but also entitle them to GPC, since the amount that it is considered they need to live on rises from £159.35 to £221.80 for a single person and from £243.25 to £368.15, if both members of a couple qualify. (The financial rewards of the original application for Attendance Allowance would not stop there, since Guarantee Pension Credit provides an automatic gateway to an array of state benefits, such as Council Tax Reduction, *as explained below.*)

However, there are two main restrictions on who may receive the Severe Disability amount. First, there must be no 'non-dependants' living in the household, such as a grown-up son or daughter, who would be assumed to be sharing the expenses of the household. However, if there is a non-dependant adult who is receiving a qualifying disability benefit or is registered blind, Severe Disability addition can be claimed. The qualifying benefits in this situation are Attendance Allowance, the daily living component of Personal Independence Payment, the middle or highest rate of the care component of Disabled Living Allowance, Armed Forces Independence Payment, Constant Attendance Allowance and Severe Disablement Allowance.

Second, you cannot receive the Severe Disability amount if someone who is looking after you is receiving Carer's Allowance *(see page 845).* However, if they are entitled to Carer's Allowance but not actually receiving it (because they are earning more than £110 per week or are receiving a state retirement pension, *as explained on page 846),* Severe Disability premium can be paid.

In the case of a couple, if both receive a qualifying disability benefit, the couple will receive the couple's rate of the Severe Disability addition (£124.90), so long as there are no non-dependant adults in their household and no one receives Carer's Allowance in respect of either of them. The premium is paid at the single rate if Carer's Allowance is paid in respect of one of the couple.

All this means that if both members of a couple are entitled to the Severe Disability premium, they are entitled to receive a weekly amount that has increased by more than £120 from the basic available through GPC.

Extra help for carers

As noted above, the other group who can benefit from additional payments through Guarantee Pension Credit is carers. The initial financial reward from a successful claim is not as great as with the Severe Disability premium, but it is certainly worth considering.

To receive the Carer's Additional Amount, you must be entitled to the main carers' benefit, Carer's Allowance. As explained earlier *(on page 845)*, this is a benefit specifically for the unpaid carers of people who are receiving a disability benefit such as Attendance Allowance. Many older people do not receive Carer's Allowance because the government has stipulated that people cannot receive it and the state retirement pension at the same time. However, as long as someone is entitled to receive Carer's Allowance, even if they do not actually get it, they are entitled to the Carer Premium of GPC, whether they are receiving a state pension or not.

If an older couple were caring for each other in a way that would qualify them for Carer's Allowance (although they did not actually receive it) and were both receiving the standard amount under GPC plus the Severe Disability premium on top of their basic GPC, they would see the amount to which they were entitled under GPC rise further, to £430.45 per week.

Pension Credit as a means of getting other goods and services

Not only does Guarantee Credit provide a guaranteed minimum income, it also entitles the recipient to an array of separate services and goods. These include:

- the maximum rate of Council Tax Reduction *(see pages 849–50)*

- the top rate of Housing Benefit *(pages 861–3)*

- the top rate of grants to improve insulation and heating *(pages 193–6)* and discounts on energy bills *(page 192)*

- a voucher towards the cost of spectacles. You can pay an additional top-up yourself if the glasses (or contact lenses) you wish to purchase cost more than the voucher.

- free dental treatment, check-ups and equipment such as false teeth provided by an NHS dentist *(see page 306)*

- free wigs, support tights and fabric support aids, such as surgical bras and spine and abdomen supports
- help with the cost of travelling to and from hospital for NHS treatment *(page 933)*
- Discretionary Loans
- the Cold Weather Payment *(page 864)*

Universal Credit

The equivalent for adults who are too young to qualify for Guarantee Pension Credit is Universal Credit. Like GPC, this is awarded on grounds of low income and does not require National Insurance contributions to qualify. Similarly, the amount received varies from person to person. At the time of writing, Universal Credit was not available everywhere. Introduced in 2013, it is being rolled out across the UK gradually, area by area – a process that will not be complete until late 2017 at the earliest. Until then, the benefits it replaces will continue to be available to new applicants in the areas that Universal Credit has not reached.

Universal Credit replaces the following benefits:

- Employment and Support Allowance (the key benefit for people who are off work and unable to work because of ill health)
- Job Seeker's Allowance (for people who are looking for work)
- Income Support (a means-tested benefit for people on a low income who are not in full-time work)
- Working Tax Credit *(see page 881)*

The idea of Universal Credit is to introduce flexibility, so that instead of someone having to apply for a completely different benefit should they get a job, their credit can be adjusted. In other words, as people move into or out of work, Universal Credit is a sort of self-adjusting benefit.

People who are helped by it include those who have lost their job, those who do not earn much and those who rely on savings and investments which do not yield much money. To qualify, a person's total savings must not exceed £6,000 (although some capital is ignored).

The Department for Work and Pensions expects people to apply to it for Universal Credit online; it has said that claimants can use the internet at their local Jobcentre Plus office if they do not have internet access themselves. If you cannot use a computer or need support for some other reason, you can use a phone service through which a DWP advisor will complete a form on your behalf; these calls are not free. The numbers are 0845 600 0723 or textphone 0845 600 0743. In exceptional circumstances, the DWP may help you fill in the form on a home visit.

Everybody who receives Universal Credit gets a basic amount called a 'standard allowance'. But in certain circumstances, they may receive more. They will receive a higher amount for each child for whom they are responsible; if a child is disabled, they receive a higher amount still. There is also provision for paying a higher amount if health problems or disabilities mean that the person involved has 'limited capability for work' or has 'limited capability for work-related activity', much in the way that the amount someone receives through GPC is higher if they have health or disability problems.

Carers may also qualify for a higher than the standard amount of Universal Credit. To do so, they must be caring for a severely disabled person for at least 35 hours each week. This will probably mean that the person for whom they are caring is receiving Attendance Allowance, Disability Living Allowance or Personal Independence Payment and the carer is receiving Carer's Allowance, but it need not. Some people will be eligible for Carer's Allowance but not receive it because they are earning more than the limit allowed for that benefit (£110 per week), yet they might nonetheless qualify for a carer element to add to their standard allowance within Universal Credit.

Despite its name, Universal Credit is not actually universal. Several key benefits remain outside it, such as the Personal Independence Payment.

Savings Pension Credit

Savings Pension Credit (SPC) is a second arm of Pension Credit. It seeks to reward people aged 65 or over of modest means who have made some provision for their retirement on top of their state pension and who reached state pension age before 6 April 2016. The amount SPC offers is small, but can be useful. It is claimed by only around 1 per cent of eligible individuals.[2] Many people are probably unaware that they would qualify.

The income eligibility works as follows. Your weekly income must be at least £133.82 The corresponding figure for a couple is £212.97. Under SPC, you would receive 60p for every £1 by which your income exceeds the threshold, up to a maximum additional weekly sum of £13.07 (for a single person) and £14.75 (for a couple).

In other words, this is an inverse means-tested benefit: the higher your private pension income, the more you receive in Savings Credit, up to a certain limit. Some people will be entitled to Savings Credit, but not Guarantee Credit, because their savings disqualify them from the latter.

Others will qualify for Guarantee Credit, but their income is too low for Savings Credit. Some people will qualify for both.

If you struggle to calculate how much you might receive under Savings Credit, try using a benefits calculator on the website turn2us.org.uk or entitledto.co.uk, or ask a benefits advisor.

Although Savings Credit is not available for people who reach state pension age on or after 6 April 2016, you may still receive it if you are part of a couple and if one of you reached state pension age before 6 April 2016 and you were getting Savings Credit up to 6 April 2016.

Help with rent: Housing Benefit and Local Housing Allowance

For people who have to pay rent to a local authority or housing association, Housing Benefit can be a godsend. It is administered not by the DWP but by local authorities. They forward cash to people whose income is considered too low to pay their rent.

When someone needs help to pay rent to a private landlord, whether an individual or a company (for instance, in a retirement housing scheme), the similar benefit is known as Local Housing Allowance.

Housing Benefit or Local Housing Allowance can include help to pay service charges. These include charges for lifts, gardens, entry phones, communal laundry facilities and fuel charges for communal areas. Service charges that are excluded include water charges, charges for care and support, personal alarms and charges for meals.

The amount of Housing Benefit (or Local Housing Allowance) paid varies according to the financial means of the person (or a couple) responsible for paying the rent and the amount of rent they have to pay. To qualify, you must:

- be liable for rent at the property you normally live in; and
- already be receiving Guarantee Pension Credit; or
- have savings of less than £16,000; or
- have a low income, whether from benefits, work, or both

If you are already receiving the Guarantee element of Pension Credit (*see above*), you will automatically be entitled to Housing Benefit at the maximum rate, and you ought to receive it automatically.

For people below pension age, Housing Benefit is in the process of being subsumed within Universal Credit (*see above*). They may receive Housing Benefit as a separate benefit or, if Universal Credit has been introduced in their area, they may receive a higher amount than the basic rate of Universal Credit to help them pay their rent.

The amount somebody receives depends partly on their income, partly on the amount of rent they have to pay and partly on whether they have an illness or disability. As with other benefits, such as GPC, you can obtain a larger amount of benefit if you are considered to have a disability and if you are a carer. However, entitlement to Housing Benefit is reduced if applicants have a 'non-dependant' living with them, such as an adult child.

Limits on the amount of benefit

Housing Benefit does not enable people to live in spacious, expensive accommodation with their local authority footing the bill. For tenants of private landlords, the rent officer of the local council sets an average rent for each size of accommodation in its area (one-bedroomed, two-bedroomed and so on). That is the maximum eligible rent on which someone can claim help. These Local Housing Allowance rates are shown on every council's website. Or you could phone and ask the housing department of your council.

That maximum eligible rent is then applied to the size of the property considered appropriate for the household in question. It is assumed that an adult couple needs one bedroom and any other person over the age of 16 needs a separate bedroom. So, if you are single or a member of a couple and living in a four-bedroom property, the council would be likely to say that the rate on which you can claim benefit is for a one-bedroom property. You would therefore have to make up any shortfall out of your own resources. However, you can claim allowance for an extra bedroom to accommodate an overnight carer if you or your partner need regular care at night.

A similar rule applies to tenants of council and other social housing. If somebody seems to have more bedrooms than they need, their property must be under-occupied; their Housing Benefit will cover only the number of rooms they are considered to need. So someone's Housing Benefit would be reduced by 14 per cent if they had one extra bedroom and by 25 per cent if two or more. This under-occupancy charge has been called the 'bedroom tax'.

Housing Benefit is one of the benefits that count towards the benefit cap that applies to people of working age *(see below)*.

You can obtain an application form for Housing Benefit from your council or at a local benefits officer or by downloading the form from the government's website (gov.uk). You must send your completed form to the Housing Benefit office of your local authority within 28 days. You can apply for both Housing Benefit and Council Tax Reduction on the same form. If you post the form, do so by recorded delivery, or through a proof of posting receipt (which is free). If you deliver it by hand, make sure you get a receipt. You can ask for any supporting documents you wish to enclose to be photocopied.

The charity Shelter offers advice about obtaining housing-related benefit on its website, helpline and at advice centres.

Local councils have the power to make discretionary housing payments to help people who are receiving Housing Benefit yet still struggling to pay their rent, perhaps because of additional costs related to health problems, travelling to hospital or acting as a carer. Councils vary in the rules they use in allocating these payments, which are made for short periods. If you are having difficulties, ask your council for a claim form and explain why you are struggling with your rent.

The benefit cap

People who are receiving Housing Benefit or Universal Credit are subject to a total limit on the amount any person or couple can receive in benefits, called the 'benefit cap'. The benefits that can be added up in the cap include not just Housing Benefit and Universal Credit but also Carer's Allowance, the benefits that Universal Credit replaces (Income Support, Jobseeker's Allowance and Employment and Support Allowance), Severe Disablement Allowance and Bereavement Allowance.

If you receive a total sum from these benefits that exceeds £257.69 per week (for a single person with no children) or £384.62 (for a couple or a lone parent), the amount of your Housing Benefit or Universal Credit is reduced to bring the total down to the level of the benefit cap. (The equivalent figures for people living in Greater London are £296.35 and £442.31.)

You can receive benefits such as Carer's Allowance without their being subject to the cap: it is triggered only if you are receiving Housing Benefit or Universal Credit.

Fortunately, the majority of the benefits considered in this part, including Pension Credit, Attendance Allowance and the Personal Independence Payment, are completely excluded from the cap.

Funeral Expenses Payments

The Department for Work and Pensions gives grants to people of modest means who have responsibility for arranging a funeral. These can be invaluable.

If you are the partner of a person who has died, or there is someone else, such as a close relative, for whose funeral it is reasonable to expect you should take responsibility, you can apply to the DWP for a grant to help cover the costs. The payment can cover the cost of burial or cremation, local authority fees, certain necessary travel expenses and up to £700 for other costs, such as a coffin.

To qualify for a Funeral Expenses Payment, you must be receiving a means-related benefit, such as Guarantee Pension Credit, Universal Credit or Housing Benefit. Your savings are disregarded when your application is assessed. However, assets of the deceased person such as occupational pensions and payments from insurance policies, burial clubs and pre-paid funeral plans are taken into account.

You should apply for a payment within three months of the funeral. You cannot usually get a payment if there is someone closer or equally close to the person who has died who is not receiving a means-tested benefit.

To apply, obtain a form from the government website (gov.uk) or phone the Bereavement Service on 0845 606 0265, textphone 0845 606 0285 or collect a form from a Jobcentre Plus office.

Applicants in Northern Ireland should go to a local Social Security or Jobs and Benefits office or phone the Social Security Agency's Bereavement Service on 0800 085 2463 or download a form from the government website (nidirect.gov.uk).

Cold Weather Payments

Cold Weather Payments are made during periods when the average temperature is below freezing to people who already receive a qualifying benefit.

This may be Guarantee Pension Credit. People receiving GPC are given £25 per week if the average temperature recorded or forecast over seven consecutive days in their area is zero degrees Celsius or less and they do not live in a care home.

For younger people, it is not enough to receive a means-tested benefit such as Income Support or Universal Credit: they must also receive a disability premium on top of this means-tested benefit, or they must be responsible for a child under the age of five or a disabled child.

NHS Low Income Scheme

Some people of modest means have never applied for Guarantee Pension Credit for one reason or another, although their income is low. They too may be entitled to help with the cost of those goods and services for which the NHS makes a charge.

To apply, you have to make a claim yourself in which you set out your income and your expenses, just as you would were you applying for Income Support or Pension Credit. The assessors work out whether your income exceeds your expenditure by more than a small amount (half the current English prescription charge). If it does, you may nonetheless qualify for partial help. Your savings must not exceed £16,000; for care home residents the limit is £23,250 for those in England, Scotland and Northern Ireland, and £24,000 for residents in Wales.

When working out your weekly expenditure requirements, the assessors take into account council tax, rent less any Housing Benefit, mortgage interest and capital payments on housing-related loans, a personal allowance and also additional sums if you are disabled and/or a carer. Inclusion of housing and council tax costs in the assessment means that you could get help with your health costs even though your income is deemed too high to qualify you for Income Support.

Help through this scheme can be particularly valuable if you have high ongoing costs to go to hospital for treatment. Ask at the hospital to which you have to travel for an application form for the Low Income Scheme. Or you can order a form (HC1) online or pick one up at your local Jobcentre Plus office; your doctor, dentist, pharmacist or optician may also be able to give you one. If you need help in completing the form, call the NHS Help with Health Costs unit on 0300 330 1343 and ask to speak to an advisor. They can fill in the form for you and then post it to you to sign and return.

The form in Northern Ireland is HC11 and it is available from the government website (nidirect.gov.uk) and Social Security offices as well as Jobs and Benefits offices.

Apart from hospital fares, the scheme can also help pay for dental treatment and appliances such as dentures, glasses and contact lenses, wigs and fabric supports. It can also help pay for prescriptions, although these are free on a non-means-tested basis for various groups in the different countries of the UK *(as explained on page 280)*.

In addition, war pensioners who have a war pension exemption certificate can claim back money for dental treatment, travel costs and glasses, so long as the reason for the cost is their disablement. Veterans UK, which is part of the Ministry of Defence and administers war pensions, can provide further information.

If you or your partner already receive Guarantee Pension Credit, Income Support, Income-based Jobseeker's Allowance, Income-related

Employment and Support Allowance or you are named on or entitled to an NHS Tax Credit Exemption Certificate, you do not need to apply for these exemptions from health charges: proof of receipt of the benefit in question entitles you to them.

Discretionary Loans

People who are receiving a means-tested benefit such as Guarantee Pension Credit or Universal Credit can apply to the Department for Work and Pensions (or in Northern Ireland, the Social Security Agency) for a loan for specific purposes. 'Budgeting Loans', as they are known, which range from £100 to £1,500 can help pay for:

- removal expenses or rent in advance to order to go and live in different accommodation
- the expenses of obtaining work
- travelling expenses (perhaps to hospital or to visit someone in hospital)
- the purchase of furniture and household equipment
- the purchase of clothing and footwear

Only people receiving a qualifying benefit are eligible and they must be able to repay the loan. These benefits are: Pension Credit (Guarantee or Savings), Income Support, Income-based Jobseeker's Allowance and Income-related Employment and Support Allowance. Loans are repaid through deductions from these benefits. There is a similar provision for people receiving Universal Credit to obtain loans, administered through Universal Credit (see page 859–60).

Application forms for budgeting loans can be obtained from local benefits offices or downloaded from gov.uk. They are discretionary, so there is no automatic entitlement to one, however desperate your circumstances.

A similar arrangement is linked to Universal Credit. If you receive that benefit and are struggling with particular expenses, such as the purchase of household equipment or essential furniture, you may be able to obtain a 'Budgeting Advance'. This is essentially a loan from the DWP that you repay through deductions on your future Universal Credit payments.

Discretionary grants

In Scotland and Wales, there are national schemes administered by local authorities that provide financial help in specific circumstances. They replace grants that used to be UK-wide. All these grants are discretionary.

The **Welsh** government has placed money in its Discretionary Assistance Fund *(listed in Useful Contacts),* providing two categories of grant. One is designed to help people in an emergency (such after a flood) or when there is an immediate threat to their health or well-being. The other type aims to help people to remain or begin to live independently in the community. An individual assistance payment could help someone of modest means to cover the costs of setting up home again after a period in a care home, for example.

The **Scottish** Welfare Fund is similar, with Crisis Grants for help in a disaster or health emergency situation and Community Care Grants that seek to help people who wish to live independently, either by helping them establish an independent home or continue living independently and preventing the need to move to a care home. These grants may also help families facing exceptional pressure.

In **Northern Ireland,** a similar scheme was being set up at the time of writing.

In **England,** no similar national pot of money exists. Local authorities may – or may not – offer help, whether through cash grants or goods, such as furniture, bedding, clothing and food.

Wherever you live in the UK, ask your local council whether anything exists in your area. The website turn2us.org.uk provides links to all the schemes throughout the UK.

Benefits, administration and advice

Benefits are administered in Great Britain by the Department for Work and Pensions. This has a number of different departments, which handle different benefits. You can key in the name of a benefit into the government's website, gov.uk, and obtain basic information about it together with an application form. Local offices that provide information about benefits are called Jobcentre Plus, and they are listed in phone directories.

In Northern Ireland, benefits are administered separately, although there is parity between them. They are the responsibility of the Social Security Agency. Local offices are called Social Security or Jobs and Benefits Offices, and they are listed in the phone book.

The Department for Work and Pensions offers information and advice helplines about the various benefits described in this part, all of which it is responsible for, apart from council tax-related matters and Housing Benefit. If you contact the DWP, you should be put through to the relevant section.

However, the DWP does not usually offer suggestions about benefits for which you could usefully apply: it is essentially responsible for the administration of benefits, not benefits advice. The people on the helpline may well be trained only in one particular benefit and thus unable to take an overall view. But they should give you details about the benefit about which you are enquiring and tell you the mechanism for making an application.

The DWP publishes leaflets about benefits and a useful guide to pensions and other benefits called *Pensioners' Guide: Making the Most of Government Help and Advice*. You can obtain a copy (or the slightly different one for Scotland) over the telephone and at Jobcentre Plus offices, Citizens Advice and other centres that offer benefits advice. Leaflets are also often available at other places such as public libraries, post offices and doctors' surgeries.

Much information and advice about benefits is provided by non-government organisations online, often with the facility for sending in questions. I have found the following websites to be especially useful:

> turn2us.org.uk
> savvywoman.co.uk
> rightsnet.org.uk
> disabilityrightsuk.org
> welfarerights.net
> entitledto.co.uk
> hertsdirect.org/benefits

Organisations that provide benefits advice over the phone as well as through the internet include the little-known but most useful Pensions Advisory Service *(see page 831)*, Age UK, Carers UK, Shelter and Independent Age.

If you are looking for an encyclopaedia that provides detailed information about all the benefits available, have a look at the Child Poverty Action Group's *Welfare Benefits Handbook*. This is updated in print form every year. A weighty tome, it is expensive, but available at a much reduced price for people who are receiving or applying for benefits. It contains more detail than is provided in this chapter on appealing against benefits decisions, for instance.

However, what many people want is someone who will sit down alongside them and talk to them in confidence about benefits and help them fill in the forms. Although this is time-consuming work, several organisations provide it and it is well worth seeking it out. The result could be a doubling of your income.

Several charitable organisations that support people with particular medical conditions offer one-to-one help with obtaining benefits, which may involve a support worker visiting you and helping you fill in forms. These groups include Macmillan Cancer Support, the Parkinson's Society and the Royal National Institute of Blind People (RNIB). Local voluntary groups for disabled people often also have welfare rights officers.

Citizens Advice provides benefits advice through a helpline and also one-to-one consultations. Trained volunteers at its local bureaux, backed up by paid experts, run benefit checks, put forward suggestions for benefits for which someone could usefully apply and also ways in which their overall income might be increased, perhaps through discounts on energy bills *(page 192)*. They also look for ways in which higher amounts could be received from existing benefits, such as the high rather than low rate of Attendance Allowance. Help is given to fill in application forms and fight appeals against the refusal of benefits, if necessary. The Citizens Advice website contains information about benefits specific to the different countries of the UK.

Local authorities also often offer welfare benefits advice at welfare centres. So too do local carers' centres (part of the Carers Trust network), many housing associations, and local Age UK organisations. If you are a carer, do get a benefits check at a carers' centre.

BBC Radio 4's *Moneybox* answers questions from callers and is also a valuable means of keeping abreast of developments in the whole field of personal finance, including benefits.

Tips on applying and appealing

When in doubt about whether to apply for a benefit, you should claim, claim early and claim often.

Be careful: you must not be seen to be deliberately depriving yourself of assets in order to qualify for means-tested help. But if your savings place you above the limit, you can choose to spend them on things you need, which would of course bring your assets down. The question the Department for Work and Pensions would ask is whether you would have acted in that way if the benefits system did not exist: in other words, were you depleting your resources in order to increase your entitlement to benefits? If you were spending money on much-needed house adaptations, a winter coat, winter boots or a new washing machine, tumble dryer or freezer, they might not consider that unreasonable compared with, say, making large gifts of cash to your children.

Applications can usually be submitted online or in paper form. I outline the pros and cons of each and the necessity of keeping a copy of your submission when considering applications for Attendance Allowance *(on page 839)*. If possible, send in your application by recorded delivery or, if that is too expensive, obtain proof of postage, which is free. Make sure you keep a copy for yourself.

If your application is turned down, consider appealing. Appeals are made in the first instance to the DWP, but after that they can be made to a part of the Courts and Tribunals Service. In that case, the decision is made by a judge acting independently of the DWP. You cannot appeal to the Tribunals Service without having first asked the DWP to reconsider its decision.

Asking the DWP to reconsider its decision

The decision to reject your application or turn down some aspect of it might have been made by a relatively untrained administrator, so there could be grounds of appeal on a technicality – for instance, that another benefit cannot disqualify you from the one you are seeking or that the benefit can be backdated. Or grounds for appeal might revolve around whether or not you satisfy the disability requirements for the benefit in question, for instance.

If you are appealing, prioritise lodging the appeal in the time window that the DWP imposes. For the vast majority of benefits, you have only one month to appeal against a decision and ask the DWP to reconsider it. However, you have slightly longer (one month and 14 days from the date you received your original decision letter) if you write and ask the DWP for a 'statement of reasons' for their decision.

Whether or not you obtain a statement of reasons, when you write and ask the DWP to reconsider their decision, you should include:

✓ your full name, address and National Insurance number

✓ a summary of the DWP's decision and the date on which it was made

✓ an explanation of why you think the DWP's decision was wrong. If you have been turned down for a disability benefit, explain why you consider you meet the assessment criteria for that benefit. If your condition has worsened since you lodged the application, say so and link the worsening of your condition to the assessment requirement.

✓ any evidence that supports your claim. *(On pages 839–40, I discuss the sort of supporting evidence you might submit for an application for a disability benefit.)*

If you cannot send in the evidence within the one-month limit, send in your request for reconsideration and say on the form that a particular submission will follow.

Expect an acknowledgement from the DWP that it has received your request for reconsideration. After that, an official from the DWP will probably phone you. Be ready for this call. Don't say you are fine: be ready to explain the difficulties you face and why you consider the DWP's decision to be wrong. Tell the official about any further supporting evidence; they should wait a month for it to arrive before making the decision.

The DWP will notify you in writing of its verdict, with two copies of a 'mandatory reconsideration notice'. Keep both copies. If it says you should have received the benefit after all, it should backdate the amounts you should have received to the date of its original decision.

Appealing to a tribunal

If the DWP has not shifted its position, you can appeal to a tribunal. You do not need a solicitor to help you, but it is certainly worth getting advice *(from one of the organisations listed on page 869)*, if possible at an advice centre.

If you decide to appeal, you must do so within one month of the date the DWP has written on its mandatory reconsideration letter. If you have difficulty in meeting this deadline, ask a benefits advisor to help you appeal against it.

You send in your appeal on a special form called SSCS1 to Her Majesty's Courts and Tribunal Service *(address in Useful Contacts)*. This form is in a leaflet called *Notice of Appeal against a Decision of the Department for Work and Pensions.*

The Appeals Service Northern Ireland provides appeals forms and handles the administrative process in Northern Ireland.

Enclose any supporting evidence you wish and also one of the copies of your mandatory reconsideration notice. On the form you will be asked whether you would like your case to be decided at a face-to-face hearing or by paperwork. More appeals succeed through face-to-face hearing; this is probably because at a hearing the appellant has another chance of putting forward their case, greater opportunity to give practical examples of the difficulties they face, and the opportunity to address particular questions and doubts the panel may have. Appellants can also call witnesses, and they can take someone to the appeal for emotional support and ask the judge on the tribunal panel for consent for any supporter to prompt them should they forget to bring up particular points.

You can send in further supporting evidence up till the hearing itself, although the earlier you send it in, the better, and you risk a delay if you give it in on the day of the hearing.

As well as a judge, the tribunal panel for Attendance Allowance and Personal Independence Payment contains a doctor and a professional expert in disability matters, such as an occupational therapist, nurse or social worker. They ask you questions about your condition and the difficulties it poses in enabling you to live independently.

The Tribunals Service must inform you at least 14 days in advance of your hearing. It has the discretion to reimburse your expenses in attending a hearing, including travel by public transport or taxi if you cannot use buses and trains, and the expenses incurred by a companion, if you need one, and any witnesses, as well as meals and lost earnings.

The panel usually comes to a decision on the day of the hearing; if not, it sends its decision by first-class post.

Appeals against a tribunal decision can only be made on the grounds of a legal error. If you wish to appeal, ask the tribunal for a written statement of the reasons for its decision and try to obtain specialist advice. If you phone Civil Legal Advice (0845 345 4345), they can tell you whether you would be entitled to financial help to pay for legal advice.

If your appeal is successful, the DWP should send you the benefit amount you have missed out on. To ensure you get paid as soon as possible, send a copy of the tribunal decision to the relevant DWP office.

Details of appeal procedures about government benefits are set out in a leaflet called *If You Think your Decision is Wrong*, GL24, which is available from the DWP (post or internet), Jobcentre Plus offices and some Citizens Advice and other advice centres.

Local authorities provide information about appealing against their benefit decisions on council tax matters and Housing Benefit. Organisations such as Shelter provide information and advice about appealing against these decisions.

Disability Rights UK provides helpful summaries of tribunal decisions on its website.

Change of circumstances

It is important to notify the Department for Work and Pensions, or the Social Security Agency in Northern Ireland, of any change in your circumstances that could affect your entitlement to any benefit you receive. In the original award notice, you will be told which changes of circumstances you should report. Report these as soon as possible and also any you might reasonably expect might affect your award of a benefit. Do so in writing to the DWP or ask at a local Jobcentre Plus office.

The change might not necessarily involve finance, such as an increase in your earnings. For instance, a basic rule for many means-tested benefits is that you must not share your household with an able-bodied adult, as it is assumed that these 'non-dependant adults' will contribute to your household income. If for instance, you are receiving Guarantee Pension Credit, perhaps with the additional Severe Disability premium, and your son or daughter comes to live with you, you must tell the Department for Work and Pensions lest you flout the rules and commit fraud. If you go into hospital, your benefit may be affected. Check on the paperwork you are sent when you receive the award. For instance, Attendance Allowance stops after a four-week stay in hospital, and any Carer's Allowance and Severe Disability addition for Pension Credit contingent upon that Attendance Allowance will also stop then.

Means-tested benefits

* You must proactively apply for means-tested benefits – they won't automatically turn up, even if you are eligible.

* Get a free benefits check and help with filling in the forms from an advice centre, if you can.

* Guarantee Pension Credit provides a substantial top-up to the pre-April-2016 state retirement pension and also qualifies you for help with housing-related mortgages and loans.

* Disability entitles you to Guarantee Pension Credit even if you would otherwise have too much income or too many savings.

* Guarantee Pension Credit qualifies you for the top rate of Housing Benefit and 100 per cent relief on council tax.

* Carers too can benefit from free benefits checks.

* Acting as an unpaid carer can open to the way to:

    * a reduction in council tax
    * credits in lieu of earnings in your National Insurance record
    * a specific benefit (Carer's Allowance)
    * extra payments on other benefits

Chapter 37

Earning, investing and bestowing

There is a lot of emphasis on publicly-provided benefits for older people. However, for most people, the fruits of their own provision will be more or at least as important. It is therefore essential to attend carefully to the disposition of such assets, income and potential income-generating capabilities you possess.

Inevitably, the extent of these will be determined largely by decisions taken long before you reach later life. Nonetheless, there is still much you can do to get the most out of such resources as remain available to you. At the same time, you may wish to generate new cash through employment, perhaps setting up your own business or taking a job.

In this chapter I first look at some of the main decisions that may face us in later life, involving private pensions, investment (including the release of cash through equity release), and work. I also outline some of the factors to be taken into account in deciding whether to give away our money.

However much or little we have, the daily task of handling money can be difficult. Perhaps we have relied on someone else, such as our father and later our partner, to handle all our financial affairs. Fine while the finance-savvy person is available, but should they leave or die, what then? We may be unaware of basic financial matters, such as the meaning of a notional rate of return, let alone whether we should invest in an ISA.

Some people, familiar with the world of finance, are searching for top-end financial advice. Others are struggling with basic arithmetic. Many older people not only find it difficult to make sense of money but get into debt. Debt does not only cause real practical problems: it affects us psychologically, sapping our confidence, leaving us too nervous to open the post. And what if we cannot see well or easily wield a pen? Today's world of online banking can make transactions truly scary.

Fortunately, in all these areas of difficulty, some help is available. This chapter therefore examines:

- ▶ private pensions
- ▶ working in later life
- ▶ investment
- ▶ equity release
- ▶ inheritance
- ▶ sources of advice and support on money matters, including debt
- ▶ coping with financial affairs if you have a disability

Private pensions

Most older people not wholly dependent on the state for their incomes will be relying mainly on private pensions, either occupational or personal. Most of the crucial decisions in this area will have been made long before retirement, however unwittingly, and many will be irrevocable. However, any that remain to be made should be taken seriously because of the huge difference they can make to financial standing.

So too should any errors once your pension is being paid. If your pension provider fails to provide your payments as it should or has made a mistake in its calculations and you cannot resolve the matter with them, contact the Pensions Ombudsman – an independent organisation which investigates complaints about the administration of pensions, for free. The Ombudsman can tell a pension provider to sort out a difficulty and to pay compensation for any distress and inconvenience it has caused.

Defined-benefit pensions

If you have a defined-benefit pension, you will be paid a particular sum based on your salary, your years of service and an 'accrual rate', that is, the rate of pension to which you are entitled for each year of service.

Unlike the state pension, which you cannot take before the age laid down by government, you can usually start taking money from a private pension scheme from the age of 55. Many schemes allow retirees to take a lump sum when they reach that age, which usually means the regular income they receive from the scheme is less.

If you want to retire before the normal age at which your firm or organisation pays a pension, talk to it about when this might be possible, how much you would receive and by how much your future pension would be reduced from not building up contributions until the normal retirement age for that organisation.

Money purchase/defined contribution schemes

The other kind of pension scheme built up while working is called a money purchase pension scheme or a defined contribution scheme. A pot of money is built up and then becomes available for the person involved to deal with as they wish.

In the past, the law required people receiving these pension pots to convert them into an annuity (a product that provides a regular income usually for life), apart from 25 per cent, which could be taken tax-free as soon as the pension was taken. Since April 2015, the requirement to buy an annuity on retirement has been withdrawn. Instead, savers can withdraw the money in their pension pot and use it entirely as they please. They can, if they wish, take their entire fund as a lump sum from the age of 55 – although 75 per cent of this would be taxable at their marginal income tax rate.

Retirees with a pension pot to spend face a decision with far-reaching consequences. Freeing up cash will enable them to spend on cruises or the like, or perhaps invest in fields like buy-to-let which they may feel will offer better returns that an annuity. However, buying an annuity *(see below)* still probably offers the most secure way of providing a regular income to the end of life.

Advice on disposal of a pension pot

Pension Wise is a free service which gives people aged 50 or over who have a defined contribution pension guidance on their decisions about how to dispose of it. The government introduced Pension Wise in 2015 shortly before removing the obligation always to buy an annuity.

Pension Wise has not been widely publicised and only one in ten people who accessed their pension pots used it during the early months after its introduction and the change in the rules on buying an annuity. Yet Pension Wise's advice is potentially very valuable. You can choose between a 45-minute phone consultation or face-to-face interview. It also publishes information on its website.

Your Pension Wise advisor would give you general guidance on the options open to you together with details about where you could go for further information and/or one-to-one bespoke advice. (In 2016 the government said it would merge the Pension Wise, the Pension Advisory Service and Money Advice Service into a new unified body.)

Pension Wise advisors do not give advice related to someone's wider financial circumstances, referring to, say, their existing investments. So seek further help from a financial advisor on your own situation *(see page 890 for finding an advisor)*. They should be able to discuss your options within a wider canvas, including your wealth in property, entitlement to benefits, care costs and liability for inheritance tax.

Beware of scammers! Since the relaxation over the disposal of pension pots, scammers have been busy inviting unsuspecting investors to buy assets such as overseas property or fine wine. If someone cold calls you with the offer of advice and the opportunity to invest, be wary, especially if they claim to be from the government. The government never contacts someone unprompted to discuss their pension options.[1]

The Telephone Preference Service (TPS) is a free service which maintains an official, central opt-out register on which you can record your preference not to receive unsolicited sales or marketing calls. It is against the law for all organisations (including charities, voluntary organisations and political parties) to make such calls to numbers registered with the TPS, unless they have your consent to do so. Some scammers will not be deterred, but registration should help reduce the numbers of businesses trying to get their hands on your pension pot. The TPS applies to both landline and mobile calls, but cannot prevent text messages. Registration is straightforward. The TPS is not associated with any company that may contact you claiming to stop unsolicited calls and which charges a fee.

Annuities

If you buy an annuity, you transfer money from your pension pot to an insurance company or other financial provider, which then provides you with regular payments for the rest of your life. These will be subject to tax if, together with any other income, they add up to more than your annual personal allowance.

There are a number of different ways in which money can be paid out. You can opt to receive a fixed monthly sum (which will of course be eroded by inflation), an inflation-indexed sum or a sum rising each year by a fixed percentage. The latter choices may sound tempting, but of course you pay heavily for asking the provider to take the financial risk you will be avoiding.

Most people opt for an annuity that ends when they die. But you can buy an annuity that pays an income to your partner should they outlive you. Arranging for a proportion to go to a surviving partner will of course drive the rate down further, as the provider will expect to have to pay out for longer.

Another option is an investment-linked annuity. This allows the pension fund to be invested in the stock market while payments are made, increasing the possibility of higher payments if the investments do well but risking a fall in income if they fare badly.

The amount an annuity provider pays varies from person to person according to such factors as the type of annuity they choose, their life expectancy, their gender (as women are expected to live longer than men) and their health. So-called 'enhanced annuities' or 'impaired annuities' pay a larger than normal sum to people with serious ongoing health conditions, such as heart disease, diabetes and kidney failure, on the assumption that payment will be needed for a shorter period. If you have a health condition, do find out what your rate would be through an enhanced annuity – if you die within the period the annuity provider expects, you will have benefitted from a higher rate than you would get with a standard annuity. But if you win your bet with the annuity provider on the length of time you live, you also gain. In that case, you continue to receive an annuity, but at a lower rate.

Buying an annuity is one of the most important decisions many of us ever take. First it determines our income (and possibly that of a partner) for the rest of our life. Second, once an annuity has been set up, it can be very difficult and often impossible to change it, although, as with most financial products, the purchaser has the right to a cooling-off period.

So how do you choose an annuity? Many people simply buy one offered by the financial provider with whom they built up their pension pot. But you do not need to do so. Indeed, you have a legal right to choose whichever provider you wish, under the so-called 'open market option', which simply means you can shop around and compare rates.

Many people fail to shop around, but this can mean they forego considerable sums. Annuity rates vary greatly and it is worth getting different quotes from different providers. Research carried out in 2014 by the Financial Conduct Authority (FCA), which issues useful factsheets on annuities, showed that eight out of ten people who purchased an annuity from the provider of their pension pot would have received a higher income from an annuity had they shopped around.[2] The consumer organisation Which? says that shopping around can increase annuity income by up to 20 per cent.[3]

However, if your pension pot provider operates a 'guaranteed annuity rate' that guarantees you a rate that is higher than any rate you would find elsewhere, it may well be best to stick with the original provider. Check the terms and conditions of its guaranteed annuity rate and also that the annuity being offered is one that meets your circumstances and needs.

The importance of doing checks such as these is explained by the Pensions Advisory Service in guidance it provides about annuities on its website. This organisation was mentioned in the previous chapter in connection with information and guidance about the state pension. It offers free, impartial information and advice about all types of private pension schemes too, including annuities. On its website, there are tools to help you estimate your life expectancy, calculate the tax you would pay on lump sums and work out how long your pension pot will last, for example. You can also talk to an expert over the phone or by webchat or write in about your individual situation. The Pensions Advisory Service is an independent organisation grant-aided by the Department for Work and Pensions.

Though beneficiaries are able to make the choice about which way to go from the age of 55, they can put it off if they choose. If you die before you cash in, however, the whole sum in your fund may become available to your heirs entirely free of inheritance tax, unlike, say, your house. This can be particularly valuable: not only do your life savings not disappear with you (if you have a lifetime annuity), but the money can be used to pay the inheritance tax on your estate. As this tax has to be cleared up before any legacies can be paid out, it can come in very handy.

Bear in mind that a high level of annuity income will disqualify you from means-tested benefits for which you might otherwise become eligible (see Chapter 36).

Paid work

Some older people work purely for financial reasons, but there may be other reasons why work is attractive: the sense of self-worth that comes from knowing that somebody is prepared to pay you for your efforts, a social world, an opportunity to get out of the house and perks, from a company car to use of the photocopier.

Receipt of the state retirement pension does not depend on stopping work, although if you work and receive your pension, much of both may be creamed off in tax. Anybody can receive a state and/or an occupational pension and continue to work either on a self-employed basis or for an employer, whether part or full time, when they are over state retirement age. Those who work after that age do not have to pay National Insurance contributions. If you decide to continue working, consider deferring receipt of your state pension (see page 831).

The Pensions Act 2008 requires all employers to offer workplace pension schemes and to enrol eligible workers into their schemes; this has become known as automatic enrolment. Employers enrol these workers into a workplace pension scheme and deduct any contributions that the worker is required to pay from their wages or salary, and then pay into the pension scheme on their behalf. To be eligible for automatic enrolment, you must be under state pension age, earning a salary of at least £10,000 per year and working in the UK under a contract of employment.

Less well known is the fact that individuals between state pension age and 74 who earn at least £5,876 (2017–8 figure) can ask to be admitted to a pension scheme, in which case the employer must contribute. This right to opt in is a valuable benefit.

Self-employment in later life is popular. There is much to be said for setting up your own business in later life to control both the financial aspects of the business but also the environment in which you work. Do make arrangements for someone else to take charge in your place should you become unwell, through an ordinary or a lasting power of attorney.

Many people seem unaware that Working Tax Credit can be claimed by people even if they are receiving their state pension. It provides up to £1,960 per year to top up low earnings, whether from employment or self-employment. Unlike most means-tested benefits, there is no savings threshold above which an applicant becomes ineligible. For younger adults only, it is being replaced by Universal Credit *(page 859)*.

Age discrimination at work

Some older people wish to carry on in their existing job, while others wish to find another. Fortunately, the rights of older people in the workplace have increased significantly in recent years.

It is unlawful for an employer to force an employee to retire at 65. It is also unlawful to insist that someone must stop work at a particular age specified by a company or organisation – its own 'mandatory retirement age', say, 67. Retirement against an employee's wishes is considered to be age discrimination unless the employer can show that the mandatory retirement age or the age at which the employer wishes the employee to go (if no such mandatory age is in place and the employee is over 65) can be 'objectively justified', if necessary at an employment tribunal. This means that the employer would have to provide sound reasons for the age he or she specifies and evidence to back them up.

'Intergenerational fairness' is often argued by employers in these circumstances; it means that the mandatory retirement age seeks to promote access to employment in the organisation for younger people. If an employer wishes to justify mandatory retirement on grounds of intergenerational fairness in order to create turnover of senior staff so as to recruit and retain younger workers, they must demonstrate that they do in fact have problems in recruiting and retaining younger workers. They must also show that the retirement age they have chosen rather than another, higher age is a proportionate way of meeting that aim.

The employer also has to show that the retirement of the employee in question is a proportionate means of meeting the aims of mandatory retirement and that is not more than is required in the circumstances.

The Ministry of Justice has set a mandatory retirement age for its judges of 70. A judge, Mr White, wished to continue past this age and took the Ministry of Justice to an employment tribunal in 2014. At the tribunal, the Ministry sought to justify its mandatory retirement age by arguing that this was necessary on grounds of inter-generational fairness, the preservation of the judge's dignity and the maintenance of public confidence in the service.

The employment tribunal agreed with the Ministry of Justice that the aims of its mandatory retirement age were legitimate. The tribunal then looked at the extent to which the retirement age was a proportionate means of achieving these aims in relation to the discriminatory effect it could have upon Mr White and other judges. Mr White was unable to show that he would suffer any significant harm if he retired at 70 as opposed to his suggested age of 72 or 75 and the tribunal therefore ruled that the retirement age of 70 was a proportionate means of achieving the aims, dismissing Mr White's claim.[4]

If an employer does not stipulate a mandatory retirement age, it has to show on a case-by-case basis that it acted fairly when dismissing someone and that the dismissal was not tainted with age discrimination.

The actions that are outlawed in the workplace because they are considered to constitute discrimination on grounds of someone's age go far beyond dismissal or making someone redundant. Employers can be hauled over the coals and required to answer to an employment tribunal in a wide range of other areas, including:

- the recruitment of staff [5]
- the denial of training
- the denial of promotion
- giving adverse terms and conditions
- the application of a provision, criterion or practice that disadvantages people of a particular age
- harassment – this is behaviour that is offensive, frightening or in any way distressing. It may constitute intentional bullying; it can also be unintentional, subtle and insidious. It does not

have to be targeted at an individual: it may consist of a general culture that tolerates, say, the telling of ageist jokes.

In addition, victimisation is outlawed. This involves treating someone detrimentally either because they themselves have made a complaint about discrimination or intend to do so, or because they have given evidence or intend to give evidence relating such a complaint.

The rules are set out in the Employment Equality (Age) Regulations 2006 and the Employment Equality (Repeal of Retirement Age Provisions) 2011. Various guides to the law are available. For instance, the Equality Commission for Northern Ireland has published *Age Discrimination Law in Northern Ireland: A Short Guide*.

If you are concerned about any form of unlawful age discrimination at work, you probably will not wish to go straight to an employment tribunal. What can you do instead?

You might first make your concerns known to the person responsible for what you consider age discrimination. Harassment, for instance, can occur through thoughtlessness; mentioning it can be enough to secure an apology and reassurance that it will not be repeated. You may be able to resolve matters amicably without upsetting your relationship with your manager.

You may, however, wish to seek a formal meeting with the person involved and perhaps ask someone to go along to provide support; this could be a colleague, friend or trade union official.

If you fail to obtain satisfaction about your concerns, you could take up the matter through the grievance procedure of your organisation. In doing this, you have a legal right to be accompanied to any hearing by a trade union rep or a work colleague. You do not need to be employed by the organisation to take up this procedure.

What if the employer in question does not have a grievance procedure? In that case – or if you fail to obtain satisfaction even though there is such a procedure and you have made use of it – you could take your complaint to an employment tribunal. Any such complaints have to be brought within three months of the act that is the subject of the complaint.

The Advisory, Conciliation and Arbitration Service (ACAS) has published a useful guide called *Age and the Workplace: Putting the Employment Equality (Age) Regulations 2006 into Practice*, which can be downloaded free from its website and provides a clear explanation of the law on age discrimination in employment.

As in so many fields, Citizens Advice is an excellent source of free, expert help. It may even help you take your case to a tribunal.

Applying for a job

Despite these rules and regulations, many employers prefer to employ younger people. If you fear you will be ruled out because of your age at an early stage, avoid including information about your age in your application if you can. Do not offer your date of birth and beware of talking about your, say, '30-years experience'.

The National Careers Service offers guidance to people looking for work that includes one-to-one interviews with advisors on the ground. They help people draw up a CV, give tips on how to behave at interviews and offer follow-up advice when necessary. You might imagine this service is available only for much younger people, such as school-leavers, but in fact any adult in England can use it. Skills Development Scotland, Careers Wales and the Careers Service Northern Ireland perform a similar role.

Living off your house or flat: equity release

In a country which has chosen to put so much of its wealth into bricks and mortar, many older people, after a lifetime spent paying off a mortgage, end up 'asset-rich, income poor'. Especially in the south of England, it is easy to end your days living in a home that seems like a gold-mine, disproportionately valuable compared to the meagre lifestyle enjoyed by its inhabitant. Is there not some way of siphoning off some of the cash locked into that brickwork and spending it while you are still able to enjoy it?

There is. 'Home equity release' schemes enable homeowners to receive cash immediately in return for pledging all or part of their house to a financial institution. You usually have to be at least 60 to participate. There are two main types of scheme.

Mortgage roll-ups are currently the most popular arrangement. Essentially, you take out a mortgage against your house and pocket the sum borrowed, but instead of paying off the interest each month, you allow it to 'roll up' into a lump sum. This is paid back, along with the capital borrowed, when the house is sold, usually on the death of the mortgagee. This would also happen if the mortgagee moved into a care home or sheltered housing. There is usually a limit on the amount you can borrow of 50 per cent of the value of your home. The equity release company provides you with a lump sum and/or smaller amounts regularly or when you request them.

So far, so good (unless you need a larger sum than the equity release company is prepared to give you). But beware! The interest that is charged is compound. This means that if you borrow, say, £100,000 and interest is charged at, say, 4.75 per cent a year, your debt fifteen years later would have more than doubled. In addition the company will levy various charges – when the scheme is set up, when it is terminated, and if and when you take the smaller, so-called drawdown payments.

On the other hand, schemes usually guarantee that even if you live so long that what you end up owing is more than the value of your home, you can still live in it until you die or move into care. There will also be no outstanding mortgage debt to be deducted from your estate, so long as you have met the conditions in the contract.

If you take the maximum amount that the equity release company will give you as a lump sum, you can then spend or invest it as you wish. The money released from equity release is free of capital gains and income tax. However, any interest generated or growth received from the lump sum whether invested or deposited at the bank would be potentially liable to tax.

If you instead take smaller sums over time you will only attract interest on the amount you have taken, say, £2,000. However, that advantage has to be set against the charges the equity release company imposes. These vary as do the other details I have described, but schemes are devised on the assumption that all the money will be taken at the start so the equity release company will stipulate the minimum amount you can take as drawdown and the prior notice you need to give it. You have to apply for drawdown – it will not necessarily be granted.

When you die or move into care and your property is sold, your heirs should be able to bank the difference between the sum raised from the sale and the amount you then owe the equity release company. But it might not be very much, particularly if house prices have stagnated. If the sale of your property raises less than the loan, plus the interest, they will receive nothing.

So if you are contemplating equity release, talk to your heirs. If the need for home improvements is your reason for embarking on equity re-lease, perhaps they can stump up the cash you need since they may hope to inherit. At least tell them what you are doing: it can come as a shock after a parent's death to discover that the substantial sum they thought they would inherit has disappeared.

It is usually a condition of an equity release contract that the property is kept in good repair. If you fail to, say, replace the roof or sort out the drains, the company can do this itself and recoup the costs from you, or add the sum to the balance of your loan. If repairs are not attended to, the value of your estate could be reduced.

Plainly the main advantage of equity release is that it delivers money when you want or need it, but it is an expensive means of borrowing and it narrows options later on.

Say, for instance, you decide you would like to move house. It is easy to say you would like to remain where you are until you die, but then a neighbour from hell moves in next door. Or you wish to move closer to your offspring. Or perhaps the property proves unsuitable should you become unable to climb stairs or walk easily. You will have to obtain the approval of the equity release company to transfer your mortgage to another property – you and the new property must meet the company's lending criteria. The equity release company will send along an independent valuer, and you will have to pay for their services as well as a property transfer fee, an administration fee and the company's legal fees (as well as your own moving, legal and other costs). But a greater barrier is likely to be your dwindling finances. You may have too little money left (in view of your debt to the equity release company) after your existing property is sold to be able to afford to buy another.

You may also have too little money to meet new claims on your wallet later on. Perhaps you will need care, which does not come cheap. As explained in Part Seven *(pages 563 and 655–63)*, the state provides a safety net to pay care home fees or the costs of help in the home for people who cannot afford them. But you may prefer to be a self-funder, not reliant on the state, and enjoy more choice in where and how you are looked after.

It can also be annoying to discover after the event that the sum of money neatly tucked into your bank account through equity release increases your liability to income tax on the interest or profits generated when an increase in the value of your home would not have been taxed. Also, capital and the income it generates might disqualify you from valuable means-tested benefits, as it will be taken into account in assessing your eligibility for benefits such as Council Tax Reduction and Guarantee Pension Credit. Your local council will also take into account these assets if it assesses you for any contribution it will make to your care home bills or homecare charges.

On the other hand, perhaps you win the lottery and wish to free yourself from your equity release obligations by repaying the loan. Earlier repayment will attract an 'early repayment fee'. If you repay a loan of £100,000 within five years of taking it out, you could be looking at a fee of £25,000.

Home reversion, the other main type of equity release scheme, is different. You surrender the ownership of your property, or part of it, to a reversion company. In return, the company pays you a percentage of the current market value of your home and then sells it when you die or move into care. At that point it makes its money, particularly if house prices have risen. During the remainder of your life or if and when you move into care, you can live in the property as a lessee, rent-free or at a peppercorn rent.

The equity release industry (providers, lawyers, financial advisors, surveyors and so on) has set up the Equity Release Council. Safeguards and guarantees for consumers set down by the Council seek to ensure that problems created with earlier schemes, such as those that led to repossession in some early cases, are not repeated. Look for a scheme operating under the Equity Release Council's Rules, Guidance and Principles (formerly known as SHIP rules).

Don't think of going ahead with any form of equity release without consulting an independent financial advisor with expertise in equity release. *I discuss how to find a financial advisor below.* Choose your advisor carefully. A Which? Investigation into financial advice for equity release in 2012 provided by some of the biggest providers of equity release products as well as independent advisors found that only the national debt charity StepChange passed all the tests that the Which team had set.[6] StepChange has a freephone advice line and webchat facility. Also ask a solicitor, acting for you alone, for his or her advice on the contract before you sign.

It is usually best to see equity release as a last resort and consider other options first, such as taking in a lodger; seeking help through a Care and Repair agency to pay for home improvements *(see pages 176–81);* selling your home and releasing cash by moving to a smaller house or flat; taking out a personal bank loan without roll up of interest; or asking friends and family for assistance.

Nonetheless, some older people want to stay in the home they have grown used to, whatever happens, and other options for raising cash are not available. As long as they do not also want to pass it on to their children, equity release may be the means of providing just the boost to their lifestyle that they want, or indeed, of enabling them to pay the maintenance costs of what may be a much larger property than they could otherwise afford to keep up.

Most goods and services for the home including other mortgages are covered by a cancellation or cooling-off period in which you can cancel the contract should you change your mind. There is no cooling-off period once a contract for equity release is signed. If you later manage to cancel the contract, the process of withdrawal is likely to be very expensive, incurring hefty penalties. So you need to be absolutely sure you are doing the right thing before you sign up.

Protecting inheritance

Younger people are often surprised to find that their older relatives are concerned about the implications their financial affairs may have for their heirs. It is sometimes assumed that older people have enough to worry about without thinking of those who will outlive them. Yet throughout history human beings have shown a keen desire to pass on their wealth, perhaps as a means of ensuring they can still influence events after their own death.

Some older people seem willing to put up with considerable hardship in their own lives for the sake of the beneficiaries of their will. If this is their choice, fair enough. Naturally, some younger relatives are only too happy to go along with this attitude. Surprisingly often, however, they would rather see their older relatives spending their money on themselves. If you find yourself in this position, you might as well make your feelings clear rather than waiting for a legacy you do not need and which is going to be tainted by guilt.

The tax spectre

Once safeguarding inheritance has become an issue, the tax problems of achieving this will quickly come into view. Where legacies greater in total than around £325,000 are in prospect (including the value of a house), the taxman will walk away with 40 per cent of the proceeds above that figure in inheritance tax, if nothing is done to stop him. There is an exception for leaving your house to your children (including adopted, foster or stepchildren) or grandchildren, which boosts the exemption to £425,000. Still, escaping inheritance tax can develop into something of an obsession, not only for older people but also of course for their relatives. Even assuming that heirs have their older relatives' best interests rather than their own at heart, everybody involved needs to beware.

King Lear syndrome

The obvious way to beat the taxman may seem to be for the older person to give away their assets while still alive. Older people are all too likely to find themselves surrounded by others only too ready to drop hints that this would be an extremely good idea. After all, they don't really need much money, do they? Not in comparison, perhaps, to the burgeoning demands of their nieces and nephews, who will be bullied unless transferred to private schools, or whose lives will be worthless without ponies or ballet lessons. And surely a home made over to a son or daughter may be kept from the council's clutches if its older owner has to go into care, and the son or daughter can take over those increasingly burdensome home maintenance problems. Beware, beware!

The Department for Work and Pensions and a local authority can claim the value of the house anyway if it considers ownership has been shifted in order to offload liability for care home or domiciliary care bills. But there are other considerations to bear in mind too.

You may feel certain of the strength and health of family relationships. But, like King Lear, you can be mistaken. People change, even close relatives, and the arrival or prospect of wealth is exactly the kind of thing that makes this happen. However much older people love their children, they can be shocked by the experience of coming within their power. Those who really care for their older relatives need to keep an eye on siblings and in-laws. 'Gold,' said Shelley, 'is the old man's sword. He should be careful before he relinquishes it.'

The most obvious problem is that an older person may develop unexpected needs for cash which they have prematurely given away. Frailty can make you yearn for a couple of months in the sun in midwinter; the purchase of a car adapted for disability can cost many thousands of pounds. Paying for 24-hour care because a major stroke has clipped your wings might cost a sum undreamt of when you handed over your spare cash to pay for your grandchildren's gap years. You could find that although you have offloaded a great deal of your income and savings, what you have left nonetheless disqualifies you from the help your council might have provided. In any case, many items, such as a mobility scooter or a yacht adapted for disability, are rarely available through the state.[7]

What is for sure is that the relatives who accepted your cash years before are not going to be in a position to return it later. As a result, what seemed like an act of spontaneous generosity can sow the seeds of resentment and guilt.

Giving money away may not provide a way round inheritance tax anyway. Only £3,000 a year may be given away without tax implications. Any gift above that level is only a 'potentially-exempt' transfer and inheritance tax will be payable on it unless the donor survives for at least seven years after making it. If an older person continues to live in a house after giving away the freehold, it will be considered a 'gift with reservation' and inheritance tax will still be payable.

There are better ways to avoid inheritance tax that do not require you to be stripped clean before death. Being married or entering into a civil partnership is one. You can leave as much as you like to a spouse or civil partner without paying a penny in tax. Otherwise, if you want to escape as much inheritance tax as possible, your best bet is to set up a trust designed to achieve this. This is surprisingly cheap and easy: it will mean giving some control of the assets involved to the trustees, but the loss of autonomy involved can be minimised. Independent financial advisors will be only too happy to explain the products involved.

Advice

There are many easily available sources of personal financial information and guidance. Apart from books and newspapers, useful websites include thisismoney.co.uk and MoneySavingExpert.com. The Radio 4 programme *Moneybox Live* provides up-to-the-minute information and responds to listeners' questions. Which? has a money helpline where you can obtain advice on any personal financial matter over the phone; however, you have to become a member to use it.

Citizens Advice provides information and guidance through a website, web chat facility and a phone helpline as well as printed information sheets. Perhaps most useful of all, Citizens Advice provides free, face-to-face advice on tax, employment, debt and other money matters at its local bureaux dotted up and down the country.

Financial advisors

Some people prefer to use a financial advisor who can give more bespoke advice in the light of their particular needs and circumstances. The Society of Later Life Advisers (SOLLA) keeps a list of people who give financial advice relevant to older people. If you type a postcode into SOLLA's search facility, you should find information about advisors nearby.

When selecting any financial advisor, check that they are registered with the Financial Conduct Authority (through the FCA's website) and that they have the right qualifications. They should have a qualification of level 4 or above in financial advice of the National Qualifications and Credit Framework. In addition, they should have a Statement of Professional Standing. To obtain this statement, they must have signed up to a code of ethics and completed at least 35 hours of professional training each year. The statement should be renewed every year; check that it is up to date.

The SOLLA list will tell you whether an advisor has SOLLA accreditation. The Society considers applicants for accreditation if they already have a level 4 qualification in financial advice, a certificate in long-term care insurance and a qualification demonstrating knowledge of equity release. Then they must demonstrate good practice over a year in the way they deal with clients, through providing sample material from their consultations. They must also show they are developing their professional knowledge and that they work in an environment which supports them in doing this. Finally, they sit a 45-minute viva which tests whether they have a good, broadly-based knowledge of older people's matters and the soft skills to discuss with their clients and/or their families the wider financial options, taking into account any hearing or other impairment. Once accredited, the applicant must continue to develop their knowledge and abide by SOLLA's code of practice. Five years on, they must go through the process of seeking accreditation again.

An independent advisor with SOLLA accreditation should therefore be well placed to give advice on, say, assembling the resources to pay for care (in a care home or taken in someone's own home), choosing an annuity to help fund care, setting up trusts perhaps for grandchildren or involving wills, choosing an equity release scheme, working out what to do with a pension pot, and minimising inheritance tax. They should not only have up-to-date expertise in particular areas, but also the ability to foresee the consequences of taking particular courses of action.

Some of the advisors on SOLLA's list are described as 'independent financial advisors'; they should give impartial advice about all the different products that are available from different companies. 'Restricted advisors' normally offer advice only about products from a limited number of product providers. If you are interested in an obtaining help from a restricted advisor, ask them to explain the nature of the restriction. However, it is usually best to seek advice about the widest possible range of financial options.

You could look for an advisor who will give you one-off advice but it is often a good idea to have one who will give ongoing advice in the light of your changing circumstances. You may receive advice on funding care only to find that your health deteriorates and you need more money to fund more care, perhaps live-in care (difficult to pay for if you are not selling your home as you probably would if moving into a care home). It is often a good idea to have an advisor whom you see every year and who can see how you are faring health- and finance-wise and to advise you accordingly.

Don't assume SSOLA members only help people with considerable resources. However, when you are looking for one, it is worth finding out whether they specialise in helping people with the level of resources you can command.

The drawback of seeking advice is that it can be very expensive. However, different financial advisors charge their clients in different ways and some wish to keep a kindly eye on their clients rather than extract hefty sums from them. On the method of charging, some levy a fixed price for the work to be carried out; others an hourly rate for their time; others do not charge for consultations but instead the advisor is paid commission by the provider of any financial product, such as an annuity, which their client buys; in that case, the client thus pays the advisor indirectly. You may find that an advisor charges in several ways. You may also find that costs are open to negotiation. Some offer a free first consultation.

It is a legal requirement that a financial advisor has to provide a copy of their 'service and cost disclosure' before they start work for anyone, so their method of charging should be clear in this. It is also important to be clear about the way an advisor charges reimbursement for expenses.

Help with money management

It is easy to be taken in by the image portrayed in the press of older people well versed in finance. These images are often aspirational: on the ground, many people struggle with money matters.

Perhaps mathematics is not your strongest subject and you suddenly find yourself having to manage your money after a lifetime in which somebody else has shouldered that task for you. Ask at your public library about adult education courses in your area. A course in basic maths can be useful and can also give a real sense of achievement as well as the pleasure of learning with a group of other people.

If you are currently in a situation in which someone else, perhaps your partner or a relative, handles all your financial affairs, make sure you learn how to take the reins, should that ever be necessary. If you now find yourself without the finance-savvy person on whom you have relied, consider whether they have a friend who could help you. Or is there someone else who could provide some basic explanations without giving actual advice on what you should do with your money? Or perhaps you know someone who used to work in some field of finance who could help you, such as the treasurer of a society or faith group of which you are a member.

Many people who do not wish to continue to shoulder the responsibility of running their own financial affairs grant a lasting power of attorney to a trusted friend, relative, partner or professional, and register the attorneyship immediately. The attorney(s) and donor then hold concurrent powers over the donor's affairs. *(I outline how to grant power of attorney in this way in Chapter 31.)*

Debt

It is easy to imagine that debt mainly afflicts younger people, but high costs, low income and zero or very low-hours contracts, which can lead to debt, affect people of any age. Citizens Advice helps thousands of people each year with debt issues. Go and talk to an advisor at one of its many local offices. They will help you address each debt, if necessary sending letters on your behalf, tell you which debts should have priority (for instance, council tax, as failure to pay can result in imprisonment), and help you work out a strategy for managing your debt. They can also see whether there are opportunities you have missed for maximising your income. For instance, there may be scope for reducing your heating bills through discounts on bills and the provision of free insulation and other long-term heating improvements. The National Debt Helpline, the Debt Foundation and StepChange for Debt also provide invaluable help to many people, although only over the phone or internet, not face-to-face.

The sheer numbers of people seeking help on debt mean that organisations such as Citizens Advice are not in a position to give as much support as people with debt problems often need. One organisation that does is Christians Against Poverty (CAP). This charity, set up in Bradford in 1996 by a businessman who was struggling with debt himself, now has 250 debt centres across the UK. Managers at these centres go and visit people who have contacted them and help them draw up a budget and work out how they can stick to it, so that they will eventually become debt-free. They will make phone calls on behalf of individuals to try to secure more favourable repayment terms. Then the person in debt pays an agreed amount into an account held by CAP, which in turns pays money to creditors. These debt centres also have befrienders who can provide help with the psychological aspects of debt. There is no need to have any Christian affiliation to become a client.

If you need help with your taxes and are on a low income, you could approach Tax Help for Older People. This is an independent, free tax advice service for people over 60 and with a household income of less that £20,000 per year. It has a network of more than 450 volunteers across the UK. If a face-to-face meeting is not possible, it will offer advice by phone, post or email.

Disability and handling money

Sight impairment, hearing impairment, problems with dexterity and mental health conditions, including dementia, can all make handling money difficult. However, help is available.

Banks, building societies and organisations such as the Post Office are service providers under the Equality Act 2010. This means they are required by law to take steps to ensure that their services are accessible, so that people with disabilities are not treated 'less favourably' than non-disabled customers *as explained on page 689.*

Failure to implement reasonable adjustments, for instance for customers who are deaf or partially sighted, can result in a bank or building society having to pay compensation for their failure and for 'injury to feelings' if they have treated the customer brusquely, as well as putting the matter right. In 2014 Kiruna Stamell, an actress with dwarfism, successfully sued the Post Office for discriminating against her in the use of its services. Her height meant she could not reach chip-and-pin machines at post office counters. Staff had tried to help her by providing boxes on which she could stand, but she argued in court that this was demeaning.

To comply with the Act and pre-empt legal action, banks and building societies have introduced a range of measures to make their facilities accessible to everyone. These include: the provision of bank statements in large print, Braille or audio; an audio service at cash machines; and hi-vis debit cards.

If you find you are disadvantaged in using your bank or building society or post office's facilities in any way on account of a disability, raise the matter with the manager. *(I explain how to use the disability discrimination legislation in more detail on pages 691–3.)*

Earning, investing and bestowing

* Pension Wise gives free, impartial guidance about the options for disposal of a pension pot.

* Shop around for an annuity: you could forego tens of thousands of pounds otherwise.

* Consider an enhanced annuity if you have a serious health condition.

* You cannot be forced to retire at 65.

* You don't have to pay National Insurance if you work after state pension age.

* Allowing an employee's age to influence their recruitment, training or promotion is unlawful.

* You don't have a cooling-off period if you sign a contract for equity release.

* Don't give your money away without careful consideration of the consequences.

* Consider sharing responsibility over your financial affairs with someone you trust through a lasting (or in Scotland continuing) power of attorney.

* Banks and building societies must ensure their facilities are accessible to people with disabilities.

HOSPITALS

> **"** *If you live in England and are going into hospital as a planned admission, you have the right to choose which hospital you go to under a system called Choose and Book. So, if you are being referred by your GP to hospital for a knee replacement operation, for example, you ought to be able to choose any hospital in England, whether it be NHS or a private hospital which carries out NHS work, on your doorstep or far away.* **"**

PART ELEVEN
HOSPITALS

When my mother went into hospital after suffering a stroke in her late eighties, she had not been admitted to hospital since bouncing along the winding lanes of west Cornwall in an ambulance while in labour with me half a century before. Fifty years on, she and I were signally unprepared for what lay ahead.

Many of us who rely on our television screens for an inside view of life in today's hospitals probably believe that most of the beds are filled by children with cancer, women giving birth, people with sports injuries or those suffering from the ill-effects of binge-drinking. In fact, more than 60 per cent of patients in acute hospitals are over the age of 65. They show up in the statistics not just because people are more likely to go into hospital when they are older: they are also more likely to remain there for longer.

To some extent this is inevitable: the older body takes longer to recover from physical trauma than the younger. But older people also fall victim to hazards once in hospital – such as falls in an unfamiliar environment and pressure sores because their skin is fragile and pressure on it is not given the necessary relief. This means that when we are getting on, we need to know whether we can avoid going into hospital, as well as how to survive both physically and psychologically when we do stay there.

For hospital administrators, getting older people out of their beds and home or to another care setting, such as a care home, is a major preoccupation, since hospital care of older people costs a lot of money. But if you are one of those older patients, it is important not to be pushed out of hospital before you are ready to leave, and not to be pushed into a care home (or for a family member to feel forced to become your home carer), if that is not what you or they wish.

This part is divided into a chapter on going into hospital and making the most of a hospital stay and a second on ensuring that the help and support someone needs when they leave hospital – medical as well as practical – is provided. It offers tips not only on healthcare but also finance. Are you aware that free healthcare and practical help in the home may be provided for six weeks after an accident, illness or operation? (This is known as Intermediate Care.) If you or a loved one are seriously ill, perhaps with a combination of illnesses such as heart failure and Parkinson's disease, are you sure you have been assessed for NHS Continuing Healthcare, which pays the full fees in a nursing home, or for health and social care within your own home, if you fit the criteria?

One of the biggest challenges of a hospital stay can be psychological. Some older people relish being in hospital if they have struggled alone with worrying health problems and now find reassuring help at hand. Others, particularly if they have sight, hearing or mental health problems, find a hospital stay dull and frustrating. People with dementia may find the experience confusing and even frightening. As I explain, their visitors can do much to help them.

Chapter 38

Staying in hospital

Why does being in hospital often seem to lodge in our memory, often less on account of the injury or illness than the stay itself? Is it the sudden relocation to a completely different environment, with its array of busy staff in different uniforms working to a routine into which we must fit? Or perhaps a feeling that we have been transported to a world in which we have little control of our own destiny and in which we may be faced with unsettling tests and treatments?

Unless the situation is an emergency, consider whether a hospital stay is really necessary before you agree to go into hospital. If it is, should you go to the hospital your doctor suggests or another? Once there, how can you ensure you receive first-rate care, from consultants, nurses, radiologists, doctors, healthcare assistants and many more?

Even the journey to hospital can loom large, not to mention the cost of parking in the hospital car park. How can you make the journey to and from hospital – or perhaps repeat journeys for a course of treatment – as easy and inexpensive as possible?

Once in your hospital bed, without easy access to the internet and perhaps a phone as well, it can be difficult to know just what your rights are as a patient and how they can be upheld. How can visitors help you assert your rights? What other support can they offer? And is there any way in which hospital can come to seem a more congenial, less alien environment?

In this chapter, I examine:

▶ the different types of hospital

▶ the drawbacks of going into hospital

▶ preventing admission

- getting to the best hospital
- securing good care
- safeguarding your rights
- the role of visitors
- support from visitors and chaplains
- transport to and from hospital

Types of hospital

The most familiar type of hospital is the acute district general hospital or general infirmary. This is likely to have general medical wards, an acute medical ward, a general surgery ward, an Accident and Emergency (A&E) department and a range of other specialist wards such as stroke, cancer, cardiology and dermatology. It is also likely to have care-of-older-people as well as maternity and paediatric wards.

While general hospitals are usually large, often employing well over 3,000 staff with many teams of specialist healthcare professionals, community hospitals or cottage hospitals are much smaller and very much the province of GPs and nurses, who provide general medical care for patients; visiting consultants from a nearby district hospital may offer outpatient clinics. Community hospitals can be pleasant, small-scale places with a homely atmosphere in which to receive round-the-clock nursing and perhaps physiotherapy and some medical care, but they are not usually geared up to deliver high-tech medical interventions. They often take patients for recuperation and rehabilitation and also end-of-life care.

There are also specialist regional hospitals, such as those dedicated to orthopaedics or cardiology or the care of people who have had a major stroke. Hospices specialise in palliative care for people with terminal illnesses and those who are dying, *and are discussed on pages 997–1002.*

Drawbacks of a hospital stay

Many people assume that planned admission to hospital is a good thing. A doctor has secured a sought-after hospital bed so expert treatment can be provided. Hospital stays are of course frequently very beneficial. Yet although hospital can provide life-saving treatment and excellent care, it holds dangers. There is the risk of picking up an infection *(see page 915)*, for example, or of having a fall in an unfamiliar environment. People with dementia may be confused by their change of scene and lose the skills they need to remain independent *(see pages 919–21).*

Also, would an absence affect your ability to return to the place you are currently living? If you are living in someone else's home without any security of tenure, might they refuse to accept you back? Does your contract with your care home contain a clause which would allow the home to ask you to leave should you remain in hospital for more than a a specified period perhaps a fortnight?

In view of these factors, discuss with your hospital consultant and your GP whether you really need to go into hospital. Perhaps the proposed assessment or treatment could be provided instead in your home or in the care home in which you are living?

Preventing admission through Intermediate Care

One of the chief objectives of Intermediate Care is the prevention of unnecessary hospital admissions. It is a type of NHS funding (and thus free to the user) which involves the provision of intensive healthcare – such as physiotherapy – and practical help in a person's home or in a care home, perhaps supplemented by day visits to hospital. It usually lasts for up to six weeks.

If you think you might need intensive therapy and perhaps also practical help for a relatively short period, raise the possibility of Intermediate Care with your GP or consultant. It could fund short bursts of preventative care, for instance at a day hospital and through therapy brought into your home. *(I discuss Intermediate Care in more detail in Chapter 39: Leaving hospital.)*

In encouraging health bodies to consider Intermediate Care as an alternative to a hospital stay, the Department of Health has drawn attention to a scheme in Bradford in which older people with mental health problems considered at risk of admission to hospital or a care home were given intensive support over a period of between six and 12 weeks. This intervention was considered to have prevented 13 per cent of them being admitted to hospital and more than a quarter having to relocate permanently to a care home.[1]

Which hospital?

Hospitals vary greatly. In some, staff on the wards are well led, know precisely what are about, communicate readily with patients, medical care is good and the food appetising; in others the reverse. How can you ensure you go to the hospital which will deliver the best treatment and in which your stay will be as comfortable and pleasant as possible? Several sources of information can help you compare the quality of medical and nursing care in different establishments.

The care in all hospitals (NHS and independent) is critically examined by national agencies, which publish the reports of their inspections. The agencies are the Care Quality Commission (in England), Healthcare Improvement Scotland, Healthcare Inspectorate Wales and the Regulation and Quality Improvement Authority (in Northern Ireland). If you type, say, 'CQC inspection' or 'HIS inspection' and the name of the hospital into your search engine, the most recent inspection report should appear.

This facility is invaluable for comparing hospitals to which you might be sent. In Scotland, Wales and Northern Ireland you should be offered a choice of hospital for treatment, as patient choice underpins the NHS Constitution *(see page 285);* in England, choice of hospital has been formalised into a system called Choose and Book, which we explore in a moment.

Several additional sources of information may help inform your choice. The website My NHS enables comparisons to be made of hospitals and consultants in England. You can find a consultant in a particular field on this site and compare their performance with that of other consultants (although only in a very general way). You can also compare hospitals – in terms of mortality rates, performance on infection control and cleanliness and the proportion of patients seen within four hours in A&E; hyperlinks are provided to the latest CQC inspection reports.

The respected research team Dr Foster Intelligence, based at Imperial College London, regularly compares the performance of hospital foundation trusts in England and draws general conclusions about the care they provide. It indicates whether mortality rates are higher or lower than expected in four different situations: after surgery; following other hospital treatment; as a result of about 60 different medical conditions; and involving conditions from which patients normally survive.[2]

In addition, data is published about how well individual hospitals perform in some areas of medicine. For instance, the National Hip Fracture Database collates patient records sent in by hospitals in England, Wales, Northern Ireland and the Channel Islands which show how they have treated patients with hip fractures.[3] The Welsh government publishes an annual National Cancer Patient Experience Survey that collates the reported experience of cancer patients within each health board, so patients can compare those experiences with national averages and the situation in other boards, although not individual hospitals.[4] The Royal College of Physicians examined the care of people who were dying in hospitals in England in 2013 and again in 2015 and published an analysis of its findings, hospital by hospital *as discussed on page 996.*[5] Useful information is also provided by the Health and Social Care Information Centre.[6]

However, data such as this will not tell you what life is actually like as a patient. To find out, keep an eye on stories in local newspapers. Ask around. Perhaps a local Healthwatch *(page 329)* or other patients' group has published a report about the hospital? Take up the opportunity to set foot inside hospitals and attend public meetings about them.

Choose and Book

If you live in England and are going into hospital as a planned admission, you have the right to choose which hospital you go to *(see page 287)*. So, if you are being referred by your GP to hospital for a knee replacement operation, for example, you ought to be able to choose any hospital in England, whether it be NHS or a private hospital which carries out NHS work, on your doorstep or far away. Strictly speaking, 'Choose and Book', as it is called, does not apply to situations in which speed of access is important, as for instance when patients are being referred for urgent cancer or chest-pain appointments. In practice, choice may also be limited by the availability of beds or outpatient appointment slots.

Choose and Book is potentially extremely valuable. Many referrals by GPs these days go through it, including if cancer is suspected. But it is important to be ready to exercise your power to choose if it is not offered.

Supposing you need an endoscopy (to check for signs of abnormalities in your oesophagus, including the development of cancerous cells, by sending down a camera to have a look). Perhaps your GP says they will book you an appointment at a local diagnostic clinic under Choose and Book, omitting to explain the extent of the choice you enjoy. At home, on the internet, you discover that the one consultant who undertakes endoscopies at this centre is not a specialist in the part of your digestive system that might need attention and combines the provision of this service with running a large health system abroad. A few minutes of further investigation brings up an endoscopy unit in a well-respected hospital and whose team of consultants, some of whom teach endoscopy, include specialists in the relevant part of your anatomy, so they should be better placed to interpret the results. If you think you would prefer treatment at this centre, phone your GP practice and ask them to change the name of the facility you have chosen. They should inform the national Choose and Book system and you can then ring and book your appointment or do so yourself over the internet.

Under Choose and Book, transport should be provided free to get you to the hospital you have chosen if your GP considers you have a clinical need for transport. Similarly, you should receive help towards your travel costs to that hospital if your income is low *(as explained in the section on hospital transport below)*.

Of course, you have to be careful with Choose and Book. If the facility at which you would like treatment is situated far from your home, you may run into difficulties if your appointment is at a time that you would find difficult to make, or you have to go for frequent follow-up treatment. If you subsequently spend time as an in-patient, you may be too far away for your visitors to travel.

Should you face a delay in getting treatment through Choose and Book, you could ask whether the facility you have found also provides services to private patients. One of the consultants in, say, the endoscopy unit may provide care at a local private hospital as well as practise within the NHS, and a consultation and diagnostic test with a consultant as a private self-funding patient may not be as expensive as you might imagine. You could check the quality of care at any private hospital at which they practise through referring to a Care Quality Commission inspection report before you go ahead.

Since 2015, attempts have been made to rename Choose and Book as the NHS e-Referral System, to coincide with the introduction of a new computer programme through which referrals by GPs are made. However, the old name, embodying as it does the principle of patient choice on which the system is based, fortunately remains in use as well.

Treatment at weekends

Consider your options carefully before you agree to have surgery towards the end of the week. Studies have shown that hospital mortality rates rise at weekends for patients who go in for emergency admissions as well as those who have elective surgery.[7] The reasons are likely to include lower numbers of consultants and diagnostic and nursing staff on hand at these times. That said, whether, if so, by how much, and the reasons for any increase in weekend mortality have been much disputed, and the chances of dying after surgery at any time of the week are very low. The government said in 2015 that it plans to make hospitals operate with all facilities in place on seven days a week, but implementing this vision is likely to take a considerable amount of money and effort.

Going to A&E

There is no formal system for offering patients choice when being conveyed by paramedics to Accident and Emergency (A&E). This is understandable. If you have, say, an eye injury, paramedics will probably wish to take you to a specialist facility. Some emergency departments will be struggling to cope with the numbers of patients, so even if you would prefer to go to one hospital rather than another, the one you say you favour would struggle to see you quickly. The overriding need may be to get you to any A&E as swiftly as possible. However, there is nothing to stop you telling paramedics which hospital you would prefer to go to. And of course if you are going to A&E under your own steam, you will go to the one you prefer – although in an emergency it is often best to get to any A&E as quickly as possible.

It is therefore worth working out which hospitals in your area would best suit if you were suddenly taken ill. Does one local hospital have a stroke unit fully staffed at weekends but another not, for instance? Is one hospital likely to have consultants on call seven days a week who would come in to perform an operation but another rely on general surgeons or junior doctors at weekends? People living in rural areas may have no choice of hospital to which they would go in an emergency. But if you have a choice, it is worth bearing these considerations in mind.

Once in A&E, you may have to wait for long periods either in the waiting room or in a curtained-off cubicle. Staff may be overstretched, the hospital specialist you need to see may be working in the operating theatre or there may be difficulty in finding a bed for you on a ward.

If you wait for long periods without drinking, you will become dehydrated; that can cause serious changes in your body and so make your medical condition worse *(as explained in Chapter 2)*. You also risk suffering harm if you miss taking medication that you would normally take, unless there is a medical reason for not doing so. As a result, you might go into A&E for a straightforward condition but go on to develop complications because you have failed to take your medication on time.

Waiting around can increase the risk of developing pressure sores. These develop on the skin of parts of the body which are subject to a lot of pressure when lying or sitting, such as the buttocks and heels. They can form in as little as 30 minutes. Expect a nurse to assess your risk and to take preventative action if necessary, *as explained on page 914.*

If you are worried about any of these matters, ask a nurse or doctor. If you can take somebody with you to A&E, so much the better. They can chase up any problems as well as keep you company and provide reassurance. They can also make sure you take any medication you need with you – not just pills but also perhaps creams you need to prevent your skin from cracking.

Which ward?

We noted above that general hospitals have general medical wards, wards for acute care and specialist wards for particular systems of the body or particular ailments. They also have care-of-older-people or care-of-the-elderly wards (formerly known as geriatric wards). In the ideal care-of-older-people ward, doctors take a holistic view of patients, perhaps because they have multiple problems or because they are frail and therefore present a more complex medical picture. Such wards are overseen by consultant geriatricians who summon, say, heart specialists from another part of the hospital when necessary. But in some care-of-older-people wards, staff will not do much more than make you or your relative comfortable and it may be hard to get heart, stroke, palliative care and other consultants brought in.

To which ward can you reasonably expect to be sent if you are being admitted to a general hospital? If you have a single medical problem, expect to be treated by specialists in that condition in the same way as somebody 30 years younger. Deploy, if necessary, pledges by government that the NHS will not be ageist, such as Standard One of the *National Service Framework for Older People (see pages 297 and 300).*

However, specialist and general medical wards can be difficult places in which to stay if you need help with moving around, washing, eating and so on. If you have complex medical needs and are frail, a care-of-older-people ward will probably be best, as long as it offer a multi-disciplinary approach, enjoys ready access to specialists and in which the nursing staff provide competent and compassionate care. But bear in mind that sometimes pressure on beds means that patients can be admitted only to any ward that happens to have a vacancy, rather than the specialist ward they need, so they may not be able to be too choosy.

Personnel

The different types of professional and their relationship one to another can be confusing from a hospital bed, particularly if you are feeling unwell. Here are the main types in a general hospital.

Doctors

Consultants: specialists in heart conditions, cancer, orthopaedics, geriatric medicine or palliative care, for example. They normally head a team of junior doctors.

Specialist registrars: doctors training to work in specialist fields which will allow them to apply for consultant posts

House officers and *senior house officers:* newly qualified doctors who are spending several years working in a variety of fields in hospitals so they can decide in which area they would like to specialise. These are the people who staff A&E units during the evenings and at weekends.

Pre-registration house doctors: people who have obtained their medical degree and are spending one year in hospital in order to be able to register as a doctor

The responsible consultant or *responsible clinician:* the person who has overall responsibility for the management, coordination and continuity of a patient's care through their stay in hospital, including during the process of discharging them. The idea is that the buck stops with this person, who should be available to respond to questions and concerns by a patient or their family. Not all hospitals operate a system of responsible clinicians, however. The body that brings together expertise in the royal colleges of medicine in the UK, the Academy of Medical Royal Colleges, urged in 2014 that this system be made universal throughout the UK.[8]

Nursing staff

The sister, or, if male, *the senior charge nurse:* the most senior nurse on a ward. They act as the manager of the ward and oversee the work of staff nurses, healthcare assistants, any nurses in training and any volunteers on the ward.

Staff nurses: liaise with doctors and tell healthcare assistants what to do. If you are concerned about the competence of a healthcare assistant, ask to speak to the staff nurse who has delegated tasks to that assistant.

Named nurses: coordinate and hold information about particular patients in wards. They are thus the first port of call if a patient has questions. Not all hospitals use this system, however.

Healthcare assistants: do anything from performing simple tests to chatting to patients to helping with personal care such as using the lavatory. It is important to be sure that you consider the assistant is competent before you grant consent for them to help you.

Matrons: or 'modern matrons', as they are sometimes called, may be responsible for several wards or a section of a hospital, such as surgery or A&E. Their remit ranges across nursing matters but also hospital cleanliness, general care facilities, hygiene, food and drink. If you are concerned about any of these matters and cannot resolve the issue with the sister or ward manager, ask to speak to the matron. The government has said matrons should be 'easily identifiable to patients, highly visible, accessible and authoritative figures to whom patients and their families can turn for assistance, advice and support and upon whom they can rely to ensure that the fundamentals of care are right'.[9] In other words, they should be problem-solvers. About three-quarters of hospitals in England have a matron, although sometimes they are given some other title.[10] Ask to talk to the matron or matron equivalent.

The government announced in 2015 that it would introduce **nurse associates** to work alongside healthcare assistants and registered nurses in England. At the time of writing, the scope of their role was being examined at a number of test sites.

If you are unsure of the status or function of any of the nursing staff, ask. A clue to status is the colour of uniform. Often the uniform of a ward sister is dark or royal blue, that of a staff nurse a lighter blue or striped, and that of a healthcare assistant a different colour, such as pink or green. Nursing staff should also wear badges which indicate their role. *(I discuss the role and training of nurses, doctors and healthcare assistants, whether working in hospital or elsewhere in Chapter 15.)*

There will also be executives responsible for particular aspects of care within a hospital, such as a **director of nursing** and a **director of infection control** (although infection control often comes within the remit of the director of nursing). There will also be **unit general managers,** who oversee several wards and are accountable for what goes on in all of them.

Finally, any hospital trust will have a **chief executive.** Other health professionals working in hospitals include physiotherapists, occupational therapists, clinical psychologists and speech and language therapists *(their roles are outlined in Chapter 15)*. Social workers in hospitals operate mainly in the field of hospital discharge *(see Chapter 39)*.

On the ward

When a person goes onto a ward, it is easy for relatives to imagine that their main concern should be to ensure swift diagnosis and treatment from a doctor. This is, of course, extremely important. But it is also important to be aware of the quality of care delivered by the staff – nurses, healthcare assistants and people serving food and drink.

Public concern and debate prompted by the inquiry into hospitals in mid-Staffordshire in 2013 by Robert Francis, QC, have raised the level of consciousness about the quality of nursing in hospitals, as it contributed to many of the failings at mid-Staffs.[11] Hospital staff should be aware of these concerns and of the importance of good, all-round nursing care. If they slip up, raise the matter with the ward manager or modern matron.

Should you expect nurses to have time not only to care competently for you but also talk to you and show you compassion? Emphatically: yes. The NHS for England has told nurses and healthcare assistants in England that they should base their behaviour on 'the six Cs'. These are:

- care
- compassion
- competence
- communication
- commitment (to patients and the wider population) and
- courage (to do the right thing for patients and to speak up when they have concerns)[12]

Below I focus on four areas in which the quality of care by ward staff can make a significant difference. Try to anticipate problems before they arise.

Eating and drinking

When we are unwell, ensuring we consume nutritious food and plenty of fluid is crucially important. If we cannot give ourselves a drink and nobody else helps us, we increase our risk of dehydration, other serious conditions and, of course, death *(as explained on page 48)*. In 2011 the

Health Service Ombudsman for England published a damming report about the care of older people in hospitals, using ten cases in which her team had upheld complaints by patients or their families. Half of the patients involved had not consumed adequate water or food during their time in hospital. She wrote, 'I hear of food removed uneaten and drinks or call bells placed out of reach.'[13]

If ward staff fail to give adequate help if you or your relative need assistance to drink, talk to the ward manager. A NICE guideline about safe staffing in hospitals issued in 2014 confirmed that help with eating and drinking (as well as washing and other personal care) is the responsibility of nursing staff. NICE says nursing care in wards should include ensuring that food and drink is provided and consumed; this should involve helping patients to eat and drink when necessary.[14] Doctors too should take an interest. The General Medical Council (which regulates doctors – *see page 305)* has told them that:

> All patients are entitled to food and drink of adequate quantity and quality and to the help they need to eat and drink. ... You should be satisfied that nutrition and hydration are being provided in a way that meets your patients' needs, and that if necessary patients are being given adequate help to enable them to eat and drink.[15]

Many older people who go into hospital are already suffering from malnutrition. In view of this, NICE has recommended that screening for malnutrition should take place for all older people as a matter of course *(see Chapter 2),* so you should expect such screening on entry. If the results show you are malnourished, steps should be taken to improve your intake of nutrients; this might be through the provision of fortified drinks, a consultation with a dietitian or investigation of any medical reason for the problem.

What can you expect in terms of quantity and choice of food and help to consume it? The Care Quality Commission, which regulates hospitals in England, is unequivocal on the need for hospitals to deliver in all three areas. It has said that hospitals must ensure that patients are provided with:

- a variety of nutritious and appetising food and fluid in sufficient quantities to meet their needs;

- food and drink that meet any reasonable requirements arising from a patient's religious or cultural background; and

- support, where necessary, to enable patients to eat and drink sufficient amounts for their needs.[16]

If you or your relative might have difficulty in eating or drinking, make sure that staff are aware of this from the start. They should give whatever help is necessary. For instance, if you are partially sighted or blind, the help you might reasonably expect staff to offer would include:

- ✓ filling in your menu preference sheet
- ✓ telling you whenever any food or drink is being served
- ✓ providing a spoon instead of a knife and fork, if that is what you prefer
- ✓ providing a deep bowl, if that is your preference, or a plate fitted with a high rim or a plate guard
- ✓ making sure your food is safe for you to eat
- ✓ making sure that you have been given what you asked for
- ✓ removing any wrapping
- ✓ cutting up your food
- ✓ telling you what is on your plate and where it is
- ✓ serving soup in cups instead of bowls
- ✓ providing drinks in suitable cups
- ✓ providing puréed food, if this is appropriate for you
- ✓ telling you if you have missed any food on your plate
- ✓ helping you to eat if you have difficulty feeding yourself
- ✓ prompting and, if necessary, helping you to drink regularly

Pressure sores

Pressure sores (or pressure ulcers) are open wounds which develop in areas of skin such as on the buttocks and heels which are subject to pressure from sitting or lying or from shear forces *(as explained on page 17)*. They can develop quickly, even within 30 minutes, and anyone (even an infant) can develop one. However, the risk is much greater for seriously ill, poorly nourished people who are lying or sitting for prolonged periods and unable to reposition themselves. Pressure ulcers normally affect the skin and underlying tissue, but can invade muscle, tendon and even bone. Coping with the pain of the ulcer and the side-effects of pain-relief medication can be distressing. Furthermore, a pressure sore can take a long time to heal. Should it become infected, for instance with MRSA *(see page 916),* healing will take longer. People with pressure sores can be unwell for a long time and find that the energy they need to recover from other conditions is sapped.

However, in most cases pressure sores are not inevitable. Straightforward steps can be taken to prevent them. Assessment of your risk is important. The National Institute for Health and Care Excellence (NICE), which has published guidance on the prevention and management of pressure sores, recommends that every adult who is admitted to hospital be assessed for their risk of developing one.[17] The risk should be reassessed if there is a change in the patient's clinical status, such as after surgery, the worsening of an underlying condition or a change in mobility. In A&E too, expect a prompt assessment particularly if you might be at high risk and precautions to be taken.

Steps that staff should be considering include:

✓ encouraging you and/or helping you to reposition yourself at regular intervals and recording this on a turning chart

✓ taping protective padding to especially vulnerable areas, such as the buttocks, hip area, elbows and heels

✓ ensuring you are lying on a surface on which either your weight is dispersed over a large area or, if that would not be enough, a surface which itself moves to redistribute your weight. (In the former category come high-specification foam mattresses; in the latter a dynamic support surface, which alters the level of pressure in little chambers within the device, through the inflation and deflation of air or the movement of fluid.)

(I also discuss the prevention of pressure sores within the context of people waiting for treatment for a broken hip on pages 398–9.)

If you should develop a pressure sore, similar steps to these should be taken to try to prevent it getting worse. If you are sitting, perhaps in a wheelchair, you should reposition yourself (if necessary with help) regularly, limit sitting times and use a pressure-relieving cushion.

Any pressure ulcer should be carefully measured and an assessment made of the stage it has reached and its relative severity. Gauze dressings should not be used, according to NICE, but modern dressings such as hydrocolloids, which create a moist environment that benefits healing and helps reduce pain when the dressing is changed. NICE says that patients and, if appropriate their families or carers, should be involved in taking decisions about the type of dressing to be used. It also recommends that patients with an ulcer should be offered a nutritional assessment by a dietician or other specially trained professional, to ensure they consume the nutrients essential for body healing *(see page 34).*[18] The equivalent guidance for Scotland is also well worth looking at if you or your relative has or might develop a pressure sore.[19]

Pressure sores are considered preventable in most cases. If you develop one in hospital (or in a nursing home), it is worth considering whether you could claim compensation on grounds of clinical negligence *(see page 812).*

Falls

Falls are the most commonly reported incident involving patient safety in hospitals in England.[20] They can happen very easily. A patient admitted for perhaps a minor condition for a day or two falls as she hurries to the lavatory in unfamiliar surroundings and, as she has osteoporosis, fractures her hip or shoulder. Suddenly she faces an operation and a period of rehabilitation from the fracture – on top of treatment for her pre-existing condition. As a result, a stay of a few days can lengthen into one of weeks, even months. If the injury has been serious, she may now face being discharged from hospital to a care home rather than returning to her own home, at least initially.

Although some falls cannot be avoided, many could be.[21] If you are at all nervous about moving around in hospital, particularly at first when the environment is unfamiliar, ask for a nurse or healthcare assistant to accompany you. Many people instinctively want to move unaided: think again! Also, make sure that all relevant factors to prevent falls *listed in Chapter 18: Falls* have been applied – such as not wearing ill-fitting slippers.

Some hospitals carry out an assessment of the likelihood of new patients having a fall and take action to prevent this, but by no means all.

Urinary catheters

On a hospital ward, somebody (perhaps a doctor, perhaps a nurse) may suggest that you should be fitted with a urinary catheter. This involves the insertion of a tube into your bladder. Urine passes down the tube into a bag outside your body, which you (or an assistant) empty periodically by turning on a tap. The catheter might remain in place for a day or two, several weeks or even longer.

The insertion of a catheter has many potential ramifications. Catheters can introduce infection to the body and, if left in for a long period, can make returning to normal urination difficult. Be ready to use your right to grant – or withhold – consent for the insertion of a catheter. *I discuss the pros and cons of having a catheter, the types of catheter used and how they are managed in Chapter 19: Continence.*

Hygiene and infection control

One of the risks we face if we go into hospital is of picking up infections. The problem is not confined to the common cold. There are other potentially more serious infections we can pick up in hospital which prove difficult to treat because the bacteria in question have become resistant to many antibiotics. These infections are more likely to take hold in patients whose resistance is already low, such as frail, elderly people.

MRSA

The family of bacteria *Staphylococcus aureus* is known to have existed for centuries, but since the widespread use of penicillin, several strains have developed which are resistant to the antibiotic methicillin.

Methicillin-resistant *Staphylococcus aureus*, or MRSA, lives on the skin of many people without causing them any harm. However, if bacteria manage to enter the body through a cut in the skin, they can give rise to an infection. Frail, elderly people are more likely to be infected than younger people because their skin is more fragile and tears more easily *(see page 17)*. To make matters worse, wounds which heal very slowly, such as leg ulcers and pressure sores, mean that the open tissue (a possible entry point for infection) can be exposed for a long time.

Although MRSA bacteria in a wound may interrupt the healing process, they do not usually cause somebody to feel unwell. Some people throw off the infection with the help of antibiotics, while others live with it as an infection in a wound, where it remains confined. However, occasionally the bacteria manage to get further into the body. They may enter the bloodstream and cause septicaemia or blood poisoning, which in severe cases can be fatal. Or they may spark off pneumonia.

Cross-infection poses a major danger in hospitals. Any activity there (or elsewhere, such as in a care home) involving an operation wound, pressure sore, other type of skin tear or entry point for drips and catheters should be carried out in extremely hygienic conditions. Staff who are about to carry out tasks such as dressing wounds or dealing with catheters should use special alcohol-based hand sanitisers.

Visitors should play their part too. The alcohol gel offered to visitors in hospitals and care homes is designed to kill MRSA. In laboratory conditions, gel kills 99 per cent of pathogens, including MRSA.[22] Use it when you enter the hospital, when you enter the ward and when you leave. Rub it into your hands, then through your fingers, interlacing them so that it gets between the fingers and covers your hands and fingers. If you are visiting and have an open cut, you must cover it with a plaster. This applies even to paper cuts.

Clostridium difficile

Clostridium difficile (or *C diff*) is more easily transmitted than MRSA and the symptoms are extremely debilitating and unpleasant.

C diff lives in the gut of about 3 per cent of adults (the figure is slightly higher for people over 65) and gives rise to no symptoms. But it can give rise to serious symptoms, mainly in frail, elderly people or those in a much weakened condition, if they should start taking antibiotics. This is because antibiotics wipe out some of the healthy bacteria in the gut, thus allowing *C diff* bacteria to multiply. The symptoms of a *C diff* infection range from a few loose stools to explosive diarrhoea, as well as a raised temperature. In the most serious cases patients feel very unwell and become severely dehydrated. Antibiotics are administered to beat the *C diff* bacteria, and patients often recover in a few weeks. However, in some severe cases, they die.

C diff bacteria live in spores with hard casings. Those in diarrhoea may land on beds, door handles, lavatory seats and so on, where their protective casing enables them to survive outside the human body. If they find themselves in an environment in which they can develop and multiply, perhaps because somebody has touched a surface on which spores have been allowed to remain and then put their finger in their mouth, the hard casing disintegrates. So patients must not only be isolated, but the environment around them kept scrupulously clean.

As with MRSA, a nurse may have been touching a patient with *C diff* or a surface on which germs lurk. Hand hygiene is thus crucially important. It is important to be aware that alcohol gel is not a cleaning agent nor does it kill *C diff* bacteria, or indeed some other germs. So hands should be washed with soap and water, thus removing the dirt in which the micro-organisms live.

The incidence of both MRSA and *C diff* infection in hospitals has dropped significantly in recent years. But it is nonetheless worth being aware of the practices you should expect to see on a ward to reduce the chances of contamination.

Expect to see staff washing their hands at any time when cross-infection might arise, for instance:

- after contact with a patient or their surroundings
- after handling laundry or making a bed

- after using a computer keyboard
- after using the toilet
- before giving medication
- before preparing, handling or eating food

Hand-washing should involve:

- the use of soap; bacteria can lurk in the cracks of bars of soap, so expect a liquid soap dispenser
- washing hands palm to palm with interlaced fingers
- washing the backs of hands with one palm over the back of the other hand and interlacing the fingers
- washing the backs of fingers with opposing palms and interlaced fingers
- rotational rubbing of the left thumb clasped in the right palm and vice versa
- rotational rubbing, backwards and forwards of right hand by clasped fingers in left hand and vice versa
- washing the wrists
- rinsing hands and wrists with warm water
- turning off the taps with the elbows or by covering them with a paper towel
- drying the hands thoroughly, but not touching the disposal bin[23]

You may spot a diagram showing how hands should be washed over the basin.

Staff often use disposable gloves. These should be worn whenever a nurse or healthcare assistant might come into contact with blood, urine and other body fluids, mucous membranes or damaged skin. Gloves should be donned immediately before the task is to be performed, then removed and thrown away as soon as it is finished. The nurse should then wash their hands. Gloves should never be kept on during routine nursing care.[24] Someone who keeps their gloves on, running them under the tap between patients, is putting patients at great danger of infection.

If a nurse approaches your father yet has failed to carry out necessary hand hygiene or don a clean pair of gloves, refuse to allow them to touch him and explain why. That may not make you popular, but it could save your father's life.

As a patient or visitor, be alert to dirt around you. Are the table and other surfaces by the bed clean? If not, germs will breed – perhaps because another patient has sneezed, or you have touched your catheter and not washed your hands. Are there dirty cups around? They should be cleared away, as stagnant fluid creates a breeding ground for germs.

If you are concerned about the cleanliness of the hospital environment, ask to speak to the cleaning supervisor; they, rather than the ward sister, are likely to be responsible for cleaning. These days, wards do not tend to have their own cleaner, as cleaners move around the building. You could also bring in Dettol wipes, which kill many germs.

In any event, precautions should be taken on the ward to prevent the spread of other infections. Patients, health professionals and visitors should cough or sneeze into tissues, dispose of them immediately and wash their hands thoroughly with soap and water after they have done so. Tissues should be readily available on the ward. Patients and visitors should also be ready to wash their hands thoroughly, for instance before eating and after using the lavatory, and also to use an alcohol gel. If a patient cannot wash their hands, they should be given a hand cleaner. Visitors should refrain from visiting if they have any infections such as tummy bugs, coughs and colds.

Patients living with dementia

Many older patients in hospital wards have dementia, although it is usually not their dementia but some other medical problem such as a chest infection or leg ulcers that has brought them into hospital. Once there, they are at higher risk of many different misfortunes.

This arises because people with dementia may be confused about their new surroundings. They may move around, unaware of the danger of an obstruction, and fall over. They may forget to wash their hands after using the toilet. They may not eat or drink as they should, because they cannot remember whether they have had a meal nor comprehend that the food or drink on their table is for them. Removal from their usual environment and difficulty in adjusting to their new surroundings may also lead them to lose previous abilities, such as to wash and dress, prepare food or entertain themselves. In addition, if their behaviour is perceived as challenging or disruptive, they are at risk of being given anti-psychotic medication to calm them down (the dangers of these drugs are explained on page 448–50).

But it is not always possible for people with dementia to avoid a hospital stay. They may be ill or have broken a bone and need treatment that can only be provided in hospital. If so, do all you can to ensure that the hospital environment is adapted to suit the patient.

Be prepared to ask for help and champion the interests of your relative in whatever way is called for. In the year 2000, when my mother had dementia, she spent several months as a patient in the mental health assessment ward of a general hospital, where she received good all-round care. One day, she had a stroke. Hospital procedures dictated that patients suffering strokes should go to the main part of the hospital, so she was wheeled out of the assessment ward to A&E; here she remained for about three hours, in extreme distress but without any treatment. Finally she was admitted to a general medical ward.

The nurses on the medical ward had little time for and perhaps little expertise in providing care for patients with dementia. My mother did not fare well there: she could not understand where she was, or why she was there; she had difficulty in feeding herself (compounded by poor vision); and she repeatedly tried to pull out her urinary catheter and intravenous drip. The problems that arose were so constant and manifold that family members took it in turn to remain at her bedside throughout the day.

However, when I asked her doctor for a transfer back to the mental health ward, he said that hospital procedures dictated that he see stroke patients only on the general medical ward, not the mental health ward (although it was only three minutes' walk away). Furthermore, he said he could not discharge my mother back to mental health until a brain scan had established whether she had actually had a stroke. As she was not considered high priority, she had to wait a week for a scan (although a patient should be scanned within hours of a stroke, *as explained in Chapter 16: Strokes*). This seemed a far cry from the person-centred, seamless care which we are told we should expect in hospital.

Confronted with that situation today, I should take up the matter with the ward manager and if necessary other parts of the hierarchy up to the chief executive, pointing out that the *National Service Framework for Older People* asserts an older person's right to 'person-centred care' and explaining that this should mean that, 'NHS and social care services treat older people as individuals and enable them to make choices about their own care.'[25] I should challenge the long delay on conducting a brain scan on grounds of age discrimination *(see pages 297–9)*.

I should expect that my mother's care be coordinated and informed by the special needs arising from her dementia. The National Institute for

Health and Care Excellence has said that hospitals which provide acute services

> should ensure that all people with suspected or known dementia using inpatient services are assessed by a liaison service that specialises in the treatment of dementia. Care for such people in acute trusts should be planned jointly by the trusts' hospital staff, liaison teams, relevant social care professionals and the person with suspected or known dementia and his or her carers.[26]

Above all, I should also expect much greater awareness among staff throughout the hospital of the nature of dementia and how they should adjust their procedures and behaviour to take it into account.

Concern at lack of understanding of dementia by hospital staff has led to a concerted drive to improve matters. The Royal College of Psychiatrists found that 60 per cent of general hospitals in England were including dementia awareness training in their staff induction programmes in 2013.[27] This is obviously good news – although plainly the figure should be 100 per cent.

But what does this heightened awareness actually mean on the ground? Less than half of the hospitals surveyed by the Royal College of Psychiatrists had any system in place to ensure that staff were aware of a patient's dementia when they went off ward to get treatment in other parts of the hospital.[28] The situation may have improved since this survey. Thus a growing number of hospitals are using the butterfly symbol to denote that a particular patient has dementia (after obtaining the consent of the patient or their representative to display it). This means that whether a patient is on the ward or moving elsewhere in the hospital, staff should be aware of their illness. However, not all staff may be well-briefed about how to relate to and care for people with dementia.

If you run into problems, from a lack of practical help on the ward to overall arrangements for care, speak initially to your or your relative's named nurse, responsible clinician and/or the ward manager. If you fail to get a satisfactory response, ask to speak to a dementia champion. These are people working in health or social care who are charged with improving the experience of people with dementia and their families and carers in hospital. There may be a dementia champion on the ward; there may be one or more in other parts of the hospital. Sometimes dementia champions in hospitals are seen to be people who restrict themselves to advising staff, not responding to concerns from individual patients or their families. But you could try.[29]

Despite the improvements, many carers wish to be present on the ward with their loved one, just as I did. In 2014, the writer Nicci Gerrard launched 'John's campaign', in memory of her father, to encourage hospitals to make better provision for the carers of people with dementia. During a five-week hospital stay (when visiting was restricted partly because of an outbreak of Norovirus), John's condition had declined steeply – he lost the ability to move around, to control his bladder and to recognise his loved ones. He also lost a great deal of weight.

In response to John's campaign, the government asked hospitals to improve their provision for the carers of patients with dementia, and by 2016 over 200 had publicly committed themselves to doing so. Steps that acute hospitals can and some do take include: allowing carers of people with dementia to visit outside normal visiting hours; offering reduced-rate or free parking for them; and overnight accommodation.[30] Find out whether your hospital has publicly pledged to improve provision for the carers of patients with dementia and use any commitment as a stick with which to try to secure the provision you consider you need.

Safeguarding your rights in hospital

Asserting your rights from a hospital bed can be a lot more challenging than doing so from your own home, with a phone (plus charger), computer, address book and notebook to hand. Take items such as this in with you.

But there are psychological reasons too which can induce a certain passivity when we are in hospital – quite apart from the fact that we feel unwell. In hospital, as in other environments in which care is given, recipients are at the weak end of a power relationship. They need help, and those in a position to give it are highly trained, laden with superior knowledge, armed with various pieces of impressive technical wizardry and operating in a world which offers few visible challenges to their authority. As we shed our daytime clothes and don nightwear, perhaps even a hospital robe, and sit up in bed as the doctor above us dispenses wisdom, it is easy to feel disempowered and depersonalised.

But it is important to be discerning. Remember that consent is needed for any medical treatment *(see page 283–5)*, that patients have a range of rights and expectations as set down, for instance, in the NHS Constitution *(page 279)*, and that the relationship between the giver and the receiver of medical care is a fluid one. Today, the doctor-patient relationship on the average maternity ward is far more equal than it was 30 years ago. A similar change in ethos and attitude may affect the care of older people eventually: meanwhile, it is important not to accept medical dictatorship as an unchangeable norm.

Knowing what is happening

I often visit people in hospitals that are impressively clean and in which patients say they enjoy their meals and are well cared for. Yet, they tell me, they have no idea what conclusions doctors have reached about their condition, what tests or treatment have been or might be given to them, let alone how long they are likely to be in hospital.

This situation can breed worry in the patient and their relatives. It can also cause patients to surrender concern for themselves. Perhaps they live alone and are now enjoying being waited on hand and foot. The food is good, they look better. Fine – unless that leads them to push aside planning for their future after hospital and engaging seriously with their recovery and rehabilitation, for instance through exercising.

As soon as a patient has been admitted to hospital, staff start to think about when they can safely discharge them *(as explained in the following chapter)*. To ensure you are as fit as possible when you return home, remain focussed on your condition during your hospital stay and engage with the professionals in your recovery or rehabilitation. If you let others look after you more than you need, you may lose the skills and the psychological motivation to live independently.

Expect to know what is happening and likely to happen to you during your hospital stay. We saw in Chapter 14 that a key element of the NHS Constitution is a right to be involved in decisions about your care. The National Institute for Health and Care Excellence (NICE) has issued a useful list of the information it says hospitals should provide to patients with social care needs when they are admitted. (No level of social care need is specified, so this guidance should apply to many older people.) NICE says that the staff who admit a patient to hospital should explain to them:

- the reason for their admission
- how long they might need to be in hospital
- the treatment and options for care they can expect
- when they can expect to see the doctors
- the name of the person who will be their main contact
- possible options for life at home when they are discharged from hospital
- their treatment and care after discharge.[31]

If a nurse tells you they cannot fill you in on matters such as these, ask to speak to someone who can. This should be your 'named nurse', whose name should be above your bed. If they or another senior nurse cannot help you, ask them whether they could ensure the consultant speaks to you next time they are on the ward. If you still get no joy, ask to speak to the ward manager or the modern matron; as noted above *(page 910)*, modern matrons should involve themselves in resolving difficulties. *As we see in the following chapter,* a discharge coordinator (often a social worker based in the hospital) should oversee planning for your discharge from hospital.

Tests

On a hospital ward we expect routine tests for pulse, temperature, blood pressure and so on, and perhaps some others such as X-rays and CT scans, and these are often vital if we are to be treated correctly. Yet sometimes we may be unaware that we are being formally assessed for a condition, still less that the result could have considerable implications for our future. While any physical test requires a patient's consent, the situation is not so clear cut for mental and also social care assessments.

For example, one elderly woman whom I used to visit, who had been in hospital for several months recuperating from an operation to mend a broken hip, had been asked by the hospital's occupational therapist if she would like to go to the kitchen and make a cup of tea with her. The woman said that she would not; thereupon a refusal to take what was in fact a highly significant test was recorded in her notes. The reason for the test's importance was as follows: the social services care manager responsible for ensuring that this lady received adequate support once she left hospital was considering whether she could manage at home, where she had been living independently with the help of regular visits by care assistants, or whether she should relocate to a care home. If she could make a cup of tea successfully, a home visit would be tried at which the occupational therapist would assess how well she could cope with other everyday tasks in her home environment.

I asked the woman why she had refused to take the test. She explained that she could see no reason to go and make tea when cups were delivered to her bedside. Her deafness and a speech impediment had probably hindered the communication necessary to clarify not only the purpose of the test but also her reasons for declining to take it. Fortunately, I was able to persuade staff to approach her again. After I had explained the test's significance to her, she was very keen to take it.

Don't be bullied into taking tests such as this only in the hospital's facilities, such as a pretend kitchen, if you would feel uncomfortable there, perhaps because you have vision problems. Say you would like an assessment at home instead. After all, the key consideration is whether you could make yourself a cup of tea in your own kitchen using equipment and in surroundings with which you are familiar.

Another potentially life-changing assessment which can be put to an unwitting patient is an assessment which concludes that they lack mental capacity or the ability to take a particular decision or to convey a decision *(see page 774)*. Any incapacity must arise from an impairment of the brain, so the first stage of any assessment of mental capacity must be identification of brain damage arising, say, from a stroke or dementia and the second whether that damage prevents the decision from being made.

Assessments for dementia often involve questions and puzzles *(as explained on page 433)*, so that somebody might easily not realise they are being formally tested, if the health professional carrying out the assessment has not explained clearly what they are doing. They might carry out such an assessment, arrive at the conclusion – rightly or wrongly – that the person is suffering from a brain impairment, such as dementia, ask a few further questions and go on to assert that the impairment renders them incapable of taking major decisions about their future.

In that situation, another person, such as their legal representative or an official from social services or the NHS, can lawfully take the decision for them. The decision could be, for example whether someone should move from their own home to a care home or receive medical treatment which carries significant risks, even against their will.

A diagnostic test for dementia followed by a test of mental capacity thus has huge implications for somebody's ability to have agency over their own future and it is of the utmost importance that they should:

● know that such a test is proposed

● ensure that the precepts of the mental capacity legislation are observed when it is conducted

● if possible have an independent person with them to check that they are, and

● know the result at once, so that they can challenge it if they wish *(see pages 774–81 for more information about this process)*.

It is well worthwhile writing clearly on a sheet of paper to keep at your bedside that you wish the name and purpose of any test which is proposed to be carried out to be written down. If you are concerned, insist

925

on talking to the ward manager, the modern matron and/or a patients' organisation which can give advice – in England: PALS, in Scotland: PASS, in Wales: your local community health council and in Northern Ireland: the Patient and Client Council *(see pages 332–4)*. If a test has been carried out, insist that you are immediately given a written record of who carried it out, its purpose, the date and the result.

Hospital notes

In a major report of the experiences of patients compiled by the Patients Association in *Patient Stories 2013: Time for Change*, problems arising from inaccurate or incomplete medical records arose time and again.[32]

As a patient, you have a legal right to see your medical records *(see page 281)*. Those added in hospital will be compiled by the doctors and nurses who assess and treat you. Ask to see what they have written down. Make sure your records are accurate and complete. Expect them to contain a record of requests by you as patient perhaps for a second opinion, as well as any serious comments or concerns you raise. Any discussions between you and hospital staff, for instance about your wish to be resuscitated in the event of a cardiac arrest *(see Chapter 41)* should be fully recorded. If there are errors or omissions, point these out and ask that the records be corrected accordingly.

In hospital you will often have some notes at the end of your bed. These will consist of charts of basic observations involving perhaps blood pressure, pulse and respiration, as well as any basic nursing notes – for instance, if you were turned to prevent pressure sores while asleep. They are not your complete records – indeed, they should not be, as the latter should be kept out of the public gaze and certainly not left in a place where any passer-by can peruse them.

Ageism

Many older people worry that their age will mean they are denied the tests and treatments that are offered to younger people. This does happen. For example, a survey on cancer and older people by Macmillan Cancer Support in 2012 found that nearly half of the 150 health professionals questioned said they had dealt with a cancer patient who had been refused treatment on the grounds that they were too old.[33]

Yet age is not an accurate means of predicting how somebody will respond to treatment. As this study noted, 'Chronological age and performance status alone are poor predictors of cancer treatment tolerance and life expectancy.'[34] Because of this variability, doctors should consider a person's 'physiological' or 'biological age', which is reflected in their physical condition and the state of their main bodily functions, separately from their chronological age. As a result, they might conclude that a 90-year-old is sufficiently fit to survive, say, a major operation or chemotherapy, but somebody much younger but in poorer health is not. The Macmillan study recommends doctors assess the patient's overall physical and also mental well-being in deciding whether to offer treatment.

If you fear that age is proving a barrier to the best treatment, try to find out what medical care is usually given to someone in their twenties with the same condition. For instance, if a young man develops pneumonia, what is provided in the way of drugs, physiotherapy and other therapy? Does your 75-year-old aunt get the same? If not, do sound medical reasons account for the discrepancy, or is ageism to blame? Perhaps you have had surgery to deal with a tumour in your breast but are not being offered radiotherapy. Why not? Has an assumption been made about your willingness to cope with the treatment? Or is a doctor rationing care based on grounds of age?

Age discrimination in the provision of healthcare by the NHS, or an agency acting for it, is against the law under the provisions of the Equality Act 2010. If you are puzzled as to why you are not being offered treatment, talk to the doctor involved. If unconvinced, challenge the doctor on grounds of age discrimination *(as outlined on pages 297–9)*. Acquaint yourself with the ways in which the medical condition in question should be treated by referring to authoritative guidance, such as the recommendations of NICE or its equivalent in Scotland *(pages 289–9)*.

Waiting lists

Perhaps the main way in which people fear that ageism will affect their treatment is that the year of their birth will assign them low priority on the waiting list for an operation. But doctors are supposed to consider not chronological but functional age when they consider both suitability for and timing of an operation. They should not put people low on waiting lists simply because they are old.

To make sure this does not happen, check that your name has actually been entered on the relevant list. Keep in touch by phone with the medical secretary in charge of that list to monitor progress if you can. In England, you could check through the Choose and Book service, if your need for treatment has been processed in this way.

Mistreatment and neglect

You visit somebody in hospital who has clearly been lying for some time in urine-soaked sheets. Or the ward staff are consistently failing to provide the help the patient needs to eat or drink. Or you think the patient may have been physically or mentally mistreated, through slapping, unnecessary rough treatment or verbal abuse, such as intimidation or disparaging remarks.

All these forms of behaviour could be classed as elder abuse. They should be taken seriously by the ward manager. Indeed, if the mental abilities of the patient are impaired and they have been ill-treated or a member of staff has deliberately failed to do something that they were aware they were under a duty to perform, a prosecution followed by a fine or imprisonment could result.[35] Some forms of abuse, such as assault, are also criminal acts in their own right, whether or not the victim has limited mental powers. *(I discuss elder abuse in more detail on pages 565–71).*

The hospital should have staff with special responsibility for dealing with and preventing elder abuse. They (together with members of the local police) will be members of an adult protection team which is co-ordinated by the social services department of the local authority. So, if you suspect elder abuse and fail to make satisfactory headway with the hospital, telephone social services and ask to speak to adult protection. Explain your concern and ask them to investigate. They ought to do so immediately if they consider that the safety of the patient is at risk. You could also contact the police.

Should you or your loved one suffer neglect on the ward and come to harm as a result, consider approaching a solicitor *(see pages 810–5)* and/or lodging an official complaint. The development of pressure sores because steps have not been taken to prevent them, infections as a result of poor hospital hygiene and dehydration because a patient has been denied the help they need to drink are all events that should not take place in hospital. You may well have a case for suing the hospital should one occur to you or your loved one *(see page 812).* But plainly, it is best to anticipate problems before they arise.

Visitors

Family and friends can feel redundant when a loved one is in hospital. In fact, though, visitors have an invaluable role to play.

Why visit?

Many people assume that they can do nothing for a parent who has, say, suffered a major stroke. Yet it is difficult to put into words the value of somebody simply holding your hand if you are very ill, particularly if they are a kindred spirit. Patients can feel frightened and alone, especially if they have hearing and/or sight problems. In that situation, to know that somebody else is there alongside you, sharing to some extent any fear, pain, frustration or confusion, can make a huge difference.

Sometimes relatives and friends believe that visiting is pointless if the patient is unlikely to remember the visit afterwards, or to recognise them as individuals, perhaps because of dementia. Yet the same people are often keen to give care and attention to a baby, even though the baby cannot name them and may or may not recall the interaction later. Why should older people in just as much need of comfort be left to cope alone? Why should the memory of an event hold greater importance than the quality of the moment? As explained earlier *(on page 429)*, people with advanced dementia who may not be able to think clearly nonetheless usually retain their emotions, and can therefore feel fear, as well as pleasure from a reassuring kiss or squeeze of their hand.

Practical tasks

Hospital radio can be a godsend. It may be available for 24 hours, with light music playing at night to help patients sleep. During the day, there may be music and chat, poems, comedy clips and a religious service, for instance. Televisions, too, can be invaluable. Some hospitals provide radio and television for free; others do not provide any of these services; often they impose charges, which can soon mount up.

Sorting out bedside entertainment is one of the many practical tasks with which visitors can help. Perhaps they can bring in a radio, television, CD player, laptop or tablet, with a headset. Anything that is to be plugged in will need to be screened first by hospital staff so items that rely on batteries will probably be more suitable if the hospital stay is brief. Consider the size of any gadgets you bring in for a patient: tiny control buttons can be difficult to use. *(On page 248 I discuss the various uses to which a tablet can be put from a hospital bed.)*

Countless other practical tasks arise in hospital, from dealing with laundry and bringing in shopping to mending spectacles and obtaining hearing-aid batteries with which visitors' help can be invaluable.

Raising issues with staff

There may also be important issues to raise with the staff, particularly if your loved one finds it difficult to convey their views and wishes. Could staff ensure that drinks are always within reach? Could they empty a catheter bag more often? Could the patient have white/brown bread in sandwiches? Could staff always help them to remove the wrapping?

Sometimes it emerges that a hospital is not covering an aspect of the patient's care which most patients and relatives would assume is being looked after and which the patient might to be unable to attend to themselves, such as the care of nails, hair or beard. If so, how will those aspects of personal care be attended to and by whom? If nails need attention, say so to the nurse or ward manager. Most hospitals contain a podiatry department and although its staff will spend most of their time on the premises seeing outpatients, there is usually a little time for paying visits to patients in wards.

Visitors may also be able to play a vital role in helping a patient's rehabilitation, perhaps after a stroke *(as outlined in Chapter 16)*.

Helping with activities

Visitors can also play a vital role in helping a patient carry on with the activities that are a part of their normal life, through bringing in books, newspapers, writing materials, craft materials and so on, if the patient has not had the opportunity of bringing them themselves. As I write this, I have just heard that a friend who was seriously ill with heart failure has died. Two days before, I had visited Muriel in hospital and, to help her cope with her alien, clinical surroundings, had brought in an assortment of rocks, fossils and wild flowers. She found them utterly absorbing, turning them over, feeling them and smelling them; indeed, they seemed to act like Proust's madeleine, transporting her back to the fields and woods which she loved to explore.

Visitors can also help ensure that the patient makes the most of all the opportunities the hospital offers. Perhaps the person you are visiting would like to see a chaplain but does not know who to ask? Is there a day-room in which they could spend time? Perhaps the hospital's occupational therapist could visit and work out what the patient can and would like to do and provide some activity meaningful to them?

Patients' rights

Visitors can also check that the patient's rights are being upheld, such as their right to know what diagnostic tests are being carried out *(as explained above)*.

If the patient has no representatives who will be consulted about what is in their best interests should they lack the capacity to make some decisions, the visitor may wish to consider whether to put themselves forward as somebody interested in their welfare *(as explained on pages 782–4)*.

And if a patient who lacks the necessary mental capacity to make decisions and has no representative or close family is to be deprived of their liberty in order to receive care or treatment, the visitor might consider putting themselves forward as somebody interested in their welfare under the deprivation of liberty safeguards *(see page 788)*.

Visiting times and phone contact

In some wards, times for visiting are short; in others much longer. Shorter times allow longer for patients to rest and also ensure they can eat their meals undisturbed. Try not to irritate staff by visiting before or after these set times (and indeed, of course, abide by other ward rules). But at the same time, if you never see your patient eat their meals, question staff about whether they are eating properly and ask to see any charts which monitor their food intake.

Perhaps you live far away and wish to ring in regularly to ask about your loved one's condition. Ask the sister or charge nurse to tell you the best time of day to do this: it will depend partly on change of shift times. Often late afternoon is a good moment – by then, day staff will have seen for themselves how patients are faring and any medical treatment is likely to have been carried out. Nurses tend not to be so busy at that time compared with, say, mid-morning.

If you will have to nurse a relative yourself when they leave hospital, ask the ward sister if you can watch staff carry out tasks which you will have to perform, such as moving the patient in bed or handling a bedpan, so that you can learn how they are best carried out. Allowing relatives to learn these tasks is at the discretion of the ward sister, but a hospital ward can be an ideal place to pick up tips. Also, if you are happy to come and help, for instance with feeding your loved one, tell the ward manager.

If you and your family and friends cannot provide sufficient visiting yourselves, perhaps because you live far away, perhaps local faith groups or voluntary organisations which offer befriending services *(see pages 218–23 and 236)* could help out? Or perhaps a PALS or equivalent holds lists of volunteer visitors?

Chaplaincy

Chaplains are appointed by NHS trusts in consultation with local faith groups to meet the spiritual and religious needs of the population that the trust in question serves.

One of the main tasks of chaplaincy teams is to ensure that patients who wish to practise their religion are able to do so. This should mean that a Roman Catholic, for example, can receive mass regularly, if necessary on the ward, a Methodist receive a visit from a Methodist minister or a Muslim can pray regularly, in a prayer room with facilities for washing beforehand and an indication of the direction in which they should face. Chaplaincy teams also ensure that patients' religious beliefs and practices are respected. They have their own core staff but are also able to call on the services of honorary chaplains, who are often retired ministers of religion.

Most large acute hospitals hold religious services, although not necessarily always on Sundays. Any help needed to get to a service should be provided by a nurse or member of the auxiliary staff or a volunteer. It is a good idea to give as much notice as you can if you are going to need help.

Chapels should be available 24 hours a day and large enough to accommodate beds and wheelchairs, as well as at least 20 seated people. Whether you have a religious affiliation or none, these places can be a valuable resource, offering a quiet space away from the busy clinical world.

But facilitating religious activity for people of faith who are practising their religion is only one element of what chaplains actually do. They are trained in pastoral care and counselling and should be able to offer general emotional help as well. So they can be invaluable to agnostics and atheists too. They are trained to respect others' belief systems and their professional code of conduct forbids them from seeking to impose their own, although they can answer questions about it.

In hospital we can feel very vulnerable. Cut off from our normal environment, we may be facing the prospect of a major operation or other painful treatment. It can be very helpful to discuss the situation with somebody who is not involved in the clinical decision-making but can be used as a confidential sounding board for thoughts, feelings and hopes. A dialogue with a chaplain need not involve any reference to religion or spirituality.

There are also practical matters with which a chaplain might be able to help. If you find yourself in hospital and have no visitors but would like some, a chaplain may be able to rustle up some volunteers through links with local faith groups.

If you do not encounter a chaplain but would like to see one, ask a nurse to make arrangements or phone the chaplain's office yourself or ask a relative to do so. A chaplain will not turn up at your bedside just because you have indicated on your admission form that you profess a particular religious faith. This information is not automatically passed on to chaplains and they do not have a right of access to it.

Chaplains with the same role as those in hospitals can also be found in other parts of the health service, such as ambulance trusts, hospices, mental health trusts and community hospitals.

Transport

Tests, treatments, outpatient appointments, attendance at clinics and visiting patients all require journeys which may be long, complicated and expensive. For people who need to visit hospital often, perhaps with a carer, the costs can be daunting. So, what are the options?

Free transport

Of course, we should all expect free transport in an NHS ambulance in an emergency. But free transport to and from hospital should also be available in non-emergency situations if you fall into one of two groups.

Some people are eligible on grounds of clinical need. They might be unable to use public transport because of a medical condition including sight, hearing or mental health problems. They may have a condition which would get worse if they made the journey other than in an ambulance. They might be unable to walk without relying on another person yet have no one to accompany them.

If you wish to know whether you would be eligible, telephone the passenger transport service section of the hospital in question. Or the PALS officials in the hospital (or their equivalent elsewhere in the UK) might be able to help *(see pages 332–4)*. The government's instructions to health bodies on patient eligibility say that free transport should be provided by the hospital in the following circumstances:

> Where the medical condition of the patient is such that they require the skills or support of passenger transport service staff on/after the journey and/or where it would be detrimental to the patient's condition or recovery if they were to travel by other means. Or where the patient's medical condition impacts on their mobility to such an extent that they would be unable to access healthcare and/or it would be detrimental to the patient's condition or recovery to travel by other means.[36]

Health bodies have the discretion also to provide free transport for a patient's escort or carer 'where their particular skills and/or support are needed'.[37]

If you are not eligible for free transport on grounds of medical need, you might perhaps be eligible for reimbursement of your travel costs. Eligibility for this help depends not on illness or disability but on financial means. If you are receiving the Guarantee element of Pension Credit *(see page 854),* you will automatically be eligible. Or you might meet the criteria for support through the NHS Low Income Scheme, which provides help with various NHS costs *(as explained on page 865).* Naturally enough, you will be expected to use the cheapest form of transport, whether bus, train or car or, in exceptional cases where no alternative exists, taxi or volunteer car. If a car is used, any parking charges are also included.[38]

Ask at the hospital to which you have to travel for an application form for the Low Income Scheme if your savings do not exceed £16,000, or £23,250 if you are living permanently in a care home. Or you can order a form online; your doctor, dentist or pharmacist may also be able to give you one. You can claim a refund for up to three months after the date of travel. Patients eligible for help with their travel costs can also claim the travelling costs of escorts where this is considered medically necessary by their GP or consultant.

If you are denied free hospital transport and you consider that it should have been granted, talk to a patients' organisation and consider lodging a formal complaint *(as outlined on page 336)*. This is clearly especially important if you face making many more journeys in the future.

If you do not qualify for transport to hospital on medical grounds, consider using public transport. Driving to a hospital can mean not only negotiating busy roads, perhaps at night, but also finding somewhere to park. The existence of free bus travel for older people means this is often the cheapest (and least stressful) way to travel.

Some hospitals, particularly private ones, are not served by frequent bus services, but general and community hospitals usually are. You can find out what is available by telephoning the public transport information lines *(described on page 702–3)* or by ringing the hospital itself or looking at its website.

Another possibility is to use any volunteer car scheme in your area. Such schemes involve a volunteer driving a patient or visitor, with the patient or visitor reimbursing the driver for petrol or paying an amount suggested by the scheme. This can work well and can sometimes involve quite long journeys. In one case of which I became aware, a volunteer regularly drove a woman in her eighties who wished to visit her twin sister in hospital 70 miles from her home. The driver took her several times; while she was at the hospital, he would go and explore the local area. However, in another case which came to my attention involving short trips to a local hospital for appointments, the volunteer always turned up with her petrol tank empty, expecting the patient to pay to fill it and buy her lunch. So, establish beforehand just how the trip will work and which costs will be covered.

Parking charges

Parking charges can be a real headache for patients and visitors, particular people who need to make frequent visits to hospital over a long period, perhaps for kidney dialysis or cancer treatment.

Some degree of charging for hospital parking takes place throughout the UK. However, the Scottish and Welsh administrations have responded to fierce public criticism of hospital parking charges by introducing free parking at the majority of hospital car parks, apart from those which have agreements with private contractors such as through private-finance-initiative (PFI) schemes. In Northern Ireland, many patients with cancer and other serious long-term conditions are entitled to free parking at hospitals. In England, car parking charges remain, and they vary widely according to the approach of the hospital trust involved.

Wherever you live in the UK, it is worth asking whether special exemptions for parking charges might apply in your case: sometimes trusts will consider certain patients for free parking, for instance, patients who must attend outpatient appointments over a long period.

Readers in England may care to make the most of recommendations drawn up by the Health Select Committee of the House of Commons in 2006, which the Department Health has urged trusts to implement, although they are not forced to do so. If your hospital trust has not done this and you are unhappy with parking charges, you could write to the trust's chief executive and its governors (a majority of whom must be elected), with copies to the chief executive of the clinical commissioning group. The recommendations were that trusts should:

- issue all regular patients, or their visitors, with a season ticket that allows them reduced price or free parking

- introduce a weekly cap on parking charges for patients

- provide free parking for patients who have to attend for treatment every day

- inform patients before their treatment begins of the parking charges, exemptions and reduced rates that will apply[39]

Outpatient appointments

If you find travelling to hospital for outpatient appointments unduly disruptive or expensive, talk to your consultant or GP about whether they are really necessary. Might the same result be achieved just as well through visits to your GP, so long as he or she is in close touch with the consultant? For instance, if your outpatient appointment involves your being given a blood test and your consultant possibly adjusting your treatment accordingly, perhaps the test could be administered at your GP practice and your GP told whether your treatment should be tweaked?

The journey to and from outpatient appointments – the means by which you travel, how long the journey takes, whether you are likely to arrive on time and whether you are likely to return home exhausted afterwards – are very important. It is worth pulling out all the stops to ensure these arrangements suit you – *see suggestions on pages 933–4.*

Staying in hospital

* Choose and Book gives you the choice to avoid poor care and/or expertise in your local hospital by choosing to be treated elsewhere.

* Intermediate Care – intensive therapy and practical support, free for up to six weeks – can aid convalescence.

* Expect help to eat and drink if you need it in hospital.

* Ensure steps are taken to prevent pressure sores, particularly in A&E.

* Weigh up the pros and cons before you accept a urinary catheter.

* Patients with dementia who go into acute hospitals should expect special attention.

* If a test for dementia or mental capacity is proposed, try to get an independent person to be present.

* Take your mobile phone and charger and the phone numbers of people and organisations you might need to contact when you go into hospital.

* Chaplains can be helpful sounding boards and comforters; religion need not be mentioned.

* You may be eligible for free transport to hospital on grounds of your clinical need or low income.

Chapter 39

Leaving hospital

When we are older, our body may take longer to recover from illness, injury or an operation. At the same time, recovery may be delayed by other conditions from which we are suffering. Indeed, our medical condition may stabilise at a level different from that before the illness or whatever prompted our hospital stay. So, for many of us, it is important to see hospital discharge as the movement from one setting to another – not the end of a process.

Alongside our body's natural recovery and attempts by doctors to aid recovery further, the practical tasks of everyday life have to be addressed. Some of us will be able to look after ourselves in a matter of days, even hours. For others, this may take a few weeks, or the period may be longer – indeed, we may never fully recover the ability to look after ourselves without help. If we are in this last category, we can find ourselves pitched into a decision about our future care and perhaps living arrangements while waiting for discharge from hospital. This may involve discussion with family carers and/or social services about help at home or entry into a care home.

In this chapter I offer tips for settling in at home after a hospital stay if recovery is going to be quite rapid. I go on to address situations in which further treatment, therapy and/or practical support are needed. Fortunately, the state provides certain kinds of help in these situations, but it is important to know what your rights are, since a wrong decision can have all sorts of implications.

This chapter therefore examines:

▶ the issue of medical fitness for discharge

▶ the discharge process that hospitals should use

▶ readjusting at home after a hospital stay

▶ the provision of free medical and practical support for up to six weeks after a hospital stay through Intermediate Care or Reablement

▶ the provision of extra ongoing help at home after a hospital stay

▶ the position of unpaid carers when arrangements post-discharge are being considered

▶ a move to a care home after a hospital stay

▶ the rights of people with mental impairment to determine their own future

▶ the provision of NHS Continuing Healthcare

Hospital discharge

You may be desperate to return home, but it is important not to allow the hospital to let you go if you are too ill or will lack the practical support you will need. Especially at a time of pressure on NHS budgets, hospitals may be tempted to send patients home too soon. It can be helpful to know just what rights you have as a patient and what you can expect from the discharge process.

Medical fitness

Hospitals owe patients a duty of care. This means they must satisfy themselves before discharging someone that discharge would not be negligent or, in other words, expose the patient to an unnecessary risk of harm. The first stage in discharge involves a declaration by the medical team that the patient is medically fit to leave that hospital.

In her report in 2011, the Health Service Ombudsman in England described several cases in which patients had been discharged when hospitals should have continued to care for them. For example, Mr W, who was suffering from dementia and depression, was admitted to hospital with pneumonia and recurrent dehydration in 2010. On Christmas Eve, the hospital discharged him to a care home. His daughter had not been given notice of the move and, when she found out, was appalled. Her father was malnourished and dehydrated, he had developed an infection – suspected *Clostridium difficile*, which can be serious *(see page 917)* – and his weight had dropped to six-and-a-half stones. She raised his case with the Ombudsman, who concluded that he had been medically unfit for discharge and that the discharge had been unsafe.[1]

The case of Mr D illustrated another common problem – that of being sent home without the medication, medical equipment or healthcare you need. Mr D was suffering from advanced stomach cancer and needed painkillers. His date of discharge was brought forward to the Saturday of a bank holiday weekend, but when his family brought him home, they discovered that the hospital had failed to provide him with sufficient painkillers or in a form which he could take, as he was unable to swallow. Thereupon, his daughter spent much of the weekend driving round in a desperate attempt to get prescription forms signed and permission for district nurses to administer morphine through injection. Her father died on the following Tuesday and part of her distress arose from her inability to spend time with him just before his death.[2]

So, check carefully that you have all the medication, medical equipment and/or healthcare services you will need at home. The National Institute for Health and Care Excellence tells hospitals they should, 'Give people information about their diagnoses and treatment and a complete list of their medicines when they transfer between hospital and home (including their care home). If appropriate, also give this to their family and carers.' NICE says this information should be given not only verbally and in a written form but also in other formats that are easy for the person to understand, such as Braille or their own language.[3]

If you do not think you or your loved one is well enough to leave hospital on the proposed date, make this clear to the consultant and other doctors. We do not have a right to remain indefinitely in our hospital bed of course, but the hospital knows it should not be discharging anybody who is not medically fit or has not been given the equipment and drugs they need or adequate medical or nursing care in place outside hospital. The hospital knows it could be taken to task by the Ombudsman for failings in this area, as well as being criticised in the press. It might also face a claim for compensation.

Practical support

In fact, discharge is not actually the prerogative of a consultant or other doctor. By declaring the patient is medically fit for discharge, they are turning the first key in a two-stage process. The second stage involves a social services official (usually called a hospital care manager or discharge manager) establishing whether the patient will need practical help when they return home so the discharge is safe. If they do, social services must ensure arrangements are in place. In England, a hospital trust works out whether a patient will need or may need practical support and formally communicates its decision to social services, together with the date on which it plans to discharge the patient in an 'assessment notice'.

So, if a nurse, hospital-based social worker or other official turns up at your bedside and starts asking you about your support arrangements at home, take the interview seriously. These officials are not enquiring out of the goodness of their heart – they must assess patients to see whether practical support will be necessary lest the patient is unsafe on their return home. The Care Act 2014 states that before giving an assessment notice, the NHS body responsible for the patient must consult the patient and, where it is feasible to do so, any carer they have.[4] So you may wish to ask any carer you have to be present at this assessment.

Beware of automatically reassuring officials that you have plenty of help at home. This can seem a matter of pride – perhaps you have four children. But they may not be able or willing to give you the help you require. Also, family, friend and neighbour relationships are so complex that it is often difficult to insist on help that has been offered. If you tell social services that you will be able to rely on help from family and friends, social services will feel under less of an obligation to organise care and support for you. Do not leave your hospital bed until any arrangements you need have been put in place. Otherwise, you might find yourself back in A&E in a day or two.

The discharge plan

Every patient who leaves hospital should have some kind of discharge plan. This is especially important when the patient has needs for practical or emotional help when they leave hospital. The National Institute for Health and Care Excellence has drawn up guidance on the form such a plan should take for patients with social care needs. (The guidance does not specify the level of care need so should apply to many older people.)

NICE says that hospitals should ensure there is a single member of staff (with expertise either in health or social care) who is responsible for coordinating the discharge from hospital of every patient with social care needs. A named replacement should always cover their absence. Hospitals should, 'Ensure that the discharge coordinator is a central point of contact for health and social care practitioners, *the person and their family* during discharge planning.'[5] (my emphasis)

NICE explains that, 'The discharge coordinator should work with the hospital- and community-based multidisciplinary teams and the person receiving care to develop and agree a discharge plan.' The plan should 'take account of the person's social and emotional wellbeing, as well as the practicalities of daily living'. It should include:

- details about the person's condition
- information about their medication
- information about staff who can be contacted once the person has been discharged
- arrangements for continuing healthcare and social care support
- details of services provided by local organisations which might be useful to them[6]

As well as working out how to ensure you can manage safely when you return home, social services (and also the NHS) will be having other possibilities in mind for your support once you leave your hospital bed. This means you could face a range of other assessments that relate to several different follow-up services:

i) Intermediate Care: This is the provision of healthcare, therapy and also practical support for up to six weeks usually immediately after a patient leaves hospital. It can be provided in the person's own home or in a care home or community hospital. All the provision is free, including practical care and support which would in other circumstances be classed as social care, for which a charge could otherwise be made. *(I discuss Intermediate Care below, on pages 957–63.)*

ii) NHS Continuing Healthcare: This also involves free practical care as well as healthcare, but in this case for people who are very unwell. Patients must have serious, complex healthcare needs to qualify. For example, my mother received NHS Continuing Healthcare for the last four-and-a-half years of her life. She was suffering from advanced dementia, which meant that she could neither stand nor feed herself and was often anxious and agitated; her agitation was exacerbated by near-blindness. *(See below for more information about NHS Continuing Healthcare. It is also provided to people who are terminally ill, as explained on page 961.)*

iii) Ongoing practical and emotional support: Some people will need not only practical help to ensure they are safe at home but ongoing practical support with day-to-day tasks such as washing and dressing. They are not so unwell as to be eligible for NHS Continuing Healthcare, but they need help for a longer period than would be provided through Intermediate Care. Or perhaps they have a range of needs, including emotional and social ones, which Intermediate Care is not designed to address.

We will look at each of these three ways forward in more detail. But before doing so, here are a few tips for patients lucky enough to recover quickly who will not need much practical help at home.

Settling in at home

✓ Ask the hospital to give you a copy of your discharge plan before you leave, setting out any medication, dressings or equipment you need, details of any follow-up care and healthcare services which have been arranged, and the name of the person responsible for ensuring these arrangements are coordinated. Expect a copy to be sent to your GP.[7] Make sure these medical notes contain accurate information about your diagnosis and treatment. If the doctors have been unable to work out what you were suffering from, make sure they say so and do not simply give information about some pre-existing condition, such as diabetes.

✓ Make sure you know who to chase up about any specialist aftercare. If you have been referred for, say, physiotherapy, but this means your name has been added to a long waiting list, you should know. You could then consider pressing your hospital trust or other health body for faster treatment or hiring therapy privately, if you have the money. *(Rehabilitation services after a stroke are discussed on pages 355–62, and healthcare professionals you might perhaps hire privately in Chapter 15.)*

✓ Before you leave, make sure that you have the phone number of the ward and the social worker based in the hospital, so that you can ring back if you have any concerns. Keep the phone number of your local district nurse and GP handy for emergencies when you have returned home.

✓ Ask nurses to show you and anybody who may be going to help you any techniques which could be useful, such as how to help you transfer from bed to a chair. There is no set method for helping somebody move – the help they need depends on their own physical condition as well as that of the helper. Anybody who is going to look after you as your carer should be told by the social services discharge manager about any support services (including training) which they could access. If they are not, they should enquire. *(See also page 947 below.)* A carer means anybody who provides unpaid help. They might be a friend or your partner, son or daughter. The help does not have to be heavy-duty, 24-hour care.

✓ Press the hospital to arrange transport home if necessary. Even when people have been in hospital for only a short time and are perfectly able to look after themselves, the hospital should ensure they have transport to get home and somebody to accompany them if necessary. If you are making your own arrangements, you may be able to reclaim the cost if you are on a low income *(see page 933)*.

✓ You may be delighted to be returning home, but could you get yourself to the hospital exit and a waiting car? In large hospitals, the distances can be daunting. Ask ahead of time for the loan of a wheelchair to get you to the door or for a porter who could wheel you down.

✓ The arrival home itself is important. If you live alone, try to make sure that somebody, perhaps a neighbour, brings in bread, milk and welcoming flowers. Some voluntary organisations, such as local Age UKs and British Red Cross branches, run schemes to give people returning home from hospital practical help. This can involve, for instance, taking the patient home from hospital, collecting prescriptions, cooking a meal and helping with shopping.

✓ Go and talk to your local pharmacist if you have any queries about the medication you should be taking. Perhaps you are unclear whether you should carry on taking a medicine prescribed by the hospital now you are home, or continue to take medication prescribed before you went into hospital. In the future, hospital pharmacies will probably send information direct to patients' local pharmacies when they leave hospital (as well as to their GP). In the meantime, your local pharmacy ought to have information about the medication you have been taking in the past and any allergies you may have and will be in a position to contact the hospital pharmacy with any questions.

✓ A hospital stay can sap confidence in the ability to live life as you used to. Build it up again gradually, perhaps by tackling a small task every day to give yourself a sense of achievement. Try to plan something to look forward to.

Employees' rights

It is worth considering briefly the position of friends and family members who might care for loved ones coming out of hospital or arrange care for them. If you are likely to have to spend time making arrangements for somebody who is leaving hospital, bear in mind that one of the types of emergency for which employees enjoy a legal right to take 'reasonable' time off work is 'to make longer-term arrangements for a dependant who is ill or injured'. A dependant includes your partner, child, parent or someone living with you as part of your family (not a lodger or tenant). Your employer can choose whether to pay you during the time you are away.

The situations in which you could take leave are:

- a disruption or breakdown in care arrangements

- the death of a dependant

- illness, assault or an accident affecting a dependant

- making longer-term arrangements for a dependant who is ill or injured (but not providing long-term care yourself)

To use this right to time off, you must inform your employer as soon as possible after the emergency has arisen.[8]

Carers

Carers are family, friends or neighbours who provide unpaid care and support for somebody who needs help. They can easily be exploited when somebody is coming out of hospital, taking on more care and general support than they wish. They should be aware that they have special rights in the process of hospital discharge.

Spouses and civil partners have a legal obligation to support each other financially. But they are not legally obliged to provide care. Of course, many spouses, partners, sons and daughters do give all the care their loved one needs. But some take on the role of carer reluctantly, without realising that they are not legally required to do so. In Britain, the ultimate responsibility to care for adults who cannot look after themselves rests with the state.

Social care authorities are aware of this position, but they may none-theless put pressure on a potential carer to provide care, despite the latter's reluctance to do so. If you are in this position, stand your ground. The Department of Health has told health and social care organisations they, 'Should not assume that others are willing or able to take up caring roles.' This applies also to people who have been the patient's carer: 'Don't assume that a person's carer will necessarily be able to, or want to, continue in a caring role. Patients and their carers may have different needs and aspirations.'[9]

If there is talk of your becoming a carer, make sure you are given time to consider your options. If the person needs a lot of support, you will be making what may be a life-changing decision. Consider how much and what type of care you are willing to give and the impact that caring is likely to have on your life as a whole.

It is worth discussing the logistics and impact of caring and also the financial consequences with an advisor at a carers' centre. There are nearly 150 such centres, under the umbrella of the Carers Trust, dotted across the UK *(see page 630)*. An advisor should be able to talk through with you what you would feel happy doing and also give you a sense of the sort of support you could most usefully request.

At the same time, if you are going to be involved in providing care, make sure you receive all the help the state will give you to support you in your role as a carer. Not only should this make your life easier: you are more likely to be able to carry on if you feel as happy as possible in the role and get regular breaks.

The National Institute for Health and Care Excellence says that a member of the hospital discharge team should provide carers with information and support and that this could include:

- printed information
- face-to-face meetings
- phone calls
- hands-on training including practical support and advice.[10]

Carers have a legal right to an assessment from social services of the support they need to help them care. As the Department of Health has pointed out in the context of discharge, 'Carers have a right to their own assessment and to any services they may need to support them in their caring role.'[11] *(I discuss carers' rights, carers' assessments and support for carers in Chapter 27.)*

Intermediate Care

Here is a scenario I have come across several times. Someone emerges from hospital after an operation, a fall or an infection with nobody to look after them at home. They assume there is no option but to spend their savings on a three-week stay in a private convalescent home. Alas, this can mean that they return home thousands of pounds poorer and perhaps far from recovered.

Or somebody goes into hospital for a knee replacement operation. They are discharged within days. Their partner, perhaps far from fit themselves, assumes they must provide all the help they need. They put their life on hold for weeks while shouldering all the household tasks, helping their other-half with personal care and trying to keep their spirits up.

Whenever I come across these situations, I invariably find that the person involved and their family are unaware of a state entitlement which was designed to help people get back on their feet after illness, injury or an operation. Intermediate Care provides people who are considered eligible with all the help they need for free for up to six weeks to re-cover their abilities to perform various essential tasks, often (but not ex-clusively) after a hospital stay. During this period of recuperation, the care offered typically involves physiotherapy, occupational therapy and, if someone has had a major stroke, speech and language therapy. Often people also need practical help: they get this too, free of charge, regardless of their financial means. If someone needs a lot of practical help while building up their strength and abilities, they may go into a care home, where they will receive round-the-clock support but also various kinds of therapy. Their health body will pay the care home bills.

An example from my own experience: in 2004, while en route to ad-dress a carers' conference in Durham, I slipped and fractured two bones in my leg. The local hospital set the bones and encased my leg in plaster, but, back home in Surrey (after a journey in which station officials armed with ramps and wheelchairs had cheerfully transferred me on and off trains), how was I to manage? Both hands had to manipulate crutches, so I could not carry a cup of tea, let alone shower or go shopping. I phoned social services (I could have phoned the local health body) and an assessor from the Intermediate Care team based at my local district hospital came straight over to work out what equipment and help I would need.

Here is another example, cited by the Department of Health in its guidance to health bodies in England on how Intermediate Care should work on the ground:

A man living in Bradford, aged 91, had a stroke while out walking his dog and as a result needed surgery on a fractured hip bone; the stroke left him with slight weakness down his left side and problems with concentrating and planning tasks. After he was discharged from hospital, an Intermediate Care team called on him at home four times a day. Care assistants helped him with personal care and household tasks. Other members of the team helped him to practise walking safely indoors using two sticks and to exercise in order to strengthen the muscles around his hip.

Once he could safely wash and dress himself, prepare hot drinks and snacks and carry them safely on a trolley, he and the team set new goals: walking safely outdoors with two sticks; bathing himself, with a bath lift to get in and out; preparing hot meals; getting on and off a bus; going shopping; and taking his dog for short walks with the help of a four-wheeled walker.

After six weeks, he was able to master all these skills, and Intermediate Care was withdrawn.[12]

The purpose of Intermediate Care is to enable someone 'to maintain or regain the skills needed to live independently in their own home'.[13] So it can also be used in a preventative way, funding intensive therapy and support for a short period to try to prevent someone's abilities from declining. They might go into a care home for a couple of weeks for this additional help and support, then return home better able to cope long term. *(See page 903.)*

The Intermediate Care team commissioned by a health authority is likely to contain nurses, physiotherapists, occupational therapists, social workers, community psychiatric nurses and care assistants. An Intermediate Care plan should be drawn up for everybody who is to be given Intermediate Care. The individual involved and any carers they may have 'should be key participants in any decisions made', according to the Department of Health.[14] This is very important: you and any family, friends or carers you may have need to know just what the goals are for your Intermediate Care, how they are to be achieved and the facilities and services that are to be provided to help you.

Each NHS health organisation publishes information on Intermediate Care for its own area. It will set out the aims of Intermediate Care, the sort of help that can be obtained and where it is provided. This information need not be set out in a particular form of words and can be misleading through omission. For instance, it may omit that Intermediate Care is free for those assessed as needing it. Yet the government has made clear in a statutory regulation that in England, 'A local authority must not make a charge for intermediate care and reablement support services for the first 6 weeks of the specified period or, if the specified period is less than 6 weeks, for that period.'[15] Indeed, the government has made clear that while Intermediate Care is time-limited, the 'period of time for which the support is provided should depend on the needs and outcomes of the individual. In some cases, for instance, a period of rehabilitation for a visually impaired person ... may be expected to last longer than 6 weeks.'[16] Yet I heard in 2016 that some people were being told that their health body had been instructed that Intermediate Care could only ever be provided for two or three weeks. This is wrong.

Nor should Intermediate Care be withheld because somebody has dementia. If they meet the criteria, they should receive the Care.

Intermediate Care is not intended to provide general care for people coping with long-term chronic conditions, but a person with, say, osteoporosis or Parkinson's disease might receive Intermediate Care for a short period while recovering from, perhaps, a bone fracture or a chest infection.

Reablement

You may find that officials talk about Reablement rather than Intermediate Care. This is similar in many ways to Intermediate Care. It too focuses on outcomes so that the individual involved is aiming for certain goals to be accomplished within the six-week maximum period usually provided for free support, such as regaining their ability to wash and dress themselves or to walk to the shops without fear of falling over. Like Intermediate Care, Reablement is free to those who receive it.

There are differences. Reablement is funded by social care authorities, not the NHS. It tends to focus more on achieving independence, so that a person can, for example, make themselves a meal; while Intermediate Care tends to focus more on the delivery of various types of health therapy. The eligibility criteria for obtaining Reablement tend to be lower than of Intermediate Care. In other words, you have to be more disabled by circumstance to receive Intermediate Care. But the distinction between the two is often blurred and some of the services involved may be delivered jointly by the NHS and social services. *(I discuss Reablement in more detail on pages 612–5.)*

An official from the Department of Health told me in 2011:

Reablement essentially does the same thing as Intermediate Care – a short (up to six weeks) period of intervention to maximise independence. The NHS and councils deliver a number of step-down services, some of which are provided jointly, following discharge from hospital. ... Reablement services are likely to fall within the definition of Intermediate Care services and should not be charged for the first six weeks.[17]

Intermediate Care operates in a similar fashion, with similar objectives through the UK. In Scotland, for instance, the Scottish government set out the purpose of Intermediate Care and the way it should work in a detailed paper in 2012.[18]

Plan ahead

If you know you are going to be entering a period of disability and recuperation, most obviously after a planned operation, do not wait until the day before you are going to be discharged from hospital before you enquire about entitlement to Intermediate Care. Do so as soon as you go in – after all, the officials will be planning your discharge from the moment you enter a hospital bed – or beforehand, if you go in for planned treatment such as a knee or hip replacement operation. Plans may already be in hand to assess you for Intermediate Care, but on the other hand, they may not. It is no fun struggling at home while you wait for services to be put in place, yet people often find themselves doing this. A study of Intermediate Care provision in Leeds in 2005 found that as many as 44 per cent of patients receiving Intermediate Care did not do so until more than ten days after they had left hospital.[19]

No reasons were given in the study, but it is not difficult to work out why people sometimes experience delays. Sometimes it takes a while to put services in place, as care assistants and physiotherapists have to be found. Some hospital patients might not have been assessed for Intermediate Care when they should have been, and it is only once they are back home that a GP refers them to the Intermediate Care team or they ask for a referral themselves. Sometimes health authorities will see Intermediate Care as a field in which they can save money and for this reason will be disinclined to offer it to as many patients as they should, or even mention the fact that it exists. In these circumstances, only patients who know of the service and, if necessary, demand to be assessed for it, end up receiving it.

A fourth possible reason is that people have had operations in private hospitals that have no direct link with Intermediate Care teams. Patients may assume that if they are going to have a procedure carried out in a private hospital, they won't be eligible for Intermediate Care. Not so. The qualifying criteria for Intermediate Care make no reference to whether any previous healthcare has been publicly or privately provided. So, if you are planning to have an operation in a private hospital and are not intending to remain in it afterwards to recuperate, check that the hospital is in touch with Intermediate Care or ask your GP to put you in touch with the Intermediate Care team before you go in. That way, therapy, equipment and practical help can be put in place ready for your return, or at least officials can be ready to assess you for Intermediate Care as soon as you have had your operation. Expect equipment such as a raised toilet seat and bath or shower aids to be delivered to your home before you go into hospital for, say, a hip replacement operation.

In a care home

Intermediate Care can work well in the care home setting. You receive the therapy you need to help to recover and regain your independence, you do not have to worry about doing the cooking and cleaning and you receive help with personal care tasks like washing, dressing, bathing and using the lavatory. What is more, you have the reassurance that such help is on hand day or night.

The national minimum standards for care homes in Wales set out how Intermediate Care should work in a care home:

> Service users assessed and admitted solely for intermediate care are helped to maximize their independence and return home. ... Staff are deployed, and specialist services from relevant professions including occupational therapists and physiotherapists are provided or secured in sufficient numbers, and with sufficient competence and skills, to meet the assessed needs of service users admitted for rehabilitation. ... Staff are qualified and/or are trained and appropriately supervised to use techniques for rehabilitation including treatment and recovery programmes, promotion of mobility, continence and self-care, and outreach programmes to re-establish community living.[20]

This standard should represent best practice throughout the UK, although strictly speaking it does not apply outside Wales.

But before you allow hospital staff to send you to a care home for Intermediate Care, you need be sure that it really can cope in, say, an unexpected emergency, or with a complex ongoing medical condition such as diabetes or Parkinson's disease.

One woman of whose situation I became aware had a fall at home and injured her knee. After a month in an acute hospital, she was transferred to a nursing home *(defined in the Glossary)* for Intermediate Care. There, daily visits from a visiting physiotherapist worked well and helped her to regain her mobility. However, she was already suffering from a chronic lung condition and needed a constant supply of oxygen. The home had difficulty in installing the supply and securing the technicians necessary to maintain it. On two occasions the oxygen supply ran out and the woman nearly died. Fortunately, one of her sons happened to arrive on the scene in time on each occasion and managed to save her life.

So check you are happy with a proposed nursing home before you agree to be transferred *(see pages 963–5)*. Once there, expect the same facilities and services as those given to permanent residents. You enjoy the same rights as they do.[21]

Reassessment

Wherever you are receiving Intermediate Care, you are likely to be assessed to see whether you still need help. If not, your care will be ended; if you do still need it, your Intermediate Care plan may be adjusted in the light of changes in your needs.

It is tempting to put on a brave face and do all you can to show that you have regained your practical skills. Beware: don't try too hard! You may be able to make a cup of tea in the middle of the morning with the reassurance of professionals standing close by, but what you need to have regained is not just the physical and mental agility, but also the stamina to make that cup of tea on your own in the middle of the night. The assessors are bound to have an eye on their budgets, but you want to be absolutely sure you can manage and have benefited as much as you need from Intermediate Care services before you relinquish them.

If the Intermediate Care manager says that care will stop and you consider this conclusion premature, challenge it. If necessary, raise the matter with their line manager. You may need to lodge, or threaten to lodge, an official complaint, or take any of the other steps open to people unhappy with NHS (or in the case of Reablement, local authority) decisions described earlier *(on pages 336–41 and 578–80)*.

If you need practical help once Intermediate Care has finished, ask your social services authority for a social care needs assessment *(as explained in Chapter 26)*. This is the gateway to ongoing practical support.

NHS Continuing Healthcare

NHS Continuing Healthcare is a special kind of funding for people who are very ill and need ongoing healthcare, and often also practical help because their medical condition means they are unable to look after themselves. NHS Continuing Healthcare enables their NHS health body – a clinical commissioning group, health board or health and social care trust – to pay a care home (usually a nursing home) to look after them. But this funding can also be taken in the patient's home, with nursing care and practical help brought in, or in an NHS facility (though not usually an acute hospital). All this care and support is entirely free of charge, regardless of financial means.

Patients have to be very unwell to qualify for NHS Continuing Healthcare funding. For example, someone might have, say, advanced Parkinson's disease and a very serious pressure sore. Or perhaps advanced dementia is causing someone to be very distressed and at the same time they have to cope with heart failure or cancer. NHS Continuing Healthcare can involve health bodies paying out a lot of money – to cover care home bills in their entirety, or a place in a long-stay NHS unit or hospice, or heavy-duty support in the patient's own home or that of a relative. They ration provision very tightly through eligibility criteria. That said, nearly 60,000 people were eligible for NHS Continuing Healthcare in England in 2016, for example.[22]

There are three reasons for applying for NHS Continuing Healthcare. First, your care or that of your relative will be free of charge, and this might be in a nursing home, thus relieving you of paying substantial fees. It could also mean that money is thereby released which could fund additional support. Thus, when my mother was receiving NHS Continuing Healthcare, my brother and I arranged for her to be visited for two hours daily during the week in order to provide additional one-to-one interaction. These visits, which my mother seemed to enjoy at a time when she took little pleasure in life were paid for from her estate; my brother and I held power of attorney. Without the benefit of Continuing Healthcare funding, we would not have been able to hire this support.

The second reason is that the care provided under NHS Continuing Healthcare may be better than you would get elsewhere. When I was looking for a care home for my mother in 1999, I certainly considered that the long-stay NHS unit, staffed by NHS personnel, to which she finally went to live offered better care than that offered by the 50 or so private nursing homes that I toured at that time. However, this is purely anecdotal experience. In any case, since that time, health bodies have closed many NHS units and sent patients to selected nursing homes with which they have entered into a contract to provide Continuing Healthcare. Those homes may be better than other homes which have not been chosen.

The third reason for trying to obtain Continuing Healthcare is that you wish to continue living in your own home and need a lot of care, but your financial position rules out any help towards the cost from social services. In this situation, Continuing Healthcare can be a godsend, as the funding can be received in your own home and can pay for the attention of district nurses, healthcare specialists and care assistants (*as explained in more detail below*).

Hospital trusts should be considering whether patients might be eligible for NHS Continuing Healthcare before they discharge them from hospital. So, if you are in hospital, likely to be discharged soon and you think you might be eligible for Continuing Healthcare, ask whether an assessment is planned. If not, ask why not, and, if no convincing reason is forthcoming and you cannot persuade the official to agree to give you an assessment, write to the chief executive of the trust and ask for one. Set out briefly the reasons why you consider you might be eligible (*after reading the guidance offered below*). You could plead your case for a Continuing Healthcare assessment with a social worker such as the discharge manager: they are well placed to nudge the hospital trust into assessing you and will have a vested interest in the outcome, since if the health service ends up paying for your care, social services will escape the burden of organising and paying for it themselves or, if you are a self-funder, giving you advice and assessing you. If there is a chance that you will be eligible, you should at least obtain a preliminary screening to see whether a full assessment should be conducted.

Who is awarded Continuing Healthcare?

It is not a particular medical condition or conditions that determines whether somebody will be granted NHS Continuing Healthcare. Rather, it is the physical and/or mental health problems with which they have to contend arising from medical conditions.

This is understandable: illnesses and ongoing conditions affect people in widely different ways. While one person may seem relatively untroubled and content if they have dementia, and remain able to walk and enjoy outings outdoors, another may be distraught most of the time and unable to carry out most of the ordinary tasks of daily living.

Any assessment of an individual for NHS Continuing Healthcare therefore tries to work out the extent of the difficulties to which serious illnesses give rise in any individual and thus the need for care. What is considered is not the adequacy or the location of any care the person happens to be receiving at the time of the assessment, but the characteristics of their needs and the impact these have on the care they require.

In England, Scotland and Wales, national eligibility criteria for NHS Continuing Healthcare have been drawn up. Health bodies publish their own criteria, but these are expected to conform to the relevant national framework. Below I use the example of the framework issued for England by the Department of Health. Its approach is broadly similar to those taken by the Scottish and Welsh governments. Northern Ireland's health and social care trusts use criteria similar to those on the British mainland, although no framework for the whole of Northern Ireland had been published at the time of writing.

To work out whether somebody is eligible for Continuing Healthcare, the Department of Health says that health bodies should apply a matrix. This offers a range of scores in 12 areas of possible need, which are called 'care domains'. These are:

mobility	cognition
breathing	skin (including tissue viability)
nutrition – food and drink	drug therapies and symptom control through drugs
altered states of consciousness	psychological and emotional needs
continence	behaviour
communication	other significant care needs

An assessment for Continuing Healthcare involves two or more professionals from different disciplines (who may call themselves a panel or a multidisciplinary team) proceeding through the various care domains or assessment subjects, entering a score for the level of need in each one – from low through moderate, high and severe to priority.[23]

When assessing the level of need in a particular domain, the assessors should examine:

● the nature of the need and its effect upon the individual, as well as the kind of steps required to manage it

● the intensity of the need – in other words, the extent or quantity of the need and its severity, as well as the need for sustained care

● the complexity of the need

● the unpredictability of the need[24]

Sometimes needs in just one or two care domains will be so serious as to qualify the individual for NHS Continuing Healthcare. In other cases, a fairly high level of need in several domains interact one with another and thus affects the patient's overall care requirement. For instance, if somebody who is very unwell also has to cope with continence and breathing difficulties, the additional impact could tip them over into eligibility, even if the continence and breathing issues could not be classed as very severe in themselves.

The needs assessment does not give the last word on eligibility for Continuing Healthcare. The experience and judgement of the professionals can also be brought to bear. The fundamental question is: are the needs of this individual primarily related to their health, in which case the NHS should be responsible for meeting them? If they are, 'The NHS is responsible for providing all of that individual's assessed health and social care needs – including accommodation, if that is part of the overall need'.[25]

In **Wales,** domains of need are also used, while in **Scotland** a tool called Single Shared Assessment (SSA) is deployed. This also involves proceeding through various considerations, as occurs with the domains matrix described above.

Your involvement in your assessment

Expect to be fully involved in your assessment. The Department of Health has said that the person who is the subject of the assessment or their representative, 'Should be given every opportunity to participate in the assessment'.[26]

Go to the meetings well briefed. Obtain the guidance on eligibility for Continuing Healthcare issued by your own health authority; ask the hospital for this, and if you draw a blank, summon PALS or its equivalent *(pages 332–4)* for assistance. Also, read carefully the government guidance that the health authority should be following in whichever country of the UK the assessment is to take place.[27] Try to acquaint yourself fully with the details of your or your relative's medical condition and the precise effects these have.

You have a right to read and obtain photocopies of your health records or those of someone you represent legally or who has given you permission to see them *(see page 281)*. Do not put off applying to see them until the last moment. It is also worth keeping your own record of your or your relative's condition. Include events, symptoms and signs of distress (with the date and time), which might not be recorded in the notes kept by doctors and nurses.

Go to the meetings confident of your own unique contribution to the process. If you have kept comprehensive records (or have a good memory) and have spent a fair amount of time with the patient, you will probably know a great deal more about them than do the professionals. This is because close observation and deep knowledge over a long period will give you a unique understanding of the impact of the symptoms of, say, your partner's Parkinson's disease on their ability to perform a range of functions, as well as on their emotional state. You will be well equipped to challenge the assertions of others at assessment meetings, and perhaps remind them of events which they have forgotten.

This may sound unlikely, since the nurse and/or social worker who knows you or your relative best should be present and have full records to hand at the assessment meeting. Yet nurses with years of experience of one person can forget many incidents – infections, even strokes – not unnaturally, as they will have been dealing with other patients at the same time. Or the nurse who knows you or your relative well might have been called away and been substituted by somebody who has only recently met you.

Be prepared to fight long and hard. Interrupt, clarify, explain and question whenever necessary. In my own case, I think sheer obstinacy on my part was crucial in securing Continuing Healthcare for my mother (who had dementia, severe osteoarthritis, could not stand up and was nearly blind). A fortnight after she had been admitted to a general hospital mental health ward for assessment in 1999, I was summoned to what I initially found a daunting situation: a case conference in which a circle of about ten professionals sat facing me across a small room. There, the consultant who presided over the meeting ordered me to move my mother out of hospital within two weeks and place her in a care home. Over the following months, I scoured her local area as well as mine, quizzing care home managers. Time and again, I would return to the case conference and say that I had not found any home which I considered capable of caring properly for my mother. As time passed, I expect that it became clear that I was not going to budge over this. Finally, the mental health trust involved agreed to care for her itself in its own Continuing Healthcare unit, which was far better equipped to deal with her needs than any of the care homes I had toured.

Four years later, my mother's health trust decided that it would review all patients in receipt of Continuing Care. It had changed the eligibility criteria under which my mother had initially received funding and the new ones seemed to her rule out: they gave priority to people whose mental illness gave rise to very challenging behaviour and my mother, though very unwell, remained sweet-natured, although she was almost constantly distressed. However, having visited her frequently, I found myself ideally placed to argue over every aspect of her health needs as the various domains were explored. I was also able to explain the ways in which her needs interacted to make her care more challenging. The government instructions to NHS health bodies stresses the need for assessments to look, 'At all of the individual's needs in the round – including the way in which they interact with one another'.[28]

The assessment took place over several meetings, each of several hours. No conclusion was reached, as my mother died during these weeks, but I suspect I would have prevailed in the end. The assessor would have been aware that I would undoubtedly have appealed against a decision to withdraw my mother's funding.

Screening or a full assessment?

If your health body decides to assess you for Continuing Healthcare, it may carry out a full assessment there and then. Or it may do a shorter assessment designed to screen out patients who would be unlikely to qualify; if the patient gets through that filter, then they will be the subject of a full assessment.

Screening is a less elaborate, less in-depth process than a full assessment for Continuing Healthcare. Rather than a multidisciplinary team, it may involve only one professional, such as a nurse, going through a checklist. It is important to find out if you are being screened in this way, so that you can make representations. Although the assessor should tell you what they are about, take no chances and tell them that you wish to know if screening is proposed. Otherwise, you might never know that you have been screened, or might hear only on receiving a letter that tells you and gives information about how you can appeal against the decision not to consider you for a full assessment.

In hospital, screening should not take place until the person involved is ready for safe discharge *(page 940)*. It can also take place when a health or social care official is considering or reviewing somebody's needs for help in any context: the Department of Health has said, 'As a minimum, whenever an individual requires a care home placement or has significant support needs, a Checklist would be expected to be completed.'[29]

If you are turned down for a full assessment as a result of a screening, the health body should inform you of the outcome of the screening, give you a copy of the Checklist and details of how to ask the clinical commissioning group to reconsider its decision. You should also be given the opportunity for your case to be referred to social services for social care support.[30]

Should you wish to challenge a decision not to proceed to a full assessment, you might find the following arguments relevant:

✓ Perhaps nobody told you in advance that you were going to be screened. Yet the Department of Health says, 'The individual should be given reasonable notice of the need to undertake the Checklist. … In an acute hospital setting or where an urgent decision is needed notice may be only a day or two days.'[31]

✓ Perhaps you or your representative were excluded from the screening. Point out that the Department has said, 'The individual themselves should normally be present at the completion of the Checklist, together with any representative.'[32]

✓ The Department of Health has said health bodies should explain the reasons why they have decided not to proceed to a full assessment: 'The rationale contained within the completed Checklist should give enough detail for the individual and their representative to be able to understand why the decision was made.'[33] If the reasons for turning you down are unclear, ask for more detail. Look for flaws in the assessor's statement.

✓ Try to think of information of which the assessor was probably unaware when making their assessment. Perhaps they failed to seek out important information or the views of particular professionals. The evidence assessors use for a Checklist screening is not usually very detailed.

A full assessment – your rights

The Department of Health is unequivocal in the importance it considers should be given to enabling the person being considered for funding, or their representative, to take part in a full Continuing Healthcare assessment.

You should not have to represent yourself if you do not wish to do so or feel that you cannot: 'The individual should be given the option of being supported or represented by a carer, relative or advocate, if they so wish.'[34] (*I explain the role of advocates on pages 804–8.*)

Some people will have a legal entitlement to an advocate. This is because social care authorities in England are legally required to provide an independent advocate to anybody who would have substantial difficulty in being involved in a social care assessment, if there is nobody (such as a family member or friend) suitable and prepared to facilitate their involvement. The eminent lawyer Professor Luke Clements has pointed out that this requirement also applies to Continuing Healthcare assessments, so long as the funding is likely to result in the person involved staying in hospital for 28 days or more or a care home for a period of eight weeks or more.[35] No medical diagnosis of, say, dementia, is required for this provision to be used, *which I also describe on pages 598–9 and 834–5.*

Perhaps English is not your first language, or you are deaf or blind, or you feel under the weather and thus need more time to get your head around the process of assessment. Expect your health body to take all necessary steps to enable you to play a full part, such as providing material in large-print form or in your own language, the services of an interpreter or simply a patient and understanding attitude to your involvement.[36]

If you consider that the views and knowledge of members of your family would be useful, you should ask that they be taken into account and give your consent to the health body to seek them. The health body must, as far as reasonably practicable, consult with the relevant social services department before making a decision about eligibility for Continuing Healthcare, so it is worth making sure that your social worker understands your needs fully. All these professionals, social workers included, come and go. Or a case may be passed to somebody else to deal with, so you will need to make sure that any matters you consider relevant are on your social services file.

Good luck!

Care of people who are dying

One category of people who are often granted Continuing Healthcare are those who are likely to die fairly soon and have intense and complex care needs. The Continuing Healthcare system provides a means of fast-tracking patients who need funding quickly without going through the care needs domain in great detail. A 'fast-track pathway tool' is used, enabling the health body to obtain immediate access to Continuing Healthcare funding – a facility particularly important for people who are deteriorating rapidly.[37]

Continuing Healthcare funding can support such people while living in a care home, hospice or hospital (including a community hospital), or in their own home or that of a close friend or family member. *(I discuss the advantages and drawbacks of the different locations for dying on pages 996–1002.)* Many people prefer to die at home *(as noted in the following chapter).* The government has specifically said that NHS Continuing Healthcare funding could help them in the following circumstances:

> If an individual has a rapidly deteriorating condition that may be entering a terminal phase, they may need NHS Continuing Healthcare funding to enable their needs to be met urgently (e.g. to allow them to go home to die or appropriate end-of-life support to be put in place).[38]

Appeals and reviews

Once it has come to its decision in the light of the recommendation by the professionals who conducted the assessment, the health body should send the person being considered for funding or their representative the decision to grant or withhold Continuing Healthcare funding and the reasons which led them to that conclusion. It should also send details of whom to contact for further clarification or to request a review of the decision.

Each clinical commissioning group draws up its own local procedures for handling appeals against Continuing Care decisions. These usually involve the clinical commissioning group taking another look at its decision and also the possibility of referral to an independent review panel, which would examine the case and make its own recommendation to the commissioning group.

If you remain dissatisfied with the outcome of your appeal to the health body, you could contact the Parliamentary and Health Service Ombudsman. Appeals on two separate fronts are also possible elsewhere in the UK. In **Scotland** aggrieved applicants could lodge an official complaint about their health board and also approach the Scottish Public Services Ombudsman. Those in **Wales** could a lodge an official complaint and contact the Public Services Ombudsman for Wales. In **Northern Ireland,** they could approach the Northern Ireland Ombudsman *(see pages 340–1)*.

If you decide not to appeal, you could seek a review of the decision at a later date. Clinical commissioning groups should have their own procedures for reviews, setting out the timescale within which decisions will be regularly reviewed. But you can request a review of a decision at any time. It is up to your health body to explain why you should not be assessed.

The most obvious situation where you might consider requesting a review is if your medical condition has worsened since an earlier assessment. Or you might ask for one when a nurse from your health body is visiting a nursing home where you are living to see whether you fulfil the criteria for what is known as 'free nursing care'. This is a flat-rate payment from central government to people living in nursing homes, regardless of their financial means; the amount varies in the different countries of the UK; in England, for instance, it was £156.25 per week in 2017. The payment (officially called the Registered Nursing Care Contribution) is supposed to represent the weekly cost of the nursing care that the home provides, on the grounds that residents should not have to pay for the healthcare element of their fees. The vast majority of nursing home residents are eligible for this payment and nurses from the local health bodies that channel these funds visit homes to see whether new residents are eligible and to review eligibility for people already receiving the payment.

These nurses should consider each person's eligibility for NHS Continuing Healthcare before reaching a decision on their eligibility for free nursing care. As the government has said, '*In all cases* individuals should be considered for eligibility for NHS Continuing Healthcare before a decision is reached about the need for NHS-funded nursing care.'[39] (my emphasis)

The location of Continuing Healthcare

In the past, patients seem to have been given little choice over the location in which the Continuing Healthcare they have been awarded could be received. Certainly according to accounts of which I have heard, health bodies have simply given a relative the name of three local nursing homes and suggested that they should look round each and decide which one would best suit. The relative has gone away grateful for the award of funding and with an illusion of choice: as many as three possible locations have been offered in which this free care can be received! In fact the three homes will be ones with which the health body happens to have a contract for the provision of Continuing Healthcare and there are other possible locations:

- in a care home different from those suggested by the Continuing Healthcare team
- in a facility run by the NHS
- in the patient's own home or that of a relative or friend

In a care home

First, look at the nursing homes proposed by the Continuing Healthcare team. They may be perfectly fine. Look at the most recent inspection report on each one, which you should be able to obtain either in the home or through the national agency that prepared the report – the Care Quality Commission (in England), the Care Inspectorate (in Scotland), the Care Standards Inspectorate for Wales and, in Northern Ireland, the Regulation and Quality Improvement Authority.

However, in their focus on safety, inspection reports can overlook assessment of what it is like actually to live in a home, minute by minute. So as well as considering whether the home would really be able to look after you, bearing in mind your physical and mental condition, also ask yourself: would the activities the home offers appeal to me? Would I get on well with the other residents? Would I feel at home there?

What can matter almost as much as good physical care is emotional support.

In a case of which I became aware, an elderly man was discharged from hospital into a nursing home for Continuing Healthcare. He had been receiving impressive care in hospital and perhaps assumed that this would be replicated in the nursing home. As the home involved had received a top rating from the Care Quality Commission and been selected by the health authority as one to which people with NHS Continuing Healthcare funding would be sent, his family also assumed his care would be of a high quality. It was not. I was unimpressed by the physical care he received when I visited almost daily and the home itself lacked a friendly or homely atmosphere.

Furthermore, the man had to take on board the reality that the tiny bedroom in which he was now living would be his final home – not the flat in which he had lived happily and now would probably never see again. This change of living environment requires massive psychological adjustment and yet the nursing home seemed to offer little or no psychological support to help him to make the change and to begin to see this new place as 'home'.

Try to find someone who will go and look round the homes the Continuing Healthcare team have put forward, if you cannot do so yourself. If they consider these homes unsatisfactory, ask them to track down alternative nursing homes in the area in which you would like to live and the inspection reports on them.[40] If any look promising, they should ring them and ask if they have Continuing Healthcare beds and, if so, whether there are any vacancies. If they do, your supporter could ask if they could go and have a look round, explaining that you have been awarded Continuing Healthcare and that they would like to examine possible locations on your behalf.

Discuss your questions about homes with experts on the helplines of Age UK, Independent Age and/or the Relatives and Residents Association. The latter focuses only on helping older care home residents and their families. The first two publish free guides on choosing a home.

In a moment, we see that people going into care homes whose fees will be shouldered by their social services authority have a right to a choice of home. This legal right does not apply to people whose place will be paid for by their health body under Continuing Healthcare. That said, if you would prefer one location rather than another, a Continuing Healthcare team would be hard put to refuse to let you go there, unless the home in question clearly was not capable of looking after you or was substantially more expensive than would be normal for a Continuing Healthcare bed. If the team objected, you could point to the emphasis on patient choice embodied in the NHS Constitution *(see page 285)*. When deciding on the location of Continuing Healthcare, the Department of Health says: 'The individual's wishes and expectations of how and where the care is delivered … should be … taken into account.'[41]

In an NHS unit

My mother received Continuing Healthcare in an NHS 12-bedded unit for elderly people with mental health problems. Such self-contained units or long-stay NHS wards can be reassuring places in which to receive NHS Continuing Healthcare. The units are staffed by NHS personnel who usually earn more and enjoy better conditions of employment than staff in private care homes. However, the numbers of these NHS long-stay facilities have been drastically cut. This is the reason why many NHS Continuing Healthcare beds are now provided in nursing homes.

My mother's experience suggested to me that long-stay NHS units provided better care than nursing homes. But such facilities can vary. A unit that forms part of a larger NHS establishment might well benefit from a stream of specialists keen to apply the latest knowledge on how to care for and communicate with, say, people with dementia. Or the facility might consist of a small unit located on its own far from any centre of medical excellence. It might be visited by only one or two consultants, themselves not apprised of the latest thinking, and with day-to-day healthcare and palliative care supplied through a GP who has received no special training in the particular conditions involved. In this sort of isolated situation, the atmosphere, quality of care and sense of blazing a trail in a challenging medical situation will much depend on the personality, motivation and interest of the ward manager. You might find good care, but you might not.

Perhaps the main drawback to receiving Continuing Care in an NHS facility compared to a nursing home is the underlying culture. The origins of these facilities lie in the NHS system, so the emphasis tends to be on healthcare, not on creating an environment which has a homely feel and in which activities are offered – crafts, sing-songs, outings and so on. So a care home which provides NHS Continuing Healthcare on behalf of a health authority may have the edge on an NHS facility in providing a homely and stimulating place to live.

Continuing Healthcare at home

Funding can also be provided to people living in ordinary housing. In this case, healthcare workers such as district nurses come into the person's home, along with care assistants to help with practical tasks. Again, the person receiving the care does not have to pay for any of this.

Of course the advantage for the patient of receiving Continuing Healthcare at home is usually that they remain in the place they would prefer to live. The drawback is that, unlike the situation in a nursing home or an NHS establishment, a qualified nurse is not on site 24 hours a day. That said, medical help could be summoned in the normal way, by calling the GP, a district nurse or an ambulance.

Another aspect of Continuing Healthcare at home is that there will be times, probably mainly in the middle of the night, when personal care tasks have to be performed by whoever happens to be available, such as a partner, unless some live-in care is provided (which is unusual).

Anybody living with the recipient of Continuing Healthcare should discuss fully with the Continuing Healthcare team how their role is to dovetail with those of the professionals. In England, control by a carer could be facilitated through the provision of a 'personal health budget'. This tool involves the NHS giving the person or their representative a sum of money which they can use to hire care and support themselves, choosing what services and when best suit them. The Department of Health has singled out Continuing Healthcare as one of the types of healthcare provision for which a personal budget should be offered in England. Indeed, it says that patients have a right to have a personal health budget for NHS Continuing Healthcare.[42]

If you have a personal budget for Continuing Healthcare in your home, make absolutely sure that the NHS body is providing all the items that should be provided entirely free of charge. Plainly, all visits by healthcare professionals should be free, as should visits by care workers. The health body should also provide all the healthcare equipment – hoists, bath seats, pressure-relieving mattresses and so on – which would be available in a long-stay hospital or nursing home, including any bespoke equipment.

However, although all costs in care homes are covered under Continuing Healthcare, anybody receiving it at home has to pay for their own food and accommodation. As the Department of Health says, in your own home (or that of a friend or relative), 'The NHS is responsible for funding health and personal care costs, not rent, food and normal utility bills'.[43]

What of the additional household costs arising from your care, such as for laundry, additional heating, special food, extra cleaning and housework or additional power to run special equipment such as a pressure-relieving mattress?

Many of these should be covered. The Department of Health has said in practice guidance that for people receiving Continuing Healthcare at home it expects clinical commissioning groups to be:

> Financially responsible for all health and personal care services and associated social care services to support assessed health and social care needs and identified outcomes for that person, e.g. equipment provision, routine and incontinence laundry, daily domestic tasks such as food preparation, washing up, bed-making, support to access community facilities, etc (including additional support needs for the individual whilst the carer has a break).[44]

So if, for instance, you have to pay higher electricity bills to cope with the costs of running a pressure-relieving mattress, your health body ought to reimburse you.

If you are receiving NHS Continuing Healthcare in your home and you have an unpaid carer, that carer will be bound to be helping out with your care, not least at night. They will also probably be giving you emotional support and running your household. This essential support will not be covered by the Continuing Healthcare funding. However, your local authority might be prepared to provide complementary support of its own. To seek this out, ask your local social services department for a carer's assessment. The Department of Health's practice guidance says that a local authority might provide additional support such as adapting your property and providing 'carer support services that may include additional general domestic support'.[45] *(In Chapter 27 I explain the sort of support carers may be given both through social services and also the advice they may receive at carers' centres. On page 540 I discuss the way in which paid, live-in care might dovetail with Continuing Healthcare.)*

If you would like to receive a personal health budget to manage Continuing Healthcare, you may need to ask for one. It seems unlikely that all health bodies will offer one to people who are eligible; they may not even mention its existence.

Welsh government guidance also discusses the provision of Continuing Healthcare at home, making similar points to that provided for England.[46] However, the **Scottish** government's guidance for health boards places greater emphasis than the English or Welsh on its provision in a hospital, care home or hospice. People living in Scotland ought to be able to receive Continuing Healthcare in their own home if they would like to and the health body considers it can be delivered there. However, they may need to press harder. Furthermore, the Scottish guidance does not discuss the allocation of costs if Continuing Healthcare is received in the person's home, other than to say that the NHS is responsible for meeting the costs of their healthcare.[47] Personal care is of course free in Scotland to everybody aged 65 or over assessed as needing it *(see pages 659–60)*.

Ongoing practical help

The vast majority of older people who leave hospital are not awarded NHS Continuing Healthcare. Some of these patients will have already been receiving help in the home, perhaps with personal care and/or housework, after an initial needs assessment by their social care authority before they went into hospital. After their hospital stay, their needs for this support may have changed. Check with social services that it will be carrying out a formal review of your previous assessment, so that additional help can be provided if necessary. *(I outline how to get the most from these assessments in Chapter 26.)*

Others will not have had this kind of help before, but find they need some now. We saw at the start of this chapter that a form of free care called Intermediate Care can be given to people for up to six weeks while they are building up their strength and practical abilities. But some people need practical help into the foreseeable future, quite separate from any short-term help with rehabilitation.

You could arrange this homecare support yourself. However, if you have no family or friends to help you, this can be difficult from a hospital bed. (That is why in the previous chapter I suggest you take into hospital all the phone numbers you might possibly need.)

You could ask to speak to the social worker based in the hospital and seek their help. That way, you should benefit from the advice and expertise of a professional. If you need only a little support, they ought to explain what kind of services and equipment would help you manage and how you could obtain them. However, unless your needs are minimal, they ought to carry out a social care needs assessment that will tease out how you can best be supported long-term. After that, you could organise the necessary care and support yourself or social services might organise it for you. If you have a level of need for help which exceeds the threshold your local authority social services department has set, and you are of modest means, it will subsidise the cost of meeting your care needs.

If you are planning to put the arrangements in place yourself, perhaps with the help of family or friends, turn to Chapter 23. If you wish to use social services, ask the social worker in the hospital for a social care needs assessment, as outlined in Chapter 26. Rich or poor, we all have a right to have an assessment if we might need some social care services, irrespective of whether we or social services might end up paying for them. The assessments are free.

Your rights in the assessment process are explained in Chapter 26. For example, your council should examine a wide range of needs, including social and emotional ones. You should be fully involved in your assessment and be able to have other people present during it, if you wish.

I outline the way in which care services can be delivered after some involvement by social services and also the rules by which care services are either free or means-tested in Chapter 28.

The help that can result from a social care needs assessment (or a review of an earlier one) includes:

1. Gadgets and adaptations to the home to cope with disability: A wide range of equipment might be provided to help you cope when you return home, for example, a walker, a wheelchair or an aid to get in and out of the bath *(see Chapter 21)*. In addition, your home could be adapted, through anything from grab rails or an outside ramp to a stairlift *(see Chapter 8)*. These can be obtained independently or through the NHS or social services. Equipment and adaptations obtained through the state are often free of charge, regardless of financial means *(see pages 480–2, 178 and 187)*.

2. Human help: This can involve regular help once or twice a week or several times a day, again obtained entirely independently or with some social services involvement. If you need a lot of help, subsidy from social services can be a lifeline, enabling you to continue to live in your own home. You are unlikely to receive live-in care paid for by social services, but you might perhaps be able to use a subsidy from social services and top-up with the help of friends and family in order to pay for a live-in care-giver. *(I discuss live-in care in Chapter 24 and help obtained through social services in Part Seven.)*

Unlike Intermediate Care and Continuing Healthcare, ongoing practical support obtained via social services is means-tested. However, some social care services are free, such as help with personal care for people aged 65 and over in Scotland, homecare for anyone over the age of 75 in Northern Ireland, and homecare charges over £60 per week for any adult in Wales *(see pages 655–64)*.

To a care home?

We saw above that some people move to a care home temporarily to receive Intermediate Care and others because they have been awarded NHS Continuing Healthcare.

More common than either of these is a permanent move when somebody finds they need quite a lot of help and prefer to have it on hand rather than only at pre-set times, as with paid help sent into their own home. Or perhaps they have dementia and need round-the-clock supervision, as well as practical assistance.

A permanent move to a care home can work well. Many people live happily in care homes, with the help they need, the company of other people, and activities and diversions laid on by the home. Others, however, fail to settle and hanker to return to their own home.

There are many factors to consider in the decision to enter a care home permanently. Consider whether the home would be able to look after you. Would you find the activities it offers interesting? Would you get on well with other residents? Do you like the general ambience of the place? Would you feel at home there?

Older patients approaching the date of planned hospital discharge can feel under huge pressure to make a quick decision about a care home. Their relatives and/or social services may be insisting that it is unlikely that they could manage in their own home and that it would be best to relocate to a particular care establishment. Yet people in this situation need time to look round possible homes, or get people they trust and who know them well to do so. They also need to be sure that a move to any care home is wise.

Do not be pressured into a quick decision. Once you have moved into a care home, moving back to your own home or into another care home is not easy – you will face the upheaval of another move and you or your representatives or social services will have signed a contract with the home which you or they will have to terminate. If you wish to move quickly, you or social services will lose out financially, as the home will expect payment during a notice period.

There are many factors to consider. Do you wish to continue to live in your existing home? Could you manage to look after yourself there? Might your ability to carry out practical tasks around the home improve in the future, perhaps after a period of therapy? Could any care home look after you better than paid carers, whether calling regularly or live-in?

These questions may be unrealistic. Perhaps you are very frail and need a lot of help. But unless it is clear to you that you should go to a care home as a permanent resident immediately, you could ask for

Intermediate Care in a care home setting. This would mean that you go and live in a home for up to six weeks in order to recuperate and perhaps regain practical skills you had lost. The Department of Health has told health bodies, 'Too many older people enter residential and nursing homes direct from acute care', and that they should consider what can be done to help someone in this situation, with rehabilitation and Reablement as the first option.[48]

If you can get Intermediate Care in a care home to which you consider you might move as a permanent resident, it should give you a real insight into what life would be like there, while also giving you therapy and support to help you get back your strength.

If Intermediate Care is not appropriate, press for a return home to make the decision about a permanent move, or at least for a visit to your home with a social worker and/or an occupational therapist at which you work out whether you could manage, with support such as equipment, house adaptations and regular human help brought in.

Concerned that older people should have the opportunity to evaluate coolly a decision about a move to a care home, the Department of Health has said, 'There is evidence that too many older people inappropriately enter long-term residential care direct from an acute hospital. *Such decisions should not be made in an acute hospital other than in very exceptional circumstances.*'[49] (my emphasis)

The National Institute for Health and Care Excellence has told health and social care authorities that they should, 'Ensure that people do not have to make decisions about long-term residential or nursing care while they are in crisis'.[50]

Neither the NHS nor social services can actually force anyone to transfer to a care home without their agreement, unless the person involved lacks the mental capacity to make the decision. In that situation, they must comply with rules and procedures designed to safeguard the human rights of the person involved *(see pages 781–92)*.

Choice of home

Obviously people who will be paying their own care home bills can choose which home to go to, so long as it is within their financial means and space is available. It is worth these self-funders obtaining a social care needs assessment from their local social services department nonetheless. In coming to a conclusion on the nature and extent of their needs for practical help, the social worker will indicate whether they actually need to be in a care home and, if they do, the type.

I have come across several people who were paying the higher fees of a nursing home when in fact a residential home (which provides less care and therefore charges lower fees) would have been perfectly adequate for them. Other people are living in care homes when they could in fact manage to live independently, if they were given information about the support they could obtain in their own home. This is not surprising if people rely solely on the opinion of the proprietors of the (mainly commercial) homes they visit, who have a financial incentive to enter into a contract for the place in their establishment they want to sell, rather than the accommodation and care the person actually needs.

A second reason for self-funders to obtain an assessment from social services is in order to qualify for various state subsidies. Those in Scotland will need one to qualify for the state's provision of free personal care. People throughout the UK need an assessment of their need for nursing care if they wish to claim a payment from the state called 'free nursing care' in a nursing home *(page 962)*. This assessment is carried out by nurses; ask at the hospital when it will be conducted.

Many patients awaiting discharge from hospital are not self-funders. If a prospective care home resident's savings (including the value of their home) amount to less than about £23,000,[51] their social services department must step in and pay at least part of the bill, *as explained on page 563.* In other words, the social services authority will be responsible for the care home fees of residents whose savings fall below certain thresholds (which vary country by country in the UK). However, while these residents can keep their savings, they are expected to pay part of the care home charges from their ongoing income, such as their State Retirement Pension.

In these cases, it is social services, not the resident, who will enter into a contract with a care home to provide them with their care and accommodation. The local authority must try to find a place which can meet the person's assessed needs and is generally suitable for them. But it must also try to meet any preferences the prospective resident or their representative expresses. This resident's 'right to choose', as it is often known, is a long-standing provision restated most recently for England in the Care Act 2014. This lays down that if an adult for whom accommodation is going to be provided by social services expresses a preference for a particular home, then the local authority must provide or arrange for the provision of their accommodation there, so long as the establishment:

- is capable of providing the care necessary to meet their assessed needs

- is capable of providing accommodation that satisfies the local authority's usual terms and conditions
- is actually available, and
- the cost of the home does not exceed what the local authority would usually pay to provide for someone with the same assessed needs[52]

The right to choose is not strictly speaking a legal right: the local authority has a duty to make effective use of public funding so you cannot absolutely insist upon a particular home if the local authority will be contributing towards the cost, but you should certainly expect to be consulted about the choice of home and for your views to be taken into account. If the home you prefer is more expensive than the ones social services propose, there are two possible ways in which the shortfall could be met.

I explained earlier *(in Chapter 26)* that if a council establishes that somebody's social care needs meet certain levels of eligibility, social services must meet those needs, even if it has to foot the cost itself. These social care needs include not only physical ones such as help with moving around but also social and emotional ones. So, if your assessment indicates a need for you to remain in close contact with your cultural or religious community and the home you prefer would enable this far better than one social services suggests, it ought to cough up the money. Or if, say, one of your eligible needs is to remain in close touch with your family and they live in another part of the country and you wish to go and live close to them, social services should pay what is necessary to enable you to do so.

The other possibility is a so-called 'top-up' by a third party. Care home residents are not allowed to top up the payments social services are making from their own resources: instead, they must find somebody else, or perhaps an organisation such as a charitable foundation, to top up for them. Such top-ups enable somebody to live in a home which is more expensive than one social services is prepared to offer, or to enjoy better facilities within a home, such as a larger bedroom. However, the person contributing the top-up has to be prepared to commit to a regular payment, perhaps over a number of years. It could be quite high – say, £150 per week – and it will rise if the fees rise (as they usually do).

Beware of social services insisting that it never pays more than a certain amount for a care home place and that if you do not want to go to the home or homes it is pointing you towards, you must find a 'top-up' – in other words, the difference. The reality is that social services pay different amounts to homes for different residents, depending on the amount of support needed. And, as noted above, social services must meet your eligible needs, even if this means paying more than it says it usually pays for a care home place.

Leaving hospital

* Be ready for discharge: hospitals plan for it as soon as they admit a patient.

* Employees have the right to time off to make arrangements for a dependant who is ill or injured.

* Take seriously any tests of your practical, physical or mental abilities before discharge.

* Intermediate Care provides free practical help, treatment and therapy for up to six weeks after a hospital stay.

* Intermediate Care is available for people who have had an operation privately.

* Make sure you are assessed for NHS Continuing Healthcare if you might qualify.

* Make sure you are involved in your assessment for Continuing Healthcare.

* Do not allow yourself to be discharged from hospital into a care home if you do not want to go there.

* Live-in care may be an option, perhaps with Continuing Healthcare funding

* If social services is organising a care home place for you, you can choose which home you go to.

THE END OF LIFE

" ** *You matter because you are you, and you matter to the end of your life.* **"

**Dame Cicely Saunders,
founder of the hospice movement**

PART TWELVE
THE END OF LIFE

When I was a child in the 1960s, sudden death amongst middle-aged adults was not uncommon. The parent of a classmate at school might die unexpectedly, usually from a heart attack or stroke. Nowadays, however, only about 15 per cent of the half a million deaths that occur every year in the UK are unexpected. The majority of us die after struggling, perhaps for years, with conditions which cannot be cured.

Today, deaths arising from the same cardiovascular disease that often killed people unexpectedly 50 years ago can be postponed for decades through inventions such as triple bypass operations and stents (which keep furred-up arteries open). Medical advances also keep alive many people with kidney disease and various types of cancer for far longer than in the past. So, many of us can expect to live for a prolonged period with a medical condition which may well kill us eventually, but not immediately.

Many people fear death, as they think it will be painful, but they are mostly mistaken. A study of 486 hospital deaths in the United States in 1908 revealed that 11 patients experienced anxiety and 90 experienced pain, but for the remaining 385, 'Death was nothing more than falling asleep'.[1] If you are in pain before you are dying, that pain is likely to remain (unless measures are taken to alleviate it), but there is nothing intrinsically painful about the process of dying.

Pain relief has of course advanced massively since the American study was conducted. What has also happened is the development of a new field of expertise called palliative care. End-of-life care is a division of palliative care – it is a multi-discipline in which nurses, doctors, social workers, chaplains, counsellors and other professionals work to maximise physical comfort and emotional and spiritual support during the final weeks and days of life.

Palliative care is also offered to people who are not at the end of their lives but have illnesses from which they may not get better and which may give rise to troublesome symptoms, such as cancer, emphysema and heart failure. This care can be given alongside treatment designed to cure. These types of palliative care are different from end-of-life care – although plainly people who receive the first may also come to need the second.

In the first chapter of this part, I examine the sort of care and support that people who are dying as well as those who have life-limiting illnesses can expect to be offered. Britain is a world leader in palliative care – the discipline has a huge knowledge base and much of that expertise has been built up in the hospitals and hospices of the UK. Yet on the ground, provision of palliative care (including end-of-life care) is uneven.[2] It is therefore worth knowing what support should be provided, in case you need to prompt.

I also examine how we can exercise choice over where and how we die. Of course, some people take matters into their own hands. In the film *Venus,* an ageing actor played by Peter O'Toole ignores the ambulance sent to take him to hospital when he is gravely ill and instead takes a train to Whitstable with a teenage girl with whom he is infatuated and dies suddenly – and happily – after paddling in the cold sea.

But for people not intending or able to try to pre-empt death, important questions present themselves. Would you wish to die in your own home or somewhere else? With or without your family around you? With maximum pain relief, even if that might make you drowsy? Would you wish to know that you were dying? Would you wish others to know? 'A good death' means different things to different people.[3]

Pressure has built up to permit healthcare professionals to give people help to kill themselves, should they come to lack the physical ability to do so themselves. Assisted dying is unlawful in the UK. However, anybody can opt to refuse life-sustaining treatment. If they are not in a fit state to do so at the time, they can refuse it in advance, and it is well worth thinking about making an 'advance directive to refuse treatment' if you are concerned that you might be kept alive against your will. Advance directives, assisted dying and other matters which may concern us as our lives ebb towards their close are discussed in the second chapter of this part.

Part Twelve therefore examines:

▶ the nature of end-of-life care
▶ where we may be cared for when we are dying
▶ how to get good end-of-life care
▶ palliative care for illness
▶ medical decisions arising at the end of life
▶ the choices we might like to consider beforehand
▶ how to make our wishes known
▶ advance directives to refuse treatment

Chapter 40

End-of-life care

Most of us are familiar with the sort of medical and nursing expertise available to us at the beginning of life. We know less about how we should be cared for as our life moves towards its close. It is worth knowing, in case we need to ask for help. This matters not only to the person who is dying; loved ones are likely to remember the occasion for the rest of their own lives.

In this chapter I look first at the nature of end-of-life care and contrast the different places in which it may be given. I also examine palliative care for different illnesses that may eventually result in death, even though death may be months, if not years away. I go on to discuss financial matters and support for carers when someone is coming to the end of their life. This chapter therefore addresses:

▶ the care and support we might seek at the end of life

▶ the help that family and friends can give

▶ spiritual support

▶ where we might choose to spend our final weeks and days

▶ palliative care for certain medical conditions

▶ how people with dementia can best be helped

▶ the position of carers

▶ financial support during end stages

What is end-of-life care? Well, it does not aim to cure somebody but to ensure that they die as comfortably as possible, with all the relief from pain and other discomfort they desire, and with the emotional and spiritual support that they choose. It also seeks to support the person's loved ones during the dying process and afterwards.

In many cases, good, everyday nursing – no more and no less – is the end-of-life care that someone needs, and, if they wish, the company of particular friends and relatives. However, in some cases, where people are facing troublesome symptoms or finding their situation difficult to deal with psychologically, more specialist help may be needed.

The World Health Organisation has teased out the hallmark features of palliative care given at the end of someone's life. It says that palliative care:

- affirms life and regards dying as a normal process
- intends neither to hasten or postpone death
- provides relief from pain and other distressing symptoms
- integrates the psychological and spiritual aspects of care
- aims to enhance quality of life
- uses a multi-disciplinary team approach to address the needs of patients and their families
- offers a support system to help patients live as actively as possible until death and to help the family cope during the patient's illness and in their own bereavement, with bereavement counselling if necessary[1]

Let us look first at the sort of tools available to modern medicine to handle the physical discomfort that can arise when someone is drawing towards the end of their life.

Symptom control

As noted in the introduction to this part, many people do not experience any troublesome symptoms during the final days or hours of their lives. But if they should, what are the sorts of steps that doctors, nurses and other care-givers should be considering to reduce any distress or discomfort?[2]

Such symptoms overlap with several which might develop in any very frail or unwell person who is spending a lot of time in bed, such as pressure sores. Some are more common in people who have very advanced cancer than in people who are succumbing to other conditions.

Bladder and bowel problems

Constipation is common amongst all older people who are unwell: 63 per cent of elderly people in hospital have been found to be constipated, compared with 22 per cent of the same age group living at home.[3] Some people who are coming to the end of their lives may be constipated, or have continence problems, just as they might if death were not imminent. Constipation is more common in people with terminal cancer than in those dying from other causes, as opiate drugs often cause constipation, while people with cancer often have poor appetites and so do not eat much.

A doctor should assess the reasons for the condition and, unless the patient is very frail, help should be provided to use the lavatory (rather than a commode or bedpan) and to increase physical activity. The addition of fibre to the diet and plenty of fluid to drink should help, but laxatives may be needed as well. *(See also Chapter 19.)*

Insertion of a urinary catheter may be suggested for incontinence or to relieve certain symptoms, but do not give consent unless you are convinced that this is the best option for you or the person you are representing. Pads may be more comfortable. *(For a discussion of the pros and cons of using a catheter, see pages 419–23.)*

Dehydration

Some people become dehydrated but find drinking difficult and an intravenous drip uncomfortable. A subcutaneous infusion of fluid can be a relatively painless means of ensuring they receive fluid. A needle is inserted into a layer of fatty tissue under the skin, often in the stomach region or in an arm or thigh, and the fluid seeps into this tissue, where it is absorbed. A nurse could set up an infusion for somebody overnight and they might feel much better the following day. *(See page 995 for ways in which relatives can help keep the mouth and lips moist.)*

Loss of appetite, nausea and vomiting

If somebody has lost their appetite, the reason can often be addressed successfully – it may be sore gums, nausea, a dirty mouth or unappetizing food, for instance. Perhaps a different dish, a little alcohol or the sharing of a meal would make the person more likely to eat and drink?

People with very advanced cancer may be disinclined to eat. Or they may feel nauseous. In either case, the causes should be investigated and action taken accordingly. A range of drugs that treat nausea (known as anti-emetic drugs) may prove useful.

Breathlessness

Steps which can help are mentioned below in connection with specialist palliative care for emphysema *(see page 1003)*. Medication to reduce anxiety may help too, as anxiety often exacerbates breathlessness.

Coughing

This can be irritating and exhausting. End-of-life care would aim to lessen and soothe it. The most obvious treatment is a simple syrup linctus; other treatment could take the form of steam inhalations or medication, such as drugs to suppress the cough reflex in the brain and bronchodilators, which keep open the bronchi (the tubes that lead into the lungs). Drugs to reduce excess sputum can also be useful *(as explained under the next sub-heading)*.

Respiratory secretions

Excessive secretions are common in people with cancer, pneumonia and bronchitis; the noise known as the death rattle results from saliva secretions building up in the throat when somebody becomes too weak to cough. Secretions can be reduced through gentle suction and the use of drugs which inhibit them. A change of position often helps, such as turning the patient on their side, if they can tolerate this.

Fever

Somebody who has an infection may have a fever. Ibuprofen and paracetamol can bring this down, as can a fan, a tepid cloth applied to the forehead, drinking water or sucking small ice chips. Very cold cloths and ice bags are unhelpful as they cause shivering, which generates heat.

Pressure ulcers

These can develop if somebody has been sitting or lying for long (or sometimes short) periods *(as I explain on page 18)*. Nurses should be alert to the possibility of these painful sores and take steps to prevent and treat them *(as described on pages 387–9 and 913–5)*.

Pain

Pain varies greatly in its nature and also from person to person, because it is a subjective sensation. This means that the optimum dose of an analgesic has to be carefully worked out for each patient, rather than adopting a one-size-fits-all approach. A decision also has to be made about whether to maintain that dose at a constant level rather than giving doses of analgesics only when the patient experiences pain. Pain assessment tools have been developed so that particular analgesic drugs can be selected carefully and at the correct dosage, while minimising side-effects such as drowsiness.

Insomnia

The first step with insomnia should be to work out the cause – such as a noisy ward, pain *(see above)* or breathlessness *(see above)* – and address it. Sleep-inducing drugs are another option.

Agitation

The cause of any agitation should be identified and addressed, if possible. Sometimes it is physical – for example, a distended bladder arising because somebody is unable to urinate. Or it may arise as a side-effect of medication, in which case the latter should be changed. At other times it is due to anxiety or emotional distress. The presence of loved ones and continuity of the staff providing care can reduce agitation arising from anxiety or emotional distress.

The administration of drugs

A fortnight before she died in 2005 in an NHS Continuing Care unit *(see page 965),* my mother, then with very advanced dementia, suddenly developed excruciating stomach pain and bleeding. This happened at a weekend and all my efforts went into finding a GP who would call. When he did, I was so relieved to have obtained some morphine that it did not occur to me to ask how it was going to be delivered. In fact, my mother struggled to swallow the tablets he prescribed and then had to endure additional distress while waiting for the next dose. Be ready to question and to press. Is morphine going to be given in a suitable form? How will its effects be monitored? What happens when they wear off? When will the dosage and method of delivery be reviewed?

Drugs can be delivered in several different ways – as tablets, in liquid form, as a skin patch, in the back passage as a suppository, intravenously, and as an infusion under the skin. It is important that they are delivered in the form in which the patient can most easily absorb them. Thus for instance, an injection or a patch would be better for somebody with severe nausea or difficulty in swallowing. Also a patch can ensure steady, continuous administration of a drug.

So too can a syringe driver. This is a device by which one or several different drugs can be given under the skin together, continuously and with the rate of delivery precisely controlled. Palliative care experts with special expertise in cancer Professor John Ellershaw and Susie Wilkinson have said: 'A single continuous subcutaneous infusion containing up to three drugs will control the vast majority of symptoms which a dying patient is likely to experience.'[4]

If somebody is likely to develop troublesome symptoms, expect a doctor to consider giving drugs in anticipation of their appearance: clearly, inadequate medication or pain relief that is given late or not at all leaves people needlessly distressed and anxious. 'Just-in-case' anticipatory prescribing of medication to patients in their own homes ensures that if and when symptoms develop, immediate treatment is available. This can prevent hospital admissions, thus allowing patients the choice of remaining at home. However, it is important that the drugs are not actually given to the patient unless and until they need them or are highly likely to do so, as they may cause side-effects, such as drowsiness.

Individual end-of-life care plans

Although end-of-life care can consist simply of good nursing care, healthcare professionals should be absolutely clear about what is needed. Perhaps a frail, elderly person has received treatment for pneumonia, but it has become clear that this will not work and they will therefore probably die. If it seems likely that death will come within days or hours, medical professionals should draw up an end-of-life care plan. This should set out how to ease any pain or other type of discomfort and provide psychological and spiritual support, and it should be drawn up in close consultation with the patient and/or their legal representatives and consultees (see pages 782 and 789).

These plans are intended to replace an approach developed in the late 1990s and over the following ten years called the Liverpool Care Pathway.[5] This sought to give people who were considered to have no more than days or hours to live all-round care and support. If someone was placed on the Pathway, treatment designed to cure their illness would stop and instead steps would be taken to make them comfortable. The provision of any emotional and spiritual support they wished to receive was also a key feature.

Surveys indicated that the Pathway was well respected by professionals in the field: 89 per cent of palliative medicine consultants considered it represented best practice for dying patients and the same proportion said they would choose it for themselves if dying from a terminal illness.[6]

However, concerns were raised about the way in which the Pathway was being implemented. Establishing whether somebody is dying and what sort and dose of medication can help them is a task for specialists. Yet sometimes junior staff had to take the decision to put somebody on the Pathway, as no consultant was available. Their decision might have been incorrect.

Another concern was that untrained personnel might fail to adjust the care of someone in the light of their individual needs and wishes and changes in their physical condition. They would assume that once a patient had been placed on the Pathway there was no chance of recovery and, what is more, that food and fluid should be withheld. As a result, someone might die feeling very thirsty and/or their death might actually be caused by the withholding of fluid. Had they been given fluid, they might have lived for some time. Yet in fact there was nothing in the Pathway that said fluid should automatically be withheld, and the monitoring of a person's condition and the reviewing of their care in the light of changing circumstances were integral elements of it.

Concerns such as these were explored in a review of the Liverpool Pathway by a team led by Baroness Julia Neuberger in 2013.[7] In the light of this team's findings, the Department of Health told health trusts in England to stop using the Pathway and instead ensure that individual end-of-life care plans were drawn up. Thereupon more than 20 organisations involved in end-of-life care came together to provide guidance for health organisations on the form these plans should take. Their recommendations were duly set out in the pithily-titled document *One Chance to Get it Right.*[8]

In the meantime, the body that draws up guidance on how particular health conditions and situations should be handled and has particular status in the health service, the National Institute for Health and Care Excellence, or NICE, had been preparing a more detailed guideline, which was published in 2015.[9] This contains many useful recommendations.

In view of all this, here are steps you could reasonably expect people who are caring for someone who is dying to take:

1. Deciding that someone is dying

This decision should not be taken by one healthcare professional alone: it should involve people from different disciplines, who record the person's changing physical symptoms, talk to them about how they feel and also talk to those close to the patient. If doctors and nurses are uncertain whether someone is entering the last days of their life, they should seek advice from professionals with greater experience in end-of-life care.[10]

In other words, if you are living in a nursing home, a nurse on the staff there should not be deciding on their own that you are dying: they should consult a doctor. If together they remain uncertain, they should consult professionals with more experience and expertise.

2. Preparation of an individual plan of care

A team of professionals from various disciplines should talk to the patient and those close to them to create an individual plan of care. Refraining from a one-size-fits-all approach, they should focus on the particular circumstances and needs of the individual in front of them and their loved ones, and they should set out how the person involved should be cared for. Their plan should include the following items of information:

- the place where the person would prefer to be cared for
- the resources needed to meet this preference
- the person's views on the way in which any troublesome symptoms they develop should be managed
- the person's other goals and wishes: these might include a desire to live as normally as possible for a limited period, even if that might shorten their life; it might include a desire to end their life in a particular place and with particular people. The patient's goals and wishes may well already have been set down in an advance care plan *(see page 993–4)*. If so, that plan should be borne in mind.
- needs for the person's care that are likely to arise in future
- any needs for care of the body after death[11]

3. Giving fluid

Health and care personnel who are looking after someone who is dying should recognise that when someone is dying they may or may not need as much fluid as before. They should ensure that the person is physically comfortable and that they die with dignity. If the person wishes to drink and is able to, every help should be given to them to do so. This should be the default course of action.[12]

If somebody cannot drink in the normal way, doctors and nurses should discuss with them (or their representatives if they are unable to take the decision themselves) whether or not they should receive fluid artificially and, if so, by what means. This might be through an intravenous drip or through an infusion of fluid under the skin *(see above)*.

The temporary alliance of organisations that drew up *One Chance to Get it Right,* which included the Royal College of Physicians, NICE, Marie Cure Cancer Care and the College of Health Care Chaplains stated unequivocally:

Even if it has been determined that someone may be dying, health and care staff must continue to offer them food and drink, provided eating and drinking would not harm the person. If the person wants this and needs helps to eat and drink, health and care staff must provide that help.[13]

4. Monitoring and readiness to change direction

Healthcare professionals should be monitoring the patient closely and adjusting their care in the light of changing circumstances. They should always be alert to the possibility that their original conclusion that the person was dying was incorrect and be ready to give them treatment to cure their medical condition if it becomes apparent that they are not dying after all.

5. Basic principles

You may be looking after a friend or relative who is dying in your own home; you or a relative or friend may be spending their final days in a care home or a hospital. You may face a variety of different medical situations. It is impossible to predict what all these might be, but the Leadership Alliance for the Care of Dying People's report contains a short, useful set of basic principles that should underlie care planning at the end of life. The Alliance says the aim should be that all care given in the last hours and days of life in England:

- ✓ is compassionate
- ✓ is based on and tailored to the **needs, wishes and preferences of the dying person** and, as appropriate, their family and those identified as important to them
- ✓ includes regular and effective **communication** between the dying person and their family and health and care staff and between health and care staff themselves
- ✓ involves **assessment of the person's condition** whenever that condition changes and timely and appropriate responses to those changes
- ✓ **is led by a senior responsible doctor and a lead responsible nurse,** who can access support from specialist palliative care services when needed; and
- ✓ is delivered by doctors, nurses, carers and others who have high professional standards and the **skills, knowledge and experience** needed to care for dying people and their families properly (my emphases)[14]

Separate guidance expressing broadly similar sentiments has been published for Scotland.[15]

If you consider any aspect of your or your relative's care falls short of any of these principles, say so. For instance, if your relative is in a nursing home and is considered to be dying, but the home is failing to monitor their condition closely and the GP to visit sufficiently frequently, raise the matter immediately with the GP and the home's manager. Or if a care home is leaving someone who is dying on their own when they would plainly benefit from the company of someone else, ask how this can possibly be called compassionate care. If the person has said they would prefer to be alone, the home should nonetheless check frequently that there is nothing they can do to help them. Be prepared to threaten to lodge a complaint if necessary.

Telling the family what is happening

The death of a loved one remains with the living for the remainder of their lives, not least if it has been traumatic. One of the ways in which long-lasting harm can occur is through a failure on the part of doctors to communicate that somebody is close to death.

My father, who was coping with emphysema, fought off pneumonia about four times over the last four or five years of his life. When, just before Christmas 1974, he went into hospital with the infection that was to kill him, my family and I fully expected him to survive. Perhaps we were in denial. Certainly, no doctor had ever filled in my mother on her husband's prognosis or on the pattern that emphysema takes in its final stages *(see page 1003)*. And so it was that when, on Boxing Day, we visited my father in hospital and the consultant afterwards drew me and my mother aside and told us that my father's lungs were worn out, we did not take this to mean that he was about to die. We understood that they had been worn out for several years. So, when the hospital rang us in the early hours of the next morning to say that he had just died, we were not only shocked but dismayed that we had not spent the night at his bedside. More than 40 years on, I continue to be haunted by concerns that his death was not a peaceful one and that his family was not at his side.

Doctors are not always good communicators about imminent death. If you suspect that a doctor is talking to you in euphemisms, such as 'making the patient comfortable', ask for clarification: 'Are you saying she is dying?' If you are unhappy with the place in which the doctor is talking to you about your relative's prognosis and future care, ask to move to a private space. Ask specific questions and demand answers (if you are prepared to hear them). Do not allow ignorance of impending death to make the passing of a loved one any worse than it might otherwise be. As consultants John Ellershaw and Chris Ward point out, 'If relatives are told clearly that the patient is dying they have the opportunity to ask questions, stay with the patient, say their goodbyes, contact relevant people and prepare themselves for the death.'[16]

In view of criticisms in this area, the Leadership Alliance for the Care of Dying People has explained that:

> **Open and honest communication** between staff and the person who is dying, and those identified as important to them, including carers, is critically important to good care. Clear, understandable and **plain language** must be used ... Communication must be **regular and pro-active**, i.e. staff must actively seek to communicate ... It must be two-way, i.e. staff must listen to the views of the person and those important to them, not simply provide information. It should be conducted in a way that **maximises privacy.** Communication must be **sensitive, respectful** in pace and tone and **take account** of what the dying person and those important to them want and feel able to discuss at any particular point in time. Staff must **check the other person's understanding** of the information that is being communicated, and **document this.**[17] (my emphases)

Advance care plans

We saw when we considered individual plans for care at the very end of life that some people would already have an 'advance care plan'. These are documents that doctors or other healthcare professionals may draw up in advance, typically a few months before it seems likely that someone will deteriorate. They seek to find out the person's wishes ahead of time in case their ability to take decisions on the sort of care they would like becomes impaired.

The preparation of advance care plans is not mandatory, nor are patients obliged to engage with the discussions involved if they would rather not. But in the world of end-of-life care, the preparation of advance care plans is regarded as good practice. Thus the Department of Health recommends that doctors draw up these plans.[18] The National Gold Standards Framework Centre for End-of-Life Care (a national organisation founded by a GP that promotes consistent and high-quality palliative care in hospitals, GP practices and care homes) says, 'Advance care planning is the key means of improving care for people nearing the end of life and of enabling better planning and provision of care to help them live and die in the place and the manner of their choosing.'[19]

Patient choice should underpin advance care plans, as with other areas of medicine, so your doctor should fully involve you in drawing up yours. Indeed, the involvement of patients in planning for end-of-life care was singled out for special mention in the NHS Constitution *(see page 279)*. Your doctor should ensure you have a copy of your advance care plan and that it is shared with other people likely to be involved, if you agree.[20] In the Medway towns in Kent, for instance, an electronic record is stored for authorised local doctors to access when needed; this is known as the My Wishes Register.

If you move into a care home to live, someone such as a nurse on the staff may ask you about your views on the way you would like to be cared for at the end of your life. If so, ask them whether they are doing so in order to prepare an advance care plan. If you are unhappy with the professional drawing up the plan, ask for someone else to do it instead or at least to be involved. The plan should range over scenarios which might arise towards the end of life and if you think the person drawing up the plan is ill-equipped to consider these, ask to speak to someone better qualified.

Advance care plans are not set in stone. They can be reviewed regularly or when circumstances change. You may well change your mind. For instance, some people say they would like to die at home but come to feel more secure in a hospital environment. Also, the extent to which your wishes are fulfilled will depend partly on whether any support you need is in place. If you go into hospital, need a lot of medical care to control pain and other symptoms and suddenly announce you wish to go home to die, you may have to cope with the fact that the health staff will find it difficult to muster the support you need immediately, and indeed some of it may be impossible to provide in your home. So, if you wish to die at home and have a serious medical condition, say so early, in time for all the necessary support to be marshalled.

Advance care plans thus provide a framework for thinking about the future. They are not legally binding documents – unlike advance directives to refuse treatment or conditions imposed in a power of attorney. *In Chapter 41, I set out some of the matters you may wish to set down in an advance care plan.*

Spiritual support

If you are a patient or relative of somebody who is edging towards the end of their life, you should not be embarrassed about asking for any spiritual support you feel you or they may need. It is an important part of the role of chaplains in hospitals (sometimes known as the Pastoral Care Team) to provide emotional and spiritual support to people who are dying and their loved ones before and immediately after the death. Chaplains are trained to provide emotional and general spiritual support ('spiritual' is defined as anything which someone considers gives their life meaning and is certainly not confined to religion). If you think you might benefit from the help of a chaplain, you need to ask for it *(as explained on page 931)*. Nursing homes do not usually have chaplains, but they ought to be able to put you in touch with local faith and humanist organisations.

Support from family and friends

Many people do not wish to be much involved in a loved one's end-of-life care, for one reason or another. They may reason that there is no point in visiting someone who is dying, as there is nothing they can do. In fact, there is usually a great deal.

Perhaps more than anything else, 'The mere presence of a familiar face raises morale, and sometimes raising morale is all you can do', retired GP Dr Justin Robbins told me in an interview in 2012.

The presence of visitors makes somebody who is coming to the end of their life also feel valued and reassured. Visitors can offer support through subtly reminding their loved one of the ways in which they are valued and the range of things they are bequeathing. I am not thinking here of money, businesses and property, but values, interests, family traditions and stories *(as discussed on page 91)*. Visitors can also play music to their loved one; hearing is usually the last sense to be lost.

But there may also be practical steps that could help. For instance, some people develop a very dry mouth when they are dying. Or they may develop this beforehand – for instance if they are receiving extra oxygen to help them overcome a chest infection. Not only is a dry mouth uncomfortable, it makes talking more difficult. Helping to keep the mouth moist is a task which relatives may welcome, as it is something they can do for their loved one themselves. Steps include:

- giving regular drinks
- helping with brushing teeth
- giving regular sips of water
- giving chips of ice to suck
- giving small chunks of pineapple in juice (not syrup)
- administrating water through a spray or blunt-ended syringe
- applying Vaseline or a lip salve

(I also discuss the value of visiting any patient in hospital on page 928–31.)

Where to die?

Just as pregnant women expect to be offered choice on where they will give birth, so we can expect choice to be offered at the end of our life. Our preferred place of death should be one of the questions about which our GP or another professional consults us during the preparation of our advance care plan. That said, as with pregnant women, sometimes circumstances mean patient choice is not always met.

In a general hospital

Half of deaths each year in England (nearly a quarter of a million) occur in hospital, many of these in general hospitals. Any large, general hospital is likely to have a palliative care team which includes palliative care consultants and specialist palliative care nurses, who should have up-to-the-minute knowledge of the latest techniques and drugs. The team is also likely also to include a social worker, who should offer a range of practical advice and help, including information on state benefits. Expertise may be brought in, such as the hospital psychiatric team, whose clinical psychologists or psychotherapists could be asked to give emotional and psychological support *(see pages 316–7)*. Chaplains, too, may be consulted *(page 928)*.

A survey by the Royal College of Physicians with the Marie Curie Palliative Care Institute in Liverpool found there had been steady improvement in the care of dying people in general hospitals in England between 2013 and 2015.[21] In three-quarters of cases in the hospitals studied, staff had undertaken a holistic assessment of patients' needs to draw up an individual plan of care, and (while drinking is not always desirable as explained above), 39 per cent of patients were drinking during their last 24 hours of life while 45 per cent were being helped to drink. The hospitals were also trying to improve care further, with 63 per cent of them training their medical staff in relevant communication skills. Room for improvement remained – in particular, fewer than 40 per cent of the hospitals could provide specialist palliative care staff at weekends.

Whatever the quality of care, hospitals remain large buildings, and inevitably have some institutional feel. And although they usually have professionals who specialise in palliative care, the focus of an acute or a general hospital is on carrying out investigations and giving treatments that aim to cure. Perhaps because of this, it is not always easy to persuade hospital doctors to switch to palliative care when it is clear that their patient is not going to get better. Researchers interviewed 29 cancer and palliative nurse specialists from five hospitals about end-of-life care in an acute hospital in 2006. Several of the nurses involved reported that it was often difficult to persuade doctors to stop giving curative treatment and start end-of-life care. Some of the doctors in question felt that palliative care equated to giving up on a patient. Others were disinclined to embark on what might be difficult discussions with patients and their relatives about end-of-life matters, and so carried on treating the patient, even though recovery was very unlikely. As a result, patients did not receive end-of-life care or, if a decision was made to give it to them instead of continuing to try to cure the condition, by then it was too late.[22] Clearly this study involved only a small number of people, but it is worth bearing its findings in mind. You may need to engage in some straight talking with your doctor and prompt them to summon palliative care expertise if the treatment to cure you or your relative seems to be on a hiding to nothing.

In a hospice

The size, nature and ethos of hospices differ from those of general hospitals. Usually far smaller in size and purpose-built, the focus of hospices is on giving people who are not going to get better as high a quality of life as possible and supporting their relatives during the dying process and afterwards. Of the 220 complaints about end-of-life care that the Parliamentary and Health Service Ombudsman examined for the period 2011–2014, virtually none involved care within a hospice.[23]

The people who pass away in hospices tend to be those whose final weeks or days call for especially sophisticated care. Admission in that final period can come as a great relief to both patient and family: they may have been struggling to cope at home, but in the hospice they know that all the help they may need is at the end of a call bell.

Patients may also stay in a hospice building well before the last weeks of their life while undergoing treatment to manage difficult symptoms; once they stabilise, they return home, or perhaps go to a care home, where their care is overseen by GPs. Whether patients are staying at a hospice or attending only for the day, psychological and spiritual support is an integral element of what the hospice offers, as for instance at St Catherine's Hospice in West Sussex.

St Catherine's Hospice is housed in an attractive, one- and two-storey, brick-and-tile building with ample car parking a few minutes' walk from the centre of Crawley. You enter through glass doors leading into the reception area, which opens onto to a large atrium occupying the centre of the complex. This is well-lit – indeed, the whole building seems flooded with natural light.

From the atrium, four wings radiate like wide spokes of a wheel. Two of these are bedroom wings and they look out onto the gardens that encircle much of the building and in which patients and their visitors can sit at tables with parasols, amongst well-tended plants. These wings provide accommodation for a total of 18 in-patients in two four-bed bays and single rooms.

The widest arm leading off the atrium contains a coffee shop, which leads into a large and welcoming conservatory, which gives onto the garden. Next to this, and also looking onto the garden, is a space for day-patients' communal activities. The fourth arm is smaller and contains the kitchen and an office. Other offices and meeting rooms for staff are housed in a separate building close by.

The 'quiet room' also leads off the atrium. It contains sofas, books, CDs and an open outer door, which faces Mecca. Gina Starnes, the patient services director, told me, 'Here you can kick off your shoes and curl up on the sofa with a book. Patients can sleep in here, if they wish.'

The quiet room can also be used for family meetings, including weddings and christenings, for meetings between family and staff, and for remembering. There are candles and a memories book. 'Mum, I miss you', reads Starnes explaining, 'The place where somebody died is important – people like to return'.

Visiting in hospices tends to be more flexible than in hospitals, with more support for visitors. At St Catherine's, visitors have the use of their own kitchen, which includes a microwave, so they can heat meals round the clock. There are two rooms for overnight accommodation and 'Staff will always make visitors tea and toast at night', according to Starnes. Visitors can bring in pets; once a goat was brought in to visit a farmer.

In hospitals too, there may, of course, be empathy and support for visitors, but the chances of finding these in a hospice are probably greater. In some ways, comparison between the two types of institution is unfair: hospitals have a far lower ratio of staff to patients than hospices; also, hospices tend to be relatively small, with their own garden, kitchen, café and spaces for patients and their visitors to use.

'Day hospice' is another element of support which hospices usually offer. Somebody who has been diagnosed with leukaemia, say, might attend day hospice one day each week at which, in company with other people with life-limiting illnesses, they might do craftwork or some other activity, enjoy a talk or another form of entertainment, have a lunch cooked on the premises with a drink beforehand, and chat to other attenders. Should they need medical advice, this can also be provided while they are on the premises. Day hospice at St Catherine's is 'a time out for attenders', says Gina Starnes: 'There's quite a nice, jovial environment. Crucially, they talk together – they get great strength from being with people in a similar situation. So it's not purely social and it's not purely medical.'

In fact, as in the majority of hospices, most of the work at St Catherine's is carried out by staff in the community. It provides support to 500 families each year in their homes. There, nurses offer training and advice to family carers and also hands-on care, often taking over from a family carer, who can then go shopping or enjoy a good night's sleep. They work in close touch with other professionals based on the ground, such as GPs and district nurses.[24]

Where no local hospice exists, national hospice services such as Sue Ryder Care and Marie Curie Care and Support through Terminal Illness provide a similar service. As with most local hospices, they provide help mainly through a peripatetic team of nurses who minister to people day and night in their own homes, usually as a planned service rather than an emergency one, and with care in their own hospice buildings for a limited number of patients. (Macmillan nurses tend to provide specialist advice rather than hands-on care.)

Patients are referred to hospices through their GP, district nurse or hospital consultant. Hospices are regulated and inspected by the Care Quality Commission in England, Healthcare Improvement Scotland, the Healthcare Inspectorate Wales and the Regulation and Quality Improvement Authority in Northern Ireland. The national standards or guidance that set out what is expected from hospices, as well as inspection reports on individual facilities, are available from these organisations.

Information about hospice and palliative care services throughout the UK is also available from the voluntary organisations Dying Matters *(see page 1023)* and Hospice UK; the latter publishes an annual *Hospice and Palliative Care Directory* covering the UK and Ireland.

In a community hospital

In fact, many people die not in hospices or general hospitals but in community hospitals and care homes. The advantage of community hospitals *(defined on page 902)* is that they tend to be situated closer to where patients and their circle of friends and family live than district hospitals and hospices. Also, they are smaller than general hospitals and tend to have a more homely feel. Of course community hospitals vary across the country, but they can provide a congenial environment for somebody who needs care in the final weeks of life (longer than the time for most hospice in-patients). Thus, for example, in a survey involving six community hospitals in 2007, all 51 bereaved carers were positive about the care their loved ones had received in these hospitals.[25] The carers particularly appreciated the location of the hospital (close to their homes), the availability of parking, the pleasant environment and the support that they themselves received from the staff.

In a care home

A care home can also be an agreeable place in which to spend one's final weeks. It is likely to have a more intimate atmosphere than a general hospital, with staff knowing how the resident is faring and recognising relatives when they visit (though these are broad generalisations and may not apply in a large home that relies heavily on agency staff).

Some older people die in care homes because they have been living in them for a while and deteriorate. Other people die in care (usually nursing) homes after being transferred to them following a spell in hospital, because they are too incapacitated to return to their own home. Some people are moved from hospices to care homes if their condition stabilises. In both cases these will probably be nursing homes – in other words, care homes with a registered nurse on duty all the time *(as explained in the Glossary)*. All told, more than one fifth of people aged over 65 die in care homes.

If you are considering entering a care home at the end of your life, do check that it could look after you well and that you would feel at home there.[26] The Scottish Partnership for Palliative Care has considered how care homes should provide end-of-life care, and wherever you live in the UK, it is worth getting hold of the booklet that distils its conclusions.

Although you could not press that the 'good practice statements' it lists should be met outside Scotland, it gives a useful sense of what you could reasonably expect:

- nursing homes should have at least one nurse on the staff who has a degree-level qualification which contains modules in palliative care

- care staff have or are working towards a qualification in palliative care, such as a Scottish Vocational Qualification in Social Services and Healthcare at level 3 *(see page 514)*

- provision will be made for relatives or friends to be accommodated overnight in the home so that they can be with a resident at the end of life, if that is their and the resident's wish

- there will be one member of staff who can provide spiritual support, for example by saying a prayer with a resident or reading a text

- staff will assist residents in seeking help to settle any outstanding affairs, including legal ones

- if a resident who is approaching the end of life does not want to eat or drink as much as before, staff will know the importance of offering small amounts of tasty food and drink, and these will be available at all times during the day or night

- staff will help residents keep their mouth clean, fresh and comfortable[27]

The amount of training in specialist end-of-life care that care home staff receive varies greatly. The Gold Standards Framework Centre in End-of-Life Care provides training to care facilities. By 2015, it had given special accreditation in end-of-life care to more than 500 care homes (a small proportion of the total number of homes). The Framework publishes a list of accredited homes on its website, together with a search facility for finding one in any particular area.[28] A good home will have this accreditation or be ensuring that a high proportion of its staff are taking courses in palliative care. It will also welcome links with a local hospice, many of which offer training in care homes. Thus in 2010 Highland Hospice reported to a conference that it was training staff in more than 40 care homes on best practice in end-of-life care and also providing helplines so that homes could obtain advice from hospice staff.[29]

Good care homes will do whatever they can to care for residents who become very unwell, helped by visiting doctors, district nurses and other health professionals. Some residents fear that if they are facing death, a care home manager may say that the home can no longer look after them so they must relocate to hospital or to another home. If the reason given is that particular equipment is needed, such as an intravenous drip or an additional supply of oxygen, how do you know whether the manager is behaving reasonably? The Scottish Partnership for Palliative Care says that equipment which can be deployed outside hospital includes a drip stand, oxygen provision, pressure-relieving mattresses, a portable nebuliser and a nasal-gastric feeding pump.[30] Plainly, it is important to check that the staff in the care home know how to operate the equipment.

It is also worth asking a nursing home about its approach to the deaths of residents if you are considering moving in. How does it help other residents to cope with the death of one of their number? Does it welcome back loved ones who wish to retain a link with the home? Does it encourage them to visit residents with whom their loved one was close?

At home

Many people say they would prefer to die at home. Others do not wish to do so, citing the frailty of family care-givers and fear of leaving behind sad memories in their homes.[31] Although dying at home can seem ideal, many people change their mind and opt to die in hospital as their condition deteriorates.[32]

It is important to talk to your doctor early on, particularly if you wish to die in your own home or in a care home, so that there is time for support arrangements to be put in place, such as training for a family carer and support from a hospice. Although most people would prefer to die at home, Professor Keri Thomas, a GP with a special interest in palliative care who pioneered the development of the Gold Standards Framework, believes the main reasons why many people end up going into hospital in their final days despite their wish to do otherwise include breakdown in the provision of homecare services and other support for family carers, such as night-sitters.[33] Doctors know that they should be planning ahead in this area; the General Medical Council has told them:

> As treatment and care towards the end of life are delivered by multi-disciplinary teams often working across local health, social care and voluntary sector services, you must plan ahead as much as possible to ensure timely access to safe, effective care and continuity in its delivery to meet the patient's needs.[34]

Palliative care

End-of-life care is not the only type of palliative care. Palliative care can also be given over days, weeks, months or years to people who have been diagnosed with an incurable, progressive condition such as cancer, chronic heart or lung disease, motor neurone disease or multiple sclerosis. Treatment aimed to cure can be given alongside palliative care – as well as treatment for other ailments, such as toothache. In this case, palliative care would seek to manage any pain or other troublesome physical symptoms and also to support the person in the round, providing any psychological and spiritual care they might wish to receive and enabling them to live as active a life as they wished. At the beginning, the focus would be on active therapies to enable them to maintain and improve their physical and mental capabilities.

When my father was suffering from emphysema in the early 1970s, he had to face the difficulties of walking and climbing stairs, the anxiety of not being able to catch his breath and the psychological challenge of increasing immobility pretty well unaided by the health service. Little in the way of equipment, drugs or even suggestions to cope with his condition was offered. Now, however, somebody with emphysema should expect palliative care, probably including a range of drugs, the administration of extra oxygen, and instruction, perhaps by a respiratory specialist nurse, on how to breathe in order to lessen the severity of the symptoms. Techniques can include breathing through pursed lips, leaning forward while sitting and supporting the upper arms on a table, and sitting near an open window or in front of a fan, so that a flow of cold air passes onto the face.[35] Relaxation techniques can also help control breathlessness: in one study, patients were less breathless and more able to do everyday activities after they had been taught breathing exercises, relaxation and coping strategies in three to six weekly sessions by a specialist nurse.[36] These sorts of techniques have the potential to much improve the quality of life of people with chronic lung disease.

But although considerable palliative care expertise exists, it is not always offered, particularly if the illness is not cancer. For instance, the Scottish Partnership for Palliative Care has pointed out that people with chronic heart failure often have limited access to palliative care. It says that it should be introduced at the early stages of the disease, 'gradually and seamlessly, overlapping and complementing active treatment'.[37]

The Department of Health has drawn attention to the need for doctors to ensure that palliative care is provided for a wide range of terminal conditions.[38] If you have not been offered specialist palliative care, raise the matter with your GP.

Cancer, chronic lung diseases, heart failure and motor neurone disease all typically follow different trajectories in their final stages. People with terminal cancer tend to go downhill suddenly and have particular needs for care during the last fortnight of life. In contrast, people suffering from heart or lung failure tend to show a continuous gradual decline over two to five years. This is punctuated by sudden problems which often require emergency hospital admission but from which they recover; in one of these, death usually seems sudden. On the other hand, people who are very frail and have dementia go downhill gradually and may recover a little along the way.

Dying with dementia

Dementia itself can cause death: as brain cells are progressively damaged, the heart, lungs and other organ systems of the body come to lose the direction they need. Eventually, damage to the brain is so serious that parts of the body start to shut down. This can take a very long time. Often the immediate cause of the death of someone with dementia is another illness such as pneumonia or cancer which they develop on top of their dementia and which their dementia may – or may not – have predisposed them to develop. All told, one in three people over 65 die with some degree of dementia.

Dementia can make coping with any illness more difficult, whether it is one of the ailments that afflicts us throughout life such as the common cold and toothache, or a serious illness which kills. If someone with dementia cannot put into words how they feel, they will be unable to convey the nature and extent of their symptoms or the impact of treatment. Ascertaining the level of pain and its location is therefore difficult, as is determining the presence and severity of other symptoms, such as nausea or constipation.

Yet alleviating distressing symptoms is all the more important because people with advanced dementia will be unable to help themselves cope with discomfort by deliberately distracting themselves with new thoughts or a diverting activity. Nor will they be in a position to put their immediate situation in the context of happier times or deeply held beliefs. So their response to pain, anxiety and so on is essentially unmediated, just as it is for an infant.

If your relative has dementia, it is therefore important to ensure that they have all the end-of-life care that might be beneficial. In the past, people with dementia have often received less attention to their palliative care needs than other people. A study in 2002 and 2003 of older people dying on an acute medical ward of a London hospital found that those with dementia were less likely to be referred to palliative care teams (9 per cent of them as opposed to 25 per cent of people without dementia) or to be prescribed palliative care drugs (28 versus 51 per cent).[39] In recent years, there has been growing recognition of the special attention that should be paid to the care of people with dementia who are dying. For instance, the Select Committee of the House of Commons on Health has urged parity of access to end-of-life care for people with dementia and those dying of physical health conditions.[40]

Talk to your loved one's GP or hospital consultant beforehand about how palliative care will be provided. Consider whether you should press their GP to seek advice on how to act: the average GP sees only about 20 patients a year who die, so may not have much experience of providing palliative care to somebody with dementia. You may wish to suggest that your relative should receive end-of-life care in a local hospice if they have or are likely to have symptoms which would be difficult to manage in the environment in which they are living. However, this factor has to be weighed against the reality that it is often better to keep people with dementia in an environment with which they are familiar, if possible.

Anybody treating a person with dementia should be taking steps to work out how they are going to comprehend the nature and severity of any symptoms and the effect of any treatment. Cards with simple questions such as 'Do you have a pain?' can be helpful *(see page 264)*. Expect doctors and nurses to consult with relatives so that they fully understand any pre-existing conditions which might cause pain or other symptoms.

For people with advanced dementia, health and care staff should look for clues to any discomfort. These might take the form of:

- body language
- facial movements and expression
- moaning or muttering
- poor sleep
- agitation
- loss of appetite
- the extent to which somebody can be consoled[41]

Caring for loved ones

Some close friends or family members wish to care for loved ones who can no longer look after themselves and are in the final stages of a life-limiting illness and/or dying. Others do not. The state cannot force somebody –

including a spouse – to do this: the ultimate legal responsibility to care for adults who cannot look after themselves rests with the state.

If you are prepared to provide practical help, make sure that:

✓ social services gives you an assessment of any needs you may have for practical help to support you. The result of this carer's assessment *(see page 621)* might include help with housework and the provision of personal care for the person for whom you are caring. Some carers do not wish to help with personal care themselves, lest that should undermine their relationship with the person involved. No assumptions should be made about the type or level of support carers will provide *(see page 626–7)*.

✓ your GP practice enters your name on any register of carers it holds. Everybody in the practice, not just your doctor, should know you are a carer. So, for instance, you could mention your status when booking consultations and expect receptionists to appreciate any difficulties you may encounter in attending surgery at particular times, most obviously if you are caring for someone who cannot be left alone.

✓ your GP practice or other health professionals give you all the training you need. Many cared-for people need help to get out of their chair and to transfer between chairs, to lavatory seats and so on. You cannot learn how to provide assistance from a book: the way you help the person for whom you are caring to move will depend on their physical condition and yours, as well as your relative weights. Expect instruction, perhaps from a district or practice nurse. If helping the person to move would threaten your own health, demand a hoist or other lifting equipment. Such equipment should be provided free under the NHS if you and they are assessed as needing it *(see page 279–80)*.

✓ you are given any respite support you need, through somebody else caring for your loved one. If your loved one has troublesome symptoms which keep them awake at night, you will have your work cut out simply staying the course. You may be able to obtain respite from peripatetic hospice nurses, for example.

✓ you receive advice on state benefits for you and your loved one. For example, you might be entitled to Carer's Allowance *(see page 844–6)*.

Financial support during end stages

Anybody who has a progressive illness and is not expected to live for more than six months as a result of that disease is entitled to be fast-tracked to the higher rate of Attendance Allowance. *As explained on page 835,* Attendance Allowance is a benefit granted on grounds of disability or illness to people aged 65 and over; it is not means-tested. Under this special provision for Attendance Allowance for people who are terminally ill, applicants simply have to produce a form from their doctor or consultant which describes their medical condition and explains that they are terminally ill. Awards under these 'claims under the special rules' are usually made for a fixed period of three years; they can be withdrawn by the Department for Work and Pensions if somebody's condition or prognosis improves so they are no longer considered to be 'terminally ill'. A claim under special rules may be made by somebody other than the person involved and without their knowledge or say-so.

There is also a fast-tracking provision for receipt of the equivalents of Attendance Allowance for people below the age of 65 – Disability Living Allowance and the Personal Independence Payment *(see page 840–4).*

NHS Continuing Care is a different sort of funding which can be given to people who are terminally ill. It covers both their healthcare costs and the costs of providing the practical help they need, and can be provided in a hospital, hospice, care home, the person's own home or that of a friend or family member. People who are deteriorating rapidly and are expected to die fairly soon can be fast-tracked to NHS Continuing Healthcare so that the support can be provided very quickly. This can enable them to leave hospital and die in their own home, if that is their wish. *(I discuss this funding for people who are dying on page 961.)*

End of life care

* Dying is not intrinsically painful or distressing.

* Palliative care enables any troublesome symptoms which may arise to be managed and provides emotional and spiritual support to the patient and their friends and family.

* If you have only hours or days to live, expect health professionals to have drawn up an end-of-life plan for your care and to review it frequently.

* If you wish to know, ask a doctor to clarify whether they are telling you that you or a loved one are dying.

* Relatives and friends can do much to provide moral support when someone is dying and also perform practical tasks such as helping to keep the mouth moist.

* Chaplains can be helpful sounding boards and comforters; religion need not be mentioned.

* If you wish to return home from hospital to die and will need care, give your GP or hospital plenty of notice so that equipment and services can be put in place before you arrive.

* A third of people over 65 die with dementia. They need special understanding and support.

* People who have only weeks or months to live can be fast-tracked for Attendance Allowance, Disability Living Allowance, the Personal Independence Payment and NHS Continuing Healthcare.

Chapter 41
Final decision-making

A t any stage in our life, doctors may have to decide whether to prevent our death by offering us life-saving treatment. This might involve stopping bleeding from a wound, providing antibiotics to fight a potentially fatal infection or resuscitating us after a heart attack. In normal circumstances, we do not have a right to receive any medical treatment, but a doctor should offer it to us so long as it would not be futile.

Decisions on whether to give potentially life-prolonging treatment are more complex when someone is very unwell and/or very old. The fragility and perhaps frailty of their body may mean that the steps involved to save their life are less likely to work. Also, the measures involved might cause more distress than in a younger, fitter person.

Take ventricular defibrillation. Familiar from hospital TV dramas, this involves giving a massive electric shock to restart a heart which has stopped beating, thereby saving life. However, the procedure is traumatic. The patient has to be placed on a hard surface and intravenous tubes have to be inserted to give them drugs. The paddles through which the current passes may burn the skin. The procedure can cause bruising, and frail patients may suffer fractures of the ribs or breastbone. Patients may come round afterwards with soreness around the throat, as a plastic tube airway is usually inserted into the windpipe to provide more effective ventilation of the lungs. Pain can be treated and bruises fade, but if there has been an interruption in blood flow to the brain despite the procedure, the patient may wake up permanently brain-damaged.

Advanced dementia is often the reason why decisions over whether or not to administer life-prolonging interventions can be very difficult. A radio programme in 2014 discussed the case of a woman who had had a pacemaker inserted to make her heart beat at the normal rate.[1] Years later, she developed dementia and the question arose whether the batteries in her pacemaker should be replaced when they wore out. Neither her dementia nor any other condition was threatening to kill her within a year, yet without a working pacemaker she would be likely to die at some stage in the not too distant future. Replacement of pacemaker batteries usually involves a simple medical procedure with a local anaesthetic, but this woman would not have been able to understand that she should lie still, so would have had to be brought into hospital against her will, restrained, given a general anaesthetic, woken up from that and then prevented, over several weeks, from tampering with the wound. In the event, her doctors, taking into account the views of her attorneys, decided it was not in her best interests to replace the batteries. When they did run out, her pulse slowed, then her heartbeat, and she died, at the age of 93.

But in many cases, lay people are unaware that treatment could be given that would avert death. For example, an elderly person in the advanced stages of a serious lung disease starts going blue in the face and slipping in and out of consciousness. An onlooker might assume nothing can be done. In fact, this condition is the result of a dramatic rise in blood carbon dioxide, which can often be treated by measuring the amount of gases in the blood and then adjusting the concentration of oxygen. The machine that performs this (which can be taken home) allows breathing to be effective even at night, when it naturally becomes shallower. A ventilator might also be needed.

While publicity tends to focus on people's efforts to ensure they would not be given life-saving treatment against their will, it is important to be aware of the desire of others to remain alive for as long as possible, even though they might be at death's door and appear to others to have a very low quality of life.

How can we ensure that the decisions made about offering or withholding life-saving interventions are those we would wish, particularly if we are not in a fit state at the time to grant or withhold our consent?

In this chapter, I set out:

▶ the rules governing the behaviour of doctors in end-of-life decision-making

▶ how patients can secure the medical treatment they would like

▶ advance directives to refuse treatment

▶ non-medical end-of-life choices

▶ where you could set down your wishes

Compulsory rules for doctors at the end of life

The General Medical Council, which regulates what doctors can do in the interests of the general public *(page 305)*, has issued guidance on how doctors should take decisions on whether or not to offer life-prolonging treatment to patients who are likely to die within the following 12 months.[2] This guidance is available free on the internet and it is worth getting hold of a copy. It applies throughout the UK. Any serious or persistent failure to follow it which comes to the attention of the GMC puts the registration of the doctor involved at risk.

In normal circumstances, doctors should offer treatment to patients likely to die within 12 months without hesitation, unless it plainly will not work. But where somebody is likely to die soon, they can decide to withhold it. The GMC has said: 'Decisions concerning potentially life-prolonging treatment must not be motivated by a desire to bring about the patient's death, and must start from a presumption in favour of prolonging life'. However, 'There is no absolute obligation to prolong life irrespective of the consequences for the patient, and irrespective of the patient's views, if they are known or can be found'.[3]

The GMC sets out a two-stage process for doctors considering whether to offer life-prolonging treatment to somebody likely to die within 12 months. They should consider, 'Which investigations or treatments are clinically appropriate and likely to result in overall benefit for the patient' and also take into account 'the patient's views and understanding of their condition'.[4]

1. Weighing up whether treatment would benefit a patient

In deciding whether treatment is clinically appropriate and likely to result in overall benefit to a patient, doctors would be expected to ask themselves:

- Would this treatment actually work in terms of saving this person's life?

- If it did, would the effect last or would the treatment have to be repeated soon afterwards?

- What is the nature of the pain and the other downsides the treatment would be likely to inflict on the patient?

- What sort of quality of life would the patient enjoy once any short-term effects of the treatment had worn off?

Let us take the example of ventricular fibrillation again. Suppose a healthy young person suffers a cardiac arrest after a routine operation. In this case, a doctor will have a fairly high chance of restarting the heart. However, the situation is different when a patient is very sick. People suffering from major illnesses such as heart or lung disease or cancer are much less likely to have their heart restarted successfully, and the chance is lower still if they are also very old. In these instances, if the heart were restarted, an arrest might happen again within minutes, and yet again if the heart were restarted once more.

But of course this has to be set against the fact that the patient might go on to survive and return to the life they had been living before this episode, even though that life might involve much illness and disability.

How is a doctor supposed to evaluate the quality of life a patient might enjoy once the short-term effects of the life-saving treatment have subsided? That is very difficult – none of us can assess the quality of life of another human being, as Professor Sam Ahmedzai, who led the Royal College of Physicians' audit of end-of-life care in hospitals in 2016, explained to me:

> Doctors cannot and should not try to estimate the quality of life of another person. They can't even reliably estimate how much pain a patient is having: they frequently underestimate pain. They underestimate nearly all symptoms. And they underestimate psychological problems. Routinely when we do a direct head-to-head comparison with what the patient says about quality of life on a questionnaire or interview with what the doctor says, we find the doctor has underestimated. Of course the more training a doctor has, the better he or she gets it; the longer the doctor knows the person, the better they get it. So a GP who had had training in communication skills would be very good at knowing whether a patient would want artificial resuscitation or not. But how often do doctors in a hospital or hospice or nursing home even think of ringing up the GP to ask whether such and such a person would want resuscitation? [5]

Just how wrong any of us can be in our estimation of the quality of life of another individual has been demonstrated by Ian Basnett, a doctor who was paralysed in all four limbs after a sports accident. He has pointed out that:

> Research on the attitudes of accident and emergency doctors found that only a fifth imagined they would be glad to be alive if they were quadriplegic, whereas over 90 per cent of people with quadriplegia reported they were glad to be alive. [6]

In view of these uncertainties, the GMC has told doctors:

You must be careful not to rely on your personal views about a patient's quality of life and to avoid making judgments based on poorly informed or unfounded assumptions about the healthcare needs of particular groups, such as older people and those with disabilities.[7]

2. The patient's view

The second general area that a doctor must consider is the view of the patient. Usually, before doctors can give any treatment, they must obtain the consent of the patient. However, if emergency treatment is needed to save somebody's life, a doctor can proceed without the patient's consent.

Normally fit people can usually weigh up the pros and cons of receiving treatment, state their view and thus give or withhold consent for any treatment offered by a doctor. But some people may not be in a mentally fit state to do that. Their mental powers might be impaired, either because they are suffering from a condition such as dementia or because those powers are affected temporarily by illness: as we saw earlier *(on page 30)*, elderly people are more likely to become confused than younger people if they are unwell. These impairments will clearly affect a person's mental capacity, or their ability to take a decision at the time it needs to be taken or to communicate their views, even through blinking.

In accordance with the principles of the mental capacity legislation *(explained on pages 770–4)*, the GMC has told doctors that they, 'Must work on the presumption that every adult patient has the capacity to make decisions about their care and treatment'.[8] If there is a chance that the patient may lack capacity, doctors, 'Must provide the patient with all appropriate help and support to maximise their ability to understand, retain, use or weigh up the information needed to make that decision or communicate their wishes'.[9]

If a doctor concludes that their patient lacks the mental capacity to come to a decision about whether to receive life-prolonging treatment, then they should explain the options to somebody the patient has appointed to speak on their behalf, most obviously through a personal welfare attorneyship *(see page 751)*. If such a person has been appointed and has been given the power to refuse life-prolonging treatment, they can act as the patient's proxy in granting or withholding consent for any treatment offered.

The other set of circumstances in which a doctor would refrain from giving treatment they would otherwise offer involves an advance directive to refuse treatment (ADRT). If one of these has been signed by the patient and it is valid and relevant to the circumstances, a doctor would not give the treatment in question, even if the patient would die without it. *(ADRTs are discussed on pages 1017–20.)*

If there is no legal proxy and no advance directive in place, the doctor must consult certain individuals associated with the patient, before coming to a final decision, if it is reasonable and practical to do so. *(These people are listed on page 782 and 789.)* Their views are fed into the decision-making process and the doctor must bear them in mind but does not have to go along with them: it is ultimately up to the doctor to consider what is in the best interests of their patient.

'Do not resuscitate' notices

In most situations in which decisions have to be made on whether to give or withhold life-sustaining treatment, there is some time in which the patient and/or other people can be consulted. But with ventricular defibrillation, time is of the essence. Once the heart stops beating and fresh blood therefore fails to reach the brain, the patient loses consciousness within a matter of seconds. Within minutes, brain cells start to die. Within about four minutes, irreversible brain damage is likely to occur. After a further two or three minutes, the brain will fail to respond to electrical stimuli and the patient will then be judged to be clinically dead.

Artificial resuscitation, in which somebody manually gives heart compressions and breathes into the patient's mouth, can, if successful, restore partial flow of oxygenated blood to the heart and brain, thus keeping them alive. This extends the window of opportunity for successful ventricular defibrillation without permanent brain damage.

As these steps must be taken immediately in the event of a cardiac arrest, an instruction is usually drawn up ahead of time if there is any doubt about whether the treatment should be offered. This is in the form of a 'Do not resuscitate' or 'Do not attempt cardio-pulmonary resuscitation' notice. It is kept in the patient's medical records and on a hospital ward you may well see a drawer labelled 'DNAR' or 'DNACPR' at the nurses' station. The instructions 'DNAR' are entered into a patient's notes by a doctor (usually a consultant), and it is only a doctor who can alter or rescind them. However, the patient or their representatives should be consulted before such an instruction is drawn up.

It is important to check your DNAR status, just in case it says you should be resuscitated when you would rather not be – or, conversely, that artificial resuscitation would not be attempted when you would prefer that every effort should be made to keep you alive. As noted *(on page 281)*, we all have a legal right to see our medical records, and representatives such as attorneys can also access them.

If you are unhappy with an instruction on resuscitation in your medical notes, go and see your GP or, if in hospital, ask to speak to a member of the medical staff (preferably a consultant or registrar) or, if none is available, a senior nurse. Ask for the instruction to be changed. If you are concerned about someone else, such as a close relative, ask on what grounds the decision was made. Was it the result of a conversation with the patient, and if so, when did this conversation take place? If there has been no recorded conversation, you are in a good position to challenge the decision. Speak to the consultant or a representative of the consultant such as a senior registrar, either of whom should have enough authority to agree that the DNAR order should be rescinded.

Of course, the consultant may say they consider the order should remain in force, as it is judged to be in the patient's best interests. Legally, doctors have a duty of care to the patient, not to the family, so if they maintain that the decision is in the patient's best interests, they can still act on it, regardless of what the relatives think (unless they are attorneys whose powers specifically include the right to refuse life-prolonging treatment). All a relative can do is to lodge a formal objection through the hospital complaints system. Go to the hospital trust's medical director to speed things up, because delay can (literally) be fatal.

If you are neither the patient nor have legal authority to speak up for them, probably your best card to play in seeking to overturn an instruction is that you consider, in view of your knowledge of the patient, it would run contrary to their wishes, views and beliefs.

Institutions such as hospices and care homes are not allowed to adopt blanket policies which deny all their residents certain types of treatment, so they cannot automatically write 'DNAR' on the notes of every patient or resident. Each case must be considered on its merits. But it is, of course, well worth the patient checking that they have not been made subject to any blanket policy, just in case.

People with chronic heart failure may have devices implanted which give an electric shock to stimulate the heart if the beat becomes irregular; these are implantable defibrillators. However, at the end of life they can cause a more prolonged, uncomfortable death. If you are in this position, discuss with your doctor the possible deactivation of your defibrillator.

What patients can do to influence end-of-life decision-making

As we have seen, we can only give or withhold our consent for treatment that is offered. At the end of life, we may not be in a fit state to do this.

What many people fear is that they will be given treatment, such as artificial resuscitation which they would have turned down had they been compos mentis.

A specific tool has been devised for this eventuality, to which I will turn in a moment. First, it is worth saying that a welfare attorney can be invaluable. If you grant one or more people the proxy power to take decisions on your behalf should you come to lose the ability to make or convey them (or in Scotland also to remember or act on decisions), you should stand a good chance of getting what you want. You can grant your welfare attorney the right to refuse consent for treatment, even if refusal would be likely to result in your death. If a particular treatment were being offered that could save your life, your attorney would consider what your best interests would be, bearing in mind your wishes and views; this might result in their refusing consent for life-saving treatment on your behalf.

The form in which one grants power of welfare attorney contains a section called 'statement of wishes'. Many people seem to ignore this, but it provides the opportunity to set down the various ways in which you would like to be treated, should you become mentally incompetent, perhaps as a result of brain injury or dementia, or unable to convey your wishes and feelings, perhaps after a major stroke. Your attorney or attorneys should take these wishes into account whenever they are acting or taking decisions in your best interests. You can put down pretty well whatever you like. It could include medical and nursing matters, but also, for instance, whom you would welcome as a visitor should you become very ill and whether you would like a piece of music to be played if you were dying. *(I discuss welfare attorneyships in Chapter 31.)*

Health (and social care) professionals in England and Wales have a legal duty to consult certain people associated with a patient should they be unable to speak up for themselves or lack the mental capacity to take the decision in question. These include any welfare attorney, but also any deputy *(see Chapter 32)*, unpaid carer, anyone 'interested in the welfare' of the person involved and 'anyone named by the person as someone to be consulted on the matter in question or on matters of that kind'.[10] These people may – or may not be – the person's next-of-kin. *(I explain these requirements on consultation on pages 782–92.)*

It is well worth nominating one or more people in that final category: they could be an old school or work friend, for instance. Being such a consultee usually involves a one-off contribution only and so should not be an onerous responsibility; acting as a welfare attorney sometimes can be.

Whoever represents you, make sure that they know your views beforehand, and that doctors, nurses, care home managers and anybody else who might be present at the time have clear information on the status of these people and their contact details. If you secure people whom you trust to take part in medical decision-making, you stand a better chance of securing the treatment you wish.

Advance directives to refuse treatment and living wills

Whether or not you nominate welfare attorneys or other people to be consulted in healthcare decision-making, you may wish to make an 'advance directive to refuse treatment' (ADRT). This provides a means for patients to refuse a particular medical treatment if they lack the mental capacity to grant or withhold consent at the time, perhaps because they are too ill or under anaesthetic or have serious brain impairment. Formerly known as the similar 'living will', an ADRT is usually used in the case of treatment that could save a patient's life. The authorisation involves only the withholding of consent for specified types of treatment – it does not give doctors, or anybody else, any other power over someone's treatment. An ADRT is legally binding: if one has been made and it is valid and applicable to the circumstances, doctors are required to follow it, even if death will probably result.[11]

An ADRT cannot be couched in general terms – it must specify the treatment or treatments the person wishes to refuse. You might wish to decline artificial resuscitation, for example, should your heart stop beating; or the use of a machine to enable you to continue to breathe; or antibiotics in the event of an infection; or kidney dialysis; or a blood transfusion; or artificial feeding, perhaps through a tube. If you have a particular medical condition, there may be other forms of treatment that could prolong your life that you would wish to refuse. Discuss with your doctor the circumstances in which an advance directive might be relevant and the treatment that might be offered before you complete it. Your doctor will be able to explain the implications of refusing treatment. For instance, you might consider saying you refuse the offer of (potentially lifesaving) thrombolytic drugs should you suffer a major stroke *(see page 351)*. But you might find that the stroke did not kill you but left you paralysed down one side of your body – an effect that the drugs might well have reversed. In other words, in some situations refusing a particular treatment in all circumstances may cause additional distress.

Two further conditions must be met for an ADRT to be valid:

✓ the person involved must have mental capacity when they sign the form (in other words, they must be mentally capable of making the decision and understanding the implications of it; *see page 774 or the Glossary for a fuller explanation of the meaning of mental capacity*)

✓ the ADRT must include a statement that the instructions in the directive are to apply even if the person's life is at risk

An ADRT made verbally is valid, but to refuse treatment necessary to sustain life, the decision must be in writing, and witnessed, and expressly state that it applies even if the person's life is at risk.

If an advance decision to refuse treatment is not valid or is not applicable to the circumstances in question, doctors do not necessarily ignore it. They must decide whether or not to give treatment based on what they consider is in the patient's best interests *(as outlined on page 773)*. As part of this process, they must consider even an invalid ADRT if they have reasonable grounds to believe that it is a true expression of the patient's wishes.[12]

Unlike the lasting power of attorney, no standard form has been published by the Office of the Public Guardian for use as an ADRT. However, the voluntary organisation Compassion in Dying publishes 'Helpful Questions to Consider when Making an Advance Decision' as part of its Advance Decision Pack, available free on its website or by post, including in large-print form. Macmillan Cancer Support also publishes suggested clauses for an ADRT and explanatory notes.

Do remember to include in your ADRT an instruction about continuing steps to keep you alive specific to your situation, such as the replacement of pacemaker batteries. *(I mention the sort of circumstances in which this decision could arise on pages 1009–10.)*

It is clearly important to make sure that your ADRT is flagged up in your medical notes and that any relevant health professionals with whom you come into contact, from a paramedic to a locum doctor, know of its existence. An ADRT could form an important part of an advance care plan *(see page 993)*.

Clearly, there is no need to involve anybody else such as a relative in making an ADRT, as is necessary with powers of attorney. However, do make sure that any welfare attorney, relatives and other people who will be consulted if you are not in a position to consent to medical treatment have a copy of your ADRT or know where to find one. According to research at the University of Nottingham in 2014, almost half the people who had made an ADRT had not shared this information with other people.[13] If you fear treatment which might be given in a hurry, wear some highly visible instruction on your person.

You can withdraw or alter your advance decision at any time and neither the withdrawal nor the alteration need be in writing. However, you must have the mental capacity to do so. If you do not, a proposed rescinding or alteration would be invalid.

It is important to review your ADRT regularly. The life-or-death circumstances you think you might face could change over time. Advances in medical science could alter the picture radically. You might change your views about the circumstances in which you would find life intolerable.

If somebody has specifically granted a welfare attorney the power to give (or withhold) consent for the same life-sustaining treatment decisions *after* making an ADRT, the latter becomes invalid. But if an advance directive is made after conferring welfare power of attorney and at a time when the person still possesses the mental capacity to do so, the advance directive overrules the power in the attorneyship.

Ultimate authority in the field of ADRTs is wielded by the Court of Protection, which can rule on whether an ADRT exists, is valid and is applicable to a particular form of treatment. Deputies may not refuse life-sustaining treatment: if such a question arises, the matter must be referred to the Court of Protection.

The **Scottish** legislation does not include provision for an advance decision to refuse treatment along the lines discussed above. However, according to Scottish law, when health professionals are deciding what if any treatment to give somebody who cannot consent, they should take account of the patient's past and present wishes.[14]

The Mental Capacity **(Northern Ireland)** Act 2016 gives advance directives to refuse treatment statutory recognition. It says (at Section 11) that someone who gives treatment to a patient contrary to their wishes as expressed in an advance statement does not have an exemption from liability. This would mean that a doctor who gave someone life-saving treatment when they had expressly said in an ADRT that they wished to refuse it would be breaking the law. The Act says that to be valid in these circumstances an advance statement must have been made by someone who had the mental capacity to make the decision, and that they would make the decision to refuse treatment in the current circumstances were they able to do so. In other words, the person must not have done anything since making their statement that contravenes it and they would not have changed their decision had they known more about their current circumstances. If they conferred the power to refuse life-sustaining treatment onto an attorney after making an ADRT, that step would also be likely to invalidate the advance decision. *As noted on page 729,* no commencement date on which the Mental Capacity (Northern Ireland) Act 2016 would come into force had been agreed at the time of writing. However, many of the Act's provisions are reflected in common law and so might well be upheld before the Act comes into force.

Fudging and transparency

Plainly, an advance directive to refuse treatment enables somebody to refuse a particular treatment that a doctor offers. But what it does not do is to enable the patient or their loved ones to ensure that a doctor offers that treatment, still less to know that it exists.

In the past doctors may have taken it upon themselves to play God. They looked at a patient, perhaps with at an advanced stage of an incurable illness, considered their quality of life to be poor and decided against offering to provide a treatment that might extend their life; if the patient was unaware that the treatment might be provided, they were not in a position to ask why it was not being offered.

Nowadays, doctors are supposed to consult patients about all the decisions they take about their care, including those at the end of their lives. But do they still retain an instinct not to consult, a sense that their superior knowledge in the medical field trumps all other considerations? We do not know. However, in a large-scale study in 2003 involving six European countries, a large proportion of end-of-life decisions were taken with doctors consulting neither the patient nor their relatives – more than half of such decisions in Italy and Sweden.[15] The decisions frequently involved doctors deciding either not to treat on the one hand or to administer medication to alleviate symptoms while appreciating that the hastening of death was a possible side-effect on the other.

Decisions towards and at the end of life can be complex. Interventions can give some people extra time that they value; for other people, they can result in great suffering, both for them and their loved ones. But if you are concerned that decisions are being taken without your being consulted, ask: does a treatment exist for the condition? Could it be tried? What would be the likely drawbacks?

The area where the absence of transparency in end-of-life care has probably been most prevalent in the past has been dealing with thirst. Plainly, if a patient who is too unwell to raise a cup to their lips is not given help to drink, they will die. But whether or not the provision of fluid should be viewed as a form of medical treatment has been debated. In the past it was seen as good nursing practice, but not necessarily a matter with which doctors should concern themselves. However, as we have seen *(on page 716)*, it is now firmly viewed as a matter on which doctors and nurses have real responsibility. Furthermore, any withdrawal or withholding of fluid or omission of help with drinking when someone seems to be dying should only happen if an active decision has been taken that this would be in that person's best interests: it should never be automatic *(see page 773)*. This decision should involve the patient or their representatives and any other people who ought to be consulted *(see pages 782, 789 and 792)*.

In the past it seems likely that withholding fluid by omitting to provide someone very ill with the help they needed to drink was used to end life and perhaps also to fudge end-of-life decision-making. In a case of which I became aware, a frail woman in her late eighties who was suffering from advanced dementia and living in a healthcare facility developed pneumonia. A doctor was called, who duly prescribed antibiotics. A week later, when the manager of the facility returned from leave, she expressed amazement to a daughter who was visiting that her mother had survived the infection. One key difference between this case and others is likely to have been that, during the manager's absence, the woman's daughter and other members of her family had been sitting at her bedside for long periods, helping her to drink.

A matron of a nursing home told a colleague of mine in 2001 that a large proportion of residents in nursing homes die from dehydration. Whether or not this is true, it is easy to see how it would happen if it were. A resident becomes ill and a doctor provides treatment for the illness, thus avoiding any discussion with relatives about whether treatment should be given. But for one reason or another, the manager of the care home refrains from providing the necessary staff time to help the enfeebled resident to drink and therefore stay alive. In other words, allowing a person to die of thirst provides a convenient means of ducking a difficult decision.

Whether or not this situation still exists remains unknown, save anecdotally. But help to drink remains different from other life-sustaining measures such as dialysis or resuscitation in that it takes effort over a period. If someone has a fever and therefore needs more fluid that usual, it takes a lot of sips to keep them hydrated. Relatives will need to check that adequate help is being given or give it themselves (making sure it can be done safely without fluid accidentally entering the lungs), if they wish to do all they can to aid recovery.

Assisted dying

Many people fear the long-term disability and illness they may face and are keen to shorten any suffering by ensuring they are given any help they need to die if they should come to lack the physical ability to kill themselves. Dementia is feared in particular, so much so that Terry Pratchett (who had a rare form of early-onset Alzheimer's) declared in 2010 that, 'People are frightened about the future. ... Suddenly we find a growing interest in assisted dying. Fear is the spur, fear of hell before death.'[16]

Assisted dying can take two forms. In assisted suicide, which Pratchett (who died in 2015) supported but did not in the event use, somebody is given the help they request to die, although they must be able to perform a deliberate act to deliver it, such as raising the cup containing poison or pressing a button or lever. They must also have the mental ability to understand what they are doing.

In an act of euthanasia, somebody deliberately kills a person who is unable to ask for help to die. The killing must be for the benefit of the person whose life is to be ended; it can involve a deliberate act or omitting to give somebody the help they need to remain alive. Plainly someone who cannot make the decision to end their own life, such as someone with advanced dementia, could not benefit from assisted suicide, but they could benefit from euthanasia, were it to become legal.

Both forms of assisted dying are currently unlawful throughout the UK. Strenuous efforts are regularly made to change this. Equally strenuous efforts are made to retain the existing legal situation.

Britons who opt for assisted suicide may choose to travel to countries such as Switzerland, where the practice is lawful. However, they are usually too unwell to get themselves there, so must find at least one person to help them. They must then consider whether that person might later face prosecution in the UK and also how they will deal with such practical matters as the disposal of the body. If the person who accompanies them is a loved one, everyone must consider how the bereaved will deal emotionally with the whole experience.

Who will look after the goldfish?

As they approach the end of their lives, many people worry about what will happen to their pets, whether they will see a particular person before they die, and what form their funeral will take.

They may also be concerned about unfinished business. Adela Austin, a psychotherapist with many years' experience, emphasised to me in an interview in 2016 the importance of trying to make peace with those close to us with whom we have unresolved difficulties. If it is not possible to do this in person, writing a letter can also be helpful. Austin believes such action can enable someone who is dying to develop greater peace of mind and gain a sense of completion and well-being. This benefits not only the person at the end of their life, but also those they will leave behind.

As well as considering whether there are particular people with whom you wish to try to make up, here are some questions you might like to address *(others are mentioned in the context of advance care plans on pages 1010–2):*

- ✓ whom you would like to be told of your death or that you are dying
- ✓ whether you wish your organs to be donated or your body used in medical training
- ✓ what kind of funeral you would like
- ✓ where you would like to be buried or your ashes placed
- ✓ to which organisations, if any, you would like mourners to send donations
- ✓ whether you would like a seat or other facility donated in your memory and if so, where *(see page 674)*
- ✓ whether your will expresses your current wishes
- ✓ what should happen to anyone for whom you are caring
- ✓ what should happen to your pets

Talk to your loved ones as frankly as possible about your final wishes. The one certainty is that at some point it will be too late. A voluntary organisation called Dying Matters, which has a local presence in many places as well as a national one, seeks to get us all talking more openly about death, dying and bereavement, using a powerful video on its website called *I Didn't Want That*. 'Death cafés', which have sprung up in several towns, involve occasional discussions about such matters in which an organiser facilitates debate over tea and cake.

Some of the most challenging end-of-life decisions that can arise involve what to tell loved ones about their or our own end. If you know your mother is dying but she does not, and she asks you about her prognosis, what do you say? Have a look at the website at healthtalk.org.uk *(see page 327)*. It features video testimonies from people and carers facing illnesses and medical situations, including the end of life.

Final decision-making

* Doctors must consider the extent to which any life-saving intervention for someone likely to die within 12 months would result in overall benefit to the patient.

* In doing this, they must take into account the patient's views and understanding of their condition.

* Check that any 'Do not attempt resuscitation' instructions in your medical notes conform to your wishes.

* Make an advance directive to refuse treatment (ADRT) if you fear being given life-saving treatment that you would rather forego.

* Specify in your ADRT the treatment or treatments you wish to refuse.

* Review your ADRT regularly.

* Make sure your ADRT will be seen by healthcare personnel, not least in an emergency.

* Fluid should only be withheld or withdrawn if that seems the best course for that particular person. It should never be withheld simply because the person does not seem to have long to live.

* If you are contemplating assisted suicide, consider carefully the likely practical and emotional implications for relatives or friends who help you travel to a country where this step is legal.

* Make your wishes known about where you wish to die and what should happen after your death.

Glossary

ABUSE

Elder abuse involves the infliction of harm on someone who is considered vulnerable or at risk by one or more other people who are in a position of trust, such as their care assistant, unpaid carer *(see below)* or attorney *(see below)*. It may involve the deliberate infliction of physical, sexual, financial or psychological harm, or harm through an omission – so neglecting to provide adequate food, drink, heating, medication or care is also a form of abuse.

ADVOCATE

This word has had several meanings. In the field of eldercare in the UK, it refers to somebody who provides one-to-one support to help somebody else to make decisions about their life; support may be for a short time or long-term. The advocate may represent the person in question, if that is what the latter would like. Advocacy is usually free.

INDEPENDENT MENTAL CAPACITY ADVOCATE

An independent mental capacity advocate is a special type of advocate. Health and social care authorities in England and Wales have to appoint an IMCA to represent the views and interests of somebody who lacks the mental capacity *(see below)* to make certain major decisions about their life and there is nobody suitable to act on their behalf. This provision will also apply in Northern Ireland once legislation passed there in 2016 is brought into force.

ATTORNEY

An attorney is someone who has been given legal authority by a 'donor' under a 'lasting power of attorney', an 'enduring power of attorney' or, in Scotland, a 'continuing power of attorney' to make decisions on behalf of the donor. Attorneys can act only within the scope of the authority the donor has given them, and their behaviour must conform to principles laid down in law. Donor and attorney may act in tandem. Or, if the donor should lose mental capacity, the attorney serves as their proxy on finance and property and/or health and welfare matters, perhaps for many years.

An ordinary power of attorney involves the delegation to someone else of the power to sign legal forms or make financial decisions by someone who retains their mental capacity throughout. The power is often granted for a limited period, perhaps while the donor is on holiday.

CARE-GIVER

In this book, this term embraces anyone who gives care, paid or unpaid. I use it most often to describe paid staff who live on the premises, to distinguish them from unpaid carers (see below) and paid, visiting care assistants.

CARE HOME

This is a facility which provides accommodation, meals and personal care (and often other types of support) to its residents. If it also provides nursing care, it is called a nursing home. Otherwise it is called a residential care home. There are also specialist care homes which care for people with particular disabilities and illnesses, such as blindness or dementia. The majority of care homes are privately owned and run to make a profit.

CARER

Somebody who provides or intends to provide unpaid care to a relative, partner or friend who needs help because of illness, disability or frailty is called a carer. The term does not therefore apply to a paid care assistant. Some authors use the term 'carer' to cover both groups, but I have restricted my use to unpaid carers, mainly because the term has that meaning in law. The care that carers give (and which social care authorities may support them to provide) can consist of practical and/or emotional support.

DEPUTY

Some people lack the mental capacity to make decisions but have not appointed an attorney or attorneys. In that case, the Court of Protection can step in and appoint someone as their 'deputy' with ongoing legal authority as set out by the Court to make decisions on the person's behalf. A deputy may be a professional, such as a solicitor, or a lay person, such as a relative or friend of the person who lacks capacity.

DIRECT PAYMENT

A direct payment is a sum of money allocated by social services (or in Scotland, social work or Northern Ireland, a health and social care trust) to someone to pay for the care and support it has assessed them as needing and which the person can use in whichever way they wish, so long as the money is spent on meeting their assessed needs. They may choose to use the money to hire assistants direct, to commission help through a care agency and/or buy other kinds of help, such as attendance at a day centre. Direct payments are also given to carers to choose the support they wish to receive to help them provide care and to sustain their own health and well-being.

DISABILITY

The Equality Act 2010, which applies in England, Scotland and Wales, defines 'disability' as a physical or mental impairment which has a substantial and long-term adverse effect on somebody's ability to carry out normal day-to-day activities. 'Long-term' is defined as having existed for at least 12 months or likely to last for at least 12 months or for the rest of the life of the person affected. This means that someone with heart disease who becomes breathless on exertion, someone with continence difficulties who needs to visit the toilet often, someone who cannot handle objects easily because osteo-arthritis has impaired their manual dexterity, and somebody with a mental condition such as a learning disability or dementia which hampers their ability to, say, go shopping can all be said to have a disability, so long as the impairment has a substantial and long-term adverse effect on their ability to carry out normal day-to-day activities.

Other, slightly different definitions of disability, explained in the text, are used in other circumstances, such as for the provision of state benefits or grants to adapt homes to cope with disability.

DOMICILIARY CARE AGENCY

This is an organisation which provides care assistants who go out to people's homes where they provide them with practical help. The help may involve housework, ironing, gardening, paperwork, shopping, driving, sitting with someone while their carer is occupied elsewhere and personal care, *which is defined below.* Some agencies specialise, such as in the provision of live-in care.

GUARANTEE PENSION CREDIT

This is the Guarantee element of Pension Credit. It tops up the weekly income of a man or woman who reaches the age at which a woman becomes entitled to her state pension to a set level, regardless of whether they have a

National Insurance contribution record. Apart from providing a guaranteed income, Guarantee Credit also provides eligibility to several other, valuable benefits, such as Housing Benefit at the maximum rate.

GUARDIAN

In Scotland, a local sheriff court can appoint someone who is not represented by an attorney and lacks mental capacity as their guardian, performing a similar role to a deputy in England and Wales *(see above)*.

MENTAL CAPACITY

Someone is said to lack mental capacity if they are unable to make a decision about a particular matter at the time the decision needs to be taken and this inability arises from an impairment in their brain. An assessment which concludes someone is mentally incapable of making a decision must be two-stage. On its own a diagnosis of dementia or other brain impairment is insufficient: there must be a second stage which shows that the person is unable to make that particular decision as a result of their brain impairment. Much more rarely, someone may be deemed to lack mental capacity if they are capable of making a decision but completely unable to convey their wishes, even through blinking. In Scotland, someone is also said to lack mental capacity if they are unable to retain the memory of a decision or to act upon it.

NHS CONTINUING HEALTHCARE

This is a type of funding provided by the NHS for the care of somebody with serious healthcare needs. It may be provided in an NHS unit, a nursing home, hospice or the patient's own home or that of a friend or relative. It covers the provision of healthcare by doctors, district nurses, specialist nurses and doctors, and other members of primary healthcare teams. But unusually (as social care is usually means-tested so wealthier people must pay for it), Continuing Healthcare also covers the provision of any social care services somebody needs, including practical help provided by care assistants, regardless of the recipient's financial means.

If NHS Continuing Healthcare is provided in a nursing home, the NHS pays the fees for accommodation, board and care in full.

NURSING HOME

A care home *(see above)* which provides nursing care and has at least one registered nurse on duty at all times is termed a nursing home.

PERSONAL BUDGET

If a social care authority decides that someone has needs for care and support which should be met, it works out how much money is needed to meet those needs; that sum is known as the person's personal budget. Social services then calculate the proportion the local authority will pay and the amount (if any) the recipient of care and support will pay.

PERSONAL CARE

This is usually considered to consist of help with any of the following activities: washing, mouth care, bathing, dressing, eating, drinking, using the toilet, managing continence and the care of skin, hair and nails. It also means prompting someone to carry out these tasks themselves and supervising them while doing so, if they are unable to decide to undertake them themselves. In Scotland the definition of personal care also includes help with moving around and the preparation of food.

PERSONAL HEALTH BUDGET

An NHS health organisation in England can give a patient or their representative a sum of money to buy the healthcare services it would otherwise have arranged on their behalf, thus giving them greater choice over the way the money allocated for their care is spent. These budgets are not used for routine aspects of care, such as GP appointments, but for the treatment of ongoing illnesses, palliative care and NHS Continuing Healthcare *(defined below)*. A budget might, for instance, fund fitness classes, physiotherapy, equipment, personal care and attendance at a day hospice, as well as treatment by doctors and nurses.

SELF-FUNDER

This is someone whose means rule them out of financial help from their social care authority. As self-funders have to contribute towards their social care costs, someone may hire domiciliary care or go into a care home as a self-funder, but in time their savings be depleted to a threshold below which social services must pick up the tab.

SOCIAL CARE

This is support usually provided or commissioned by local authorities in the form of information, advice, equipment and services (both in the home and outside it) to help people cope with practical and emotional needs. In older people, these needs usually arise from illness, disability, frailty, family issues, elder abuse, a learning disability, mental health problems, sight and/hearing difficulties, and acting as an unpaid carer. While, as a general rule, healthcare is free and social care means-tested, social care is often provided free or with a subsidy from the social care authority.

Useful contacts

AbilityNet
25 Angel Gate, Office 4,
London EC1V 2PT
Tel: 020 3714 8230
Helpline: 0800 269 545
abilitynet.org.uk

Abuse
If you have experienced or fear imminent abuse, phone the main social services department number of your local authority or, if out of office hours, its emergency duty team; the numbers should be in your telephone directory. Social services may make an immediate visit. Or you could make your first call to the police: they and social services should be working closely together in this field. For advice only you could ring Action on Elder Abuse's helpline (office hours) or The Silver Line.

Access NI
Tel: 0300 200 7888
nidirect.gov.uk

Action Against Medical Accidents
Christopher Wren Yard, 117 High Street, Croydon CR0 1QG
Tel: 020 8688 9555

Action for Blind People
105 Judd Street,
London WC1H 9NE
Tel: 0303 123 9999
rnib.org.uk

Action on Elder Abuse
PO Box 60001,
Streatham SW16 9BY
Tel: 020 8835 9280
Helpline: 0808 808 8141
elderabuse.org.uk

Action on Hearing Loss
1–3 Highbury Station Road,
London N1 1SE
Tel: 0207 359 4442
Textphone: 0207 296 8001
Helpline: 0808 808 0123;
Textphone: 0808 808 9000
SMS: 0780 0000 360
actiononhearingloss.org.uk

Advisory, Conciliation and Arbitration Service (ACAS)
Tel: 0300 123 1100
Textphone: 18001 0300 123 1100
acas.org.uk

Age Cymru
Tŷ John Pathy, 13–14 Neptune Court, Vanguard Way,
Cardiff CF24 5PJ
Tel: 029 2043 1555
Helpline: 0800 0223 444
ageuk.org.uk/cymru

Age NI
3 Lower Crescent,
Belfast BT7 1NR
Tel: 028 9024 5729
Helpline: 0808 808 7575
ageuk.org.uk/northern-ireland

Age Scotland
Causewayside House,
160 Causewayside,
Edinburgh EH9 1PR
Tel: 0333 32 32 400
Helpline: 0800 12 44 222
ageuk.org.uk/scotland

Age UK
Tavis House, 1–6 Tavistock Square, London WC1H 9NA
Tel: 0800 169 8787
Helpline: 0800 678 1174
ageuk.org.uk

Ageing Without Children
awoc.org

Almshouse Residents Action Group
justiceforalmshousevictims.org.uk

Alzheimer's Disease International
64 Great Suffolk Street,
London SE1 0BL
Tel: 020 7981 0880
alz.co.uk

Alzheimer Scotland
160 Dundee Street,
Edinburgh EH11 1DQ
Tel: 0131 243 1453
Helpline: 0808 808 3000
alzscot.org

Alzheimer's Society
58 St Katharine's Way,
London E1W 1LB
Tel: 020 7423 3500
Helpline: 0300 222 1122
alzheimers.org.uk

Alzheimer's Society Northern Ireland
Unit 4 Balmoral Business Park,
Boucher Crescent,
Belfast BT12 6HU
Tel: 028 9066 4100
Helpline: 0300 222 1122
alzheimers.org.uk

Alzheimer's Society Wales
16 Columbus Walk, Atlantic Wharf, Cardiff CF10 4BY
Tel: 0292 0480 593
Helpline: 0300 222 1122
alzheimers.org.uk

Animal Welfare Trust
Tyler's Way,
Watford Bypass WD25 8WT
Tel: 0208 950 0177
nawt.org.uk

Anxiety UK
Zion Community Centre,
339 Stretford Road, Hulme,
Manchester M15 4ZY
Tel: 0161 226 7727
Helpline: 0844 4775 744
Textphone: 0753 7416 905
anxietyuk.org.uk

Appeals Service Northern Ireland
12 Wellington Place,
Belfast BT2 7AQ
Tel: 028 9054 4000
courtsni.gov.uk/en-GB/Tribunals/
AppealsServices

Arthritis Care
Floor 4, Linen Court, 10 East
Road, London N1 6AD
Helpline: 0808 800 4050
arthritiscare.org.uk

Arthritis Research UK
Copeman House, St Mary's Court,
St Mary's Gate,
Chesterfield S41 7TD
Tel: 0800 5200 520
arthritisresearchuk.org

Association of British Dispensing Opticians
199 Gloucester Terrace,
London W2 6LD
Tel: 01227 733 905
abdo.org.uk

Association of British Introduction Agencies
Suite 109, 315 Chiswick High Rd,
London W4 4HH
Tel: 07919 612 975
abia.org.uk

Association of Retirement Housing Managers
c/o EAC, 3rd Floor, 89 Albert
Embankment, London SE1 7TP
Tel: 020 7463 0660
arhm.org

Association of Speech and Language Therapists
Speen,
Princes Riseborough HP27 0SZ
Tel: 01494 488 306
helpwithtalking.com

Automobile Association
Tel: 0800 316 3983
Textphone: 07860 027 999
theaa.com

Bladder and Bowel Foundation
SATRA Innovation Park,
Rockingham Road,
Kettering, Northants NN16 9JH
Tel: 01536 533 255
Helpline: 0845 345 0165
bladderandbowelfoundation.org

Blue Cross
Shilton Road, Burford OX18 4PF
Tel: 0300 777 1897
bluecross.org.uk

Board of Community Health Councils in Wales
3rd Floor, 33–35 Cathedral Road,
Cardiff CF11 9HB
Tel: 02920 235 558
wales.nhs.uk

British Association for Counselling and Psychotherapy
15 St John's Business Park,
Lutterworth,
Leicestershire LE17 4HB
Tel: 01455 883 300
Textphone: 01455 560 606
bacp.co.uk

British Association of Social Workers
16 Kent Street,
Birmingham B5 6RD
Tel: 0121 622 3911
basw.co.uk

British Bankers' Association
Pinners Hall, 105–108 Old Broad Street, London EC2N 1EX
Tel: 020 7216 8800
bba.org.uk

British Dental Association
64 Wimpole Street,
London W1G 8YS
Tel: 020 7935 0875
bda.org

British Dietetic Association
5th Floor, Charles House, 148–9 Great Charles Street, Queensway, Birmingham B3 3HT
Tel: 0121 200 8080
bda.uk.com

British Gas
PO Box 227, Rotherham S98 1PD
Tel: 0800 048 0202
Textphone: 18001 0800 072 8626
Emergencies: 0800 111 999
britishgas.co.uk

British Geriatrics Society
31 St John's Square,
London EC1M 4DN
Tel: 020 7608 1369
bgs.org.uk

British Heart Foundation
Greater London House,
180 Hampstead Road,
London NW1 7AW
Tel: 0300 330 3322
Textphone: 18001 020 7554 0000
bhf.org.uk

The British Medical Association
Tavistock Square,
London WC1H 9JP
Tel: 020 7387 4499
Helpline: 0300 123 1233
bma.org.uk

British Orthopaedic Association
35–43 Lincoln's Inn Fields,
London WC2A 3PE
Tel: 020 7405 6507
boa.ac.uk

British Psychological Society
48 Princess Road East,
Leicester LE1 7DR
Tel: 0116 254 9568
bps.org.uk

British Society of Gerontology
PO Box 2265,
Pulborough RH20 6BB
Tel: 01798 875 653
britishgerontology.org

British Standards Institute
389 Chiswick High Road,
London W4 4AL
Tel: 0345 080 9000
bsigroup.com

British Toilet Association
Enterprise House, 2–4 Balloo
Avenue, Bangor, County Down,
Northern Ireland BT19 7QT
Tel: 02891 477 397
btaloos.co.uk

Building Research Establishment
Bucknalls Lane,
Watford WD25 9XX
Tel: 01923 664 262
bre.co.uk

**Campaign Against Retirement
Leasehold Exploitation**
Tel: 07808 328 230
carlex.org.uk

Car Plus
Tel: 0113 410 5260
carplus.org.uk

Care and Repair Cymru
2 Ocean Way, Cardiff CF24 5TG
Tel: 029 2067 4830
careandrepair.org.uk

Care and Repair England
3 Hawksworth Street,
Nottingham NG3 2EG
Tel: 0115 950 6500
careandrepair-england.org.uk

Care and Repair Scotland
135 Buchanan Street,
Glasgow G1 2JA
Tel: 0141 221 9879
careandrepairsscotland.co.uk

Care Council for Wales
South Gate House, Wood Street,
Cardiff CF10 1EW
Tel: 0300 30 33 444
ccwales.org.uk
Information hub: ccwales.org.uk/
getting-in-on-the-act-hub

Care Inspectorate
11 Riverside Drive,
Dundee DD1 4NY
Tel: 0345 600 9527
careinspectorate.com

Care Quality Commission
Citygate, Gallowgate,
Newcastle upon Tyne NE1 4PA
Tel: 03000 616 161
cqc.org.uk

**Care and Social Services
Inspectorate Wales**
Welsh Government office,
Rhydycar Business Park,
Merthyr Tydfil CF48 1UZ
Tel: 0300 7900 126
cssiw.gov.wales

Careers Service Northern Ireland
56 Ann Street, Belfast BT1 4EG
Tel: 0300 200 7820
nidirect.gov.uk/contacts/contacts-
az/careers-service

Careers Wales
Unit 1, Brecon Close, William
Browne Close, Llantarnam Park,
Cwmbran, Torfaen NP44 3AB
Tel: 0800 028 4844
Textphone: 0800 0029 489
careerswales.com

Carers Northern Ireland
58 Howard Street, Belfast BT1 6JP
Tel: 02890 439 843
carersuk.org

Carers Scotland
21 Pearce Street,
Glasgow G51 3UT
Tel: 0141 445 3070
carersuk.org

Carers Trust
32–36 Loman Street,
London SE1 0EH
Tel: 0300 772 9600
carers.org

Carers UK
20 Great Dover Street,
London SE1 4LX
Tel: 020 7378 4999
carersuk.org

Carers Wales
River House, Ynys Bridge Court,
Cardiff CF15 9SS
Tel: 029 2081 1370
carersuk.org

Carry on Gardening
The Geoffrey Udall Centre,
Beech Hill, Reading RG7 2AT
Tel: 0118 988 5688
carryongardening.org.uk

Cats Protection
Chelwood Gate,
Haywards Heath RH17 7TT
Tel: 01825 741 330
cats.org.uk

CAUSE
Leslie Office Park, 393 Holywood
Road, Belfast BT4 2LS
Tel: 028 90 650650
Helpline: 0845 60 30 29 1
cause.org.uk

Central Services Agency
2 Franklin Street,
Belfast BT2 8DQ
Tel: 028 9032 4431
centralservicesagency.com

**Centre for Accessible
Environments**
Holyer House, 20–21 Red Lion
Court, London EC4A 3EB
Tel: 020 7822 8232
cae.org.uk

Centre for Policy on Ageing
Tavis House, 1–6 Tavistock
Square, London WC1H 9NA
Tel: 020 7553 6500
cpa.org.uk

Chambers and Partners
39–41 Parker Street
London WC2B 5PQ
Tel: 020 7606 8844
chambersandpartners.com

Chartered Institute of Housing
Octavia House, Westwood Way,
Coventry CV4 8JP
Tel: 024 7685 1713
cih.org

Chartered Society of Physiotherapy
14 Bedford Row,
London WC1R 4ED
Tel: 020 7306 6666
csp.org.uk

Chest, Heart and Stroke Scotland
Rosebery House, 9 Haymarket Terrace, Edinburgh EH12 5EZ
Tel: 0131 225 6963
Helpline: 0808 801 0899
chss.org.uk

Child Poverty Action Group
30 Micawber Street,
London N1 7TB
Tel: 020 7837 7979
cpag.org.uk

Christians Against Poverty
Jubilee Mill, North Street,
Bradford BD1 4EW
Tel: 01274 760 720
capuk.org

Christians on Ageing
'Stoneway', Hornby Road,
Appleton Wiske,
Northallerton DL6 2AF
Tel: 01609 881 408
christiansonageing.org.uk

Chartered Institute of Library and Information Professionals
7 Ridgmount Street,
London WC1E 7AE
Tel: 020 7255 0500
cilip.org.uk

Cinnamon Trust
10 Market Square, Hayle,
Cornwall TR27 4HE
Tel: 01736 757900
cinnamon.org.uk

Citizens Advice
Contact your local office.
Adviceline
For England: 03444 111 444
For Wales: 03444 77 20 20
TextRelay: 03444 111 445
For Northern Ireland: 0300 123 3233
Consumer inquiries
Helpline: 03454 04 05 06
Textphone: 18001 03454 04 05 06
Welsh-speaking phone:
03454 04 05 05
Welsh-speaking textphone:
18001 03454 04 05 05

Letters about post or energy problems only
Citizens Advice consumer service
2nd Floor, Fairfax House,
Merrion Street, Leeds LS2 8JU
citizensadvice.org.uk

Citizens Advice Scotland
Tel: 0808 800 9060
cas.org.uk

Civil Aviation Authority
45–59 Kingsway,
London WC2B 6TE
Tel: 01293 567 171
caa.co.uk

Civil Legal Advice
Tel: 0345 345 4345
Textphone: 0345 609 6677
gov.uk/civil-legal-advice

College of Health Care Chaplains
128 Theobald's Road,
London WC1X 8TN
Tel: 020 3371 2004
healthcarechaplains.org

College of Occupational Therapists
106–114 Borough High Street,
London SE1 1LB
Tel: 020 7357 6480
cot.co.uk

College of Optometrists
42 Craven Street,
London WC2N 5NG
Tel: 020 7839 6000
college-optometrists.org

College of Podiatry
207 Providence Sq, Mill Street,
London SE1 2EW
Tel: 020 7234 8620
scpod.org

College of Sexual and Relationship Therapists
PO Box 13686,
London SW20 9ZH
Tel: 020 8543 270
cosrt.org.uk

Compassion in Dying
181 Oxford Street,
London W1D 2JT
Tel: 020 7479 7731
Helpline: 0800 999 2434
compassionindying.org.uk

Conquest Art
Office 92, Trident Court,
1 Oakcroft Road, Surbiton,
Chessington KT9 1RH
Tel: 020 3044 2731
conquestart.org

Consumer Council for Northern Ireland
Floor 3, Seatem House, 28–32
Alfred Street, Belfast BT2 8EN
Tel: 028 9025 1600
Textphone: 028 9025 1600
consumercouncil.org.uk

Contact the Elderly
2 Grosvenor Gardens,
London SW1W 0DH
Tel: 0207 240 0630
Helpline: 0800 716543
contact-the-elderly.org.uk

Continence Foundation
Hatton Square, 16 Baldwins
Gardens, London EC1N 7RJ
Tel: 020 7404 6875
continence-foundation.org.uk

Convention of Scottish Local Authorities
Verity House, 19 Haymarket
Yards, Edinburgh EH12 5BH
Tel: 0131 474 9200
cosla.gov.uk

Countryside Mobility
Living Options Devon, Ground
Floor Units, 3–4 Cranmere Court,
Lustleigh Close, Matford Business
Park, Exeter, Devon EX2 8PD
Tel: 01392 459 222
countrysidemobility.org

Court of Protection

PO Box 70185, First Avenue
House, 42–49 High Holborn,
London WC1A 9JA
Tel: 0300 456 4600
gov.uk/courts-tribunals/court-of-
protection

Crossroads: Caring for Carers

7 Regent Street,
Newtownards BT23 4AB
Tel: 028 9181 4455
crossroadscare.co.uk

Crown Prosecution Service

Rose Court, 2 Southwark Bridge,
London SE1 9HS
Tel: 020 3357 0899
cps.gov.uk

Cruse Bereavement Care

Unit 01, One Victoria Villas,
Richmond TW9 2GW
Helpline: 0844 477 9400
crusebereavementcare.org.uk

Debt Advice Foundation

Tel: 0800 043 40 50
debtadvicefoundation.org

Dementia Engagement and Empowerment Project

Tel: 01392 420 076
dementiavoices.org.uk

Dementia Services Development Centre

Iris Murdoch Building,
Stirling FK9 4LAl
Tel: 01786 467 740
dementia.stir.ac.uk

Dental Complaints Service

Stephenson House, 2 Cherry
Orchard Road, Croydon CR0 6BA
Tel: 020 8253 0800
gdc-uk.org

Department for Transport

33 Horseferry Road,
London SW1P 4DR
Tel: 0300 330 3000
gov.uk/government/organisations/
department-for-transport

Department for Work and Pensions

(DWP) Caxton House, Tothill
Street, London SW1H 9NA

Benefits Helplines
Attendance Allowance
Tel: 0345 605 6055; Textphone:
0345 604 5312

*Benefit Enquiry Helpline
Northern Ireland*
Tel: 0800 220 674
Textphone: 028 9031 1092

Bereavement benefits
Tel: 0345 608 8601
Textphone: 0345 608 8551

Carers Allowance
Tel: 0345 608 4321
Textphone: 0345 604 5312

Disability Living Allowance
Tel: 0345 605 6055
Textphone: 0345 604 5312

*Employment and Support
Allowance*
Tel: 0800 055 6688
Textphone: 0800 023 4888
Welsh-speaking: 0800 012 1888

NHS Low Income Scheme
152 Pilgrim Street,
Newcastle-upon-Tyne NE1 6SN
Tel: 0300 330 1343
or 0191 279 0565
Textphone: 18001 0300 330 1343

Pension Credit
Tel: 0800 99 1234
Textphone: 0800 169 0133

Pensions
Tel: 0345 606 0265
Textphone : 0345 606 0285
To claim state pension:
Tel: 0800 731 7898
Textphone 0800 731 7339
For online technical help:
Tel: 0345 604 3349
Textphone: 0345 604 3412
To find out the size of your pension:
Tel: 0345 300 0168
Textphone: 0345 3000 169

Personal Independence Payment
Tel: 0345 850 3322
Textphone: 0345 601 6677

Universal Credit
Tel: 0345 600 0723
Textphone: 0345 600 0743

Winter Fuel Payments Centre
Tel: 03459 15 15 15
Textphone: 0345 606 0285

Department of Communities and Local Government
2 Marsham Street,
London SW1P 4DF
Tel: 0303 444 0000
gov.uk

Department of Health
Richmond House, 79 Whitehall,
London SW1A 2NS
Tel: 020 7210 4850
Textphone: 0207 451 7965
gov.uk/government/organisations/
department-of-health

Department of Health Publications
PO Box 777, London SE1 6XH
Tel: 0300 123 1002
Textphone: 0300 123 1003

Department of Health, Social Services and Public Safety, Northern Ireland Executive
Castle Buildings, Stormont,
Belfast BT4 3SJ
Tel: 028 9052 0500
health-ni.gov.uk

Depression Alliance
9 Woburn Walk,
London WC1H 0JE
Tel: 0207 407 7584
depressionalliance.org

Diabetes UK
10 Parkway, London NW1 7AA
Tel: 0345 123 2399
Helpline: 0345 123 2399
diabetes.org.uk

Disability Action
Portside Business Park 189 Airport Road West, Belfast BT3 0ED
Tel: 028 9029 7880
Textphone: 028 9029 78822
disabilityaction.org

Disabled Living Foundation
34 Chatfield Road,
London SW11 3SE
Tel: 020 7289 6111
Helpline: 0300 999 0004
dlf.org.uk

Disabled Motorists Federation
Volunteers' Centre,
Clarence Terrace,
Chester-le-Street DH3 3DQ
Tel: 0191 416 3172
dmfed.org.uk

Disabled Persons Railcard Office
PO Box 6613,
Arbroath DD11 9AN
Tel: 0345 605 0525
Textphone: 0345 601 0132
disabledpersons-railcard.co.uk

Disabled Persons Transport Advisory Committee
c/o Department for Transport,
Great Minster House,
33 Horseferry Road,
London SW1P 4DR
Tel: 020 7944 6441

Disabled Ramblers
14 Belmont Park Road,
Maidenhead SL6 6HT
Tel: 01628 621 414
disabledramblers.co.uk

DisabledGo
Unit 7, Arlington Court,
Arlington Business Park,
Stevenage SG1 2FS
Tel: 01438 842 710
disabledgo.com

Disability Rights UK
Ground Floor, CAN Mezzanine,
49–51 East Rd, London N1 6AH
Tel: 020 7250 8181
disabilityrightsuk.org

Disclosure and Barring Service
PO Box 3961,
Royal Wootton Bassett SN4 4HF
Helpline: 03000 200 190
Textphone: 03000 200 192
In Welsh: 03000 200 191
From abroad: 44 151 676 9390
gov.uk/government/organisations/
disclosure-and-barring-service

Disclosure Scotland
PO Box 250, Glasgow G51 1YU
Helpline: 0300 0200 040
disclosurescotland.co.uk

Dogs Trust
17 Wakley Street,
London EC1V 7RQ
Tel: 020 7837 0006
dogstrust.org.uk

DVLA (Drivers and Vehicles Licensing Authority)
Swansea SA6 7JL
Tel: 0300 790 6806
dvla.gov.uk

Dying Matters
34–44 Britannia Street,
London WC1X 9JG
Tel: 0800 021 4466
dyingmatters.org

The Eaga Trust
25 Main Street, Ponteland,
Northumberland NE20 9NH
Tel: 07887 415 388
eagatrust.com

Elderly Accommodation Counsel
3rd Floor, 89 Albert Embankment,
London SE1 7TP
Tel: 020 7820 1343
Helpline: 0800 377 7070
eac.org.uk

Energy Saving Trust
21 Dartmouth Street,
London SW1H 9BP
Tel: 0300 123 1234
energysavingtrust.org.uk

Energy Watch UK
1C Mitre Court, Lichfield Road,
Sutton Coldfield B74 2LZ
Tel: 0121 354 7676
energywatchuk.com

Equality and Advisory Support Service
Freepost FPN 4431
Tel: 0808 800 0082
Textphone: 0808 800 0084
equalityadvisoryservice.com

Equality and Human Rights Commission
Fleetbank House, 2–6 Salisbury Square, London EC4Y 8JX
Tel: 020 7832 7800
Helpline: 0808 800 0082
Textphone: 0808 800 0084
equalityhumanrights.com

Equity Release Council
3rd Floor, Bush House,
North West Wing, Aldwych,
London WC2B 4PJ
Tel: 0844 669 7085
equityreleasecouncil.com

Euan's Guide
29 Constitution Street,
Edinburgh EH6 7BS
Tel: 0131 510 5106
euansguide.com

Experience Community
Tel: 07958 591 841
experiencecommunity.co.uk

Extend
2 Place Farm, Wheathampstead,
Hertfordshire AL4 8SB
Tel: 01582 832 760
extend.org.uk

Fieldfare Trust
7 Volunteer House, 69 Crossgate,
Cupar, Fife KY15 5AS
Tel: 01334 657 708
fieldfare.org.uk

Financial Conduct Authority
25 North Colonnade,
London E14 5HS
Tel: 020 7676 1000
Helpline: 0800 111 6768 / 0300 500 8082
fsa.gov.uk

Firststop Care Advice
3rd Floor, 89 Albert Embankment,
London SE1 7TP
Tel: 0203 519 6002
Helpline: 0800 377 7070
firststopcareadvice.org.uk

Fish Insurance
12 Sceptre Court, Sceptre Way,
Bamber Bridge, Preston PR5 6AW
Tel: 0333 331 3770
fishinsurance.co.uk

Fitness League
14 Graylands Estate,
Langhurstwood Road, Horsham,
West Sussex RH12 4QD
Tel: 01403 266 000
thefitnessleague.com

Fold Housing Association
3 Redburn Square, Hollywood,
County Down BT18 9HZ
Tel: 028 9042 8314
foldgroup.co.uk

Foundations
The Old Co-op Building,
11 Railway Street, Glossop,
Derbyshire SK13 7AG
Tel: 0300 124 0315
foundations.uk.com

Friends of the Elderly
40–42 Ebury Street,
London SW1W 0LZ
Tel: 020 7730 8263
fote.org.uk

Future Pension Centre
Tel: 0345 3000 168
Textphone: 0345 3000 169
gov.uk/future-pension-centre

Gardening for the Disabled
PO Box 285,
Tunbridge Wells, Kent TN2 9JD
gardeningforthedisabledtrust.org.uk

General Dental Council
37 Wimpole Street,
London W1G 8DQ
Tel: 020 7887 3800
Helpline: 0845 222 4141
gdc-uk.org

General Medical Council
3 Hardman Street,
Manchester M3 3AW
Tel: 0161 923 6602
gmc-uk.org

General Optical Council
10 Old Bailey,
London EC4M 7NG
Tel: 020 7580 3898
optical.org

General Pharmaceutical Council
25 Canada Square,
London E14 5LQ
Tel: 020 3713 8000
pharmacyregulation.org

Gold Standards Framework Centre
Victoria Mews,
8–9 St Austin's Friars,
Shrewsbury, Shropshire SY1 1RY
Tel: 01743 291 891
goldstandardsframework.org.uk

Good Care Group
The Tower Building, York Road,
London SE1 7NQ
Tel: 020 3728 7575
thegoodcaregroup.com

Gransnet
gransnet.com

Health and Care Professions Council England
Park House, 184 Kennington Park
Road, London SE11 4BU
Tel: 0300 500 6184
hcpc-uk.co.uk

Health and Safety Executive
Redgrave Court, Merton Road,
Bootle, Merseyside L20 7HS
Tel: 0151 922 9235
Helpline: 0300 003 1747
hse.gov.uk

**Health and Social Care
Information Centre**
Tel: 0300 303 5678
content.digital.nhs

Health Education England
1st Floor, Blenheim House,
Duncombe Street, Leeds LS1 4PL
Tel: 0113 295 2155
hee.nhs.uk

**Healthcare Improvement
Scotland**
1 South Gyle Crescent,
Edinburgh EH12 9EB
Tel: 0131 623 4300
healthcareimprovementscotland.org

Health Inspectorate Wales
Welsh Government,
Rhydycar Business Park,
Merthyr Tydfil CF48 1UZ
Tel: 0300 062 8163
hiw.org.uk

Healthwatch
National Customer Service Centre,
Citygate, Gallowgate,
Newcastle upon Tyne NE1 4PA
Tel: 03000 683 000
healthwatch.co.uk

Help my Mobility
PO Box 312, Lymington, Hants
Helpline: 0845 838 7085
Tel: 020 3137 5857
help-my-mobility.org

**Her Majesty's Courts and
Tribunal Service**
102 Petty France,
London SW1H 9AJ
Tel: 020 3334 3555
gov.uk/government/organisations/
hm-courts-and-tribunals-service

**Her Majesty's Revenue and
Customs (HMRC) New
Employer Helpline**
Tel: 0300 200 3211
Textphone: 0300 200 3212

**HMRC Employer Enquiries and
Support**
Customer Operations Employer
Office, BP4009,
Chillingham House,
Benton Park View NE98 1ZZ
Tel: 08457 143 143
Textphone: 0845 602 1380
hmrc.gov.uk

Home Energy Scotland
Tel: 0808 808 2282
energysavingtrust.org.uk

Homeshare
11 Divinity Road,
Oxford OX4 1LH
Tel: 01865 497 095
homeshare.org

Hospice UK
34–44 Britannia Street,
London WC1X 9JG
Tel: 020 7520 8200
hospice.org.uk

Housing Ombudsman Service
81 Aldwych, London WC2B 4HN
Tel: 0300 111 3000
housing-ombudsman.org.uk

IBS Network
14 Knutton Road,
Sheffield S5 9NU
Tel: 0114 272 3253
theibsnetwork.org

Inclusive Mobility and Transport Advisory Committee for Northern Ireland
Enterprise House, 55–59 Adelaide Street, Belfast BT2 8FE
Tel: 028 9072 6020
Textphone: 028 9072 6020
imtac.org.uk

Independent Age
6 Avonmore Road,
London W14 8RL
Tel: 020 7605 4200
Helpline: 0800 319 6789
independentage.org

Information Commissioner's Office
Wycliffe House, Water Lane,
Wilmslow, Cheshire SK9 5AF
Helpline: 0303 123 1113
Tel: 01625 545 745
Textphone: 01625 545 860
ico.org.uk

Inspire
Lombard House, 10–20 Lombard Street, Belfast BT1 1RD
Tel: 028 9032 8474
inspirewellbeing.org

Institute for Fiscal Studies
7 Ridgmount St,
London WC1E 7AE
Tel: 020 7291 4800
ifs.org.uk

International Longevity Centre
11 Tufton St, London SW1P 3QB
Tel: 020 7340 0440
ilcuk.org.uk

Irish Advocacy Network Northern Ireland Office
Knockbracken Healthcare Park,
Saintfield Road, Belfast BT8 8BH
Tel: 028 9079 8849
irishadvocacynetwork.com

Jewish Care
221 Golders Green Road,
Colindale, London NW11 9DQ
Tel: 020 8905 5229
Helpline: 020 8922 2222
jewishcare.org

King's Fund
11–13 Cavendish Square,
London W1G 0AN
Tel: 020 7307 2400
kingsfund.org.uk

Kingston Centre for Independent Living
31–35 High Street,
Kingston-upon-Thames KT1 1LF
Tel: 020 8546 9603
kcil.org.uk

Land and Property Services Agency
Clare House, 303 Airport Road,
Belfast BT3 9ED
Tel: 028 9081 6000
finance-ni.gov.uk

Law Society of England and Wales
113 Chancery Lane,
London WC2A 1PL
Tel: 020 7242 1222
lawsociety.org.uk

Law Society of Northern Ireland
96 Victoria Street,
Belfast BT1 3GN
Tel: 028 9023 1614
lawsoc-ni.org

Law Society of Scotland
Atria One, 144 Morrison Street,
Edinburgh EH3 8EX
Tel: 0131 226 7411
lawscot.org.uk

Legal Aid Agency
Unit B8, Berkley Way,
Viking Business Park, Jarrow,
South Tyneside NE31 1SF
Tel: 0300 200 2020
gov.uk/government/organisations/
legal-aid-agency

Lifetime Homes
Holyer House, 20–21 Red Lion
Court, London EC4A 3EB
Tel: 020 7822 8700
lifetimehomes.org.uk

Live-in Homecare Information Hub
stayinmyhome.co.uk

Living Streets
Floor 4, Universal House,
88–94 Wentworth Street,
London E1 7SA
Tel: 020 7377 4900
livingstreets.org.uk

Local Government Ombudsman England
PO Box 4771,
Coventry CV4 0EH
Tel: 0300 061 0614
lgo.org.uk

Local Government Ombudsman Wales
1 Ffordd yr Hen Gae,
Pencoed CF35 5LJ
Tel: 0300 790 0203
ombudsman-wales.org.uk

London Underground Customer Services
Tel: 0343 222 1234
tfl.gov.uk

Macmillan Cancer Support
89 Albert Embankment,
London SE1 7UQ
Tel: 020 7840 7840
Helpline: 0808 808 00 00
macmillan.org.uk

Macular Disease Society
Crown Chambers, South St,
Andover, Hampshire SP10 2BN
Tel: 01264 350 551
Helpline: 0300 3030 111
macularsociety.org

Marie Curie Care and Support through Terminal Illness
89 Albert Embankment,
London SE1 7TP
Tel: 020 7599 7777
Helpline: 0800 090 2309
mariecurie.org.uk

Marion Shoard
P.O. Box 664, Rochester, ME1 9JB
marionshoard.co.uk

Mark Bates Ltd
Premier House,
Londonthorpe Road,
Grantham, Lincs NG31 9SN
Tel: 01476 512 190
markbatesltd.com

Mencap
123 Golden Lane,
London EC1Y 0RT
Tel: 020 7454 0454
Helpline: 0808 808 1111
mencap.org.uk

Mencap Northern Ireland
4 Annadale Avenue,
Belfast BT7 3JH
Tel: 028 9049 2666
Helpline: 0808 808 1111
mencap.org.uk

Mental Health Foundation
Colechurch House, 1 London
Bridge Walk, London SE1 2SX
Tel: 020 7803 1100
mentalhealth.org.uk

Mental Welfare Commission for Scotland
Thistle House, 91 Haymarket
Terrace, Edinburgh EH12 5HE
Tel: 0131 313 8777
Helpline: 0800 389 6809
mwcscot.org.uk

Mind
15–19 Broadway, Stratford,
London E15 4BQ
Helpline: 0300 123 3393
Tel: 020 8519 2122
mind.org.uk

Mobility and Access Committee for Scotland
Tel: 0131 244 0848

Mobility and Support Information Service
20 Burton Close, Telford TF4 2BX
Tel: 07774 405 734
masis.org.uk

Money Advice Service
120 Holborn, London EC1N 2TD
Tel: 0800 138 7777
themoneyadviceservice.org.uk

Motability
City Gate House, 22 Southwark
Bridge Road, London SE1 9HB
Tel: 0300 456 4566
Textphone: 0300 037 0100
motability.co.uk

Multiple Sclerosis Society
372 Edgware Road,
London NW2 6ND
Tel: 0808 800 8000
mssociety.org.uk

National Association for Providers of Activities for Older People
Unit 5.12, 71 Bondway,
London SW8 1SQ
Tel: 020 7078 9375
napa-activities.co.uk

National Audit Office
157–197 Buckingham Palace
Road, London SW1W 9SP
Tel: 020 7798 7264
nao.org.uk

National Careers Service
PO Box 1331,
Newcastle upon Tyne NE99 5EB
Tel: 0800 100 900
Textphone: 0800 0968 336
nationalcareersservice.direct.gov.uk

National Debt Helpline
Tel: 0808 808 4000
nationaldebtline.org

National Federation of Shopmobility
2–4 Meadow Close,
Ise Valley Industrial Estate,
Wellingborough NN8 4BH
Tel: 01933 229 644
shopmobilityuk.org

National Federation of Women's Institutes
104 New Kings Road,
London SW6 4LY
Tel: 020 7371 9300
thewi.org.uk

National Institute for Health and Care Excellence
10 Spring Gardens,
London SW1A 2BU
Tel: 0300 323 0140
nice.org.uk

National Kidney Federation
The Point, Coach Road, Shireoaks,
Worksop, Notts S81 8BW
Tel: 0845 601 0209
kidney.org.uk

National Mental Capacity Forum
Social Care Institute for
Excellence, First floor,
Kinnaird House, 1 Pall Mall East,
London SW1Y 5BP
Tel: 020 7766 7400
scie.org.uk

National Osteoporosis Society
Camerton, Bath BA2 0PJ
Tel: 01761 471 771
Helpline: 0808 800 0035
nos.org.uk

National Pensioners Convention
10 Melton Street,
London NW1 2EJ
Tel: 020 7383 0388
npcuk.org

National Rail Enquiries
Freepost RSEH-TBGE-HBJJ,
Plymouth PL4 6AB
Tel: 08457 48 49 50
Textphone: 0845 605 0600
nationalrail.co.uk

National Trust
Heelis, Kemple Drive,
Swindon SN2 2NA
Tel: 0344 800 1895
nationaltrust.org.uk

Natural England
County Hall, Spetchley Road,
Worcester WR5 2NP
Tel: 0300 060 3900
gov.uk/government/organisations/
natural-england

Natural Resources Wales
Ty Cambria, 29 Newport Road,
Cardiff CF24 0TP
Tel: 0300 065 3000
naturalresources.wales

Nest (Welsh Government Warm Homes Scheme)
Innova One,
Tredegar Business Park NP22 3EL
Tel: 0800 294 1945
nestwales.org.uk

Next Generation Text Service
Tel: 0800 7311 888
Textphone: 0800 500 888
ngts.org.uk

NHS 24 (Scotland)
Helpline: 111
Information line: 0800 22 44 88
Switchboard: 0141 337 4501
nhs24.com

NHS 111
Tel: 111
Textphone: 18001 111
nhs.uk/111

NHS Improvement
Tel: 0300 123 2257
improvement.nhs.uk

NHS Wheelchair Service
Tel: 111
wheelchairmanagers.nhs.uk

Northern Ireland Association for Mental Health
80 University Street,
Belfast BT7 1HE
Tel: 028 9032 8474
niamhwellbeing.org

Northern Ireland Chest, Heart and Stroke
21 Dublin Road, Belfast BT2 7HB
Tel: 028 9032 0184
nichs.org.uk

Northern Ireland Executive
Stormont Castle, Belfast BT4 3TT
Tel: 028 9052 8400
northernireland.gov.uk

Northern Ireland Housing Executive
The Housing Centre,
2 Adelaide St, Belfast BT2 8PB
Tel: 0344 892 0900
Helpline: 03448 920 900
Textphone: 18001 03448 920 900
nihe.gov.uk

Northern Ireland Pensioners Parliament
Age Sector Platform,
Merrion Business Centre,
58 Howard Street, Belfast BT1 6PJ
Tel: 028 9031 2089
agesectorplatform.org

Northern Ireland Social Care Council
7th Floor Millennium House,
19–25 Great Victoria Street,
Belfast BT2 7AQ
Tel: 028 9536 2600
niscc.info

Nursing and Midwifery Council
23 Portland Place,
London W1N 3AF
Tel: 020 7637 7181
nmc.org.uk

Office for Gas and Electricity Markets (Ofgem)
Tel: 020 7901 7295
ofgem.gov.uk

Office for the Ombudsman of Northern Ireland
33 Wellington Place,
Belfast BT1 6HN
Helpline: 0800 34 34 24
Tel: 02890 233821
Textphone: 028 90897789
ni-ombudsman.org.uk

Office of Care and Protection
The Royal Courts of Justice,
Chichester Street, Belfast BT1 3JF
Tel: 028 9072 4733
nidirect.gov.uk

Office of Fair Trading
Fleetbank House, 2–6 Salisbury Square, London EC4Y 8JX
Tel: 0845 722 4499
gov.uk/government/organisations/office-of-fair-trading

Office of the Public Guardian England and Wales
PO Box 16185,
Birmingham B2 2WH
Tel: 0300 456 0300
Textphone: 0115 934 2778
gov.uk/government/organisations/office-of-the-public-guardian

Office of the Public Guardian Scotland
Hadrian House, Callendar Road,
Falkirk FK1 1XR
Tel: 01324 678 300
publicguardian-scotland.gov.uk

Open Britain
Tourism for All UK,
7A Pixel Mill, 44 Appleby Road,
Kendal, Cumbria LA9 6ES
Tel: 0845 124 9971
openbritain.net

Our Organisation Makes People Happy!
2nd Floor, Admel House,
24 High Street, Wimbledon,
London SW19 5DX
Tel: 020 3601 6363
Helpline: 0845 689 0066
oomph-wellness.org

Outdoor Swimming Society
Tel: 01865 770 381
outdoorswimmingsociety.com

Overseas Healthcare Team
Tel: 0191 218 1999

Parkinson's Disease Society UK
215 Vauxhall Bridge Road,
London SW1V 1EJ
Tel: 020 7931 8080
Helpline: 0808 800 0303
Textphone: 18001 0808 800 0303
parkinsons.org.uk

Parliamentary and Health Services Ombudsman
Millbank Tower, 30 Millbank,
London SW1P 4QP
Tel: 0345 015 4033
Textphone: 0300 061 4298
ombudsman.org.uk

PALS
Tel: 111 for the address and phone number of your local office.

PASS
cas.org.uk/pass
Contact your local Citizens Advice for details of your local service.

Patient and Client Council
1st Floor, Ormeau Baths, 18
Ormeau Avenue, Belfast BT2 8HS
Tel: 0800 917 0222
Textphone: 028 9032 1285
patientclientcouncil.hscni.net

Patients Association
PO Box 935,
Harrow, Middlesex HA1 3YJ
Tel: 020 8423 9111
Helpline: 0845 608 4455
patients-association.com

Pension Wise
PO Box 10404, Ashby de la
Zouch, Leicestershire LE65 9EH
pensionwise.gov.uk

Pensions Advisory Service
11 Belgrave Road,
London SW1V 2RB
Helpline: 0300 123 1047
For women
Tel: 0345 600 0806
For self-employed
Tel: 0345 602 7021
gov.uk/pensions-advisory-service

Pensions Ombudsman Service
11 Belgrave Road,
London SW1V 1RB
Tel: 020 7630 2200
pensions-ombudsman.org.uk

People's Dispensary for Sick Animals
Whitechapel Way,
Telford, Shropshire TF2 9PQ
Tel: 01952 290 999
Helpline: 0800 731 2502
pdsa.org.uk

Pets as Therapy
Clare Charity Centre,
Wycombe Road, Saunderton,
High Wycombe HP14 4BF
Tel: 01494 569 130
petsastherapy.org

Playlist for Life
Touchbase Glasgow, 43 Middlesex
Street, Glasgow G41 1EE
Tel: 0141 418 7184
playlistforlife.org.uk

Policy Research Institute on Ageing and Ethnicity
1st Floor Abbey House, 270–272 Lever Street, Bolton BL3 6PD
Tel: 01204 386 305
priae.org

Professional Standards Authority
157–197 Buckingham Palace Road, London SW1W 9SP
Tel: 020 7389 8040
professionalstandards.org.uk

Public Law Project
150 Caledonian Road, London N1 9RD
Tel: 020 7843 1260
publiclawproject.org.uk

Public Services Ombudsman for Wales
1 Ffordd yr Hen Gae, Pencoed CF35 5LJ
Tel: 0300 790 0203
ombudsman-wales.org.uk

Red Cross Society
44 Moorfields, London EC2Y 9AL
Tel: 0344 871 11 11
Textphone: 020 7562 2050
redcross.org.uk

Regulation and Quality Improvement Authority
9th Floor Riverside Tower, 5 Lanyon Place, Belfast BT1 3BT
Tel: 028 9051 7500
rqia.org.uk

Relate
Premier House, Carolina Court, Lakeside, Doncaster DN4 5RA
Tel: 0300 100 1234
relate.org.uk

Relatives and Residents Association
1 The Ivories, 6–18 Northampton Street, London N1 2HY
Tel: 020 7359 8148
Helpline: 020 7359 8136
relres.org

Rica
Unit G03, The Wenlock Business Centre, 50–52 Wharf Road, London N1 7EU
Tel: 020 7427 2460
Textphone: 020 7427 2469
rica.org.uk

Royal British Legion
199 Borough High Street, London SE1 1AA
Tel: 020 3207 2100
Helpline: 0808 802 8080
britishlegion.org.uk

Royal College of General Practitioners
30 Euston Square, London NW1 2FB
Tel: 020 3188 7400
rcgp.org.uk

Royal College of Nursing
20 Cavendish Square, London W1G 0RN
Tel: 020 7409 3333
rcn.org.uk

Royal College of Physicians
11 St Andrew's Place,
Regent's Park, London NW1 4LE
Tel: 020 3075 1649
rcplondon.ac.uk

Royal College of Speech and Language Therapists
2 White Hart Yard,
London SE1 1NX
Tel: 020 7378 1200
rcslt.org

Royal College of Surgeons
35–43 Lincoln's Inn Fields,
London WC2A 3PE
Tel: 020 7405 3474
rcseng.ac.uk

Royal National Institute of Blind People
105 Judd Street,
London WC1H 9NE
Tel: 0303 123 9999
rnib.org.uk

Royal Society for the Prevention of Cruelty to Animals
Wilberforce Way, Horsham,
West Sussex RH13 7WN
Tel: 0300 1234 555
rspca.org.uk

Royal Voluntary Service
Beck Court, Cardiff Gate Business Park, Cardiff CF23 8RP
Helpline: 0845 608 0122
royalvoluntaryservice.org.uk

Sage Traveling
3319 Stoney Brook Drive,
Houston, Texas, 77063 USA
Tel: 020 3540 6155
sagetraveling.com

Samaritans
Helpline: 116 123
samaritans.org

Scientific Advisory Committee on Nutrition in Britain
Public Health England, 2nd Floor
Skipton House, 80 London Road,
London SE1 6LH
Tel: 020 7654 8400
sacn.gov.uk

Scottish Association for Mental Health
Brunswick House, 51 Wilson Street, Glasgow G1 1UZ
Tel: 0141 530 1000
samh.org.uk

Scottish Social Services Council
Compass House, 11 Riverside Drive, Dundee DD1 4NY
Tel: 0345 60 30 891
sssc.uk.com

Scottish Government
St Andrew's House, Regent Road,
Edinburgh EH1 3DG
Tel: 0131 244 2529
Helpline: 0300 244 4000
gov.scot

Scottish Government Justice Directorate
Area 2W, St Andrew's House,
Regent Road,
Edinburgh EH1 3DG
Tel: 0131 244 3581
gov.scot

Scottish Government Publications
BookSource, 50 Cambuslang
Road, Cambuslang Investment
Park, Glasgow G32 8NB
Tel: 0845 370 0067
booksource.net

Scottish Helpline for Older People
Motherwell, Lanarkshire
Tel: 0845 125 9732

Scottish Independent Advocacy Alliance
Mansfield Traquair Centre,
15 Mansfield Place,
Edinburgh EH3 6BB
Tel: 0131 524 1975
siaa.org.uk

Scottish Intercollegiate Guidelines Network
8–10 Hillside Crescent,
Edinburgh EH7 5EA
Tel. 0131 623 4720
sign.ac.uk

Scottish Older People's Assembly
Hayweight House, 4th Floor,
23 Lauriston Street,
Edinburgh EH3 9DQ
Tel: 0131 281 0875
scotopa.org.uk

Scottish Natural Heritage
Leachkin Road,
Inverness IV3 8NW
Tel: 01463 725 000
snh.gov.uk

Scottish Partnership for Palliative Care
24 Canning Street,
Edinburgh EH3 8EG
Tel: 0131 272 2735
palliativecarescotland.org.uk

Scottish Public Services Ombudsman
4 Melville Street,
Edinburgh EH3 7NS
Helpline: 0800 377 7330
Tel: 0131 556 8400
spso.org.uk

Scottish Qualifications Authority
Lowden, 24 Wester Shawfair,
Dalkeith, Midlothian EH22 1FD
Tel: 0345 279 1000
sqa.org.uk

Scottish Seniors Alliance
Park Lane House, Suite 3–4, 47
Broad Street, Glasgow G40 2QW
Tel: 0141 551 0595
spanglefish.com/
ScottishSeniorsAlliance

Self-Directed Support in Scotland
selfdirectedsupportscotland.org.uk

Sense
9a Birkdale Avenue, Selly Oak,
Birmingham B29 6UB
Tel: 020 7520 0972
Helpline: 0300 330 9256
Textphone: 0300 330 9256 / 020
7520 0971
sense.org.uk

Share and Care Homeshare
265–269 Kingston Road,
London SW19 3NW
Tel: 0208 875 9575
Textphone: 07477 102 444
shareandcare.co.uk

Shared Lives Plus
G04 The Cotton Exchange,
Old Hall Street, Liverpool L3 9JR
Tel: 0151 227 3499
sharedlivesplus.org.uk

Shelter
88 Old Street, London EC1V
9HU
Tel: 0808 800 4444
shelter.org.uk

Sheltered Housing UK
The Little House,
Marldon, Devon TQ3 1SL
shelteredhousinguk.co.uk

Shopmobility
PO Box 6641,
Christchurch BH23 9DQ
Tel: 0844 41 41 850
shopmobilityuk.org

Silver Line
Minerva House, 42 Wigmore
Street, London W1U 2RY
Tel: 020 7224 2020
Helpline: 0800 4 70 80 90
thesilverline.org.uk

Skills Development Scotland
Monteith House, 11 George
Square, Glasgow G2 1DY
Tel: 0800 917 8000
skillsdevelopmentscotland.co.uk

Skills for Care
West Gate, Grace Street,
Leeds LS1 2RP
Tel: 0113 245 1716
Helpline: 0113 241 1275
skillsforcare.org.uk

Skills for Health
4th Floor, 1 Temple Way,
Bristol BS2 0BY
Tel: 0117 922 1155
Helpline: 020 7388 8800
skillsforhealth.org.uk

**Social Care Institute for
Excellence**
First floor, Kinnaird House, 1 Pall
Mall East, London SW1Y 5BP
Tel: 020 7766 7400
scie.org.uk

Society of Later Life Advisers
PO Box 590,
Sittingbourne, Kent ME10 9EW
Tel: 0333 2020 454
societyoflaterlifeadvisers.co.uk

Solicitors for the Elderly
Mill Studio Business Centre,
Crane Mead,
Ware, Hertfordshire SG12 9PY
Tel: 0844 567 6173
sfe.legal

Solicitors Regulation Authority
The Cube, 199 Wharfside Street,
Birmingham B1 1RN
Tel: 0370 606 2555
sra.org.uk

Solid Fuel Association
7 Swanwick Court, Alfreton,
Derbyshire DE55 7AS
Helpline: 01773 835400
solidfuel.co.uk

Sport England
21 Bloomsbury Square,
London WC1B 4SE
Tel: 020 7273 1551
Helpline: 0345 8508 508
sportengland.org

Sport Scotland
Doges, 62 Templeton Street,
Glasgow G40 1DA
Tel: 0141 534 6500
sportscotland.org.uk

Sports Council for Northern Ireland
2a Upper Malone Road,
Belfast BT9 5LA
Tel: 028 9038 1222
sportni.net

Sports Council for Wales
Sophia Gardens,
Cardiff CF11 9SW
Tel: 029 2030 0500
Helpline: 0300 3003123
sportwales.org.uk

Stationery Office
Mandela Way, London SE1 5SS
Tel: 0333 202 5070
tso.co.uk

StepChange Debt Advice
Wade House, Merrion Centre,
Leeds LS2 8NG
Tel: 0800 138 1111
stepchange.org

Stonewall Housing
2A Leroy House, 436 Essex Road,
London N1 3QP
Tel: 020 7359 6242
Textphone: 020 7359 8188
bonalatties.org

Strathclyde Partnership for Transport
131 St Vincent Street,
Glasgow G2 5JF
Tel: 0141 332 6811
spt.co.uk

Stroke Association
240 City Road, London EC1V 2PR
Tel: 020 7566 0300
Textphone: 020 7251 9096
Helpline: 0303 3033 100
stroke.org.uk

Sue Ryder Care
16 Upper Woburn Place,
London WC1H 0AF
Tel: 020 7554 5900
Helpline: 0845 050 1953
sueryder.org

Tax Help for Older People
Unit 10, Pineapple Business Park,
Salway Ash,
Bridport, Dorset DT6 5DB
Tel: 0845 601 3321
taxvol.org.uk

Telecare Services Association
Wilmslow House, Grove Way,
Wilmslow, Cheshire SK9 5AG
Tel: 01625 520 320
telecare.org.uk

Telephone Preference Service
DMA House, 70 Margaret Street,
London W1W 8SS
Tel: 0845 070 0707
tpsonline.org.uk

Thrive
The Geoffrey Udall Centre,
Beech Hill, Reading RG7 2AT
Tel: 0118 988 5688
thrive.org.uk

Translink Northern Ireland
Falcon Rd, Belfast BT12 6PU
Tel: 028 9066 6630
Textphone: 028 9038 7505
translink.co.uk

Transport for London
Access and Mobility Department,
42–50 Victoria Street,
London SW1H 0TL
Tel: 020 7941 4600
Helpline: 0343 222 1234
Textphone: 0800 112 3456
tfl.gov.uk

Traveline
Drury House, 34–43 Russell
Street, London WC2B 5HA
Tel: 0114 22 11 282
Helpline: 0871 200 22 33
Textphone: 84268
traveline.info

TV Licensing
Darlington DL98 1TL
Tel: 0300 555 0286
Textphone: 0300 790 6050
Welsh language textphone: 0300
790 6053
tvlicensing.co.uk

UK Cohousing Network
cohousing.org.uk

UK Council for Psychotherapy
2 Wakley Street,
London EC1V 7LT
Tel: 020 7014 9955
ukcp.org.uk

UK Men's Sheds Association
Tel: 0793 3954 061
menssheds.org.uk

University of the Third Age
19 East Street, Bromley BR1 1QE
Tel: 020 8466 6139
u3a.org.uk

Welsh Government
Cathays Park, Cardiff CF10 3NQ
Tel: 01443 845500
Helpline: 0300 0603300 / 0845
010 3300
wales.gov.uk

Which? (Consumers' Association)
2 Marylebone Road,
London NWI 4DF
Tel: 020 7770 7000
Helpline: 01992 822 800
which.net

Wood Green Animal Shelters
King's Bush Farm, London Road,
Godmanchester,
Cambridgeshire PE29 2NH
Tel: 0300 303 9333
woodgreen.org.uk

World Health Organisation
Avenue Appia 20,
1211 Geneva 27, Switzerland
Tel: 00 41 22 791 21 11
who.int

YMCA
10–11 Charterhouse Square,
London EC1M 6EH
Tel: 020 7186 9500
ymca.org.uk

Notes

Chapter 1: The ageing body

1. Kirkwood, T (1999) *Time of our Lives: The Science of Human Ageing,* London: Phoenix Press
2. See for instance, Wikipedia, *Ageing;* and Michelitsch, T et al 'Aging as a consequence of misrepair – a novel theory of aging', *Nature Proceedings,* April 2009, DOI: 10.1038/npre.2009.2988.2
3. There is a large body of literature which examines the impact of ageing on the human body. I have found the following especially useful: Pathy, J, Sinclair, A and Morley, J (eds) (2006) *Principles and Practice of Geriatric Medicine,* Chichester: John Wiley, and Grimley Evans, J et al (eds) (2003) *Oxford Textbook of Geriatric Medicine,* Oxford University Press.
4. Rosenbloom, A (ed) *Vision and Aging,* St Louis, Missouri: Butterworth Heinemann Elsevier, p 36
5. Ibid, p 40
6. This is because the material of the lens which increases in thickness as we age is yellow, and the pigment involved absorbs short rather than long wavelengths of light.
7. In particular changes to the optic nerve and the gradual fusion of three small bones which transmit sound waves within the ear and which need to be able to move freely to do so.
8. Zhan, W et al (2010) 'Generational differences in the prevalence of hearing impairment in older adults', *American Journal of Epidemiology,* Vol. 171, no. 2, pp 260–66
9. Methven, L et al (2012) 'Ageing and taste', *Proceedings of the Nutrition Society,* Vol. 71, pp 556–65
10. Murphy, C et al (2002) 'Prevalence of olfactory impairment in older adults', *Journal of the American Medical Association* Vol. 288, no. 18, pp 2307–12, as quoted by Boyce, J and Shone, G 'Effects of ageing on smell and taste', *Postgraduate Medical Journal,* April 2006, 82(966), pp 239–41
11. Zylicz, Z, Twycross, R and Jones, E (2004) *Pruritus in Advanced Disease,* Oxford University Press
12. Some experts maintain that loss of about one-fifth of subcutaneous fat is a universal feature of ageing, others that it is caused by disease or loss of appetite in some individuals.
13. Craig, R and Mindell, J (2005) *Health Survey for England 2005, Vol. 1: The Health of Older People,* National Statistics and NHS, p 104
14. Aronow, W et al (2008) *Cardiovascular Disease in the Elderly,* London: Informa Healthcare, p 3
15. Hedden, T and Gabrieli, J 'Insights into the ageing mind: a view from cognitive neuroscience', *Nature Reviews: Neuroscience,* 5 February 2004, pp 87–96

16. Selkoe, D 'Aging brain, aging mind', *Scientific American,* September 1992, pp 97–103

17. Carstensen, L and Mikels, J (2005) 'At the intersection of emotion and cognition', *Amercian Psychological Society,* Vol. 14, no. 3, pp 116–21

18. Schaie, K (1996) *Intellectual Development in Adulthood: The Seattle Longitudinal Study,* Cambridge University Press

19. Maylor, E A (2005) 'Age-related Changes in Memory' in Johnson, M (ed) *The Cambridge Handbook of Age and Ageing,* Cambridge University Press, pp 200–8

20. See Hedden and Gabrieli, op. cit. *(note 15),* p 89.

21. Rabbitt, P (2014) *The Aging Brain: an Owner's Manual,* London: Routledge

22. To the broadcaster Sîan Williams in an interview on BBC1's *Breakfast,* 2 December 2011.

23. Salthouse, T (1998) 'Relation of successive percentiles of reaction time distributions to cognitive variables and adult age', *Intelligence* 26, pp 153–66, quoted by Sternberg, R and Grigorenko, E (2005) 'Intelligence and Wisdom' in Johnson, M (ed) *The Cambridge Handbook of Age and Ageing,* Cambridge University Press, p 211

24. The theory of these two types of intelligence was developed by Professor Raymond Cattell and Dr John L Horn.

25. Salthouse T (1984) 'Effects of age and skill in typing', *Journal of Experimental Psychology: General,* Vol. 113, no. 3, pp 345–71

26. Figures from Alzheimer's Society (2014) *Dementia UK*

27. Stern, Y (ed) (2007) *Cognitive Reserve,* London and New York: Taylor and Francis

28. Gordon, J et al (2012) *Delirium: Factsheet,* London: Royal College of Psychiatrists

Chapter 2: Food, drink and temperature

1. British Association for Parenteral and Enteral Nutrition (2006) *Malnutrition among Older People in the Community*

2. Holmes, S 'Nutrition matters for older adults', *Journal of Community Nursing,* Vol. 20, February 2006, p 24

3. Lipschitz, D (2000) 'Nutrition and Ageing' in Grimley Evans, J et al (eds) *Oxford Textbook of Geriatric Medicine,* Oxford University Press, p 140

4. Deutz, N et al (2001) 'Protein intake and exercise for optimal muscle function with aging: recommendations from the ESPEN Expert Group', *Clinical Nutrition,* Vol. 33, no. 6, pp 929–36

5. NICE (2014) *Vitamin D: Increasing Supplement Use in At-risk Groups,* NICE Guideline PH56

6. SACN (2016) *Vitamin D and Health,* London: Public Health England. SACN recommends 10 micrograms per day.

7. The British Dietetic Association publishes many useful factsheets, from which this figure was drawn; so too does the Food Standards Agency.

8. World Health Organisation (2015) *Guideline: Sugars Intake for Adults and Children.* The Scientific Advisory Committee on Nutrition advises Public Health England.

9. Public Health England (2014) *National Diet and Nutrition Survey: Results from Years 1–4 (combined of the Rolling Programme (2008/2009-2011/21), Executive Summary,* p 11

10. NICE (2010) *Prevention of Cardiovascular Disease at Population Level,* NICE Public Health Guidance 25, p 10

11. Emly, M and Rochester, P (2006) 'A new look at constipation management in the community', *British Journal of Community Nursing,* Vol. 11, no. 8, pp 328–32

12. Bendich, A and Deckelbaum, R (2010) *Preventive Nutrition,* New York: Humana Press, p 537

13. Studies quoted by Kearney, M et al (2005) 'Mainstreaming prevention: prescribing fruit and vegetables as a brief intervention in primary care', *Public Health,* Vol. 119, pp 981–6

14. Ibid.

15. Public Health England, op. cit. *(note 9),* p 10

16. 'Vegetables to die for help village's men to reach ripe old age', *The Times,* 4 December 2009, p 41

17. The study is known as the Age-related Eye Disease Study (AREDS) and took place in two stages. A useful source of reference is its Wikipedia page. Further details can be found at 'Lutein + zeaxanthin and omega-3 fatty acids for age-related macular degeneration: the Age-Related Eye Disease Study 2 (AREDS2) randomized clinical trial', *Journal of the American Medical Association,* 15 May 2013, Vol. 309, no. 19

18. Action for Blind People *Nutritional Supplements for Age-related Macular Degeneration, factsheet,* undated, downloaded 2016. Action for Blind People is a partner organisation of the Royal National Institute for Blind People.

19. NICE (2016) *Clinical Knowledge Summaries: Macular Degeneration – Age-related*

20. 'Older People Food Survey', *Envisage,* Spring 2005, No. 4, Cardiff: Age Concern Cymru (now Age Cymru)

21. Reader's Digest (1972) *Family Health Guide,* London: Reader's Digest Association, pp 70–1

22. Sahyoun, N et al (2003) 'Nutritional status of the older adult is associated with dentition status', *Journal of the American Diet Association,* Vol. 103, no. 11, pp 61–6, quoted by Holmes, S 'Nutrition matters for older adults', *Journal of Community Nursing,* Vol. 20, February 2006, p 24

23. Prince, M et al (2014) *Nutrition and Dementia: a Review of Available Research,* London: Alzheimer's Disease International, p 49

24. Ibid, p 7

25. Ibid, pp 57–8

26. Lang, I et al 'Obesity, physical function and mortality in older adults', *Journal of the American Geriatrics Society,* Vol. 56, no. 7, August 2008, pp 1,474–8

27. Rayman, M and Callaghan, A (2006) *Arthritis and Nutrition,* Oxford: Blackwell, p 47

28. Winter, J et al 'BMI and all-cause mortality in older adults: a meta-analysis', *American Society for Nutrition,* 22 January 2014

29. Lipschitz, D, op. cit. *(note 3),* p 145

30. Holmes, op. cit. *(note 2)*

31. NICE (2006) *Nutrition Support in Adults, Clinical Guideline* 32, paras 1.2.2–5

32. British Dietetic Association *Diet and Hypertension* and *Salt and Health,* Food Fact Sheets, BDA website, undated, downloaded 2016

33. Food Standards Agency 'Eat well, be well: salt tips and myths', FSA website, 2010

34. British Dietetic Association *Fluid,* Food Fact Sheet, BDA website, undated, downloaded 2016

35. Seymour, D et al (1980) 'Acute confusional states and dementia in the elderly: the role of hydration, volume depletion, physical illness and age', *Age and Ageing,* Vol. 9, pp 137–46, quoted by McLaren, S and Crawley, H (2000) *Promoting Nutritional Health in Older Adults,* London: EMAP Healthcare Ltd

36. Lipschitz, op. cit. *(note 3),* p 140

37. Royal College of Nursing and NHS National Patient Safety Agency, *Hospital Hydration Best Practice Toolkit: Practical tips for Encouraging Water Consumption,* undated, downloaded in 2016

38. Wilson, M M (2006) 'Dehydration' in Pathy, J, Sinclair, A and Morley, J (eds) *Principles and Practice of Geriatric Medicine,* Chichester: John Wiley, p 321

Chapter 3: Physical activity

1. Bassey, J (2005) 'The benefits of physical activity for health in older people – an update', *Reviews in Clinical Gerontology,* Vol. 15, p 2

2. Wannamethee, S et al 'Changes in physical activity, mortality, and incidence of coronary heart disease in older men', *The Lancet,* Vol. 351, 30 May 1998, pp 1,603–8

3. *New England Journal of Medicine,* 1999, Vol. 341, pp 650–58, as quoted by Tho-

mas, P 'Exercise: the marathon myths', *What Doctors Don't Tell You,* Vol. 12, no. 11, February 2002, p 4

4. Larson, E et al 'Exercise is associated with reduced risk for incident dementia among persons 65 years of age and older', *Annals of Internal Medicine,* Vol. 144, no. 2, 17 January 2006, pp 73–81

5. Bassey, J (2000) 'The benefits of exercise for the health of older people', *Reviews in Clinical Gerontology,* Vol. 10, p 23. See also Bassey, J (2005) 'The benefits of exercise for the health of older people – an update', *Reviews in Clinical Gerontology,* Vol. 10, pp 1–8.

6. Diabetes UK (2015) *Diabetes Facts and Stats,* p 6

7. Wannamethee et al, op. cit. *(note 2)*

8. Bassey, op. cit. *(note 5),* p 3

9. Seiler, W (2003) 'Consequences of immobility' in Grimley Evans, J et al *Oxford Textbook of Geriatric Medicine,* Oxford University Press, p 1,175

10. Department of Health (2011) *Stay Active: A Report on Physical Activity from the Four Home Countries' Chief Medical Officers,* p 43

11. Ibid, p 47

12. Ibid, p 49

13. Ibid, p 61

14. Ibid, p 60

15. Office for National Statistics (2011) *Social Trends No. 41*

16. Crombie, I et al (2004), 'Why older people do not participate in leisure time physical activity: a survey of activity levels, beliefs and deterrents', *Age and Ageing,* Vol. 33, pp 287–92

17. NICE (2008) *Osteoarthritis: The Care and Management of Osteoarthritis in Adults,* NICE Clinical Guideline 59, para 1.3.1

18. Many types of exercise, including resistance training, are described in Dinan, S, Sharp, C and YMCA Fitness Industry Training (2002) *Fitness for the Over 60s,* London: Piatkus Books

19. Hillman, M (1992) *Cycling: Towards Health and Safety,* London: British Med-

ical Association together with Oxford University Press, p 16

20. Abercrombie, L (1940) 'For Bicycling' *Lyrics and Unfinished Poems* Newtown, Powys: Gregynog Press, p 15. The 'green and golden land' refers to the Dymock area of Gloucestershire, famous for its wild daffodils, in which the poet lived just before World War One.

21. Young, A and Dinan, S (2005) 'Activity in later life', *British Medical Journal,* Vol. 330, p 189

22. Interview with the author, 22 March 2012

23. NICE (2006) *Parkinson's Disease: National Clinical Guideline for Diagnosis and Management in Primary and Secondary Care,* NICE Clinical Guideline 35, p 141

24. Gray, M (2015) *Sod 70! The Guide to Living Well,* London: Bloomsbury

Chapter 4: Psychological well-being

1. Coleman, P and O'Hanlon, A (2004) *Ageing and Development,* London: Hodder Arnold, p 156

2. Maslow, A (1954 and 1970, second edition) *Motivation and Personality,* New York: Harper & Row. Many other people have developed Maslow's thinking, such as Richard Gross in *Psychology: The Science of Mind and Behaviour,* London: Hodder and Stoughton, 2010.

3. Home Office (2011) *Home Office Statistical Bulletin: Crime in England and Wales 2010/11,* HOSB: 10/11, p 48

4. Department for Transport (2014) *Reported Road Casualties Great Britain: 2013 Annual Report, complete report,* p 136

5. BBC Radio 4, *Today* programme, 'Thought for the Day', 2 November 2007. See also Billings, A (2002) *Dying and Grieving: A Guide to Pastoral Ministry,* London: Society for Promoting Christian Knowledge

6. See for instance Bennett, K et al (2010) 'Loss and restoration in later life: an examination of the dual process model of

coping with bereavement', *Omega,* Vol. 61 no. 4, pp 315–22

7. Glass, T et al (1999) 'Population-based study of social and productive activities as predictors of survival among elderly Americans', *British Medical Journal,* Vol. 319, pp 478–83

8. Bennett, K (2002) 'Low-level social engagement as a precursor of mortality among people in later life', *Age and Ageing,* Vol. 31, pp 165–8

9. Griffin, J (2010) *The Lonely Society?* London: Mental Health Foundation, p 11

10. Office for National Statistics (2015) *Labour Force Survey,* quoted by Age UK (2016) *Later Life in the United Kingdom,* p 23

11. Green, J et al (2014) 'More than A to B: the role of free bus travel for the mobility and well-being of older citizens in London', *Ageing and Society,* Vol. 34, pp 472–94

12. Age UK (2011) *Loneliness and Isolation, Evidence Review,* p 8

13. McCrae, N et al '"They're all depressed, aren't they?" A qualitative study of social care workers and depression in older adults', *Aging and Mental Health,* Vol. 9, no. 6, November 2005, pp 508–16

14. Traies, J (2014) *The Lives and Experiences of Lesbians over 60 in the UK,* University of Sussex: unpublished PhD thesis, p 70; Dr Traies has also set out her findings in (2016) *The Lives of Older Lesbians,* Basingstoke: Palgrave Macmillan

15. Williamson, T (2010) *My Name is not Dementia,* London: Alzheimer's Society, p 25

16. Robins, W et al (2002) 'Global self-esteem across the life-span', *Psychology and Aging,* Vol. 17, pp 423–34, as quoted by Coleman, P 'Spirituality, Health and Ageing: David Hobman Memorial Lecture, 2006', in Burke, G (2007) *Spirituality: Roots and Routes,* London: Age Concern, p 49

17. Coleman, P, op. cit. *(note 15),* p 50

18. Dr Sadie Wearing of the London School of Economics discussed this subject in a lecture at Oxford University's Institute of Population Ageing on 1 December 2011.

19. Figures from British Association of Aesthetic Plastic Surgeons obtained in 2013.

20. Figures from American Society for Aesthetic Plastic Surgery obtained in 2013.

21. BBC Radio 4, *Woman's Hour,* 28 December 2010

22. Telephone conversation with the author on 11 September 2006. See Harbottle, E (1999) *Learning through Losses,* Derby: Christian Council on Ageing.

23. Woods, R (1999) *Psychological Problems of Ageing: Assessment, Treatment and Care,* London: John Wiley and Sons, p 62

24. Kenneth Agar suggests some of these activities in his book *How to Make your Care Home Fun* (2009) London: Jessica Kingsley

25. Maslow, A (1970) *Motivation and Personality* (second edition), New York: Harper & Row, p 159

26. 'Rebel and grandmother Anneli joins protestors against war', *Isle of Thanet Gazette,* 26 January 2007

27. Information about Len Clark obtained in 2015.

28. Loretto, W and Vickerstaff, S 'The Relationship Between Gender and Age' in Parry, E and Tyson, S (2011) *Managing an Age-diverse Workforce,* Basingstoke: Palgrave Macmillan

29. Department of Health (2016) *Annual Report of the Chief Medical Officer 2015 on the State of the Public's Health: Baby Boomers: Fit for the Future?*

30. Tornstam, L 'Gerotranscendence: a theoretic and empirical exploration', quoted by Erikson, E and Erikson, J (1997) *The Life Cycle Completed,* London: W Norton and Co, p 124

31. Ibid, p 126

Chapter 5: Shall I move?

1. Percival, J (2002) 'Domestic spaces: uses and meanings in the daily lives of older people', *Ageing and Society,* Vol. 22, pp 729–49

2. Ibid, p 734

3. Nicholls, M 'Millions hit by dentist shortage', *Healthcare Today,* 16 January 2008

4. Doheny, S and Milbourne, P (2014) 'Older people, low income and place: making connections in rural Britain' in Hagan Hennessy, C, Means, R. and Burholt, V. (eds) *Countryside Connections: Older People, Community and Place in Rural Britain,* Bristol: Policy Press, pp 193–220

5. Lowe, P and Speakman, L (2006) *The Ageing Countryside,* London: Age Concern Books, p 148

6. A report by the Commission for Rural Communities in 2010 entitled *State of the Countryside Update 10: Sparsely Populated Areas* also cited transport and fuel as significant extra costs for people living in remote places in England.

7. Oliver, C (2008) *Retirement Migration: Paradoxes of Ageing,* Abingdon: Routledge, p 1

8. Ibid, p 157

9. Lifetime Homes (2010) *Revised Lifetime Homes Standard,* available from Lifetime Homes *(see Useful Contacts).*

10. Thorpe, S, and Habinteg Housing Association (2006) *Wheelchair Housing Design Guide,* Watford: Building Research Establishment

11. Information about Homeshare schemes and the organisations that run them is available from Shared Lives Plus *(see Useful Contacts).*

Chapter 6: Retirement and sheltered housing

1. Information downloaded from the website of Sheltered Housing UK in 2014

2. R (Boyejo and others) v Barnet London Borough Council and R (Smith) v Portsmouth Borough Council [2009] EWHC 3261 (admin), [2009] All ER (D) 169 (dec)

3. RNIB Factsheet (2014) *Designing Gardens and Nature Trails*

4. Age UK, *Making It Work for Us: A Residents' Inquiry into Sheltered and Retirement Housing,* undated, downloaded 2013, p 41

5. Healthwatch Lambeth (2015) *Review of Extra Care Services,* Table 1

6. Law Commission (2015) *Change of Occupancy and Other Events: Consultation Paper 226,* London: Law Commission

7. For an excellent explanation of these powers, see Department for Communities and Local Government (2009) *Residential Long Leaseholders: A Guide to Your Rights and Responsibilities.*

8. In the Title Conditions (Scotland) Act 2002.

9. For instance, in Plumb, R 'How to handle your "right to manage" – by a leading management agent', 14 September 2012, available on the website of CARLEX.

10. Age UK, op. cit. *(note 4),* p 20

11. In 2015 the government said it would bring the Local Government Ombudsman within a new Public Service Ombudsman. The Housing Ombudsman is likely to remain separate – see The Cabinet Office (2015*) A Public Service Ombudsman: Government Reponses to Consultation.*

12. The Association of Retirement Housing Managers (2013) *Code of Practice,* para 4.1

13. Healthwatch Lambeth, op. cit. *(note 4),* p 8

14. See Department for Communities and Local Government (2015) *Your Right to Buy Your Home,* p 22

15. Traies, J (2014) *The Lives and Experiences of Lesbians over 60 in the UK,* University of Sussex: unpublished PhD thesis, p 220

16. Ibid, p 223

Chapter 7: Retirement Villages

1. I obtained information about Belong Warrington from a visit in 2015.
2. Bernard, M et al (2007) 'Housing and care for older people – life in an English purpose-built retirement village', *Ageing and Society*, Vol. 27, p 564
3. Ibid, p 570
4. Liddle, J et al (2014) 'Exploring the age-friendliness of purpose-built retirement communities: evidence from England', *Ageing and Society*, Vol. 34, issue 9, pp 1601–1629

Chapter 8: Staying put

1. The account of the work of Care and Repair Cardiff and the Vale is based on information obtained on a visit in 2015.
2. Councils are governed in this area by the Regulatory Reform (Housing Assistance) (England and Wales) Order 2002.
3. This would amount to fettering their discretion, which is unlawful *(as explained on page 571).*
4. Heywood, F et al (2001) *Housing and Home in Later Life,* Buckingham: Open University Press, p 112
5. Statutory Instrument 2014 No. 2672 The Care and Support (Charging and Assessment of Resources) Regulations 2014, para 3
6. Scottish Government Circular No. CCD 2/2001: Guidance Package Index Ref: F2 *Free Home Care for Older People Leaving Hospital. See also page 660.*
7. Information given to the author by Stannah in 2011.
8. The events involving Ruth and her house took place during 2016.
9. Housing Grants, Construction and Regeneration Act 1996, Section 100 (1)
10. Scottish Government (2009) *Help with Adaptations to your Home: A Guide for Disabled People in Private Housing in Scotland*
11. Age UK (2015) *Don't Leave Park Homes out in the Cold*

Chapter 9: Relationships

1. Office for National Statistics 'The number of people aged 60 and over getting divorced has risen since the 1990s', press release, 6 August 2013
2. Greene, G (1971) *A Sort of Life,* London: The Bodley Head, preface
3. Newlyn, J and Cuthbertson, G (2008) *Branch Lines: Edward Thomas and Contemporary Poetry,* London: Enitharmon Press, p 126
4. Whitty, M and Buchanan, T (2012) *The Psychology of the Online Dating Romance Scam,* University of Leicester
5. Reported in Shoard, M (2007) 'It's never too late for romance', *Woman's World* 2007/2008, London: National Federation of Women's Institutes
6. Doka, K (1989) *Disenfranchised Grief,* Lexington, Massachusetts: Lexington Books, quoted by Ward, R et al (2011) *Lesbian, Gay, Bisexual and Transgender Ageing,* London: Jessica Kingsley, p 119
7. Cardozo, L et al (1998) 'Meta-analysis of estrogen therapy in the management of urogenital atrophy in postmenopausal women', *Obstetric Gynaecology,* Vol. 92, pp 722–7, quoted by Evans, A (2009) 'Vaginal dryness: break the silence', *Geriatric Medicine,* December 2009, Vol. 39, no. 12, p 658
8. Davidson, K 'Gender differences in new partnership choices and constraints for older widows and widowers' in Davidson, K and Fennell, G (eds) (2004) *Intimacy in Later Life,* New Brunswick, New Jersey: Transaction Publishers, pp 73–4
9. Gierveld, J de J (2003) 'Social Networks and Social Well-being', in Arber, S et al *Gender and Ageing: Changing Roles and Relationships,* Maidenhead: Open University Press, p 98
10. Stonewall (2011) *Lesbian, Gay and Bisexual People in Later Life,* London: Stonewall, referred to by Traies, J (2014) *The Lives and Experiences of Lesbians over 60 in the UK,* University of Sussex: unpublished PhD thesis, p 80

11. Borell, K and Karlsson, S (2003) 'Reconceptualising Intimacy and Ageing' in Arber, S et al, op. cit. *(note 9)*

12. Knowles, D as quoted by Shoard, M, op. cit. *(note 5)*

13. 'My love for two women: carer Bruce Covill speaks about feelings of loss and loneliness, and the two loves in his life', *Share*, August 2006, London: Alzheimer's Society, pp 8–9

14. Mrs Johnson had worked most recently at the Leveson Centre for the Study of Spirituality and Ageing near Birmingham. She discusses family commitments and retirement in Chapter 13 of Woodward, J (2008) *Valuing Age: Pastoral Ministry with Older People*, London: SPCK.

15. Shoard, M 'The art of recovery', *Plus,* the quarterly journal of the Christian Council on Ageing, August 2006

16. Bolton, M (2012) *Loneliness – The State We're In,* Oxford: Age UK Oxfordshire, p 12

17. Ibid.

18. Cockburn, J (1988) *Lonely Hearts: Love among the Small Ads,* London: Guild Publishing, p 194

19. Bury, M and Holme, A (1991) *Life after Ninety,* London: Routledge, p 102

20. Andrews, G et al (2003) 'Assisting friendships, combating loneliness: users' views on a befriending scheme' *Ageing and Society,* Vol. 23, pp 349–62

21. Befriending Network (2011) *Quality of the Moment: Working 1:1 with People with Dementia,* Edinburgh: Befriending Network & Alzheimer Scotland

22. Steer, C, NHS Highland, 'Loneliness and Health', paper given at conference on *Tackling Loneliness and Isolation in Later Life,* in Edinburgh on 22 March 2017, organised by Holyrood Policy Events of Edinburgh

Chapter 10: Group activities

1. Quotation on website at claremontproject.org

2. I obtained information about the Farncombe Day Centre from visits, most recently in 2013.

3. Davidson, K (2006) *Investigation into the Social and Emotional Wellbeing of Lone Older Men,* Guildford: Age UK Surrey

4. I obtained information about the Guru Nanak Day Centre from a visit in 2012.

5. I discuss this case, together with other ways in which faith groups support carers, in Shoard, M 'Caring for carers', *Church of England Newspaper,* 8 December 2005.

6. I talked to Ray, Netta and Alan about their voluntary work in 2015.

7. Nazroo, J and Matthews, K (2012) *The Impact of Volunteering on Well-being in Later Life* London: WRVS (Women's Royal Voluntary Service, now the Royal Voluntary Service)

Chapter 11: Computers and the internet

1. Department of Health (2016) *Annual Report of the Chief Medical Officer 2015 on the State of the Public's Health: Baby Boomers: Fit for the Future*, p 31

Chapter 12: Communication

1. Statistics provided on the website of the RNIB, 2016.

2. Hétu, R et al (1993) 'The impact of acquired hearing impairment on intimate relations: implications for rehabilitation', *Audiology,* Vol. 32, pp 363–81

3. Pentland, B et al (1987) 'The effects of reduced expression in Parkinson's disease on impression formation by health professionals', *Clinical Rehabilitation,* Vol. 1, pp 307–13, quoted in Parkinson's UK (2007) *Factsheet on Communication*

4. Allan, K and Killick, J (2001) *Communication and the Care of People with Dementia,* Buckingham: Open University Press and Killick, J (2013) *Dementia Positive,* Edinburgh: Luath Press

5. Allan, K and Killick, J, op. cit. *(note 4)*, p 176

6. Killick, J, op. cit. *(note 4)*, p 66

7. Allan, K and Killick, J, op. cit. *(note 4)*, p 164
8. Magnusson, S (2014) *Where Memories Go: Why Dementia Changes Everything*, London: Hodder and Stoughton, as quoted by Killick, J, op. cit. *(note 4)*, p 140
9. Clark, C et al 'Altered Sense of Humor in Dementia', *Journal of Alzheimer's Disease*, Vol. 49, no. 1, 2016, pp 111–119
10. Allan and Killick, op. cit. *(note 4)*, p 54
11. James, O (2008) *Contented Dementia*, London: Vermilion
12. Naomi Feil, who trained as a social worker, wrote *The Validation Breakthrough* (Baltimore, Maryland: Health Professions Press, 2012).
13. Killick, op. cit. *(note 4)*, p 57
14. Details of Sam Dondi-Smith's device are at interactiveme.org.uk
15. Bryden, C (2016) *Nothing About Us, Without Us!* London: Jessica Kingsley, p275

Chapter 13: Animal Magic

1. McNicholas, J et al 'Pet ownership and human health: a brief review of evidence and issues', *British Medical Journal*, Vol 331, 24 November 2005 (BMJ 2005;331:1252)
2. Gray-Davidson, F (1998) *Alzheimer's: A Practical Guide for Carers*, London: Piatkus, pp 174–5
3. The management of pets in care homes is explored in McNicholas, J et al (1993) *Pets and People in Residential Care: Towards a Model of Good Practice*, available from the Department of Psychology, University of Warwick

Chapter 14: The NHS: rights and pledges

1. The law in question is the Public Bodies (Joint Working) (Scotland) Act 2014.
2. These are the Health and Social Care Directorate of the Scottish Executive, the Health, Social Services and Children Directorate of the Welsh Government and the Department of Health, Social Services and Public Safety of the Northern Ireland Executive. You can find information about the activities of these arms of government, including the guidance they have issued and pronouncements about healthcare on their websites *(see Useful Contacts for their addresses)*.
3. The NHS Constitution and the Handbook that accompanies it are frequently updated. I refer to the versions that were published in 2015.
4. Health and Social Care Act 2012, Sections 203 and 316
5. NHS (2015) *The NHS Constitution for England*, p 6
6. The maximum that health bodies in England can charge is £10 for viewing records and £50 for viewing and photocopying records held in part on computer and in part on paper.
7. The rules on the provision of access to health records are set out in Department of Health (2010) *Guidance for Access to Health Records Requests*.
8. NHS (2015) *The Handbook to the NHS Constitution for England*, pp 31–34
9. Ibid, p 27
10. Scottish Government (2012) *Charter of Patient Rights and Responsibilities*, pp 6–7
11. Under Article 20 of European Community Regulation 883/2004 on the coordination of social security systems
12. NHS (2015) *The NHS Constitution for England*, Section 3a. This right is explained in *The Handbook to the NHS Constitution for England*, pp 27–9. See also Scottish Government (2012) *Charter of Patient Rights and Responsibilities*, p 6.
13. The relevant case is R (on the application of Yvonne Watts) v Bedford Primary Care Trust and Secretary of State for Health: see (2003) EWHC 2228 and (2004) EWCA 166 and Case C 372/04/. Jonathan Herring discusses this case in *Older People in Law and Society* (2009), Oxford University Press, p 297.
14. This would be considered good practice. It is also required under the Equality Act

2010 and the Patient Rights (Scotland) Act 2011, Schedule: Principle 15

15. This is the situation in England and Wales, under Section 1(5) of the Mental Capacity Act 2005. In Scotland the legal requirement is to consider whether treatment 'benefits' a patient, under the Adults with Incapacity (Scotland) Act 2000, Section 1 (2). *See page 774.* This legislation also applies to other professionals such as social workers who often take decisions on behalf of people whose mental powers are impaired *(as explained in Chapter 33).*

16. NHS, op. cit. *(note 5),* Section 3a (called 'informed choice')

17. NHS (2015) *The NHS Constitution for England,* Section 3a. This is explained in the *Handbook to the NHS Constitution,* pp 68–9.

18. NHS (2015) *The NHS Constitution for England,* Section 3a

19. British Medical Association, NHS Employers and NHS England (2015) *General Medical Services (GMS) Contract Guidance for GMS Contract 2015/16,* pp 9–10; the reference to a care coordinator is in a template letter for GP practices to use, on p 87.

20. Ibid, p 8

21. Ibid, pp 32–3

22. NHS Confederation (2015) *Personal Budgets in Mental Health, Briefing Issue 284,* p 1

23. Ibid.

24. NHS (2015) *The NHS Constitution for England,* Section 3a; see also the *Handbook to the NHS Constitution,* pp 47–8

25. The National Institute for Health and Care Excellence replaced the National Institute for Health and Clinical Excellence in 2013. The guidance and recommendations it prepared before 2013 continue to apply. As befits its new name, since 2013 NICE has been developing guidance and quality standards to inform social care, as well as healthcare.

26. Patient Rights (Scotland) Act 2011, Schedule: Principle 9

27. NHS England *Standard General Medical Services Contract (2014)* Gateway reference: 01538, para 7.9

28. Brown, K et al 'Problems found in the over-75s by the annual health check', *British Journal of General Practice,* Vol. 47, no. 422, January 1997

29. British Geriatrics Society (2011) *Quest for Quality: An Inquiry into the Quality of Healthcare Support for Older People in Care Homes,* p 19. The survey was carried out by the multi-professional Older People's Specialists' Forum, which is hosted by the BGS.

30. Steel, N et al 'Self reported receipt of care consistent with 32 quality indicators: national population survey of adults aged 50 or more in England', *British Medical Journal,* Vol. 337, no. 23, August 2008, pp 441–5

31. The Pharmaceutical Services Negotiating Committee explains the NHS contract for community pharmacists on its website *(see Useful Contacts).*

32. Ibid.

33. Research quoted in Welsh Assembly Government (2006) *National Service Framework for Older People,* p 160

34. Human Rights Act 1998, Section 6

35. Equality Act 2010, Part 2

36. Government Equalities Office (2012) *Equality Act 2010: Banning Age Discrimination on Services, Public Functions and Associations: Government Response to the Consultation on Exceptions,* para 1.7

37. Moser, K et al (2007) 'Do women know that the risk of breast cancer increases with age?' *British Journal of General Practice,* Vol. 57, pp 404–6

38. Equality Act 2010, Section 118

39. Welsh Assembly Government (2006) *National Service Framework for Older People,* p 15

40. Ibid, p 25

41. Department of Health (2001) *National Service Framework for Older People*

Chapter 15: Practitioners, organisations and concerns

1. Royal Pharmaceutical Society (2013) *Medicines Optimisation: Helping Patients to Make the Most of Medicines*
2. Ibid, p 3
3. General Pharmaceutical Council (no date, downloaded in 2016) *The Right Prescription: A Call to Action: Reducing the Inappropriate Use of Anti-psychotic Drugs for People with Dementia*
4. Patients Association (2015) *Survey of Medicines-related Care of Residents with Dysphasia in Care Homes,* p 4
5. Abdelhafiz, A and Austin, C (2003) 'Visual factors should be assessed in older people presenting with falls or hip fracture', *Age and Ageing,* Vol. 32, pp 26–30
6. This is known as peripheral neuropathy and I also refer to it in the context of falls *(see page 389)*.
7. Department of Health (2013) *Review of the Regulation of Cosmetic Interventions*
8. These would probably involve the recommendations drawn up in 2014 by the Scottish Cosmetic Interventions Expert Group chaired by Andy Malyon (the Chief Medical Officers' Speciality Adviser in Plastic Surgery).
9. *As explained on pages 321–3 and 514.*
10. Royal College of Nursing (2011) *Delegation: A Pocket Guide*
11. Skills for Care, Skills for Health and NHS England, *The Care Certificate Framework Document: Guidance Document,* undated, downloaded in 2016.
12. National Health Service, England, Social Care, England, Public Health, England The Health and Social Care Act 2008 (Regulated Activities) Regulations 2014: Statutory Instruments 2014 No. 2936, Schedule 1
13. Health and Social Care Act 2008 (Regulated Activities) Regulations 2010, Schedule 1
14. Care Quality Commission 'CQC prosecutes cosmetic surgery company for failure to register', CQC press notice, 4 May 2012
15. Care Quality Commission *Guidance for Providers on Meeting the Regulations Health and Social Care Act 2008 (Regulated Activities) Regulations 2014 (Part 3) (as amended)*
16. CQC's address is in Useful Contacts. You can read more about the way in which the CQC registers and inspects services in the handbooks it publishes for different types of service – for instance, *How CQC Regulates: NHS and Independent Acute Hospitals: Provider Handbook,* 2015 and *How CQC Regulates: Residential Adult Social Care Services: Provider Handbook,* 2015.
17. *Medway Messenger,* 1 February 2013, p 53
18. Health and Social Care Act 2012, Section 182 (6)
19. Health and Social Care Act 2012, Section 181 (5)
20. Grahame-Clarke, W 'Ex-nurse's victory in battle for hospital bed', *East Anglian Daily Times,* 23 September 2005, as quoted by Mandelstam, M (2009) *Community Care Practice and the Law,* London: Jessica Kingsley
21. NHS (2015) *The NHS Constitution for England,* pp 85, 87, 90
22. Statutory Instrument 2009 No. 309 National Health Service, England Social Care, England, The Local Authority Social Services and National Health Service Complaints (England) Regulations 2009, para 5 (b)

Chapter 16: Strokes

1. The Stroke Association (2016) *Facts and Figures,* p 17
2. Ibid, p 4
3. NICE (2008) *Stroke and Transient Ischaemic Attack in Over-16s: Diagnosis and Initial Management,* CG 68, paras 1.4.1.1 and 1.4.2.1
4. NHS and Quality Improvement Scotland (2009) *Management of Patients with Stroke or TIA: Assessment, Investigation, Immediate Management and Secondary Prevention*

5. NICE (2016) *Mechanical Clot Retrieval for Treating Acute Ischaemic Stroke: Interventional Procedures Guidance,* IPG 548

6. NICE op. cit. *(note 3)* paras 1.6.2.7 and 1.6.2.1

7. NICE op. cit. *(note 3)* paras 1.6.1

8. Royal College of Physicians (2016) National Clinical Guideline for Stroke, para 4.5.1 B

9. Ibid, para 5.1.1

10. See for instance 'Treating atrial fibrillation' on the NHS Choices website, at: nhs.uk/Conditions/Atrial-fibrillation

11. Stephens, M (2008) *The Diary of a Stroke,* London: Psychology News Press

12. Kalra, L 'Stroke and Stroke Rehabilitation' in Sinclair, A, Morley, J and Vellas, B (2012) *Principles and Practice of Geriatric Medicine,* Chichester: John Wiley & Sons, p 678

13. Literature review in *Stroke Review,* Vol. 8, no. 1, 2004, pp 17–20

14. 'Stroke campaign partners call for better communication therapy and support for stroke survivors', Royal College of Speech and Language Therapists, press release, 19 November 2008

15. For a description of stroke units and an examination of their benefits, see Langhorne, P and Wright, F (2003) 'Organisation of acute stroke care', *Stroke Review,* Vol. 7, no. 1, pp 8–12

16. NICE (2013) *Long-term Rehabilitation after Stroke,* Clinical Guideline 162

17. Starkstein, S and Robinson, R (2006) 'Psychiatric Complications of Strokes' in Jeste, D and Friedman, J (eds) *Current Clinical Neurology: Psychiatry for Neurologists,* New Jersey: Human Press. The drugs used are selective serotonergic re-uptake inhibitors (SSSRIs) and tricyclic antidepressants. See also Scottish Intercollegiate Guidelines Network, op. cit. *(note 4),* para 4.15.4.

18. Birns, J and Seetharaman, S 'Early supported discharge after stroke', *Neurology,* October 2009

19. Literature review in *Stroke Review,* Vol. 7, no. 4, 2003, pp 103–4

20. Sackley, C et al (2006) 'Cluster randomised pilot controlled trial of an occupational therapy intervention for residents with stroke in UK care homes', *Stroke,* Vol. 37, pp 2,336–41

21. Royal College of Physicians, op. cit. *(note 9),* para 2.7.1K

22. NICE, op. cit. *(note 16)* para 1.1.14

Chapter 17: Anxiety and depression

1. Chew-Graham, C et al (2002) 'The management of depression in primary care', *Family Practice,* Vol. 19, no. 6, pp 632–7, quoted by Hughes, M and Edgar, F 'Beating the lows in later life: evaluation of a mental health awareness-raising campaign aimed at older adults', *Faculty for the Psychology of Older People Newsletter,* No. 125, January 2014, Leicester: British Psychological Society

2. Dr Edgar's research is reported in Hughes, M and Edgar, F, op. cit. *(note 1)*

3. Cully, J and Stanley, M (2008) 'Assessment and treatment of anxiety in later life', in Laidlaw, K and Knight, B *Handbook of Emotional Disorders in Later Life,* Oxford University Press, p 236

4. Loder, B 'Depression in later life: a personal account', *Quality in Ageing,* Vol. 10, Issue 1 March 2009, pp 47–48

5. The symptoms of depression are discussed in, for instance, Rodda, J, Boyce, N and Walker, Z (2008) *The Old Age Psychiatry Handbook,* Chichester: John Wiley and Sons, pp 60–1

6. NICE (2009) *Clinical Guideline on Depression in Adults with a Chronic Physical Health Problem: Recognition and Management,* CG 91, p 5

7. Beeston, D (2006) *Older People and Suicide,* Stoke-on-Trent: Centre for Ageing and Mental Health, Staffordshire University

8. Woods, B (2008) 'Suicide and attempted suicide in later life' in Woods, B and Clare, L (2008) *Handbook of the Clinical Psychology of Ageing,* Chichester: John Wiley and Sons, p 114. Professor Woods points out that other factors shown in various studies to be significant in older

people deciding to commit suicide are pain, poor adjustment to a stroke and fear of being placed in a nursing home.

9. Ibid.

10. Sharon, A et al 'Psychiatry disorders and other health dimensions among Holocaust survivors six decades later', *British Journal of Psychiatry*, Vol. 195, no. 4, October 2009, pp 331–5

11. Kuwert, P et al 'Impact of forced displacement during World War II on the present day mental health of the elderly: a population-based study', *International Psychogeriatrics*, Vol 21, No 4, August 2009, pp 748–53

12. Mann, A (1997) 'Depression: often missed amongst older people in long-term care', *Relatives and Residents Association Conference Report*, London: Relatives and Residents Association

13. Nordhus, I (2008) 'Depression and anxiety in older adults' in Woods and Clare, op. cit. *(note 8)*, p 101

14. NICE (2009) *Clinical Guideline on Depression in Adults with a Chronic Physical Health Problem: Recognition and Management*, p 5

15. Scottish Intercollegiate Guidelines Network (2010) *Non-pharmaceutical Management of Depression*, Guideline No. 114

16. Serotonin-specific re-uptake inhibitor drugs aim to increase the level of serotonin, which is involved in the transmission of messages from nerve cells to other cells. SSSRIs tend to be used rather than the older tricyclic anti-depressants, which have more harmful side-effects. For information about medication for depression and anxiety, see Rodda, J, Boyce, N and Walker, Z, op. cit. *(note 5)*

17. NICE, op. cit. *(note 14)*, p 9

18. Gilbert, P (2009) *Overcoming Depression: A Self-help Guide using Cognitive Behavioural Techniques;* Fennell, M (2009) *Overcoming Low Self-esteem;* Kennerley, H (2014) *Overcoming Anxiety using Cognitive Behavioural Techniques*

19. NICE (2009) *Depression in Adults: the Treatment and Management of Depression in Adults,* Clinical Guideline 90, para 1.4.4.1

20. Ibid, para 1.5.1.2

21. Department of Health (2001) *National Service Framework for Older People,* para 7.31

22. The five stages of grief were identified by the psychiatrist Elizabeth Kübler-Ross (denial, anger, bargaining, depression and acceptance); she never intended that they should form a rigid framework.

Chapter 18: Falls

1. Swift, C 'Falls in late life and their consequences: implementing effective services', *British Medical Journal* 322, 7 April 2001, pp 855–7

2. Royal College of Physicians (2016) *Falls and Fragility Fracture Audit Programme: National Hip Fracture Database Annual Report 2015,* p 1

3. Joanna Downton discusses the psychological effects of falls in her book *Falls in the Elderly,* London: Edward Arnold, 1993, pp 16–8.

4. Ibid, p 21

5. Shaw, F and Kenny, R (1998) 'Can falls in patients with dementia be prevented?' *Age and Ageing,* Vol. 27, p 7

6. Welsh Assembly Government (2008) *National Service Framework for Older People in Wales,* p 111

7. Minns, J et al (2004) 'Assessing the safety and effectiveness of hip protectors', *Nursing Standard,* Vol. 18, pp 33–8

8. NICE (2013) *Falls: Assessment and Prevention of Falls in Older People,* para 1.1.12.6

9. Downton, op. cit. *(note 3)*, p 5

10. World Health Organisation *Health Evidence Network 2007*

11. Audit Commission (1995) *United They Stand: Co-ordinating Care for Elderly Patients with Hip Fracture,* London: Audit Commission

12. Audit Commission (2000) *United They Stand: Co-ordinating Care for Elderly Patients with Hip Fracture, Update,* February 2000, London: Audit Commission

13. The full title is Darowski, A (2007) *The Care of Patients with Fragility Fracture* ("Blue Book"), London: British Orthopaedic Association and British Geriatrics Society

14. Various annual reports of the National Hip Fracture Database; this material is available only on the internet, at nhfd.co.uk

15. Scottish Intercollegiate Guidelines Network (2009) *Management of Hip Fracture in Older People,* a National Clinical Guideline, para 3.1

16. Department of Health (2009) *National Dementia Strategy,* p 62

17. British Orthopaedic Association, op. cit. *(note 13),* p 32

18. Scottish Intercollegiate Guidelines Network, op. cit. *(note 15),* para 4.2

19. British Orthopaedic Association, op. cit. *(note 13),* p 32

20. Ibid, p 6

21. Audit Commission (1995) *United They Stand: Co-ordinating Care for Elderly Patients with Hip Fracture,* London: Audit Commission, p 29

22. British Orthopaedic Association, op. cit. *(note 13),* p 34

23. Ibid.

24. Department of Health (2001) *National Service Framework for Older People,* para 6.3.2

25. NICE, op. cit. *(note 8),* para 1.1.2.1

26. NICE has published several guidelines on various aspects of osteoporosis, for instance 'primary prevention', 'secondary prevention' and 'osteoporotic fractures' (guideline numbers TA 160, 161 & 204 respectively). The SIGN guidance is Scottish Intercollegiate Guidelines Network (2003) *Management of Osteoporosis: A National Clinical Guideline.*

27. NICE, op. cit. *(note 8),* para 1.1.4.1

Chapter 19: Continence

1. Craig, R, and Mindell, J (2005) *Health Survey for England 2005,* National Centre for Social Research, p 6

2. NICE (2006) *Urinary Incontinence: The Management of Urinary Incontinence in Women,* p 1

3. Williams, D and Moran, S (2006) 'Use of Urinary Sheaths in Male Incontinence', *Nursing Times,* Vol. 102, issue 47, p 42

4. Royal College of Physicians (1995) *Incontinence: Causes, Management and Provision of Services,* London: RCP

5. Heath, H, and Schofield, I (1999) *Healthy Ageing: Nursing Older People,* London: Mosby, p 199

6. NICE, op. cit. *(note 2),* p 12

7. Ibid, para 2.1

8. Bassey, J (2000) 'The benefits of exercise for the health of older people', *Reviews in Clinical Gerontology,* Vol. 10, pp 17–31

9. Scottish Intercollegiate Guidelines Network (2004) *Management of Urinary Incontinence in Primary Care: National Clinical Guideline 39*

10. NICE, op. cit. *(note 2),* para 4.3

11. Wagg, A (2010) 'Urinary Incontinence' in Fillit, H, Rockwood, K and Woodhouse, K (eds) *Brocklehurst's Textbook of Geriatric Medicine and Gerontology,* 7th edition, Philadelphia: Saunders Elsevier

12. Williams and Moran, op. cit. *(note 3)*

13. Harari, D (2009) 'Faecal incontinence in older people', *Reviews in Clinical Gerontology,* Vol. 19, pp 87–101

14. Royal College of Physicians (2010) *National Audit of Continence Care,* p 6

15. Department of Health (2000) *Good Practice in Continence Services,* p 38

16. Loveday, H et al 'Epic3: National evidence-based guidelines for preventing healthcare-associated infections in NHS hospitals in England', *Journal of Hospital Infection* 86S1 (2014), pp S1–S70

17. Royal College of Nursing (2012) *Catheter Care: RCN Guidance for Nurses,* p 19

18. Ibid.

19. Ibid, p 21

20. Ibid.

21. Ibid, p 51

22. Community Care and Health (Scotland) Act 2002, Schedule 1, Sections 1 and 2
23. Department of Health (2009) *NHS-funded Nursing Care Practice Guide,* para 50

Chapter 20: Dementia

1. The Alzheimer's Society publishes a wide range of free factsheets on aspects of dementia, such as *Dementia and the Brain* and *Genetics of Dementia.*
2. Godwin, B and Poland, F 'Bedlam or bliss? Recognising the emotional self-experience of people with moderate to advanced dementia in residential and nursing care', *Quality in Ageing and Older Adults,* Vol. 16, no. 4, 2015, pp 235–47
3. Barrett, E and Burns, A (2014) *Dementia Revealed: What Primary Care Needs to Know: A Primer for General Practice,* NHS England, Department of Health and Royal College of General Practitioners, p 11
4. The Alzheimer's Society covers England, Wales and Northern Ireland. These booklets are relevant wherever you live in the UK. Both societies publish much useful free information and advice.
5. Hilton, C 'Dementia, screening, targets and incentives: *Primum non nocere*', *British Journal of General Practice,* August 2015 pp 388–9
6. Dr Matthew Jones Chesters of the University of East London discusses the limitations of assessments of cognitive ability in 'Psychological Interventions', in Walker, Z and Butler, R (eds) (2001) *The Memory Clinic Guide,* London: Taylor and Francis.
7. MRI stands for magnetic resonance imaging, PET for positron emission tomography and SPECT for single-photon emission computed tomography.
8. *Mapping the Dementia Gap: Study produced by Tesco, Alzheimer's Society and Alzheimer Scotland,* 2011. Discrepancies in diagnosis in England are also shown in the Department of Health's *Dementia*

Care Atlas, an online tool set up in 2016 at shapeatlas.net/dementia

9. NICE (2011) *Dementia: Supporting People with Dementia and their Carers in Health and Social Care,* Clinical Guideline 42, para 1.4.5.1
10. Scottish Government and Alzheimer Scotland (2011) *Standards of Care for Dementia in Scotland: a Guide for People with Dementia and their Carers,* p 5
11. *See pages 781–9 for the additional safeguards in place, including in Scotland.*
12. NICE, op. cit. *(note 9),* para 1.1.1.6
13. These drugs include donepezil, galantamine and rivastigmine.
14. See for instance Fewkes, R et al (2011) 'Initial assessment and management of cognitive impairment', *CME Geriatric Medicine* Vol 13, no 2, 58–66
15. See Meccoci, P et al (2009) 'Effects of memantine on cognition in patients with moderate to severe Alzheimer's disease', *International Journal of Geriatric Psychiatry,* Vol. 24, issue 5, May
16. Suggestions for sessions are proposed in Spector, A et al (2005) *Making a Difference,* London: Journal for Dementia Care.
17. NICE, op. cit. *(note 9),* para 1.6.1.1
18. Graff, M, Vernooij-Dassen et al (2006) 'How can occupational therapy improve the daily performance and communication of an older patient with dementia and his primary caregiver? A case study', *Dementia,* Vol. 5, pp 503–32
19. Clare, L and Wilson, B (1997) *Coping with Memory Problems: A Practical Guide for People with Memory Impairments, their Relatives, Friends and Carers,* Bury St Edmunds, Suffolk: Thames Valley Test Company, pp 28–9
20. See Mackenzie, L et al (2007) 'Guidelines on using dolls', *Journal of Dementia Care,* January/February 2007, pp 26–7
21. Kitwood, T (1997) *Dementia Reconsidered: The Person Comes First,* Buckingham: Open University Press
22. May, H et al (2009) *Enriched Care Planning for People with Dementia: Bradford*

Dementia Group Good Practice Guides, London: Jessica Kingsley

23. NICE, op. cit. *(note 9),* paras 1.1.4.4 and 1.1.4.5

24. Ibid, para 1.1.4.2

25. Alzheimer Scotland (2012) 'One year post-diagnostic support – guaranteed', *Dementia in Scotland,* Issue 75, March, pp 1–3

26. NICE, op. cit. *(note 9),* para 1.1.1.1

27. *Body language in people with advanced dementia is discussed in more detail on page 1005.*

28. NICE, op. cit. *(note 9),* paras 1.8.1 and 1.8.2.1

29. Holmes, C and Cotterrell, D (2009) 'Role of infection in the pathogenesis of Alzheimer's disease: implications for treatment', *CNS Drugs,* Vol. 23, no. 12, pp 993–1,002

30. Husebo, B et al 'Efficacy of treating pain to reduce behavioural disturbances in residents of nursing homes with dementia: cluster randomized clinical trial', *British Medical Journal,* Vol. 343, 17 July 2011, d4065

31. Banerjee, S (2009) *The Use of Antipsychotic Medication for People with Dementia: Time for Action,* Department of Health

32. Ibid.

33. NICE, op. cit. *(note 9),* paras 1.7.2.1 and 1.7.1.1

34. NICE, op. cit. *(note 9),* para 1.7.1.1 (I have paraphrased this list, not quoted it.)

35. Department of Health (2012) National Dementia and Antipsychotic Prescribing Audit

36. See, for instance, Alzheimer Scotland's *Drugs used during Dementia* and the Alzheimer's Society's *Dementia: Drugs used to Relieve Depression and Behavioural Symptoms*

37. Alzheimer's Society (2011) *Optimising Treatment and Care for People with Behavioural and Psychological Symptoms of Dementia – a Best Practice Guide for Health and Social Care Professionals*

Chapter 21: Equipment

1. Craig, R and Mindell, J (eds) (2007) *Health Survey for England 2005: The Health of Older People,* London: National Centre for Social Research, Vol. 1, p 5

2. House of Commons *Hansard,* Invalid Vehicles: Accidents: Written Question – 10859, 9 October 2015, question asked by The Rt Hon. Kate Hollern, MP

3. In a statutory instrument called the Cancellation of Contracts made in a Consumer's Home or Place of Work etc. Regulations 2008.

4. Her Majesty's Revenue and Customs, *VAT Reliefs for Disabled People,* HMRC Reference Notice 701/7, August 2002

5. Statutory Instrument 2014 No. 2672 The Care and Support (Charging and Assessment of Resources) Regulations 2014, para 3 6.

6. Ibid.

7. Community Care and Health (Scotland) Act 2002, Schedule 1, para 5

8. Convention of Scottish Local Authorities *National Strategy and Guidance for Charges Applying to Non-residential Social Care Services 2014/5*

9. Scottish Government Circular No. CCD 2/2001: Guidance Package Index Ref: F2 *Free Home Care for Older People Leaving Hospital. See also page 466.*

10. British Standards Institute standard BS EN 12182:2012 Assistive Products for Persons with Disability: General Requirements and Test Methods

Chapter 22: Telecare

1. I interviewed Careline in Carlisle in 2007 and checked the information they had given me in 2015.

Chapter 23: Human help

1. Personal care is defined in The Health and Social Care Act 2008 (Regulated Activities) Regulations 2014, Statutory Instrument 2014 No. 2936, para 2 (1) *The definition of personal care is slightly different in Scotland, as explained on pages 659–60.*

2. Care Act, 2014, Section 73. For Scotland, *see note 1*.
3. Scottish Social Services Council (Registration) Rules 2014
4. The Health and Social Care Act 2008 (Regulated Activities) Regulations 2014, Statutory Instrument 2014 No. 2936, para 9
5. Disclosure and Barring Service, *Referral guidance: frequently asked questions,* undated, downloaded in 2016
6. Herring, J (2009) *Older People in Law and Society,* Oxford University Press, p 174
7. The Disclosure and Barring Service, Disclosure Scotland and Access Northern Ireland publish explanations of the way in which this system works. The legal basis of those for England is set down in National Health Service, England, Social Care, England, Public Health, England, The Health and Social Care Act 2008 (Regulated Activities) Regulations 2014, Statutory Instrument 2014 No. 2936.
8. The rules on registration are set down in the Health and Social Care Act 2008, Sections 8–19
9. Care Act 2014, Section 4
10. See for instance Welsh government (2004) *National Minimum Standards for Domiciliary Care Agencies in Wales* (2004) Standard 1
11. The easiest way to get hold of the domiciliary care regulations together with the standards that lay out how the regulations should be implemented in each country of the UK is through the website of the relevant national organisation – the Care Quality Commission, Care Inspectorate (in Scotland), Care and Social Services Inspectorate Wales and, in Northern Ireland, the Regulation and Quality Improvement Authority.
12. NICE (2015) *Home Care: Delivering Personal Care and Practical Support to Older People living in their own Homes*
13. The Health and Social Care Act 2008 (Regulated Activities) Regulations 2014, Statutory Instrument 2014 No. 2936, para 18
14. Humphries, R et al (2016) *Social Care for Older People: Home Truths,* London: King's Fund and Nuffield Trust, p 7
15. Skills for Care, Skills for Health and NHA Health Education England, *The Care Certificate Standards,* undated, downloaded in 2016
16. The Health and Social Care Act 2008 (Regulated Activities) Regulations 2014, Statutory Instrument 2014 No. 2936, para 9. See also Care Quality Commission (2015) *Guidance for Providers on Meeting the Regulations Health and Social Care Act 2008 (Regulated Activities) Regulations 2014 (Part 3) (as amended),* Regulation 9: Person-centred care.
17. Ibid.
18. Welsh Government (2004) *National Minimum Standards for Domiciliary Care Agencies in Wales,* Standards 2 and 4
19. *See pages 659–60.*
20. Care Quality Commission, op. cit. *(note 16),* Regulation 10
21. Care Inspectorate inspection report for Symphony Home Care Housing Support service, Dumfries, inspection completed on 24 November 2015, p 29

Chapter 24: Live-in Care

1. Care Quality Commission (2015) *Thinking about using a Hidden Camera or other Equipment to Monitor Someone's Care?* (an information leaflet)

Part Seven: Help from the Council

1. Humphries, R et al (2016) *Social Care for Older People: Home Truths,* London: King's Fund and Nuffield Trust, pp 41–2

Chapter 25: The world of social care

1. British Association of Social Workers (2012) *The Code of Ethics for Social Work*
2. Care Act 2014, Section 4 (1)
3. Department of Health (2016) *Care and Support Statutory Guidance to Implement the Care Act 2014,* para 3.3

4. Ibid, para 22.2
5. Care Act 2014, Section 35
6. Care Act 2014, Section 42 (1) and Social Services and Well-being (Wales) Act 2014, Section 126 (1)
7. Safeguarding Vulnerable Groups (Northern Ireland) Order 2007, Section 3
8. Adult Support and Protection (Scotland) Act 2007, Section 3
9. Keeffe, M et al (2007) *UK Study of Abuse and Neglect of Older People: Prevalence Survey Report*, Department of Health
10. Care Act 2014, Section 42
11. Ibid, Section 43. The safeguarding boards often publish the procedures they use when tackling abuse. In London, for instance, there is a pan-London set of procedures – see Social Care Institute for Excellence with the Pan London Adult Safeguarding Editorial Board (2011) *Protecting Adults at Risk: London Multi-agency Policy and Procedures to Safeguard Adults from Abuse*
12. Ibid, Section 68 (2)
13. There is a helpful summary of the legal remedies in Brammer, A (2010) *Social Work Law* Longman, pp 501–2
14. Adult Support and Protection (Scotland) Act 2007, Section 19
15. Mental Capacity Act 2005, Section 44
16. Adults with Incapacity Act (Scotland) Act 2000, Section 83 and Mental Capacity Act (Northern Ireland) 2016, Section 267 (this latter law had not been brought into force at the time of writing).
17. 'Nurse gave patients drugs and removed all bells for an easy night', *The Daily Telegraph,* 26 January 2010
18. Some equipment and services might result from an assessment of his wife's needs for care, which would take place in tandem with the assessment of his needs as her carer.
19. This is called the Personal Expenses Allowance.
20. Department of Health (2003) *Guidance for Access to Health Records Requests under the Data Protection Act 1998,* para 5.4
21. That is not to say that this is an ideal system. Thus in 2013 a group of MPs and peers urged the introduction of an independent tribunal to examine complaints and appeals involving social care services – see House of Lords, House of Commons Joint Committee on the Draft Care and Support Bill (2013) *Draft Care and Support Bill: Report,* Session 2012–13, paras 259–63.
22. Dr Jackie Gulland interview with the author, 4 March 2010
23. Local Government Ombudsman *Liverpool City Council (05C08592) press release,* 30 January 2009
24. See the 'precedent letters' section on the resources page of Professor Clements' website, at lukeclements.co.uk
25. Public Law Project (2007) *How to fund a judicial review claim when public funding is not available,* Public Law Project Information Leaflets for Practitioners, No. 2, p 1

Chapter 26: Social care assessments

1. The equivalent in Scotland is the social work department of a local authority and in Northern Ireland the health and social care trust.
2. The definition of personal care varies a little across the UK and where a difference is important, I highlight it.
3. The preparation and serving of food is included in the definition of personal care in Scotland, but not in England, Wales or Northern Ireland.
4. Care Act 2014, Section 9 (1)
5. For Scotland, the legislation and guidance on assessment and care planning are set down in Section 12A of the Social Work (Scotland) Act 1968, Social Care (Self-directed Support) (Scotland) Act 2013 and Scottish Government (2014) *Statutory Guidance to Accompany the Social Care (Self-directed Support) (Scotland) Act 2013*

The relevant legislation for Wales is the Social Services and Well-being

(Wales) Act, 2014; Social Care, Wales: The Care and Support (Eligibility) (Wales) Regulations 2015; and Welsh Government (2015) *Social Services and Well-being (Wales) Act 2014: Part 4 Code of Practice (Meeting Needs)*. The Care Council for Wales's web hub is a useful resource for finding material about the care legislation.

For Northern Ireland, the legislation and guidance on assessment and care planning are set down in the Health and Personal Social Services (NI) Order 1972, as amended by the Health and Personal Social Services (NI) Order 1991, the Health and Personal Social Services (NI) Order 1994 and the Health and Social Care (Reform) Act (NI) 2009. The main guidance is Department of Health, Social Services and Public Safety *Care Management, Provision of Service and Charging Guidance,* Circular HSC (ECCU) 1/2010. There is a useful explanation of social care law in Northern Ireland on the website of the Law Centre (NI) entitled *Introduction to Community Care: Encyclopaedia of Rights.*

6. The eligibility criteria for England are set down in Statutory Instrument 2015 No. 313, Social Care, England the Care and Support (Eligibility Criteria) Regulations 2015, Section 2. These are explained in Department of Health (2016) *Care and Support Statutory Guidance, Issued under the Care Act 2014,* paras 6.98–6.112. This para refers to section 2 (2) of the Regulations and para 6.104 of the Guidance.

7. Department of Health (2016) *Care and Support Statutory Guidance, Issued under the Care Act 2014,* para 6.103. This is not a direct quote.

8. Care Act 2014, Section 1 (2). (I have paraphrased rather than quoted.)

9. Department of Health, op. cit. *(note 6),* para 6.105

10. Samuel, M 'Social workers "more generous" to clients in high-threshold councils', *Community Care,* 2 August 2012

11. This list is based partly on the elements that the Department of Health has stipulated must always be incorporated in a care and support plan, as set out in its guidance Department of Health *Care and Support Statutory Guidance 2016, Issued under the Care Act 2014,* para 10.36. (I have paraphrased rather than quoted.)

12. Department of Health, op. cit. *(note 7),* para 10.26

13. Welsh Government, Welsh Statutory Instruments 2015 No. 1578 Social Care, Wales: The Care and Support (Eligibility) (Wales) Regulations 2015, and Welsh Government (2015) *Social Services and Well-being (Wales) Act 2014: Part 4 Code of Practice (Meeting Needs).*

14. Welsh Government (2015) *Social Services and Well-being (Wales) Act 2014: Part 4 Code of Practice (Meeting Needs),* para 49

15. Ibid, para 47

16. Ibid, para 44

17. Department of Health, Social Services and Public Safety Circular HSS (ECCU) 2/2008: *Regional Access Criteria for Domiciliary Care,* para 13. (I have paraphrased rather than quoted.)

18. Scottish Government (2014) *Self-directed Support: Practitioner Guidance,* p 19

19. Care Act 2014, Section 78 (1)

20. R v Haringey LBC ex p Norton, as quoted by Clements, L and Thompson, P (2011) *Community Care and the Law,* London: Legal Action Group, p 72

21. Welsh Government (2014) Social Services and Well-being (Wales) Act, Section 2

22. Scottish Government (2014) *Statutory Guidance to Accompany the Social Care (Self-directed Support) (Scotland) Act 2013,* para 1.2

23. Scottish Government (2011) *Standards of Care for Dementia in Scotland*

24. Department of Health, Social Services and Public Safety Circular HSC (ECCU) 1/2010 *Care Management, Provision of Services and Charging Guidance,* p 4

25. Denise Platt, speaking in a phone-in on BBC Radio 4's *You and Yours* on 15 January 2008. At the time, Ms Platt headed the Commission for Social Care Inspection, which was replaced by the Care Quality Commission in 2009.

26. Care Act 2014, Section 37

27. Ibid, Section 1 (3) (paraphrased, not a direct quotation)

28. Department of Health, op. cit. *(note 7)*, para 6.30

29. Ibid, para 6.9

30. Social Care Institute for Excellence (2010) *At a Glance 30: Personalisation Briefing*, p 1

31. Social Care (Self-directed Support) (Scotland) Act 2013, Section 1 (2)

32. Department of Health, op. cit. *(note 7)*, paras 7.10–7.15

33. Ibid, para 10.4

34. Ibid, para 6.30

35. Care Act 2014, Section 9 (5)

36. Department of Health, op. cit. *(note 7)*, para 6.87

37. Department of Health, Social Services and Public Safety Circular HSC (ECCU) 1/2010 *Care Management, Provision of Services and Charging Guidance*, p 2

38. Department of Health, op. cit. *(note 6)*, para 1.19

39. at Section 6 (3) (b); *see note 22.*

40. See Department of Health, op. cit. *(note 6)*, paras 2.4–2.11

41. Department of Health, op. cit. *(note 6)*, para 2.44

42. See R v Bristol CC ex p Penfold (1997–98) 1 CCLR 315, QBD, quoted by Clements, L, and Thompson, P (2011) *Community Care and the Law*, London: Legal Action Group, p 67

43. Care Act 2014, Section 25 (9)

44. Department of Health, op. cit. *(note 6)*, para 10.29

45. As quoted by Rowlings, C 'Community Care for Older People' in (eds) Shardlow, S and Nelson, P (2005) *Introducing Social Work* Lyme Regis: Russell House Publishing Ltd, p 42

46. Care Act 2014, Section 9 (4)

47. Samuel, M 'The rise of non-qualified social care staff under personalisation', *Community Care*, 25 May 2011

48. Equality and Human Rights Commission (2011) *Close to Home: An Inquiry into Older People and Human Rights in Home Care*, p 52

49. Ibid.

50. Department of Health, op. cit. *(note 6)*, para 6.23

51. Dunning, J 'Bureaucracy is damaging personalisation, social workers say', *Community Care*, 25 May 2011

52. Department of Health, op. cit. *(note 6)*, para 6.44

53. See R v Cornwall County Council ex p Hickinbottom, J (2009) 12 CCLR 381, para 68, as quoted by Clements, L and Thompson, P, op. cit. *(note 42)* p 77

54. Social Care, England Statutory Instrument 2014 No. 2673 The Care and Support (Preventing Needs for Care and Support) Regulations 2014, para 4

55. Ibid.

56. Care Act 2014, Section 27 (1)

57. Ibid, para 13.15

58. Ibid, para 13.27

Chapter 27: Support for carers

1. Care Act 2014, Section 10 (3)

2. Social Services and Well-being (Wales) Act 2014, Section 3 (4)

3. Community Care and Health (Scotland) Act 2002, Section 8, and Carers and Direct Payments Act (Northern Ireland) 2002, Section 10

4. Scottish Government (2014) *Self-directed Support: A Guide for Carers*, p 7

5. Care Act 2014, Section 10 (1)

6. The social care legislation for carers is contained in the Care Act 2014, the Community Care and Health (Scotland) Act 2002 and the Social Care (Self-directed Support) (Scotland) Act 2013; the Social Services and Well-being (Wales) Act; and the Carers and Direct Payments Act (Northern Ireland) 2002.

   The rights and reasonable expectations of carers during their assessment are set out for England in Department of Health *Care and Support Statutory Guidance 2016, Issued under the Care Act 2014,* chapters 6 and 11; for Scotland in Scottish Government (2014) *Self-directed Support: A Guide for Carers;* for Wales in Welsh Government (2015) *Social Services and Well-being (Wales) Act 2014: Code of Practice, Part 3 (Assessing the Needs of Individuals)* and *Part 4 (Meeting Needs);* and for Northern Ireland in Department of Health, Social Services and Public Safety (2005) *Carers Assessment and Information: Guidance for Trusts and Boards.*

7. Department of Health, Social Services and Public Safety (2005) *Carers Assessment and Information: Guidance for Trusts and Boards,* p 17

8. The eligibility criteria for carers are set out in Statutory Instrument 2015 No. 313, Social Care, England the Care and Support (Eligibility Criteria) Regulations 2015, section 3. These are explained in Department of Health (2016) *Care and Support Statutory Guidance, Issued under the Care Act 2014,* paras 6.114–6.129. This para refers to section 3 (1) of the Regulations and para 6.115 of the guidance.

9. The government guidance gives as an example: 'The carer might be a grandparent with caring responsibilities for their grandchildren while the grandchildren's parents are at work.' (para 6.121)

10. Department of Health (2016) *Care and Support Statutory Guidance, Issued under the Care Act 2014,* para 6.121; the list in the text is not a direct quote

11. Ibid, para 6.119 (this list is not a direct quotation)

12. Ibid, para 6.126

13. See *The Care and Support (Eligibility) (Wales) Regulations 2015.* The official guidance on how these should be put into effect had not been published at the time of writing.

14. Scottish Government (2014) *Self-directed Support: A Guide for Carers,* p 5

15. Ibid.

16. Ibid.

17. *See pages 946–7.*

18. Care Act 2014, Section 7 (2)

19. Department of Health (2016) *Care and Support Statutory Guidance, Issued under the Care Act 2014,* para 10.40

20. Ibid, para 6.17

Chapter 28: Organising and paying for care and support

1. Department of Health (2016) *Care and Support Statutory Guidance Issued under the Care Act 2014,* para 11.3; the rules on which this guidance is based are set out in the Care Act 2014 and statutory instruments associated with it.

2. Scottish Government (2014) *Statutory Guidance to Accompany the Social Care (Self-directed Support) (Scotland) Act 2013.*

3. Social Services and Well-being (Wales) Act, 2014, Section 6 (2)

4. Department of Health, op. cit. *(note 1),* para 12.3

5. Scottish Care *Care Inspectorate and Self-directed Support Workshop,* Glasgow Hilton Hotel, 11 February 2013

6. Scottish Executive *Self-directed Support – New National Guidance, Circular No. CCD7/2007,* para 254

7. The rules on direct payments are explained in Department of Health (2016) *Care and Support Statutory Guidance Issued under the Care Act 2014,* chapter 12; Scottish Government (2014) *Statutory Guidance to Accompany the Social Care (Self-directed Support) (Scotland) Act 2013;* Welsh Assembly Government *Direct Payments Guidance Community Care, Services for Carers and Children's Services (Direct Payments) (Wales) Guidance 2011;* and Department of Health and Social Services and Public Safety of Northern Ireland (2004) *Direct Payments Legislation & Guidance for Boards & Trusts.*

8. Department of Health, op. cit. *(note 1),* para 12.36

9. Ibid, para 12.46

10. Ibid, para 12.41

11. Ibid, para 12.60

12. The information about the Kingston Centre for Independent Living was correct in April, 2015.

13. See the page of Disability Rights UK's website that lists its membership organisations.

14. Care (Self-directed Support) (Scotland) Act 2013, Section 6 (3) and Community Care, Services for Carers and Children's Services (Direct Payments) (Wales) Regulations 2011, Regulation 9

15. See Department of Health, Social Services and Public Safety (2008) *A Guide to Receiving Direct Payments,* pp 4 and 9 and Section 282 of the Mental Capacity Act (Northern Ireland) 2016

16. See for instance surveys reported in Poole, T (2006) *Direct Payments and Older People,* London: King's Fund

17. The Scottish Government (2012) *Self-directed Support (Direct Payments) Scotland: A National Statistics Publication for Scotland*

18. Swift, P 'Why is direct payments uptake so low?' *Community Care,* 5 September 2007

19. Care Act 2014, Sections 31 and 32

20. Ibid, Section 31 (6)

21. Department of Health, op. cit. *(note 1),* paras 12.18 and 12.22

22. Ibid, para 12.2

23. Care Act 2014, Section 31 (4) (b)

24. Department of Health, op. cit. *(note 1),* para 12.5

25. Ibid, para 12.27

26. Ibid, para 12.33

27. Ibid, para 12.29

28. Ibid, paras 12.36 and 12.37

29. Ibid, para 12.3

30. Ibid, 12.6

31. Social Care (Self-directed Support) (Scotland) Act 2013, Section 7. See the excellent publication Scottish Government (2014) *Self-directed Support: A Guide for Carers.*

32. The legal provision for a carer to receive a direct payment is contained in the Social Care (Self-directed Support) (Scotland) Act 2013, Section 7; Social Services and Well-being (Wales) Act, 2014, Section 52; and the Carers and Direct Payments Act (Northern Ireland) 2002, Section 8. In England, the Care Act 2014 omits to include a specific power for local authorities to give direct payments to carers. However, the power is implied in the Act, in Section 33 (3). Furthermore, the Department of Health says that the statutory guidance on direct payments 'applies to people in need of care and support and carers equally, unless specifically stated'. – Department of Health (2016) *Care and Support Statutory Guidance Issued under the Care Act 2014,* para 12.6.

33. 'Home care charges lottery revealed by Which?', Which? press notice, 20 January 2011

34. Survey by consultants L E Wales, quoted by Huggins, A in 'Social Care Charges (Wales) Measure 2010', published on the website of Howells Solicitors, South Wales, accessed in 2014

35. The rules on charging in England are set down in Statutory Instrument 2014 No. 2672 The Care and Support (Charging and Assessment of Resources) Regulations 2014. Councils must follow these regulations and have regard to the guidance on charging in Department of Health (2016) *Care and Support Statutory Guidance Issued under the Care Act 2014,* chapters 8 and 9: Charging and financial assessment.

36. Statutory Instrument 2014 No. 2672 The Care and Support (Charging and Assessment of Resources) Regulations 2014, Part 4

37. Ibid, Part 5 and Schedule 2. This is explained in Department of Health, op. cit. *(note 1),* para 8.43.

38. Ibid, Part 4, para 14 (This point is also explained in the Department of Health's Statutory Guidance *(see note 1),* para 8.43)

39. Ibid, Part 2, para 3

40. Ibid.

41. Pitt, V 'One in five councils illegally charge for reablement services', *Community Care,* 20 September 2010

42. Statutory Instrument, op. cit. *(note 36),* Part 4 and Schedule 1

43. Ibid, Schedule1,para 4

44. Ibid.

45. Ibid, Schedule 1, para 17

46. Ibid, Schedule 1, part 1

47. Statutory Instrument 2014 No. 2673 Care and Support (Preventing Needs for Care and Support) Regulations 2014, para 3.3

48. Community Care and Health (Scotland) Act 2002, Schedule 1

49. Community Care and Health (Scotland) Act 2002 (Amendment to Schedule 1) Order 2009, para 2

50. COSLA (2015) *National Strategy and Guidance: Charges Applying to Non-residential Social Care Services 2016/17,* para 7.44

51. Scottish Executive *Free Home Care for Older People Leaving Hospital,* Circular No. CCD 2/2001, para 9

52. Community Care and Health (Scotland) Act 2002, Schedule 1, 5 (d)

53. COSLA, op. cit. *(note 51),* para 7.36

54. Scottish Government (2014) *Statutory Guidance to accompany Section 3 of the Social Care (Self-Directed Support) (Scotland) Act 2013,* para 14.28 and the Carers (Waiving of Charges for Support) (Scotland) Regulations 2014, para 4.28

55. The legal provisions are set out in Welsh Assembly Government The Social Care Charges (Means Assessment and Determination of Charges) (Wales) Regulations 2011 and explained in Welsh Government (2011) *Introducing More Consistency in Local Authorities' Charging for Non-Residential Social Services: Guidance for Local Authorities,* number WAG10–12408. The cap figure of £50 was raised to £60 in 2015.

56. Welsh Government (2011) *Introducing More Consistency,* op. cit. *(note 55),* para 115

57. Ibid, para 117; this list is not a direct quotation

58. Department of Health, Social Services and Public Safety Circular HSS (SS) 1/80 *The Future Provision of the Home Help Service in Northern Ireland,* Appendix 1, para 3

59. Ibid, Appendix 4

60. Under the Carers and Direct Payments Act (Northern Ireland) 2002, Section 2 (5)

61. Care Act 2014, Section 4

62. Department of Health, op. cit. *(note 1),* paras 8.55–8.58. The right to request does not extend to arranging care in a care home – a council can choose to do this for people whose financial resources rule them out of council subsidy, but it is not required by law to do so.

Part Eight: Out and About

1. Scott, Sir Walter in a letter. This quotation was displayed in a plaque on Edinburgh Waverley station in 2016.

2. *Experiences of Outdoor Environments* Inclusive Design for Getting Outdoors (I'DGO), OPENspace Research Centre, School of Art, University of Edinburgh

3. Ibid, 'How Does the Outdoor Environment Affect Older People's Quality of Life?'

Chapter 29: On foot

1. Craig, R and Mindell, J (eds) *Health Survey for England 2005: The Health of Older People* National Statistics and NHS, Vol. 1, p 5

2. Department for Transport and the British Healthcare Trades Association (2005) *A guide to best practice on access to pedestrian and transport infrastructure: Inclusive Mobility,* para 3.4.

3. Ibid, para 3.4

4. Ibid, para 3.13

5. Highways Act, 1980, Section 41. Other elements of highways law in England and Wales are set down mainly in this Act and the Countryside and Rights of Way Act 2000.

6. Department of Transport (2009) *Reported Road Casualties,* table 2

7. *Manual for Streets* by the Department for Transport, Department for Communities and Local Government and the Welsh Assembly Government published

in 2007 by The Stationery Office gives a sense of how those who design streets think and thus some of the improvements you could usefully suggest.

8. Quoted by Age UK (2011) *Pride of Place: How Councillors Can Improve Neighbourhoods for Older People,* p 10

9. Help the Aged (2007) *Nowhere to Go: Public Provision in the UK,* p 5 (In 2009, Help the Aged joined with Age Concern to form Age UK.)

10. Further information, with a photograph, in my article 'Way to go', *Woman's World,* summer 2005.

11. House of Commons Select Committee on Communities and Local Government *Twelfth Report: The Provision of Public Toilets,* Session 2007–08, paras 59–73

12. Information largely from interview with Dr Joyce Lesson, vice-chair of North Tyneside Older People's Forum, 29 November 2011.

13. The cities are Belfast, Leeds, Sheffield, Manchester, Newcastle, Stoke-on-Trent, Brighton and Hove, Edinburgh, Cardiff, Nottingham, Glasgow and the London Borough of Camden.

14. Lincolnshire County Council's approach is set down in its *Countryside Accessibility Guidance,* published in 2009.

15. Under the Countryside and Rights of Way Act 2000, Section 60 (2) (c)

16. Ibid, Schedule 2

17. Scottish Natural Heritage (2005) *Scottish Outdoor Access Code,* para 2.14

18. Equality Act 2010, Section 6

19. Ibid, Schedule 1, para 2

20. Equality and Human Rights Commission (2014) *What Equality Law Means for your Business*

21. The legislation in Northern Ireland is the Disability Discrimination Act, 1995, as amended by the Disability Discrimination Act, 2005; the Equality Commission for Northern Ireland provides ample information on this and other aspects of disability discrimination laws and procedures in the province.

22. Chartered Institute of Library and Information Professionals (2006) *Library and Information Services for Older People: Professional Guidance, Policy and Research*

23. Equality Act 2010, Section 149

Chapter 30: On wheels and water

1. Cited in Kitchen, P 'Older Driver MOT', *Woman's World 2007/2008,* London: National Federation of Women's Institute, pp 86–8

2. Institute of Advanced Motorists *Motoring Facts 2008,* p 13. See also Department for Transport *Road Casualties Great Britain 2008.*

3. There are alternative possible qualifying conditions involving being both deaf and blind or being severely mentally impaired and having severe behavioural problems. Details are available from the Department for Work and Pensions.

4. Regulation (EC) No 1107/2006 of the European Parliament and the Council of 5 July 2006 Concerning the Rights of Disabled Persons and Persons with Reduced Mobility when Travelling by Air

5. Civil Aviation Authority Consumer Protection Group (2007) *EC Regulation No 1107/2006 Concerning the rights of disabled persons and persons with reduced mobility when travelling by air*

6. Department for Transport (2003) *Access to Air Travel for Disabled People – Code of Practice*

7. Ibid, para 4.9

8. Ibid, para 4.15

9. Regulation (EU) 1177/2010 Concerning the Rights of Passengers when Travelling by Sea and Inland Waterways; this was brought into force in 2012

10. Rica (2013) *Public Transport: A Guide for Older and Disabled People*

11. Equality Act 2010, Section 168

12. Ibid, Section 165

13. They are set out in Statutory Rules of Northern Ireland 2014 No. 302 Road Traffic and Vehicles, The Taxi Licensing Regulations (Northern Ireland) 2014

Chapter 31: Powers of attorney

1. The laws in this area that apply in England and Wales are the Mental Capacity Act 2005 and the Mental Health Act 2007.
2. The relevant laws are the Adults with Incapacity (Scotland) Act 2000 and the Adult Support and Protection (Scotland) Act 2007.
3. See The Scottish Government (2008) *Code of Practice for Continuing and Welfare Attorneys; Code of Practice: Access to Funds; Guardianship and Intervention Orders – Making an Application: A Guide for Carers; Revised Code of Practice for Persons Authorised under Intervention Orders and Guardians* and *Code of Practice for Local Authorities Exercising Functions under the 2000 Act.*
4. In 2001 in Scotland and 2007 in England and Wales.
5. The procedures are set down in the Mental Capacity Act 2005, Schedule 4.
6. There is a set order of priority for informing relatives of the application for registration.
7. The *Enduring Powers of Attorney (Northern Ireland) Order 1987* provides for the creation of enduring powers of attorney.
8. The powers involving lasting power of attorney are contained in Part 5 of the Mental Capacity Act (Northern Ireland) 2016.
9. Ibid, Part 7 for the powers involving the Public Guardian
10. Ibid, Sections 130–1
11. House of Lords Select Committee on the Mental Capacity Act 2005, Report of Session 2013–14 *Mental Capacity Act 2005: Post-legislative Scrutiny*, HL Paper 139, 2014, para 95
12. Interview with the author, 22 July 2013. In 2015 the Care Quality Commission rated Amherst Court as outstanding.
13. Department for Constitutional Affairs *Mental Capacity Act 2005 Code of Practice issued by the Lord Chancellor on 23 April 2007 in Accordance with Sections 42 and 43 of the Act,* para 7.57

14. The Scottish Government (2008) *Code of Practice for Local Authorities Exercising Functions under the 2000 Act*

Chapter 32: Deputies and guardians

1. The legal powers governing deputies in England and Wales are set out in the Mental Capacity Act 2005, Sections 15–21. Explanatory material about deputies is available from the Office of the Public Guardian.
2. Mental Capacity Act 2005, Section 19 (9) (b)
3. The rules governing the behaviour of deputies are set out in Department for Constitutional Affairs (2007) *The Mental Capacity Act 2005 Code of Practice, issued by the Lord Chancellor on 23 April 2007,* London: The Stationery Office, chapter 8 and in later documents by the Public Guardian, in particular *Deputies: Make Decisions for Someone who Lacks Capacity* (undated, accessed online in 2015)
4. Public Guardian (2012) *Public Guardian Practice Note: Gifts: Deputies and EPA/LPA Attorneys,* No 02/2012
5. Department for Constitutional Affairs, op. cit. *(note 3),* paras 8.38–9
6. Scottish Government (2008) Adults with Incapacity (Scotland) Act 2000 *Revised Code of Practice for Persons Authorised under Intervention Orders and Guardians*
7. See for instance, Alzheimer's Scotland (2013) *Dementia – Money and Legal Matters: A Guide* (two volumes) and Dementia Services Development Centre (2014) *10 Questions about the Law and Dementia in Scotland*
8. See Part 6, Mental Capacity Act (Northern Ireland) 2016.
9. Northern Ireland Courts and Tribunals Service (2012) *Handbook for Controllers Appointed under the Mental Health (Northern Ireland) Order 1986.* The legal provisions for controllers are contained in *The Mental Health (Northern Ireland) Order 1986.*

Chapter 33: How representatives should behave

1. Mental Capacity Act 2005, Section 1
2. Department for Constitutional Affairs (2007) *The Mental Capacity Act 2005 Code of Practice, issued by the Lord Chancellor on 23 April 2007,* London: The Stationery Office
3. Mental Capacity Act 2005, Section 42
4. Ibid, Sections 1 (2) and (5)
5. Department for Constitutional Affairs, op. cit. *(note 2),* Chapter 3
6. Public Guardian (2007) Lasting Power of Attorney Property and Affairs, form LPA PA 10.07, prescribed information, note 4
7. Adults with Incapacity (Scotland) Act 2002, Section 1 (5)
8. *See note 3 of Chapter 31.*
9. Mental Capacity Act 2005, Section 2 (1)
10. Ibid, Section 3 (1)
11. Ibid, Section 3 (3) and note 4 (Mental Capacity Code), para 4.20
12. See Jacoby, R and Steer, P 'How to assess capacity to make a will', *British Medical Journal,* 21 July 2007, Vol. 335, pp 155–7 and Frost, M, Lawson, S and Jacoby, R (2015) *Testamentary Capacity,* Oxford University Press
13. Mental Capacity Act 2005, Section 42 (1) (a)
14. Adults with Incapacity (Scotland) Act 2002, Section 1 (6)
15. Ibid.
16. Williams, V et al (2012) *Making Best Interests Decisions: People and Processes,* London: Mental Health Foundation, p 7 and para 3.3
17. House of Lords Select Committee on the Mental Capacity Act 2005, *Report of Session 2013–14 Mental Capacity Act 2005: Post-legislative Scrutiny,* HL Paper 139, 2014, paras 133 and 139
18. Department for Constitutional Affairs, op. cit. *(note 2),* Section 8.8
19. Social Care Institute for Excellence (2014) *Good Practice Guidance on Accessing the Court of Protection,* SCIE Guide 42
20. Adults with Incapacity (Scotland) Act 2000, Section 14
21. Mental Capacity Act 2005, Section 4 (7)
22. Explanatory Notes to Mental Capacity Act 2005, para 33
23. The requirements about IMCAs are set out in the Mental Capacity Act 2005, Sections 35–41, and explained in Chapter 10 of the Department for Constitutional Affairs' *Code of Practice,* op. cit. *(note 2).*
24. House of Lords, op. cit. *(note 21),* para 166
25. Ibid, paras 167 and 170
26. Mental Health Act 2007, Schedule 7
27. The case is P v Cheshire West and Cheshire County Council and P and Q v Surrey County Council. It was issued by the Supreme Court on 19 March 2014. You can read the judgment at supremecourt.uk/decided-cases/docs/UKSC_2012_0068_Judgment.pdf.
28. Lord Chancellor (2008) *Deprivation of Liberty Safeguards: Code of Practice,* Ministry of Justice. See also Court of Protection (Amendment) Rules 2015 SI 548.
29. There has been some questioning about whether the powers and provisions in the Adults with Incapacity (Scotland) Act of 2000 were sufficient to allow someone to be placed in a situation in which they are effectively deprived of their liberty in a way that is compatible with Article 5 of the European Convention on Human Rights. The Scottish Law Commission reported on this in October 2014 and produced a draft Bill amending the 2000 Act. At the time of writing, debate was continuing on whether the Commission's suggestions were correct and the response of the Scottish Government was awaited.
30. Adults with Incapacity (Scotland) Act 2000, Section 1 (4)
31. A named person has a right to be consulted only within the context of people detained under mental health legislation

in Scotland, not in the context of mental capacity legislation.

32. Under the Mental Health (Care and Treatment) (Scotland) Act 2003, Section 259 (1)

33. Mental Health (Care and Treatment) (Scotland) Act 2003, Section 259

34. Mental Capacity Act (Northern Ireland) 2016, Sections 35 and 36

35. Ibid, Sections 19 and 69

36. Ibid, Section 73

37. See, for instance, Northern Health and Social Care Trust (2010) *Consent for Examination, Treatment or Care,* Reference number NHSCT/10/332

Chapter 34: Limited authorisation, advisors and advocates

1. Scottish Government (2008) *Code of Practice: Access to Funds*

2. Ibid.

3. Scottish Government (2008) *Guardianship and Intervention Orders – Making an Application: A Guide for Carers,* Appendix 3

4. Scottish Government (2008) *Revised Code of Practice for Persons Authorised under Intervention Orders and Guardians*

5. *See notes 3 and 4.*

6. Care Act 2014, Section 67

7. Department of Health (2016) *Care and Support Statutory Guidance to Implement the Care Act 2014,* Chapter 7: Independent advocacy

8. Statutory Instrument No. 2824 Social Care, England, The Care and Support (Independent Advocacy Support) No. 2 Regulations 2014, para 3

9. Welsh Government (2015) *Social Services and Well-being (Wales) Act, 2014, Code of Practice,* Part 10: Advocacy, paras 47 and 50

10. Ibid, paras 77 and 80

Chapter 35: Universal state benefits

1. The government publishes papers on various aspects of the Single-tier Pension, from the way it affects self-employed people to National Insurance credits and the pension. These are available on the government's website (gov. uk). Other useful explanations include Department for Work and Pensions (2013), *The Single-tier Pension: A Simple Foundation for Saving,* Cmnd 8528 and Institute for Fiscal Studies (2013) *A Single-Tier Pension: What Does it Really Mean?*

2. Crawford, R and Tetlow, G (2016) *The New (not yet) Flat-rate State Pension,* London: Institute for Fiscal Studies

3. You can find the relevant Council Tax Reduction Regulations, first made in 2012 and amended frequently since then, on the websites of the Scottish and the Welsh governments.

4. The Council Tax Reduction Schemes (Default Scheme) (England) Regulations 2012. Citizens Advice produces information about Council Tax Reduction schemes in England, Scotland and Wales on its website.

Chapter 36: Means-tested benefits

1. Department for Work and Pensions (2014) *Estimates of the take-up of the main income-related benefits by caseload and expenditure in Great Britain,* p 15

2. Figure obtained from the website rightsnet.org.uk, 2015.

Chapter 37: Earning, investing and bestowing

1. House of Commons Work and Pensions Committee (2015) *Pension Freedom Guidance and Advice First Report of Session 2015-16* HC 371, para 27

2. Financial Conduct Authority 'FCA finds annuity market not working for consumers – Competition Market Study launched', press notice, 14 February 2014

3. Which? website page on buying an annuity, downloaded in 2015

4. Mr G B N White v Ministry of Justice, 24 November 2014, London Central Employment Tribunal, case number 2201298/2013

5. Unless the person is older than or within six months of the employer's mandatory

retirement age, or 65 if the employer does not have one.

6. 'Which? tests equity release advice', *Which?* magazine, February 2012, pp 22–5

7. You may be able to avoid paying VAT on these purchases, however – *see page 479.*

Chapter 38: Staying in hospital

1. Department of Health (2009) *Intermediate Care – Halfway Home,* Best Practice Guidance, p 31. *I discuss Intermediate Care in more detail in Chapter 39: Leaving hospital.*

2. Dr Foster Intelligence *Inside Your Hospital: Dr Foster Hospital Guide 2001–2011*

3. The results of research by the National Hip Fracture Database are provided online at nhfd.co.uk

4. See for instance Welsh Government, Macmillan and GIG Cymru NHS Wales *Wales Cancer Patient Experience Survey 2013 Cwm Taf University Health Board.*

5. Royal College of Physicians (RCP) in collaboration with the Marie Curie Palliative Care Institute Liverpool (2014 and 2016) *National Care of the Dying Audit for Hospitals*

6. The website of the Health and Social Care Information Centre, at hscic.gov. uk, provides useful information; however, it is aimed at professionals and can be difficult for lay people to understand.

7. See for instance Aylin, P et al 'Day of week procedure and 30 day mortality for elective surgery: retrospective analysis of hospital episode statistics', *British Medical Journal,* Vol. 346, f2424, 28 May 2013 but also Boseley, S 'Fewer people die in hospital at weekends, study finds', *Guardian,* 6 May, 2016

8. Academy of Medical Royal Colleges (2014) *Guidance for Taking Responsibility: Accountable Clinicians and Informed Patients*

9. Department of Health Service Circular 2001/010 *Implementing the NHS Plan – Modern Matrons*

10. The Royal College of Nursing Institute and The University of Sheffield School of Nursing and Midwifery (2004) *Evaluation of the Modern Matron Role in a Sample of NHS Trusts: Final Report to the Department of Health,* p ii

11. The Mid Staffordshire NHS Foundation Trust Public Inquiry (2013) *Report of the Mid Staffordshire NHS Trust Public Inquiry (Chair: R Francis),* London: Stationery Office

12. NHS England (2012) *Compassion in Practice – Our Culture of Compassionate Care*

13. *Care and Compassion? Fourth report of the Health Service Commissioners for England,* Session 2010–2011, HC 778, London: The Stationery Office, p 10

14. NICE (2014) *Safe Staffing for Nursing in Adult Inpatient Wards in Acute Hospitals:* NICE Safe Staffing Guideline, p 14

15. General Medical Council (2010) *Treatment and Care towards the End of Life: Good Practice in Decision-Making,* para 109 (Although this guidance was issued for patients at the end of their lives, there seems no reason why the precepts to which I refer should not apply to other patients.)

16. Care Quality Commission (2015) *Guidance for Providers on Meeting the Regulations Health and Social Care Act 2008 (Regulated Activities) Regulations 2014 (Part 3) (as amended) Care Quality Commission (Registration) Regulations 2009 (Part 4) (as amended),* pp 53–7

17. NICE (2014) *Pressure Ulcers: Prevention and Management,* para 1.1.2

18. Ibid, para 1.4.4

19. NHS Quality Improvement Scotland (2009) *Best Practice Statement for Prevention and Management of Pressure Ulcers,* made available by Healthcare Improvement Scotland

20. Alderwick, H et al (2015) *Better Value in the NHS,* London: King's Fund, p 67

21. Ibid, p 68

22. Grice, J et al 'The effect of posters and displays on the use of alcohol gel', *Brit-*

ish Journal of Infection Control, Vol. 9, issue 5, September 2008, p 24

23. Royal College of Nursing (2012) *Wipe it Out: Essential Practice for Infection Prevention and Control: Guidance for Nursing Staff,* p 10

24. Ibid, p 13

25. Department of Health (2001) *National Service Framework for Older People,* p 23

26. National Institute of Health and Clinical Excellence (2006, amended 2011) *Dementia: Supporting People with Dementia and their Carers in Health and Social Care,* Clinical Guideline 42, para 1.1.11.2

27. Royal College of Psychiatrists (2013) *National Audit of Dementia Care in General Hospitals 2012–13, Second Round Audit Report and Update,* eds: Young, J et al, London: Healthcare Quality Improvement Partnership, p 58

28. Ibid, p 55

29. They are different from 'dementia friends champions' – volunteers who give talks to members of the public to encourage greater dementia awareness in society at large.

30. You can read about John's Campaign at johnscampaign.org.uk The website that lists hospitals' attitudes to visiting by the carers of people with dementia is at theguardian.com/society/series/johns-campaign

31. NICE (2015) *Transition between Inpatient Hospital Settings and Community or Care Home Settings for Adults with Social Care Needs,* NICE Guideline, para 1.3.5

32. Coles, S and Watson, M (2013) *Patient Stories 2013: Time for Change,* Patients Association

33. Macmillan Cancer Support 'Ageism in NHS stopping older cancer patients getting treatment', press notice, 20 December 2012. See also Lievesley, N (2009) *Ageism and Age Discrimination in Secondary Health Care in the United Kingdom: A Review from the Literature,* London: Centre for Policy on Ageing, and Clark, A (2009) *Ageism and Age Discrimination in Primary and Community Health Care in the United Kingdom: A review from the Literature,* London: Centre for Policy on Ageing

34. Macmillan Cancer Support (2012) *Cancer Services, Coming of Age: Learning for the Improved Cancer Treatment Assessment and Support for Older People Project,* Age UK and the Department of Health, para 1.42

35. Under the Mental Capacity Act 2005, Section 44; the Adults with Incapacity Act (Scotland) Act 2000, Section 83; and the Mental Capacity Act (Northern Ireland) 2016, Section 267. (The Northern Ireland provision had not been brought into force at the time of writing.)

36. Department of Health (2007) *Eligibility Criteria for Patient Transport Services,* para 8

37. Ibid, para 9

38. Department of Health (2006) *Income Generation Car Parking Charges – Best Practice for Implementation*

39. House of Commons Health Committee (2006) *NHS Charges Third Report of Session 2005–06, Vol. I: Report, together with formal minutes,* HC 815–I, p 57

Chapter 39: Leaving hospital

1. *Care and compassion? Fourth report of the Health Service Commissioners for England, Session 2010–2011,* HC 778, London: The Stationery Office, pp 29–30

2. Ibid, pp 13–14

3. NICE (2015) *Transition between Inpatient Hospital Settings and Community or Care Home Settings for Adults with Social Care Needs,* NICE Guideline, NG27, paras 1.1.5 and 1.1.6. This guideline strictly speaking applies to adults with social care needs. However, the level or type of social care need *(which includes emotional as well as practical needs, as explained in Chapter 26)* is not specified so the guideline should apply to many older people.

4. The formal procedures by which hospitals in England discharge patients and involve social services in doing so are

set out in the Care Act 2014, Schedule 3; these are explained in Department of Health *Care and Support Statutory Guidance 2016 Issued under the Care Act 2014*, Annex G.

5. NICE, op. cit. *(note 3)*, para 1.5.2

6. Ibid, para 1.5.15 (I have paraphrased rather than quoted.)

7. Department of Health (2010) *Ready to Go? Planning the Discharge and Transfer of Patients from Hospital and Intermediate Care*, Good Practice Guidance. The NICE guideline *(see note 3)* at para 1.5.6 recommends for adults with social care needs that the discharge plan should be available to their GP within 24 hours.

8. Employment Rights Act 1996, Section 57; for Northern Ireland, see The Employment Rights (Northern Ireland) Order 1996

9. Department of Health *Care and Support Statutory Guidance 2016, Issued under the Care Act 2014*, para 2.49

10. NICE, op. cit. *(note 3)*, para 1.5.7

11. Department of Health, op. cit. *(note 7)*, p 12

12. Department of Health (2009) *Intermediate Care – Halfway Home: Best Practice Guidance*, p 31

13. Statutory Instrument 2014 No. 2672 The Care and Support (Charging and Assessment of Resources) Regulations 2014, Section 3 (3) (c)

14. Department of Health, op. cit. *(note 12)*, p 12

15. Statutory Instrument, op. cit. *(note 13)*, Section 3 (1) and (2)

16. Department of Health, op. cit. *(note 9)*, para 2.62

17. Email to the author from John Crook, Reablement Inquiries, Department of Health, 8 December 2010.

18. Scottish Government (2012) *Maximising Recovery, Promoting Independence: An Intermediate Care Framework for Scotland*. Provision for Intermediate Care to be free for people aged 65 and over in Scotland is set down in Convention of Scottish Local Authorities (2015) *National Strategy and Guidance: Charges Applying to Non-residential Social Care Services 2016/17*, para 7.44.

19. Young, J et al (2005) 'A whole systems study of Intermediate Care services for older people', *Age and Ageing*, Vol. 34, pp 577–83

20. Welsh Assembly Government (2004) *National Minimum Standards for Care Homes for Older People*, Standard 13: Intermediate Care

21. All care homes in the UK have to conform to regulations enforced by the Care Quality Commission (in England), the Care Inspectorate (in Scotland), the Care Standards Inspectorate for Wales and, in Northern Ireland, the Regulation and Quality Improvement Authority. These regulations, as well as the standards that explain how care home providers should comply with them do not say that those for people staying in care homes while receiving Intermediate Care should be less rigorous than those applying to permanent residents.

22. Department of Health (2016) *NHS Continuing Healthcare Activity Statistics for England, Quarter 1 2016-17 Report*

23. Department of Health (2012) *National Framework for NHS Continuing Healthcare and NHS-funded Nursing Care*, para 84

24. Ibid, para 35 (this list is not a direct quotation)

25. Ibid, para 33

26. Ibid, para 80

27. For England, see Department of Health (2012) *National Framework for NHS Continuing Healthcare and NHS-funded Nursing Care*, para 84; for Scotland, see Scottish Government *NHS Continuing Healthcare* CEL 6 (2008); for Wales, see Welsh Assembly Government *Continuing NHS Health Care: Framework for Implementation in Wales 2004*.

28. Department of Health, op. cit. *(note 23)*, para 60

29. Ibid, para 16.1

30. Ibid, para 22.2

31. Ibid, para 20.1

32. Ibid, para 20.2

33. Ibid, para 21.1
34. Ibid, para 80
35. Ibid, para 4.3
36. Clements, L (2017) *Community Care and the Law*, London: Legal Action Group, p 89
37. Department of Health, op. cit. *(note 23)* para 97
38. Ibid, para 38
39. Ibid, para 14
40. The Care Quality Commission (in England), the Care Inspectorate (in Scotland), the Care Standards Inspectorate for Wales and, in Northern Ireland, the Regulation and Quality Improvement Authority publish the reports of their inspections on their websites.
41. Department of Health, op. cit. *(note 23)*, para 42
42. NHS England (2014) *Guidance on the Right to have a Personal Health Budget in Adult NHS Continuing Healthcare and Children and Young People's Continuing Care*, p 11
43. Department of Health, op. cit. *(note 23)*, para 88.1
44. Ibid, para 85.1
45. Ibid.
46. Welsh Assembly Government *Continuing NHS Health Care: Framework for Implementation in Wales 2004*, section 7.5
47. Scottish Government *NHS Continuing Healthcare* CEL 6 (2008), para 107
48. Department of Health, op. cit. *(note 7)*, p 20
49. Ibid, p 15
50. NICE, op. cit. *(note 3)*, para 1.5.11
51. The figures differ slightly in the different countries of the UK.
52. Statutory Instrument 2014 No. 2670 Social Care, England: The Care and Support and Aftercare (Choice of Accommodation) Regulations 2014, para 3 (I have paraphrased not quoted.)

Part Twelve: The end of life

1. Cited in Steinhauser, K and Tulsky, J 'Defining a good death' in Hanks, G et al (2010) *Oxford Textbook of Palliative Medicine*, Oxford University Press, p 135
2. Personal Social Services Research Unit, London School of Economics and Political Science (2015) *Equity in the Provision of Palliative and End of Life Care in the UK* London: Marie Curie Care and Support through Terminal Illness
3. Paddy, M (2011) 'Understanding nurse and patient perceptions of a "good death"', *End of Life Journal*, Vol. 1, no. 2, pp 1–10. See also Hanks, G et al, op. cit. *(note 1)*.

Chapter 40: End-of-life care

1. World Health Organisation (2003), *WHO Definition of Palliative Care.* I have selected elements from this list which refer to palliative care used at the end of life. The WHO says palliative care may also be used early in the course of an incurable illness in conjunction with other treatment intended to prolong life, such as radiation therapy.
2. End-of-life care is a complex discipline; the material in Chapter 40 is a basic account. There are several works of reference, such as Hanks, G et al (2010) *Oxford Textbook of Palliative Medicine*, Oxford University Press. For details about palliative care for frail, elderly people, see the evidence-based guidelines on palliative care in care homes that were endorsed by the Australian government in 2006 and are available on the internet: Edith Cowan University and Australian Government National Health and Medical Research Council (2006) *Guidelines for a Palliative Approach in Residential Aged Care.*
3. Sykes, N 'Constipation and diarrhoea' in Hanks, G et al, op. cit. *(note 2)*, p 834
4. Ellershaw, J and Wilkinson, S (2003) *Care of the Dying: A Pathway to Excellence,* Oxford University Press, p 51
5. Marie Curie Palliative Care Institute Liverpool (2009) *Liverpool Care Pathway for the Dying Patient, version 12*
6. Chinthapalli, K 'The Liverpool Care Pathway: what do specialists think?'

British Medical Journal, Vol. 346, 2 March 2013, pp 18–9

7. Independent Review of the Liverpool Care Pathway chaired by Baroness Julia Neuberger (2013) *More Care, Less Pathway: A Review of the LCP,* Department of Health

8. Leadership Alliance for the Care of Dying People (2014) *One Chance to Get it Right,* available on the government's website (gov.uk)

9. NICE (2015) *Care of the Dying Adult:* NICE Guideline, Short Version

10. Ibid, para 1.1

11. Ibid, para 1.3.5 (This is not a direct quotation: I have paraphrased and explained NICE's recommendations.)

12. Ibid, para 1.4.

13. See Leadership Alliance for the Care of Dying People, op. cit. *(note 8),* para 20

14. Ibid, pp 7–8

15. NHS Scotland (2014) *Caring for People in the Last Days and Hours of Life: National Statement*

16. Ellershaw, J and Ward, C 'Care of the dying patient: the last hours or days of life', *British Medical Journal,* Vol. 326, 4 January 2003, pp 30–34

17. Leadership Alliance for the Care of Dying People, op. cit. *(note 8),* paras 23–6.

18. Department of Health (2008) *End of Life Care Strategy,* para 3.31. The General Medical Council has also emphasised the need for advance planning – see the report it drew up for doctors in 2010 entitled *Treatment and Care Towards the End of Life: Good Practice in Decision-Making.*

19. *Gold Standards Framework Advance Care Planning,* downloaded from the Framework's website in 2015. The Gold Standards Framework Centre in End-of-Life Care was originally developed in 2000 as a grass roots initiative to improve palliative care within primary care by Dr Keri Thomas, who is now the Framework's National Clinical Lead *(see also note 33).* Gold Standards Framework accreditation has been endorsed by NICE and the Department of Health.

20. Department of Health, op. cit. *(note 18),* para 3.32. Various organisations have published best practice suggestions that make points such as this. See for instance, Henry, C and Seymour, J (2008) *Advance Care Planning: A Guide for Health and Social Care Staff,* NHS England and University of Nottingham and Royal College of Physicians (2009) *Concise Guidance to Good Practice: Number 12: Advance Care Planning.*

21. Royal College of Physicians, Marie Curie Cancer Care (2016) *National Care of the Dying Audit for hospitals, England,* London: Royal College of Physicians

22. Willard, C and Luker, K (2006) 'Challenges to end of life care in the acute hospital setting', *Palliative Medicine,* Vol. 20, pp 611–15

23. Evidence given to House of Commons Health Committee and referred to in *End of Life Care, Fifth Report of Session 2014-15,* HC 805, para 56

24. The information about St Catherine's Hospice is based on a visit I made in 2011 and was checked in 2012.

25. Payne, S et al (2007) 'Experiences of end-of-life care in community hospitals', *Health and Social Care in the Community,* Vol. 15, no. 5, pp 494–501

26. *For suggestions for points to consider, see page 970.* Age UK and Independent Age publish factsheets and guides; see also my article 'Choosing and Living in a Care Home', published in 2006 by Care Select and available on my website. Amaranth Books will be publishing a companion volume in 2019 about choosing a care home.

27. Scottish Executive and Scottish Partnership for Palliative Care (2006) *Making Good Care Better: National Practice Statements for General Palliative Care in Adult Care Homes in Scotland,* pp 17–44. This list is not a direct quotation.

28. See the accreditation page of the Framework's website.

29. This was described by Paula McCormack of Highland Hospice at the conference 'Care Homes: A Good Place to

Live, a Good Place to Die', organised by Scottish Care and held in Glasgow on 30 September 2010.

30. Scottish Executive and Scottish Partnership for Palliative Care, op. cit. *(note 27)*, p 57

31. Steinhauser, K and Tulsky, J 'Defining a "good death"' in Hanks, G et al (2010) *Oxford Textbook of Palliative Medicine*, Oxford University Press, p 138

32. Barclay, S 'Place of death – how much does it matter?', *British Journal of General Practice*, April 2008, pp 229–31

33. Thomas, K *Community Palliative Care*, downloaded from the website of the Gold Standards Framework in 2015. *See also note 19.*

34. GMC (2010) *Treatment and Care Towards the End of Life: Good Practice in Decision-making*, para 50

35. Since cold against the cheek or through the nose can alter the pattern of breathing and reduce the perception of breathlessness.

36. Corner, J et al 'Non-pharmalogical intervention for breathlessness in lung cancer', *Palliative Medicine*, Vol. 10, pp 299–303. This and other management approaches are described in Ferrell, B and Coyle, N (2006) *Textbook of Palliative Nursing*, Oxford University Press, pp 254–5.

37. Scottish Partnership for Palliative Care (2008) *Living and Dying with Advanced Heart Failure: A Palliative Care Approach*, pp 4 and 16

38. Department of Health, op. cit. *(note 18)*, para 4.47

39. Sampson, E et al (2006) 'Differences in care received by patients with and without dementia who died during acute hospital admission: a retrospective case note study', *Age and Ageing*, Vol. 26, pp 187–9

40. House of Commons Health Committee (2015) *End of Life Care: Fifth Report of Session 2014-15*, HC 405, recommendation 6, p 43

41. This difficult area is explored in Edith Cowan University, op. cit. *(note 2)*.

Chapter 41: Final decision-making

1. *Inside the Ethics Committee,* presented by Dame Joan Bakewell, BBC Radio 4, 31 July 2014

2. General Medical Council (2010) *Treatment and Care Towards the End of Life: Good Practice in Decision-Making*

3. Ibid, para 10

4. Ibid, para 14

5. Interview with Professor Sam Ahmedzai, 16 February 2001, comment confirmed in 2016

6. Paper presented by Dr Ian Basnett, Labour Party fringe conference 2004, quoted by Campbell, J 'Disabled people and the right to life' in Clements, L, and Read, J (eds) *Disabled People and the Right to Life* (2008), London: Routledge

7. General Medical Council, op. cit. *(note 2)*, para 46

8. Ibid, para 11

9. Ibid, para 12

10. Mental Capacity Act 2005, Section 4 (7)

11. The legislation is contained in Mental Capacity Act 2005, Sections 24–6.

12. This is explained in Royal College of Physicians (2009) *Advance Care Planning: National Guidelines*, Figure 1, p 3

13. Cited in House of Lords Select Committee on the Mental Capacity Act 2005, *Report of Session 2013–14 Mental Capacity Act 2005: Post-legislative Scrutiny*, HL Paper 139, 2014, para 197

14. Adults with Incapacity (Scotland) Act 2000, Section 1 (4)

15. der Heide, A et al 'End-of-life decision-making in six European countries: descriptive study', *The Lancet*, 17 June 2003

16. Foreword by Sir Terry Pratchett to *My Name is Not Dementia*, Alzheimer's Society, 2010. Sir Terry suffered from posterior cortical atrophy, in which areas at the back of the brain begin to shrink and shrivel.

Index

Note: Numbers in **boldface** indicate key discussions of a topic.

A

B

G

M

O

R

U

ABOUT THE AUTHOR

MARION SHOARD was born in 1949 and grew up in Cornwall and Kent. After reading zoology at Oxford University, she studied countryside planning and went to work for the Council for the Protection of Rural England. Concerned about the impact of modern agriculture on England's landscape, she left to write her first book, *The Theft of the Countryside,* which was published in 1980 and sparked nationwide debate.

Marion went on to investigate and campaign about land ownership, writing *This Land is Our Land* in 1987; access to the countryside, writing *A Right to Roam* in 1999; and landscape tastes, writing 'Edgelands' in 2002. In 2006 she was named one of the 100 most influential environmentalists by the Guardian and in 2009 received the Golden Eagle lifetime achievement award from the Outdoor Writers and Photographers Guild.

Just as *A Right to Roam* was being published, it became clear Marion's mother was fast developing dementia. Thrust into the world of eldercare, Marion found a dearth of straight-talking guidance for people in similar situations. Once she had organised good care for her mother, she decided to try to provide some.

Marion soon realised her mother's plight and that of many other older people sprang largely from decisions they had taken or failed to take years before about where to live, what to do with their money and how they might remain healthy. Her first book in this field, *A Survival Guide to Later Life,* was published in 2004.

Since then she has been deepening her understanding with further research and involvement with individuals and organisations such as the Alzheimer's Society, the Relatives and Residents Association and Healthwatch Medway. *How to Handle Later Life* is the result.